RUSSELL-CLARKE AND HOWE
ON
INDUSTRIAL DESIGNS

RUSSELL-CLARKE AND HOWE
ON
INDUSTRIAL DESIGNS

EIGHTH EDITION

BY

MARTIN HOWE, Q.C.

SWEET & MAXWELL

THOMSON REUTERS

First Edition 1930 by A.D. Russell-Clarke
Second Edition 1951 by A.D. Russell-Clarke
Third Edition 1960 by A.D. Russell-Clarke
Fourth Edition 1968 by A.D. Russell-Clarke and Michael Fysh
Fifth Edition 1974 by Michael Fysh
Sixth Edition 1999 by Martin Howe
Seventh Edition 2005 by Martin Howe
Eighth Edition 2010 by Martin Howe

Published in 2010 by Thomson Reuters (Legal) Limited
(Registered in England & Wales Company No 1679046
Registered Office and address for service:
100 Avenue Road London NW3 3PF)
trading as Sweet & Maxwell

Typeset by Interactive Sciences Ltd, Gloucester
Printed and bound in Great Britain by CPI Anthony Rowe, Chippenham
and Eastbourne

*For further information on our products and services visit
www.sweetandmaxwell.co.uk.

No natural forests were destroyed to make this product; only farmed
timber was used and re-planted.

A CIP catalogue record for this book is available from
the British Library
ISBN Hardback 978 1 847 03891 3

Thomson Reuters and the Thomson Reuters logo are
trademarks of Thomson Reuters Sweet & Maxwell® is a registered
trademark of Thomson Reuters (Legal) Limited.

100619661X

CONTENTS

Chapter 1

Overview and Historical Introduction to Design Righ n the United Kingdom

Chapter 2

Community Designs and EU Harmonised UK Design

Chapter 3

Pre-2001 UK Registered Designs

Chapter 4

UK National Unregistered Design Right

Chapter 5

Copyright Protection for Industrial Designs

Chapter 6

Infringement and Validity Disputes: Remedies and Procedures

Chapter 7

Actions for Threats of Proceedings for Infringement

Chapter 8

Compulsory Licensing and Crown User

Chapter 9

European Community Law and Competition

Chapter 10

Protection of Semiconductor Topographies

Chapter 11

Countries with Historical Connections with UK Registered Designs

Appendices

Appendix A: UK Registered Designs

Appendix B: Community Designs

Appendix C: UK Unregistered Design Right

Appendix D: Copyright

Appendix E: Court, Tribunal and Procedural Rules

Appendix F: International Materials

TABLE OF CASES

References are to paragraph number.

TABLE OF COUNCIL DECISIONS

*References are to paragraph number. Those in **bold** type indicate reproduction in full.*

TABLE OF STATUTES

References are to paragraph number. Those in **bold** *type indicate reproduction in full.*

NATIONAL TABLE OF STATUTES

*References are to paragraph number. Those in **bold** type indicate reproduction in full.*

TABLE OF STATUTORY INSTRUMENTS

References are to paragraph number. Those in **bold** *type indicate reproduction in full.*

1

TABLE OF CIVIL PROCEDURE RULES

References are to paragraph number. Those in **bold** *type indicate reproduction in full.*

TABLE OF PRACTICE DIRECTIONS

References are to paragraph number. Those in **bold** *type indicate reproduction in full.*

TABLE OF EUROPEAN AGREEMENTS, CONVENTIONS AND INTERNATIONAL TREATIES

*References are to paragraph number. Those in **bold** type indicate reproduction in full.*

TABLE OF EUROPEAN DIRECTIVES

References are to paragraph number. Those in **bold** *type indicate reproduction in full.*

TABLE OF EUROPEAN REGULATIONS

References are to paragraph number. Those in **bold** *type indicate reproduction in full.*

TABLE OF ABBREVIATIONS

CDPA 1988—Copyright, Designs and Patents Act 1988: Apps C1 (unregistered design right) and D1 (copyright extracts) below.

Cth—Commonwealth of Australia (in parentheses after name of Act).

The Directive—Directive 98/71/EC on the legal protection of designs of October 13, 1998 (OJ L 289, 28.10.98, p.28): App.A1 below.

The Green Paper—Green Paper on the Legal Protection of Industrial Design, EC Commission Working Document, 111/F/5131/91–EN, June 1991.

OHIM—the Office for Harmonisation in the Internal Market (Trade Marks and Designs)

RDA 1949—Registered Designs Act 1949.

RDA(A)—Registered Designs Act 1949 as amended, as it stood prior to its amendment to conform with the Directive (App.A5 below).

RDA(E)—Registered Designs Act 1949, as amended to conform with the EC Designs Directive (App.A2 below).

The Regulation—Council Regulation (EC) No.6/2002 on Community designs of December 12, 2001; OJ L 3, 5.1.2002, p.1)—App.B1 below.

CHAPTER 1

OVERVIEW AND HISTORICAL INTRODUCTION TO DESIGN RIGHTS IN THE UNITED KINGDOM

1. The Five Different Rights

The five rights which protect industrial designs

Industrial designs are protected under the present day law of the United **1–001**
Kingdom by no less than five legal rights: Community registered designs,
Community unregistered design right, UK registered designs, UK unregistered design right, and artistic copyright. Changes in the law resulting
from EU single market harmonisation measures have added two further
legal rights, the Community registered design and the Community
unregistered design right, to the three legal rights which previously
existed in this field. The upshot is an area of law of labyrinthine
complexity. From the point of view alike of businesses seeking to protect
their new designs against copying, and of businesses seeking to adapt
their products to competition in the market while staying within the legal
limits of what they are entitled to do, this situation cannot be healthy. The
complexity and cost of taking legal advice, and the seemingly random
differences in the scope and term of the different kinds of protection,
must surely mean that it is often uneconomic to pursue protection for
designs when they ought to be protected, or to resist accusations of
infringement when the law in theory ought to allow the activities
complained of. However, the law is as it is, and the main purpose of this
work is to try to cover the field comprehensively and to provide a guide
through the labyrinth.

1–002 The governing pieces of legislation in the field are as follows. Council Regulation (EC) No.6/2002 on Community designs has direct effect within the member states of the European Union and provides for Community registered designs and for the Community unregistered design right. Directive 98/71/EC on the legal protection of designs required member states to harmonise the essential features of their substantive law of registered designs, and the Registered Designs Act 1949 was radically amended in consequence of this Directive by Regulations made under s.2(2) of the European Communities Act 1972.[1] To distinguish that Act in its present form from the previous versions, which still remain relevant for a variety of purposes, the 1949 Act as amended to conform with the EC Directive will be referred to in this work as the "RDA(E)".

1–003 The previous major changes to the law governing protection of designs were made by the Copyright Designs and Patents Act 1988 ("the CDPA 1988"). That Act repealed and replaced the previous copyright law (the Copyright Act 1956),[2] created a new right, the unregistered design right,[3] which still exists in parallel with the Community unregistered design right created by the EC Regulation, and amended the Registered Designs Act 1949 in a number of important respects. The Registered Designs Act 1949, as amended by the CDPA 1988, will be referred to in this work as the "RDA(A)"; the RDA(A) is still relevant as the law governing the validity of designs applied for before December 9, 2001, and will therefore need to be considered by practitioners until 2026. Even the RDA 1949 in its original form, i.e. before amendment by the CDPA 1988, continues to apply to registered designs applied for before August 1, 1989, and so will need to be considered by practitioners until 2014. For this reason, in the Appendices[4] to this work are printed the RDA(E), relevant to new designs and the RDA(A), relevant to designs filed between 1989 and 2001, which is annotated to allow the reader to see the old RDA 1949 in its form before amendment by the CDPA 1988.

1–004 These five rights have their own separate rules for subsistence, ownership, scope of infringing acts and term. Although there is alignment of the substance of the Community and UK registered design rights, they obviously differ in their geographical coverage, and also differ in their application procedure. The unregistered design right has a special form which applies to the specialist field of the protection of semi-conductor topographies.[5] All this gives rise to a structure of legal protection of great complexity, particularly with regard to the boundary

---

[1] For a description of these Regulations, see Ch.2 below.
[2] CDPA 1988 Pt I governs copyright; App.D, below.
[3] CDPA 1988 Pt III governs unregistered design right; App.C, below.
[4] The RDA(E) is set out in App.A2 below and the RDA(A) in App.A5 below. The Registered Designs Act 1949, when it is necessary to refer to its provisions before the extensive amendments made by the 1988 Act, will be referred to simply as the RDA 1949.
[5] This subject is covered at paras 10–001 et seq.

between the coverage of artistic copyright and of unregistered design right, where aspects of the design of a single article will often be the subject of different rights: in general, with unregistered design right protecting three-dimensional shapes, and copyright protecting surface patterns. Even within the scope of artistic copyright, there is an important distinction between designs that effectively receive copyright protection for the full term of the copyright, and those that receive protection for a limited term of 25 years.[6]

Summary of the attributes of the five rights

It may be helpful to introduce the broad picture before proceeding to the details, with the inevitable complexities. Accordingly, on the following page, in tabular form, are the principal attributes and fields of coverage of these five legal rights. 1–005

2. Inter-Relationships

General picture as regards overlap of rights

The broad legislative policy can be stated simply: in general, both of the Community rights (registered and unregistered) and UK registered design coverage may freely overlap with artistic copyright on the one hand, and UK unregistered design right on the other. 1–006

However, there is a clear legislative policy to separate the coverage of the two UK unregistered rights (design right and artistic copyright) from each other. It will frequently be of critical importance to decide which of these two unregistered rights is the relevant one. Because of the radical differences between the rules governing ownership, subsistence and terms of the two rights (see table on the following page), there will be many cases where an action based on one right (usually copyright) will succeed, but an action based on the other right (usually design right) would fail. In general, the rules governing subsistence and term of unregistered design right are more restrictive than those for copyright. Thus, it is better to rely on artistic copyright, if it is available. 1–007

---

[6] In some cases this boundary is defined by exceptions to exceptions: for probably the worst example, see the position on the protection of sculptures which are intended to be multiplied on an industrial scale, considered at para.5–079 below.

	UK Registered Designs	Community Registered Designs	Community Unregistered Design Right	Unregistered Design Right	Artistic Copyright
Basic nature of right	Obtained by application (very limited substantive examination) at UK designs registry; requires absolute novelty and "individual character"; confers monopoly right (i.e. no need to prove copying if similar design is adopted).	Obtained by deposit (no substantive examination) at Community Designs Office; requires absolute novelty and "individual character"; confers monopoly right (i.e. no need to prove copying if similar design is adopted).	No formalities for subsistence; requires absolute novelty and "individual character"; copying is an essential ingredient for infringement.	No formalities for subsistence; requires originality but not absolute novelty; copying is an essential ingredient for infringement.	No formalities for subsistence; requires originality but not absolute novelty; copying is an essential ingredient for infringement.
Conditions for subsistence	National of any country may apply for registration; if from a Paris Convention country, may obtain early priority based on application in home country.	Same as for UK registered designs.	Right acquired by publication of the design (by public sale of products embodying it or otherwise) so as to become known to circles specialised in the sector concerned within the Community; actual sale or publication need not be within the EC nor is there any nationality requirement for the designer or product manufacturer.	Very restrictive rules apply to nationality of designer, their employer or person commissioning design. Most designs originating outside the EC will not qualify for subsistence.	Wide rules apply to nationality or residence of author or publisher, nationals of most countries in the world, including all major economies, will qualify for subsistence of artistic copyright.

4

	UK Registered Designs	Community Registered Designs	Community Unregistered Design Right	Unregistered Design Right	Artistic Copyright
What it covers	Two-dimensional and three-dimensional features of the appearance of products which are industrial or handicraft items or of parts of such products. Features which are dictated by function are excluded.	Same as for UK registered Designs.	Same as for Community registered Designs.	Three-dimensional features of design of industrial articles, whether aesthetic or functional. Surface decoration is excluded from scope of this right.	(1) Three-dimensional articles and two-dimensional design features (i.e. surface markings and decorations) on industrial articles. (2) Reproduction of three-dimensional articles which are themselves artistic works; i.e. works of sculpture and "works of artistic craftsmanship". (3) Both two- and three-dimensional aspects of the design of buildings and other structures.
Term	Maximum 25 years from date of application to register.	Same as for UK registered Designs.	Three years from publication of the design.	Ten years from first marketing of articles to the design; during last five years any competitor may obtain a "licence of right" royalties set by the Patent Office.	(A) Life of the author plus 70 years; or (B) If design is applied industrially (normally by making 50 or more articles) effective term of copyright in industrial design field limited to 25 years from first marketing of articles.

1–008   At some risk of over-simplifying a complex picture, the protection of the three-dimensional features of the design of "ordinary" industrial articles is within the scope of unregistered design right and outside the scope of copyright. Thus, a person who copies the shape of a competitor's industrial article need worry (subject to searching for a UK or Community registered design) only about the risk of infringing UK unregistered design right with its more limited 10-year term, or Community unregistered design right with its even more restricted three-year term. However, there are exceptions. Some industrially manufactured articles fall into categories which the legislature presumably regards as being more "artistic" than ordinary run of the mill articles; and the three-dimensional shape of these articles is covered by copyright in the underlying work (usually a drawing or a prototype), rather than by unregistered design right. These copyright-protected articles are items which are "works of sculpture" and "works of artistic craftsmanship". The precise boundaries of that latter category are particularly hard to define.[7] In addition, the three-dimensional design of buildings and other structures is firmly within the field of artistic copyright and outside the field of unregistered design right.[8]

1–009   With two-dimensional designs, the position is different. Two-dimensional designs, whether consisting of the whole design of essentially two-dimensional articles, or of surface decorations or markings applied to three-dimensional articles, are outside the scope of UK unregistered design right and within the scope of artistic copyright. There will in most cases be an underlying drawing or other graphic work used as the basis of replication of such design features, the copyright in which can be enforced against competitors who copy such features. Two dimensional designs may also be within the scope of Community unregistered design right which, unlike the UK national right, covers two-dimensional as well as three-dimensional features of appearance.

Problems at the boundary between copyright and UK unregistered design right

1–010   The division between the two types of right does create problems. First, difficulties may be created in protecting a design which consists of two-dimensional and three-dimensional elements, where the relationship between those elements is the essence of the design. For example, a new garment design may consist not of a new shape on its own, or a new pattern or colour scheme on its own, but in the way in which aspects of pattern or colour are applied in relation to the three-dimensional form of

---

[7] As to what is a "work of artistic craftsmanship", see para.5–022 below.
[8] And indeed not covered by registered designs either, except possibly in the case of prefabricated structures; see para.3–036 below.

the garment. It is not easy to see how to deal with this kind of design, since the law now seems to require that two-dimensional and three-dimensional elements should be split up from each other for the purpose of considering separately the originality of, and the infringement of, two distinct legal rights.[9]

In addition, there are some difficult problems in precisely defining the boundary line between copyright and unregistered design right. Surface decorations, i.e. features applied to a surface for decorative purposes, are specifically excluded from UK unregistered design right[10] and are correspondingly retained within the scope of artistic copyright.[11] This means that even if a pattern applied to a surface has some height (and therefore might otherwise be regarded as having "shape" within the unregistered design right), it is outside design right but within copyright if it is "decoration". But what if its purpose is functional, or it has a mixed functional and aesthetic purpose? It is not totally clear which side of the line such a feature will fall as between the scope of the two rights.[12]

1–011

3. History of Copyright and Industrial Designs up to 1911

Early Copyright Acts

The first Act dealing with copyright was passed during the reign of Queen Anne in 1709. This Act[13] provided that authors of books and their assigns should have the sole liberty of printing the same for 14 years from the date of first publication. Following on from the Statute of Anne, the year 1734 saw the introduction of the first Act dealing with works of art. This was the Engraving Copyright Act 1734. It was amended by the Engraving Copyright Act 1767 and followed by the Prints Copyright Act 1777.

1–012

Textiles: the start of industrial design protection

The first Act dealing with copyright in industrial designs was the Designing and Printing of Linens, etc. Act 1787. It was concerned with designs for certain specified textile materials, namely linens, cottons, calicos and muslins, and followed much the same lines as the earlier Act relating to engravings and prints. It gave to designers, printers and

1–013

---

[9] See the consideration given to this problem at paras 5–086 to 5–087 below; and see the problems caused in *Lambretta Clothing Co Ltd v Teddy Smith (UK) Ltd* [2004] EWCA Civ 886; [2005] R.P.C. 6 regarding a sketch showing different components of a tracksuit top with different colours.
[10] CDPA 1988 s.213(3)(c).
[11] CDPA 1988 s.51(3).
[12] See para.4–034 below, for consideration of this problem.
[13] The Copyright Act 1709.

proprietors of new and original patterns for the materials in question the sole right and liberty of printing and reprinting them for two months from the date of first publication, provided the name of the proprietor was marked on each piece. An infringer was liable to a special action on the case, damages and costs. This Act was in the nature of an experiment, and was only to continue in force for one year. In 1789 (by the Designing and Printing of Linens Act) it was, however, continued in force till July 1, 1794 and in 1794[14] it was made perpetual, and the period of protection extended to three months from the date of first publication.

Sculptures

1–014   The next branch of endeavour to be dealt with was sculpture. In 1797 the first Sculpture Copyright Act was passed. This was, however, largely superseded by a second Act dealing with sculpture which was passed in 1814. This Act, the Sculpture Copyright Act 1814, provided that any person who should:

> "make or cause to be made any new and original Sculpture, or Model, or Copy, or Cast of the Human Figure or Human Figures, or of any Bust or Busts, or of any Part or Parts of the Human Figure, clothed in drapery or otherwise, or of any Animal or Animals, or of any Part or Parts of any Animal combined with the Human Figure or otherwise, or of any subject being matter of Invention in Sculpture, or of any *Alto* or *Basso Relievo* representing any of the matters or things hereinbefore mentioned . . . "

should have the sole right and property therein for 14 years from the date of first publication. The right was only to accrue if the new sculpture, model, copy, or cast, was marked by the proprietor with his name and date of publication before it was published. This Act remained in force till the passing of the Copyright Act 1911, when it was repealed.

Extension of protection for textile designs

1–015   In 1839 the legislature again turned its attention to industrial designs, and during the next 50 years a series of statutes was passed, gradually extending the boundaries of copyright in these works. The first of the series, introduced in 1839 by the Copyright of Designs Act, considerably increased the protection afforded to fabrics under the earlier Acts[15] by enacting that these should extend to fabrics composed of wool, silk or

---

[14] The Linens, etc., Act 1794.
[15] The Designing and Printing of Linens Act 1787 and the Linens, etc., Act 1794.

hair, and to mixed fabrics made up of any two or more of the following materials: linen, cotton, wool, silk or hair.

Extension of protection to articles of manufacture generally and introduction of registration

In the same year a further Act[16] extended the protection to far beyond the confines of the textile trade, and laid the foundations of the law of registered designs as it exists today. It gave protection to every new or original design, as follows: **1–016**

> "(1) For the Pattern or Print, to be either worked into, or worked on, or printed on, or painted on, any Article of Manufacture being a Tissue or Textile Fabric, except Lace, and also except Linens, Cottons, Calicoes, and Muslins ...
>
> (2) For the Modelling, or the Casting, or the Embossment, or the Chasing, or the Engraving, or for any other kind of Impression or Ornament on any Article of Manufacture, not being a Tissue or Textile Fabric ...
>
> (3) For the Shape or Configuration of any Article of Manufacture ... "

This second Act, which so far as textiles were concerned, was ancillary to the Acts already in existence dealing with fabrics, thus included not merely textiles, but "any article of manufacture", and gave protection not merely to ornamentation placed upon an article, but also to the shape in which it was made. It also introduced for the first time a system of registration. A Registrar was directed to be appointed by the Board of Trade, and, unless a design was registered before it had been published, the benefits of the Act could not be obtained. A new principle was thus introduced, which differed fundamentally from that of the previous Copyright Acts, according to which, as soon as the proprietor had published his work, copyright in it had automatically accrued to him. This principle is still central to one aspect of the protection afforded to industrial designs, although it has now been modified by the introduction under the EU harmonised law of a one-year "grace period" after first publication of a design during which the proprietor may make an application to register.[17] **1–017**

---

[16] The Copyright of Designs Act 1839.
[17] For the one year grace period, see para.2–034 below.

Substances

1–018 In 1842, the Acts of 1839, together with the earlier Acts dealing with fabrics, were repealed. This was effected by a statute entitled "An Act to consolidate and amend the Laws relating to the Copyright of Designs for Ornamenting Articles of Manufacture". This Act (known as the Designs Act 1842) replaced the legislation which it repealed by a new set of provisions which, whilst embodying most of what was contained in the earlier Acts, considerably extended their scope. In particular, protection was given, not merely to designs to be applied to articles, but also to substances. Any new and original design,

> "applicable to the ornamenting of any Article of Manufacture, or any Substance, artificial or natural . . . whether applicable for the pattern, or for the shape or configuration, or for the ornament thereof"

was now made the subject of copyright. Designs for sculpture and other things within the provisions of the Sculpture Copyright Acts, which would otherwise have fallen within the provisions of the new Act (since they would be designs applicable for the shape or configuration of a "substance") were, however, specifically excluded from its provisions. The new Act divided the possible articles of manufacture and substances into classes, and further increased the remedies for infringement, but these were as yet obtainable only if the actual application of the design had taken place within the United Kingdom.

Registration of functional industrial designs

1–019 In 1843 an amending Act[18] was passed. This Act recited that, whereas by the Act of 1842 the sole right had been given to the proprietor of certain new and original designs to apply them to the "ornamenting" of any Article of Manufacture or any Substance, it was expedient to extend the protection of the Act to designs not of an ornamental character. It, therefore, enacted that copyright should subsist in "any new or original Design for any Article of Manufacture having reference to some purpose of Utility", so far as such design should be for the shape or configuration of the Article. As in the Act of 1842, there was an express provision that the Act should not apply to designs within the Sculpture Copyright Acts.

---

[18] The Copyright of Designs Act 1843.

Overlapping protection for sculptures

The next Act was in 1850.[19] This empowered the proprietor of any **1–020** "Sculpture, Model, Copy or Cast within the protection of the Sculpture Copyright Acts" to apply to the Registrar of Designs for registration of his work, for the whole or any part of the term during which copyright might exist under the Sculpture Copyright Acts. By this Act, therefore, sculpture which had been recognised as falling within the broad terms of the Designs Acts 1842 and 1843, but which had been specifically excluded from them, was brought within their scope.

Two further Acts dealing with industrial designs were passed, in 1858 and 1861, but these were not of major importance.

Drawings, paintings and photographs

Although laws had been passed dealing with literary works, dramatic **1–021** and musical works, prints and engravings, sculpture, designs for textiles and articles of manufacture generally, no effort had so far been made to protect ordinary drawings and paintings. It was not until as late as 1862 that legislation dealing with these works was introduced. In that year, the Fine Arts Copyright Act 1862 was passed. This Act provided that the author, being a British subject, or resident within the Dominions of the Crown, of every original painting, drawing and photograph and their assigns should have the sole and exclusive right of,

> "copying, engraving, reproducing and multiplying such painting or drawing and the design thereof, or such photograph and the negative thereof by any means and of any size for the term of the natural life of such author and seven years after his death."

The proprietor could not obtain the benefit of the statute, unless and **1–022** until they had registered their copyright at Stationers' Hall. After this Act, no further legislation dealing with paintings, drawings or photographs was introduced until the Act was repealed and fresh provisions substituted by the Copyright Act 1911.

Designs transferred to Commissioners for Patents

In 1875 the powers and duties of the Board of Trade under the various **1–023** Designs Acts were by the Copyright of Designs Act 1875 transferred to

---

[19] The Copyright of Designs Act 1850.

the Patent Office, through the Designs Branch of which registration was now carried out.

1–024   Copyright in industrial designs having thus become associated with patents for inventions, in 1883 a single consolidating and amending Act was passed embracing both of these subjects, as well as Trade Marks, which were also directed to be registered at the Patent Office. Since the definition of what could be registered under the new Act contained words similar to those in the 1842 and 1843 Acts, specifically excluding works of sculpture, and since the Act of 1850, which had enabled such works to be registered, was now repealed, these works were once more relegated solely to the protection of the Sculpture Copyright Acts.

The Patents and Designs Act 1907 and the Copyright Act 1911

1–025   This brings the position up to 1912, when the Copyright Act 1911 became law. This Act was a measure of far-reaching importance. It did away with substantially all the existing copyright legislation which had been accumulating over a period of two centuries, repealing no less than 18 Acts, most of them substantially *in toto*. Every branch of the subject was now brought within the four corners of two statutes. These two Acts, the Copyright Act 1911 and the designs portion of the Patents and Designs Acts 1907–1946, regulated the position from 1911 until 1949. In that year registered designs were once more separated entirely from patents, and the law relating to registered designs was governed by the Registered Designs Act 1949. The most important alterations in the law effected by that Act were the amendment of the definition of a design and the abolition of classification, both of which materially affected the validity as well as the scope of many registered designs.

4. Historical Development of the Relationship between Copyright and Industrial Design Protection

The relationship between artistic copyright and industrial designs

1–026   Since 1797 for sculptures, and since 1862 for works of fine art, copyright has been the primary form of protection for artistic works. The extent to which artistic copyright has (whether deliberately or through legislative oversights) extended into the field of industrial designs has been the subject of frequent legislative upheaval and changes of tack over time. As already noted, in 1842 sculptures were specifically excluded from the scope of industrial design protection,[20] in 1850 they were permitted to be

---

[20] See para.1–018 above.

registered as industrial designs (thus giving the author the option of overlapping protection),[21] and then in 1875 sculptures were again excluded from registration as industrial designs.[22]

The effect of the Copyright Act 1911 on overlapping protection

The position reached before the passing of the Copyright Act 1911 was that there was not a great deal of overlapping between industrial design protection and artistic copyright. At that time six statutes were in force relating to works of any artistic nature. Five dealt with purely artistic works. These were the Engraving Copyright Acts 1734 and 1767, the Prints Copyright Act 1777, the Sculpture Copyright Act 1814 and the Fine Arts Copyright Act 1862. One Act dealt with industrial designs. This was the designs portion of the Patents and Designs Act 1907.   **1–027**

As long as these Acts were operative, such overlapping as did exist was not of great importance, as there was very little correspondence between the monopolies created. Infringement, generally speaking, was restricted to reproduction of the copyright work in a medium similar to that of the work itself. A substantial increase in overlap between industrial and other forms of artistic copyright was created by the passing of the Copyright Act 1911. To some extent this was intentional, but in part it was also by oversight.   **1–028**

First, works of sculpture acquired copyright as artistic works under the Copyright Act 1911, in place of the copyright which they had enjoyed under the Sculpture Copyright Act 1814, which was repealed. The repeal of the 1814 Act meant that the sculptures ceased to be excluded from registration under the Patents and Designs Act 1907.[23] It was thus possible for sculptures to fall within the scope of both the Copyright Act and the Patents and Designs Act 1907.[24] Secondly, the Copyright Act 1911 was framed so as to include "works of artistic craftsmanship" and "architectural works of art".[25] All works of artistic craftsmanship, and possibly some architectural works of art, would appear also to have been "designs" within the meaning of the Patents and Designs Act 1907.   **1–029**

Thirdly, under the Copyright Act 1911, the scope of artistic copyright was extended to cover reproduction of the copyright work "in any   **1–030**

---

[21] See para.1–020 above.

[22] See para.1–023 above.

[23] The definition of "design" in the Patents and Designs Act 1907 s.93 contained a specific exclusion "(not being a design for a sculpture or other thing within the protection of the Sculpture Copyright Act 1814)"; with the repeal of the 1814 Act, this exclusion ceased to apply.

[24] *Pytram Ltd v Models (Leicester) Ltd* [1930] 1 Ch. 639. For a recent and very extensive judicial survey of the historical development of the overlap between copyright protection for sculptures and registered design protection, see *Lucasfilm Ltd v Ainsworth* [2009] EWCA Civ 1328; [2010] F.S.R. 10 p.270, CA, per Jacob L.J.

[25] The Copyright Act 1911 s.35(1), definition of "artistic work".

material form whatsoever".[26] The effect of this was that before the 1911 Act, if a drawing of an article, such as a teapot, was registered, both as a drawing under the Fine Arts Copyright Act and as a design under the Patents and Designs Act, copyright under the first-mentioned Act would be infringed only by reproduction of the work in the form of another drawing, or possibly a painting or a photograph; and under the second Act only by reproduction of an actual article, i.e. a teapot. After 1911, reproduction of the drawing in the form of an industrial article would (absent the special provision discussed in the next paragraph) be an infringement, not only of industrial design right under the Patents and Designs Acts, but also of artistic copyright under the Copyright Act.

Section 22 of the Copyright Act 1911

1–031 In order to limit the extent of the overlap of artistic copyright with industrial designs, which it had potentially created by formulating the main provisions of the Copyright Act 1911 in such wide terms, the legislature inserted a special section in the Act. This section, which was s.22, gave rise to certain problems of interpretation and resulting litigation. Its terms were as follows:

> "(1) This Act shall not apply to designs capable of being registered under the Patents and Designs Act 1907 except designs which, though capable of being so registered, are not used or intended to be used as models or patterns to be multiplied by any industrial process.
> (2) General rules under section 86 of the Patents and Designs Act 1907 may be made for determining the conditions under which a design shall be deemed to be used for such purposes as aforesaid."

1–032 It will be seen that the general effect of the section was to preclude from the protection of the Copyright Act 1911, anything registrable as a design, though an exception was made in the case of a conception which, though so registrable, was not used or intended to be used as a model or pattern to be multiplied by an industrial process.

1–033 In accordance with this section, r.89 of the Designs Rules 1920[27] provided as follows:

---

[26] The Copyright Act 1911 s.1(2), and this included the reproduction of two-dimensional works in three-dimensions; *King Features Syndicate Inc v O. & M. Kleemann Ltd* [1941] A.C. 417; (1941) 58 R.P.C. 207.

[27] SI 1920/337; this subsequently became r.92 of the Designs Rules 1932, and then r.2 of the Copyright (Industrial Designs) Rules 1949 (SI 1949/2367) after the passing of the RDA 1949. It is in substance reproduced under the present law as the Copyright (Industrial Process and Excluded Articles) (No.2) Order 1989 (SI 1989/1070) art.2, set out at para.5–099 below. This provision now regulates the circumstances in which the industrial application of a copyright work will trigger the special 25-year limitation on its effective term: see para.5–099 below.

"A design shall be deemed to be used as a model or pattern to be multiplied by any industrial process within the meaning of section 22 of the Copyright Act 1911—

(a) when the design is reproduced or is intended to be reproduced in more than fifty single articles, unless all the articles in which the design is reproduced or is intended to be reproduced together form only a single set of articles, as defined by rule 5 of these Rules[28];

(b) when the design is to be applied to (1) printed paper hangings; (2) carpets, floor cloths, or oil cloths, manufactured or sold in lengths or pieces; (3) textile piece-goods or textile goods manufactured or sold in lengths or pieces; (4) lace not made by hand."

Effects of section 22

It will be seen that the effect of s.22 of the Copyright Act 1911—as interpreted by the above-mentioned rules—was that if a work was capable of registration as a design, and was reproduced or intended to be reproduced in more than 50 single articles (except in the case of a set), or was to be applied to any of the materials specified in part (b) of the rule (e.g. to carpets or textile piece-goods), it received no protection under the Copyright Act 1911. If, however, the intention was to reproduce the design in less than 50 articles, the Copyright Act still applied.[29] **1–034**

Section 22 produced an "all or nothing" effect as regards the subsistence of copyright. If a work fell within the section as interpreted by the rules, then no copyright subsisted in the artistic work, whether in the field of application to industrial designs or in the traditional methods of non-industrial exploitation of artistic works. In such a case, the only method of protection was to register it as a design under the Patents and Designs Acts, and this would not cover the non-industrial exploitation of the artistic work. **1–035**

The obvious interpretation of the effect of s.22 is that copyright is denied to an artistic work in two circumstances: first, if it is created with the original intention of embodying a design to be industrially reproduced; and secondly, if the copyright owner subsequently permits it so to be reproduced, even if it is not created with that original intention. However, the apparent harshness of the effects of the section led the House of Lords to reject the second proposition in the "Popeye" cartoon **1–036**

---

[28] The definition of a set of articles in r.5 was in substance the same as the current definition in RDA(A) s.44(1).
[29] *Chabot v Davies* (1936) 155 L.T. 525.

case, *King Features Syndicate Inc and Betts v O. & M. Kleemann Ltd.*[30] It was there held that the person to be considered was the author of the work and no one else, and that the relevant date was that of the making of the design. Lord Maugham said[31]:

> "The design, it is clear, is entitled to the benefit of the Copyright Act 1911, if it is not used or intended to be used as model or pattern . . . The questions arise: Not used by whom? At what time? Who is it that is not to have the intention to use it? When is that negative to be satisfied? My Lords, I cannot doubt that the person so referred to is the author and that the time is the time when the design comes into existence."

Lord Wright said[32]: " . . . the use or intention to use which s.22 postulates must exist at the date when the sketch was made. That is the natural time".

1–037   In the case in question, the work, in respect of which copyright was claimed, was a drawing (or a number of drawings) of a fictitious character known as "Popeye the Sailor", which had originally appeared in series of cartoons in an American newspaper first published in Canada, and later in cinematograph films. The alleged infringement consisted of reproductions of the character in the form of toys and brooches. The author, when he first produced the drawings, had no intention of industrialising them. Some years later, however, after the character of "Popeye" had become popular, he proceeded to license certain manufacturers to make articles in the form of designs such as toys, brooches, etc.

1–038   It was argued that as the author had authorised reproduction of the work in forms which were registrable as designs (i.e. brooches and toys), the Act no longer applied to the work, and it was therefore no infringement to reproduce it without authority, at least in such forms. It was, however, held (reversing the Court of Appeal) that the material date, being when the work first came into existence, nothing which happened subsequently, could affect the position, or, in any way, limit or affect the copyright. Lord Wright said[33]:

> "There is nothing in section 22 of the Copyright Act which can be construed as cutting down or destroying the full scope of the artistic copyright once it has attached under the Act . . . In my opinion clear

---

[30] (1941) 58 R.P.C. 207; [1941] A.C. 417. This case is probably a good illustration of the maxim that the House of Lords (now the Supreme Court) are right because they are final, not necessarily final because they are right.
[31] (1941) 58 R.P.C. 207 at 212.
[32] (1941) 58 R.P.C. 207 at 220.
[33] (1941) 58 R.P.C. 207 at 219.

words would be required to deprive a person in whole or in part of his full copyright without his consent once that copyright has accrued to him."

The effect of the above decision was that, although there was no   1–039
mention of time or date in s.22, there had to be read into the section a qualification that use or intention to use was only to be considered when the work was first created. The result of this was that, provided there was no intention on the part of the author to use his design as a model or pattern for industrial multiplication at the time it was created, full rights under the Copyright Act, which were far more extensive and of longer duration than those under the Designs Act, were at his disposal, even should he subsequently change his mind and proceed to industrialise his work.

In the *Popeye* case there was no intention to industrialise the work at the   1–040
time it was made, and copyright in it, therefore, subsisted. In a considerable number of other cases, however, where the design was registrable and evolved with the definite intention of being used as a model or pattern from which a large number of articles (considerably in excess of 50) could be produced, the Copyright Act 1911 was held, by virtue of s.22, not to apply, and there being no registration under the Patents and Designs Acts, proceedings to restrain infringement were dismissed.[34]

Section 22 could create a complicated state of affairs where an initial   1–041
work counted as an industrial design, but later embellishments or additional features could result in infringement, even though the copying of the underlying design did not.[35]

Reform of provisions against overlap under the Copyright Act 1956

Largely because of the interpretation placed on it by the House of Lords   1–042
in the *Popeye* case, s.22 failed in important areas to achieve the separation between the fields of artistic copyright and of industrial design, which had been the intention of the legislature in 1911. Under the Copyright Act 1956, the basic policy remained the same (i.e. to exclude the application of artistic copyright from the field of industrial designs), but, instead of the "all or nothing" approach to subsistence of copyright in s.22, a new and more subtle approach was adopted by s.10 of the Copyright Act 1956.[36]

The effect of the section (in its original 1956 form before amendment by   1–043
the Design Copyright Act 1968) may be summarised as follows:

---

[34] *Pytram Ltd v Models (Leicester) Ltd* [1930] 1 Ch. 639; *Wood v Stoddarts Ltd* M.C.C. 1930–1931, 294: *Con Planck v Kolynos Inc* [1925] 2 K.B. 804; *Ware v Anglo-Italian Commercial Agency Ltd (No.1)* M.C.C. 1917–1923, 346.

[35] *Ware v Anglo-Italian Commercial Agency Ltd (No.2)* M.C.C. 1917–1923, 371; *Masson Seeley & Co Ltd v Embosotype Manufacturing Co Ltd* (1924) 41 R.P.C. 160.

[36] Section 10 is set out both in its original form and as later amended by the Design Copyright Act 1968 at App.D2 below.

1. Where copyright subsisted in an artistic work, and a "correspond-ing design" was registered, it would not be an infringement under the Copyright Act to do anything during the registration which was within the scope of the protection under the RDA 1949. After the registered design had expired, it would not be an infringement of copyright to do anything which would have been within the scope of the design if it had notionally been registered with any possible minor variations and in respect of any possible articles to which it was capable of being applied.[37]

2. Where copyright subsisted in an artistic work, and

   (a) a "corresponding design" was "applied industrially" by or with the licence of the owner of the copyright;
   (b) articles with the design so applied were put on the market; and
   (c) no design was registered in respect of those articles,

   then it would not be an infringement of the copyright in the work under the Copyright Act:

   (a) During "the relevant period of fifteen years," i.e. 15 years from the first offer for sale or sale by the owner, to do anything which would have been within the scope of the protection of the design, if it had been registered under the RDA 1949 for "all relevant articles", i.e. for all articles which had been offered for sale or sold by the copyright owner; or
   (b) after the 15 years to do anything which would have been within the scope of the design, if its registration had been notionally extended to cover any possible minor variations, and in respect of any possible articles to which it was capable of being applied.

1–044   The phrase "applied industrially" had under the rules of the 1956 Act[37a] the same meaning as the phrase "industrial multiplication" under s.22 of the 1911 Act referred to previously. Thus, it is fulfilled by application to more than 50 articles, and, to put it briefly, to goods made in length or pieces.

1–045   The effect of this was to make the rights of the owner of the copyright in an artistic work no longer dependent upon the author's intentions at the time they made the work. Their rights of exploitation in the industrial field were now made dependent upon their obtaining registration of their work as an industrial design under the RDA 1949. So that prior publication of a design created as a purely artistic work should not

---

[37] "Associated designs and articles" as defined by s.10(6).
[37a] Copyright (Industrial Designs) Rules 1957 (SI 1957/867), App.D6 below.

destroy the novelty and originality of the design, and thus prevent its registration, the RDA 1949 was amended to protect a copyright owner against the invalidating effect of previous non-industrial exploitation of his own artistic work.[38]

The fatal flaw in the overlap provisions of the Copyright Act 1956

Section 10 of the Copyright Act 1956 was in fact fatally flawed to achieve **1–046** its intended purpose of excluding the application of artistic copyright from the industrial design field. It took many years before the extent and full implications of this flaw were appreciated. The flaw was as follows. Because the exclusion from copyright created by s.10 was tied to the registrability of designs under the RDA 1949, the shield against copyright infringement would not apply to industrial designs, which, for one reason or other, were not registrable as designs under the RDA 1949. This aspect of the shield made sense in the case of designs which were excluded from registrability because they were treated by rules as being designs for articles "of a primarily literary or artistic character".[39] However, when it came to designs at the opposite end of the aesthetic spectrum, those with no artistic or aesthetic appeal whatever, it seems to have been overlooked completely that designs were registrable only if they had "eye appeal".[40] Thus, a design which was unregistrable because it had no aesthetic merit whatsoever could be effectively protected by artistic copyright, unlike a design with greater aesthetic merit, in respect of whose industrial application copyright could not be enforced.

Designs which were unregistrable, because they were for parts of **1–047** articles only[41] likewise escaped the effect of s.10, and artistic copyright could be enforced in respect of their industrial application. In *Dorling v Honnor Marine Ltd*,[42] the claimant had designed a new sailing dinghy which he called "The Scorpion". He had made detailed plans of all the parts of the Scorpion, which were so designed that they could be sold as a "kit of parts" from which the complete craft could be assembled. The defendants, who had held a licence from the claimant, after its termination continued to make and sell kits of parts and also completed Scorpions. In an action for infringement of the artistic copyright in the plans, the defendants relied as a defence upon s.10, contending that a corresponding design had been applied industrially by the claimant; that

---

[38] RDA 1949 s.6(4).

[39] For the exclusion of such designs from registration, see para.3–033 below. See *Klarman Ltd v Henshaw Linen Supplies* [1960] R.P.C. 150, an interlocutory case, where it was held that prima facie a plastic cover together with the matter printed on it was excluded from registration by the rule, being "printed matter primarily of a literary or artistic character", and that prima facie the copyright in the drawing on the cover had been infringed.

[40] See paras 3–047 et seq., below.

[41] As for the former requirement that a design be registered only in respect of a complete article "made and sold separately", see para.3–038 below.

articles, to which the design had been so applied, had been sold; and that, as no design had been registered by the claimant, the defendants' acts complained of were not an infringement. It was held that neither the parts nor the plans were registrable as designs; that what the defendants were doing was therefore not within the scope of any design which could have been registered; and that the defendants could not therefore rely upon s.10 as a defence. It was further held that in making the infringing parts the defendants had infringed the copyright in the plans, because it was said that copyright in a two-dimensional artistic work can be infringed by making an object in three dimensions.

1–048   The case was conducted upon the assumption—which was accepted by all parties—that the completed hull of the dinghy could have been registered, the defendants arguing in this connection that the making of the parts would have been within the scope of a registered design for the complete hull, because their manufacture was making something "for enabling any such article to be made as aforesaid" within the meaning of s.7 of the RDA 1949. The Court of Appeal rejected this argument and granted the claimant relief for infringement of the artistic copyright in his plans.

1–049   To similar effect was a decision that artistic copyright could be enforced in respect of a design for the front of an electrical meter because a design for a meter front is not registrable as such, the front of the meter not being an article to be sold separately from the rest of the meter.[43]

1–050   However, in the case of a single article which has partly functional and partly aesthetic features, the design as registered is in respect of the design of the article as a whole. It would thus be taking the effects of *Dorling v Honnor* too far to argue that artistic copyright could be enforced in respect of the functional aspects of a design which is registrable, regarded as a whole.[44]

Overlapping protection permitted by the Design Copyright Act 1968

1–051   Consistent legislative intention from 1883[45] onwards was to prevent overlap between artistic copyright and industrial design protection (subject to a possible exception relating to a limited class of articles which

---

[42] [1964] R.P.C. 160.

[43] *Sifam Electrical Instrument Co Ltd v Sangamo Weston Ltd* [1973] R.P.C. 899 at 911, lines 19–31; and at 913, lines 35–914 and line 33, per Graham J.

[44] This seems to follow from *Interlego AG v Tyco International Ltd* [1988] R.P.C. 343 at 354, PC appeal from Hong Kong. This case (concerning Lego bricks) was in fact an attempt by the copyright owner to escape from the effects of s.22 of the 1911 Act, which continued in force as part of the law of Hong Kong until January 1, 1973, by arguing that its designs, or at least aspects of them, were not registrable designs. On this aspect, the same reasoning seems to apply to s.10 of the 1956 Act as to s.22 of the 1911 Act.

were essentially artistic in character[46]), even if that intention was ineffectively carried into effect because of drafting flaws. However, the Design Copyright Act 1968 reflected a positive parliamentary intention to permit overlapping protection between artistic copyright and registered designs. It amended s.10 of the Copyright Act 1956[47] to permit artistic copyright to be enforced without restriction for a period of 15 years from the date when the article concerned was first marketed, whether or not a corresponding design had been registered, or whether or not such a design had been industrialised but not registered. However, at the end of 15 years, no act which would infringe a design registration if the design had been notionally registered, would any longer infringe the copyright subsisting under the 1956 Act. Thus, artistic copyright could be freely enforced in the industrial sphere, but the effective term of it *in that sphere* was limited to 15 years from when the copyright owner first marketed articles to the design, which was the same as the term of a registered design which the copyright owner could have applied for. To the extent that artistic copyright still extends into the industrial design field,[48] this principle of limiting its effective term has been carried through to the present law, although the period is now 25 years to correspond with the increased maximum term of a registered design.[49]

It should be noted that the effect of the Design Copyright Act 1968 was **1–052** to diminish the effect of, but not to eliminate, the serious anomaly exposed to view in *Dorling v Honnor*. Industrial designs, which were unregistrable because they had no eye appeal, did not fall within the new s.10 at all, so that the enforcement of artistic copyright relating to them was not restricted to the 15-year period which would have applied if they had been registrable designs. Nor did the enforcement of artistic copyright in such (functional) designs fall within the scope of the Design Copyright Act 1968 which limited protection in the industrial sphere to 15 years. Thus, designs which lacked any aesthetic merit whatsoever obtained effective protection for the life of the author plus 50 years. The single most important industrial design right existing under the law before 1988, which was undoubtedly artistic copyright in functional design drawings, arose through legislative oversight, not on purpose. The perceived inappropriate nature and disproportionate extent of protection for functional designs through artistic copyright in drawings was a major impetus behind the extensive reforms of the law of industrial designs introduced by the CDPA 1988.

---

[45] When works of sculpture were specifically excluded from registration as industrial designs, having previously been specifically included since 1850; see para.1–020 above.

[46] Articles which counted as "sculptures" or "works of artistic craftsmanship": see *Lucasfilm Ltd v Ainsworth* [2009] EWCA Civ 1328; [2010] F.S.R. 10 p.270, CA and paras 5–019 et seq. and 5–022 et seq., below.

[47] For this section as amended by the Design Copyright Act 1968, see App.D2 below.

[48] Its application in that field has been greatly curtailed: see para.5–068 below.

5. Amendments Made by EU Harmonisation Measures

1–053   The next significant changes to the law after the CDPA 1988 were made in consequence of measures intended to reduce distortions in the European single market by harmonising the registered designs laws of the member states and by creating a parallel Community registered design right which is a unitary right applying to the territory of the Community as a whole. The opportunity was also taken to create the short lived (three years from first publication) Community unregistered design right. Since this has been created effectively as an adjunct of the Community registered right, it is in many ways a curious legal beast. Unlike other unregistered rights such as copyright and the UK unregistered design right, its subsistence depends upon absolute novelty and difference in overall impression from the prior art, rather than upon the subjective originality exercised by the designer. However, unlike the registered right, it can only be infringed by copying. These new Community rights, and the changes to the law of UK registered designs, are explained in the next chapter.

1–054   Three very important changes, as compared with the previous UK law of registered designs, have been made. These are: (1) the scope of infringement of registered designs has in general been widened, and the test of validity in relation to the prior art been made correspondingly more stringent, by the introduction of the concept that comparisons with prior art or with alleged infringements are to depend upon a difference in *overall impression*; (2) a design registered for one product can now be infringed by the application of the design, or a similar one, to any product, in contrast with the previous law which restricted infringement to application of the design to the same kind of article; and (3) designs can now be registered for parts of products, whether separable or not, in contrast to the old law when registered designs applied to the design of an article as a whole. By contrast with registered design law, the law relating to artistic copyright and to UK unregistered design right is largely unchanged from that laid down by the CDPA 1988. This means that there are now two unregistered rights (Community and UK) running in parallel, which are very different in nature, scope and term from each other.

CHAPTER 2

COMMUNITY DESIGNS AND EU HARMONISED UK DESIGN

Contents

1. The European Harmonised System

Harmonisation in the EU internal market

National laws protecting industrial designs within the different member **2–001**
states of the European Community (now the European Union) used to
differ widely from each other. As part of the programme of harmonisation
intended to create a single "internal market"[1] for the EC, measures have
been adopted with the aim of removing many, but not all, of the
differences[2] between the laws of the member states. As a result, there are
now parallel systems of national and Community registered designs, but
with the essential features of the Community rights and of the national
rights in each member state being the same everywhere. In addition, there
is a Community unregistered design right, although no attempt has been

---

[1] The creation of the "internal market" was laid down a;s an objective of the Community
by the Single European Act of 1986, which inserted art.7a into the Treaty of Rome. That
has become art.26 TFEU under the amendments to the European Treaties made by the
Treaty of Lisbon which came into effect on December 1, 2009.
[2] The internal market objectives are set out in recitals (1) to (3) of the Directive and recitals
(1) to (4) of the Regulation: see App.A1 and B1 below.

made to harmonise the still widely differing national systems of protec-tion for unregistered rights.[3]

2–002   The EU harmonised law applies to UK registered designs which were applied for on and after December 9, 2001.[4] Most of the old law continues to apply to UK registrations filed before that date, whether granted before or after that date.[5] The Community registry at OHIM began accepting applications for Community designs from April 1, 2003. Unregistered Community design right attaches to designs first made available to the public within the Community or put on the market from March 6, 2002.[6]

The Directive and the Regulation

2–003   The two main EU measures which have been adopted are a Directive and a Regulation. Directive 98/71/EC on the legal protection of designs[7] requires member states to harmonise the essential features of their substantive law of registered designs. Other aspects of registered designs law, such as remedies for infringement[8] and procedure for registration,[9] are not, however, covered by the Directive and continue to be covered by differing national laws. Council Regulation (EC) No.6/2002 on Commu-nity designs[10] provides for Community registered designs and for the Community unregistered design right. Community designs are of unitary character and extend throughout all EU member states. Community registered designs are acquired by application[11] through the Office for Harmonisation in the Internal Market (Trade Marks and Design), which is located in Alicante, Spain.

---

[3] See recital (7) of the Directive. For this reason, unregistered design rights in the UK are dealt with separately in Ch.4 below.

[4] The date of coming into force of the Registered Designs Regulations 2001 (App.A3 below) which transposed the Directive into UK law. There is a possible argument that the new EU harmonised law of validity should apply to all designs filed after October 28, 2001 because that was the last possible date for Member States to implement the Directive, and the UK was in breach of Community law by failing to implement it until December 9: see *Oakley Inc v Animal Ltd* [2005] EWHC 210 Ch; [2005] R.P.C. 30, Peter Prescott Q.C. (reversed as to the main point by the Court of Appeal at [2005] EWCA Civ 1191; [2006] R.P.C. 9, see para.2–004 below). It is believed that the preliminary reference to the ECJ relating to this point suggested by the deputy judge was not pursued.

[5] The continuing law relating to pre-2002 UK registered designs is covered in Ch.3 below.

[6] The 60th day after the publication of the Regulation in the EC Official Journal, as directed by art.111(1): App.B1 below.

[7] Of October 13, 1998, [1998] O.J. L289/28; the full text of the Directive is printed in App.A1 below.

[8] See recital (5) of the Directive. However, remedies for infringement have since then been subject to a certain amount of EU harmonisation under Directive 2004/48/EC on the enforcement of intellectual property rights.

[9] See recital (6) of the Directive, App.A1 below.

[10] [2001] O.J. L3/1. The Regulation is printed at App.B1 below.

[11] For application procedure, see paras 2–143 et seq. below.

The Directive and national implementing measures

Directive 98/71/EC does not, as such, create rights and obligations as **2–004** between private businesses and individuals, such as owners of registered designs and potential infringers. This is because: "A directive shall be binding, as to the result to be achieved, upon each Member State to which it is addressed, but shall leave to the national authorities the choice of form and methods".[12] Thus, a directive has "vertical" effect, i.e. it is binding in Community law on the member state itself, but does not have "horizontal" effect, i.e. it does not bind individuals or non-State entities. In order to achieve such an effect, the provisions of the Directive need to be "transposed" into national law. In the United Kingdom, such "transposition" has been carried out by means of regulations[13] under s.2(2) of the European Communities Act 1972 which have heavily amended the Registered Designs Act 1949 in order to implement the Directive.[14] This use of regulations to make wholesale amendments to primary legislation, rather than passing a Bill through Parliament, represents part of an ever increasing trend.[15] The lawfulness of this extensive use of regulations under s.2(2) of the 1972 Act to amend the Registered Designs Act 1949, and in particular the lawfulness of the implementation by those regulations of the transitional provision in art.11(8) of the Directive permitting Member States to apply the old law of validity to designs applied for before the Directive was transposed into national law, was upheld by the Court of Appeal in *Oakley Inc v Animal Ltd*.[16]

Despite the fact that the Directive does not *as such* have horizontal **2–005** effect and directly bind anyone other than the State, it is a principle of EU

---

[12] Article 288 TFEU, formerly art.249 EC.

[13] The Registered Designs Regulations 2001 (SI 2001/3949) which are printed at App.A3 below.

[14] The Registered Designs Act 1949 as so amended is printed at App.A2 below. The Act as so amended is referred to throughout this text by the abbreviation "RDA(E)", in order to distinguish it from previous versions of the Act.

[15] During passage of the Bill which led to the European Communities Act 1972, Parliament was assured that the regulation-making powers in s.2(2) would only be used for comparatively minor matters. For example, Geoffrey Rippon in the second reading debate, HC col.282 (February 15, 1972), said: "I fully appreciate the concern of the House at any new general power to make subordinate legislation, but I should like to reassure hon. Members about the prospect. On the basis of existing Community instruments, we foresee a need for not more than four instruments under clause 2(2) in 1972 and about another 12 in 1973." He then went on to suggest that any important changes would be incorporated in "the ordinary programme of departmental legislation". And Sir G. Howe, Solicitor-General, HC col.1313 (June 13, 1972): "It is therefore sensible, in the interests of Parliament, that consequential amendments of a small, minor and insignificant kind should be capable of being effected by orders under clause 2(2)." However, it now seems clear that there is no legally binding restriction on the importance of the amendments to primary legislation that may be made under s.2(2): *Thoburn v Sunderland City Council* [2003] Q.B. 151, para.76 of the judgment.

[16] [2005] EWCA 1191; [2006] R.P.C. 9. For a discussion of the wider implications of this case and a criticism of the obiter dicta of two members of the court about the inapplicability of authorities relating to "Henry VIII" powers to s.2(2) of the 1972 Act, see Martin Howe *"Oakley Inc v Animal Ltd*: Designs create a constitutional mess": [2006] E.I.P.R. 192.

law that national legislation passed to implement a Directive should be construed, so far as possible, in accordance with the Directive concerned.[17] The interpretation of the Directive itself is a matter of EU law, and national courts may refer questions of interpretation of the Directive to the European Court when it will assist them in applying national legislation based on the Directive.[18] By this indirect route, the European Court in effect becomes the ultimate interpreter of the national legislation which implements the Directive.

2–006   The Directive contains a series of recitals which, although not part of its substantive text, seek to explain the purposes to be served by the substantive articles of the Directive and therefore may cast light on the meaning of those substantive articles. For this reason, in the text which follows, relevant recitals will be set out or referred to in connection with the substantive articles to which they relate.

The effect of the Regulation

2–007   No similar mechanism of transposition is required for Regulation (EC) No.6/2002. This is because "A regulation shall have general application. It shall be binding in its entirety and directly applicable in all Member States".[19] There is thus no need for any national implementing legislation in order for the provisions of the Regulation to have direct effect[20]: they directly create rights which can be sued upon.[21] The European Court has jurisdiction to interpret the provisions of the Regulation either on a preliminary reference where such questions arise in the course of proceedings in national courts, or on a judicial review of decisions of OHIM or of its Boards of Appeal.[22] The key provisions of the Regulation are identically worded to the corresponding provisions of the Directive and the scheme of the Directive and Regulation intends that they shall have identical effect.[23] For this reason, in the text which follows, each provision of the Directive (together with its transposed version in UK national legislation) will be considered in parallel with the corresponding provision of the Regulation.

2–008   The Council Regulation itself contains the substantive law of validity and infringement of Community designs. Some more minor matters

---

[17] Case C-106/89 *Marleasing SA v La Comercial Internacional de Alimentacion SA* [1990] E.C.R. I-4135; [1992] 1 C.M.L.R. 305, ECJ.

[18] Under the preliminary reference procedure under art.267 TFEU (formerly art.234 EC): see para.6–009 below.

[19] Article 288 TFEU, formerly art.249 EC.

[20] In the UK, this is the result of s.2(1) of the European Communities Act 1972: see the analysis in *Thoburn v Sunderland City Council* [2003] Q.B. 151.

[21] There are rules laid down within the Regulation itself as to which courts have jurisdiction over questions of infringement and validity of Community design rights: see paras 6–002 to 6–004 below.

[22] For these procedures see paras 6–009 and 2–151 below.

[23] See recital (9) of the Regulation, App.B1 below.

(principally procedures before OHIM) are dealt with in an implementing Regulation issued by the Commission under delegated powers.[24] In the United Kingdom, although national legislation is not required to give effect to the EC Council Regulation, regulations have been made under s.2(2) of the European Communities Act 1972 in order to deal with the impact of Community designs on UK registered designs: e.g. to provide that an earlier filed application for a Community registered design can count as prior art against a later filed application for a UK design,[25] and to make certain other consequential provisions relating to Community designs such as extending "threats" actions to cover threats of proceedings for infringement of a Community design.[26]

Interpretation of the new corpus of law

There is at present only limited judicial authority giving guidance on the interpretation of the Regulation, the Directive, and the corresponding national legislation, although a number of the more obscure points of interpretation have been answered by national courts if not yet by the ECJ.[27] The structure of the Regulation and the Directive is closely modelled on the earlier system relating to trade marks, which likewise has provision for harmonised national registrations[28] and Community registrations.[29] A considerable corpus of judicial decisions has grown up relating to the interpretation of the trade marks Directive and Regulation, including a number of important decisions of the ECJ. Where these relate to procedural, jurisdictional or structural matters, these authorities are probably good guidance to the interpretation of the corresponding provisions of the designs Directive and Regulation.[30] However, authorities relating to the interpretation of the substantive provisions of the

2–009

---

[24] Commission Regulation (EC) No.2245/2002 of October 21, 2002 implementing Council Regulation (EC) No.6/2002 on Community design: see App.B2 below. In addition, there is a Commission Regulation on fees in OHIM: Commission Regulation (EC) No.2246/2002, App.B3 below.

[25] The Registered Designs Regulations 2003 (SI 2003/550) printed at App.A4 below.

[26] The Community Design Regulations 2005 (SI 2005/2339) App B5 below. As to "threats" actions, see paras 7–002 et seq. below.

[27] At the date of this edition going to press, there have been two reported decisions of the General Court (formerly Court of First Instance) on the interpretation of the Regulation, Case T-9/07 *Grupo Promer Mon Graphic SA v OHIM* March 18, 2010, [2010] E.C.D.R. 7 and Case T-148/08 *Beifa Group Co. Ltd v OHIM* [2010] E.C.D.R. 9 which was an appeal from an OHIM Board of Appeal, and one by the ECJ itself on the interpretation of the ownership provisions in art.14 of the Regulation: Case C-32/08 *FEIA v Cul de Sac Espacio Creativo SL* [2009] E.C.D.R. 327; [2010] R.P.C. 13, ECJ.

[28] First Council Directive 89/104/EEC of December 21, 1988 to approximate the laws of the member states relating to trade marks ([1989] O.J. L40/1).

[29] Council Regulation (EEC) No.40/94 of December 20, 1993 on the Community trade mark ([1994] O.J. L11/1).

[30] A good example of where such carry-across of authorities seems to be clearly justified is in relation to the rules relating to parallel imports into the European Economic Area: see paras 9–007 et seq. below.

trade marks Directive and Regulation should be treated with considerably more caution, even where they appear to be dealing with
similar words or phrases, having regard to the different objects and
purposes of the legal rights involved.[31]

2–010   Clearly, previous national case law cannot be applied directly to the
interpretation of the law under the Directive and the Regulation, which is
intended to be a new harmonised European system of law not based on
any particular previously existing national law. However, it does not
follow that previous national authorities should be ignored altogether.
Elements of the new system may be seen to have roots in the previous
national laws of one or more member states, in which case previous
national authorities from those states may be particularly helpful.[32]
Alternatively, previous national authorities may throw light on points of
principle relating to the general nature of design right protection.[33]

2–011   Apart from judicial authorities, some guidance on interpretation of the
Directive and Regulation may be gained from their legislative and pre-
legislative history. This has been lengthy and tortuous, starting with a
Commission Green Paper in 1991,[34] which was followed by a series of
formal Commission proposals for these measures which are accompanied
by explanatory memoranda discussing many of the changes made from
draft to draft.[35] The Green Paper is particularly useful in discussing some
of the concepts which were intended, at least by the Commission, to
underlie some of the broadly or vaguely defined terms in the substantive
legislation.[36] However some care should be taken in assuming that the
Green Paper is necessarily an accurate guide to how the legislation will be
interpreted. First, there have been very considerable changes in drafting
between the preliminary drafts attached to the Green Paper and the final
versions of the Directive and the Regulation. Secondly, the courts will not
necessarily accept that the Commission's words, like the words of

---

[31] The purpose of a trade mark right is to serve as an indication of the trade origin of goods
or services to which it is applied; for the nature of design right, see paras 2–009 et seq.
below. The fact that trade marks and designs have different objects and purposes led to
the English Court of Appeal deciding (probably incorrectly) that the exclusion from
protection of designs dictated by function is of much narrower scope than the
corresponding exclusion in the Trade Marks Directive: see para.2–028 below.

[32] A clear example of this approach from the field of patents can be seen in *Pioneer
Electronics v Warner Music Manufacturing* [1997] R.P.C. 757 (CA), where the English courts
interpreted the concept of direct product of a process in art.64(2) of the European Patents
Convention by reference to German, Austrian and Swiss authorities since those countries
had had almost identical phraseology in their patent laws since the 19th century.

[33] e.g. the distinction between functional and non-functional features: see para.2–028
below.

[34] Green Paper on the Legal Protection of Industrial Design, EC Commission Working
Document, 111/F/5131/91-EN, June 1991. The Green Paper annexed preliminary draft
proposals for the Regulation and the Directive.

[35] Directive proposal and amended proposal: [1993] O.J. C345/1 and [1996] O.J. C142/7;
Regulation proposal and amended proposal: [1994] C29, 31/20 and [2000] C248/3.

[36] For example, it discusses boundaries between "products" (protected by design right) and
e.g. "interior design" (considered not to be protected): see para.2–010 below.

Humpty-Dumpty, mean exactly what the Commission intends them to mean.

Relationship with other rights

In general, the rights conferred by registered designs can overlap with other forms of protection such as unregistered design rights and copyrights. In the history of UK registered designs law, there have been periods of time when the legislative policy was to seek to prevent overlap between registered design rights and copyrights.[37] No such legislative policy exists under the EU harmonised law, and indeed art.16 of the Directive provides: **2–012**

> "The provisions of this Directive shall be without prejudice to any provisions of Community law or of the law of the Member State concerned relating to unregistered design rights, trade marks or other distinctive signs, patents and utility models, typefaces, civil liability or unfair competition."

In the United Kingdom, unregistered design protection continues to exist and is unaffected by the Directive.[38]

Relationship with copyright protection

In respect of copyright, the Directive seems to goes further than in relation to other rights. Article 17 provides: **2–013**

> "A design protected by a design right registered in or in respect of a Member State in accordance with this Directive shall also be eligible for protection under the law of copyright of that State as from the date on which the design was created or fixed in any form. The extent to which, and the conditions under which, such a protection is conferred, including the level of originality required, shall be determined by each Member State."

One reading of this provision is that any subject matter which is protectable as a design should also, at least in principle, be protectable under copyright law and the member states should amend their laws to achieve this result. However, recital (8) sets out the rationale of this provision as follows: **2–014**

> "Whereas, in the absence of harmonisation of copyright law, it is important to establish the principle of cumulation of protection

[37] See para.1–032 above.
[38] See Ch.4 below.

29

under specific registered design protection law and under copyright law, whilst leaving member states free to establish the extent of copyright protection and the conditions under which such protection is conferred;"

2–015   Thus, it appears that member states are not required to extend copyright law to cover anything which is protectable as a design if their copyright law does not extend that far; however, member states are no longer permitted to introduce a provision similar to that of s.10 of the Copyright Act 1956 before it was amended by the Design Copyright Act 1968, which specifically restricted the copyright in an artistic work when a "corresponding design" was registered.[39] If this interpretation is correct, it is still permissible for the United Kingdom to exclude three-dimensional shape designs from effective copyright protection.[40]

2. What is a Protectable Design?

Requirements for protection

2–016   In order to be protectable (whether as a registered UK national or Community design, or as a Community unregistered design), it is necessary for a design to satisfy the following requirements:

(1) it complies with the definition of "design";
(2) it relates to a "product";
(3) it does not relate to features which are dictated by function;
(4) it is new;
(5) it has "individual character"; and
(6) it is not contrary to public policy or morality.

Apart from these basic requirements relating to designs generally, there are special rules relating to designs for parts of so-called "complex products", and an exclusion from protection of design features needed to interconnect with other parts of products (a "must fit" exception). These requirements will be dealt with successively in the paragraphs following. There are also some other miscellaneous grounds[41] upon which registered designs can be invalidated[42] after grant, and upon which Community unregistered designs can be invalidated.

---

[39] See paras 1–044—1–054 above.
[40] The effect of s.51 CDPA 1988 is to exclude the reproduction of artistic works in the form of three-dimensional industrial articles from the scope of copyright protection; instead, such acts will generally infringe UK unregistered design right which has a much shorter term of protection and is not available to nationals of many countries which do not confer design right protection on British nationals: see paras 5–059—5–063 below.
[41] See paras 2–046 and 2–047 below.
[42] Applications for Community registered designs are subjected to formal examination

Definition of "design": essence is the *appearance* of a product

Article 1(a) of the Directive defines "design" as follows: 2–017

> "'design' means the appearance of the whole or a part of a product resulting from the features of, in particular, the lines, contours, colours, shape, texture and/or materials of the product itself and/or its ornamentation."

This definition has been transposed word for word into RDA(E) s.2(2), and the same definition is contained in the Regulation in art.3(a). The same basic definition of "design" thus applies to UK registered designs, to Community registered designs and to Community unregistered designs.

This makes clear that the essence of design protection is the protection   2–018
of the *appearance* of a product. The concern of design protection with appearance is emphasised by recital (10) of the Directive, which reads:

> "Whereas protection is conferred by way of registration upon the right holder for those design features of a product, in whole or in part, which are shown visibly in an application and made available to the public by way of publication or consultation of the relevant file."

Function as such is not protected, and indeed there is a specific   2–019
exclusion from protection of features which are dictated by function (see para.2–025 below). As the definition makes clear, protection of appearance extends both to the shape of the product and to surface decoration or ornamentation, and indeed to features which are on the borderline between shape and surface decoration such as "texture".[43] Protection also

---

only, so most grounds of invalidity only arise if a third party takes proceedings to invalidate the registered design after grant. In the UK, the former practice of substantive examination has been abandoned to bring the UK Registry practice into line: see para.2–130 below.

[43] The Green Paper even appears to suggest that the "touch" of a texture can be part of the "appearance" of a product: para.5.4.7.2. A more orthodox interpretation of the words used in the substantive provisions would suggest that "texture" in only part of a "design" to the extent that texture can be seen. There does not seem to be room in the context of designs for the registration of noises or smells, both of which it seems can in principle be registered as trade marks subject to the formal requirement that they must be capable of being represented graphically with sufficient precision and certainty: Case C-283/01 *Shield Mark BV v Joost Kist hodn Memex* [2004] R.P.C. 315, ECJ: noise of cock-crow registrable as trade mark if represented in musical notation; Case C-273/00 *Sieckmann v Deutsches Patent und Marken Amt* [2003] R.P.C. 685, ECJ: trade mark alleged to consist of a distinctive smell not capable of registration because it could not satisfactorily be represented in graphical form by a chemical formula (of methyl cinnamate), by a description in written words, or by deposit of an odour sample.

extends to the materials of which a product or part of a product is made, insofar as these are reflected in its appearance.[44]

What is a "product"?

2–020   What constitutes a product is defined by art.1(b) of the Directive as follows:

> "(b) 'product' means any industrial or handicraft item, including inter alia parts intended to be assembled into a complex product,[45] packaging, get-up, graphic symbols and typographic typefaces, but excluding computer programs."

This definition is transposed into RDA(E) s.1(1)(3) with some rearrangement of the order of the subclauses in the definition,[46] presumably intended to make clear that the exclusion of computer programs applies across the board and not just to graphic symbols and typefaces. Whether this alteration of wording will lead to any difference of interpretation in the United Kingdom is doubtful, having regard to the principle of EU law that national legislation which gives effect to directives should be interpreted in accordance with the directive concerned.[47] In the Regulation, art.3(b) defines "product" in identical words to art.1(b) of the Directive.

2–021   It is important to realise that, whilst a design at its inception relates to a product, the scope of protection is not limited to that product or even similar products but extends to any product in which the design is used. In this respect, the new law represents a radical departure from the old UK registered design law where a design had to be registered in respect of a specific type of article, and infringement could only take place through the application of the design to that type of article.[48] Thus, although an application for a Community registered design is required to indicate the products in which the design is intended to be incorporated or to which it is to be applied,[49] and to specify the class of those products

---

[44] e.g. glass or marble or brushed metal have a distinctive appearance which is more than can be described simply in terms of colour. If the Commission's thought in the Green Paper (Green Paper on the Legal Protection of Industrial Design, EC Commission Working Document, 111/F/5131/91-EN, June 1991) is correct that "appearance" can include matters which are perceived by touch rather than sight, then e.g. the softness or hardness of materials would count as part of the "design".

[45] "Complex products" are considered in para.2–051 below.

[46] See App.A2, para.A2–001 below.

[47] See para.2–005 above.

[48] See paras 3–181—3–183 below.

[49] Regulation art.36(2).

under the Locarno Convention,[50] those indications do not affect the scope of protection of the design.[51]

The definition of "product" is broadly worded. Whilst in many cases **2–022** there will be no difficulty in saying whether a particular article is an "industrial or handicraft item", there are some areas where the borderline is not clear, and where there has been some difficulty deciding under the previous law whether or not something is an "article" for the purposes of registered design law. Whether something is an article on the one hand or a building or structure on the other has been a cause of some difficulty.[52] The Green Paper appears to assume that buildings and structures and similar things are not "products" since it suggests that "interior decoration" and "landscape architecture" are appropriately protected under copyright laws rather than by the design right.[53] However, it goes on to suggest that there are grey areas, and that, for example, a kitchen consisting of units, etc. should be protectable under design law.[54] If this general approach is correct, it may be that the new design law will adopt an approach not dissimilar to that adopted by the old UK registered design law, where a distinction was drawn between objects which were delivered to the customer in finished form (which were industrial "articles"), and structures and the like which had to be built on site.[55]

A greater area of difficulty has been the exclusion from registration of **2–023** articles which have no existence apart from carrying the design itself,[56] and articles of a "primarily literary or artistic character".[57] There is no

---

[50] Regulation art.1(3)(d). The Locarno Convention classification is at App.F4, paras F4–016 et seq. below.

[51] Regulation art.36(6). It appears however that the type of product to which the design relates, gathered either from the indication on the application or from the characteristics of the design itself, may affect who is to be regarded as the informed user and what degree of design freedom they will regard the designer as having; this in turn may indirectly affect the scope of protection (as well as validity): see para.2–038 below and *Case T-9/07 Grupo Promer Mon Graphic SA v OHIM* March 18, 2010 [2010] E.C.D.R. 7.

[52] See paras 3–036—3–037 below, for discussion of this subject under the previous UK law. Pre-formed poultry and animal sheds were considered to be articles in respect of which designs could be registered, but a design for an air raid shelter was refused registration, the distinction drawn being that the air raid shelter was to be built on site but the animal sheds were for delivery to the customer in their finished state.

[53] Paragraph 5.4.14.1.

[54] Paragraph 5.4.14.2: "The Commission is aware that there are a number of cases which constitute a grey zone, where it is difficult to say whether the support of the design [sic: means the thing to which the design is applied] is a "product" in the traditional sense or something different. For instance, a kitchen designed by using a number of elements (cupboards, chairs, table, refrigerator, washing machine, gas-stove and sink) combined together to form a pleasant, new and unitary set could be considered both as an example of interior decoration or as a complex product. It seems to the Commission that protection under a Community design in such cases should be possible."

[55] See para.3–037 below.

[56] e.g. watercolour paintings on paper, and oil paintings on canvas: it was not accepted that the paper or canvas would count as an "article" to which a design had been applied: see paras 3–028—3–032 below.

[57] See paras 3–033—3–035 below. Such items were excluded from registrability by rules made under s.1(5) of RDA 1949. Thus, items such as book jackets, calendars, dress making patterns, greeting cards, playing cards, etc. were excluded from registration.

corresponding explicit exclusion in the new law, but presumably some similar exclusion is implicit in the words "industrial or handicraft" item, and the boundaries of that exclusion will need to be worked out in Office and judicial decisions. Article 36(2) of the Regulation requires an applicant for a Community design to indicate "the products in which the design is intended to be incorporated or to which it is intended to be applied". This suggests that there must be some actual product or intended product to carry the design which has an existence and purpose, apart from merely carrying or embodying the design itself. The Green Paper refers to the "industrial character of design" and suggests that "design" is the appearance which can be given to a product by using some technical device in accordance with industrial proceedings.[58] If some form of "industrial process" (in its extended form as extending to hand-crafted items) is indeed implicit in the definitions of "design" and of "product", then the end result may be not dissimilar to the exclusion under the old UK law from registrability of "articles" which consist of, or which merely serve to carry, the design itself.[59]

2–024   The inclusion of graphic symbols and typographic typefaces in the definition of "product" is something of an anomaly and can only be explained by an anomaly of history. Under present day technology, symbols and typefaces are intangible shapes generally held in computer or electronic memory, which are then rastered out onto printing plates or onto paper or screens as required. It might therefore be thought that such shapes are appropriately within the field of copyright protection, rather than industrial design protection.[60] However, historically, typefaces were made and produced in the form of metal type pieces or moulds for setting type, and the design of the typefaces could be registered in respect of such physical articles. The specific inclusion of graphic symbols and typefaces in the definition of "product" can therefore be regarded as reflecting a policy decision to continue to allow the protection of these items under designs law, despite the changes in technology which have taken place. However, whilst "industrial and handicraft items" in general would appear to be actual physical objects, symbols and typefaces on the face of

---

[58] "5.4.12. The Industrial Character of Design. 5.4.12.1. A 'design' is the appearance which can be given to a product by using some technical device in accordance with industrial proceedings. For the purposes of this Green Paper the 'Industrial' character of design will be understood to cover also 'craftmanship' [sic], where the same prototype is reproduced by hand, inevitably with small variations in the shape of the various products. For this reason the Commission prefers to use the word 'product' without qualifying it by the adjective 'industrial', as do many legislations."

[59] The logic of this line of reasoning would suggest that the "design" of a sculpture would not be protectable under the new design law, because there must be an underlying product to which the design is attached. Sculptures are covered by copyright. Sculptures were excluded from protection under the old UK registered designs law, although apparently by virtue of the specific statutory exclusion of articles of primarily literary or artistic character rather than on the more fundamental ground that they had no existence apart from the design itself: see para.3–035 below.

[60] There is indeed overlapping protection under copyright law: note the exclusion of typefaces from s.51(1) CDPA 1988, discussed at para.5–059 below.

it are intangible shapes which exist independently of a physical printing plate or piece of paper or computer screen on which they appear.[61] It is, therefore, fairly anomalous to define them as "products".

Exclusion of features which are dictated by technical function

Article 7(1) of the Directive provides that: **2–025**

> "A design right shall not subsist in features of appearance of a product which are solely dictated by its technical function."

This provision has been transposed in almost identical words into   **2–026** s.1C(1) of RDA(E).[62] Article 8(1) of the Regulation is identical to art.7(1) of the Directive.[63] Further elucidation of this provision is given by recital (14) of the Directive[64]:

> "Whereas technological innovation should not be hampered by granting design protection to features dictated solely by a technical function; whereas it is understood that this does not entail that a design must have an aesthetic quality; . . . whereas features of a design which are excluded from protection for these reasons should not be taken into consideration for the purpose of assessing whether other features of the design fulfil the requirements for protection."

The wording employed, "solely dictated by its technical function", is   **2–027** virtually identical to the wording used in the old UK law in RDA 1949 s.1(1)(b)(i)[65]: "are dictated solely by the function which the article has to perform". These words contained an ambiguity. If a wholly functional article can be made in a variety of shapes, can it be said that no specific choice of shape is "dictated" by the article's function, and therefore that no such specific choice of shape is excluded from protection because other functional alternatives are available? Such an interpretation was rejected by the House of Lords in *Amp Inc v Utilux Pty Ltd*,[66] which held that "dictated solely by function" meant "attributable to or caused or prompted by function": where a shape is adopted by a designer upon the sole requirement of functional ends, i.e. to make the article work and not to appeal to the eye, then it is excluded from protection. Thus, in relation to the electrical terminals in that case, the fact "that other shapes of terminals might also be dictated by the function to be performed by them

---

[61] So, in a typographical design case, the prior art "Frutiger" typeface was distributed on CD-ROMs: see *Microsoft Corp's Design* [2006] E.C.D.R. 29, OHIM Invalidity Division.
[62] See App.A2, para.A2–004 below.
[63] See App.B1 below.
[64] Recital (10) of the Regulation is substantially identical: see App.B1 below.
[65] See App.A5, para.A5–001 below.
[66] [1972] R.P.C. 103.

will not alter the fact that the shape of Amp's terminals was dictated only by functional considerations . . . "[67]

2–028   The English Court of Appeal however has held that the phrase as used in the Directive and Regulation is to be interpreted differently from the corresponding phrase in the old UK national law as interpreted by the House of Lords in *Amp v Utilux*,[68] and that this phrase only operates to exclude where the technical function dictates that that shape and no other may be used.[69] The Court of Appeal declined to follow in the context of designs the interpretation placed by the ECJ on the phrase "the shape of goods which is necessary to obtain a technical result" in art.3(1)(e) of the Trade Marks Directive.[70] In this regard it appears that the English Court of Appeal may have fallen into error by attempting to be "more European than the Europeans", because the OHIM Third Board of Appeal has subsequently rejected the Court of Appeal's approach in *Landor & Hawa* and preferred the earlier UK approach in *Amp v Utilux* as representing the correct interpretation of the exclusion in the Regulation and the Directive.[71] This conflict of view between the English Court of Appeal and the OHIM Board of appeal will need to be resolved by a decision of the ECJ, either upon a preliminary reference from a national court or on an appeal to the ECJ from an OHIM Board of Appeal. The Board of Appeal extensively surveyed the differing national approaches to the issue of technical function under pre-harmonised national laws, and went on to reason as follows:

> "29 The multiplicity-of-forms theory has been adopted by courts in the United Kingdom (see the judgment of the Court of Appeal in *Landor & Hawa International Ltd v Azure Designs Ltd* [2006] EWCA Civ 1285) and Spain (Juzgado de lo Mercantil PTO Número Uno de Alicante, Auto No 267/07, 20 November 2007, in *Silverlit Toys Manufactory Ltd v Ditro Ocio 2000 SL and others.*
>
> 30 There is nonetheless a major flaw in the multiplicity-of-forms theory. If it is accepted that a feature of a product's appearance is not 'solely dictated by its function' simply because an alternative product configuration could achieve the same function, Article 8(1) CDR will apply only in highly exceptional circumstances and its very purpose will be in danger of being frustrated. That purpose, as was

---

[67] [1972] R.P.C. 103 per Lord Morris at 115. The case is more fully analysed at paras 3–054—3–060 below.

[68] *Landor & Hawa Intnl Ltd v Azure Designs Ltd* [2006] EWCA Civ 1285; [2007] F.S.R. 9; [2006] E.C.D.R. 413, CA at para.39; it is not apparent from the report that the Court of Appeal was addressed with any argument to the effect that the phrase as it appears in the Directive and Regulation was drawn from pre-existing UK national law and accordingly the *Amp v Utilux* interpretation might still be relevant from that perspective: see para.2–010 above.

[69] *Landor & Hawa Intnl Ltd v Azure Designs Ltd* [2006] EWCA Civ 1285; [2007] F.S.R. 9; [2006] E.C.D.R. 413, CA, at paras 31–38 and 62.

[70] Directive 89/104/EEC.

[71] *Lindner Recyclingtech GmbH v Franssons Verkstader AB* (R690/2007–3) [2010] E.C.D.R. 1.

noted above, is to prevent design law from being used to achieve monopolies over technical solutions, the assumption being that such monopolies are only justified if the more restrictive conditions imposed by patent law (and in some countries by the law of utility models) are complied with. If a technical solution can be achieved by two alternative methods, neither solution is, according to the multiplicity-of-forms theory, solely dictated by the function of the product in question. This would mean that both solutions could be the subject of a design registration, possibly held by the same person, which would have the consequence that no one else would be able to manufacture a competing product capable of performing the same technical function (see W. Cornish and D. Llewelyn, *Intellectual Property: Patents, Copyright, Trade Marks and Allied Rights* (5th edition, London, Sweet & Maxwell 2003) at p.549). This leads to the conclusion that the multiplicity-of-forms theory cannot be correct.

31 The principal alternative, discussed by academic authors, to the multiplicity-of forms theory has its origin in English case law. The case of *Amp v Utilux* [1971] FR 572 concerned the interpretation of a provision of the Registered Designs Act 1949 which denied protection to the features of a design that were solely dictated by a product's technical function. The House of Lords held that a product's configuration was solely dictated by its technical function if every feature of the design was determined by technical considerations. The striking similarity between section 1(3) of the 1949 Act and Article 8(1) CDR does not of course mean that the approach of the House of Lords in *Amp v Utilux* must necessarily be adopted in relation to the Community provision. Indeed, as was noted above in paragraph 29, the multiplicity-of-forms theory has now been adopted by the English Court of Appeal in *Landor & Hawa International v Azure Designs*. Thus the Court of Appeal must have thought that the approach taken in *Amp v Utilux* was no longer valid, following harmonization, in spite of the similar wording of the Community provisions and the 1949 Act. The approach taken in *Amp v Utilux* would, however, have the advantage of allowing the purpose of Article 8(1) CDR to be achieved. No one would be able to shut out competitors by registering as Community designs the handful of possible configurations that would allow the technical function to be realised. This may explain why the French courts, which formerly espoused the multiplicity-of-forms theory, began to abandon that theory at the beginning of the 21st century in favour of an interpretation which closely resembles the *Amp v Utilux* approach (see the judgments cited by Cohen, op. cit., at pp.23–24).

32 In addition to being supported by a teleological interpretation, the approach discussed in the previous paragraph is also supported by the wording of Article 8(1) CDR. That provision denies protection to features of a product's appearance that are 'solely dictated by its

technical function'. Those words do not, on their natural meaning, imply that the feature in question must be the only means by which the product's technical function can be achieved. On the contrary, they imply that the need to achieve the product's technical function was the only relevant factor when the feature in question was selected.

33 Good design involves two fundamental elements: the product must perform its function and it should be pleasant to look at. In the case of some products, such as pictures and ornaments, their very function is to please the eye. In the case of other products, such as the internal working parts of a machine, the visual appearance is irrelevant. That is why the Community design legislation denies protection to component parts that are not visible in normal use. In the case of most products the designer will be concerned with both the functional and the aesthetic elements. That applies also to large items of industrial equipment, such as shredders for use in recycling plants. The shredder must, in the first place, perform its function effectively and safely and without creating excessive noise, but it is also desirable that the shredder should be pleasing to the eye and thus enhance the working environment of the people who operate it and see it in use. For that reason there is no objection in principle to granting design protection to industrial products whose overall appearance is determined largely, <u>but not exclusively,</u> by functional considerations."

2–029   In *Philips v Remington*,[72] the national court (the English Court of Appeal), had asked:

"whether Article 3(1)(e), second indent, of the [Trade Marks] Directive must be interpreted to mean that a sign consisting exclusively of the shape of a product is unregistrable by virtue of that provision if it is established that the essential functional features of the shape are attributable only to the technical result. It also seeks to know whether the ground for refusal or invalidity of the registration imposed by that provision can be overcome by establishing that there are other shapes which can obtain the same technical result."[73]

The ECJ answered that:

"The rationale of the grounds for refusal of registration laid down in Article 3(1)(e) of the Directive is to prevent trade mark protection

---

[72] Case C-299/99 *Koninklijke Philips Electronics NV v Remington Consumer Products Ltd* [2003] R.P.C. p.14.

[73] This question is very similar to the question which was before the House of Lords in *Amp v Utilux*, and the parties' respective arguments as set out in paras 67 and 68 of the ECJ's judgment closely echo the arguments of the parties in *Amp v Utilux*.

from granting its proprietor a monopoly on technical solutions or functional characteristics of a product which a user is likely to seek in the products of competitors . . .

79 . . . that provision is intended to preclude the registration of shapes whose essential characteristics perform a technical function, with the result that the exclusivity inherent in the trade mark right would limit the possibility of competitors supplying a product incorporating such a function or at least limit their freedom of choice in regard to the technical solution they wish to adopt in order to incorporate such a function in their product."

It concluded at para.83:

"Where the essential functional characteristics of the shape of a product are attributable solely to the technical result, Article 3(1)(e), second indent, precludes registration of a sign consisting of that shape, even if that technical result can be achieved by other shapes."

However, in his Opinion Advocate-General Colomer suggested[74] that there is a difference in wording between the Trade Marks Directive and the Designs Directive which might lead to a different result, and this passage in the Opinion led the Court of Appeal in *Landor*[75] not to apply the ECJ's reasoning in the trade mark case to designs. With respect, the Court of Appeal appears to have given excessive weight to an observation by Advocate-General Colomer which, as pointed out by the OHIM Board of Appeal,[76] was clearly an obiter dictum, and further is inherently unconvincing in seeking to suggest that there is any real difference in the wording between the exclusions in the trade marks and designs directives and regulations. Further, the respective exclusions of functional features from protection in the Trade Marks and the Designs Directives appear to be intended to achieve a similar purpose of preventing the hampering of technical innovation, judged by recital (14) of the Designs Directive, as quoted above. If there is to be a difference in interpretation of this provision as compared with the corresponding trade mark exclusion, it must presumably lie in it being somehow less objectionable to monopolise one of a number of possible technical solutions under designs law as compared with trade mark law, but it is difficult to think

2–030

---

[74] A-G's Opinion at para.34.
[75] *Landor & Hawa Intnl Ltd v Azure Designs Ltd* [2006] EWCA Civ 1285; [2007] F.S.R. 9; [2006] E.C.D.R. 413, CA, paras 36–37; see also *Bailey (t/a Elite Anglian Products) v Haynes* [2007] F.S.R. 10, PCC at paras 70–73.
[76] In *Lindner Recyclingtech GmbH v Franssons Verkstader AB* (R690/2007–3) [2010] E.C.D.R. 1 at para.28.

of a convincing policy reason for such a difference.[77] Under the TRIPS Agreement art.25(1),[78] member states are entitled to deny protection to "designs dictated essentially by technical or functional considerations", a phrase clearly based on a wider *Amp v Utilux* type approach, so that a wider reading of the exclusion in art.7(1) of the Directive would be consistent with the international obligations of the EU and its members. Notwithstanding the decision of the English Court of Appeal in *Landor*, it would appear that this is a point which merits the attention of the ECJ on a preliminary reference.

Design must be new

2–031   Article 3(2) of the Directive provides that:

> "A design shall be protected by a design right to the extent that it is new and has individual character."

This provision is transposed in substantially identical words into s.1B(1) of RDA(E). Article 4(1) of the Regulation is substantially identical. The requirement of novelty is further expanded in art.4 of the Directive, which reads:

> "A design shall be considered new if no identical design has been made available to the public before the date of filing of the application for registration or, if priority is claimed, the date of priority. Designs shall be deemed to be identical if their features differ only in immaterial details."

This provision is transposed into RDA(E) s.1B(2) in wording which has been rearranged but seems to have identical effect.[79] The question of what is the relevant date, and what counts as having been "made available to the public", so as to count as prior art for this purpose, is expanded on in a later section of this chapter.[80] Article 5 of the Regulation is of identical effect insofar as it relates to Community registered designs.

2–032   Obviously, unregistered designs do not have application dates or priority dates and, in respect of those, art.5(1) of the Regulation provides:

---

[77] One possible reason is that design law is limited in term but trade mark law provides perpetual protection, so long as the mark stays in use and is renewed. However, the 25-year term of a registered design is lengthy and effective protection of one of a number of possible technical solutions would be obtained without reference to the merit or inventiveness of the technical solution concerned: the protection would arise simply from being different in appearance (overall impression) from what has gone before.
[78] See App.F2, para.F2–012 below.
[79] See App.A2, para.A2–003 below.
[80] Paragraphs 2–057 et seq. below.

"A design shall be considered to be new if no identical design has been made available to the public:

(a) in the case of an unregistered Community design, before the date on which the design for which protection is claimed has first been made available to the public".

The requirement of novelty applies to Community unregistered designs as well as to registered designs. It is important to note that the requirement of novelty is different from the requirement of *originality*, which applies to UK unregistered designs[81] and to copyright.[82] Something may be original even if it is identical, or very similar to, a piece of prior art, so long as its author has created it independently and has not copied from the prior art concerned. However, a later design, even if original in that sense, may be deprived of novelty by an earlier design, regardless of whether it played any part in the later designer's design process or whether he was even aware of its existence. In this respect, Community unregistered design right may be "knocked out" in circumstances where it is perfectly possible to rely on UK unregistered design right or copyright.

Differing only in "immaterial details"

This phrase is familiar since it is substantially the same as s.1(4) of RDA   2–033
1949—indeed, it may well have been in effect copied into the Directive and Regulation from the old UK law. There is a considerable amount of judicial exposition of this phrase in UK law, which is considered in the next chapter in the context of old registered designs law.[83] In essence, one asks whether the two designs are substantially similar in appearance, considering the designs not only side by side but also apart, and a little distance away.[84] It may be that the test in the Directive and Regulation is a stricter test than that prevailing under the old UK law, the reason being that under the EU law there is the additional requirement for protection that a design should have "individual character", considered in the next paragraph. It is, therefore, not so necessary as under the old law to give a wide meaning to what counts as "immaterial details" in order to deprive a meritless and barely novel design of protection. It has been held that the assessment of novelty, i.e. the assessment of whether a design differs from prior art only in "immaterial" details, is not to be carried out through the eye of the "informed user",[85] unlike the assessment of

---

[81] See paras 4–042—4–044 below.
[82] See paras 5–037—5–042 below.
[83] See paras 3–151—3–153 below.
[84] See para.3–152 below, and, in particular n.12.
[85] *Normann Copehagen APS v Paton Calvert Housewares Ltd* [2010] E.C.D.R. 3, OHIM Third Board of Appeal.

"individual character."[86] But whilst the Directive and Regulation do not explicitly state that the "informed user" is to play a part in this exercise, it would be surprising if an exercise of judgement deciding whether or not difference of detail are "immaterial" is to be carried out by any other person, and the correctness of this proposition must be doubted.

"Individual character"

2–034   The requirement that a design should have "individual character" is additional to the requirement that it should merely be new. The provisions imposing the requirements of novelty and individual character are set out in para.2–031 above; however, the requirement of "individual character" is further defined in art.5 of the Directive:

> "1. A design shall be considered to have individual character if the overall impression it produces on the informed user differs from the overall impression produced on such a user by any design which has been made available to the public before the date of filing of the application for registration or, if priority is claimed, the date of priority.
>   2. In assessing individual character, the degree of freedom of the designer in developing the design shall be taken into consideration."

2–035   Article 5(1) is transposed in identical wording into s.1B(3) RDA(E), and art.5(2) is transposed into s.1B(4).[87] Article 6 of the Regulation is in identical terms, save that it refers to the date when the design was first made available to the public in the case of Community unregistered designs.[88] In addition to these substantive provisions, recital (13) of the Directive (to which recital (14) of the Regulation is effectively identical) states:

> "Whereas the assessment as to whether a design has individual character should be based on whether the overall impression produced on an informed user viewing the design clearly differs from that produced on him by the existing design corpus, taking into consideration the nature of the product to which the design is applied or in which it is incorporated, and in particular the industrial sector to which it belongs and the degree of freedom of the designer in developing the design."

---

[86] As to which, see para.2–034 below.
[87] Save that the designer is referred to as the "author", in conformity with the terminology used elsewhere in the Act.
[88] See App.B1, para.B1–007 below.

The requirement of "individual character" focusses more on overall   2–036
impression rather than on details. Thus, detailed differences will not be
enough to give validity to a new design if it produces the same overall
impression as an earlier design.

The old UK registered design law required that a design should be new,   2–037
which meant that it should differ from any earlier design in more than
immaterial details[89] or in features which are variants commonly used in
trade.[90] As noted above, the "immaterial details" provision also forms
part of the test of novelty under the EU harmonised law. The "trade
variants" provision has gone, but has been replaced with the new
requirement of "individual character". It would appear that in most
cases, the new law will impose a higher threshold before protection can
validly be claimed through the imposition of the new requirement that
the design should possess "individual character", i.e. that it should
produce a different overall impression on the informed user from any
prior design. This will not always be the case. There may be cases where
the substitution of one common trade variant for another in one feature
of the prior design does produce a substantial difference in overall
impression. In such a case, the new design will be protectable under the
EU harmonised law, but would not have been protectable under the old
UK registered designs law.

Assessing the difference in overall impression

The substantive provisions state that the degree of freedom of the   2–038
designer shall be taken into account in assessing whether a design
possesses individual character. This presumably means that where a
designer's freedom is highly constrained by the nature of the product,
smaller differences will be sufficient to confer "individual character" than
would be the case if the designer had more freedom to make variations.[91]
In order to work out what is the designer's degree of freedom, it may be
necessary to identify what type of product the design relates to, since the
nature of the product might impose particular constraints on the designer's freedom. The General Court has held[92]:

"56. Accordingly, it follows from Article 36(6) of Regulation No
6/2002 that, in order to ascertain the product in which the contested
design is intended to be incorporated or to which it is intended to be

---

[89] See para.3–151 below.
[90] See para.3–154 below.
[91] *Procter & Gamble Co v Reckitt Benckiser* (UK) Ltd [2007] EWCA Civ 936; [2008] F.S.R. 8, CA
at paras 29–30. The same approach would also apply when assessing the difference in
overall impression in the context of infringement: see para.2–097 below.
[92] Case T-9/07 *Grupo Promer Mon Graphic SA v OHIM* [2010] E.C.D.R. 7, March 18, 2010.

applied, the relevant indication in the application for registration of that design should be taken into account, but also, where necessary, the design itself, in so far as it makes clear the nature of the product, its intended purpose or its function. Taking into account the design itself may enable the product to be placed within a broader category of goods indicated at the time of registration and, therefore, to determine the informed user and the degree of freedom of the designer in developing his design."

2–039   The court went on to reason that the severe design constraints which applied to the particular sub-category of products[93] to which the design related meant that comparatively smaller differences might suffice to produce a different overall impression, although on the facts of that case, even taking into account that factor, the differences were not sufficient to give rise to a different overall impression.[94]

2–040   In addition to the designer's freedom, the recitals quoted above (but not the substantive provisions) mention two further factors to be taken into account in assessing whether there is a difference in overall impression. One is the product to which the design is applied, and the other is the industrial sector to which the design belongs. It is not clear whether these factors would affect the assessment by widening it or narrowing it. Further, these recitals appear to assume that a design is being compared with one applied to a product of the same type within the same industrial sector, and it is not clear how the assessment will be affected if a design applied to a product of one type is compared with a design applied to a product of a different type in a different industry.[95]

Evidence relating to assessment of overall impression

2–041   What evidence, if any, should be adduced before the court or tribunal considering the question on the issue of whether or not the overall impression produced by one product differs from that of another? This is a procedural matter and will depend upon the rules of evidence of the court or tribunal which is carrying out the assessment. However, even in the case of the English court system, with its heavy reliance on the oral evidence of witnesses and its willingness to entertain live evidence from

[93] Case T-9/07 *Grupo Promer Mon Graphic SA v OHIM* [2010] E.C.D.R. 7, March 18, 2010, paras 66–70: "rappers" within the broader category of promotional items for games.
[94] Case T-9/07 *Grupo Promer Mon Graphic SA v OHIM* [2010] E.C.D.R. 7, March 18, 2010, paras 71–85.
[95] *Procter & Gamble Co v Reckitt Benckiser (UK) Ltd* [2007] EWCA Civ 936; [2008] F.S.R. 8, CA at para.21; the Court of Appeal observed that in such a case there may be difficulty in identifying the attributes of the informed user, but did not find it necessary to express a view in order to deal with the case in front of it.

expert witnesses instructed by the parties, the Court of Appeal has said that the place for evidence on this question is "very limited indeed"[96]:

> "By and large it should be possible to decide a registered design case in a few hours. The evidence of the designer, e.g. as to whether he/she was trying to make, or thought he/she had made, a break-through, is irrelevant. The evidence of experts, particularly about consumer products, is unlikely to be of much assistance: anyone can point out similarities and differences, though an educated eye can sometimes help a bit. Sometimes there may be a piece of technical evidence which is relevant—e.g. that design freedom is limited by certain constraints. But even so, that is usually more or less self-evident and certainly unlikely to be controversial to the point of a need for cross-examination still less substantial cross-examination."

This is consistent with the courts' approach to evidence under the pre-2001 registered design law. Evidence from an "expert" witness on the subject of how an ordinary consumer will perceive ordinary consumer goods is unlikely ever to be useful[97]; and the courts will use their increased powers under the Civil Procedure Rules to prevent the admission of non-useful expert evidence of this character.[98] Because the role of evidence in the assessment of overall impression is so limited, it may in an appropriate case be made the subject of a successful summary judgment application.[99] There are however other issues, such as on whether or not something forms part of the design corpus deemed to be known to the informed user[100], where expert evidence is admissible and potentially useful.[101] However, disclosure will not normally be ordered

2–042

---

[96] *Procter & Gamble Co v Reckitt Benckiser (UK) Ltd* [2007] EWCA Civ 936; [2008] F.S.R. 8, CA, para.4.

[97] *Isaac Oren v Red Box Toy Factory Ltd* [1999] F.S.R. 785, Jacob J., at 791.

[98] *Thermos Ltd v Aladdin Sales and Marketing Ltd* [2000] F.S.R. 402, Jacob J. It was also suggested that registered design cases are generally suitable for the abbreviated procedure where written evidence is submitted and there is no cross examination. If the only questions in the case are questions of substantiality and similarity (between registered design, alleged infringement, and the prior art) to be judged by the eye of the court, then indeed there may be little point in cross examination of witnesses which simply degenerates into arguments about what is similar or what is substantial. These observations from *Thermos* were reiterated again by Jacob L.J. in *Proctor & Gamble Co v Reckitt Benckiser (UK) Ltd* [2007] EWCA Civ 936; [2008] F.S.R. 8, CA at para.5, with the added observation at para.6 that they applied equally to EU harmonised designs law.

[99] *J Choo (Jersey) Ltd v Towerstone Ltd* [2008] EWHC 346 (Ch); [2008] F.S.R. 19, Floyd J., involving comparison of designs for handbags. The court was also willing, on the facts of that case, to grant summary judgment on the issue of whether the defendant's design of handbags had been copied from the claimant's handbags, an issue it needed to decide since there was a claim for infringement of an unregistered Community design as well as a registered right.

[100] See para.2–043 below.

[101] Under the pre-harmonised law, a comparable question was that of whether or not design variants are "common to the trade", and consideration of this issue would normally involve evidence from experts in the trade: *Grafton v Watson* (1885) 51 L.T. 141; *Cooper v Symington* (1893) 10 R.P.C. 264.

on this very broad issue, assuming that the courts follow the practice adopted in relation to disclosure on the subject of whether a design is "commonplace" in the context of a UK unregistered design case.[102] Evidence on the subjective design history of the design in question or on whether one design has in fact been copied from another is irrelevant and inadmissible in the assessment of overall impression, but evidence that a design has received independent accolades may be of secondary relevance.[103]

The "informed user"

2-043   The "informed user" is an important person, since this notional person is employed as the benchmark for assessing whether a design has "individual character" for the purpose of enjoying protection, and also whether one design differs in overall impression from another for the purpose of infringement.[104] This notional person is design law's equivalent of the notional "person skilled in the art" who plays such a large part in patent law. Design law's "informed user" however would appear not be a manufacturer or designer, but someone on the customer or consumer side.[105] They are taken to be "informed", which must mean at least reasonably well informed as to the range of products and designs available on the relevant market, and specifically are taken to be aware of the "existing design corpus"[106]. This means, according to a number of decisions of the OHIM invalidity division, that "the informed user is familiar with all designs that are known in the the normal course of business in specialist circles in the sector in question".[107] They are also

---

[102] *Ultraframe Ltd v Eurocell Building Plastics Ltd* [2003] EWHC 3258 (Ch); [2005] F.S.R. 2, Pumfrey J.; as to the requirement that a UK unregistered design should not be "commonplace", see para.4–045 below.

[103] *Proctor & Gamble Co v Reckitt Benckiser* (UK) Ltd [2007] EWCA Civ 936; [2008] F.S.R. 8, CA, at para.7; evidence on whether or not the defendant copied the claimant's design is of course directly relevant to the question of infringement of an unregistered Community design (see para.2–099 below), but even in that context should not affect the assessment of whether the overall impression is the same or different.

[104] See para.2–097 below.

[105] *Woodhouse UK PLC v Architectural Lighting Systems* [2005] EWPCC (Designs) 25; [2006] R.P.C. 1, PCC (Judge Fysh Q.C.). "Informed" adds a notion of familiarity with the field rather higher then might be expected from an average consumer but does not require an archival mind or eye or more than an average memory. In relation to street lighting, the "informed user" would be a regular member of an urban development team who was interested in the appearance of street furniture.

[106] As mandated by recital (13) of the Directive (quoted in para.2–035 above) and recital (14) of the Regulation. Although these recitals specifically refer to the characteristics of the "informed user" in the context of validity, the same attributes are carried over into the context of infringement: *Proctor & Gamble Co v Reckitt Benckiser* (UK) Ltd [2007] EWCA Civ 936; [2008] F.S.R. 8, CA at paras 16–17. The "informed user" is familiar with design issues, and is not the same as the "average consumer" who features in trade mark law: see para.24.

[107] *Sunstar Suisse SA v Dentaid SL* (OHIM ref: 420; June 20, 2005, an interdental brush) at para.18; *Eredu v Arrmet* (OHIM ref: ICD 24; April 27, 2004, a bar stool) at para.18.

informed enough to understand the factors which affect a designer's freedom, since this factor is supposed to play a part in the assessment exercise. However, it has been said that they are not that technically experienced or particularly interested in the technical design of the product concerned[108]; but, presumably, the informed user must be taken to be aware of technical matters which constrain the designer's freedom. According to the General Court,[109] the informed user of a promotional game toy (a "rapper") could either be a child in the approximate age range of 5 to 10 or a marketing manager in a company that makes goods which are promoted by giving away "rappers", but the court thought it makes "little difference": the important point is that both those categories of person are familiar with the phenomenon of "rappers" (and their features). But what if it does make a difference: which type of "informed user" should the court then select, or should the court take a user at the more informed end of the range when a range of different types of users will use a product?

According to the established case law of the OHIM Boards of Appeal, the "informed user" is identified on the basis of the class of products within which, according to the application for registration, the design is intended to be incorporated.[110] However, this cannot provide an answer in the case of unregistered Community designs where presumably one must look at either the intrinsic nature of the design itself or possibly at the type of product on or in which the design was first marketed on the occasion which gave rise to subsistence of Community unregistered design right. But where a design initially registered or used in relation to one kind of product is said to have been used in relation to a very different kind of product, for example in the context of an allegation of infringement, it may be a more difficult question whether the "informed user" should be a user of products of the first kind or of the second kind.[111]   **2–043A**

The concept of the "informed user" does not seem all that different from the customer whose eye was the touchstone of assessing the validity   **2–044**

---

[108] *Normann Copehagen APS v Paton Calvert Housewares Ltd* [2010] E.C.D.R. 30, OHIM Third Board of Appeal.

[109] *Case T-9/07 Grupo Promer Mon Graphic SA v OHIM* March 18, 2010 [2010] E.C.D.R. 7, at paras 61–65.

[110] *Wuxi Kipor Power Co v Honda Giken KK* [2009] E.C.D.R. 4, OHIM Third Board of Appeal.

[111] It has been held, in a case where a prior design has been been applied to a different kind of product from the product to which the design in suit is applied, that the question of whether or not that prior design is available as prior art should be assessed by reference to "circles specialised in the sector" of the prior art product rather than specialised in the sector of the product to which the design in suit has been applied: see paras 2–076 to 2–077 below. But when it comes to the judgemental exercise of comparing the design in suit with the prior art design, or the comparable judgemental exercise of comparing the design in suit with an alleged infringement applied to a different kind of product, from which sector should the "informed user" be drawn?

of a design (and infringement as well[112]) under the old UK registered designs law, although he or she may possibly be deemed to have a slightly more comprehensive knowledge of the designs which are known in the normal course of business.[113]

Public policy and morality as a ground for refusal or invalidation

2–045   A right in a UK registered design does not subsist if the design is contrary to public policy or to accepted principles of morality.[114] This means that the Registry should refuse an application for such a design,[115] and if registered it is vulnerable to a declaration of invalidity.[116] The concept of public policy and morality is explicitly not the subject of harmonisation,[117] so that specifically British conceptions of public policy and morality should be applied rather than any attempt at a European harmonised conception. A Community application may be refused by OHIM if it happens to "notice" this ground of objection in the course of formal examination of the application[118]; OHIM must necessarily attempt to apply a Europe-wide conception of public policy and morality.[119]

Miscellaneous grounds for refusal: flags and emblems, etc.

2–046   There are provisions for the refusal of registration of a UK design which involves the use of the Royal arms, the Crown or other Royal symbols, or representations of the Queen or a member of the Royal family, or words, letters or devices likely to lead persons to think that the applicant has had or recently has had Royal patronage or authorisation, unless consent is given by or on behalf of the Queen or the member of the Royal Family concerned.[120] Similar provisions apply to arms to which a person is entitled by virtue of a grant of arms from the Crown,[121] and to protected Olympic symbols.[122] A design which involves the Union Jack or the flags

---

[112] See para.3–208 below.
[113] See para.3–048 below.
[114] RDA(E) s.1D.
[115] RDA(E) s.1A(1)(b). Examination of applications on this ground is maintained, even though substantive examination on other grounds has been abolished: see para.2–130 below.
[116] RDA(E) s.11ZA(1).
[117] Directive recital (16).
[118] Regulation art.47(1)(b).
[119] The Commission's original Green Paper proposal would have invalidated a design if it had offended the public policy or morality in any part of the Community: see draft Regulation annexed to the Green Paper art.6.
[120] RDA(E) Sch.A1, para.1(1).
[121] RDA(E) Sch.A1, para.1(3).
[122] Sch.A1, para.1(4).

of England, Wales, Scotland or the Isle of Man, and is misleading or grossly offensive, should also be refused registration.[123] Certain flags and emblems of Paris Convention countries, and of international organisations protected under the Paris Convention, should also not be incorporated into a registered design without the consent of the relevant authority.[124] Community designs may be invalidated on application by a member state on Paris Convention grounds, or on the grounds of making improper use of badges, emblems and escutcheons which are of particular interest in a member state.[125]

Grounds for invalidation on objection by owner of conflicting rights

There are several grounds upon which a design may be declared invalid on the application of the owner of conflicting rights. (In the case of UK registered designs they did not constitute grounds for refusal of the application even before substantive examination was abolished, and Community registered designs have never been substantively examined.) These are: (1) that the registered proprietor is not the proprietor of the design and the real proprietor objects[126]; (2) the design involves the use of an earlier distinctive sign (e.g. a trade mark) and the owner of that earlier sign has the right to prevent its use and objects to the registration[127]; and

2–047

---

[123] RDA(E) Sch.A1, para.1(2).

[124] RDA(E) Sch.A1, paras 2–5.

[125] Regulation art.25(1)(g).

[126] RDA(E) s.11ZA(2); Regulation art.25(1)(c). The true proprietor may instead seek the transfer of the registration to his name: see para.2–110 below. It should be noted that under the new harmonised law, this ground of objection to validity can only be put forward by the true proprietor, unlike under the pre-2001 law where any person aggrieved (including a third party alleged infringer) could invalidate the registered design if it was applied for by a person who was not in fact the proprietor: see *Woodhouse UK Plc v Architectural Lighting Systems* [2005] EWPCC (Designs) 25; [2006] R.P.C. 1, PCC (Judge Fysh Q.C.) and para.3–216 below. It should be borne in mind that this wider ability to attack the validity of registrations on ownership grounds continues to apply to registered designs in force today which were granted on applications made under the pre-harmonised law.

[127] RDA(E) s.11ZA(3); Regulation art.25(e); see e.g. *OOO Business-Alliance v Vitec Global Ltd* [2009] E.C.D.R. 7, OHIM Invalidity Division: registered design prominently contained the word "VITEC", and "Vitek" was registered by the objector as a Community trade mark. This kind of objection may become increasingly common in view of the growing trend for graphic trade marks to be registered as designs in order to obtain extra protection at low cost. See also Case T-148/08 *Beifa Group Co. Ltd v OHIM* [2010] E.C.D.R. 9 in which the General Court annulled the decision of the OHIM Third Board of Appeal because it had failed to carry out a comparison of the actual representation of the prior sign as registered for a German national trade mark) with the design in suit. Interestingly, both the General Court and the Board of Appeal regarded it as relevant that the prior trade mark was registered for the same goods as the products for which the applicant indicated that it wished to use the design: but this surely must be irrelevant because the exclusive rights conferred by the design cover all products so a similar trade mark registered for any goods ought to invalidate the design.

(3) the design constitutes an unauthorised use of a copyright work and the owner of the copyright objects.[128]

3. Partial Designs and Designs of Parts

Designs need not relate to a whole product

2–048   The definition of "design"[129] states that it includes the appearance of "the whole *or a part* of a product". This represents a significant departure from the old UK registered designs law, under which a design had to relate to a specific article, being an article made and sold separately.[130] In considering infringement, one had to ask whether the alleged infringement was substantially the same as the registered design looked at as a whole.[131] Thus, a new design of chair back could not be protected as such, but had to be included in an application for registration of a design for a chair as a whole. Although the novel features of the design (i.e. the new back) would be given greater weight when assessing infringement, the other features of the chair could not be ignored altogether and someone who adopted a similar chair back might escape infringement because differences in the other features of the chair were great enough to make the design as a whole "substantially different".[132]

2–049   Under the EU harmonised law, there seems no reason why the design of the chair back cannot be registered by itself. In practice, this would be achieved by filing a representation which portrays only the chair back and does not portray the rest of the chair. This would mean that when it came to infringement, only the back of the defendant's chair would be compared with the registration and it would be irrelevant how different or similar, for example, the legs of the defendant's chair are to the design of the proprietor's own product on the market. This suggests a registration strategy, in the case of products which have novel parts and features as well as being novel overall, of applying for a series of registrations directed to different features or parts of the product. The limitation on this strategy is that each of the registrations of parts would have to satisfy the requirements of novelty and individual character when considered in isolation. Thus, this strategy could not be used in the case of a design consisting of a novel combination of elements each of which are old when taken in isolation.

---

[128] RDA(E) s.11ZA(4); Regulation art.25(f).
[129] Set out at para.2–017 above.
[130] See para.3–038 below.
[131] See paras 3–211—3–212 below. Purely functional features which did not fall within the statutory definition of design could be disregarded: see paras 3–191—3–192 below.
[132] See para.3–211 below.

Community unregistered design right and parts of products

This raises the question of to what extent parts of products are protected by Community unregistered design right. There is no registration which serves to define what is the "design" to which protection attaches: is it the design of the whole product, or the design of a part or parts, or does first marketing of a product give rise to a bundle of unregistered design rights attaching to the whole and to each eligible part of the product? This latter "bundle" solution has received judicial approval in the case of UK unregistered design right,[133] and there seems no reason why similar logic should not apply to the Community unregistered right. If, for example, a manufacturer produces a new chair which has a design of back which is new in its own right, a design of legs new in their own right, and overall a design of chair which is a new combination of features (even if the seat is old), there seems no policy reason why he should not be entitled to unregistered design right protection in each of these three designs, provided each of the designs considered in isolation satisfies the requirements of novelty and individual character. Otherwise, a competitor would be able to copy[134] the novel chair back, but would escape infringement because he attached it to a different seat and legs so that the chair as a whole would produce a different "overall impression".

2–050

Component parts and "complex products"

Component parts are specially provided for in the legislation. Articles 3 and 4 of the Directive provide:

2–051

> "3. A design applied to or incorporated in a product which constitutes a component part of a complex product shall only be considered to be new and to have individual character:
>
> (a) if the component part, once it has been incorporated into the complex product, remains visible during normal use of the latter, and
> (b) to the extent that those visible features of the component part fulfil in themselves the requirements as to novelty and individual character.
>
> 4. 'Normal use' within the meaning of paragraph (3)(a) shall mean use by the end user, excluding maintenance, servicing or repair work."

Article 1 defines a complex product as follows:

---

[133] See para.4–005 below.
[134] Copying is an essential element of *unregistered* design right infringement: see para.2–099 below.

"(c) 'complex product' means a product which is composed of multiple components which can be replaced permitting disassembly and reassembly of the product."

The above provisions are transposed into subss.1B(8) and (9), and subs.1(3) of RDA(E). Articles 4(2), (3) and 3(c) of the Regulation are in substantially identical terms. Some further light is cast on these provisions by recital (12) of the Directive,[135] which states that features of design that are excluded from protection by these provisions should not be taken into consideration for the purpose of assessing whether other features of the design fulfill the requirements for protection. This does seem to be rather stating the obvious.

Designs of interconnections: the "must fit" exclusion

2–052   Article 7(2) of the Directive provides that:

"2. A design right shall not subsist in features of appearance of a product which must necessarily be reproduced in their exact form and dimensions in order to permit the product in which the design is incorporated or to which it is applied to be mechanically connected to or placed in, around or against another product so that either product may perform its function."

This is transposed into s.1C(2) of RDA(E). Article 8(2) of the Regulation is in the same terms. The rationale of this exclusion is explained in recital (14) of the Directive[136] on the basis that "whereas . . . the interoperability of products of different makes should not be hindered by extending protection to the design of mechanical fittings".

2–053   This provision is very similar to the "must fit" exclusion from UK unregistered design right[137] and the drafting is clearly based on that provision. The UK "must fit" exclusion has received some judicial consideration.[138] In that context, it has been held that a human eyeball counted as an "article", so that the shape of a contact lens fell within this exclusion.[139] Even if that proposition is correct in relation to the exclusion in the UK legislation,[140] it does not seem possible to carry it over to the EU harmonised provision, because "product" is defined as an "industrial or

---

[135] Recital (12) of the Regulation is substantially identical.
[136] Recital (10) to the Regulation is in the same terms.
[137] Under s.213(3)(b)(i) of the CDPA 1988. See App.C1, para.C1–001 below.
[138] See paras 4–015—4–024 below for an extensive discussion of the UK provision and the cases.
[139] *Ocular Sciences Ltd v Aspect Vision Care Ltd* [1997] R.P.C. 289 at 425, lines 1–35.
[140] As to which doubts are expressed, see para.4–019 below.

handicraft item",[141] and on no view is a human eyeball or other body part a "product". The provision is concerned with the interconnection between industrial items, so that products of different makes can "inter-operate", not with the interconnection between a product and the environment in which it operates.

Modular products

An exception from the "must fit" exclusion is made in the case of so-called "modular products". Article 7(3) of the Directive provides: **2–054**

> "3. Notwithstanding paragraph 2, a design right shall, under the conditions set out in Articles 4 and 5, subsist in a design serving the purpose of allowing multiple assembly or connection of mutually interchangeable products within a modular system."

This provision has been transposed into s.1C(3) of RDA(E), and art.8(3) of the Regulation is identical.

It is extremely difficult to understand the rationale for the exemption of   **2–055**
"modular products" from the "must fit" exclusion, except by reference to the lobbying power and influence on the Community legislative process of certain modular product manufacturers. The relevant recitals[142] merely assert that:

> "the mechanical fittings of modular products may nevertheless constitute an important element of the innovative characteristics of modular products and present a major marketing asset and therefore should be eligible for protection".

The first part of that statement may be true, but the second half of the proposition is a non-sequitur if the interconnection means of non-modular products are not similarly protected.

However, this provision may ultimately prove to have limited scope.   **2–056**
Article 7(3) excludes "modular products" from the application of the "must fit" exclusion in art.7(2). It does not exclude them from the application of the exclusion in art.7(1) of features which are solely dictated by the technical function of a product. The technical function of a modular product may include the need for it to interconnect with its neighbour, and its design will be excluded from protection to the extent

---

[141] See para.2–020 above.
[142] Recital (15) to the Directive, and recital (11) to the Regulation.

that its features are dictated by the technical function of connecting to the next modular element.

4. Available Prior Art

Date at which novelty and individual character are to be assessed

2–057   As already discussed above, in order to be protectable, a design must possess novelty and "individual character" at its relevant date. In the case of a UK[143] or Community registered design, that date is normally the date when the application is filed, or an earlier "priority date" if priority is claimed from an earlier application.[144] To this general rule, there are two exceptions.

2–058   First, it is possible to modify an application in the course of prosecution. If a modification is made to a UK design application which significantly alters the design, the registrar may direct that the application be treated for this purpose as having been made on the date on which it was so modified.[145] The purpose of this provision is to prevent an applicant from getting an unfair head-start over a competitor or potential infringer by retrospectively altering the scope of his design right protection. There is no corresponding provision relating to applications for Community registered designs; instead, the representation of the design may only be amended if the "identity of the design is retained".[146] Thus, an applicant for a Community design who wishes to alter the identity of the design will need to file a fresh application, which will of course attract a new and later filing date.

2–059   Secondly, it is possible to make an application for multiple designs within one application. It may be necessary or desirable then in effect to divide the multiple application into one or more separate applications. This is done by cancelling out one or more of the designs from the parent application, and then filing a new application or applications containing the designs cancelled out from the parent. If this is done, the new applications can be allowed to retain the filing date of the parent

---

[143] A UK design is normally treated as having been registered on its filing date, unless one of the exceptions below applies: RDA(E) s.3C.

[144] Directive art.4; RDA(E) s.1B(7); Regulation art.5(1)(b). In the case of a Community design, the application can be filed either at OHIM itself or at a national designs registry as receiving office (Regulation art.38). To receive a valid filing date, the application must comply with a number of formal requirements set out in art.36 (see App.B1, para.B1–037 below).

[145] RDA(E) s.3B(2). An application which is modified in a way which does not alter the identity of the design retains its original filing date: RDA(E) s.3B(4). The Directive art.11(7) permits a design right to be retained in amended form if the identity of the design is retained.

[146] The Implementing Regulation art.11(2), which restricts the apparently wide right to amend the application under art.47(2) of the Regulation.

application.[147] In the Community registry, the original multiple application is divided, rather than a new application being filed.[148]

As regards Community unregistered designs, the relevant date is the date when the design was first "made available to the public".[149] The three-year term of the unregistered design right runs from this date.[150]

2–060

Claims to an earlier priority date

When an application for protection is made in a Paris Convention[151] country, the applicant or his successor in title may, within six months, file an application for a UK registered design and claim priority from his Convention application.[152] A valid claim to priority has the effect that novelty and individual character are assessed as of the priority date, rather than the filing date of the UK application.[153] Similarly, a Community design right application at OHIM may claim priority from a design right or utility model application filed in or for a Paris Convention state,[154] in which case the priority date counts as the date of filing of the application.[155] The member states of the EU are Paris Convention countries; thus, priority may be claimed at OHIM from a UK or other national filing within the Community. A Community design may also claim so-called "exhibition priority", where the design has been exhibited within six months before the filing date at a recognised international exhibition falling within the Paris Convention on International Exhibitions.[156]

2–061

For the purposes of these provisions, any filing which is equivalent to a regular national filing under the national law of the state where it was made, or under bilateral or multilateral agreements, counts as a Convention application.[157] It appears that this must mean that priority may be claimed in the UK registry from Community applications,[158] as well as from international applications filed under the Hague Agreement.[159]

2–062

The concept of priority can obviously have no application to Community unregistered design right.

2–063

[147] RDA(E) s.3B(3).
[148] Regulation art.37(4); Implementing Regulation art.2.
[149] Regulation art.5(1)(a). As to what constitutes making a design available to the public, see para.2–067 below.
[150] Regulation art.11(1).
[151] See below, paras 2–141—2–142, for more details of the Paris Convention and of the formalities required for claiming priority.
[152] RDA(E) s.14(1); the Designs (Convention Countries) Order 2007: see App.A11 below.
[153] RDA(E) s.14(2).
[154] Regulation art.41(1).
[155] Regulation art.43.
[156] Regulation art.44.
[157] Regulation art.41(2); RDA(E) s.14(4).
[158] Article 39 of the Regulation provides that a Community application which has been accorded a date of filing is to be treated in the member states as equivalent to a regular national filing, including where appropriate the priority claimed from it.
[159] For international applications under the Hague Agreement, see para.2.–152 below.

Conflicting registrations with earlier application or priority dates

2–064   When an application is made to register a design, it is possible that someone else may have applied to register a similar design with an earlier filing or priority date. If that earlier design has been published (whether through publication of the registration by the relevant designs registry, or by commercial sale of products) before the filing or priority date of the later application, then the earlier design will be available to be cited against the validity of the later application in the normal way. However, it might still be unpublished at the relevant date of the later design, and in this case special rules need to be invoked to deal with the conflict. Article 11(1)(d) of the Directive provides that registration of a design shall be refused or declared invalid:

> "(d) if the design is in conflict with a prior design which has been made available to the public after the date of filing of the application or, if priority is claimed, the date of priority, and which is protected from a date prior to the said date by a registered Community design or an application for a registered Community design or by a design right of the Member State concerned, or by an application for such a right."

2–065   However, this ground of refusal or invalidity may be invoked only by the holder of the earlier registration or application.[160] These provisions were transposed into s.1A(2) RDA(E) as regards refusal of the application (now repealed following the abolition of substantive examination), and into s.11ZA(1A) as regards invalidity. Because these provisions render a granted design invalid, a design which escapes refusal on this ground because the earlier design has not been published at the date when the application is determined will still be rendered invalid if the earlier design is subsequently published. The holder of the earlier right will presumably take steps to publish it if he has not done so, in order to support his attack on the later design. In consequence of the accession by the EU to the Hague System of international registration of designs,[161] this ground of attack may be based on an international application which designates the EU with an earlier filing or priority date in exactly the same way as on an earlier application for a Community registered design.[162]

2–066   Article 25(1)(d) of the Regulation provides that a Community design may be declared invalid if it is in conflict with a prior design, and the wording is substantially identical to art.11(1)(d) of the Directive quoted above. This ground of invalidity may be invoked only by the owner of the

---

[160] Directive art.11(4).
[161] Under the Geneva Act of the Hague Agreement; see paras 2–152 et seq. below.
[162] Regulation art.25(1)(d)(iii); and as regards UK designs, RDA(E) s.11ZA(1A)(b)(ii).

earlier registered design or application.[163] On the face of it, this ground of invalidity applies to unregistered Community designs as well as registered designs, since the whole of art.25 sets out the grounds of attack on both species of right. However, curiously, it refers to the earlier design being protected prior to the later design's date of filing or its priority date, and an unregistered right will obviously not have either of these dates. It might have been thought that there was no need for an earlier filed design right to invalidate an unregistered right, for the following reason. An unregistered right is infringed only through copying, and the owner of the earlier application can freely exploit his earlier filed design without being accused of copying the later published unregistered right. This may provide a policy reason for interpreting art.25(1)(d) as not applying to unregistered design rights, but if so, the drafting could have been clearer.

Making a design available to the public

The concept of making a design available to the public is critical both for the purpose of asking what earlier published designs are available as prior art against a design with a later date, and also for fixing the date at which an unregistered Community design right comes into existence. The concept is defined in essentially the same way in both contexts. Article 6(1) of the Directive reads: **2–067**

> "1. For the purpose of applying Articles 4 and 5 [novelty and individual character], a design shall be deemed to have been made available to the public if it has been published following registration or otherwise, or exhibited, used in trade or otherwise disclosed, except where these events could not reasonably have become known in the normal course of business to the circles specialised in the sector concerned, operating within the Community, before the date of filing of the application for registration or, if priority is claimed, the date of priority. The design shall not, however, be deemed to have been made available to the public for the sole reason that it has been disclosed to a third person under explicit or implicit conditions of confidentiality."

Article 7(1) of the Regulation is in substantially identical terms to art.6(1) of the Directive. Article 11(1) of the Regulation, which defines publication for the purpose of fixing the date of inception of an unregistered Community design right, has converted the double negative ("except where these events could not reasonably have become known") into a positive ("in such a way that . . . these events could reasonably have become known"). This, however, appears to be a mere drafting **2–068**

---

[163] Regulation art.25(3).

difference not intended to produce any difference between the substance of the two provisions.

2–069   Article 6(1) of the Directive has been transposed into RDA(E) s.1B(5) and 1B(6)(a). The Act refers to the European Economic Area rather than the Community.[164]

2–070   The definition of "making available to the public" in the new designs law is a new concept which differs in important ways from the old law of registered designs and the law of patents. It introduces a number of uncertainties, and its interpretation and application will no doubt prove to be a fruitful field for the legal profession and the courts for many years. The different aspects of the new concept will be explored in the following paragraphs.

Need the disclosure of the design be in relation to a product?

2–071   These provisions are apt to cover the disclosure of a design by way of public sale or exposure of a product to which the design has been applied or in which it has been incorporated. The disclosure need not be an exposure of an actual product, but could, for example, be a photograph of a product or a drawing of an intended product. However, what if no product at all is involved in the disclosure? For example, a painting is published and the subject of the painting is later applied as surface decoration to a product. Will the earlier publication of the painting as such invalidate the later registered or unregistered right in respect of the picture in the painting applied to the surface of the product? Under the old UK law, to count as prior art the earlier design must have been published "in respect of the same or any other article",[165] so that the publication of a pattern would not invalidate a later design registration if it did not suggest the application of the pattern to an article at all. Although the law has been changed so that a design right now covers any product, rather than a specific article, it would seem that similar logic ought still to apply under the new law when an earlier publication does not relate to any product at all.

Geographical scope

2–072   Under the old UK law of registered designs, prior art had to be published within the United Kingdom in order to be available.[166] Historically, the same rule applied in patent law but, under the Patents Act 1977 (which was passed to give effect to the European Patents Convention), this rule was swept away and matter published anywhere in the world was

---

[164] Under the European Economic Area Agreement, the Directive extends to the EEA countries as well as to the Community itself; see para.9–001 below.

[165] See para.3–118 below.

[166] See para.3–142 below.

available as prior art. The new design law concept appears to be a compromise between these two positions. On the one hand, something published outside the EEA which never comes to the attention of anyone within the EEA is not available as prior art. On the other hand, a design published at e.g. a major international exhibition in the United States which is attended by businessmen from the EEA will count. The advent of the world wide web may have changed the impact of this provision. Something published on a website anywhere in the world is available to be viewed anywhere; the issue as to whether it could reasonably have become known to the relevant persons within the EEA may depend upon how well it was indexed in search engines. It has been held that publication in an international (PCT) patent application is likely to become known to the sector concerned within the Community because it would be in the normal course of business for companies in the sector to monitor such applications, irrespective of the national origin of the applicant for the patent.[166a]

In the Green Paper, the Commission's original thinking behind the new test was stated as follows[167]:   **2–073**

> "The circle of relevant persons is limited to those operating within the Community, but their knowledge is not subject to any territorial limitation as, for obvious reasons, they do not operate in a closed system. The specialists will therefore be asked to say whether to their knowledge a design has been already disclosed, inside or outside the Community. If the design is unknown to them, then it should be eligible for protection even if in fact there is an identical prior design in some remote country in the world or if an identical design has existed in the past and has completely vanished from the collective memory."

One further geographical point arises: is it necessary that the design should be reasonably known to business circles throughout the EEA, or is it sufficient that it should be known to business circles within one country only, or within one part of a country only? Policy reasons would suggest the latter. If a design has been prior published in or to a part of the EEA and is therefore available to be used by trade circles within that part, the holder of a later registered right should not be able to prevent them from utilising it.   **2–074**

[166a] *Unistraw Asset Holdings Pty Ltd v Felföldi Edesseggyarto KFT* [2010] E.C.D.R. 10, Case R417/2009-3, OHIM Third Board of Appeal. A PCT application filed by an Australian national; quaere whether the result would have been different if it has been an Australian national filing.

[167] See para.5.5.5.2.

How wide need publication be?

2–075   Under the previous UK registered design law (and under patent law), something is considered to have been published if it has been communicated to a single person without a fetter of confidence.[168] The new design law provisions, with their reference to "the circles specialised in the sector concerned", suggest that the publication needs to be more widespread, actually or at least potentially. However, the wording does not seem to suggest that actual knowledge by a number of people in the relevant "circles" is required to be proved: the phrase "could reasonably have become known" suggests that the circumstances of the "publication" must have been such that it was objectively reasonably likely that its subject matter would become known to a number of persons in the relevant "circles", and it is not necessary to go further and prove that it was actually known in those circles. Thus, the display of a design at an exhibition in the United States which traders from the EEA are wont to attend, or publication on a website which relevant persons within the EEA are reasonably likely to look at, would seem to count.[168a] Whether any of the visitors from the EEA actually happened to walk over and look at the individual exhibit would appear not to be necessary.

What is the "sector concerned"?

2–076   In order to count, the publication needs to be to "circles specialised in the sector concerned", but what this means is less straightforward than might be thought. Where one is considering a registered design and a piece of prior art which relate to the same kind of product, the concept of the "sector concerned" is reasonably straightforward. However, what if the registered design being considered and the prior art come from widely different sectors of industry? Because the structure of the new legislation does not limit designs to particular products or ranges of products, either for the purpose of validity or of infringement, this creates a problem of some difficulty. What if the registered design is applied to a widget, but a virtually identical design has previously been applied to a sprocket? The earlier design may be very well known to sprocket makers, but unknown to makers of widgets. Is the "sector concerned" the sector concerned with the registered or unregistered design in issue, or is it the sector concerned with the posited prior publication?

2–077   Although the first solution might be superficially attractive, deeper consideration favours the second solution, which the English Court of

---

[168] See paras 3–129—3–130 below.

[168a] See *Crocs Inc. v Holey Soles Holdings Ltd* [2010] E.C.D.R. 11, Case R-9/2008-3, OHIM Third Board of Appeal. Shoes were marketed in Florida and Colorado with a launch campaign involving extensive internet use and shown at a major show in Florida; observed that "The Internet . . . is a formidable information tool and was certainly used by designers of footwear as well as in any other field" (para.85).

Appeal has emphatically endorsed,[169] mainly because of the absurd consequences that would result from adopting the first solution. Because infringement of a Community design is not limited by type of product as declared on the application to register, in the example given above the prior art sprocket would infringe (if manufactured again) the registered design for the widget. If the sprocket were not available as prior art against the widget design because it would be unknown to widget makers, the widget registered design would arbitrarily curtail the freedom of sprocket makers to use and develop prior art in their own field even if that prior art was very well known. The Court of Appeal also considered that its preferred approach was supported by the legislative history of the wording in art.7 of the Regulation,[170] and was so clearly of the view that its interpretation was correct that it regarded it as *acte claire* and so there was no need to refer the point of interpretation to the ECJ.[171] This approach also has the advantage of applying a consistent test to the question of publication, whether one is considering it in the context of prior publication against the validity of a design, or as a first publication which founds an unregistered design right: one asks whether the event is likely to have become known to the circles specialised in the type of product to which the prior publication relates.

Confidential disclosures

Confidential disclosures expressly do not count as publications. This is probably no more than stating the obvious, and in this respect there is no change from the previous law.[172]   2–078

Period of grace: disclosures by the proprietor with 12 months before filing

Publication of a design of a third party, even a day before the priority date or filing date, will invalidate a later design. However, as a special exception to this rule, people are allowed to publish their own design for up to 12 months without such publications invalidating a subsequent application for registration. The purpose of this is to allow products to be   2–079

---

[169] *Green Lane Products Ltd v PMS International Group Ltd* [2008] EWCA Civ 358; [2008] F.S.R. 28; [2008] E.C.D.R. 15, CA: a case where soft spiky plastic massage balls were prior art but the same shape was later registered as a design for putting into a tumble dryer and softening fabric. The Court of Appeal upheld the ruling at first instance of Lewison J. at [2007] EWHC 1712 (Pat); [2008] F.S.R. 1 who at para.14 referred to this paragraph of the 7th edition of this work in support of the conclusion he reached.

[170] Paragraphs 64–74.

[171] Paragraph 11. At paras 51–52, the Court of Appeal rejected a suggestion in a Board of Appeal decision that an alteration to the indication of the type of product to which a registered design is intended to be applied might affect inter alia the extent of the exclusive rights and the determination of the prior art, pointing out that art.36(6) says "quite the opposite": see *Casio's App Case R 1421/2006–3* [2007] E.C.D.R. 13.

[172] See paras 3–131—3–134 below.

tested on the market for a time before the expense of registration need be incurred. This represents a departure from the old UK law. Article 4(2) of the Directive states:

> "2. A disclosure shall not be taken into consideration for the purpose of applying Articles 4 and 5 [novelty and individual character] if a design for which protection is claimed under a registered design right of a Member State has been made available to the public:
>
> (a) by the designer, his successor in title, or a third person as a result of information provided or action taken by the designer, or his successor in title; and
>
> (b) during the 12-month period preceding the date of filing of the application or, if priority is claimed, the date of priority."

This provision has been transposed into RDA(E) s.1B(6)(c) and (d). Article 7(2) of the Regulation makes identical provision in relation to Community registered designs. By its nature, this provision has no application to Community unregistered designs.

2–080   It should be seen that this provision extends to publications not only by the designer (or their successor in title), but also to publications by third parties in consequence of information provided or action taken by the designer or his successor. Thus, this provision is apt to cover e.g. circulation of photographs of the designer's own product in a publication in consequence of the placing on the market of the designer's product, or copying and reproduction of the design by a competitor, even if that adoption does not itself infringe any legal right of the designer.

2–081   However, it is not clear how this provision applies where the product marketed by the designer, and the design which he registers, are different; e.g. because he has improved the design of the product by the time he files his design application. A broader reading of this provision, having regard to its purposes, would suggest that the designer should be protected in such an instance. The earlier, different, design has in effect partially made available to the public the design later filed, and to the extent that it has so partially made it available, the grace period should apply. The contrary interpretation would lead to the result that the designer could only register the exact thing that he had earlier put on the market, and the addition of new developments or improvements to it would lead to loss of protection. (Of course, if the developments or improvements were big enough to alter the overall impression of the design, then the later design would be valid in its own right and would not require the "grace period" protection.)

Publication in abuse of the designer's rights

2–082   The 12-month period of grace also applies if a design has been made available to the public in consequence of "an abuse in relation to the designer or his successor in title".[173] Under the previous UK law, a similar provision applied in respect of disclosures made in breach of good faith.[174] The terms "abuse" and "breach of good faith" are not precisely the same, but are of similar general import. What amounts to bad faith (in the context of making an application) has been the subject of a reasonable amount of judicial discussion under the Trade Marks Act 1994 s.3(6),[175] and under the Trade Marks Regulation.[176]

5. Infringement of Registered UK and Community Designs and of Unregistered Community Designs

Requirements for infringement

In order to infringe a design, a defendant must (1) perform an act of a kind which is capable of constituting infringement, and (2) do that act in relation to a design which is the same as or sufficiently close to the first design to fall within the scope of the protection. These two aspects of infringement will be considered in turn. The law of infringement of UK and Community registered designs is the same although, obviously, the territorial scope of infringement differs. In the case of unregistered Community designs, there is the important additional requirement that in order to infringe, the defendant's design must have been copied from the design that is the subject of the unregistered design right.

2–083

Acts which constitute infringement of designs

Article 12(1) of the Directive provides:

2–084

> "1. The registration of a design shall confer on its holder the exclusive right to use it and to prevent any third party not having his consent from using it. The aforementioned use shall cover, in

---

[173] Directive art.6(3); transposed into RDA(E) s.1B(6)(e); Regulation art.7(3).

[174] See para.3–135 below.

[175] *Gromax Plasticure Ltd v Don & Low Nonwovens Ltd* [1999] R.P.C. 367: one of two parties involved in an informal joint enterprise applied for the trade mark in its own name; held (by Lindsay J. at 379) that this did not to amount to "bad faith", which he defined as including dishonesty "and some dealings which fall short of the standards of acceptable commercial behaviour observed by reasonable and experienced men in the particular area being examined".

[176] *Trillium TM: Harte-Hans Data Technologies v Trillium Digital Systems Ltd* Case C000053447/1, March 28, 2000 (reported only in unsatisfactory note form at [2000] E.T.M.R. 1054), the Cancellation Division of OHIM said as follows at § 11: "Bad faith is a narrow legal concept in the CTMR system. Bad faith is the opposite of good faith, generally implying or involving, but not limited to, actual or constructive fraud, or a design to mislead or deceive another, or any other sinister motive. Conceptually, bad faith can be understood as a 'dishonest intention'. This means that bad faith may be interpreted as unfair practices involving lack of any honest intention on the part of the applicant of the CTM at the time of filing."

particular, the making, offering, putting on the market, importing, exporting or using of a product in which the design is incorporated or to which it is applied, or stocking such a product for those purposes."

This provision has been transposed into RDA(E) s.7(2) in conjunction with s.7(1). Article 19(1) of the Regulation is the same as art.12(1) of the Directive.

2–085   The wording of these provisions is substantially based on the acts of primary infringement laid down in the Community Patent Convention in respect of patents for products,[177] upon which s.60(1)(a) of the Patents Act 1977 is based. However, unlike in the case of patents, there is no provision creating secondary or contributory infringement on the part of persons who supply components or means (e.g. moulds or printing plates) for creating infringing products. In these respects, the new law of infringement has been narrowed in comparison with the previous law of UK registered designs.[178]

2–086   Whilst "use" of a product is an infringing act, this is tempered in the case of products purchased from the design right owner or his licensee by the so-called "exhaustion of right" provisions, which prevent a design right owner from enforcing their rights in respect of products which have been put on the market within the EEA by him or with his consent.[179]

Limitations on infringement

2–087   Article 13(1) of the Directive provides:

"1. The rights conferred by a design right upon registration shall not be exercised in respect of:

(a) acts done privately and for non-commercial purposes;
(b) acts done for experimental purposes;
(c) acts of reproduction for the purposes of making citations or of teaching, provided that such acts are compatible with fair trade practice and do not unduly prejudice the normal exploitation of the design, and that mention is made of the source."

These limitations on infringement are transposed into RDA(E) s.7A(2)(a)–(c) and (3). The same limitations in relation to Community

---

[177] Article 29(a) of the 1975 Luxembourg text; the substantial change is that exportation is made an infringing act.
[178] Under s.7(3) RDA(A), it was an infringement to make or sell, etc. "anything for enabling" a primary infringing article to be made, so that moulds or special tools would be caught; and s.7(4) RDA(A) made it an infringement to do anything in relation to a kit of parts that would have been an infringement in relation to the assembled article.
[179] Directive art.15; RDA(E) s.7A(4); Regulation art.21. The impact of these provisions on parallel imports is discussed in Ch.9 below.

designs are contained in art.20(1) of the Regulation. There is a similar experimental use defence in the patent field which has been the subject of a certain amount of judicial authority. It is necessary to distinguish between experiments on the one hand, and commercial trials and demonstrations on the other.[180]

Ships and aircraft from another country

Article 13(2) of the Directive provides: 2–088

"2. In addition, the rights conferred by a design right upon registration shall not be exercised in respect of:

(a) the equipment on ships and aircraft registered in another country when these temporarily enter the territory of the Member State concerned;

(b) the importation in the Member State concerned of spare parts and accessories for the purpose of repairing such craft;

(c) the execution of repairs on such craft."

This provision has been transposed into RDA(E) s.7A(2)(d) to (f). Article 20(2) of the Regulation is in similar terms, but refers to ships and aircraft registered in a third country (i.e. a non-member state) which temporarily enter the territory of the Community.

A ferry which shuttles repeatedly between different countries of the   2–089 European Union could not be sued for infringement under the national registered design law of any country which it visits, unless one of those countries is its flag state.[181] However, such a ship would infringe a Community registered or unregistered design right because it would be permanently, rather than temporarily, within the territory of the Community.

Territorial scope of infringement of UK registrations

The right conferred by registration of a design is a territorial monopoly   2–090 similar to a patent monopoly and therefore, although s.7 of the RDA(E) does not expressly say so, in order for acts to amount to infringement they must take place within the territory within which the Act applies. This comprises the United Kingdom, i.e. England, Wales, Scotland and

---

[180] The Court of Appeal held in *Monsanto v Stauffer* [1985] R.P.C. 515 that the experimental use defence did not extend to trials conducted for commercial or regulatory purposes to prove a product.

[181] This is because a ship which repeatedly visits a country is still making a temporary visit on each occasion: see *Stena Rederi AB v Irish Ferries Ltd* [2003] EWCA Civ 66; [2003] R.P.C. 36.

Northern Ireland, together with the Isle of Man,[182] the territorial waters of the United Kingdom[183] and structures and vessels engaged in mineral exploitation in the UK sector of the continental shelf.[184] Certain countries and territories for historical reasons permit enforcement or re-registration of design registrations obtained in the United Kingdom, but this is by virtue of their own laws and is not as such infringement of the legal right conferred by the UK design registration.

2–091   Thus, the making of articles abroad, which are within the scope of the registered design, does not amount to an infringement of the right conferred by the UK registration, even if acts are performed within the United Kingdom which assist, facilitate or lead to the making of such articles. If the acts performed abroad amount to infringement of a corresponding design registration under the laws of that country, it is possible that action could be taken either there or in the courts of the United Kingdom in such circumstances; however, the rules as to when action can be taken here in respect of committing or facilitating the commission of tortious acts abroad is a complex subject which is outside the scope of this work.[185]

Territorial scope of Community design right

2–092   A Community design right extends, and has equal effect, throughout the European Union.[186] The territorial scope of the European Union is defined by art.52 of the Treaty on European Union in conjunction with art.355 TFEU. It consists of the home territories of the member states, together with certain overseas territories and dependencies as defined in art.355. The EU Treaties apply to the Channel Islands and to the Isle of Man only to the extent necessary to ensure the implementation of the arrangements for the islands set out in the 1972 Accession Treaty under which the United Kingdom joined the EEC.[187]

Temporal limits of infringement

2–093   For an act to amount to infringement, it must take place within the temporal limits of the monopoly conferred by the design registration. In the case of a UK registration, this starts on the date on which the

---

[182] The Registered Designs (Isle of Man) Order 2001 (SI 2001/3678).
[183] RDA(E) s.47A(1).
[184] RDA(E) s.47A(2).
[185] See *Lucasfilm Ltd v Ainsworth* [2009] EWCA Civ 1328; [2010] F.S.R. 10; [2010] E.C.D.R 5, CA: broadly, an intellectual property right arising under foreign law is not justiciable in the English courts, with the exception of rights under the laws of EEA states which can sometimes be enforced under the Brussels Regulation.
[186] Regulation art.1(3).
[187] TFEU art.355(5)(c).

certificate of registration is granted,[188] despite the fact that for other purposes the design once registered is treated as having been registered as of the date of application.[189] As to the end point, the registered design will only be infringed by acts performed before it expires, so it is not an infringement to import articles from abroad after expiry, even if those articles were made abroad before expiry.

A Community registered right takes effect upon its registration by OHIM, and it appears, although the wording of the provision[190] is not totally clear, that once registered it takes effect retrospectively as from its filing date. An applicant may in certain circumstances ask OHIM to defer publication of his application and registration of the design for up to 30 months after the filing or priority date.[191] If he does so, his infringement rights are limited to cases where someone has copied from his design in the same way as is the case of an unregistered right.[192] This implies that in the general case where deferment is not requested, the design once registered has unrestricted effect from its date of filing. **2–094**

A Community unregistered right runs for a period of three years "as from" the date on which the design is first made available to the public.[193] **2–095**

Scope of protection

The scope of protection, i.e. what designs are covered by a registration, is governed by the following provisions. Article 9 of the Directive provides: **2–096**

"1. The scope of the protection conferred by a design right shall include any design which does not produce on the informed user a different overall impression.
2. In assessing the scope of protection, the degree of freedom of the designer in developing his design shall be taken into consideration."

This provision is transposed into RDA(E) s.7(1) and 7(3). Article 9 of the Regulation is in identical terms.

The test of infringement uses the same phrase, "different overall impression", as that used in the comparison test which is performed between the design and prior art in order to decide whether or not the **2–097**

---

[188] RDA(E) s.7A(6).
[189] See para.2–025 above.
[190] Regulation art.12. Although art.10 of the Directive is similarly worded to art.12 of the Regulation, it would appear that s.7A(6) of RDA(E) has the overriding effect of preventing suit in respect of UK registered designs for acts committed before the date of grant.
[191] Regulation art.50.
[192] Regulation art.19(3).
[193] Regulation art.11(1).

design is valid. The nature of that comparison, the evidence which may appropriately be adduced, and the characteristics of the "informed user", are discussed earlier in this chapter.[194] However it seems that the test is not quite the same in the two contexts. In the context of validity the relevant Recitals[195] state that the impression produced by the new design on the informed user must "clearly differ" from the impression produced by the prior art, but the Court of Appeal has held[196] that no such requirement that the overall impression must "clearly" differ applies in order to escape infringement.

2–098   In the *Procter & Gamble* case (which concerned air freshener sprayers), the Court of Appeal gave general guidance on applying the "different overall impression" test in the context of infringement.[197] One should identify the notional "informed user" correctly[198] and what he would know about the design corpus, and then ask whether the accused product produces a "different overall impression" on such a person. This test is inherently rather imprecise and a considerable margin is left to the judgement of the tribunal. Having said that, the Court made some general observations about applying the test:

"(i) The test is 'different' not 'clearly different.'

(ii) The notional informed user is 'fairly familiar' with design issues.

(iii) Next is not a proposition of law but a statement about the way people (and thus the notional informed user) perceive things. It is simply that if a new design is markedly different from anything that has gone before, it is likely to have a greater overall visual impact than if it is 'surrounded by kindred prior art.'[199] It follows that the 'overall impression' created by such a design will be more significant and the room for differences which do not create a substantially different overall impression is greater. So protection for a striking novel product will be correspondingly greater than for a product which is incrementally different from the prior art, though different enough to have its own individual character and thus be validly registered.

---

[194] See paras 2–038—2–042 above.

[195] Recital (13) of the Directive and Recital (14) of the Regulation.

[196] *Procter & Gamble Co v Reckitt Benckiser* (UK) Ltd [2007] EWCA Civ 936; [2008] F.S.R. 8, CA at paras 18–19: the explanation for the phrase "clearly different" in the recitals is that policy requires that there should be "clear blue water" between a design which is registered and the prior art, but there is no policy requirement that the difference be "clear" in order to avoid infringement: it is enough if the design differs in overall impression.

[197] *Procter & Gamble Co v Reckitt Benckiser* (UK) Ltd [2007] EWCA Civ 936; [2008] F.S.R. 8, CA, at paras 33–35.

[198] For the characteristics of the "informed user", see para.2–043 above.

[199] Adopting Judge Fysh's "pithy phrase" in *Woodhouse UK PLC v Architectural Lighting Systems* [2005] EWPCC (Designs) 25; [2006] R.P.C. 1, PCC at para.58.

(iv) On the other hand it does not follow, in a case of markedly new design (or indeed any design) that it is sufficient to ask 'is the alleged infringement closer to the registered design or to the prior art', if the former infringement, if the latter not. The tests remains 'is the overall impression different?'

(v) It is legitimate to compare the registered design and the alleged infringement with a reasonable degree of care. The court must 'don the spectacles of the informed user' to adapt the hackneyed but convenient metaphor of patent law. The possibility of imperfect recollection has a limited part to play in this exercise.[200]

(vi) The court must identify the 'overall impression' of the registered design with care. True it is that it is difficult to put into language, and it is helpful to use pictures as part of the identification, but the exercise must be done.

(vii) In this exercise the level of generality to which the court must descend is important. Here, for instance, it would be too general to say that the overall impression of the registered design is 'a canister fitted with a trigger spray device on the top.' The appropriate level of generality is that which would be taken by the notional informed user.[201]

(viii) The court should then do the same exercise for the alleged infringement.

(ix) Finally the court should ask whether the overall impression of each is different. This is almost the equivalent to asking whether they are the same—the difference is nuanced, probably, involving a question of onus and no more."

Copying in the case of unregistered Community design right

In the case of unregistered Community design right, there is an additional **2–099** requirement for infringement that the defendant's design should have been copied from the design sued upon. This is laid down in the Regulation, art.19(2):

> "2. An unregistered Community design shall, however, confer on its holder the right to prevent the acts referred to in paragraph 1 only if the contested use results from copying the protected design.

---

[200] See also *Procter & Gamble Co v Reckitt Benckiser (UK) Ltd* [2007] EWCA Civ 936; [2008] F.S.R. 8, CA at para.25: what matters for overall impression is what strikes the mind of the informed user *when* it is carefully viewed, rather than what sticks in the mind *after* it has been carefully viewed. For the pre-2001 approach to "imperfect recollection" in designs cases, see paras 3–209—3–210 below.

[201] It has been said (applying this approach when comparing mowing machines) that "generality must not be taken too far": *Rolawn Ltd v Turfmech Machinery Ltd* [2008] EWHC 989 (Pat); [2008] R.P.C. 27; [2008] E.C.D.R. 13, Mann J. at para.125.

> The contested use shall not be deemed to result from copying the protected design if it results from an independent work of creation by a designer who may be reasonably thought not to be familiar with the design made available to the public by the holder."

2–100 The second paragraph of this provision is puzzling. If an independent work is made in the circumstances contemplated in that paragraph, it clearly is not the result of copying the protected design, and the paragraph appears to be pure surplussage. However, it could perhaps have the effect of undermining or restricting the scope of the first paragraph. If a second designer did not in fact copy and was not in fact aware of the protected design, could it be argued that he is nonetheless liable because the circumstances are such that he might "reasonably be thought" to be familiar with it?

> "In deciding the factual question of whether or not there has been copying, the British courts will presumably follow the same approach that they have always applied in deciding the issue of copying in copyright and UK unregistered design right cases. Thus, in an appropriate case, a claimant can rely upon 'similar fact evidence' of previous instances of copying by a defendant, although the court will need to ensure that the burden of investigating such secondary issues does not outweigh the probative value of the results of such investigations".[202]

Spare parts

2–101 The Directive provides for the continuation for a transitional period of indeterminate duration of differing national treatments on the subject of spare parts.[203] Under this provision, the United Kingdom continues to permit the making and supply of spare parts for the purpose of repair of a "complex product", even if there is a UK registered design covering the component part itself.[204]

Right to continue prior use

2–102 Article 22 of the Regulation provides that:

> "1. A right of prior use shall exist for any third person who can establish that before the date of filing of the application, or, if a priority is claimed, before the date of priority, he has in good faith commenced use within the Community, or has made

---

[202] *Mattel Inc v Woolbro (Distributors) Ltd* [2004] F.S.R. 217, Laddie J.
[203] Directive art.14.
[204] RDA(E) s.7A(5).

serious and effective preparations to that end, of a design included within the scope of protection of a registered Community design, which has not been copied from the latter.

2. The right of prior use shall entitle the third person to exploit the design for the purposes for which its use had been effected, or for which serious and effective preparations had been made, before the filing or priority date of the registered Community design.

3. The right of prior use shall not extend to granting a licence to another person to exploit the design.

4. The right of prior use cannot be transferred except, where the third person is a business, along with that part of the business in the course of which the act was done or the preparations were made."

If a prior user of a design has published it, the effect of publication will   **2–103**
be to render invalid any registration which it might infringe with a later filing or priority date. This prior use defence can therefore only be needed when non-public use has been made of the earlier design, e.g. by manufacturing products to the design prior to public launch, or where "serious and effective preparations" have been made for such use which have not resulted in a publication of the intended design.

6. Property Rights and Licensing

UK registered designs and applications

The law relating to proprietary rights in, and licensing of, national   **2–104**
registered designs and applications for registration is not covered by the Directive. Consequently, member states are not required to harmonise this aspect of their law. In the United Kingdom, the previous law has been retained with only minor amendments consequential on the change to the substantive nature of the registered design right.[205] Because the law is essentially unchanged, the subject of property rights and licensing of EU harmonised UK registered designs and applications is dealt with in Ch.3.[206]

---

[205] Under the old UK law, the registered design consisted of the right to apply the design to a specific article. Under the new law, the registered design covers the application of the design to, or its incorporation in, any product (see para.2–021 above). In consequence, RDA s.2(2), which regulates the transmission of rights in a design, now omits the previous reference to "or the right to apply a design to any article": compare App.A2 below, with App.A5 below.
[206] See paras 3–216 et seq. below.

Property law relating to Community designs and applications

2–105 Community registered and unregistered design rights are unitary rights, which have equal effect throughout the EU. They cannot be transferred or otherwise dealt with save in respect of the whole Community,[207] so that, for example, it is not possible to split up the ownership of a Community design into different countries or areas of the EU. Because of the EU-wide character of these rights, it was deemed necessary to create a framework of law at EU level governing property matters: entitlement to apply in the case of registered rights, and ownership of unregistered rights, and transmission and licensing. However, the EU based system of property law is not complete, and for some purposes national systems of law are imported.[208]

First ownership of a Community design right

2–106 The legal ownership of a Community unregistered design right, and the right to apply to register a Community design right, are regulated by the same provisions. The originator of a new design may place it on the market, so generating a Community unregistered design right, and may then choose to apply to register the design taking advantage of the 12-month grace period.[209] It is obviously sensible that the ownership of the unregistered right, and the right to apply for the registered right, will generally be in the same hands. Article 14 of the Regulation provides:

"Right to the Community design

1. The right to the Community design shall vest in the designer or his successor in title.
2. If two or more persons have jointly developed a design, the right to the Community design shall vest in them jointly.
3. However, where a design is developed by an employee in the execution of his duties or following the instructions given by his employer, the right to the Community design shall vest in the employer, unless otherwise agreed or specified under national law."

2–107 This Article of the Regulation (unlike e.g. UK national law on registered and unregistered designs) contains no provision under which the commissioning of a design outside the employment relationship (i.e. under a contract for services as distinct from a contract of service) will vest the right to the design in the person commissioning the design rather than

---

[207] Regulation art.1(3).
[208] Such a solution was adopted in respect of European Patent applications under the European Patent Convention.
[209] For the grace period, see para.2–079 above.

the designer. However, the ECJ has held that the reference in art.14(1) to the "successor in title" to the designer implies that a contract between the designer and the commissioner of the design may have the effect of transferring title from the designer to the commissioner and that whether a contract has such an effect is to be assessed by reference to the relevant national law of contract.[210] Presumably, the national law for this purpose is the proper law of the contract under which the design was commissioned and that referred to in para.3 is the proper law of the contract of employment, which will regulate the ownership of the design right as between employer and employee across the Community as a whole. This could produce the result that the Community design right vests in, say, the employee (because the law of the country of employment of the designer is generous to employees), but the right to apply for a national registered design in the United Kingdom vests in the employer.[211] The national law referred to could be the law of a non-EU country, if the designer is employed outside the Community.

A designer (or a team of designers if the design was made by a team) 2–108 has the right to be cited as such in the register.[212] This right exists even if ownership of the design is vested in an employer or some other person.

Persons who commission the making of designs

It should also be noted that the Regulation does not, unlike UK law, 2–109 automatically vest the right to a design in a person who commissions the creation of a design for money or money's worth.[213] In order to claim ownership of a Community design right, such a person would have to establish that it was an express or implied term of the contract under which the design was created that the right to the design should vest in them. This will not be so in all circumstances, and in this respect the ownership provisions on Community design right resemble the UK ownership provisions relating to copyright,[214] rather than those relating to registered or unregistered design right.

Disputes over entitlement to a Community design

Disputes over the ownership of unregistered Community design rights, 2–110 or over applications for or registrations of registered rights, are governed

---

[210] Case C-32/08 *FEIA v Cul de Sac Espacio Creativo SL* [2009] E.C.D.R. 327; [2010] R.P.C. 13, ECJ.
[211] Because s.2(1B) of RDA(E) vests the right to apply for a UK design in the employer, and does not import the design ownership law of the country where the designer is employed.
[212] Regulation art.18.
[213] See para.3–222 below.
[214] As to these, and the case law on implied terms, see paras 5–148—5–149 below.

by art.15 of the Regulation. Legal proceedings[215] must be started within three years of the date when the unregistered design was disclosed or the registered design was published, unless the person against whom the claim is made was acting in bad faith.[216] In the case of a registered Community design, mention of any such proceedings is entered in the register and a note of the final determination of the proceedings and any change of ownership that may be effected.[217] There is a special provision safeguarding the position of a person who is displaced as owner of a registered Community design and his licensees. Unless he acted in bad faith at the time, the displaced owner or licensee who has exploited the design within the Community, or made serious and effective preparations to do so, is entitled to a non-exclusive licence under the design "for a reasonable period on reasonable terms".[218]

Recordal of interests in the register

2–111   The person in whose name a Community design is registered, or, before registration, the person in whose name an application stands, is deemed by art.17 of the Regulation to be the person entitled to the design or application in any proceedings before OHIM or elsewhere. Although the article is headed *"Presumption* in favour of the registered holder of the design", the actual text of the article appears to create more than a presumption and it appears that the person named on the register is entitled to the right unless and until he is displaced and the register is corrected under art.15(4)(c).

2–112   A person to whom a registered Community design is transferred may not invoke the rights arising from the registration until the transfer has been recorded in the register.[219] Certain important legal acts relating to registered Community designs, such as transfers, mortgages and licences, do not have effect against third parties, except for third parties who have actual knowledge of the transaction, until after the transaction has been entered in the register.[220] A licence or a transfer of a licence shall, at the request of one of the parties, be entered in the register and published.[221]

Dealings with and transfers of Community design rights

2–113   Because EU law does not provide a complete framework of law regulating property rights and transfers, national laws are imported subject to

---

[215] As to which courts have jurisdiction over such claims, see Ch.6 below.
[216] Regulation art.15(3).
[217] Regulation art.15(4).
[218] Regulation art.16(2).
[219] Regulation art.28(b).
[220] Regulation art.33(2). The procedure for registration is laid down in arts 23 to 26 of the Implementing Regulation.
[221] Regulation art.32(5).

certain overriding provisions within the Regulation. There is a set of rules which seeks to allocate a specific national law to every design right. That national law governs the impact of dealings in Community design rights on third parties.[222]

The first overriding provision is that a Community design right as an **2–114** object of property shall be dealt with in its entirety and for the whole area of the EU.[223] This would appear to mean that not only is it impossible to divide a Community design right geographically, but it is also not possible to divide it in any other way, e.g. by transferring the right to apply it to some kinds of products to one person and the right to apply it to other products to someone else.

The national law which is imported to govern a Community design **2–115** right as an object of property is the national design right law[224] of the member state in which the holder has his seat or domicile on the relevant date.[225] If that does not apply, it is the country where the holder has an establishment.[226] In the case of a registered right, these provisions are governed by what is stated in the register.[227] Where there are joint holders in different member states, in the case of a registered right the law of the country of the first named proprietor applies.[228] In the case of an unregistered right, it is the law of the country of whichever joint holder they designate by agreement.[229] If they fail to designate one of them by agreement, then the law of the country in which OHIM has its seat, i.e. Spain, applies.[230] This catch-all provision also applies in any other case in which the law of a specific member state does not apply by reference to the domicile or place of establishment of the holder or joint holders of the right. The most common instance where this catch-all provision will apply is to non-EU owners of Community design rights who will find their property rights subject to Spanish law much to their surprise.

A security interest or other rights in rem may be created in a **2–116** Community registered design, and such rights shall be entered in the register and published at the request of one of the parties.[231] A registered Community design may be levied in execution, but the courts of the country whose law applies to the right have exclusive jurisdiction.[232] Although the Regulation does not specifically provide for it, it would

---

[222] Regulation art.33.
[223] Regulation art.27(1).
[224] Presumably, this is the national registered design right law when it is a Community registered design, and the national unregistered design right law if it is an unregistered Community design right. Fortunately, the property laws governing these classes of right in the UK are similar if not identical.
[225] Regulation art.27(1)(a).
[226] Regulation art.27(1)(b).
[227] Regulation art.27(2).
[228] Regulation art.27(3)(b).
[229] Regulation art.27(3)(a).
[230] Regulation art.27(4).
[231] Regulation art.29.
[232] Regulation art.30.

seem likely that unregistered Community design rights may be levied in execution in the same way as any intangible moveable property whose proper law is that of the country concerned.

2–117   Community design rights may only be involved in insolvency proceedings in the member state within whose territory the centre of a debtor's main interests is situated.[233] This provision creates rather a conundrum when the debtor's main interests are not situated in any member state because the debtor is not an EU national or company.

Licensing of Community design rights

2–118 A Community registered or unregistered design right may be licensed in respect of the whole or part only of the EU,[234] and a licence may be exclusive or non-exclusive. Thus, although the design itself can only be transferred in respect of the whole EU, it is possible to divide up the right to exploit the design geographically by creating licences. The creation of such licences is, of course, subject to the EU's general law of competition, which may restrict the circumstances in which it is permissible to do this.

2–119   A licensee who operates outside the scope of his licence as regards duration, the form in which the design may be used, or the range and quality of products to which it may be applied can be sued for infringement, as well as for breach of contract.[235] The regulation confers certain quasi-proprietary rights on a licensee. An exclusive licensee may bring proceedings against a third party for infringement if the owner, having been given notice to do so, does not himself bring proceedings in an appropriate period.[236] A non-exclusive licensee may bring proceedings if the owner gives him permission to do so.[237] A licensee, whether exclusive or non-exclusive, may join in to an infringement action brought by the owner of the right for the purpose of obtaining compensation for damage suffered by him.[238]

Law governing applications for registration as objects of property

2–120 The same rules govern applications for registration as govern designs once they are registered.[239] In the case of applications, the relevant entries in the register are made upon registration of the resulting Community design.[240]

---

[233] Regulation art.31.
[234] Regulation art.32(1).
[235] Regulation art.32(2).
[236] Regulation art.32(3).
[237] Regulation art.32(3).
[238] Regulation art.32(4).
[239] Regulation art.34(1).
[240] Regulation art.34(2).

7. Application Procedure

Application for a UK registered design

National procedures for the registration of design rights are not subject to   **2–121**
harmonisation by the Directive. For this reason, the application procedure
for registration of a design in the United Kingdom was initially largely
unchanged, except in some respects resulting from changes in the
substantive rights granted by registration.[241] However, as from October 1,
2006 the RDA 1949 was amended[242] to abolish substantive examination of
UK national registered design applications, so bringing the UK system
more into line with the system for registration of Community designs at
OHIM (see paras 2–130 et seq. below).

The Designs Registry

The functions of the Registrar of Designs under the RDA(E) are per-   **2–122**
formed by the Comptroller-General of Patents, Trade Marks and
Designs.[243] The Designs Registry is a branch of the UK Intellectual
Property Office (previously called the Patent Office) under the overall
direction of the Comptroller, who now enjoys the rather more modern
title of Chief Executive of the UK IPO. An application to register a design
may be made by an applicant in person, or more usually is made through
a firm of patent attorneys.

Method of application

The application is made on Designs Form DF2A,[244] which, when com-   **2–123**
pleted, must be sent to the Intellectual Property Office in Newport. A
single Designs Form DF2A can include an application to register multiple
designs. Designs Form DF2A no longer contains a declaration which
must be signed by or on behalf of the applicant to the effect they claim to
be the proprietor of the design and believe it has individual character.[245]
However, it is still a statutory requirement imposed by RDA(E) s.3(3) that
an application for registration "shall be made by the proprietor of the
design or designs", so presumably the filing of Designs Form DF2A must
be taken as an implicit claim to proprietorship of the design or designs to
which it refers. In addition, although substantive examination for novelty

---

[241] For example, the fact that design registrations no longer relate to a specific kind of
article.
[242] By the Regulatory Reform (Registered Designs) Order 2006 (SI 2006/1974), below.
[243] RDA(E) s.44(1), definition of "registrar".
[244] RDA(E) s.3(1) requires that an application for a registered design shall be made in the
prescribed form. For the prescribed Form DF2A, see App.A10 below.
[245] Such a declaration was included on the previous Designs Form 2A which was prescribed
by the Registered Designs Rules 2006 (SI 2006/3950).

and individual character has been abolished, these still remain grounds of invalidity on which the design can be revoked. However, the absence on the application form of a declaration that the applicant believes that the design has individual character would seem to imply that an applicant who knows that the design sought to be registered is old or lacks individual character and applies to register it simply to cause trouble for competitors is not (at least expressly) making any kind of false statement.

2–124   Section 3(3) of RDA(E) states that an application for registration of a design or designs in which national unregistered design right subsists shall be made by the person claiming to be the (unregistered) design right owner. Despite this statutory provision, Designs Form DF2A[246] does not contain any formal declaration that the applicant is the owner of any unregistered design right subsisting in the design which he seeks to register. Presumably the filing of a Designs Form DF2A must be regarded by the UK IPO as an implicit claim that the applicant is the proprietor of any national design right.

2–125   The omission of this declaration and the declaration of proprietorship of the registered design from the Form presumably follow from the amendments to RDA(E) which were made at the time when substantive examination was abolished.[247] Before these amendments, s.3A(3) required the Registrar to refuse an application for the registration of a design unless the applicant claimed to be proprietor of the registered design and also, if UK unregistered design right subsisted, of the unregistered right as well as the registered right.[248] RDA(E) s.3A(3) was amended[249] to require the Registrar to refuse the application if "it appears to the registrar that" the applicant is not entitled to apply under either of these grounds. Thus it seems that the Registrar must refuse the application if some information is brought to his attention which indicates that these grounds of refusal arise, but is no longer under any positive duty to take steps to check for these grounds.

Representations or specimens of the design

2–126   A representation or specimen of each design must be included in or accompany the application form.[250] Specimens will be disregarded if they are hazardous or perishable,[251] or too large or thick.[252] A representation or specimen of a design which consists of a repeat pattern (e.g. for

---

[246] Unlike its predecessor, Designs Form 2A.

[247] By the Regulatory Reform (Registered Designs) Order 2006 (SI 2006/1974): see App.A9 below.

[248] RDA(E) s.3(3).

[249] By ibid, art.12(4).

[250] Registered Designs Rules 2006 r.4(1)(b).

[251] Rule 4(6).

[252] Rule 5(3)–(4); the specimen must not exceed 29.7cm x 21cm x 1cm.

wallpaper) must include the complete pattern and a sufficient portion of the repeat in length and width to show how the pattern repeats, and the application must contain a statement that it relates to a repeating surface pattern.[253] Representations are normally drawings or photographs of the design. The representation or specimen must show clearly what the design is, as the scope of the monopoly must be made clear to the public.[254] A "statement of novelty" is no longer filed for post-2001 registrations, but instead a "partial disclaimer" may, but need not, be filed.[255] This indicates that the design is in the appearance of part only of a product or limits the scope or extent of the protection of the design conferred by the registration.

In *Ford Motor Co Ltd's Application*,[256] the representation lodged in support of an application showed a car wheel from one view only. Under the pre-2001 law then in force, a registered design had to relate to a whole article and could not be for part of a product as under the present law. Further illustrations of the wheel were called for, but the applicants contended these were both unnecessary and in practice unobtainable since at the time when the design was made, it was no more than an artist's conception. In holding that the application ought nevertheless to proceed, Whitford J. in the Registered Designs Appeal Tribunal said[257]:

2–127

> "In design cases, the really important and significant question . . . is: Does this application adequately show the design features which the applicant desires to protect in such a way that when he has secured his monopoly there will be no difficulty in ascertaining, when you look at the representation, what the design features are? . . . In this case, it is . . . clear that the appearance of the wheel from the side or back is utterly irrelevant from the point of view of a claim to a design . . . and . . . inclusion of pictures of the side and the back would be a positive disadvantage."

Since the design is only that which can be seen by the eye, sectional drawings will only be admissible provided they only illustrate features which can be seen in the finished article without dismemberment or severance. An exception exists in the case of articles (such as Easter eggs) that are intended to be broken up in the course of normal use or consumption; in such a case, internal features which are only visible on breakup may form part of a design registration.[258]

2–128

---

[253] Rule 4(7).

[254] *Re English Electric Co's Application* (1933) 50 R.P.C. 359; *Pugh v Riley Cycle Co* (1912) 29 R.P.C. 196 at 202. Even if the Office is happy with the filed representations of a design, an unclear representation may cause serious problems when it comes to suing for infringement, or even result in the design registration being invalid.

[255] This is an option permitted by r.6. As to the old statements of novelty, see paras 3–253 et seq. below.

[256] [1972] R.P.C. 320.

[257] [1972] R.P.C. 320 at 330.

[258] *Ferrero SpA's Application* [1978] R.P.C. 473, RDAT.

Illegal or immoral, etc. designs

2–129 Before 2001, the Registrar was neither required nor authorised to register a design the use of which would, in his opinion, be contrary to law or morality.[259] For post-2001 registrations, it is provided that "a right in a registered design does not subsist in a design which is contrary to public policy or to accepted principles of morality".[260] This formulation presumably means that an immoral, etc. design can be challenged by way of invalidity proceedings as well as by the Registrar at the application stage. Former rules have been repealed[261] which allowed the refusal of designs depicting portraits of the Royal Family, armorial bearings, etc. or the name or portrait of a living or recently deceased person in the absence of consent from that person or his personal representatives,[262] but these have been replaced by broadly similar grounds for refusal of an application in the newly inserted Sch.A1 to the RDA(E).[263]

Examination of applications and Office objections

2–130 As has previously been mentioned, examination of applications for UK registered designs for most substantive grounds of invalidity has been abolished.[264] However, applications are still examined for compliance with formal requirements and for compliance with the limited grounds specified in RDA(E) s.3A(4). These grounds are:

(a) that an application does not comply with s.1(2) of the Act, i.e. that it does not comply with the definition of "design" meaning the appearance of the whole or a part of a product resulting from the features of, in particular, the lines, contours, colours, shape, texture or materials of the product or its ornamentation;

(b) that it does not comply with s.1C (designs dictated by their technical functions) or 1D (public policy or morality) of the Act;

(c) that there is a ground of refusal under Sch.A1 to the Act. Schedule A1 provides for refusal of applications for designs containing representations of the Royal and other arms, national

---

[259] RDA(A) s.43(1). However, a design should not be refused solely because a section of the public is likely to be offended: *Masterman's Design* [1991] R.P.C. 89, RDAT at 103: furry doll with male genitalia.

[260] RDA(E) s.1D. This is a non-harmonised standard so the principles applied may differ from state to state of the EU.

[261] By the 2001 Regulations.

[262] Former rr.24 and 25 of the 1995 Rules.

[263] See para.2–046 above.

[264] See para.2–121 above.

flags, or portraits of members of the Royal family or other persons unless appropriate consent is obtained.

In fact, the practice of the Office in the past has been not to refuse a **2–131** registration if there exists at the date of application for registration some reasonable doubt as to the registrability of a design: it was the practice to resolve the doubt in the applicant's favour.[265] The justification for this practice was that it is possible for the validity of a wrongly granted registration later to be challenged in court, but a wrongly refused application cannot later be revived.[266] Whether it is appropriate to continue this generous practice in relation to the much narrower grounds of refusal which now remain is yet to be seen.

Hearing on the Registrar's objections

If there appears to the Registrar to be any objection to the application, a **2–132** statement of objections is sent to the applicant and the applicant then has two months in which he may apply to the Registrar for a hearing, or make observations in writing on those objections.[267] Hearings are normally conducted not by the Registrar in person,[268] but by a senior official of the Designs Registry acting on his behalf. Where the Registrar decides to refuse an application, he must send his written reasons to the applicant, and the date when they are sent is deemed to be the date of the decision.[269]

Appeal from the Registrar's decision

An appeal lies against a decision of the Registrar to refuse to register a **2–133** design.[270] Such an appeal (as well as any appeal against a decision of the Registrar under other provisions of the Act, such as decisions on declarations of invalidity) lies to the Registered Designs Appeal Tribunal ("the RDAT").[271] The applicant has six weeks from the date of the decision (which is the date when the written reasons are sent to him[272]),

---

[265] *McMillan's Design* [1972] R.P.C. 294.
[266] However the applicant can appeal against the refusal; see para.2–133 below.
[267] Rule 8.
[268] Who is the Comptroller-General of Patents, Trade Marks and Designs, now styled the Chief Executive of the Intellectual Property Office; see para.2–122 above.
[269] Rule 8(5) and (6).
[270] RDA(E) s.3D. An appeal also lies under this subsection against a decision of the Registrar relating to the modification of an application: as to modification, see para.2–058 above.
[271] RDA(E) s.28(1).
[272] Rule 8(6), which deems the date of the decision to be the date when the Registrar's written reasons are *sent* to the applicant.

or 14 days in the case of a decision on a matter of procedure, to appeal to the RDAT.[273]

2–134   The RDAT is an anomalous body. Although nominally it is an administrative tribunal rather than a court, it is required to consist of judges of the English High Court nominated by the Lord Chancellor, together with one judge of the Court of Session.[274] In practice, the English High Court judges who are nominated are the judges of the Patents Court, a special sub-division within the Chancery Division.[275] The Patents Court hears appeals from the Comptroller in patent matters,[276] and hears patent infringement and validity proceedings,[277] and registered design infringement and validity proceedings.[278] Thus, the same judge sitting in the same courtroom will hear appeals from the Comptroller in registered design proceedings, except that he will sit as the Tribunal and not as the High Court.[279] The parallel is completed by the inclusion of a judge of the Court of Session as a member of the RDAT, since he will hear appeals in the rare cases when the Intellectual Property Office conducts Designs Registry hearings in Scotland.[280]

2–135   On an appeal, the RDAT may exercise any power which could have been exercised by the Registrar in the proceedings from which the appeal is brought.[281] The procedure of the RDAT is regulated by its own procedural rules,[282] including rules regulating the right of audience.[283] The RDAT may examine witnesses on oath,[284] and has the same powers as the High Court to award costs.[285]

---

[273] RDAT Rules 1950 (as amended) r.1(2). It used to be the case that the time appeal ran from the date when the written reasons were *received* by the applicant, but the Registered Designs Rules 2006 have changed that (by r.8(6)). The view of the Registry as expressed in Patent Office Practice Note 1/2003 (Revised) on Appeals to the Court from the Comptroller [2003] R.P.C. 817, at para.12, reflects the previous position. The Registrar has jurisdiction to extend the time for appealing to the RDAT prior to its expiry.

[274] RDA(E) s.28(2).

[275] CPR Pt 63.

[276] The Patents Act 1977 s.97.

[277] CPR 63.1(1)(a)(i).

[278] See para.6–001 below.

[279] Apart from the sartorial effect that the judge and other participants will not be robed, this means that the rules of the High Court restricting rights of audience to barristers and specially qualified solicitors do not apply; however, in the Patents Court's parallel patent appellate jurisdiction, special provision is made allowing for patent attorneys and others such as employed lawyers to appear; Patents Act 1977 s.102A.

[280] If the Office conducts a patent hearing in Scotland, the appeal from its decision lies to the Court of Session, instead of to the Patents Court which is part of the English High Court: Patents Act 1977 s.97(4).

[281] RDA(E) s.28(7).

[282] Registered Designs Appeal Tribunal Rules 1950 (SI 1950/430), as amended; see App.A10 below.

[283] RDA(E) s.28(8). RDAT r.5A restricts the right of audience before the RDAT to solicitors or counsel qualified in any part of the United Kingdom, or patent attorneys.

[284] RDA(E) s.28(4).

[285] RDA(A) s.29(5); or in Scotland, the same power as the Court of Session to award expenses. However, its powers to award costs are in practice exercised on more restrictive principles; see *Re Stilton Trade Mark* [1967] R.P.C. 173; and *Re Brampton's Designs* (1926) 43 R.P.C. 55, for the older practice.

In *Re Game Balls Co Ltd's Application*,[286] it was held that unless it can be   **2–136**
shown on appeal that the Registrar has been proceeding upon some
wrong principle, he must be the prima facie judge of the question in front
of him, and as he had done nothing wrong in principle the appeal was
dismissed.[287]

Further challenge to a decision of the RDAT

There is no provision for any statutory appeal from decisions of the   **2–137**
RDAT. In this respect, the RDAT is anomalously different from the
Patents Court when exercising the parallel jurisdiction on patent appeals,
where there is a statutory appeal to the Court of Appeal.[288] However,
despite the composition of the RDAT, appeals before it are explicitly
stated not to be proceedings of the High Court,[289] and in consequence of
its nominal status as an "inferior" tribunal[290] its decisions may the subject
of judicial review under the common law jurisdiction exercised by the
Administrative Court, a sub-division of the Queen's Bench Division of
the High Court. A review of the scope of and procedure for judicial
review is outside the scope of this book, but for present purposes the
most important potential ground of judicial review is that the Tribunal's
decision is based on an error of law.[291]

The existence of this ground of judicial review does allow what is in   **2–138**
effect an appeal to the higher courts from decisions of the RDAT on points
of law,[292] albeit by a circuitous route.[293]

Grant of certificate and inspection of registration

When a design is registered the Registrar must issue a certificate of   **2–139**
registration to the proprietor.[294] The right of the proprietor to sue
infringers dates from the issue of this certificate, not from the date of
registration (which is normally the same as the date of application).[295]

---

[286] (1928) 45 R.P.C. 26.
[287] cf. *Gutta Percha & Rubber (London) Ltd's Application* (1935) 52 R.P.C. 383 overruled on
another point in the House of Lords in *Stenor v Whitesides (Clitheroe) Ltd* (1948) 65 R.P.C.
1.
[288] The Patents Act 1977 s.97(3).
[289] RDA(E) s.28(9).
[290] As distinct from a superior court of record such as the High Court, whose proceedings
are not subject to judicial review.
[291] Judicial review can also take place on the ground of breach of natural justice in the
procedure of the Tribunal; see *R. v Patents Appeal Tribunal, ex p. Geigy* [1963] R.P.C. 341
and *Baldwin and Francis Ltd's Application* [1959] R.P.C. 221.
[292] For example, the judicial review of the decision of the RDAT which went on appeal to the
House of Lords in *Ford Motor Co Ltd's Design Appns* [1995] R.P.C. 167.
[293] The route involves the initial review of the decision of a specialist judge of the High
Court sitting in the RDAT by non-specialist judges at the same judicial level sitting in the
Administrative Court, before the case can go up to the Court of Appeal.
[294] RDA(E) s.18(1).
[295] RDA(E) s.7A(6).

2–140   It used to be the case that certain categories of design could be kept secret for a time even after they had been registered.[296] The rules prescribed that in the case of a design for textile goods, for three years, and in the case of a design for wallpaper and lace for two years, the design as registered was kept secret, and was not open to inspection by the public.[297] As regards designs for all other articles, the design will be kept secret only from the date of application until registration is effected.[298] The only exception under the present law relates to designs which are relevant for defence purposes where publication would be prejudicial to the defence of the realm.[299]

Convention applications

2–141   There is power to declare by Order in Council with a view to fulfilment of a treaty, convention, arrangement or engagement that any country specified in the order is a Convention country for the purposes of the Act.[300] The relevant convention is the Paris Convention for the Protection of Industrial Property.[301] Any person who has applied for protection for a design in a Convention country, or his legal representatives or assignee, is entitled to registration of his design in this country based on the date of his application in the Convention country.[302] The application must (by art.4(C)(1) of the Convention) be made here within six months of the date of application in the Convention country. The documents required to be lodged with a normal application will be required on a Convention application, and in addition, there must be lodged with the application or within three months thereafter a copy of the representation of the design filed or deposited in respect of the first application in the Convention country; this representation must be duly certified by the authority with

---

[296] RDA(E) s.22(2) (now repealed) authorised rules to be made prescribing classes of products in which the representation or specimen would not be open to inspection for a period after registration.

[297] The Registered Designs Rules 1995 as amended (now revoked) r.69.

[298] From this date, the design itself, together with any evidence filed by the applicant in support of the contention that the appearance of the article is material, are open to public inspection; RDA(E) s.22(1).

[299] RDA(E) s.5(1); and see paras 8–012 to 8–015 below.

[300] RDA(E) s.13(1).

[301] Original version signed on March 20, 1883, as revised at Brussels on December 14, 1900 at Washington on June 2, 1911, at the Hague on November 6, 1925 at London on June 2, 1934, at Lisbon on October 31, 1958 and at Stockholm on July 14, 1967. See App.F4 below.

[302] RDA(E) s.14(2). Where the design is applied for in a country (in the case in question, Germany) whose law does not require the applicant to specify any particular article or article to which the design is to be applied, then it seems that Convention Priority could validly be claimed in the UK for a series of applications relating to any articles which are within the scope of the overseas application: *Deyhle's Design Applications* [1982] R.P.C. 526, RDAT. Although UK law does not now require that a design is restricted to a particular article, this point is still relevant to the validity of Convention priority claims of pre-2001 designs.

which it was filed or verified to the satisfaction of the Registrar,[303] and the applicant may be directed to provide a translation.[304]

It is to be noticed that r.39 which gives the Registrar a general discretion to extend periods of time prescribed by the rules, does not extend to the six-month time limit for filing Convention applications, which is laid down by the statute,[305] which in turn reflects the requirements of the Convention: art.4(C)(1). **2–142**

Application for registration of a Community design

The system for registration of Community designs is effectively a deposit system only. There is no substantive examination of the application to see, for example, if it is novel and has individual character. The UK registration system has now been brought into line[306] after an initial period during which the deposit-only Community system ran side by side with the examination based UK system. Somebody who wishes to harass competitors by registering obviously invalid designs is now free to make use of either system. **2–143**

The application to register a Community design is made to OHIM: the Office for Harmonisation in the Internal Market (Trade Marks and Designs). The Office is located in Alicante, Spain. The Office was established by the Community Trade Mark Regulation, and the Community Designs Regulation entrusted the Office with the additional task of registering and administering the Community design system.[307] Most of the administrative and structural provisions governing the Office, its Divisions and its Boards of Appeal are to be found in the Community Trade Mark Regulation rather than in the Community Designs Regulation. This work deals with those provisions only where they directly impinge on the procedures for registration, ownership or invalidation of Community designs. **2–144**

Filing the application form

The form of application is prescribed by the President of OHIM.[308] The application form may be filed either at OHIM itself or at a national designs registry or the Benelux Design Office as receiving office.[309] **2–145**

---

[303] Rule 7.
[304] Rule 7(6).
[305] RDA(E) s.14(1) proviso.
[306] See para.2–130 above.
[307] Regulation art.2.
[308] The current form of application is downloadable as a PDF from the OHIM website at *http://www.oami.europa.eu* [Accessed August 24, 2010] and the form can be completed and sent to OHIM or to a receiving office; as an alternative an application may be made online on the OHIM website at *http://oami.europa.eu/ows/rw/pages/QPLUS/forms/electronic/fileApplicationRCD.en.do* [Accessed June 10, 2010].
[309] Regulation art.35.

Arrangements are in place for the direct electronic filing of applications with OHIM over the internet for users who register to make such applications.[310] The Regulation requires applications to contain certain basic information: this is the identity of the applicant,[311] a representation[312] of the design suitable for reproduction (or a sample in the case of a two-dimensional design if a request for deferment of publication is made), and an indication of the products to which the design relates.[313] In addition, the application may contain a description explaining the representation or the specimen,[314] a request for deferment of publication,[315] the identity of the representative (normally a patent attorney) if the applicant has appointed one, the classification (under the Locarno Convention classes) of products to which the design is intended to be applied, and the citation of the designer or teams of designers or a statement that they have waived the right to be cited.[316] The identification of the intended product and the Locarno classification does not affect the scope of protection of the design, which extends to any product in which the design is used.[317] An application fee and publication fee is payable.[318] The application should include a claim for Convention or exhibition priority, if these are claimed.[319]

2–146   OHIM has five working languages; English, French, German, Spanish and Italian. An application may be filed in any Community language, but if it is not one of the languages of the Office then the applicant must

---

[310] Details at *http://www.oami.europa.eu* [Accessed August 23, 2010].

[311] The application must state the name, address and nationality of the applicant and the State in which the applicant is domiciled or in which it has its seat or establishment: Implementing Regulation art.1(b); it must also contain the signature of the applicant or his representative: art.1(i).

[312] Detailed rules as to the form of the representation, which may be filed on paper or electronically, are set out in the Implementing Regulation art.4.

[313] Regulation art.36(1) and (2).

[314] The description may not exceed 100 words: Implementing Regulation art.1(2)(a). Its purpose is to explain the representation: it shall not contain statements as to the purported novelty or individual character of the design or its technical value.

[315] As to deferment of publication, see para.2–042 above.

[316] Regulation art.36(3). These requirements are specified in more detail in art.1 of the Implementing Regulation.

[317] Regulation art.36(6): in *Green Lane Products Ltd v PMS International Group Ltd* [2008] EWCA Civ 358; [2008] F.S.R. 28; [2008] E.C.D.R. 15, CA, the Court of Appeal at paras 51–52 rejected a suggestion in an OHIM Board of Appeal decision that an alteration to the indication of the type of product to which a registered design is intended to be applied might affect inter alia the extent of the exclusive rights, pointing out that art.36(6) says "quite the opposite": see *Casio's App Case R 1421/2006–3* [2007] E.C.D.R. 13 at para.20. However, the General Court in Case T-9/07 *Grupo Promer Mon Graphic SA v OHIM* March 18, 2010, [2010] E.C.D.R. 7 suggested that the indication of the product may affect the identity of the notional "informed user" of the design, and if so this may have an indirect effect on issues of validity and scope of protection: see para.2–043 above. The Locarno classification serves purely administrative purposes (assisting searching): Implementing Regulation art.3(2). For the Locarno classification, see App.F4 below; a far more detailed listing of current OHIM guidance on classification is available on the OHIM website.

[318] Regulation art.36(4); for the level of fees, see Commission Regulation (EC) No.2246/2002, App.B3 below.

[319] Implementing Regulation art.1(1)(f) and (g).

indicate one of those languages into which the application is to be translated and which becomes the language of proceedings in the Office relating to that application.[320]

Multiple applications

Several designs may be combined in one multiple application, as long as all of the products to which the designs relate are within the same Locarno class and additional fees are paid.[321] OHIM will require a multiple application to be divided up if it relates to more than one class.[322] A multiple application gives rise to multiple Community registered rights each of which may be dealt with separately.[323]   **2–147**

Formal examination only

The application is examined for compliance with formal requirements, and if it is in order it is accorded a date of filing.[324] If in the course of carrying out this formal examination, OHIM notices either that the design is not a design as defined by art.3(a) of the Regulation,[325] or that it is contrary to public policy or to accepted principles of morality, it shall refuse the application.[326] It should be noted that this examination is extremely limited: OHIM is not mandated to examine for these matters at all; it only refuses on these grounds if it happens to "notice" that they are applicable in the course of examining for other matters. In addition, the only substantive ground is that what is applied for is not a design at all; there is no search for prior art and no right to refuse on the ground that the design applied for is not new or does not have individual character.   **2–148**

The effect of this lack of substantive application is to remove a filter against the registration of obviously invalid designs and transfer the burden of removing them onto trade competitors who will need to commence invalidation proceedings.   **2–149**

Registration

If the formal requirements relating to the application form have been satisfied and OHIM has not "noticed" that one of the grounds in the   **2–150**

---

[320] Regulation art.98; Implementing Regulation art.1(1)(h).
[321] Regulation art.37.
[322] Implementing Regulation art.2(2).
[323] Regulation art.37(4).
[324] Regulation art.45; Implementing Regulation art.10.
[325] See para.2–009 above.
[326] Regulation art.47(1).

preceding paragraph applies, then the design is automatically regis-tered.[327] Upon registration, the design is published in the Community Designs Bulletin.[328]

Appeals against decisions of OHIM

2–151   A decision to refuse an application or other administrative decisions relating to an application may be the subject of an appeal from OHIM to a Board of Appeal.[329] An appeal has suspensive effect.[330] A decision of a Board of Appeal may be challenged by an action brought before the Court of Justice of the European Union: such an action will be dealt with initially by the General Court (formerly known as the Court of First Instance) which is attached to that Court.[331] The action before the General Court is a review of the legality of the decision of the Board of Appeal, not to review the facts in the light of documents or evidence produced for the first time in the General Court. It follows that new documents or evidence are not admissible in the General Court (and by extension on any further appeal to the ECJ), even if the applicant wishes to adduce them in the light of points raised in the decision of the Board of Appeal.[332]

International applications under the Hague Agreement

2–152   As an alternative to making an application to OHIM for a Community registered design, it is possible to make an international application under the Hague System for the international registration of designs, which is administered by the World Intellectual Property Organisation (WIPO). The countries or international bodies from which such an application can be made are those which are signatories to the Geneva Act[333] of the Hague Agreement.[334] The European Union became a party to the Geneva Act with effect from January 1, 2008. It has made provision for giving effect to Hague System international registrations by Council Regulation (EC) No.1891/2006 "amending Regulations (EC) No.6/2002 and (EC) No.40/94 to give effect to the accession of the European Community to the Geneva Act of the Hague Agreement concerning the international registration of industrial designs" which has inserted new

---

[327] Regulation art.48.
[328] Regulation art.49; the Bulletin is provided for in art.73(1) and in practice is published electronically: *http://oami.eu.int/bulletin/ctm/ctm_bulletin_en.htm* [Accessed June 10, 2010].
[329] Regulation art.55(1).
[330] Regulation art.55(1).
[331] Regulation art.61.
[332] Case T-9/07 *Grupo Promer Mon Graphic SA v OHIM* March 18, 2010, [2010] E.C.D.R. 7, paras 22–25.
[333] For the Geneva Act, see App.F5 below.
[334] For an up to date list, see the WIPO website at *http://www.wipo.int/treaties/en/documents/pdf/hague.pdf* [Accessed June 10, 2010].

arts 106a to 106f into the Community Design Regulation.[335] A number of EU Member States (at the time of this edition Bulgaria, Croatia, Denmark, Estonia, France, Germany, Hungary, Latvia, Lithuania, Poland, Romania, Slovenia and Spain) are signatories to the Geneva Act and part of the Hague System, but the United Kingdom is not.

Any person who is a national of, domiciled or habitually resident in, or has a real and effective industrial or commercial establishment in one of the Contracting Parties to the Geneva Act may file an international application.[336] The Contracting Parties are either individual states or intergovernmental organisations such as the European Union. The international application is filed either directly with the International Bureau,[337] or via the office of a Contracting Party'[338] unless that Contracting Party has declared that it is not willing to act as a receiving office for international applications.[339] The European Union has so declared[340] and accordingly OHIM will not act as a receiving office for international applications. Thus, a UK citizen or resident, etc. will need to file an international application with the International Bureau; a citizen or resident of an EU Member State which is itself a signatory to the Geneva Act may have the choice of filing either at the International Bureau or at the national designs registry of the Member State.

2–153

An international application designates the Contracting Parties (which are countries or intergovernmental organisations) in the territory of which the applicant seeks registered design protection.[341] Registration by the International Bureau takes place virtually immediately upon only minimal examination for compliance with formal requirements and payment of the correct fees[342]; the onus is then on the national or intergovernmental designs offices designated in the application to examine the international registration and object to it if it does not comply with the requirements of their own law for registered design protection and communicate a refusal. International registrations which designate the EU are examined by OHIM on the same limited grounds as applications filed directly with OHIM and the refusal (if there is one) is communicated within six months of publication.[343] Unless there is such a refusal, an international registration takes effect (if it designates the EU) within the

2–154

---

[335] See App.B1, paras B1–108—B1–113 below.

[336] Geneva Act art.3; see App.F5, para.F5–003 below.

[337] Geneva Act art.4(1)(a). The International Bureau is a branch of WIPO in Geneva. Applications can be filed either on paper or electronically, although if filed electronically they must contain a representation of the design rather than a specimen. An application filed at the International Bureau must be in one of the Bureau's official languages which are English, French or Spanish.

[338] Geneva Act art.4(1)(a).

[339] Geneva Act art.4(1)(b).

[340] Regulation art.106b.

[341] Regulation art.5(1)(v).

[342] Regulation art.10(1). Publication of the application may in some circumstances be deferred: see art.11.

[343] Regulation art.106e.

EU as if it were a Community registered design,[344] and the same procedures apply as regards enforcement and invalidation.[345]

2–155   International applications should not be confused with Convention applications under the Paris Convention under which an application for a Community or UK registered design may claim priority from a previous filing.[346] In fact, an international application may claim Paris Convention priority in exactly the same way as an application for a Community design made directly to OHIM or a UK application made to the UK IPO.[347]

8. Term of Protection

Registered rights

2–156   UK and Community registered designs have a term of up to 25 years from their filing date, obtained in five-year increments.[348] There are provisions for the restoration of lapsed rights if a belated application is made after a failure to renew.[349] A registered design may be cancelled or surrendered which prematurely brings its term to an end.[350]

Unregistered Community rights

2–157   An unregistered Community design has a term of three years from the date when it was first made available to the public within the Community.[351]

---

[344] Regulation art 106d.

[345] Regulation art 106f; see paras 6–035 et seq. below.

[346] See para.2–061 above.

[347] Geneva Act art.6.

[348] Directive art.10; transposed to RDA(E) s.8; Regulation art.12.

[349] RDA(E) s.8A and 8B; Regulation art.13(3).

[350] Note that in this respect a cancellation or surrender differs from a declaration of invalidity, which has retrospective effect. Cancellation of UK registrations is governed by RDA(E) s.11, and surrender of Community registrations by Regulation art.51.

[351] Regulation art.11; for the concept of making a design available to the public, see para.2–070 above.

CHAPTER 3

PRE-2001 UK REGISTERED DESIGNS

1. Application of the Old Law to Existing Registered Designs

The harmonised EU law of registered designs came into force on December 9, 2001,[1] and that new law, set out in Ch.2, applies to all registered designs resulting from an application filed in the UK Registry on or after that date. However, major aspects of the old law continue to apply to designs granted or applied for before that date. Most importantly, the old law of validity applies to the determination of applications pending on that date and to granted designs.[2] Since there are major differences between the old and new body of law, and since the new law is meant to be a new European harmonised system rather than a development of old domestic law, the law of validity of pre-2001 designs is presented separately in this chapter rather than attempting to interweave it with the exposition of the new law in Ch.2. In addition, the old and new versions of the Registered Designs Act are printed separately in the Appendices.[3]

3–001

[1] The date of coming into force of the Registered Designs Regulations 2001 (SI 2001/3949) (App.A3 below). This was later than the latest date permitted by the Directive for Member States to transpose its provisions into national law (October 28, 2001), so there is an argument that the owner of a registered design granted on an application filed after October 28, 2001 is entitled to have its validity decided according to the new rather than the old law: see *Oakley Inc v Animal Ltd* [2005] EWHC 210 Ch; [2005] R.P.C. 30, Peter Prescott Q.C. (reversed on appeal on main issue at [2006] R.P.C. 9) and para.2–004 above.
[2] 2001 Regulations regs 10, 11 and 12 (App.A3, paras A3–004—A3–006 below).
[3] Apps A2 and A5 below.

3–002   In fact, there are not two but effectively three different versions of the 1949 Act now in force and applying to different categories of extant designs of different vintages. New designs applied for from December 9, 2001 onwards are governed by the version of the Act amended to conform with the new European harmonised law under the Directive.[4] That version of the Act is referred to in this work as RDA(E). Designs whose application date was before December 9, 2001, but on or after August 1, 1989 have their validity governed by the Registered Designs Act 1949 as amended by the Copyright, Designs and Patents Act 1988. That version of the Act is referred to in this work as RDA(A). Designs applied for before August 1, 1989 still have their validity governed by the version[5] of the 1949 Act before it was amended by the 1988 Act. The amendments made by the 1988 Act were quite substantial, and are noted on the RDA(A) version of the Act in the Appendices so as to avoid cluttering up the RDA(E) version.[6] Since registered designs have a maximum term of 25 years, it will still be necessary to look at the pre-1989 version of the Act until 2014, and at the pre-2001 version until 2026.

3–003   The effect of the transitional provisions is that, subject to some small qualifications, the validity of every registered design in force today is governed by the law that was in force at its date of application. By contrast, there are no transitional provisions which restrict the application of the new *infringement* law and so the new European harmonised law applies to the infringement of all existing designs as well as to new designs granted since 2001. This is capable of producing some startling and quite unfortunate consequences, because the scope of designs under the new law is in general broader than under the old: overall impression rather than substantial difference of design. Each system of law is internally self consistent when it comes to infringement and validity. Under the old law, it was always safe to reproduce a prior art design, because either the scope of the registered design was too narrow to cover it, or the registered design was invalid. The same is true under the new law because, although the scope of infringement is probably wider than under the pre-2001 national law, the same test[7] is applied as to the necessary difference of the registered design from the prior art. However, when these two different standards are mismatched together in the case of an existing pre-2001 registered design, it now becomes possible, and indeed likely in many cases, that a registered design will not be invalidated by a piece of prior art (because it will be materially different from it under the old law), but will cover that prior art as a matter of infringement (because it produces the same overall impression). The only saving grace is that there is a transitional provision which protects people

---

[4] For an exposition of the Directive, see Ch.2 above.
[5] 2001 Regulations reg.13 (App.A3, para.A3–006 below).
[6] At App.A5 below.
[7] Or the test may possibly be slightly more stringent in the case of validity than in the case of infringement: see para.2–097 above.

who continue to perform acts which were not infringements before December 9, 2001.[8] However, it is no longer necessarily safe to go back and reproduce a prior art design, even one of one's own designs, unless it has been in continuous production since before December 9, 2001.

In addition to widening the scope of infringement in the manner set out above, the new law also widens the scope of infringement of existing registered designs by removing the restriction that the infringement must be an article of the kind for which the design is registered.[9] It follows that existing registered designs can be infringed by applying the design to any kind of article. This may in practice be impossible in the case of designs consisting of the shape and configuration of an article, but surface patterning designs may well be applicable to a wide range of articles. **3–004**

Although the old law of infringement of registered designs is no longer in force, the existing body of law is retained for reference in this chapter because as yet there is only limited case law relating to the new harmonised European infringement test and because it is still of practical interest in certain jurisdictions whose law is historically linked with UK registered design law—see Ch.11 below. The major differences between the new and the old law will need to be borne in mind when drawing on the old authorities. **3–005**

Apart from infringement and validity, the law relating to property rights in registered designs has not been the subject of European harmonisation and remains essentially unchanged. The law on this subject as set out in this chapter therefore applies to both old and new designs. **3–006**

The amendments to the 1949 Act were not made by Act of Parliament but instead by regulations under the European Communities Act 1972 implementing, or purporting to implement, the United Kingdom's obligations under the Directive.[10] It is therefore in principle possible for the validity of the changes made by regulation to the 1949 Act to be challenged either on the grounds of disconformity with the obligations imposed by the Directive when properly construed, or on the grounds that they go beyond what the Directive requires.[11] Such an attack on the validity of the regulations was however rejected by the Court of Appeal.[12] The application of the new law of infringement onto existing registered designs, despite the anomalies which it creates, does appear to be required by the Directive, at least by implication, since art.11(8) expressly permits member states to retain the old law of validity for old designs **3–007**

---

[8] 2001 Regulations reg.14(3), based on art.12(2) of the Directive.
[9] 2001 Regulations reg.12(5) and 13(7) and see para.2–021 above.
[10] See para.2–004 above.
[11] Because the European Communities Act 1972 s.2(2) does not confer a general power to amend Acts of Parliament as the bureaucracy wishes, but only a power to amend in order to implement a treaty right or obligation of the UK or to deal with matters arising out of such obligations or rights: see R. (Orange Personal Communications Ltd) v Secretary of State for Trade and Industry [2001] 3 C.M.L.R. 36.
[12] See para.2–004 above.

and makes no mention of the law of infringement, and art.12(2) protecting continuing acts appears to assume that the law of infringement will change on the coming into force of the Directive.

2. What was a "Design" Capable of Registration?

The nature of registered design protection

3–008   An exclusive right was conferred by registration of a design under the Registered Designs Act 1949, as amended by CDPA 1988. This right was in the nature of a monopoly right, which means that it was infringed by another party who employed that design or a design not substantially different[13] from it, regardless of whether that other party copied from the owner of the registered design, or created his own design entirely independently. In this respect, the registered design right is fundamentally different from unregistered design right and copyright. For both of those rights, copying is an essential element of the test of infringement.[14]

3–009   Old UK registered designs are limited to the protection of aesthetic as opposed to functional designs,[15] again in this respect differing from the unregistered design right and copyright. The right lasts for a maximum period of 25 years[16] from the date of registration.[17] Registration is prima facie evidence of validity of the monopoly right. Validity is frequently challenged by alleged infringers in infringement proceedings.[18]

---

[13] RDA 1949 s.7(1). For the meaning of "not substantially different" in this context, see para.3–184 below. As explained in paras 3–003—3–004, in respect of acts of infringement from December 9, 2001 onwards the old "not substantially different" test has been replaced by the "different overall impression" test under the new European harmonised law: see para.2–043 above.

[14] See paras 4–001 and 5–121. The RDA 1949, before it was amended by the CDPA 1988, continued to use the old phrase of "copyright in a registered design", presumably for historical reasons. This phrase misleadingly implied that copying was an element of infringement of the registered design right, which ceased to be true under the RDA 1949. As part of the extensive amendments to the RDA 1949 made by CDPA 1988, the phrase "copyright in a registered design" was replaced by references simply to an "exclusive right" and "the right in the registered design." Compare RDA 1949 s.7 before and after amendments; App A5, para.A5–007 below.

[15] See para.3–047 below.

[16] RDA s.8(2); for designs registered before the amendments made by CDPA 1988, the maximum term was 15 years, although those which survived past December 8, 2001 may be extended by up to 25 years: see para.3–237 below, regarding the transitional arrangements.

[17] The term runs from the date of application to register, since RDA s.3(5) provides that a design when registered is registered as of the date when the application is made. This is so despite the fact that s.7(5) prevents proceedings for infringement being taken for acts done in the period between the date of application and the date of grant of the certificate of registration.

[18] See para.6–025 below.

Definition of "design" for purposes of registration

To have been registrable, a design must first conform to the definition of "design" given in s.1(1) of the RDA(A). Secondly, it must, at the date of registration, have been "new" within the meaning of s.1(2) of the RDA(A).[19] Section 1(1) defined "design" as follows: **3–010**

"(1) In this Act, 'design' means features of shape, configuration, pattern or ornament applied to an article by any industrial process, being features which in the finished article appeal to and are judged by the eye, but does not include

(a) a method or principle of construction or
(b) features of shape or configuration of an article which—

(i) are dictated solely by the function which the article has to perform, or
(ii) are dependent upon the appearance of another article of which the article is intended by the author of the design to form an integral part."

This definition contains a cumulative series of requirements, many of which have been the subject of judicial decision and analysis. The historical process by which this definition has evolved is of importance to its present day interpretation and application. Some of the more important embellishments to the definition, such as those dealing with eye appeal and methods or principles of construction, have found their way into the pre-2001 statutory definition as a result of the explicit adoption by the legislature of judicial phraseology used in earlier cases, in which such requirements were held to be implicit in the earlier and less elaborate statutory definitions of "design". This manifests an intention by the legislature to adopt and make explicit the principles developed in those cases. **3–011**

The elaborate statutory definition of "design" is at the heart of all aspects of pre-2001 registered design law, and its requirements will be successively analysed in the following paragraphs. **3–012**

Design must have had reference to some article

The words of the section are: "... design means features of shape, configuration, pattern or ornament *applied to an article* ... " (emphasis added). Thus a registrable design, as defined by the RDA(A), must have reference to some specific article to which it is to be applied.[20] The design **3–013**

---

[19] The subject of novelty is dealt with in paras 3–089 et seq. below.
[20] *Saunders v Wiel* (1893) 10 R.P.C. 29 at 32; *Re Clarke's Registered Design* (1896) 13 R.P.C. 351. This is no longer a requirement under the post-2001 European harmonised law: see paras 2–021 and 3–004 above.

to be registered "is a shape, configuration or pattern to be applied to a particular specified article".[21-22] It can be readily seen that a particular pattern of surface ornamentation could be applied to a wide range of different articles. An application for registration was not in respect of the pattern as such, but in respect of its application to the specific article named. If it was desired to register the same design, e.g. a surface pattern or decoration, in respect of a series of different articles (apart from the special case of articles which together form a set), then a separate application had to be made in respect of each article, and each application to register was numbered separately and treated as a separate and distinct application.[23]

3–014   In the case of designs consisting of features of shape or configuration, there may of course be cases where the design is intrinsically applicable only to a specific kind of article. The article itself does not, however, constitute the design.[24] In *Dover v Nurnberger Celluloid Waren Fabrik Gebruder Wolff*,[25] Buckley L.J. said[26]:

> "Design means, therefore, a conception or suggestion or idea of a shape or of a picture or of a device or of some arrangement which can be applied to an article by some manual, mechanical or chemical means. It is a conception, suggestion, or idea, and not an article, which is the thing capable of being registered . . . It is a suggestion of form or ornament to be applied to a physical body."[27]

3–015   Accordingly, it is submitted that a design is an idea or conception as to features of shape, configuration, pattern or ornament applied to an article. Although that idea, while still in the author's head, may be potentially capable of registration, in fact it must be reduced to visible form to be identifiable, and until it is so reduced there is nothing capable of registration. It may be so rendered either by its being embodied in the actual article, or by its being placed upon a piece of paper in such a way that the shape or other features of the article to be made are clear to the eye.[28] Whatever the means of identification (under some of the old Acts, provision was made whereby a mere verbal description could in some cases be accepted as sufficient), as soon as the idea is reduced to a form which is identifiable, there is something which is a "design", and which, if new, may be registrable.

[21-22] *Interlego AG v Tyco International Ltd* [1988] R.P.C. 343 at 353 line 50 to 354 line 1, per Lord Oliver of Aylmerton.

[23] Registered Designs Rules 1989 r.13 (revoked).

[24] *Walker, Hunter & Co v Falkirk Iron Company* (1887) 4 R.P.C. 390 at 393.

[25] (1910) 27 R.P.C. 498.

[26] (1910) 27 R.P.C. 498 at 503.

[27] See also *Pugh v Riley Cycle Co Ltd* (1912) 29 R.P.C. 196 at 202; *Wood v Stoddarts Ltd* M.C.C. 1930–1931, 294.

[28] *King Features Syndicate Inc and Betts v O. & M. Kleemann Ltd* (1941) 58 R.P.C. 207 at 228.

It may be an obvious point, but it is important to distinguish the design   **3–016**
from the medium on which it is carried or the physical form in which it
is presented. A piece of paper or printed publication showing a new
shape of article, or an article with a new pattern applied to it, may
embody or depict a design which is registrable *as a design to be applied to
that article*. Thus, the features shown would not embody a registrable
design when viewed as features applied to the paper or publication
itself,[29] but would be registrable when viewed as—and sought to be
registered as—features applied to the article depicted.[30]

Design may be two- or three-dimensional

According to s.1 of the RDA(A), four kinds of features may constitute a   **3–017**
design, namely, shape, configuration, pattern and ornament. For all
practical purposes, however, these may be reduced to two categories of
features, those in two dimensions and those in three. In a classic
statement of what constitutes a design (at that time according to the
definition in the Patents and Designs Acts 1907 to 1939),[31] Lord Wright in
King Features Syndicate Inc and Betts v O. & M. Kleemann Ltd (the *Popeye*
case) said[32]:

> " . . . thus a design may be the shape of a coal scuttle, a basin, a motor
> car, a locomotive engine or any material object, it may be the shape
> embodied in a sculptured or plastic figure which is to serve as a
> model for commercial production, or it may be a drawing in the flat
> or a complex pattern intended to be used for the manufacture of
> things such as linoleum or wallpaper."

Thus a design may consist either of a shape which is in three   **3–018**
dimensions, or of a pattern which is in two dimensions, and that shape or
pattern must be applied to an article or articles. An article can quite well
exist without any pattern upon it, whereas it can have no existence at all
apart from its shape or configuration. Thus, where the design is for a
shape, it is really applied to the article by being incorporated into it,

---

[29] For the exclusion from registration of designs applied to articles of a primarily literary or
artistic character, see paras 3–028 et seq. below.
[30] See *Riego de la Branchardiere v Elvery* (1849) 18 L.J. Ex. 381 and *Masson Seeley v Embosotype
Co* (1924) 41 R.P.C. 160, where Tomlin J. held that the pages of a catalogue showing
various sizes and shapes of type were not capable of registration as a design. The
conception as to the various shapes of type which were depicted were designs, though
they were on the facts of the case unregistrable, since they were not new. Cf. the New
South Wales case of *Buzacott v Dutch* M.C.C. 1930–1931, which was, however, it is
thought, wrongly decided.
[31] For the statutory definition of "design" then in force, see the Patents and Designs Acts
1907 to 1939 s.93 in App.A7 below.
[32] (1941) 58 R.P.C. 207 at 219.

rather than applied to it in the literal sense of the word. As Lindley L.J. put it in *Re Clarke's Registered Design*[33]: "A design applicable to a thing for its shape can only be applied to the thing by making it in that shape."

3–019   Shape and configuration have long been regarded as synonymous,[34] although something has recently been suggested (in the unregistered design right context) as being configuration but not shape, namely the topological interconnection of electronic components in accordance with a circuit diagram.[35] Shape and configuration both signify something solid, in three dimensions[36]; in fact, the form in which the article itself is fashioned. Again, it has been said that pattern and ornament can in the majority of cases be treated as synonymous.[37] A pattern or ornament, though it may stand out to a certain extent from the article to which it is applied, as in embossing or engraving, may to all intents and purposes be considered as something in two dimensions only, which is placed upon the article simply for the purpose of its decoration. A typical example would be a pattern for a wallpaper or a chintz. However, surface features, particularly if they are pronounced, may be treated as features of shape or configuration, as in *Cow & Co Ltd v Cannon Rubber Manufacturers Ltd*,[38] where it was held that a series of ribs on the surface of a hot water bottle were features of configuration within the scope of the statement of novelty which claimed such features. However, it is possible that the features in that case would alternatively have counted as pattern or ornament, i.e. there is an overlap between shape and configuration, and pattern and ornament, and some features are capable of falling within either category.[39]

[33] (1896) 13 R.P.C. 351 at 359.

[34] *Saunders v Wiel* (1893) 10 R.P.C. 31; *Re Clarke's Registered Design* (1896) 13 R.P.C. 351 at 358–61; *Dover v Nurnberger Celluloid Waren Fabrik Gebruder Wolff* (1910) 27 R.P.C. 498 at 504; *Wells v Attache Case Manufacturing Co Ltd* (1932) 49 R.P.C. 113; *Kestos Ltd v Kempat Ltd and Kemp* (1936) 53 R.P.C. 139. Cf. however, *Re Rollaston's Design* (1898) 15 R.P.C. 441; *Re Bayer's Design* (1907) 24 R.P.C. 65, and *Amp Inc v Utilux Pty Ltd* [1972] R.P.C. 103 at 108 and 111 (configuration may have a meaning slightly different from shape; per Lord Reid). See also the observations of Lloyd-Jacob J. on this point in *Schmittzehe v Roberts* (1955) 72 R.P.C. 122 at 124. For a recent review of the authorities on the meaning of "configuration", see *Lambretta Clothing Co Ltd v Teddy Smith (UK) Ltd* [2004] EWCA (Civ) 886; it was held that "configuration" did not include the colouration of the parts of a garment, a proposition from which there was a surprising dissent by Sedley L.J.

[35] *Mackie Designs Inc v Behringer* [1999] R.P.C. 717, Pumfrey J.; see para.5–035 below, where the correctness of the proposition that "configuration" can extend to abstract concepts like electronic circuit interconnections is doubted.

[36] Although it has been suggested that the design of a doyly consists of features of shape and configuration, even though most people would ordinarily regard a doyly as a flat or two-dimensional object: *Lambretta Clothing Co Ltd v Teddy Smith (UK) Ltd* [2004] EWCA (Civ) 886, per Jacob L.J. at para.24.

[37] *Kestos Ltd v Kempat Ltd and Kemp* (1936) 53 R.P.C. 139 at 152.

[38] [1959] R.P.C. 240 at 347. See also *Sommer Allibert (UK) Ltd v Flair Plastics Ltd* [1987] R.P.C. 599, CA, at 621 where it was held that grooves moulded into plastic garden chairs constituted part of the "shape and configuration" of the chairs.

[39] See paras 4–029 and 4–031 below, for discussion of this distinction in the context of unregistered design right.

Designs combining two- and three-dimensional elements

Although it is unusual, there is no reason in principle why a registered   **3–020**
design cannot consist of a combination of elements, some of which are
two-dimensional and some of which are three-dimensional. Such a
possibility was considered by Jessel M.R. in *Barran v Lomas*[40]:

> "In designs for china and pottery it frequently happens that the main
> portion of the design is the new shape of the vessel, and it also
> frequently happens that for a new shaped vessel a new kind of
> ornament is proposed suitable for that new shaped vessel, the whole
> is registered as one design. The answer would be, you have not
> registered your shape or your ornament alone, you have registered
> the whole, and that is what you claim—you claim a vessel of a
> particular shape and with a particular kind of pattern on it. If the
> person who registered the design did not claim the ornament itself,
> or, if I may say so, did not disclaim the use of the ornament as
> applied to merely one shape of vessel, he could be treated as having
> registered the whole design, i.e. the shape as well as the ornament, or
> rather the combination of the shape and ornament."

Directing registration to shape or to pattern

One way in which a distinction between shape, configuration, pattern   **3–021**
and ornament may be important is in construing the ambit of a registration. In registering a design it is, therefore, important to decide whether
it is the pattern, the shape, or the combination of the two, which it is
desired to protect. If the novelty of the design lies only in the combination
of the elements of pattern and shape each of which, taken separately, is
not new, then the applicant may have no choice but to register the
combination as his design. In this case, his right to sue infringers will be
correspondingly limited to cases where the elements of pattern and shape
are both substantially present.

If both shape and pattern are new, and it is desired to protect each of   **3–022**
them separately, two registrations would have to be taken out, one for
shape and the other for pattern.[41] If a single registration is taken out
which relates only, say, to pattern, there will be no infringement if the
shape only is taken, and vice versa. If it is desired to limit a design to
features of shape only, the safest course is to submit a representation
which does not depict a pattern, and vice versa.

An alternative which was conventionally adopted in practice was to   **3–023**
make use of the statement of novelty under r.15[42] in order to claim either

[40] (1880) 28 W.R. 972.
[41] *Pearson v Morris Wilkinson & Co* (1906) 23 R.P.C. 738.
[42] Registered Designs Rules 1989 (now revoked).

the features of shape and configuration, or the features of pattern and ornament, shown on the filed representation. This rule required an applicant[43] to submit "a statement ... of the features of the design for which novelty is claimed" on the representations filed in connection with his application to register. However, whilst it seems that features identified in the statement of novelty are to be given special weight in determining the ambit of the monopoly conferred by the registered design (whether for the purposes of validity or of infringement), it is far from clear that other features of the design which are depicted on the representation on the register, albeit not themselves claimed as being novel, can be wholly disregarded for the purpose of imposing a limitation on the ambit of the monopoly. In *Interlego AG v Tyco International Ltd* Lord Oliver said[44]:

> "In approaching the definition it is always to be borne in mind what is to be registered. It is a shape, configuration or pattern to be applied to a particular specified article and it is the shape or configuration of the whole article in respect of which there is to be a commercial monopoly. That necessarily involves taking the design and the article as a whole."

3–024   The question of the effect of the statement of novelty on the ambit of the monopoly conferred by the registered design is explored in more detail later as a separate topic.[45]

What is an "article"?

3–025   As already noted,[46] a design, in order to have been registrable, must have had reference to some specific "article". "Article" is not a word of clearly defined scope, and it must take much of its meaning from the context in which it is used. It should first be noted that the word "article" is introduced in s.1 of the RDA(A) as part of the requirement that the features constituting the design must be "applied to an article by any industrial process". It is therefore implicit that the finished article (i.e. the article once the design has been applied to it) must be an object of a kind which results from an industrial process. What precisely constitutes an "industrial process" in this context is considered in more detail below.[47] Secondly, s.44(1) of the RDA(A) includes the following definition of

---

[43] Except in the case of an application to register the pattern or ornament to be applied to textile articles or wallcoverings, in which case a statement of novelty is not required; r.15(1).

[44] [1988] R.P.C. 343 at 353.

[45] See paras 3–253 et seq. below.

[46] See para.3–013 above.

[47] See para.3–045 below.

"article": "'article' means any article of manufacture and includes any part of an article if that part is made and sold separately".

This effectively imposes two requirements in order for an object to **3–026** count as an article for the purposes of design registration. First, it must be an "article of manufacture" and, secondly (by implication), it must be "made and sold separately". These requirements will be considered in turn.

"Article of manufacture"

The Act does not explicitly define what is meant by an "article of **3–027** manufacture". The broad purpose of the RDA(A) is to give protection to designs which are applied to the products of manufacturing industry. Therefore, for example, buildings and structures, which are the result of building activities rather than manufacturing industry, are outside the ambit of "articles of manufacture" for the purpose of registered design protection.[48] Designs for buildings and structures are protectable under the laws of copyright rather than registered designs, by reason of the copyright which subsists in architects' drawings and in buildings or models for buildings.[49] "Article of manufacture" can include artificial substances which result from manufacturing processes—for example, linoleum,[50] cloth[51] or wallpaper.[52] It would, however, presumably not include a natural substance such as clay.

Article must have a purpose other than merely carrying the design

A problem which may be posed is whether, for example, a piece of paper **3–028** or canvas is "an article of manufacture" and if so, whether every drawing or watercolour sketch done on paper, and every oil painting done on canvas, is a registrable design, since in each case there is something which constitutes a pattern applied to an article of manufacture. In part, this problem is solved by the provisions of r.26,[53] which was made under s.1(5) of the RDA(A) authorising the exclusion from registration of articles of a primarily literary or artistic character.[54]

However, such objects are excluded from registration on more funda- **3–029** mental grounds, since it was held even under the 1907 to 1919 Acts that paper and canvas as such were not "articles of manufacture" (nor

---

[48] See para.3–036 below.
[49] CDPA 1988 ss.4(1)(a) and (b).
[50] Class 8 under the 1907–46 Acts.
[51] Class 13 under the 1907–46 Acts.
[52] Class 7 under the 1907–46 Acts.
[53] The Registered Designs Rules 1989.
[54] Considered in more detail in para.3–033 below.

"substances"[55]) within the meaning of the definition.[56] Not every drawing or painting placed upon a piece of paper or canvas was a design.[57] An article of manufacture, or a substance, had to have some purpose other than that of merely carrying the ornament.[58] This proposition must be even more true under the RDA 1949, where it is only the application of the design to an "article of manufacture", and not to a "substance", which has to be considered.

3–030   Where the article has no purpose beyond merely carrying the ornament, as, for instance, in the case of a drawing, painting or photograph upon an ordinary piece of paper, the article is so subordinate to the ornament that it may be disregarded as such. Thus, in the case of a drawing of, say, a landscape or hunting scene on a piece of paper, although there is a pattern, that pattern is not applied to any "article of manufacture" within the meaning of the Act, and so there is no "design" which can be registered. However, the same picture of a hunting scene would be registrable as a design to be applied to say, a cigarette box, a tray or a lampshade.

3–031   In the context of present day technology, the question arises as to whether a "design" can be applied to the screen of a general purpose computer. Is the screen of a general purpose computer to be treated as analogous to paper, and merely a medium for carrying pictures or designs which cannot be said to have been "applied" to an article? Or can a picture on the screen be said to be a decorative feature applied to the computer itself, albeit that it only becomes visible when the power is switched on, unlike a picture painted onto the outside of the computer? It has been held that at least in some circumstances a logo appearing on a computer screen is capable of being a design "applied" to the computer,[59] but the reasoning appears to be restricted only to "icons which appear on a machine into which they are inherently built. I am not concerned with icons, trade marks, devices or characters which appear temporarily whenever a particular computer program is loaded."[60] In the Tribunal's view, the programming of software in order to generate the appearance of an icon on the screen did amount to the application of the designs "by an industrial process" within RDA(A) s.1(1).

3–032   Other cases of considerable doubt and difficulty are bound to arise. It is clear, on the one hand, that an ordinary piece of paper upon which a

---

[55] The definition of an article under the Patents and Designs Acts 1907 to 1919 s.93 was, "any article of manufacture and any substance artificial or natural, or partly artificial and partly natural". It was thus wider than the definition in the RDA 1949, since a design could be applied to "any substance", which could include a natural substance.

[56] *Masson Seeley v Embosotype Co* (1924) 41 R.P.C. 160; see also under earlier legislation, *Riego de la Branchardiere v Elvery* (1849) 18 L.J. Ex. 381.

[57] *King Features Syndicate Inc and Betts v O. & M. Kleemann Ltd* (1941) 58 R.P.C. 207 at 222.

[58] *Re Littlewoods Pools Ltd's Application* (1949) 66 R.P.C. 309.

[59] *Apple Computer Inc's Design Appns* [2002] F.S.R. 602, RDAT (Jacob J.).

[60] *Apple Computer Inc's Design Appns* [2002] F.S.R. 602, RDAT (Jacob J.) at 604, para.5.

painting or drawing is made is not "an article of manufacture"[61] within the meaning of the Act. On the other hand, paper in the form of wallpaper has always been treated as registrable as "an article of manufacture",[62] the justification advanced being that the wallpaper, unlike the ordinary piece of paper, has a function beyond merely carrying the ornament, its purpose being to cover the walls of a room.[63] There may, nevertheless, be intermediate cases in which it may be difficult to say whether the article is or is not merely carrying the ornament.[64]

Exclusion of designs for articles of a "primarily literary or artistic character": rule 26

Section 1(5) of the RDA(A) authorised the Secretary of State to make rules   **3–033** excluding from registration designs for articles of a primarily literary or artistic character. Rule 26[65] was made under this power, and provided:

"26. There shall be excluded from registration under the Act designs to be applied to any of the following articles, namely:

(1) Works of sculpture, other than casts or models used or intended to be used as models or patterns to be multiplied by any industrial process;

(2) Wall plaques, medals and medallions[66];

(3) Printed matter primarily of a literary or artistic character, including book jackets, calendars, certificates, coupons, dressmaking patterns, greetings cards, labels, leaflets, maps, plans, playing cards, postcards, stamps, trade advertisements, trade forms and cards, transfers and similar articles."

Rule 26 had the effect of excluding from registration a number of   **3–034** articles which were borderline cases under the 1919 Act.[67] In *Usher v*

[61] *King Features Syndicate Inc and Betts v O. & M. Kleemann Ltd* (1941) 58 R.P.C. 207 at 222.
[62] See *Wallpaper Manufacturers Ltd v Derby Paper Staining Co* (1925) 42 R.P.C. 443.
[63] *Re Littlewoods Pools Ltd's Application* (1949) 66 R.P.C. 309.
[64] For such a case, see *Con Planck v Kolynos Inc* [1925] 2 K.B. 804; an advertisement cut-out.
[65] This rule was originally made as r.26 of the Designs Rules 1949 and only minor amendments were made to it by subsequent revisions of the Registered Designs Rules prior to 2001.
[66] The word "medallion" was added by amendment; this was presumably to put beyond doubt what had already been decided by Vaisey J. in *Reliance (Name-plates) Ltd v Art Jewels Ltd* (1953) 70 R.P.C. 86, where an applicant unsuccessfully argued that a Coronation medallion was not a "medal" within the former text of r.26(2).
[67] For example, see *Con Planck v Kolynos Inc* [1925] 2 K.B. 804, decided under the 1919 Act. Probably the advertisement cut-out which was the subject of that case would be excluded from registration by r.26. See, however, the very strange decision of the RDAT (Whitford J.) in *Lamson Industries Ltd's Application* [1978] R.P.C. 1, which held that computer printout paper carrying alternating bands of colour was not excluded from registration under r.26(3), although it was excluded because it was functional. The correctness of this decision (on both grounds) must be open to the most serious question.

Barlow[68] the validity of r.26 was challenged unsuccessfully on the ground that it was ultra vires, and it was held that a wall plaque published before 1950 was excluded from registration by virtue of the rule.

3–035   It should be noted that r.26(1) purported to exclude some but not all works of sculpture from the category of articles to which a design can be applied.[69] By implication, it suggests that designs are registrable in respect of casts or models used or intended to be used as models or patterns to be multiplied by an industrial process. This produces an oddity, since it would appear that the design as applied to the actual articles industrially multiplied from the cast or model would be excluded from registration. It is, therefore, unclear what would be the value of a registration simply covering the casts or models. It appears to have been generally assumed, under the 1907–1919 Acts, that works of sculpture (at least if multiplied on an industrial scale) were articles in respect of which a design could be registered.[70] This, however, is difficult to reconcile with the reasoning set out in para.3–021, above, under which a piece of paper or canvas carrying a picture was excluded from registration. The justification for this distinction advanced in previous editions of this work was as follows:

> "Although in certain cases, where a pattern or an ornament is applied to, say, paper or canvas, the substance is subordinate to the ornament, so that the article may be said virtually to disappear, where features of shape are concerned, the features are actually embodied in the substance, so that the substance cannot be subordinate to the features. If this is correct, designs involving shape may be capable of registration even though the article to which they are applied serves no strictly useful purpose."

Buildings and structures

3–036   How far buildings and structures can be "articles of manufacture" was considered in *Re Concrete Ltd's Application*.[71] The application there was for a design for an air-raid shelter constructed of reinforced concrete. It was stated that the practice of the Patent Office was to accept designs for structures such as poultry or animal sheds which are pre-formed and portable, in that they are delivered to purchasers as finished articles, and that this would include a case where, for convenience, the article was delivered in sections to be bolted together. However, the Registered

---

[68] (1952) 69 R.P.C. 27.

[69] See *Lucasfilm Ltd v Ainsworth* [2009] EWCA Civ 1328; [2010] F.S.R. 10; [2010] E.C.D.R 5, CA.

[70] *Pytram Ltd v Models (Leicester) Ltd* [1930] 1 Ch. 639 (model of a wolf cub's head); *Wood v Stoddarts*, M.C.C. 1930–1931, 294.

[71] (1940) 57 R.P.C. 121. This case was considering the definition in the 1907 Act s.93, App.A below, which is not materially different for present purposes.

Designs Appeal Tribunal (RDAT) (Morton J.), in dismissing the appeal from the decision of the Assistant Comptroller, who had refused the application, said:

> "There are, in my view, certain indications in the Acts and the Rules that the article to which the design is to be applied must be something which is to be delivered to the purchaser as a finished article."

He also approved the remarks of the Assistant Comptroller in *Re Collier & Co's Application*,[72] in which registration of a design for a petrol filling station was refused on the ground that the various operations incidental to the erection of the building or structure in question were merely analogous to those involved in ordinary building, and that these would not constitute the application of a design to an article by an industrial process in the sense contemplated by the Acts. Morton J. expressly stated, however, that he did not decide that a building or structure could never be an article within the meaning of the then s.93 (later s.44(1) of the RDA(A)).   **3–037**

Spare parts and parts of articles

The definition of "article" in s.44(1) of the RDA(A) contemplates that an article in respect of which a design is registered can be a part of another article. Thus, such items as handles for wardrobes, or fancy steering wheels for cars, can be the subject of design registrations in their own right (as distinct from merely forming part of the design of the greater article into which they are incorporated), so long as the part concerned is "made and sold separately". The House of Lords has decided that, in order to satisfy this requirement, it is not sufficient that the part concerned is made and sold simply as a spare part for the greater article; it must in addition "have an independent life as an article of commerce and not be merely an adjunct of some larger article of which it forms part".[73]   **3–038**

In applying this test, the House dismissed an appeal against the rejection of applications to register designs in respect of components for cars such as main body panels, doors, bonnet lids, boot lids and windscreens. In doing so, the House appeared to approve the distinction   **3–039**

---

[72] (1937) 54 R.P.C. 253, cf. *Staples v Warwick* (1906) 23 R.P.C. 609, where registration had been obtained for an amusement tower in the form of a lighthouse built of timber and having on its outside a spiral track to enable persons to slide down from top to bottom. An interim injunction to restrain infringement was granted, but validity of the design was not questioned.

[73] *Ford Motor Co Ltd's Design Appns* [1994] R.P.C. 545 at 554 lines 20–25, per McCowan L.J., QB Div Ct; approved by Lord Mustill in *Ford Motor Co Ltd's Design Appns* [1995] R.P.C. 167 at 179 lines 3–6, HL.

drawn by the lower courts[74] between this category of items which would be sold simply as spare parts, and items such as wing mirrors, seats and steering wheels, where customers might buy fancy designs for their own sake and not simply as replacement spare parts. These latter were referred to as "proprietary articles", which by their nature were susceptible to being made and sold separately.[75] The designs in the latter category were, however, not formally before the House, since there was no appeal before the House against their registrability.[76] It appears that such items as umbrella cases, cases for spectacles, shotgun and camera cases, etc. are separately registrable articles, and are not merely adjuncts of the articles to which they relate.[77]

3–040   The House in Ford[78] cited with apparent approval the observations of Graham J. in *Sifam Electrical Instruments Co Ltd v Sangamo Weston Ltd*, who was considering whether the fronts of electrical meters were registrable under the Registered Designs Act[79]:

"The meter front here is not now and never has been sold separately nor was it ever intended that it should be . . . If an article or part of an article is in fact being sold at the time of the application to register that in itself would invalidate the registration because the design would have been published and would not be 'new or original' within subsection (2). What then do the words mean? The defendants say they mean 'susceptible of being sold separately,' which they say this meter front is. But here again any part of any article is susceptible of being sold separately even if, for example, the part has to be forcibly removed from the whole of the article of which it forms part . . . Why should designs not be registrable for such parts which are susceptible of industrial design and of being dealt with as articles of commerce? However to give the words such a meaning would have the result that any part of any article could then be registered and thus would defeat the apparent intention of the Act. One might also then ask: When is part of an article not an article in its own right?

---

[74] Decision of the Registered Designs Appeal Tribunal (RDAT), *Ford Motor Co Ltd's and Iveco Fiat SpA's Design Appns* [1993] R.P.C. 399 and decision of the Queen's Bench Divisional Court, *Ford Motor Co Ltd's Design Appns* [1994] R.P.C. 545.

[75] *Ford Motor Co Ltd's and Iveco Fiat SpA's Design Appns* [1993] R.P.C. 399 at 420 lines 21–30, RDAT.

[76] See however observations of Lord Mustill in *Ford Motor Co Ltd's Design Appns* [1995] R.P.C. 167, at 176, lines 6–14, HL.

[77] *A Fulton Co Ltd v Totes Isotoner (UK) Ltd* [2003] R.P.C. 499 at para.31, Pat Cty Ct.

[78] *Ford Motor Co Ltd's and Iveco Fiat SpA's Design Appns*, cited above at n.71 at 175, per Lord Mustilll.

[79] *Sifam Electrical Instruments Co Ltd v Sangamo Weston Ltd* [1973] R.P.C. 899 at 913. The question of whether the meter fronts would have been registrable under the RDA was relevant to whether copyright in drawings of the meter fronts would be infringed, because of the then overlap provisions of the Copyright Act 1956; see para.1–049 above.

... The intention must be to grant registration only for such articles as are intended by the proprietor of the design to be put on the market and sold separately, such as for example a hammer handle, or a bit for a bradawl ...

The words used are 'if that part is made and sold separately', and the phrase as a whole, to my mind, confirms that both the manufacture and sale of the part in question must be operations which are distinct from the manufacture and sale of the whole article of which the 'part' forms a component. It is necessary to imply the words 'to be' in order to construe the phrase as not including sale of the part prior to or at the date of the application for registration since this would produce an absurd result contrary to section 1(2), and cannot possibly have been the intention of the legislature."

Parts of articles and the "must match" exclusion

Even where parts of articles satisfy the test that they are "made and sold separately" and so are in principle capable of registration in their own right, s.1(1)(b)(ii) excluded features of shape and configuration from the statutory definition of "design" which: "(b) ... (ii) are dependent upon the appearance of another article of which the article is intended by the author to form an integral part".   **3–041**

This exclusion is colloquially referred to as the "must match" exclusion, and was introduced into the definition of design in s.1(1) of the RDA by the amendments made by the CDPA 1988. It therefore does not apply to designs registered before those amendments took effect.[80] The effect of this exclusion can be either total or partial. If the design of the part consists entirely of features which are "dependent upon the appearance of" the greater article in which it was to be included, then the design is unregistrable as a design applied to that part; i.e. the design of the part cannot be registered *as such*. (It may, of course, be registrable as an aspect of the design applied to the greater article, if sought to be registered as such.) Alternatively, there may be some features of the design of the part which are dependent upon the appearance of the greater article, and others which are not. If so, the registration of the design as applied to the part comprises only those features in respect of which there is design freedom independent of the greater article. The main policy reason behind this exclusion is apparently to prevent the monopolisation of the supply of spare parts through the registration of designs in respect of parts of articles.[81]   **3–042**

---

[80] For the amendments made by the CDPA 1988 and the position of designs registered before the effective date of those amendments, see para.3–270 below.

[81] Note however that the Divisional Court in *Ford* (*Ford Motor Co's Design Appns* [1994] R.P.C. 545 at 554 lines 39–51, QBD) considered it unnecessary to look at Ministerial statements in *Hansard* made during the passage of the Bill for the CDPA 1988, because

3-043   This effect of this exclusion was considered by the courts in *Ford Motor Co's Design Appns*, although the House of Lords itself declined to consider this ground of exclusion because of their conclusion that the parts sought to be registered were not in any event articles "made and sold separately" within the definition of "article" in s.44(1) of the RDA(A).[82] However, both the RDAT[83] and the Queen's Bench Divisional Court on a judicial review of the RDAT's decision,[84] considered that the designs of components for cars such as main body panels, doors, bonnet lids, boot lids and windscreens consisted only of features which fell within the "must match" exclusion. These parts, according to the reasoning of the RDAT,[85] form part of and contribute to the overall shape and appearance of the vehicle. As the Divisional Court put it, there is no "design freedom" for the suppliers of this category of parts, having regard to the need to comply with the overall design of the car as a whole.[86]

3-044   This category of parts are to be distinguished from parts which, while in situ are contributing features to the appearance of the vehicle, are subsidiary to its essential shape and include wing mirrors, wheels, seats and the steering wheel, where substitutions are possible while leaving the general shape and appearance unchanged; i.e. in these cases the supplier of the spare part has design freedom to provide, e.g. sportier looking wheels or more comfortable seats, without detracting from the design of the car as a whole.[87]

Application of the design "by an industrial process"

3-045   It was part of the statutory definition of a registrable design[88] that the features constituting the design should be "applied to an article by any industrial process". What an "industrial process" is, is not explicitly

they did not consider the legislation to be ambiguous or obscure. A similar exclusion applies to unregistered design right: see para.4–026 below. Since unregistered design right covers functional aspects of design, in addition to the "must match" exclusion, there is also a "must fit" exclusion.

[82] *Ford Motor Co Ltd's Design Appns* [1995] R.P.C. 167 at 179, line 21 to 180, line 3, per Lord Mustill, HL. See para.3–038 for consideration of the question of when a spare part is an article "made and sold separately".

[83] *Ford Motor Co Ltd's and Iveco Fiat SpA's Design Appns* [1993] R.P.C. 399, RDAT.

[84] *Ford Motor Co Ltd's Design Appns* [1994] R.P.C. 545, QBD. For the mechanism of effective appeal by way of judicial review of decisions of the Registered Designs Appeal Tribunal, see para.2–137 below.

[85] *Ford Motor Co Ltd's and Iveco Fiat SpA's Design Appns* [1993] R.P.C. 399 at 417 lines 34–43, RDAT.

[86] *Ford Motor Co Ltd's Design Appns* [1994] R.P.C. 545 at 554 lines 27–37. It should be noted that for this purpose, the design of the article as a whole is the design of the car *including* the part concerned, not the design of the car minus the part. It does not matter whether the part is designed before the car or vice versa: *Valeo Vision SA v Flexible Lamps Ltd* [1995] R.P.C. 205 at 218, ChD, per Aldous J.; the design of the part becomes subordinated to the design of the whole, whichever order the design process takes place in.

[87] *Ford Motor Co Ltd's and Iveco Fiat SpA's Design Appns* [1993] R.P.C. 399 at 420 lines 25–30, RDAT.

[88] Section 1(1) of the RDA 1949 (as amended), quoted in full at para.3–010 above.

defined in the RDA(A). However, it has traditionally been considered that this requirement entails nothing more than this, that it must be possible to reproduce the design upon articles en masse. The actual process used may be of any description whatsoever. A particular shape may be given to an article by turning it upon a lathe or by pouring it into a mould. A particular pattern may be placed upon it by printing, painting or engraving, or possibly sewn or woven upon it. Although often it will be done by machinery, it need by no means necessarily be so. For instance, a man may design a special pattern for a lampshade, and numbers of lampshades may thereafter have that design applied to them by hand painting.

It would appear that a series of operations such as are involved in building does not constitute the application of a design to an article by an industrial process in the sense contemplated by the Acts.[89]   **3–046**

Eye appeal

The statutory definition of "design" restricted the definition to features   **3–047**
"which in the finished article appeal to and are judged by the eye".[90] This positive part[91] of the definition of "design" cannot be considered in isolation from its negative counterpart, the exclusion from "design" (by s.1(1)(b)(i) RDA(A)[92]) of features which are dictated by function. The words "judged by the eye" will exclude cases where it is shown that the customer is not influenced in choice by appearance, but only by criteria of suitability for a purpose. In reaching this conclusion, both of these aspects (positive and exclusionary) of the definition of design were considered together by the House of Lords in *Amp Inc v Utilux Pty Ltd*, a case concerning an attempt to register the design of an electrical spade connector[93]:

> "Those who wish to purchase an article for use are often influenced in their choice not only by practical efficiency but by appearance. Common experience shows that not all are influenced in the same way. Some look for artistic merit . . . Many simply choose the article

---

[89] *Re Collier & Co Ltd's Applications* (1937) 54 R.P.C. 253; *Re Concrete Ltd's Application* (1940) 57 R.P.C. 121; and see para.3–036 above, concerning the registrability of designs for buildings and structures.

[90] RDA 1949 s.1(1). Before the amendments made by the CDPA 1988, the words were "appeal to and are judged *solely* by the eye"; (RDA 1949 s.1(3) before amendment). It is not however easy to see that the omission of the word "solely" was intended to effect any change in the definition of design. It should be noted that features which are only intermittently visible, such as symbols which appear on the front of a digital watch only when it is switched on, may count as part of a design: *Suwa Seikosha's Design Application* [1982] R.P.C. 166, RDAT; so also may features of an Easter egg which are visible only when the egg is broken open: *Ferrero SpA's Application* [1978] R.P.C. 473, RDAT.

[91] See *Harvey (G. A.) & Co (London) Ltd v Secure Fittings Ltd* [1966] R.P.C. 515, Ct of Sess.

[92] For consideration of this exclusion, see para.3–054 below.

[93] [1972] R.P.C. 103 at 107, per Lord Reid.

which catches their eye. Whatever the reason may be, one article with a particular design may sell better than one without it: then it is profitable to use the design. And much thought, time and expense may have been incurred in finding a design which will increase sales."

3–048 The eye to which appeal must be made, and the eye which is to judge, is not the eye of the court but the eye of the customer.[94] The underlying purpose of design registration is to give to the owner of the design the commercial value resulting from customers preferring the appearance of articles which have the design, to those which do not have it.[95] This can be contrasted with the commercial value arising from the functional benefits of the design, whose protection is outside the purpose of the registered design system.[96]

3–049 The explicit requirement for eye appeal was first inserted into the statutory definition by the 1919 Act.[97] The incorporation of this wording into the statutory definition however reflected what had already been stated to be the law in many decided cases.[98]

3–050 Thus in *Re Bayer's Design*, Fletcher Moulton L.J. said[99]:

"Designs apply to nothing but that which the eye can tell entirely. Nothing in my opinion is a good design but that of which full knowledge is given when you have once shown to the eye what your design is. It may be shape or configuration; that is given by a specimen or proper drawing, and the eye can see it, and the eye can recognise whether it has been imitated ... the Act contemplates something which is applicable to an article, and which is defined by a representation. Just look at the definition in clause 60[100] ... It deals entirely with the shape or configuration, or ornament, or pattern; they are all things which the eye has the complete power of learning from representation ...

If the eye be the judge of infringement, it must be because the eye is the competent judge of that which is to be infringed. I am satisfied, therefore, that nothing but that which can be matter for the eye to see can be a good subject of design."

---

[94] [1972] R.P.C. 103 at 109 lines 10–12, per Lord Reid.

[95] [1972] R.P.C. 103 at 108 lines 17–25, per Lord Reid.

[96] Other aspects of industrial design and patent law may provide protection for functional designs: see para.4–01 below.

[97] Patents and Designs Act 1907 and 1919 (consolidated) s.93, App.A7, para.A7–005 below: "'Design' means only the features of shape, configuration, pattern or ornament applied to any article by any industrial process or means, whether manual, mechanical or chemical, separate or combined which in the finished article appeal to and are judged solely by the eye; but does not include any mode or principle of construction or anything which is in substance a mere mechanical device."

[98] *Cooper v Symington* (1893) 10 R.P.C. 264 at 267; *Re Bayer's Design* (1907) 24 R.P.C. 65 at 74, 77 and 80; *Harrison v Taylor* (1859) 4 H. & N. 815 at 819.

[99] *Re Bayer's Design* (1907) 24 R.P.C. 65 at 77.

[100] The Patents and Designs and Trade Marks Act 1883 s.60.

Eye appeal is not the same as artistic merit

Though a particular design may appeal to the aesthetic sense or to the sense of the beautiful, it has always been considered that a design need not possess any artistic merit.[101] Such an interpretation would cause problems because of the difficulty which would arise of judging between what is and what is not artistic,[102] since that which appeals to one man as artistic and beautiful may in no way please another.   **3–051**

> "It could not reasonably be supposed that the court was to be required to decide on such a vague criterion an aesthetic or artistic appeal."[103]

The impression resulting from the design may influence choice and selection on the part of a person desiring to acquire the finished article carrying the design, and if it influences such a person, then the design may be considered to have "eye appeal" for the purposes of the statutory definition. The design may be "calculated to attract the attention of the beholder", regardless of whether or not it makes a favourable impression upon him.[104]   **3–052**

On the other hand, the test of appeal is not simply that of mere visual appreciation, i.e. to the lower sense which takes account of the thing seen without any particular reaction being generated thereby[105]: the design must have individuality of appearance, which makes it not merely visible, but noticed.[106]   **3–053**

Features dictated by function

Section 1(1)(b) of the RDA(A) excluded from the statutory definition of design: **3–054**

[101] *Re Clarke's Design* (1896) 13 R.P.C. 351 at 361; *Walker Hunter & Co v Falkirk Iron Co* (1887) 4 R.P.C. 390 at 391.

[102] Such difficulty does arise, and has to be grappled with by the courts, in deciding what counts as "a work of artistic craftsmanship" for the purpose of s.4(1)(c) of the CDPA. The difficulties of this question gave rise to five differing interpretations on the part of the members of the House of Lords in *Hensher (George) Ltd v Restawile Upholstery (Lancs) Ltd* [1975] R.P.C. 31, HL. For discussion of this problem, see para.5–022 below.

[103] *Amp Inc v Utilux*, cited above at 109, per Lord Reid.

[104] *Amp Inc v Utilux* at 112, per Lord Morris.

[105] As was the appellant's contention in *Amp Inc v Utilux Pty Ltd* [1970] R.P.C. 397 at 423, CA.

[106] In *Stenor Ltd v Whitesides (Clitheroe) Ltd* (1946) 63 R.P.C. 81, Romer J. held that if a design were so small that its features could not be properly discerned or appreciated by the naked eye, there could be no design within the meaning of the definition. The Court of Appeal and the House of Lords, however, refused to decide the question of whether in judging with the eye, normal or aided vision was to be relied upon; see *Stenor Ltd v Whitesides* (1948) 65 R.P.C. 1. The same question arose in *Amp Inc v Utilux* [1970] R.P.C. 397 at 406 at first instance, Lloyd-Jacob J. holding that in normal circumstances unmagnified vision was the criterion. The point was passed over in the Court of Appeal (*Amp Inc v Utilux* [1970] R.P.C. 397 at 423) and not mentioned in the House of Lords judgments.

"features of shape or configuration of an article which—

>   (i) are dictated solely by the function which the article has to perform".

The underlying policy of this exclusion is to prevent registered designs being used to obtain monopolies which in effect cover the functional aspects of the design of articles.[107] By contrast, the unregistered design right does cover the functional aspects of shape and configuration, but is tempered by being of shorter duration,[108] and by the fact that it is a right against copying rather than a monopoly right.[109]

3–055   This exclusion did not apply to features of pattern or ornament. However, this is probably because such surface features are less likely to be functional in the first place, rather than because of any legislative policy in favour of permitting monopolies in functional surface features.[110] Such features would, in any event, have to satisfy the positive requirement of the definition that they have eye appeal,[111] and the above quoted exclusion of features dictated by function probably does no more than make explicit what is already implicit in the positive part of the definition requiring eye appeal.[112]

3–056   The effect of the words "dictated solely by the function" was considered by the House of Lords in *Amp Inc v Utilux Pty Ltd*[113] in relation to a design for electrical terminals for washing machines. It was argued that the exclusion only applies in cases where the designer has no option but to design an article in a particular shape because of the function it has to perform: if the function required the article to be made in one shape only, then and only then were its features dictated solely by function. It was shown that in relation to electrical terminals, numerous alternative shapes of terminal could have been used for the relevant washing machines and it was therefore argued that the respondent's terminal was outside the exception.

---

[107] New functional designs of articles can in principle obtain protection through the patent system, but to do so they must satisfy the requirement of "inventive step": the Patents Act 1977 s.1(1)(b). There is an obvious public policy for the registered design system not to be used to obtain monopolies over new functional designs which may not even satisfy the requirement of inventiveness which they would have to satisfy under the patent system, particularly since the monopoly period for registered designs (25 years) is now longer than the 20 years of a patent monopoly.

[108] 10 years only, of which the second five years is subject to "licences of right"; see para.4–133 below.

[109] See para.1–005 above.

[110] Such surface features might, for example, include the pattern of electrical connections on a printed circuit board.

[111] See para.3–047 above.

[112] This appears to have been the view which Lloyd-Jacob J. expressed on this point in *Kent & Thanet Casinos Ltd v Bailey's School of Dancing Ltd* [1965] R.P.C. 482 at 488, lines 1–7. The case concerned the pattern on the rotor of a roulette wheel.

[113] [1972] R.P.C. 103.

These arguments were rejected since, if they were correct, the statutory   3–057
exclusion would have virtually no practical effect. Lord Reid said[114]:

> "If the purpose of the Act was to give protection to a designer where
> design has added something of value to the prior art then one would
> expect an exclusion from protection of those cases where nothing has
> been added because every feature of the shape sought to be protected
> originated from purely functional considerations."

Viscount Dilhorne said, drawing on both the positive (eye appeal), and   3–058
exclusionary aspects of the definition[115]:

> "Why though should such a terminal appeal to the eye of an
> electrician? A silver teapot may be made in different shapes. Some
> will attract some customers and some others. They will be attracted
> by a particular shape, not because one teapot serves the purpose for
> which it is made better than another. But a terminal will appeal to the
> eye of an electrician only if he thinks it best for his purpose. It is its
> suitability for its function that will decide his choice and the last part
> of the definition makes it clear that if its shape and configuration are
> dictated solely by its function, as in my opinion it was in this case, it
> is not registrable as a design under the Act."

The phrase "dictated solely by the function" was held to mean   3–059
"attributable to or caused or prompted by". Where a shape is adopted by
a designer upon the sole requirement of functional ends, i.e. to make the
article work and not to appeal to the eye, then the provision excludes it
from statutory protection. Lord Morris said[116]:

> "In the present case the terminal was simply devised so that it would
> 'do the job.' It was to perform the function that was defined by
> Hoover's requirements. The terminal is . . . to be looked at as a unit.
> But if its constituent parts are considered, I think that on the evidence
> each one was solely devised so that it should correctly perform its
> own particular function. There was nothing extra. There was nothing
> that could be regarded as any kind of embellishment. First and last
> and all the time the key-note was success. The terminals . . . would be
> judged by performance and not by appearance."

He added[117]:

> " . . . that other shapes of other terminals might also be dictated by
> the function to be performed by them will not alter the fact that the

[114] [1972] R.P.C. 103 at 109, line 40.
[115] [1972] R.P.C. 103 at 118.
[116] [1972] R.P.C. 103 at 113.
[117] [1972] R.P.C. 103 at 115.

shape of Amp's terminals was dictated only by functional considerations . . . "

3–060   The negative exclusion of features dictated by function may in some circumstances prevent the registration of a design which does satisfy the positive requirement of having eye appeal. This could happen if every feature of the shape is one attributable solely to the function which the finished article is to perform, even though the shape may also have eye appeal.[118]

"Eye appeal" and articles which are partly functional

3–061   Where a designer sets out to produce an article that would perform a particular function, but where in producing it he has added or applied some features of shape that are additional to or supplementary to what is functionally needed, with the result that in the finished article there are features that appeal to the eye, there may be a design which is registrable within the statutory definition.[119] Similarly, if for example, some advantage, whether mechanical or otherwise, apart from the main purpose of the article, is incidentally derived from the adoption of a particular shape, that does not of itself exclude that shape from registration as a design.[120] Whether any such advantage is obtained or not is quite immaterial.[121]

3–062   In order to be excluded from registration under this exception to the definition of design (features dictated solely by function) it is necessary that all of the features of the design should be so dictated. If some features are dictated by function and others are not, it appears that the whole shape or configuration is registrable, assuming that it has eye appeal. Thus in the case of Lego toy bricks, the registration extended to cover functional aspects of the shape and configuration of the bricks as well as aesthetic aspects[122]:

[118] *Interlego AG v Tyco International Ltd* [1988] R.P.C. 343 at 355–356, particularly at 355, lines 19–21, considering the effect of *Amp v Utilux*. See also *Allibert SA v O'Connor* [1981] F.S.R. 613, Irish High Ct, where fishboxes were held to be excluded from registration because every feature of their design was solely attributable to functional considerations.
[119] *Amp v Utilux* [1972] R.P.C. 103 at 113. And in *Gardex Ltd v Sorata Ltd* [1986] R.P.C. 623, ChD, it was held that strengthening ribs applied to the underside of a shower tray constituted a protectable aspect of a registered design because the claimant gave evidence that the designer had in mind the eye of the plumber or the builder's merchant to whom "the thing must look good" (p.637). This decision seems, with respect, far fetched, and, if correct, it would rob the exclusion from registrability of functional designs of most of its effect.
[120] *Kestos Ltd v Kempat Ltd and Kemp* (1936) 53 R.P.C. 139 at 151; *Walker, Hunter & Co v Falkirk Iron Co* (1887) 4 R.P.C. 390 at 393; *Hecla Foundry Co v Walker Hunter & Co* (1889) 6 R.P.C. 554 at 558 and 559; *Re Bayer's Design* (1907) 24 R.P.C. 65 at 74; *Rogers v Driver* (1851) 20 L.J.Q.B. 31.
[121] *Hecla Foundry Co v Walker, Hunter & Co* (1889) 6 R.P.C. 554 at 558; *Re Clarke's Registered Design* (1896) 13 R.P.C. 351 at 358; *Moody v Tree* (1892) 9 R.P.C. 233 at 235.
[122] *Interlego AG v Tyco International Ltd* [1988] R.P.C. 343 at 354, per Lord Oliver. Followed in *Valeo Vision SA v Flexible Lamps Ltd* [1995] R.P.C. 205 at 215–6, ChD, per Aldous J.

"What is contemplated here is that an article—and that must mean the whole of the article and not simply part of it—is to be made in a particular shape or configuration. Thus, the shape or configuration as a whole is being 'applied' to the article as a whole. It then has to be asked, is *that* shape or configuration (i.e. the shape or configuration of the whole article) dictated solely by the functional purpose? Moreover, it makes no sense to exclude from registration designs for articles which have—and indeed may be intended to have as their principal attraction—a distinctive and novel appearance merely because they contain also features—perhaps even very minor ones —which are dictated by the functional requirements."

With such articles, criteria both of appearance and of pure utility may come to influence a potential customer. In such cases, it has been said that those underlying features of function or construction which are common to other articles of the same type or class must notionally be excluded from consideration on an inquiry as to what are the features which possess eye appeal within the definition, "concern being had solely to the artistic variants, if any, whereby the application of the method in the construction of the article has imported any genuine design character-istics".[123] **3–063**

This exercise presupposes an imaginary article, which (for purposes of notional comparison) is to exhibit the basic features of function or construction to which "artistic variants" may have been applied. The article is the general type of article in question, the genus or species qua use or purpose, for instance, chairs as a class, or tables as a class. Its shape must be taken to be the simplest and commonest known form of that type of article. For every species of article there must be certain incidents or general characteristics of shape which are essential to get the article to work and fulfill its function. An article possessing only these incidents is the article to which the design must be imagined to be applied. It may be called the fundamental article. If a design is a design within the meaning of the section, any article in which it has been incorporated must appear to the eye to possess some incident of shape beyond those primary essential features which are the property of the fundamental article. The design by its application must have produced some visible alteration or embellishment upon this fundamental form. In *Harvey & Co Ltd v Secure Fittings Ltd*,[124] the article in respect of which the design in suit was registered was a unit comprising, in combination, cold and hot water tanks. Having stated that the eye is the judge of the design, Lord Avonside said[125]: **3–064**

---

[123] *Swain (Matthew) Ltd v Barker (Thomas) & Sons Ltd* [1967] R.P.C. 23, per Lloyd-Jacob J. The design in suit in this case was for a wire baking tray.
[124] [1966] R.P.C. 515, Ct of Sess.
[125] [1966] R.P.C. 515 at 518 see also 520.

"The design to appeal must be noticeable and have some perceptible appearance of an individual character. Where, as in the present instance, the design is for a shape or configuration of the article as a whole, the only effective application of the design rests in making an article of that shape and configuration. In that situation, in order to achieve application of design to an article, the article produced must be such as appeals to the eye as possessing, by reason of its shape or configuration, features which distinguish it from others of its type and class. There can be 'a unit comprising in combination hot and cold water tanks' which is functional and basic in that it comprises only these elements which are essential for its operation for the purpose, an 'article' without 'design'. Where design is claimed as in this case, the initial question is whether or not the making of the article in the chosen shape or configuration results in the production of an article which displays to the eye features different from those of the basic or fundamental 'unit,' and alteration or embellishment of that unit."

3–065   If an article to which an alleged design has been applied does not appear to the eye to contain any characteristics over and above the fundamental form, then there is no design within the meaning of the section. The same is the case if such characteristics are so trifling as to be almost unobservable.

3–066   But in adopting this approach, it must be borne in mind that the design has to be looked at as a whole and the question asked whether the features of shape or configuration, taken as a whole and in combination, appeal to the eye?[126]

Design features which also achieve functional purpose

3–067   The preceding paragraph has considered the case where some features of the shape of an article can be categorised as dictated by function, whilst other features can be considered as features giving rise to "eye appeal". What however of the case where a feature of shape has both functional and decorative purposes? Provided that the shape is capable of giving to the article to which it is applied a definite individuality of appearance, which renders it distinguishable from the "fundamental" or unadorned form of the article, it will be registrable as a design, even though some mechanical advantage necessarily follows from the shape in question.

3–068   In *Cow & Co Ltd v Cannon Rubber Manufacturers Ltd*,[127] the design was for a diagonal arrangement of ribs on a hot water bottle. It was held that

---

[126] Questions so posed in *Interlego AG v Tyco International Ltd* [1988] R.P.C. at 357, lines 13–19; Lego bricks held to be registrable, despite the fact that some features were dictated by the function of having to interlock. See also *Interlego AG v Alex Foley (Vic) Pty Ltd* [1987] F.S.R. 238.

[127] [1959] R.P.C. 240 at 347.

although the ribs fulfilled a very important purpose in producing radiation of the heat without discomfort to the user, such an arrangement was not dictated solely by function, and the registration was upheld. It was also argued by the defendants that since, upon the evidence, the simplest and most economical way to form the ribs was to form them diagonally, the design was for that reason invalid on the ground that its features were dictated solely by function. This argument was, however, rejected. Lord Evershed M.R. said[128]:

> "The argument is plainly attractive; but (as I have indicated) on the whole I am not satisfied that the defendants here have discharged the onus, which requires, after all, that they should establish that this distinctive feature (which, as I have said, does seem to me to appeal strikingly to the eye) is in truth a feature dictated solely by—that is to say, one adopted upon the sole requirement of—functional ends. I think that the fact that it is functionally useful may be taken as established; but I am not satisfied for myself that the defendants proved that it was that object, and that object alone, which dictated the adoption of this type of ribbing."

Thus, even if a thing is patentable, provided that it also appeals to the eye, there is no objection to its being the subject of both a patent and a registered design.[129] A device, however, the advantage of which resides not in its appearance but merely in the way it functions, if it is protectable at all, can be the subject of a patent only, and not of a design. The position was summarised by Farwell J. in *Re Wingate's Registered Design*[130]:   3–069

> "The intention of the legislature was to ensure so far as possible that only that which was in fact a design, and the merit of which lay in the design itself, that is in the appeal to the eye, should come within the Act. But, by that, I do not mean that because a design, being in fact a design, and being new and original qua design, also discloses a method of construction or a mechanical device, it cannot be registered. In my judgment so long as the design, qua design, is something which makes an appeal to the eye and is new or original, it is properly a subject-matter of registration, notwithstanding that it also involves a method of construction which may be entitled to protection as a patent . . . "

---

[128] [1959] R.P.C. 240 at 352.
[129] *Werner Motors Ltd v A. W. Gamage Ltd* (1904) 21 R.P.C. 137 at 621, see also; *Rogers v Driver* (1851) 20 L.J.Q.B. 31; *Re Bayer's Design* (1907) 24 R.P.C. 65 at 74; *Walker Hunter & Co v Falkirk Iron Co* (1887) 4 R.P.C. 390 at 394. It was also held in the case of *Re United States Playing Cards Company's Application* [1908] 1 Ch. 297 that the same thing may be the subject of both a trade mark and a design.
[130] (1935) 52 R.P.C. 126 at 131.

3–070 However, there may be a limit to this doctrine if a purely functional advantage of the article in question cannot be achieved without adopting the particular shape which is the subject of the design. In *Stratford Auto Components Ltd v Britax (London) Ltd*,[131] Lloyd-Jacob J. held that the test to be applied is whether or not the function to be subserved by the article to which the design is applied imposes such control upon the freedom of the manufacturer as in substance to leave him no option but to adopt a feature or features appearing in the representations of the registered design. He decided that, in the particular case in question, the feature of the channel section in a windscreen for a motorcycle was of this nature, and that it must therefore be excluded from any consideration of the shape or configuration of the design. In addition, since it was the only novel feature in the design compared with the prior art, the registration was invalid for lack of novelty.

Historical development of the exclusion of functional shapes

3–071 The phrase "dictated solely by the function which the article has to perform" was adopted into s.1(3) of the RDA 1949 (s.1(1) following the amendments made by the CDPA 1988) from the judgment of Luxmoore J. in *Kestos Ltd v Kempat Ltd and Kemp*[132]:

> "A mere mechanical device is a shape in which all the features are dictated solely by the function or functions which the article has to perform (see *Tecalemit Ltd v Ewarts Ltd (No.2)*).[133] In other words, if a person produces an article for a particular purpose, though that person may obtain the grant of letters patent for it, the producer cannot obtain a monopoly of that article by registration of a design for it. The only protection given by the registration is for the particular form of the article shown in the design registered. More-over, the particular form must possess some features beyond those necessary to enable the article to fulfil the particular purpose, but the fact that some advantage is derived from the adoption of a particular shape does not exclude it from registration as a design."

3–072 This phraseology of Luxmoore J. was accepted by the Court of Appeal[134] and the House of Lords[135] in *Stenor Ltd v Whitesides (Clitheroe)*

---

[131] [1964] R.P.C. 183.

[132] (1936) 53 R.P.C. 139 at 151. See also *Re Wingate's Design* (1935) 52 R.P.C. at 131; *Rosedale Associated Manufacturers Ltd v Airfix Products Ltd* [1957] R.P.C. 239 at 241, 251.

[133] (1927) 44 R.P.C. 503. See also *Infields Ltd v Rosen* (1940) 56 R.P.C. 163 at 182, where Simonds J. indicated obiter that a person who by registering two designs thereby obtained a monopoly in a particular mechanical device would probably not be entitled to protection, on the basis that the difference between the two amounted to no more than an ordinary trade variation. Considered by Viscount Dilhorne in *Amp Inc v Utilux Pty Ltd*, cited above at 115.

[134] (1945) 63 R.P.C. 81 at 91.

[135] (1948) 65 R.P.C. 1.

Ltd, as forming an accurate test of what was a "mere mechanical device" under the statutory definition of "design" then in force[136]:

> " 'Design' means only the features of shape, configuration, pattern or ornament applied to any article by any industrial process or means, whether manual, mechanical or chemical, separate or combined, which in the finished article appeal to and are judged solely by the eye; but does not include any mode or principle of construction, or anything which is in substance a mere mechanical device."

Thus, the judicial embroidery of the phrase "mere mechanical device" became incorporated into the statutory definition, and resulted in an unsatisfactory and ambiguous definition until its meaning was authoritatively expounded by the House of Lords in *Amp v Utilux*.[137]   3–073

The definition of a design in force before 1919 did not contain any express limitation against the registration of mechanical contrivances. It read[138]:   3–074

> " 'Design' means any design (not being a design for a sculpture or other thing within the protection of the Sculpture Copyright Act 1814) applicable to any article, whether the design is applicable for the pattern, or for the shape or configuration or for the ornament thereof, or for any two or more such purposes, and by whatever means it is applicable, whether by printing, painting, embroidering, weaving, sewing, modelling, casting, embossing, engraving, staining, or any other means whatever, manual mechanical, or chemical, separate or combined."

Designs where the appearance is not material

Section 1(3) of the RDA(A) provided: 3–075

> "(3) A design shall not be registered in respect of an article if the appearance of the article is not material, that is, if aesthetic considerations are not normally taken into account to a material extent by persons acquiring or using articles of that description, and would not

---

[136] Patents and Designs Acts 1907 to 1919 s.93 as amended by the 1919 Act, App.A7, para.A7–005 below.

[137] [1972] R.P.C. 103. Lord Reid at 109, lines 18–28, commented that "Much of the controversy has centred round the world 'dictated' which is a metaphorical word out of place in a statutory definition. Unfortunately the draftsman, instead of saying what he meant in his own words, chose to lift words from a judgment where metaphor may be useful and illustrative... [the word 'dictated'] is ambiguous as the draftsman would have seen if he had paused to reflect."

[138] The Patents and Designs Act 1907 s.93, App.A7, para.A7–005 below (1907 definition in italics).

be so taken into account if the design were to be applied to the article."

3–076   This subsection was introduced into the RDA by the CDPA 1988, and had no equivalent in s.1 of the RDA 1949 in its original form.[139] It should be noted that this subsection is not, strictly speaking (unlike the requirement of eye appeal and the exclusion of functional features), part of the statutory definition of design. Instead, it purports to relate to a category of designs, which satisfy all the requirements of the statutory definition of design in s.1(1), but which are to be excluded from registrability. To fall into this excluded category, a design must consist of features having "eye appeal", but, on the other hand, the appearance of the article to which the design is applied is "not material". Since the requirement of eye appeal has been interpreted[140] as requiring that the features concerned must appeal to the eye of the customer in the sense of materially influencing the customer to buy the article, it is extremely difficult to envisage any circumstances where the exclusion from registrability in s.1(3) can possibly bite. Possibly, it is to be regarded as simply a legislative backstop. It is conceivable that it might have some effect in the case of functional features of surface pattern or ornament, which are not explicitly covered by the exclusion in s.1(1)(b)(i), but even this is doubtful.[141]

Exclusion of "method or principle of construction"

3–077   Section 1(1)(a) of the RDA(A) excluded from the statutory definition of design "a method or principle of construction". The scope of this exclusion can best be understood by looking at the historical origins of this phrase. Like so many other important phrases in the definition of "design", it originated from a judicial dictum, in this case of Parker J. in *Pugh v Riley Cycle Co Ltd*.[142] Here the design was for the framework of a motor-wheel, and the statement of novelty attached to the registration was as follows:

> "The novelty consists in the disposition of the tyre rim d, in relation to the hub e, and in the cross-sectional arrangement of the spokes, a, b, c, such disposition and arrangement being shown in the accompanying drawing."

---

[139] For transitional arrangements relating to designs with an effective date of registration before the CDPA 1988, see para.3–273 below.

[140] By the House of Lords in *Amp v Utilux* [1972] R.P.C. 102; see para.3–047. The Registry appears, however, to be of the view that the test imposed under s.1(3) may be more stringent: see *Amper SA's Design Application* [1993] R.P.C. 453, RDAT.

[141] See para.3–054 above.

[142] (1912) 29 R.P.C. 196. See also *Phillips v Harbro' Rubber Co* (1920) 37 R.P.C. 233 at 242 and *Pilkington Bros Ltd v Abrahams & Son* (1915) 32 R.P.C. 61 (a surface effect on glass).

Parker J. said[143]:   **3–078**

"The second point being whether what the plaintiff registered was in fact a registrable design. A design to be registrable under the Act must be some conception or suggestion as to shape, configuration, pattern or ornament. It must be capable of being applied to an article in such a way that the article to which it has been applied will show to the eye the particular shape, configuration, pattern or ornament, the conception or suggestion of which constitutes the design . . . A conception or suggestion as to *a mode or principle of construction*,[144] though in some sense a design, is not registrable under the Act. Inasmuch, however, as the mode or principle of construction of an article may affect its shape or configuration, the conception of such a mode or principle of construction may well lead to a conception as to the shape or configuration of the completed article, and a conception so arrived at may, if it be sufficiently definite, be registered under the Act. The difficulty arises where the conception thus arrived at is not a definite conception as to shape or configuration, but only a conception as to some general construction, the definite shape or configuration being consistently with such a mode or principle of construction capable of variation within wide limits. To allow registration of a conception of such general characteristics of shape or configuration might well be equivalent to allowing the registration of a conception relating to the mode or principle of construction. Thus, in *Moody v Tree*[145] the design registered was the picture of a basket, the claim being for the pattern of the basket consisting of the osiers being worked in singly and all the butt ends being outwards. Obviously, there could be made by this method of construction any number of baskets differing in pattern except that all would have a certain common characteristic due to the method of construction and visible to the eye. It was held that the registration was bad as being an attempt to register a conception as to the mode of construction and not as to shape, configuration, pattern or ornament. A similar decision was *Re Bayer's Design*."[146]

Parker J. then went on to consider the facts of the case before him[147]:   **3–079**

"The truth seems to be that it is the precise disposition of the inner flange of the hub in relation to the rim which determines the precise cross-sectional arrangement of the spokes and makes the conception of shape and configuration involved at all definite. Once allow this

[143] (1912) 29 R.P.C. 196 at 202.
[144] Emphasis added.
[145] (1892) 9 R.P.C. 233.
[146] (1907) 24 R.P.C. 65.
[147] (1912) 29 R.P.C. 196 at 205.

disposition to be altered and you have no definite conception of shape or configuration left, but only a general characteristic of shape due to the method of construction. In my opinion the registration so construed would bring the case within the authorities I have cited and would be void as an attempt to protect a mode of construction as opposed to a conception as to shape or configuration. The validity of the registration can, therefore, in my opinion only be saved by construing the application as seeking protection for that definite shape or configuration in the completed article, which will result from its construction precisely in accordance with the registered drawing or for shape or configuration which is to the eye substantially the same, . . . and in considering whether the shape or configuration is the same, engineering evidence is, for the most part, out of place. The eye, and only the eye, must be the judge."

3–080   That case can be seen as an attempt to register as a design not one particular individual and specific shape of an article, but a range of possible shapes. Whilst a design could potentially be infringed by a range of different designs which are "not substantially different" from it,[148] the starting point for the scope of the monopoly is a single shape (or surface pattern) which is the design on the register. If the application for registration is framed in such a way that what is sought to be registered is not a single appearance (i.e. of shape or of pattern), but a range of different appearances, which all embody the general features which are claimed by the applicant, then those features are too general, and amount to a method or principle of construction. In other words, any conception which is so general as to allow several different specific appearances to be made within it, is too broad and will be invalid.[149]

3–081   The other sense in which "method or principle of construction" has been used is as being a process or operation by which a shape is produced, as opposed to the shape itself. This was the interpretation applied by the Court of Appeal in *Rosedale Associated Manufacturers Ltd v Airfix Products Ltd*.[150] There, the design was for a child's bucket with castellations in its bottom for producing sand castles (itself an old idea), and the material of which the bucket was made being of uniform thickness throughout, the castellations appeared also on the outside of the bottom of the bucket. The Court of Appeal, upholding the decision of Lloyd-Jacob J., rejected the suggestion that the design was invalid as being merely a method or principle of construction. Lord Evershed M.R. said[151]:

---

[148] As to the meaning of this test, see para.3–184 below.
[149] See *Kestos Ltd v Kempat Ltd and Kemp* (1936) 53 R.P.C. 139 at 151.
[150] [1956] R.P.C. 360; [1957] R.P.C. 239.
[151] [1957] R.P.C. 239 at 241.

"The second objection arose from the circumstance ... that if the bucket is made of plastic material, then the most economical and satisfactory method of construction would be such that the contour or configuration of the bottom of the bucket would exactly correspond both inside and out, that is the body of the bucket would be of uniform thickness throughout. There are to my mind several answers to this objection. In the first place it is not stated or to be supposed that the design is or was intended to be limited to toys of plastic material. Second, the objection seems to be directed solely to the fact that the shape of the bottom of the bucket is the same inside and out; it neglects the circumstance that the bucket bottom has that shape at all, which is an essential feature of the design as such. But, third and more important, the objection in my view misapprehends the point and significance of the disqualification implicit in the words 'method or principle of construction'. In my judgment, the quoted words are intended to exclude from the design registration (to use the language in *Kestos Ltd v Kempat Ltd*[152] of Luxmoore J., who was greatly experienced in cases of this character) the drawing or illustration of 'a process or operation by which a shape is produced as opposed to the shape itself'. In the present case the subject of the registration is a particular appearance of toy bucket, having specific features directed to attract the eye."

Romer L.J. said[153]:   3–082

"I cannot see that ... the design is 'a method or principle of construction'. It may well be that the shape of the buckets is in accord with accepted methods of plastic construction, but that seems to me to be quite a different thing. Luxmoore J. in *Kestos*[154] gave judicial authority to the following statement in Mr Russell-Clarke's book, *Copyright in Industrial Designs*. 'If it is possible to get several different appearances which all embody the general features which he claims, then those features are too general and amount to a mode or principle of construction.' In my judgment no such possibility exists in relation to the respondents' design."

In *Cow & Co Ltd v Cannon Rubber Manufacturers Ltd*,[155] it was held by   3–083
Lloyd-Jacob J. and the Court of Appeal that a design consisting of a diagonal arrangement of ribs upon a hot water bottle did not constitute a method or principle of construction, and that the registration was valid.

---

[152] (1936) 53 R.P.C. 139 at 151.
[153] [1957] R.P.C. 239 at 251.
[154] (1936) 53 R.P.C. 139 at 151.
[155] [1959] R.P.C. 240 at 347.

Letters and numerals

3–084   A particular arrangement of words, letters or numerals cannot, in the ordinary way, constitute a design, nor can they be regarded as forming any part of a design, and they must, accordingly, be entirely ignored.[156] If, however, letters or numerals were actually worked into or embroidered into a pattern, as, for instance, in the case of a monogram, they can be taken into account as forming part of the design.[157] Rule 22[158] gave the Registrar power to require, where words, letters or numerals appear in the design, that a disclaimer of any right to their exclusive use shall be made. This represented a change from the former r.22[159] which differentiated between letters and numerals which are, and which are not, of the essence of the design. The old rule required that where they were not of the essence they should be removed from any representations or specimens of the design lodged at the Patent Office, and that where they were of the essence, the Registrar might require a disclaimer of any right to their exclusive use. An example of where words and letters were ordered to be struck out from the application under the provisions of the old r.22, upon the ground that they were not of the essence of the design, is *United Africa Co's Application*.[160] Despite the change made to r.22, presumably a disclaimer should normally be required in respect of letters and numerals which are not of the essence of the design; and even if such a disclaimer is not imposed by the Registrar, such letters and numerals would not count as part of the design as a matter of general law.

Checks or stripes

3–085   A design for a pattern may consist of a mere arrangement of straight lines or stripes.[161] This was recognised in the statutory Form 2A (Application for Registration of a Design) scheduled to the Registered Designs Rules 1989 which required the applicant specifically to state if his design consists "substantially of checks or stripes".[162]

---

[156] *Re an Application by Associated Colour Printers Ltd* (1937) 54 R.P.C. 203 at 210.
[157] *Re an Application by Associated Colour Printers Ltd* (1937) 54 R.P.C. 203 at 207.
[158] Registered Designs Rules 1989.
[159] Designs Rules 1949.
[160] [1959] R.P.C. 182.
[161] See *Gottschalk & Co v Velez & Co* (1936) 53 R.P.C. 403, and *Re an Application by Associated Colour Printers Ltd* (1937) 54 R.P.C. 203, where Luxmoore J. indicated that there was nothing inherently unregistrable in the combination of lines forming the framework of a calendar. However, see the impact on this particular case of r.26(3) of the Registered Designs Rules 1989, which excluded from registration printed matter primarily of a literary or artistic character, discussed at para.3–033 above.
[162] The requirement was contained in Box 5 of Form 2A as set out in Sch.1 to the Registered Designs Rules 1989.

Colour

The question of the extent to which colour could constitute a design or at least an aspect of a design has been considered in a number of cases, but the position with regard to it remained somewhat obscure. In *Grafton v Watson*[163] Chitty J. said: "When I speak of colour I am aware that colour cannot be the subject-matter of design,"[164] and it thus seems clear that colour cannot per se constitute design.[165] In *Norton v Nicholls*, however, Lord Campbell C.J. said[166]: "The colours on both sides were essentially as much part of the shawl, or of the combination as any of the five points which he claimed at the trial,"[167] and therefore it seems that colour may in some cases form an element in a design.[168] The true principle is, it is submitted, to be found set out in the judgment of Farwell J. in the case of *Re Calder Vale Manufacturing Co and Lappet Manufacturing Co's Designs*.[169] He said:

> "I desire with regard to colours to say this, that while I am very far from suggesting that there may not be cases where differences in colour may be of importance,[170] and indeed sufficient to differentiate the designs, prima facie, in my view colour is not a matter of any great importance in considering a question of this kind, more especially in a case such as this, where the colours are for all practical purposes limited to a few, in this case four colours, where the variation of colours is not such in my judgment as materially to affect the similarity of the design, the design being the pattern, which remains the same and has the same appeal to the eye, although the arrangement of the four colours may be different in each case. Therefore, so far as colour is concerned, in my judgment no importance should be attached, for the purpose of comparing these designs, to the difference in colour."[171]

3–086

[163] (1884) 50 L.T. 420.
[164] See also the judgment of Hall V.-C. in *Nevig v Bennett & Sons* (1898) 15 R.P.C. 412 at 417.
[165] See also the decision of the Assistant Comptroller in *Re an Application by Associated Colour Printers Ltd* (1937) 54 R.P.C. 203 at 205.
[166] See also *Knowles & Co Ltd v Bennett & Sons and Bigio* (1895) 12 R.P.C. 137 at 142 and *Gottschalk & Co v Velez & Co* (1936) 53 R.P.C. 403.
[167] (1859) 28 L.J.Q.B. 225 at 227.
[168] See the Appendix to the decision in *Smith Kline and French Laboratories' Application* [1974] R.P.C. 253.
[169] (1935) 52 R.P.C. 119, at 120 and 125. Approved by Graham J. in *Smith Kline and French Laboratories' Application* [1974] R.P.C. 253 (speckled drug capsules). A summary of Designs Registry Office practice relating to the significance of colour in the registration of designs is printed as an appendix to this decision.
[170] See also p.120 of the Report, where the learned judge said in the course of the argument: "Colour cannot be disregarded; it may or may not make a material difference." See also *Kent and Thanet Casinos Ltd v Bailey's School of Dancing Ltd* [1965] R.P.C. 480 (a rotor for a roulette wheel, having coloured sectors).
[171] (1935) 52 R.P.C. 119 at 124.

3–087   This accords with the view expressed in *Re an Application by Associated Colour Printers Ltd*,[172] where the design was for a calendar pad, printed in only three colours, the background being black, the lettering white, and the lines orange. Luxmoore J. indicated, obiter, that the colours in which the design in question were printed must be ignored.

3–088   If colour was in the normal course of events taken into account as forming part of the design, as was pointed out by the Assistant Comptroller in his decision in the *Associated Colour Printers' Application*, it would be practically impossible to secure effective protection for any design for a pattern because either it would be necessary to register the pattern in all possible combinations of colours, or trade rivals would be able with impunity to apply the pattern in colours other than those shown in the registration. It would appear, therefore, that colour must, prima facie, be ignored. Ordinary differences of colour may, in other words, be regarded as mere "trade variants," which do not alter the identity of the design. In certain exceptional cases, however (e.g. a shot design for a silk handkerchief), it is possible that the colours and their arrangement might form part of the design,[173] especially if the colouring was called attention to in the statement of novelty.[174]

3. Novelty and Prior Art

Novelty a requirement for registration

3–089   There are two fundamental requirements for a pre-2001 design to be registrable. First, it must be a design falling within the statutory definition in s.1(1) of the RDA(A). That requirement, which itself has many aspects, is analysed in the preceding section. The second fundamental requirement for registrability is that the design should be new. That requirement is imposed by subss.1(2) and 1(4) of the RDA(A) in the following terms:

> "(2) A design which is new may, upon application by the person claiming to be the proprietor, be registered under this Act in respect of any article, or set of articles, specified in the application."
>
>   . . .

---

[172] (1937) 54 R.P.C. 203.

[173] *The Secretary of State for War v Cope* (1919) 36 R.P.C. 273 would appear to have been a case of a registration in which colour formed part of the design. There the design was for the British War Medal Ribbon.

[174] As regards statements of novelty, and illustrations of cases where a specific colour for part of the article was specified, see para.3–215 below. See also *Valeo Vision SA v Flexible Lamps Ltd* [1995] R.P.C. 205 at 215, ChD, where the colour of car light lenses was disregarded, the statement of novelty being limited to features of shape and configuration only.

"(4) A design shall not be regarded as new for the purposes of this Act if it is the same as a design—

(a) registered in respect of the same or any other article in pursuance of a prior application, or
(b) published in the United Kingdom in respect of the same or any other article before the date of application,

or if it differs from such a design only in immaterial details or in features which are variants commonly used in the trade."

The above quoted requirement that a design should be "new" differs **3–090** from the wording of the RDA 1949 before the amendments made by the CDPA 1988. Prior to those amendments, the requirement for registrability was that a design should be "new or original". How, if at all, the pre-1989 test of "new or original" differed from the pre-2001 test of "new" is discussed below.[175] It should be noted that the old requirement (if it is different) still governs the validity of designs registered under the pre-1988 Act law.[176]

Date at which novelty is to be assessed

The date at which the novelty of a design is to be assessed is normally at **3–091** the date of application. Thus, self evidently, publications which take place later, even if very shortly afterwards, are irrelevant; and the inquiry as to novelty is restricted to the body of "prior art" published before that date.

There are special cases where novelty is assessed as at a different date **3–092** from the date of application. When the appearance of a design is altered in the course of prosecution, the Registrar may direct that novelty is assessed as at the date when the alteration was made instead of at the original filing date of the application.[177] If a single application is filed which in the view of the Registrar contains multiple designs, then the applicant may be allowed effectively to split up his application into the requisite number of new single applications, but retain his original filing date for all of them.[178] In both these cases, the maximum term of the registered design is reckoned from the altered date rather than the original application date.[179]

In addition to these two special cases where the Registrar directs a **3–093** different filing date, there is the case of a Convention application. The date of application will normally be considered to be the date on which the application for registration of the design was filed in the United

---

[175] See para.3–160 below.
[176] As to the transitional provisions affecting such designs, see para.3–270 below.
[177] Registered Design Rules 1989 r.34(1)(a).
[178] Rule 34(1)(b).
[179] See para.3–249 below.

Kingdom Designs Registry.[180] However, it is possible for an application filed in the United Kingdom to claim priority from an earlier application filed in a Convention country.[181] If Convention priority is validly claimed, then the date at which the novelty of the design filed in the United Kingdom is assessed is not the date of the UK filing, but as at the date of filing of the earlier application in the Convention country.[182]

Conflicting registrations with earlier application dates

3–094 The first of the two bases upon which the novelty of a design can be attacked, under s.1(4)(a) of the RDA(A) quoted above, is by reason of another design registration (whether in respect of the same or a different article[183]) which enjoys an earlier effective application date. In order to provide a basis of attack under this provision, it is necessary that the potentially conflicting design which is cited should either (1) already be on the register at the date of application[184] for the design in suit, or (2) be put on the register later but be based on an application with an earlier effective date than that of the design in suit.[185] Where the cited registration is itself derived from a Convention application, its application date for this purpose will be the date of the original filing in the Convention country, rather than its filing date in the United Kingdom Registry.[186]

3–095 If there is a potentially conflicting application which has an earlier date, it will only be available to cite against the novelty of a design with a later application date if it does go on to be registered itself. A potentially conflicting application which is abandoned or refused will not found an attack of lack of novelty under this head.[187] Nor will a registration which is itself invalid,[188] although it may be necessary as a matter of procedure for the owner of the design against which such a registration is cited to take the step of rectifying the register to expunge the invalid registration before it ceases to be available as an attack on the novelty of his own design.[189] In these respects, it can be seen that an attack of lack of novelty based on a design registration with an earlier application date is similar

---

[180] For the requirements needed for an application to establish a date of filing, see para.3–249 below.

[181] As to which, see para.2–141 above.

[182] RDA(A) s.14(2).

[183] This is made clear by the express wording of s.1(4)(a) RDA(A), quoted in para.3–089 above. A special exception exists where the owner of a registered design himself seeks to re-register his design in respect of a different article; see para.3–105 below.

[184] Which may for this purpose be the date of filing of an earlier application in a Convention country; see para.3–093 above.

[185] *Re Shallwin's Application* [1961] R.P.C. 203.

[186] The same rules apply as for determining the date of application for the design in suit; RDA(A) s.14(2); and see para.3–093 above.

[187] Under this head: if it is published, it could of course found an attack based on prior publication, but then only as of the date of publication, not as of its date of application.

[188] *Chudzikowski v Sowak* [1957] R.P.C. 111 at 116 lines 4–27, per Lord Evershed M.R., CA.

[189] As to rectification of the register to remove invalid entries, see para.6–026 below.

to the old "prior claiming" attack under the pre-1977 British patent system.[190] It is different from the "deemed publication" attack under the post-1977 harmonised European patent system, under which the validity or otherwise of the cited earlier application is irrelevant.[191]

The Registrar is not entitled to refuse an application for registration on the ground that an application for a similar design has previously been refused, since novelty is determined by publication, and there would be no publication in such a case, as rejected or abandoned design applications are kept secret.[192]   **3–096**

What constitutes prior publication?

What counts as "published" for the purpose of calling into question the novelty of a later design registration? This is broader than the word at first suggests. It is by no means limited to the publishing of a design in a printed publication, although it includes that. In practical terms, there are two main ways in which a design can be published: by prior use of the design, by selling or displaying to the public articles to which the design has been applied; and by paper publications of one sort or another.[193] It is not, in fact, necessary that publication should be on paper; an oral disclosure, provided it is non-confidential, will amount to publication.[194]   **3–097**

In general, the law as to what constitutes a prior publication for registered design purposes is that same as the law of prior publication under the pre-1977 patent law, and pre-1977[195] patent authorities on the subject have consistently been treated as applicable to registered design cases.[196]   **3–098**

In order to be relied upon for the purpose of attacking the novelty of a pre-2001 design registration, the publication concerned must have been   **3–099**

---

[190] Patents Act 1949 s.32(1)(a) lists as a ground of invalidity "that the invention ... was claimed in a valid claim of earlier priority date ... of another patent granted in the United Kingdom".

[191] European Patent Convention art.54(3); Patents Act 1977 s.2(3). These provisions make available, for the purpose of attacking the novelty of a patent or application with a later filing date, the matter contained in conflicting applications with an earlier filing date, provided that those conflicting applications go on to be published. It is not necessary that they should go on to give rise to valid patents themselves or even that they should proceed to grant.

[192] *Re Brampton's Designs* (1926) 43 R.P.C. 55, and see RDA(A) s.22(4).

[193] *Plimpton v Malcolmson* (1876) 3 Ch.D. 531.

[194] See para.3–129 below.

[195] The Patents Act 1977 replaced the previous patent law, which was of domestic origin, with a harmonised European system of patent law deriving from the European Patent Convention (EPC). This lays down the test for prior art that it should have been "made available to the public" (EPC art.54(2); Patents Act 1977 s.2(2)). The authorities which interpret this test of harmonised European origin are not necessarily a good guide to the meaning of "publication" under the Registered Designs Act, whose jurisprudence developed in parallel with the pre-1977 British patent law.

[196] See, e.g., *Rosedale Assoc Mfrs Ltd v Airfix Products Ltd* [1957] R.P.C. 239 at 244, line 21 and 249, line 21, CA.

within the United Kingdom.[197] This limitation has important practical consequences.[198]

Publication by prior use

3–100 Prior publication of a design by prior use can be said to take place when the design has been applied to articles, and those articles have been used in such a way that the design becomes disclosed to the public before the date of application for registration of the design in suit. It should be noted that it is sufficient if the design is used on any kind of article, and it need not be the same article, or even in the same category, as the article in respect of which the design is registered or sought to be registered.[199]

3–101 In general there will be publication if articles to which the design is applied are manufactured, displayed or used in such a way that members of the public will or might see them. It is not necessary that the articles should have been sold.[200] Prior use thus does not mean use by the public, but use in public as opposed to use in private.[201]

3–102 In the classic patent[202] case of *Carpenter v Smith*,[203] the patent was for a lock. The defendant produced a lock similar to the plaintiff's which he proved to have been used for 16 years on a gate adjoining a public road. It was held that there was publication. In *Stead v Anderson*,[204] the patent was for making roads with wooden blocks. The alleged prior use was the use of wooden blocks to make a private carriage-drive at the house of Sir William Worsley. Parke B. said[205]:

> "As to the alleged user, the only evidence is that a similar pavement had previously been laid down at Sir W. Worsley's . . . If the mode of

---

[197] For post 2001 designs, the rule is wider and includes all matter available to "interested circles" in the European Community: see para.2–072 above.

[198] See para.3–142 below.

[199] This is made clear by the express wording of RDA(A) s.1(4)(b) quoted in para.3–089 above. The position was different prior to the 1949 Act, since before then the novelty-destroying design had to be applied to an article in the same class as the article in respect of which the design in suit was sought to be registered; see para.3–162 below.

[200] *Betts v Neilson* (1868) L.R. 3 Ch. 429; *Gill v Coutts & Sons and Cutler* (1896) 13 R.P.C. 125.

[201] *Carpenter v Smith* (1842) 1 W.P.C. 540; *Croysdale v Fisher* (1884) 1 R.P.C. 17 at 21; *Gill v Coutts & Sons and Cutler* (1896) 13 R.P.C. 125.

[202] As is noted in para.3–097 above, the law of prior publication for the purpose of pre-2001 registered designs was the same as the law of prior publication for patent purposes which prevailed before the Patents Act 1977. However, care should be taken when looking at patent authorities not to confuse publication through use with the related but legally quite separate ground on which the novelty of a patent could be destroyed, by *prior use as such*. This meant commercial use of the invention within the UK, regardless of whether or not its details had thereby been published to anyone; *Bristol-Myers (Johnson's) Appn* [1975] R.P.C. 127, HL. This latter doctrine has no application to the law of registered designs.

[203] (1842) 1 W.P.C. 540.

[204] (1848) 2 W.P.C. 147.

[205] (1848) 2 W.P.C. 147 at 149.

forming and laying the blocks at Sir W. Worsley's had been precisely similar to the plaintiff's, that would have been a sufficient user to destroy the plaintiff's patent, though put in practice in a spot to which the public had not free access."

Thus, if the use was in such a position and in such circumstances that some members of the public would be likely to have seen the design, there will be publication, even though it is not proved that anyone did examine it.[206] **3–103**

The disclosure of the prior use need not be to a large number of the public. If there has been a disclosure of the design to any individual member of the public who is not under an obligation as to secrecy, there will be publication. Thus, in *Humpherson v Syer*,[207] a machine made substantially according to the patent was shown to a person in Syer's shop. In *Re Taylor's Patent*[208] a stove similar to the patented article was used in the hall of a private house and shown to visitors. Use in a private house may, therefore, be publication. In *Fomento Industrial SA v Mentmore Manufacturing Co Ltd*,[209] certain ballpoint pens were given as gifts to three individuals who were free to use the pens as they wished. In all these cases there was held to be publication. **3–104**

Re-registration of the same design for different articles, or a similar design for same or different articles

A special exception existed to the general rule that the novelty of a design will be destroyed by the prior registration or publication of that design as applied to any kind of article. By s.4(1) of the RDA(A), the proprietor of a registered design was entitled to apply for registration of the same design, or a design with modifications or variations not sufficient to affect its identity, in respect of another article. His own previous registration, or the publication of his design as registered, does not then destroy the novelty of his new design registration in respect of the new article, but his term of protection is limited to the term of the original design.[210] This, in effect, gave the proprietor of a design registration the ability to extend the scope of the registration during its lifetime to cover further articles, although in formal terms each application to protect his design on a new article will be a separate application leading to a separate design registration.[211] It appears that his application for registration of the design **3–105**

[206] *Gill v Coutts and Cutler* (1896) 13 R.P.C. 125 at 136; *Heath v Smith* (1885) 2 W.P.C. 268.
[207] (1887) 4 R.P.C. 407.
[208] (1896) 13 R.P.C. 482.
[209] [1956] R.P.C. 87.
[210] RDA(A) s.4(1) proviso.
[211] The Registered Designs Rules 1989 r.13. This procedure is no longer necessary under the post-2001 law, because infringement of a design registration is no longer limited to the kind of article for which it is registered.

on the new article must precede his actual use of the design on the new article. This is because, if he uses the design on an article which falls outside the scope of his earlier registration, then that will not count as a publication "of the registered design", which is all that s.4(1) of the RDA(A) shields him against as regards the novelty of his new application.

3–106 A person who makes an application to register a design and finds that it has previously been registered in respect of a different article was allowed to buy up the earlier design registration while his own application was still pending, and if he did so he could take advantage of this rule in the same way as if he had himself been the owner of the earlier registration all along.[212]

3–107 The same rule applied to the registration (whether in respect of the same article or a different article) of a design which is not exactly the same as the earlier registered design, but has "modifications or variations not sufficient to alter the character or substantially to affect the identity thereof."[213] However, this provision has been interpreted narrowly so that practically any significant change or difference between the earlier and later design will destroy the protective effect of this provision. For an applicant to rely on s.4(1)(b), the subject of his application must have substantial identity with his prior published design. In *Sebel Ltd's Application (No.1)*,[214] it was held that substitution in the old design of a different stand did substantially alter the identity of the article (a rocking horse), and that the subsection did not apply. Since the stand had already been published in an advertisement showing it applied to another horse, it was held that the design failed to qualify for novelty under s.1, the said stand being a mere trade variant. In *Sebel Ltd's Application (No.2)*,[215] a design was held not to fall within s.4 because the character of the design was different from the character of the applicant's earlier design. Thus it seems that the applicant's own earlier design may be sufficiently similar to destroy the novelty of his later application for protection of his modified design, and yet too different to allow him to take advantage of the protection of RDA(A) s.4(1). This is an odd and unfortunate result if it is indeed correct.

Publication in documents

3–108 In cases of publication of a design by prior use as applied to an article, normally the only questions which arise are whether it has been published at all (i.e. whether the articles to which it has been applied have been disclosed to the public), and whether the design is similar enough to

---

[212] RDA(A) s.4(2).
[213] RDA(A) s.4(1)(b).
[214] [1959] R.P.C. 12.
[215] [1959] R.P.C. 19.

the design in suit to destroy the latter's novelty.[216] But where the novelty of a design is tested against a prior published document, a number of additional questions can arise which do not arise in the case of a prior use.

First, it may not be clear whether or not the document discloses a **3–109** design as applied to an article at all. A trade catalogue containing photographs or illustrations of articles to which a design has been applied may be a clear enough case. But the publication in a document of a pattern or picture does not as such destroy the novelty of a design which consists of applying that pattern or picture to an article.[217] For it to destroy the novelty of such a design, the paper publication must suggest explicitly or implicitly by context that the pattern or picture should be applied to an article.

Secondly, the pattern (if it is two-dimensional) or shape (if it is three- **3–110** dimensional) of the design may not be clear from the document. Particularly in a case where it involves a written description rather than an explicit picture or illustration, there may be room for argument as to the precise nature of the design which the document discloses, before one can go on to ask whether or not it is similar enough to the later design to destroy novelty.[218]

Thirdly, a paper publication may be shielded from destroying the **3–111** novelty of a later design registration by the special provisions of subss.6(4)–(5) of the RDA(A). These provisions allowed the owner of copyright in an artistic work to exploit his work so long as he did not apply it industrially to an article, without his own exploitation of it counting against the novelty of his own later application for a design registration covering the artistic work as applied to an article.[219]

When does a document count as published?

If a design has been contained in documents, such as books or catalogues, **3–112** which have been sold or circulated, there would clearly be publication. It is not, however, necessary that large numbers of the documents should be proved to have been actually sold or circulated. In *Harris v Rothwell*,[220] Lindley L.J. said[221]:

> "It is sufficient to show that the invention was so described in some book or document, published in this country, that some English people may fairly be supposed to have known of it."

---

[216] As to which, see para.3–145 below.
[217] See para.3–118 below.
[218] See para.3–121 below.
[219] See para.3–125 below.
[220] (1887) 4 R.P.C. 225.
[221] (1887) 4 R.P.C. 225 at 230.

3–113   And in *Otto v Steel*[222] Pearson J. said[223]:

> "The question is whether or not this book has been published in such a way as to become part of the public stock of knowledge in this country. It is not, to my mind, necessary for that purpose to show that it has been read by a great many people, or that any person in particular has got from it the exact information which it is said would have enabled Dr Otto in this case to have made his engine. But, to my mind, it must have been published in such a way that there may be a reasonable probability that any person, and amongst such persons, Dr Otto, might have obtained that knowledge from it."

3–114   In *Plimpton v Malcolmson*[224] Jessel M.R. said[225]:

> " . . . if a man publishes a book, that is, a large number of copies, and sends them to booksellers for sale, and they are, for a reasonable time, exposed in the window, so that you may infer that people have known and seen them, and may reasonably so infer, though you do not prove one has been sold—if the other side cannot prove that one has not been sold, you may reasonably infer that some of those books have been sold."

3–115   The presence of even only one copy of a document in a public library has been held to constitute publication,[226] and the presence of a design in the sample library of a well-known firm, where it was open to inspection by customers of the firm, and by such members of the public as the firm was ready to allow to inspect it, has also been held to amount to publication.[227]

3–116   But if the document, though in a library, was not, in fact, in a place where it was accessible to members of the public, then there would not be publication.[228] In *United Horse-Shoe & Nail Co v Stewart & Co*[229] the alleged anticipation consisted of an American specification which had been deposited in the Patent Office library, and was in a place where it was accessible to all persons making use of the library. It was held that it constituted a prior publication. In *Harris v Rothwell*[230] two copies of German specifications had been deposited in the German department of

---

[222] (1886) 3 R.P.C. 109.
[223] (1886) 3 R.P.C. 109 at 112.
[224] (1876) 3 Ch.D. 531.
[225] (1876) 3 Ch.D. 531 at 562.
[226] *United Horse-Shoe & Nail Co v Stewart & Co* (1888) 5 R.P.C. 260; *Harris v Rothwell* (1887) 4 R.P.C. 225; *United Telephone Co v Harrison, Cox-Walker & Co* (1882) 21 Ch.D. 720.
[227] *Pressler & Co Ltd v Gartside & Co (of Manchester) Ltd and Widd & Owen Ltd* (1933) 50 R.P.C. 240.
[228] *Minter v Williams* 1 W.P.C. 137.
[229] (1888) 5 R.P.C. 260.
[230] (1887) 4 R.P.C. 225.

the Patent Office library. One had been there a year and the other six weeks, and their presence had been published in the Patent Office Journal. It was held that there was publication. Lindley L.J. said[231]:

> "Prima facie a patentee is not the first inventor of his patented invention if it be proved that before the date of his patent an intelligible description of his invention, whether in English or in any other language commonly known in this country, was known to exist in this country, either in the Patent Office, or in any other library to which the public are admitted, and to which persons in search of information on the subject to which the patent relates would naturally go for information. But if, as in the *Plimpton cases* and *Otto v Steel*, it be proved that the foreign publication, though in a public library, was not, in fact, known to be there, the unknown existence of the publication in this country is not fatal to the patent."

Of the cases referred to in the above judgment, in the *Plimpton* cases,[232] **3–117** one copy of a book had been sent to the Patent Office, but, owing to a mistake, it was not entered in the catalogue, and it was taken into a private room and left there. It was held that the book was not accessible to the public, and that there had been no publication. Similarly, in *Otto v Steel*,[233] one copy of a book was in the British Museum. It was not kept in the reading room, but in an inner room, and was catalogued only under the name of the author. It was held that, in these circumstances, it could not be relied upon as an anticipation.

Does the document disclose a design applied to an article?

In order to destroy the novelty of a design registration, an earlier design **3–118** must be published "in respect of the same or any other article".[234] Mere publication of the pattern which constitutes the design was therefore not sufficient to destroy the novelty of a design registration, which consisted of the application of that pattern to an article.[235] In principle, the same holds true of the publication of a shape, although it is less easy to envisage cases where the publication of a shape does not implicitly convey the article to which that shape is to be applied. Thus, novelty may reside in the application of an old shape or pattern to new subject-matter. This was first laid down in the leading case of *Saunders v Wiel*.[236] There,

---

[231] (1887) 4 R.P.C. 225 at 232.
[232] *Plimpton v Malcolmson* (1876) 3 Ch.D. 531; *Plimpton v Spiller* (1877) 6 Ch.D. 412.
[233] (1886) 3 R.P.C. 109.
[234] RDA(A) s.1(4)(b).
[235] As already explained, a "design" for the purposes of design registration must have reference to some article; para.3–013 above.
[236] (1893) 10 R.P.C. 29.

the design consisted of the handle of a spoon made to represent Westminster Abbey seen from a particular point of view. The design had actually been copied from a photograph of the Abbey.

3–119   The validity of the design was upheld,[237] Bowen L.J. saying[238]:

> "It seems to me that the novelty and originality in the design, within this section, is not destroyed by its being taken from a source common to mankind . . . The novelty may consist in the applicability to the article of manufacture of a drawing or design which is taken from a source to which all the world may resort. Otherwise, it would be impossible to take any natural or artistic object and to reduce it into a design applicable to an article of manufacture, without also having this consequence following, that you could not do it at all in the first place unless you were to alter the design so as not to represent exactly the original; otherwise there would be no novelty in it, because it would be said that the thing which was taken was not new. You could not take a tree and put it on a spoon, unless you drew the tree in some shape in which a tree never grew, nor an elephant unless you drew it and carved it of a kind which had never been seen. An illustration, it seems to me, that may be taken about this is what we all know as the Apostles spoons. The figures of the Apostles are figures which have been embodied in sacred art for centuries, and there is nothing new in taking the figures of the Apostles, but the novelty of applying the figures of the Apostles to spoons was in contriving to design the Apostles' figures so that they should be applicable to that particular subject-matter. How does a building differ from that? In no sense it seems to me."

3–120   It should be recalled that under the 1949 Act,[239] if a pattern (or shape) has been published in respect of any article, the publication will destroy the novelty of any design which consists of the application of that pattern (or shape) to an article of any kind, however different it is from the kind of article to which the publication suggests that the design should be applied. However, the publication will not invalidate such later design registrations if it does not suggest the application of the pattern (or shape) to an article at all. Thus, a series of pictures published in a fine art catalogue would not destroy the novelty of a later design consisting of the application of one of those pictures to, say, the back of a chair, because a painting or picture simpliciter is not an "article".[240] But the same pictures

---

[237] The old case of *Adams v Clementson* (1879) 12 Ch.D. 714 being doubted.
[238] (1893) 10 R.P.C. 29 at 33.
[239] The position before the Registered Designs Act 1949 was different; see para.3–162 below.
[240] See para.3–028 above.

published in a catalogue of patterns for application to wallpaper would destroy the novelty of such a later design registration, because wallpaper is an article.[241]

What design is disclosed by a prior published document?

Assuming that a prior published document does satisfy the requirement   3–121
that it discloses a design, i.e. a shape or pattern, as applied or to be applied to an article, the next question may be what is the shape or pattern which it discloses? In some cases this will be clear, for instance where the publication contains explicit pictures or illustrations. However, it may be less clear and the disclosure may consist in whole or in part of written text which needs to be interpreted, or general instructions which can be put into practice in a variety of ways. In such cases the test to be applied is that borrowed from the pre-1977[242] patent law of anticipation, i.e. that the prior art document must contain "clear and unmistakable directions" to make an article with the shape or pattern which is the same as, or similar enough[243] to the registered design in suit to deprive it of novelty.

This was laid down in *Rosedale Associated Manufacturers Ltd v Airfix*   3–122
Ltd.[244] Lord Evershed M.R. said[245]:

"In this respect the test of prior publication of an alleged invention should, in my judgment, be no less applicable in the case of a registered design, and as regards the former, I venture to cite once more the oft-quoted language of Lord Westbury in *Hills v Evans*[246]: 'The antecedent statement must, in order to invalidate the subsequent patent, be such that a person of ordinary knowledge of the subject would at once perceive and understand and be able practically to apply the discovery without the necessity of making further experiments.' By a like reasoning, to my mind, if a document is to constitute prior publication, then a reader of it, possessed of ordinary knowledge of the subject, must from his reading of the document be able at least to see the design in his mind's eye and should not have to depend on his own originality to construct the design from the ideas which the document may put into his head."

---

[241] Although the distinction is a fine one, wallpaper has always been treated as an article which has a purpose beyond carrying its pattern; see para.3–028 above.

[242] Patent law under the harmonised European system implemented by the Patents Act 1977 is not necessarily the same.

[243] As to what is similar enough, see para.3–151 below.

[244] [1957] R.P.C. 239.

[245] [1957] R.P.C. 239 at 244.

[246] (1862) 31 L.J. Ch. 457 at 463.

3–123   On the same point Romer L.J. said[247]:

> "In *Flour Oxidising Co v Carr & Co*[248] Parker J. (as he then was) said[249]:
> 'Where the question is solely a question of prior publication it is not,
> in my opinion, enough to prove that an apparatus described in an
> earlier specification could have been used to produce this or that
> result. It must also be shown that the specification contains clear and
> unmistakable directions so to use it.' These observations by Parker J.
> were cited with approval by Lord Dunedin in *British Thomson-
> Houston Co v Metropolitan-Vickers Electrical Co*,[250] and again (when
> delivering the judgment of the Judicial Committee) in *Pope Alliance
> Corporation v Spanish River Pulp & Paper Mills, Ltd.*[251] In the latter case
> and at the same page Lord Dunedin posed the test as follows: 'would
> a man who was grappling with the problem solved by the Patent
> attacked, and having no knowledge of that Patent, if he had had the
> alleged anticipation in his hand, have said "that gives me what I
> wish"? It is true that these citations were related to anticipations of
> inventions, but it seems to me that they apply by analogy to alleged
> anticipations by "paper publications" of registered designs'."

3–124   It is not permissible to make a mosaic of a number of prior documents
for the purpose of attacking novelty. If the attack on novelty is to succeed,
the design must be disclosed in the single prior document. If, however,
one document contains a reference to another document, the two may be
read together.[252]

Proprietor who exploits copyright in an artistic work

3–125   Subsections 6(4) and 6(5) of the RDA(A)[253] contained provisions which
are designed to protect the owner of a copyright in an artistic work
against his own exploitation of the artistic work, if he later decided to
apply for a design registration covering the application of the design in
the artistic work to an article. Basically, subs.6(4) provided a shield
against the novelty-destroying effect of the previous exploitation of the
artistic work, provided that the registered design application was made
by the proprietor of the copyright or with his consent. Subsection 6(5)
excluded from the scope of that shield any exploitation which consists of

---

[247] [1957] R.P.C. 239 at 249.
[248] (1908) 25 R.P.C. 428. See also *General Tire and Rubber Co v Firestone Tyre and Rubber Co Ltd*
[1972] R.P.C. 457 at 484–486 per Sachs L.J. "A signpost, however clear, upon the road to
the patentee's invention will not suffice. The prior inventor must be clearly shown to
have planted his flag at the precise destination before the patentee."
[249] (1908) 25 R.P.C. 428 at 457.
[250] (1927) 45 R.P.C. 1 at 23 and 24.
[251] (1928) 46 R.P.C. 23 at 52.
[252] *Rosedale Associated Manufacturers Ltd v Airfix Ltd* [1957] R.P.C. 239 at 245 and 250.
[253] Set out in App.A below.

or includes the sale of articles to which the design has been applied industrially, or other commercial dealings with such articles. Thus, the purpose seems to be to protect the artistic copyright owner, so long as he does not permit his artistic work to be applied as a design to an article before the date when he makes a registered design application.

The substance of these provisions dates from an amendment made to the RDA 1949 by the Copyright Act 1956.[254] In fact, the provisions apply not merely to the case where the artistic work is identical to the registered design, but to any case where the registered design is a "corresponding design", a concept which is considered elsewhere.[255] The shield is lost if the design in question, or a design differing from it only in trade variants,[256] has been applied industrially. What counts as industrial application for this purpose is also considered elsewhere.[257] **3–126**

However, these provisions could have a surprisingly wide effect, if the interpretation given to them in a Designs Registry decision is correct. In *Bissell AG's Design*,[258] carpet sweepers according to their design had been made and marketed by the applicants in the United States of America before the date of their registered design application in the United Kingdom. An illustration of the sweeper had appeared in a journal in the United Kingdom before that date, but there had been no manufacture or sale in this country. The Assistant Comptroller held that the illustration in the journal was the use of a copyright artistic work corresponding to the design. He further held that manufacture and sale of the actual articles in the United States did not cause that use to fall within the exception to the shield contained in subs.6(5) of the RDA(A), because[259]: **3–127**

"I am impressed by the argument that, given the general philosophy of the Registered Designs Act, section 6(4) must be read as providing that one disregards all previous use of the artistic work to which the design corresponds, made by or with the consent of the copyright owner, unless it includes the sale, letting for hire, or offer for sale or hire in the United Kingdom of articles to which the design in question had been applied industrially."

---

[254] s.44(1) of the Copyright Act 1956 inserted the substance of subss.6(4) and 6(5) RDA(A) into RDA 1949 as subs.6(4).

[255] What is a "corresponding design" is considered in the context of the overlap between registered designs and artistic copyright; see para.5–054 below.

[256] See para.3–154 below.

[257] See para.5–099 below.

[258] [1964] R.P.C. 125. A further possible extension of this argument is that even if carpet sweepers themselves had been sold in the United Kingdom, they should be disregarded, at least if 50 or fewer had been made, because selling a carpet sweeper made from design drawings is in one sense using those artistic works: *Bampal Materials Handling Co Ltd's Design* [1981] R.P.C. 44, Pat Off. This interpretation does, however, appear completely to lose sight of the legislative purposes of subs.6(4).

[259] [1964] R.P.C. 125 at 127.

3–128   It is submitted that the correctness of this decision must be open to serious doubt. Subsection 6(5) was intended to remove the shield of s.6(4) from acts of publication of the design which consist of *or include* acts of sale or offer for sale, etc. of articles. Thus, the shield is removed not just from the actual acts of sale or offer for sale, etc. of the articles, but from acts which are incidental thereto, such as the publishing of illustrations of the article in catalogues or trade papers. It can hardly deprive such acts of their character as being incidental to the sale of articles, just because the actual sale of the articles takes place outside the United Kingdom. If *Bissell* is indeed correct, it produces surprising and unwarranted effects, particularly in cases where prior publications from overseas are invoked.[260]

Disclosure to a single person is enough for publication

3–129   As has already been noted, the most common ways in which a design becomes "published" for the purpose of destroying the novelty of a later design registration is either through prior public use of the design on an article, or publication of the design in a written document. However, there is no restriction on the manner in which the design comes to be published, and the disclosure could even be purely oral. In general, there will be publication if the design is disclosed to any individual member of the public who is not under any obligation to secrecy.[261] Disclosure to merely one such person will be sufficient to constitute publication. In *Humpherson v Syer*,[262] Bowen L.J. said[263]:

> "I put aside questions of public use, and treat this as a question of whether there has been a prior publication; that is, in other words, has information been communicated to any member of the public, who was free in law or equity to use it as he pleased. Was Widmer a person to whom this communication had been made in a manner which left him free both in law and equity to do what he liked with the information . . . You must take all the circumstances of the case, and ask yourself whether there was any confidential relation estab-lished between the two parties—whether it was an implied term of the employment that the information should be kept by the shopman to himself, or whether he might afterwards, without any breach of good faith, use the matter, and use it as he chose."

3–130   In *Bristol-Myer's Application*,[264] a South African patent specification was relied upon in patent opposition proceedings. This document had been

---

[260] See paras 3–142—3–144 below.
[261] (1886) 3 R.P.C. 109.
[262] (1887) 4 R.P.C. 407. And see also the judgment of Fry L.J. at 414.
[263] (1887) 4 R.P.C. 407 at 413.
[264] [1969] R.P.C. 146 at 155.

specially obtained by a company employee and was the only copy available at the relevant time in the United Kingdom. The Court of Appeal held that in the circumstances publication had been established:

> "It seems to us that we are bound by [*Fomento v Mentmore*][265] to reject the contention that publication depends either upon anything in the nature of a dedication to the public or upon the degree of dissemination of the information alleged to have been published. On the contrary, if the information, whether in documentary form or in the form of the invention itself, has been communicated to a single member of the public without inhibiting fetter, that is enough to amount to making available to the public ... "

Confidential disclosures

On the other hand, a communication made under circumstances which impose an obligation of confidence on the recipient is not a publication.[266]   **3–131**

If the person to whom the disclosure is made has himself an interest in the design, then it may be easy to infer that the disclosure is confidential.[267] In *Blank v Footman, Pretty & Co*[268] Blank, the proprietor of a design, before registering it, showed it to Hummel, a commission agent who had the sole right of selling Blank's goods in England. Hummel, therefore, had an interest in the design, and it was held that, this being so, the communication must be regarded as confidential, and such as not to amount to publication. Kekewich J. said[269]:   **3–132**

> "Therefore, Mr Hummel has an interest in any design of Mr Blank's goods of this class, and although he is not a partner, or in any way a partner, he has that interest which makes him a person whom Mr Blank would naturally consult before endeavouring to put any of that class of goods on the market. Mr Blank, therefore, having sketched his design, shows it to Mr Hummel. I cannot conceive that in doing so he would be publishing the design in any sense which could be placed on that word. Even if that relation had not existed between the two parties, I see no reason why a designer should not

---

[265] *Fomento Industrial SA v Mentmore Mfg Co Ltd* [1956] R.P.C. 87 was a case of publication by prior use of samples of ballpoint pens, discussed at para.3–100 above.

[266] *Morgan v Seaward* (1836) 1 W.P.C. 187 at 194; *Patterson v The Gas Light & Coke Co* (1877) 3 App. Cas. 239; *Gadd and Mason v The Mayor of Manchester* (1892) 9 R.P.C. 516; *Nevill v Bennett & Sons* (1898) 15 R.P.C. 412.

[267] *Blank v Footman, Pretty & Co* (1888) 5 R.P.C. 653; *Heinrichs v Bastendorff* (1893) 10 R.P.C. 160.

[268] (1888) 5 R.P.C. 653.

[269] (1888) 5 R.P.C. 653 at 656.

call in an expert, a gentleman whom he knows to be experienced in the trade likely to advise him well and whom he can trust, for the purpose of advising him before incurring extra expense and trouble."

3–133   Mere private collaboration will generally not amount to publication.[270] If, however, the disclosure involves anything in the nature of commercial dealing, then prima facie it will not be considered confidential and will amount to publication.[271] In *Gunston v Winox Ltd*[272] Lord Sterndale M.R. said[273]: "There is ample authority that the showing of a design to a person for the purpose of getting an order is prima facie a disclosure of that design." And this will be so even though the goods are not, in fact, delivered till after the date of registration.[274]

3–134   It should be noted that s.6(1)(c) of the RDA(A) states that the registration of a design for a new or original[275] textile design is not invalidated by the acceptance of a "first and confidential order for goods bearing the design". It is not easy to see what effect this provision might have, since if the order is accepted in circumstances which place an obligation of confidence on the purchaser, the disclosure of the design to him will not in any case be a publication. Nor does this provision appear to impose an obligation of confidence in circumstances where it would not exist under the general law. This provision appears to be pure surplussage, possibly having its origin in a fear at one time that a rule similar to the patent doctrine of invalidation by prior use as such[276] might otherwise apply to registered designs.

Disclosure of a proprietor's design in breach of good faith

3–135   As already indicated,[277] a disclosure which is confidential does not amount to publication. This is the case regardless of whether it is a case of a prior disclosure by the proprietor himself of the design sought to be registered, or a disclosure of another conflicting design by a third party. However, in the case of the disclosure of the proprietor's own design

---

[270] *Nevill v Bennett & Sons* (1898) 15 R.P.C. 412.
[271] *Winfield & Son v Snow Bros* (1891) 8 R.P.C. 15; *Nevill v Bennett & Sons* (1898) 15 R.P.C. 412; *Gunston v Winox Ltd* (1921) 38 R.P.C. 40.
[272] (1921) 38 R.P.C. 40.
[273] (1921) 38 R.P.C. 40 at 52.
[274] *Winfield & Son v Snow Bros* (1891) 8 R.P.C. 15.
[275] The retention in this provision of the words "or original" appears to be a pure drafting oversight, since the test for novelty was changed from "new or original" to "new" by the amendments made by the CDPA 1988, and it should have been carried right through the RDA 1949.
[276] For an explanation of this see para.3–102 above, especially n.202.
[277] See para.3–131 above.

before the date of application, certain special statutory provisions apply.[278] These are subsections 6(1)(a) and (b) of RDA(A):

"6.—(1) An application for the registration of a design shall not be refused, and the registration of a design shall not be invalidated, by reason only of—

(a) the disclosure of the design by the proprietor to any other person in such circumstances as would make it contrary to good faith for that other person to use or publish the design;

(b) the disclosure of the design in breach of good faith by any person other than the proprietor of the design; ... "

Unless "good faith" is interpreted as extending more widely than cases where there is a legally enforceable obligation of confidence, which does not seem to be the case, subs.6(1)(a) is purely surplussage since a disclosure in circumstances covered by subs.6(1)(a) will always be confidential and hence will not amount to a publication. It simply reiterates what the law already provides, in the special case of the disclosure of the design by the proprietor himself.   **3–136**

However, subs.6(1)(b) has a wider effect, since it will prevent a design application being invalidated by a prior disclosure of the proprietor's own design which does count as a publication, if that disclosure has taken place in breach of good faith. Presumably the obligation of good faith is owed to the proprietor, although the subsection does not expressly say so. An example of where subs.6(1)(b) would bite is a case where an agent of the proprietor, in breach of good faith, inserted an advertisement disclosing the design in a publication. In such a case there would be a publication, since readers of the advertisement could not be subject to an obligation of confidence despite the breach of the rights of the proprietor of the design. However, subs.6(1)(b) would then prevent the disclosure from operating as a barrier to registration of the design.   **3–137**

In *Chudzikowski v Sowak*,[279] the defendant attacked the validity of the registered design on the ground that articles in accordance with the design which a third party had made for the plaintiff were sold by the third party to the defendant before the date of registration. The plaintiff said that these sales constituted a disclosure in breach of good faith by a person other than the proprietor. He contended accordingly that the sales did not invalidate his design. Lloyd-Jacob J. held that the third party was aware that the articles which he was selling were the property of the plaintiff, and that any disclosure of the design attaching to the sales was   **3–138**

---

[278] In addition to the provisions cited in this paragraph, there is special protection given against invalidation of a subsequent design application where the proprietor exploits an artistic work in which copyright subsists, without actually commercialising the work in the form of articles; see para.3–125 above.

[279] [1957] R.P.C. 111.

in breach of good faith, and that the design was valid. The Court of Appeal affirmed his decision, Lord Evershed M.R. saying[280]:

> "[The defendant] contended that in order to bring the case within section 6(1)(b) it is necessary to prove that the 'person' there mentioned at the time of the disclosure himself realised that what he was doing constituted a breach of good faith. I am not prepared to accept that view of the subsection. I think if it is shown that the person in question knew what he was doing and if the thing he did was in truth according to the terms of the contract, or other relation between him and the proprietor, a breach of good faith, the terms of the subsection are satisfied."

Disclosure to a government department

3–139   By subs.6(3) of the RDA(A), in the special case of the communication of a design by its proprietor to a government department to consider its merits, the registration shall not be refused or invalidated merely by reason of such communication, or anything done in consequence of such a communication.

Display of designs at exhibitions

3–140   Certain exhibitions may be certified by the Secretary of State. The display of a design at such an exhibition will not invalidate a later application by the proprietor to register the design which is made within six months of the opening date of the exhibition. Subsection 6(2) of the RDA(A) provides:

> "An application for the registration of a design shall not be refused, and the registration shall not be invalidated by reason only—
>
> (a) that a representation of the design, or any article to which the design has been applied, has been displayed, with the consent of the proprietor of the design, at an exhibition certified by the Secretary of State for the purposes of this subsection;
> (b) that after any such display as aforesaid, and during the period of the exhibition, a representation of the design or any such article as aforesaid has been displayed by any person without the consent of the proprietor; or
> (c) that a representation of the design has been published in consequence of any such display as is mentioned in paragraph (a) of this subsection,

---

[280] [1957] R.P.C. 111 at 114.

if the application for registration of the design is made not later than six months after the opening of the exhibition."

The protection of this subsection is restricted to display of the design at **3–141** the exhibition, and to any consequential re-publications by third parties. It does not cover the publication of the design in a periodical prior to display at a certified exhibition. That is not in consequence of the display at the exhibition, and is therefore not exempted by s.6(2) from invalidating the design.[281] The exhibition must have been certified by the Secretary of State in advance of its taking place, and the official practice of sometimes issuing a certificate retrospectively after the event is unlawful and ineffective to confer the protection of the subsection on persons who exhibit their designs.[282]

Prior publication must be within the United Kingdom

In order for a prior design to be available to cite against the novelty of a **3–142** design registration, the publication of the prior design must have taken place within the United Kingdom.[283] For this purpose[284] the United Kingdom is deemed to include the Isle of Man,[285] the territorial waters of the United Kingdom,[286] and structures and vessels engaged in mineral exploitation in the United Kingdom sector of the continental shelf.[287] In conditions of increasing international trade and progressive integration of national markets into a single global market in many sectors, the rule restricting relevant prior publication to the United Kingdom can be regarded as a historical hangover by the time it was replaced by the European harmonised approach in 2001. The corresponding rule in the case of patents was abolished nearly 25 years previously.[288]

Historically, one of the objectives of the patent system was to encourage **3–143** the development of new industries in the United Kingdom through, inter alia, the introduction from foreign countries of techniques known there but not previously known in the United Kingdom. Accordingly, the fact that an invention was previously known abroad did not invalidate a British patent, and indeed a person who imported an invention which he copied from the public domain abroad was entitled to be granted a British patent and was referred to as an "inventor by importation". Although the

---

[281] *Re Steel & Co's Application* [1958] R.P.C. 411.
[282] *Mod-Tap W Corp v BI Communications plc* [1999] R.P.C. 333, per Pumfrey J.
[283] RDA(A) s.1(4)(b); see para.3–089 above.
[284] And indeed generally for registered designs purposes.
[285] RDA(A) s.47.
[286] RDA(A) s.47A(1).
[287] RDA(A) s.47A(2).
[288] The Patents Act 1977, enacting the harmonised substantive rules in the European Patent Convention, permits the novelty of a patent to be attacked on the basis of prior art published anywhere. It is not restricted to prior publications in the United Kingdom, or even in the territory of the EPC member states.

registered designs system never went as far as the patent system in recognising a mere copyist of a design from abroad as being entitled to apply for the grant of a registered design in the United Kingdom,[289] it did follow the patent system to the extent of disregarding prior art published outside the United Kingdom. However, with increasing numbers of patent and design applications being made by foreign residents as Convention applications based on original applications in their home countries, the rule against the citation of prior art published outside the United Kingdom increasingly had the effect that such foreign proprietors could obtain monopolies in the United Kingdom which would have been invalid in their home countries because of prior art there, to the detriment of competing exporters from the same home country, and to home based industry which would otherwise have been able to import or copy designs in the public domain abroad. Despite these factors, the opportunity was not taken at the time of the CDPA 1988 to modify this aspect of the RDA 1949 to bring it into line with patent law.

3–144   In practice, much foreign published prior art is also published in the United Kingdom. Whilst overseas design registrations did not as such count against the validity of United Kingdom design registrations, in practice copies of them are regularly filed in the Science Reference Library[290] and thus will be available to cite against the novelty of later British design applications. Similarly, many foreign trade journals are published in libraries in the United Kingdom. Establishing the date of deposit on the shelves of a particular library may be crucial. In the case of a publication (or, indeed, a foreign design registration on the shelves of a British library) which originates from the proprietor of the British registration himself, the provisions of ss.6(4)–(5) of the RDA(A)[291] may unexpectedly prove to be an obstacle against the citation of such prior art, especially if the Designs Registry Decision in *Bissell AG's Design*[292] is indeed correct.

Assessing the novelty of a design against a prior design

3–145   The previous paragraphs of this section have considered the circumstances in which either prior published designs, or registered designs with an earlier application date, can be cited against the novelty of a design registration. Once it has been established that such a design is

---

[289] On ownership grounds, since such a copyist would not be the author of the design, i.e. "the person who creates it", as required by RDA(A) s.2(3); see para.3–230 below.

[290] Formerly called the Patent Office Library.

[291] These protect the proprietor of a copyright work from earlier exploitation of the copyright work invalidating his later design application; see para.3–125 above.

[292] [1964] R.P.C. 125: this decision is considered and its correctness doubted at para.3–128 above.

citable, and also precisely what design the prior publication or registration discloses,[293] it then becomes necessary to compare the design in
suit[294] with the prior design in order to see whether or not the former is
"new" within the meaning of subs.1(4) of the RDA(A). If this comparison
exercise is carried out, and the design in suit is identical in all respects to
a prior design, then the design in suit is obviously not "new". However,
the design in suit may be generally similar to a prior design, but there
may be certain differences. If so, two questions will need to be asked.

(1) Are the differences "immaterial details"?[295]
(2) Are the differences merely in features which "are variants
    commonly used in the trade"?[296]

If all the differences can be categorised either as immaterial details, or **3–146**
as variants commonly used in the trade, then the design in suit is not new.
These two categories of potential differences will be considered in the
following paragraphs of this section.

It should however be emphasised that before the above comparison **3–147**
exercise is carried out, it is necessary to identify what amounts in each
case to the "design" within the meaning of the Act, both in the case of the
design in suit and in the case of the prior design. The "designs" being
compared, particularly in the case of three-dimensional designs, will not
necessarily be all the features of shape of the respective articles. Thus, the
"design" consists only of features which have eye appeal and functional
features are excluded from being part of the "design".[297] Accordingly, if
the only differences between the prior article and the shape of the article
in suit are in functional features, there is then no difference between the
"design" of each, and the design in suit will not be novel.[298] Vice versa,
commonality in functional features between the registered design and the
prior art should be ignored, and attention should be focused on the
features having eye appeal which may reveal significant differences.[299]

---

[293] This may not always be easy, particularly in the case of prior publications which consist
of written matter rather than of pictures or illustrations; see para.3–121 above.

[294] The test of novelty might be applied at the application stage when a design was sought
to be registered, or in the context of proceedings after registration when its validity is
challenged. In both cases it is apt to call it the design in suit.

[295] See para.3–151 below.

[296] See para.3–154 below.

[297] The effect of this is extensively considered at paras 3–061 et seq. and 3–067 et seq.
above.

[298] Whether a design is more useful than other designs which have gone before is not to be
considered: *Walker, Hunter & Co v Falkirk Iron Co* (1887) 4 R.P.C. 390; *Moody v Tree* (1892)
9 R.P.C. 333; *Re Clarke's Registered Design* (1896) 13 R.P.C. 351 at 358; *Allen West & Co Ltd
v British Westinghouse Electric & Manufacturing Co Ltd* (1916) 33 R.P.C. 157 at 164 and *Wells
v Attache Case Manufacturing Co* (1932) 49 R.P.C. 113 at 119. However, see the remarks of
Romer J. in *Tyler & Sons v Sharpe Bros & Co* (1894) 11 R.P.C. 35.

[299] *Dalgety Australia Operations Ltd v FF Seeley Nominees Pty Ltd* (1985) 68 A.L.R. 458; 5 I.P.R.
97; *Household Articles Ltd's Registered Design* [1998] F.S.R. 676 at 684. Where different
designs are applied to the same functional items, the overall appearance of the complete
products may look similar: coffee pots.

The whole of the design need not be new

3–148   "The design may be valid within the Act, although all the parts are old except some particular part only which is new or original. The novelty or originality of the particular part may be sufficient to impart the character of novelty and originality to the whole."[300]

3–149   In fact, a design may well be novel although all the individual features are old at the date of registration,[301] for the combination of two or more old and well-known designs or parts of designs will constitute novelty, if the effect, i.e. the appearance of the combination as a whole, is new.[302] Possibly even the omission of something from an old shape or pattern might result in a new or original design which could be protected.[303]

3–150   In the case of an article consisting of several parts, if there is only one part which is new in shape, though that part may fail to give a sufficiently novel appearance to the article for it to be registrable as a whole, nevertheless, the part may be registrable by itself.[304] In order for this to be possible, the part would have to satisfy the test of being an article of commerce in its own right which is "made and sold separately",[305] and must fall outside the so-called "must match" exclusion.[306]

Differing in "immaterial details": the eye is the judge

3–151 It has always been the case that mere slight variations from articles already manufactured are not registrable,[307] that the variation from what has gone before must not be trivial or infinitesimal,[308] and that small variations which any skilled workman might make between the articles which he makes for different customers are not enough.[309] These principles have been given statutory recognition in the final words of subs.1(4)

---

[300] *Walker & Co v A. G. Scott & Co* (1892) 9 R.P.C. 482 at 485, per Chitty J.

[301] *Falk Ltd v Jacobwitz* (1944) 61 R.P.C. 116 at 126; *Lusty & Sons Ltd v Morris Wilkinson & Co (Nottingham) Ltd* (1954) 71 R.P.C. 174 at 181.

[302] *Harrison v Taylor* (1859) 4 H. & N. 815; *Re Clarke's Design* (1896) 13 R.P.C. 351 at 360; *Heinrichs v Bastendorff* (1893) 10 R.P.C. 160; *Phillips v Harbro' Rubber Co* (1920) 37 R.P.C. 233; *Staples v Warwick* (1906) 23 R.P.C. 609; *Nevill v Bennett & Sons* (1898) 15 R.P.C. 412 at 415; *Sherwood & Cotton v Decorative Art Tile Co* (1887) 4 R.P.C. 207; *Wallpaper Manufacturers Ltd v Derby Paper Staining Co* (1925) 42 R.P.C. 43; *Falk Ltd v Jacobwitz* (1944) 61 R.P.C. 116 at 126. It is not appropriate to consider the matter from the point of view of the obviousness of the combination in the patent sense; *Carr's Design Application* [1973] R.P.C. 689.

[303] *Re Clarke's Design* (1896) 13 R.P.C. 351 at 360.

[304] *Walker Hunter & Co v Falkirk Iron Co* (1887) 4 R.P.C. 390; *Re Clarke's Design* (1896) 13 R.P.C. 351; *Ford Motor Co Ltd's Design* [1972] R.P.C. 320 at 330.

[305] For the application of this test to spare parts and components of articles, see para.3–038 above.

[306] See para.3–041 above.

[307] *Wells v Attache Case Manufacturing Co* (1932) 49 R.P.C. 113 at 119.

[308] *Re Rollason's Design* (1898) 15 R.P.C. 441; *Lazarus v Charles* (1873) L.R. 16 Eq. 117.

[309] *Simmons v Mathieson & Co Ltd* (1911) 28 R.P.C. 486 at 491.

of the RDA(A) which lays it down that no design shall be regarded as new if it differs from a previous design "only in immaterial details".

The question which has to be decided is whether the two appearances **3–152** are substantially the same or not. That the eye, and the eye alone, is to be the judge of identity, and is to decide whether one design is or is not an anticipation of another, has been consistently laid down.[310] The design must be looked at as a whole,[311] the question being whether an article made according to the design under consideration is substantially similar in appearance to an article made according to the alleged anticipation. The test is not only to look at the two designs side by side, but also apart, and a little distance away.[312] The novelty should in other words be substantial,[313] and it must be substantial having regard to such matters as the nature of the article, the extent of the prior art and the number of previous designs in the field in question. Especially with fields such as clothing where there is a huge volume of prior art, there must be some clearly marked and defined differences,[314] though the actual standard of ingenuity required on the part of the author is extremely small.[315] It has been said that, by analogy with the approach in the field of patents to the assessment of the obviousness or otherwise of an invention,[316] evidence of the commercial success of the applied design, if attributable to the design itself and not to extraneous causes, may be material in determining the novelty or originality of the design.[317] This proposition is however open to question, since the obviousness or otherwise of the new design in the patent sense is not the criterion.[318] It has also been said that in an infringement action the fact that the defendant has copied the claimant's design may be good evidence tending to show that the design is novel,[319] although the logical basis of this proposition is not easy to understand.

Although the words "substantial" and "substantially similar" are used **3–153** in some of the judicial decisions referred to above, it should be noted that the Act uses the words "immaterial details" in the test of novelty, and a

---

[310] *Moody v Tree* (1892) 9 R.P.C. 333; *Pugh v Riley Cycle Co Ltd* (1912) 29 R.P.C. 196; *Jones and Attwood Ltd v National Radiator Co Ltd* (1928) 45 R.P.C. 71.

[311] *Re Clarke's Design* (1896) 13 R.P.C. 351 at 360; *Allen West & Co Ltd v British Westinghouse Electrical & Manufacturing Co Ltd* (1916) 33 R.P.C. 157 at 165.

[312] *Grafton v Watson* (1884) 50 L.T. 420.

[313] *Le May v Welch* (1885) 28 Ch.D. 24 at 34; *Allen West & Co Ltd v British Westinghouse Electric & Manufacturing Co Ltd* (1916) 33 R.P.C. 157 at 165; *Simmons v Mathieson & Co Ltd* (1911) 28 R.P.C. 486 at 491; *Re Monotype Corporation Ltd's Application* (1939) 56 R.P.C. 243 (font of type held not to be sufficiently novel).

[314] *Le May v Welch* (1885) 28 Ch.D. 24. As to coins adapted for use as pendant medallions, see *McMillan's Design* [1972] R.P.C. 294.

[315] *Walker, Hunter & Co v Falkirk Iron Co* (1887) 4 R.P.C. 390; *Vandervell & Co v Lundberg & Sons* (1916) 33 R.P.C. 60; *Wells v Attache Case Co* (1932) 49 R.P.C. 113 at 119.

[316] *Samuel Parkes & Co Ltd v Cocker Bros Ltd* (1929) 46 R.P.C. 241 at 248.

[317] *Harvey & Co Ltd v Secure Fittings Ltd* [1966] R.P.C. 515 at 520 and *Negretti & Zambra v Stanley* (1925) 42 R.P.C. 358.

[318] See *Carr's Design Application* [1973] R.P.C. 689.

[319] *Nevill v Bennett & Sons* (1898) 15 R.P.C. 412; *Cartwright v Coventry Radiator Co* (1926) 42 R.P.C. 351 at 357.

different phraseology, "not substantially different", in the test of infringement.[320] Are these two tests meant to be the same or different? If they are different, which is wider? Is it possible for a prior art design to be far enough away from the registration that it differs in more than "immaterial details", but still be close enough that it is "not substantially different", so that continued production of a prior art design could infringe a later registration? There are strong policy reasons for believing that this cannot be intended, since the purpose of the test of novelty is to permit the public to continue to use prior published designs without interference from a later monopoly.[321] In *Valor Heating Co Ltd v Main Gas Appliances Ltd*,[322] Whitford J. considered that, despite the difference in wording, "by and large the test must be the same".[323] If this is the case, the draftsman's use of the differing phraseology in subss.1(4) and 7(1) can only be explained, like so much else in registered designs legislation, on the basis of historical anomaly.

Variants commonly used in the trade

3–154   It has always been held that nothing will be counted new or original unless it differs from what has gone before by something more than ordinary trade variants,[324] or features in common use in the trade.[325] This is embodied in the statutory test of novelty in the RDA(A),[326] which specifically excludes from registration those designs which differ from prior designs only in features which are "variants commonly used in the trade". This is a distinct ground of invalidity from a variation in "immaterial details" and a design may lack novelty on this ground even if replacing one trade variant in the prior art with the common trade variant in the registered design does have a significant visual impact.[327] Consideration of this aspect of novelty will normally involve the evidence of experts in the trade.[328]

3–155   What is a trade variant was explained by Lord Moulton in *Phillips v Harbro' Rubber Co*[329]:

---

[320] RDA(A) s.7(1); see paras 3–164 and 3–206 below.
[321] See the very well known observations of Lord Moulton to this effect in the patent context in *Gillette Safety Razor Co v Anglo-American Trading Co* (1913) 30 R.P.C. 465 at 480, HL.
[322] *Valor Heating Co Ltd v Main Gas Appliances Ltd* [1973] R.P.C. 871, ChD.
[323] *Valor Heating Co Ltd v Main Gas Appliances Ltd* [1973] R.P.C. 871, ChD at 877 lines 5–20.
[324] *Phillips v Harbro' Rubber Co* (1920) 37 R.P.C. 233; *Negretti & Zambra v Stanley & Co Ltd* (1925) 42 R.P.C. 358, *Wells v Attache Case Co* (1932) 49 R.P.C. 113 at 119; *Saunders v Automotive Spares Ltd* (1932) 49 R.P.C. 450; *Infields Ltd v Rosen* (1939) 56 R.P.C. 163 at 182.
[325] *Re Travers' Application* (1951) 68 R.P.C. 255.
[326] RDA(A) subs.4(4).
[327] *J Rapee & Co Pty Ltd v Kas Cushions Pty Ltd* (1989) 15 I.P.R. 577 at 590, per Gummow J.; *Household Articles Ltd's Registration* [1998] F.S.R. 676 at 685 per Laddie J.
[328] *Grafton v Watson* (1885) 51 L.T. 141; *Cooper v Symington* (1893) 10 R.P.C. 264.
[329] (1920) 37 R.P.C. 233 at 240 HL.

"It is necessary with regard to the question of infringement, and still more with regard to the question of novelty and originality, that the eye should be that of an instructed person, i.e. that he should know what was common trade knowledge and usage in the class of articles to which the design applies. The introduction of ordinary trade variants into an old design cannot make it new or original. For example, if it is common practice to have or not to have spikes in the soles of running shoes, a man does not make a new or original design out of an old type of running shoe by putting spikes into the soles."

A trade variant is, therefore, some embellishment (useful or otherwise) which is known, and sometimes, though not always, used in connection with a particular class of article or class of work.　**3–156**

There is no reason why a main feature of a design should not, if the evidence justifies the conclusion, be a variant commonly used in the trade, but the variant must be one used and not merely published in the United Kingdom. It seems that "commonly used in the trade" means at least that it must be shown by the evidence to have been available in the United Kingdom from more than one origin.[330] That a feature is shown in a single trade catalogue is not sufficient to make it a trade variant.[331]　**3–157**

It has been said that there can be no novelty or originality where the shape is imposed upon the designer by the necessity of his task,[332] for some mental effort, small though the amount may be, is necessary upon the part of the author.[333] Some skill and labour of a draughtsmanlike nature must be involved.[334]　**3–158**

Thus, mere workshop alterations which any ordinary competent work-man might be expected to produce in carrying out their ordinary day-to-day trade, or would be likely to make in order to fit one thing upon another cannot possibly constitute novelty.[335] Mere alteration in scale is not in general sufficient to render a design new or original.[336]　**3–159**

Distinction between "new" and "original"

As has already been noted, one of the amendments made by the CDPA 1988 to the RDA 1949 was to change the test of novelty from "new or original" to "new". Did this change of wording effect any alteration in the　**3–160**

[330] Re Britvic's Application [1960] R.P.C. 201.
[331] Amp Inc v Utilux Pty Ltd [1970] R.P.C. 397 at 429, per Graham J., not considered in the House of Lords.
[332] Vandervell & Co v Lundberg & Sons (1916) 33 R.P.C. 10.
[333] Dover Ltd v Nurnberger Celluloid Waren Fabrik (1910) 27 R.P.C. 498.
[334] Harrison v Taylor (1887) 4 H. & N. 815 at 820.
[335] Allen West & Co Ltd v British Westinghouse Electric and Manufacturing Co Ltd (1916) 33 R.P.C. 157; Re Travers' Application (1951) 68 R.P.C. 255 at 258.
[336] Re Calder Vale Manufacturing Co Ltd and Lappet Manufacturing Co Ltd's Designs (1936) R.P.C. 117 at 125.

law? What distinction, if any, was to be drawn between the words "new" and "original" under the former law is doubtful. It may be that "new" means different from what has gone before. It is also possible that the view advanced by Buckley L.J. in *Dover v Nurnberger Celluloid Waren Fabrik*[337] is the correct one. There he said that "new" referred to cases where the shape or pattern was completely new in itself, whilst "original" referred to cases where, though old in itself, it was new in its application to the article in question. He said[338]:

> "If the design be new it may be registered under that expression. But the Act by section 49 seems to contemplate that it may be registered, even if it be not new, provided it be original. The explanation of this lies possibly in the fact that the novelty may consist not in the idea itself, but in the way in which the idea is to be rendered applicable to some special subject-matter. The word 'original' contemplates that the person has originated some thing that by the exercise of intellectual activity he has started an idea which had not occurred to anyone before, that a particular pattern or shape or ornament may be rendered applicable to the particular article to which he suggests that it should be applied . . . It is easier by illustration in the concrete than by words in the abstract to explain what I mean. First, a few illustrations as to shape. The traditional figure of Falstaff is as old as Shakespeare, but if a person conceived for the first time, the idea of making a wine beaker in the form of the figure of Falstaff, that would be an original design for a wine beaker. The same would be true of an Uncle Toby jug for beer. The words new, or original, involve the idea of novelty, either in the pattern, shape, or ornament itself, or in the way in which an old pattern, shape, or ornament is to be applied to some special subject-matter."

3–161   Whether or not "or" in the phrase "new or original" is used in the disjunctive sense was considered in *Aspro-Nicholas' Application*.[339] Graham J. held that it was not so used. The phrase was changed from "new *and* original" to "new *or* original" in an amendment made to s.50(a) of the Patents and Designs Act 1907 by the Patents and Designs Act 1919 s.20. In *Carr's Design Application*,[340] however, it would appear that the RDAT, relying upon words of Lord Simonds in *Stenor Ltd v Whitesides (Clitheroe) Ltd*[341] favoured the opposite point of view, although Whitford J. refrained from expressing a concluded view upon the matter. The possible distinction was also considered as arguably giving rise to considerations under

---

[337] (1910) 27 R.P.C. 498.
[338] (1910) 27 R.P.C. 498 at 503.
[339] [1974] R.P.C. 645.
[340] [1973] R.P.C. 689.
[341] (1947) 65 R.P.C. 1 at 11.

the head of "originality" analogous to questions of obviousness under the patent system.[342]

The position before RDA 1949: novelty as to class of articles

Prior to the RDA 1949, goods in respect of which designs might be   **3–162**
registered were divided into classes, and every application for registration had to state the class in which the design was to be registered.
Registration, when granted, conferred on the owner of the design the
exclusive right to apply the design to any article in the class in which the
design was registered. So far as novelty and originality were concerned,
if a similar shape or pattern had already been applied to any article in the
same class as that in which registration was sought, no matter what its
character or purpose, and the resulting design published, the later design
was thereby deprived of novelty or originality. This principle was laid
down by the House of Lords in the case of *Stenor v Whitesides (Clitheroe)
Ltd*.[343] There the prior design was a bicycle crank axle, and this was held
to anticipate a similar design for an electric fuse, both the articles in
question falling within Class 1, being "articles composed wholly of metal
or in which metal predominates".

If a prior similar design had been previously applied to an article in a   **3–163**
different class to that in which the later design was sought to be
registered, other considerations arose. In that case the question of
whether the later design was new or original compared with the earlier
one depended upon whether the articles to which the two designs had
been applied were similar in character or purpose. If they were similar or
analogous, the later design was deprived of novelty or originality by the
earlier one.[344] If, however, the nature of the articles was different, this was
not so. This principle, together with the one referred to above, were stated
by Viscount Simon in *Stenor v Whitesides (Clitheroe) Ltd*.[345]

4. Pre-2001 Infringement of Registered Designs

Requirements for infringement of a registered design

As explained in the opening paragraphs of this chapter, the old UK law   **3–164**
of registered design infringement no longer has effect in relation to acts
taking place since December 9, 2001, even in respect of designs which
were registered under the old law. However, until the body of case law
under the new European harmonised law has built up more extensively,

---

[342] *Caron International's Design Application* [1981] R.P.C. 179, RDAT (Whitford J.), at 185–186.
[343] (1948) 65 R.P.C. 1.
[344] *Walker Hunter & Co Ltd v Falkirk Iron Co* (1887) 4 R.P.C. 390; *Re Bach's Design* (1889) 6 R.P.C. 376; *Le May v Welch* (1885) 28 Ch.D. 24.
[345] (1948) 65 R.P.C. 1.

reference back to the old law may still be of some use, particularly since the practical approach to determination of infringement will remain very much the same even if the legal test has (at least in theory) altered significantly. In addition, the "not substantially different" test of infringement remains the law in some overseas jurisdictions: see Ch.11 below. Therefore, the section of this chapter on the old law of infringement is retained. What amounted to primary infringement of a registered design was governed by s.7 of the RDA(A). Subsection 7(1) reads:

"(1) The registration of a design under this Act gives the registered proprietor the exclusive right—

(a) to make or import—

(i) for sale or hire, or
(ii) for use for the purposes of a trade or business, or

(b) to sell, hire or offer or expose for sale or hire,

an article in respect of which the design is registered and to which that design or a design not substantially different from it has been applied."

3–165   Although changes were made in the arrangement and wording of the subsection, very little change of substance was made to the above quoted provision in the amendments made to the RDA 1949 by the CDPA 1988.[346] To the extent that there is any difference between the pre-2001 and the pre-1988 definitions of infringement, the pre-1988 definition still continued to apply up to 2001 to infringement of designs registered under the pre-1988 law.[347] One point however of symbolic importance was the removal by those amendments of the phrase "copyright in the registered design" which was previously contained in RDA 1949 s.7(1). As the test of infringement since the enactment of the RDA 1949 has always been objective and does not involve the necessity for any element of copying on the part of the creator of the defendant's design,[348] the phrase "copyright in a registered design" was always inappropriate and potentially misleading. The inclusion of the phrase in the 1949 Act was presumably an unthinking carry-over by the draftsman from earlier registered designs legislation under which infringement required a "fraudulent or obvious imitation".[349]

[346] For subs.7(1) before the amendments made by the CDPA 1988, see App.A5, para.A5–007 below.
[347] CDPA 1988 s.268(2); see para.3–274 below for consideration of the transitional provisions.
[348] Unlike copyright and unregistered design right, both of which require copying as an essential element of infringement.
[349] The Patents and Designs Acts 1907 to 1919 s.60(1); see App.A7, para.A7–004 below. The old law applying this statutory test is further considered in para.3–185 below and, in relation to Australia where this test continues to apply to infringement of registered designs applied for before the Designs Act 2003 (Cth), in para.11–004 below.

There are three basic elements which had to be satisfied in order for   **3–166**
there to be infringement of a registered design, and these three elements
will be considered in turn in the following paragraphs of this section. The
three elements are:

(1) *The defendant's acts*: whether a potential defendant has done an
act of a kind which can amount to infringement, such as making,
importing, etc. In addition to what can for convenience be
described as the acts of primary infringement set out in subs.7(1)
quoted above, a registered design could also be infringed by acts
of a kind which can be viewed as secondary, by acts in relation to
moulds or tools for making infringing articles,[350] or kits of parts
for such articles.[351] This aspect of infringement also involves the
question of whether the act concerned has been performed
within the territorial[352] and temporal[353] scope of the registered
design monopoly.

(2) *The kind of article*: whether the article involved in the potentially
infringing acts is an article in respect of which the design is
registered.[354] Note that this restriction has been completely
abolished under the post-2001 law of infringement, even in
respect of old designs.[355]

(3) *The design of the article complained of*: whether that article embodies a design "not substantially different" from the registered
design.[356]

There will of course be a defence if the acts in question are licensed by   **3–167**
the registered design proprietor,[357] or there may be other special defences
to infringement such as defences[358] under European Union law. These
matters are dealt with in other chapters.

Acts of primary infringement of a registered design

The acts of primary infringement were set out in subs.7(1) of the RDA(A)   **3–168**
quoted above. It should be noted that under registered designs law, a
mere dealer may be liable for an act of primary infringement as easily as
a manufacturer. Both manufacture and subsequent dealings such as
importation, sale and offer or exposure for sale, are acts of primary

---

[350] RDA(A) s.7(3); see para.3–170 below.
[351] RDA(A) s.7(4); see para.3–173 below.
[352] i.e. within the United Kingdom, Isle of Man, etc; see para.3–177 below.
[353] i.e. between the date when the registered design comes into force and its expiry; see
para.3–180 below.
[354] See para.3–181 below.
[355] 2001 Regulations reg.12(5) and reg.13(7). See App.A3 below.
[356] See paras 3–184 to 3–215 below.
[357] RDA(A), subs.7(2).
[358] See para.9–01 below.

infringement. In this respect, registered designs differ from both copyright and UK unregistered design right. In the case of copyright, manufacture[359] and initial distribution[360] are acts of primary infringement, but subsequent dealings with infringing articles are secondary infringements which require a mental element of either actual knowledge, or reason to believe, that the articles are infringing copies.[361] UK unregistered design right draws a similar distinction between manufacturers who are primary infringers,[362] and importers or other dealers who may be liable for secondary infringement if they have the necessary mental element.[363] In this respect, the RDA 1949 altered the earlier law, which drew a distinction between manufacturers and vendors.[364]

3–169   The only limitation on which acts constitute infringement is that the importation or making of an article merely for private or personal use would not be an infringement. Apart from that, no mental element is involved, and acts of making, importing or dealing in articles which turn out to be infringing articles is a tort of strict liability. The only mitigation of the harshness of this provision is a defence against damages (although not against the other potential liabilities of a person who has infringed) if the defendant proves that he was not aware that the design in suit was registered.[365]

Making of moulds and tools, etc.

3–170   It may be convenient for present purposes to refer to this as a form of secondary infringement, in order to distinguish it from the primary acts of infringement set out in subs.7(1) of the RDA(A). Subsection 7(3) of the RDA(A) provided that it was an infringement to make, or to engage in dealings of the kind falling within subs.7(1) in relation to, "anything for enabling any such article to be made", the phrase "any such article" referring back to an article within the scope of subs.7(1). The effect of this subsection was to extend liability to acts of making or dealing in such items as moulds or specially adapted tools which are intended to be or at least capable of being used to make articles falling within the scope of

---

[359] CDPA 1988 s.17.
[360] CDPA 1988 s.18.
[361] CDPA 1988 ss.22 and 23.
[362] CDPA 1988 s.226.
[363] CDPA 1988 s.227.
[364] To succeed in an action for infringement against a manufacturer it was not necessary to show that the defendant knew that what it was doing was an infringement, whereas in the case of an action against a mere vendor the plaintiff had to show that the defendant had knowledge of the fact that the design had been applied without the consent of the proprietor. Compare ss.60(1)(a) and 60(1)(b) of the Patents and Designs Acts 1907 to 1939, App.A7, para.A7–004 below.
[365] RDA(A) s.9: it thus provides no defence in circumstances where the defendant thought that the goods in which he was dealing were licensed, or otherwise thought that there was a good defence to infringement. As to other remedies, including an account of profits, see para.6–061 below.

registration. The precise scope of this provision is far from clear, although it presumably did not extend to, e.g. general purpose tools which could be used to make articles within the scope of the registration but could equally be used to make other articles.[366] In *Aberdale Cycle Co Ltd v Charles Twigg & Co Ltd*,[367] Lloyd-Jacob J. said[368]:

> "The statutory provision must rather be read as meaning that, in addition to a monopoly in the complete manufacture, the rights of the proprietor of the design extend to the manufacture of some thing which, when used in the usual manner for its usual purpose, will result in the production of the article as designed. A typical instance would be the construction of a printing roller for textiles, the surface of which could not be used for its normal purpose without producing that design."

What was subs.7(3) of the RDA(A) was derived with some modifica- **3–171**
tion from a provision of the 1907 Act,[369] which was applied in *Haddon v Bannerman*.[370] The claimants were proprietors of a registered design for a face of type. The defendants had in England made matrices by which a design like that of the claimants could be applied to articles. The matrices were, however, to be shipped to India, so that the actual application of the design would take place there, and not in England. Warrington J. held that the act of making the matrices was comprehended by the words "to do anything with a view to enable the design to be so applied", and that there had, therefore, been an act of infringement in this country of the registered design.

It should be noted that subs.7(3) expressly referred to enabling articles **3–172**
to be made "in the United Kingdom or elsewhere". Thus, it was no defence to infringement of this provision to show that there was no intention to commit a primary infringement within the territorial scope of the registered design. Subsection 7(3) was apt to cover the export of tools or dies to other countries if the use of the tools or dies there would, if carried out in the United Kingdom, have created an infringing article.[371]

---

[366] Cf. the corresponding provisions for copyright, CDPA 1988 s.99(1)—"an article specifically designed or adapted for making copies of a particular copyright work"; unregistered design right CDPA 1988 s.230(1)(b)—"anything specifically designed or adapted for making articles to a particular design".

[367] (1952) 69 R.P.C. 131. The actual decision in this case has been reversed by the introduction of RDA(A) subs.7(4) which extends infringement to kits of parts. However, the interpretation of what amounts to a thing for enabling would appear still to be good law.

[368] *ibid.* at 141.

[369] Patents and Designs Acts 1907 to 1939 s.60(1)(a); "or to do anything with a view to enable the design to be so applied".

[370] (1912) 29 R.P.C. 611.

[371] See further, para.3–177 below.

Kits of parts

3–173 Subsection 7(4) RDA(A) provided:

> "(4) The right in the registered design is also infringed by a person who without the licence of the registered proprietor—
>
> (a) does anything in relation to a kit that would be an infringement if done in relation to the assembled article (see subsection (1)), or
>
> (b) makes anything for enabling a kit to be made or assembled, in the United Kingdom or elsewhere, if the assembled article would be such an article as is mentioned in subsection (1);
>
> and for this purpose a 'kit' means a complete or substantially complete set of components intended to be assembled into an article."

3–174 This provision was introduced into RDA 1949 by CDPA 1988. It should be noted that it did not apply, in common with the other amendments to the definition of infringement made by the 1988 Act, to pre-1988 Act registered designs.[372] The inclusion of this subsection effected a statutory reversal of *Aberdale Cycle Co Ltd v Charles Twigg & Co Ltd*,[373] where a claim was rejected that the sale of components for making up into an article was "anything for enabling any such article to be made".[374] There, the plaintiffs' designs were for toy tricycles fitted with boots between the rear wheels. The defendants made tricycles some of which were sold without boots, but boots were sold separately with instructions for fitting them to the tricycles. The contention that the manufacture of the boots, coupled with the instructions, constituted an infringement, was rejected.

3–175 It was held by the Court of Appeal in *Dorling v Honnor Marine Ltd*,[375] reversing in part Cross J.,[376] that the mere making of the various parts of an article without evidence that the completed articles were for sale or for use for the purposes of any trade or business was not making something "for enabling any such article to be made as aforesaid" within the meaning of subs.7(3) RDA 1949, and therefore did not itself constitute infringement. However, subs.7(4) RDA(A) was not restricted to cases of sale of kits to be assembled for use in a business context: it would clearly, for example, cover the sale of kits to members of the public who were intending to make the articles up for recreational purposes. The members of the public would themselves not be infringers because they would be

---

[372] CDPA 1988 s.268(2): for further consideration of the transitional provisions and pre-1988 Act registered designs, see para.3–274 below.

[373] (1952) 69 R.P.C. 131. The Court of Appeal followed and effectively approved this decision in *Dorling v Honnor Marine Ltd* [1964] R.P.C. 160.

[374] See para.3–170 above.

[375] [1964] R.P.C. 160.

[376] [1963] R.P.C. 205.

making the articles for purely private purposes with no intention of resale,[377] but the sale of the kits to them would be an infringing act.

It should be noted that the subsection, in 7(4)(b), makes explicit reference to the assembly of the kit taking place "in the United Kingdom or elsewhere". Thus, in the same way as in the case of tools or dies under subs.7(3), the making of kits for export would appear to be an infringing act, even though no actual article is ever made within the United Kingdom.[378]   **3–176**

Territorial limits of infringement

In this respect, there does not seem to be any change between pre- and post-2001 infringement law as regards UK registered designs, although of course the Community registered and unregistered design rights apply to the territory of the whole Community. The right conferred by registration of a design is a territorial monopoly similar to a patent monopoly and therefore, although subs.7(1) of the RDA(A) does not expressly say so, in order for acts to amount to infringement they must take place within the territory within which the Act applies. This comprises the United Kingdom, i.e. England, Wales, Scotland and Northern Ireland, together with the Isle of Man,[379] the territorial waters of the United Kingdom,[380] and structures and vessels engaged in mineral exploitation in the UK sector of the continental shelf.[381] Certain countries and territories for historical reasons permit enforcement or re-registration of design registrations obtained in the United Kingdom, but this is by virtue of their own laws and is not as such infringement of the legal right conferred by the UK design registration.   **3–177**

Thus, the making of articles abroad which are within the scope of the registered design does not amount to an infringement of the right conferred by the UK registration, even if acts are performed within the United Kingdom which assist, facilitate or lead to the making of such articles. If the acts performed abroad amount to infringement of a corresponding design registration under the laws of that country, it is possible that action could be taken either there or in the courts of the United Kingdom in such circumstances; but the rules as to when action can be taken here in respect of committing or facilitating the commission of tortious acts abroad is a complex subject which is outside the scope of this work.   **3–178**

However, there are two particular ways in which a person performing acts wholly within the United Kingdom could incur liability for what are,   **3–179**

---

[377] See para.3–168 above.
[378] See para.3–177 below.
[379] RDA(A) s.47. The Act extends to the Isle of Man subject to certain modifications: the Registered Designs (Isle of Man) Order 2001 (SI 2001/3678).
[380] RDA(A) s.47A(1).
[381] RDA(A) s.47A(2).

in effect the facilitation of acts of applying the registered design to articles abroad. First, the making or sale within the United Kingdom of "anything for enabling any such article to be made" was an infringement, whether the article is to be made "in the United Kingdom or elsewhere".[382] Secondly, the making or sale within the United Kingdom of a kit of parts would appear also to have been an infringement, even if the kit was to be assembled outside the United Kingdom.[383] The provisions can be likened to the so-called "contributory infringement" provisions of patent law[384]; however, in patent law, contributory infringement is limited to cases of supply of articles to persons putting the patented invention into effect within the United Kingdom, and it is not an infringement to supply "essential means" to persons abroad for the purpose of making articles falling within the claims of the patent outside the United Kingdom.[385] Quite why Parliament felt it necessary to depart from its approach under patent law and to subject British manufacturers and exporters to the competitive disadvantage of prohibiting them from supplying tools or kits for the making of articles in places where the making of those articles may be perfectly lawful, can only be regarded as a subject of bafflement.

Temporal limits of infringement

3–180   For an act to amount to infringement, it must take place within the temporal limits of the monopoly conferred by the design registration. This starts on the date on which the certificate of registration is granted,[386] despite the fact that for other purposes the design once registered is treated as having been registered as of the date of application.[387] As to the end point, the registered design will only be infringed by acts performed before it expires,[388] so it is not an infringement to import articles from abroad after expiry even if those articles were made abroad before expiry. It would appear that it was an infringement to make moulds or tools, or

---

[382] RDA(A) s.7(3): see para.3–171 above.

[383] This would appear to follow from the inclusion of the words "in the United Kingdom or elsewhere" in RDA(A) s.7(4)(b). Although subs.7(4) does not say in terms that the intended assembly referred to in the final phrase of the subsection can take place outside the UK, it would be irrational to prohibit in sub-paragraph (b) anything enabling the kit to be assembled "in the United Kingdom or elsewhere" if this were not the case. As to this provision generally, see para.3–173 above.

[384] Patents Act 1977 s.60(2) makes it an infringement to supply "means relating to an essential element of the invention for putting the invention into effect".

[385] Patents Act 1977 s.60(2) concludes with the words "that those means are suitable for putting, and are intended to put, the invention into effect *in the United Kingdom*".

[386] RDA(A) s.7(5).

[387] RDA(A) s.3(5). In this respect, registered designs differ from patents and trade marks, in respect of which infringement proceedings can be taken after grant in respect of acts committed before grant: Patents Act 1977 s.69; Trade Marks Act 1994 s.9(3).

[388] The maximum of a registered design under the RDA(A) is 25 years from the date of application; the proprietor must renew it for successive terms to achieve this. See para.3–248 below.

kits of parts for assembly, even if the actual making of the articles would take place after expiry.[389]

The article for which the design is registered

As has already been noted, a registered design did not consist of the shape or pattern as such, but of the shape or pattern as applied to some specific article in respect of which the design is registered.[390] Special provisions existed which facilitated the proprietor of design registered in respect of one article to expand his registration at a later stage to cover the same shape or pattern as applied to other articles.[391] A design registration was only infringed before 2001 by the application of the design to an article in respect of which the design was registered. Unless the defendant's article does so correspond there was no infringement. **3–181**

There is little case law on this requirement. One illustration was *Bourjois Ltd v British Home Stores Ltd*.[392] There, the article for which the design was registered was "a container for a perfume bottle". The container consisted, as the representations showed, of a bucket with a removable top simulating ice with a champagne bottle which formed part of the top sticking out of it. In articles sold according to the registered design a bottle of perfume was secreted in the bucket beneath the top, and was therefore invisible and formed no part of the article registered. The defendant's article, which was alleged to infringe, consisted of a bucket with an actual bottle of perfume in the shape of a champagne bottle lodged in some packing simulating ice. The defendant contended that there was no infringement as his article was a composite article partly consisting of the perfume bottle itself, and not a container for the perfume bottle. Upon a motion, an application for an interlocutory injunction was refused. **3–182**

Before the 1949 Act it was a necessary element of infringement that the article complained of should fall within the "class" in respect of which the design was registered.[393] By the 1949 Act classes were abolished. Between 1949 and 2001 the article complained of must, in order to infringe, have been the article in respect of which the design was registered. Now the law of infringement has been widened again and the application of a design to any article at all can infringe. **3–183**

---

[389] This seems to follow from the wording of RDA(A), subs.7(3) and 7(4) and is reinforced by the fact that the making of moulds or tools, or kits, for the making of articles outside the territorial ambit of the monopoly is an infringement; see para.3–177 above.

[390] See para.3–013 above.

[391] RDA(A) s.4(1); see para.3–097 above.

[392] (1951) 68 R.P.C. 280.

[393] The Patents and Designs Acts 1907 to 1939 s.60(1)(a): "apply . . . to any article in any class of goods in which the design is registered . . . " See App.A8 below.

Degree of resemblance for infringement of registered design

3–184   The final, and often in practice the most debatable aspect of infringement, was the question of whether the design applied to the allegedly infringing article was sufficiently similar to the registered design to infringe. The statutory test, as laid down by the concluding words of subs.7(1) of the RDA(A) was that the infringing article is one to which "that design [i.e. the registered design] or one not substantially different from it has been applied".

3–185   This test was first introduced in the RDA 1949 and was not altered by the amendments made by the CDPA 1988. It represented a radical departure from the previous law, under which infringement occurred by applying to an article "the design or any fraudulent or obvious imitation thereof".[394] It was a radical departure in two respects. First, the 1949 Act test was purely one of objective comparison and involved no requirement that the defendant's design should have been arrived at by copying; whilst the pre-1949 test at least prima facie required that there should be copying if not actual dishonesty. In this respect, the post-1949 test was wider. However, in a second respect, the post-1949 test may well have been narrower. Provided there are differences between the registered design and the alleged infringement which cannot be dismissed as insubstantial, there was no infringement. Under the old test, one article could be said to be an "obvious imitation" of another if the key or main features of its design had been copied, regardless of substantial differences in less prominent features. In this respect, the pre-2001 test of infringement was in principle narrower; now the post-2001 test of "overall impression" takes us back closer to the pre-1949 UK test. In this as in many other respects a historical perspective on the law of designs reveals a zig-zag progression in which the law changes direction, probably at each stage without any understanding of the reasons why the previous change was made.

3–186   It is submitted that the post-1949 test of infringing resemblance was so radically different in concept, and at least potentially so different in application case by case, that extreme caution should be exercised before treating pre-1949 authorities as applicable after the 1949 Act. Unfortunately, in the 50 years from the RDA 1949 to the 2001 Regulations, there was very little judicial comment on the change in the nature of the test of infringement, and cases largely proceeded on a *sub-silentio* assumption that things were largely the same as under the old law. Perhaps that assumption now becomes more true with the wider and more general test of infringement under the post 2001 law based on overall appearance.

3–187   With these cautionary words, the following paragraphs of this section will now explore the pre-1949 authorities on this aspect of infringement, and the post-1949 authorities, such as they are.

---

[394] The Patents and Designs Acts 1907 to 1939 s.60(1)(a); App.A7, para.A7–004 below.

How does one look for infringing resemblance?

The statutory test required that it is necessary to decide whether a design **3–188**
applied to an article was the same as, or not substantially different from,
the registered design. It can be seen that this exercise will involve a
number of steps. It is submitted that the basic structure of the exercise
required is still the same under the post 2001 law, even if the legal test
applied is different:

(1) Identifying at a purely physical level what needs to be looked at
and compared with what;
(2) Identifying the features which constitute the design in each
case;
(3) Identifying the similarities and differences between the two
cases;
(4) Unless there are no differences between the features which
constitute the design in each case, the final step involves attribut-
ing some degree of importance or weighting to those features
which are similarities, and those features which are differences. If
the differences can then be regarded as unimportant, there will
be infringement.

What needs to be compared

In order to ascertain what the registered design is, so that it may be **3–189**
compared with the alleged infringement, it is necessary to examine the
representation of the design on the register. A copy of this is in practice
attached to the certificate of registration.[395] An actual manufactured
article embodying the design may also be looked at to assist the process
of comparison,[396] although if this course is adopted, care should be taken
to avoid introducing further features which are not present on the
representation on the register.

In the case of articles which are flexible, or parts of which are movable, **3–190**
the appropriate course is normally to manipulate the alleged infringing
article into the position shown in the representations of the registered
design. In *Schmittzehe v Roberts*,[397] the registered design consisted of a doll
with movable head, legs and arms. Dealing with this point, Lloyd-Jacob
J. said[398]:

"There is no question that that figure can readily be manipulated into
positions similar to those which form the illustration to the design

[395] *Re Rollason's Registered Design* (1898) 15 R.P.C. 441 at 445; (1897) 14 R.P.C. 909 at 912;
Jackson v Testar (1919) 36 R.P.C. 289.
[396] *Dunlop Rubber Co Ltd v Golf Ball Developments Ltd* (1931) 48 R.P.C. 268 at 277, 280; *Benchairs
Ltd v Chair Centre Ltd* [1973] F.S.R. 123 at 126.
[397] (1955) 72 R.P.C. 122.
[398] *Schmittzehe v Roberts* cited above at 125.

registration, and if so manipulated they are in substance indis-
tinguishable from that which forms the plaintiff's monopoly, but Mr
Whitford, counsel for the defendant, has submitted that, unless the
defendant can be fixed with knowledge of such manipulation of her
figures as to resemble the illustrations in the design registrations, the
plaintiff has not made out a case of infringement. In my judgment
that submission proceeds upon a mistaken appreciation of the scope
of the Registered Designs Act. A registration, if valid, gives to the
registered proprietor an exclusive right in relation to articles to which
the registered design, or a design not substantially different from it,
has been applied, and in my judgment the manufacture and offer for
sale of a figure which, qua its characteristic features is indistinguish-
able from the registered design, is sufficient to establish infringement
of the statutory monopoly, wholly irrespective of whether by manipulation the precise attitude chosen for the purposes of representation
can be avoided."

In addition, where an article (a foldable mattress) was shown in both
folded and unfolded configurations in the representation, although it
appeared to be accepted that in principle both the folded and unfolded
configurations formed part of the registration and so the alleged infringement had to be compared with it in both forms, it was held that the eye
of the consumer would not attach any particular significance to the
appearance of the article in its folded form so it was the unfolded form
which mattered.[399]

Isolating the features which constitute the "design"

3–191   The exercise being carried out involves comparing the "design" applied
to the alleged infringing article with the "design" on the register. In each
case this need not be all the features of shape (or pattern) applied to the
article, but only those features which have "eye appeal".[400] Furthermore,
features of shape which are dictated by function,[401] methods or principles
of construction,[402] and features of a part intended for inclusion in a
greater article which "must match" the overall design of the article of
which the part is to form part,[403] are all specifically excluded from
forming part of the "design" according to the statutory definition.[404] It
follows that differences between the article depicted on the register and
the alleged infringing article in features which do not form part of the

---

[399] *Isaac Oren v Red Box Toy Factory Ltd* [1999] F.S.R. 785, Jacob J., at 794, paras 21–22.
[400] See para.3–047 above.
[401] See para.3–054 above.
[402] See para.3–077 above.
[403] See para.3–041 above.
[404] i.e. the definition contained in RDA(A) s.1(1) analysed extensively in paras 3–010 et seq.
above.

"design" in each case according to the statutory definition, are irrelevant to the question of infringement and are to be disregarded. Thus, the comparison exercise should concentrate on the features which have eye appeal,[405] and functional considerations and features which are there for wholly functional purposes should generally be ignored.[406] In this respect, the approach is similar to that adopted in comparing the registered design with the prior art for the purpose of assessing novelty.[407]

The above rule was further reinforced by subs.7(6) of the RDA(A),[408] **3–192** which provided:

"(6) The right in a registered design is not infringed by the reproduction of a feature of the design which, by virtue of section 1(1)(b), is left out of account in determining whether the design is registrable."

The features covered by s.1(1)(b) are functional features and features **3–193** falling within the "must match" exclusion. Subsection 7(6) contained a drafting misconception, since s.1(1)(b) did not in fact direct that certain features of a design are to be left out of account in determining registrability; rather, s.1(1)(b) excludes the stated features from counting as part of the "design" at all for any purpose. Thus, subs.7(6) was in fact a wholly redundant provision, although it can be said that it did no harm.

No infringement if difference is in essential features

Once the features of the registered design and of the alleged infringement **3–194** which count as part of the "design" have been identified, it was then necessary to compare them to see whether or not any differences between those features are substantial. If a feature of the registered design which is an essential feature of that design is not present on the alleged infringement, then there could be no infringement.[409] Before proceeding further, it should be noted that the converse did not follow, since the statutory definition of infringement in the 1949 Act, that the design as a whole is "not substantially different", would not appear to warrant the course of boiling a registered design down merely to a set of features

---

[405] *Holdsworth v M'Crea* (1867) L.R. 2 H.L. 380; *Hecla Foundry Co v Walker Hunter & Co* (1889) 6 R.P.C. 554 at 559; *Staples v Warwick* (1906) 23 R.P.C. 609; *Hothersall v Moore* (1892) 9 R.P.C. 27.

[406] *Leatheries v Lycett Saddle & Motor Accessories Co Ltd* (1909) 26 R.P.C. 166.

[407] See para.3–145 above.

[408] This subsection was introduced by the CDPA 1988, and had no precursor in the RDA 1949 before amendment.

[409] *Harper & Co Ltd v The Wright & Butler Lamp Manufacturing Co Ltd* (1895) 12 R.P.C. 483 at 488; *Staples v Warwick* (1906) 23 R.P.C. 609; *Gramophone Co Ltd v Magazine Holder Co* (1910) 27 R.P.C. 152 at 157; and see *Barran v Lomas* (1880) 28 W.R. 973.

which can be regarded as "essential" and disregarding all its other features.

3–195   In *Dunlop Rubber Co Ltd v Golf Ball Developments Ltd* Farwell J. said[410]:

> "Now in a case where the registered design is made up of a pattern which has no striking feature in it, but it appeals to the eye as a whole, it may very well be that another design may be an imitation of it which makes the same appeal to the eye, notwithstanding that there are many differences in details. It may well be that is so; but I think conversely it is true to say that, if a design has in it a striking feature which catches and holds the eye, and which is the one thing that strikes the eye when one looks at the design, a design which otherwise may be like a registered design but which eliminates the striking feature or alters it so that it is not recognisable, in such a case it seems to me it is impossible to say that one is an imitation of the other."

Essential features may be identified by reference to prior art

3–196   It has long been the law that where the alleged infringement only has that part of the registered design which was old and has not taken that which is new, there will be no infringement.[411] Thus, where the registered design differs from what has gone before only by some one particular feature, then unless the alleged infringement embodies that feature, it cannot possibly be an infringement.[412] Thus in *Walker & Co v Scott & Co Ltd*,[413] where the design was for an oil can, which differed from previous oil cans only in that it had rounded edges instead of sharp edges, an oil can the edges of which were not round was held not to be an infringement. Where the design is registered with a statement of novelty which sets out the particular feature which is claimed to be new, it would seem that any infringing design would need to contain the feature so claimed.[414]

3–197   More generally, the scope of a design may depend upon the state of the prior art at the date of registration. In *Hecla Foundry Co v Walker, Hunter & Co*, Lord Herschell said[415]:

> "It seems to me, therefore, that the eye must be the judge in such a case as this, and that the question must be determined by placing the

---

[410] (1931) 48 R.P.C. 268 at 281 note that in this case he was applying the pre-1949 "fraudulent or obvious imitation" test.

[411] *Staples v Warwick* (1906) 23 R.P.C. 609. See also *Gramophone Co Ltd v Magazine Holder Co* (1910) 27 R.P.C. 152 at 159 and *Repetition Woodwork Co Ltd v Hilton & Briggs* (1924) 41 R.P.C. 449.

[412] *Staples v Warwick* (1906) 23 R.P.C. 609.

[413] (1892) 9 R.P.C. 482.

[414] More generally on the effects of a statement of novelty, see para.3–253 below.

[415] (1889) 6 R.P.C. 554 at 559.

designs side by side, and asking whether they are the same, or whether the one is an obvious imitation[416] of the other. I ought perhaps to qualify this by saying that, as a design to be registered must, by section 47,[417] be a 'new or original design not previously published in the United Kingdom,' one may be entitled to take into account the state of knowledge at the time of registration, and in what respect the design was new or original, when considering whether any variations from the registered design which appear in the alleged infringement are substantial or immaterial."

If only small differences separate the registered design from what has gone before, then equally small differences between the alleged infringement and the registered design will be held to be sufficient to avoid infringement.[418] **3–198**

In *Simmons v Mathieson & Co Ltd*[419] Swinfen Eady J. said: **3–199**

" . . . and I think under these circumstances, seeing what the defendants have done in producing something independently, something bearing some resemblance to it, but I think differing as much from the plaintiff's as the plaintiff's differ from any of its predecessors, it would be impossible to hold that there was sufficient novelty in the plaintiff's design to sustain his registration as a new and original design, without at the same time deciding that the defendants' is so different that it cannot be held to infringe. I think, therefore, on the question of infringement, that the defendants have not infringed the plaintiff's registered design."

And on appeal, Fletcher Moulton L.J. said[420]: **3–200**

"The only possible way in which this registration could be good would be to magnify the importance of minute details so as to give it novelty or originality, and then if you magnify the importance of small details for that purpose, you must also keep them on that scale for the purpose of deciding whether there is an infringement."

Thus, where the novelty is small, the court may refuse to hold anything to be an infringement, unless it is almost exactly like the registered **3–201**

---

[416] The then test under s.58(a) of the Patents, Designs and Trade Marks Act 1883; see App.A8, para.A8–004, below.

[417] Patents, Designs and Trade Marks Act 1883; see App.A8, para.A8–003 below.

[418] *Simmons v Mathieson & Co Ltd* (1911) 28 R.P.C. 486 at 490; and see *Re Plackett's Design* (1892) 9 R.P.C. 436.

[419] (1911) 28 R.P.C. 486.

[420] (1911) 28 R.P.C. 486 at 496.

design.[421] This was made particularly clear in the case of *Negretti and Zambra v WF Stanley & Co Ltd*, where Astbury J. said[422]:

> "In a design of this very humble character, where the design itself is very close to the designs which have gone before, as Lord Halsbury said in the Gramophone case,[423] the plaintiffs, in order to succeed in infringement, must show that the article complained of is an exact reproduction of the plaintiffs' design, and that any difference, however trifling or unsubstantial, will, or may, protect it from infringement."

3–202   Thus, it may be said that a registered design which is possessed of substantial novelty and originality will have a broader reading given to the monopoly which it affords than will a design which is barely novel or original.[424] It does not however follow that a registered design which has no close prior art is to be given a very wide ambit which can ignore substantial differences between the registered design and the alleged infringement.[425] Even under the potentially wider test under the pre-1949 law of obvious imitation, the fact that the alleged infringement was nearer the registered design than the anticipations was not necessarily indicative of infringement.[426]

Design based on a very well known subject

3–203   It has been said that[427]:

> "Of course the better known the subject of the design is, the narrower the scope of protection. If you have a view of Westminster Abbey you can only protect the precise view taken."

3–204   That reference to a view of Westminster Abbey is a reference to *Saunders v Wiel*,[428] where it was held that a pattern need not be novel as such in order to constitute a novel design as applied to an article.[429] The

---

[421] *Gramophone Co Ltd v Magazine Holder Co* (1911) 28 R.P.C. 221; *Repetition Woodwork Co v Hilton & Briggs* (1924) 41 R.P.C. 449.

[422] (1925) 42 R.P.C. 358 at 365.

[423] *Gramophone Co Ltd v Magazine Holder Co* (1911) 28 R.P.C. 221 at 226.

[424] *Chudzikowski v Sowak* [1957] R.P.C. 111 at 117.

[425] *Gaskell & Chambers Ltd v Measure Master Ltd* [1993] R.P.C. 76, ChD: optic for dispensing spirits which was a substantial departure from the prior art. The alleged infringement had a "family resemblance" to it, but that was not enough to amount to infringement. The fact that it was similar enough that an objective observer might infer copying was not relevant; it was for the court to decide whether the objective similarity of the designs was sufficient: Aldous J. at 81, lines 9–25.

[426] *Dunlop Rubber Co Ltd v Golf Ball Developments Ltd* (1931) 48 R.P.C. 268 at 280.

[427] *Dean's Rag Book Co v Pomerantz* (1930) R.P.C. 485 at 491, per Luxmoore J.

[428] (1893) 10 R.P.C. 29.

[429] *Saunders v Wiel* is discussed at para.3–118 above.

above principle was stated and applied by Luxmoore J. in *Dean's Rag Book Co Ltd v Pomerantz & Sons*,[430] which was an action for infringement of the copyright in a registered design for a toy in the form of "Mickey Mouse". In that case the prior art consisted not in anything which was itself registrable as a design, but in representations of "Mickey Mouse" which had appeared in films. The action was dismissed on the following basis[431]:

> "It follows that the subject of the design may be well known; it may come from a source common to mankind, yet if its application to a particular class of article, for example, a toy, is novel, the actual design can then be protected. Of course the better known the subject of the design is, the narrower the scope of protection. If you have a view of Westminster Abbey, you can only protect, I think, the precise view taken. In the same way if you adapted to a particular class of article the portrait of a well-known man, or a figure from a well-known picture, you could only protect the particular representation as registered. My attention has been called to a number of authorities, such as *The Gramophone Co Ltd v Magazine Holder Co*[432]; *Jackson v Testar*[433] and *Phillips v Harbro' Rubber Co*.[434] Those cases are not entirely like the present, but I think they do show a principle that, where the subject of the registered design is well known, there is less room for deviation from the registered design than there is in cases where the design does not relate to a well-known subject-matter. As I have already said, the subject of this particular registered design is well known. By registering the design of Mickey the Mouse the plaintiff company has not obtained a monopoly in all designs of Mickey the Mouse, and if anyone wants to apply Mickey the Mouse to a toy he can, in my opinion, do so, provided he does not apply the registered design or a colourable imitation of it. Where the subject-matter of the design, as in this case, is well known, small differences may be sufficient to prevent infringement. Here, looking at the article complained of, and the registered design as shown in the pictures attached to the certificate, I can see there are many differences. Of course there is a general similarity between the representation and the defendants' article; both are representations of Mickey the Mouse; to this extent they resemble each other, as they each in their turn resemble the original as shown on the films, but I think an examination of the defendants' article with the pictures of the registered design reveals many differences; slight perhaps in themselves, but sufficient with the other evidence to satisfy me that there

[430] (1930) 47 R.P.C. 485.
[431] (1930) 47 R.P.C. 485 at 491.
[432] (1911) 28 R.P.C. 221.
[433] (1919) 36 R.P.C. 289.
[434] (1920) 37 R.P.C. 233.

has been no copying in fact, and in view of what I have said with regard to registration of designs relating to well-known subject-matter the differences are such as you would expect where two people have made independent designs of the same subject-matter; that is, Mickey the Mouse."

3–205 The above principle applies to protection which may be obtained by way of registration of a design in respect of an article. It should be noted that the originator of a character such as Mickey Mouse may well have much wider protection against the application of representations of his character to articles under the law of copyright.[435]

Whether differences are substantial

3–206 As has been set out in the preceding paragraphs, if the alleged infringement lacked what, by reference to the prior art or otherwise, must be categorised as an essential feature of the registered design, then there was no infringement. If this cannot be said, but there are differences, it remained finally to be decided whether or not, having regard to the differences and to the features which are the same, the design of the alleged infringing article is substantially different.

3–207 Guidance on this test can only be given by illustration. Having regard to the radical change in the nature of the test of infringement effected by the 1949 Act,[436] caution should be exercised in treating pre-1949 authorities as applicable to cases under the RDA 1949 or RDA(A). The question has been put as: Has the alleged infringement substantially the same appearance as the registered design?[437] In one early case, it was said that you must compare the registered design and the alleged infringement and decide whether or not the general effect is the same[438]; although it is questionable whether similarity in general effect is enough under the "not substantially different" test even though this formulation almost precisely foreshadows by 100 years the "different overall impression" post-2001 test. The test of infringement was "by and large the same" as the test applicable to the question of whether a design is different enough from a prior art design to count as new.[439]

3–208 As an aid to carrying out the process of evaluation to assess whether or not differences are substantial, it may be of assistance to look at the registered design and the alleged infringement not only together, but

---

[435] As was in fact held to be the case in the *Popeye* case, *King Features Syndicate Inc v O. M. Kleeman Ltd* (1941) 58 R.P.C. 207. For copyright protection for patterns applied to articles, see para.5–084 below.

[436] See para.3–185 above.

[437] *Hecla Foundry Co v Walker, Hunter & Co* (1889) 6 R.P.C. 554 at 559; *Manchester v Unfreville & Son* (1907) 24 R.P.C. 782 at 788.

[438] *Nevill v Bennett & Sons* (1898) 15 R.P.C. 412 at 417, Hall V.-C.

[439] *Valor Heating Co Ltd v Main Gas Appliances Ltd* [1973] R.P.C. 871 at 887 lines 5–20, per Whitford J., ChD; as regards the test in the context of novelty, see para.3–152 above.

separately, spaced apart in time, and a little way off.[440] The eye for this purpose, will be the eye of the customer.[441] To decide this question, the court must "adopt the mantle" of an interested customer and decide the question for itself, and the decision cannot be delegated to witnesses.[442]

In *Valor Heating Co Ltd v Main Gas Appliances Ltd*,[443] it was argued that **3–209** the trade mark doctrine of "imperfect recollection"[444] had application to the question of infringement in design cases. The argument was based mainly on pre-1949 authorities.[445] Whitford J. gave no clear answer to the question of whether the "imperfect recollection" doctrine is as such applicable to registered design cases, but observed that those authorities suggested that[446]:

> "you must consider infringement not merely on the basis of a side by side comparison, but also upon the basis of having had a look at the registered design, then having gone away and come back and perhaps been put in a position of deciding whether some other article is the one you originally saw. . . . Quite plainly if the design is seen on one occasion and something not substantially different is seen on another occasion, then the one is going to be taken for the other."[447]

The doctrine of imperfect recollection in trade mark and passing off **3–210** cases is based on the fact that a customer may fall victim to confusion in circumstances in which he cannot compare the defendant's and the claimant's trade marks (or distinctive get up) side by side. Thus, the customer may at the point of encountering the defendant's mark (or get up) recollect the salient features of the claimant's trade mark (or get up) but have an imperfect recollection of less prominent details. Thus, he may be confused despite the fact that if he had had the opportunity to compare the marks side by side, he would not have been confused. When the statutory test of design infringement included the phrase "fraudulent

---

[440] *Grafton v Watson* (1884) 50 L.T. 420; *Wallpaper Manufacturers Ltd v Derby Paper Staining Co* (1925) 42 R.P.C. 429 at 449; *Dunlop Rubber Co Ltd v Golf Ball Developments Ltd* (1931) 48 R.P.C. 268 at 281. See also, e.g. the approach adopted by the Court of Appeal in *Benchairs Ltd v Chair Centre Ltd* [1974] R.P.C. 429 at 445 lines 5–14; and Lloyd-Jacob J. in *Watson v Smith Bros* [1965] R.P.C. 147 at 154, lines 5–10.

[441] *Benchairs Ltd v Chair Centre Ltd* [1974] R.P.C. 429.

[442] *Gaskell & Chambers v Measure Master Ltd* [1993] R.P.C. 76, Aldous J., at 79.

[443] *Valor Heating Co Ltd v Main Gas Appliances Ltd* [1973] R.P.C. 871, ChD.

[444] Derived from remarks made by Luxmoore L.J. in a dissenting judgment in *Rysta Ltd's Application* (1943) 60 R.P.C. 87, and later approved by the House of Lords in *Aristoc v Rysta* (1945) 62 R.P.C. 65.

[445] See para.3–185 above.

[446] *Valor Heating Co Ltd v Main Gas Appliances Ltd* [1973] R.P.C. 871 at 878, line 35. See also *Sommer Allibert (UK) Ltd v Flair Plastics Ltd* [1987] R.P.C. 599, CA, at 624, where the CA appear to have proceeded on the basis of counsel's concession that the pre-1949 Act authorities were still applicable, but approved the proviso that the hypothetical customer through whose eyes the court is looking should be regarded as a customer who is interested in the design of the particular article which he is purchasing.

[447] But does the converse follow?

imitation",[448] then imperfect recollection may have had a direct bearing on the question of fraudulence; however, it is submitted that the doctrine of imperfect recollection as elaborated in trade mark cases has no direct application either to the test of design infringement under the 1949 Act or to the post 2001 harmonised approach. Unlike trade marks, this is not a context where the purpose of designs is to operate as indicia of trade origin. Viewing the designs spaced apart in time may simply be a helpful exercise for the court, since features which do not stick in the mind may be more readily dismissed as insubstantial.

Designs must be compared as a whole

3–211 Subject to the considerations which may arise if there is a special statement of novelty,[449] the registration of a design in respect of an article is for the thing as a whole, and no other design could be an infringement unless it was substantially the same as the registered design looked at as a whole.[450] In *Jones and Attwood v National Radiator Co Ltd* Tomlin J. said[451]:

> "Further, they have not claimed novelty or originality in respect of any special feature. It is in the shape or configuration of the boiler, as a whole, as shown in the registered representation, that the novelty or originality rests, and I do not think that they can successfully allege infringement because any particular feature is reproduced in the article complained of. They must rest upon imitation in respect of the shape or configuration of the whole."

3–212 It is a fallacy to fasten on the novel features of the registered design and argue that there is infringement because the essential novelty of the registered design is embodied in the alleged infringement. Although it is certainly the case that a design which does not adopt the features of the registered design that give it novelty will not infringe,[452] the registered design includes all its features, both those which are novel and those which are not, and the comparison exercise conducted against the alleged infringement must have regard to the designs as a whole.[453]

3–213 If an article as registered has not only a shape but also has a particular pattern upon it, the registration may be deemed to cover both these features in combination,[454] in which case there will be no infringement

---

[448] See para.3–185 above.

[449] See para.3–214.

[450] *Holdsworth v M'Crea* (1867) L.R. 2 H.L. 380 at 388; *Sackett & Barnes v Clozenberg* (1910) 27 R.P.C. 104 at 108; *Wilson v Chalco Ltd* (1922) 39 R.P.C. 252 at 256.

[451] *Jones & Attwood v National Radiator Co Ltd* (1928) 45 R.P.C. at 83.

[452] See para.3–196 above.

[453] *Benchairs Ltd v Chair Centre Ltd* [1974] R.P.C. 429 at 445 15–21, CA.

[454] *Barran v Lomas* (1880) 28 W.R. 973; *Manchester v Umfreville & Son* (1907) 24 R.P.C. 782, where the claim was for "shape and pattern".

unless both features are taken. It is, however, possible for an applicant to restrict his application solely to shape or solely to pattern, in which case the protection extends to the appropriate aspect.[455] If both the shape and pattern are new, the applicant may have two registrations, one directed to the shape and the other to the pattern.[456] In such a case the design for shape may be infringed but not the design for pattern, and vice versa.[457]

Impact of the statement of novelty

The history and effects of the so-called statement of novelty are con- **3–214** sidered in more depth in a later section.[458] Most registered designs were filed with statements of novelty which claimed as novel either the shape and configuration, or pattern and ornament, in general terms. If there was a general statement of novelty directed to shape and configuration, or pattern and ornament, the court would have regard to the features of the design as a whole in determining questions of infringement, and would have to work out from the prior art and other evidence what features of the registered design were essential, what were of some importance but perhaps by themselves not essential, and what were immaterial. It was, however, open to an applicant by their statement of novelty to identify any particular feature or features, as being the features which they regard as novel.[459] A comparable function is now performed by statements of partial disclaimer under r.15[460] although that serves simply to delimit the matter for which protection is sought and does not make or imply any statement as to which features are or are not novel. The precise effect of a specific statement of novelty was not clear, since there was no warrant under the statute for wholly disregarding features which form part of the design because they are not novel; in other words, the registered design could not be treated as if it were a monopoly covering all possible articles so long as they possess the feature or features claimed as novel. However, it does seem that the court would lay greater emphasis on the features claimed as being novel when it came to assess what is and what is not a substantial departure from the design as registered; and correspondingly less emphasis on other, non-novel, features of the design.[461] It is open to question precisely how the court should take into account a specific statement of novelty when applying the new post-2001 law of infringement to a pre-existing registered design. Presumably it should continue to

---

[455] In *Re Rollason's Registered Design* (1898) 14 R.P.C. 909 at 916.
[456] See para.3–021 above.
[457] *Pearson v Morris Wilkinson & Co* (1906) 23 R.P.C. 738.
[458] See paras 3–253 et seq.
[459] Under the old terminology, they were "claiming" these features; *Sackett & Barnes v Clozenburg* (1910) 27 R.P.C. 104 at 108.
[460] Of the Designs Rules 2006, at App.A10, para.A10–006 below.
[461] *Sommer Allibert (UK) Ltd v Flair Plastics Ltd* [1987] R.P.C. 599, CA, at 619, line 37 to 620, line 30.

emphasise features claimed as novel when applying the new "overall impression" test even though there is no mechanism for doing so in respect of a post-2001 design: the new partial disclaimer performs a different function.

3–215   An illustration of a specific statement of novelty is *Portable Concrete Buildings Ltd v Bathcrete Ltd.*[462] There, the article in respect of which the design was registered was "a portable building primarily for use as a garage", and the statement of novelty read as follows: "Novelty lies in the shape of the article having the ends coloured blue as shown in the representation." Lloyd-Jacob J. said[463] with regard to the question of infringement:

> "Treated solely as fronts for garages, I myself entertain no doubt that these two differ in no substantial particular . . . But the real distinction . . . arises, as I see it, from the presence of the design feature at both ends in the construction to which the registered design relates and only at the entrance end in the defendants' Senator construction."

5. Property Rights and Licensing

Persons who may apply to register a UK design

3–216   The law relating to who may apply for registered designs and property rights in them has not been harmonised by the Directive. It therefore remains the same in respect of pre- and post-2001 registered designs. It has always been the case that an applicant who claims to be the proprietor of the design must in fact be proprietor, in accordance with the rules set out below.[464]

---

[462] [1962] R.P.C. 49. See also *Cook & Hurst's Design Application* [1979] R.P.C. 197, RDAT, where an application was allowed on appeal of a design for football shirts with a statement of novelty directed to stripes of particular colours.

[463] [1962] R.P.C. 49 at 53. But where the statement of novelty is in conventional form limited to features of shape or configuration, then colours will be disregarded: *Valeo Vision SA v Flexible Lamps Ltd* [1995] R.P.C. 205, ChD: lens colours in car light clusters.

[464] *AL BASSAM Trade Mark* [1995] R.P.C. 511, CA, concerning the interpretation of the same phrase in the Trade Marks Act 1938 s.17(1). This phraseology ("the person claiming to be the proprietor") has a common legislative origin in the case of registered designs and trade marks: in ss.47(1) and 62(1) respectively of the Patents, Designs and Trade Marks Act 1883; see at 523, per Morritt L.J. The Court of Appeal confirmed that the same approach does indeed apply to registered designs in *Ifejika v Ifejika* [2009] EWCA Civ 563; [2010] F.S.R. 29; but it is sufficient if the applicant for registration has an equitable rather than a legal title at the time of application. Further, if the person currently on the register as proprietor is in fact the proprietor of the design then the court will normally exercise its discretion not to cancel the registration despite the fact that he was registered erroneously as a result of a void assignment from a party which in fact did not have title at the time of application, since to do so would be a "triumph of form over substance" (per Patten L.J. at para.30); reversing *Ifejika v Ifejika* [2009] EWHC 3343 (Pat); [2010] F.S.R. 7, Judge Fysh Q.C. who had granted summary judgment cancelling the registration. Where the applicant for registration in fact had no title, even where the application was made in good faith but in the wrong name, it is susceptible to cancellation by the court:

The proprietor is defined by s.2 of the RDA(E). This section is as fol- **3–217**
lows:

"(1) The author of a design shall be treated for the purposes of this
     Act as the original proprietor of the design, subject to the
     following provisions.

(1A) Where a design is created in pursuance of a commission for
     money or money's worth, the person commissioning the design
     shall be treated as the original proprietor of the design.

(1B) Where, in a case not falling within subsection (1A), a design is
     created by an employee in the course of his employment, his
     employer shall be treated as the original proprietor of the
     design.

(2) Where a design, or the right to apply a design to any article,
    becomes vested, whether by assignment, transmission or opera-
    tion of the law, in any person other than the original proprietor,
    either alone or jointly with the original proprietor, that other
    person, or as the case may be the original proprietor and that
    other person, shall be treated for the purposes of this Act as the
    proprietor of the design or as the proprietor of the design in
    relation to that article.

(3) In this Act the 'author' of a design means the person who
    creates it.

(4) In the case of a design generated by computer in circumstances
    such that there is no human author, the person by whom the
    arrangements necessary for the creation of the design are made
    shall be taken to be the author."

These provisions are identical to the provisions governing the owner- **3–218**
ship of UK unregistered design right, it being the clear legislative intent
that the right to apply for a design registration and the unregistered
design right in the same design should normally vest in the same person.[465]

Woodhouse UK Plc v Architectural Lighting Systems [2005] E.W.P.C.C. (Designs) 25; [2006]
R.P.C. 1, PCC (Judge Fysh Q.C.): this was a post-2001 case but concerned a registration
whose validity was governed by the pre-2001 law; in the case of a registered design
granted under the EU harmonised law, a validity challenge on ownership grounds can
only be made by the true proprietor: see para.2–048 above. Under the pre-2001 law, if it
came to the Registrar's attention that an applicant claiming to be proprietor was not in
fact the proprietor then the application could be refused: *Leara Trading Co Ltd's Design*
[1991] R.P.C. 453, RDAT.

[465] For the provisions relating to ownership of unregistered design right, see paras 4–104 et
seq. below. Given this sensible legislative policy, it is a pity that it has not been carried
through in the case of designs which are protected by artistic copyright, to which
different ownership rules apply, in particular the copyright does not vest in a person
commissioning the design; see para.5–147 below. This may mean that in the case of a
single article, the right to reproduce the surface pattern (the subject of artistic copyright)

Author as proprietor of registered design right

3–219 Primarily, then, it is the author of the design who is the proprietor and who is entitled to apply for registration. The actual designer is the author,[466] i.e. the author is the person who conceives the idea or invents it, and gives visible expression to it with his hands, e.g. by drawing or by making a model.[467] The person who is, in this way, responsible for the novelty is the author.[468] In order to be the author a man need not, however, work out every detail in its final form. If he conceives the features and reduces them to visible form he will be the author, even though he instructs someone else to give the finishing touches, and actually to embody the design in its precise form.[469] If, however, the instructions are such that the person who is to carry them out might, in accordance with them, produce a number of different designs, and he contributes the only features which give novelty to the design over the prior art, then that person will be really responsible for evolving the design, and he will be the author to the exclusion of his instructor.[470]

Joint authorship of registered designs

3–220 The RDA(E) makes no explicit provision for joint authorship of designs, unlike the case of unregistered designs[471] or copyright works.[472] However, there seems no reason in principle why there cannot be joint authorship of a design for the purposes of registration, where two or more persons collaborate together to produce the design; nor does it seem necessary that authorship should be restricted "merely to who pushed

---

may vest in a different person from the right to reproduce the three-dimensional shape (unregistered design right); the right to apply for a design registration, which is capable of covering surface pattern and/or shape (see para.3–017 above) may therefore be in different hands from the copyright covering the surface pattern.

[466] *Lazarus v Charles* (1873) L.R. 16 Eq. 117.

[467] *Kenrick & Co v Lawrence & Co* (1890) 25 QBD 99.

[468] *Pearson v Morris Wilkinson & Co* (1906) 23 R.P.C. 738; *Pressler & Co Ltd v Gartside & Co* (1933) 50 R.P.C. 240.

[469] *Pearson v Morris Wilkinson & Co* (1906) 23 R.P.C. 738. See also *Cala Homes (South) Ltd v Alfred McAlpine Homes East Ltd* [1995] F.S.R. 818, ChD, a copyright case where it was said that "to have regard merely to who pushed the pen is too narrow a view of authorship", discussed at para.5–145 below.

[470] *Pressler & Co Ltd v Gartside & Co* (1933) 50 R.P.C. 240. This result depended on the finding (at 245, line 5) that on the instructions given to him, the weaver might just as well have produced a sample of cloth exactly similar to one or other of the prior art designs, so he alone contributed the features of the design which gave it novelty. If the person instructing him had suggested features which were themselves novel, and the weaver had then worked out the details of the design, it is probable that they would have been joint authors, by analogy with the approach in copyright cases, where authorship requires the contribution of a significant part of the original skill and labour which is protected by the copyright: see *Cala Homes*, considered at para.5–145 below.

[471] CDPA 1988 s.259(1); see para.4–107 below.

[472] CDPA 1988 s.10(1); see para.5–144 below.

the pen",[473] or alternatively merely to who physically embodies a design in tangible form. There seems every reason why the law of joint authorship of designs for registration purposes should be interpreted as being the same as that for the purposes of the unregistered design right, given Parliament's evident intention that registered and unregistered design rights shall by and large vest in the same person or persons.

In *Re Vredenburg's Registered Design*[474] the position where two persons   **3–221** produce a similar design more or less simultaneously and communicate the fact of authorship to each other was considered. It was held that even assuming the communication was confidential it was impossible for either person alone to be the proprietor, and a registration obtained by one such person was expunged.

Designs created pursuant to a commission

Where a design is created in pursuance of a commission for money or   **3–222** money's worth, the person commissioning the designer becomes the person entitled to apply to register that design.[475] This provision takes precedence over the provision giving designs created by an employee to an employer,[476] so that a person who commissions the creation of a design will be entitled to register it regardless of whether he places the commission directly with the individual designer, or with a company which in turn employs the designer. Where a chain of commissions is placed, e.g. by a customer who commissions a manufacturer who in turn commissions a specialist designer, the person in whom the design right will vest is the person ultimately placing the commission, i.e. the end customer.[477]

This provision (and the provision relating to employees considered in   **3–223** the next paragraph) are in substance the same as, although differently worded from, the relevant provisions of the RDA 1949[478] before its amendment by the CDPA 1988. The old provisions still apply to proprietorship of designs created before the commencement of the CDPA 1988.[479]

---

[473] Phrase taken from the judgment of Laddie J. in *Cala Homes*, a copyright case where an architect who directed another architect regarding the features he wanted in the drawings was held a joint author together with the person who physically drew them.

[474] (1935) 52 R.P.C. 7.

[475] RDA(E) s.2(1A), see para.3–217 above.

[476] RDA(E) s.2(1B), see para.3–217 above.

[477] *Arnold (James) & Co Ltd v Miafern Ltd* [1980] R.P.C. 397 at 404, ChD. A copyright case under the 1956 Act, which provided that copyright in commissioned engravings and photographs belonged to the person commissioning them; a rule no longer present in the CDPA 1988; see para.5–147 below.

[478] RDA 1949 s.2(1) proviso. This uses the phrase "for good consideration" rather than "for money or money's worth". It is arguable that a purely non-financial consideration was within the scope of the old provision but outside the scope of the new.

[479] See para.3–270 below.

Designs created in the course of employment

3–224 By RDA(E) s.2(1B), quoted above, when a registrable design is created by an employee in the course of his employment, the right to register it belongs to the employer.[480] This is defined as meaning "employment under a contract of service or apprenticeship".[481] This definition of employment is identical to those relating to unregistered design right[482] and copyright.[483] For a more extensive discussion of what constitutes employment for this purpose, and in what circumstances a design is considered to be created in the course of employment, see the discussion relating to the corresponding copyright provisions.[484]

Assignee or transferee of the right to register

3–225 Section 2(2) of the RDA(E) quoted above, deals with the transmission of the right to register a design to persons other than the original proprietor. The subsection implicitly acknowledges that the right to apply for a design is a piece of intangible legal property which exists and is transmissible, even before it has been crystallised by the filing of the application to register it.[485]

3–226 There is one difference between pre- and post-2001 registered designs which arises from a change in the nature of the rights. A pre-2001 registration had to relate to a specific article—it could not be registered in general or *in vacuo*.[486] Therefore one could have different registrations of the same design in respect of different articles, and potentially a right to apply a design in respect of different articles might be assigned to different persons. Subsection 2(2) of RDA(A) therefore contemplated transmission of either "the design", which presumably meant the right to apply the design to all and any articles to which it is capable of application, or of "the right to apply a design to any article", which contemplated the case where the right to apply a design is split up between different owners by reference to the articles or categories of articles to which it is to be applied.[487] Section 2(2) of RDA(E) has been amended to omit the reference to the right to apply the design to any articles, and now permits only the assignment of the right to apply for the design as such (i.e. in respect of all and any articles). It is an interesting conundrum what happens in cases where there are existing designs on the register in different hands for the same design for different articles, as

---

[480] This has always been the position; *Lazarus v Charles* (1873) L.R. 16 Eq. 117.
[481] RDA(E) s.44(1), definition of "employee", "employment" and "employer".
[482] CDPA 1988 s.263(1); see para.4–112 below.
[483] CDPA 1988 s.178.
[484] See para.5–150 below.
[485] See *AL BASSAM Trade Mark* [1995] R.P.C. 511, CA.
[486] See para.3–013 above.
[487] Such partial assignments can also be made in the case of unregistered design right (see para.4–123 below) and copyright (see para.5–157 below).

a result of a division of rights to apply the design which was permissible under the old law. Following the amendment, the new law of infringement applies and neither of the registrations are restricted to any particular article. Presumably the registrations now overlap each other and neither owner can make and sell his articles without the consent of the other, subject to the "continuing act" defence in the transitional provisions.[488]

The subsection makes no reference to the formal means by which the **3–227** right to apply for a registered design can be transmitted. Clearly, a formal document by the original proprietor which on its face irrevocably conveys all his interest (or all his interest in respect of application of the design to a particular article or articles under the pre-2001 law) to an assignee would be sufficient. The reference to "operation of law" covers the case of transmission to the personal representatives of a deceased original proprietor, or to a trustee in bankruptcy. However, the question arises of what transactions, short of a formal assignment, will serve to "vest" the "right" in such a way as to make a person, other than the original proprietor, entitled to apply to register. For example, if the original proprietor enters into a contract with a manufacturer under which he allows the manufacturer to make articles to his design, but agrees not to make them himself, is the manufacturer then entitled to register the design?

It is clear that a contract which does not give any right to manufacture **3–228** cannot serve to convey the right to register. Thus, a contract giving a person the exclusive "right" to sell or import a particular article, without any right to manufacture it, since he has acquired no right to apply the design, cannot make him a proprietor, and any registration obtained by him would be invalid.[489]

What of a person who is permitted to manufacture under a contract **3–229** from the original proprietor of the design? There is some old authority that even a mere licensee, so long as he has a licence to manufacture,[490] is a proprietor within the meaning of the section, and can, therefore, apply to have the design registered. It is submitted however that such a result is not correct. Subsection 2(2) refers to a "right" being "vested", and such language is not apt to cover a case where one person gives another permission to apply his design, even if that permission is exclusive, i.e. he covenants that he will not apply it himself. It is submitted that it is only if the transaction concerned is, when properly analysed, intended to amount to an absolute grant rather than being a licence (even if exclusive) or a mere contractual arrangement giving permission, that the terms of subs.2(2) can be satisfied so as to allow the assignee rather than the

[488] 2001 Regulations reg.14(3).
[489] *Re Guiterman's Registered Designs* (1886) 55 L.J. Ch. 309; *Jewitt v Eckhardt* (1878) 8 Ch.D. 404.
[490] *Jewitt v Eckhardt* (1878) Ch.D. 404.

original proprietor to be registered as proprietor of the design. Whilst it is possible that a document purporting to be a licence can, when properly construed, be found to be an assignment, it is still necessary that it should have the essential characteristic of being an absolute grant.[491]

Registering a design copied from abroad

3–230 The question arises as to how far, if at all, someone who merely imports a design from abroad can obtain registration for it in the United Kingdom. (In the case of post-2001 designs, this would mean importing it from outside the EU.) In this connection, there is no right, such as used to exist in patent law, whereby it was possible to apply for a patent as true and first importer of an invention, knowledge of which has been acquired abroad.[492] In the case of designs, unless the applicant can show that he has acquired a right to the design itself, or a right to apply it to the article in question, he cannot, merely on the basis of having acquired knowledge of the design abroad, qualify as an applicant for its registration. He is not in a position to pass muster as proprietor. Thus, where the sole agent in the United Kingdom of an American company had applied and obtained registration of designs for three of the toys which he sold under the agency, although the company consented to his registering the designs in his own name it was held that, as he had not obtained any right to apply the designs, he was not the proprietor, and the designs were expunged from the register.[493] Where, however, a British manufacturing firm received designs from an agent in Constantinople, which the agent considered suitable for the Persian market, and the firm, after working them up into a practical form, registered them, and made and supplied the resulting goods to the agent as sole agent for Persia, but retained the designs for themselves in other markets, it was held that the registrations were valid.[494] Assuming the agent was the author, the firm had acquired rights in the designs for valuable consideration, and had thereby become proprietors. The only way, therefore, in which it may be possible to register a design imported from abroad, is on the same basis as it is possible to register designs originating in the United Kingdom, namely, if a right to the design or to apply it has been acquired.[495]

---

[491] *Messager v British Broadcasting Co Ltd* [1928] 1 K.B. 660.

[492] A person who copied an invention abroad was regarded as an "inventor by importation" in the UK and entitled to obtain a valid patent for it in this country. This rule dates from the 17th century when it was considered to be in the public interest to encourage English citizens to steal inventions from abroad and so establish new industries in England. Invention by importation was abolished by the Patents Act 1977.

[493] *Re Guiterman's Registered Designs* (1886) 55 L.J. Ch. 309; see also *Jewitt v Eckhardt* (1878) 8 Ch.D. 404.

[494] *Nevill v John Bennett & Sons* (1898) 15 R.P.C. 412.

[495] Cf. *Barker v Associated Manufacturers (Gowns and Mantles) Ltd* (1933) 50 R.P.C. 332, where the registration of a dress design acquired abroad was in fact held to be invalid on the grounds of prior use by the defendants rather than on the ground of lack of proprietorship. It appears however that lack of proprietorship was not argued. Maugham J. at 337

Assignments of registered designs

A registered design is property which may be assigned or mortgaged, or   **3–231**
may be transmitted by operation of law, according to the general law of
property.[496] However, RDA(E) s.19(1) provides for the registration at the
Designs Registry of the title of any person who becomes entitled by
assignment, transmission or operation of law "to a registered design or to
a share in a registered design, or becomes entitled as mortgagee, licensee
or otherwise to any other interest in a registered design". It seems that
such registration is not a condition precedent to obtaining (in the case of
an outright assignment) the legal title to the property in a registered
design. However, certain potentially adverse consequences follow from a
failure to register.

First, only the person who is actually recorded on the register as   **3–232**
proprietor of the design can sue third parties for infringement, because
the exclusive right is conferred by s.7 on the "registered proprietor".[497]
Thus, while an assignment remains unregistered, the legal title to sue
third parties (although probably not the legal title to the property in the
design as such) remains vested in the old proprietor on the register, who
must be made a party to the action if the assignee is to sue.[498] Secondly,
except for the purposes of an application to rectify the register, evidence
of an unregistered transaction cannot be given in court without special
leave.[499] Thirdly, subject to any rights vested in any other person of which
notice is entered in the register, the person who is registered as proprietor
has the power to assign, grant licences under or otherwise deal with the
design.[500] This means that the rights of an unregistered assignee may be
defeated by a later assignment to another person made by the old
proprietor.[501] However, the later assignment may be defeasible if the later
assignee has actual or constructive notice of the earlier inconsistent
assignment.[502]

---

suggested that "you might . . . apply for and obtain registration of a design which was
used by the Ancient Egyptians 6,000 years ago". This however rests on his willingness to
assume for the purpose of the case that one is entitled to register the design of a dress
merely by importing it from abroad (at 336, line 50 to 337, line 2), an assumption which
is, had the point been argued before him, not correct.

[496] This is the implication of RDA(E) s.19(1), which provides for registration of assignments
etc. "when any person becomes entitled by assignment, transmission or operation of law
to a registered design . . . "

[497] See para.6–012 below regarding who may sue for infringement.

[498] See para.6–012 below.

[499] RDA(E) s.19(5).

[500] RDA(E) s.19(4).

[501] *Performing Right Society Ltd v London Theatre of Varieties* [1924] A. C. 1; cf. *Ward, Lock & Co
Ltd v Long* [1906] 2 Ch. 550.

[502] This is probably the effect of RDA(E) s.19(4) proviso, which says that "any equities in
respect of a design may be enforced in like manner as in respect of any other personal
property". An unregistered assignment is probably an equity for this purpose.

3–233   The procedure for applying to register assignments and other instruments and events under s.19 is set out in the Registered Designs Rules 2006 r.27.[503]

Assignments to be together with unregistered design right

3–234   The RDA(E) contains certain provisions designed to avoid the property in a registered design becoming separated from the ownership of the unregistered design right in the same design, both before and after registration. Where design right subsists in a design which is sought to be registered, the registrar is required not to entertain an application to register the design unless it is made by the person claiming to be owner of the unregistered design right.[504] Furthermore, once a design has been registered, the registrar is required to refuse registration of any interest in the registered design unless he is satisfied that the person entitled to that interest is also entitled to a corresponding interest in the unregistered design right.[505] This latter provision seems intended to discourage not only the separation of ownership of the two parallel rights, but the separation of any lesser interests such as licences. In many cases, no parallel unregistered right will subsist, either because the registered design is pattern or ornamentation rather than shape or configuration[506]; or because the applicant is foreign and does not possess the correct national qualifications for subsistence of unregistered design right.[507]

3–235   There is a statutory presumption when an unregistered design right is assigned that it acts also as an assignment of the registered design, unless the contrary intention appears.[508] There is also a mirror image statutory presumption that when a registered design is assigned, the assignment will carry with it any unregistered design right in that design.[509]

3–236   But while these provisions are designed to facilitate and even encourage registered and unregistered rights in respect of the same design staying in the same hands, they do not absolutely prevent them from being assigned into different hands, whether deliberately or accidentally. The question then arises of what happens next. The Registrar is prohibited from registering the transaction or event by which the proprietor of the registered design became entitled to his interest: the subsection is in mandatory terms and gives the Registrar no discretion to register in these circumstances.[510] Because he cannot register, the proprietor of the

---

[503] SI 2006/1975, App.A10 below.

[504] RDA(E) s.3(2).

[505] RDA(E) s.19(3A).

[506] Because unregistered design right covers only features of shape and configuration; see paras 4–003 and 4–029 below.

[507] See paras 4–055 et seq. below.

[508] RDA(E) s.19(3B).

[509] CDPA 1988 s.224; see para.4–126 below.

[510] RDA(E) s.19(3A): "the registrar *shall not* register an interest . . . unless he is satisfied that the person entitled to that interest is also entitled to a corresponding interest in the design right" (emphasis added).

registered design is unable to sue for infringement, although no such inhibition would affect the owner of the unregistered right. Thus it seems the practical effect of the provisions, if the ownership of the registered and unregistered rights become divorced from each other, is to stultify the registered right.

The prohibition on registration also applies to a lesser interest than **3–237** ownership, such as a licence. A person who obtains a licence only under the registered right but not under the corresponding unregistered right will not be able to exploit his licence without the consent of the owner of, or possibly a licence of right in respect of, the unregistered right. In addition, he will not be able to register his licence; presumably, this is intended to provide some sort of legislative sanction against taking such a licence on top of the inherent disadvantages of such a course. Oddly, there are no statutory presumptions in the case of licences which mirror those applying in the case of assignments. Thus, there is no statutory presumption that a licence under a registered design will also grant to the licensee a licence under the unregistered design right in that design; or vice versa in the case of a licence under an unregistered design right. However, in a case where failure to license the unregistered design right in parallel with the registered right (or vice versa) would result in stultification of the licence, it may be appropriate to imply such a parallel licence as a matter of necessity to give business efficacy to the licence transaction.[511]

Licences under registered designs

A licence is merely a permission granted by the owner of the registered **3–238** design to one or more persons to do some act or acts which, but for the permission, will constitute an infringement of the registered design.[512] As in the case of an assignment, a licence may cover the entire range of rights which go to make up the registered design right, or it may cover only some specific right or particular occasion, or even only a particular portion of the area to which the right extends. No particular formalities are laid down for the grant of a licence under a registered design, and therefore such a licence could be a formal written licence, an informal oral licence, or an implied licence.

In *Dorling v Honnor Marine Ltd*,[513] a letter was sent by the claimant, who **3–239** was a copyright owner, telling the second defendant that he had no licence under the copyright and must stop manufacture. The court, having found that an oral licence had in fact been granted by the claimant to the second defendant without any period being mentioned, decided

---

[511] For the implication of licences to give business efficacy to a transaction, see, *e.g* the implication of a licence to repair an article sold by the licensor: *Solar Thomson Engineering Co Ltd v Barton* [1977] R.P.C. 537, CA, and para.5–133 below.

[512] *Steers v Rogers* (1883) 10 R.P.C. 245 at 251.

[513] [1963] R.P.C. 205; [1964] R.P.C. 160.

that the letter was not a nullity, but operated as a notice under the licence serving to determine the licence within a reasonable period, which was, in the circumstances, six months.[514] It was also held that, in view of the surrounding facts, the licence was personal, and that the second defendant could not assign his interest under it.

3–240   The most usual covenants by a licensee are those whereby he undertakes to pay royalties, to furnish accounts to the licensor and to grant him the right of inspection and of taking copies of the relevant documents. Provision is often made for minimum royalties, that is to say, if the royalties payable in any one year shall not have amounted to a specified sum, then the licensee is to pay the licensor such further sum as, with the amount of royalties payable for that year, amounts to the specified sum. Other covenants by a licensee which may be inserted relate to marking of articles with the design number, to give notice of infringement or suspected cases of infringement to the licensor and to use "best endeavours" to promote the exploitation of the design.[515]

3–241   Usual covenants by the licensor are for payment of renewal fees so as to maintain the registered design in existence, and it is often provided that should the licensor omit to do this, the licensee may make the payment and deduct the amount in question from the royalties which he owes. The licensor may also undertake to institute proceedings for infringement of the registered design, or to permit the licensee to do so in the name of the licensor if he so desires. It is important that in a clause of this nature the question of who is to pay for proceedings should be covered. It is also desirable to provide for proceedings not to be instituted by the licensor at the request of the licensee unless it appears that there is a good chance of success (e.g. unless a favourable opinion from counsel has been obtained), as otherwise the licensor may find himself forced to bring proceedings which are almost certain to end unsuccessfully. The licensor will usually undertake to defend proceedings brought by any third party for cancellation of the design or rectification of the register. He should, however, under no circumstances, covenant as to the validity of the registration, since it is impossible ever to guarantee that any registration is necessarily a valid one.

3–242   If the licensee does not agree to a minimum royalty clause on the lines indicated above, the licensor should obtain from him an undertaking at least to use his best endeavours to apply the design to articles of the type for which it is registered on a commercial scale to such an extent as is reasonable in all the circumstances of the case.

3–243   It is usual to have a clause whereby the licence is to determine if the registration of the design is declared to be invalid by a court of competent jurisdiction, but without prejudice to any rights accrued to either party at the date of termination. Power is often embodied in the licence for the

---

[514] See *Martin Baker Aircraft Co Ltd v Canadian Flight Equipment Ltd* (1955) 72 R.P.C. 236.
[515] *Terrell v Mabie Todd & Co Ltd* (1952) 69 R.P.C. 234.

licensor to put an end to the licence if royalties are unpaid for a stated time, or if the licensee breaks any of his covenants.

Exclusive licences under registered designs

A licence may be non-exclusive or exclusive. By a general non-exclusive licence, though the licensee is permitted by the licence to do any of the acts restricted by the registered design, he has no guarantee that he will be the only person permitted to do these things, and the proprietor of the design may grant similar rights to other persons, or may exercise them himself. In an exclusive licence, however, the registered design owner grants the licence to the other party and covenants, either expressly or impliedly, that no one else (including himself[516]) will be permitted to exercise the rights in question. The exclusive licensee is thus the only person in the field. **3–244**

The exclusive licensee of a UK registered design has a right, concurrent with the right of the owner of the registered design, to sue third parties who infringe the registered design.[517] These recently adopted provisions are modelled on the comparable provisions allowing exclusive licensees under UK unregistered design right and copyright to sue third parties for infringement.[518] Before this recent statutory change, an exclusive licensee under a UK registered design, anomalously and in contrast to the position under all the other UK and Community rights, had no right to sue. **3–245**

Registration of licences and other interests

Any form of licence under a registered design is capable of registration at the Designs Registry. Although registration of a licence is less essential than registration of proprietorship (since an unregistered proprietor cannot enforce his rights against infringers[519]), it is prudent to register a licence under a registered design unless it is informal or very short lived. The register stands as prima facie evidence of anything required or authorised to be entered in it.[520] An unregistered licence is still effective as a licence. However, RDA(E) s.19(5) provides that unregistered licences (together with other transactions creating or conveying interests under registered designs) shall not be admitted in court as evidence of the title of any person to the interest concerned unless the court otherwise directs. **3–246**

---

[516] A licence which prohibits the licensor from granting licences to any other party, but still permits the licensor to perform acts within the scope of the licensed rights himself, is conventionally called a "sole" rather than an "exclusive" licence.

[517] RDA(E) s.24F.

[518] For a description of the special statutory rights given to exclusive licensees, see para.4–129 below (unregistered design right) and para.5–162 below (copyright).

[519] See para.6–012 below.

[520] RDA(E) s.17(8).

There is therefore a risk, however theoretical, that the licensor might sue an unregistered licensee for infringement, deny that he has granted a licence, and the licensee would then be at the mercy of the court as to whether it would allow him to prove the existence of his licence in defence of the infringement action.

3–247   Of more practical concern is the protection which registration of a licence gives in cases when the licensor conveys the registered design to some other person, either voluntarily or involuntarily, for example in the case of an insolvency. The power of the person registered as proprietor of the design to assign or grant licences under it is subject to any rights vested in any other person of which notice is entered in the register,[521] thus providing protection to licensees whose interests are entered on the register. An exclusive licensee has a special statutory right to enforce the terms of the licence (i.e. effectively the covenant of exclusivity) against a successor in title to the registered design.[522]

6. Term of Protection

Term of registered design

3–248   The maximum term of protection of a registered design is 25 years[523] from the date of registration, which is normally the date when the application to register was filed. The registration when obtained gives a registered design right for an initial period of five years from the date of registration.[524] The proprietor of the design can, if he applies within the existing term and on payment of the requisite fee, obtain extension of his registered design right for successive periods of five years up to the maximum permitted term.[525] If an application for a further five-year term is not made before the end of the existing term, the registered design lapses but can be retrospectively revived as a matter of right within the following six months.[526] Even after expiry of this six-month extended period, there is a procedure for restoring a lapsed design if the proprietor can show that it lapsed despite the fact that he took reasonable care to have it extended.[527] In the event of such restoration, there are special provisions to protect the interests of persons who commence acts which are retrospectively converted into infringements by such a restoration.[528]

---

[521] RDA(E) s.19(4).
[522] RDA(E) s.15C.
[523] The maximum term was only 15 years in the case of applications under the RDA 1949 before the amendments made by the CDPA 1988; see para.3–275 below.
[524] RDA(E) s.8(1).
[525] RDA(E) s.8(2).
[526] RDA(E) s.8(4).
[527] RDA(E) s.8A.
[528] RDA(E) s.8B.

Special cases where term is not reckoned from the date of application

The date from which the term of a registered design is reckoned is the 3–249 date of registration. By s.3C(1), subject to certain exceptions, a design when registered is registered as of the date on which the application for registration was made.[529] These exceptions are, first, when an application for a design is altered in such a way as to alter the appearance of the design: in such a case the Registrar will treat the date of application as being the date when the application is amended to alter the appearance.[530] Secondly, a multiple application can effectively be divided up: one or more new additional applications can be filed which take the date of the original filing.[531]

In the case of a Convention application, the application for a registered 3–250 design is treated for the purpose of determining novelty as if made on the date when the application from which priority is claimed was made in the Convention country, rather than the UK filing date which may be up to six months later.[532] However, for a post 2001 registered design, its term is reckoned from the date of filing of the application in the United Kingdom.[533] There are special provisions in the transitional provisions which allow the terms of extant pre-2001 registrations to be extended so as effectively to run from their UK filing date rather than from their Convention filing date.[534]

Special cases in which term is curtailed for some pre-2001 designs

There are some special cases in which the term of a registered design is 3–251 curtailed to a shorter maximum period than the normal 25 years from the date of registration. These special rules only apply to pre-2001 designs. The first case is the re-registration of the same design in respect of different articles,[535] or of a similar design in respect of the same or a different article.[536] Only the proprietor of the earlier design was given the special privilege of doing so, but when he invoked that privilege the price

[529] RDA(E) s.3C.
[530] RDA(E) s.3B(2). Whilst this later dating is advantageous to the applicant in giving him a longer term of protection, it may be disadvantageous in that the novelty of his design will now be assessed as of the later date when he amends it, and it may be invalidated by intervening publications or registrations; see para.3–091 above.
[531] RDA(E) s.3B(3). Whilst this limits the term of the registered design, it is normally advantageous to him since the novelty of his designs will still be judged as at his original filing date.
[532] RDA(E) s.14(2).
[533] This is the effect of RDA(E) s.3C(3)(a). This represents a change from the previous law, when the term of a design based on a Convention application ran from its Convention date rather than its UK filing date under s.3(5) of RDA(A).
[534] 2001 Regulations regs 11(7), 12(7) and 13(10).
[535] See para.3–105 above.
[536] See para.3–107 above.

he paid was that the maximum term of the new registration was limited to the expiry of the original registration.[537] This is based on the actual term, not the maximum possible term, of the original registration, so if he fails to renew the original registration this will curtail the term of his dependent registrations as well. This special rule continues to apply so as to restrict the term of pre-2001 registered designs which have survived past December 8, 2001.[538]

3–252   The second case was when the proprietor of copyright in an artistic work took advantage of the special protection which permitted him to register the work as a design in cases when he had not himself exploited the work industrially.[539] In such a case, the term of his registered design was limited to the expiry of his artistic copyright.[540] There is a special provision in such a case enabling any person interested to apply for a registered design to be cancelled from the register on the ground that the corresponding copyright had expired.[541] However, this ground of cancellation no longer applies after December 8, 2001.[542]

7. The Pre-2001 Statement of Novelty

Basis of the statement of novelty

3–253   The former r.15[543] required that, except in the case of an application to register the pattern or ornament to be applied to textiles, wall coverings or lace, "a statement satisfactory to the registrar of the features of the design for which novelty is claimed" shall appear on the filed representations or specimens.[544] Although the rule was in mandatory terms, there was no statutory basis in the RDA(A)[545] for the imposition of this requirement. Nor was there any statutory statement (whether in Act or Rules) of what legal effect such a "statement of novelty" (as it is colloquially called) was supposed to have.

3–254   Historically, the practice of including such statements with registered design applications grew up in the 19th century in parallel with the practice of including claims in patent applications. In many of the older cases, statements of novelty are referred to as "claims", as if they were the equivalent of patent claims. There is however a very important difference which makes such a parallel potentially misleading. An applicant for a

---

[537] RDA(A) s.4(1) proviso and s.8(6).
[538] 2001 Regulations regs 11(9), 12(9) and 13(12).
[539] RDA(A) s.6(4): see para.3–125 above.
[540] RDA(E) s.8(5).
[541] RDA(E) s.11(3).
[542] 2001 Regulations reg.11(2), 12(2) and 13(3)—note the words in brackets at the end of each of these provisions.
[543] Registered Designs Rules 1989 (SI 1989/1105) (revoked).
[544] The current r.6 of the 2006 Rules allows the applicant to submit a partial disclaimer: which has a different function from the old statement of novelty.
[545] Whether before or after its amendment by the CDPA 1988.

patent is free to define his monopoly by reference to his claims as he chooses. Anything having the combination of features set out in a claim will infringe his patent. By including fewer features in his claim, or defining them more broadly, an applicant for a patent may make his monopoly as broad as he wishes. Of course, by doing so he increases the risk of invalidity, prompting refusal of the application by the Patent Office or revocation after grant by the court.

But the applicant for a registered design is not free to craft his **3–255** monopoly as he chooses. He can register only a single design, not a class of designs defined by reference to a feature or range of features.[546] Infringement was defined as applying a design which is the same as the design which is registered, or one not substantially different from it.[547] But the statement of novelty was merely a unilateral statement by the applicant asserting that certain features shown on his representation were novel; that statement did not exclude other features also shown on the representation from forming part of the design (i.e. the whole collection of features shown) as registered. In *Interlego AG v Tyco International Ltd*, Lord Oliver said[548]:

> "In approaching the definition it is always to be borne in mind what is to be registered. It is a shape, configuration or pattern to be applied to a particular specified article and it is the shape or configuration of the whole article in respect of which there is to be a commercial monopoly. That necessarily involves taking the design and the article as a whole."

Thus, it is a logical non sequitur to suppose that the statement of **3–256** novelty could exclude features of the registered design, even though not stated to be novel, from consideration as forming part of the design which is on the register, whether for the purposes of assessing novelty or for the purposes of assessing infringement.

To take an example, an applicant may file an application depicting a **3–257** design for a chair. His statement of novelty may say that the novelty of the design resides in the shape of the back of the chair. Thus, he is implicitly acknowledging that the shape of the seat and legs is old. However, the shape of the seat and legs is still part of the whole combination of features which together makes up the design which he has placed on the register. If a competitor makes a chair with the same back (thereby copying the features said to be novel alone) but combining that back with a seat and legs which are radically different from those shown in the representation of the registered design, so that the appearance of the chair as a whole is markedly different, does he infringe? On the face of it, there is no statutory authority for disregarding, when

[546] See para.3–077 above.
[547] See paras 3–184 et seq. above.
[548] At 353, line 51 to 354, line 3.

applying the test of infringement, any of the features which form part of the design which is on the register according to the statutory definition. What therefore is the effect of the "statement of novelty"?

Impact of the statement of novelty on what is "substantial"

3–258 Despite the exiguous statutory basis for its existence, and the logical difficulties which seem to attend its invocation, the "statement of novelty" became too well entrenched in the history and practice of registered designs for its effects to be dismissed. The best view seems to be that the statement of novelty could have an important impact on what is regarded as "substantial" when it comes to assessing similarity for the purposes of infringement, and what is "material" for the purposes of assessing novelty over similar prior art.[549] Presumably, it is still relevant to determining the scope of infringement of pre-2001 registered designs when applying the "overall impression" test under the new law of infringement,[550] even though the concept of what is "substantial" does not directly appear in the new test. Thus, although there is no statutory basis for disregarding any feature which forms part of the registered design, similarities or dissimilarities in features which are identified as novel in the statement of novelty are to be given greater weight when applying these tests, and similarities or dissimilarities in features not identified as novel are to be given correspondingly less weight.[550a] The object of having a statement of novelty is to call attention to any special or outstanding novel feature or features upon which the author desires to lay stress, as forming the kernel of his idea or conception.[551] Its function of creating what amounts to an estoppel against the proprietor was stated in the following terms by the Court of Appeal: "While the court does not

[549] The tests of what is "insubstantial" for infringement purposes, and what are "immaterial details" for novelty purposes are probably the same tests despite the difference in wording; see para.3–151 above.

[550] This appears to have been the assumption of the court and both counsel in *Woodhouse UK PLC v Architectural Lighting Systems* [2005] EWPCC (Designs) 25; [2006] R.P.C. 1, PCC (Judge Fysh Q.C.) at para.55, although the question of whether the statement of novelty can be taken into account at all under the new EU harmonised test of infringement (which applies to old designs as well as new ones) does not seem to have been the subject of argument.

[550a] This proposition was essentially accepted in the Australian case *Chiropedic Bedding v Radburg* (2010) 83 I.P.R. 275, where Jessup J. considered the effect of a statement of novelty under the Designs Act 1906 (Cth) and extensively reviewed the Australian and British authorities. At [22], he said that there is "much to be said" for the view expressed in this paragraph (in the seventh edition of this book).

[551] This sentence has formed part of this work since the first edition. Another formulation of the effect of the statement of novelty, in a passage from a different textbook referred to without apparent dissent by the Court of Appeal, is as follows: "The effect of the [statement of novelty] is both to define more closely and to broaden the scope of the registration, so that the essential features of the design become those set out in the statement, and the representation becomes a mere illustration of the design." From T.A. Blanco White, *Patents for Inventions and the Registration of Industrial Designs* (2nd edn, 1955) at pp.242–3; referred to by Russell L.J. in *Benchairs v Chair Centre Ltd* [1974] R.P.C.

have to assume that [the statement of novelty] is correct, it precludes the proprietor, who has obtained his registration on the grounds that certain features of the design give novelty to it, from thereafter denying their novelty and asserting their immateriality, so as to extend the scope of the protected design."[552]

This does not however mean that it is permissible wholly to disregard   **3–259** the other features of the design as shown in the illustration; the statement of novelty directs special attention to the part or parts of the design identified in the statement of novelty, but it wholly misconceives the purpose of such as statement to read it as if restricting the design to only those features specified.[553] In this respect, a partial disclaimer filed in respect of a post-2001 does perform the function, if appropriately framed, of totally disregarding features which are not then treated as forming part of the design for any purpose. In the example previously given, the applicant could file a partial disclaimer indicating that his design related only to the design of the chair back.

It has been suggested that the statement of novelty did not absolutely   **3–260** bind the proprietor of the registered design; in other words, if there are in fact novel features in his design other than those included in the statement of novelty, he may not be absolutely bound to treat all those other features as lacking in novelty.[554]

Statement of novelty in general terms

It was quite usual to frame a statement of novelty merely in general   **3–261** terms, such as that "the novelty resides in the features of shape or configuration of the article as shown in the attached drawings". This general form did not amount to a claim to any particular feature (beyond referring the design to three-dimensional as distinct from two-dimensional design features), but merely to the article as a whole, thus leaving the matter in just the same position as if there had been no statement at all. The design will be taken to be for the shape or pattern as a whole,[555] giving no particular emphasis to any feature or features beyond the impact which the features inherently make on the eye. It will not then be possible to prevent a person taking any special feature of the design and

---

429 at 445, line 30. However, the reference to the representation becoming a "mere illustration" probably goes a little too far, if it is taken to suggest that the features which are illustrated in the representation but not included in the statement of novelty can be wholly disregarded.

[552] *Sommer Allibert (UK) Ltd v Flair Plastics Ltd* [1987] R.P.C. 599, CA, at 619, line 45 to 620, line 3, per Slade L.J. giving the judgment of the court.

[553] Such an approach would "rob the illustrations which accompany the design of any real value for the ascertainment of the design features"; per Lloyd-Jacob J. in *Kent & Thanet Casinos Ltd v Bailey's School of Dancing Ltd* [1965] R.P.C. 482 at 486, lines 35 et seq.

[554] So suggested by Lord Evershed M.R. in *Cow & Co Ltd v Cannon Rubber Manufacturers Ltd* [1959] R.P.C. 344 at 350 lines 4–15, but explicitly without deciding the point.

[555] *Wilson v Chalco Ltd* (1922) 39 R.P.C. 252.

copying it, unless he has taken the thing when viewed substantially as a whole.[556]

3–262   In *Holdsworth v M'Crea*[557] Lord Westbury said:

> "The only thing which it is here necessary to point out, as well for warning to inventors as for the protection of the public, is this, that if a design, as exhibited in a pattern, is filed and registered by an inventor, without any farther limitation or description than that which is given by the design itself, it protects the entire thing, and the entire thing only, and the protection cannot, at pleasure, be made applicable, one day to the entirety, and another day to the separate integral parts or elements of the entire design. It must be considered that the protection of the statute is invoked for the entire thing that appears upon the register and is applicable to nothing but the exact copy of the thing so registered."

3–263   The words "exact copy" are of course subject to the later statutory test which permitted infringement as well by designs which are "not substantially different". Experience possibly shows, that for many good industrial designs, the novelty does not reside in any particular feature or features which can be isolated or described in words, but in the general appearance of the article as a whole. In such cases it would be impossible and in fact wrong to single out any particular feature or features in a statement of novelty, and the applicant will be well advised to comply with the rule by lodging a bare statement indicating that the novelty is in the design as a whole by using the words, "the novelty lies in the shape or configuration of the article as shown in the representations."

Statement of novelty identifying a special feature or features

3–264   If a special feature was indicated on the statement of novelty as being that to which the proprietor particularly assigns value, then it might well be that someone adopting that feature as part of their design would infringe, although if special emphasis had not been given that feature, he would not have come so near the registered design as a whole as to be an infringer.[558] But it must be remembered that the counterpart of this effect is that any statement of novelty laying claim to some particular feature

---

[556] *Holdsworth v M'Crea* (1867) L.R. 2 H.L. 380; *Jones and Attwood v The National Radiator Co Ltd* (1928) 45 R.P.C. 71 at 84, per Tomlin J.; *Thom v Sydall* (1872) 26 L.T.(N.S.) 15; *Benchairs Ltd v Chair Centre Ltd* [1974] R.P.C. 429 at 445.

[557] (1867) L.R. 2 H.L. 380.

[558] See *Sackett and Barnes v Clozenberg* (1910) 27 R.P.C. 104; where Neville J. said, at 108; "It appears to me that if it is desired to protect a particular feature in the general design of a sideboard, it must, under the Act of 1883, be registered or claimed separately." This formulation however may proceed on the old false misconception that a statement of novelty is equivalent to a patent claim. See also *W. Lusty & Sons Ltd v Morris Wilkinson* (1954) 71 R.P.C. 169 at 179.

will exclude anything which does not contain this feature from any possibility of being held to be an infringement of the registered design.

In *Phillips v Harbro' Rubber Co*,[559] Lord Moulton indicated how essential   **3–265** he thought it was that there should be a statement of the novelty. He said[560]:

> "This strikingly illustrates, as I have said, the difficulty of the task which is imposed upon a court dealing with a registered design when the person registering it has not availed himself of his right to file with his application a statement of the matters which, he claims, constitute its novelty. Your lordships might easily have failed to observe this feature and to give it its true importance, and grave injustice might have been done to the public by treating heel pieces which do not possess this feature as being within the ambit of the registered design."

Formulating a statement of novelty

The old forms of claim, typified in such cases as *Pugh v Riley Cycle Co*   **3–266** *Ltd*[561] and in *Re Bayer's Design*,[562] were wrong, because they were framed on the same lines as a claim in a patent specification, and amounted to claims for modes or principles of construction.[563] An example of a good form of statement of novelty is to be found in *Re Gutta Percha and Rubber (London) Ltd's Application*,[564] although this case was later overruled on other grounds unconnected with the form of the statement.[565]

Thus, the design can be regarded as the representation interpreted in   **3–267** the light of the statement of novelty which is attached thereto, which cannot be disregarded.[566]

Two or more features independently novel

There would seem to be no reason why two or more features should not   **3–268** be singled out by the claim as constituting the novelty in a registration. There would, however, presumably be no infringement unless both were

---

[559] (1920) 37 R.P.C. 233.

[560] (1920) 37 R.P.C. 233 at 241.

[561] (1912) 29 R.P.C. 196. The claim was to "the disposition of the tyre rim d, in relation to the hub e, and the cross-section arrangement of the spokes a, b, c . . . "

[562] (1907) 24 R.P.C. 65. The claim was to the gores or gussets of a corset being "cut horizontally from front to back". See also *Moody v Tree* (1892) 9 R.P.C. 233.

[563] *Pugh v Riley Cycle Co Ltd* (1912) 29 R.P.C. 196; *Kestos Ltd v Kempat Ltd & Kemp* (1936) 53 R.P.C. 139. These cases are discussed in the context of "methods or principles of construction" at para.3–077 above.

[564] (1935) 52 R.P.C. 383.

[565] *Stenor v Whitesides (Clitheroe) Ltd* (1948) 65 R.P.C. 1.

[566] See *Smout v Slaymaker* (1890) 7 R.P.C. 90; *Moody v Tree* (1892) 9 R.P.C. 233; *Cooper v Symington* (1893) 10 R.P.C. 264.

taken. (Under post-2001 law, the applicant could file two applications with partial disclaimers restricting each application to one of the features. He could then independently sue on the two registrations.) If the novelty is pointed out as residing in one or more features, then clearly it cannot reside also in the whole, and two statements of novelty, one claiming a particular feature or features and one directed to the article as a whole, should be, it would appear, inconsistent. This would appear to be the justification for the decision in *Re Evered & Co's Applications*,[567] where two applications were made for registration of the same article, the applications differing only in their statements of novelty, whereby each claimed a different feature as the novel one, the applications were refused on the ground that the effect was to imply in one application that the shape of one particular part was novel, and at the same time, in the other application, that it was not novel, and that this, if allowed, would be tantamount to granting registration for a part or parts of an article, which would be contrary to the provisions of s.44, if the part was not sold separately.[568] Now that parts of articles can be registered, this principle has no application under the current law.

3–269   If, however, two features in a particular article are each sufficiently novel to be independently susceptible of protection, it is hard to see why two independent and valid registrations each emphasising one of the features in the statement of novelty should not be obtainable as suggested in some of the older cases.[569] Possibly the objection is that by a series of such registrations, the effect could be to create a wide monopoly in the type of article itself.[570]

8. Transitional Provisions Applying to Pre-CDPA 1988 Registration

Pre-and post-1988 Act registered designs

3–270   The CDPA 1988 made a large number of amendments, some of them very important, to the Registered Designs Act 1949. The CDPA 1988 contained transitional provisions which made most of the features of the old law continue to apply in respect of "old" designs. The watershed is the date on which the application to register was filed. The old law of registered designs continued to apply to registered designs the application for which was filed before the commencement of the CDPA 1988, i.e. before

---

[567] [1961] R.P.C. 105.

[568] As regards the non-registrability of designs for parts of articles, see para.3–038 above.

[569] *Pearson v Morris Wilkinson & Co* (1906) 23 R.P.C. 738; *Harper v Wright and Butler* (1895) 12 R.P.C. 483.

[570] See, e.g. *Infields Ltd v Rosen* (1939) 56 R.P.C. 163 at 182, where a proprietor had several registered designs which together covered all possible combinations.

August 1, 1989, in respect of what constitutes a design and its validity,[571] authorship and first ownership,[572] the scope of infringement,[573] and maximum term of design right.[574] Most but not all of these special rules have been carried over into the post-2001 law by the transitional provisions.[575]

Definition of "design" and registrability

As indicated, the old law (i.e. the RDA 1949 in its unamended form) continues to regulate the validity of registered designs applied for before August 1, 1989. There is, however, a special category of designs applied for between January 12, 1988 and August 1, 1989 to which special treatment is given. Subject to specific exceptions, the special treatment given to these old registrations under the pre-2001 law is carried forward into the post-2001 law.[576] **3–271**

A significant change in the law which was made by the 1988 Act was the introduction of the "must match" exclusion.[577] This exclusion did not apply to old registered designs. However, it was still necessary for such designs to satisfy the requirement that they are in respect of articles which are "made and sold separately", a requirement of the old law.[578] **3–272**

The exclusion from registrability of articles whose appearance is not material was newly introduced by the 1988 Act and this exclusion was not in explicit terms present in the old law[579]; however, as already discussed, it is hard to see what this exclusion adds to the requirement of eye appeal as interpreted by the House of Lords in *Amp v Utilux*.[580] A further change is that RDA(A) required that designs be "new"; before amendment, it required that they be "new or original".[581] In theory there might be some old designs which are "original" but not "new"; however, **3–273**

---

[571] CDPA 1988 s.265(2). However, a "divisional" application filed on or after August 1, 1989 which is divided out of an original application filed before that date is dealt with under the old law: *Amper SA's Design Application* [1993] R.P.C. 453, RDAT. For "divisional" applications generally, see para.2–059 above.

[572] CDPA 1988 s.267(4). Although in this respect there do not appear to have been substantive changes to the law, despite some changes of wording.

[573] CDPA 1988 s.268(2).

[574] CDPA 1988 s.269(2).

[575] 2001 Regulations reg.13, which refers to pre-1988 Act registrations as "pre-1989 registrations". In fact, registrations applied for in the first seven months of 1989 fall into this category as well because the cut off date is August 1, 1989 when CPDA 1988 came into force.

[576] 2001 Regulations reg.13(2).

[577] Considered in para.3–041 above.

[578] See para.3–038 above.

[579] As RDA(A) new subs.1(3).

[580] [1972] R.P.C. 102. In para.3–075 above, the opinion is expressed that the exclusion of designs from registrability purportedly effected by RDA(A) s.1(3) has no effect, because it covers a null class: anything falling within s.1(3) cannot fall within the statutory definition of "design" in the first place, which in this respect is unchanged from the old law.

[581] RDA 1949 s.1(2).

the better view is probably that this change of formulation has no effect.[582]

Infringement of pre-1988 Act registered designs

3-274   The old law of infringement continued to apply to old registered designs up to December 2001. The most important respect in which the new law was different was in relation to kits of parts. Under the RDA(A) it was an infringing act to make or offer for sale a kit of parts for making up into an article in accordance with the registered design.[583] This was not so under the RDA 1949 before amendment,[584] and the old law continued to apply in respect of infringements of old registered designs. However, the new law of infringement now applies without distinction to existing registered designs, whether applied for before or after the 1988 Act; and the supply of kits of parts is no longer (at least explicitly) an infringing act.

Maximum term was limited to 15 years

3-275   The CDPA 1988 increased the maximum term of protection of a registered design from 15 years to 25 years.[585] However, this amendment did not apply to designs applied for under the pre-1988 Act law, which remained limited to a maximum term of 15 years.[586] However, any such designs which have managed to survive past the coming into force of the new European harmonised law may benefit from an increase in maximum term to 25 years.[587]

---

[582] The possible distinction between "new" and "original" is discussed at para.3–160 above.

[583] RDA(A) s.7(4).

[584] See the cases referred to at para.3–173 above.

[585] By amending s.8(2) to permit the registration to be renewed for up to five five-year terms instead of three.

[586] CDPA 1988 s.269(2).

[587] 2001 Regulations reg.13(8).

CHAPTER 4

UK NATIONAL UNREGISTERED DESIGN RIGHT

Contents

1. Nature of Unregistered Design Right

Nature of unregistered design right

UK national unregistered design right—called in the Act simply "design right"[1]—is a right to prevent the copying by others of the shape and configuration (if original) of manmade articles.[2] It is of comparatively short duration—usually 10 years after the first marketing of articles to which the design has been applied (although longer than the three years of Community unregistered design right); during the last five years of which competitors are entitled to copy the design provided they pay royalties under a licence of right. Unlike registered designs, the unregistered design right protects functional as well as aesthetic features of shape and configuration. It does not protect surface pattern and ornament—these fall within the ambit of registered designs or copyright. UK national unregistered design right is far more different from UK national registered designs than is Community unregistered design right from the corresponding Community registered right.   **4–001**

Unregistered design right, like copyright, subsists without formalities. In a marked difference from copyright, there are important limitations in practice in the case of design rights of foreign origin. Authors from most parts of the world are entitled to copyright in the United Kingdom because of international conventions providing for reciprocal protection,   **4–002**

---

[1] CDPA 1988 s.213(1). App.C1 below.
[2] As to precisely what is an "article" for this purpose, see para.4–010 below.

but there are industrially important countries whose products do not enjoy unregistered design right protection in the United Kingdom because of lack of reciprocity. Design right can only subsist in designs which were first embodied in a design document or an actual article on or after August 1, 1989[3–4]; designs pre-dating that date could for a period now expired still be protectable under the law of copyright under the transitional provisions.

Definition of "design" for unregistered design right

4–003   Section 213(2) of the CDPA 1988 provides:

"(2) In this Part 'design' means the design of any aspect of the shape or configuration (whether internal or external) of the whole or part of an article."

4–004   This definition of "design" (and the exclusions from it which are dealt with later[5]) is to some extent modelled on the pre-2001 definition of "design" for registered design purposes.[6] However, there are some very important differences from the registered design definition. The first is that unregistered design right is relevant only to the three-dimensional aspects of the design of an article and it does not cover such matters as surface pattern, ornamentation or colour.[7] Secondly, unregistered design right is not restricted to protecting features of a design which have "eye appeal"[8]—it will protect purely functional as well as aesthetic features of shape or configuration. Indeed, there seems no reason to think that design right will not protect visually insignificant or even invisible features of shape or configuration, provided that they are of functional importance.[9]

[3–4] CDPA 1988 s.213(7).

[5] See para.4–007 below.

[6] RDA(A) s.1(1); considered extensively at paras 3–010 et seq.

[7] See para.4–029 below. Registered designs can protect the shape and configuration of an article, and/or a pattern or decoration applied to it; see paras 3–017 to 3–021 above.

[8] For this concept in the context of registered designs, see para.3–047 above.

[9] So held in *Ocular Sciences Ltd v Aspect Vision Care Ltd* [1997] R.P.C. 289 at 422, lines 35 to 15, Pat Ct, concerning detailed dimensions of contact lens designs. In this respect, it seems that unregistered design right goes further than copyright, under which features which are not visually significant in the drawing relied upon cannot be protected, irrespective of the technical significance of those features: *Interlego AG v Tyco International Ltd* [1988] R.P.C. 343, PC; and see para.4–103 below. Although the *Interlego v Tyco* approach was applied in an unregistered design case *Volumetric Ltd v Myriad Technologies Ltd* unreported April 10, 1995 (ChD) Sir John Vinelott, that approach was said to be too narrow as a general rule by the Court of Appeal in *A Fulton Co Ltd v Totes Isotoner (UK) Ltd* [2004] R.P.C. 301; [2003] EWCA Civ 1514, at paras 15–16, although not for that case or for cases concerned solely with the visual appearance of the design. In *Dyson Ltd v Qualtex (UK) Ltd* [2006] EWCA Civ 166; [2006] R.P.C. 31, CA at paras 22–23, it was said that the question is whether feature is "discernible" or "recognisable", rather than whether it is "visually significant".

It has been suggested that, since an unregistered design right protects a shape, mere changes of scale do not produce different designs.[10]

Thirdly, unlike a pre-2001 registered design, which protects the design applied to a whole article,[11] unregistered design right subsists in the shape or configuration of part of an article, or indeed in "any aspect"[12] of the shape or configuration of the whole or part of the article. Thus, a single article (or a design document recording the design of an article) will normally embody not a single design right, but a large bundle of different design rights subsisting in the whole and every part and every aspect of the shape and configuration of the article, provided that the part or aspect concerned is original[13] and is not otherwise excluded from enjoying design right by one of the exceptions considered in the following paragraphs. This concept of a bundle of design rights becomes significant when the question of infringement is considered, because, except in the case of slavish copying of the whole article, the design right proprietor will seek to match a design right which he can contend subsists in a part or aspect of the design of his article with the features of the alleged infringing article which he contends have been copied.[14] **4–005**

The concept that a single article or design document will normally embody a bundle of design rights subsisting in the whole and in every part and aspect of the shape and configuration of an article was unsuccessfully challenged in *A Fulton Co Ltd v Totes Isotoner (UK) Ltd*,[15] a case in which the defendants were held to have copied part of an article (an umbrella case). The claimants had a registered design which related to the whole article,[16] and it was held that the difference in the part of the article that had not been copied rendered the design of the defendants' article as a whole substantially different so that their umbrella case did not infringe either the registered design,[17] or the unregistered design right subsisting in the design of the whole case. However, the defendants' article was held to infringe the unregistered design right subsisting in the part of the case which they had copied, the claimants being entitled to plead and rely upon that partial design right. In the course of its judgment, the Court of Appeal quoted the text of para.4–005 above in the sixth edition with apparent approval.[18] **4–006**

[10] *Ocular Sciences Ltd v Aspect Vision Care Ltd* [1997] R.P.C. 289.
[11] In order for there to be infringement, there must be identity, or sufficient similarity, between the registered design and the infringing article as a whole: see para.3–211 above.
[12] It appears that an "aspect" of a design is any feature of shape or configuration which is discernible or recognisable: *Dyson Ltd v Qualtex (UK) Ltd* [2006] EWCA Civ 166; [2006] R.P.C. 31, CA.
[13] See para.4–042 below.
[14] See para.4–098 below.
[15] [2004] R.P.C. 301.
[16] Under the old UK law of registered designs, a registration had to be in respect of a whole article which was "made and sold separately": see para.3–38 above.
[17] The application of the test of infringement of registered designs involved comparing the alleged infringement with the registered design *as a whole*: see para.3–211 above.
[18] At para.20 of the judgment of Jacob L.J., giving the judgment of the court.

What is an "article"?

4–007 Part III of the CDPA 1988 contains no explicit definition of the word "article." For registered designs purposes, the word "article" (under the pre-2001 law) was defined as "any article of manufacture and includes any part of an article if that part is made and sold separately".[19] What constitutes an "article of manufacture" for this purpose has been the subject of a body of case law, as a result of which buildings and structures have been held not to be "articles" for registered designs purposes.[20] The question arises whether or not the word "article" has a similar meaning in the unregistered design context, despite the omission of an express definition of the word.

4–008 It seems likely that the word "article" in the unregistered design context does not extend to embrace such objects as buildings and structures. First, to refer to a building as an "article" is not in accordance with ordinary usage of the word: nobody would call a house an article. Secondly, the CDPA 1988 has taken considerable trouble to separate out the fields of application of unregistered design right and of copyright[21]: and buildings and structures are clearly within the field of copyright protection.[22] However, there seems no real reason to import into the meaning of "article" in the unregistered design context any implication arising from the use of the word "manufacture" in the registered design context that articles should be made or at least be capable of being made en masse[23]; it would seem to be enough so long as the article is an object which can be designed and made, even if it is a "one off". There seems no basis, as is the case with registered designs,[24] for excluding spare parts from counting as "articles" for unregistered designs purposes. It is clear that an article can be a part of a larger article,[25] and there seems no reason

---

[19] RDA(A) s.44(1).

[20] The registered designs cases on this point are summarised at para.3–036 above.

[21] CDPA 1988 s.51(1), which excludes from the scope of copyright infringement the making of articles which are not themselves artistic works (see para.5–050 below); and CDPA 1988 s.236 excepts from infringement of design right anything which is an infringement of copyright (see para.4–088 below).

[22] Curious as it may seem, buildings and structures and parts of them are themselves "artistic works" for copyright purposes; CDPA s.4(1)(b) and s.4(2). Thus, even if "article" were construed to cover buildings and structures, the reproduction of a building design would still fall within the field of copyright infringement, rather than design right infringement, because of the continued application in CDPA s.51(1) of copyright infringement to designs for articles which are themselves artistic works. There therefore seems little point in giving a strained construction to the word "article" which would make it cover a building or structure. However, the Court of Appeal has rejected an argument that an object which becomes incorporated into a building, such as a specially designed door, thereby becomes consumed into the realty and ceases to be an "article" for the purposes of copyright law (CPDA s.23) upon incorporation: *Pensher Security Door Co Ltd v Sunderland County Council* [2000] R.P.C. 249 at 280, lines 18–26. Presumably the same principle would apply for unregistered design right purposes.

[23] See para.3–045 above.

[24] For the meaning of this, see para.3–038 above.

[25] The "must fit" and "must match" exclusions (CDPA 1988 s.213(3)(b)) considered below make it clear that an "article" can be part of a larger article.

to import the aspect of the registered design definition which refers to articles being "made and sold separately".

It has been held that the word "article" is wide enough to embrace a **4–009** part of the human body such as the eyeball, at least when considering the "other article" against which the article whose design is in issue must fit in the context of the "must fit" exclusion.[26]

Exclusions from scope of design right

Subsection 213(3) of the CDPA 1988 provides that: **4–010**

"(3) Design right does not subsist in—

(a) a method or principle of construction,
(b) features of shape or configuration of an article which—

(i) enable an article to be connected to, or placed in, around or against, another article so that either article may perform its function, or
(ii) are dependent upon the appearance of another article of which the article is intended by the designer to form an integral part, or

(c) surface decoration."

These exclusions will be considered in turn.

Method or principle of construction

This is based upon the identically worded exclusion in the definition of **4–011** design for registered designs purposes in the 1949 Act.[27] However, it may in practice have considerably greater significance, because the unregistered design right, unlike registered designs, is intended to protect functional features of design as well as aesthetic features. Thus, it may impose a real limitation on what would otherwise be the scope of the rights conferred by a functional design.

In the registered design context, it has been held that the exclusion of **4–012** a "method or principle of construction" denies registration to "a process or operation by which a shape is produced as opposed to the shape itself"[28]; i.e. an attempt to register as a design a range or class of differing shapes, rather than a single shape (which is what a "design" must consist

---

[26] *Ocular Sciences Ltd v Aspect Vision Care Ltd* [1997] R.P.C. 289 at 425 Pat Ct: contact lenses designed to fit against another "article", the human cornea. This decision and the "must fit" exclusion generally are considered at para.4–015 below.
[27] RDA(A) s.1(1)(a).
[28] *Kestos Ltd v Kempat Ltd* (1936) 53 R.P.C. 139 at 151, per Luxmoore J.; for fuller discussion of the registered design cases, see para.3–077 above.

of). A similar distinction applies in the unregistered design field between the principle or method of construction (which cannot be monopolised) and a particular shape achieved through the application of that method:

> "It is certainly true that there are methods of construction involved in the creation of the Miniflat case. One is the method whereby the case retains its rectangular box-like shape when the umbrella is not contained within it. Another is the stitching technique which creates the outward-pointing seams on the edges and at the corners of the case. However, the design of the case is the shape or configuration produced by those methods of construction, not the methods by which that shape or configuration is produced. The fact that a special method or principle of construction may have been used in order to create an article with a particular shape or configuration does not mean that there is no design right in the shape or configuration. The law of design right will not prevent competitors using that method or principle of construction to create competing designs (of course other areas of the law, like patents, might prevent competitors doing that), as long as the competing designs do not have the same shape or configuration as the design right owner's has."[29]

It follows that s.213(3)(a) does not preclude a design from being protected merely because it has a functional purpose[30] or indeed if every individual element of the design can be said to have a functional purpose.[31] Therefore, even if there is some method or principle of construction involved in the design in question, if it is possible to make a device which is visually different but works in a different way "it follows that there is no principle monopolised here—only a visual embodiment of a device constructed in accordance with the principle."[32] But where an article embodying a design is copied only at the level of copying general principles or ideas, there will be no infringement, since the "design" in which design right subsists is the actual physical shape of the article (or a part or aspect of that shape), not a more general concept, idea or

---

[29] *A Fulton Co Ltd v Grant Barnett & Co Ltd* [2001] R.P.C. 257 at 278, para.70, Park J. Approved by the Court of Appeal in *Landor & Hawa Intnl Ltd v Azure Designs Ltd* [2006] EWCA Civ 1285; [2007] F.S.R. 9; [2006] E.C.D.R. 413, CA at para.12. Note that para.13 cites a passage to similar effect from a previous edition of this work. The passage quoted is in fact the first paragraph on p.27 of the 5th Edition relating to methods or principles of construction in relation to *registered* designs, but is described by Neuberger L.J. as from the seventh edition and relating to s.213(3)(a); this glitch makes no difference, because the analysis of what is a "method or principle of constuction" is effectively the same in both contexts.

[30] *Landor & Hawa Intnl Ltd v Azure Designs Ltd* [2006] EWCA Civ 1285; [2007] F.S.R. 9; [2006] E.C.D.R. 413, CA at paras 10–11.

[31] *Landor & Hawa Intnl Ltd v Azure Designs Ltd* [2006] EWCA Civ 1285; [2007] F.S.R. 9; [2006] E.C.D.R. 413, CA at para.16.

[32] *Isaac Oren v Red Box Toy Factory Ltd* [1999] F.S.R. 785, Jacob J., at paras 14–15.

principle embodied in that physical shape.[33] Another way of putting this point is to say that unregistered design right does not protect ideas, and when copying is only at the level of ideas there will be no exact or substantial reproduction of the design.[34]

When a new functional principle is devised which can only be put into **4–013** practice by the use of a particular shape in an article, or at least that shape or a shape which cannot substantially differ from it, it appears that s.213(3)(a) will operate to prevent design right being enforced .[35] The authorities cited in the preceding paragraph also by implication support this conclusion.[36] Thus, if the functional method or principle can only be adopted by a competitor through reproducing that specific shape, this exclusion means that the design right owner cannot stop competitors from copying the shape of his article to the extent necessary to put into practice the new functional principle. A possible refinement of this principle is that unregistered design right does not prevent a competitor from deducing from an article a method or principle, and then working out the shape of his own article from the method or principle; and provided that he goes through this process, and does not take the short cut of simply saving himself design work by copying the shape without going back to first principles, he does not infringe even if he ends up with a shape which is the same or similar. An illustration of this approach in the copyright context is given in *Catnic Components Ltd v Hill & Smith Ltd*.[37] There, the plaintiffs devised a new form of steel lintel embodying a novel principle, which was indeed the subject of a patent which was sued upon in the action. They contended that the defendants, in addition to infringing the patent,[38] had in creating their own lintel infringed the copyright in the design drawings for the plaintiff's lintel. It was conceded that the defendant derived the idea of a box girder type of lintel from the claimant's brochure.[39] Buckley L. J. said[40]:

---

[33] *Rolawn Ltd v Turfmech Machinery Ltd* [2008] EWHC 989 (Pat); [2008] R.P.C. 27; [2008] E.C.D.R. 13, Mann J., see at paras 80–83.

[34] *Virgin Atlantic Airways v Premium Aircraft Interiors* [2009] EWHC 26 (Pat); [2009] E.C.D.R. 11, Lewison J. at paras 31–33 and 134.

[35] *Bailey (t/a Elite Anglian Products) v Haynes* [2007] F.S.R. 199, PCC, at para.68; the basic appearance of the design in that case, which related to anglers' bait nets, was generated by the "Atlas warp stitch" method which was used to make them.

[36] See *Landor & Hawa Intnl Ltd v Azure Designs Ltd* [2006] EWCA Civ 1285; [2007] F.S.R. 9; [2006] E.C.D.R. 413, CA at para.17: the proposition may be as a matter of fact very difficult to establish.

[37] *Catnic Components Ltd v Hill & Smith Ltd* [1982] R.P.C. 183, CA, HL. See also *Kleeneze Ltd v DRG (UK) Ltd* [1984] F.S.R. 399, ChD, where the defendants copied the idea of a letterbox draught excluder with brushes but worked out their own detailed design starting from the idea; no infringement even though the end product had a lot of similarities arising from design constraints.

[38] The decision of the Court of Appeal on the patent infringement claim was reversed by the House of Lords; but there was no appeal from the dismissal by the Court of Appeal of the copyright infringement claim.

[39] *Catnic Components Ltd v Hill & Smith Ltd* [1982] R.P.C. 183 at 220, line 39, CA, HL.

[40] *Catnic Components Ltd v Hill & Smith Ltd* [1982] R.P.C. 183 at 222, lines 32 et seq.

" . . . [The evidence] effectively rebutted any inference that the defendants had copied anything of the plaintiffs other than the idea of a box girder type of lintel. The dimensional similarities were due . . . to the functions which the lintels were designed to perform and the normal dimensions of materials used in building cavity walls and of the cavities in such walls."

4–014   The Court of Appeal rejected the argument that the defendants had infringed by copying the idea itself, and accordingly rejected the allegation of infringement.[41] Although the analogy is not exact between an idea in the copyright context,[42] and a "method or principle of construction" in the context of unregistered design right, it appears that a similar approach will be applied by the courts.

The "must fit" exclusion from design right

4–015   Section 213(3)(b)(i)[43] of the CDPA 1988 excludes certain features of the design of an article from the scope of design right. These are broadly speaking the features of an article which enable it to interface or interfit with another article, either a greater or composite article in which it is placed, or an article with which it connects or physically interrelates. (There is no equivalent of this "must fit" exclusion in the case of registered designs, because functional features are not protectable as part of a registered design in the first place.[44]) The "must fit" provision was clearly inserted into the Act with (amongst other things) spare parts in mind. However, the Court of Appeal has expressed the view that it is not possible to approach this provision with any clear legislative purpose in mind, given the extremely complex and conflicting economic arguments which were involved in its legislative history. On the one hand Parliament refused to create a general exception for spare parts, and on the other hand did not intend that manufacturers of original equipment should have absolute control over the manufacture of spares. Accordingly the court must construe the language of the statute as it stands, as it would be understood by a reasonable reader.[45] Some examples might help to illustrate the points which arise.

4–016   (1) A crankshaft for a car engine. The bearing surfaces would need to be precisely positioned relative to the axis of rotation of the crankshaft and precisely dimensioned, in order to work correctly against the bearing surfaces in the engine cylinder block and in the piston big-ends. There

---

[41] *Catnic Components Ltd v Hill & Smith Ltd* [1982] R.P.C. 183 at 222, lines 46 to 223 and line 23.

[42] As to copying of ideas in the copyright context, see paras 5–131 et seq. below.

[43] Set out in para.4–010 above.

[44] See paras 3–047 and 3–054 above.

[45] *Dyson Ltd v Qualtex* (UK) Ltd [2006] EWCA Civ 166; [2006] R.P.C. 31, CA at para.11 per Jacob L.J.

would be some room for variation in the precise shape of the crankshaft in between its bearing surfaces, but even in that respect its general shape would be fairly closely dictated by the need to fit and operate within the engine block. It would appear that design right cannot subsist at all in the shape and configuration of the bearing surfaces; design right can subsist in the precise shape and dimensions of the portions of the crankshaft intermediate the bearing surfaces, but presumably the effect of the exclusion is that that design right cannot be infringed by someone who copies the general shape of the shaft to the extent necessary to make it work in the engine block, but does not copy the shape and dimensions in more detail.

(2) An electrical plug, designed to fit in with an electrical socket. It would appear in this case that the shape and dimensions of the pins of the plug is excluded from design right (as would the corresponding apertures in the socket). However, other aspects of the plug, such as its shape at the rear, would not be excluded. **4–017**

One purpose of this "must fit" exclusion would appear to be to prevent monopolisation of replacement parts by a maker of original equipment. Replacement parts may be needed to repair a machine by replacing a part which is worn out or broken, or there may be consumable parts which need periodical replacement, such as printer or photocopier cartridges.[46] But the provision is not wide enough to permit a spare parts manufacturer simply to copy the spare parts of the maker of the original equipment: he is effectively able to copy only those aspects of the spare parts which are necessary to allow the parts to fit and function properly within the rest of the machine, and must design for himself without copying those aspects of the original equipment manufacturer's parts which are not dictated by the surrounding parts of the machine.[47] Apart from spare parts, there are also wider potential problems of compatibility in contexts such as that of plugs and sockets, where the devisor of a bespoke system of sockets might otherwise be in a position to monopolise all items which are connected to his outlets. This problem was illustrated in the artistic copyright context in *LB Plastics v Swish*, where one of the defences advanced was that the defendants wished to make their drawers compatible with an existing drawer and carcase system devised by the plaintiffs. However, since the plaintiffs' own carcase had been derived in turn from their drawers (which in turn were based on design drawings), **4–018**

[46] Cf. *Canon Kabushiki Kaisha v Green Cartridge Co (Hong Kong) Ltd* [1997] F.S.R. 817, PC.
[47] *Dyson Ltd v Qualtex (UK) Ltd* [2006] EWCA Civ 166; [2006] R.P.C. 31, CA. Assessing this question in relation to a large number of parts was an enormously detailed and difficult exercise, since each part raised multiple issues of fact and law. The Court of Appeal restricted its consideration to 6 parts as a matter of case management. It would also appear that the exercise which the law requires a spare parts maker to go through—to copy features necessary to interfit but not to copy other features—is enormously difficult and complex, and probably more difficult than the design task faced by the maker of the original equipment. Observed by Jacob L.J. at para.126: "trying to navigate by the chart provided by this crude statute is a risky business."

"the requirement of interchangeability was not ... so much a badge of respectability as an incitement to copy".[48] One can see in the insertion of the "must fit" exclusion from design right a legislative intent to prevent an effective monopoly arising in a situation where articles have to be compatible with each other, whether that monopoly is based on the design of features of the compatible article being sold by the defendant (i.e. the drawers in the example just considered) or based on rights in the design of the other article (i.e. the carcase in the example given). An illustration of the effect of this provision in a "compatibility" case is that of leather cases for mobile phones, where features of the cases which made them fit around the mobile phones for which they were designed were held excluded from design right.[49] However, in a case about umbrella cases, it was pointed out that it was unacceptable to construe the "must fit" exclusion as denying protection to any article that is shaped so as to contain or cover another article; many shapes having similar approximate dimensions would have succeeded in the task of containing the umbrellas, and the particular features which gave the case in issue its unique shape or configuration were not designed so as to enable it to perform the function of containing the umbrella.[50]

4–019   However, it has been held that the exclusion goes further, and that the exclusion applies even if the other "article" against which the first article must fit is a part of the human body such as the cornea, or it seems any object natural or artificial.[51] It is submitted that the correctness of this decision is open to doubt. In a case where one party designs an article to fit against a part of the human body, any competitor is free to measure up the body part himself and devise his own article, without needing to copy the other design. This is quite unlike the case where an article must fit an existing artificially created article, where it may be impossible to avoid copying directly or indirectly an article in which (apart from the exclusion) design right would subsist. Thus, the legislative policy behind the exclusion does not necessarily justify extending the scope of the exclusion from the need to fit against artificially created articles to all natural things. Nor, it is submitted, is it natural to read the word "article" as covering natural things in the context of legislation conferring unregistered design right on manufactured articles.[52]

4–020   Assuming that it is the legislative purpose of the exclusion to provide a defence in spare parts and other "compatibility" cases, the legislative

---

[48] *LB Plastics Ltd v Swish Products Ltd* [1979] R.P.C. 551 at 630 lines 2–20, per Lord Hailsham, HL. Lord Wilberforce said that the desire to achieve interchangeability "tells against [the defendants] by suggesting a causal [*casual* in the report] connection between the design of their drawer and (via [a common customer's] furniture) the plaintiff's drawer". At 621, lines 25–32.

[49] *Parker v Tidball* [1997] F.S.R. 680, ChD.

[50] *A Fulton Co Ltd v Grant Barnett & Co Ltd* [2001] R.P.C. 257 at 279 paras 74–75, Park J.

[51] *Ocular Sciences Ltd v Aspect Vision Care Ltd* [1997] R.P.C. 289 at 425, lines 1–35, Pat Ct.

[52] For discussion of the meaning of the word "article" in the context of unregistered design right, see para.4–007 above.

route chosen for achieving it seems rather strange. That purpose could have been achieved by creating a defence against infringement in cases where a spare part is made and supplied or in other cases where physical compatibility is needed in order to market a part which interfits with an established piece of equipment.

However, instead of providing a defence against infringement, what has been done is to create an exception to subsistence of the right. The exception will apply regardless of the purpose for which another party may copy the features concerned and this can produce a rather strange result. Take the example of the crankshaft referred to above. Obviously a person who makes and sells crankshafts as spare parts will escape infringement of the design right, if he only copies the crankshaft to the extent needed to make it fit. However, what if a competing engine maker copies the crankshaft end of the cylinder block and the crankshaft in his own engine? It would appear that, provided he does not copy more closely than is necessary to make the crankshaft and its bearings interfit, he does not infringe design right. And yet, the design of the bearing surfaces of these components may constitute a significant part of the original engine manufacturer's design effort. However, because the exception relates to subsistence of the design right regardless of the purpose of the copying, rather than being an exception tied to the purpose for which the competitor copies, there seems no escape from such anomalous results[53]: **4–021**

> "If a feature of shape or configuration of one article enables that article to be connected to, or placed in, around or against another article so that either article may perform its function, the feature is excluded from protection under the design right provisions of the Act. If the policy of the Act is to prevent such interface features from qualifying for design right, I can see no reason why that policy should not apply merely because the two interfitting articles carrying the features are in fact assembled together and form the whole or part of another, larger, article."

This leads to a further question which was considered in the same case: what is the impact of the "must fit" exception on the design right in a larger article of which a smaller article forms part? Many features of a smaller article may be needed for it to fit into a larger composite article and perform its function there. Those features are clearly excluded by the "must match" exception from forming part of the design right subsisting in the design of the smaller article itself. But what of the design right in the larger article? Can features of the smaller article be effectively protected under the design right subsisting in the larger article? **4–022**

---

[53] *Electronic Techniques (Anglia) Ltd v Critchley Components Ltd* [1997] F.S.R. 401 at 419, per Laddie J., ChD.

4–023   It is clear from the provisions relating to kits of parts[54] that an "article" in which design right subsists can be a composite article consisting of many smaller parts. Thus, to take the example discussed above, the engine as a whole enjoys design right. Under s.213(2), the design of the engine will include the shape of the crankshaft, since the crankshaft is a part of the composite article. If the word "article" in subs.213(3)(b) is interpreted as having to refer to the same article as that to which subs.213(2), refers i.e. the engine as a whole, then the features of the crankshaft are not relevant to the way the engine connects to any other article. Thus, those features are not excluded from forming part of the design right in the engine as a whole. If this were right, then the design of the crankshaft would be effectively protectable as part of the design right in the design of the engine as a whole, even if it is not protectable when viewed as design right in the crankshaft as an article in its own right. This interpretation is consistent with the wording of the two subsections, but would appear to undermine the legislative purpose of the "must fit" exclusion. It appears to be on this policy ground that an argument relying on the design right in the composite article to overcome this "must fit" problem was rejected.[55] However, a later case about child safety barriers consisting of a number of components appears to have proceeded on the basis that the "must fit" exclusion applied to the design rights subsisting in the component parts, but did not apply to the design right in the parts when viewed as component parts of the composite article,[56] and the Court of Appeal has declined to resolve the conflict between these two decisions because on the facts of the case it would be obiter.[57] The policy reason for this distinction was said to be because the "must fit" exception was intended to deny protection to articles such as spare parts.[58] The difficulty with this distinction is that if the "must fit" exclusion does not apply to the interfacing aspects of the component part when viewed as a component of a larger article, it would then be an infringement to make and supply the component part whether as part of a composite article or on its own as a spare part. The reason for this is that the spare part manufacturer would still be reproducing the whole of the design in question, namely the design of the *part* of the composite article. The fact that he did not reproduce other parts of the composite article would not help him, because that would only be relevant to infringement

---

[54] CDPA 1988 s.260; and see para.4–040 below.

[55] *Electronic Techniques (Anglia) Ltd v Critchley Components Ltd* [1997] F.S.R. 401 at 416–8, ChD.

[56] *Baby Dan AS v Brevi SRL* [1999] F.S.R. 377.

[57] *Ultraframe (UK) Ltd v Eurocell Building Plastics Ltd* [2005] EWCA Civ 761; [2005] R.P.C. 36, CA at paras 68–69: it would have been obiter because design right subsisted in the assembly as a whole apart from the manner of interconnections and that design right was infringed. At first instance, *Ultraframe (UK) Ltd v Eurocell Building Plastics Ltd*, Lewison J. had simply followed the later of the two conflicting decisions under the rules of precedence without himself preferring one view or the other.

[58] *Ultraframe (UK) Ltd v Eurocell Building Plastics Ltd* [2005] EWCA Civ 761; [2005] R.P.C. 36, CA at 382.

or non-infringement of quite different design rights forming part of the bundle of design rights subsisting in the design of the composite article and all its parts and aspects.[59]

The concept that a single article will give rise not just to one design **4–024** right but a bundle of them, in the whole and in each and every part and every aspect of every part of it, is challenging enough. To that must be added the concept that one particular physical part, if it is a separable component of a larger composite article, will enjoy two legally distinct design rights: one design right in its shape when viewed as an article in its own right, and a legally different design right relating to that same shape when it is viewed as a 'part' of the larger composite article.[60] In these circumstances, whilst it would be possible as a matter of logic for the "must fit" exclusion to apply to one of the legal rights (the design right in the component itself) but not to the other legal right (the design right in the component when viewed as part of the larger article), that would appear to negate the legislative purpose of the exclusion by allowing the design right in the part of the larger article to be enforced against spare parts.

To resolve this problem, one possible interpretation of the statute is to **4–025** say that the article ("an article") referred to in s.213(3)(b) can be any article, and need not be the specific article from whose design right the features are excluded. Alternatively, the puzzle might be better solved by treating the reference to "another article" in s.213(3)(b)(i) as referring to any component of itself when it is the design right of a composite article which is under consideration, as well as to articles which are external to that composite article. There is nothing in the wording of the section which says that the "another article" referred to cannot be a component part within the article whose design right is under consideration. Thus, on this interpretation, if one is considering the design right in the engine as a whole, "another article" in s.213(3)(b)(i) can refer to the crankshaft, so that features of the engine as a whole (including the configuration of the engine block) which interfit with the crankshaft are excluded from the design rights in the engine and its parts (viewed as parts of the engine). Equally, on this interpretation, the engine block is "another article", so that any feature of the composite engine (including features of the crankshaft when viewed as part of the design right in the composite engine) which fits the engine block is excluded from design right. It is

---

[59] For discussion of the concept of a bundle of design rights, see para.4–097, below.

[60] In fact, the position is even more complex than that, because every aspect of every part of the component will be covered by two legally distinct design rights, one being the design of that aspect when viewed as part of the component article and one being the design of that aspect when viewed as a (proportionately smaller) part of the composite article. In the case of an article which is a component of a sub-assembly within a larger article, there could even be three design rights per aspect: for example, a crankshaft within and engine within a car. The bearing surface of the crankshaft is still an aspect of a part of the car, as well as being an aspect of part of the engine and an aspect of a part of the crankshaft.

submitted that this interpretation, whilst the matter is of mind-boggling complexity, is consistent both with the policy and with the wording of these provisions.

The "must match" exclusion

4–026   Subsection 213(3)(b)(ii) of the CDPA 1988 excludes from the scope of design right features of shape or configuration "which are dependent upon the appearance of another article of which the article is intended by the designer to form an integral part". It is the aesthetic counterpart of the "must fit" exception which was considered in the last paragraph. The "must fit" exception covers the case of spare parts etc. which need to be made in a certain shape for functional reasons; the "must match" exception covers the case where they need to be made in a certain way for aesthetic reasons to fit in with the appearance of the greater article of which they are to form part. The "must match" exclusion is narrower in that it only applies to an article which is intended to be an "integral part" of another article; thus it is not enough if an article needs to match another article against which it is placed but does not form part of, as for example a kitchen unit which needs to match the kitchen units against which it is placed.[61] It seems that in order for the exception to apply, there must be a sufficient degree of need to adopt the features concerned, and the fact that adopting certain features helps to achieve a consistent theme is not necessarily sufficient to engage the "must match" exclusion.[62] There is a precisely equivalent exclusion in the case of pre-2001 registered designs,[63] which was considered by the RDAT[64] and the Queen's Bench Divisional Court on a judicial review of the RDAT's decision.[65] The designs of components for cars such as main body panels, doors, bonnet lids, boot lids, and windscreens were held to consist only of features which fell within the "must match" exclusion. These parts, according to the reasoning of the RDAT,[66] form part of and contribute to the overall shape and appearance of the vehicle. As the Divisional Court put it, there is no "design freedom" for the suppliers of this category of parts, having regard to the need to comply with the overall design of the car as a whole. For this purpose, the overall design was the design of the car *including* the

---

[61] *Mark Wilkinson Furniture Ltd v Woodcraft Designs (Radcliffe) Ltd* [1998] F.S.R. 63, ChD. At 73, the court rejected an argument that the fitted kitchen as a whole was to be regarded as an "article" of which each unit was an integral part.

[62] *Ultraframe UK Ltd v Fielding* [2003] R.P.C. 435 at 460, para.79 per Laddie J.; it appears that the conservatory parts there under consideration were of "little visual impact."

[63] RDA(A) s.1(1)(b)(ii): see para.3–041 above.

[64] *Ford Motor Co Ltd's and Iveco Fiat SpA's Design Appns* [1993] R.P.C. 399, RDAT (Julian Jeffs Q.C.).

[65] *Ford Motor Co Ltd's Design Appns* [1994] R.P.C. 545, QBD. For the mechanism of effective appeal by way of judicial review of decisions of the Registered Designs Appeal Tribunal, see para.2–137 above.

[66] *Ford Motor Co Ltd's and Iveco Fiat SpA's Design Appns* [1993] R.P.C. 399 at 417 lines 34–43, RDAT (Julian Jeffs Q.C.).

part concerned, not the design of the car minus the part.[67] The Court of Appeal has held that the approach of the RDAT in that case is to be followed in the context of unregistered design right, and that as a practical matter the design of the part concerned must be dependent upon the appearance of the overall article so that if there is design freedom there is no dependency.[68]

This category of parts are to be distinguished from parts which, while   **4–027** in situ are contributing features to the appearance of the vehicle, are subsidiary to its essential shape and include wing mirrors, wheels, seats, and the steering wheel, where substitutions are possible while leaving the general shape and appearance unchanged; i.e. in these cases the supplier of the spare part has design freedom to provide, e.g. sportier looking wheels or more comfortable seats, without detracting from the design of the car as a whole.[69]

In the context of unregistered designs, it is important to decide whether   **4–028** one is considering design right in the composite article of which the smaller article forms part (of which the design of the smaller article may potentially form a protectable aspect because its shape is the shape of part of the composite article falling within s.213(2) of the CDPA 1988), or the design right in the part viewed as an article in its own right. This point is discussed in the last paragraph in relation to the "must fit" exception, and similar arguments would appear to apply. In addition, the same point can be made as in relation to the "must fit" exception, that the exclusion does not simply protect the makers of spare parts as such, but, being an exclusion from subsistence rather than an exception to infringement, it applies to shield persons who copy the excluded features regardless of the purpose for which they do so.

Unregistered design right does not cover surface decoration

As has already been pointed out,[70] unregistered design right differs from   **4–029** registered designs in that it only relates to the "shape and configuration" of an article, i.e. the three-dimensional aspects of its design. Registered designs can relate either to shape and configuration, or to pattern and ornament, or indeed to a combination of two-and three-dimensional elements.[71]

---

[67] *Ford Motor Co Ltd's Design Appns* [1994] R.P.C. 545 at 554, lines 27–37, QBD. And see *Valeo Vision SA v Flexible Lamps Ltd* [1995] R.P.C. 205, ChD, at 218 (car light cluster lenses).

[68] *Dyson Ltd v Qualtex (UK) Ltd* [2006] EWCA Civ 166; [2006] R.P.C. 31, CA, paras 58–64. Thus, the design of the handle of a vacuum cleaner wand was not dependent upon the appearance of the wand to which it was attached or of the overall machine, and the "must match" exclusion did not apply.

[69] *Ford Motor Co Ltd's and Iveco Fiat SpA's Design Appns* [1993] R.P.C. 399 at 420, lines 25–30, RDAT.

[70] See para.4–003 above.

[71] See paras 3–017 to 3–024 above.

4–030   It is thus implicit in the definition of design in CDPA 1988 s.213(2) that unregistered design right is concerned with three-dimensional design only. However, in addition, s.213(3)(c) specifically excludes "surface decoration" from the scope of the right. This is presumably because decorative patterns can be applied to surfaces as slightly raised lines or grooves, or as other features which have depth in space. Such patterns would at least arguably consist of features of shape, and could therefore fall within the scope of unregistered design right if this specific exclusion had not been inserted in the Act. It is the intention of the Act that surface decoration should be protectable by way of copyright, not unregistered design right.[72] In general, this is more beneficial because copyright protection will give rise to a far longer effective term of protection.[73]

4–031   It is implicit in the use of the word "decoration" that the surface features should have an aesthetic purpose rather than a functional one. Surface features which are primarily decorative but have a limited functional purpose still count as surface decoration,[74] but surface features which have significant function do not count as "surface decoration" even if they have some aesthetic appeal.[75] But surface features which are purely functional would not count as "surface decoration" and would not be within this specific exclusion. However, there is still room to argue that functional features which are applied to a surface and have some height, but are essentially a two-dimensional pattern, are not "features of shape or configuration" which fall within the definition of design[76] to begin with. In the registered design[77] context, there has been some consideration of the distinction between shape and configuration on the one hand, and pattern and ornament on the other hand.[78] In *Cow & Co Ltd v Cannon Rubber Manufacturers Ltd*,[79] the ribbing applied to the surface of a hot water bottle was held to fall within the statement of novelty which referred to "shape or configuration" of the article. However, on the

---

[72] CDPA 1988 s.51 prevents the making of articles (other than artistic works) to a design falling within the scope of copyright infringement. However, s.51(3) specifically excludes "surface decoration" from the definition of design for that purpose, meaning that copyright in, e.g. a drawing, can be infringed by the application of surface decoration to an article. See para.5–084 below.

[73] In this context, effectively 25 years after first marketing of articles to which the pattern has been applied; see para.5–808 below.

[74] *Helmet Integrated Systems Ltd v Mitchell Tunnard* [2006] EWPCC 1; [2006] F.S.R. 41, H.H. Judge Fysh: scalloping incorporated in order to improve the helmet's appearance, and the incidental effect of stiffening the visor cover was incidental and did not take this feature of the helmet outside the "surface decoration" exclusion: paras 99–102. And see *Dyson Ltd v Qualtex (UK) Ltd* [2006] EWCA Civ 166; [2006] R.P.C. 31, CA at para.38(c).

[75] *Dyson Ltd v Qualtex (UK) Ltd* [2006] EWCA Civ 166; [2006] R.P.C. 31, CA at paras 83–84: e.g. ribbing on a handle which provides grip.

[76] CDPA 1988 s.213(2), para.4–003 above.

[77] Of course, surface features which were entirely functional would not fall within the scope of the registered design at all, because they would lack eye appeal; see para.3–047 above.

[78] See para.3–017 above.

[79] [1959] R.P.C. 240. See also *Sommer Allibert (UK) v Flair Plastics Ltd* [1987] R.P.C. 599, CA: grooves moulded into the surface of plastic garden chairs.

reasoning of the Court,[80] this appeared to rest on the conclusion that there is an overlap between "shape and configuration" and "pattern and ornament", and these particular features could be regarded as falling within either.

If it is right to consider that features such as surface ribbing are "shape **4–032** or configuration" (even if they are capable of counting as "pattern or ornament" as well), then it would seem that purely functional surface features will fall within the scope of design right provided that they have some height perpendicular to the surface: for example, the pattern formed by the copper conductors on a printed circuit board. The copper conductors genuinely have some height, albeit a small one, above the underlying insulating board, and it is the shape of the copper which performs the function of making the correct electrical connections for the circuit to function.[81]

But what if the surface features have a mixed purpose which is both **4–033** aesthetic and functional, such as an ornate pattern of heating conductors laid onto the surface of a hot plate for keeping dinner dishes warm? In the registered design context, features which serve both a functional and an aesthetic purpose are treated as having "eye appeal" and therefore can form part of what is protected by the registered design.[82] It has been held in the unregistered design right context that features which are decorative and also have a functional purpose are "surface decoration" and that such features need not be wholly decorative.[83] If such mixed-purpose features are excluded from design right, they will normally enjoy the greater protection of copyright; purely functional surface features consisting of shape necessarily fall within the scope of design right and so enjoy its more limited protection.

What is a "surface feature"?

A feature which is truly three-dimensional, rather than a surface feature, **4–034** will fall outside the scope of the exclusion from design right (i.e. will therefore be covered by design right), regardless of whether its purpose is functional or decorative. The fact that a design feature exists in a third dimension, but only in a small third dimension, does not mean that it must be surface decoration: there is a value judgment for the court to make.[84]

---

[80] Lloyd-Jacob J. at 244 lines 12–28.
[81] This point is considered further in the context of the special rules applying to unregistered designs in semiconductor topographies; see para.10–004 below.
[82] See para.3–061 above.
[83] *Mark Wilkinson Furniture Ltd v Woodcraft Designs (Radcliffe) Ltd* [1998] F.S.R. 63. Surface decoration includes both decoration lying on the surface of the article and decorative features formed in the surface itself.
[84] *A Fulton Co Ltd v Grant Barnett & Co Ltd* [2001] R.P.C. 257 at 280 paras 78–79, Park J.,

4–035   In the registered design case already referred to in the previous paragraph, *Cow & Co Ltd v Cannon Rubber Manufacturers Ltd*[85] the ribbing on the surface of a hot water bottle was held to count as part of the "shape or configuration" of the hot water bottle, but apparently on the basis that certain features can be regarded both as "shape and configuration" and "pattern and ornament".[86] If this is right, then the ribbing on the hot water bottle is a very good example of features which count as "shape or configuration" and so fall within the definition of "design" in s.213(2) of the CDPA 1988, but are also "surface decoration" and are therefore excluded from the scope of unregistered design right by virtue of s.213(3)(c) of the CDPA 1988.

4–036   Some further guidance on the distinction between two-and three-dimensional shapes may be gleaned from cases under the now repealed subs.9(8) of the Copyright Act 1956, the so-called "non-expert recognition" test.[87] The subsection only applied to the reproduction in three dimensions of a two-dimensional work. It is worth considering two contrasting examples.

4–037   (1) *Lerose Ltd v Hawick Jersey Intl Ltd.*[88] Infringement was alleged of drawings which consisted of "point patterns" for knitting. The defendants argued that the knitted fabric was a reproduction of the point patterns in three dimensions, because the different stitches represented on the point pattern drawing resulted in a pattern in the knitted fabric which had height and depth. It was held that subs.9(8) was intended to apply to things which were "essentially" three-dimensional objects, and that fabrics of this kind "are no more three dimensional objects than would be woven fabrics on which patterns were printed".

4–038   (2) *Guilford Knapwood Ltd v Embsay Fabrics Ltd.*[89] The defendants copied a method of reinforcing the edges of the holes in warp-knitted fabric which involved an asymmetrical arrangement of threads. Walton J. considered this to be a reproduction of the claimant's lapping diagram in three dimensions, so falling within the ambit of subs.9(8).

4–039   The distinction between the two cases is that in *Lerose*, the copyright work was concerned with producing a decorative pattern on the knitted fabric, the fact that this consisted of raised and lowered areas being a means to this end. In the *Guilford* case, the copyright work was essentially concerned with a way of arranging the threads in three dimensions. Thus,

---

holding that raised seams at the edges and corners of an umbrella case were not surface decoration but were significant aspects of the shape or configuration of the case, serving to accentuate its rectangular box-like character. See also *Mark Wilson Furniture Ltd v Woodcraft Design (Radcliffe) Ltd* [1998] F.S.R. 63.

[85] [1959] R.P.C. 240.
[86] Lloyd-Jacob J. at 244 lines 12–28.
[87] See para.5–104 below.
[88] [1974] R.P.C. 42 at 50, per Whitford J.
[89] [1983] F.S.R. 567, Ch D.

although the works in each case were presumably of comparable thickness, the essential difference in the nature of the designs embodied in the copyright works in each case made it right to treat one as essentially two dimensional and the other as essentially three dimensional. While the courts are not bound to follow authorities under the repealed subs.9(8) when they come to approach the question of what is or is not shape or configuration, or surface decoration, in the context of unregistered design right, it is submitted that the approach adopted in these two cases is likely to prove helpful.

Unregistered design right and kits of parts

For the purposes of unregistered design right, a kit of parts is treated for all purposes in the same way as if it had been an assembled article. This follows from s.260 of the CDPA 1988, which applies the provisions of Pt III of that Act to kits in the same way as they apply to the assembled article. It defines a kit as "a complete or substantially complete set of components intended to be assembled into an article".[90] Thus, for the purposes of subsistence of design right, the bundle of design rights subsisting in a kit will include the shape and configuration of the assembled article as a whole. Subsection 260(2) specifically states that the section "does not affect the question whether design right subsists in any aspect of the design of the components of a kit as opposed to the design of the assembled article." As has already been pointed out,[91] the design of a component which is a part of a greater article can qualify for design right either viewed as a part of the greater article (since "design" includes the shape of any part of an article[92]) or viewed as an article in its own right, and therefore in this respect the deeming provision of s.260 would not affect the protectability of the design of a component even without this exclusion in subs.260(2). A more complex question is whether the application of the "must match" exception[93] to an article which is a component of a greater article can depend upon whether one is considering its design as the design of a part of the greater article, or as an article in its own right. The provisions of s.260 would appear to put a kit of parts for assembly into a composite article in precisely the same position as an assembled composite article, whatever is the correct answer to this problem. **4–040**

Section 260 will also have the effect of applying the provisions of the Act on infringement to kits of parts as if they were assembled articles. **4–041**

---

[90] CDPA 1988 s.260(1).
[91] See para.4–023 above.
[92] CDPA 1988 s.213(2).
[93] CDPA s.213(3)(b)(i), considered in para.4–026 above.

2. Originality and Qualification for Subsistence

Originality of a design

4–042   Unregistered design right will subsist in a design only if the design is "original".[94] There is a partial definition of what is original in CDPA 1988 s.213(4):

> "(4) A design is not 'original' for the purposes of this Part if it is commonplace in the design field in question at the time of its creation."

4–043   It should be noted that this does not purport to be a comprehensive definition of "original". In other words, it does not say that any design which is not "commonplace" is automatically original. Rather, this subsection is either inserted out of an abundance of caution, or it is excluding a certain category of designs, those that are "commonplace", from attracting design right even if they would otherwise have counted as being original. The latter interpretation is now the established judicial view.[95]

4–044   It has been held that "original" here is being used in the same sense as in the law of copyright.[96] Unregistered design right, like copyright, is an unregistered right and copying is an essential element of infringement. Thus, "original" means that the design has been originated by the author, in the sense of not having been copied from a previous design, and the author has expended sufficient skill or labour on its creation that it can fairly be counted as original.[97] It is therefore irrelevant (subject to the exclusion of "commonplace" designs considered below[98]) that a design is not novel, in the sense that it exists already, provided that the author has originated the same design independently and has not copied from it.[99] Of course, to infringe the author's unregistered design right, a third party

---

[94] CDPA 1988 s.213(1).

[95] *Ocular Sciences Ltd v Aspect Vision Care Ltd* [1997] R.P.C. 289 at 429, considered further at para.4–042 per Laddie J., Pat Ct; *Farmer's Build Ltd v Carier Bulk Materials Handling Ltd* [1999] R.P.C. 461, CA, per Mummery L.J. at 482 lines 24–28.

[96] *Farmer's Build Ltd v Carier Bulk Materials Handling Ltd* [1999] R.P.C. 461, CA, at 475 lines 13–23 per Mummery L.J.; *C & H Engineering v F. Klucznik & Sons Ltd* [1992] F.S.R. 421 at 427, Aldous J; *Parker v Tidball* [1997] F.S.R. 680 at 689, ChD; *Sales v Stromberg* [2005] EWHC 1624 (Ch); [206] F.S.R. 7, R.Wyand Q.C. at paras 34 et seq. For the authorities on originality in the copyright context, see para.5–037 below.

[97] Simplicity of the design as such does not prevent it counting as original: *Sales v Stromberg* [2005] EWHC 1624 (Ch); [206] F.S.R. 7, R.Wyand Q.C. at para.24: a simple geometric shape might or might not be commonplace in the design field in question: see para.4–45 below. For protection of very simple works in the copyright context, see paras 5–009 et seq. below.

[98] See para.4–045 below.

[99] Unregistered Community design right is different: in order for that right to subsist, the design in question must be objectively new and satisfy the test of individual character having regard to all available prior art, whether or not the designer copied from it or even knew of its existence: see para.2–011 above.

must be shown to have copied from the author's design rather than from the previous third party design.[100] Little assistance is to be derived from the meaning of the word "original" as part of the phrase "new or original" which existed in the requirement for a registrable design in the RDA 1949 before its amendment by the CDPA 1988.[101]

Exclusion from protection of "commonplace" designs

Subsection 213(4) of the CDPA 1988[102] excludes from counting as "original", and hence excludes from enjoying unregistered design right protection, any design which is "commonplace in the design field in question". There is no statutory definition of the word "commonplace". Therefore the word is presumably to be given its ordinary dictionary definition of something which is common or trite. The word has no domestic legislative history, but its use can be traced back[103] to its use in the 1987 EEC Directive,[104] which required member states to give protection to semiconductor topographies.[105] In the light of this background, Laddie J. has said[106]:   **4–045**

> "Any design which is trite, trivial, common-or-garden, hackneyed or of the type which would excite no peculiar attention in those in the relevant art is likely to be commonplace. This does not mean that a design made up of features which, individually, are commonplace is necessarily itself commonplace. But to secure protection, the combination must itself not be commonplace ... In many cases the run of the mill combination of well known features will produce a design which is itself commonplace."

The exercise of deciding whether or not a design is commonplace is necessarily an objective[107] exercise of comparing the design with earlier well known designs in "the design field in question at the time of its creation". In this respect (in contrast with the requirement of originality which is subjective as regards what was known to the designer and what he based his work on) it has been described as introducing a consideration that is "akin to novelty".[108] In considering this issue, "the design field   **4–046**

---

[100] See para.4–093 below.
[101] For consideration of the judicial dicta on this point, see para.3–160 above.
[102] Quoted in para.4–042 above.
[103] *Ocular Sciences Ltd v Aspect Vision Care Ltd* [1997] R.P.C. 289 at 429, line 1, per Laddie J., Pat Ct.
[104] Council Directive 87/54/EEC, Art.2(2); see App.C4 below.
[105] The special design right pertaining to semiconductor topographies, which originated from a special international treaty, is considered at paras 10–001 et seq., below.
[106] *Ocular Sciences Ltd v Aspect Vision Care Ltd* [1997] R.P.C. 289 at 429 line 48; he went on to hold that certain designs for contact lenses were commonplace (430, lines 7–34).
[107] *Farmers Build Ltd v Carier Ltd* [1999] R.P.C. 461 at 482, line 29, per Mummery L.J.
[108] *C & H Engineering v F. Klucznik & Sons Ltd* [1992] F.S.R. 421 at 428, per Aldous J., ChD.

in question" is to be considered broadly, and should not be over-narrowed, for example by distinguishing between the field of sports clothing and the field of leisure clothing.[109] Nor should the design field be over-broadened and it should have reference to the purpose of the article.[110] Nor should old designs be disregarded, at least in a case where there exists a trend for present-day designers to look back at "vintage" products,[111] or where old designs could still be seen day to day by members of the public as features of old buildings.[112] It has been suggested in the Court of Appeal that products made by the parties to the action or persons connected with the parties are to be disregarded when considering the issue of whether a design is commonplace.[113] With respect, it is difficult to understand the rationale for such an exclusion, which gains no support from the statutory language. It should be recalled that the question of whether or not a design is commonplace is, by s.213(4), to be assessed "at the time of its creation".[114] If a designer creates a new article which subsequently becomes very popular, that does not undermine the validity of his design because nothing that happens later can retrospectively make it commonplace at the time of its creation. If he subsequently creates a different design which adopts features from his

[109] *Lambretta Clothing Co Ltd v Teddy Smith (UK) Ltd* [2004] EWCA (Civ) 886 at paras 43–47; *Ultraframe (UK) Ltd v Eurocell Building Plastics Ltd* [2005] EWCA Civ 761; [2005] R.P.C. 36, CA at paras 51–55: it is not appropriate for an expert witness to give evidence as to what is "the design field in question", which is a matter for the court, but the court will take into account evidence about the perspective of typical designers of articles of the kind in question, e.g. what range of articles would such designers expect to be familiar with, and what trade exhibitions they would be likely to attend. Thus, a designer of conservatory roofs would have a wider perspective than just conservatory roofs and would be familiar with all aspects of conservatory design and with windows and doors outside the conservatory field.

[110] *Sales v Stromberg* [2005] EWHC 1624 (Ch); [206] F.S.R. 7, R.Wyand Q.C. at paras 49 et seq.: the articles were decorative pendants used in complementary medicine and the court rejected an suggestion by the defendant that the design field be broadened to "artefacts referencing imagery associated with ancient and indigenous cultures ... and alternative/New Age interests such as healing."

[111] *Sales v Stromberg* [2005] EWHC 1624 (Ch); [206] F.S.R. 7, R.Wyand Q.C. at para.52.

[112] *Scholes Windows Ltd v Magnet Ltd* [2002] F.S.R. 172, CA; window designs: "The statutory question [of what is commonplace] does not depend on when other designs in the design field with which comparison is made were first produced or on when they were in use or whether they have fallen into disuse and become 'historical designs' ... There is nothing in these provisions which expressly or impliedly excludes from consideration existing designs, which were first produced at an earlier time than the design in suit, if they can be fairly and reasonably regarded as included in the design field in question at the time of creation of the design in suit. The fact that they could still be seen by designers and members of the public as a feature of windows on many houses in July 1994 is a relevant factor in deciding whether or not they were in the design field at the date of creation and were commonplace within the meaning of subsection (4)." para.44, per Mummery L.J.

[113] *Farmer's Build Ltd v Carier Ltd* [1999] R.P.C. 461, CA, at p.482 lines 21–23.

[114] There seems to be some confusion on this point within the *Farmer's Build* judgment, since at p.482, lines 13–15 it is suggested that the design of the article in which design right is claimed should be compared with the design of other articles in the same field "including the alleged infringing article". However, the alleged infringing article cannot possibly exist at the time of creation of the design in which design right is claimed: if it did, the action would fail at the outset because it could not possibly have been copied from it.

first design, there seems no reason either on the statutory wording or for reasons of policy to disregard his own prior product in the assessment of whether or not those features are commonplace: the same design cannot, at the same date, be commonplace when created by one person and not commonplace when created by someone else.[115] Nor is there any reason to disregard a defendant's prior designs in the assessment of what is commonplace, unless perhaps they are actually unlawful as infringements.

In considering what effect is to be given to the exclusion of protection of "commonplace" designs, it should be borne in mind that design right is capable of subsisting not merely in the shape or configuration of a whole article, but in any aspect of the whole or any part of that shape or configuration. It may be rare that the entire design of a complete article with all its details can be said to be "commonplace"; however, unless an article is of a wholly new kind, or of a very rare kind, there will almost always be aspects of the design of an article which are commonplace, particularly if its features are looked at at a high enough level of generality. The fact that a table has four legs, one at each corner, could be said to be an aspect of its design, but stated as such it is clearly commonplace for tables. It can therefore be seen that the exclusion of "commonplace" designs from counting as original has the effect of restricting the level of generality of the features in which the author of a design is entitled to claim design right. Thus, competitors may copy an article, provided they copy only at such a general level that the features they have copied are commonplace. However, design right may still subsist in the more detailed implementation of features which are commonplace at a general level: **4–047**

"Nevertheless, while I accept that it could be said to be commonplace for a flat folding umbrella to have a roughly rectangular handle, that does not mean that the shape or configuration of any particular handle is commonplace merely because it is roughly rectangular. Within the broad parameters of size and shape which [the defendant] says are to be expected of handles for flat folding umbrellas, there is considerable scope for detailed design work to be undertaken, and for the creation of a shape or configuration which has its own special qualities and which is not commonplace."[116]

---

[115] It can of course be original when created by one designer without reference to a previous design, and unoriginal when created by another designer who copied it from prior art.

[116] *A Fulton & Co Ltd v Grant Barnett & Co Ltd* [2001] R.P.C. 257 at 275 para.28 per Park J.; and see *Scholes Windows Ltd v Magnet Ltd* [2000] F.S.R. 432 at 442, ChD, where it was held that small shifts to a line or an angle or an arc may in some contexts make a difference between a design working and not working, in which case such small differences may make a design non-commonplace as compared with other superficially similar designs.

In addition to the case where the overall shape of an article is common-place when considered at a certain level of generality, there will be cases where small details or embellishments or other features will be com-monly used in the industry. The effect of the exclusion of "commonplace" designs is that such features may freely be copied, with the proviso that the particular way in which commonplace details are deployed may be the subject of valid design right and so protectable.[117]

4–048   Given that it is now settled that the word "original" has the meaning ascribed to it in para.4–044, it may be asked what (if any) additional restriction is placed on the word "original" by the exclusion of common-place designs. If an aspect of a design is commonplace, it is very likely that the author of the design of an article will have copied that aspect from pre-existing articles. If so, that aspect will not in any event be original, i.e. will not have originated with the author. The exclusion of commonplace designs would however bite even in a case where the author has devised that aspect of the design for himself, not knowing that it is in commonplace use already and not having himself copied it from a preceding article or articles. What legislative purpose is served by such an exclusion? The answer is twofold. First, it obviates the need to prove that the author of the design sued upon has in fact derived commonplace design features from previous articles; it can therefore be viewed effec-tively as an irrebuttable presumption which obviates the need to prove something which is normally wholly within the knowledge of the opposing party and easy to deny.[118] Secondly, it provides reasonable certainty to a person who wants to copy a competitor's product that, provided he restricts himself to copying features which are known by him to be commonplace, he does not risk infringement of design right because of a quirk in the subjective way in which the particular designer has created his design.

4–049   The evidence required to show that some feature, or a design as a whole, is commonplace, will require the court to survey, normally with the assistance of expert evidence, the prior designs available in the design field in question and then ask itself, as a matter of fact and degree, whether or not it is "commonplace",[119] that being an ordinary English word which does not benefit from further judicial elaboration.[120] Although under registered designs law there are a number of authorities on the possibly related concept of what counts as a "variant commonly used in the trade",[121] the courts have resisted the application of that

---

[117] *Farmer's Build Ltd v Carier Ltd* [1999] R.P.C. 461, CA at 476, line 11: "A new and exciting design could be produced out of trite ingredients and the application of the simplest engineering principles."

[118] The history of litigation shows that in certain industries—the garment industry being the best known example—false claims to having originated design features, or whole designs, are frequently made.

[119] *Farmer's Build Ltd v Carier Ltd* [1999] R.P.C. 461, CA, at 481.

[120] *Farmer's Build Ltd v Carier Ltd* [1999] R.P.C. 461, CA at 479 lines 31–44.

[121] See para.3–154 above.

concept to the different test of "commonplace" for unregistered design right purposes.[122]

One question left open by the Act is whether the design concerned **4–050** needs to be commonplace within the United Kingdom, or whether one can consider the "design field in question"[123] across the world. In the registered design field, consideration of prior art was restricted to that available within the United Kingdom,[124] but this is for historical reasons, and has been abandoned in the context of patents since the Patents Act 1977. However, in one case it has been held that the inquiry as to what is commonplace is limited to what is available *in the United Kingdom* at the time the design was created.[125] It appeared that the court was primarily concerned with the fact that the territorial scope of a design right is limited to the United Kingdom and asked why a design should be deprived of protection here because it is commonplace in Vanuatu? However, it should be noted that in the case of registered designs the RDA 1949 expressly limited consideration of prior art to the territory of the United Kingdom[126] but the unregistered design right provisions of CDPA 1988 contain no such express limitation. Furthermore, a design created anywhere in the world can qualify for design right protection (even though there are restrictive requirements regarding the nationality of the designer or first owner of the design). And an alleged infringing design can be created in any country of the world and the articles subsequently imported to the United Kingdom at which point the question of infringement arises. What if a design is commonplace in its country of origin where articles of that kind are widely made and used, but is not commonplace within the United Kingdom because they are not extensively imported here at the time? What if certain design features are commonplace in the country where the defendant's design originated so that the designer of the defendant's article legitimately assumed that those features could freely be copied? Is it appropriate that the designer of the claimant's article gets wide protection because commonplace features become a rarity on importation of articles into the United Kingdom—in effect, a kind of quasi "patent of importation"?[127] It would

---

[122] *Farmer's Build Ltd v Carier Ltd* [1999] R.P.C. 461, CA at 481 lines 28–32 per Mummery L.J.: "Section 213(4) is not an indirect imposition of novelty as a condition for the subsistence of design right. In this context 'commonplace' does not mean 'not novel'. It is also inappropriate to apply in this context related concepts of registered design and patent law, such as 'variants commonly used in the trade' (s.1(4) R.D.A. 1949) and 'the state of the art.'"

[123] Words used in CDPA 1988 s.213(4).

[124] See para.3–143 above.

[125] *A Fulton Co Ltd v Totes Isotoner (UK) Ltd* [2003] R.P.C. 499 at paras 68–74, Pat Cty Ct. This point was not included in the appeal to the Court of Appeal.

[126] Since amended under the harmonised European system to what was available to interested trade circles in the European Community—see para.2–072 above.

[127] When available patent prior art was limited to the territory of the UK, it was possible to obtain a patent of importation by obtaining an invention overseas and patenting it here: indeed, the patent system positively encouraged the stealing of foreigners' inventions in order to put them into use in the United Kingdom.

be startling, for example in a case about Iranian-style garment designs if the court were limited to looking only at those Iranian garments that happened to have been imported into the United Kingdom when it considered what was commonplace.[128] It is submitted that the trend has increasingly been to look at intellectual property rights on a global basis in conjunction with the increasing trend towards globalisation of trade, and that even by 1988 the territorial restriction on prior art under the RDA 1949 was a historical relic which had been swept away from the field of patents by the Patents Act 1977. It is therefore hard to justify the introduction of a new territorial limitation on the consideration of prior art in the CDPA 1988 merely by implication.

Prerequisites for subsistence of design right

4–051 Design right does not subsist unless and until the design has been recorded in a design document or an article has been made to the design.[129] Thus, the design of an intended article which exists just as an idea in someone's head, or is the subject of oral discussion, does not enjoy design right until the design has been fixed in one of these ways. A "design document" is defined as[130] "any record of a design, whether in the form of a drawing, a written description, a photograph, data stored in a computer or otherwise".

4–052 One question which arises is whether design right subsists when a mould is made for an article, assuming that the mould was made without any pre-existing drawing or other record of the design of the intended article. Clearly, design right will subsist once the first article is struck from the mould. However, it seems that design right will not subsist from the making of the mould itself, unless the mould is to be regarded as a "design document". Whilst the mould is clearly in one sense a record of the design of the intended article, it is hard to envisage it as falling into the category of a design "document".

4–053 In the case of an article which is to be assembled, design right will subsist as soon as a complete or substantially complete set of components intended for its assembly is brought together: this is the effect of the provision treating kits of parts as if they were assembled articles.[131]

4–054 Apart from the requirement that the design be fixed in the way set out above, in order for design right to subsist, the right qualifications must be fulfilled as regards the national connections of the design. The requirements are complex, and have the underlying policy purpose of denying design right protection to individuals and businesses from countries

---

[128] See *Guild v Eskander Ltd* [2003] F.S.R. 23, CA. The point was not argued in the case, presumably because to argue that investigation of prior art should be limited to the United Kingdom is such a case would have exposed the absurdity of the argument.

[129] CDPA 1988 s.213(6).

[130] CDPA 1988 s.263(1).

[131] CDPA 1988 s.260; see para.4–040 above.

under whose laws British designs do not enjoy similar protection. There are three alternative bases on which a design can qualify: (1) by reference to the nationality (or country of habitual residence) of the designer or his employer or the person who commissioned the design[132]; or (2) by reference to the country where articles made to the design were first marketed[133]; or (3) by reference to the nationality (or habitual residence) of the person carrying out the first marketing.[134] In addition, the Act confers a general power by Order in Council to widen the grounds of qualification for subsistence of design right in accordance with international treaty obligations, but this power has not yet been exercised.[135]

Nationality of designer, employer or commissioner

When a design is not made in the course of employment, and has not been commissioned for money or money's worth, it is the nationality or the other national connections of the designer which are relevant. It may be worth calling such a design a "freelance" design. Alternatively, if a design has been created in the course of employment or under commission, then it is the nationality or national connections of the employer or commissioner which is relevant. It should be noted that in this latter category of "non-freelance" designs, the nationality of the designer is irrelevant.[136] Thus, if a designer who has qualifying nationality is commissioned to create the design by, or is employed by, a company or individual who does not have qualifying nationality, then design right will not subsist.[137]   **4–055**

A "freelance" design will qualify for unregistered design right if the designer is a qualifying individual.[138] Who will count as a qualifying individual is explained below.[139] In the case of a design which is either made in the course of employment or under commission, design right will subsist if the employer or the commissioner, as the case may be, is a qualifying individual or a qualifying body corporate.[140] In order to decide which of these two mutually exclusive tests of qualification for subsistence are to be applied, it will be necessary to work out the sometimes   **4–056**

---

[132] See para.4–055 below.
[133] See para.4–065 below.
[134] See 87, para.4–067 below.
[135] CDPA 1988 s.221.
[136] CDPA 1988 s.218(1) provides that qualification by reference to designer, applies only to designs which are not made in pursuance of a commission or in the course of employment.
[137] It may come to subsist later, if articles are first marketed in a qualifying country.
[138] CDPA 1988 s.218(2).
[139] See para.4–061 below.
[140] CDPA 1988 s.219(1).

difficult question of whether the design was made in pursuance of a commission[141] or in the course of employment.[142]

4–057   It is not totally clear what happens if a design is made both in pursuance of a commission and in the course of employment. This can happen where someone commissions a company or other employer to create a design, and the actual work of creating the design is done by an employee. On a literal reading of the Act, it should be enough if either the employer or the commissioner is a qualifying person.[143] However, it is clear in such a case that the design right (assuming it subsists) vests in the person giving the commission to the exclusion of both the employer and the designer employee.[144] It is therefore not easy to see why as, a matter of policy, the qualifying status of the employer should remain relevant, since the qualifying status of a self employed designer from whom the same design had been commissioned would not be relevant. Certainly, if it is possible to rely on the qualifying status of the intervening employer in addition to the status of the commissioner in such a situation, it does represent an anomaly.

Qualification in the case of computer generated designs

4–058   If a design is created by a computer rather than by an individual, then the person by whom the arrangements are undertaken is treated as being the designer.[145] The rules as to qualification for subsistence are applied by reference to the status of that person in "freelance" cases where it is the status of the designer that is relevant,[146] and in non-freelance cases by reference to the status of the commissioner and/or employer in the same way as if the design had been made by a human being. Where the computer is programmed and operated by an individual acting in the course of his employment, there could be some doubt as to whether it is the individual who is deemed to be the designer or the employer who is the designer. In most cases, this would make no difference because subsistence would depend upon the qualifying status of the employer rather than the employee in either case. However, it could make a difference where the design is commissioned if the anomaly discussed above is correct, and it is then permissible to rely on the status of both the commissioner and the employer if the employer was the designer; however, alternatively, if the employee himself is the "designer" of the computer generated work then it would clearly not be possible to rely on the employer's status.

[141] See para.4–109 below.
[142] See para.4–112 below.
[143] CDPA 1988 s.219(1) provides for design right to subsist "if it is created in pursuance of a commission from, or in the course of employment with, a qualifying person".
[144] CDPA 1988 s.215(2) and (3); see also as to ownership of design right, para.4–109 below.
[145] CDPA 1988 s.214(2).
[146] CDPA 1988 s.218(2).

Joint designers, employers or commissioners

Special provisions apply where a design is created jointly[147] by more than one person, but one or more but not all of the joint designers are qualifying persons. Basically, unregistered design right does subsist as long as at least one of the joint designers qualifies, but the design right vests only in the designer or designers who do qualify, to the exclusion of those who do not.[148]

4–059

Similar provisions apply where a design is jointly commissioned, and one or more but not all the commissioners are qualifying persons.[149] The same principle also applies when a design is created in the course of employment by joint employers, as might happen is a case where the employer is a partnership.[150]

4–060

Qualifying countries and qualifying persons

It has been explained that the basic purpose of the complex set of rules which make subsistence of unregistered design right depend upon qualifications to do with nationality, is to give design right in the United Kingdom only to designs with an appropriate connection with a country which gives suitable protection under its own laws to designs of British origin. The starting point of the scheme is therefore the list of "qualifying countries" by reference to which design right may subsist. "Qualifying countries" consist, first, of the United Kingdom itself.[151] Secondly, there is a power, not yet exercised, to extend the unregistered design right provisions of the Act, i.e. Pt III of the CDPA 1988, to dependent territories of the United Kingdom by Order in Council.[152]

4–061

Thirdly, the other member states of the European Union[153] count as qualifying countries. In this case, there is a departure from the principle of requiring reciprocal protection for British designs, since all EU member states qualify regardless of the protection or lack of it which they give to designs under their own laws. These countries were all included presumably out of fear that the legislation might otherwise fall foul of what is now art.18 of the TFEU which prohibits discrimination on the ground

4–062

---

[147] Joint design is defined by CDPA 1988 s.259; see para.4–107 below.
[148] CDPA 1988 s.218(3) and (4).
[149] CDPA 1988 s.219(2) and (3).
[150] CDPA 1988 s.219(2) and (3).
[151] CDPA 1988 s.217(3)(a). For the purposes of unregistered design right, the United Kingdom is not deemed to include the Isle of Man: cf. registered designs, para.3–147 above. The Isle of Man is however a "qualifying country" by Order in Council: see n.12 below.
[152] CDPA 1988 s.255(2) confers the power (which has not yet been exercised as of September 2010) but if it is exercised CDPA s.217(3)(b) then has the effect of treating the dependent territory to which Pt III has been extended as a "qualifying country" for the purposes of the subsistence provisions.
[153] CDPA 1988 s.217(3)(c).

of nationality.[153a] Fourthly, there is a list of countries designated by Order in Council as providing reciprocal protection.[154] The countries designated under this provision at present are the Channel Islands and the Isle of Man,[155] Hong Kong,[156] and a number of British colonies and former colonies. The only major independent country at present designated is New Zealand. The limited list of qualifying countries for design right purposes should be contrasted with the much longer list of qualifying countries for copyright purposes.[157] In the case of copyright, it can generally be assumed that works originating from almost all major economies of the world will be entitled to copyright protection in the United Kingdom, but this is far from so in the case of design right.

4–063   Individuals who are citizens of a qualifying country are "qualifying individuals" for design right purposes, as also are individuals who are habitually resident[158] in a qualifying country.[159] Citizens of British colonies were treated differently from full British citizens[160]—they were qualifying individuals only if the colony concerned had had the design right provisions[161] extended to it by Order in Council[162] or if the colony had been designated in the same way as a foreign country under the provisions relating to reciprocal protection.[163]

4–064   Analogous rules apply to companies and other bodies corporate,[164] which for this purpose includes any body having legal personality.[165] A corporation is a qualifying person if it is formed under the law of a qualifying country,[166] or if has a place of business in a qualifying country at which "substantial business activity is carried on".[167] For the purpose of determining whether or not substantial business activity is carried on in a country, no account is to be taken of dealings in goods which at all

---

[153a] See joined cases C-92/92 and C326/92 *Phil Collins v Imtrat* [1993] E.C.R. I-5145, where the ECJ held that denial of performer's right on the grounds that the plaintiff was not a German national was a breach of the then art.12 of the EC Treaty.

[154] CDPA 1988 s.217(3)(d); refers to Orders in Council made under s.256.

[155] The Design Right (Reciprocal Protection) (No.2) Order 1989 (SI 1989/1294), App.C5 below. It should be noted that an order under s.256 merely provides design right protection within the United Kingdom to designs connected with those territories. An Order in Council under s.255 would have the additional effect of extending the British design right provisions to become part of the internal law of the territories concerned.

[156] Presumably the effect of the designation of Hong Kong continues after its reversion to Chinese rule.

[157] See para.5–047 below.

[158] For some reason, in the case of unregistered design right, the qualification is based on habitual residence; this contrasts with the corresponding copyright provision, CDPA 1988 s.154(1)(b), which is based on citizenship, domicile or residence; i.e. qualifying residence need not be habitual for copyright purposes.

[159] CDPA 1988 s.217(1).

[160] CDPA 1988 s.217(4).

[161] i.e. Pt III of the CDPA 1988.

[162] CDPA 1988 s.255.

[163] i.e. by Order in Council under s.256.

[164] Which for this purpose include the Crown and foreign governments; CDPA s.217(2).

[165] CDPA 1988 s.217(1).

[166] CDPA 1988 s.217(1)(a).

[167] CDPA 1988 s.217(1)(b).

material times are outside that country.[168] This is presumably to avoid a company acquiring qualification merely by conducting headquarters or similar activity in a qualifying country.

Qualification for subsistence of design right by first marketing

If a design does not qualify for design right by virtue of the qualifying **4–065** status of the designer, commissioner or employer as discussed above,[169] then an alternative basis is provided on which it may qualify for subsistence of design right. In order for this to happen, two conditions must be satisfied. First, articles to which the design has been applied must be first marketed in the United Kingdom, elsewhere in the European Union, or in a territory to which the unregistered design right provisions, i.e. Pt III of the CDPA 1988, has been extended by Order in Council.[170] It should be noted that this does not include "qualifying countries" which are designated as giving reciprocal protection under s.256 of the CDPA 1988[171]: first marketing in those countries does not count for this purpose.

"Marketing" for this purpose means selling or letting for hire, or **4–066** offering or exposing for sale or hire, in the course of a business.[172] However, no account is to be taken for this purpose of marketing "which is merely colourable and not intended to satisfy the reasonable require- ments of the public."[173] This latter qualification on the definition of marketing is intended to prevent someone qualifying for design right protection by a merely nominal effort at first marketing, and is modelled on the corresponding provision relating to subsistence of copyright.[174] It should be noted that, unlike under copyright law, there is no provision allowing for so-called "simultaneous" publication within a limited period in different countries, so that the first marketing in the qualifying territory must indeed be the first occasion on which articles made to the design are presented to the market anywhere in the world.

The second condition is that these articles should be put on the market **4–067** by a qualifying person, and that that person is "exclusively authorised" to do so by the person who would (had he been qualified) be the first owner of the design right.[175] Exclusive authorisation has an extended meaning[176] which seems intended to include a case where a non- qualifying designer purports to transfer the exclusive right to apply the

---

[168] CDPA 1988 s.217(5).
[169] See para.4–056 above.
[170] CDPA 1988 s.220(1)(b). Part III has not yet been extended to anywhere but the UK; see para.4–061 above.
[171] As to which, see para.4–061 above.
[172] CDPA 1988 s.263(2).
[173] CDPA 1988 s.263(2).
[174] CDPA 1988 s.175(5), although that provision has been so construed by the courts as to leave it without any teeth at all.
[175] CDPA 1988 s.220(1)(a).
[176] What amounts to "exclusively authorised" is defined by s.220(4).

design to the qualifying person who then carries out the first marketing. Since the unregistered design right at this stage does not subsist, there can be no transfer of property in it as such; but presumably it contemplates the case where the original designer either by contract or in equity becomes legally bound[177] not to exploit the design as against the other party.[178]

3. Infringement of Unregistered Design Right

Infringement of unregistered design right

4–068 There are two elements which have to be satisfied in order for there to be an infringement of an unregistered design right, which will be considered in turn in the following paragraphs. These two elements are:

(1) *The defendant's acts:* whether a potential defendant has done an act of a kind which can amount to infringement. In addition to the "primary" acts of infringement set out in s.226(1) quoted above, "secondary" infringement can be committed by such acts as importations and other dealings.[179]

(2) *The design of the article complained of:* whether that design reproduces the design in which design right subsists.[180]

4–069 There will of be a defence if the acts in question are licensed by the design right proprietor, or there may be special defences such as defences under EU law.

Acts of primary infringement

4–070 What amounts to a primary infringement of an unregistered design right is governed by s.226(1) of the CDPA 1988, which provides:

"(1) The owner of design right in a design has the exclusive right to reproduce the design for commercial purposes—

(a) by making articles to that design, or—

(b) by making a design document recording the design for the purpose of enabling such articles to be made."

---

[177] A legally binding obligation on the part of the notional first owner of the notional right not to exploit the design himself is an essential requirement of the definition of exclusive authorisation under s.220(4)(b).

[178] As to first ownership and transmission of unregistered design right, see para.4–123 below.

[179] See paras 4–077 et seq., below.

[180] See paras 4–090 et seq., below. It has surprisingly been held that the test of what amounts to a reproduction differs between whether one is considering reproduction under s.226(1)(a) or (b): see *Soc Esplosivi Industriali SpA v Ordnance Technologies (UK) Ltd* [2007] EWHC 2875 (Ch); [2008] R.P.C. 12, Lindsay J., considered further and criticised at para.4–096 below.

The first act of primary infringement laid down by s.226(1)(a) of the **4–071** CDPA 1988 is that of "making articles" to the design concerned. This is the physical manufacture or bringing into existence of an article in accordance with an infringing design. It should be noted that in the case of an article made up from a number of parts, it is not necessary actually to assemble the parts together in order to "make" the article. The article will have been "made" once a kit of parts for its final assembly has been brought together. This consequence follows from s.260(1) of the CDPA 1988, which applies the design right provisions of the Act to a kit of parts as they apply to a complete article.[181]

In order for there to be infringement, the object made must be an **4–072** "article". It is not clear whether or not a building or structure is an "article" for the purposes of unregistered design right.[182] Usually, this question will arise at the stage of determining whether or not design right subsists at all in a design for the "article" in question, rather than at the stage of deciding whether there is infringement.[183]

The alternative form of primary infringement, contrary to s.226(1)(b), is **4–073** the making of a "design document". This provision seems designed to catch infringements at the stage anterior to actual physical production of articles, so long as the infringing design has been sufficiently recorded on paper, as computer data or otherwise.[184] This provision could have important practical application in a case where an infringing design is originated within the United Kingdom, but actual physical manufacture of articles were contracted out in another country. In such a case, liability for primary infringement would attach to the person doing design work in the United Kingdom. However it has been held that the intention to make actual articles from the design document must be fairly definite at the time when the design is recorded, so that recording designs for the purpose of further development in the course of future design work is not sufficient to come within the scope of s.226(1)(b).[185]

It should be noted that primary infringement of design right does not **4–074** involve any requirement of knowledge or other mental element in order for a person to be guilty of infringement. In this respect, primary

---

[181] For more extensive consideration of the provisions relating to kits of parts, see para.4–040 above.

[182] For consideration of this question, see para.4–007 above. It is clear that a building or structure is not an "article of manufacture" for the purposes of registered designs, but the position regarding unregistered designs is less clear.

[183] Although it is possible that a design for something which clearly is an "article" might be copied in the form of a part of a building or structure: in that case it would be necessary to decide for the purpose of determining infringement whether or not the construction of the building or structure had involved the making of an "article".

[184] For fuller treatment of what counts as "design document", see para.4–051 above.

[185] See *Soc Esplosivi Industriali SpA v Ordnance Technologies (UK) Ltd* [2007] EWHC 2875 (Ch); [2008] R.P.C. 12, Lindsay J. at paras 56–62. This involves reading s.226(1)(b) is requiring an actual subjective purpose on the part of the maker of the document of manufacturing articles at the time of recording the design, as distinct from the reading it simply as requiring the design document to have the objective purpose of *enabling* the making of articles to the design in question, which is what the words of the section actually say; i.e.

infringement differs from secondary infringement.[186] Thus, a person such as a manufacturing subcontractor who innocently executes an order from a customer for what turns out to be an infringing design is an infringer: there is a limited "innocence" defence for acts of primary infringement against damages (but not other remedies)[187] but this depends on proving that the defendant had no reason to believe that design right *subsisted* in the design concerned.

Authorising acts of primary infringement

4–075   Section 226(3) of the CDPA 1988 provides that:

> "(3) Design right is infringed by a person who without the licence of the design right owner does, or authorises another to do, anything which by virtue of this section is the exclusive right of the design right owner."

4–076   The effect of this subsection is that design right is infringed not only by a person who physically makes an infringing article or who physically creates an infringing "design document", but also by any person who "authorises" another person to do these acts. This provision is modelled on the long standing prohibition in copyright law against "authorising" acts of primary infringement.[188] Under copyright law, "authorising" would catch as a primary infringer the publisher who places an order with a printer for the printing of a book, and under unregistered design right law this provision will catch by analogy a customer who places an order with a manufacturing sub-contractor according to a design specified by the customer.[189]

Secondary infringement of design right

4–077   Secondary infringement is concerned with importation, possession, and other dealings with infringing articles. Unlike primary infringement, liability for secondary infringement involves a mental element: the infringer must know or have reason to believe that the articles concerned are infringing articles. Section 227(1) of the CDPA 1988 provides:

for the purpose of *enabling*, not for the purpose of *making*. This interpretation of s.226(1)(b) may create real difficulties in case where an initial sketch or outline design is produced which will normally pass through a number of stages before sufficiently detailed and exact production drawings are produced which can be put into the hands of workshop operatives.

[186] See para.4–077 below.
[187] CDPA 1988 s.223(1): see para.6–040 below.
[188] Now contained in CDPA 1988 s.16(2), but dating back to the Copyright Act 1911 s.1(2).
[189] For fuller discussion of what counts as "authorising" for the purposes of infringement of copyright, see para.6–023 below.

"227.—(1) Design right is infringed by a person who, without the licence of the design right owner—

(a) imports into the United Kingdom for commercial purposes, or
(b) has in his possession for commercial purposes, or
(c) sells, lets for hire, or offers or exposes for sale or hire, in the course of a business,

an article which is, or which he knows or has reason to believe is, an infringing article."

This subsection is closely modelled on the corresponding provisions covering secondary infringement of copyright.[190] **4–078**

What is an "infringing article"?

An infringing article is first and most obviously defined (by CDPA 1988 s.228(2)) as an article whose making to that design was an infringement of the design right in question. However, a design document is specifically excluded from counting as an infringing article, even though its making might have amounted to an infringement of the design right in question.[191] **4–079**

This definition of infringing article adequately deals with the case of an article which has been made within the United Kingdom, since one can then ask whether or not the making of the article amounted to primary infringement. If its making did not infringe for the reason that it was made by the design right owner or with his consent, then it is not an "infringing article" and subsequent dealings with it cannot amount to secondary infringements even if the design right owner does not consent or actively objects. Thus, secondary infringement in the case of articles made within the United Kingdom does not give the design right owner the ability to control subsequent dealings with a lawfully made article in the way in which registered design infringement can do.[192] **4–080**

The making of an imported article will not have constituted infringement of design right for the simple reason that the act of making will have taken place outside the territorial scope of the right, i.e. the United Kingdom.[193] To decide whether an imported article (or an article which is proposed to be imported) is an "infringing article" for the purpose of secondary infringement, Parliament has laid down a hypothetical question in s.228(3)(b) that "its making to that design in the United Kingdom would have been an infringement of design right in the design or a **4–081**

---

[190] CDPA 1988 ss.22 and 23. See para.5–109 below.
[191] CDPA 1988 s.228(6).
[192] See para.3–168 above. This, of course, is subject to the constraints imposed by EU and competition law.
[193] See para.4–086 below.

breach of an exclusive licence agreement relating to the design". This hypothetical question raises no difficulty of application in cases where the imported article was made by a party unconnected with the owner of the design right in the United Kingdom, but does raise some questions of interpretation in a potential "parallel import" case: that is, a case where a third party is seeking to import into the United Kingdom an article which was made by the design right owner in a foreign country or by someone connected with him such as a licensee, assignee or associated or subsidiary company. This subject is more comprehensively dealt with later.[193a]

Dealings in articles after expiry of design right

4–082   The life of unregistered design right is comparatively short,[194] and the transitional effects of the infringement provisions on articles made before expiry may be of significant commercial importance. It seems clear that it is a secondary infringement of design right (provided that the requisite mental element is present) to import or deal with articles even after the design right has expired, provided that the articles concerned were made before expiry of the right. That this is so is suggested by s.228(4) of the CDPA 1988, which provides:

> "(4) Where it is shown that an article is made to a design in which design right subsists or has subsisted at any time, it shall be presumed until the contrary is proved that the article was made at a time when design right subsisted."

4–083   This provision, which applies without distinction to domestic and imported articles, also strongly suggests that the hypothetical test relating to imported articles[195] is to be applied as at the date when the articles were actually made in their country of origin, and not on some later date such as the date of importation to the United Kingdom.

Infringing act must be done for commercial purposes

4–084   All forms of infringement of unregistered design right involve commercial activity. Thus, a primary infringement (of making an article or design document) must be done "for commercial purposes" to amount to infringement.[196] Both the secondary infringements of importation and possession must likewise be "for commercial purposes" in order to

---

[193a] At paras 9–009—9–014 below.
[194] 10 years, for some purposes effectively cut to five by the licence of right provisions, compared with copyright which may last for the life of the author plus 70 years.
[195] See para.4–079.
[196] CDPA 1988 s.226(1), quoted in para.4–068 above.

amount to infringement[197]; whilst sale, letting for hire etc. must be "in the course of a business." The definition of "commercial purposes" is restrictive: it says that the acts must be done "with a view to the article in question being sold or hired in the course of a business."[198] "Business" is defined as including a trade or profession.[199]

The definition of "commercial purposes" does not cover all activities **4–085** that one would think of as being commercial. For example, if a manufacturer builds a machine which he intends to use as a piece of capital equipment in his own factory, with no intention of selling it or hiring it out, the making of the machine would appear to fall outside the definition of "commercial purposes" and so the making and subsequent use of the machine would not amount to infringement. Furthermore, one consequence of the definition of infringing article (as being an article whose making is or would be an infringement of design right[200]) is that an article made for private and non-business purposes would not be an infringing article. Its subsequent commercial sale, even if clearly in the course of a business, would not amount to infringement of design right.[201]

Territorial scope of infringement

To amount to infringement of design right, acts generally need to take **4–086** place within the territorial scope of Pt III of the CDPA 1988, which is the United Kingdom (including for this purpose territorial waters and fixed Continental Shelf installations[202]). In addition, there is a power to extend Pt III to dependent territories of the United Kingdom which has not yet been exercised.[203]

However, there are certain exceptions. There seems no reason why a **4–087** person who is physically abroad cannot be liable for primary infringement by authorising an act (such as making an article) which takes place within the United Kingdom.[204] In addition, a person can incur liability for joint tortfeasance through the agency of another, and need not be physically present in order to incur liability of this nature.[205]

---

[197] CDPA 1988 s.227(1), quoted in para.4–075 above.

[198] CDPA 1988 s.263(3).

[199] CDPA 1988 s.263(1).

[200] See paras 4–079 and 4–082 above.

[201] For example, a model made by a private model maker for his own collection which is subsequently auctioned after his death. However, in most cases where an article is commercially sold, it would normally be presumed that the maker had commercial sale in mind when he made the article.

[202] CDPA 1988 s.257; but not the Isle of Man, unlike the Registered Designs Act; see para.3–134.

[203] CDPA 1988 s.217(3)(b). No such Order has yet been made as of November 1, 2004.

[204] See para.4–075 above.

[205] See Ch.6 below.

Overlap with infringement of copyright

4–088   CDPA 1988 s.236 provides that:

> "Where copyright subsists in a work which consists of or includes a design in which design right subsists, it is not an infringement of design right in the design to do anything which is an infringement of the copyright in that work."

4–089   This catch all provision seems designed to take care of cases where copyright protection and design right protection would otherwise co-exist. It would seem to have little practical effect in cases where both copyright and design right are in the hands of the same owner, since it will merely mean that such a person has one cause of action instead of two. However, in a case where the ownership provisions are such as to give copyright to one person and design right to another,[206] this provision may have a real impact. The question of overlap between copyright and design right is addressed more extensively elsewhere.[207]

What amounts to an infringing design

4–090   Having discussed the question of what acts will potentially amount to infringement of unregistered design right, the second (and often the most important) aspect of what amounts to infringement is to decide whether or not the design of the allegedly infringing article amounts to a reproduction of the claimant's design.

4–091   It is important to appreciate the central part played by the concept of reproduction. This means that the question of infringement is determined not just by an objective comparison of the claimant's and defendant's designs, but also by asking how the defendant's design was originated and in particular whether or not it was copied directly or indirectly from the claimant's design.

4–092   Secondly, it is important to realise that, as already discussed in the context of subsistence of design right,[208] a design for an article will normally embody not a single "design" which enjoys design right protection, but a large bundle of such designs subsisting in each part and aspect of the overall design of the article. The task of deciding whether or not there is infringement will therefore involve not a single overall comparison of the two articles (claimant's and defendant's) but detailed

---

[206] Such as will often happen in the case of a commissioned work, where the commissioner will normally enjoy design right (see para.4–055 above) but may well not be entitled to copyright.

[207] See para.5–059 below.

[208] See para.4–003 above.

consideration of each part or aspect where there are similarities which may arise as a result of reproduction.[209]

The concept of reproduction

Infringement of design right must involve reproduction, i.e. copying. This concept is derived from copyright law. The essential nature of the test of infringement of design right is therefore far more similar to infringement of copyright than to infringement of registered design, which is a true monopoly right.[210] It is essential for the claimant to prove a chain of copying leading from his own design, to the design alleged to infringe. Of course, the similarity of that design to his own, if it came into existence later in time, can itself be powerful evidence from which the likelihood of copying can be inferred.[211] A claimant should set out the points of similarity upon which he relies to prove copying in advance of the trial and not seek to take the defendant by ambush in circumstances where the defendant may have difficulty in properly investigating the allegation and possibly producing an innocent explanation for what at first sight may be a damaging point of similarity.[212] But if a design is genuinely created independently, however similar it is to the design of the claimant, it cannot infringe his design right. If a chain of copying is established, it is irrelevant whether the copying took place directly from the claimant's own articles, or indirectly via articles of third parties.[213] In principle it is possible for reproduction to take place via the medium of written or oral instructions without the maker of the infringing article having had sight of the claimant's article or even of a drawing or picture of it.[214]

4–093

---

[209] *A Fulton Co Ltd v Totes Isotoner (UK) Ltd* [2004] R.P.C. 301; [2003] EWCA Civ 1514. "Subject to complying with the general qualifications for subsistence of unregistered design right, a designer is entitled to prevent the copying exactly or substantially of part only of his design, unless that part is excluded from protection because it is not original (i.e. is copied or is commonplace) or falls within the must fit/must match exceptions or any combination of these." Paragraph 39 per Jacob L.J. giving the judgment of the court.

[210] Although this has not always been so—until 1949, registered design law imposed a requirement of copying; see paras 3–185—6 above.

[211] A close similarity between the claimant's design and the alleged infringing article, coupled with the opportunity of the alleged copier to have had access to the work, raises an inference of copying: *A Fulton Co Ltd v Grant Barnett & Co Ltd* [2001] R.P.C. 257 at 284 para.95 per Park J.; in this respect, the approach in unregistered design cases is no different from that in copyright cases where this proposition was stated to be "not so much one of law as of plain rational thought": *Ibcos Computers Ltd v Barclays Finance Ltd* [1994] F.S.R. 275 at 297, per Jacob J.

[212] *Lambretta Clothing Co Ltd v Teddy Smith (UK) Ltd* [2004] EWCA (Civ) 886 at para.65; a point about the type of fabric used to make the defendant's garment was gratuitously raised for the first time by the claimant's designer in the witness box when under cross-examination.

[213] CDPA 1988 s.226(4) explicitly provides that "reproduction may be direct or indirect, and it is immaterial whether any intervening acts themselves infringe design right". This provision is probably surplussage, since it has always been unquestioned in the case of copyright infringement that reproduction can take place via an indirect route.

[214] See the cases discussed in the context of copyright infringement, para.5–122 below.

4–094   In many cases, the question of reproduction will be interwoven in a complex way with other aspects of the question of infringement. A defendant may admit having seen the claimant's article and admit having taken some ideas or features from it, but claim that he worked out the detailed shape and configuration of his own design for himself.[215] It is not enough to show that the defendant has gone through an independent though very similar design exercise and has arrived at very similar designs, even if it involves copying some of the basic dimensions of the claimant's design, so long as the dimensions copied are not themselves enough (taken together) to constitute a design in which design right subsists.[216] In such cases, the extent to which the defendant has in fact done his own design work rather than copying from the claimant becomes a (frequently difficult) question of fact.

Exact or substantial reproduction

4–095   CDPA 1988 s.226(2) provides that:

> "(2) Reproduction of a design by making articles to the design means copying the design so as to produce articles exactly or substantially to that design . . . "

4–096   It has surprisingly been held that this reference in s.226(2) to the design being reproduced "exactly or substantially" applies only to infringement under s.226(1)(a) (making articles to the design), whilst infringement under s.226(1)(b) (making a design document) requires there to be exact reproduction of the design.[217] With respect, such a conclusion is not supported by the wording of the section when properly analysed whilst as a matter of policy it is verging on the irrational. Section 226(1)(b) contemplates the making of articles from the design document in question within the phrase "for the purpose of enabling *such articles* to be made". The words "such articles" refer back to the words in para.(a) "articles to that design", which words are expressly defined in subs.226(2) as embracing articles "exactly or substantially" to that design. Accordingly it is clear on the wording of the section that para.226(1) embraces design documents which record designs which "exactly or substantially"

---

[215] See *Rolawn Ltd v Turfmech Machinery Ltd* [2008] EWHC 989 (Pat); [2008] R.P.C. 27; [2008] E.C.D.R. 13, Mann J.; some copying of general ideas not sufficient to support inference that details had been copied.

[216] *Ocular Science Ltd v Aspect Vision Care Ltd* [1997] R.P.C. 289 at 423 lines 34–50: "In taking some or all of [certain dimensions] and feeding them into their spreadsheet, they were not copying the package of numerous dimensions which the plaintiffs assert constitute the total design in which their monopoly right resides." For a case involving rather similar questions in the artistic copyright context, see *Billhofer Maschinenfabrik GmbH v T. H. Dixon & Co* [1990] F.S.R. 105, ChD, discussed at para.5–123 below.

[217] *Soc Esplosivi Industriali SpA v Ordnance Technologies (UK) Ltd* [2007] EWHC 2875 (Ch); [2008] R.P.C. 12, Lindsay J.

reproduce the claimant's design. As to policy, it is hard to think of any reason why the legislature should wish to confine infringement under s.226(1)(b) to "exact" reproductions (whatever that may mean in the real world) and as far as the editor of this work is aware it has never before been suggested at any point in the legislative or pre-legislative process leading to the enactment of this section, or in any commentary or previous judicial decision, that paragraphs (a) and (b) of s.226(1) might have different scope as regards what designs will infringe them. It is submitted that this decision is manifestly erroneous and should not be followed.

Leaving aside that point which can relate to subs.226(1)(b) only, the **4–096A** requirement for "exact or substantial" reproduction appears to impose a fairly strict test as regards the degree of resemblance needed to infringe an unregistered design right. There is an important conceptual difference between this provision and the corresponding provisions relating to copyright, which render it an infringement to copy the whole or a "substantial part" of a work.[218] It is *not* an infringement to reproduce a substantial part of a design, and a judgment which proceeds on such a basis is in error.[219] However, the difference between the two approaches in more apparent than real. A copyright work (e.g. a drawing) is normally treated as a single work and copying of part only is caught by the "substantial part" provision. By contrast, in the case of design rights, there is no provision for infringement by copying of a substantial part of a design, but a single design drawing or prototype article will normally embody a large bundle of design rights, subsisting potentially in each and every aspect of the shape or configuration (whether internal or external) of the shape or configuration of an article.[220] The question of "part" thus comes at the stage of subsistence of the right, rather than at the stage of infringement. In principle, the question of infringement must be asked in relation to each and every such possible design right in each and every aspect of the whole or part of the claimant's article. It would appear to follow from the wording of the statute that if the design right in part of an article is sued upon, it is irrelevant to infringement of that particular design right how similar or different are the other parts of the two articles concerned, although the contrary has been suggested judicially.[221]

[218] CDPA s.16(3)(a).
[219] *L Woolley Jewellers Ltd v A & A Jewellery Ltd* [2003] F.S.R. 15, CA, where a case in which the trial judge had applied such an approach was remitted to the Patents County Court for reconsideration. Upon reconsideration applying the correct test of comparing the designs as a whole, the Patents County Court still held there to be infringement: see *L Woolley Jewellers Ltd v A & A Jewellery Ltd (No.2)* [2003] EWPCC (Des) 1; [2004] F.S.R. 47, H.H. Judge Fysh Q.C.
[220] CDPA 1988 s.213(2); and see para.4–003 above.
[221] In *Parker v Tidball* [1997] F.S.R. 680 at 691, where the deputy judge said that "in a case where a design of part of an article is reproduced in part of an allegedly infringing article, one should ask oneself what by way of comparative design would be suggested to the interested observer but to do so in the light of the entirety of the allegedly infringing article, not just by confining attention to the corresponding parts". In adopting this

4–097   In clear cut cases where there has been exact or substantial copying of the whole design of the claimant's article, there will be no difficulty in deciding the question of infringement. However, in many cases it may be possible to identify only an aspect or part of the design of the claimant's article which can be said to have been embodied in the defendant's article. In such a case (assuming it can be shown that the similarities concerned do indeed arise from copying rather than independent design), the question of infringement may in effect convert into a question of subsistence: having identified the collection of features which can be said to have been copied from the claimant's design into the design of the defendant's article, can it be said that that collection of features amounts to an aspect of the shape or configuration of the whole or part of the claimant's article in which design right subsists? A claimant may, of course, be required to identify and plead the design rights which he relies upon, rather than being allowed to advance at the trial a wide range of alternative contentions without warning.[222] However, subject to the rules of pleading, there seems no reason why a claimant should not choose to rely upon a large number of alternative design rights in a single article, such as the design right in the article as a whole, and the design rights in the various individual parts or aspects which he considers may have been infringed.[223]

Does design right subsist in the features which have been copied?

4–098   If the question of infringement of design right is recast in terms of whether design right subsists in the collection of features which have been copied, it then becomes necessary, having identified that collection

proposition, the learned deputy judge was seeking to follow *C & H Engineering v F. Klucznik & Sons Ltd* [1992] F.S.R. 421 at 428, but it is submitted that this case does not support that proposition since there is no indication that Aldous J. was considering (or was asked to consider) a design right in part of an article rather than in the whole article. Where the design right sued upon is the design right in a part of an article, it is submitted that there is no statutory warrant for taking into account matter extraneous to that particular design right, i.e. other parts of the article, in applying the test of infringement. Of course, it may be that a claimant by limiting the design right sued upon to a small part of an article with few features will end up with a design right of so little substance that it fails the tests of originality or of subsistence, or in respect of which a slight departure can be regarded as "substantial"; however, that is a different point which does not involve taking into account other parts of the articles being compared.

[222] In *Ocular Sciences Ltd v Aspect Vision Care Ltd* [1997] R.P.C. 289, Laddie J. at 422 emphasised the importance of pleading the design right: "This means that the proprietor can trim his design right to most closely match what he believes the defendant to have taken. The defendant will not know what the alleged monopoly resides in until the letter before action or, more usually, the service of the statement of claim. This means that a claimant's pleading has particular importance. It not only puts forward the claim but is likely to be the only statement of what is asserted to be the design right."

[223] For an example of a case where the claimant pleaded design rights in the whole and in various combinations of parts of an article (an umbrella), all of which were considered to be satisfactory as a matter of pleading, see *A Fulton Co Ltd v Grant Barnett & Co Ltd* [2001] R.P.C. 257 at para.38.

of features, to consider whether or not that collection of features does or does not satisfy the cumulative series of statutory criteria under which it may qualify as a design in which design right subsists. These criteria have been dealt with in an earlier section of this chapter[224]; however, briefly, the copied collection of features must consist of three-dimensional shape and configuration rather than of surface decoration[225]; must not be a "method or principle of construction"[226]; must be original[227] and not commonplace[228]; and must not fall within the "must match" or "must fit" exclusions from design right.[229]

Thus, it may well be necessary to consider the originality or otherwise   **4–099** of the collection of features which have been copied; and, although the design of the claimant's article regarded as a whole may rank as original and not commonplace, it may be that the only features which have been copied are not original or are commonplace.[230] This type of inter relationship between subsistence of the right and infringement is already familiar from copyright law, where it has long been recognised that in order to decide whether or not an alleged infringement is a reproduction of a substantial part of the copyright work, one important factor to take into account is whether or not the features which have been copied from the copyright work are themselves sufficiently original for copyright to subsist in them.[231]

The "must match" and "must fit" exclusions are primarily intended to   **4–100** cover the case of spare parts and other contexts where one article must be made compatible with another. However, because of what seems to be a drafting anomaly, these exceptions have been framed in terms of exceptions to subsistence of the right, rather than as defences to infringement. This means that they will effectively operate as defences to infringement in a far wider context than the legislature can have intended.[232]

Approach to the question of substantiality

As has already been noted, s.226(2) of the CDPA 1988 provides that   **4–101** reproduction of a design for the purposes of infringement requires

---

[224] See paras 4–003 et seq., above.
[225] See paras 4–029 and 4–034 above.
[226] See para.4–011 above.
[227] See para.4–042 above.
[228] See para.4–045 above.
[229] See paras 4–015 and 4–026 above.
[230] To give a trite example, it is commonplace for a table to have four legs. If the claimant creates an original design of table, but the only feature of his design which the defendant copies is the feature of having four legs, one at each corner, then the defendant will not have reproduced any "design" of the claimant in which design right subsists; see para.4–045 above.
[231] For consideration of this issue in the context of copyright infringement, see para.5–124 below.
[232] See the example of the crankshaft copied by a competing engine manufacturer discussed at para.4–015 above.

producing articles "exactly or substantially to that design". Where the allegedly infringing design is similar but not exactly the same, the court will need to decide whether or not such differences as are present can be disregarded as being insubstantial or insignificant, or whether they are significant enough to take the allegedly infringing design out of the scope of infringement. At the time of preparing this edition, there is still limited authority on the question of substantiality of reproduction in the context of infringement of unregistered design right. In one case it has been said that the test is to be applied by comparing the designs "through the eyes of the person to whom the design is directed".[233] That test is essentially similar to the test applied for registered design infringement,[234] and is no doubt a suitable test in cases where the design consists of elements having eye appeal; however, it is not clear that it is a suitable test in cases where the features of the design which have been copied are said to be important functionally, rather than being important to the eye appeal of the finished article.

4–102   Thus, some guidance can be gleaned from looking at the approach of the courts to deciding whether or not as a design is "not substantially different" from a registered design,[235] and in deciding whether or not an alleged infringement is a reproduction of a substantial part of a copyright work.[236] There are, however, some important differences in the likely approach of the courts, which flow from the differences in the nature of unregistered design right from the nature of the respective interests protected by registered designs and artistic copyright. Thus, because registered designs are intended to protect features which have "eye appeal",[237] rather than functional designs as such, the courts' approach to infringement of registered designs gives weight to the similarity or dissimilarity of aesthetic features, and little or no weight to functional similarities. By contrast, unregistered design right is intended to protect purely functional designs (as well as decorative three-dimensional designs) and therefore it is to be expected that the court will give weight to the copying of important functional features of shape or configuration, even if those features are not visually prominent or indeed are visually insignificant.[238] In one case it has been suggested that a visual comparison should be carried out through the eye of a "notional addressee" of the

---

[233] *C & H Engineering v F. Klucznik & Sons Ltd* [1992] F.S.R. 421 at 428 per Aldous J.; pig fender designs notionally compared through the eyes of pig farmers. Followed (by concession of counsel and in a case where the designs were aesthetic rather than functional) in *Parker v Tidball* [1997] F.S.R. 680.

[234] Where the designs are looked at and compared "through the eye of the customer": see para.3–227 above.

[235] See paras 3–184 et seq., especially 3–206 and 3–211: the pre-2001 test.

[236] See paras 5–123—5–136 below.

[237] See para.3–047 above.

[238] Since unregistered design right will protect visually insignificant or even invisible features (see para.4–03 above), it follows that such features cannot be dismissed when considering the question of substantiality of reproduction of the design.

design,[239] and the court apparently rejected a suggestion that small features should be compared under magnified conditions.[240] With respect, this approach seems difficult to justify in the case of design right in a functional design where differences or similarities in microscopic features might be functionally of great significance.[241]

Artistic copyright, unlike registered designs, protects functional fea- **4–103** tures of articles depicted in drawings and gives weight to their functional importance in the context of substantiality of reproduction.[242] However, artistic copyright imposes a threshold test, in that it does not protect features which are visually insignificant in the copyright drawing sued upon.[243] There seems no reason in principle why unregistered design right should impose any such test,[244] and it would seem to follow that features which are a functionally important part of a design should be given weight when it comes to assessing infringement, even if they are visually insignificant or even invisible to the naked eye. Thus, for example, the tiny and visually insignificant radii on the Lego bricks in *Interlego*[245] would be treated as substantial features of a design for the purposes of deciding whether or not there had been infringement in an unregistered design case.

4. Property Rights and Licensing

First ownership of design right by designer

Who becomes the first owner of an unregistered design right depends **4–104** upon whether the design is the work, on the one hand, of a freelance designer or, on the other hand, has been created in the course of employment or pursuant to a commission. In the case of a freelance designer, the design right becomes vested in the designer himself.[246] The designer is defined as being "the person who creates it".[247]

---

[239] *Bailey (t/a Elite Anglian Products) v Haynes* [2007] F.S.R. 199, PCC at paras 34–36: comparison of meshes of nets used for anglers' bait.
[240] *Bailey (t/a Elite Anglian Products) v Haynes* [2007] F.S.R. 199, PCC at para.34.
[241] The court appears to have followed the observation of Aldous J. in *C & H Engineering* (n.219 above); however Aldous J. in that context was dealing with the issue of what aspects of the designs of pig fenders should be regarded as substantial or insubstantial and his reference to the "eye" of a pig farmer was essentially referring to the background knowledge of pig fenders that such a person would bring with him to the exercise of comparison rather than to the mechanics of the process of visual comparison.
[242] See para.5–125 below.
[243] *Interlego AG v Tyco International Ltd* [1988] R.P.C. 343, PC; see para.5–124 below.
[244] *Ocular Sciences Ltd v Aspect Vision Care Ltd* [1997] R.P.C. 289 at 422, lines 35–423 and line 15; detailed dimensions of contact lenses.
[245] [1988] R.P.C. 343, PC.
[246] CDPA 1988 s.215(1).
[247] CDPA 1988 s.214(1).

4-105   In the case of designs which are computer generated, the designer is defined as "the person by whom the arrangements necessary for the creation of the design are undertaken".[248] "Computer generated" is defined as meaning that the design is generated in circumstances such that there is no human designer.[249]

4-106   The Act appears to contemplate that the designer will be an individual or individuals, rather than a body corporate; however, the use of the word "person", rather than "individual", normally implies that the word is capable of covering corporations as well as individuals. It is conceivable that there could be cases, particularly in the case of computer generated designs, where no particular individual or individuals can be identified as the designer, and a company could be regarded as being the "designer" itself. However, in the more normal case, a company's relevant individual employees will be the designers and the company may be entitled to ownership on that basis.

Joint designers

4-107 The Act contemplates that a design may be created jointly by more than one designer working together. Section 259(1) provides that:

> " . . . a 'joint design' means a design produced by the collaboration of two or more designers in which the contribution of each is not distinct from that of the other or others".

4-108   This definition of joint design is modelled on the corresponding copyright provision defining joint authorship of a copyright work,[250] and there seems no reason why it should not be construed in the same way.[251] Leaving aside the case of commissioned designs and designs created in the course of employment, the design right in a design created by joint designers will normally vest in the designers together. This assumes that all of the joint designers have the correct national qualifications in order for design right to subsist[252]; if they do not, then, so long as at least one of the joint designers does qualify, the design right will belong only to the designer or designers that do possess such correct qualifications.[253]

---

[248] CDPA 1988 s.214(2).
[249] CDPA 1988 s.263(1).
[250] CDPA 1988 s.10(1).
[251] This was the approach adopted (apparently by agreement between counsel) in *Parker v Tidball* [1997] F.S.R. 680 at 701, following the architectural copyright case *Cala Homes (South) Ltd v Alfred McAlpine Homes East Ltd* [1995] F.S.R. 818 at 835. For the copyright authorities in which joint authorship has been considered, see para.5–144 below.
[252] See paras 4–055 to 4–061 above.
[253] CDPA 1988 ss.218(3) and (4).

Designs created pursuant to a commission

Where a design is created in pursuance of a commission, the person **4–109** commissioning the designer becomes the first owner of the design right subsisting in it.[254] This provision takes precedence over the provision giving design right in designs created by an employee to an employer,[255] so that a person who commissions the creation of a design will take the design right regardless of whether he places the commission directly with the individual designer, or with a company which in turn employs the designer. Where a chain of commissions is placed, e.g. by a customer who commissions a manufacturer who in turn commissions a specialist designer, the person in whom the design right will vest is the person ultimately placing the commission, i.e. the end customer.[256]

A commission for this purpose is defined as a commission for money **4–110** or money's worth.[257] The unregistered design right provisions governing commissioned designs are essentially identical to those governing proprietorship of registered designs,[258] and it would seem in general that first ownership of unregistered design right, and of the right to apply for registration of a design, are intended to vest in the same person.[259] There has been little case law so far on commissioning of designs for the purposes of unregistered design right.[260]

One important consequence of a design having been created pursuant **4–111** to a commission, is that it is the national connections of the person placing the commission, rather than of the designer, which becomes relevant for the purposes of qualification for subsistence of design right.[261]

Designs created in the course of employment

Where a design is created by an employee in the course of his employ- **4–112** ment, first ownership of design right will vest in the employer rather than in the employee[262] (unless the design has been commissioned, in which

---

[254] CDPA 1988 s.215(2).

[255] CDPA 1988 s.215(3); see para.4–112 below.

[256] *Arnold (James) & Co Ltd v Miafern Ltd* [1980] R.P.C. 397 at 404, ChD. A copyright case under the 1956 Act, which provided that copyright in commissioned engravings and photographs belonged to the person commissioning them; a rule no longer present in the CDPA 1988.

[257] CDPA 1988 s.263(1).

[258] RDA(A) s.2(1A).

[259] For the corresponding registered design provisions, see para.3–222 above.

[260] For one example, see *Apps v Weldtite Products Ltd* [2001] F.S.R. 703, an unremarkable case on its facts, where a consultant who was engaged by the defendant for a fee to answer the question "How can we produce a suitable stabiliser to cover [the defendant's] bikes?" was held to have been commissioned to produce an improved stabiliser design which he then came up with.

[261] See para.4–055 above.

[262] CDPA 1988 s.215(3).

case the design right will vest in the person placing the commission rather than the employer[263]). An employee is defined as a person employed under a contract of service or apprenticeship.[264] This definition is essentially identical to the long standing corresponding definition in copyright law,[265] and presumably is intended by Parliament to be interpreted to the same effect.[266] The registered design provisions are also effectively identical.[267] For more extensive discussion of the circumstances in which a design is created in the course of employment, see the discussion on the corresponding copyright provisions.[268]

4–113   It should be noted that there is no reference in CDPA 1988 s.215 to the operation of its rules (automatically vesting design right in the commissioner of a design or in the employer of the designer) being excluded by an agreement to the contrary. This contrasts with the corresponding section vesting copyright in the employer of the author, which is explicitly subject to any agreement to the contrary.[269] Furthermore, it was thought necessary when providing for design rights in semiconductor topographies explicitly to modify the application of s.215 to those designs so as to permit a written agreement to exclude the operation of these automatic ownership rules.[270] This does raise the possibility, however odd, that under the Act an agreement to the contrary cannot oust the automatic vesting of design right in the commissioner or employer. If there is an explicit agreement to the contrary and this interpretation is right, it will mean that the legal title will vest in the employer or commissioner in accordance with the rules laid down in s.215, but the designer will be the equitable owner, because by contract he has the right to require the legal owner to vest the design right back in him. The consequences are somewhat perverse, and it is arguable that s.215 is to be interpreted as implicitly subject to agreement to the contrary.

4–114   However, if this is right, it might provide a means for artificial escape from the rules governing qualification for subsistence, and this may be a possible policy reason for interpreting s.215 so as not to permit exclusion from its operation by agreement. One important consequence of a design having been created in the course of employment is that it is the national connections of the employer, rather than of the designer-employee, which become relevant for the purposes of deciding whether or not the design satisfies the rules on national qualification for subsistence of design right.[271]

---

[263] See para.4–109 above.
[264] CDPA 1988 s.263(1).
[265] CDPA 1988 s.178; previously Copyright Act 1956 s.4(4).
[266] For provisions relating to copyright works created by employees, see para.5–150 below.
[267] RDA(E) s.2(1B) and s.44(1), definition of "employee". See para.3–224 above.
[268] Paragraphs 5–150 et seq. below.
[269] CDPA 1988 s.11(2).
[270] See para.10–011 below.
[271] See para.4–055 above.

Special rule of ownership where right subsists by virtue of first marketing

It is possible that a design does not qualify for design right in the United **4–115** Kingdom when it is first created, because the designer, commissioner or employer (as the case may be) does not satisfy the correct national qualifications.[272] In such a case, the design may later qualify for unregistered design right by virtue of being first marketed in a qualifying territory by an appropriately qualified person.[273] In such a case, a special rule applies as regards first ownership of the design right. Instead of the design right vesting in the original designer (or his commissioner or employer), first ownership of the design right vests in the qualifying person who first markets articles made according to the design.[274]

Prospective ownership of future design rights

The normal rules relating to first ownership of design right can be **4–116** displaced by agreement. A prospective owner of design right can make an agreement under which he purports to assign the future design right (either individually or as part of a class of designs) to another person. If the agreement satisfies the required formalities, which are that it is in writing and is signed by the prospective owner, then the design right or rights concerned will vest in the assignee rather than in the prospective owner upon their creation.[275] This provision does not affect subsistence of design right: it is still the national connections of the designer or (if applicable) the commissioner or employer which are relevant for the purposes of qualification for subsistence, not the national status of the assignee.

This provision only operates if the assignee is by virtue of the **4–117** agreement concerned entitled against all other persons to require the right to be vested in him.[276] Thus, for example, a purported assignment entered into by a designer in breach of a contractual obligation with a third party would not be effective to vest design right in the assignee. Quite apart from this special statutory provision, the normal rules of contract law, specific performance and equity apply to the ownership of design right. Thus, if a contract obliges a designer expressly or impliedly to hold a design he creates for the benefit of another person, then that contract may be specifically enforceable even if for example it fails to satisfy the formal requirements of an assignment of prospective rights because it is not in writing. The difference is that, if a prospective assignment falls within s.223, legal title to the design right will vest in the

---

[272] See para.4–055 above.
[273] For details of these requirements, see para.4–065 above.
[274] CDPA 1988 s.215(4); see para.4–065 above.
[275] CDPA 1988 s.223(1).
[276] CDPA 1988 s.223(1).

assignee without the need for any further action. A person relying on a contract falling outside s.223 will at best acquire an equitable title to the design right and may need to take further steps to perfect his title or to enforce his rights against third parties.

Special jurisdiction of the IP Office over first ownership, subsistence and term of design right

4–118   A special jurisdiction is conferred on the IP Office to determine disputes about the subsistence or term of an unregistered design right, or the identity of the person in whom the design right first vested.[277] This jurisdiction has been rarely used to date, but provides a lower cost method of determining disputed questions about the scope as well as subsistence of design rights although questions of infringement cannot be directly entertained.[278] The decision of the IP Office on such a dispute is expressed to be binding on the parties to the dispute. Thus, such a decision would seem to have the same effect of creating binding issue estoppels and res judicata as the judgment of a court of law.

4–119   It should be noted that the jurisdiction given to the IP Office to decide these questions is exclusive, in the sense that, subject to specific exceptions, no other court or tribunal is permitted to decide these issues.[279] Thus, either the dispute procedure must first be started at the IP Office which then itself refers the dispute to the English High Court or the Court of Session,[280] or the parties themselves or the IP Office must agree that the IP Office procedure can be by-passed.[281]

4–120   The important exception to the exclusive nature of the IP Office jurisdiction arises when any of the matters above (subsistence, term or first ownership) arises incidentally in the course of infringement or other proceedings before the courts.[282] In an ordinary infringement action, it would be quite common for all these issues to be in dispute, and it would obviously be absurd if issues of subsistence (which are often closely interrelated with the scope of infringement) were hived off for decision in separate proceedings in the IP Office.

---

[277] CDPA 1988 s.246(1).

[278] See *Christopher Tasker's Design Right References* [2001] R.P.C. 39: a designer of sliding mirrored door wardrobes referred questions as to subsistence of design right in his designs to the Registry, and joined two of his competitors as respondents to the reference. The hearing officer gave a detailed ruling as to the particular features in which design right subsisted, and which were excluded as principles or methods of construction, by the "must fit" exclusion, as surface decoration and on other grounds.

[279] CDPA 1988 s.246(2).

[280] CDPA 1988 s.251. This procedure could be invoked if the Patent Office considers the dispute too complicated for its own procedures; however, given the tendency of all tribunals to try to gather business to themselves, it may in practice be harder to obtain such a reference than it ought to be.

[281] CDPA 1988 s.246(2)(c).

[282] CDPA 1988 s.246(2)(b).

The IP Office jurisdiction is limited to determining who was the first **4–121** owner of a design right, so that disputes about how design right has devolved under assignments or commercial agreements are outside this jurisdiction. However, the IP Office may well be involved in deciding upon the effect of assignments or of disputed commercial contract terms if there is an argument as to whether or not the making of the design was pursuant to a commission,[283] or where it is said that there was an assignment of prospective design rights before the design was created.[284] The IP Office has jurisdiction to decide any incidental question of fact or law arising in the course of a dispute under this jurisdiction.[285] An appeal lies from a decision of the IP Office under this jurisdiction to the courts.[286]

Nature of property in design right

CDPA 1988 s.222(1) provides that: **4–122**

> "(1) Design right is transmissible by assignment, by testamentary disposition or by operation of law, as personal or moveable property."

Thus, the ordinary laws of personal property will apply to design right. **4–123** Design right will pass upon death or in an insolvency according to the same rules as any other personal property. There is, however, a minimum formality for an effective assignment: the assignment must be in writing and be signed by or on behalf of the assignor.[287] An assignment that fails to satisfy these formal requirements will not serve to convey legal title in the design right to the assignee, but may be effective as an equitable assignment, and is likely to be so if supported by consideration.

The design right in a single design is divisible by assignment or **4–124** transmission into partial rights covering different classes of acts covered by the design right, or different periods of time.[288] For example, design right may be assigned in respect of the application of the design to some particular kind of article but not articles in general, in a similar way to that in which copyrights can be divided up, e.g. into the hard cover and paperback rights.[289] Alternatively, a design right may be assigned for a period of two years only, in which case it would then revert to the assignor at the end of the two year period without need for an assignment

---

[283] See para.4–109 above.
[284] See para.4–116 above.
[285] CDPA 1988 s.246(3).
[286] i.e. the English High Court or the Court of Session; CDPA 1988 s.251(4).
[287] CDPA 1988 s.222(3). If the assignor is a corporation, the assignment can be under seal instead of signed; s.261.
[288] CDPA 1988 s.222(2).
[289] CDPA 1988. s.222(2) is modelled on the corresponding copyright provisions, under which copyrights can be divided up into parcels. See para.5–158 below.

back. If a third party infringes the design right which has been divided up, it is the person whose partial right covers the acts of the infringer who is entitled to sue.[290]

Assignment of unregistered right in conjunction with registered design

4–125   When a registered design is assigned, there is a statutory presumption that the assignment is also intended to convey the unregistered design right in the design unless the contrary intention appears.[291] Read literally, this provision applies only to the design right in the actual design which is the subject of the registration, i.e. the design of the whole article, and not to the bundle of design rights which are likely to subsist in aspects or parts of the design of the article.[292] However, there is scope for arguing for a purposive interpretation of this provision, which would extend the presumption of conveyance of unregistered design rights at least to the rights in designs which embody the major or essential features of the registered design.

Joint ownership of design right

4–126   Design right can be jointly owned, most frequently when the design has been created by joint designers.[293] In such a case, for a third party to do acts which require the licence of the design right owner, requires the licence of all the joint owners.[294] Thus, each joint owner can sue a third party for infringement, although the extent of his financial remedies may be limited to the damage sustained by his own interest in the design right.[295]

Licensing of design right

4–127   Licence merely means consent or permission, and no specific require- ments are laid down as to how a design right owner may license another person or persons to do acts which would otherwise infringe a design right. Thus, a licence may be conferred by a formal written document, by a contract, by express written or oral permission to do an act, or by implication. Licences under a design right (however granted) are given

---

[290] CDPA 1988 s.258(1).
[291] CDPA 1988 s.224.
[292] For discussion of this topic, see para.4–003 above.
[293] See para.4–107 above.
[294] CDPA 1988 s.258(2).
[295] See para.6–011 below for remedies and procedure applicable to joint owners.

by statute a quasi-proprietory status, in that such a licence is binding upon the successors in title to the proprietor who granted the licence.[296] The exception is that a licence granted by a predecessor in title does not bind a purchaser in good faith of the design right for valuable consideration without notice (actual or constructive) of the licence, or a successor in title to such person.[297] This effectively treats a licence under a design right as if it were an equitable interest in, or under, the design right. A similar provision applies to a licence granted by a prospective owner of a design right.[298] Although licences, even exclusive licences, of design right do not create a proprietary interest in the design right, such licences can amount to "an interest in property" for the purposes of s.320 of the Companies Act 1985.[299]

Exclusive licences of design right

Exclusive licensees of design right are given a special status. For this purpose, an exclusive licence is defined as a licence which authorises the licensee to exercise part or all of the rights conferred by the design right, to the exclusion of all other persons, including the person granting the licence. In addition, it must fulfil the formal requirements of being in writing and being signed[300] by or on behalf of the design right owner.[301] An exclusive licence which fails to satisfy these formal requirements (for example, because it is oral) may be perfectly effective contractually, at least as against the original grantor, but will not be accorded the special privileges which the Act confers upon exclusive licences and exclusive licensees. **4–128**

These privileges are, first, that the terms of the exclusive licence are enforceable against a successor in title to the grantor.[302] Secondly, the exclusive licensee may be effectively protected against parallel imports from other countries of goods made by or under the licence of the design right owner.[303] Thirdly, an exclusive licensee has the right to bring infringement proceedings against third parties in his own name.[304] **4–129**

---

[296] CDPA 1988 s.222(4).

[297] CDPA 1988 s.222(4).

[298] CDPA 1988 s.223(3).

[299] *Ultraframe Ltd v Fielding (No.2)* [2005] EWHC 1638 (Ch); [2006] F.S.R. 7, Lewison J.

[300] Or alternatively in the case of a corporation being under seal; CDPA 1988 s.261.

[301] CDPA 1988 s.225(1).

[302] CDPA 1988 s.225(2). This is so long as the successor in title is bound by the exclusive licence, i.e. that he is not a purchaser for value without notice; see para.4–127 above. Without this special statutory provision, there could be difficulty in enforcing the negative covenant implicit in the exclusive licence against a successor in title who may have no privity of contract with the exclusive licensee.

[303] This follows from the reference to an exclusive licence agreement in the definition of "infringing article" in CDPA 1988 s.228(3)(b); see para.4–081 above.

[304] This is subject to certain procedural safeguards; see para.6–016 below.

5. Term of Protection

Duration of design right

4–130 Unregistered design right is of comparatively short duration. It will normally last 10 years from the first making available for sale or hire of articles to which the design has been applied,[305] anywhere in the world.[306] Where orders are taken in advance for the delivery of articles at a later date, those articles are "made available" for the purposes of the 10-year term beginning to run at the date when they are delivered and therefore physically made available to customers and not at the date when orders are taken.[307] However, it will in any event expire 15 years after the design right first came into existence (when the first design document or article embodying the design was made).[308] This means that the effective period of commercial protection from first marketing may be shorter than 10 years in the case of an article which was designed more than five years before it was placed on the market.

4–131 It should be noted that the period of protection (whether limited by first marketing or by first design) will expire not on the relevant anniversary date, but at the end of the calendar year concerned, in the same way as copyrights generally do. This is a rule of convenience designed to avoid the need to investigate the precise date during a year when a design was first marketed or created.

Availability of licences of right during the last five years of the term

4–132 The term of protection for an unregistered design right is subject to the important practical limitation that "licences of right" are available during the last five years of the design right term.[309] This means that the period of exclusive protection conferred by a design right is five years[310] and thereafter it effectively converts into a right to receive royalties rather than an exclusive right. The royalties and other terms of a licence of right are set by the IP Office in default of agreement.[311]

---

[305] CDPA 1988 s.216(1)(b).

[306] CDPA 1988 s.216(2).

[307] *Dyson Ltd v Qualtex* (UK) Ltd [2006] EWCA Civ 166; [2006] R.P.C. 31, CA at paras 115–119.

[308] CDPA 1988 s.216(b).

[309] CDPA 1988 s.237(1).

[310] Plus a number of months up to the end of the calendar year concerned; see para.4–132 above.

[311] For procedure and other aspects of licences of right, see paras 8–002 et seq., below.

CHAPTER 5

COPYRIGHT PROTECTION FOR INDUSTRIAL DESIGNS

1. Copyright in Artistic Works Relevant to Industrial Designs

Scope of copyright protection for industrial designs

The relative importance of copyright for the protection of industrial **5–001**
designs was reduced by the CDPA 1988. Before that Act, copyright in
design drawings constituted the principal effective means by which the
copying of industrial articles could be prevented. This form of protection
was based on the realisation that if an industrial article is made from a
design drawing, then a competitor who copies the article will in turn
indirectly be copying the design drawing on which the article is based,
and thereby infringing the copyright in the drawing. It is a little
surprising that industrial articles should be protected by a form of
protection intended for "artistic works"; and, indeed, it does appear that
this form of protection arose through an oversight on the part of the
legislature rather than deliberate intent.[1]

The changes made by the CDPA 1988 removed much of the field of **5–002**
industrial design protection from the realm of copyright.[2] However,
copyright protection does remain of considerable importance. First,
copyright continues to protect aspects of design which do not consist of

---

[1] See para.5–055 below.
[2] See para.5–059 below.

three-dimensional shape and configuration—principally surface decoration of articles.[3] (These also can be protected by the short-lived Community unregistered design right, which unlike UK national unregistered design right, covers surface decorative features as well as three dimensional shapes.) Secondly, copyright rather than design right continues to apply to the protection of certain categories of three-dimensional objects which are themselves "artistic works" such as (surprisingly) buildings and structures, and (less surprisingly) works of sculpture and works of artistic craftsmanship.[4]

5–003   Because of the central importance of copyright in "artistic works" to all these areas of protection, the following paragraphs set out the relevant categories of artistic work in which copyright can subsist. In addition, the potential relevance of literary copyright to the field of industrial design is briefly considered.[5]

Categories of artistic work

5–004   The categories of artistic works in which copyright can subsist are defined by CDPA 1988 s.4(1) as follows:

"4.—(1) In this Part 'artistic work' means—

(a) a graphic work, photograph, sculpture or collage, irrespective of artistic quality,

(b) a work of architecture being a building or a model for a building, or

(c) a work of artistic craftsmanship."

Section 4(2) expands on the definition of "graphic work" as follows:

" 'graphic work' includes—

(a) any painting, drawing, diagram, map, chart or plan, and

(b) any engraving, etching, lithograph, woodcut or similar work."

5–005   Although there has been some re-arrangement of the definitions, the categories of artistic work are in substance the same as those under the Copyright Act 1956,[6] except that there may have been some widening of the categories of graphic work which are capable of enjoying copyright protection.[7] It may be helpful to consider first the categories of artistic

---

[3] See para.5–084 below.
[4] See para.5–051 below.
[5] Paragraph 5–033 below.
[6] Copyright Act 1956 s.3(1), taken in conjunction with the definitions of "drawing", "engraving", and "photograph" in s.48(1).
[7] See para.5–006 below.

work which are essentially two-dimensional, i.e. graphic works, photographs and collages, and then move on to consider the categories which are or may be three-dimensional, which are sculptures, works of artistic craftsmanship and works of architecture.

Graphic works

The 1956 Act enumerated paintings, drawings and engravings as distinct (and exhaustive) categories of artistic work,[8] while the 1988 Act lists all these types of work as part of a non-exhaustive definition of a wider category of "graphic work". This suggests that objects which might have been regarded as not falling strictly within any of the categories of painting, drawing, etc., or engraving, etc., but are of a similar general nature, will be regarded as graphic works under the 1988 Act. All the categories of graphic work enumerated in subs.4(2) share the characteristic that they present in one way or other a visual image, although the techniques by which that image is produced are widely differing. The image can be a representation of some thing or person, real or imaginary, or could be abstract or, e.g. a pleasing pattern. It can, however, be argued that there must be a visual image which can be appreciated or understood by the eye. It can also be noted that the enumerated kinds of graphic work are all generally two-dimensional, and so presumably in order to count as a graphic work an object may need to be essentially two-dimensional.   **5–006**

The individual categories of graphic work will now be considered in turn, but bearing in mind the possibility of copyright subsisting in works in the wider general category.   **5–007**

Drawing, diagram, map, chart or plan

This group of categories of artistic work[9] were all included under the definition of "drawing" in the Copyright Act 1956.[10] It is still convenient to consider them together, since in any event the categories merge into each other.   **5–008**

In the context of industrial designs, almost any drawing or diagram of an industrial article which possesses any degree of complexity is in principle capable of counting as an artistic work for copyright purposes. It should be borne in mind that CDPA 1988 s.4(1)(a) provides that these works (as well as photographs, collages and sculptures) are to count as artistic works "irrespective of artistic quality",[11] so that the court is not concerned to judge whether or not such works fall within any wider   **5–009**

---

[8] Copyright Act 1956 s.3(1).
[9] All listed in sub-para.(a) of the definition of "graphic work" in CDPA 1988 s.4(2) set out in para.5–004 above.
[10] Section 48(1).
[11] As did the Copyright Act 1956 s.3(1)(a).

conception of being "artistic".[12] As it was put by Megarry J. in *British Northrop Ltd v Texteam Blackburn Ltd*[13]:

5–010 "The [1956] Act merely provides, by section 48(1), that 'drawing' includes any diagram, map, chart or plan, and so *prima facie* if there is anything which can fairly be called a diagram, it is a drawing and may be the subject of copyright. It may indeed be that some thing may be drawn which cannot fairly be called diagram or a drawing of any kind: a single straight line drawn with the aid of a ruler would not seem to me to be a very promising subject for copyright. However, apart from cases of such barren and naked simplicity as that, I should be slow to exclude drawings from copyright on the mere score of simplicity. I do not think that the mere fact that a drawing is of an elementary and commonplace article makes it too simple to be the subject of copyright.

In this case I have been taken through the drawings in question seriatim, and I have been able to consider them again after the conclusion of the argument. I accept that some of them are indeed simple. They include a rivet, a screw, a stud, a bolt, a metal bar, a length of wire with a thread cut at one end, a length of cable with nipples at each end, a block of leather, a washer and a collar. They are all carefully drawn to scale, with precise dimensions, and I cannot extract from the statute any indication that these drawings should not be able to qualify for copyright. If simplicity were a disqualification, at some point there would come enough complexity to qualify. It is not that I am unable to see exactly where the Act draws the line: it is that I cannot see that there is any intention to draw any line at all."

5–011 It has been held that a point pattern for a fabric design is a drawing or diagram.[14]

Paintings

5–012 Prima facie, paintings involve the application of paint or colour to a surface in order to produce a visual image. In the context of industrial design, their main practical importance arises from the application of designs based on paintings as surface decoration of industrial articles.

---

[12] In contrast to "works of artistic craftsmanship", where the court is concerned with this difficult task; see para.5–022 below.

[13] [1974] R.P.C. 57 at 68, lines 37 et seq.

[14] *Lerose Ltd v Hawick Jersey International Ltd* [1974] R.P.C. 42. This contrasts with the approach adopted before the Copyright Act 1911; see *Hollinrake v Truswell* [1894] 3 Ch. 421 (Cardboard Pattern Sleeve).

Photographs

A photograph is defined by CDPA 1988 s.4(2), as follows: **5–013**

> " 'photograph' means a recording of light or other radiation on any medium on which an image is produced or from which an image may by any means be produced, and which is not part of a film."

The effect of the exclusion of "film" from this definition is to exclude   **5–014**
only moving images,[15] not to exclude still photographs taken on traditional film material. It is clear under the 1988 Act definition[16] that there is
no restriction to the traditional techniques by which photographs used to
be produced, so that, for example, a visual image captured in binary pixel
form in the memory of a computer would count as a "photograph".
However, the definition does require that the image has been recorded
from light or other radiation, so that a generated "virtual reality" image,
however real it might look, would not count as a photograph. Such an
image would however almost certainly count as a graphic work.

In the context of industrial design, photographs are potentially impor-   **5–015**
tant because they can form part of a number of industrial processes by
which the design of articles is produced, such as the photographic
printing of the layout of conductors on a printed circuit board or the
masks used to produce semiconductor devices. There may therefore be
situations where it needs to be considered whether the copying of such
finished articles can amount to the indirect copying of a copyright work
(the photograph) in which copyright can subsist.

Engravings, etchings, lithographs, etc.

This category of works, specified in subpara.(b) of the definition of   **5–016**
"graphic work" in CDPA 1988 s.4(2), are all works which are traditionally
associated with methods of printing or replicating, particularly of pictures or images. Works in this category are likely to be, but need not
necessarily be, derivative works, for example an engraving taken from a
drawing for the purpose of replicating the picture by a printing process.
A potential source of importance for the inclusion of such derivative
works amongst the categories of "artistic works" is that such derivative
works may enjoy a copyright[17] quite independent of the copyright in the

---

[15] CDPA 1988 s.5(1).

[16] The Copyright Act 1956 s.48(1) defined a photograph as "any product of photography or any process akin to photography", leaving some scope for argument as to whether images produced by new processes radically different from traditional photography would or would not qualify.

[17] So long as they count as "original". However, an engraving or similar work taken from an original drawing or painting will normally itself rank as original because it is a work of an essentially different kind; see para.5–043 below.

work from which they are drawn, which may have expired or be in different hands.

5–017   "Engraving" in ordinary speech can and usually does mean an image produced from an engraved plate (usually by printing on paper), but in the context of the Act it embraces not only the image made from the engraved plate but the engraved plate itself.[18]

5–018   In one New Zealand case it was held that a three-dimensional cavity made in a metal injection mould by a process of cutting out the metal with a machine tool constituted an "engraving" within the corresponding New Zealand statute[19]; this had the consequence in that court's view that the plastic toys made in the mould were also "engravings" by analogy with prints made from an engraved plate.[20] However it is submitted that in this surprising decision, the court fell into the fallacy of treating any object made by a process that could be described as "engraving" as an "engraving" in the context of this enumerated category of copyright works; this genus all share the essential characteristic that they are essentially two-dimensional objects whose purpose is to bear visual images for replication.[21] Indeed in the Australian case *Greenfield Products Pty Ltd v Rover-Scott Bonnar Ltd*[22] the wide approach in *Wham-O* was rejected and it was said that engraving "has to do with marking, cutting or working the surface—typically the flat surface—of an object". This latter approach has been followed in one English case concerning transitional copyrights under CPDA 1988.[23]

Sculptures

5–019   This is the first of the three-dimensional categories of artistic work. In ordinary usage, sculpture is the art of forming representations of objects[24]

---

[18] *Arnold (James) & Co Ltd v Miafern Ltd* [1980] R.P.C. 397, ChD. In this case it was held that rubber printing plates, described as "rubber stereos" and made by a photolithographic process, were "engravings" for this purpose; 403–404.

[19] *Wham-O Mfg Co v Lincoln Industries Ltd* [1985] R.P.C. 127 CA of NZ.

[20] *Wham-O Mfg Co v Lincoln Industries Ltd* [1985] R.P.C. 127 CA of NZ at 154: "There appears currently to be no good reason why an article produced by injection moulding from a mould which is an engraving should not be itself an engraving if it is produced from that mould."

[21] See the reasoning of the NZ Court of Appeal at 153, lines 10–18. The reasoning of this case on the subject of "sculpture" is also criticised below; see para.5–19.

[22] (1990) 17 I.P.R. 417, Fed Ct of Australia, Pincus J.

[23] *Hi-Tech Autoparts Ltd v Towergate Two Ltd* [2002] F.S.R. 16, Pat Cty Ct, at 265. The non-slip mat moulds in issue in that case would now secure protection under unregistered design law rather than copyright. However, *decorative* surface ribbing applied to a mat would probably be outside the scope of design right because of the specific exclusion of 'surface decoration' from CDPA s.213(3)(c), and it would be necessary to rely on copyright to protect the design. If there were no antecedent drawing, it would be necessary to seek to rely on the mould plate as a copyright work and contend that it is an engraving: although, as already noted, "engraving" is now just one example of a broader category of "graphic works" within CDPA s.4(2).

[24] Which may of course not be real objects, since sculpture can consist of abstract shapes.

in the round or in relief by chiselling stone, carving wood, modelling clay casting metal, or similar processes.[25] "Sculpture" for copyright purposes is defined[26] as including "a cast or model made for purposes of sculpture". This extension to the definition is apt to cover for example such things as a wooden pattern for a sand mould used for casting a bronze sculpture.

What counts a "sculpture" for copyright purposes was considered in depth by the Court of Appeal in the *Lucasfilm* case[27] where the court rejected the argument that a stormtrooper's helmet created for the film "Star Wars" was protectable as a work of sculpture. Whilst indicating that it was not possible or wise to attempt to devise a comprehensive definition of "sculpture" sufficient to determine the issue in any given case,[28] the court approved the trial judge's approach of having regard to a series of factors as follows[29]:

5–020

"(i) Some regard has to be had to the normal use of the word.
(ii) Nevertheless, the concept can be applicable to things going beyond what one would normally expect to be art in the sense of the sort of things that one would expect to find in art galleries.
(iii) It is inappropriate to stray too far from what would normally be regarded as sculpture.
(iv) No judgment is to be made about artistic worth.
(v) Not every three dimensional representation of a concept can be regarded as a sculpture. Otherwise every three dimensional construction or fabrication would be a sculpture, and that cannot be right.
(vi) It is of the essence of a sculpture that it should have, as part of its purpose, a visual appeal in the sense that it might be enjoyed for that purpose alone, whether or not it might have another purpose as well. The purpose is that of the creator. This reflects the reference to "artist's hand" in the judgment of Laddie J. in *Metix*, with which I respectfully agree. An artist (in the realm of the visual arts) creates something because it has visual appeal which he wishes to be enjoyed as such. He may fail, but that does not matter (no judgments are to be made about artistic merit). It is the underlying purpose that is important. I think that this encapsulates the ideas set out in

---

[25] *Concise Oxford English Dictionary*, 5th edn; essentially this definition was adopted by the Court of Appeal of New Zealand in *Wham-O Mfg Co v Lincoln Industries Ltd* [1985] R.P.C. 127 at 155 to 156.
[26] CDPA 1988 s.4(2).
[27] *Lucasfilm Ltd v Ainsworth* [2009] EWCA Civ 1328; [2010] F.S.R. 10; [2010] E.C.D.R 5, CA.
[28] Paragraph 77.
[29] Paragraph 54, setting out para.118 of the judgment of Mann J. at first instance.

the reference works referred to in *Wham-O* and set out above (and in particular the Encyclopaedia Britannica).

(vii) The fact that the object has some other use does not necessarily disqualify it from being a sculpture, but it still has to have the intrinsic quality of being intended to be enjoyed as a visual thing. Thus the model soldier in Britain might be played with, but it still, apparently, had strong purely visual appeal which might be enjoyed as such. Similarly, the Critters in *Wildash* had other functions, but they still had strong purely visual appeal. It explains why the Frisbee itself should be excluded from the category, along with the moulds in *Metix* and *Davis*. It would also exclude the wooden model in *Wham-O* and the plaster casts in *Breville*, and I would respectfully disagree with the conclusions reached by the judges in those cases that those things were sculptures. Those decisions, in my view, would not accord with the ordinary view of what a sculpture is, and if one asks why then I think that the answer is that the products fail this requirement and the preceding one—there is no intention that the object itself should have visual appeal for its own sake, and every intention that it be purely functional.

(viii) I support this analysis with an example. A pile of bricks, temporarily on display at the Tate Modern for 2 weeks, is plainly capable of being a sculpture. The identical pile of bricks dumped at the end of my driveway for 2 weeks preparatory to a building project is equally plainly not. One asks why there is that difference, and the answer lies, in my view, in having regard to its purpose. One is created by the hand of an artist, for artistic purposes, and the other is created by a builder, for building purposes. I appreciate that this example might be criticised for building in assumptions relating to what it seeks to demonstrate, and then extracting, or justifying, a test from that, but in the heavily subjective realms of definition in the artistic field one has to start somewhere.

(ix) The process of fabrication is relevant but not determinative. I do not see why a purely functional item, not intended to be at all decorative, should be treated as a sculpture simply because it is (for example) carved out of wood or stone."

5–020A Mann J. went on to observe[30]:

"Those factors are guidelines, not rigid requirements. The question: "What is a sculpture?" has some of the elements about it of the

---

[30] *Lucasfilm Ltd v Ainsworth* [2008] EWHC (Civ) 1878 (Ch); [2009] F.S.R.2; [2008] E.C.D.R. 17, Mann J., at para.119.

unanswerable question: "What is Art?" However, they do, in my view, represent what one can extract from the cases, definitions and statutes in order to assist in answering the question whether any particular article is a sculpture or not. They are an attempt to extract elements from what plainly are sculptures, to distinguish what makes something plainly not a sculpture, and to arrive at some factors which result from that exercise. I would no more attempt a definition than any of the judges in the other authorities."

Both Mann J.'s last guideline (ix) and the Court of Appeal's judgment make it clear that it is not correct to construe the word "sculpture" in this context as including any three-dimensional object made by a process of sculpting, so that, e.g. wooden patterns made for the purpose of casting machine parts would count as sculptures. In this regard, the English Court of Appeal disagreed with[31] an approach along these lines was adopted by the Court of Appeal of New Zealand, which held that wooden models from which moulds were made for casting children's plastic throwing discs (Frisbees) were sculptures.[32] The addition of the qualifying words "for the purposes of sculpture" in the extension of the statutory definition to casts or models suggests that the legislature intended to exclude casts or models made for general industrial purposes and to include only those whose ultimate purpose is the production of an object which can itself be regarded as a sculpture.[33] The Court of Appeal approved previous English cases where models and casts for making dental impression trays, and moulds for making cartridges for flow mixers, were held not to be sculptures,[34] and disapproved a suggestion in one case that models of the plates of a sandwich toaster intended to produce scallop-shaped toasted sandwiches could count as works of sculpture.[35] Although sculptures are one of the categories of works[36] which enjoy copyright "irrespective of artistic quality",[37] these words do not warrant disregarding the requirement that sculptures must serve an

---

[31] Paragraph 65.
[32] *Wham-O Mfg Co v Lincoln Industries Ltd* [1985] R.P.C. 127.
[33] Interestingly, the Court of Appeal of New Zealand in *Wham-O* declined to hold that either the metal injection moulds, or the moulded plastic discs themselves, were sculptures: *Wham-O Mfg Co v Lincoln Industries Ltd* [1985] R.P.C. 127 at 157.
[34] *J & S Davis v Wright Health Group Ltd* [1988] R.P.C. 403, ChD, Whitford J. distinguished the *Wham-O* case, noting (at 412 line 26) that "a carved wooden model is one thing. A model fashioned in plasticine or some other suitable modelling material, which it was never intended to have any permanent existence, being no more than a stage in production, is another". However, the distinction between permanent and impermanent objects may not be sound, and the Court of Appeal in Lucasfilm approved the result of this case on broader grounds. For flow mixer cartridges, see *Metix (UK) Ltd v G. H. Maughan (Plastics) Ltd* [1997] F.S.R. 718, ChD.
[35] *Breville Europe PLC v Thorn EMI Domestic Appliances Ltd* [1995] F.S.R. 77, Falconer J.
[36] In common with drawings and other graphic works.
[37] CDPA 1988 s.4(1)(a).

artistic or representational purpose, and not merely a functional purpose as moulds or patterns in an industrial production process.[38]

5–021   More generally, the policy of the CDPA 1988 is to protect three-dimensional industrial articles via the medium of unregistered design right, and anomalous results would arise if industrial patterns for end products which are not themselves sculptures were to count as such. The shield against copyright infringement conferred by CDPA 1988 s.51[39] would be pierced.

Works of artistic craftsmanship

5–022   This constitutes an ill-defined category, not falling within any of the specific categories already dealt with, of works which are artistic works entitled to copyright protection if original. There is obviously a considerable potential for overlap with industrial articles which are the subject of unregistered design right protection, and it may therefore be important to pin down what distinguishes this special category of articles from run of the mill industrial articles. As is the case with works of architecture,[40] it will be seen that the definition of this category of works is not qualified by the words "irrespective of artistic quality" in CDPA 1988 s.4(1)(a). Therefore it is presumably intended that the courts shall pay some regard to artistic quality in assessing what works fall under this head. Operations involving "craftsmanship" would clearly seem to include work in a variety of different media such as precious metals, wood, leather and cloth and in addition to include embroidery, pottery etc. The central difficulty then lies in what further qualification is imposed by the adjective "artistic" in the context.

5–023   The leading authority, in which this problem was extensively considered by the House of Lords, is *Hensher v Restawile*,[41] where a claimant was unsuccessful in contending that a prototype for a mass-produced sofa was a "work of artistic craftsmanship".[42] Although the House was unanimous in reaching this conclusion, there was considerable divergence of approach between the five reasoned opinions. Lord Reid gave a broad meaning to the word artistic, which went beyond the views of the majority of the House. He considered that if any substantial section of the public genuinely admires and values a thing for its appearance and gets pleasure or satisfaction, whether emotional or intellectual, from looking at it, then he would accept that it is artistic even though many others might think it meaningless or common or vulgar.[43] Lord Morris and

---

[38] *Lucasfilm*, para.70.
[39] See para.5–059 below.
[40] See para.5–029 below.
[41] *Hensher (George) Ltd v Restawile Upholstery (Lancs) Ltd* [1975] R.P.C. 31, HL.
[42] Under the Copyright Act 1956 s.3(1)(c). But there is no material difference in the wording of the 1988 Act.
[43] *Hensher (George) Ltd v Restawile Upholstery (Lancs) Ltd* [1975] R.P.C. 31 at 54, lines 39, et seq.

Viscount Dilhorne considered that "artistic" was an ordinary English word which required no interpretation, and what was artistic should be decided as a question of fact in the light of the evidence, including evidence from art experts.[44] By contrast, Lord Kilbrandon considered that what is artistic is a question of law for determination by the judge and not a matter for evidence by witnesses, whilst the question of what is artistic depends upon whether the author had a conscious purpose of artistic creation which can be deduced from the work itself or from the surrounding circumstances.[45] Lord Simon of Glaisdale emphasised the point that the Act contains a composite phrase "work of artistic crafts-manship" which must be construed as a whole; and a pertinent test is whether the work can be regarded as a work of an artist-craftsman.[46]

The need for both the aspects of craftsmanship and artistry to be united in the production of the work was recognised in the earlier case of *Burke and Margot Burke Ltd v Spicers Dress Designs*,[47] where it was alleged that a frock was a work of artistic craftsmanship under the Copyright Act 1911. Clauson J. dismissed the action, holding as follows[48]:

5–024

> "The manner in which they claim copyright in this frock is this. They say that the frock, having been made by their workwomen, is a frock of which they are the authors for copyright purposes. . . . They claim that it is an original work of artistic craftsmanship, and that they are, therefore, under the Copyright Act entitled to prevent the defendants from reproducing that original work of artistic craftsmanship. The first difficulty in their way is that all that their workwomen have done is to do certain acts of craftsmanship and thus produce a work of craftsmanship. It is said that, having regard to the beauty of this frock when completed, it is not only a work of craftsmanship, but a work of artistic craftsmanship. For the moment, though I am not satisfied that that is correct, I will assume that it is. But where did the artistic element which has become connected with this work of craftsmanship originate? It certainly did not originate in the work-people. All they did was by purely mechanical processes to produce this article; they are crafts-women, but they were not 'artistic' craftswomen; they borrowed the artistic qualities of the article from the inspiration of Mrs Burke in her sketch, and accordingly, although

[44] *Hensher (George) Ltd v Restawile Upholstery (Lancs) Ltd* [1975] R.P.C. 31 at 56–57 and 62–63.
[45] *Hensher (George) Ltd v Restawile Upholstery (Lancs) Ltd* [1975] R.P.C. 31 at 72–73.
[46] *Hensher (George) Ltd v Restawile Upholstery (Lancs) Ltd* [1975] R.P.C. 31 at 65–6.
[47] [1936] Ch. 400. See also *Merlet v Mothercare PLC* [1986] R.P.C. 115, CA, where a prototype baby cape was held not to be a work of artistic craftsmanship. See also *Komesaroff v Mickle* [1988] R.P.C. 204, Victoria Supreme Ct, where it was held that "moving sand pictures" consisting of a mixture of liquid, coloured sands and air bubbles between two glass sheets were not works of artistic craftsmanship because the designer's action did not directly bring about the sand landscapes which resulted from turning the product upside down; they could not be regarded as the product of craftsmanship.
[48] [1936] Ch. 400 at 407.

I can well understand that it might be said that the frock was an original work of craftsmanship, the craftsmanship being original, it is not, in my view, an original work of artistic craftsmanship, because the artistic element did not originate in those who made the work. It is not original in so far as it is artistic; in so far as it is not artistic it is not protected by the Act."

A similar approach was adopted in a later garment case where it was held that machine made prototype garments were neither works of craftsmanship nor works of art[49]; nor were samples of patchwork spreads and bedcovers.[50] Models of a stormtrooper's helmet and armour were works of craftsmanship but lacked the necessary artistic quality,[51] as did a "plug" for forming a mould for a yacht hull.[52] On the other hand, wire models of animals with a predominantly representational purpose were held to be works of artistic craftsmanship despite some of them having functional purposes of acting as table or wall candle holders.[53]

5–025   The meaning of a work of artistic craftsmanship has been considered in two cases brought by the same claimant in Australia[54] and in Canada.[55] In both countries it was decided that a set of wooden rods ("Cuisenaire rods") to be used for teaching mathematics to children were not a work of artistic craftsmanship; the rods were neither works of craftsmanship, nor were they artistic. In the Australian case Pape J. said[56]:

"The addition of the adjective 'artistic' requires that the craftsman, in exercising his skill and labour in creating the article, must set out to produce something which possesses those attributes suggested by the word itself, even if the article also possesses functional character, such as a Chippendale chair or table. The type of work to which protection is given is something akin to Chippendale's chairs, Grimling Gibbons' carvings, Cellini's candelabra, and the tapestry recently made in France for the new Coventry Cathedral. The idea was well expressed in the 1952 Report of the Copyright Committee, Cmnd No.8662, paragraph 260, where it is said: 'We are not here concerned with articles manufactured under conditions of ordinary industrial production (artistically meritorious as many of these are) which can secure their own protection under the Registered Designs Act, but with the works of craftsmen working in many media

---

[49] *Guild v Eskander Ltd* [2001] F.S.R. 638, Rimer J.; the finding of copying was reversed on appeal at [2003] F.S.R. 23 but the finding in respect of works of artistic craftsmanship was not challenged.

[50] *Vermaat & Powell v Boncrest Ltd* [2001] F.S.R. 45, ChD.

[51] *Lucasfilm Ltd v Ainsworth* [2008] EWCA 1878 (Ch); [2009] F.S.R.2; [2008] E.C.D.R. 17 per Mann J. at paras 134–5.

[52] *Burge v Swarbrick* [2007] H.CA 17; [2007] F.S.R. 27, High Ct of Australia.

[53] *Wildash v Klein* (2004) 61 I.P.R. 324, Australian Northern Territory Sup Ct.

[54] *Cuisenaire v Reed* [1963] V.R. 719.

[55] *Cuisenaire v South West Imports Ltd* [1968] Ex.C.R. 493.

[56] *Cuisenaire v Reed* [1963] V.R. 719 at 729, 730.

(silversmiths, potters, woodworkers, hand embroiderers and many others) in circumstances for which that Act [i.e. the Registered Designs Act] does not provide appropriate protection . . .

In my opinion the words 'artistic' and 'craftsmanship' each refer to some quality in the acts performed by the maker or author of the article in which copyright is alleged to subsist in the course of performing the physical operation of making that article as distinct from the earlier cogitation and thought which produced the idea upon which the work was based. The true test, I think, is whether the author, in making the article in which copyright is alleged to subsist, was applying his skill and taste to its production with the main object of creating an article which, even if it be utilitarian, nevertheless will have a substantial appeal to the aesthetic tastes of those who observe it. Put another way, it may be said that the test is whether the author was, in creating the article, cultivating one of the fine arts with the main object of appealing to the aesthetic tastes of those who view it, provided that the expression 'the fine arts' is given the wide meaning of any application of skill and taste to the production of articles which are beautiful in themselves or which have an appeal to aesthetic taste."

He continued: 5–026

"The emphasis is thus upon the object of the author in creating the work, rather than on the reaction of the viewer to the completed work, for it is commonplace in copyright law that it is immaterial whether the work has any merit: *Walter v Lane.*[57] In stating that the emphasis is on the object of the author, I do not desire to be taken as saying that the sole test of whether the work of a craftsman is a work of artistic craftsmanship is the intention or object of the craftsman at the time he made the work. As a general rule, the court adjudicating on the matter will apply a purely objective test by an examination of the article itself. When, however, as in this case, such an objective test may be thought to deny that the work is one of artistic craftsman-ship, and it is sought to establish the contrary, the object of the creator of that work must, in my view, play a dominant part in the resolution of the question. The best evidence concerning that is the evidence of the creator of the work himself . . . "

The proposition that what is "artistic" largely depends upon the 5–027 subjective intention of the author was, however, doubted in a New Zealand case on the grounds that:

"I have some difficulty with the proposition that the author can have tried to be artistic and failed, yet the product, because this was the

[57] [1900] A.C. 539 at 549, per Lord Halsbury L.C.

intention of the author, is nevertheless to be regarded as a work of artistic craftsmanship".[58]

Although both the elements of craftsmanship and artistry must be present, it is possible for them to be provided by two individuals working together and they need not necessarily be combined in the person of a single individual.[59]

5–028   In the Canadian Cuisenaire rod case Noel J. said[60]:

> "Although they are coloured in a manner such as to interest or please children, the same as blocks for instance, they were never intended primarily as an article regarded as artistic or beautiful in itself even if the artistic requirements required here are not too great. Indeed, even if artistic merit is not a matter of importance in copyright law, the word artistic must still be given its ordinary meaning although, may I add, there could be considerable debate as to the merit of a particular work.
>
>   It is true, as pointed out by counsel for the plaintiff, that there is originality in the colouring and size, selection and arrangement within the sets and the choice of the colours may well have been arrived at with a view to applying the method he conceived to teach children arithmetic. It is, however, the artistic work itself which is entitled to protection and not the idea behind it. These rods indeed are tools and nothing more . . .
>
>   An artistic work, in my view, must to some degree at least, be a work that is intended to have an appeal to the aesthetic senses—not just an incidental appeal, such as here, but as an important or one of the important objects for which the work is brought into being. The plaintiff's rods may have a certain attraction to children, but this, in my view, is a very secondary purpose which, I am afraid, is not a sufficient basis for a finding that the rods are artistic."

Works of architecture

5–029   CDPA 1988 s.4(1)(b) includes in the definition of artistic works "a work of architecture being a building or a model for a building". "Building" is defined as including "any fixed structure, and any part of a building or

---

[58] *Bonz Group (Pty) Ltd v Cooke* [1994] N.Z.L.R. 216, NZ High Ct, per Tipping J. at 223, a case concerning hand knitted woollen sweaters and cardigans. Cited with approval in *Vermaat & Powell v Boncrest Ltd* [2001] F.S.R. 45, ChD and also cited with approval by Mann J. in *Lucasfilm Ltd v Ainsworth* [2008] EWCA 1878 (Ch); [2009] F.S.R. 2; [2008] E.C.D.R. 17, Mann J. at para.131.

[59] *Vermaat & Powell v Boncrest Ltd* [2001] F.S.R. 43, ChD at 49, following *Bonz Group (Pty) Ltd v Cooke* [1994] N.Z.L.R. 216, NZ High Ct.

[60] *Cuisenaire v South West Imports Ltd* [1968] Ex.C.R. 493 at 514. The relevant section of the Canadian Act being construed included, "works of painting, drawing, sculpture and artistic craftsmanship, and architectural works of art and engravings and photographs".

fixed structure".[61] It is strange to think of a house or an industrial plant being "an artistic work", but that is the effect of the statutory provision. It should be noted that this category of artistic work is quite distinct from architectural plans, which will normally enjoy copyright as "drawings". Thus, copying of a building or structure will normally involve infringement of copyright in the architectural drawings according to which it was built, as well as infringement of the separate and distinct copyright in the building itself.

One important consequence of classing buildings as being themselves "artistic works" is that the statutory provisions intended to avoid overlap between copyright and design right will not operate to exclude the construction of buildings from being an infringement of copyright,[62] because the exclusion applies only to designs for things which are not themselves artistic works.   **5–030**

It should be noted that buildings and structures are generally not "articles" for the purpose of design registrations, unless perhaps they are pre-fabricated[63]; and it is doubtful whether they are "articles" for the purposes of unregistered design right.[64] In any event, the statutory scheme is that the protection of designs of buildings, whether by way of reliance on copyright in architects' drawings or in the buildings themselves, is fully within the field of copyright rather than that of registered or unregistered design rights. One consequence is that designs of buildings will enjoy a much longer effective period of protection[65] than designs for industrially produced articles.[66]   **5–031**

---

[61] CDPA 1988 s.4(2). Presumably, a distinction is to be drawn between parts of a structure as such, and objects, such as radiators or doors or bathroom fittings, which are fabricated separately and retain their identity even though they are incorporated into a structure. The Court of Appeal has rejected an argument that an object which becomes incorporated into a building, such as a specially designed door, thereby becomes consumed into the realty and ceases to be an "article" for the purposes of CPDA s.23 upon incorporation: *Pensher Security Door Co Ltd v Sunderland County Council* [2000] R.P.C. 249 at 280, lines 18–26. Although such an object may become upon incorporation a part of the structure, it would be an extremely odd result if the shield against infringement of copyright under s.51 were thereby to be lost, since rationally the protection of the designs of such building fittings should belong to the field of unregistered design right rather than copyright. The answer presumably is that a design for, say, a radiator, is not to be regarded as "a design for" a part of a building when it is created because a radiator has an independent existence as an article. The fact that the radiator may later, after it has travelled through builders' merchants, end up incorporated into a building does not render the design drawing for it a design *for* part of a building. This is to be distinguished from, say, an architectural drawing for a room or a balcony, which all along will only come into existence and be constructed as part of a building. Similarly, the design of a new kind of brick would be the subject of design right rather than copyright, despite the fact that most such bricks after they had been made and sold would ultimately be incorporated into a building or other structure.

[62] [2001] F.S.R. 113 s.51, considered in depth at para.5–059 below.

[63] See para.2–010 (post-2001 harmonised law) and 3–036 above.

[64] See para.4–007 above.

[65] Normally 70 years after the death of the author; see para.5–160 below.

[66] Which enjoy an effective period either of 10 years under industrial design right (see paras 4–131 and 4–133 above), or a copyright term effectively limited to 25 years; see para.5–088 below.

5–032   A building or structure is not confined merely to houses. In *Vincent v Universal Housing & Co Ltd*[67] copyright was successfully claimed in a garden consisting of a particular arrangement of a lily pond, stone steps and walls, lawn, paths, flower beds and shrubberies. Romer L.J. held that the walls, pond and steps were "structures", and that the garden as a whole was a "structure".

Literary copyrights and industrial designs

5–033   Literary copyrights may of course be relevant to industrial design cases, since the copying of the design of an industrial article may be accompanied by copying of catalogues, brochures and other written material. If the literary material which is copied is original and sufficient to count as substantial, then infringement of literary copyright may occur. Unlike the case where articles or designs for articles are reproduced, there is no provision cutting down the scope or the effective term of literary copyright in the industrial field, so that if literary material is reproduced, that will normally remain an infringing act for a very long time; normally 70 years after the death of the author of the work.

5–034   There may be some circumstances in which the effect of literary copyright could go beyond affecting catalogues, brochures and written material, and possibly impinge on the design of an article itself. It has been held that circuit diagrams, or at least the symbolically recorded information contained in them as to the components in the circuit viewed as a table, amount to a literary work in which copyright subsists.[68] It followed that the defendants' "net list", a circuit design document of the defendants which listed the components in the defendants' circuitry and their interconnections, infringed the literary copyright, although it was expressly not decided whether or not the defendants' actual circuits would infringe the literary copyrights.[69] Unfortunately it would appear that, presumably because the defendant was not represented, the potential exclusionary effect of s.51 CDPA was not considered. Section 51 applies without distinction to any kind of copyright (whether artistic, literary or of any other kind) in a design document or model.[70]

5–035   That case has since been considered in a case where there was full argument on both sides.[71] It was said that it went no further than saying

---

[67] M.C.C. 1930–1, 275.

[68] *Anacon Corp Ltd v Environmental Research Technology Ltd* [1994] F.S.R. 659, ChD. It should be noted however that the defendant was not represented, and Jacob J. at 663 indicated that he "would have preferred not to have decided the circuit diagram point at all in the absence of argument from the other side. It may well be that in some subsequent case where the matter is fully argued a different view might be taken".

[69] The argument that they would do so was apparently based on the fact that visible indications of the nature of the components appeared on the defendants' circuit itself; *Anacon Corp Ltd v Environmental Research Technology Ltd* [1994] F.S.R. 659 at 663.

[70] For a fuller discussion of the exclusionary effect of CDPA 1988 s.51, see paras 5–059 et seq. below.

[71] *Electronics Techniques (Anglia) Ltd v Critchley Components Ltd* [1997] F.S.R. 401, ChD.

that literary copyright subsists in a list of notations even if they happen to appear in an artistic work,[72] but it does not follow that matter which is presented in diagrammatic form, such as the interrelationship between the components, can be regarded as part of the literary work: that is part of the artistic work and the two are mutually exclusive.[73] The latter case did not deal with the "net list" infringement point. These conflicting decisions were the subject of consideration in *Mackie Designs Inc v Behringer*.[74] That did not resolve the conflict as to whether only one kind of copyright, or both literary and artistic copyright, could subsist within a single work[75]; however, it did decide that the shield against copyright infringement under s.51 applied because the method of interconnection of components in the circuit diagram was an aspect of the "configuration" of the circuit and so fell within the scope of unregistered design right.[76] This proposition, if correct, provides an example of something which is "configuration" but which does not amount to "shape".[77] However, this proposition faces serious difficulties. It appears to conflict with the well known and established principle that design right subsists in an actual physical object and not in some generalised concept embodied in it.[78] This interpretation of the word "configuration" has been subject to criticism in another textbook which has been judicially noted.[79] Whilst it might have been tempting from a policy point to bring circuit diagrams fully within the ambit of unregistered design right, it is submitted that this approach cannot be supported as a correct interpretation of the law relating to design right. Design right is concerned with shape and configuration and can protect only circuit *layout* diagrams (i.e. diagrams which show the physical setting out of the components), assuming that they do not count as "surface decoration".[80] Circuit diagrams and net interconnection lists (i.e. documents detailing the *topology* or electrical interconnection of the circuit components as distinct from their *topography*) are outside the scope of design right and for this reason cannot be excluded from the field of

---

[72] *Electronics Techniques (Anglia) Ltd v Critchley Components Ltd* [1997] F.S.R. 401, ChD at 414, per Laddie J.

[73] *Electronics Techniques (Anglia) Ltd v Critchley Components Ltd* [1997] F.S.R. 401, ChD at 412–413. But see *Aubrey Max Sandman v Panasonic UK Ltd* [1998] F.S.R. 651, ChD, where Pumfrey J. at 658 preferred the view that both literary and artistic copyrights could subsist in a single work which contained both literary and artistic elements.

[74] [1999] R.P.C. 717, Pumfrey J.

[75] 720 at lines 2–19.

[76] [1999] R.P.C. 717 at 721–723.

[77] Until this rather surprising decision it had previously been considered that "shape" and "configuration" were virtual synonyms, both for registered design (see para.3–019 above) and unregistered design (see para.4–004 above) purposes.

[78] See, for example, *Rolawn Ltd v Turfmech Machinery Ltd* [2008] EWHC 989 (Pat); [2008] R.P.C. 27; 2008] E.C.D.R. 13, Mann J.

[79] See Laddie, Prescott and Vitoria, *The Modern Law of Copyright and Designs* 3rd edn (Lexis Nexis Butterworths, 2000), paras 53–6—53–10; this criticism of *Mackie* was noted, without being resolved, in the Court of Appeal in *Lambretta Clothing Co Ltd v Teddy Smith (UK) Ltd* [2004] EWCA (Civ) 886; see paras 26–27.

[80] As to the exclusion of "surface decoration" and its relationship with functional surface features with some depth, see para.4–030 above.

copyright by reason of the application of s.51. This potentially would lead to the anomaly that the copyright in circuit diagrams might be enforceable for the life of the author plus 70 years, if "reproduction" of them in the form of a physical circuit counts as a reproduction at all for copyright purposes.

5–036   The creation of an industrial article may frequently involve the use of information recorded in a literary work, but it does not follow that the article is a reproduction of the literary work, any more than a cake is a reproduction of the recipe for making it.[81] However, there may be cases where the information contained in a literary work reappears in such similar form on an article that it might be possible to argue that the article is a reproduction of the literary work. If, however, the literary work is, or comprises part of, a design document for an article which is not itself an artistic work,[82] then the shield provided against copyright infringement in the industrial sphere by s.51 will apply.[83] However the position is different regarding aspects of the article which are not part of the shape or configuration, such as surface decoration or other markings. If the names and characteristics of components were printed on a circuit board (say, to aid assembly) then such material, if it does reproduce a literary work, would not be excluded from copyright infringement by s.51 or by the "recipe for a cake" point. But if the printed matter were derived not directly from similar material printed on the claimant's article, but by reverse engineering from the claimant's actual components, it would appear to be excluded from being an infringement.[84]

2. Originality and Other Requirements for Subsistence

The concept of originality

5–037   It is a requirement of CDPA 1988 s.1(1)(a) that in order for copyright to subsist in an artistic work, the work must be "original". This is a requirement shared by literary, dramatic and musical works, although

---

[81] *Brigid Foley Ltd v Ellott* [1982] R.P.C. 433, ChD, per Megarry V.-C. at 434, lines 27–37; *Interlego AG v Tyco Industries Inc* [1988] R.P.C. 343 at 373 (obiter); but see *Autospin (Oil Seals) Ltd v Beehive Spinning* [1995] R.P.C. 683, ChD, at 699–700, per Laddie J., who considered that it might be a reproduction of a literary work consisting of a computer data file which precisely identified the dimensions of an article, to make an article to those dimensions. However, a possible alternative view is that such a data file *is* an artistic work, since CDPA 1988 s.17(1) implies that a work can be stored in any medium by electronic means.

[82] CDPA 1988 s.51; considered extensively at paras 5–058 et seq. below.

[83] CDPA 1988 s.51(3) defines a "design document" as including, amongst other things, a "written description" and "data stored in a computer", both categories capable of falling within the realm of literary rather than artistic copyright.

[84] See *Purefoy Engineering Co Ltd v Sykes Boxall & Co Ltd* (1955) 72 R.P.C. 89, CA, where the Court of Appeal rejected an argument that "reproducing" the claimant's catalogue of parts by selecting the same list of parts to sell and then writing standard descriptions of those parts would infringe copyright in the catalogue. is excluded from infringement, even if it is converted into a form which no longer consists of features of shape and

not at least expressly by the other categories of copyright work protected by the Act.[85]

The requirement of originality applies across the board to literary, dramatic, musical and artistic works and therefore many of the important decisions interpreting the principles to be applied are outside the field of artistic copyright. In essence, "original" is used simply in the sense of "originating from the author". However similar the work is to a pre-existing work, it will still be original so long as it is created independently without derivation from the pre-existing work. Novelty in the patent or registered design sense is not necessary.[86] But the work of a copier, however diligent and industrious,[87] will not qualify in this context, as he is not the author[88]; a copied work is not "original". This is subject to the principle that a derivative work, such as an engraving or photograph made from a painting, can count as original because of the difference of form from the work from which it was derived.[89]

5–038

The standard required of a work to qualify as being original would always seem to be modest. No originality of thought or expression in the popular sense of being out of the ordinary, worthy of notice or still less of being meritorious, is required.[90] A work qualifies as original, rather as a result of the expenditure of time and effort upon it and irrespective of the quality of achievement. Being concerned not with ideas but with the form in which those ideas are expressed, the law of copyright has been interpreted to accord originality to a mere modicum of labour.

5–039

Quantum of originality required for derivative works

It is when the author of a work has drawn upon existing subject matter that difficulties are most likely to arise. The question has arisen for

5–040

---

configuration. See also *BBC Worldwide Ltd v Pally Screen Printing* [1998] F.S.R. 665, Laddie J., where the defendant created two-dimensional reproductions of "Teletubbies" on t-shirts which had presumably been derived from watching the three-dimensional articles (dressed up actors in Teletubby constumes) on television.

[85] CDPA 1988 s.1(1)(b) and (c); sound recordings, films, broadcast or cable programmes and the typographical arrangement of published editions.

[86] Cf. *Kenrick & Co v Lawrence & Co* (1890) 25 Q.B.D. 99.

[87] *Interlego AG v Tyco International Ltd* [1988] R.P.C. 343 at 372, per Lord Oliver; "Of course, even a relatively small alteration or addition quantitatively may, if material, suffice to convert that which is substantially copied from an earlier work into an original work. Whether it does so or not is a question of degree having regard to the quality rather than the quantity of the addition. But copying, per se, however much skill and labour may be devoted to the process, cannot make an original work. A well executed tracing is the result of much labour and skill but remains what it is, a tracing".

[88] *Walter v Lane* [1900] A.C. 539; *British Northrop v Texteam Blackburn Ltd* [1974] R.P.C. 57 at 68; *Macmillan v Cooper* (1923) 40 T.L.R. 186.

[89] See para.5–043 below.

[90] *University of London Press Ltd v University Tutorial Press Ltd* [1916] 2 Ch. 601 at 608. See below. See also *Martin v Polyplas Manufactures Ltd* [1969] N.Z.L.R. 1046 (three-dimensional engravings made from photographs of coins).

example in relation to compilations of various kinds,[91] tables,[92] selections,[93] adaptations, and so on.

5–041   In each case the requisite quantum of originality will be a question of fact and degree.[94] In *University of London Press Ltd v University Tutorial Press Ltd*,[95] having held that examination papers were literary works, Peterson J. went on to consider originality:

"Assuming that they are 'literary work,' the question then is whether they are original. The word 'original' does not in this connection mean that the work must be the expression of original or inventive thought. Copyright Acts are not concerned with the originality of ideas, but with the expression of thought, and, in the case of 'literary work,' with the expression of thought in print or writing. The originality which is required relates to the expression of the thought. But the Act does not require that the expression must be in an original or novel form, but that the work must not be copied from another work—that it should originate from the author. In the present case it was not suggested that any of the papers were copied. Professor Lodge and Mr Jackson proved that they had thought out the questions which they set, and that they made notes or memoranda for future questions and drew on those notes for the purposes of the questions which they set. The papers which they prepared originated from themselves, and were, within the meaning of the Act, original. It was said, however, that they drew upon the stock of knowledge common to mathematicians, and that the time spent in producing the questions was small. These cannot be tests for determining whether copyright exists. If an author, for purposes of copyright, must not draw on the stock of knowledge which is common to himself and others who are students of the same branch of learning, only those historians who discovered fresh historical facts could acquire copyright for their works. If time expended is to be the test, the rapidity of an author like Lord Byron in producing a short poem might be an impediment in the way of acquiring copyright, and, the completer his mastery of his subject, the smaller would be the prospect of the author's success in maintaining his claim to copyright. Some of the questions, it was urged, are questions in book work, that is to say, questions set for the purpose of seeing whether the student has read and understood the book prescribed by the syllabus. But the questions set are not copied from the book; they

[91] e.g. Trade catalogues. *Collis v Cater* (1898) 78 L.T. 613; *Purefoy Engineering Co Ltd v Sykes Boxall & Co Ltd* (1955) 72 R.P.C. 89 at 95 and 102, CA (standard parts catalogue).
[92] *Bailey v Taylor* (1830) 1 Russ. & My. 73 (mathematical tables).
[93] *Harman Pictures NV v Osborne* [1971] 1 W.L.R. 723.
[94] *G. A. Cramp & Sons Ltd v F. Smythson* [1944] A.C. 329 at 335, per Viscount Simon L.C., accepting the principle stated by Lord Atkinson in *Macmillan & Co Ltd v Cooper (K. & J.)* (1923) 40 T.L.R. 186.
[95] See n.90 above.

are questions prepared by the examiner for the purpose of testing the student's acquaintance with the book, and in any case it was admitted that the papers involved selection, judgment, and experience. This objection has not, in my opinion, any substance; if it had, it would only apply to some of the questions in the elementary papers, and would have little, if any, bearing on the paper on advanced mathematics. Then it was said that the questions in the elementary papers were of common type; but this only means that somewhat similar questions have been asked by other examiners. I suppose that most elementary books on mathematics may be said to be of a common type, but that fact would not give impunity to a predatory infringer. The book and the papers alike originate from the author and are not copied by him from another book or other papers. The objections with which I have dealt do not appear to me to have any substance, and, after all, there remains the rough practical test that what is worth copying is prima facie worth protecting."

The question or originality must also be approached by considering the **5–042** particular work as a whole. In *Ladbroke (Football) Ltd v William Hill (Football) Ltd*,[96] a case involving a compilation for football pool coupons, the House of Lords stated that it was not permissible to dissect the particular work for which copyright was claimed into small parts and then try to show that each individual part was not original and not entitled to copyright.[97]

Derivative work of a new kind

Although there is no copyright in a work which is a mere copy of another **5–043** work, because it does not count as "original", it is possible for originality to reside in the conversion of a work into a new form. Thus, in *Graves' Case*[98] it was held that some photographs of engravings taken in turn from paintings were original photographs under the Fine Arts Copyright Act 1862, since they were original as photographs. However, this concept of originality does involve some difference in nature between the derivative work and the principal work on which it is based, and it does

---

[96] [1964] 1 W.L.R. 273; [1964] 1 All E.R. 465.
[97] See *Warwick Film Productions v Eisinger* [1969] 1 Ch. 508 where part of the work was pirated by the claimant in unedited form. This part of the work attracted copyright merely by its collocation in the whole. Cf. also *Purefoy Engineering Co Ltd v Sykes Boxall & Co Ltd* (1955) 72 R.P.C. 89 at 103 and 104. (part of the defendants' catalogue for component parts not copied from claimant's catalogue, but from castings drawings). *Industrial Furnaces Ltd v Reaves* [1970] R.P.C. 605 at 624. And *Biotrading & Financing Oy v Biohit Ltd* [1998] F.S.R. 109, CA; although the copying of an unoriginal shape might not amount to the copying of a substantial part, it was likely to do so when the amount copied included the context in which the shape was portrayed, and the author's originality included the placing of that shape into that context.
[98] *Graves' Case* (1869) L.R. 4 QB 715 at 723, per Blackburn J., Ct of QB.

not follow that all photographs taken from other works are necessarily original. For example, if a photograph were taken of a black and white original graphic work of the intended layout of circuitry on a printed circuit board, the photograph consisting then of a mere replication of the original pattern, it is hard to see that there would be any scope for originality in the photograph. The relevant copyright would be (if at all) the copyright in the original graphic work.

Simplicity of work and originality

5–044   Mere simplicity will not necessarily exclude a work from being original. This situation may arise with drawings. In *British Northrop Ltd v Texteam Blackburn Ltd*,[99] the drawings relied upon related to parts for looms and weaving machinery. Some of these drawings were alleged to be too simple to be capable of being original. The reasoning of Megarry J. rejecting this submission is quoted earlier in this chapter.[100]

Physical existence of artistic work

5–045   CDPA 1988 s.3(2) explicitly provides that copyright does not subsist in a literary, dramatic or musical work "unless and until it is recorded, in writing or otherwise". Since there is no corresponding provision relating to artistic works, it raises the question whether an artistic work need exist or be recorded in physical form before copyright can subsist: is it enough, for instance, for it to exist as a concept in someone's head which is orally described or illustrated by gestures? This would seem unlikely to be the legislative intent. Rather, it seems implicit in the definitions of the various categories of artistic work that they should all have some tangible form of physical existence; although there seems no reason for example why a drawing or other graphic word should not exist in the form of data in a computer from which a visual representation of it can if required be generated.

5–046   This interpretation would keep the law relating to subsistence of copyright in artistic works in line with that pertaining to unregistered design right, where it is necessary for a design to have physical existence in the form of an article to which the design has been applied or a "design document" before the design right can subsist.[101]

---

[99] [1974] R.P.C. 57; this case has already been considered in the context of whether or not very basic or simple drawings count as artistic works at all; see para.5–009 above.

[100] At paras 5–010—5–011 above.

[101] CDPA 1988 s.213(6) and see para.4–051 above. It may be that Parliament considered that a design, in contrast to an artistic work, could exist as an abstract concept so that it was necessary specifically to exclude design right from subsisting in unrecorded designs.

Qualification for subsistence of copyright

Copyright only subsists in artistic (and other) works if the correct national **5–047** qualifications concerning the nationality or national residence of the author, or the place of first publication of the work, are satisfied. These provisions are complex, and their overall purpose is to deny copyright protection to nationals of foreign countries that do not confer reciprocal protection under their own laws on works of British origin. However, thanks to the progressive expansion of the Berne Convention and the Universal Copyright Convention, it is now the case that almost all countries in the world—and virtually all those having significant industrial activity—fall within the qualification provisions of the CDPA 1988 and Orders in Council made under it.

This is in sharp contrast to the position pertaining to unregistered **5–048** design right, where designs originating in only a very limited number of foreign countries and British dependent territories qualify for protection.[102] The current provisions concerning qualification of foreign works for copyright protection are contained in CDPA 1988 s.154 and in the Copyright and Performances (Application to Other Countries) Order 2008 as amended.[103] In general, it can be assumed that artistic works originating from most industrial countries will qualify for copyright protection. In cases of difficulty it is suggested that the reader consult a reference work on general copyright law, since space does not permit more extensive treatment of this subject in this specialist work.

3. When Copyright can Protect the Shape of Three-Dimensional Articles

Artistic copyright and three-dimensional articles

Before the coming into force of the CDPA 1988, artistic copyright in **5–049** drawings was the most important right preventing the copying of the three-dimensional shapes of industrial articles. This was because it was an infringement of the copyright in a drawing of an industrial article to make the article depicted in that drawing, since that was regarded as a reproduction in three dimensions of the drawing. It followed that it was also an infringement to make a copy of the plaintiff's article on the market, because to do so would amount to a reproduction by the copyist (albeit indirect) of the drawings from which the claimant's article had been manufactured. Before coming to consider the authorities pertaining to this doctrine,[104] it must be appreciated that the scope of this doctrine has been very greatly restricted by the CDPA 1988, which replaced artistic

---

[102] See para.4–61 above.
[103] SI 2008/677, App.D4 below.
[104] See following paragraphs; these are mainly decided under the Copyright Act 1956.

copyright protection with unregistered design right protection across much of the industrial field.

5–050   The circumstances in which artistic copyright, in drawings or in three-dimensional objects such as sculptures or sculptural models, continues to be available to protect the shape and configuration of three-dimensional objects can be summarised as follows:

(1) Where a design drawing depicts a three-dimensional object which is itself an artistic work, such as a sculpture or a work of artistic craftsmanship. In such a case, a three-dimensional copy made by a third party whether directly from the drawing or indirectly from the claimant's own sculptures or works of artistic craftsmanship will infringe the copyright in the drawing.[107]

(2) Where the claimant's work in which copyright subsists is itself a three-dimensional artistic work such as sculpture or a work of artistic craftsmanship, and it is copied.[108]

(3) In the case of buildings and structures: because a building or structure is itself an "artistic work",[109] making a copy of a building or structure will infringe copyright.

(4) Where the copyright work was created before August 1, 1989 (a category now expired). In these circumstances the old law under the Copyright Act 1956 continued to apply, and copyright in drawings of three-dimensional articles could still be enforced against industrial articles copied directly from the drawings or indirectly from articles made from them. The right to continue to enforce copyrights in this way continued until 10 years after the commencement of the CDPA 1988, i.e. until August 1, 1999.[105] During the last five years of this period, such copyrights were subject to the grant of licences of right.[106]

5–051   Leaving aside the special case of buildings and structures, it can be seen that there is a special category of articles, which themselves rank as being artistic works, whose protection remains in the field of copyright. The three-dimensional shape of more mundane industrial articles is left to the lesser protection afforded by unregistered design right. However, even in the case of "artistic" articles which are protected by copyright, there is a distinction between those which are exploited on an industrial scale and those that are not. If the copyright owner exploits his copyright by making articles by an industrial process and selling them, then his

---

[105] CDPA 1988 Sch.1, para.19(1), considered in para.5–172 below.
[106] CDPA 1988 Sch.1, para.19(3), and see para.5–173 below.
[107] See para.5–062 and 5–079 below.
[108] See para.5–062 below.
[109] See para.5–019 above.

copyright ceases to be effective,[110] for this purpose 25 years,[111] after they first market such articles. On the other hand, a copyright owner who never exploits their copyright by making articles on an industrial scale retains the right to prevent others from copying his work in the form of industrial articles for the full term of the copyright.

The summary set out above relates to the shape of three-dimensional **5–052** objects. It does not cover the subject of the protection of surface patterns or surface decorations, which is considered separately in the next section.[112] In general, artistic copyright continues to be the primary form of protection relating to surface pattern and decoration, since that is outside the scope of unregistered design right.

Development of the doctrine of three-dimensional reproduction of copyright drawings

The possibility that copyright in drawings could be used to prevent the **5–053** making of three-dimensional objects from the drawings first came to prominence in the *Popeye* case.[113] There, the House of Lords held that three-dimensional figurines infringed the copyright in cartoon drawings of Popeye the Sailor. The case was primarily concerned with the interpretation of the provisions of the Copyright Act 1911 which were intended to exclude copyright from the field of industrial design: s.22(1) stated that copyright did not subsist in works which were designs capable of being registered under the then registered designs legislation[114] which were used or intended to be used as designs or patterns to be multiplied by any industrial process. Since the Popeye cartoon drawings were not at the time of their creation intended to be used for such a purpose, the House ruled that s.22(1) did not apply to them, copyright subsisted in them, and that copyright was infringed by the making of the defendant's Popeye figurines.

That decision had only limited application, because most designs for **5–054** industrial articles are intended for that purpose at the time of creation and would have been excluded from copyright by s.22(1) of the Copyright Act 1911. That provision itself is probably now only of historical interest.[115] The Copyright Act 1956 radically altered this provision. Instead of the "all or nothing" test of s.22(1) of the 1911 Act, under which copyright either subsisted for all purposes in a work or did not subsist at all for any purpose, s.10 of the Copyright Act 1956 did not exclude design

---

[110] See para.5–088 and 5–169 below.
[111] In the case of articles first marketed before the commencement of the CDPA 1988, the period is 15 years; see para.5–170 below.
[112] See para.5–084 below.
[113] *King Features Syndicate v O. M. Kleeman Ltd* [1941] A.C. 417.
[114] The Patents and Designs Acts 1907–1919, App.A7 below.
[115] Although it might continue to be relevant to a case where an old copyright work is relied upon which was created before the commencement of the Copyright Act 1956.

drawings for industrial articles from copyright protection, but instead excluded acts of industrial exploitation from the scope of copyright.[116] It did so by excluding from the scope of infringement of copyright any acts which would have infringed a corresponding design registration, had the copyright work been registered as a design under the RDA 1949.

5–055   There was a serious anomaly in the drafting of this exclusion, which came to light in *Dorling v Honnor Marine Ltd*[117] where the plaintiff sued for infringement of copyright in drawings for kits of parts for making into boats. The defendants contended that their acts were excluded from the scope of copyright protection by s.10 of the Copyright Act 1956 because the designs embodied in the drawings had been applied industrially. The Court of Appeal held that the exclusion from the scope of copyright created by s.10 was co-extensive with any notional design registration that could have been obtained, and since the making and sale of a kit of parts (as distinct from the complete boat) would not have infringed such a notional registered design,[118] then the defendants were outside the shield provided by s.10 and did infringe copyright in the drawings. The implication of this decision was far wider than just in relation to kits of parts. Since a functional design was not registrable under RDA 1949 unless and to the extent that it has "eye appeal",[119] it followed that copyright in drawings embodying unregistrable functional designs could be fully enforced.[120]

5–056   This resulted in a glaring anomaly. Industrial designs which had eye appeal and therefore some artistic merit were excluded from the scope of artistic copyright protection. However, designs that were purely functional and therefore even less artistic enjoyed full effective copyright protection under the law of artistic copyright, via the indirect means of enforcing the artistic copyright in their design drawings. This anomaly was reduced in extent, but not removed, by the Design Copyright Act 1968, which amended s.10 of the Copyright Act 1956[121] to permit the enforcement of copyright in registrable industrial designs for the 15-year period for which a notional design registration would have lasted, but not afterward. The anomaly persisted to the extent that fully functional industrial designs enjoyed unrestricted copyright protection for the full term of the copyright.[122]

---

[116] See s.10 in its original unamended form, App.D2, para.D2–006 below.

[117] [1964] R.P.C. 160, CA.

[118] The actual decision concerning the infringement of registered designs by making and supplying kits of parts was effectively reversed by the amendments made to the RDA 1949 by the CDPA 1988: RDA(A) s.7(4), and see para.3–173 above.

[119] See para.3–047 above.

[120] So held in *Allibert SA v O'Connor* [1981] F.S.R. 613, under the corresponding Irish legislation; a case about fishboxes all of whose features were held to be functional, hence not registrable, hence copyright in drawings could be fully enforced.

[121] See s.10 as amended by the Design Copyright Act 1968, App.D2, para.D2–006 below.

[122] See the trenchant comments of Lord Templeman on this anomaly in *British Leyland Motor Corp v Armstrong Patents Co Ltd* [1986] R.P.C. 279 at 372, lines 19–31, HL; also Oliver L.J. in the Court of Appeal in the same case, at 296, lines 21–32.

Decision of the House of Lords in the *British Leyland* case

The correctness of the doctrine that the copying of functional industrial **5–057** articles constituted infringement of artistic copyright in their design drawings, by reproducing those drawings in three dimensions, was upheld after exhaustive argument by a majority decision in the House of Lords in the *British Leyland* case.[123] The majority in favour of the decision was four to one, with Lord Griffiths dissenting on this point.[124] In view of the settled rights and expectations which have been founded upon this interpretation of the law, it became too late to re-open the correctness of the decision of the House in *British Leyland*.[125]

Thus, to the extent that its application has not been restricted by statute **5–058** by the CDPA 1988, the doctrine must be regarded as settled law.

Exclusion of industrial designs from scope of artistic copyright

A major restriction of the *British Leyland* doctrine has been effected by **5–059** CDPA 1988 s.51(1), which provides:

> "51.—(1) It is not an infringement of any copyright in a design document or model recording or embodying a design for anything other than an artistic work or a typeface to make an article to the design or to copy an article made to the design."

---

[123] *British Leyland Motor Corp v Armstrong Patents Co Ltd* [1986] R.P.C. 279, HL.

[124] Lord Griffiths' dissenting argument was elegant and intellectually attractive, *British Leyland Motor Corp v Armstrong Patents Co Ltd* [1986] R.P.C. 279, HL at 385–386: "The purpose of a drawing [of a functional object] is not to use artistic skill to produce an object of attraction to the public. The draughtsman applies his skill and labour in order to produce a drawing from which the object it depicts had been manufactured; it is in effect an instruction to those in the machine room who have to make the object . . . I can see that the skill and labour of the draughtsman should be protected by preventing direct copying of the blueprints . . . The draftsman's skill is merely the conduit by which the designer's ideas are communicated to the constructional engineers on the shop floor. In such circumstances, to construe reproducing as including indirect copying is to transfer the protection of artistic copyright from the draftsman to the manufacturer which is not the purpose of artistic copyright. The courts have, however, so construed the Act in recent years. . . . I believe this to have been a false step and to have brought about a result never intended by Parliament." The majority, however, considered that they were not justified in departing from the earlier decision of the House in *L.B. Plastics Ltd v Swish Products Ltd* [1979] R.P.C. 551, HL.

[125] So held by the Privy Council (on appeal from Hong Kong) in *Canon Kabushiki Kaisha v Green Cartridge Co (Hong Kong) Ltd* [1997] 3 W.L.R. 13. The board (opinion delivered by Lord Hoffmann) indicated their view that "a strong case" could be made for saying that the decisions of the House of Lords in *British Leyland* and in *L.B. Plastics* above, were wrong, since they failed sufficiently to distinguish between the reproduction of an artistic work, and the use of the information contained in an artistic work, but that it was now far too late to depart from the construction of the Act which had been adopted in the earlier cases.

5–060   The purpose of this provision was to effect a sweeping reversal[126] of the *British Leyland* doctrine over most of the field of industrial design, and to restrict the applicability of industrial copyright only to those industrial articles which can themselves be regarded as "artistic".[127] The rest of the field is covered by the more limited protection afforded by unregistered design right. It is very important, however, to realise that "design" for this purpose only includes three-dimensional shape and configuration, meaning that, subject to a complication considered in para.5–068 below where surface patterns and decorations are created within the same design drawing as the shape of the article, surface patterns and decorations are still in principle within the field of artistic copyright.

5–061   *Illustration 1:* A designer makes a drawing of a teapot. On the drawing of the teapot, he includes a decorative picture to be applied to the side of the teapot. He makes teapots according to the drawing and places them on the market. A competitor who copied the shape of his teapot would infringe design right (the drawing being a design document in which design right subsists) but not copyright. It is submitted that a competitor who copied the decorative picture, whether by placing it on a teapot or anything else, would infringe copyright in the drawing.[128] That copyright would cease to be enforceable against the placing of the picture on articles 25 years after the designer first placed his own teapots on the market.[129]

5–062   *Illustration 2:* A jeweller makes a design sketch of a new intricately worked piece of jewellery, and then handcrafts the piece from his sketch. Assuming that the piece of jewellery is sufficiently artistic to qualify as a "work of artistic craftsmanship", a competitor who makes his own copy of the piece infringes the copyright in both the design drawing and in the prototype work of artistic craftsmanship. Whether the effective period of copyright protection is 25 years or the normal term of life plus 70 years depends upon whether the jeweller makes his own pieces on a sufficient scale to count as "making by an industrial process".[130] In fact, there is also an unregistered design right subsisting in the design of the jewellery piece, but this is academic because infringement of copyright ousts infringement of design right.[131]

---

[126] *Lucasfilm Ltd v Ainsworth* [2009] EWCA Civ 1328; [2010] F.S.R. 10; [2010] E.C.D.R 5, CA at paras 83–85.

[127] i.e. the object recorded or embodied in the design document or model is itself an artistic work such as a sculpture or a work of artistic craftsmanship. The Court of Appeal in *Lucasfilm Ltd v Ainsworth* [2009] EWCA Civ 1328; [2010] F.S.R. 10; [2010] E.C.D.R 5, CA clarified the limited scope of what counts as a sculpture in rejecting a contention that a model for a stormtrooper's helmet for the film "Star Wars" was a sculpture: see para.5–020 ante.

[128] This appears to be implicit in the reasoning of the Court of Appeal in *Lambretta Clothing Co Ltd v Teddy Smith (UK) Ltd* [2004] EWCA (Civ) 886, a decision which is more fully considered in para.5–069 below.

[129] See para.5–088 below.

[130] CDPA 1988 s.52(1); see para.5–099 below.

[131] CDPA 1988 s.236; see para.4–088 above.

Illustration 3: A cartoonist creates a series of cartoon drawings of   **5–063**
Popeye the Sailor, with the sole intention at that stage of publishing them
in periodicals and books. Later, he decides to merchandise products
based on his cartoons and instructs a designer to make a design drawing
of a figurine of Popeye. Figurines are made from the design drawing and
are placed on the market. A competitor who copies the figurines on the
market will infringe the design right, but not the copyright, in the design
drawing; and by itself, the design right would leave the Popeye figurines
free to be copied after 10 years. But what of the copyright in the original
cartoon drawings? They were not intended to be designs for figurines (or
for anything) when created, so do they fall within the exclusionary words
of s.51? If they do not, then copying the figurines will infringe the
copyright in the cartoon drawings, and the legislature in 1988 has
unwittingly reproduced the same anomaly as that which was revealed in
the Copyright Act 1911 by the *Popeye* case.[132]

Whether design purpose need be present

The third illustration in the preceding paragraph raises the question of   **5–064**
whether, in order for the exclusion from copyright of s.51(1) to bite, the
purpose that the artistic work be intended to act as a design document
needs to be present when it is created. Such a requirement may be
suggested by the words "a design for anything" in s.51(1). On this
interpretation, a drawing that is created without the purpose of acting as
a design for anything, but which is later used at the basis of a design, falls
outside the ambit of s.51(1) and copyright in it remains enforceable.

On the other hand, looked at objectively, it could be said that the   **5–065**
Popeye cartoon drawings referred to in the illustration embody all along
a design for a figurine, in the sense that features of shape and configuration that could be used for a figurine are present in the cartoon drawings
when they are created. Thus, when s.51(1) speaks of "a design for
anything", it merely means that design features (i.e. features of shape and
configuration) are present that could objectively be used for the creation
of an article, regardless of the subjective intention of the author of the
drawing at the time of its creation. Thus, regardless of subjective intent at
the time of creation, to the extent that any artistic work is capable of being
used for the creation of three-dimensional articles which are not themselves artistic works, the shield against copyright infringement provided
by s.51(1) applies, and the author of the artistic work is left with his
remedies in unregistered design right alone. This latter interpretation
probably makes better sense of the overall policy of the CDPA 1988.

---

[132] See para.5–049 above.

Other acts excluded from infringing copyright

5–066   As already discussed, s.51(1) excludes from copyright infringement the making and copying of articles. The exclusion applies whether the reproduction from the article is in the form of another article, or two-dimensional picture such as a catalogue photograph of the defendant's article or even a picture on a T-shirt or in a book.[133] In order to complete the ambit of the exclusion from infringement, so that it is not unlawful to deal in other ways with articles whose making is rendered lawful by s.51(1), CDPA 1988 s.51(2) provides:

> "(2) Nor is it an infringement of the copyright to issue to the public, or include in a film, broadcast or cable programme service, anything the making of which was, by virtue of subsection (1), not an infringement of that copyright."

5–067   This subsection excludes from infringement all possible restricted acts, or potential primary infringements, that could apply to a copy of an artistic work.[134] Since secondary infringements can occur only if the making of the article is a primary infringement (or in the case of imported articles if its making in the United Kingdom would have been an infringement),[135] it follows that it is not possible to commit a secondary infringement of copyright by dealing with an article whose making is rendered lawful by s.51(1), and no special exclusion is necessary.

Scope of "design" for the purposes of section 51(1)

5–068   Section 51(1) excludes from infringement of copyright in an artistic work the making or copying of an article made to the "design" recorded or

---

[133] See *BBC Worldwide Ltd v Pally Screen Printing* [1998] F.S.R. 665, Laddie J., where the defendant created two-dimensional reproductions of "Teletubbies" on T-shirts which had presumably been derived from watching the three-dimensional articles (dressed up actors in Teletubby costumes) on television. If, however, the defendant had gone back and copied direct from the claimant's original two-dimensional concept drawings for the Teletubbies, then the shield in s.51 would not apply and he would infringe copyright in the drawings. Thus, in the Popeye example considered above, a third party who created a cartoon strip in a newspaper based upon seeing a figurine on the market would presumably not infringe copyright because he was shielded by s.51, but a third party who created his own cartoon strip by copying directly from the original Popeye cartoons would infringe.

[134] See CDPA 1988 ss.18 and 20. The section appears to make no distinction between direct copying of an article (in the form of other articles) and indirect copying in another form, such as producing two-dimensional pictures of the article in another medium: see *BBC Worldwide Ltd v Pally Screen Printing Ltd* [1998] F.S.R. 665, ChD, where pictures of "Teletubbies" printed on T-shirts would appear to be excluded from copyright infringement by s.51 so long as the defendant's pictures were derived from the three-dimensional Teletubbies themselves and not from the claimants' own two-dimensional pictures of them.

[135] CDPA 1988 s.27(1) and (2).

embodied in the artistic work. When an artistic work, e.g. a drawing of a machine part, consists and consists only of matter which constitutes a record of a "design", then the exclusion is easy to apply: reproduction of the artistic work in the form of articles falls entirely within the domain of design right and outside the domain of copyright.[136] However, the exclusion causes more difficulty in the case of an artistic work which consists partly of matters which form part of a record of a "design", and partly of other matters such as depictions of colouration or surface decoration. The most important point, which has already been noted, is that "design" for this purpose includes only features of shape or configuration, i.e. the three-dimensional design of an article. The definition of design for the purposes of s.51(1) is laid down by s.51(3) as follows:

" 'design' means the design of any aspect of the shape or configuration (whether internal or external) of the whole or part of an article, other than surface decoration."

This definition is to all intents and purposes identical to the basic **5–069** definition of "design" for the purposes of unregistered design right,[137] and since the purpose of s.51 is to mark the boundary between the domains of unregistered design right and of artistic copyright, there is a clear legislative intent that both definitions of design shall be interpreted in the same way. It should be remembered that certain important matters are excluded from the scope of unregistered design right for policy reasons. These are methods or principles of construction,[138] and features which "must fit"[139] or "must match".[140] These are not excluded from the definition of design in s.51(3)[141] so that the shield against copyright infringement provided by s.51 will apply to these features as much as to features which are the subject of design right. The legislature on this occasion has avoided repeating the anomaly under the Copyright Act 1956 which was revealed by *Dorling v Honnor Marine.*[142]

A case where a design drawing consisted both of matter constituting a **5–070** "design" within s.51 and of additional matter was considered by the Court of Appeal in *Lambretta Clothing Co Ltd v Teddy Smith (UK) Ltd.*[143]

---

[136] Photocopying the drawing however would still be a matter of infringement of artistic copyright.

[137] CDPA 1988 s.213(2), discussed at para.4–003 above.

[138] See para.4–011 above.

[139] See para.4–015 above.

[140] See para.4–026 above.

[141] Nor indeed are they excluded from the definition of "design" for design right purposes in s.213(2); rather, they are excluded from enjoying design *right* by s.213(3).

[142] See para.5–055 above.

[143] [2004] EWCA (Civ) 886, on appeal from Etherton J. at [2003] R.P.C. 41. A much simpler case where design drawings consisted of the outline shape of badges and the surface pattern on the front of the badges was considered in *Flashing Badge Co Ltd v Groves* [2007] EWHC 1372 (Ch); [2007] F.S.R. 36, Rimer J.: see para.5–087 below.

The designs in issue were for track tops and consisted of making different parts (body, sleeves, trim stripes, zips, pockets) of various different colours and applying a logo to the front and back. There was no originality in the shapes of the track top or its parts, which were simply copied from an existing garment. Both Etherton J. at first instance and the majority of the Court of Appeal (Jacob and Mance L.JJ.) held that the colouration of the various parts did not form part of the "design" under s.51, or in any event consisted of "surface decoration" which is explicitly excluded from "design" by s.51(3). It is submitted that this conclusion is undoubtedly correct. There was then a divergence of view as to whether s.51 operated to prevent the claimant asserting copyright infringement in respect of alleged copying of the colouration. Jacob L.J. said as follows in para.39:

> "39. Now, apart from the colourways, there is no doubt that Mr Harmer's drawing is a 'design document'. Does the fact that 'surface decoration' is excluded from the definition of 'design' for the purpose of s.51 make any difference? I think not. For these colourways are not just colours in the abstract: they are colours applied to shapes. Neither physically nor conceptually can they exist apart from the shapes of the parts of the article. It is not as though this surface decoration could subsist on other substrates in the same way as, for instance, a picture or logo could. If artistic copyright were to be enforced here, it would be enforced in respect of Mr Harmer's whole design drawing. But that is not allowed by s.51. I think the judge put it elegantly when he said (para.74):
>
>> 'Such an approach . . . would appear to give rise . . . to an impossible task. It would require the Court to consider the existence and infringement of copyright in respect of the juxtaposition of colourways divorced from the shape or configuration of the article in question, even though the shape and configuration of Lambretta's garment provide the borders of the colourways and the means by which the colourways are juxtaposed.' "

5–071   By contrast, Mance L.J. reasoned on this point at paras 80 to 82:

> "80. . . . in order 'to make an article to the design' or 'to copy an article made to the design' embodied in a drawing, it is, because of the definition in s.51(3), still necessary to conclude that the article was made, or was a copy of an article made, to the design, meaning 'the design [as embodied in the drawing] of any aspect of the shape or configuration . . . of the whole or part of an article, other than surface decoration'. Only if it was, does s.51 prevent there being any copyright infringement. And, even if it was, I do not see any basis for reading s.51 as going further than preventing any copyright infringement to the extent that it was made, or was a copy of an article made,

to the design in that limited sense. The alternative is that, as soon as any design right is infringed in a drawing by making an article, or copying an article made, to the shape or configuration shown in a drawing, there can be no infringement of any copyright in respect of that drawing, no matter what the relative importance of the shape or configuration and of the other aspects copied. That would seem arbitrary. . . .

82. In any event, however, s.51 requires one to ignore any copying of the shape or configuration of the track-suit top, when assessing whether Teddy Smith copied the whole or any substantial part of Mr Harmer's drawing for the purposes of s.16. What Teddy Smith did copy, if they copied anything, was the colourways and surface decoration. The relevant question in the light of ss.16 and 51 is therefore whether, in doing this, they copied the whole or a substantial part of Mr Harmer's drawing. I do not see that this is or becomes an impossible question, merely because, in asking whether Teddy Smith copied a substantial part of Mr Harmer's drawing, one is required to ignore any copying (if there had happened to be any) of the shape or configuration of the article embodied in Mr Harmer's drawing. Distinctions between shape and configuration and other aspects are inherent in s.51 and indeed s.213, and discrimination between "substantial" and lesser parts of a work is inherent in s.16(3). . . . The position regarding surface decoration appears to me consistent with my conclusion as to the law. Surface decoration can have no design right protection under s.213, but it is excluded by s.51(3) from the concept of design for the purposes of s.51(1). So copyright in a drawing showing an article with surface decoration may still be infringed, if (putting aside any copying of the design of the shape or configuration of the article) there has, by virtue of the copying of the surface decoration, been copying of a substantial part of the drawing. I do not see any basis for limiting the copyright protection in case of surface decoration to a situation where the surface decoration could be said itself to constitute a separate drawing."

Unfortunately, the third member of the court, Sedley L.J. held that the s.51 defence applied on the diametrically opposite (and, it is submitted, erroneous) ground that the colouration of the parts was part of the "configuration" of the article and so part of the "design" within s.51. This decision of the Court of Appeal is therefore unsatisfactory, in that it does not appear to provide a majority for the reasoning of either Jacob L.J. or Mance L.J. Jacob L.J. appears implicitly to allow for artistic copyright to be enforced in a case where a surface picture or logo appears within a design drawing,[144] apparently on the basis that such drawings could exist

5–072

---

[144] As in the example of a drawing of a teapot with a decorative picture on its side

physically or conceptually apart from the shapes of the parts of the article. Thus, both judgments appear to have the following propositions in common:

(1) the "design document" for the purposes of s.51 is not the same thing as the physical drawing which embodies the design document, where that drawing contains additional matter which does not form part of a record of a "design" (i.e. features of shape and configuration) as defined in s.51. This is also implicit in the opening sentence of Jacob L.J.'s para.39 (quoted in full above) which states that *"apart from the colourways* [emphasis added], there is no doubt that Mr Harmer's drawing is a design document"; i.e. the colourways *are* additional matter which does not form part of the "design document" under s.51;

(2) the fact that the drawing is a single artistic work in which only one copyright subsists does not mean that s.51 then operates, in the case where the drawing is only partly a "design document", as an absolute bar to the enforcement of that copyright. In such a case, where the copyright work is partially within and partially outside s.51, the copyright in the work may be enforced in respect of those aspects of the work which fall outside s.51.

The difference of view lies in whether (per Jacob L.J.) the copyright in those aspects of the work can only be enforced where the additional matter is independent of the features of shape and configuration and could in principle exist on some different substrate, e.g. it is a picture or logo; or whether (per Mance L.J.) one ignores any copying of features of shape and configuration when assessing whether a substantial part of the drawing has been copied. The approach of Mance L.J. does seem to admit of having regard to the position on the article from which and to which a surface feature is copied: e.g. the fact that a stripe is shown on a sleeve on the drawing, and is copied onto a sleeve rather than some other part of the garment on the alleged infringement, is to be taken into account. In deciding between these two approaches it cannot be said that the legislature has set the courts an easy task, since the draftsman of s.51 seems simply to have assumed that a drawing will fall wholly within or wholly outside the section, and the status of drawings consisting partly of a "design document" and partly of additional matter such as surface decoration has not been considered or addressed. Accordingly, the wording of s.51 does not provide a clear guide one way or the other

considered in para.5–059 *Illustration 1* above. If the picture for the side of the teapot is drawn on a separate drawing from the drawing of the shape of the teapot, then the copyright in the drawing of the picture can be fully enforced (subject to the time limitation in s.52) against copyists. It would be illogical and anomalous if such protection were lost simply because the designer chose to put his picture down in the same drawing as that in which he defined the shape of the teapot.

between the two approaches; however it is submitted that the approach of Mance L.J. accords better with the legislative intent of the CDPA 1988, which was to give three-dimensional features of design the less advantageous protection of unregistered design right but to retain copyright protection for surface decoration—hence its explicit exclusion from s.51(3). The approach of Jacob L.J. would lead to significant numbers of designs of surface decoration losing protection because they fall down a legislative gap between the two different rights. It is submitted that this is a conclusion which the courts should be slow to reach unless the wording of the Act actually compels it, and that the wording of s.51 can be fully respected and satisfactorily applied through Mance L.J.'s formulation that it prevents copyright infringement "to the extent that" an article is being made to the "design" embodied in the drawing.

Section 51 and surface patterns or decorations

As has already been noted, s.51(3) explicitly excludes "surface decoration" from the scope of "design". The distinction between what counts as surface decoration and what counts as shape or configuration is discussed more fully in the context of unregistered design right.[145] The effect of the exclusion from "design" in s.51 is to exclude surface patternings which do have some three-dimensional aspect, for example because they are produced by etching or raising lines or patterns on the surface, but which are decorative rather than functional.[146] Thus, *decorative* surface patterns involving some three dimensional height from the surface are protectable by way of copyright rather than by way of design right. One would have thought that this would mean that *functional* surface patterning involving some three dimensional height would be within the field of design right rather than copyright.   **5–073**

However, it has been suggested that at least some such surface features may escape from s.51 through quite a different route, on the grounds that they are produced from a mould which counts as an "engraving", because it is a plate into which the surface features have been engraved and therefore the objects which the plate is used to create are also "engravings" and are therefore artistic works. On this ground it has been held that moulded rubber floor mats for cars are "artistic works" so that s.51 does not apply to them.[147] This end result seems so bizarre that the reasoning which leads to it must be open to question. It is submitted that its fallacy is as follows. CDPA s.4(2) defines, within the category of artistic works, a subclass "(b) any engraving, etching, lithograph, woodcut or similar work". All of these are different methods by which pictures may   **5–074**

---

[145] See para.4–029 above.
[146] Or at least *primarily* functional: see *Hi-Tech Autoparts Ltd v Towergate Two Ltd (No.2)* [2002] F.S.R. 270, Pat Cty Ct.
[147] See *Hi-Tech Autoparts Ltd v Towergate Two Ltd (No.2)* [2002] F.S.R. 16, Pat Cty Ct.

be produced (if necessary in quantity) by printing onto paper, and they form part of the category of "graphic work". The essence of them is that although the plates are three-dimensional in the sense of having raised portions, their purpose is to produce a two-dimensional pattern on a surface by putting ink onto it at the points where they make contact with the surface. In that context it may be appropriate in ordinary usage to refer to, say, a "woodcut" as embracing both the actual wooden plate carved by the artist and the prints which are produced from it. However, just because flat prints on paper can in accordance with reasonable linguistic usage be referred to as engravings, etchings, woodcuts, etc., it does not follow that industrial articles such as rubber floor mats fall within the scope of the words "engraving, etching, woodcut or similar work", nor that they are "graphic works", simply because some process of engraving or etching etc has been used to create the moulds in which they are made. This is really just another form of the pernicious fallacy originated in the New Zealand *Wham-O* case,[148] which held that a plastic moulded "Frisbee" was an engraving because the mould in which it was made was created by a process involving engraving or cutting the required three-dimensional shape into the metal of the mould.

Restriction of copyright term where articles are made by an industrial process

5–075   Even in cases where copyright in an artistic work can be enforced in respect of the three-dimensional design of an article, a further layer of complication arises. That is that in some circumstances, copyright can be fully enforced for its unrestricted term (normally life of the author plus 70 years[149]), whilst in other circumstances the enforceability of the artistic copyright against its reproduction in the form of industrial articles is restricted to an effective term of 25 years[150] after the copyright owner first markets his own industrial articles. This is the effect of CDPA 1988 s.52, the overall purpose of which is to align the period of protection conferred by those aspects of artistic copyright which continue to remain relevant to industrial articles to the term of protection that would be offered by a corresponding registered design. The background and purpose of this section is more fully considered below in the context of the protection of surface patterns, which is the aspect of industrial design to which artistic copyright primarily continues to apply.[151] At this point therefore only those aspects of s.52 which are particularly pertinent to three-dimensional designs will be considered.

---

[148] Discussed and criticised in para.5–018 above.
[149] See para.5–164 below.
[150] The restriction is to the shorter term of 15 years in the case of articles first marketed before the coming into force of the CDPA 1988; see para.5–170 below.
[151] See para.5–088 below.

Section 52 bites (and in consequence restricts copyright protection to 25 years) when the owner of the copyright in an artistic work exploits the work by making or licensing the making of articles which are copies of the work "by an industrial process".[152] What counts as making by an industrial process is prescribed by statutory instrument,[153] and means if 50 or more articles (not forming a set) are made or goods are made by machine in lengths or pieces.[154] For this purpose the making of the articles can take place either inside or outside the United Kingdom and an argument that s.52 (and its predecessor s.10(2) of the Copyright Act 1956) are by implication restricted to cases where the making by an industrial process takes place within the United Kingdom has been rejected in robust terms.[155] In addition, the statutory instrument excludes from the scope of s.52 (and therefore keeps within the realm of full unrestricted copyright) certain articles which are regarded as of "primarily literary or artistic character".[156] The exclusions made for this purpose mirror the exclusions from registrability under the RDA(A) of designs for articles of a primarily literary or artistic character, in which respect the statutory instrument is in identical terms.[157] Thus, articles which are classed as of "primarily literary or artistic character" are both excluded from registrability under the RDA(A) and enjoy the full unrestricted term of copyright, further emphasising that the underlying policy of s.52 is to align the effective term of protection under artistic copyright law of works which are capable of registration as designs with the term of protection that they would have enjoyed if registered.

5–076

The exclusions that relate to three-dimensional[158] articles are laid down in art.3 of the Order[159] as follows:

5–077

"3.—(1) There are excluded from the operation of section 52 of the Act—

---

[152] CDPA 1988 s.52(1)(a).

[153] The Copyright (Industrial Process and Excluded Articles) (No.2) Order 1989 (SI 1989/1070) made under CDPA 1988 s.52(4).

[154] More fully considered in para.5–099 below.

[155] *Lucasfilm Ltd v Ainsworth* [2008] EWCA 1878 (Ch); [2009] F.S.R.2; [2008] E.C.D.R. 17, Mann J. at paras 159–166: "The place of manufacture seems to me to be supremely irrelevant to the question—I can detect no point of principle which would indicate that it should matter whether the articles were made in the UK as opposed to elsewhere. Such a distinction would be arbitrary." The Court of Appeal did not need to deal with this point: *Lucasfilm Ltd v Ainsworth* [2009] EWCA Civ 1328; [2010] F.S.R. 10; [2010] E.C.D.R 5, CA 1 at para.98.

[156] Under a power conferred by CDPA 1988 s.52(4)(b).

[157] Rule 26 of the Registered Designs Rules 1989, made under RDA(A) s.1(5). This is set out and considered at para.3–033 above.

[158] The exclusions relating to printed matter and other two-dimensional articles are considered in para.5–94 below.

[159] Copyright (Industrial Process and Excluded Article) (No.2) Order 1989 (SI 1989/1070), App.D5 below.

(a) works of sculpture, other than casts or models used or intended to be used as models or patterns to be multiplied by any industrial process;

(b) wall plaques, medals and medallions;"

5–078   The applicability of these provisions to sculptures and to wall plaques and medallions are discussed in the next two following paragraphs.

Industrial articles which are themselves sculptures

5–079   It has already been pointed out that because a sculpture is an artistic work, in consequence a design for an object which is itself a sculpture falls outside the exclusion from copyright laid down by s.51(1) of the CDPA 1988. When does a finished industrial article rank as a "sculpture"? It seems that the essential feature of sculpture is that it is a branch of representational art,[160] and that implies that the essential purpose of the object concerned must be to portray or represent the shape which it bears, rather than being functional. An elegant teapot may be deliberately shaped to be beautiful, but even so it is hardly a "sculpture". On the other hand, it may well be that an object with a dominant[161] representational purpose need not be particularly beautiful in order to rank as a sculpture.[162] In one case, a wolf cub's head originally modelled in clay and then reproduced on a large scale in the form of papier-mâché replicas, was considered to be a sculpture.[163]

5–080   In one New Zealand case, it was held that a wooden model which was used as the basis for making an injection mould for making plastic children's toys ("Frisbees") was a sculpture, but the actual plastic toys made from the mould were not.[164] The correctness of the view that the wooden model is a sculpture has been doubted by the English Court of

---

[160] Paragraphs 5–019 to 5–020A above.

[161] The object need not be entirely non-functional: e.g. the Australian case *Wildash v Klein* (2004) 61 I.P.R. 324, Australian Northern Territory Sup Ct, where three-dimensional representations of animals made in wire and designed to have aesthetic appeal to potential purchasers were held to be sculptures even though some of them acted as wall and table candle holders and "mozzie coil" holders; cited with approval by the Court of ·Appeal in *Lucasfilm Ltd v Ainsworth* [2009] EWCA Civ 1328; [2010] F.S.R. 10; [2010] E.C.D.R 5, CA at para.69.

[162] e.g. a bad plaster statue of a saint considered by the Court of Appeal in *Lucasfilm Ltd v Ainsworth* [2009] EWCA Civ 1328; [2010] F.S.R. 10; [2010] E.C.D.R 5, CA at para.74. It should be recalled that CDPA 1988 s.4(1)(a) includes sculptures among the categories of artistic work which count as such "irrespective of artistic quality".

[163] And therefore an artistic work within s.35(1) of the Copyright Act 1911: *Pytram Ltd v Models (Leicester) Ltd* [1930] 1 Ch. 639. However, this appears to proceed on the concession of counsel, nor was it necessary in that case to distinguish between the question of whether the original clay model was a sculpture, and whether the papier-mâché replicas were. The actual decision in the case concerns whether the model was for a design capable of registration under the Patents and Designs Act 1907, and this aspect, as well as the position under the present law, is discussed at para.3–033 above.

[164] *Wham-O Mfg Co v Lincoln Industries Ltd* [1985] R.P.C. 127, CA of NZ; the decision of this court on the former point is criticised at para.5–020 above.

Appeal,[165] but even assuming that that decision is right, to what extent can artistic copyright apply to copying of the finished plastic articles on the market? Since the wooden model is a model embodying a design for an object which is itself not a sculpture (the plastic Frisbee), it would appear that s.51 will apply to exclude artistic copyright (whether in the wooden model itself or in any pre-existing sketches on which the wooden model was based) from covering reproduction of the finished articles. The owner is left to his remedy in design right alone, so that the question of the application of s.52 does not arise.

But suppose that the finished article is itself an object that counts as a **5–081** sculpture, such as (assuming that *Pytram* is right on this point) a replicated figure of a wolf cub's head. In such a case, s.52 can apply only if the copyright owner authorises its reproduction on an industrial scale, i.e. in 50 or more copies. If he does not do this, then he can enforce his sculpture copyright for its full term. If he does do this, the further question arises of whether the operation of s.52 is excluded by article 3(1)(a) set out above.[166] That excludes sculptures, but only if they are not "casts or models used or intended to be used as models or patterns to be multiplied by any industrial process." But the original clay model must necessarily be a model or pattern intended to be multiplied by an industrial process or the question of the application of s.52 would not have arisen in the first place. Thus, at first sight it would appear that the excluding words in art.3(1)(a) will necessarily apply in all cases where a sculpture is multiplied by an industrial process (i.e. in 50 or more copies), thereby rendering art.3(1)(a) nugatory.

However, it may be more correct to interpret art.3(1)(a) as referring **5–082** only to the articles placed on the market themselves. This interpretation is supported by the wording of CDPA 1988 s.52(4)(b). If this is right, since the wolf's cubs heads placed on the market are themselves sculptures, and are not themselves models or patterns intended for further replication, art.3(1)(a) does apply to exclude them from the ambit of s.52 and artistic copyright in works embodying the design for them (whether a drawing or an initial model) can be enforced for its unrestricted term.

This interpretation would mean that the exclusion from art.3(1)(a) would apply only when the articles placed on the market are themselves models or patterns intended to be further replicated by the customers. Thus, a company that produced on an industrial scale casting patterns that were intended to be used by customers for casting their own end products would find that the effective copyright protecting its casting patterns would be limited to 25 years.[167] The difficulties of interpretation

---

[165] In *Lucasfilm Ltd v Ainsworth* [2009] EWCA Civ 1328; [2010] F.S.R. 10; [2010] E.C.D.R 5, CA at para.65.

[166] In para.5–077 above.

[167] It is not necessary that each customer should replicate the casting pattern that they buy 50 times, because art.3(2) provides: "Nothing in article 2 of this Order shall be taken to limit the meaning of 'industrial process' in paragraph 1(a) of this article."

caused by exclusions to exclusions to exclusions seem to be endemic to industrial design law.

Wall plaques and medallions

5–083   The position of wall plaques, medals and medallions is more straightforward. Although the design of these objects is three-dimensional, in the sense that the patterns on them are generally formed in relief or by indentation, the patterns are clearly "surface decoration". Thus, s.51 does not operate to exclude them from the scope of artistic copyright nor do their surface patterns fall within the scope of unregistered design right.[168] The further effect of art.3(1)(b) quoted above is that artistic copyright remains effectively enforceable for its full term and is not restricted to the 25-year limited period.

4. Copyright as a Protection for Surface Patterns

Artistic copyright and surface patterns

5–084   Artistic copyright still retains its pre-eminence when it comes to the protection of industrial articles that are two-dimensional, and the surface patterns of articles that are three-dimensional. Unregistered design right applies only to features of shape and configuration, as does the corresponding exclusion of application of artistic copyright to the design of industrial articles contained in CDPA 1988 s.51.[169] Surface patterns and features which are strictly three-dimensional because they are raised or indented nevertheless are outside the scope of design right and within the scope of copyright, provided that they are decorative rather than functional.[170]

5–085   This leaves artistic copyright (in parallel with registered designs which can apply to pattern and ornament as well as shape and configuration[171]) as the right providing effective protection to two-dimensional pictures and patterns as applied to industrial articles. In order for artistic copyright to arise and to be relevant, there must (as in the *British Leyland* doctrine discussed above)[172] be an artistic work upon which the pattern or picture is based, since a prototype article will not itself qualify for subsistence of copyright except in exceptional cases: such as where it is a "work of artistic craftsmanship".[173] But the application of a pattern or

---

[168] See para.5–066 above.
[169] See para.5–068 above.
[170] See para.4–026 above as regards exclusion of surface decoration from unregistered design rights; and para.5–068 above as regards the exclusion of surface decoration from the application of CDPA 1988 s.51, and the continued application of artistic copyright.
[171] See paras 3–017 to 3–021 above.
[172] Paragraph 5–057 above.
[173] See para.5–022 above.

picture to an industrial article will normally involve the preparation of some form of drawing or other graphic work which is then replicated.[174]

Cases where elements of two- and three-dimensional designs are inter-linked

It is easy to understand the concept of surface pattern or decoration as distinct from three-dimensional shape in cases like the example given of a picture on the side of a teapot. The shape of the teapot could be copied without copying the picture; or the picture could be copied onto a completely different teapot, or indeed onto another article altogether or onto a piece of paper. However, there may be cases where the whole essence of the design resides in the inter-relationship between features of shape and features of pattern, so that the pattern is virtually meaningless without the three-dimensional shape to which it relates. For example, a dress design might make the sleeves one colour, the torso another and the skirt another; or consider the track-top design which was the subject of the decision of the Court of Appeal in the *Lambretta* case.[175] Viewing the pattern alone without reference to the shape of the three-dimensional article to which it is intended to be applied is very difficult indeed—must it be viewed simply as a block of three colours on the paper? Regarded as such, will it be sufficiently original to qualify for copyright protection? If it does, will a competitor who copies the three colours but applies them to completely different parts of their garment infringe the copyright?

5–086

It is apparent from the divergence of judicial reasoning in the *Lambretta* case that the courts have been unsuccessful so far in overcoming the inherent logical difficulties created by Parliament's decision to protect two different aspects of what in lay terms counts as design through two distinct rights having different attributes. In reality, the creation of the two- and three-dimensional aspects of a new article may be a single act of creative design in which it may be difficult to disentangle the two- and three-dimensional elements from each other and impossible for each of those aspects to make sense on its own if artificially divorced from the other. However, this exercise of artificial division is required by the law and the courts will have to continue to struggle with its implications. An intermediate case of less difficulty than *Lambretta*—although not as simple as the picture on the teapot example given above—was where the

5–087

---

[174] The original graphic work could even be on the surface of a prototype article. For example, if a new design of teapot is created with a decorative picture on its side, the designer might hand paint the prototype article with his original picture from which it is then replicated. The original picture would then undoubtedly be a graphic work in which copyright will subsist if it is original, despite the fact that the substratum on which it is created is a prototype teapot.

[175] [2004] EWCA (Civ) 886: the facts are set out and the reasoning analysed in paras 5–070 above, et seq.

claimant relied on copyright in drawings of decorated badges whose outline shape followed the outline of the artistic design on the front of the badge.[176] Granting summary judgment, Rimer J. held that the surface decoration on the front of the badges was excluded from the scope of s.51, and therefore copyright in the drawings could be enforced against the reproduction of the surface decoration on the front of the defendant's badges. However, s.51 did apply to the drawings insofar as they depicted the outline shapes of the badges. Presumably, the claimant could have relied on unregistered design right as regards that aspect of its complaint.[177]

Restriction of copyright term where the design is applied industrially

5–088   Where an artistic work is applied as an industrial design,[178] in most cases the effective term for which the copyright can be enforced in respect of industrial application is restricted to 25 years after first marketing of the industrial articles. This is the effect of CDPA 1988 s.52(1) and (2), which provide:

> "52.—(1) This section applies where an artistic work has been exploited, by or with the licence of the copyright owner, by—
>
> (a) making by an industrial process articles falling to be treated for the purposes of this Part as copies of the work, and
> (b) marketing such articles, in the United Kingdom or elsewhere.
>
> (2) After the end of the period of 25 years from the end of the calendar year in which such articles are first marketed, the work may be copied by making articles of any description, or doing anything for the purpose of making articles of any description, and anything may be done in relation to articles so made, without infringing copyright in the work."

---

[176] *Flashing Badge Co Ltd v Groves* [2007] EWHC 1372 (Ch); [2007] F.S.R. 36, Rimer J. The judge analysed the differing reasoning of the members of the Court of Appeal in *Lambretta*.

[177] It does not appear from the report that unregistered design right was relied upon, nor is the reason why it was not relied upon clear. It may be that on the facts of that case, a "win" on the surface designs was good enough for the claimant and there was no real prospect of the defendant continuing to make the shaped badges and putting a different design on the front.

[178] "Design" is used here to cover both two-dimensional and three-dimensional aspects of the design of an article. The sidenote to s.52, "Effect of exploitation of design derived from artistic work", confusingly uses "design" in this wider sense, immediately after s.51 which uses "design" in the narrower sense of three-dimensional features only. Great care is needed to avoid confusion.

As can be seen, the restriction on the enforceability of copyright applies from January 1 of the year following the 25th anniversary of the date when the articles are first placed on the market, rather than the 25th anniversary date itself. This rule is for convenience, in order to avoid the difficulties in proving the precise date when articles were first placed on the market. In the case of articles first placed on the market before the coming into force of the CDPA 1988 (August 1, 1989) the restriction on the scope of copyright laid down by s.52 comes into force 15 years after the first marketing.[179] However, that is 15 years exactly from the first marketing, not the end of the calendar year.[180]   **5–089**

The overall purpose of this provision is to align the effective period of copyright protection for artistic works which are applied as industrial designs with the period of protection that would have been enjoyed by a corresponding registered design. Thus, the 25-year period is based on the current maximum term of registered design protection,[181] whilst the 15 years correspond to the 15-year life of registered designs under the RDA 1949 before it was amended by the CDPA 1988.[182]   **5–090**

Where only part of an artistic work is exploited in this way, the restriction on the effective term of copyright imposed by this section applies only to that part of the work.[183]   **5–091**

Scope of restriction on copyright

If s.52(2) comes into force at the end of 25 years, it greatly restricts the effective scope of the copyright in the artistic work, but does not eliminate the copyright completely. For example, a painter creates a painting. He later authorises teapots to be made with a reproduction of his painting on the side. After 25 years, from January 1 of the following year onwards he can no longer prevent his painting being copied onto competing teapots or indeed any other kind of article. However, the copyright does continue to subsist (for his lifetime plus 70 years) and he can continue to enforce it in some contexts: for instance, he can still sue for infringement if his painting is reproduced without his permission in a book or calendar.   **5–092**

The extent of the residual enforceability of his copyright depends on two factors: the explicit exclusions in and under s.52, and limitations on its scope inherent in the use of the word "article". These will be dealt with in turn.   **5–093**

---

[179] CDPA 1988 Sch.1 para.20(1); and see para.5–170 below.
[180] This is because the effect of the transitional provisions is to preserve the date which was laid down by the old s.10 of the Copyright Act 1956, which expired on the 15th anniversary of first marketing: see s.10(3), as amended by the Design Copyright Act 1968, App.D2, para.D2–006 below.
[181] See para.3–274 above.
[182] See para.3–301 above.
[183] CDPA 1988 s.52(3).

Articles of a primarily literary or artistic character, and films

5–094   Section 52(4) of the CDPA 1988 provides for the exclusion from the operation of s.52 by statutory instrument of articles "of a primarily literary or artistic character". Under this power has been made the Copyright (Industrial Process and Excluded Articles) (No.2) Order 1989.[184] Article 3 of this Order excludes certain three-dimensional objects from the operation of this section, which are dealt with in the section dealing with the application of artistic copyright to three-dimensional designs.[185] So far as relevant to two-dimensional designs, it reads as follows:

> "3.—(1) . . .
>
> (c) printed matter primarily of a literary or artistic character, including book jackets, calendars, certificates, coupons, dressmaking patterns, greetings cards, labels, leaflets, maps, plans, playing cards, postcards, stamps, trade advertisements, trade forms and cards, transfers and similar articles."

5–095   This list of matter which is excluded as being of primarily literary or artistic character is the same as the list of articles which were excluded on the same basis from registrability for registered designs purposes.[186] This is intentional, having regard to the fact that the 25-year cut-off of copyright is not intended to apply to designs that are not registrable because they are deemed too "literary" or "artistic". They are left entirely within the domain of copyright protection, and enjoy an unrestricted term.

5–096   In addition to the classes of articles excluded from s.52 by statutory instrument, s.52(6)(a) states that "references to articles do not include films". In the example of the painter given previously, he would still be able to prevent his painting from being shown in a film.[187] Further, if he had himself authorised his painting to be included in a film rather than placed on a teapot, he would not have caused the beginning of the 25-year period under the section to be triggered.

Scope of section 52 limited to "articles"

5–097   Section 52 is also limited, both as regards what kinds of acts by the copyright owner trigger its application as well in respect of what acts the copyright owner still retains the power to restrain, by any limitation

---

[184] SI 1989/1070, App.D5 below.
[185] See paras 5–075 to 5–079 above.
[186] Under RDA(A) s.1(5) and r.26 of the Registered Design Rules 1989; discussed at para.3–034 above.
[187] Subject to the "incidental inclusion" fair dealing defence in CDPA 1988 s.31(1).

inherent in the word "article". The section applies (subject to the specific exclusions already mentioned) to "articles of any description".[188] Unfortunately neither the section nor the Act as a whole contains any relevant definition of the word "article".[189] One interpretation is to say that "article" in s.52 means the same as "article" in the context of registered designs under the pre-2001 law. This would make sense, given that the whole purpose of s.52 is to align copyright protection with the term of registered design protection. Furthermore, the predecessor to s.52, which was s.10 of the Copyright Act 1956, clearly used "article" in the same sense as the RDA 1949, and it is hard to see any reason why Parliament should have intended to adopt a different meaning in s.52.[190]

Assuming that this is correct, there are two important consequences. **5–098** The first is that there is authority that for registered design purposes, for an object to count as an "article" it must have some purpose beyond merely carrying the design.[191] Thus, an oil painting on canvas is not an "article" because it is in substance the design itself and not an article to which the design has been applied. Thus, objects of this nature would be excluded from s.52 on fundamental grounds even without the explicit exclusion of articles of a primarily literary or artistic character discussed above.[192] A second consequence is that buildings and structures would not be "articles"[193]: a question giving rise to more doubt if "article" in this section is to be construed independently of its meaning for registered design purposes.

Making articles by an industrial process

The start of the 25-year period in s.52 is triggered when articles are "made **5–099** by an industrial process"[194] and then marketed. What is to count as making by an industrial process for this purpose is defined by statutory instrument made under s.52(4)(a). The Copyright (Industrial Process and Excluded Articles) (No.2) Order 1989[195] art.2 provides as follows:

---

[188] CDPA 1988 s.52(2) quoted above.
[189] Section 178 contains a definition of an article in a periodical.
[190] As regards interpretation, see CDPA 1988 s.172(2).
[191] Discussed at para.3–028 above.
[192] If this is right, then one consequence is that the word "article" has a different meaning from the sense in which it is used elsewhere in the copyright provisions (Pt I) of the CDPA 1988. For instance, s.27 refers to "articles" which are infringing copies, and it would clearly be absurd if for this purpose a painting did not count as an article. However, there is inevitably an inconsistency between the meaning of "article" in s.52 and s.27, or there is an inconsistency between its meaning in s.52 and in the Registered Designs Act as amended by CDPA 1988. On a purposive interpretation of these provisions, the greatest sense and consistency is created by interpreting "article" in s.52 as having the same meaning as in the RDA(A).
[193] See para.3–036 above.
[194] CDPA 1988 s.52(1)(a).
[195] SI 1989/1070, App.D5 below.

"2. An article is to be regarded for the purposes of section 52 of the Act (limitation of copyright protection for design derived from artistic work) as made by an industrial process if—

(a) it is one of more than fifty articles which—

(i) all fall to be treated for the purposes of Part I of the Act as copies of a particular artistic work, but

(ii) do not all together constitute a single set of articles as defined by section 44(1) of the Registered Designs Act 1949; or

(b) it consists of goods manufactured in lengths or pieces, not being hand-made goods."

5–100   As regards registered designs and sets of articles, see the previous discussion. One difficulty raised by this provision is what happens if more than 50 articles are made over lengthy period of time. It is easy to see that if more than 50 articles are all made at once before any are sold, as soon as the first one of them is placed on the market the 25-year period begins running. However, what if the copyright owner makes and sells five or 10 articles every year? Once he reaches 50, is the very first one that he made and sold then treated as having been made by an industrial process, so triggering the application of s.52 as from its marketing date, as it were retrospectively? Or can the period only begin to run once the fiftieth article has been made?

5. Acts Amounting to Infringement of Copyright

Acts of primary infringement

5–101   The acts of primary infringement of copyright (so-called "restricted acts") that are relevant to artistic copyright are:

(1) Copying the work, which means "reproducing the work in any material form"[196];

(2) Issuing copies of the work to the public, in the sense of being the first originator on the market of the copies rather than a subsequent distributor[197];

(3) Broadcasting the work or including it in a cable programme service.[198]

---

[196] CDPA 1988 s.17(2).
[197] CDPA 1988 s.18.
[198] CDPA 1988 s.20. This category of primary infringement has only incidental relevance to the field of industrial design and will not be considered further.

Copying by reproducing the work in any material form

This means the creation in some physical form of an object which is a **5–102** copy of the whole or a substantial part of the work. For an object to be a copy of a work, it is necessary that there should be a causal link between the work and the copy; similarity that results from co-incidence, or from independent design, is not the result of copying. The degree of resemblance necessary for it to amount to a reproduction of a substantial part is dealt with in the next section.[199] What counts as a material form for this purpose includes "storing the work in any medium by electronic means".[200] Thus, an electronic image of a drawing in a computer memory, or a representation of a sculpture in the form of a set of co-ordinates in three dimensions stored in a computer, would count as a material form. Although normally reproduction will involve the creation of an inanimate physical object, it is possible to reproduce a work in material form by posing human beings in a position or manner where they resemble the depiction of the work.[201]

Of particular importance in the field of industrial design is that CDPA **5–103** 1988 s.17(3) provides:

"(3) Copying in relation to an artistic work includes the making of a copy in three dimensions of a two-dimensional work, and the making of a copy in two dimensions of a three-dimensional work."

This aspect of the definition of copying is in substance the same as the **5–104** definition in the Copyright Act 1956.[202] However, the troublesome "non-expert recognition test" laid down by subs.9(8)[203] of that Act is not carried forward into the 1988 Act. The *British Leyland* doctrine already discussed[204] rests on the proposition that a two-dimensional drawing can, for copyright purposes, be "reproduced" by making the three-dimensional article depicted in it. But although the former (in practice limited)

---

[199] Paragraphs 5–118 et seq. below.
[200] CDPA 1988 s.17(2).
[201] In *Bradbury Agnew & Co v Day* (1916) 32 T.L.R. 349, a case under the Copyright Act 1911, an injunction was granted to restrain infringement of copyright in a cartoon by representing it on the stage in the form of a burlesque, on the ground that a substantial part of the cartoon had been reproduced in a material form.
[202] Copyright Act 1956 s.48(1), definition of "reproduction".
[203] Copyright Act 1956 s.9(8) says; "The making of an object of any description which is in three dimensions shall not be taken to infringe the copyright in an artistic work in two dimensions, if the object would not appear, to persons who are not experts in relation to objects of that description, to be a reproduction of the artistic work." In practice, subs.9(8) virtually never operated to provide a defence, and probably had a far more limited effect than was intended by the draftsman of the 1956 Act. For an extensive discussion of the purpose and effect of subs.9(8), and a history of its interpretation by the courts in successive cases, see *British Leyland Motor Corp v Armstrong Patents Co Ltd* [1986] R.P.C. 279 at 369, line 23 to 372, line 31.
[204] See para.5–057 above.

restriction in the former subs.9(8) has been abolished, CDPA 1988 s.51 creates far more sweeping circumstances in which the reproduction of a work in three dimensions (whether the copied work is itself two-dimensional or three-dimensional) will not infringe artistic copy-right.[205]

Primary infringement by issuing copies to the public

5–105   The effect of this provision is to impose liability for primary infringement on the person who is the first issuer of an infringing article in a chain of distribution. Subsequent distributors in the chain are liable (if at all) for secondary infringement.[206] Secondary infringement involves a mental element[207] whereas a primary infringer incurs strict liability, whether or not he knows or has reason to believe that he is infringing copyright.

5–106   It was held under the Copyright Act 1956 that the issue to the public of three-dimensional articles which were derived from drawings constituted publication of those drawings[208]; so undoubtedly such an act would amount to the issue to the public of copies of the two-dimensional work for the purposes of s.18 of the CDPA 1988. However, the extent to which issue of such works to the public will constitute infringement has been heavily restricted by CDPA 1988 s.51, discussed above.[209]

Authorising acts of primary infringement

5–107   Section 16(2) of the CDPA 1988 provides:

> "(2) Copyright in a work is infringed by any person who without the licence of the copyright owner does, or authorises another to do, any of the acts restricted by the copyright."

5–108   The effect of this subsection is that copyright is infringed not only by a person who physically makes an object which is an infringing copy or physically issues such copies to the public, but also by any person who "authorises" another person to do these acts. This provision goes back to similar wording in the Copyright Act 1911.[210] "Authorising" would catch as a primary infringer the publisher who places an order with a printer

---

[205] The effect of this provision, which aims by and large to exclude artistic copyright from the field covered by the unregistered design right, is extensively discussed at paras 5–059 et seq. above.

[206] See CDPA 1988 s.18(2). This subsection has been purportedly amended in a way which (if the amendment is intra vires and valid) could impinge on the case of works imported into the EEA from elsewhere: see para.9–015 below.

[207] See para.5–107 below.

[208] *British Northrop Ltd v Texteam (Blackburn) Ltd* [1974] R.P.C. 57 at 65 lines 21–27.

[209] See para.5–059 above.

[210] The Copyright Act 1911 s.1(2).

for the printing of a book, and in the context of industrial design this provision will catch a customer who places an order with a manufacturing sub-contractor according to a design specified by the customer.[211]

Secondary infringements of copyright

Secondary infringement is concerned with importation, possession, and other dealings with infringing articles. Unlike primary infringement, liability for secondary infringement involves a mental element: the infringer must know or have reason to believe that the articles concerned are infringing articles. Section 22 of the CDPA 1988 provides:

> "22. The copyright in a work is infringed by a person who, without the licence of the copyright owner imports into the United Kingdom, otherwise than for his private or domestic use, an article which is, or which he knows or has reason to believe is, an infringing copy of the work."

5–109

Section 23 goes on to provide:

5–110

> "23. The copyright in a work is infringed by a person who, without the licence of the copyright owner—
>
> (a) possesses in the course of a business,
> (b) sells or lets for hire, or offers or exposes for sale or hire,
> (c) in the course of a business exhibits in public or distributes, or
> (d) distributes otherwise than in the course of a business to such an extent as to affect prejudicially the owner of the copyright,
>
> an article which is, or which he knows or has reason to believe is, an infringing copy of the work."

What is an "infringing copy"?

An infringing copy is first and most obviously defined (by CDPA 1988 s.22(2)) as an article whose making constituted an infringement of the copyright in the work in question.

5–111

This definition of an infringing article adequately deals with the case of an article which has been made within the United Kingdom, since one can then ask whether or not the making of the article amounted to primary infringement. If its making did not infringe for the reason that it

5–112

---

[211] For fuller discussion of what counts as "authorising" for the purposes of infringement of copyright, see para.6–023 below.

was made by the copyright owner or with his consent, then it is not an "infringing copy" and subsequent dealings with it cannot amount to secondary infringements even if the copyright owner does not consent or actively objects. Thus, secondary infringement in the case of articles made within the United Kingdom does not give the copyright owner the ability to control subsequent dealings with a lawfully made article in the way in which registered design infringement can do.[212]

5–113   The making of an imported article will not have constituted infringement of the copyright for the simple reason that the act of making will have taken place outside the territorial scope of the right, i.e. the United Kingdom.[213] To decide whether an imported article (or an article which is proposed to be imported) is an "infringing copy" for the purpose of secondary infringement, Parliament has laid down a hypothetical question in s.22(3)(b) that:

> "its making in the United Kingdom would have constituted an infringement of the copyright in the work in question, or a breach of an exclusive licence agreement relating to that work".

This hypothetical question raises no difficulty of application in cases where the imported article was made by a party unconnected with the owner of the copyright in the United Kingdom, but does raise some questions of interpretation in a potential "parallel import" case: that is, a case where a third party is seeking to import into the United Kingdom an article which was made by the copyright owner in a foreign country or by someone connected with him such as a licensee, assignee or associated or subsidiary company. This subject is more comprehensively dealt with later.[214]

Dealings in articles after the expiry of copyright

5–114   It may sometimes be necessary to consider the transitional effects of the infringement provisions on articles made before expiry of a copyright. It would appear that it is a secondary infringement of copyright (provided that the requisite mental element is present) to import or deal with articles even after the copyright has expired, provided that the articles concerned were made before expiry of the right. This seems to follow from the wording of s.27. In the case of imported articles, this assumes that the hypothetical test relating to imported articles[215] is to be applied

---

[212] See para.3–168 above. This of course is subject to the constraints imposed by EU free movement of goods and competition law.
[213] See para.5–116 below.
[214] See para.9–009 below.
[215] See para.5–111.

as at the date when the articles were actually made in their country of origin, and not on some later date such as the date of importation to the United Kingdom. This seems clearly to be the case under the corresponding provisions relating to design right.[216]

Slightly more doubtful is the position that applies when the period of artistic copyright comes to be limited under s.52 of the CDPA 1988, normally 25 years after the first exploitation of the copyright work in the form of industrially produced articles.[217] Subsection 52(2) states that after the expiry of that period, "anything may be done in relation to articles so made, without infringing copyright in the work". On the face of it, this would suggest that articles may be lawfully dealt with after the expiry of the 25-year period, even if they were made during that period, whether in the United Kingdom or outside it. This interpretation produces an anomalous difference from the rule relating to copyright expiry and to unregistered design right; but interpreting it to the opposite effect would produce an anomalous difference from the position pertaining to registered designs, where articles made abroad during the term of the design may be lawfully imported after expiry.[218] Since s.52 is meant to align the effective term of copyright with that of registered designs, the former anomaly may be preferable to the latter anomaly.

5–115

Territorial scope of infringement

To amount to infringement of copyright, acts generally need to take place within the territorial scope of Pt I of the CDPA 1988, which is the United Kingdom (including for this purpose territorial waters and fixed Continental Shelf installations,[219] and things done on British ships, aircraft and hovercraft[220]). In addition, there is a power to extend Pt I to dependent territories of the United Kingdom[221] which has not yet been exercised.

5–116

However, there are certain exceptions. A person who is physically abroad can be liable for primary infringement by authorising an act (such as making an article which is an infringing copy) which takes place within the United Kingdom.[222] In addition, a person can incur liability for joint tortfeasance through the agency of another, and need not be physically present in order to incur liability of this nature.[223]

5–117

---

[216] See para.4–082 above.
[217] For extensive discussion of this provision, see paras 5–088 et seq. above.
[218] See para.3–180 above.
[219] CDPA 1988 s.157(1) and s.161.
[220] CDPA 1988 s.162.
[221] CDPA 1988 s.157(2).
[222] See para.6–024 below.
[223] See para.6–022 below.

6. What Amounts to Reproduction

What amounts to an infringing reproduction

5–118   Often, the most substantial question in an industrial design copyright case is whether the defendant's article does or does not constitute a "reproduction in material form"[224] of the claimant's copyright work. In theory, this divides into two questions: (1) was the design of the defendant's article copied, directly or indirectly, from the claimant's copyright work, and (2) if so, are the resulting similarities between the claimant's work and the defendant's article such that the latter counts as a reproduction of the former? In practice, these two questions will often be mixed up together; it may be the case that the defendant admits copying some features or aspects of his article from the claimant's work, such as its general idea, but denies that he has copied other aspects, such as the more detailed working out of those ideas.

5–119   CDPA 1988 s.16(3) provides:

> "(3) References in this Part to the doing of an act restricted by the copyright in a work are to the doing of it—
>
> (a) in relation to the work as a whole or any substantial part of it, and
>
> (b) either directly or indirectly,
>
> and it is immaterial whether any intervening acts themselves infringe copyright."

5–120   Thus, to copy a "substantial part" of a work is as much an infringement as to copy the whole of it. The tests applied to determine what counts as a "substantial part" are dealt with below.

Direct or indirect copying

5–121   In referring in this way to direct or indirect copying, s.16(3) makes explicit what was always accepted to be the case under the previous law. Thus, it does not matter the route by which the defendant copies the claimant's copyright work, so long as a chain of causation leading from the copyright work to the alleged reproduction can be shown to exist. In industrial design cases, it will only be in exceptional cases that direct copying will occur. More usually, the defendant will copy from the claimant's article on the market, which in turn will have been copied (by the claimant) from the design drawing or prototype work in which copyright subsists. Sometimes, a third party may copy from the claimant and in turn the defendant may copy the third party's article. In such a

---

[224] CDPA 1988 s.17(2).

case (whether he knows it or not) the defendant has indirectly reproduced the claimant's work.

In the case of artistic works, reproduction normally takes place **5–122**
visually: by the maker of the defendant's article looking at and visually
copying the design of the claimant's article. But this is not strictly
necessary, so long as the chain of causation exists. If verbal instructions
derived from looking at the claimant's article are given to a designer, the
article which the designer produces will be a reproduction of the
claimant's article, at least if the instructions are such as to give the
designer little latitude in the design which he produces.[225] On the other
hand, verbal instructions which merely convey a general idea of the
design of the article concerned may not be sufficient to constitute
reproduction of the claimant's design.[226]

Visual significance of features which are copied

Whether nor not a copied article constitutes a reproduction of a copyright **5–123**
work depends upon the extent and nature of the features that are copied.
It is therefore important to identify what kinds of features are regarded as
significant for copyright purposes. In other words, by copying what kinds
of features does the defendant end up reproducing a substantial part of
the copyright work?

The first and most fundamental point is that in the context of artistic **5–124**
copyright, the features must have visual significance. However technically important a feature might be, if it does not have visual significance
then it will not be an infringement of copyright[227] to copy it by itself, nor,

---

[225] *Solar Thomson Engineering Co Ltd v Barton* [1977] R.P.C. 537, CA, where a designer was
given instructions "independently" to design an elastomeric ring to fit the plaintiff's
pulley wheel in order for the defendants to avoid having to buy replacement rings when
they wore out. The design produced by the independent designer closely resembled the
plaintiff's own design of ring. Given the constraints imposed by the design of the
plaintiff's pulley wheel which it had to fit, and the other constraints in his instructions,
the court held that the "independent" designer's instructions were such that it was
"virtually inevitable" that he would produce a design having the essential features of the
claimant's design. Therefore, there was a sufficient causal link to give the designer's
version of an indirect reproduction of the plaintiff's article and therefore of his
underlying copyright work; at 560, lines 17–27.

[226] *Gleeson v H. R. Denne Ltd* [1975] R.P.C. 471, CA: Instructions were given to a shirt maker
to produce a clerical shirt "with a fly front and a tunnel collar with a front opening, but
not to take a full clerical collar but rather to take a relatively small plastic insert". The
instructions were not "in any such detail as might justify a contention that [the shirt
maker] was in substance producing a copy of the shirt". The fact that the instructions
might be communicating an *idea* which was derived from the plaintiff's shirt was held to
be irrelevant; at 490 at 5–37. And see *Stoddard Intnl PLC v Wm Lomas Carpets Ltd* [2001]
F.S.R. 848, Pumfrey J., where a concept only was communicated to a carpet designer and
this was insufficiently constraining on the results of what the designer might produce to
amount to infringement.

[227] This rule is specifically an aspect of artistic copyright, and there seems no reason why it
should apply to unregistered design right. In that context, there seems no reason to
suppose that technically significant features of shape and configuration are not fully part
of the "design" even if visually insignificant: see para.4–103 above.

by extension of reasoning, will a defendant by copying such a feature in conjunction with others bring himself closer to the borderline of reproducing a substantial part of the work. This principle was stated in *Interlego*,[228] where small changes in tolerances and dimensions in Lego toy bricks were treated as not visually significant.[229] The reasoning which this is based is that the essence of an artistic work is what is visually significant.[230] Thus, a small step and lip shown on a sectional drawing of a traffic cone, which was held to have been a significant functional design feature copied by the defendant, was not of sufficient visual significance (having regard to other differences in the overall appearance of the cones) that the defendant could be said to have copied a substantial part of the claimant's cone drawing.[231]

5–125   On the other hand, if features are depicted which are of visual significance, the question whether they are sufficiently important to be a substantial part must depend upon their significance to the kind of person to whom the artistic work is addressed, which would be an engineer in the case of an engineering drawing.[232] The fact that critical and important dimensions have been copied is significant in deciding whether or not there has been a reproduction of a substantial part of the work[233]:

> "Appellants' counsel was able to establish, at least to my satisfaction, that the dimensions so minutely copied were precisely the critical dimensions necessary to reproduce the appellants' design in a form acceptable to [the respondents' customer]. Substantiality for the purposes of the Copyright Act is to be judged by the quality rather than the quantity, and the critical dimensions can hardly be judged to be less than substantial just because they are measured only in millimetres."

5–126   But the copying of functionally important or critical dimensions and spatial arrangements by themselves may not be qualitatively sufficient to constitute reproduction of a substantial part if the overall visual appearance of the two designs is too different from each other.[234]

---

[228] *Interlego AG v Tyco International Ltd* [1988] R.P.C. 343, PC.

[229] *Interlego AG v Tyco International Ltd* [1988] R.P.C. 343, PC at 374; the claimants could not rely on the basic design of the bricks as shown in their drawings because that basic design was copied from older drawings that were out of copyright.

[230] *Interlego AG v Tyco International Ltd* [1988] R.P.C. 343 at 374, lines 18 et seq.

[231] *Johnstone Safety Ltd v Peter Cook (Intl) Plc* [1990] F.S.R. 161, CA.

[232] *Billhöfer Maschinenfabrik GmbH v T. H. Dixon & Co* [1990] F.S.R. 105, ChD.

[233] *L.B. Plastics Ltd v Swish Products Ltd* [1979] R.P.C. 551 at 628, lines 10–16, per Lord Hailsham; see also at 621, per Lord Wilberforce; however, this is in a context where the two designs were held to have "striking general similarity" (619, line 18 and 624, line 43) and where the copying was held to have gone beyond the critical dimensions themselves; at 630 lines 13–20.

[234] *Billhöfer Maschinenfabrik GmbH v T. H. Dixon & Co* [1990] F.S.R. 105 at 123.

Significance of written matter in graphic works

Graphic works, particularly design drawings, will frequently contain   **5–127**
written matter such as descriptions of the parts or of the views of them
that are depicted, figures indicating dimensions and other information
which would be used by a person making the article from the drawing to
assist him. To what extent can such written matter be taken into account
in assessing whether an article is a reproduction of the graphic work?

On the one hand, explanatory figures and legends should not be   **5–128**
ignored as part of the drawing in considering whether there is a causal
link between the three-dimensional article and the drawing.[235] There was
a series of cases under which it was held that such explanatory material
should be taken into account in applying the so-called "non-expert
recognition" test under s.9(8) of the Copyright Act 1956,[236] but it does not
necessarily follow from that proposition that written matter is also to be
taken into account in the context of assessing whether a substantial part
has been reproduced. Where there are two drawings on one sheet
showing different views of an object, the different views may be
considered together and in the light of words written on the sheet which
describe the relationship of the views to each other[237]:

> " . . . where as here two sketches or drawings are included on a sheet
> and obviously relate to the same article they can both be looked at,
> both for the purpose of establishing the scope of copyright and for
> considering purposes of infringement. Equally . . . it is quite unreal
> when a section of an article is shown in a drawing to ignore the fact,
> as is clear from the wording, including the use of the word
> 'diameter,' that it is a section of a circular article."

On the other hand, a case where there is a detailed manufacturing   **5–129**
drawing where the dimensions are an integral part of the drawing is
different from a case where a drawing is a schematic representation of an
object in rudimentary form which is a mere appendage to a table of
dimensions which actually embody the features copied. In such a case it
would seem unlikely that an article made to those dimensions could be

---

[235] *British Leyland Motor Corp v Armstrong Patents Co Ltd* [1986] R.P.C. 279 in the Court of
Appeal at 293 per Oliver L.J.; further discussed by him in *Interlego AG v Tyco International
Ltd* [1988] R.P.C. 343 at 373.

[236] *Temple Instruments Ltd v Hollis Heels Ltd* [1973] R.P.C. 15; *Merchant Adventurers Ltd v Grew*
[1973] R.P.C. 1; and *L.B. Plastics Ltd v Swish Products Ltd* [1979] R.P.C.

[237] *Temple Instruments Ltd v Hollis Heels Ltd* [1973] R.P.C. 15 at 18. It appears that although
Graham J. most explicitly took into account the written matter for the purpose of
applying the subs.9(8) test, he was also willing to regard it as forming part of the artistic
work more generally for the purpose of assessing its originality and for the purposes of
assessing whether or not there had been a reproduction of a substantial part.

said to reproduce the drawing viewed as an artistic work.[238] In one case a drawing depicted the intended colours of the squares on a patchwork quilt by means of marking each square with a number, and a key needed to be consulted to convert the numbers into their corresponding colours. The court held on a preliminary issue that copyright subsisted in the drawing as it was at least a "diagram".[239] In this respect the court followed an earlier case where it had been held that a knitting point pattern was a drawing under the 1956 Act.[240] The slightly more subtle question of whether the colours represented by these notations formed part of the subject matter of the artistic work protected by the copyright was not directly addressed. It is submitted however that they did. Whilst in a painting one would represent colours directly, there are recognised categories of drawings or diagrams where colours are represented in other ways, for example by conventional heraldic shadings in black and white depictions of coats of arms. In addition, a coloured picture projected on a computer display would be represented in memory as a bitmap in which the colour of each pixel would be represented by numerical values indicating the red, green and blue components of a colour. It would be hard to say that the bitmap in memory is not a graphic work, even though an intermediate process of interpretation has to take place before it is converted into colours visible to the human eye.

Copying of ideas and principles

5–130   It is conventionally said that it is not enough for infringement merely to copy the general idea conveyed by the copyright work; and that unless the particular way of representing or treating the idea is also taken, there will be no infringement.[241] This proposition however depends upon what one counts as being an idea, and what one considers to be a way of treating or representing an idea, not necessarily an easy dividing line to apply.[242]

5–131   The proposition may be of assistance to a defendant who deduces from an article an idea or principle, and then genuinely works out the design

---

[238] See *Duriron Co Inc v Hugh Jennings & Co Ltd* [1984] F.S.R. 1 at 14, per Dillon L.J. Although the Court of Appeal decided the case on the basis that there had been no reproduction in fact, they came close to deciding the case on this ground. See the drawing relied up at p.3 of the report. Of course, such a table of dimensions coupled with a rudimentary picture would clearly be a "design document" for unregistered design right purposes, in which it becomes unnecessary to attempt to distinguish between artistic and non-artistic components.

[239] *Vermaat & Powell v Boncrest Ltd* [2001] F.S.R. 45, ChD, at 50; the drawing appears at 51 of the report.

[240] *Lerose Ltd v Hawick Jersey Intnl Ltd* [1973] F.S.R. 15 at 21.

[241] *Hanfstaengl v Baines & Co Ltd and Mansfield* [1895] A.C. 20 at 24 and 27; *Kenrick & Co v Lawrence & Co* (1890) 25 Q.B.D. 99; *McCrum v Eisner* (1918) 117 L.T. 536; *Burke and Margot Burke Ltd v Spicer's Dress Designs* [1936] Ch. 400.

[242] "But, of course, as the late Professor Joad used to observe, it all depends on what you mean by 'ideas'." Per Lord Hailsham in *L.B. Plastics Ltd v Swish Products Ltd* [1979] R.P.C. 551 at 629, line 33.

of his own article from the idea or principle. Provided that he goes through this process, and does not take the shortcut of simply saving himself design work by copying the shape as well as the idea without going back to first principles, he does not infringe, even if he ends up with a shape which is the same or similar to that of the article from which he has copied the idea. An illustration of this approach is *Catnic Components Ltd v Hill & Smith Ltd*.[243] There, the plaintiffs devised a new form of steel lintel embodying a novel principle, which was indeed the subject of a patent which was sued upon in the action. They contended that the defendants, in addition to infringing the patent,[244] had in creating their own lintel, infringed the copyright in the design drawings for the plaintiff's lintel. It was conceded that the defendant derived the idea of a box girder type of lintel from the plaintiff's brochure.[245] Buckley L.J. said[246]:

" ... [The evidence] effectively rebutted any inference that the defendants had copied anything of the plaintiffs other than the idea of a box girder type of lintel. The dimensional similarities were due ... to the functions which the lintels were designed to perform and the normal dimensions of materials used in building cavity walls and of the cavities in such walls."

The Court of Appeal rejected the argument that the defendants had infringed by copying the idea itself, and accordingly rejected the allegation of infringement.[247] It seems that the courts will adopt a similar approach in the unregistered design right context when interpreting the exclusion from design right of a "method or principle of construction",[248] although the analogy is not necessarily exact.

    5–132

Degree of similarity needed to count as reproduction

Bearing in mind as discussed above the kind of features which are and which are not to be taken into account in assessing whether or not an object is a reproduction of an artistic work, it then has to be decided whether the degree of similarity is or is not sufficiently great. In *King Features Syndicate Inc v O. & M. Kleeman Ltd*,[249] the *Popeye* case, it was said that what is a copy is a question of fact and when the copy is not exact the

    5–133

---

[243] *Catnic Components Ltd v Hill & Smith Ltd* [1982] R.P.C. 183, CA, HL.

[244] The decision of the Court of Appeal on the patent infringement claim was reversed by the House of Lords; but there was no appeal from the dismissal by the Court of Appeal of the copyright infringement claim.

[245] *Catnic Components Ltd v Hill & Smith Ltd* [1982] R.P.C. 183 at 220, line 39.

[246] *Catnic Components Ltd v Hill & Smith Ltd* [1982] R.P.C. 183 at 222, lines 32 et seq.

[247] *Catnic Components Ltd v Hill & Smith Ltd* [1982] R.P.C. 183 at 222, line 46 to 223 and line 23.

[248] See para.4–011 above.

[249] [1941] A.C. 417 at 424.

court must examine the degree of resemblance in accordance with the principles set out in *Hanfstaengl v Baines & Co*[250] and *West v Francis*.[251] There must be:

> "such a degree of similarity as would lead one to say that the alleged infringement is a copy or reproduction of the original of the design—having adopted its essential features and substance".[252]

Reproduction does not imply exactitude of likeness between that which is reproduced and the reproduction itself.[253]

5–134   A case of inexact reproduction of an artistic work (a design for fabric) was considered by the House of Lords in *Designers Guild Ltd v Russell Williams (Textiles) Ltd*.[254] It could be said that the claimant's and the defendant's designs of fabrics were similar in design concept, having vertical stripes which were not sharply defined but applied with a "brushstroke" technique and having flowers with leaves scattered across them—although different flowers differently arranged.[255] The trial judge found that the defendants had copied and then, as is often the case when trial judges reject a case of independent design as untruthful, gave short shrift to the defendant's alternative submission that if they had copied, then they had not reproduced a substantial part of the claimant's work. When the case came before the Court of Appeal it was in no doubt, principally as a matter of impression on comparing the designs, that the defendant's work, although similar in concept and using similar techniques, did not amount to a reproduction of a "substantial part" of the claimant's work.[256] The House of Lords reversed the decision of the Court of Appeal. However, it decides less than it might at first sight appear to do, because the decision of the House appears to be principally based upon the respective roles of a trial judge and the Court of Appeal in the appellate system and did not involve the House itself re-evaluating the substantive question of whether or not there had been a reproduction of a substantial part of the copyright work; instead, the House considered that the Court of Appeal should not have interfered with the trial judge's conclusion on this issue.[257] The House pointed out that the question is

---

[250] [1895] A.C. 20. See also *Hanfstaengl v W. H. Smith & Sons* [1905] 1 Ch. 519 at 524; "a copy is that which comes so near to the original as to suggest that original to the mind of every person seeing it", per Kekewich J.

[251] (1822) 5 B. & Ald. 737.

[252] [1941] A.C. 417 at 424.

[253] *British Northrop Ltd v Texteam Blackburn Ltd* [1974] R.P.C. 57 at 72. *Daily Calendar Supplying Bureau v United Concern* [1967] A.I.R. Madras 381.

[254] [2001] F.S.R. 11.

[255] Colour reproductions of the designs in issue, without which it is not really possible to understand the case, are reproduced within the report of the case in the Court of Appeal [2000] F.S.R. 121 at 136–137.

[256] [2000] F.S.R. 121, per Morritt L.J. at paras 22 and 30, and per Clarke L.J. at 135. The initial reaction of the Lords Justices was that the defendant's fabric did not involve the reproduction of a substantial part of the claimant's fabric design.

[257] [2001] F.S.R. 11.

whether the copied features form a substantial part of the claimant's work, so that other (non-copied) features in the defendant's work which produce a different overall appearance can be disregarded and it is even suggested that it is not necessary to look at the defendant's work for the purpose of assessing whether or not the copied features in the claimant's work (once identified) do or do not form a substantial part of that work.[258] This, however, is quite a difficult intellectual exercise to perform when it is not possible to say yes or no as to whether a particular feature has been copied, but rather it has been re-executed in a rather different way—how can one then determine whether it has been substantially reproduced without comparing the manner of execution and evaluating how similar or different they are?[259] Only one of their Lordships directly addressed the issue of inexact (or "altered") copying of the whole of the work, as distinct from exact copying of a distinct part of the work,[260] which surely was the central point in the case. It was observed that if the similarities between two works are sufficient to justify an inference of copying, then they are likely to be sufficiently substantial to satisfy the "substantial part" test as well.[261] With respect to the high authority of the tribunal in which these observations were expressed, it is submitted that this proposition cannot be taken in general to be correct and potentially it will mislead. The reason is, as pointed out by Hoffmann J. (as he then was) in *Billhöfer Maschinenfabrik v Dixons*[262]:

> "In considering the question of causal connection, i.e. whether the alleged infringement was copied from the copyright work, it is the resemblances in *inessentials*, the small, redundant, even mistaken elements of the copyright work, which carry the greatest weight. This is because they are least likely to have been the result of independent design. Such resemblances may lead the court to conclude that everything in the alleged infringement was copied. On the other hand, when the court has decided that some parts were copies and the others were not, the question of whether they amounted to a substantial part depends upon whether they were sufficiently important".

He went on to hold that the factors which in that case had been copied were not sufficiently important to be a substantial part of the plaintiff's copyright drawing. It is thus clear that the court may give quite different relative weights to features of similarity in the two distinct exercises of establishing causal connection (copying) and of assessing substantial

---

[258] [2001] F.S.R. 11 at para.41, per Lord Millett.
[259] [2001] F.S.R. 11. See Lord Scott of Foscote's observations on this point at para.65.
[260] [2001] F.S.R. 11, Lord Scott at paras 61 et seq.
[261] [2001] F.S.R. 11 per Lord Millett at para.43; and per Lord Scott at para.67.
[262] [1990] F.S.R. 105 at 123.

part. To attempt to conflate the two exercises will only lead to muddle and confusion.

Degree of resemblance with simple works

5–135   In a case where the copyright work is of a very simple character it is comparatively easy to hold that the defendant is taking no more than the mere idea and is, therefore, not guilty of infringement, unless he has copied the work very closely. Thus, in *Kenrick & Co v Lawrence & Co*,[263] Willes J. said[264]:

> "It may be also that even the coarsest or the most commonplace, or the most mechanical representation of the commonest object is so far protected on registration that an exact reproduction of it, such as photography for instance would produce, would be an infringement of copyright. But in such a case it must surely be nothing short of an exact literal reproduction of the drawing registered that can constitute the infringement . . . If a new and very simple tea caddy were represented first by A in a drawing which he registered, I cannot conceive that he could during his whole life prevent B from drawing the same tea caddy, and even from drawing it from his recollection of A's picture, nor that A could claim copyright, except in the extremely limited and useless sense in which I have suggested that a copyright might exist for a registered drawing of even such a subject . . . It seems to me, therefore, that although every drawing of whatever kind may be entitled to registration, the degree and kind of protection given must vary greatly with the character of the drawing and that with such a drawing as we are dealing with, the copyright must be confined to that which is special to the individual drawing over and above the idea—in other words, the copyright is of the extremely limited character which I have endeavoured to describe."

The right to repair and spare parts

5–136   Quite apart from the fact that copyright is not infringed by acts which are done with the express licence of the copyright owner, it has long been recognised that the owner of a copyright or patent or other intellectual property right may impliedly license certain acts by placing articles of his own on the market. One respect in which a licence may be implied arises from the normal expectation of a customer that he will be permitted to repair articles which he purchases, without being effectively prevented from doing so by the exercise by the vendor of rights which would

---

[263] (1890) 25 Q.B.D. 99.
[264] (1890) 25 Q.B.D. 99 at 102–104.

prevent the customer from doing so. This doctrine has long been recognised in the field of patents, and was recognised as applying also to copyright in *Solar Thomson*,[265] a case where the defendant made pulley wheel inserts to repair pulley wheels on a machine sold to it by the plaintiff. That was a case where the customer himself made or had made the articles which would, apart from implied licence, have infringed the plaintiff's copyright.

In *British Leyland*,[266] the House of Lords held that this doctrine applied **5–137** also to the case where a manufacturer makes spare parts, not to the order of any particular customer, but so as to have a stock of spare parts available to supply to a general class of customers who have bought goods from the copyright owner. The doctrine of the "right to repair" may be based, according to the reasoning of the House of Lords in that case, on some broader or different common law principle than just consensual implied licence. This doctrine is now of less practical relevance than it was, since it has been replaced by a different (statutory) protection for makers of spare parts under the unregistered design right.[267]

The scope of and justification for the spare parts exception in *British* **5–138** *Leyland* was later examined by the Privy Council,[268] who described ascertaining the principle on which it is based as "no easy matter". The opinion of the board contains an extensive criticism of the intellectual basis of the "right to repair" as expressed in the speeches in the House of Lords, and concluded that the spare parts exception "cannot be regarded as truly founded on any principle of the law of contract or property", but instead on what the House perceived as "overriding public policy". In view of its basis, it should not be further extended to cover "consumables": that is, components which have to be replaced as a regular part of the operation of a machine (such as photocopier cartridges), as distinct from components that have to be replaced in the course of repairing a machine because they break or wear out.[269]

Fair dealing and related defences

There is a defence of specific relevance to artistic works, and therefore at **5–139** least potentially of relevance to industrial designs. That is the defence relating to the "incidental inclusion" of a work in an artistic work, sound

---

[265] *Solar Thomson Engineering Co Ltd v Barton* [1977] R.P.C. 537, CA.

[266] *British Leyland Motor Corp v Armstrong Patents Co Ltd* [1986] R.P.C. 279, HL.

[267] The "must fit" and "must match" exceptions: see paras 4–015 et seq. and 4–026 et seq. above.

[268] *Canon Kabushiki Kaisha v Green Cartridge Co (Hong Kong) Ltd* [1997] W.L.R. 13.

[269] *Canon Kabushiki Kaisha v Green Cartridge Co (Hong Kong) Ltd* [1997] W.L.R. 13. See also *Dennison Mfg Co v Alfred Holt & Co Ltd* (1987) 10 I.P.R. 612, NZ, a New Zealand case in which an applicator gun was given away free, and supplies of consumables (plastic price label tags) were sold.

recording, film, broadcast or cable programme.[270] Thus, a film maker who includes a scene in which industrial articles are lying around does not thereby at least in normal circumstances infringe the artistic copyrights that may subsist in the designs for those articles. It might be different if an article bearing a design which is the subject of artistic copyright were made a central feature in a film, photograph or other artistic work; in such a case its inclusion might well be outside the defence because its inclusion was not "incidental".[271]

5–140   In addition, the fair dealing defences of research or private study,[272] and criticism or review and reporting current events,[273] apply to artistic works which are the basis of industrial design protection as to other categories of artistic works. For more extensive treatment of these defences, it is suggested that a general work on copyright be consulted.

7. Property Rights and Licensing

Authorship and first ownership of copyright

5–141 The author of an artistic work is defined as being "the person who creates it".[274] In the case of artistic works which are computer generated, the author is defined as "the person by whom the arrangements necessary for the creation of the work are undertaken".[275] "Computer generated" is defined as meaning that the work is generated in circumstances such that there is no human author.[276]

5–142   The Act appears to contemplate that the author will be an individual or individuals, rather than a body corporate; however the use of the word "person" rather than "individual" normally implies that the word is capable of covering corporations as well as individuals. It is conceivable that there could be cases, particularly in the case of computer generated designs, where no particular individual or individuals can be identified as the author and a company could be regarded as being the "author" itself. However, it may be that the word "person" is used because it is possible that there could be corporate authors of works such as broadcasts and films,[277] and the word person is simply used so that it can comprehend all categories of copyright works.

---

[270] CDPA 1988 s.31.

[271] See *Football Association Premier League Ltd v Panini UK Ltd* CA [2004] F.S.R. 1, where club badges were not "incidental" in photographs of footballers.

[272] CDPA 1988 s.29.

[273] CDPA 1988 s.30.

[274] CDPA 1988 s.9(1).

[275] CDPA 1988 s.9(3).

[276] CDPA 1988 s.178.

[277] See CDPA 1988 s.9(2), which defines the author of broadcasts artificially as the person making the broadcast: that person could well be a company.

Joint authors

The Act contemplates that a work may be created jointly by more than **5–143** one author working together. Section 10(1) provides that:

> " . . . a 'work of joint authorship' means a work produced by the collaboration of two or more authors in which the contribution of each author is not distinct from that of the other author or authors."

This definition lays down no particular restriction on the way in which **5–144** the authors work together in order to produce a work of joint authorship. It is not necessary for example in the case of a drawing that each of the joint authors should wield a pen. One author can suggest the general layout and contents of the drawing while the other actually executes the drawing work. It has been held that where two or more people collaborate in the creation of a work and each contributes a significant part of the skill and labour protected by the copyright, then they are joint authors. It is wrong to think that only the person who carries out the mechanical act of fixation is an author.[278]

Leaving aside the case of works created in the course of employment, **5–145** the copyright in a work created by joint authors will normally vest in the authors together.[279]

Works created pursuant to a commission

It is now no longer the case under the CDPA 1988 that the copyright in **5–146** any categories of artistic works created pursuant to a commission vests automatically in the person giving a commission. This is a significant change from the Copyright Act 1956, which provided that the copyright in photographs, engravings and paintings or drawings that were portraits, should vest in a person commissioning them for money or money's worth.[280] This provision still has to be borne in mind in the case of works created before the coming into force of the CDPA 1988, August 1, 1989,[281] and indeed to works created after that date but in respect of which the commission was given before that date.[282]

---

[278] *Cala Homes (South) Ltd v Alfred McAlpine Homes East Ltd* [1995] F.S.R. 818, at 835: "to have regard merely to who pushed the pen is too narrow a view of authorship." In that case, the person who gave instructions according to which architectural drawings were drawn by another person under his supervision was not only held to be a joint author, but the major author (p.836). See also *Murray v King* (1983) 2 I.P.R. 99 and *Prior v Lansdowne Press Pty Ltd* [1977] R.P.C. 511.

[279] CDPA 1988 s.11(1), applied in the light of s.10(3).

[280] The Copyright Act 1956 s.4(3).

[281] The law then in force applies to questions of ownership; CDPA 1988 Sch.1 para.11(1).

[282] CDPA 1988 Sch.1, para.11(2)(a).

5–147   In the case of both registered and unregistered designs, the design right vests in the person commissioning the work rather than in the designer.[283] The present state of the law can therefore produce the rather unfortunate consequence in the field of industrial design that the right to apply for a registered design, in respect of an article, and the unregistered design right in its shape and configuration, will vest in one person, but associated artistic copyright (which in most cases will mainly be relevant to the protection of surface pattern) will vest in another person.

5–148   However, quite apart from any special statutory provision, the normal rules of contract law, specific performance and equity apply to the ownership of artistic copyright. Thus, if a contract obliges a designer expressly or impliedly to hold a copyright in a design he creates for the benefit of another person, then that contract may be specifically enforceable. Where a court in the United Kingdom has jurisdiction to interpret and enforce the contract in question, it can order the designer to assign to the commissioner copyrights arising all over the world.[284] In the case of an implied term, the test is whether or not it is necessary in order to give business efficacy to the contract for the designer to hold the copyright for the benefit of the commissioner and to the exclusion of himself; if an exclusive or non-exclusive licence will suffice for the purposes of business efficacy, then only a licence will be implied.[285] An important practical difference is that a commissioner relying on an express or implied contractual term with the author of the design will at best acquire an equitable title to the copyright and may need to take further steps to perfect his title or to enforce his rights against third parties.

---

[283] Registered designs para.3–222 above; unregistered design right para.4–109 above.

[284] *R Griggs Group Ltd v Evans (No.2)* [2004] EWHC 1088 (Ch); [2004] F.S.R. 48, ChD, P Prescott Q.C.; in this respect it seems that an order for an assignment of foreign copyrights based on *in personam* jurisdiction differs from an attempt to enforce a foreign copyright through the courts of the UK, which not permissible except in the special case of EU and Lugarno Convention countries: *Lucasfilm Ltd v Ainsworth* [2009] EWCA Civ 1328; [2010] F.S.R. 10; [2010] E.C.D.R 5, CA, paras 174–183.

[285] *Ray v Classic FM plc* [1998] F.S.R. 622; summary of the law set out in *Ray* approved by the Court of Appeal in *R Griggs Group Ltd v Evans* [2005] EWCA Civ 11; [2005] F.S.R. 31, CA, where commissioner was held entitled to copyright in a commercial logo. See also *Ironside v Att Gen* [1998] R.P.C. 197, ChD, where the claimant accepted a fee for designs for coins after winning a competition; however, the reasoning of this case, and why in particular payment of a fee was held to give rise to outright ownership rather than a licence, is very unclear. See also *Nichols Advanced Vehicle Systems Inc v Rees* [1979] R.P.C. 127, ChD, at 139, lines 20–25; and *Cyprotex Discovery Ltd v University of Sheffield* [2004] R.P.C. 43, at paras 136–9, where works were created (computer programs) which embodied underlying work of the person commissioning the writing of the programs. Similar reasoning was applied in *Lucasfilm Ltd v Ainsworth* [2008] EWCA 1878 (Ch); [2009] F.S.R.2; [2008] E.C.D.R. 17, Mann J. at paras 184–185, where the defendant created three-dimensional models of stormtroopers' helmets and other items working from sketches and paintings supplied to him; since he was working to render into three-dimensional form the copyright designs of others this was a "classic case" for saying that there was an implication that the commissioner would have copyright in the helmet (if there was any—see para.5–20 above).

Copyright works created in the course of employment

Where a work is created by an employee in the course of his employment, **5–149** first ownership of copyright will vest in the employer rather than in the employee.[286] An employee is defined as a person employed under a contract of service or apprenticeship.[287] This definition is the same as that for the purpose of unregistered design right,[288] which presumably is intended by Parliament to be interpreted to the same effect. The registered design provisions are also effectively identical.[289] At least in this respect, all three kinds of right will vest, or not vest, in an employer in the same circumstances. There is a special provision relating to copyright in works created for governmental or parliamentary purposes vesting such copyright in the Crown or Parliament.[290]

For these provisions to apply, it is first necessary that the employee **5–150** should be employed under a contract of service (or apprenticeship) as distinct from a looser relationship under which work is done, such as a contract for services. The distinction is a question of fact[291] which must be resolved by a consideration of the details of the relationship. The test of whether or not a contract is a contract of service for these purposes is the same as the test under the general law, since "where Parliament has used language in its definitions well understood in other contexts it would take clear words to produce a result where those definitions did not retain their well understood meaning".[292]

The scope to be given to the phrases "contract of service" or "contract **5–151** of employment" has been considered on numerous occasions (although only rarely in connection with the ownership of copyright or design right). The tests to be applied have been recently reviewed and summarised by the Court of Appeal in the context of ownership of design rights in *Ultraframe Ltd v Fielding*.[293] The relevant tests are (1) that the employee agrees that, in consideration of a wage or other remuneration, he will provide his own work and skill in the performance of some service for his employer; (2) he agrees, expressly or impliedly, that in the performance of that service he will be subject to the other's control in a sufficient degree to make that other employer; (3) the other provisions of the contract are consistent with it being a contract of service. Applying these principles, it was held that a controlling shareholder and director of a company was not an employee of that company even though he drew

---

[286] CDPA 1988 s.11(2).
[287] CDPA 1988 s.178; previously the Copyright Act 1956 s.4(4).
[288] See para.4–112 above.
[289] RDA(E) s.2(1B) and s.44(1), definition of "employee". See para.3–216 above.
[290] CDPA 1988 s.11(3), s.163 and s.165. There is also a similar provision relating to copyright works made for or published by specified international organisations; s.168.
[291] *Smith v General Motor Cab Co Ltd* [1911] A.C. 188 at 193. See also *Ray v Classic FM plc* [1998] F.S.R. 622.
[292] *Ultraframe Ltd v Fielding* [2004] R.P.C. 479, CA, per Waller L.J. at para.19.
[293] *Ultraframe Ltd v Fielding* [2004] R.P.C. 479, CA, per Waller L.J. at para.19.

remuneration from it and did work for it, largely because the element of control was not present. However, the relevant design rights were still held in trust for the company. One earlier statement of the test to be applied in resolving the question in a case where the context was one of copyright was to invite consideration as to whether on the one hand the employee is employed as part of their employer's business and his work is a normal and integral part of that business, or whether his work is not integrated into the business but is only accessory to it.[294]

5–152   The second requirement, assuming a contract of employment to exist, is that the copyright work should have been created in the course of that contract. This creates no difficulty where the employee's job is specifically to design or to create copyright works of that type, but can pose more difficulties where the creating of the work is outside the employee's normal activities but nonetheless relevant to the employer's business. Whether the work was created in the course of employment is a question of fact.[295] Assistance in approaching this question may be gained by considering the analogous cases which have arisen in connection with employees' inventions.[296] A company director will often be an employee of the company, but sometimes may hold a "mere" directorship, that is a directorship without a parallel contract of service. In *Antocks Lairn Ltd v I. Bloohn Ltd*,[297] the managing director of the plaintiff company, who was not a party to the action and had no service agreement with his company, was said by the plaintiffs to have acted as a servant of the company in the preparation of drawings: he had two capacities, one as director and another as manager. Graham J., holding that the copyright in the drawings were nevertheless owned by the director said[298]:

> " . . . I think the intention of the section is to give the copyright in drawings to the author who makes them, unless he is what perhaps may be called a normal employee who is employed for that purpose. I do not think the intention was to include in subsection (4) a managing director who, as part of his management activities, from time to time acted as if he was a servant or employee of the company rather than as a director, particularly where . . . no service agreement as such, whether formal or informal, to do this particular work was proved. Such a managing director would, of course, hold the drawings he made in trust for his company and would have to assign

---

[294] *Beloff v Pressdram Ltd* [1973] R.P.C. 765 at 772 per Ungoed-Thomas J. Many of the leading cases on this topic are reviewed in this judgment.

[295] *Byrne v Statist Co* [1914] 1 K.B. 622; *Stevenson Jordan & Harrison Ltd v Macdonald & Evans* [1952] 1 T.L.R. 101.

[296] See *Patchett v Sterling Engineering Co* (1955) 72 R.P.C. 50 at 56; *Worthington Pumping Engine Co v Moore* (1903) 20 R.P.C. 41.

[297] [1972] R.P.C. 219.

[298] [1972] R.P.C. 219 at 222. See also *Amplaudio Ltd v Snell* (1938) 55 R.P.C. 237 (mandatory injunction granted to enforce employee's obligations: patent).

the copyright in them to his company if and when called upon to do."

The assumption made by Graham J. in the final sentence was in effect validated, and its basis explained, by the Court of Appeal in *Ultraframe Ltd v Fielding*[299] where designs were created by an individual who was the controlling shareholder and director or shadow director of a group of companies. The Court held that he was not an employee (see para.5–147 above), but nonetheless found that he held the design rights on trust for the companies. The trust arose not simply from his position, but from the use in the creation of the designs of all the assets of the companies, including confidential information obtained in conducting the companies' business which would have been utilised in creating the designs.[300] Once the circumstances of creation of the design rights vested their beneficial title in the companies, it was not possible thereafter for the companies to waive or transfer their entitlement to the individual even though he was a 100 per cent shareholder because such a transaction would have been ultra vires the companies and a fraud against creditors, being an alienation of the company's property otherwise than by way of a valid distribution of profits or reduction of capital in a manner authorised by company law.

Both the *Antocks Lairn* and *Ultraframe* cases appear to rest on the **5–152A** director concerned doing the work in company time, or making use of company property, materials and confidential information in the course of creating the drawings or designs in question. If a director/shareholder of a company creates a copyright work or design in circumstances where its creation genuinely owes nothing to the use of company property or information obtained in the course of the company's business, does the director hold it on trust for the company simply on the ground that it would be useful for the company to acquire it, and that as director he owes the company a duty not merely to run its business as it stands but to look for new business opportunities? It may be that it would be taking the law too far to impose a duty on a director to give up in favour of the company a potentially valuable piece of property created by him, in the absence of any use of company property or information or payment for his time by the company.

Prospective ownership of future copyright

The normal rules relating to first ownership of copyright can be displaced **5–153** by agreement. A prospective owner of copyright can make an agreement under which he purports to assign the future copyright (either individually or as part of a class of works) to another person. If the agreement

---

[299] [2004] R.P.C. 479.
[300] [2004] R.P.C. 479 at para.34 per Waller L.J.

satisfies the required formalities, which are that it is in writing and is signed by the prospective owner, then the copyright or rights concerned will vest in the assignee rather than in the prospective owner upon the creation of the works.[301]

5–154   This provision only operates if the assignee is, by virtue of the agreement concerned, entitled against all other persons to require the right to be vested in him. So, for example, a purported assignment entered into by an author in breach of a contractual obligation with a third party would not be effective to vest copyright in the assignee.

5–155   Quite apart from this special statutory provision, the normal rules of contract law, specific performance and equity apply to the ownership of copyright. Thus, if a contract obliges a designer expressly or impliedly to hold the copyright in a design he creates for the benefit of another person, then that contract may be specifically enforceable even if, for example, it fails to satisfy the formal requirements of an assignment of prospective rights because it is not in writing. However, legal title will not vest in that other person without further action.[302]

Nature of copyright as a property right

5–156   CDPA 1988 s.90(1) provides that:

> "(1) Copyright is transmissible by assignment, by testamentary disposition or by operation of law, as personal or moveable property."

Thus, the ordinary laws of personal property will apply to copyright. Copyright will pass upon death or in an insolvency according to the same rules as any other personal property. There is however a minimum formality for an effective assignment: the assignment must be in writing and be signed by or on behalf of the assignor.[303] An assignment that fails to satisfy these formal requirements will not serve to convey legal title in the copyright to the assignee, but may be effective as an equitable assignment, and is likely to be so if supported by consideration.

5–157   The copyright in a single work is divisible by assignment or transmission into partial rights covering different classes of acts covered by the copyright, or different periods of time.[304] For example, copyright may be assigned in respect of the application of the design to some particular kind of article but not articles in general; in the literary field it can be divided up, e.g. into the hard cover and paperback rights. Alternatively, a copyright may be assigned for a period of two years only, in which case

---

[301] CDPA 1988 s.91(1).
[302] See para.5–142 above.
[303] CDPA 1988 s.90(3). If the assignor is a corporation, the assignment can be under seal instead of being signed; s.176(1).
[304] CDPA 1988 s.90(2).

it would then revert to the assignor at the end of the two-year period without need for an assignment back to that assignor. If a third party infringes a copyright which has been divided up, it is the person whose partial right covers the acts of the infringer who is entitled to sue.[305]

Copyright in an unpublished work which is left by a will

When a work in which copyright subsists, i.e. the original physical object itself, passes under a bequest and the work has not been published, there is a statutory presumption that the copyright in the work passes with the bequest as well, unless a contrary intention is indicated.[306] While this provision seems mainly aimed at such things unpublished manuscripts of books left by authors, it will also apply to artistic works embodying industrial designs.   **5–158**

Joint ownership of copyright

Copyright can be jointly owned, most frequently when the work has been created by joint authors.[307] In such a case, for a third party to do acts which require the licence of the copyright owner would require the licence of all the joint owners.[308] Thus, each joint owner can sue a third party for infringement,[309] although the extent of their financial remedies may be limited to the damage sustained by their own interest in the copyright.[310]   **5–159**

Licensing of copyright

Licence merely means consent or permission, and no specific requirements are laid down as to how a copyright owner may license another person or persons to do acts which would otherwise infringe a copyright. Thus, a licence may be conferred by a formal written document, by a contract, by express written or oral permission to do an act, or by implication.[311] Licences under a copyright (however granted) are given by statute a quasi-proprietory status, in that such a licence is binding   **5–160**

---

[305] CDPA 1988 s.173(1).

[306] CDPA 1988 s.93.

[307] See para.5–144 above.

[308] CDPA 1988 s.173(2).

[309] See, for example, *Cala Homes (South) Ltd v Alfred McAlpine Homes East Ltd* [1995] F.S.R. 818, ChD, where the client of an architect who was the joint author of drawings prepared by the architect was able to sue another customer of the architect who used the drawings. The other customer had the licence of the architect, but not of the other joint owner.

[310] See para.6–011 below for remedies and procedure applicable to joint owners.

[311] An important application of implied licences is in the context of making spare parts to repair articles sold by the copyright owner: see para.5–137 above.

upon the successors in title to the proprietor who granted the licence.[312] The exception is that a licence granted by a predecessor in title does not bind a purchaser in good faith of the copyright for valuable consideration without notice (actual or constructive) of the licence, or a successor in title to such person.[313] This effectively treats a licence under a copyright as an equitable interest in or under the copyright. A similar provision applies to a licence granted by a prospective owner of a copyright.[314]

Exclusive licences of copyright

5–161   Exclusive licensees of copyright are given a special status. For this purpose, an exclusive licence is defined as a licence which authorises the licensee to exercise part or all of the rights conferred by the copyright, to the exclusion of all other persons, including the person granting the licence; and it must fulfil the formal requirements of being in writing and being signed[315] by or on behalf of the copyright owner.[316] An exclusive licence which fails to satisfy these formal requirements (for example because it is oral) may be perfectly effective contractually, at least as against the original grantor, but will not be accorded the special privileges which the Act confers upon exclusive licences and exclusive licensees.

5–162   These privileges are, first, that the terms of the exclusive licence are enforceable against a successor in title to the grantor.[317] Secondly, the exclusive licensee may be effectively protected against parallel imports from other countries of goods made by or under the licence of the design right owner.[318] Thirdly, an exclusive licensee has the right to bring infringement proceedings against third parties in their own name.[319]

8. Term of Protection and 1988 Transitional Provisions

Term of copyright

5–163   The normal term of copyright in an artistic work of any kind is 70 years after the death of the author, at least when the author is a national of a

---

[312] CDPA 1988 s.90(4).

[313] CDPA 1988.

[314] CDPA 1988 s.91(3).

[315] Or alternatively in the case of a corporation being under seal; CDPA 1988 s.176(1).

[316] CDPA 1988 s.92(1).

[317] CDPA 1988 s.92(2). This is so long as the successor in title is bound by the exclusive licence, i.e. that they are not a purchaser for value without notice. Absent this special statutory provision, there could be difficulty in enforcing the negative covenant implicit in the exclusive licence against a successor in title who may have no privity of contract with the exclusive licensee.

[318] This follows from the reference to an exclusive licence agreement in the definition of "infringing article" in CDPA 1988 s.27(3)(b); see para.5–113 above.

[319] This is subject to certain procedural safeguards; see paras 6–016—6–017 below. This right to sue third parties is also enjoyed by licensees under certain non-exclusive licences: see para.6–015 below.

member state of the European Economic Area.[320] This term was increased from 50 years after the author's death by regulations under the European Communities Act 1972 to give effect to Directive 93/98/EEC harmonising the term of protection of copyright and certain related rights. There are transitional provisions whose general effect is that if the work was still in copyright in the United Kingdom or another member state when the regulations came into effect, it enjoys the increased term.[321] It should be noted that for reasons of convenience, the copyright expires on December 31 in the relevant anniversary year.

Where the work is a work of joint authorship, the 70 years runs from **5–164** the death of the last of them to die.[322]

Where the author cannot be identified, and remains unidentified **5–165** throughout that period, the copyright expires 70 years after the work was first made available to the public.[323] If the work is computer generated and so has no human author, the copyright expires 70 years after it was made.[324]

In the case of authors who are not nationals of an EEA member state, **5–166** the term of copyright in the United Kingdom is restricted to the term enjoyed in the country of origin of the work.[325]

Under the Copyright Act 1956, although copyright in most types of **5–167** artistic work lasted for the life of the author plus 50 years, the term of copyright in photographs expired 50 years after first publication (without regard to the date of death of the author), and a special rule applied to engravings.[326] The effect of the transitional provisions is that copyright in old published photographs taken before June 1, 1957 has the same expiry date as they would have done under the 1956 Act,[327] whilst unpublished photographs taken after that date received a new fixed copyright term of 50 years after the end of the year in which the new Act came into force, i.e. until the end of 2039.[328] The same rules applies to engravings unpublished at the date of the author's death.[329]

In the industrial design field, only a minority of works enjoy the full **5–168** effective period of copyright protection under the rules governing the term of copyright. Two further important rules apply to cut down the effective term.

---

[320] CDPA 1988 s.12(2), as amended by the Duration of Copyright and Rights in Performances Regulations 1995 (SI 1995/3297).
[321] See SI 1995/3297, regs 12–35; detailed consideration of these provisions is outside the scope of this work.
[322] CDPA 1988 s.12(8) as amended by SI 1995/3297.
[323] CDPA 1988 s.12(3) as amended by SI 1995/3297.
[324] CDPA 1988 s.12(7) as amended by SI 1995/3297.
[325] CDPA 1988 s.12(6) as amended by SI 1995/3297.
[326] The Copyright Act 1956 s.3(4) proviso.
[327] CDPA 1988 Sch.1 para.12(2)(c).
[328] CDPA 1988 Sch.1 para.12(4)(c).
[329] CDPA 1988 para.12(4)(b).

Restriction of copyright protection when an artistic work is exploited as an industrial design

5–169   Section 52 of the CDPA 1988 applies to restrict the effective period of artistic copyright protection in an industrial context to 25 years after articles bearing the design are first marketed by the copyright owner. The circumstances in which this rule comes into operation have already been extensively dealt with.[330] The effective term to which the copyright is limited in the industrial context by this provision is until December 31 of the 25th year after the articles were first marketed. The copyright does not expire: it continues to subsist until the end of its normal term, but it can no longer be enforced in the industrial context.[331] The purpose of this provision is to align the period of artistic copyright protection to the same period as would have been enjoyed if the artistic work had been registered as a design under the RDA(A).[332]

5–170   There is an important transitional provision that continues to apply to articles which were made industrially and first marketed before the CDPA 1988 came into effect, i.e. before August 1, 1989. Such articles were covered by s.10 of the Copyright Act 1956, which was the predecessor to s.52 of the 1988 Act. Although s.10 of the 1956 Act is differently drafted,[333] in general[334] it will apply in the same circumstances as s.52 of the new Act does. The difference is that s.10 laid down a period of 15 years from the date of marketing of the articles, rather than 25 years, and if the s.10 period did begin to run before commencement, the copyright owner is still limited to the 15 years; they do not get the benefit of the increased term under the new Act.[335] Indeed, he is restricted to the precise 15th anniversary of the date when the articles were first marketed, and does not get the benefit of the December 31 expiry.[336]

Transitional enforcement of artistic copyright in respect of three-dimensional articles

5–171   As has already been discussed,[337] the CDPA 1988 made a major change in the pre-existing law by heavily restricting the circumstances in which the

---

[330] See paras 5–088—5–091 above.

[331] See para.5–092 above.

[332] For maximum term of a registered design, see para.3–274 above.

[333] It is based on the concept of a "corresponding design": a design which, when applied to an article, would result in a reproduction of the artistic work.

[334] The limitation of s.10 of the 1956 Act, removed by the drafting of s.52, was that it did not apply at all to designs for articles which were wholly functional because such designs were not registrable under the RDA 1949: see para.5–052 above. In such a case, the 25-year period in s.52 begins to apply only if such articles are marketed after commencement; CDPA 1988 Sch.1, para.20(2).

[335] CDPA 1988 Sch.1, para.20(1); see *Lucasfilm Ltd v Ainsworth* [2009] EWCA Civ 1328; [2010] F.S.R. 10; [2010] E.C.D.R 5, CA, paras 93–95.

[336] This is the effect of CDPA 1988 Sch.1, para.20(1) when read together with s.10 of the Copyright Act 1956.

[337] See paras 5–059 et seq. above.

copyright in artistic works can be enforced in respect of three-dimensional industrial articles. It was necessary to have transitional provisions to deal with existing copyrights, many of which would have been licensed or dealt with on the basis of the law as it then stood. On the other hand, it was perceived as undesirable and unwarranted to allow such existing copyrights to retain an effective period of protection of the life of the author plus 50 years, since such a length of protection was viewed as one of the defects in the existing law which needed to be rectified.

The solution adopted was to permit such existing copyrights to **5–172** continue to be enforced in respect of three-dimensional industrial reproduction for the fixed period of 10 years after the coming into force of the 1988 Act. This provided the same effective term of protection as unregistered design right gives from first marketing. Thus, the new unregistered design right only covers designs which are brought into physical existence, either by the making of an article embodying them or a "design document", after commencement.[338] On the other side of the coin, the transitional provisions provided that s.51, which excludes three-dimensional industrial articles from the scope of most artistic copyright,[339] did not apply for 10 years after commencement to a design recorded or embodied in a design document before commencement.[340] Thus, the copyright in such existing artistic works which embody designs could be enforced in the same way as under the old law for 10 years, i.e. until July 31, 1999. Indeed, in one respect such old artistic copyrights could be enforced more extensively than they could under the old law, since the old "non-expert recognition test" no longer applied to limit the scope of infringement.[341]

However, again bringing such transitionally enforceable copyrights **5–173** into line with the term of the new unregistered design right, the transitional provisions rendered such copyrights subject to "licences of right" for the last five years of their term (i.e. as from August 1, 1994) under the same rules and procedures as apply to unregistered design right.[342] Such licences of right apply only to acts which are excluded from infringement by s.51: if it is a copyright work which remains effectively enforceable under the new law, then neither the licences of right provision, nor indeed the 10-year period, will affect it.[343]

---

[338] CDPA 1988 s.213(7).

[339] See paras 5–509 et seq. above.

[340] CDPA 1988 Sch.1, para.19(1).

[341] The Copyright Act 1956 s.9(8); although in practice it had very limited application—see para.5–104 above.

[342] CDPA 1988 Sch.1, paras 19(2), (3) and (6).

[343] For such circumstances, when the industrial article is itself an "artistic work", see para.5–050, points (2) to (4) above. The scope of the licence of right is restricted to acts which would be excluded from copyright by s.51; CDPA 1988 Sch.1, para.19(7).

CHAPTER 6

INFRINGEMENT AND VALIDITY DISPUTES: REMEDIES AND PROCEDURES

1. Courts in which Proceedings may be Brought

Courts in which civil proceedings may be brought

6–001   Civil proceedings for infringement are the primary means by which the five principal rights which protect designs can be enforced. Actions for infringement of a UK registered design in England and Wales must be brought in the High Court[1] or in the Patents County Court.[2] If brought in the High Court, registered design proceedings are assigned to the Chancery Division and within that division are taken by the Patents Court.[3] In Scotland, registered design proceedings are brought in the

---

[1] RDA(E) s.27(1)(a). This defines "the court" for the purposes of applications under the RDA(E), but an infringement action arguably is not such an application. However, the jurisdiction of ordinary county courts has always excluded patent infringement actions, a patent being regarded as a "franchise" within the meaning of the County Courts Act 1959 s.39, and it is probable that a registered design monopoly also falls under this head. Even if an ordinary county court were theoretically to have jurisdiction to entertain a registered design infringement action, it would clearly have no jurisdiction to deal with validity (*Figorski Ltd v Smith Seymour Ltd* (1939) 56 R.P.C. 135; and see now RDA(E) s.27) and so in practice would have to stay any such action in which invalidity was raised. As to the position of the Court of Chancery of the County Palatine of Lancaster (now assimilated into the High Court), see *British Insulated and Helsby Cables Ltd v London Electric Wire Co and Smiths* (1913) 30 R.P.C. 620.
[2] For the jurisdiction of the Patents County Court, see para.6–006 below.
[3] CPR r.63.3.

Court of Session,[4] and in Northern Ireland in the High Court.[5] Proceedings concerned with the registration or validity of registered designs are specifically excluded from the normal rules which apply to the allocation of jurisdiction to the courts of the different parts of the United Kingdom in civil and commercial cases.[6] Those rules however apply to the bringing of infringement actions.[7]

Actions for infringement of a Community registered or unregistered   **6–002**
design right must be brought in a Community Design Court, which member states are required to designate.[8] The United Kingdom has designated[9] as Community Design Courts the High Court and the Patents County Court[10] in England and Wales, the Court of Session in Scotland, and the High Court of Northern Ireland. These are the same courts as those which exercise jurisdiction over UK registered designs[11]. These designated Community design courts have exclusive jurisdiction over actions for infringement or threatened infringement, declarations of non-infringement and counterclaims or actions for a declaration of invalidity.[12] A judgment that a design is invalid given by a Community Design Court in any member state has effect throughout the Community.[13] Applications for a declaration of invalidity of a registered (but not an unregistered) Community design may also be made to the Community Designs Office in Alicante.[14]

Within the English High Court, claims relating to Community regis-   **6–003**
tered designs, like UK registered designs, are assigned to the Patents Court within the Chancery Division[15]; however, curiously and anomalously in view of the near identity of the law governing them, it appears that Community unregistered designs may be sued upon in the general Chancery Division (although marked in the Intellectual Property list) outside the Patents Court, and that in such cases general Chancery judges may exercise the jurisdiction of the High Court to act as a Community Design Court.[16]

---

[4] RDA(E) s.27(1)(b).
[5] RDA(E) s.27(1)(c).
[6] The Civil Jurisdiction and Judgments Act 1982 (as amended), Sch.5, para.2.
[7] The Civil Jurisdiction and Judgments Act 1982 (as amended), Sch.4, arts 2 and 5(3).
[8] The Community Designs Regulation art.80.
[9] The Community Designs (Designation of Community Design Courts) Regulations 2005 (SI 2005/696) App E4 below.
[10] Although CPR r.63.13(c) implies that Community unregistered design right claims might be brought in other County Courts where there is a Chancery District Registry, this cannot be the case because only the Patents County Court is designated as a Community Design Court by the Regulations.
[11] See previous para.6–001.
[12] Community Designs Regulation art.81.
[13] Community Designs Regulation art.87.
[14] Community Designs Regulation art.52.
[15] CPR r.63.2(1)(b)(i)—see App E1 below.
[16] This appears to be the effect of CPR r.63.13 coupled with para.16.1(5) of Practice Direction 63 (App E2 below). Whilst this might seem logical in aligning the power to try

6–004   The jurisdiction of Community design courts in different member states is controlled by rules based on the Brussels Convention and Regulation on the recognition and enforcement of judgments.[17] Such a court may exercise EU-wide jurisdiction over infringements if the defendant is domiciled in its territory or, if not domiciled in any member state, if the defendant has a place of establishment there.[18] If the defendant is neither domiciled nor has a place of establishment in any member state, jurisdiction may be assumed by the court where the claimant has its domicile or establishment.[19] If neither the claimant nor the defendant has a domicile or establishment in any member state, then the courts of Spain, being the seat of the Office, can exercise jurisdiction.[20] The parties may agree to the exercise of full jurisdiction by the courts of a particular member state.[21] Alternatively to these rules providing for the exercise of full Community wide jurisdiction, the courts of the state where an infringing act is committed or threatened may exercise jurisdiction, but if jurisdiction is exercised on this ground it is not Community-wide but is limited to that particular territory.[22] Jurisdiction to grant provisional measures such as interim injunctions is conferred on any courts of the member states, whether or not a Community design court, which have power to grant such measures in respect of national design rights, and even if the courts of some other member state have jurisdiction over the substantive dispute.[23]

6–005   Wider rules of jurisdiction relate to proceedings for UK unregistered design right[24] and copyright than in respect of registered designs. If brought in the English High Court, copyright and design right proceedings are assigned to the Chancery Division, where they are taken as Intellectual Property matters.[25] In the county court in England, actions for infringement must be brought in one of the county courts where there is also a Chancery district registry,[26] and they must satisfy the normal financial and other criteria regarding county court jurisdiction.

Community unregistered design cases with the power to try UK unregistered design and copyright cases (see para.6–005), those latter two rights are very different in their nature from either Community registered or unregistered design rights, which are almost identical to each other and should be governed by the same procedures.

[17] Community Designs Regulation art.82.
[18] Community Designs Regulation art.82(1) and art.83(1).
[19] Community Designs Regulation art.82(2).
[20] Community Designs Regulation art.82(3).
[21] Community Designs Regulation art.82(4).
[22] Community Designs Regulation arts 82(5) and 83(2). However, pronouncements on validity still have Community wide effect: see art.87.
[23] Community Designs Regulation art.90.
[24] With the exception of claims relating to semiconductor topography rights (see Ch.20 below) which CPR r.63.2(1)(b)(ii) (see App E1 below) allocates to the Patents Court or the Patents County Court.
[25] The Supreme Court Act 1981 Sch.1, para.1(i); Practice Direction, paras 18 and 19, see App.E2 below.
[26] Practice Direction, para.18–1—18–2, see App.E2 below.

The Patents County Court

In order to provide a cheaper and more rapid forum for the determination   **6–006**
of disputes than the English High Court, particularly in smaller cases,
CDPA 1988 s.287 authorised the establishment of patents county courts
having special jurisdiction to deal with patents, designs and ancillary
matters. So far, a single Patents County Court has been established, which
sits at the Central London County Court.[27] It is not bound by the ordinary
geographical rules of county courts, and can exercise its jurisdiction
throughout England and Wales.[28] It can exercise the same powers as the
High Court, and therefore has the power to rectify invalid registered
designs.[29] Like the High Court, it has been designated as a Community
design court.[30] The Patents County Court is probably now the forum of
choice in England and Wales for all but very heavy or commercially high
value registered or unregistered design infringement cases.[31] In the
Patents County Court, patent attorneys have the right to go on the record
and a right of audience,[32] as well as counsel and solicitors.

The Patents County Court has special jurisdiction to entertain any   **6–007**
proceedings "relating to patents or designs",[33] as well as proceedings
"ancillary to, or arising out of the same subject matter as, proceedings
relating to patents or designs".[34] This clearly includes proceedings for
infringement of registered designs and of unregistered design right, but
it is probable that it does not include proceedings for infringement of
artistic copyright that are in respect of the design of an article.[35] Even if
such a claim as such is not a "designs" proceeding for this purpose, it can
be brought in the Patents County Court either if it is included together
with a design right claim (in which case it is "ancillary"), or if it falls

---

[27] The Patents County Court (Designation and Jurisdiction) Order 1994 (SI 1994/1609). The
Patents County Court was for a time at Edmonton County Court under the previous 1990
Order.
[28] CDPA 1988 s.287(2).
[29] 1994 Order art.3.
[30] See para.6–002 above.
[31] Apart from other considerations, starting an action in the Patents County Court will
virtually guarantee that the case is heard by a judge with specialist knowledge of designs
law, compared with pot luck on this score in the Chancery Division of the High Court.
At the time of this edition going to press, the judge of the Patents County Court was H.H.
Judge Michael Fysh Q.C., the previous editor of this work, although shortly due to retire.
In the High Court, there has been a tendency, particularly for smaller unregistered design
cases, to be heard by deputy High Court judges with no specialist expertise in the
subject.
[32] CDPA 1988 s.292.
[33] CDPA 1988 s.287(1)(a); 1994 Order art.3.
[34] CDPA 1988 s.287(1)(b).
[35] *McDonald v Graham* [1994] R.P.C. 407, CA, at 435 lines 7–10, per Ralph Gibson L.J. The
Patents County Court Users Guide, published by that Court, appears to assume that the
special jurisdiction relating to "designs" is limited to registered and unregistered design
rights.

under the ordinary geographical and financial jurisdiction rules of the Central London County Court.[36]

Appellate Courts

6–008   In England and Wales, appeal lies from decisions of the Chancery Division of the High Court or of the Patents County Court[37] to the Court of Appeal (Civil Division). It has also been designated as a second tier (appellate) Community design court under art.80(1) of the Regulation.[38] Appeals are now much more difficult to pursue than in the past and it is more difficult to overturn decisions of a trial judge. Procedurally, there is now a filtering mechanism under which permission to appeal needs to be obtained from either the trial judge or, if he refuses, from a judge of the Court of Appeal.[39] In substantive terms, the Court of Appeal is now supposed to act by way of review of the decision of the lower court rather than by way of rehearing and this means that it will be reluctant to overturn a decision of a trial judge on a question of mixed fact and law which involves applying a standard after evaluating and giving weight to a variety of factors, unless it can be shown that there is an error of principle in his approach. In the field of industrial designs, questions on which the Court of Appeal will now adopt this approach include: whether or not one design is "not substantially different" from another so as to infringe a registered design[40]; whether or not a fabric design reproduces a substantial part of another design in infringement of

---

[36] Any county court under its ordinary jurisdiction rules was able to hear actions for a statutory tort such as copyright infringement: see *Minerstone Ltd v Be Modern Ltd* [2002] F.S.R. 807 where it was held that it had jurisdiction to entertain an action for trade mark infringement. However, since that decision, CPR r.63.13 in combination with para.16.1 of the Practice Direction (Apps.E1 and E2 below) has restricted other intellectual property claims to the Chancery Division, the Patents County Court or to county courts which are also Chancery district registries, and para.16.3 of the Practice Direction has limited trade mark proceedings to a subset of the courts with Chancery District registries.

[37] Assuming that the case is allocated to the "multi-track", which most contested designs cases will be; otherwise appeal from the County Court lies to the High Court.

[38] The Community Designs (Designation of Community Design Courts) Regulations 2005 (SI 2005/696) App E4 post, reg.2(2), which also designates the Court of Session (in practice, the Inner House), and the Northern Ireland Court of Appeal as second-tier Community Design Courts for hearing appeals.

[39] CPR r.52.3.

[40] *Thermos Ltd v Aladdin Sales and Marketing Ltd* [2002] F.S.R. 184, CA. But cf. *Procter & Gamble Co v Reckitt Beuckiser (UK) Ltd* [2007] EWCA Civ 936; [2008] F.S.R. 8, CA where the Court of Appeal departed from the trial judge's assessment of whether the alleged infringement produced a "different overall impression" from the registered design, on the ground that he had erred in principle inter alia by approaching the "dominant features" of the design at too general a level which did not convey in words the overall impression which would be given to an informed observer. In effect, this seems to be a finding that the judge got to the wrong answer by applying too loose a test of infringement.

copyright[41]; and whether or not a design or design feature is "commonplace" for unregistered design right purposes.[42]

Further appeal from the Court of Appeal lies to the UK Supreme Court, **6–009** with permission either of the Court of Appeal or from the Supreme Court itself. In addition, a separate route for the determination of questions of EU law lies by way of a preliminary reference under art.267 TFEU which may be made by a court or tribunal at any level (including e.g. the RDAT). Such preliminary references obviously assume greatly increased practical importance in the field of designs now that the Community design rights have been introduced and the law of UK registered designs has been harmonised. However, a detailed description of the procedures for making preliminary references and the procedures of the European Court of Justice in dealing with them,[43] and of the General Court (formerly Court of First Instance) in dealing with appeals from OHIM, is outside the scope of this work.

2. Parties

Action by a proprietor of unregistered rights

Actions for infringement of copyright and of UK unregistered design **6–010** right may be brought by a proprietor or by an exclusive licensee.[44] An action for infringement of a Community unregistered right may be brought by its holder.[45] An exclusive licensee may sue if the holder, having been given notice to do so, does not himself bring proceedings in an appropriate period.[46] A non-exclusive licensee may bring proceedings if the holder gives him permission to do so.[47] Since there is no register of proprietors of any of these unregistered rights, a claimant alleging that he is the proprietor of such a right will normally need to prove the facts giving rise to subsistence of the right[48] and, unless he is the author, the

---

[41] *Designers Guild v Russell Williams (Textiles) Ltd* [2001] F.S.R. 113, HL, at paras 27–30 per Lord Hoffmann: " . . . the application of a not altogether precise legal standard to a combination of features of varying importance."

[42] *Scholes Windows Ltd v Magnet Ltd* [2002] F.S.R. 172, CA.

[43] The reader may wish to consult D. Anderson and M. Demetriou, *References to the European Court*, 2nd edn (London: Sweet & Maxwell, 2002).

[44] As to exclusive licensees, see para.6–015 below.

[45] Community Designs Regulation art.19(1), explicitly confers the exclusive rights arising from a Community design on its "holder".

[46] Community Designs Regulation art.32(3).

[47] Community Designs Regulation art.32(3).

[48] In the case of a Community unregistered design right, it is clear that the proprietor of the right does not have to go beyond that and show that the design is novel and has individual character: the burden of raising and proving allegations that the design lacks novelty or individual character rests on the defendant and this must be done by the proper procedure of a counterclaim for invalidity: Regulation, art.85 *Karen Millen Ltd v Dunnes Stores Ltd* [2007] I.E.H.C. 449; [2008] E.C.D.R. 11, Irish High Ct (Finlay Geoghegan J.).

events or chain of title by which he has become proprietor. In the case of copyright, his task may be assisted by certain statutory presumptions.[49]

6–011   Where the copyright or design right has been divided up by partial assignments,[50] the proprietor who is entitled to sue is the one within whose partial assignment the acts of the infringer fall.[51] When a copyright or unregistered design right is jointly owned, a third party needs the licence of all joint owners to do acts within the scope of the right, so each joint owner can sue separately, even in a case where the third party is acting with the consent of one of them.[52]

Action by a proprietor of registered design

6–012   With UK registered designs, the right of action for infringement is vested by statute explicitly in the registered proprietor.[53] The registered proprietor is the person whose name at the time in question is entered upon the register as proprietor. Thus, entry of the name of the proprietor on the register is a condition precedent for his right to sue third parties for infringement.[54] A person who has taken an assignment of a registered design but who has not been entered on the register as proprietor cannot maintain an action for infringement without joining the registered proprietor to the action.[55] Such an assignee will normally be recognised as proprietor in equity, and as such he will be able to sue if the registered proprietor, as owner of the legal title, is also joined to the action,[56] though the court might grant him an interim injunction pending him obtaining the legal estate or getting himself upon the register, or pending the joining of the legal owner as a party to the action.[57]

---

[49] CDPA 1988 s.104. The most relevant of these are subss.(2) and (4), which raise presumptions in favour of a purported author if they are named on the work when made or on copies as published, or in favour of a purported publisher if they are named as such on copies of the work as published. Sale of an industrial article will normally be regarded as a publication of the artistic works on which it is based and although one would not ordinarily use the word "publisher" outside the literary field, there seems no reason why this should not cover the person under whose name industrial articles are placed on the market.

[50] See paras 4–123 and 5–157 above.

[51] CDPA 1988 s.173(1) and s.258(1).

[52] See paras 4–127 and 5–160 above; see also *Cala Homes (South) Ltd v Alfred McAlpine Homes East Ltd* [1995] F.S.R. 818, ChD.

[53] RDA(E) s.24A(1) (formerly s.7(1) prior to the amendments made by the Intellectual Property (Enforcement, etc.) Regulations 2006 (SI 2006/1028).

[54] *Woolley v Broad* (1892) 9 R.P.C. 208; *Winkle & Co Ltd v Gent & Son* (1914) 31 R.P.C. 17.

[55] In *Winkle & Co Ltd v Gent & Son* (1914) 31 R.P.C. 17, a firm who owned a registered design had turned itself into a limited company, to which the partners assigned the assets of the business including the registered design. However, they failed to register the assignment until after the defendants' acts of infringement. The action was brought in the name of the company, who were required to amend to join the partners as claimants in order to sustain their title to sue.

[56] *Winkle & Co Ltd v Gent & Son* (1914) 31 R.P.C. 17 at 21; see para.6–018 below.

[57] *E. M. Bowden's Patents Syndicate Ltd v Herbert Smith & Co* [1904] 2 Ch. 86; *University of London Press Ltd v University Tutorial Press Ltd* [1916] 2 Ch. 601; *Performing Right Society Ltd v London Theatre of Varieties* [1924] A.C. 1.

In requiring registration as proprietor as a condition precedent to the **6–013** right to sue for infringement, registered designs differ from patents: under the Patents Act 1977, a person who has taken an assignment of a patent is the proprietor and can sue as such[58]; registration is merely prima facie evidence of the identity of the proprietor,[59] although there are penalties for late registration of assignments.[60]

The right to sue on a Community registered design is conferred on its **6–014** holder,[61] and the person in whose name it is registered or, prior to registration, the person in whose name the application is filed, is deemed to be the person entitled in proceedings before the Office and also in any other proceedings.[62]

Actions by exclusive and certain non-exclusive licensees

Persons who are exclusive licensees under copyrights and UK unregis- **6–015** tered and registered design rights have, by statute, a right to sue third parties for infringement which is concurrent with that of the proprietor.[63] The right of exclusive licensees of registered designs to sue was introduced in 2006,[64] and before that date exclusive licensees of registered designs had no right to sue. There is also an additional provision[65] which allows some non-exclusive licensees under copyrights (but not design rights) to sue concurrently with the proprietor if "the infringing act was directly connected to a prior licensed act of the licensee." The licence agreement must be in writing and signed by or on behalf of the copyright owner, and it must expressly grant the non-exclusive licensee a right of action under the section. Both registered and unregistered Community designs may be sued upon by an exclusive licensee if the owner fails to bring proceedings, and by a non-exclusive licensee if the owner[66] gives permission. In order for the copyright and UK unregistered and registered design right licence provisions to apply, the licence concerned must

---

[58] The Patents Act 1977 s.61(1).

[59] The Patents Act 1977 s.32(9).

[60] The Patents Act 1977 s.68.

[61] The Community Designs Regulation art.19. As regards actions by exclusive or non-exclusive licensees, the same rules apply to Community registered designs as to Community unregistered design rights: see para.6–010 above.

[62] The Community Designs Regulation art.17.

[63] CDPA 1988 s.101 and s.234 and RDA(E) s.24F. The provisions relating to copyright and to design right are identical and those relating to registered designs are very similar.

[64] Section 24F was inserted into the RDA(E) by the Intellectual Property (Enforcement, etc.) Regulations 2006 (SI 2006/1028), which implemented the Intellectual Property Enforcement Directive 2004/48/EC.

[65] CDPA 1988 s.101A, which was inserted in the Act by reg.28 of the Copyright and Related Rights Regulations 2003 (SI 2003/2498) in pursuance of Directive 2001/29/EC on the harmonisation of certain aspects of copyright and related rights in the information society, purportedly in order to give effect to art.8 of the Directive.

[66] See para.2–054 above.

satisfy the formal and other requirements of the Acts,[67] so that, for example, an exclusive licence which is oral would not satisfy the terms of the Act and the licensee would not have the statutory concurrent right to sue.

6–016   In such an action, the alleged infringer may avail himself of any defence that would be available if he were sued by the proprietor.[68] Where a design right or copyright owner and a licensee have concurrent rights of action under these provisions, both must be joined as parties to the action unless the court gives leave to the contrary.[69] The purpose of these provisions is to ensure that both copyright owner and licensee are bound by the outcome of the action, so that defendants are not exposed to the risk of multiple actions for the same alleged infringements. To satisfy this requirement, the owner and licensee may be co-claimants; or one may be a claimant and the other added as a (nominal) defendant. An owner or licensee who is added as nominal defendant in this way will normally not be liable for costs unless he takes part in the proceedings.[70] Interim relief however may be granted without waiting to join the missing owner or licensee.[71]

6–017   There are provisions designed to prevent the double recovery of damages or accounts of profits by owner and licensee, and for the fair apportionment of pecuniary relief between them.[72]

Equitable owners and licensees

6–018   Sometimes a person who has no legal right to sue (because he is not the owner or exclusive licensee of a copyright or unregistered design right, or not the registered proprietor of a registered design) may have a right to sue in equity. The historical principle on which this is based is that, before the fusion of law and equity, he would have been entitled to ask the Court of Chancery to compel the person having the legal title to bring an action in the common law courts. Under modern procedure, it is merely necessary that the person with the legal title to sue should be made a party to the litigation, either as co-claimant or as nominal defendant.

6–019   Examples of circumstances where a person may have an equitable title to sue are: an assignee of a registered design who has not yet been placed on the register as proprietor[73]; a company whose director has created a design or copyright work in the course of his duties as director but where

---

[67] See paras 4–129 and 5–162 above, and see RDA(E) s.15C which requires an exclusive licence under a registered design to be in writing signed by or on behalf of the proprietor in order to count as such under the Act.
[68] CDPA 1988 s.101(3) and s.234(3) and RDA(E) s.24F(3).
[69] CDPA 1988 s.102(1) and s.235(1) and RDA(E) s.24F(5).
[70] CDPA 1988 s.102(2) and s.235(2) and RDA(E) s.24F(5).
[71] CDPA 1988 s.102(3) and s.235(3) and RDA(E) s.24F(6).
[72] CDPA 1988 s.102(4) and s.235(4) and RDA(E) s.24F(7).
[73] See para.6–012 above.

the relationship with the company is not a contract of employment[74]; a person to whom a future copyright or unregistered design right has purportedly been assigned, but where the assignment fails to fulfil the formal statutory requirements of a prospective assignment of copyright or design right[75]; copyright works created pursuant to a commission in circumstances where it is expressly or impliedly agreed that the benefit of the copyright shall belong to the commissioner[76]; and more generally in cases where expressly or impliedly by contract or by reason of the fiduciary relationship of the parties, equity treats the legal proprietor as holding his rights in trust for another person.[77]

Apart from cases of an equitable owner, and of licensees of copyrights **6–020** and registered and unregistered design rights which fall within the statutory provisions, a licensee has no title to sue for infringement.[78] It has been suggested that it might be possible to join a licensee to an action brought by a proprietor and this might affect the quantum of damages, but this seems difficult to reconcile with principle.[79] However, in the case of Community registered and unregistered design rights, the Regulation expressly permits an exclusive or non-exclusive licensee to join into an action brought by the owner for the purpose of claiming damages.[80]

Who may be sued for infringement

The persons who are liable for infringement of copyright, design right or **6–021** registered design are determined by the ordinary rules of tort. Thus, not only the person physically performing the infringing act is liable, but also the person or persons under whose direction or on whose behalf the act is done under normal principles of agency.

Under normal tortious principles, directors and other persons who **6–022** exercise de facto control over companies can incur personal liability if they personally commit or are personally involved in infringing acts of

---

[74] See para.5–150 above.

[75] See paras 4–116 and 5–154.

[76] Unlike in the case of a registered or unregistered design, legal title to a copyright in a work created pursuant to a commission does not vest in the person placing the commission: see para.5–150 above.

[77] See para.5–147 above.

[78] Before the insertion of s.24F into the RDA(E), an exclusive licensee of a registered design did not have title to sue and the fact that his exclusive licence was entered on the register was irrelevant for this purpose: *Heap v Hartley* (1889) 6 R.P.C. 495; L.R. 42 ChD 461, CA, a case of an attempt by an exclusive licensee under a patent to bring an action: "I think therefore that an exclusive licensee has no title whatever to sue"; per Fry L.J. at 501, line 45. See also *Isaac Oren v Red Box Toy Factory Ltd* [1999] F.S.R. 785, Jacob J.; nor could he overcome the absence of a statutory right to sue by alleging that a third party infringer had interfered with contractual relations between the registered design owner and the licensee. See also *Newby v Harrison* I.J.&H. 393. Note that in the case of patents, exclusive licensees have long had a statutory right to sue, now under the Patents Act 1977 s.67.

[79] *Trico Folberth Ltd v Romac Motor Accessories Ltd* (1934) 51 R.P.C. 90.

[80] Reg., art.32(4); and see para.2–119 above.

their company.[81] Similarly, persons who engage in a joint venture with other persons who physically commit acts of infringement in the course of the joint venture will incur liability for infringement; for example, a parent company which gives instructions to a subsidiary to perform an infringing act,[82] or a manufacturer who is involved in directing the activities of its distributor on the market.[83] If the physical infringing act is committed within the territory of the right concerned, it does not matter that the other party to the joint venture physically never enters the territory; it is enough if they involve themselves in the activity, e.g. by giving instructions from abroad.[84]

Liability for "authorising" restricted acts

6–023   Quite apart from potential liability under the common law principles discussed in the preceding paragraph, by statute a person who authorises another to do an act which is a primary infringement of a copyright[85] or unregistered design right[86] himself commits an act of primary infringement. There is no corresponding provision relating to registered designs.

6–024   It has been held by the House of Lords that "authorise" in the context of the Copyright Act means to grant or purport to grant expressly or by implication the right to do the act complained of.[87] Thus, a customer who placed an order with a manufacturer to make goods according to a design specified by the customer would be liable for "authorising" if use of the design infringed a copyright or design right of a third party; however, that would not appear to be the case if the customer left it to the manufacturers to provide the design of the product concerned and left it to the manufacturers to satisfy themselves that they had the relevant rights to use it. In one earlier case it was said that where a customer places an order with a manufacturer for the supply of a quantity of a particular article and the articles are then made and supplied to the order, it is impossible to say that the customer has not authorised the making of those articles.[88] That proposition must be regarded as being too widely stated to be consistent with the decision of the House of Lords in *CBS v Amstrad*, although it may have been a correct conclusion on the facts of

---

[81] *MCA Records Inc v Charly Records Ltd* [2002] F.S.R. 402, CA, which considers the previous authorities on the question; *Evans (C) & Sons Ltd v Spritebrand Ltd* [1985] F.S.R. 267, CA; *Performing Right Society Ltd v Ciryl Theatrical Syndicate* [1924] 1 K.B. 1, CA.
[82] *Unilever v Gillette* [1989] R.P.C. 583, CA.
[83] *Morton-Norwich Products v Intercen Ltd* [1978] R.P.C. 501, ChD.
[84] *Unilever v Gillette*, above.
[85] See para.5–107 above.
[86] See para.4–075 above.
[87] *CBS Songs Ltd v Amstrad Consumer Electronics Plc* [1988] R.P.C. 567 at 604 line 40 et seq., HL.
[88] *Standen Engineering Ltd v A. Spalding & Sons Ltd* [1984] F.S.R. 554 at 557, ChD.

that case.[89] There is no territorial limitation on the place where an authorisation may be given in order for liability to be incurred: it is only necessary that the acts to be authorised should occur within the territorial scope of the design right or copyright.[90]

3. Invalidity of UK Registered Designs

Mode of challenging validity of rights relied upon

No special steps need to be taken by a defendant who challenges the existence or validity of a copyright or UK unregistered design right, beyond putting in issue the allegations of subsistence in his pleadings. However, when the validity of a UK registered design is challenged, a special procedure applies. A defendant who puts in issue the validity of a registered design may counterclaim for an order that the register be rectified by cancelling or varying the entry relating to the design.[91] The former rules of court[92] appeared to allow a defendant the option of disputing validity without counterclaiming for rectification; but in practice this was virtually never done and indeed would present the court with a serious difficulty if it were to make a finding of invalidity. It is

6–025

---

[89] The customer in fact sent out specifications asking for goods to be made to designs identified by him: *Standen v Spalding* [1984] F.S.R. 554 at 558. The case would be quite different if a customer had ordered off goods from a manufacturer's standard catalogue. In *Pensher Security Door Co Ltd v Sunderland County Council* [2000] R.P.C. 249, the Court of Appeal held that a housing authority was liable for authorising the making of doors because they commissioned the making of a particular design of door "thereby sanctioning and impliedly purporting to grant the right to manufacture doors to that design": per Aldous L.J. at 278, line 45 to 279, line 10. Whilst this may be the right interpretation of the facts of that particular case, it is submitted that there are many circumstances where the commissioning of the making of articles to a particular design does *not* impliedly purport to grant rights in respect of the design of the article. For example, a customer who orders the making of 100 articles depicted in a manufacturer's catalogue is plainly expecting the manufacturer to be responsible for having or securing any necessary rights in the design and is not himself purporting to grant any rights of his own in respect of the design and should not, in accordance with the reasoning of the House of Lords in *CBS v Amstrad*, be held liable for "authorising." Aldous L.J. in *Pensher* quoted a paragraph from the judgment of Falconer J. in *Standen* containing the over-wide reasoning mentioned above, and whilst he commented (at 278, line 48) that Falconer J. did not have the advantage of reading the speech of Lord Templeman in *CBS*, he did not explicitly overrule Falconer J.'s over wide reasoning. It is submitted that it would have been preferable had he done so.

[90] *ABKCO Music & Records Inc v Music Collection International Ltd* [1995] R.P.C. 657, CA. This means, for example, that a customer who places an order with a UK manufacturer from abroad could be liable for "authorising" if the goods are made to an infringing design.

[91] RDA(E) s.20(1) confers jurisdiction on the court. An application to rectify may be made, subject to certain exceptions (see below) by any "person aggrieved" (s.20(1A)(d)) and a person who has been sued on a registered design will necessarily count as a person aggrieved by the entry in the register. CPR 63.5(b) provides that applications of this nature may be made in existing proceedings under CPR Pt 20, i.e. by way of counter-claim.

[92] RSC ord.104, r.23(1).

open to question whether it is even possible to challenge the validity of a registered design by way of defence only (i.e. without seeking rectification of the register) because the wording of the Act appears to confer exclusive rights on the design so long as it is on the register.[93] Most applications to rectify are made by defendants in response to being sued on a registered design, but a freestanding application may be made to one of the courts[94] having jurisdiction over registered designs.[95]

6–026   Where an application is made to rectify the register, the claim form and the accompanying documents must be served on the Registry at the same time as on the other party or parties, and the Registrar is then entitled to take part in the proceedings and shall appear if so directed by the court.[96] In practice, the registrar only appears and takes part when he considers that some point of public interest or registry practice is involved. Whether the attack on validity is initiated by way of counterclaim or as a free-standing application, the court will, if it makes a finding of invalidity, make an appropriate order cancelling the design from the register, so that the public generally cannot thereafter be sued on an invalid design. The order of the court in then transmitted to the registrar for entry on the register.[97]

6–027   As an alternative to making a free-standing application to rectify the register to one of the courts having jurisdiction, an application may be made to the registrar for a declaration of invalidity.[98] The general rule is that such an application may be made by "any person interested",[99] a more modern sounding phrase which is presumably intended to have the same meaning as a "person aggrieved" in the case of an application to a court to rectify.[100] In the case of a number of grounds of invalidity, only certain specified persons may mount the attack in the registry and these correspond to the categories who may make the attack in court.[101] These provisions however apply only to post-2001 registered designs. In the case of pre-2001 registrations, the old provisions relating to cancellation on application to the registrar still apply.[102] These allow for cancellation of the registration on any ground on which its registration could have been

---

[93] RDA(E) s.7. Contrast the wording of the Trade Marks Act 1938 s.4(1) which stated that the registration "if valid" conferred exclusive rights.

[94] Or an application may be made to the Registrar: see below.

[95] In England and Wales, CPR 63.5(a) provides that such an application is made by issuing a claim form under CPR Part 7.

[96] RDA(E) s.20(3).

[97] RDA(E) s.20(4).

[98] RDA(E) s.11ZA.

[99] RDA(E) s.11ZB(1).

[100] The same phrase, "any person interested", was used in the now-repealed s.11(2) of RDA(A) which allowed applications to be made to the registrar to cancel a registration.

[101] See para.6–028 below. The provisions of s.11ZB substantially correspond to those of s.20(1A).

[102] 2001 Regulations reg.12(2).

refused, and contain no restriction on who may apply for cancellation other than it should be by "any person interested".[103]

Who may challenge validity

The general rule is that the validity of a registered design may be challenged by any "person aggrieved".[104] This phrase has been liberally construed by the courts and extends to any person whose actual or potential commercial activities may be adversely affected by the presence of the design on the register.[105] However, in the case of attacks on some grounds, only certain people are entitled to make the attack. These are: **6–028**

(1) *Royal Arms and other emblems:* Schedule A1 of RDA(E)[106] prohibits the registration of designs using the Royal arms or other symbols, representations of members of the Royal Family or devices suggesting patronage by them, the national flags of the United Kingdom or of its parts, or the arms of other persons under a grant of arms from the Crown. It also has similar protection for the emblems of Paris Convention countries and international organisations. Invalidity on these grounds can only be alleged by a person concerned by the use of the emblem etc in question.[107]

(2) *Unpublished designs with earlier priority date:* On this ground[108] only the owner of, or applicant for, the earlier registration can allege invalidity.[109]

(3) *Wrong proprietor registered:* Only the true proprietor of the design may object to validity on this ground.[110]

(4) *Infringement of earlier distinctive sign or copyright:* Only the holder of rights to the sign or the owner of the copyright may attack validity on this ground.[111]

It should be noted that the above restrictions on who is entitled to attack validity were introduced by the 2001 Regulations which implemented the Directive. Under the previous law, the registration of a design could be attacked on any ground by any person, so long as he was a **6–029**

---

[103] RDA(A) s.11(2).

[104] RDA(E) s.20(1A)(d).

[105] *British Insulated and Helsby Cables Ltd v London Electric Wire Co and Smiths Ltd* (1913) 30 R.P.C. 620; *Rose v Pickavant & Co Ltd* (1923) 40 R.P.C. 320; *Smith v Grigg Ltd* (1924) 41 R.P.C. 149; *Re Abraham Margolin's Registered Design* (1937) 54 R.P.C. 1.

[106] Inserted by the 2001 Regulations before Schedule 1 to the Act.

[107] RDA(E) s.20(1A)(a).

[108] See para.2–065 above.

[109] RDA(E) s.20(1A)(b) and 20(1B).

[110] RDA(E) s.20(1A)(c) and s.11ZA(2).

[111] RDA(E) s.20(1A)(c) and s.11ZA(3) and (4).

"person aggrieved".[112] Thus, a design could be attacked e.g. on the ground that the wrong person had been entered on the register as proprietor, by a third party who was sued for infringement, not just by the true owner.[113] This remains the position when a pre-2001 registration is attacked today; in other words, the restrictions on who may attack validity apply only to post-2001 EU harmonised national registrations.[114]

Grounds of challenge to validity

6–030 A person who challenges the validity of a registered design is required to serve a document separate from his statement of case headed "Grounds of Invalidity" specifying the grounds upon which the validity of the registered design is challenged.[115] Full particulars must be given of any prior designs relied upon to attack the novelty or individual character of the registration. In the case of a design alleged to be made available to the public by written description, the date on which, and the means by which, it was made available must be specified unless this is clear from its face.[116] In the case of a design alleged to have been made available by use, the date(s) of such use, the name of all persons making such use, any written material which identifies such use, the existence and location of any apparatus employed in such use, and all facts and matters relied on to establish that the design was made available to the public, must be specified.[117] Evidence of particular designs which have not been specifically pleaded cannot be introduced under an allegation of common general knowledge.[118]

6–031 But this practice does not generally apply to the identification of matters alleged to be in common use in the trade, as distinct from particular prior designs. In *Scripto Inc v Tallon Ltd*,[119] where the defendants had pleaded that the registered designs in suit differed from prior published designs which they had particularised only in immaterial details, "or in features being variants commonly used in the trade", an application for further and better particulars on the ground that a plea of a particular prior user was involved was refused, it being held that this was a plea of common user of which no particulars need be given.

---

[112] RDA(A) s.20(1).

[113] See *AL BASSAM Trade Mark* [1995] R.P.C. 511, CA, a trade mark case. See also para.3–216 above, n.67.

[114] 2001 Regulations reg.12(2).

[115] Practice Direction para.4.2(2).

[116] Practice Direction para.4.4(1).

[117] Practice Direction para.4.4(2). Rather curiously, the Practice Direction is drafted so that the court's power to order inspection of any such apparatus is specified in para.4.5 to apply only in relation to patent cases. However the court would have power to order such inspection (if the apparatus is within the jurisdiction or out of the jurisdiction but within the power of one of the parties) under its general powers in any case.

[118] *Gottschalck & Co v Velez & Co* (1936) 53 R.P.C. 403.

[119] [1960] R.P.C. 262.

Although "trade variants" is an issue which applies only to pre-2001 registered designs, presumably the same practice would be applied in respect of evidence directed to general questions under the new law such as what is known to the "informed user",[120] as distinct from specific designs relied upon to attack novelty or distinctive character. It has been held in the context of UK unregistered design right that disclosure will not normally be ordered in relation to what designs are "commonplace",[121] by analogy with the practice normally adopted in relation to pleas of reliance on common general knowledge in a patent action, because it is a vague and broad issue and the defendant will normally be in as good a position to work out what is commonplace as the claimant.[122] Presumably the same practice will apply where reliance is placed on the general design corpus[123] in UK registered design or Community registered or unregistered design cases.

It is not usual to order further particulars of general averments that the **6–032** design is solely a method of construction or dictated by function, since the defendant's position will depend upon what the claimant argues to be the essential features of his design.[124] A similar practice has been adopted in relation to general pleas that the registered design is ambiguous.[125]

Where grounds of invalidity are amended by a defendant who relies on **6–033** additional prior art, the claimant may be given the option of abandoning his design in the light of the new prior art and collecting his costs since the date of the original grounds of invalidity from the defendant who failed to plead it earlier.[126] The practice of making this kind of order in registered design cases[127] is not however as settled as the practice in patent actions.[128]

---

[120] Who is taken to be familiar with the "existing design corpus", i. e. with "all designs that are known in the the normal course of business in specialist circles in the sector in question" see para.2–043 above.

[121] As to "commonplace" and unregistered design right, see paras 4–045 et seq.

[122] *Ultraframe Ltd v Eurocell Building Plastics Ltd* [2003] EWHC 3258 (Ch); [2005] F.S.R. 2, Pumfrey J.

[123] As to the "existing design corpus" and the "informed user's" deemed knowledge of it, see para.2–043 above.

[124] *Sebel & Co Ltd v Lines Bros Ltd* (1954) 71 R.P.C. 373.

[125] In *Scripto, Inc. v Tallon Ltd* [1960] R.P.C. 262, the defendants pleaded that each of the registered designs was ambiguous, because it did not indicate how it differed from the other registered designs otherwise than by features dictated solely by function. It was held that, anyhow in the absence of any statements of novelty in respect of the designs, such a plea need not be further particularlised by stating the features alleged to be so dictated. "Ambiguity" as such is not a ground of invalidity of a registered design under current law.

[126] This at any rate may be the practice if the action is complicated; *Photax (London) Ltd v Lustro Distributors Ltd* (1951) 68 R.P.C. 176; or if a considerable period of time has elapsed between service of the particulars and the application to amend: see *Rose and Hubble Ltd v L. Hart (Stockport) Ltd* [1966] R.P.C. 217.

[127] *Woolley v Broad* (1892) 9 R.P.C. 429; *Wilson and Wilson Bros Bobbin Co Ltd v Wilson & Co Ltd* (1899) 16 R.P.C. 315. For form of order, see *Rose and Hubble Ltd*, above.

[128] The form of the order in patent actions is that in *Baird v Moule's Patent Earth Closet Co*, set

Effect of order for rectification

6–034   Unless the court or the registrar orders otherwise, an order rectifying the Register of Designs or a declaration of invalidity has retrospective effect, so that in particular when an entry is deleted it is deemed never to have been made.[129] This means that if a registered design is cancelled because it is invalid, it is treated as if it always had been void. It is usual practice to stay an order for rectification made at trial pending an appeal by the registered design proprietor; if such a stay is not applied for at the time of judgment at first instance, it is doubtful whether the registered design can later be revived on appeal.[130]

4. Invalidity of Community Designs

6–035   Community registered designs may be declared invalid either by the Office, or by a Community design court.[131] Community design courts can only declare a registered design invalid on the basis of a counterclaim in infringement proceedings, and accordingly have no jurisdiction to entertain free-standing applications attacking the validity of such registered designs.[132] Such free-standing applications can only be launched in the Office.

6–036   Only Community design courts have jurisdiction to declare an unregistered Community design right to be invalid,[133] and the Office has no jurisdiction in this regard. Accordingly, Community design courts can entertain applications for a declaration of invalidity either if they arise in a counterclaim in infringement proceedings, or as free-standing applications.[134] Such free-standing applications will generally need to be brought in the courts of the state where the owner of the right is domiciled etc, since the rules conferring special jurisdiction on the courts of a state where an infringement is committed or is threatened do not apply to such an application.[135] Whilst in an action for alleged infringement of an

---

out in *Edison Telephone Co v India Rubber Co* (1881) 17 ChD. 137; see also *Morris Wilson & Co v Coventry Machinists Co* (1891) 8 R.P.C. 853. For form of order where proceeding is a motion to expunge, see *Re John Glen & Sons Designs* (1933) 50 R.P.C. 41, 51 or if there is a counterclaim for rectification as in *See v Scott Paine* (1933) 50 R.P.C. 56.

[129] RDA(E) s.20(5) (court) or s.11ZE(2) (registrar).

[130] See *Pavel v Sony Corp* [1995] R.P.C. 500, CA, a patent case.

[131] The Community Design Regulation art.24(1). The same procedures apply to the invalidation of designs granted on the basis of international applications under the Hague Agreement—see art.106f and para.2–154, above.

[132] The Community Design Regulation art.24(1).

[133] The Community Design Regulation art.24(3).

[134] The Community Design Regulation art.24(3).

[135] The Community Design Regulation art.82(5) only applies to actions under arts 81(a) and (d). The rules relating to jurisdiction of different national Community design courts are outlined in para.6–004 above.

unregistered Community design, the claimant must prove the necessary facts that are said to give rise to subsistence of the Community design right under art.11 of the Regulation, i.e. when and where the design was made available to the public in the Community, and must "indicate" what constitutes the individual character of the unregistered Community design, there is no onus on the claimant to disprove grounds of invalidity such as that the design is not novel or lacks individual character: the burden lies on the defendant or other person challenging validity to raise and prove such grounds.[136] In the case of an unregistered Community design right, the challenge to validity may be made either by way of a counterclaim for a declaration of invalidity, or "by way of a plea".[137]

The general rule is that any person may apply for a declaration of invalidity; there is no "person aggrieved" or "person interested" threshold as required in the case of UK national registrations.[138] However, in the case of specific grounds of invalidity, such as an attack on proprietorship, only certain persons may apply and these restrictions correspond to those which apply to post-2001 UK registrations.[139]   **6–037**

Where invalidity proceedings are brought in a Community design court, it will in general apply the same procedure as it applies to national designs.[140] Thus, in England and Wales, similar rules apply with regard to service of grounds of invalidity and what must be specified in those grounds regarding prior publications or uses which are relied upon.[141] One procedural difference is that it is the court itself, rather than the parties, which informs the Office of the filing of a counterclaim relating to a registered Community design or a court order disposing of such a counterclaim.[142] Very oddly, there appear to be at present no explicit   **6–038**

---

[136] The Community Design Regulation art.85(2); and *Karen Millen v Dunnes Stores Ltd* [2007] I.E.H.C. 449; [2008] E.C.D.R. 156, Irish High Ct (Finlay Geoghegan J.).

[137] The wording of the Community Design Regulation art.85(2). Presumably "by way of a plea" means that the issue is raised by way of defence without a claim for a declaration of invalidity; however, it seems that the onus still rests on the defendant to establish invalidity whether validity is challenged by way of a plea or by counterclaim.

[138] See paras 6–027 and 6–028 above. The fact that there is no "person aggrieved" threshold is implied by the fact that art.25 of the Regulation does contain restrictions on who may apply to invalidate on certain specified grounds, but contains no general restriction in other cases. In the case of applications to the Office, art.52(1) explicitly states that "any natural or legal person" may apply, subject only to the explicit restrictions in art.25.

[139] These are set out in para.6–028 above; the restrictions are imposed by art.25(2), (3) and (4) of the Regulation and the UK law implements the corresponding provisions of the Directive which are intended to mirror the Regulation.

[140] Article 88(1) of the Regulation requires Community design courts to apply the same rules of procedure as those applying to the same type of action relating to a national design right, except where otherwise provided in the Regulation.

[141] See para.6–030 above. The Practice Direction is written in this regard without distinction between UK and Community registered designs.

[142] The court is required to inform the Office of counterclaims and of orders by art.86 of the Regulation. Under the Practice Direction, para.17, the parties are supposed to inform the court in writing that they are filing a counterclaim or asking for an order which ought to be sent to the Office, presumably in case the court is unable to work this out for itself.

requirements requiring the pleading of grounds of invalidity of Community unregistered designs.[143] However, art.88(1) of the Regulation states in mandatory terms that:

> "Unless otherwise provided in this Regulation, a Community design court shall apply the rules of procedure governing the same type of action relating to a national design right in the Member State where it is situated."

It seems almost certain that the "national design right" referred to in this article must be a harmonised national design right under the Directive, and cannot be an unharmonised national law having quite different characteristics such as UK unregistered design right. It follows that it is a mandatory requirement of EU law under art.88(1) that the UK courts must apply the same procedure to Community unregistered designs as they apply to UK *registered* designs, and not the procedures they apply to UK unregistered design right.

6–039   Applications to the Office are governed by arts 52 et seq. of the Regulation, supplemented by more detailed provisions in arts 28 et seq. of the Implementing Regulation.[144] A written reasoned statement of the grounds of invalidity must be filed with the application,[145] and there are detailed requirements as to the particulars which must be supplied in respect of the different grounds of invalidity.[146] The Office informs the registered proprietor and invites written representations from the parties as often as necessary, and the Invalidity Division renders its decision.[147] A third party who is being sued for infringement of the design in question is entitled to join in to the invalidity proceedings in the Office.[148]

6–040   An appeal as of right lies from decisions of the Invalidity Division to a Board of Appeal. Such an appeal has an automatic suspensive effect, so there is no need (unlike in the case of UK court decisions) to apply for a stay if the decision is to invalidate the design.[149] A party who is dissatisfied with the decision of a Board of Appeal can bring an action before the Court of Justice of the European Union to annul or alter the decision.[150]

---

[143] This is because CPR r.63.6, which applies the detailed requirements in the Practice Direction to serve Grounds of Invalidity, refers in terms only to claims in which "the validity of a patent or a registered design is challenged."

[144] Commission Regulation (EC) No.2245/2002 of October 21, 2002 implementing Council Regulation (EC) No.6/2002 on Community Designs: see App.B2 below.

[145] Regulation art.52(2).

[146] Implementing Regulation art.28(1)(b).

[147] Regulation art.53(2).

[148] Regulation art.54.

[149] Regulation art.55(1). The procedure on appeal in governed by arts 55 to 60 of the Regulation and arts 34 to 37 of the Implementing Regulation.

[150] Regulation art.61. Such an action comes before the General Court (formerly Court of First Instance), with a further tier of appeal to the Court of Justice itself in some cases.

There are provisions which are designed to prevent conflicting deci- **6–041** sions by different Community design courts or by the Office on the validity of the same design. An application to the Office is not admissible if an application relating to the same subject matter and cause of action, and involving the same parties, has been adjudicated on by a Community design court and has acquired the authority of a final decision.[151] No counterclaim for a declaration of invalidity of a registered design may be made in a Community design court if an application relating to the same subject matter and cause of action, and involving the same parties, has already been determined by the Office.[152]

A declaration of invalidity may be partial rather than total and a **6–042** registered Community design may be maintained on the register in amended form to meet the grounds of invalidity as found by the court or the Office.[153] The effect of a declaration of invalidity is that the design is deemed not to have had from the outset the effects specified in the Regulation to the extent that it has been declared invalid.[154] Unlike in the case of UK registrations, there appears to be no power for the court or Office to modify this provision or to direct a different date.

5. Remedies in Civil Proceedings

Nature of remedies that can be claimed

The remedies available for infringement of registered designs, copyright **6–043** and unregistered design right are, with some special additions and modifications, those available for infringement of a proprietary right under the general law of tort. Thus, CDPA 1988 s.96(2) states that:

> "(2) In an action for infringement of copyright all such relief by way of damages, injunctions, accounts or otherwise is available to the plaintiff as is available in respect of the infringement of any other property right."[155]

In respect of Community designs (registered and unregistered), the **6–043A** Regulation specifies that the Community design court should, subject to special reasons for not doing so, award an injunction against infringement, seizure of infringing products and:

> "materials and implements predominantly used in order to manufacture the infringing goods, if their owner knew the effect for which

---

[151] Regulation art.52(3).
[152] Regulation art.86(5).
[153] Regulation art.25(6).
[154] Regulation art.26(1).
[155] Section 229(2) relating to unregistered design right is in identical terms, as is s.24A(1) of the RDA(E).

such use was intended or if such effect would have been obvious in the circumstances",

and

"other sanctions which are provided by the law of the member state in which the acts of infringement or threatened infringement are committed, including its private international law".[156]

The provisions of the Regulation have now been supplemented by a new para.1A(2) of the Community Design Regulations 2005,[157] which gives to the holder of a Community (registered or unregistered) design right "all such relief by way of damages, injunctions, accounts or otherwise ... as is available in respect of the infringement of any other property right".[158] Whilst it is clear that damages or an account of profits should be awarded in respect of infringements within the United Kingdom on the same basis as for infringement of UK design rights, it may be that a court in the United Kingdom acting as a Community design court should look to the principles applied under the local laws of other member states in determining pecuniary remedies relating to infringements in those states in cases where it is adjudicating on such infringements.[159] However, at least in theory, the remedies available for infringement under the laws of the different member states should now have been substantially harmonised.[160]

6–044   Thus, the general rules relating to tortious remedies apply to all five of the relevant types of right which protect designs, subject to certain specific modifications. The right to obtain an injunction for infringement of copyright and design right is curtailed during the "licences of right" period. The right to obtain damages is subject to "innocence" defences in relation to all three kinds of right under UK law. Although there is an argument that the court should apply those defences by analogy to infringements of Community registered and unregistered rights, the contrary has been held.[161] There is a special statutory head of damages ("additional" damages) available for infringement of copyright and

---

[156] Regulation art.89(1).

[157] See App.B5, para.B5.003: reg.1A together with regs 1B to 1D dealing with the delivery up of infringing articles were inserted into the 2005 Regulations by the Intellectual Property (Enforcement, etc.) Regulations 2006 (SI 2006/1028) which implemented the Intellectual Property Enforcement Directive 2004/48/EC.

[158] As to whether or not the insertion of this general paragraph without making explicit provision for the "innocence" defences which would apply to infringements of the corresponding rights under national law has the effect of excluding the "innocence" defences which would arise in the case of infringement of corresponding rights under national law, see para.6–052 below.

[159] This would appear to be the consequence of art.89(1) of the Regulation; otherwise the substantive relief available for an act of infringement might depend upon the forum in which the claim was pursued.

[160] By the Intellectual Property Enforcement Directive 2004/48/EC.

[161] See para.6–052 below.

unregistered design right (but not registered designs) which may be awarded to successful claimants if the infringement is "flagrant", and on other grounds. Special statutory remedies are given to secure the delivery up or destruction of infringing articles, as well as moulds and other items which could be used to make further infringing copies. These and other detailed matters are dealt with in the following paragraphs.

Disclosure and pre-action disclosure

Normal disclosure is in the nature of an interim remedy leading to an adjudication on the merits of the case, rather than being part of the final relief sought in its own right. Disclosure is available in actions for enforcement of rights relating to designs on the same basis as other kinds of actions in the courts of England and Wales under CPR Pt 31. In principle it is possible for a party which is unsure whether it has a cause of action, or has insufficient information properly to plead a claim, to seek pre-action disclosure under CPR r.31.16. However a wide-ranging claim to pre-action disclosure has been rejected on the ground that pre-action disclosure should not be allowed to become: **6–044A**

> "a means of examining a competitor's otherwise secret designs on the basis that some kind of infringement might have occurred . . . unless there is at least a clear and convincing evidential basis for the belief that acts of infringement may have occurred and the court can then be satisfied that the pre-action disclosure sought is highly focussed."[162]

Quite apart from ordering disclosure in the course of an action for the purpose of assisting in the adjudication of the claims in the action, the courts of England and Wales have long been willing to order disclosure of the identities of suppliers of infringing goods or customers to whom infringing goods have been shipped for the purpose of permitting the claimant to take action against those persons and to prevent the further manufacture or distribution of infringing goods.[163] Because of doubts about the extent of the powers of the Scottish courts in this respect, there is now a statutory right to apply to courts in Scotland for disclosure of "information regarding the origin and distribution networks of goods or services which infringe an intellectual property right".[164]   **6–0044B**

---

[162] *BSW Ltd v Balltec Ltd* [2006] EWHC 822 (Ch); [2007] F.S.R. 1, Patten J. at para.83; unsupported assertions that the intended defendant could not have developed its products in the time available without resorting to infringement are not sufficient to satisfy this burden.

[163] *Norwich Pharmacal Co v Customs and Excise Commissioners* [1974] A.C. 133, and cases following.

[164] Regulation 4 of the Intellectual Property (Enforcement, etc.) Regulations 2006 (SI 2006/1028).

Injunctions

6–045 In most design cases, an injunction to restrain further infringements is the principal remedy sought by the claimant, surpassing in importance even the award of damages. An injunction is an equitable remedy and therefore its grant in any case is a matter for the discretion of the court; however the normal practice under which that discretion is exercised is that an injunction to restrain further infringement will be granted as a matter of course, as it is presumed from the fact of infringement that there is a likelihood of its recurrence.[165] The fact that the defendant says that he will not do it again will not necessarily prevent an injunction being granted against him,[166] although exceptionally, if it can be definitely shown that there is no such likelihood of any recurrence, then an injunction may be refused.[167] In the case of infringement of Community design rights, art.89(1)(a) of the Regulation provides for the court to make an order preventing infringement "unless there are special reasons for not doing so". This formulation would appear to leave it open to the courts to apply the same principles to the award of injunctions in Community design right cases as they have heretofore applied to national design rights or copyright.

6–046 As in all cases of threatened invasion of a property right, an injunction can be granted *quia timet* to restrain infringement in the absence of an actual act of infringement, if it is shown that the defendant has the intention of infringing or has threatened to infringe.[168]

Effect of "Licences of Right" on relief

6–047 The availability of injunctions is restricted in cases where the right concerned is subject to the grant of licences of right. This is the case with all unregistered design rights during the final five years of their term,[169] and was the case with transitional artistic copyrights during the last five years of their term in respect of acts that would be excluded from

---

[165] *Proctor v Bayley & Son* (1889) 6 R.P.C. 538. The presumption in favour of the grant of an injunction is now further reinforced by the Intellectual Property Enforcement Directive 2004/48/EC.

[166] *Losh v Hague* (1839) 1 W.P.C. 202; *Savory (E.W.) Ltd v World of Golf Ltd* [1914] 2 Ch. 566.

[167] *Proctor v Bayley & Son* (1889) 6 R.P.C. 538: an injunction was refused, even though infringement was proved, as there the defendants had only used the infringing article on one occasion, five years previous to the action, and had ever since abandoned its use, as they found it did not work satisfactorily.

[168] *Cooper v Whittingham* (1880) 15 Ch.D. 501; *Shoe Machinery Co Ltd v Cutlan* (1895) 12 R.P.C. 342 at 357: a patent case, Romer J. said: "Two kinds of action may be brought by a plaintiff patentee. The one is based on this, that the defendant has infringed before action brought, and in respect of this the plaintiff is entitled to claim damages, or an account and an injunction to prevent similar infringements in the future. The other action is based not on the fact that the defendant has infringed, but that he threatens and intends to infringe; and in this case the plaintiff may claim an injunction to restrain the threatened infringement. Of course you may find both kinds of action combined in one . . . "

[169] See para.4–133 above.

infringement of copyright by s.51 of the CDPA 1988.[170] In addition, there are powers under anti-monopoly procedures to impose licences of right on specific design rights.[171] Where a licence of right is available, no injunction or order for delivery up can be granted against a defendant who undertakes to take a licence on terms to be settled by the Comptroller in default of agreement, and damages or the amount recoverable on an account of profits will be limited to double the amount that would have been payable under a licence of right.[172] Such an undertaking can be given by a defendant even after the relevant design right has expired, if he is being sued for acts done before expiry.[173] However, it seems that in order to take advantage of this provision the defendant must reasonably expect to be able to honour the terms of such a licence and if it cannot, for example if it is a £2 company with no available assets to pay the royalties, then the court retains the power to impose an injunction.[174] This provision remedies the defect in the old licences of right provisions of the Patents Act 1977, which gave patentees an incentive to spin out proceedings in the Patent Office in order to deny a licence to applicants for as long as possible. Such an undertaking can be offered at any time before the final order in the proceedings, and without an admission of liability.[175] This means that a defendant who denies infringement can safeguard his position in case he loses by giving an undertaking to take a licence. If he wins he need pay nothing, because he will have been found to have done no acts within the scope of the licence; if he loses, he cannot be put out of business by an injunction and must merely pay licence fees for the future and damages for the past. His liability for damages or an account of profits is capped (at twice the level of licence fees ultimately determined) from the moment that licences of right became available.[176] Furthermore, from the moment that he makes an application to the Patent Office to settle the terms of the licence, his liability is limited to the royalties set by the Patent Office, because the licence once its terms are settled dates back

---

[170] See para.5–173 above.

[171] CDPA 1988 s.238(1). See para.9–020 below.

[172] CDPA 1988 s.239(1). This double-royalty cap applies to acts carried out before the date of application for the licence of right; from then onwards the licence (once terms are settled) will retrospectively cover acts done from the date of application onwards and only the single royalty will be payable on those acts. For settlement of terms by the Comptroller, see para.8–005 below.

[173] *Ultraframe (UK) Ltd v Eurocell Building Plastics Ltd* [2005] EWCA 761; [2005] R.P.C. 36, CA, per Neuberger L.J. at paras 104–118. Jacob L.J. at para.71 expressed the view that the normal level of damages for infringement during the licence of right period would in any case be the appropriate royalty rate (by analogy with damages cases in which a rights owner regularly licenses out the rights in question, see e.g. the cases mentioned in sub-para.(4) of para.6–049 below). If this observation is correct, it would mean that the "double royalty" cap in s.239 could never apply to a damages claim, although at least in theory it might apply to restrict what is recoverable on an account of profits if the claimant is very successful in demonstrating that the defendant has made large profits from the infringement..

[174] *Dyrland Smith AS v Turberville Smith Ltd* [1998] F.S.R. 774, CA, at 778–9.

[175] CDPA 1988 s.239(2).

[176] CDPA 1988 s.239(1)(c) and 239(3).

to the date of application.[177] The court may grant an interim injunction in circumstances where the defendant is prepared to undertake to apply for a licence of right only conditionally if it loses at trial.[178]

Damages

6–048   The measure of damages is prima facie the loss which the proprietor of the design has suffered owing to the infringement and is as Lord Blackburn stated in *Livingstone v Rawyards Coal Co*[179]:

> "that sum of money which will put the party who has been injured . . . in the same position as he would have been if he had not sustained the wrong for which he is now getting his compensation or reparation."

6–049   More specifically, damages will normally be claimed under a number of heads[180]:

(1) Where the defendant has made sales which the claimant showed he would otherwise have made, the claimant is entitled to their loss of profits on the assumption that they would have made the sales in fact made by the defendant. Unless it is a case where it can be shown that every single sale by the defendant was at the expense of the defendant, the court will apply a percentage figure to reflect the chance that the claimant would, but for the infringement, make the sales in fact made by the defendant.[181]

(2) Where the defendant has undercut the claimant's prices and the latter had to reduce his prices to compete, the claimant is entitled to be recompensed for the diminution in his profits.[182]

(3) In case of sales by the defendant which the evidence shows the claimant would not himself have made, the claimant is entitled to a fair and proper royalty at the price or hire which should have been paid for the use of his design to legalise those sales.[183]

(4) As a general alternative to these methods, the design owner can if he wishes claim all his damages for all sales made by the

---

[177] CDPA 1988 s.248(6): see para.8–005 below.
[178] *Dyrlund Smith AS v Turberville Smith Ltd* [1998] F.S.R. 774, CA. Presumably, the defendant's tactical mistake in this case was not to agree to take a licence immediately and then contend that his royalty obligation was zero because his products did not fall within the scope of the licensed rights.
[179] (1880) 5 App. Cas. 25.
[180] Generally, the assessment of damages in design cases (whether design copyright, design right or registered design) will follow the principles worked out in patent cases: *Blayney (T/a Aardvark Jewelry) v Clogau St David's Gold Mines Ltd* [2003] F.S.R. 360, CA.
[181] *Gerber Garment Technology Inc v Lectra Systems Ltd* [1997] R.P.C. 443, CA.
[182] *Gerber Garment Technology Inc v Lectra Systems Ltd* [1997] R.P.C. 443, CA.
[183] See *Gerber Garment Technology Inc v Lectra Systems Ltd* [1997] R.P.C. 443, CA.

defendant on the basis of a fair and proper royalty. Royalty is estimated from the point of view of what royalty would have been fixed for the use of the design by a willing licensor and willing licensee bargaining on equal terms in a neutral atmosphere with a knowledge that the design is valid.[184]

The basis on which damages are calculated in all kinds of intellectual property cases is now potentially affected by general rules laid down in reg.3 of the Intellectual Property (Enforcement, etc.) Regulations 2006.[185] This provision was introduced in order to transpose into UK law the damages provisions of the Intellectual Property Enforcement Directive 2004/48/EC. It provides that when: **6–049A**

"the defendant knew, or had reasonable grounds to know, that he engaged in infringing activity, the damages awarded to the claimant shall be appropriate to the actual prejudice he suffered as a result of the infringement."

It goes on to set out a number of criteria which should be taken into account in awarding such damages which are taken verbatim from the Directive, including inter alia the "moral prejudice" caused to the claimant by such the infringement. It is not clear whether reg.3 will affect the basis upon which the courts of the United Kingdom have previously awarded damages in intellectual property cases, and reg.3(3) specifically states that the regulation does not affect the operation of any enactment or rule of law relating to remedies for infringement of intellectual property rights "except to the extent that it is inconsistent with the provisions of this regulation." Thus it appears that reg.3 has been made as a fail-safe to ensure that if the rather unclear provisions of the Directive are interpreted in a way which is inconsistent with previous UK practice then the courts should apply the Directive.

In *Cow & Co Ltd v Cannon Rubber Manufacturers Ltd (No.2)*,[186] damages were assessed on the basis of a reasonable royalty upon all infringing articles made and sold by the defendants. In some cases this may be the only practical method of assessment.[187] If, however, loss of profit is taken as the basis, the principle is to ascertain as far as possible how far the sale of the defendant's infringing articles has interfered with the sale of the claimant's goods,[188] and to compensate him for the loss of any orders which the defendant obtained which would have otherwise gone to them. **6–050**

---

[184] *General Tire & Rubber Co v Firestone Tyre & Rubber Co* [1976] R.P.C. 197, HL; *Meters Ltd v Metropolitan Gas Meters Ltd* (1911) 28 R.P.C. 157 at 164; *Watson, Laidlaw & Co Ltd v Pott, Cassels and Williamson* (1914) 31 R.P.C. 104 at 120.
[185] SI 2006/1028.
[186] [1961] R.P.C. 236.
[187] *B. T.-H. v C. Peebles* (1923) 40 R.P.C. 119 at 128.
[188] *Pneumatic Tyre Co Ltd v Puncture Proof Pneumatic Tyre Co Ltd* (1899) 16 R.P.C. 209.

But it does not always necessarily follow that the claimant would have sold a quantity of articles equal to that sold by the defendant.

6–051   The computation of damages may be subject to the damages "cap" which applies in cases where the defendant undertakes to take a licence of right.[189] The cap is unlikely to be relevant to damages assessed on a royalty basis (because it is set at twice the royalty rate determined for the licence of right) but could in some cases restrict considerably the damages that might be obtainable on a loss of profits basis.

Innocence defences

6–052   The right to receive damages is subject to "innocence" defences in the case of all three kinds of design right under UK law. In the case of copyright and primary[190] infringement of UK unregistered design right, if an infringer shows that he did not know, and had no reason to believe, that the copyright or design right concerned existed, then he is not liable for damages.[191] Similarly, it is a defence against damages for an infringer of a registered design to show that he was not aware, and had no reasonable grounds for supposing, that the design was registered.[192] As regards Community registered and unregistered design rights, art.89(1)(d) of the Regulation which lays down sanctions in an action for infringement provides for "other sanctions appropriate under the circumstances which are provided by the law of the Member State". This appears to suggest that the member state should apply its own law of damages relating to analogous national rights and accordingly should apply by analogy any innocence defences which form part of that law. If this is right, then the innocence defences applying to UK national designs should be applied by analogy to cases of infringement of Community registered and unregistered design rights. However, it has rather surprisingly been held that Community registered and unregistered design rights are not subject to a corresponding innocence defence.[193]

---

[189] CDPA 1988 s.239(1)(c); see para.6–047 above.
[190] There is a more extensive defence in the case of secondary infringement of UK unregistered design right: see para.6–056 below.
[191] CDPA 1988 s.97(1) and s.233(1).
[192] RDA(E) s.24B. Section 24B was inserted into the RDA(E) by the Intellectual Property Enforcement Regulations 2006 (SI 2006/1028) but effectively re-enacted the previous s.9(1) of the Act without making any changes of substance.
[193] *J Choo (Jersey) Ltd v Towerstone Ltd* [2008] EWHC 346 (Ch); [2008] F.S.R. 19, Floyd J. The court's reasoning is based on the fact that the Intellectual Property Enforcement Regulations 2006 (SI 2006/1028) inserted a new reg.1A into the Community Design Regulations 2005 (see App.B5, para.B5–003 below) which gives "all such relief by way of damages . . . as is available in respect of the infringement of any other property right", and the same Regulations inserted s.24B into the RDA 1949 providing for the innocence defence in respect of UK registered designs. With respect, the court seems to have attached undue significance to the fact that s.24B (see App.A2, para.A2–049 below) was inserted into the RDA 1949 by the 2006 Regulations, and to have overlooked the fact that the new s.24B merely re-enacted without any change of substance the previous innocence defence in s.9(1) of the RDA 1949. Since the Intellectual Property Enforcement Directive 2004/48/EC mandates the award of damages only in cases where a defendant "knows

It is important to appreciate that these innocence defences only go to **6–053** innocence as regards the existence of the right concerned, and do not provide a defence to a defendant who is morally "innocent" on other grounds. Thus, a manufacturing subcontractor who innocently executes an order from a customer in the genuine belief that the customer either owns or is licensed under the relevant right, will have no defence under these provisions. In general, there is reason to suppose that copyright or design right will subsist in aspects of the design of an industrial article, unless perhaps it is believed to be an old article in which design right must have expired, or perhaps a design of foreign origin.[194] In respect of Community unregistered design right, subsistence depends upon the design having been made public within the Community[195] and the question of whether the defendant knows or has reason to suspect that such publication has occurred will be relevant to the defence.

In the case of registered designs, the defence may offer more scope,[196] **6–054** since to overcome it the infringer may have to be shown to have some positive reason to suppose that the design is registered,[197] or at least be engaged in an activity where it is a matter of prudent business practice for him to search the register.[198] It is specifically provided that marking an article with the word "registered" or such like, does not put a defendant on notice for the purpose of losing their innocence defence unless the number of the design registration is also given.[199] However, since the defence goes to awareness of the existence of the design rather than awareness of infringement, it is enough to destroy the defence if a complaint is made identifying the registered design by number even if it

or has reasonable grounds to know that he is engaged in an infringing activity" (see para.6–049A above), it is very strange indeed that the regulations intended to transpose that Directive into UK national law have been construed as having the effect of depriving a defendant of an innocence defence available under the corresponding national law in circumstances to which the Directive does *not* apply. Nor does it appear that any broader arguments were presented to the court based on the possible market distorting effect of such discrimination in the remedies attached to Community and UK registered designs, although the court could see "no possible policy reason" (para.33) for the difference in treatment.

[194] In view of the very large gaps in the availability of design rights to designs of foreign origin: see para.4–062 above.

[195] See paras 2–067 et seq. above.

[196] See, e.g. *Byrne v Statist Co* [1914] 1 K.B. 622.

[197] See *Schmittzehe v Roberts* (1955) 72 R.P.C. 122 at 126, where innocence in respect of a registered design of a toy figure was established, and *Wilbec Plastics Ltd v Wilson Dawes Ltd* [1966] R.P.C. 513.

[198] The section was considered by the Privy Council in the case of *Khawam (John Khalil) & Co v Chellaram & Sons (Nigeria) Ltd* [1964] R.P.C. 337. The respondents, who were traders in textiles in Lagos, had an office in Manchester where a branch of the Designs Registry is situated. It was held that if they had made a search there, they would have discovered the registration in question, but having failed to make the necessary investigation, which a prudent man of business would have made, the courts below were right in rejecting the respondents' defence of innocent infringement.

[199] RDA(E) s.24B(2).

does not identify which of the defendant's goods are alleged to infringe it.[200]

6–055   A defendant who succeeds in establishing one of these defences does not escape other relief. The claimant may be entitled to claim an account of profits as an alternative to damages and his right to do so is not automatically restricted by these provisions. Nor is the claimant's right to seek an injunction[201]; although of course the facts giving rise to a successful innocence defence may also affect the exercise of the court's discretion on whether to grant injunctive relief.

6–056   Apart from the general defence of innocence as regards subsistence of the right (which applies to primary infringers), there is a special defence available to secondary[202] infringers of unregistered design right (but not of copyright) who "innocently" acquire infringing articles and then wish to continue to hold in stock or re-sell them after they have been imputed with knowledge of their infringing character. Since knowledge or reason to believe that an article is infringing is a necessary ingredient of secondary infringement,[203] a person in any event will not be liable for acts of importing, possessing, selling, etc. at a time when he does not have such knowledge or reason to believe and therefore no specific defence is necessary to cover that situation. But further, when a defendant shows that an infringing article was innocently acquired by him or by a predecessor in title, the only remedy against him for acts of secondary infringement is damages not exceeding a reasonable royalty.[204] This means that a dealer who innocently[205] buys articles which he later discovers infringe a design right cannot be prevented from selling off his stock. No injunction or order for delivery up can be granted against him—he is simply liable to pay the design right owner a reasonable royalty. But this does not prevent the grant of an interim injunction against a person in possession of infringing article who claims to have acquired them innocently if the fact of innocent acquisition is disputed.[206] This defence probably does not apply in respect of infringement of

---

[200] *Carlis Ware v Radford* [1959] R.P.C. 38 at 40, where Vaisey J. said of s.9: " . . . it limits the right of a plaintiff complaining of an infringement by saying that damages shall not be awarded to a plaintiff against a defendant who proves—that is proves affirmatively —that at the date of the infringement he was not aware and had no reasonable grounds for supposing that the design was registered."

[201] See the express words of RDA(E) s.24B(3).

[202] For the meaning of secondary infringement, see para.4–077 above.

[203] CDPA 1988 s.227(1).

[204] CDPA 1988 s.233(2). The subsection places the burden on the defendant to raise the defence and to prove it on the balance of probabilities: *Badge Sales v PMS Intul Group Ltd* [2004] EWHC 3382 (Ch); [2006] F.S.R. 1, Lewison J.

[205] The definition of "innocence" in s.233(3) is that he "did not know and had no reason to believe that it was an infringing article": the inverse of the definition of the mental element required for secondary infringement in s.227(1).

[206] *Badge Sales v PMS Intul Group Ltd* [2004] EWHC 3382 (Ch); [2006] F.S.R. 1, Lewison J.: in such circumstances, if there is an arguable case that the defendant was not innocent at the time of acquisition of the articles, an interim injunction will be granted on classic "irreparable harm/balance of convenience" grounds and the claimant will be required to give a cross-undertaking in damages.

Community unregistered design right because the Regulation specifically provides for an order for seizure of infringing products as one of the sanctions for infringement.[207]

Additional damages

In respect of both copyright infringement[208] and unregistered design right infringement,[209] the court is given power to award "such additional damages as the justice of the case may require" having regard to all the circumstances, and in particular to: **6–057**

"(a) the flagrancy of the infringement, and
(b) any benefit accruing to the defendant by reason of the infringement."

There has been considerable discussion in the authorities as to whether such "additional" damages awarded under the predecessor to these provisions in the Copyright Act 1956[210] allowed the award of what would be classified in English common law as "exemplary" damages, or only "aggravated" damages.[211] It is doubtful to what extent a statutory provision which has force throughout the United Kingdom should be constrained by reference to specially English common law concepts. This question may no longer be relevant, since the wording of CDPA 1988 s.97(2)[212] was deliberately widened as compared with the 1956 Act.[213] It is probably better to regard "additional" damages as being a head of relief sui generis. It was clearly intended that it should in appropriate circumstances give the court power to award damages to penalise a defendant which go beyond the loss suffered by the claimant, as well as giving the court greater power to reflect intangible factors (such as intangible damage to the reputation of a copyright work or design caused by low quality plagiarism) than can be adequately reflected in ordinary compensatory damages. **6–058**

In accordance with normal procedure, liability in a copyright or design right case will be determined at the trial and the quantum of damages will be assessed at a subsequent inquiry. The question of whether or not **6–059**

---

[207] Regulation art.89(1)(b); this is a separate provision from art.89(1)(d) considered in para.6–052 above under which national law is applied by analogy. However, it would still be open to an innocent retailer to argue that there are "special reasons" for not ordering seizure under the opening words of art.89(1).

[208] CDPA 1988 s.97(2).

[209] CDPA 1988 s.229(3).

[210] The Copyright Act 1956 s.17(3).

[211] See the discussion of the legislative history in *Cala Homes South Ltd v Alfred McAlpine Homes East Ltd (No.2)* [1996] F.S.R. 36, ChD.

[212] To which s.229(3) relating to unregistered design right infringement is identical.

[213] See *Intellectual Property and Innovation*, Cmnd 9712 (1986), para.12–3.

the infringement is flagrant is normally more appropriate for determination at the trial than on an inquiry; however, a decision to award additional damages can only be taken having regard to all the circumstances of the case, including flagrancy if present. Accordingly, the approved procedure is for the trial judge to find flagrancy and to direct the inquiry that:

> "in considering whether the justice of the case requires an award of additional damages under section 97(2) of the 1988 Act, the court taking the inquiry should have particular regard to the findings as to the flagrancy of the infringement made in the judgment".[214]

If additional damages are to be sought, the claimant is required to state that he claims such damages and the grounds for claiming them in his particulars of claim.[215]

6–060　　If a claimant opts for an account of profits in place of his ordinary "compensatory" damages, he cannot seek additional damages as well as the account of profits.[216]

Account of profits

6–061　As an alternative to claiming damages, a claimant whose copyright, design right or registered design is infringed may claim an account of the profits made by the defendant from his acts of infringement. This may indeed be the only available pecuniary remedy when a successful "innocence" defence bars him from recovering damages. There can be a large difference in the amount recoverable from the two alternative remedies. In the case of damages, the amount recovered is measured by the claimant's loss, whilst in an account of profits it is measured by the profits of the infringer regardless of the claimant's loss. Thus, if the infringer has conducted his relevant activities in such a way as to make little or no profit, the claimant will recover little or nothing even if his own losses from the infringement are large. In order to mitigate the risks faced by a claimant to some extent in choosing whether or not to elect to seek an account of profits, the courts have introduced the practice of directing a defendant who has been found to infringe to produce basic information on revenues and costs before requiring the claimant to elect.[217]

---

[214] *MCA Records Inc v Charly Records Ltd* [2002] F.S.R. 401, CA. Obviously, that particular form of words relates to copyright and the reference would be to s.229(3) in an unregistered design right case.

[215] Practice Direction para.22.1, App.E2, para.E2–013, below.

[216] *Redrow Homes Ltd v Betts Brothers Plc* [1998] F.S.R. 345, HL; overruling on this point Laddie J. in *Cala v Alfred McAlpine (No.2)* [1996] F.S.R. 36.

[217] *Island Records Ltd v Tring International plc* [1995] 3 All E.R. 444.

Where a defendant has made and sold goods which infringe a **6–062** claimant's rights, the usual form of order is that the defendant is directed to account for his profits from making and selling the goods concerned,[218] as distinct from only such additional profit as can be identified as arising from the use of the infringing design. However, this approach is not necessarily appropriate in all cases, since the infringing design could sometimes be only a small or subsidiary feature in the whole article, and play little or no part in achieving sales. In such a case it is doubtful whether the court would award all the profits arising from making and selling the article, rather than an apportionment which reflects the benefit obtained by use of the design, for the merely technical reason that the sale of the article as a whole is a tortious act.[219] The principle upon which the distinction is made has been stated as follows[220]:

> "If one man makes profits by the use or sale of some thing, and that whole thing came into existence by reason of his wrongful use of another man's property in a patent, design or copyright, the difficulty disappears and the case is then, generally speaking, simple. In such a case the infringer must account for all of the profits which he thus made."

A refinement of the principle thus stated, is that an infringer may have **6–063** to pay the whole of the profits arising from making and selling his article, even where only a part of it actually infringes, if the infringing part is the essential part and the rest is subordinate.[221] Where the infringement relates to an identifiable portion of an article (such as a certain proportion of the pages of a book), then it is appropriate to order an account of profits based on the infringing proportion.[222]

---

[218] *Peter Pan Mfg Corp v Corsets Silhouette Ltd* [1963] R.P.C. 45; *Edelsten v Edelsten* (1863) 1 De GJ & S 185, CA; *Ford v Foster* (1872) 7 Ch. 611; *Lever v Goodwin* (1887) 36 ChD. 1, CA; *Weingarten Bros v Charles Bayer & Co* (1905) 22 R.P.C. 341, HL.

[219] For an extensive review of the authorities relating to the circumstances in which the court will award an apportionment of profits, rather than the whole profits arising from the infringing act, see the judgment of Windeyer J. in *Colbeam Palmer Ltd v Stock Affiliates Pty Ltd* [1972] R.P.C. 303, High Ct of Australia. See also Slade J. in the "Chicago Pizza" case *My Kinda Town Ltd v Soll (Chicago Pizza)* [1983] R.P.C. 15, ChD. Other cases where an apportionment of profits has been ordered (mainly cases where a patented invention effects only a limited improvement to a larger article) are; *Crossley v Derby Gas-Light Co* (1838) 3 My & Cr 428; *Cartier v Carlile* (1862) 31 Beav 292 (trade mark); *Goodlet v Fowler* (1876) 14 S.C.R. (N.S.W.) 496; *Siddell v Vickers* (1892) 9 R.P.C. 152, CA; *United Horse Shoe and Nail Co Ltd v Stewart* (1888) 5 R.P.C. 260, HL; and *United Horse Shoe and Nail Co Ltd v Stewart* (1886) 3 R.P.C. 143.

[220] *Colbeam Palmer Ltd v Stock Affiliates Pty Ltd* [1972] R.P.C. 303, High Ct of Australia.

[221] *Dart Industries Inc v Decor Corp Pty Ltd* [1994] F. s.R. 567, Full Ct of High Ct of Australia, where a patent related to "the essential feature of a single item . . . without which this particular container would not have been produced at all" (at 579). There seems no reason why the same principle should not apply to designs cases.

[222] *Blackie & Sons Ltd v Lothian Book Publishing Co Pty Ltd* (1921) 29 C.L.R. 396; *Bailey v Taylor* (1829) 1 Russ. & My. 73.

6–064   An account of profits is an equitable discretionary remedy, and the question of whether to award an account of profits at all, as well as the form of the account which is ordered, is at the end of the day a matter for the discretion of the court in seeking to achieve a fair apportionment, so that neither party shall have what justly belongs to the other.[223]

Delivery up of infringing articles, moulds, etc.

6–065   Statutory powers are laid down for the delivery up of articles which infringe a copyright,[224] a UK registered design[225] or a UK unregistered design right.[226] As well as the infringing articles themselves, these powers extend to "anything specifically designed or adapted" for making articles which infringe the particular copyright or design right concerned.[227] This seems intended to cover such things as moulds, transfers or printing plates intended for making infringing articles, but would not cover general purpose machinery which could make infringing articles but which could make non-infringing articles as well. When an order for delivery up is applied for under these provisions, the court has power to order the articles concerned to be forfeited to the claimant, destroyed or otherwise dealt with[228]; or the court has a discretion to make no order, particularly if it is of the view that other remedies available to the claimant will be adequate.[229] It must make no order in a case where a defendant undertakes to take a licence of right,[230] or in a case where the special limited "innocence" defence applying to secondary infringers of design right applies.[231]

6–066   A limitation period applies to the right to seek delivery up of articles under these provisions, and there are procedural safeguards designed to protect the interests of third parties in the goods concerned.[232]

6–067   In respect of Community registered and unregistered design rights, the Regulation provides specifically that sanctions for infringement include an order for seizure of infringing products[233] and an order:

> "to seize materials and implements predominantly used in order to manufacture the infringing goods, if their owner knew the effect for

---

[223] *My Kinda Town Ltd v Soll (Chicago Pizza)* [1983] R.P.C. 15 at 58, ChD.
[224] CDPA 1988 s.99(1).
[225] RDA(E) s.24C, inserted by the Intellectual Property (Enforcement, etc.) Regulations 2006 (SI 2006/1028).
[226] CDPA 1988 s.230(1).
[227] CDPA 1988 s.99(1)(b) and s.230(1)(b), and RDA(E) s.24C(A)(b).
[228] CDPA 1988 s.114(1) and s.231(1), and RDA(E) s.24D(1).
[229] CDPA 1988 s.114(2) and s.231(2), and RDA(E) s.24D(2).
[230] See para.6–047 above.
[231] See para.6–052 above.
[232] See CDPA 1988 ss.113–15 and ss.230–2.
[233] Regulation art.89(1)(b).

which such use was intended or if such effect would have been obvious in the circumstances".[234]

This formula is apt to cover moulds and similar articles specifically adapted to make products to the design in question, but the word "predominantly" also leaves some room for argument that more general purpose implements can be seized if their predominant use has in fact been to make infringing articles. An order for seizure, whether of infringing products or materials and implements, is discretionary in that the court is not required to make such orders if there are "special reasons for not doing so".[235] These provisions in the Regulation have now been fleshed out by explicit and detailed statutory provisions for delivery up of infringing articles and moulds, etc. in relation to Community registered and unregistered designs which correspond closely to the statutory provisions described above for UK copyright and registered and unregistered designs.[236]

Prior to the 2006 Regulations,[237] the RDA(E) made no provision for delivery up in respect of UK registered designs, but delivery up or destruction of infringing articles was ordered in the exercise of the common law jurisdiction of the court.[238] An order for delivery up or destruction on oath was almost invariably obtainable by a successful claimant.[239] Delivery up of moulds could also be ordered.[240] But delivery up would only be awarded as against the defendants themselves, and not against third parties.[241]

6–068

The exercise of the common law power to order delivery up or destruction is largely rendered unnecessary by the statutory powers described above. Furthermore, it would probably be wrong for the courts to exercise the common law jurisdiction in a way which contradicts Parliament's intention as to how the statutory powers should be applied, for example by making a common law order for delivery up in circumstances where an order under the statutory power would be refused.

6–069

---

[234] Regulation art.89(1)(c).

[235] Regulation art.89(1), opening paragraph.

[236] Regulations 1B to 1D were inserted into the Community Design Regulation 2005 (App. B5, paras B5–004—B5–006 below) by the Intellectual Property (Enforcement, etc.) Regulations 2006 (SI 2006/1028) in order to implement the Intellectual Property Enforcement Directive 2004/48/EC into UK national law.

[237] See previous footnote.

[238] *Hole v Bradbury* (1879) 12 Ch.D. 886; *Chappell v Columbia Gramophone Co* [1914] 2 Ch. 124 and 745; *Macrea v Holdsworth* (1848) 2 De G. & Sm. 496.

[239] See *Gordon and Munro v Patrick & Hill* (1895) 12 R.P.C. 22; *Ingram and Kemp Ltd v Edwards Bros* (1904) 21 R.P.C. 463; *Gunston v Winox Ltd* (1921) 38 R.P.C. 40; *Cartwright v Coventry Radiator Co* (1925) 42 R.P.C. 351; *Wallpaper Manufacturers Ltd v Derby Paper Staining Co* (1925) 42 R.P.C. 449; *Dunlop Rubber Co v Booth & Co Ltd* (1926) 43 R.P.C. 139.

[240] *Rosedale Associated Manufacturers Ltd v Airfix Products Ltd* [1956] R.P.C. 360 at 368.

[241] In *Knowles & Co Ltd v John Bennett & Sons* (1895) 12 R.P.C. 137, where the infringing goods were in the hands of shipowners, Robinson V.-C. said at 148: "I can order the defendants to deliver the goods to the plaintiffs, but I cannot make anyone else deliver them. The shipowners might be added as defendants, so as to restrain them from parting with the goods except to the plaintiffs."

However, there could be residual cases falling outside the statutory framework where it might be possible and even appropriate to invoke the common law jurisdiction.[242]

6. Criminal Proceedings

Criminal proceedings for the infringement of copyright

6–070 It is possible to institute criminal proceedings in a design case which involves infringement of artistic copyright. It is a criminal offence to make for sale or hire an article which the maker knows or has reason to believe is an infringing copy of a copyright work.[243] In addition, it is an offence to do any of the acts amounting to secondary infringement of copyright[244] knowing or having reason to believe that the article concerned is an infringing copy of a copyright work.[245] The penalty is up to six months' imprisonment on summary conviction, or up to two years on conviction on indictment.[246]

6–071 The criminal court before whom proceedings are brought has similar powers to order delivery up or destruction of infringing articles and moulds, etc. as a civil court does in civil proceedings.[247] A search warrant may be obtained by the police in cases of suspected offences.[248] Directors and managers are criminally liable for acts of a company which are committed with their consent or connivance.[249]

6–072 These offences are very widely drawn and extend far beyond such people as record pirates who were their primary target. No provision is made to cover the case where there is a bona fide dispute as to whether an article infringes or not. Criminal liability is not limited to cases where the defendant knows that what he is doing is an infringement: it is enough if he "has reason to believe".[250] It is at least arguable that a

---

[242] See, e.g. *Chappell v Columbia Graphophone Co* [1914] 2 Ch. 745, where the Court of Appeal ordered the delivery up of articles (copies of sound recordings) which were not themselves infringements of copyright, upon the grounds that their making had been the direct result of an infringing act, the copying out of musical scores for the orchestra which had conducted the recording session. Assuming that the principle exemplified in this case is right at all, as to which it is possible to argue, the power of the court to order delivery up of articles falling outside the statutory powers may still be exercisable in the case of copyright and design right infringement.

[243] CDPA 1988 s.107(1)(a).

[244] As to what constitutes secondary infringement, see para.5–109 above.

[245] CDPA 1988 s.107(1)(b)–(e).

[246] CDPA 1988 s.107(4).

[247] CDPA 1988 s.108(1); see para.6–065 above.

[248] CDPA 1988 s.109. And where infringing copies of a copyright work or articles specifically designed or adapted for making such copies (such as moulds), come into the possession of any person (such as the police or trading standards officers) in connection with the investigation or prosecution of a relevant offence, a court can make an order for forfeiture of such copies or articles: CDPA 1988 s.114A.

[249] CDPA 1988 s.110(1).

[250] The same test as for secondary infringement; see para.5–109 above.

defendant who is notified of an allegation of infringement, which turns out at the end of the day to be correct, has sufficient "reason to believe" to make him criminally liable, even if he believes on bona fide grounds that there are good reasons for contesting the allegation. These criminal provisions are therefore capable of abuse; particularly since they could be deployed against dealers or retailers, so driving a manufacturer's goods off the market without challenging him directly.

There are no corresponding provisions relating to unregistered design rights or to registered designs; only civil remedies are available to enforce those rights. **6–073**

Criminal proceedings relating to registered designs

There is no offence corresponding to that of infringement of copyright by which a registered design can be enforced through the criminal courts. However, it is an offence for a person to represent falsely that a design applied to or incorporated in any product sold by him is registered either as a UK registered design[251] or as a Community registered design,[252] including in either case by marking it as such. Continuing to mark products as "registered" after expiry of a registration is an offence in the case of both UK[253] and Community[254] registrations. It is also an offence to cause a false entry to be made in the UK Register of Designs.[255] This offence is quite broad, since causing a design to be registered when knowing it to be invalid would presumably count; however, its scope is limited by the fact that the required *mens rea* is actual knowledge of the falsity of the entry which is made. **6–074**

It is also an offence to fail to comply with a direction of the Secretary of State suppressing the publication or registration of designs which are deemed relevant for defence purposes.[256] Directors and managers are liable for offences committed by companies with their consent or connivance.[257] **6–075**

7. Other Miscellaneous Remedies

Self-help remedy

In the case of infringements of copyright, including artistic copyright, there is a "self-help" remedy. The copyright owner, or an agent authorised by him, is entitled to seize and detain infringing copies which are **6–076**

---

[251] RDA(E) s.35(1).
[252] Community Designs Regulations 2005 (SI 2005/2339) reg.3, App.B5, para.B5–008 below.
[253] RDA(E) s.35(2).
[254] Community Designs Regulations 2005 (SI 2005/2339) reg.3(2).
[255] RDA(E) s.34.
[256] RDA(E) s.33; defence directions are given under RDA(E) s.5.
[257] RDA(E) s.35A.

exposed or immediately available for sale or hire, provided he gives prior notice to a local police station and leaves a notice at the place of seizure identifying himself and the grounds of seizure.[258] There seems no reason why this provision should not extend to industrial articles which are infringing copies of artistic works.

6–077   This "self help" remedy is primarily intended for use against itinerant vendors, market traders with no regular pitch, and such like, since the copyright owner may not seize anything in the possession of somebody at his permanent or regular place of business.[259] Force may not be used to effect the seizure.[260] A person disputing such a seizure can apply to the court, which can order that the goods be forfeited to the copyright owner, destroyed or otherwise dealt with, or returned to the person from whom they have been seized.[261] The same principles and procedure apply as when an order is sought for delivery up or destruction in a civil action.[262]

6–078   Under the Goods Infringing Intellectual Property Rights (Customs) Regulations 2004,[263] and EC Council Regulation No.1383/2003, goods which infringe or which are suspected of infringing a copyright, or a Community or UK registered or unregistered design right may be seized while passing through customs. Moulds or matrices may also be seized.[264] A procedure is laid down under which the rights holder gives notice to customs to institute the seizure.

---

[258] CDPA 1988 s.100.
[259] CDPA 1988 s.100(3).
[260] CDPA 1988 s.100(3).
[261] CDPA 1988 s.114.
[262] See para.6–061 above.
[263] SI 2004/1473: see App.E8 below.
[264] Article 2(3) of Regulation 1383/2003.

CHAPTER 7

ACTIONS FOR THREATS OF PROCEEDINGS FOR INFRINGEMENT

Contents

1. Statutory Action for Threats

Threats of proceedings

It is possible for serious commercial damage to be done by threats of legal   **7–001**
proceedings for infringement of intellectual property rights, regardless of
whether the threats have any justification. Threats made to dealers or
retailers may well deter them from dealing in the goods which are alleged
to infringe, simply in order to avoid the trouble and expense of being
dragged into litigation which does not concern them. This obviously can
cause serious losses to the supplier of the allegedly infringing article. At
common law, the rule was that losses resulting from such threats, as long
at least as there was some bona fide basis for making the allegation of
infringement, were not recoverable,[1] nor in consequence could the
making of such threats be restrained by injunction.

In order to deal with the problem revealed by the *Halsey* case, the   **7–002**
Patents, Designs and Trademarks Act 1888[2] provided with regard to
patents, that anyone who was aggrieved by the issue of threats of legal
proceedings or liability which were groundless should have the right to
institute proceedings to restrain their continuance. The successor to this
provision[3] was amended in 1932 to make it applicable also to threats of

---

[1] *Halsey v Brotherhood* (1881) 19 Ch.D. 386, CA, a patent case. Nor will an action for
unlawful interference with contractual relations lie, where a contract is broken as a result
of a threat of infringement proceedings, so long as the legal right is asserted in good faith:
Granby Marketing Services Ltd v Interlego AG [1984] R.P.C. 209, ChD, a copyright case.
[2] Section 32.
[3] Patents and Designs Act 1907 s.36.

infringement of registered designs. The CDPA 1988 which created unregistered design right, at the same time introduced a provision dealing with threats of infringement of the new right.[4] In the case of copyright, there is no similar provision; so that the maker of industrial articles who is damaged by threats of artistic copyright infringement proceedings made against his customers will have to rely on the far more limited remedies provided at common law.[5] Provision has now been made by Regulations under the European Communities Act 1972 for threats actions in respect of unjustified threats of proceedings for infringement of Community registered and unregistered design rights[6].

Statutory action for unjustified design threats

7–003   A statutory remedy for threats of unjustified proceedings for UK registered design infringement is provided by RDA(E) s.26:

> "26.—(1) Where any person (whether entitled to or interested in a registered design or an application for registration of a design or not) by circulars, advertisements or otherwise threatens any other person with proceedings for infringement of the right in a registered design, any person aggrieved thereby may bring an action against him for any such relief as is mentioned in the next following subsection.
>
> (2) Unless in any action brought by virtue of this section the defendant proves that the acts in respect of which proceedings were threatened constitute or, if done, would constitute, an infringement of the right in a registered design the registration of which is not shown by the [claimant] to be invalid, the [claimant] shall be entitled to the following relief, that is to say—
>
> (a) a declaration to the effect that the threats are unjustifiable;
> (b) an injunction against the continuance of the threats; and
> (c) such damages, if any, as he has sustained thereby.
>
> (2A) Proceedings may not be brought under this section in respect of a threat to bring proceedings for an infringement alleged to consist of the making or importing of anything.[7]
>
> (3) For the avoidance of doubt it is hereby declared that a mere notification that a design is registered does not constitute a threat of proceedings within the meaning of this section."

---

[4] CDPA 1988 s.253.
[5] See para.7–043 below.
[6] The Community Design Regulations 2005 (SI 2005/2339) App.B5, para.B5–007 below, reg.2.
[7] Subsection 2A was introduced as part of the amendments made by the CDPA 1988 to the RDA 1949.

CDPA 1988 s.253 provides a similar remedy in respect of threats of   **7–004**
proceedings for UK unregistered design right infringement. The Community Designs Regulations 2005[8] now also provide a similar remedy for threats of proceedings for infringement of Community registered and unregistered design rights. Both s.253 and the relevant part of these Regulations are effectively word for word the same as s.26 of the RDA(E) quoted above, so all three provisions will be discussed together.

These provisions are effectively identical to each other and also closely   **7–005**
correspond to the analogous provision relating to patents threats.[9] That however was amended into a slightly different form in 2004.[10] The purpose of the predecessor of that section[11] has been stated as follows[12]:

"Actions for infringement of letters patent notoriously take up a great deal of time and money and persons who have actions of this type brought against them, or who have the threat of actions of this type hanging over them, might well think it better to concede victory than to embark upon the lengthy and costly business of defending themselves. It was no doubt with considerations of this sort in mind that those who framed the Patents Acts have over the years thought it necessary to introduce into the statute some provision which makes it an offence for people to make groundless threats of infringement against others."

Statutory threats action: who may sue?

From the wording of the sections, "any person aggrieved" by the threats   **7–006**
may bring the action. It need not be the person to whom the threats are addressed, and indeed one of the main purposes of these provisions is to provide a remedy to third parties who suffer commercial damage as a result of threats made to other parties. The manufacturer of the articles alleged to infringe would, for example, be a person aggrieved as the threats would tend to stop the sale of his goods.[13] A principal shareholder and director of a company is capable of being a person aggrieved in respect of threats made in relation to the company's activities.[14]

The question of whether or not someone is a person aggrieved is in the   **7–007**
main a question of fact to be established by the evidence; if the threat is not made to the person himself, then he must establish by evidence that

---

[8] The Community Design Regulations 2005 (SI 2005/2339) reg.2, App.B5, para.B5–007 below.
[9] The Patents Act 1977 s.70.
[10] By the Patents Act 2004.
[11] The Patents Act 1949 s.65.
[12] *Alpi Pietro e Figlio & Co v J. Wright & Sons (Veneers) Ltd* [1972] R.P.C. 125 at 129, per Whitford J.
[13] *Challender v Royle* (1887) 4 R.P.C. 363 at 371.
[14] *Brain v Ingledew Brown Bennison & Garrett (No.3)* [1997] F.S.R. 511 at 524, ChD.

the threats have or are likely to cause him damage which is not minimal.[15] Thus, when a threat was made to a customer in respect of products supplied a long time in the past but about which there was no evidence that the customer had any present or future intention of ordering them again (quite apart from the threat), this was not enough to make the supplier of the products a "person aggrieved".[16] But the fact that a trader is able to assuage the fears of his threatened customers so that the threat does not produce an identifiable loss, does not mean that he is not aggrieved by it; in such a case, he has a real commercial interest which has been interfered with and has a grievance which the court will recognise.[17]

Who may be sued for making threats?

7–008   Any person who makes a threat may be sued, regardless of whether or not he does or claims to own or have any interest in the design right concerned. Indeed, the provision relating to registered design threats[18] specifically states that the person making the threats is liable; irrespective of whether he is or is not entitled to or interested in a design or an application for a design. Apart from making it clear that a person who makes threats of infringement proceedings of a non-existent registered design will not escape liability on that ground, it also means that the section is apt to cover such people as, e.g. a British distributor of a foreign manufacturer, who takes it upon himself to make threats in the market place relating to registered designs which in fact belong not to him but to the foreign manufacturer.[19]

Solicitors, patent attorneys and other agents

7–009   A person who acts as agent for another would therefore appear to be himself liable for any threat which he may issue. Thus it appears that a solicitor or a patent attorney who writes a letter on behalf of his client which contains a threat, is personally liable if the threat turns out to be

---

[15] *Brain v Ingledew Brown Bennison & Garrett* [1996] F.S.R. 341 at 351, per Aldous L.J., CA. However, this does not mean that the claimant need prove concrete loss of contracts to the standard necessary for proving a claim to damages, in order to be a person aggrieved by the threat and therefore entitled to the injunctive and declaratory relief provided by these sections; *Brain v Ingledew Brown Bennison & Garrett (No.3)* [1997] F.S.R. 511 at 520, ChD.

[16] *Reynes-Cole v Elite Hosiery Co Ltd* [1965] R.P.C. 102, CA.

[17] *Brain v Ingledew Brown Bennison & Garrett (No.3)* [1997] F.S.R. 511, ChD.

[18] RDA(E) s.26(1) (App.A2, para.A2–056 below).

[19] In this respect, the RDA 1949 made an important change from the 1919 Act. Under the 1919 Act, a person issuing a threat was liable only if they were "claiming to have an interest" in a design, so under that Act an agent or distributor who did not possess or claim any interest in a design in respect of which they were threatening proceedings could not presumably have been sued.

unjustified. In *Earle's Utilities Ltd v Harrison*,[20] which was an action against a solicitor, Farwell J., whilst deciding the case upon the ground that the particular letter in question was not worded so as to constitute a threat, said[21]:

> "I am not aware that there is anything in section 36 [of the 1907–1938 Acts] which specifically protects a solicitor who chooses to disregard the provisions of the section."

7–010 Whilst in such circumstances the client will be liable to indemnify the solicitor or patent attorney who incurs liability by making threats on the client's instructions, a serious practical problem may arise in acting for overseas clients (or insolvent clients) against whom a right of indemnity for the solicitor or other agent may be worthless. But the court does now have power under the Civil Procedure Rules to decline to join a solicitor as a co-defendant to a threats claim, or even possibly to stay a threats action brought against him, if it appears that the predominant purpose of the party making the threats claim is to sow dissension between solicitor and client rather than to obtain relief any real value.[22]

Manner in which the threat is communicated

7–011 The section states that an action will lie where any person threatens another "by circulars, advertisements or otherwise". The words "or otherwise" have been construed broadly, and are not confined to such things as circulars or advertisements *ejusdem generis*[23] Thus, oral threats are within the sections.[24]

7–012 The fact that the threats complained of are contained in a letter marked "without prejudice" will not prevent them from being actionable threats within the meaning of these provisions.[25]

Threat made to one person to sue another

7–013 The most usual case is one of direct threats, i.e. where the person to whom the threats are uttered is himself the person threatened with the proceedings. For example, where a statement is made to a manufacturer that they

---

[20] (1935) 52 R.P.C. 77.

[21] (1935) 52 R.P.C. 77 at 80.

[22] *Reckitt Benckiser UK v Home Pairfum Ltd* [2004] EWHC 302 (Pat); [2004] F.S.R. 37, Laddie J.: a patent and registered design threats counterclaim. It should be noted that the court refused to stay or strike out the claim made by the defendant against the claimant itself, even though the relief might be of little value, because it is not per se abusive for a party to pursue a claim of low value which is conferred on that party by statute.

[23] *Skinner & Co v Perry* (1893) 10 R.P.C. 1.

[24] *Ellis & Sons v Pogson* (1923) 40 R.P.C. 62, 179; *Luna Advertising Co Ltd v Burnham & Co* (1928) 45 R.P.C. 258.

[25] *Kurtz v Spencer* (1888) 5 R.P.C. 161 at 173.

will be sued, or to their customers that they will be sued. The statutory threats action is, however, not limited to these cases. An action may be brought to restrain the issue of indirect threats, i.e. of statements in which proceedings are threatened, not against the person to whom the statement is made, but against his agent or against a third person. Thus, a statement made to a customer or a potential customer of a manufacturer that proceedings will be brought not against him but against the manufacturer gives rise to an action.[26] The customer may be put in fear that the legal proceedings against the manufacturer may result in his source of supply being cut off, and this perceived risk may cause him to turn to a different supplier.

Mere general warning distinguished from specific threat

7–014 A mere general warning to infringers not to infringe, and to warn the public that the monopoly is one which the owner intends to enforce, does not fall within the section.[27] In *Johnson v Edge*,[28] Lindley L.J. said:

> "I cannot suppose that the section prevents a patentee from saying that which the patent itself implies—that anyone infringing must expect legal proceedings to be taken against him. I do not think it can mean that. This is merely saying what everybody knows already. That is not a threat against anybody in particular."

7–015 And Kay L.J. said[29]:

> "I think that all Lord Justice Bowen intended in his judgment in *Challender v Royle* was merely this, that if a man stated, 'I have got a patent, and I mean to protect that patent by enforcing all my legal rights under it,' a general warning of that kind, not pointed against any particular person, which would not be by the public understood to apply to any particular person, might not be within this 32nd section at all; I do not think his language was meant to go further than that."

7–016 In *Johnson v Edge*, the threat complained of was as follows:

> "Notice to grocers and others. Information of extensive violation of Mr William Edge's patent rights has been received. All parties are warned not to infringe these rights."

---

[26] *John Summers & Sons Ltd v Cold Metal Process Co* (1948) 65 R.P.C. 75; *Surridge's Patents Ltd v Trico-Folberth Ltd* (1936) 53 R.P.C. 420.
[27] *Johnson v Edge* (1892) 9 R.P.C. 142; *Boneham and Hart v Hirst Bros & Co Ltd* (1917) 34 R.P.C. 209; *Challender v Royle* (1887) 4 R.P.C. 363.
[28] (1892) 9 R.P.C. 142 at 148.
[29] (1892) 9 R.P.C. 142 at 149.

It was held that this was a threat of legal proceedings within the meaning of the section, and was not a mere general warning. Lindley L.J. said[30]:

> "Now this is addressed to the trade; what would they understand by it? If they had turned their attention to it after Mr Johnson sent out these things, they would say: 'Oh, that is addressed to Harrison and Johnson—we know those two; they are making more or less things like Mr Edge; it must be those things.' It must be, therefore, an intimation—it would be construed to be an intimation by Mr Edge—that he considered these things an infringement of his patent."

7–017

Thus, the threat need not actually name any particular person. It will be sufficient if it is implied from the wording and circumstances that a specific person or persons are referred to. In *Boneham and Hart v Hurst Bros & Co Ltd*[31] the threat complained of was an advertisement to the effect that a certain registered design for a guard for the face of a wristwatch had "evoked some rubbishy imitations," and that legal proceedings would be taken against any infringer. It was held that there was a threat within the meaning of the section, for the warning was clearly directed against somebody: it was not merely a warning against infringement in the future, but included a definite statement that some persons had already infringed.

7–018

Threat need not identify a particular design right or product

According to the sections for a threat to be actionable it must be a threat of "proceedings for infringement of the right in a registered design"[32] or "of a design right".[33] However, this does not mean that the threat must identify a specific registered design or specific unregistered design right in order to be actionable. Unspecific threats to sue for "registered design infringement" or "infringement of my design rights" would be caught. That this is so is made clear from the legislative history of RDA(E) s.26,[34]

7–019

---

[30] At 148.
[31] (1917) 34 R.P.C. 209. See also *Miles and Martin Pen Co v Selsdon Fountain Pen Co* (1949) 66 R.P.C. 193 and *Alpi Pietro e Figlio & Co v J. Wright & Sons (Veneers) Ltd* above.
[32] RDA(E) s.26(1).
[33] CDPA 1988 s.253(1).
[34] Under the Patents and Designs Act 1919 s.36, the words were: "Where any person claiming to have an interest in a patent . . . threatens any other person with any legal proceedings or liability in respect of any alleged infringement of the patent . . . "; so that under that Act the threat had to be in respect of a particular patent or design. In the RDA 1949, the requirement that the threatener claim an interest in the design was replaced with specific wording "(whether entitled to or interested in . . . or not)"; and this seems apt to cover the case of an unspecified registered design that does not exist as well as the case of a person who makes threats by reference to a specific registered design in which they have no interest.

and it can hardly have been intended that CDPA 1988 s.253 should be interpreted differently. Furthermore, the purpose of these sections would be severely undermined if it were the case that the threatener could escape liability by not mentioning any specific design right, but merely alleging infringement in general terms.

7–020   An unjustified threat of infringement proceedings which is unspecific may be even more damaging than one which is specific, because it is harder to investigate the merits of it. A threat which is unspecific about which products it relates to is an actionable threat unless it can be justified across the full range of the products to which the recipient of the threat may reasonably take it to relate.[35]

What amounts to a threat of proceedings

7–021   Although it is only actionable to threaten a person with "proceedings for infringement", it is not essential in order to fall within the section that there should be any specific mention of proceedings. If from what is said any ordinary person would infer that proceedings were being threatened, an action will lie.[36] Thus, in *Luna Advertising Co Ltd v Burnham & Co Ltd*, where a representative of the defendants had called upon customers of the claimants and intimated that a certain daylight sign erected by them was an infringement of his firm's patent and had requested them to take it down immediately, Clauson J., deciding that a threat of legal proceedings or liability had been made, said[37]:

> "I think that an interview of this kind, a serious interview between business men, although nobody speaks of solicitors and writs, has no real meaning except to convey to the person whom I regard as having been threatened, that the threatener has legal rights and means to enforce them."

7–022   In *Kurtz v Spence*[38] the threat was to this effect:

> "We are the owners of a patent for the manufacture of alum and other salts of alumina, which is dated the 11th August 1882: your working is an infringement of it, which we cannot allow."

It was held that this constituted a threat of legal proceedings.

7–023   Again, in *Rosedale Associated Manufacturers Ltd v Airfix Products Ltd*,[39] a letter had been written to the plaintiffs on behalf of the defendants stating

---

[35] *Grimme Landmaschinefabrik GmbH v Scott* [2009] EWHC 2691 (Pat); [2010] F.S.R. 11, Floyd J.

[36] *Luna Advertising Co Ltd v Burnham & Co Ltd* (1928) 45 R.P.C. 258; *Willis & Bates Ltd v Tilley Lamp Co* (1944) 61 R.P.C. 8.

[37] (1928) 45 R.P.C. 258 at 260.

[38] (1888) 5 R.P.C. 161.

[39] [1956] R.P.C. 360.

that the writers were given to understand that the plaintiffs were supplying castellated toy buckets, that the defendants were the proprietors of a registered design for a castellated toy bucket of which they enclosed a representation, and contained the following two sentences:

> "In these circumstances our clients have thought it right to instruct us to advise you of the position. You must understand that our clients are prepared to protect their interests with the utmost vigour."

Lloyd-Jacob J. held[40]:   **7–024**

> "In my judgment, it is impossible to suppose that that paragraph in the letter was concerned merely with giving an intimation that a registered design was the property of Airfix. Coupled with the statement in the first paragraph that Airfix had reason to suppose that there was an offer for a supply of castellated toy buckets by Rosedale at the time the letter was written, the letter is to my mind a threat of proceedings. Let me examine it a little more closely by asking: 'What is a threat?' Here again there is no difficulty in expressing as a matter of words what constitutes a threat. The use of any language such as would be understood by a normal reader if it was a letter, or hearer if it was a statement, to mean that the writer, or, if an agent had written the letter, his principal, intended to take proceedings in respect of the act complained of must necessarily constitute a threat of proceedings. Is it any the less a threat of proceedings if it is expressed in general language stating that the complainants will protect their interests with the utmost vigour?"

On the other hand, in *Paul Trading Co Ltd v Marksmith & Co Ltd*[41] a letter,   **7–025**
a telephone conversation and an oral communication were all held not to embody any threats. The letter, after drawing the recipients' attention to the existence of a registered design, stated that the article sold by the recipients was a "copy", and asked for the name of the manufacturer or supplier so that the writer could contact him. The telephone conversation was a request to remove from the window of Boots' premises in Regent Street an advertisement referring to the plaintiffs' article because it militated against sales of the defendants' articles at premises nearby. The oral communication, which also contained a request for removal of the advertisement, made it plain, however, that there was no question of issuing proceedings against Boots. Lloyd-Jacob J., in giving judgment for the defendants, drew a distinction in the case of the verbal communication between a routine call by a commercial traveller and a special visit

---

[40] [1956] R.P.C. 360 at 363.
[41] (1952) 69 R.P.C. 301.

for conveying a warning. Following *Surridge's Patents Ltd v Trico-Folberth Ltd*,[42] he held that this state of affairs was the very antithesis of a threat of proceedings.

7-026   A notification that legal proceedings have been started against another party is capable of amounting to an implied threat to sue the person to whom the notification is addressed as well: *O. and M. Kleemann Ltd v Rosedale Associated Manufacturers Ltd*.[43] There the defendants in an infringement action counterclaimed for an injunction, damages and other relief against the plaintiffs by reason of their having issued a circular letter to customers of the defendants. The plaintiffs applied to strike out this allegation in the pleading as disclosing no reasonable cause of action. The letter which was particularised in the pleading was as follows:

> "We refer to our items Nos.X100, X200, and X300 which are the subject of our Registered Designs numbers... We are writing to inform you that on Tuesday, 5th May 1953, we commenced an action in the High Court of Justice claiming an injunction, damages, costs and other relief against Rosedale Associated Manufacturers Ltd. for infringement of these Registered Designs by their List Items Nos.5807, 5805 and 5808."

On an application to strike out this allegation, the circular was held to be capable of amounting to a threat of proceedings.

7-027   A threat to bring legal proceedings must of course be distinguished from actually commencing proceedings. The statutory action relates to threats, not to actually starting proceedings. Damage caused, whether to the actual defendant sued or to a third party, by the bringing of unjustified proceedings is not actionable under the statutory threats proceedings, nor is it actionable in any other way, except possibly at common law as an abuse of process if the claimant can be shown to have started the proceedings with no bona fide belief that he had an arguable claim. This distinction is important, because in a case where a customer is sued for registered design infringement and stops buying a manufacturer's product after service of proceedings on him, it will not be possible for the manufacturer to recover the financial loss caused by the cessation of trade even if the allegation of infringement made in the proceedings fails.[44]

---

[42] (1936) 53 R.P.C. 420.

[43] (1953) 71 R.P.C. 78.

[44] *Carflow Products (UK) Ltd v Linwood Securities (Birmingham) Ltd* [1998] F.S.R. 691, Laddie J. In that case, the service of the writ had been preceded by threatening letters which were actionable but on the facts the customer's decision to suspend trade followed and was caused by the actual service of the writ. Since the decision was not causally connected to the preceding threats, the aggrieved party was not able to recover substantial damages under the threats provisions.

A mere statement that a person would have a theoretical legal liability 7–028
for infringement is not enough. There must be a definite threat (express or
implied) that proceedings will, at any rate in certain contingencies, be
brought.[45]

Though no one single letter in a series contains a threat, the cumulative 7–029
effect of the correspondence looked at as a whole may nevertheless
constitute a threat within the meaning of the section.[46]

2. Exceptions and Justification

Exception for threats in respect of making or importation

Both sections and the regulation contain an exception which renders it 7–030
not actionable to make a threat in respect of "an infringement alleged to
consist of making or importing anything".[47] This exception to the scope of
the "threats" action was first introduced in the patent context by the
Patents Act 1977,[48] with the policy purpose of allowing threats of
proceedings safely to be made against the originator (manufacturer or
importer) of infringing articles, but retaining the protection of the threats
action when threats are made against customers and others lower down
the distribution chain. Unfortunately, the exception is ineptly drafted[49] to
achieve its intended purpose, since it is couched in terms of the way the
threat is expressed rather than the person to whom it is addressed.

Thus, a threat addressed to a manufacturer which threatens proceed- 7–031
ings in respect of promotion, marketing, advertisement and sale, as well
as manufacture, does not fall within the exception and is actionable[50]
(unless justified). A person who wishes to take advantage of this
exception in order to escape liability in case his threat turns out to be
unjustified, must couch his threat in terms which fall inside the exception,
and so must complain only of making or importing.

This leaves open the question of what happens if a person threatens a 7–032
mere retailer, making a threat which in its literal terms falls within the
exception; i.e. threatening the retailer with proceedings for making the
articles complained of, but not for selling them. Presumably the court
could then quite readily infer that, despite the way the threat is worded,

---

[45] *Earle's Utilities Ltd v Harrison* (1935) 52 R.P.C. 77; *Desiderio v Currus Ltd* (1935) 52 R.P.C.
201. cf. *Berkeley & Young Ltd and A. & M. Goodman Ltd v Stillwell, Darby & Co Ltd and Konig*
(1940) 57 R.P.C. 291.
[46] *Willis & Bates Ltd v Tilley Lamp Co* (1944) 61 R.P.C. 8.
[47] RDA(A) s.26(2A); CDPA 1988 s.253(3).
[48] Section 70(4).
[49] The drafting of the Patents Act 1977 has been subject to much criticism over the years, on
this and many other points.
[50] *Cavity Trays Ltd v RMC Panel Products Ltd* [1996] R.P.C. 361, CA. However, the Patents Act
2004 has since amended this provision to allow threats in respect of any kind of
infringement to be made against manufacturers and importers.

it would in the circumstances be understood and received as a threat in respect of selling the articles, and so was outside the exception.[51]

7–033   A further problem arises from the inept drafting of these exceptions. What happens when a threat is made against a retailer, not that he will be sued himself, but that proceedings will be brought against his manufacturing or importing supplier which will put his source of supply at risk, so deterring the retailer from continuing to stock the product? Absent the exception, such a threat to one person to sue another person does fall within the scope of the "threats" action.[52] However, it would appear that a threat couched in terms of suing the supplier for manufacturing or importing would fall within the literal terms of the exception to the threats action, allowing such threats to be made with impunity.

Notification of existence of design right

7–034   Both sections and the regulation contain exceptions which explicitly declare that a mere notification that a registered design[53] or an unregistered design right[54] exists does not constitute a threat of proceedings. The reason for this provision is the existence of the "innocence" defences under which a defendant can escape liability for infringement if he is not aware of the existence of the registered design or unregistered design right.[55] The owner of such a right may legitimately wish to bring its existence to the attention of traders in order to overcome such potential defences, and as long as he does so without coupling the notification of existence expressly or implicitly with a threat of proceedings, he is safe to do so.

7–035   It is a question for decision on the facts as to whether there has been a "mere" notification of existence, or whether the notification has been communicated in such a way as to imply a threat. Thus, where a patent agent stated in a letter that a certain article would infringe his client's patent when granted and added: "Incidentally, our client also has a registered design covering this article"; it was held that this did not amount to a threat of legal proceedings in respect of the registered design.[56] On the other hand, when a notification of the existence of a registered design was contained "as a separate matter" in a letter which threatened proceedings for infringement of copyright in the design drawings which formed the basis of the registered design, it was

---

[51] The approach to the assessment of what amounts to a threat is based on how it will in practical terms be understood, not precise analysis of its language: see para.7–021 above.

[52] See para.7–013 above.

[53] RDA(E) s.26(3); Community Design Regulation 2005 reg.2(6)(a).

[54] CDPA 1988 s.253(4); Community Design Regulation 2005 reg.2(6)(b).

[55] See para.6–052 above.

[56] *Finkelstein v Billig* (1930) 47 R.P.C. 516.

considered that any businessman receiving the letter might think that he was being threatened with everything, including the registered design.[57]

Justification of threats

If there is a threat falling within these provisions, it is defence for the **7–036** person making the threats to show that the threats are justified. The test of justification is objective. It is not enough for the threatener to show that he had a bona fide belief that the threat was justified; he must demonstrate that the acts in respect of which he makes the threats are (or in the case of potential acts would be if done) infringements of a registered design[58] or of an unregistered design right,[59] or of a Community design,[60] as the case may be. The infringement which he proves need not be an infringement of *his* registered design or design right; this is a corollary of the fact that the sections cover threats made in respect of rights which do not belonging to the threatener. Obviously, in such a case, the threatener may wish to defend himself by proving that the acts concerned did indeed infringe the rights of the third party concerned.

In respect of registered designs, there is a further qualification to the **7–037** defence of justification. RDA(E) s.26(2) provides that the person making the threats may justify them by proving "that the acts in respect of which the proceedings are threatened constitute, or if done would constitute, an infringement of the right in a registered design the registration of which is not shown by the plaintiff to be invalid". That phrase covers the case of a threat relating to a registered design which is indeed infringed but which is invalid. Such a threat is in the end actionable in the same way as a case where there is no infringement, but the onus shifts. The claimant has to prove that the threat was made by the defendant in the first place; the defendant has to prove (in order to justify) his allegation of infringement; and if the claimant contends that the design is invalid, the onus of doing so reverts again to him.

In the case of a registered Community design, it is provided that[61] if the **7–037A** defendant proves that the acts in respect of which proceedings were threatened constitute or, if done, would constitute an infringement of a

---

[57] *Jaybeam Ltd v Abru Aluminium Ltd* [1976] R.P.C. 308 at 313. Whitford J. described the letter as: "perhaps an over-ingenious attempt by solicitors no doubt experienced in this field of law to take advantage of specific provisions of the Act in such a way that they might make a threat or what would be understood to be a threat by any businessman without in fact contravening the provisions of the statute."

[58] RDA(A) s.26(2).
[59] CDPA 1988 s.253(2).
[60] The Community Designs Regulations 2005 reg.2(3).
[61] The Community Designs Regulations 2005 reg.2(3).

registered Community design the claimant shall be entitled to the relief claimed *only if he shows that the registration is invalid*. This conforms with the position on UK registered designs and is consistent with the fact that the burden of establishing invalidity of a registered Community design rests on the person attacking it.[62]

7–038   The above provisions relating to registered UK and Community designs are in accordance with the normal burdens in an infringement action, when the onus of proving infringement rests on the claimant, and the onus of establishing invalidity then lies on the defendant. A threats action is similar to an infringement action with the roles of the parties reversed. If the threat is admitted, it is for the defendant to open his case first on infringement and validity.[63] It is quite usual for a defendant to a threats action who pleads justification, assuming he is the owner of the design right concerned, to counterclaim for infringement in the threats action. If it is a registered design case, the claimant would then dispute validity by delivering a counterclaim to the counterclaim seeking rectification of the register.[64]

7–038A   There is however an anomaly in the case of a threat of proceedings for infringement of an *unregistered* Community design. The defence of justification of a threat in respect of an unregistered Community design states that the claimant shall not be entitled to the relief claimed "if the defendant proves that the acts in respect of which proceedings were threatened constitute or, if done, would constitute an infringement of an unregistered Community design"[65] but, unlike the provision relating to registered Community designs,[66] makes no mention of what happens if the unregistered Community design is invalid. Presumably, this difference in wording flows from a difference between the presumptions of validity relating to Community registered and unregistered design rights. A registered Community design is presumed valid and its validity can only be challenged by way of a counterclaim[67]; but the validity of an unregistered Community design right can be challenged either with a counterclaim or "by way of a plea".[68] Presumably, reg.2(5) of the Community Design Regulations 2005 is to be construed as not providing justification for the threat in a case where the defendant establishes either by way of plea or by way of a counterclaim that the unregistered Community design right sued upon is invalid.

---

[62] See para.6–035 above.
[63] *Falk Ltd v Jacoburtz* (1944) 61 R.P.C. 116; *Lusty & Sons Ltd v Morris Wilkinson & Co (Nottingham) Ltd* (1954) 71 R.P.C. 174.
[64] See para.6–025 above.
[65] The Community Designs Regulation 2005 reg.2(4).
[66] The Community Designs Regulation 2005 reg.2(3).
[67] Regulation art.85(1)—subject only to a special exception in the case of a challenge based on a prior national design right by the owner of that right.
[68] Regulation art.85(2).

3. Relief Granted for Threats

Remedies in a threats action

If the claimant succeeds in establishing that the threats have been made, **7–039**
and the defendant fails to show that they are justified, the claimant may
then obtain a declaration that they are unjustifiable, an injunction against
their continuance,[69] and may also recover such damage as he may have
suffered by reason of the threats.[70]

In a motion for judgment in default of defence in a threats action, the **7–040**
court will not grant a declaration that the threats were unjustifiable
without first hearing argument from both sides.[71] Neither will a declaration be made by consent.[72]

Interim injunctions to restrain threats

It is often of importance for a person who is suffering from threats to put **7–041**
a stop to them as quickly as possible. For this purpose an interim
injunction is the appropriate and frequently granted remedy. Such
injunctions are granted on the normal principles applicable to the grant of
interim relief: assuming that there is a seriously arguable case that threats
falling within the section have in fact been made[73] and are damaging to
the claimant, the court will consider whether the balance of convenience
favours the grant of interim relief to restrain further threats until trial.

To justify injunctive relief, there must be some reasonable expectation **7–042**
of the threats being repeated.[74] Unless the case is very clear-cut, the court
will not go into the question of justification of the threats in depth on an
interim application.[75]

---

[69] If an undertaking is offered the court will not usually grant an injunction: *Corn Products Co Ltd v Naamlooze Vennootschap W. A. Scholten's Chemische Fabriken* (1939) 56 R.P.C. 59.

[70] Such damages can include abortive legal costs incurred by the party against whom the threat is made if proceedings are threatened but never commenced; *Cavity Trays Ltd v RMC Panel Products Ltd* [1996] R.P.C. 361, CA.

[71] *R. Demuth Ltd v Inter-Pan Ltd* [1967] R.P.C. 75.

[72] *Corn Products Co Ltd v N. V. Scholton* (1939) 56 R.P.C. 59.

[73] See *Luna Advertising Co Ltd v Burnham & Co* (1928) 45 R.P.C. 258; *Desiderio v Currus Ltd* (1935) 52 R.P.C. 201.

[74] Thus an interlocutory injunction was refused in *Alpi Pietro e Figlio v John Wright & Sons (Veneers) Ltd* [1972] R.P.C. 125 at 132. In this case the plaintiffs' agent visited the defendants, sought an interview with a director and informed the director of his intentions with regard to the sale of certain veneers. This information prompted from the director what was accepted to be a threat. Whitford J., refusing interlocutory relief, held that there had to be a reasonable expectation that the threat would be made to others and that was not the case in those circumstances.

[75] Older interlocutory cases in which the merits of the plea of justification were considered in depth no longer reflect the modern practice, under which rapid progress towards a full trial on the merits is preferred to attempting to investigate the merits in depth on an interim injunction application; see; *International Sales Ltd v Trans-Continental Trading Co Ltd and Benno Maisel* (1935) 52 R.P.C. 107; cf. *Stringer v Platnauer* (1933) 50 R.P.C. 60; *Cerosa Ltd v Poseidon Industrie A.B.* [1973] F.S.R. 223.

4. Common Law Proceedings for Threats

Common law remedies for threats of proceedings

7–043 Apart from the special statutory remedies which apply in the case of UK and Community registered and unregistered designs, but not artistic copyright, the common law remedy of an action for slander of goods or slander of title (often referred to as trade libel) is also potentially available. This cause of action is far more difficult to succeed in establishing than the statutory remedies. It may, however, be necessary to invoke it in cases where untrue statements are made which do not actually amount to threats of proceedings, or which fall outside the statutory remedies for other reasons, or in the case of threats of copyright infringement where the common law remedy is the only possible remedy available.

7–044 In order to succeed in such an action it is necessary to prove, the onus on both allegations resting throughout on the claimant:

(1) that the statements were untrue;
(2) that they were made maliciously.

7–045 At common law it was also necessary to show that special damage had resulted.[76] By the Defamation Act 1952 this is however no longer necessary, for s.3(1) of the Act provides:

"In an action for slander of title, slander of goods or other malicious falsehood, it shall not be necessary to allege or prove special damage—

(a) if the words upon which the action is founded are calculated to cause pecuniary damage to the plaintiff and are published in writing or other permanent form; or

(b) if the said words are calculated to cause pecuniary damage to the plaintiff in respect of any office, profession, calling, trade of business held or carried on by him at the time of the publication."

---

[76] *Wren v Wield* (1869) L.R. 4 Q.B. 730 at 734; *Dicks v Brooks* (1880) 15 Ch.D. 22 at 40; *Halsey v Brotherhood* (1881) 19 Ch.D. 386 at 388; *Greers Ltd v Pearman & Corder Ltd* (1922) 39 R.P.C. 406; cf. the statement of Jessel M.R. in *Halsey v Brotherhood* (1880) 15 Ch.D. 514 at 520 and 523, where he indicated that malice might not be necessary for an action for an injunction as opposed to an action for damages, if the claimant makes out that the defendant intends to persevere in the representations complained of, though untrue.

Malice

Malice in this connection means that the statements were made *mala fide*, **7–046**
i.e. with dishonest motive or without reasonable or probable cause.[77] In
Greers Ltd v Pearman & Corder Ltd, Scrutton L.J. said[78]:

> "The only question in this case is—is there evidence on which the
> jury could find that the statements were made maliciously? 'Mali-
> ciously' not in the sense of illegally, but in the sense of being made
> with some indirect or dishonest motive. Honest belief in an
> unfounded claim is not malice, but the nature of the unfounded
> claim may be evidence that there was not an honest belief in it. It may
> be so unfounded that the particular fact that it is put forward may be
> evidence that it is not honestly believed."[79]

In that case the defendants' solicitors, on instructions, had written to **7–047**
the plaintiffs alleging that their goods were being labelled and advertised
so as to constitute an infringement of their clients' trade mark. It was
found that there was malice, as the defendants in fact knew that what the
plaintiffs were doing did not constitute an infringement. Proof of
knowledge on the part of the defendant, at the time of making the
statement, that what he was saying was untrue, is the most usual way in
which malice is established. A statement by a person that a patent,
registered design, trade mark or copyright was infringed with knowledge
that this was untrue would thus be malicious. Similarly, threats of
proceedings for infringement of patents or registered designs which do
not themselves amount to actionable threats within the sections of the
respective Acts, may nevertheless be actionable as being malicious.[80]

A more difficult question would arise where a person alleged infringe- **7–048**
ment, when the act complained of did in fact fall within the scope of his
monopoly, but where the monopoly was to his knowledge invalid. Such
a statement would appear to be malicious. The important question would
be, is it untrue? The judgment of Cotton L.J. in *Challender v Royle*[81] bears
on this point:

> " . . . I cannot see how, if a patent is invalid, there can be any act done
> in infringement of a legal right when the legal right depends only on
> the validity of that patent.[82] On the other hand it may be said that
> infringement and validity are separate questions, and that at any rate

[77] *Halsey v Brotherhood* (1881) 19 Ch.D. 386.
[78] (1922) 39 R.P.C. 406 at 417.
[79] See also *Halsey v Brotherhood* (1881) 19 Ch.D. 386 at 388. *Balden v Shorter* [1933] Ch. 427 at
430.
[80] *Mentmore Manufacturing Co Ltd v Fomento (Sterling Area) Ltd* (1955) 72 R.P.C. 12 (a case
originally brought under s.65 of the Patents Act 1949).
[81] (1887) 4 R.P.C. 363 at 371.
[82] See also *Pittevil & Co v Brackelsberg Melting Processes Ltd* (1932) 49 R.P.C. 73.

a registered design or trade mark, once granted, is valid until taken off the register."[83]

Actions for defamation

7–049   A further class of case which may give rise to an action is where statements are made which are not merely untrue, but which are also defamatory, thus amounting to a libel or slander. A mere allegation that goods infringe a design right or copyright is unlikely to amount to defamation, but an allegation that implies plagiarism or other dishonest or disreputable conduct could well be, such as an allegation that the claimant's goods are spurious.[84] The subject of libel and slander properly so-called is outside the scope of this book and specialist works should be consulted.

Position where litigation is pending

7–050   Other causes of action are potentially available if litigation which is ongoing is improperly exploited to deter traders from dealing in articles which are alleged to infringe. These are contempt of court[85] and abuse of process; further consideration of these remedies is outside the scope of this book.

7–051   However, the fact that infringement proceedings are on foot does not prevent the statutory threats remedies being invoked if threats are made of litigation against other parties, although the existence of such proceedings may affect the balance of convenience as regards the grant or refusal of an interlocutory injunction.[86] The fact that infringement proceedings are brought against a claimant after the issue of the threat does not debar the claimant from relief under the statutory provisions.

---

[83] See *Smith v Grigg* (1924) 41 R.P.C. 149, and *Re Margolin's Registered Design* (1937) 54 R.P.C. 1.

[84] *Thorley's Cattle Food Co v Massam* (1880) 14 Ch.D. 763 at 774; 780; *Thomas v Williams* (1880) 14 Ch.D. 864 at 872.

[85] *St Mungo Manufacturing Co v Hutchinson Main & Co Ltd* (1908) 25 R.P.C. 356 (a Scottish case); the pursuers were in the course of bringing action for infringement of a registered design. *Pendente lite* they issued circulars stating that the defendants had applied a fraudulent or obvious imitation of their design to golf balls, that they had commenced proceedings against the defendants, and warning retail dealers that if they sold any such golf balls they would be rendering themselves liable to proceedings. It was held that the publication of such circulars *pendente lite* constituted contempt of court, and they must accordingly be restrained.

[86] Where a defendant in an infringement action issued a writ against a patentee to restrain the issue of threats made by the patentee after the infringement action had been commenced, and it being established that the infringement action was being prosecuted with due diligence, an application for an interlocutory injunction in the threats action was refused: *Marks & Young (Trading as M. Y. Dart Co) v Scott's "Keepdrye" Dartboard Co* (1940) 57 R.P.C. 351. In *Non-Drip Measure Co Ltd v Strangers Ltd and F. W. Woolworth & Co Ltd* (1942) 59 R.P.C. 1 and 60 R.P.C. 335, where in an infringement action there was a counterclaim in respect of threats, an interim injunction to restrain threats made after issue of writ was (although unreported) granted.

CHAPTER 8

COMPULSORY LICENSING AND CROWN USER

1. Compulsory Licensing of Registered Designs

Compulsory licensing of registered designs

There used to be limited and little used powers for compulsory licences **8–001** of registered designs which could be granted on application to the Patent Office (now the UK Intellectual Property Office). These former powers should be distinguished from the powers of the Patent Office to set the terms of licences of right under unregistered design rights, described in subsequent paragraphs. Licences of right are automatic; however, it was a condition precedent to obtaining a compulsory licence to demonstrate unreasonable failure by the proprietor to exploit his registered design. These powers were repealed following the transposition of the Directive into UK law.[1]

2. Licences of Right for Unregistered Designs

Licences of right for UK unregistered designs

During the last five years of the life of an unregistered design right, the **8–002** design is subject to the grant of licences of right.[2] This is equivalent to half the effective commercial term of the design right, i.e. half of the 10-year period from first marketing.[3] During the "licences of right" period the unregistered design right effectively ceases to be a monopoly right, or at

---

[1] Transposition was effected by the 2001 Regulations; reg.6 repealed s.10 of RDA(A) which had conferred the compulsory licence powers on the Registrar.
[2] CDPA 1988 s.237(1).
[3] For term of unregistered design right, see para.4–131 above.

least a right to prevent copying of the design concerned by competitors, and becomes instead a mere right to receive royalties from use of the design by others. It should be noted that from the beginning of the "licences of right" period, it becomes impossible for the proprietor to obtain an injunction against the use of the design by any competitor who gives an undertaking to the court that he will take a licence of right on terms which are settled in the IP Office.[4]

Procedure for grant of licences of right

8–003   In default of agreement, the terms of a licence of right are settled by the IP Office.[5] A licence may be applied for in advance: up to one year before the date when licences of right become available in respect of the design right concerned.[6] It should be noted that (unlike in a case of the now-repealed power to grant a compulsory licence of a registered design on the ground of failure of the proprietor to exploit it) the Office has no discretion on whether or not to grant a licence of right, merely over the terms which will apply. Although it has been argued that the availability of licences of right is inconsistent with the United Kingdom's obligations under the Agreement on Trade-Related Aspects of Intellectual Property (the "TRIPs" Agreement) art.26,[7] it has been held that this aspect of the TRIPs Agreement does not give rise to obligations which have been incorporated into the domestic law of the United Kingdom, whether directly or via the European Union's adhesion to TRIPs,[8] so that the Office must apply the "licences of right" provisions of the CDPA 1988 regardless of arguments about the United Kingdom's international obligations.[9]

---

[4] See para.6–047 above. This greatly diminishes the incentive that existed under the licences of right procedure in the transitional provisions of the Patents Act 1977 (Sch.1, para.4(2)(c)) for the proprietor to spin out the proceedings for settlement of terms as long as possible in order to delay the moment at which the licensee gets their licence.

[5] CDPA 1988 ss.237(2) and s.247(1). Nominally the terms are settled by the comptroller, i.e. the Comptroller-General of Patents, Designs and Trade Marks (CDPA 1988 s.263(1)) but in practice by officials of the IP Office appointed to conduct hearings and act on his behalf.

[6] CDPA 1988 s.247(2); this would normally be at the end of the fourth calendar year after first marketing of articles to which the designs has been applied.

[7] Which provides that WTO members shall make industrial design protection available for a minimum 10-year term: see App.F2 below.

[8] *Azrak-Hamway Intnl Inc's Licence of Right (Design Right and Copyright) Appn* [1997] R.P.C. 134, Pat Off. See also *Re The Uruguay Round Treaties*, Op 1/94, [1995] 1 C.M.L.R. 205, ECJ.

[9] There is no provision relating to licences of right similar to that relating to compulsory licences of registered designs (RDA(A) s.10(3), now repealed) whereby the Patent Office was obliged directly to take into account the international obligations of the UK assumed by treaty or agreement. However, The European Communities (Definition of Treaties) (The Agreement Establishing the World Trade Organisation) Order 1995 (SI 1995/265) has designated the Uruguay Round agreements including the TRIPs Agreement as Community Treaties for the purposes of the European Communities Act 1972. This means that it is possible to argue that provisions of those agreements which are intended to have direct effect upon true construction of the agreements will be given direct effect in UK domestic law by the terms of s.2(1) of the 1972 Act.

The procedure followed by the Office is laid down by the Design Right   **8–004**
(Proceedings Before Comptroller) Rules 1989, as amended.[10] Proceedings
are commenced by the applicant serving a notice on the Office setting out
the terms of the licence which he seeks and identify the person he alleges
to be the owner of the design right concerned.[11] A respondent who objects
to the terms of the licence serves a notice of objection[12]; there is provision
for a counter-statement by the applicant[13] and thereafter the Office gives
directions for the further hearing of the dispute.[14] The procedure normally includes the service of evidence by statutory declaration or
affidavit, and an oral hearing at which witnesses may be cross examined.[15]

Terms and effect of licence of right

A licence of right must authorise the applicant to do all things within the   **8–005**
scope of the statutory provisions; there is no discretion to limit the scope
of the licence to some activities but not others.[16] For this reason it has
been held that a licence of right must include a right for the licensee to
sub-license if he requires it.[17] Once settled by the Office, a licence takes
effect as from the date when the application for it was filed,[18] unless it is
applied for in advance of the date when licences of right become
available, in which case it takes effect from that date.[19]

The approach to royalty rate adopted by the Office is to ask what   **8–006**
would be agreed between a willing licensor and a willing licensee in free
negotiation; as part of this exercise, it may be appropriate to estimate and
share out between licensor and licensee the profits available from the
exploitation of the design right.[20] The royalty rate will be based on
compensating the owner of the design right in his capacity as rights

---

[10] SI 1989/1130, App.C3 below.
[11] SI 1989/1130 r.10 and Sch.1, Form 3.
[12] SI 1989/1130 r.10(4).
[13] SI 1989/1130 r.10(5).
[14] SI 1989/1130 rr.10(11) and 4.
[15] SI 1989/1130 rr.5 and 6.
[16] CDPA 1988 s.247(3).
[17] *Bance's Licence of Right (Copyright) Appn* [1996] R.P.C. 667, Pat Off. A licence of right has
even been granted in which the identity of the licensee's sub-licensee has been kept
confidential from the licensor: *Sterling Fluid System Ltd's Licence of Right (Copyright) Appn*
[1999] R.P.C. 775.
[18] CDPA 1988 s.247(6)(b). There is no discretion to make the licence run from any other date;
[1996] R.P.C. 667 at 684, line 12.
[19] CDPA 1988 s.247(6)(a).
[20] *Pioneer Oil Tools Ltd's Licence of Right (Copyright) Appn* [1997] R.P.C. 573, Pat Ct, where a
royalty rate of 9% was set in respect of parts for oil drilling equipment; *Bance's Licenced
Right*, above, where royalty rates of 5–7% were set on impact wrenches and spares;
Sterling Fluid System Ltd's Licence of Right (Copyright) Appn [1999] R.P.C. 775, Pat Off,
where the licensee was mainly making pumps which were more or less identical to the
licensor's pumps and it was therefore appropriate to levy a royalty on the total price of
the products; it was suggested that a different approach would be appropriate where the
licensee's products incorporated only a small proportion of copyright material. This is an

owner and not on compensating him for profits lost by him as a potential supplier of products displaced by competition from the licensee.[21]

8–007   If the identity of the design right owner is unknown and cannot be ascertained by reasonable inquiry, there is provision for the Office to grant a licence of right on terms which are free of royalty.[22] Since the Office in such a case "may" rather than "must" grant a licence, presumably it has a discretion to order payment of royalties which would have to be paid into some kind of blocked account in case the design right owner comes forward in the future. If a design right owner later emerges, he can ask for royalties to be set,[23] but the position of the licensee is protected in the interim, even if it emerges that in fact a licence of right should not have been granted in respect of the design concerned.[24]

8–008   A licence of right is compulsory in nature. For this reason, a licensee under a licence of right is specifically prohibited from (without the consent of the design right owner) marking his goods with, or using in relation to his goods, a trade description indicating that he is the licensee of the design right owner.[25] Another consequence of the non-consensual nature of a licence of right is that the grant of such a licence does not serve to "exhaust" the rights of the design right owner and so he may maintain actions under parallel rights in other EU member states to prohibit the importation there of articles made or placed on the market in the United Kingdom under the licence.[26]

8–009   Appeal from the Office in exercising its jurisdiction to settle the terms of licences of right lies to the Registered Designs Appeal Tribunal.[27]

3. Crown User and Emergency Powers

Secrecy of registered designs for defence purposes

8–010   According to RDA(E) s.5, if an application for a registered design is made which contains a design whose publication could be prejudicial to the defence of the realm, an obligation can be imposed on the applicant to keep his design secret and it can effectively be seized or suppressed by the government for defence purposes. These provisions are similar to

example of a case where the royalty rate was fixed largely on the "profits available" approach, also applied in *E-UK Controls Ltd's Licence of Right (Copyright) Appn* [1998] R.P.C. 833, Pat Off, and in *NIC Instrument Ltd's Licence of Right (Design Right) Appn* [2005] R.P.C. 1, Pat Off.

[21] *NIC Instrument Ltd's Licence of Right (Design Right) Appn* [2005] R.P.C. 1, Pat Off, applying the same principle as that applied in Crown user patent cases in *Patchett's Patent* [1967] R.P.C. 77 and 237.

[22] CDPA 1988 s.248; SI 1989/1130, r.13.

[23] CDPA 1988 s.248(3).

[24] CDPA 1988 s.248(4).

[25] CDPA 1988 s.254. Such an act gives rise to a right of civil action on the part of the design right owner; s.254(2).

[26] *Pharmon v Hoechst*, Case 19/84 [1985] 3 C.M.L.R. 775, ECJ.

[27] CDPA 1988 s.249. As to the RDAT, see para.3–262 above.

those relating to patents[28] where they are intended to cover such things as inventions of new weapons. Given that registered designs relate only to the "eye appeal"[29] or aesthetic aspects of the design of industrial articles, it seems unlikely that these provisions are likely to be of extensive application in the registered designs context.

If the Registrar considers that a design applied for falls within any class **8–011** of design which certain government departments have classified as being of a secret nature the Registrar may give directions prohibiting or restricting the publication of information with respect to the design or the communication of such information to any person or class of persons specified.[30] While any such direction is in force, the design is not open to public inspection.[31] Provision is made for review from time to time by the government department which has prescribed the secret class of articles so that the design shall not remain secret for longer than necessary.[32]

By RDA(E) s.33(1), non-compliance with a secrecy direction made **8–012** under s.5 is made a criminal offence punishable by up to two years' imprisonment on indictment.

In order to prevent residents of the United Kingdom from escaping **8–013** these provisions by registering their designs via overseas designs registries, RDA(E) s.5(4) prohibits any UK resident from making or causing to be made any application for a registered design which is in a prescribed class outside the United Kingdom, unless application is first made here. A resident of the United Kingdom who makes an application overseas in breach of this provision is similarly guilty of an offence.[33]

Crown use of registered and unregistered designs

Detailed and elaborate provisions relating to the use of UK registered **8–014** designs for the services of the Crown and the rights of third parties in respect of such use are contained in the RDA(E). Section 12 and Sch.1 permit any government department, and any person authorised in writing by a government department, to make use of a registered design.[34] Very similar provisions apply to the use of UK unregistered designs for Crown purposes,[35] and the use of Community registered and unregistered designs.[36]

The authority of a government department may be given before or after **8–015** a registered design is registered, and in the case of both registered and

---

[28] The Patents Act 1977 s.22.
[29] See para.3–047 above.
[30] RDA(E) s.5(1).
[31] RDA(E) s.5(2).
[32] RDA(E) s.5(3).
[33] Under RDA(E) s.33(1).
[34] RDA(E) Sch.1, para.1(1).
[35] CDPA 1988 s.240.
[36] Community Designs Regulations 2005 (SI 2005/2339) reg.5 and Sch.

unregistered designs, both before or retrospectively after the acts in respect of which the authority is given are done.[37]

8–016   What can count as Crown purposes is defined widely. Any use for the supply to the government of any country outside the United Kingdom, in pursuance of any agreement or arrangement between Her Majesty's Government in the United Kingdom and the government of that country, of articles required for the defence of that country or for the defence of any other country whose government is party to any agreement or arrangement with Her Majesty's Government in respect of defence matters will be deemed to be a use for the services of the Crown.[38] Also the supply to the United Nations or to the government of any country belonging to that organisation, in pursuance of an agreement or arrangement between Her Majesty's Government and that organisation or government, of articles required for any armed forces operating in pursuance of a resolution of that organisation or any organ of it, will be deemed to be a use for the services of the Crown.[39] This can include the use of the design by commercial companies based in the United Kingdom for the purpose of supplying weapons to overseas governments pursuant to an arrangement or agreement between the British government and the overseas government, if the necessary governmental authorisation is given.

8–017   The "Crown user" provisions relating to registered and unregistered designs are modelled on those which apply in the case of patents. In practice the Crown is, however, not likely to make such substantial use of its powers in the case of designs as it does in the case of patents. It is conceivable that there could be somewhat greater use in the case of unregistered design right than in the case of registered designs, since unregistered design right protects designs which are functional in nature.

Compensation for Crown user

8–018   If a registered design has before the date of registration been recorded by or applied by a government department otherwise than in consequence of the communication of the design by the registered proprietor, any use of the design may be made free of any royalty or other payment.[40] This provision has no parallel in the case of unregistered design right because there will in any event be no use of that right unless there is a chain of causation, i.e. copying, from the owner of the design to the Crown use concerned.[41]

[37] RDA(E) Sch.1, para.1(4); CDPA 1988 s.240(6).
[38] RDA(E) Sch.1, para.1(6); CDPA 1988 s.240(3).
[39] RDA(E) Sch.1, para.1(6); CDPA 1988 s.240(3).
[40] RDA(E) Sch.1, para.1(2).
[41] This is implicit in the nature of the unregistered design right, which is a right to restrain copying rather than a monopoly right; see para.4–093 above.

If the registered design has not been so recorded or applied, Crown use   **8–019**
of the design is subject to payment of compensation, as is the Crown use
of an unregistered design. Where any Crown use of a registered[42] or
unregistered[43] design is so made, then, unless it appears to the department to be contrary to the public interest so to do, the department must
notify the proprietor as soon as possible after the use is begun, and
furnish him with such information as to the extent of the use as he may
from time to time require. Compensation is paid upon such terms as may
be agreed, either before or after use, between the government department
and the proprietor, or may in default of agreement be determined by the
court.[44] In the case of unregistered design right, if the identity of the
owner cannot be ascertained on reasonable inquiry, the government
department concerned may apply to the court for an order that no royalty
or other sum is payable for the Crown use concerned.[45]

Any dispute as to the exercise by a government department or a person   **8–020**
authorised by a government department of the Crown user provisions, or
as to the terms for the use of a design for the services of the Crown, or as
to the right of any person to receive any part of a payment made for
Crown use, may be referred to the court by either party.[46] In any
proceedings resulting from such a reference the department may, if the
proprietor is a party, apply for cancellation of a registered design, and
may, in any case, put in issue its validity without applying for actual
cancellation.[47] The court shall have regard to any benefit or compensation
which the party, or any person deriving title from him, may have
received, or be entitled to receive, directly or indirectly, from any
government department in respect of the design in question.[48] In addition, there is provision for compensation for loss of profit by the owner of
the registered or unregistered design for not being awarded a contract to
supply the goods concerned to the Crown.[49]

The principles on which compensation will be calculated in design   **8–021**
cases will be similar to those applied in the case of Crown use of patented
inventions.[50] Apart from the normal provisions relating to the use of
designs for the purposes of the Crown, there are special provisions
during periods of emergency declared by Order in Council which
effectively permit the government to authorise the use of designs for far
wider purposes during the period of the emergency.[51]

---

[42] RDA(E) Sch.1, para.1(5).
[43] CDPA 1988 s.241(1).
[44] RDA(E) Sch.1, para.1(3); CDPA 1988 s.241(2).
[45] CDPA 1988 s.241(3).
[46] RDA(E) Sch.1, para.3; CDPA 1988 s.252.
[47] RDA(E) Sch.1, para.3(2).
[48] RDA(E) Sch.1, para.3(4).
[49] RDA(E) Sch.1, para.2A; CDPA 1988 s.243.
[50] For a full survey of the question of Crown user and compensation for Crown user in
relation to a patent see *Patchett's Patent* [1967] R.P.C. 77 and 237.
[51] RDA(E) Sch.1, para.4; CDPA 1988 s.244.

Chapter 9

EUROPEAN UNION LAW AND COMPETITION

Contents

1. EU Law on the Free Movement of Goods and Parallel Imports

Free movement of goods under European Union law

9–001 In cases where goods are imported from other member states of the European Union or elsewhere in the European Economic Area,[1] the provisions of domestic legislation relating to registered and unregistered designs and copyright have to be read subject to the rules of EU law on the free movement of goods. The rules relating to Community registered and unregistered design rights are in any event framed with the intention of being consistent with those rules. Those rules stem from arts 34 to 36 TFEU (formerly arts 28 to 30 EC), as extensively interpreted and developed in the case law of the European Court of Justice. The "free movement" rules are relevant to "parallel import" cases; that is, cases where goods are imported by third parties (or "parallel traders") into the United Kingdom which have been placed on the market elsewhere in the single market either by the person who is the proprietor of the relevant design right in the United Kingdom, or by a person in some way connected with him such as a licensee, or, in the case of a group of companies, another member of the group.

9–002 Article 34 TFEU (formerly art.28 EC), prohibits the imposition on imports from other member states of "quantitative restrictions on imports

---

[1] At the time of writing, this comprises the EU Member States together with Norway, Iceland and Liechtenstein, who are parties to the European Economic Area Agreement. EEA art.6 provides that the provisions of the EEA agreement which substantially correspond with provisions of the Rome Treaty (now superseded by the TFEU), shall be interpreted in conformity with the relevant rulings of the ECJ given prior to the date of signature of the EEA Agreement (May 2, 1992).

and all measures having equivalent effect".[2] However, art.36 TFEU (formerly art.30 EC) permits the imposition of such restrictions where they are "justified on grounds of . . . the protection of industrial and commercial property". The European Court of Justice (ECJ) has established a body of case law, applying generally to all forms of intellectual property rights, that governs when such rights can and cannot be invoked against goods imported from other member states. The general rule is that once goods of a particular design have been placed on the market somewhere in the EEA by or with the consent of a person (e.g. by a licensee), he cannot invoke his design rights in any other member state to prevent the free circulation in the single market of those goods.[3] But intellectual property rights can be fully enforced against goods from an origin which is unconnected with the proprietor of the design right being enforced.[4] It has been reaffirmed by the ECJ that these rules apply even if the goods are imported from a member state where the proprietor is unable to obtain corresponding intellectual property protection, so that (from the proprietor's point of view) he is compelled by economic forces to place goods on the market there at a lower price than if he had enjoyed corresponding protection in that country.[5]

9–003 Members of a group of companies are treated as a single entity for these purposes.

Statutory enactment of EU free movement rules

9–004 In the case of copyright and UK registered and unregistered design right, there is explicit statutory recognition (although not actual enactment) of the EU free movement rules developed by the ECJ. CDPA 1988 s.27(5), dealing with circumstances in which the importation of articles will infringe copyright, provides:

> "(5) Nothing in subsection (3) shall be construed as applying to an article which may lawfully be imported into the United Kingdom by virtue of any enforceable Community right within the meaning of section 2(1) of the European Communities Act 1972."

---

[2] With regard to the member states of the EEA outside the EU, the EEA Agreement arts 10 and 14 correspond with arts 28 and 30 of the Rome Treaty.
[3] Case 187/80 *Merck & Co v Stephar Bv* [1981] E.C.R. 2063; [1981] 3 C.M.L.R. 463, ECJ, a patent case, but expounding the general principles applicable to all kinds of intellectual property.
[4] Case 119/75 *Terrapin (Overseas) Ltd v Terranova Industrie CA Kapfever & Co* [1976] E.C.R. 1039 at 1061; [1976] 2 C.M.L.R. 485 at 505 and 506, ECJ (a trade mark case).
[5] Joined cases C-267–268/95 *Merck & Co Inc v Primecrown Ltd* [1997] 1 C.M.L.R. 83; [1997] F.S.R. 237, ECJ, a patent case. This principle, however, may have quite extensive application in designs cases, in view of the considerable variations in design laws between different member states of the EEA prior to the harmonising effect of the Design Directive.

9–005   CDPA 1988 s.228(5) is in identical terms in relation to unregistered design right, and RDA(E) s.24G(5)[5a] provides the same in relation to registered designs.

9–006   In relation to UK registered designs, RDA(E) s.7A(4) provides:

> "(4) The right in a registered design is not infringed by an act which relates to a product in which any design protected by the registration is incorporated or to which it is applied if the product has been put on the market in the European Economic Area by the registered proprietor or with his consent."

This provision derives from the Designs Directive,[6] and the Community Designs Regulation makes the same provision in respect of Community registered and unregistered designs.[7] These provisions are modelled on the corresponding provisions in the Trade Marks Directive and Regulation[8] and, like those provisions, will be construed in the light of the preceding case law of the ECJ relating to free movement of goods upon which they are based. It should however be noted that these "exhaustion of rights" provisions is some respects go further than the free movement rules in that there does not need to be any element of trade between member states involved: they would apply so as to prevent a design right owner who sold his goods in Manchester from enforcing his design right against the sale of those goods in London.

Imports from outside the EEA

9–007 The rules developed by the ECJ on free movement of goods do not apply in relation to goods first marketed outside the EU or EEA.[9] For this purpose, countries which merely have association agreements[10] with the EU count as being outside the single market, despite the fact that the wording of the relevant association agreement may be similar or identical to the above mentioned provisions of TFEU (formerly the Rome Treaty).[11] In relation to Community design right (registered or unregistered) and

---

[5a] Inserted by the Intellectual Property (Enforcement, etc.) Regulations 2006 (SI 2006/1028) reg.2, Sch.1, paras 1 and 3.

[6] Article 15 of the Designs Directive. See App.A1 below.

[7] Article 21 of the Community Designs Regulation. See App.B1 below.

[8] First Council Directive 89/104/EEC to approximate the laws of the Member States relating to trade marks art.7; Council Regulation 40/94/EEC on the Community Trade Mark art.13.

[9] *EMI v CBS* [1976] E.C.R. 811; [1976] 2 C.M.L.R. 235.

[10] e.g. Switzerland.

[11] *Polydor v Harlequin Record Shop* [1982] E.C.R. 329; [1982] 1 C.M.L.R. 677, ECJ, a copyright case, where the then association agreement between the Community and Portugal was interpreted as not giving rise to a right to parallel import, despite the similarity of its wording with that of arts 30 and 36 (since renumbered 28 and 30) of the Rome Treaty, having regard to the different objects and purposes of the association agreement from the Rome Treaty.

UK registered design right which has been harmonised in accordance with the Directive, the position regarding parallel imports from outside the EEA now seems clear, in that it is likely that the ECJ will follow its decisions on the corresponding "exhaustion of rights" provisions of the Trade Marks Directive and Regulation. In that context, the ECJ has held that Community law requires member states to allow a trade mark owner to prohibit parallel imports from outside the EEA unless he has consented to the placing of the goods on the market within the EEA.[12] Furthermore, the ECJ has held that such consent cannot be implied consent save in very exceptional circumstances, so in particular the fact that the owner has sold the goods without any explicit restriction against resale into the EEA in a country whose contract law grants implied consent for resale anywhere in the world does not avail the importer.[13]

In relation to UK unregistered design right, the rules relating to importation from outside the EEA are not regulated by EU law so it becomes necessary to apply the provisions of British domestic law to "parallel import" cases in order to determine whether or not the importation concerned is lawful. In the case of copyright an amendment has purportedly been made to CDPA 1988 s.18, pursuant to an EC Directive on rental rights which on its face would appear to make it an infringement of copyright to place on the market lawfully made copies of a copyright work (or even the original) from outside the EEA.[14]   **9–008**

Parallel imports and unregistered design right

In the case of importation of articles from outside the EEA, the lawfulness   **9–009**
or otherwise of the importation is governed, in the case of UK design right, by the definition of "infringing copy" in the case of an imported article laid down in CDPA 1988 s.228(3). This reads:

"(3) An article is also an infringing article if—

(a) it has been or is proposed to be imported into the United Kingdom, and
(b) its making to that design in the United Kingdom would have constituted an infringement of design right in the design, or a

---

[12] Case C-355/96, *Silhouette International Schmied GmbH v Hartlauer Handelsgesellschaft mbH* [1998] 2 C.M.L.R. 953. Although, rather oddly, the RDA(E) was amended by the Intellectual Property (Enforcement, etc.) Regulations 2006 (SI 2006/1028) which inserted a new s.24G (see App.A2, para.A2–054 below) which defines "infringing article" in the same way as the corresponding provisions relating to copyright and unregistered design right (set out in para.9–009 below) this does not have the effect of permitting the resale in the UK of parallel imports from outside the UK because s.7(2)(a) of RDA(E) makes it an infringement to import or sell an article to which a design is applied and does not require that it be an "infringing article" as defined by s.24G.

[13] Joined cases C-414–416/99 *Zino Davidoff SA v A & G Imports Ltd* ECJ, November 20, 2001.

[14] See para.9–015 below.

breach of an exclusive licence agreement relating to that design."

CDPA 1988 s.27(3) lays down an identical definition of infringing articles for the purpose of copyright. The two provisions will be considered together.

9–010   It can be seen that the subsection lays down a hypothetical test. A notional making of the article must be assumed to have taken place—this notional making took place in the United Kingdom rather than the actual foreign country where the article was made. But who for this purpose is assumed to be the notional maker? Probably the most straightforward interpretation is to assume that the notional maker in the United Kingdom is the person who actually made the article in the foreign country. This means that if the actual maker in the foreign country was the copyright or design right owner then (assuming no exclusive licence exists) the article is not an "infringing article" and its importation into the United Kingdom is lawful, regardless of the wishes of the owner. On the other hand, if the article was made in the foreign country by a local licensee of the right owner, whose licence does not extend to allowing him to make in the United Kingdom, then the article is an "infringing article". This is indeed the interpretation of the predecessor to this subsection[15] which was adopted by the court in the *Charmdale* case.[16]

Alternative approaches to the hypothetical making in the United Kingdom

9–011   There are other approaches to applying the "hypothetical maker" test which are logically possible. One possible alternative is to assume that the person who hypothetically makes the article in the United Kingdom should be assumed to be not the actual maker in the foreign country, but the importer. This approach has indeed been adopted explicitly as the test in the relevant Australian statute.[17] Another possible alternative is to

---

[15] Which was the Copyright Act 1956 s.5(2); see also s.18(3) in similar terms relating to sound recordings. However, that subsection did not contain the reference to breach of an exclusive licence agreement which appeared for the first time in the above quoted section of the CDPA 1988.

[16] *CBS United Kingdom Ltd v Charmdale Record Distributors Ltd* [1980] F.S.R. 289, ChD, Browne-Wilkinson J. In that case, the action was brought by a UK company which was the exclusive licensee of the US company from whom the imported articles originated. On these facts, there would now be infringement, since the inclusion of the words "or a breach of an exclusive licence agreement" in the new subs.27(3)(b) of CDPA 1988 has effected a statutory reversal of the case on this point. However, the case remains unaffected in its rejection of the argument that the hypothetical maker in the UK should be assumed to be the importer, rather than the person who actually made the article in the foreign country of origin.

[17] Copyright Act 1968 (Australia) s.37 and s.38.

assume that the notional maker is some person acting without the authority of the copyright owner. This approach was adopted in a New Zealand case under a statute whose terms were the same as those of the Copyright Act 1956 (UK).[18] Either of these tests would for most practical purposes produce the same effect, since it is unlikely in a case where the right owner is taking action against parallel imported articles that the importer is acting with his authority.

These alternative interpretations have received support in some quarters before, and even after and in spite of, the *Charmdale* case. It is submitted, however, that the approach adopted in *Charmdale* as to who should be the hypothetical maker is clearly correct. First, there is no obvious support for the alternative arguments in the language of the statute. Secondly, the relevant statutory test originated in the Copyright Act 1911 s.2(2). Part I of that Act was headed "Imperial Copyright" and the Act extended effectively throughout the then British Empire. The importation test there applies to each colony or dominion.[19] It seems inconceivable that the Parliament of 1911 should have intended to impose a test which would have the effect of erecting barriers to free trade within the Empire, by empowering the owner of a single copyright throughout the Empire to prevent his own works passing from one part of the Empire to another.[20]   **9–012**

Thirdly, it is hard to see how these arguments (whatever their merits under the 1956 Act) can survive the language of CDPA 1988 ss.27(3)(b) and 228(3)(b), and in particular the inclusion in those provisions of the references to the breach of an exclusive licence agreement. On the interpretations considered above, these words would be otiose; on the other hand, if the hypothetical maker is the actual maker then those words have a clear and understandable purpose of covering the case where the article is made in the foreign country by the person who is the right owner in the United Kingdom, but where it would be a breach by him of his obligations under an exclusive licence to have made the same article here. Fourthly, it is difficult to see what the obvious purpose of Parliament was in allowing the person who is the right owner in the United Kingdom (in the absence of a division of rights or a special factor such as an exclusive licence agreement) to exclude articles of his own manufacture which he has placed on foreign markets, so allowing him to maintain artificial low and high price zones to the detriment of the British consumer.   **9–013**

[18] *Albert (J) & Sons Pty Ltd v Fletcher Construction Co Ltd* [1976] R.P.C. 615, NZ. This decision was criticised and not followed in *Charmdale* at 297–299.

[19] See s.2(2)(d).

[20] It may be that the interpretation adopted in the New Zealand case of *Albert & Sons v Fletcher Construction*, above is largely explained by cultural factors, in that the New Zealand courts are more willing to consider their national market as being isolated from other markets, as compared with the historically global trade outlook in the UK.

Examples of the application of the *Charmdale* approach

9–014 It may be helpful to consider a few example cases where importation is lawful or unlawful, on the assumption (which is submitted to be correct) that the hypothetical making/actual maker test is applied to the two subsections.

(1) The owner of a copyright or design right is the same person in the United Kingdom and in a foreign country. He places goods made by him on the market both here and in the foreign country. It would be lawful for a third party to import the articles which he has placed on the foreign market.

(2) The owner of the right is the same here and in a foreign country. He makes and sells in the foreign country, but has granted an exclusive licence to another manufacturer to use his design in the United Kingdom. It would be unlawful for a third party to import the right owner's goods from the foreign country into the United Kingdom, because of the express reference in the two subsections to "breach of an exclusive licence agreement". If, however, the licensee in the United Kingdom made under a non-exclusive licence, the right owner's goods could be lawfully imported from abroad.

(3) Rights over the design in the foreign country have been trans-ferred by assignment to a party which is unconnected with the copyright or design owner in the United Kingdom. In this case, it would be unlawful to import the goods made in the foreign country by that party into the United Kingdom.

(4) The person who owns the right in the United Kingdom has granted a licence to another party to manufacture in a foreign country. That licence (whether it is exclusive or non-exclusive) is limited to the territory of that country. It would then be unlawful to import into the United Kingdom the goods made by the licensee and placed on the market in the foreign country.[21]

Parallel imports and copyright infringement: the "distribution right"

9–015 Where the right being enforced in respect of an industrial design is copyright rather than unregistered design right, certain amendments have purportedly been made by statutory instrument to s.18 of the CDPA 1988 which, if validly made, would impact on the ability of third parties to place industrial articles which have been placed on the market by the copyright owner outside the EEA on the market within the EEA. Section

---

[21] This is because had the licensee hypothetically made the goods concerned in the UK instead of in the place where he was licensed to do so, it would have been outside the scope of his licence and therefore a breach of the copyright or design right concerned.

18 makes the issue of copies to the public a primary infringement of copyright.[22] However, this applies to the person who first places the copies on the market (the original source) and does not affect subsequent retailers or other dealers. In its form as passed by Parliament in the original Act, s.18(2) made it quite clear that if the copies were first placed on the market outside the United Kingdom, then a person who imported them into the United Kingdom (or a dealer who acquired them from that person) was not regarded as issuing the copies to the public for the purposes of the section and so could not be liable for infringement under it.[23]

However, subs.18(2) as purportedly amended[24] defines as issuing to the public: **9–016**

> "the act of putting into circulation in the EEA copies not previously put into circulation in the EEA by or with the consent of the copyright owner".[25]

(In addition, it defines it as including the act of putting into circulation outside the EEA copies not previously put into circulation in EEA or elsewhere: presumably intended to make export from the EEA into a primary infringement.)[26] The effect of the first-quoted amendment would be to render it a primary infringing act to buy up industrial articles lawfully placed on a non-EEA market (such as the United States) by the person who is copyright owner both there and in the United Kingdom, and then import them and place them on the market in the United Kingdom. This would radically change the former law regarding parallel imports, which arose from the definition of "infringing copy" in s.27.[27] However, it is submitted that there are compelling reasons for concluding that the amendment to s.18 which was purportedly made by statutory instrument is void, at least in so far as it relates to copyrights in the field of industrial design.

The amendment was purportedly made by regulations under the   **9–017**
European Communities Act 1972.[28] Regulations under the 1972 Act can amend even Acts of Parliament, if they are made "for the purpose of implementing any Community obligation of the United Kingdom".[29] The 1996 Regulations purport (so far as relevant for present purposes) to implement Council Directive 92/100 on rental right and lending right and

---

[22] See para.5–105, above.
[23] See s.18(2) in its form before amendment, App.D1 below. Note particularly that it refers to "the act of putting into circulation copies not previously put into circulation *in the United Kingdom or elsewhere*" (emphasis supplied); and also the explicit exclusion in s.18(2)(b) of "any subsequent importation of those copies into the United Kingdom".
[24] See amended text at App.D1 below.
[25] New subpara.18(2)(a).
[26] New subpara.18(2)(b).
[27] As set out in para.9–009 above.
[28] The Copyright and Related Rights Regulations 1996 (SI 1996/2967).
[29] The European Communities Act 1972 s.2(2)(a).

on certain rights related to copyright in the field of intellectual property.[30] Article 2 of the Directive requires the creation of a rental and lending right, but excludes from its ambit both buildings and works of applied art.[31] The rental and lending right has been implemented by the 1996 regulations through the insertion into the CPDA 1988 of a new s.18A; s.18A duly excludes from its ambit buildings and works of applied art and so does not appear to impinge on the field of industrial designs.[32]

9–018   The Directive also obliges member states to introduce a "distribution right".[33] The distribution right gives a right owner the exclusive right to make copies of his work, or indeed the original itself,[34] available within the EEA. It is expressly provided that the distribution right shall not be exhausted within the Community except where the first sale *in the Community* is made by the rightholder or with his consent.[35] This provision is transposed into the wording of the purported amendment to s.18(2)(a) of the CDPA 1988 summarised above.[36] However, art.9 of the Directive provides only for the creation of the harmonised "distribution right" in relation to a very limited category of works, none of them particularly relevant to the field of industrial design. These are performers' rights in fixations of their performances, sound recordings, films and fixations of broadcasts.[37] On the other hand, the purported amendment to s.18 in the 1996 Regulation extends to all categories of copyright works, not just this very limited class. To the extent that the amendment purportedly made by the 1996 Regulations extends beyond the limited classes of works specified in art.9 of the Directive, the Regulations are not made in pursuance of a Community obligation of the United Kingdom, and accordingly appear to fall outside the vires of s.2(2)(a) of the European Communities Act 1972. Section 2(2)(b) confers a wider power to make provision by regulations for the "purpose of dealing with matters arising out of or related to any such obligation". Whilst clearly there is some margin of discretion given to ministers in framing regulations whose purpose is to transpose a Directive into domestic law to deal with matters "arising out of or related to" the obligation imposed by the Directive, it is hard to see any justification for making a wholesale change to substantive copyright law as laid down in primary legislation because of a Community obligation only to amend the law relating to a very limited class of works. Whilst s.2(2)(b) has been broadly construed in obiter dicta by two members of the Court of Appeal,[38] it is still difficult to

---

[30] Directive 92/100 [1992] O.J. L346/61.

[31] Directive 92/100 [1992] O.J. L346/61 art.2(3).

[32] And hence new s.18A has not been included amongst the extracts from CDPA Pt I in App.D1 to this work.

[33] Article 9.

[34] Article 9(1).

[35] Article 9(2).

[36] In para.9–016 above.

[37] Article 9(1).

[38] *Oakley Inc v Animal Ltd* [2005] EWCA 1191; [2006] R.P.C. 9, CA. See para.2–004 above.

see how this wholesale change to the law can be reasonably justified as "arising out of or related to" the very limited changes to UK law required to be made in order to implement the distribution right. It should be noted that the question of the lawfulness or otherwise of the purported amendment to s.18 contained in the 1996 Regulations is a matter of British domestic law and not of Community law.[39]

2. Competition Law Affecting Designs

Competition law and designs

A general survey of competition law, whether that arising under arts 101 and 102 TFEU (formerly arts 81 and 82 EC) or under the Competition Act 1998, is outside the scope of this work; specialist works on those subjects should be consulted. This work, however, will deal with some special points with specific reference to designs. **9–019**

Licences of right imposed in monopolies cases

There are provisions enabling copyrights[40] and unregistered design rights,[41] to be subjected to a regime of licences of right upon the recommendation of the Monopolies and Mergers Commission where a right owner unreasonably refuses to grant licences on reasonable terms, or imposes unreasonable restrictions on the use of the design by the licensee, and these matters are considered to be operated against the public interest. Similar provisions also existed in relation to registered designs, but these powers have been reduced to more limited powers to cancel anti-competitive conditions within licences and the former powers to impose licences of right have been repealed for fear that they would contravene the Designs Directive.[42] **9–020**

When it is ordered that copyrights or unregistered design rights become subject to "licences of right" in this way, the procedure for settlement of the terms of individual licences is the same as that applying to design rights and transitional copyrights in their last five years of life.[43] **9–021**

---

[39] R. (Orange Personal Communications Ltd) v Secretary of State for Trade and Industry [2001] 3 C.M.L.R. 781, Sullivan J.
[40] CDPA 1988 s.144.
[41] CDPA 1988 s.238.
[42] RDA(E) s.11A; compare it with RDA(A) s.11A which did permit the imposition of licences of right. The repeal was carried out by the 2001 Regulations reg.6(2).
[43] See para.8–003 above.

CHAPTER 10

PROTECTION OF SEMICONDUCTOR TOPOGRAPHIES

Contents   *Para.*

1. Protection of Semiconductor Topographies

The protection of semiconductor topographies

10–001 Semiconductor topography designs are protected as a special category, since they are required to be protected by the Treaty on Intellectual Property in Respect of Integrated Circuits.[1] The EEC adhered to this Treaty and member states were directed to comply with its terms by a Community Directive.[2] In the United Kingdom, the required changes to domestic law were made by regulations under the European Communities Act 1972. That Act permits regulations made under it, even to amend Acts of Parliament, if this is done in compliance with obligations arising under Community law. Thus, amendments have been made to an Act of Parliament, the CDPA 1988, and a new variant of intellectual property right has been created, in the field of semiconductor designs without the need for any primary legislation.

10–002 The regulations concerned are the Design Right (Semiconductor Topographies) Regulations 1989.[3] According to general principles of construction, these regulations should be interpreted in the light of the Treaty and the Directive which they are seeking to implement. The method which the regulations use to provide protection to semiconductor topographies in the United Kingdom is effectively to "bolt on" these rights to the unregistered design right created by Pt III of the CDPA 1988, subject to certain specific (and important) differences. The following paragraphs

---

[1] See App.F3, below. Compliance with this Treaty is now an obligation under TRIPs art.3(1).

[2] Protection of Topography Directive 87/54/EEC at App.C4 below.

[3] SI 1989/1100, as amended; see App.C4 below.

will therefore look at the specific features in respect of which semi-conductor topography protection differs from ordinary unregistered design right protection.

Principal features of the semiconductor topography right

The semiconductor topography right possesses the fundamental features of the ordinary unregistered design right, in that it is an unregistered right which protects against copying rather than conferring a monopoly. The principal respects in which it differs from ordinary unregistered design right are: **10–003**

(1) there is a special definition of what constitutes a design for this purpose, which takes account of the specific characteristics of semiconductor designs;
(2) it has the same term of protection as unregistered design right (normally 10 years from first marketing) but there is no provision for "licences of right" during the last five years of the term;
(3) the national qualifications for subsistence of the right are far wider than in the case of ordinary design right. In particular, semiconductor designs originating in the USA and Japan, both major sources of semiconductor designs, are protected.

Definition of semiconductor topography design

Regulation 2(1)[4] defines semiconductors and their topographies as fol-lows: **10–004**

" 'semiconductor product' means an article the purpose, or one of the purposes, of which is the performance of an electronic function and which consists of two or more layers, at least one of which is composed of semiconducting material and in or upon one or more of which is a pattern appertaining to that or another function.

'Semiconductor topography' means a design within the meaning of section 213(2) of the Act which is a design of either of the fol-lowing—

(a) the pattern fixed, or intended to be fixed, in or upon—

(i) a layer of a semiconductor product or
(ii) a layer of material in the course of and for the purpose of the manufacture of a semiconductor product, or

---

[4] Of the Design Right (Semiconductor Topographies) Regulations 1989 (SI 1989/1100), App.C6 below.

(b) the arrangement of the patterns fixed, or intended to be fixed, in or upon the layers of a semiconductor product in relation to one another."

10–005   A few features of these definitions are worth noting.

A pattern "in or upon" a semiconductor layer

10–006   The definitions refer to patterns which can exist either "in" or "upon" a semiconductor layer. The concept of a pattern which is "upon" a semiconductor layer presents little difficulty. The manufacture of semiconductor devices will frequently involve the laying down of a pattern of metal conductors on the surface of the actual semiconductor chip to convey current between the semiconductor devices themselves, and between those devices and the integrated circuit's external pins. Such a pattern laid down on a surface is no different in principle from (although on a smaller physical scale than) a printed circuit board; and it is suggested that the layout of a printed circuit board does fall within the definition of "design" for the purposes of the ordinary unregistered design right.[5]

10–007   However, a slightly more difficult point arises from the reference to patterns which are "in", as distinct from "upon", a semiconductor layer. The manufacture of semiconductor devices generally involves the "doping" of regions of a crystal substrate with small amounts of impurities which create an excess of electrons (negative charges) or of "holes" (positive charges). These regions do not exist in the sense of a physical shape of an article which can be seen and touched: rather, there is a configuration of different regions within a single physical article between which there are slight differences of material: rather like light and dark woods forming a marquetry pattern. The definition in the Regulations assumes that such a configuration of internal materials, not existing as an external tangible shape, is as aspect of the "shape or configuration" of an article: this is implicit in the reference to a pattern fixed "in" the layer. This is not an obvious conclusion in the context of the general definition of what constitutes a design for "ordinary" design right purposes.[6] Whether or not the draftsman of the 1989 Regulations was correct in the assumption that a pattern existing only inside an object and consisting of differences of material between regions is a "design" for general unregistered design right purpose, the effect of the Regulation must be to deem such a thing to be a design in the semiconductor context.

---

[5] See para.4–029 above.
[6] See paras 4–003 and 4–029 above.

Other aspects of the definitions

The definition embraces both the essentially two-dimensional pattern   **10–008**
placed in or upon the semiconductor itself, and also (in sub-para.(a)(ii))
such patterns when embodied in such objects as masks which are used in
the course of semiconductor manufacture. To the extent that essentially
two-dimensional patterns are excluded from the scope of ordinary design
right,[7] such exclusion must be taken as implicitly overridden by the
Regulations in the case of semiconductor designs.

Sub-paragraph (b) makes clear that this special design right also covers   **10–009**
the inter-relationship (essentially in three dimensions) of the successive
two-dimensional patterns that are applied in the course of manufacture of
a semiconductor. For example, a first mask may be applied, through
which is doped a pattern of material giving rise to excess electrons (an N
layer) which is allowed to go quite deeply into the chip; thereafter
another dope is applied through a different mask giving rise to a P layer,
which is not as deep. The depths and relationships of the P and N layers
within the chip, as well as their relationship with any pattern of surface
conductors which are applied to it, are covered by this special type of
design right.

Special rules for qualification

Regulation 4(2) as amended[8] considerably widens the class of persons by   **10–010**
reference to whose national origins semiconductor designs qualify for
design right protection, as compared with ordinary designs.[9] The
amended Schedule to the Regulations[10] contains a list of qualifying
countries outside the European Union and European Economic Area
which includes industrially important countries such as the United
States, Japan, China, Australia and Canada. In addition, a modification is
made to the operation of the qualification rules. In the case of ordinary
designs which are created in the course of employment or under a
commission, the national qualification rules are applied by reference to
the national connections of the employer or commissioner, rather than in
those of the designer.[11] In the case of semiconductor designs, this rule is
disapplied and the national qualification rules are always applied by

---

[7] Because they are not features of "shape or configuration" (para.4–003 above), or because
they are explicitly excluded as "surface decoration"; see para.4–029 above.
[8] A new version of reg.4(2) was substituted by the Design Right (Semiconductor
Topographies) (Amendment) Regulations 2006 (SI 2006/1833) which inserted a list of
qualifying countries as the Schedule to the 1989 Regulations.
[9] The national qualification rules for unregistered design right are very restrictive, with
only a very few countries outside the EU ranking for this purpose: see para.4–061
above.
[10] See App.C4 below.
[11] See para.4–055 above.

reference to the designer, rather than an employer or commissioner.[12] A special extended rule applies to designs that do not qualify for design right on first creation, but qualify by first marketing in a correct country.[13]

First ownership of design right

10–011   The rules relating to first ownership of design right[14] are varied in the case of semiconductor designs by explicitly allowing the rules vesting design right in the employer or commissioner of the design to be excluded by agreement in writing to the contrary.[15]

Duration of design right in semiconductors

10–012   The duration of the design right in a semiconductor in most cases will be the same as that in an ordinary design, that is the end of the calendar 10 years after articles to the design are first marketed.[16] However, where a design is made and then sat on for a period before first marketing, the term appears to be different. With ordinary designs, the term is limited to 15 years after the design is first recorded or embodied, so that if the owner sits on the design for longer than five years, he cuts down his effective commercial period of protection by a corresponding amount.[17] With semiconductor designs, the effect of sitting on the design is different. If the owner fails to market designs for the 15-year period, his design right expires. However, if he manages to market the topography itself or articles made to it before the 15-year period has expired, he then enjoys the further 10 years from first marketing.[18] Thus, if he first markets articles 14 years after he first created the design, it appears he enjoys semiconductor design right for a further 10 years, i.e. a total of 24 years from first creation. If it had been an ordinary design, the right would have expired one year after first marketing in those circumstances.

10–013   In applying these rules as to term of protection, special rules apply to cases where articles are sold subject to obligations of confidence, with obligations of confidence imposed at the request of a government for the protection of security in connection with the production of arms falling into a special category.[19]

10–014   Semiconductor designs are excluded from the "licences of right" provisions which apply to ordinary unregistered designs,[20] so that the

---

[12] This is the effect of reg.4(3)
[13] See para.4–065 above; cf. the effect of reg.4(4) in the case of semiconductor designs.
[14] As to which, see paras 4–104 to 4–114 above.
[15] Regulation 5.
[16] CDPA 1988 s.216(1)(b); as effectively restated by regs 6(1) and 216(a).
[17] CDPA 1988 s.216(1)(b); see para.4–131 above.
[18] This appears to be the effect of CDPA 1988 s.216(b) as re-worded by reg.6(1).
[19] Regulation 7.
[20] Regulation 9.

owner of a semiconductor design will enjoy a full monopoly period of 10 years from first marketing, rather than the five years of monopoly which is effectively enjoyed by ordinary unregistered designs.[21]

Special rules applying to infringement of semiconductor designs

The regulations modify the ordinary rules of infringement of unregis- **10–015** tered design right, by applying a special exclusion intended to permit "reverse engineering". Regulation 8(1) inserts a new subsection 226(1A)(b) which excludes from infringement:

"(b) the reproduction of a design for the purpose of analysing or evaluating the design, or analysing, evaluating or teaching the concepts, processes, systems or techniques embodied in it."

It is also provided[22] that: **10–016**

"(4) It is not an infringement of the design right in a semiconductor topography to—

(a) create another original semiconductor topography as a result of an analysis or evaluation of the first topography or of the concepts, processes, systems or techniques embodied in it, or

(b) reproduce that other topography."

This interesting provision probably does no more than the existing **10–017** exclusion of "methods or principles of construction" from ordinary design right.[23] It is also reminiscent of the principle long recognised in copyright law that copyright does not protect ideas as such, but merely the form in which they are expressed.[24]

There is a special "exhaustion of rights" provision which is relevant to **10–018** parallel imports from EU member states.[25] Design documents are treated as infringing articles in the same way as actual articles made to the design.[26] The infringement provisions explicitly apply to a substantial part of the topography in the same way as to the topography as a whole.[27]

---

[21] See para.4–133 above.

[22] By reg.8(1), inserting a subs.226(4) into the CDPA 1988 for this purpose.

[23] For discussion of the effect of this, see para.4–011 above.

[24] For discussion of this, see para.5–131 above.

[25] Regulation 8(1) inserted subs.226(2) although it seems to do no more than restate the rules applying under TFEU arts 34 to 36. For these rules, applicable to free movement of goods within the EEA, see para.9–001 above.

[26] Regulation 8(3): this affects secondary dealers with such design documents.

[27] Regulation 8(5): this provision is probably unnecessary having regard to the nature of design right: see para.4–095 above.

CHAPTER 11

COUNTRIES WITH HISTORICAL CONNECTIONS WITH UK REGISTERED DESIGNS

11–001 This Chapter outlines the registered designs laws of a number of countries whose law is historically linked to the registered designs law of the United Kingdom. It is hoped that this will assist the reader in cross-relating the laws of these countries to the appropriate parts of the earlier Chapters of this book which deal with the corresponding current or past laws of the United Kingdom and the case law which illustrates and explains it.

1. Australia

Historical

11–002 Registered designs law in Australia is now governed by the Designs Act 2003 (Cth) which came into force on June 17, 2004. It replaced the Designs Act 1906 (Cth). The 1906 Act survived for nearly 100 years, although not without extensive amendments in the course of its life. The definition of "design" in s.4(1) of the Designs Act 1906 Act (Cth) revealed its obvious ancestry in UK legislation, although with a significant difference:

> " 'design' means features of shape, configuration, pattern or ornamentation applicable to an article, being features that, in the finished article, can be judged by the eye, but does not include a method or principle of construction."

11–003 It should be noted that under this definition, the design was required to be "judged by" the eye. But in contrast to the definition of design in e.g. s.1(1) of RDA 1949 (UK),[1] there was no requirement that the design must "appeal to" the eye, nor any exclusion of features of shape or configuration which are dictated by function. These differences from UK law were

---

[1] Appendix A5–001 below.

the result of a deliberate policy in Australia of extending protection to functional designs: s.18(1) of the Designs Act 1906 (Cth) provided that a design would not be invalid "by reason only that the design consists of, or includes, features of shape or configuration that serve, or serve only, a functional purpose."

The test for infringement under the 1906 Act was "fraudulent or obvious imitation"[2]: this is the same as the old test under the law of the United Kingdom before the RDA 1949.[3] This test of infringement was applied narrowly by the Australian courts.[4] It continues to be the test of infringement in relation to designs granted under the 1906 Act.[5] For a design to be a "fraudulent imitation", it is necessary that the application of the design be with knowledge of the existence of the registration and the absence of consent to use, or at least with reason to suspect those matters,[6] but this requirement need not be satisfied for a finding that something is an "obvious imitation".[7]

11–004

Apart from the general antiquity of the law still based on an Act passed in 1906, it was felt that registered designs in Australia were too easy to obtain but that, once obtained, their scope of protection was too narrow.[8] Hence the Designs Act 2003 (Cth) re-cast both the definition of "design", and the linked tests of validity over the prior art and of infringement. It is obvious from looking at the 2003 Act that it has drawn fairly heavily on the terminology of the new EU harmonised registered designs law so that, for example, designs are applied to "products" rather than (as under the previous Australian law), to "articles"; the test of validity is that the design is "new and distinctive"[9]; and "complex products"[10] and the "informed user"[11] make their appearances.

11–005

---

[2] The Designs Act 1906 (Cth) s.30(1).

[3] The Patents and Designs Act 1907 and 1919 s.60(1), App A7–004 below, and see para.3–185 above for the "fraudulent or obvious imitation" test under UK law and how it compares with the subsequent "not substantially different" test under RDA 1949 (UK).

[4] *Firmagroup Australia Pty Ltd v Byrne and Davidson Doors (Vic) Pty Ltd* (1987) 180 C.L.R. 483; *Dart Industries Inc v Décor Corporation Pty Ltd* (1989) 15 I.P.R. 403, Fed Ct Gen Div: despite "obvious similarities", there were "distinct and perceptible differences" such that it was plain that there was no infringement under s.30(1).

[5] *Technicon Industries Pty Ltd v Caroma Industries Ltd* (2009) 81 I.P.R. 465. The Full Court of the Federal Court upheld the primary judge's finding that the appellant's lavatory pan amounted to a "fraudulent imitation" of the registered design since the limited differences were merely there to disguise the copying.

[6] *Polyaire Pty Ltd v K-Aire Pty Ltd* (2005) 221 C.L.R. 287; 216 A.L.R. 205; 64 I.P.R. 223; [2005] H.C.A. 32 at para.[17] of the judgment of the High Court of Australia.

[7] *Chiropedic Bedding v Radburg* (2010) 83 I.P.R. 275, where it was held that the design was not a fraudulent imitation because the alleged infringer lacked such knowledge but was still an obvious imitation.

[8] Australian Law Reform Commission, "Designs" (1995), Report No.74.

[9] The Designs Act 2003 (Cth) s.15; under EU harmonised law, the design must be "new" and have "individual character": see para.2–034 above.

[10] Section 5 defines "complex product" as "a product comprising at least two replaceable component parts permitting disassembly and re-assembly of the product." Cf. "complex products" and their component parts under EU harmonised design law at paras 2–051 et seq. above.

[11] See further below.

Definition of design

11–006 Section 5 of the 2003 Act provides that "design", in relation to a product, means the overall appearance of the product resulting from one or more visual features of the product. A "visual feature" is defined[12] as including "the shape, configuration, pattern and ornamentation of the product." A visual feature may, but need not, serve a functional purpose.[13] Whilst lacking a comprehensive inclusive definition of what counts as a visual feature, the Australian Act (unusually for designs legislation) contains a non-exhaustive list of things which do not count as visual features of a product, namely the feel of the product,[14] and the materials used in the product.[15]

11–007 A "product" is a "thing that is manufactured or hand made".[16] A component part of a "complex product"[17] may be a product, if it is made separately from the product.[18]

Validity over prior art

11–008 Section 15 of the 2003 Act provides that a design is registrable if it is "new and distinctive" when compared with the "prior art base". This consists of designs publicly used within Australia, designs published in a document within or outside Australia,[19] and prior conflicting design applications. A design is "new" unless it is identical to a design that forms part of the prior art base for the design.[20] A design is "distinctive" unless it is "substantially similar in overall impression" to a prior art design.[21] The design in question is assessed for this purpose against each design in the

[12] Section 7(1).
[13] Section 7(2).
[14] Section 7(1)(3).
[15] Section 7(3)(b). Contrast the EU harmonised definition of "design", quoted at para.2–017 above, which explicitly includes the appearance resulting from, in particular, the " . . . texture and/or materials of the product". There is a distinction between the use of materials as such, and the distinctive appearance which the use of some materials gives to a product: see para.2–019 above, and fn.44. A question raised by this provision of the Australian Act is whether it goes as far as excluding from design protection the *appearance resulting from* the use of a particular material.
[16] Section 6(3).
[17] Defined by s.5 as "a product comprising at least 2 replaceable component parts permitting disassembly and re-assembly of the product."
[18] Section 6(2).
[19] Thus, designs used on a product outside Australia but not published in a document do not count. However, as long as the design is published in a document, there seems to be no requirement that the document should be likely to find its way to Australia. Cf. the EU harmonised test of what counts as prior art, which excludes matters which "could not reasonably have become known in the normal course of business to the circles specialised in the sector concerned, operating within the Community": see paras 2–072 to 2–074 above.
[20] Section 16(1).
[21] Section 16(2). Under the EU harmonised test, a design has "individual character" if the overall impression it produces on the informed user differs from the overall impression produced by the prior art design (see para.2–034 above). The Australian test is verbally

prior art base individually, and not by combining together features from various different items of prior art.[22] Like the EU approach, overall impression is assessed though the eyes of the "informed user",[23] and having regard to the freedom of the creator of the design to innovate.[24] But the Australian Act also contains as general requirement that the person making the comparison between the two designs "is to give more weight to similarities between the designs than to differences between them."[25] The precise effect of this provision is unclear, but it is presumably intended to push Australian law further towards a very high threshold of difference from the prior art before a new design can validly be registered, with a correspondingly wide scope of protection when it comes to infringement.[26]

A further feature of Australian law is that if the applicant files a **11–009** "statement of newness and distinctiveness" which identifies certain visual features of the design, particular regard is paid to those features although still in the context of the design as a whole.[27] The effect of this "statement of newness and distinctiveness" is therefore very similar to the effect of the "statement of novelty" which was sometimes used under pre-harmonised UK law despite lacking a firm statutory basis or any statutory statement of its legal effect.[28] The "statement of novelty" which could be filed under the Designs Act 1906 (Cth) had a similar effect.[29]

---

harder to satisfy because a design will be unregistrable if it is merely *similar* in overall impression to a prior art design, whereas the EU test requires that the overall impression be *the same*. Whether this verbal difference will lead to a real difference in approach in applying the two tests is harder to tell.

[22] *LED Technologies v Elecspess* (2009) 80 I.P.R. 85.

[23] Section 19(4), which defines the standard of the "informed user" as "the standard of a person who is familiar with the product to which the design relates, or products similar to the product to which the design relates". The Australian Law Commission Report which led to the 2003 Act based the concept of the informed user on the EC's then proposed Designs Regulation (para.5.18). From *Review 2 v Redberry Enterprise* (2009) 79 I.P.R. 214, *Review Australia Pty Ltd v New Cover Group Pty Ltd* (2009) 79 I.P.R. 236 and *LED Technologies v Elecspess* (2009) 80 I.P.R. 85, it appears that the Australian "informed user" as envisaged by the courts is indeed very similar in characteristics to the "informed user" under EU harmonised law and the English case of *Woodhouse UK PLC v Architectural Lighting Systems* [2005] EWPCC (Designs) 25; [2006] R.P.C. 1, PCC (Judge Fysh Q.C.) was cited in these cases.

[24] Section 19(2)(d); the corresponding EU test requires that "the degree of freedom of the designer in developing the design shall be taken into consideration": see para.2–034 above.

[25] Section 16(1).

[26] See further below.

[27] Section 19(2)(b).

[28] The UK statement of novelty was recognised in rules but not in the RDA 1949 or in any previous statute. For a description of its history and effects, see paras 3–253 et seq. above.

[29] *Chiropedic Bedding v Radburg* (2010) 83 I.P.R. 275, where Jessup J. extensively analysed the Australian and British authorities on the effects of a statement of novelty for the purpose of determining its effects under the 1906 Act which still applied to the validity and infringement of the design in suit. At [22] he concluded, drawing in part on the view expressed in para.3–284 of the 7th edition of this book (now para.3–258 above of this

Test of infringement

11–010   The test for infringement mirrors the test for validity, in that a registration is infringed by a product which "embodies a design that is identical to, or substantially similar in overall impression to, the registered design".[30] However, like the previous UK law but unlike the EU harmonised law, an Australian registered design is only infringed when such a design is embodied in a product in relation to which the design is registered.[31] Where a design is embodied in a product with the licence or authority of the registered owner, it is not an infringement to import that product into Australia.[32]

Other features

11–011   As has been mentioned in the Chapter on the EU harmonised system,[33] designs are registered without examination as to substantive validity. In this respect, the harmonised EU system represented a departure from the previous UK system under which applications for design registration were substantively examined for validity against the prior art. The examination of UK national applications for substantive validity was abandoned largely because it was untenable to maintain substantive examination when a parallel application for registration could be made to OHIM for a Community registered design which would bypass this safeguard. Thus, manifestly invalid registered designs can easily be registered and the registrations can then be used vexatiously to interfere with the activities of competitors.

11–012   In Australia, the Designs Act 2003 (Cth) creates a system which is an interesting hybrid between systems of design registration with and without substantive examination. Designs are initially placed on the

---

edition), that the court's eyes "would be open to the complete design" but "should, in my view, assess that design against the prior art with a particular emphasis upon those features that the registered owner himself or herself, at the point of registration, considered to be novel".

[30] Section 71(1). It appears that the approach in Australia is strictly to compare the alleged infringing product to the representation of the design on the register, and a comparison with the product in which the registered design has been commercialised should not play any formal part in this process: *LED Technologies v Elecspess* (2009) 80 I.P.R. 85, departing in this respect from the approach of Jacob L.J. in *Procter & Gamble Co v Reckitt Benckiser (UK) Ltd* [2007] EWCA Civ 936; [2008] F.S.R. 8, and following *Review 2; Review Australia Pty Ltd v Innovative Lifestyle Investments Pty Ltd* (2008) 166 F.C.R. 358; 246 A.L.R. 119; 75 I.P.R. 289; [2008] F.C.A. 74.

[31] Section 71(1)(a); by contrast, under EU harmonised designs law a design right will be infringed if a sufficiently close design is applied to *any* product: see para.2–084 above.

[32] Section 71(2). In this respect the law of Australia differs from EU law, which makes it an infringement to import the design right owner's own product from outside the EEA unless the design right owner has consented to that product being placed on the market inside the EEA: see para.9–007 above.

[33] Paragraph 2–143 above; now UK IP Office practice has been brought into line: see para.2–123 above.

register without substantive examination for validity. However, unlike the EU system, these registered designs cannot be enforced unless and until they have been examined.[34] Examination can be requested at any time by the owner of the registered design or by anyone else.[35] Upon examination, the Registrar will either uphold the design's validity and issue a certificate of examination,[36] possibly after a validating amendment,[37] or find it invalid and revoke it.[38] Whether this system is effective to prevent commercial uncertainty and damage arising from the abusive registration of manifestly invalid designs must depend upon the speed and effectiveness of the on-request examination process. A threat to bring infringement proceedings in relation to a registered design which has not yet been examined is automatically treated as unjustified for the purposes of the "threats" provisions of the Act.[39]

2. Hong Kong

Registered Designs in Hong Kong are protected under the Registered Designs Ordinance—Chapter 522. This was made in 1997 to replace the previous United Kingdom Designs (Protection) Ordinance under which there was a system for derivative protection in Hong Kong for designs registered in the United Kingdom. The 1997 Ordinance created a system of design registration in Hong Kong that is free-standing from the UK system. **11–013**

However, most of the substantive provisions of the 1997 Ordinance are closely modelled on the registered design legislation then in force in the United Kingdom—namely the RDA(A) before it was amended in order to conform to the new EU harmonised system. Thus, the definition of "design" under the Ordinance[40] is word-for-word identical to the definition in RDA(A) s.1(1).[41] Like the RDA(A) (UK), the Hong Kong Ordinance provides that a design must be "new" in order to be registrable,[42] and a design shall not be regarded as new if it differs from a prior design only in immaterial details or in features which are variants commonly used in the trade.[43] The test of infringement is the "not substantially different" test,[44] the same as that under RDA(A) (UK).[45] **11–014**

---

[34] Section 73(3).
[35] Section 63(1).
[36] Section 67.
[37] Section 66.
[38] Section 68.
[39] Section 77(3); the "threats" provisions of the Designs Act 2003 (Cth) are broadly similar to the threats provisions under UK law: see Ch.7 above.
[40] Section 1(1).
[41] See App A5–001 below.
[42] Section 5(1); cf. RDA(A) s.1(2).
[43] Section 5(2); cf. RDA(A) s.1(4).
[44] Section 31(1).
[45] RDA(A) s.7(1), App A5–007 below; for an extensive discussion of this test under the pre-EU UK law, see paras 3–184 et seq. above.

11–015   The Hong Kong Registry does not conduct a substantive examination of validity, and designs are registered after an examination for formalities only.

3. India

History

11–016   In India, the Designs Act 2000 repealed and replaced the Designs Act 1911. The Designs Act 2000 aimed to modernise India's registered design law and to bring it into conformity with modern international standards. However its key provisions remain modelled on UK registered design law.

Definition of "design" and conditions for registrability

11–017   The definition of "design" in s.2(d) is in substance identical to the definition introduced into UK law by the Patents and Designs Act 1919.[46] To be registrable a design must be "new or original",[47] the same requirement as existed under UK law until the amendments made by the CDPA 1988.[48] The courts of India have tended to follow the English authorities on its interpretation[49]:

> "A large body of case law has been built up during the years, to explain what is meant by 'novelty and originality'. As the English law on the subject is almost the same as in India, the English cases are also a great help in determining the principles to be applied. In fact there are very few Indian decisions on the subject. Generally, the test for novelty and originality is dependent on determining the type of mental activity involved in conceiving the design in question. If the design is original, then the designer must have conceived something new; if the design is a mere trade variation of a previous design then the designer could be said to have merely kept an existing design in view and made some changes in it."

11–018   Novelty is assessed with respect to the *class* of articles to which the article sought to be registered belongs.[50]

11–019   But, unlike the pre-1949 UK legislation, the Designs Act 2000 (India) also imposes three additional requirements for registrability over and

---

[46] See App A7–005 below.

[47] Section 4(a).

[48] In the UK, the CDPA 1988 deleted the words "or original" from the phrase "new or original": see paras 3–160 et seq. above.

[49] *Western Engineering Company v America Lock Company 2nd* (1973) II Delhi 178, a case under the Designs Act, 1911 (India).

[50] This arises from the definition of "copyright" in the registered design under s.2(c), which is "the exclusive right to apply a design to any article in any class in which the design is registered". In this respect, the Designs Act 2000 (India) follows the law of the UK before

above the basic requirement that the design shall be "new or original". These additional requirements are:

- that the design has not has been disclosed to the public anywhere in India or in any other country by publication in tangible form or by use or in any other way prior to the filing or priority date.[51] It is not clear what this requirement imposes above and beyond the requirement that the design be "new or original", apart from making it clear that worldwide prior art is available as a bar to registration and not just prior art from within India. What counts as disclosure to the public is interpreted in the same way as under the law of the United Kingdom, i.e. disclosure even to a single person who not under a legal obligation to keep it secret amounts to a disclosure to the public,[52] a case under the Designs Act 1911 (India) in which the Delhi High Court adopted as representing Indian law the relevant passages at pp.41–42 of the 4th edition of this work.[53] This provision has been interpreted as requiring, in the case of a paper publication, not mere publication of the abstract shape of the design but also that the design is disclosed as being applied to the same kind of article as the article in respect of which the design is registered[54];
- that the design is "significantly distinguishable from known designs or combination of known designs".[55] The phrase "sufficiently distinguishable" is not defined elsewhere in the Act and it is open to doubt whether and to what extent it adds anything to the "new or original" test. It has always been the case under UK law that slight variations in design or changes in "immaterial details" do not give rise to a new validly registrable design,[56] and this approach to "new and original" was followed in India under the previous Designs Act 1911.[57] On the other hand, the exclusion from registrability of a design based on a "combination of known designs" may reflect a substantial departure from UK law, under which it has always been the case that the combination of two or

---

the RDA 1949, under which validity was assessed against prior art falling within the class of articles containing the article in respect of which the design was sought to be registered, and the right conferred by registration extended to the use of the design on any articles falling within that class: see paras 3–162 and 3–163 above.

[51] Section 4(b).

[52] *Wimco Ltd, Bombay v Meena Match Industries, Sivakasi & Other* [1983] (3) P.T.C. 373 (Del.)

[53] See now paras 3–129 to 3–130 above.

[54] *Dart Industries Inc. v Techno Plast and Ors* 2007 (35) P.T.C. 285 Del, citing *Gopal Glass Works Limited v Assistant Controller of Patents and Designs and Ors* 2006 (33) P.T.C. 434, Calcutta High Court.

[55] Section 4(c).

[56] See paras 3–151 et seq. above.

[57] *B Chawla & Sons v Bright Auto Industries* AIR 1981 Delhi 95, 19 (1981) D.L.T. 323, 1981 R.L.R. 373.

more old and well-known designs or parts of designs will constitute novelty, if the effect, i.e. the appearance of the combination as a whole, is new[58];

- that the design does not comprise or contain "scandalous or obscene matter."[59]

11–020   A design must be registered in respect of an article which is made and sold separately; like the pre-harmonised UK law but unlike under the EU harmonised law, a design for a part only of an article or product cannot be validly registered.[60]

Infringement

11–021   The test of infringement under the Designs Act 2000 (India) is the use of the same design or a "fraudulent or obvious imitation" of it.[61] This is the same as the test under the law of the United Kingdom before the RDA 1949.[62] As has already been mentioned, the Designs Act 2000 (India) follows the pre-1949 UK law in allowing the owner of a registered design to sue in respect of use of designs on articles falling within the class in which the design is registered.[63]

4. Ireland

11–022   In Ireland, registered designs were protected under the Industrial and Commercial Property (Protection) Acts 1927 to 1958[64] until those Acts were replaced by the Industrial Designs Act 2001, which implemented the Designs Directive in Ireland. Accordingly, as would be expected, the substantive law relating to national registered designs in Ireland is very

---

[58] See paras 3–148 to 3–150 above.

[59] Section 4(d). Cf. RDA(A) (UK) s.43(1), under which the registrar was not authorised or required to register a design the use of which would in his opinion be contrary to law or morality: see para.2–045 above.

[60] *Glaxo Smithkline Consumer Healthcare GmbH v Amigo Brushes Pte Ltd* 109 (2004) D.L.T. 41, 2004 (28) P.T.C. 1 Del, at para.24: features of a toothbrush handle not in themselves registrable.

[61] Sections 22(1)(a) and (b).

[62] For the difference between the "fraudulent or obvious imitation" test under the pre-1949 law, and the "not substantially different" test under RDA 1949, see paras 3–185 and 3–210 above. For a more recent authority on the "fraudulent or obvious imitation" test, see the Australian case of *Dart Industries Inc v Décor Corporation Pty Ltd* (1989) 15 I.P.R. 403, Fed Ct Gen Div.

[63] Section 22(1)(a) and (b), and see para.3–162 above. Under the RDA 1949 (UK), infringement rights were narrowed to cover only use of the design on articles for which it was registered; and then under the EU harmonised law, infringement rights were expanded to cover use of the design (or a design having the same overall impression) on *any* product: see para.2–021 above.

[64] As would be expected, this legislation was closely modelled on the registered design law of the UK then in force, which was the Patents and Designs Acts 1907 and 1919 when the Irish 1927 Act was passed: see App.A7 below.

similar to the substantive law in the United Kingdom under the EU harmonised system.[65] In addition, Community registered and unregistered designs can be enforced in Ireland in the same way as in the United Kingdom.[66]

The transitional provisions of the 2001 Act state that a design which **11–023** stood registered on the day on which that Act came into force (which was July 1, 2002[67]):

> "shall continue to be registered under the Industrial and Commercial Property (Protection) Acts 1927 to 1958, and those Acts shall apply notwithstanding the coming into operation of this Act."[68]

This on the face of it purports to preserve the old law of infringement in respect of existing registered designs, contrary to the terms of the Transitional Provision in art.14 of the Directive[69] which only permits the retention of the old law on *validity* of existing designs, not the old law of infringement. It is possible that the Irish courts would construe the transitional provision in the 2001 Irish Act as only extending to matters of validity, consistently with their duty as courts of a Member State to interpret national legislation consistently with relevant EU legislation if it is possible to do so.[70]

5. New Zealand

In New Zealand, registered designs are protected under the Designs Act **11–024** 1953. The provisions of this Act are closely modelled on those of the UK legislation then in force, namely the RDA 1949 (UK) and the New Zealand Act does not reflect the substantial amendments which were made to the RDA 1949 by the Copyright Designs and Patents Act 1988 (UK).[71]

Thus, the definition of "design" in s.2(1) of the Designs Act 1953 (NZ) **11–025** is the same as that in s.1(3) of RDA 1949 (UK) before its amendment by the 1988 Act[72]; designs are registrable under s.5(2) of the Designs Act 1953

---

[65] Described in Ch.2 above.
[66] Because these rights derive from the Designs Regulation which is directly applicable within all Member States: see para.2–007 above. As regards enforcement of Community unregistered design right in Ireland, see *Karen Millen Ltd v Dunnes Stores Ltd* [2007] I.E.H.C. 449; [2008] E.C.D.R. 156, Irish High Ct (Finlay Geoghegan J.), at para.6–010 fn.48 and para.6–036 para.136, above.
[67] Industrial Designs Act 2001 (Commencement) Order 2002 (Irl).
[68] Industrial Designs Act 2001 (Irl) Sch.1, para.1.
[69] Appendix A1–015 below.
[70] Under Case C-106/89 *Marleasing SA v La Comercial Internacional de Alimentacion SA* [1990] E.C.R. I-4135; [1992] 1 C.M.L.R. 305, ECJ, and cases to similar effect: see para.2–005 above.
[71] See paras 3–296 to 3–301 above for the UK law relating to pre-1988 Act registered designs.
[72] Appendix A5–001 below.

(NZ) if they are "new or original", the same test at that under s.1(2) of the RDA 1949 (UK)[73]; the right conferred by registration is called (rather misleadingly[74]) the "copyright in the design" and is infringed by the application to any article in respect of which the design is registered of the same design or a "design not substantially different from" the registered design.[75]

11–026 Like under the pre-1988 Act UK law,[76] the maximum term of a registered design in New Zealand is 15 years from the date of application.[77] In New Zealand, registered design applications are subjected to substantive examination for validity,[78] a practice which has now been abandoned in respect of UK national registered design applications to conform with the practice of EU designs registry at OHIM.[79]

---

[73] Appendix A5–001 below.

[74] The use of the word "copyright" is misleading because copying is not a necessary ingredient of infringement: see para.3–165 above.

[75] The Designs Act 1953 s.11(1); same as RDA 1949 (UK) s.7(1). The "not substantially different" test did not change under the law of the UK between the pre-1988 Act and post-1988 Act law, and is explained at paras 3–164 et seq. above; a significant difference in the scope of infringing acts was the introduction via the 1988 Act of infringement by providing a kit of parts; this is not in the Designs Act 1953 (NZ) and in this respect it follows pre-1988 Act UK law: see para.3–300 above.

[76] See para.3–301 above.

[77] The Designs Act 1953 (NZ) s.12.

[78] The Designs Act 1953 (NZ) s.7(2).

[79] See para.2–130 above; as regards OHIM practice, see para.2–148 above.

Appendix A

UK REGISTERED DESIGNS

Contents   *Para.*

A1. Directive 98/71/EC of the European Parliament and of the Council of 13 October 1998 on the legal protection of designs

THE EUROPEAN PARLIAMENT AND THE COUNCIL OF THE EUROPEAN UNION,

Having regard to the Treaty establishing the European Community and in   **A1–001**
particular Article 100a thereof,
   Having regard to the proposal by the Commission,[1]
   Having regard to the opinion of the Economic and Social Committee,[2]
   Acting in accordance with the procedure laid down in Article 189b of the
Treaty,[3] in the light of the joint text approved by the Conciliation Committee on
29 July 1998,

[1] OJ C 345, 23. 12. 1993, p.14 and OJ C 142, 14. 5. 1996, p.7.
[2] OJ C 388, 31. 12. 1994, p.9 and OJ C 110, 2. 5. 1995, p.12.
[3] Opinion of the European Parliament of 12 October 1995 (OJ C 287, 30. 10. 1995, p.157),
   common position of the Council of 17 June 1997 (OJ C 237, 4. 8. 1997, p.1), Decision of the
   European Parliament of 22 October 1997 (OJ C 339, 10. 11. 1997, p.52). Decision of the
   European Parliament of 15 September 1998. Decision of the Council of 24 September
   1998.

(1) Whereas the objectives of the Community, as laid down in the Treaty, include laying the foundations of an ever closer union among the peoples of Europe, fostering closer relations between Member States of the Community, and ensuring the economic and social progress of the Community countries by common action to eliminate the barriers which divide Europe; whereas to that end the Treaty provides for the establishment of an internal market characterised by the abolition of obstacles to the free movement of goods and also for the institution of a system ensuring that competition in the internal market is not distorted; whereas an approximation of the laws of the Member States on the legal protection of designs would further those objectives;

(2) Whereas the differences in the legal protection of designs offered by the legislation of the Member States directly affect the establishment and functioning of the internal market as regards goods embodying designs; whereas such differences can distort competition within the internal market;

(3) Whereas it is therefore necessary for the smooth functioning of the internal market to approximate the design protection laws of the Member States;

(4) Whereas, in doing so, it is important to take into consideration the solutions and the advantages with which the Community design system will provide undertakings wishing to acquire design rights;

(5) Whereas it is unnecessary to undertake a full-scale approximation of the design laws of the Member States, and it will be sufficient if approximation is limited to those national provisions of law which most directly affect the functioning of the internal market; whereas provisions on sanctions, remedies and enforcement should be left to national law; whereas the objectives of this limited approximation cannot be sufficiently achieved by the Member States acting alone;

(6) Whereas Member States should accordingly remain free to fix the procedural provisions concerning registration, renewal and invalidation of design rights and provisions concerning the effects of such invalidity;

(7) Whereas this Directive does not exclude the application to designs of national or Community legislation providing for protection other than that conferred by registration or publication as design, such as legislation relating to unregistered design rights, trade marks, patents and utility models, unfair competition or civil liability;

(8) Whereas, in the absence of harmonisation of copyright law, it is important to establish the principle of cumulation of protection under specific registered design protection law and under copyright law, whilst leaving Member States free to establish the extent of copyright protection and the conditions under which such protection is conferred;

(9) Whereas the attainment of the objectives of the internal market requires that the conditions for obtaining a registered design right be identical in all the Member States; whereas to that end it is necessary to give a unitary definition of the notion of design and of the requirements as to novelty and individual character with which registered design rights must comply;

(10) Whereas it is essential, in order to facilitate the free movement of goods, to ensure in principle that registered design rights confer upon the right holder equivalent protection in all Member States;

(11) Whereas protection is conferred by way of registration upon the right holder for those design features of a product, in whole or in part, which are shown visibly in an application and made available to the public by way of publication or consultation of the relevant file;

(12) Whereas protection should not be extended to those component parts which are not visible during normal use of a product, or to those features of such part which are not visible when the part is mounted, or which would not, in themselves, fulfil the requirements as to novelty and individual character;

whereas features of design which are excluded from protection for these reasons should not be taken into consideration for the purpose of assessing whether other features of the design fulfil the requirements for protection;

(13) Whereas the assessment as to whether a design has individual character should be based on whether the overall impression produced on an informed user viewing the design clearly differs from that produced on him by the existing design corpus, taking into consideration the nature of the product to which the design is applied or in which it is incorporated, and in particular the industrial sector to which it belongs and the degree of freedom of the designer in developing the design;

(14) Whereas technological innovation should not be hampered by granting design protection to features dictated solely by a technical function; whereas it is understood that this does not entail that a design must have an aesthetic quality; whereas, likewise, the interoperability of products of different makes should not be hindered by extending protection to the design of mechanical fittings; whereas features of a design which are excluded from protection for these reasons should not be taken into consideration for the purpose of assessing whether other features of the design fulfil the requirements for protection;

(15) Whereas the mechanical fittings of modular products may nevertheless constitute an important element of the innovative characteristics of modular products and present a major marketing asset and therefore should be eligible for protection;

(16) Whereas a design right shall not subsist in a design which is contrary to public policy or to accepted principles of morality; whereas this Directive does not constitute a harmonisation of national concepts of public policy or accepted principles of morality;

(17) Whereas it is fundamental for the smooth functioning of the internal market to unify the term of protection afforded by registered design rights;

(18) Whereas the provisions of this Directive are without prejudice to the application of the competition rules under Articles 85 and 86 of the Treaty;

(19) Whereas the rapid adoption of this Directive has become a matter of urgency for a number of industrial sectors; whereas full-scale approximation of the laws of the Member States on the use of protected designs for the purpose of permitting the repair of a complex product so as to restore its original appearance, where the product incorporating the design or to which the design is applied constitutes a component part of a complex product upon whose appearance the protected design is dependent, cannot be introduced at the present stage; whereas the lack of full-scale approximation of the laws of the Member States on the use of protected designs for such repair of a complex product should not constitute an obstacle to the approximation of those other national provisions of design law which most directly affect the functioning of the internal market; whereas for this reason Member States should in the meantime maintain in force any provisions in conformity with the Treaty relating to the use of the design of a component part used for the purpose of the repair of a complex product so as to restore its original appearance, or, if they introduce any new provisions relating to such use, the purpose of these provisions should be only to liberalise the market in such parts; whereas those Member States which, on the date of entry into force of this Directive, do not provide for protection for designs of component parts are not required to introduce registration of designs for such parts; whereas three years after the implementation date the Commission should submit an analysis of the consequences of the provisions of this Directive for Community industry, for consumers, for competition and for the functioning of the internal market; whereas, in respect of component parts of complex products, the analysis should, in particular, consider harmonisation on the basis of possible options, including a remuneration system and a limited term of exclusivity; whereas, at the latest one

year after the submission of its analysis, the Commission should, after consultation with the parties most affected, propose to the European Parliament and the Council any changes to this Directive needed to complete the internal market in respect of component parts of complex products, and any other changes which it considers necessary;

(20) Whereas the transitional provision in Article 14 concerning the design of a component part used for the purpose of the repair of a complex product so as to restore its original appearance is in no case to be construed as constituting an obstacle to the free movement of a product which constitutes such a component part;

(21) Whereas the substantive grounds for refusal of registration in those Member States which provide for substantive examination of applications prior to registration, and the substantive grounds for the invalidation of registered design rights in all the Member States, must be exhaustively enumerated,

HAVE ADOPTED THIS DIRECTIVE:

Article 1

Definitions

A1–002   For the purpose of this Directive:

> (a) "design" means the appearance of the whole or a part of a product resulting from the features of, in particular, the lines, contours, colours, shape, texture and/or materials of the product itself and/or its ornamentation;
> (b) "product" means any industrial or handicraft item, including *inter alia* parts intended to be assembled into a complex product, packaging, get-up, graphic symbols and typographic typefaces, but excluding computer programs;
> (c) "complex product" means a product which is composed of multiple components which can be replaced permitting disassembly and reassembly of the product.

Article 2

Scope of application

A1–003   1. This Directive shall apply to:

> (a) design rights registered with the central industrial property offices of the Member States;
> (b) design rights registered at the Benelux Design Office;
> (c) design rights registered under international arrangements which have effect in a Member State;
> (d) applications for design rights referred to under (a), (b) and (c).

2. For the purpose of this Directive, design registration shall also comprise the publication following filing of the design with the industrial property office of a Member State in which such publication has the effect of bringing a design right into existence.

Article 3

Protection requirements

1. Member States shall protect designs by registration, and shall confer **A1–004** exclusive rights upon their holders in accordance with the provisions of this Directive.

2. A design shall be protected by a design right to the extent that it is new and has individual character.

3. A design applied to or incorporated in a product which constitutes a component part of a complex product shall only be considered to be new and to have individual character:

(a) if the component part, once it has been incorporated into the complex product, remains visible during normal use of the latter, and

(b) to the extent that those visible features of the component part fulfil in themselves the requirements as to novelty and individual character.

4. "Normal use" within the meaning of paragraph (3)(a) shall mean use by the end user, excluding maintenance, servicing or repair work.

Article 4

Novelty

A design shall be considered new if no identical design has been made **A1–005** available to the public before the date of filing of the application for registration or, if priority is claimed, the date of priority. Designs shall be deemed to be identical if their features differ only in immaterial details.

Article 5

Individual character

1. A design shall be considered to have individual character if the overall **A1–006** impression it produces on the informed user differs from the overall impression produced on such a user by any design which has been made available to the public before the date of filing of the application for registration or, if priority is claimed, the date of priority.

2. In assessing individual character, the degree of freedom of the designer in developing the design shall be taken into consideration.

Article 6

Disclosure

1. For the purpose of applying Articles 4 and 5, a design shall be deemed to **A1–007** have been made available to the public if it has been published following registration or otherwise, or exhibited, used in trade or otherwise disclosed, except where these events could not reasonably have become known in the normal course of business to the circles specialised in the sector concerned, operating within the Community, before the date of filing of the application for

417

registration or, if priority is claimed, the date of priority. The design shall not, however, be deemed to have been made available to the public for the sole reason that it has been disclosed to a third person under explicit or implicit conditions of confidentiality.

2. A disclosure shall not be taken into consideration for the purpose of applying Articles 4 and 5 if a design for which protection is claimed under a registered design right of a Member State has been made available to the public:

(a) by the designer, his successor in title, or a third person as a result of information provided or action taken by the designer, or his successor in title; and

(b) during the 12-month period preceding the date of filing of the application or, if priority is claimed, the date of priority.

3. Paragraph 2 shall also apply if the design has been made available to the public as a consequence of an abuse in relation to the designer or his successor in title.

Article 7

Designs dictated by their technical function and designs of interconnections

A1–008   1. A design right shall not subsist in features of appearance of a product which are solely dictated by its technical function.

2. A design right shall not subsist in features of appearance of a product which must necessarily be reproduced in their exact form and dimensions in order to permit the product in which the design is incorporated or to which it is applied to be mechanically connected to or placed in, around or against another product so that either product may perform its function.

3. Notwithstanding paragraph 2, a design right shall, under the conditions set out in Articles 4 and 5, subsist in a design serving the purpose of allowing multiple assembly or connection of mutually interchangeable products within a modular system.

Article 8

Designs contrary to public policy or morality

A1–009   A design right shall not subsist in a design which is contrary to public policy or to accepted principles of morality.

Article 9

Scope of protection

A1–010   1. The scope of the protection conferred by a design right shall include any design which does not produce on the informed user a different overall impression.

2. In assessing the scope of protection, the degree of freedom of the designer in developing his design shall be taken into consideration.

Article 10

Term of protection

Upon registration, a design which meets the requirements of Article 3(2) shall **A1–011** be protected by a design right for one or more periods of five years from the date of filing of the application. The right holder may have the term of protection renewed for one or more periods of five years each, up to a total term of 25 years from the date of filing.

Article 11

Invalidity or refusal of registration

1. A design shall be refused registration, or, if the design has been registered, **A1–012** the design right shall be declared invalid:

  (a) if the design is not a design within the meaning of Article 1(a); or
  (b) if it does not fulfil the requirements of Articles 3 to 8; or
  (c) if the applicant for or the holder of the design right is not entitled to it under the law of the Member State concerned; or
  (d) if the design is in conflict with a prior design which has been made available to the public after the date of filing of the application or, if priority is claimed, the date of priority, and which is protected from a date prior to the said date by a registered Community design or an application for a registered Community design or by a design right of the Member State concerned, or by an application for such a right.

2. Any Member State may provide that a design shall be refused registration, or, if the design has been registered, that the design right shall be declared invalid:

  (a) if a distinctive sign is used in a subsequent design, and Community law or the law of the Member State concerned governing that sign confers on the right holder of the sign the right to prohibit such use; or
  (b) if the design constitutes an unauthorised use of a work protected under the copyright law of the Member State concerned; or
  (c) if the design constitutes an improper use of any of the items listed in Article 6b of the Paris Convention for the Protection of Industrial Property, or of badges, emblems and escutcheons other than those covered by Article 6b of the said Convention which are of particular public interest in the Member State concerned.

3. The ground provided for in paragraph 1(c) may be invoked solely by the person who is entitled to the design right under the law of the Member State concerned.

4. The grounds provided for in paragraph 1(d) and in paragraph 2(a) and (b) may be invoked solely by the applicant for or the holder of the conflicting right.

5. The ground provided for in paragraph 2(c) may be invoked solely by the person or entity concerned by the use.

6. Paragraphs 4 and 5 shall be without prejudice to the freedom of Member States to provide that the grounds provided for in paragraphs 1(d) and 2(c) may also be invoked by the appropriate authority of the Member State in question on its own initiative.

7. When a design has been refused registration or a design right has been declared invalid pursuant to paragraph 1(b) or to paragraph 2, the design may be registered or the design right maintained in an amended form, if in that form it complies with the requirements for protection and the identity of the design is retained. Registration or maintenance in an amended form may include registration accompanied by a partial disclaimer by the holder of the design right or entry in the design Register of a court decision declaring the partial invalidity of the design right.

8. Any Member State may provide that, by way of derogation from paragraphs 1 to 7, the grounds for refusal of registration or for invalidation in force in that State prior to the date on which the provisions necessary to comply with this Directive enter into force shall apply to design applications which have been made prior to that date and to resulting registrations.

9. A design right may be declared invalid even after it has lapsed or has been surrendered.

Article 12

Rights conferred by the design right

A1–013   1. The registration of a design shall confer on its holder the exclusive right to use it and to prevent any third party not having his consent from using it. The aforementioned use shall cover, in particular, the making, offering, putting on the market, importing, exporting or using of a product in which the design is incorporated or to which it is applied, or stocking such a product for those purposes.

2. Where, under the law of a Member State, acts referred to in paragraph 1 could not be prevented before the date on which the provisions necessary to comply with this Directive entered into force, the rights conferred by the design right may not be invoked to prevent continuation of such acts by any person who had begun such acts prior to that date.

Article 13

Limitation of the rights conferred by the design right

A1–014   1. The rights conferred by a design right upon registration shall not be exercised in respect of:

(a) acts done privately and for non-commercial purposes;
(b) acts done for experimental purposes;
(c) acts of reproduction for the purposes of making citations or of teaching, provided that such acts are compatible with fair trade practice and do not unduly prejudice the normal exploitation of the design, and that mention is made of the source.

2. In addition, the rights conferred by a design right upon registration shall not be exercised in respect of:

(a) the equipment on ships and aircraft registered in another country when these temporarily enter the territory of the Member State concerned;
(b) the importation in the Member State concerned of spare parts and accessories for the purpose of repairing such craft;
(c) the execution of repairs on such craft.

Article 14

Transitional provision

Until such time as amendments to this Directive are adopted on a proposal **A1–015** from the Commission in accordance with the provisions of Article 18, Member States shall maintain in force their existing legal provisions relating to the use of the design of a component part used for the purpose of the repair of a complex product so as to restore its original appearance and shall introduce changes to those provisions only if the purpose is to liberalise the market for such parts.

Article 15

Exhaustion of rights

The rights conferred by a design right upon registration shall not extend to acts **A1–016** relating to a product in which a design included within the scope of protection of the design right is incorporated or to which it is applied, when the product has been put on the market in the Community by the holder of the design right or with his consent.

Article 16

Relationship to other forms of protection

The provisions of this Directive shall be without prejudice to any provisions of **A1–017** Community law or of the law of the Member State concerned relating to unregistered design rights, trade marks or other distinctive signs, patents and utility models, typefaces, civil liability or unfair competition.

Article 17

Relationship to copyright

A design protected by a design right registered in or in respect of a Member **A1–018** State in accordance with this Directive shall also be eligible for protection under the law of copyright of that State as from the date on which the design was created or fixed in any form. The extent to which, and the conditions under which, such a protection is conferred, including the level of originality required, shall be determined by each Member State.

Article 18

Revision

Three years after the implementation date specified in Article 19, the Commis- **A1–019** sion shall submit an analysis of the consequences of the provisions of this Directive for Community industry, in particular the industrial sectors which are most affected, particularly manufacturers of complex products and component parts, for consumers, for competition and for the functioning of the internal market. At the latest one year later the Commission shall propose to the European Parliament and the Council any changes to this Directive needed to complete the internal market in respect of component parts of complex products and any other changes which it considers necessary in light of its consultations with the parties most affected.

Article 19

Implementation

A1–020   1. Member States shall bring into force the laws, regulations or administrative provisions necessary to comply with this Directive not later than 28 October 2001.

When Member States adopt these provisions, they shall contain a reference to this Directive or shall be accompanied by such reference on the occasion of their official publication. The methods of making such reference shall be laid down by Member States.

2. Member States shall communicate to the Commission the provisions of national law which they adopt in the field governed by this Directive.

Article 20

Entry into force

A1–021   This Directive shall enter into force on the 20th day following its publication in the *Official Journal of the European Communities*.

Article 21

Addressees

A1–022   This Directive is addressed to the Member States.

Done at Luxembourg, 13 October 1998.

For the European Parliament	*For the Council*
The President	*The President*
J.M. GIL-ROBLES	C. EINEM

A2. The Registered Designs Act 1949 (current version, EU harmonised law)

Registration of designs

A2–001   **1.**—(1) A design may, subject to the following provisions of this Act, be registered under this Act on the making of an application for registration.

(2) In this Act "design" means the appearance of the whole or a part of a product resulting from the features of, in particular, the lines, contours, colours, shape, texture or materials of the product or its ornamentation.

(3) In this Act—

"complex product" means a product which is composed of at least two replaceable component parts permitting disassembly and reassembly of the product; and

"product" means any industrial or handicraft item other than a computer program; and, in particular, includes packaging, get-up, graphic symbols, typographic type-faces and parts intended to be assembled into a complex product.[4]

[Substantive grounds for refusal of registration

1A.— . . .][5] [6]　　　　　　　　　　　　　　　　　　　　　　**A2–002**

[Requirement of novelty and individual character

1B.—(1) A design shall be protected by a right in a registered design to the **A2–003** extent that the design is new and has individual character.

(2) For the purposes of subsection (1) above, a design is new if no identical design or no design whose features differ only in immaterial details has been made available to the public before the relevant date.

(3) For the purposes of subsection (1) above, a design has individual character if the overall impression it produces on the informed user differs from the overall impression produced on such a user by any design which has been made available to the public before the relevant date.

(4) In determining the extent to which a design has individual character, the degree of freedom of the author in creating the design shall be taken into consideration.

(5) For the purposes of this section, a design has been made available to the public before the relevant date if—

(a) it has been published (whether following registration or otherwise), exhibited, used in trade or otherwise disclosed before that date; and

(b) the disclosure does not fall within subsection (6) below.

(6) A disclosure falls within this subsection if—

(a) it could not reasonably have become known before the relevant date in the normal course of business to persons carrying on business in the European Economic Area and specialising in the sector concerned;

(b) it was made to a person other than the designer, or any successor in title of his, under conditions of confidentiality (whether express or implied);

(c) it was made by the designer, or any successor in title of his, during the period of 12 months immediately preceding the relevant date;

(d) it was made by a person other than the designer, or any successor in title of his, during the period of 12 months immediately preceding the relevant date in consequence of information provided or other action taken by the designer or any successor in title of his; or

(e) it was made during the period of 12 months immediately preceding the relevant date as a consequence of an abuse in relation to the designer or any successor in title of his.

[4] Substituted by the Registered Designs Regulations (SI 2001/3949) reg.2.
[5] Added by the Registered Designs Regulations (SI 2001/3949) reg.2.
[6] Repealed by the Regulatory Reform (Registered Designs) Order 2006 (SI 2006/1974) arts 2 and 3.

(7) In subsections (2), (3), (5) and (6) above "the relevant date" means the date on which the application for the registration of the design was made or is treated by virtue of section 3B(2), (3) or (5) or 14(2) of this Act as having been made.

(8) For the purposes of this section, a design applied to or incorporated in a product which constitutes a component part of a complex product shall only be considered to be new and to have individual character—

(a) if the component part, once it has been incorporated into the complex product, remains visible during normal use of the complex product; and

(b) to the extent that those visible features of the component part are in themselves new and have individual character.

(9) In subsection (8) above "normal use" means use by the end user; but does not include any maintenance, servicing or repair work in relation to the product.][7]

[Designs dictated by their technical function

A2–004   1C.—(1) A right in a registered design shall not subsist in features of appearance of a product which are solely dictated by the product's technical function.

(2) A right in a registered design shall not subsist in features of appearance of a product which must necessarily be reproduced in their exact form and dimensions so as to permit the product in which the design is incorporated or to which it is applied to be mechanically connected to, or placed in, around or against, another product so that either product may perform its function.

(3) Subsection (2) above does not prevent a right in a registered design subsisting in a design serving the purpose of allowing multiple assembly or connection of mutually interchangeable products within a modular system.][8]

[Designs contrary to public policy or morality

A2–005   1D.—A right in a registered design shall not subsist in a design which is contrary to public policy or to accepted principles of morality.][9]

Proprietorship of designs

A2–006   2.—(1) The author of a design shall be treated for the purposes of this Act as the original proprietor of the design, subject to the following provisions.

(1A) Where a design is created in pursuance of a commission for money or money's worth, the person commissioning the design shall be treated as the original proprietor of the design.

(1B) Where, in a case not falling within subsection (1A), a design is created by an employee in the course of his employment, his employer shall be treated as the original proprietor of the design.

(2) Where a design[...][10] becomes vested, whether by assignment, transmission or operation of law, in any person other than the original proprietor, either alone or jointly with the original proprietor, that other person, or as the case may be the original proprietor and that other person, shall be treated for the purposes of this Act as the proprietor of the design [...][11].

(3) In this Act the "author" of a design means the person who creates it.

---

[7] Added by the Registered Designs Regulations (SI 2001/3949) reg.2.
[8] Added by the Registered Designs Regulations (SI 2001/3949) reg.2.
[9] Added by the Registered Designs Regulations (SI 2001/3949) reg.2.
[10] Repealed by the Registered Designs Regulations (SI 2001/3949) Sch.2.
[11] Repealed by the Registered Designs Regulations (SI 2001/3949) Sch.2.

(4) In the case of a design generated by computer in circumstances such that there is no human author, the person by whom the arrangements necessary for the creation of the design are made shall be taken to be the author.

[Applications for registration

3.—(1) An application for the registration of a design [or designs][12] shall be **A2–007** made in the prescribed form and shall be filed at the Patent Office in the prescribed manner.

(2) An application for the registration of a design [or designs][13] shall be made by the person claiming to be the proprietor of the design.

(3) An application for the registration of a design [or designs][14] in which national unregistered design right subsists shall be made by the person claiming to be the design right owner.

(4) . . . [15].

(5) An application for the registration of a design which, owing to any default or neglect on the part of the applicant, has not been completed so as to enable registration to be effected within such time as may be prescribed shall be deemed to be abandoned.][16]

[Determination of applications for registration

3A.—(1) Subject as follows, the registrar shall not refuse [to register a design **A2–008** included in an application under this Act][17].

(2) If it appears to the registrar that an application for the registration of a design [or designs][18] has not been made in accordance with any rules made under this Act, he may refuse [to register any design included in it][19].

(3) If it appears to the registrar that [the applicant is not under section 3(2) or (3) or 14 entitled to apply for the registration of a design included in the application, he shall refuse to register that design][20].

[(4) If it appears to the registrar that the application for registration includes—

(a) something which does not fulfil the requirements of section 1(2) of this Act;

(b) a design that does not fulfil the requirements of section 1C or 1D of this Act; or

---

[12] Inserted by the Regulatory Reform (Registered Designs) Order 2006 (SI 2006/1974) arts 2 and 11.

[13] Inserted by the Regulatory Reform (Registered Designs) Order 2006 (SI 2006/1974) arts 2 and 11.

[14] Inserted by the Regulatory Reform (Registered Designs) Order 2006 (SI 2006/1974) arts 2 and 11.

[15] Repealed by the Regulatory Reform (Registered Designs) Order 2006 (SI 2006/1974) arts 2 and 4.

[16] Substituted by the Registered Designs Regulations (SI 2001/3949) reg.4.

[17] Substituted by the Regulatory Reform (Registered Designs) Order 2006 (SI 2006/1974) arts 2 and 12.

[18] Inserted by the Regulatory Reform (Registered Designs) Order 2006 (SI 2006/1974) arts 2 and 12.

[19] Substituted by the Regulatory Reform (Registered Designs) Order 2006 (SI 2006/1974) arts 2 and 12.

[20] Substituted by the Regulatory Reform (Registered Designs) Order 2006 (SI 2006/1974) arts 2 and 12.

(c) a design to which a ground of refusal mentioned in Schedule A1 to this Act applies,

he shall refuse to register that thing or that design.]²¹]²²

[Modification of applications for registration

A2–009   **3B.**—(1) The registrar may, at any time before an application for the registration of a design [or designs]²³ is determined, permit the applicant to make such modifications of the application as the registrar thinks fit.

(2) Where an application for the registration of a design [or designs]²⁴ has been modified before it has been determined in such a way that [any design included in the application]²⁵ has been altered significantly, the registrar may, for the purposes of deciding whether and to what extent the design is new or has individual character, direct that the application [so far as relating to that design]²⁶ shall be treated as having been made on the date on which it was so modified.

(3) Where—

(a) an application for the registration of [more than one design]²⁷ has disclosed more than one design and has been modified before it has been determined to exclude one or more designs from the application; and

(b) a subsequent application for the registration of a design so excluded has, within such period (if any) as has been prescribed for such applications, been made by the person who made the earlier application or his successor in title,

the registrar may, for the purpose of deciding whether and to what extent the design is new or has individual character, direct that the subsequent application shall be treated as having been made on the date on which the earlier application was, or is treated as having been, made.

(4) Where [. . .]²⁸ the registration of a design has been refused on any ground mentioned in [section 3A(4)(b) or (c)]²⁹ of this Act, the application [for the design]³⁰ may be modified by the applicant if it appears to the registrar that—

(a) the identity of the design is retained; and

(b) the modifications have been made in accordance with any rules made under this Act.

(5) An application modified under subsection (4) above shall be treated as the original application and, in particular, as made on the date on which the original application was made or is treated as having been made.

²¹ Substituted by the Regulatory Reform (Registered Designs) Order 2006 (SI 2006/1974) arts 2 and 12.
²² Added by the Registered Designs Regulations (SI 2001/3949) reg.4.
²³ Inserted by the Regulatory Reform (Registered Designs) Order 2006 (SI 2006/1974) arts 2 and 13.
²⁴ Inserted by the Regulatory Reform (Registered Designs) Order 2006 (SI 2006/1974) arts 2 and 13.
²⁵ Substituted by the Regulatory Reform (Registered Designs) Order 2006 (SI 2006/1974) arts 2 and 13.
²⁶ Inserted by the Regulatory Reform (Registered Designs) Order 2006 (SI 2006/1974) arts 2 and 13.
²⁷ Substituted by the Regulatory Reform (Registered Designs) Order 2006 (SI 2006/1974) arts 2 and 13.
²⁸ Repealed by the Regulatory Reform (Registered Designs) Order 2006 (SI 2006/1974) arts 2 and 13.
²⁹ Substituted by the Regulatory Reform (Registered Designs) Order 2006 (SI 2006/1974) arts 2 and 13.
³⁰ Inserted by the Regulatory Reform (Registered Designs) Order 2006 (SI 2006/1974) arts 2 and 13.

(6) Any modification under this section may, in particular, be effected by making a partial disclaimer in relation to the application.][31]

[Date of registration of designs

3C.—(1) Subject as follows, a design, when registered, shall be registered as of the date on which the application was made or is treated as having been made.

(2) Subsection (1) above shall not apply to an application which is treated as having been made on a particular date by section 14(2) of this Act or by virtue of the operation of section 3B(3) or (5) of this Act by reference to section 14(2) of this Act.

(3) A design, when registered, shall be registered as of—

    (a) in the case of an application which is treated as having been made on a particular date by section 14(2) of this Act, the date on which the application was made;

    (b) in the case of an application which is treated as having been made on a particular date by virtue of the operation of section 3B(3) of this Act by reference to section 14(2) of this Act, the date on which the earlier application was made;

    (c) in the case of an application which is treated as having been made on a particular date by virtue of the operation of section 3B(5) of this Act by reference to section 14(2) of this Act, the date on which the original application was made.][32]

A2–010

[Appeals in relation to applications for registration

3D.—An appeal lies from any decision of the registrar under section 3A or 3B of this Act.][33]

4.—[...][34]

A2–011

A2–012

Provisions for secrecy of certain designs

5.—(1) Where, either before or after the commencement of this Act, an application for the registration of a design has been made, and it appears to the registrar that the design is one of a class notified to him by the Secretary of State as relevant for defence purposes, he may give directions for prohibiting or restricting the publication of information with respect to the design, or the communication of such information to any person or class of persons specified in the directions.

(2) The Secretary of State shall by rules make provision for securing that where such directions are given—

A2–013

    (a) the representation or specimen of the design,
        shall not be open to public inspection at the Patent Office during the continuance in force of the directions [...].[35]

    (b) [...][36]

(3) Where the registrar gives any such directions as aforesaid, he shall give notice of the application and of the directions to the Secretary of State, and thereupon the following provisions shall have effect, that is to say—

---

[31] Added by the Registered Designs Regulations (SI 2001/3949) reg.4.
[32] Added by the Registered Designs Regulations (SI 2001/3949) reg.4.
[33] Added by the Registered Designs Regulations (SI 2001/3949) reg.4.
[34] Repealed by the Registered Designs Regulations (SI 2001/3949) Sch.2.
[35] Repealed by the Registered Designs Regulations (SI 2001/3949) Sch.2.
[36] Repealed by the Registered Designs Regulations (SI 2001/3949) Sch.2.

(a) the Secretary of State shall, upon receipt of such notice, consider whether the publication of the design would be prejudicial to the defence of the realm and unless a notice under paragraph (c) of this subsection has previously been given by that authority to the registrar, shall reconsider that question before the expiration of nine months from the date of filing of the application for registration of the design and at least once in every subsequent year;

(b) for the purpose aforesaid, the Secretary of State may, at any time after the design has been registered or, with the consent of the applicant, at any time before the design has been registered, inspect the representation or specimen of the design[...][37] filed in pursuance of the application;

(c) if upon consideration of the design at any time it appears to the Secretary of State that the publication of the design would not, or would no longer, be prejudicial to the defence of the realm, he shall give notice to the registrar to that effect;

(d) on the receipt of any such notice the registrar shall revoke the directions and may, subject to such conditions, if any, as he thinks fit, extend the time for doing anything required or authorised to be done by or under this Act in connection with the application or registration, whether or not that time has previously expired.

(4) No person resident in the United Kingdom shall, except under the authority of a written permit granted by or on behalf of the registrar, make or cause to be made any application outside the United Kingdom for the registration of a design of any class prescribed for the purposes of this subsection unless—

(a) an application for registration of the same design has been made in the United Kingdom not less than six weeks before the application outside the United Kingdom; and

(b) either no directions have been given under subsection (1) of this section in relation to the application in the United Kingdom or all such directions have been revoked:

Provided that this subsection shall not apply in relation to a design for which an application for protection has first been filed in a country outside the United Kingdom by a person resident outside the United Kingdom.

A2–014   6.—[...][38]

[Right given by registration

A2–015   7.—(1) The registration of a design under this Act gives the registered proprietor the exclusive right to use the design and any design which does not produce on the informed user a different overall impression.

(2) For the purposes of subsection (1) above and section 7A of this Act any reference to the use of a design includes a reference to—

(a) the making, offering, putting on the market, importing, exporting or using of a product in which the design is incorporated or to which it is applied; or

(b) stocking such a product for those purposes.

(3) In determining for the purposes of subsection (1) above whether a design produces a different overall impression on the informed user, the degree of freedom of the author in creating his design shall be taken into consideration.

---

[37] Repealed by the Registered Designs Regulations (SI 2001/3949) Sch.2.
[38] Repealed by the Registered Designs Regulations (SI 2001/3949) Sch.2.

(4) The right conferred by subsection (1) above is subject to any limitation attaching to the registration in question (including, in particular, any partial disclaimer or any declaration by the registrar or a court of partial invalidity).][39]

[Infringements of rights in registered designs

7A.—(1) Subject as follows, the right in a registered design is infringed by a   **A2–016** person who, without the consent of the registered proprietor, does anything which by virtue of section 7 of this Act is the exclusive right of the registered proprietor.

(2) The right in a registered design is not infringed by—

(a) an act which is done privately and for purposes which are not commercial;

(b) an act which is done for experimental purposes;

(c) an act of reproduction for teaching purposes or for the purposes of making citations provided that the conditions mentioned in subsection (3) below are satisfied;

(d) the use of equipment on ships or aircraft which are registered in another country but which are temporarily in the United Kingdom;

(e) the importation into the United Kingdom of spare parts or accessories for the purposes of repairing such ships or aircraft; or

(f) the carrying out of repairs on such ships or aircraft.

(3) The conditions mentioned in this subsection are—

(a) the act of reproduction is compatible with fair trade practice and does not unduly prejudice the normal exploitation of the design; and

(b) mention is made of the source.

(4) The right in a registered design is not infringed by an act which relates to a product in which any design protected by the registration is incorporated or to which it is applied if the product has been put on the market in the European Economic Area by the registered proprietor or with his consent.

(5) The right in a registered design of a component part which may be used for the purpose of the repair of a complex product so as to restore its original appearance is not infringed by the use for that purpose of any design protected by the registration.

(6) No proceedings shall be taken in respect of an infringement of the right in a registered design committed before the date on which the certificate of registration of the design under this Act is granted.][40]

Duration of right in registered design

8.—(1) The right in a registered design subsists in the first instance for a period   **A2–017** of five years from the date of the registration of the design.

(2) The period for which the right subsists may be extended for a second, third, fourth and fifth period of five years, by applying to the registrar for an extension and paying the prescribed renewal fee.

(3) If the first, second, third or fourth period expires without such application and payment being made, the right shall cease to have effect; and the registrar shall, in accordance with rules made by the Secretary of State, notify the proprietor of that fact.

(4) If during the period of six months immediately following the end of that period an application for extension is made and the prescribed renewal fee and

[39] Substituted by the Registered Designs Regulations (SI 2001/3949) reg.5.
[40] Added by the Registered Designs Regulations (SI 2001/3949) reg.5.

any prescribed additional fee is paid, the right shall be treated as if it had never expired, with the result that—

(a) anything done under or in relation to the right during that further period shall be treated as valid,

(b) an act which would have constituted an infringement of the right if it has not expired shall be treated as an infringement, and

(c) an act which would have constituted use of the design for the services of the Crown if the right had not expired shall be treated as such use.

(5) [...][41]

(6) [...][42]

Restoration of lapsed right in design

A2–018   **8A.**—(1) Where the right in a registered design has expired by reason of a failure to extend, in accordance with section 8(2) or (4), the period for which the right subsists, an application for the restoration of the right in the design may be made to the registrar within the prescribed period.

(2) The application may be made by the person who was the registered proprietor of the design or by any other person who would have been entitled to the right in the design if it had not expired; and where the design was held by two or more persons jointly, the application may, with the leave of the registrar, be made by one or more of them without joining the others.

(3) Notice of the application shall be published by the registrar in the prescribed manner.

(4) If the registrar is satisfied that the [failure of the proprietor][43] to see that the period for which the right subsisted was extended in accordance with section 8(2) or (4) [was unintentional][44], he shall, on payment of any unpaid renewal fee and any prescribed additional fee, order the restoration of the right in the design.

(5) The order may be made subject to such conditions as the registrar thinks fit, and if the proprietor of the design does not comply with any condition the registrar may revoke the order and give such consequential directions as he thinks fit.

(6) Rules altering the period prescribed for the purposes of subsection (1) may contain such transitional provisions and savings as appear to the Secretary of State to be necessary or expedient.

Effect of order for restoration of right

A2–019   **8B.**—(1) The effect of an order under section 8A for the restoration of the right in a registered design is as follows.

(2) Anything done under or in relation to the right during the period between expiry and restoration shall be treated as valid.

(3) Anything done during that period which would have constituted an infringement if the right had not expired shall be treated as an infringement—

(a) if done at a time when it was possible for an application for extension to be made under section 8(4); or

(b) if it was a continuation or repetition of an earlier infringing act.

---

[41] Repealed by the Registered Designs Regulations (SI 2001/3949) Sch.2.

[42] Repealed by the Registered Designs Regulations (SI 2001/3949) Sch.2.

[43] Substituted by the Regulatory Reform (Registered Designs) Order 2006 (SI 2006/1974) arts 2 and 17.

[44] Inserted by the Regulatory Reform (Registered Designs) Order 2006 (SI 2006/1974) arts 2 and 17.

(4) If, after it was no longer possible for such an application for extension to be made and before publication of notice of the application for restoration, a person—

  (a) began in good faith to do an act which would have constituted an infringement of the right in the design if it had not expired, or
  (b) made in good faith effective and serious preparations to do such an act,

he has the right to continue to do the act or, as the case may be, to do the act, notwithstanding the restoration of the right in the design; but this does not extend to granting a licence to another person to do the act.

(5) If the act was done, or the preparations were made, in the course of a business, the person entitled to the right conferred by subsection (4) may—

  (a) authorise the doing of that act by any partners of his for the time being in that business, and
  (b) assign that right, or transmit it on death (or in the case of a body corporate on its dissolution), to any person who acquires that part of the business in the course of which the act was done or the preparations were made.

(6) Where [a product]⁴⁵ is disposed of to another in exercise of the rights conferred by subsection (4) or subsection (5), that other and any person claiming through him may deal with the product in the same way as if it had been disposed of by the registered proprietor of the design.

(7) The above provisions apply in relation to the use of a registered design for the services of the Crown as they apply in relation to infringement of the right in the design.

Exemption of innocent infringer from liability for damages

9.—[. . .]⁴⁶   A2–020
10.—[. . .]⁴⁷   A2–021

[Cancellation of registration

11.—The registrar may, upon a request made in the prescribed manner by the   A2–022
registered proprietor, cancel the registration of a design.]⁴⁸

[Grounds for invalidity of registration

11ZA.—(1) The registration of a design may be declared invalid—   A2–023

  (a) on the ground that it does not fulfil the requirements of section 1(2) of this Act;
  (b) on the ground that it does not fulfil the requirements of sections 1B to 1D of this Act; or
  (c) where any ground of refusal mentioned in Schedule A1 to this Act applies.]⁴⁹

---

⁴⁵ Substituted by the Registered Designs Regulations (SI 2001/3949) Sch.1, para.2.
⁴⁶ Repealed by the Intellectual Property (Enforcement, etc.) Regulations 2006 (SI 2006/1028) reg.2, Sch.4.
⁴⁷ Repealed by the Registered Designs Regulations (SI 2001/3949) Sch.2.
⁴⁸ Substituted by the Registered Designs Regulations (SI 2001/3949) reg.7.
⁴⁹ Substituted by the Regulatory Reform (Registered Designs) Order 2006 (SI 2006/1974) arts 2 and 7.

[(1A) The registration of a design ("the later design") may be declared invalid if it is not new or does not have individual character when compared to a design which—

    (a)   has been made available to the public on or after the relevant date; but

   [(b)   is protected as from a date prior to the relevant date—

        (i) by virtue of registration under this Act or the Community Design Regulation or an application for such registration, or

       (ii) by virtue of an international registration (within the meaning of Articles 106a to 106f of that Regulation) designating the Community.][50]][51]

[(1B) In subsection (1A) "the relevant date" means the date on which the application for the registration of the later design was made or is treated by virtue of section 3B(2), (3) or (5) or 14(2) of this Act as having been made.][52]

(2) The registration of a design may be declared invalid on the ground of the registered proprietor not being the proprietor of the design and the proprietor of the design objecting.

(3) The registration of a design involving the use of an earlier distinctive sign may be declared invalid on the ground of an objection by the holder of rights to the sign which include the right to prohibit in the United Kingdom such use of the sign.

(4) The registration of a design constituting an unauthorised use of a work protected by the law of copyright in the United Kingdom may be declared invalid on the ground of an objection by the owner of the copyright.

(5) In this section and sections 11ZB, 11ZC and 11ZE of this Act (other than section 11ZE(1)) references to the registration of a design include references to the former registration of a design; and these sections shall apply, with necessary modifications, in relation to such former registrations.][53]

[Applications for declaration of invalidity

A2–024   **11ZB.**—(1) Any person interested may make an application to the registrar for a declaration of invalidity [under section 11ZA(1)(a) or (b)][54]of this Act.

(2) Any person concerned by the use in question may make an application to the registrar for a declaration of invalidity [under section 11ZA(1)(c)][55] of this Act.

(3) The relevant person may make an application to the registrar for a declaration of invalidity [under section 11ZA(1A)][56] of this Act.

(4) In subsection (3) above "the relevant person" means, in relation to an earlier design protected by virtue of registration under this Act [or the Community Design Regulation][57] or an application for such registration, the registered

---

[50] Substituted by the Designs (International Registrations Designating the European Community) Regulations 2007 (SI 2007/3378) reg.2.

[51] Inserted by the Regulatory Reform (Registered Designs) Order 2006 (SI 2006/1974) arts 2 and 7.

[52] Inserted by the Regulatory Reform (Registered Designs) Order 2006 (SI 2006/1974) arts 2 and 7.

[53] Added by the Registered Designs Regulations (SI 2001/3949) reg.7.

[54] Substituted by the Regulatory Reform (Registered Designs) Order 2006 (SI 2006/1974) arts 2 and 8.

[55] Substituted by the Regulatory Reform (Registered Designs) Order 2006 (SI 2006/1974) arts 2 and 8.

[56] Substituted by the Regulatory Reform (Registered Designs) Order 2006 (SI 2006/1974) arts 2 and 8.

[57] Inserted by the Registered Designs Regulations (SI 2003/550) reg.2.

proprietor of the design [, the holder of the registered Community design][58] or (as the case may be) the applicant.

(5) The person able to make an objection under subsection (2), (3) or (4) of section 11ZA of this Act may make an application to the registrar for a declaration of invalidity [under][59] that subsection.

(6) An application may be made under this section in relation to a design at any time after the design has been registered.][60]

[Determination of applications for declaration of invalidity

11ZC.—(1) This section applies where an application has been made to the registrar for a declaration of invalidity in relation to a registration.

(2) If it appears to the registrar that the application has not been made in accordance with any rules made under this Act, he may refuse the application.

(3) If it appears to the registrar that the application has not been made in accordance with section 11ZB of this Act, he shall refuse the application.

(4) Subject to subsections (2) and (3) above, the registrar shall make a declaration of invalidity if it appears to him that the ground of invalidity specified in the application has been established in relation to the registration.

(5) Otherwise the registrar shall refuse the application.

(6) A declaration of invalidity may be a declaration of partial invalidity.][61]

A2–025

[Modification of registration

11ZD.—(1) Subsections (2) and (3) below apply where the registrar intends to declare the registration of a design invalid [under section 11ZA(1)(b) or (c), (1A), (3) or (4)][62] of this Act.

(2) The registrar shall inform the registered proprietor of that fact.

(3) The registered proprietor may make an application to the registrar for the registrar to make such modifications to the registration of the design as the registered proprietor specifies in his application.

(4) Such modifications may, in particular, include the inclusion on the register of a partial disclaimer by the registered proprietor.

(5) If it appears to the registrar that the application has not been made in accordance with any rules made under this Act, the registrar may refuse the application.

(6) If it appears to the registrar that the identity of the design is not retained or the modified registration would be invalid by virtue of section 11ZA of this Act, the registrar shall refuse the application.

(7) Otherwise the registrar shall make the specified modifications.

(8) A modification of a registration made under this section shall have effect, and be treated always to have had effect, from the grant of registration.][63]

A2–026

[Effect of cancellation or invalidation of registration

11ZE.—(1) A cancellation of registration under section 11 of this Act takes effect from the date of the registrar's decision or from such other date as the registrar may direct.

A2–027

---

[58] Inserted by the Registered Designs Regulations (SI 2003/550) reg.2.
[59] Substituted by the Regulatory Reform (Registered Designs) Order 2006 (SI 2006/1974) arts 2 and 8.
[60] Added by the Registered Designs Regulations (SI 2001/3949) reg.7.
[61] Added by the Registered Designs Regulations (SI 2001/3949) reg.7.
[62] Substituted by the Regulatory Reform (Registered Designs) Order 2006 (SI 2006/1974) arts 2 and 9.
[63] Added by the Registered Designs Regulations (SI 2001/3949) reg.7.

(2) Where the registrar declares the registration of a design invalid to any extent, the registration shall to that extent be treated as having been invalid from the date of registration or from such other date as the registrar may direct.]⁶⁴

[Appeals in relation to cancellation or invalidation

A2–028 **11ZF.**—An appeal lies from any decision of the registrar under section 11 to 11ZE of this Act.]⁶⁵

Powers exercisable for protection of the public interest

A2–029 **11A.**—(1) Where a report of the Competition Commission has been laid before Parliament containing conclusions to the effect—

- (a) [...]⁶⁶
- (b) [...]⁶⁷
- (c) on a competition reference, that a person was engaged in an anti-competitive practice which operated or may be expected to operate against the public interest, or
- (d) on a reference under section 11 of the Competition Act 1980 (reference of public bodies and certain other persons), that a person is pursuing a course of conduct which operates against the public interest,

the appropriate Minister or Ministers may apply to the registrar to take action under this section.

(2) Before making an application the appropriate Minister or Ministers shall publish, in such a manner as he or they think appropriate, a notice describing the nature of the proposed application and shall consider any representations which may be made within 30 days of such publication by persons whose interests appear to him or them to be affected.

(3) If on an application under this section it appears to the registrar that the matters specified in the Commission's report as being those which in the Commission's opinion operate or operated or may be expected to operate against the public interest include—

- (a) conditions in licences granted in respect of a registered design by its proprietor restricting the use of the design by the licensee or the right of the proprietor to grant other licences, [...]⁶⁸
- (b) [...]⁶⁹

he may by order cancel or modify any such condition [...]⁷⁰.

(4) [...]⁷¹
(5) [...]⁷²

(6) An appeal lies from any order of the registrar under this section.

(7) In this section "the appropriate Minister or Ministers" means the Minister or Ministers to whom the report of the Competition Commission was made.

---

⁶⁴ Added by the Registered Designs Regulations (SI 2001/3949) reg.7.
⁶⁵ Added by the Registered Designs Regulations (SI 2001/3949) reg.7.
⁶⁶ Repealed (subject to savings specified in SI 2003/1397, arts 3(1) and 8) by the Enterprise Act 2002 Sch.26, para.1.
⁶⁷ Repealed (subject to savings specified in SI 2003/1397, arts 3(1) and 8) by the Enterprise Act 2002 Sch.26, para.1.
⁶⁸ Repealed by the Registered Designs Regulations (SI 2001/3949) Sch.2.
⁶⁹ Repealed by the Registered Designs Regulations (SI 2001/3949) Sch.2.
⁷⁰ Repealed by the Registered Designs Regulations (SI 2001/3949) Sch.2.
⁷¹ Repealed by the Registered Designs Regulations (SI 2001/3949) Sch.2.
⁷² Repealed by the Registered Designs Regulations (SI 2001/3949) Sch.2.

Powers exercisable following merger and market investigations

11AB.—(1) Subsection (2) below applies where—

A2–030

   (a) section 41(2), 55(2), 66(6), 75(2), 83(2), 138(2), 147(2) or 160(2) of, or paragraph 5(2) or 10(2) of Schedule 7 to, the Enterprise Act 2002 (powers to take remedial action following merger or market investigations) applies;

   (b) the Competition Commission or (as the case may be) the Secretary of State considers that it would be appropriate to make an application under this section for the purpose of remedying, mitigating or preventing a matter which cannot be dealt with under the enactment concerned; and

   (c) the matter concerned involves conditions in licences granted in respect of a registered design by its proprietor restricting the use of the design by the licensee or the right of the proprietor to grant other licences.

(2) The Competition Commission or (as the case may be) the Secretary of State may apply to the registrar to take action under this section.

(3) Before making an application the Competition Commission or (as the case may be) the Secretary of State shall publish, in such manner as it or he thinks appropriate, a notice describing the nature of the proposed application and shall consider any representations which may be made within 30 days of such publication by persons whose interests appear to it or him to be affected.

(4) The registrar may, if it appears to him on an application under this section that the application is made in accordance with this section, by order cancel or modify any condition concerned of the kind mentioned in subsection (1)(c) above.

(5) An appeal lies from any order of the registrar under this section.

(6) References in this section to the Competition Commission shall, in cases where section 75(2) of the Enterprise Act 2002 applies, be read as references to the Office of Fair Trading.

(7) References in section 35, 36, 47, 63, 134 or 141 of the Enterprise Act 2002 (questions to be decided by the Competition Commission in its reports) to taking action under section 41(2), 55, 66, 138 or 147 shall include references to taking action under subsection (2) above.

(8) An order made by virtue of this section in consequence of action under subsection (2) above where an enactment mentioned in subsection (1)(a) above applies shall be treated, for the purposes of sections 91(3), 92(1)(a), 162(1) and 166(3) of the Enterprise Act 2002 (duties to register and keep under review enforcement orders etc.), as if it were made under the relevant power in Part 3 or (as the case may be) 4 of that Act to make an enforcement order (within the meaning of the Part concerned).][73]

11B.—[...][74]

A2–031

Use for services of the Crown

12.—The provisions of the First Schedule to this Act shall have effect with respect to the use of registered designs for the services of the Crown and the rights of third parties in respect of such use.

A2–032

---

[73] Inserted (subject to savings specified in SI 2003/1397 art.12) by the Enterprise Act 2002 Sch.25, para.1(3).
[74] Repealed by the Registered Designs Regulations (SI 2001/3949) Sch.2.

Orders in Council as to convention countries

A2–033
13.—(1) His Majesty may, with a view to the fulfilment of a treaty, convention, arrangement or engagement, by Order in Council declare that any country specified in the Order is a convention country for the purposes of this Act:

Provided that a declaration may be made as aforesaid for the purposes either of all or of some only of the provisions of this Act, and a country in the case of which a declaration made for the purposes of some only of the provisions of this Act is in force shall be deemed to be a convention country for the purposes of those provisions only.

(2) His Majesty may by Order in Council direct that any of the Channel Islands, any colony, shall be deemed to be a convention country for the purposes of all or any of the provisions of this Act; and an Order made under this subsection may direct that any such provisions shall have effect, in relation to the territory in question, subject to such conditions or limitations, if any, as may be specified in the Order.

(3) For the purposes of subsection (1) of this section, every colony, protectorate, territory subject to the authority or under the suzerainty of another country, and territory administered by another country under the trusteeship system of the United Nations, shall be deemed to be a country in the case of which a declaration may be made under that subsection.

Registration of design where application for protection in convention country has been made

A2–034
14.—(1) An application for registration of a design [or designs][75] in respect of which protection has been applied for in a convention country may be made in accordance with the provisions of this Act by the person by whom the application for protection was made or his personal representative or assignee: Provided that no application shall be made by virtue of this section after the expiration of six months from the date of the application for protection in a convention country or, where more than one such application for protection has been made, from the date of the first application.

(2) Where an application for registration of a design [or designs][76] is made by virtue of this section, the application shall be treated, for the purpose of determining whether [(and to what extent)][77] that or any other design is new [or has individual character][78], as made on the date of the application for protection in the convention country or, if more than one such application was made, on the date of the first such application.

(3) Subsection (2) shall not be construed as excluding the power to give directions under [section 3B(2) or (3)][79] of this Act in relation to an application made by virtue of this section.

(4) Where a person has applied for protection for a design by an application which—

    (a) in accordance with the terms of a treaty subsisting between two or more convention countries, is equivalent to an application duly made in any one of those convention countries; or

---

[75] Inserted by the Regulatory Reform (Registered Designs) Order 2006 (SI 2006/1974) arts 2 and 14.

[76] Inserted by the Regulatory Reform (Registered Designs) Order 2006 (SI 2006/1974) arts 2 and 14.

[77] Substituted by the Registered Designs Regulations (SI 2001/3949) Sch.1, para.4.

[78] Substituted by the Registered Designs Regulations (SI 2001/3949) Sch.1, para.4.

[79] Substituted by the Registered Designs Regulations (SI 2001/3949) Sch.1, para.4.

(b) in accordance with the law of any convention country, is equivalent to an application duly made in that convention country.

he shall be deemed for the purposes of this section to have applied in that convention country.

Extension of time for applications under s.14 in certain cases

15.—(1) If the Secretary of State is satisfied that provision substantially equivalent to the provision to be made by or under this section has been or will be made under the law of any convention country, he may make rules empowering the registrar to extend the time for making application under subsection (1) of section fourteen of this Act for registration of a design in respect of which protection has been applied for in that country in any case where the period specified in the proviso to that subsection expires during a period prescribed by the rules.   **A2–035**

(2) Rules made under this section—

(a) may, where any agreement or arrangement has been made between His Majesty's Government in the United Kingdom and the government of the convention country for the supply or mutual exchange of information or [products],[80] provide, either generally or in any class of case specified in the rules, that an extension of time shall not be granted under this section unless the design has been communicated in accordance with the agreement or arrangement;

(b) may, either generally or in any class of case specified in the rules, fix the maximum extension which may be granted under this section;

(c) may prescribe or allow any special procedure in connection with applications made by virtue of this section;

(d) may empower the registrar to extend, in relation to an application made by virtue of this section, the time limited by or under the foregoing provisions of this Act for doing any act, subject to such conditions, if any, as may be imposed by or under the rules;

(e) may provide for securing that the rights conferred by registration on an application made by virtue of this section shall be subject to such restrictions or conditions as may be specified by or under the rules and in particular to restrictions and conditions for the protection of persons (including persons acting on behalf of His Majesty) who, otherwise than as the result of a communication made in accordance with such an agreement or arrangement as is mentioned in paragraph (a) of this subsection, and before the date of the application in question or such later date as may be allowed by the rules, may have imported or made [products][81] to which the design is applied or in which it is incorporated or may have made an application for registration of the design.

[The nature of registered designs

15A.—A registered design or an application for a registered design is personal property (in Scotland, incorporeal moveable property).][82]   **A2–036**

---

[80] Substituted by the Registered Designs Regulations (SI 2001/3949) Sch.1, para.5.
[81] Substituted by the Registered Designs Regulations (SI 2001/3949) Sch.1, para.5.
[82] Inserted by the Intellectual Property (Enforcement, etc.) Regulations 2006 (SI 2006/1028) reg.2, Sch.1, paras 1 and 2.

[Assignment, &c of registered designs and applications for registered designs

A2–037   **15B.**—(1) A registered design or an application for a registered design is transmissible by assignment, testamentary disposition or operation of law in the same way as other personal or moveable property, subject to the following provisions of this section.

(2) Any transmission of a registered design or an application for a registered design is subject to any rights vested in any other person of which notice is entered in the register of designs, or in the case of applications, notice is given to the registrar.

(3) An assignment of, or an assent relating to, a registered design or application for a registered design is not effective unless it is in writing signed by or on behalf of the assignor or, as the case may be, a personal representative.

(4) Except in Scotland, the requirement in subsection (3) may be satisfied in a case where the assignor or personal representative is a body corporate by the affixing of its seal.

(5) Subsections (3) and (4) apply to assignment by way of security as in relation to any other assignment.

(6) A registered design or application for a registered design may be the subject of a charge (in Scotland, security) in the same way as other personal or moveable property.

(7) The proprietor of a registered design may grant a licence to use that registered design.

(8) Any equities (in Scotland, rights) in respect of a registered design or an application for a registered design may be enforced in like manner as in respect of any other personal or moveable property.][83]

[Exclusive licences

A2–038   **15C.**—(1) In this Act an "exclusive licence" means a licence in writing signed by or on behalf of the proprietor of the registered design authorising the licensee to the exclusion of all other persons, including the person granting the licence, to exercise a right which would otherwise be exercisable exclusively by the proprietor of the registered design.

(2) The licensee under an exclusive licence has the same rights against any successor in title who is bound by the licence as he has against the person granting the licence.][84]

A2–039   **16.**—[. . .][85]

Register of designs etc

A2–040   **17.**—(1) The registrar shall maintain the register of designs, in which shall be entered—

(a) the names and addresses of proprietors of registered designs;

(b) notices of assignments and of transmissions of registered designs; and

(c) such other matters as may be prescribed or as the registrar may think fit.

(2) No notice of any trust, whether express, implied or constructive, shall be entered in the registrar of designs, and the registrar shall not be affected by any such notice.

---

[83] Inserted by the Intellectual Property (Enforcement, etc.) Regulations 2006 (SI 2006/1028) reg.2, Sch.1, paras 1 and 2.

[84] Inserted by the Intellectual Property (Enforcement, etc.) Regulations 2006 (SI 2006/1028) reg.2, Sch.1, paras 1 and 2.

[85] Repealed by the Registered Designs Regulations (SI 2001/3949) Sch.2.

(3) The register need not be kept in documentary form.

(4) Subject to the provisions of this Act and to rules made by the Secretary of State under it, the public shall have a right to inspect the register at the Patent Office at all convenient times.

(5) Any person who applies for a certified copy of an entry in the register or a certified extract from the register shall be entitled to obtain such a copy or extract on payment of a fee prescribed in relation to certified copies and extracts; and rules made by the Secretary of State under this Act may provide that any person who applies for an uncertified copy or extract shall be entitled to such a copy or extract on payment of a fee prescribed in relation to uncertified copies and extracts.

(6) Applications under subsection (5) above or rules made by virtue of that subsection shall be made in such manner as may be prescribed.

(7) In relation to any portion of the register kept otherwise than in documentary form—

(a) the right of inspection conferred by subsection (4) above is a right to inspect the material on the register; and

(b) the right to a copy or extract conferred by subsection (5) above or rules is a right to a copy or extract in a form in which it can be taken away and in which it is visible and legible.

(8) [. . .][86] The register shall be prima facie evidence of anything required or authorised by this Act to be entered in it and in Scotland shall be sufficient evidence of any such thing.

(9) A certificate purporting to be signed by the registrar and certifying that any entry which he is authorised by or under this Act to make has or has not been made, or that any other thing which he is so authorised to do has or has not been done, shall be prima facie evidence, and in Scotland shall be sufficient evidence, of the matters so certified.

(10) Each of the following—

(a) a copy of an entry in the register or an extract from the register which is supplied under subsection (5) above;

(b) a copy of any representation, specimen or document kept in the Patent Office or an extract from any such document,

which purports to be a certified copy or certified extract shall, [. . .][87] be admitted in evidence without further proof and without production of any original; and in Scotland such evidence shall be sufficient evidence.

(11) . . . [88]

(12) In this section "certified copy" and "certified extract" mean a copy and extract certified by the registrar and sealed with the seal of the Patent Office.

Certificate of registration

18.—(1) The registrar shall grant a certificate of registration in the prescribed form to the registered proprietor of a design when the design is registered.   **A2–041**

(2) The registrar may, in a case where he is satisfied that the certificate of registration has been lost or destroyed, or in any other case in which he thinks it expedient, furnish one or more copies of the certificate.

---

[86] Repealed by the Criminal Justice Act 2003 s.332, Sch.37, Pt 6.
[87] Repealed by the Criminal Justice Act 2003 s.332, Sch.37, Pt 6.
[88] Repealed by the Youth Justice and Criminal Evidence Act 1999 s.67, Sch.6.

Registration of assignments, etc

A2–042   **19.**—(1) Where any person becomes entitled by assignment, transmission or operation of law to a registered design or to a share in a registered design, or becomes entitled as mortgagee, licensee or otherwise to any other interest in a registered design, he shall apply to the registrar in the prescribed manner for the registration of his title as proprietor or co-proprietor or, as the case may be, of notice of his interest, in the register of designs.

(2) Without prejudice to the provisions of the foregoing subsection, an application for the registration of the title of any person becoming entitled by assignment to a registered design or a share in a registered design, or becoming entitled by virtue of a mortgage, licence or other instrument to any other interest in a registered design, may be made in the prescribed manner by the assign or, mortgagor, licensor or other party to that instrument, as the case may be.

(3) Where application is made under this section for the registration of the title of any person, the registrar shall, upon proof of title to his satisfaction—

  (a) where that person is entitled to a registered design or a share in a registered design, register him in the register of designs as proprietor or co-proprietor of the design, and enter in that register particulars of the instrument or event by which he derives title; or

  (b) where that person is entitled to any other interest in the registered design, enter in that register notice of his interest, with particulars of the instrument (if any) creating it.

(3A) Where [national unregistered design right][89] subsists in a registered design, the registrar shall not register an interest under subsection (3) unless he is satisfied that the person entitled to that interest is also entitled to a corresponding interest in the [national unregistered design right][90]

(3B) Where [national unregistered design right][91] subsists in a registered design and the proprietor of the registered design is also the design right owner, an assignment of the [national unregistered design right][92] shall be taken to be also an assignment of the right in the registered design, unless a contrary intention appears.

(4) [. . .][93]

(5) Except for the purposes of an application to rectify the register under the following provisions of this Act, a document in respect of which no entry has been made in the register of designs under subsection (3) of this section shall not be admitted in any court as evidence of the title of any person to a registered design or share of or interest in a registered design unless the court otherwise directs.

Rectification of register

A2–043   **20.**—(1) The court may, on the application of [the relevant person][94] order the register of designs to be rectified by the making of any entry therein or the variation or deletion of any entry therein.

[(1A) In subsection (1) above

  "the relevant person" means—

---

[89] Substituted by the Registered Designs Regulations (SI 2001/3949) Sch.1, para.6.
[90] Substituted by the Registered Designs Regulations (SI 2001/3949) Sch.1, para.6.
[91] Substituted by the Registered Designs Regulations (SI 2001/3949) Sch.1, para.6.
[92] Substituted by the Registered Designs Regulations (SI 2001/3949) Sch.1, para.6.
[93] Repealed by the Intellectual Property (Enforcement, etc.) Regulations 2006 (SI 2006/1028) reg.2, Sch.4.
[94] Substituted by the Registered Designs Regulations (SI 2001/3949) reg.8.

(a) in the case of an application invoking any ground referred to in [section 11ZA(1)(c)][95] of this Act, any person concerned by the use in question;

(b) in the case of an application invoking the ground mentioned in [section 11ZA(1A)][96] of this Act, the appropriate person;

(c) in the case of an application invoking any ground mentioned in section 11ZA(2), (3) or (4) of this Act, the person able to make the objection;

(d) in any other case, any person aggrieved.

(1B) In subsection (1A) above "the appropriate person" means, in relation to an earlier design protected by virtue of registration under this Act [or the Community Design Regulation][97] or an application for such registration, the registered proprietor of the design[, the holder of the registered Community design][98] or (as the case may be) the applicant.][99]

(2) In proceedings under this section the court may determine any question which it may be necessary or expedient to decide in connection with the rectification of the register.

(3) Notice of any application to the court under this section shall be given in the prescribed manner to the registrar, who shall be entitled to appear and be heard on the application, and shall appear if so directed by the court.

(4) Any order made by the court under this section shall direct that notice of the order shall be served on the registrar in the prescribed manner; and the registrar shall, on receipt of the notice, rectify the register accordingly.

(5) A rectification of the register under this section has effect as follows—

(a) an entry made has effect from the date on which it should have been made,

(b) an entry varied has effect as if it had originally been made in its varied form, and

(c) an entry deleted shall be deemed never to have had effect,

unless, in any case, the court directs otherwise.

[(6) Orders which may be made by the court under this section include, in particular, declarations of partial invalidity.][100]

Power to correct clerical errors

21.—(1) The registrar may, in accordance with the provisions of this section, correct any error in an application for the registration or in the representation of a design, or any error in the register of designs.   **A2–044**

(2) A correction may be made in pursuance of this section either upon a request in writing made by any person interested and accompanied by the prescribed fee, or without such a request.

(3) Where the registrar proposes to make any such correction as aforesaid otherwise than in pursuance of a request made under this section, he shall give notice of the proposal to the registered proprietor or the applicant for registration of the design, as the case may be, and to any other person who appears to him to

---

[95] Substituted by the Regulatory Reform (Registered Designs) Order 2006 (SI 2006/1974) arts 2 and 10.

[96] Substituted by the Regulatory Reform (Registered Designs) Order 2006 (SI 2006/1974) arts 2 and 10.

[97] Inserted by the Registered Designs Regulations (SI 2003/550) reg.2.

[98] Inserted by the Registered Designs Regulations (SI 2003/550) reg.2.

[99] Inserted by the Registered Designs Regulations (SI 2001/3949) reg.8.

[100] Inserted by the Registered Designs Regulations (SI 2001/3949) reg.8.

be concerned, and shall give them an opportunity to be heard before making the correction.

Inspection of registered designs

A2–045   22.—(1) Where a design has been registered under this Act, there shall be open to inspection at the Patent Office on and after the day on which the certificate of registration is [granted][101]—

(a) the representation or specimen of the design [...].[102]

(b) [...][103]

This subsection has effect subject to [subsection (4)][104] and to any rules made under section 5(2) of this Act.

(2) [...][105]

(3) [...][106]

[(4) Where registration of a design has been refused pursuant to an application under this Act, or an application under this Act has been abandoned in relation to any design—

(a) the application, so far as relating to that design, and

(b) any representation, specimen or other document which has been filed and relates to that design,

shall not at any time be open to inspection at the Patent Office or be published by the registrar.][107]

Information as to existence of right in registered design

A2–046   23.—On the request of a person furnishing such information as may enable the registrar to identify the design, and on payment of the prescribed fee, the registrar shall inform him—

(a) whether the design is registered[...][108], and

(b) whether any extension of the period of the right in the registered design has been granted, and shall state the date of registration and the name and address of the registered proprietor.

A2–047   24.— ...

[Action for infringement

A2–048   24A.—(1) An infringement of the right in a registered design is actionable by the registered proprietor.

(2) In an action for infringement all such relief by way of damages, injunctions, accounts or otherwise is available to him as is available in respect of the infringement of any other property right.

---

[101] Substituted by the Regulatory Reform (Registered Designs) Order 2006 (SI 2006/1974) arts 2 and 16.

[102] Repealed by the Registered Designs Regulations (SI 2001/3949) Sch.2.

[103] Repealed by the Registered Designs Regulations (SI 2001/3949) Sch.2.

[104] Substituted by the Regulatory Reform (Registered Designs) Order 2006 (SI 2006/1974) arts 2 and 16.

[105] Repealed by the Regulatory Reform (Registered Designs) Order 2006 (SI 2006/1974) arts 2 and 16.

[106] Repealed by the Regulatory Reform (Registered Designs) Order 2006 (SI 2006/1974) arts 2 and 16.

[107] Substituted by the Regulatory Reform (Registered Designs) Order 2006 (SI 2006/1974) arts 2 and 15.

[108] Repealed by the Registered Designs Regulations (SI 2001/3949) Sch.2, para.1.

(3) This section has effect subject to section 24B of this Act (exemption of innocent infringer from liability).][109]

[Exemption of innocent infringer from liability

24B.—(1) In proceedings for the infringement of the right in a registered design damages shall not be awarded, and no order shall be made for an account of profits, against a defendant who proves that at the date of the infringement he was not aware, and had no reasonable ground for supposing, that the design was registered.

(2) For the purposes of subsection (1), a person shall not be deemed to have been aware or to have had reasonable grounds for supposing that the design was registered by reason only of the marking of a product with—

    (a) the word "registered" or any abbreviation thereof, or

    (b) any word or words expressing or implying that the design applied to, or incorporated in, the product has been registered,

unless the number of the design accompanied the word or words or the abbreviation in question.

(3) Nothing in this section shall affect the power of the court to grant an injunction in any proceedings for infringement of the right in a registered design.][110]

A2–049

[Order for delivery up

24C.—(1) Where a person—

A2–050

    (a) has in his possession, custody or control for commercial purposes an infringing article, or

    (b) has in his possession, custody or control anything specifically designed or adapted for making articles to a particular design which is a registered design, knowing or having reason to believe that it has been or is to be used to make an infringing article,

the registered proprietor in question may apply to the court for an order that the infringing article or other thing be delivered up to him or to such other person as the court may direct.

(2) An application shall not be made after the end of the period specified in the following provisions of this section; and no order shall be made unless the court also makes, or it appears to the court that there are grounds for making, an order under section 24D of this Act (order as to disposal of infringing article, &c).

(3) An application for an order under this section may not be made after the end of the period of six years from the date on which the article or thing in question was made, subject to subsection (4).

(4) If during the whole or any part of that period the registered proprietor—

    (a) is under a disability, or

    (b) is prevented by fraud or concealment from discovering the facts entitling him to apply for an order,

an application may be made at any time before the end of the period of six years from the date on which he ceased to be under a disability or, as the case may be, could with reasonable diligence have discovered those facts.

---

[109] Inserted by the Intellectual Property (Enforcement, etc.) Regulations 2006 (SI 2006/1028) reg.2, Sch.1, paras 1 and 3.
[110] Inserted by the Intellectual Property (Enforcement, etc.) Regulations 2006 (SI 2006/1028) reg.2, Sch.1, paras 1 and 3.

(5) In subsection (4) "disability"—

(a) in England and Wales, has the same meaning as in the Limitation Act 1980;

(b) in Scotland, means legal disability within the meaning of the Prescription and Limitation (Scotland) Act 1973;

(c) in Northern Ireland, has the same meaning as in the Statute of Limitations (Northern Ireland) 1958.

(6) A person to whom an infringing article or other thing is delivered up in pursuance of an order under this section shall, if an order under section 24D of this Act is not made, retain it pending the making of an order, or the decision not to make an order, under that section.

(7) The reference in subsection (1) to an act being done in relation to an article for "commercial purposes" are to its being done with a view to the article in question being sold or hired in the course of a business.

(8) Nothing in this section affects any other power of the court.][111]

[Order as to disposal of infringing articles, &c

A2–051   24D.—(1) An application may be made to the court for an order that an infringing article or other thing delivered up in pursuance of an order under section 24C of this Act shall be—

(a) forfeited to the registered proprietor, or

(b) destroyed or otherwise dealt with as the court may think fit,

or for a decision that no such order should be made.

(2) In considering what order (if any) should be made, the court shall consider whether other remedies available in an action for infringement of the right in a registered design would be adequate to compensate the registered proprietor and to protect his interests.

(3) Where there is more than one person interested in an article or other thing, the court shall make such order as it thinks just and may (in particular) direct that the thing be sold, or otherwise dealt with, and the proceeds divided.

(4) If the court decides that no order should be made under this section, the person in whose possession, custody or control the article or other thing was before being delivered up is entitled to its return.

(5) References in this section to a person having an interest in an article or other thing include any person in whose favour an order could be made in respect of it—

(a) under this section;

(b) under section 19 of Trade Marks Act 1994 (including that section as applied by regulation 4 of the Community Trade Mark Regulations 2006 (SI 2006/1027));

(c) under section 114, 204 or 231 of the Copyright, Designs and Patents Act 1988; or

(d) under regulation 1C of the Community Design Regulations 2005 (SI 2005/2339).][112]

[Jurisdiction of county court and sheriff court

A2–052   24E.—(1) In Northern Ireland a county court may entertain proceedings under the following provisions of this Act—

---

[111] Inserted by the Intellectual Property (Enforcement, etc.) Regulations 2006 (SI 2006/1028) reg.2, Sch.1, paras 1 and 3.

[112] Inserted by the Intellectual Property (Enforcement, etc.) Regulations 2006 (SI 2006/1028) reg.2, Sch.1, paras 1 and 3.

section 24C (order for delivery up of infringing article, &c),

section 24D (order as to disposal of infringing article, &c), or

section 24F(8) (application by exclusive licensee having concurrent rights),

where the value of the infringing articles and other things in question does not exceed the county court limit for actions in tort.

(2) In Scotland proceedings for an order under any of those provisions may be brought in the sheriff court.

(3) Nothing in this section shall be construed as affecting the jurisdiction of the Court of Session or the High Court in Northern Ireland.][113]

[Rights and remedies of exclusive licensee

24F.—(1) In relation to a registered design, an exclusive licensee has, except against the registered proprietor, the same rights and remedies in respect of matters occurring after the grant of the licence as if the licence had been an assignment. **A2–053**

(2) His rights and remedies are concurrent with those of the registered proprietor; and references to the registered proprietor in the provisions of this Act relating to infringement shall be construed accordingly.

(3) In an action brought by an exclusive licensee by virtue of this section a defendant may avail himself of any defence which would have been available to him if the action had been brought by the registered proprietor.

(4) Where an action for infringement of the right in a registered design brought by the registered proprietor or an exclusive licensee relates (wholly or partly) to an infringement in respect of which they have concurrent rights of action, the proprietor or, as the case may be, the exclusive licensee may not, without the leave of the court, proceed with the action unless the other is either joined as a claimant or added as a defendant.

(5) A registered proprietor or exclusive licensee who is added as a defendant in pursuance of subsection (4) is not liable for any costs in the action unless he takes part in the proceedings.

(6) Subsections (4) and (5) do not affect the granting of interlocutory relief on the application of the registered proprietor or an exclusive licensee.

(7) Where an action for infringement of the right in a registered design is brought which relates (wholly or partly) to an infringement in respect of which the registered proprietor and an exclusive licensee have concurrent rights of action—

(a) the court shall, in assessing damages, take into account—
  (i) the terms of the licence, and
  (ii) any pecuniary remedy already awarded or available to either of them in respect of the infringement;
(b) no account of profits shall be directed if an award of damages has been made, or an account of profits has been directed, in favour of the other of them in respect of the infringement; and
(c) the court shall if an account of profits is directed apportion the profits between them as the court considers just, subject to any agreement between them;

and these provisions apply whether or not the proprietor and the exclusive licensee are both parties to the action.

(8) The registered proprietor shall notify any exclusive licensee having concurrent rights before applying for an order under section 24C of this Act (order for

---

[113] Inserted by the Intellectual Property (Enforcement, etc.) Regulations 2006 (SI 2006/1028) reg.2, Sch.1, paras 1 and 3.

delivery up of infringing article, &c); and the court may on the application of the licensee make such order under that section as it thinks fit having regard to the terms of the licence..][114]

[Meaning of "infringing article"

A2–054   **24G.**—(1) In this Act "infringing article", in relation to a design, shall be construed in accordance with this section.

(2) An article is an infringing article if its making to that design was an infringement of the right in a registered design.

(3) An article is also an infringing article if—

    (a) it has been or is proposed to be imported into the United Kingdom, and

    (b) its making to that design in the United Kingdom would have been an infringement of the right in a registered design or a breach of an exclusive licensing agreement relating to that registered design.

(4) Where it is shown that an article is made to a design which is or has been a registered design, it shall be presumed until the contrary is proved that the article was made at a time when the right in the registered design subsisted.

(5) Nothing in subsection (3) shall be construed as applying to an article which may be lawfully imported into the United Kingdom by virtue of an enforceable Community right within the meaning of section 2(1) of the European Communities Act 1972.][115]

Certificate of contested validity of registration

A2–055   **25.**—(1) If in any proceedings before the court the validity of the registration of a design is contested, and it is found by the court that the design is[, to any extent,][116] validly registered, the court may certify that the validity of the registration of the design was contested in those proceedings.

(2) Where any such certificate has been granted, then if in any subsequent proceedings before the court for infringement of the right in the registered design or for [invalidation][117] of the registration of the design, a final order or judgment is made or given in favour of the registered proprietor, he shall, unless the court otherwise directs, be entitled to his costs as between solicitor and client: Provided that this subsection shall not apply to the costs of any appeal in any such proceedings as aforesaid.

Remedy for groundless threats of infringement proceedings

A2–056   **26.**—(1) Where any person (whether entitled to or interested in a registered design or an application for registration of a design or not) by circulars, advertisements or otherwise threatens any other person with proceedings for infringement of [the right in a registered design] any person aggrieved thereby may bring an action against him for any such relief as is mentioned in the next following subsection.

(2) Unless in any action brought by virtue of this section the defendant proves that the acts in respect of which proceedings were threatened constitute or, if done, would constitute, an infringement of the right in a registered design the

---

[114] Inserted by the Intellectual Property (Enforcement, etc.) Regulations 2006 (SI 2006/1028) reg.2, Sch.1, paras 1 and 3.

[115] Inserted by the Intellectual Property (Enforcement, etc.) Regulations 2006 (SI 2006/1028) reg.2, Sch.1, paras 1 and 3.

[116] Substituted by the Registered Designs Regulations (SI 2001/3949) Sch.1, para.8.

[117] Substituted by the Registered Designs Regulations (SI 2001/3949) Sch.1, para.8.

registration of which is not shown by the [claimant][118] to be invalid, the [claimant][119] shall be entitled to the following relief, that is to say—

    (a) a declaration to the effect that the threats are unjustifiable;

    (b) an injunction against the continuance of the threats; and

    (c) such damages, if any, as he has sustained thereby.

(2A) Proceedings may not be brought under this section in respect of a threat to bring proceedings for an infringement alleged to consist of the making or importing of anything.

(3) For the avoidance of doubt it is hereby declared that a mere notification that a design is registered does not constitute a threat of proceedings within the meaning of this section.

The court

27.—(1) In this Act "the court" means—   **A2–057**

    (a) in England and Wales the High Court or any patents county court having jurisdiction by virtue of an order under section 287 of the Copyright, Designs and Patents Act 1988,

    (b) in Scotland, the Court of Session, and

    (c) in Northern Ireland, the High Court.

(2) Provision may be made by rules of court with respect to proceedings in the High Court in England and Wales for references and applications under this Act to be dealt with by such judge of that court as the [Lord Chief Justice of England and Wales may, after consulting the Lord Chancellor, select][120] for the purpose.

[(3) The Lord Chief Justice may nominate a judicial office holder (as defined in section 109(4) of the Constitutional Reform Act 2005) to exercise his functions under subsection (2).][121]

The Appeal Tribunal

28.—(1) Any appeal from the registrar under this Act shall lie to the Appeal **A2–058** Tribunal.

(2) The Appeal Tribunal shall consist of—

    (a) one or more judges of the High Court nominated [by the Lord Chief Justice of England and Wales after consulting the Lord Chancellor,][122] and

    (b) one judge of the Court of Session nominated by the Lord President of that Court.

(2A) At any time when it consists of two or more judges, the jurisdiction of the Appeal Tribunal—

    (a) where in the case of any particular appeal the senior of those judges so directs, shall be exercised in relation to that appeal by both of the judges, or (if there are more than two) by two of them, sitting together, and

    (b) in relation to any appeal in respect of which no such direction is given, may be exercised by any one of the judges;

[118] Substituted by the Intellectual Property (Enforcement, etc.) Regulations 2006 (SI 2006/1028) reg.2, Sch.1, paras 1 and 4.

[119] Substituted by the Intellectual Property (Enforcement, etc.) Regulations 2006 (SI 2006/1028) reg.2, Sch.1, paras 1 and 4.

[120] Substituted by the Constitutional Reform Act 2005, s.15(1) Sch.4, Pt 1, paras 35 and 36.

[121] Inserted by the Constitutional Reform Act 2005, s.15(1) Sch.4, Pt 1, paras 35 and 36.

[122] Substituted by the Constitutional Reform Act 2005, s.15(1) Sch.4, Pt 1, paras 35 and 37.

and, in the exercise of that jurisdiction, different appeals may be heard at the same time by different judges.

(3) The expenses of the Appeal Tribunal shall be defrayed and the fees to be taken therein may be fixed as if the Tribunal were a court of the High Court.

(4) The Appeal Tribunal may examine witnesses on oath and administer oaths for that purpose.

(5) Upon any appeal under this Act the Appeal Tribunal may by order award to any party such costs [...]^{123} as the Tribunal may consider reasonable and direct how and by what parties the costs [...]^{124} are to be paid; and any such order may be enforced—

    (a) in England and Wales or Northern Ireland, in the same way as an order of the High Court;

    (b) in Scotland, in the same way as a decree for expenses granted by the Court of Session.

(6) ...

(7) Upon any appeal under this Act the Appeal Tribunal may exercise any power which could have been exercised by the registrar in the proceeding from which the appeal is brought.

(8) Subject to the foregoing provisions of this section the Appeal Tribunal may make rules for regulating all matters relating to proceedings before it under this Act including right of audience.

(8A) At any time when the Appeal Tribunal consists of two or more judges, the power to make rules under sub-section (8) of this section shall be exercisable by the senior of those judges: Provided that another of those judges may exercise of that power if it appears to him that it is necessary for rules to be made and that the judge (or, if more than one, each of the judges) senior to him is for the time being prevented by illness, absence or otherwise from making them.

(9) An appeal to the Appeal Tribunal under this Act shall not be deemed to be a proceeding in the High Court.

(10) In this section "the High Court" means the High Court in England and Wales; and for the purposes of this section the seniority of judges shall be reckoned by reference to the dates on which they were appointed judges of that court or the Court of Session.

[(11) The Lord Chief Justice may nominate a judicial office holder (as defined in section 109(4) of the Constitutional Reform Act 2005) to exercise his functions under subsection (2)(a).]^{125}

Exercise of discretionary powers of registrar

A2–059   **29.**—Without prejudice to any provisions of this Act requiring the registrar to hear any party to proceedings thereunder, or to give to any such party an opportunity to be heard, rules made by the Secretary of State under this Act shall require the registrar to give to any applicant for registration of a design an opportunity to be heard before exercising adversely to the applicant any discretion vested in the registrar by or under this Act.

---

^{123} Repealed by the Intellectual Property (Enforcement, etc.) Regulations 2006 (SI 2006/1028) reg.2 and Sch.4.

^{124} Repealed by the Intellectual Property (Enforcement, etc.) Regulations 2006 (SI 2006/1028) reg.2 and Sch.4.

^{125} Inserted by the Constitutional Reform Act 2005, s.15(1) and Sch.4, Pt 1, paras 35 and 37.

Costs and security for costs

30.—(1) Rules made by the Secretary of State under this Act may make   **A2–060**
provision empowering the registrar, in any proceedings before him under this
Act—

- (a) to award any party such costs as he may consider reasonable, and
- (b) to direct how and by what parties they are to be paid.

(2) Any such order of the registrar may be enforced—

- (a) in England and Wales or Northern Ireland, in the same way as an order
  of the High Court;
- (b) in Scotland, in the same way as a decree for expenses granted by the
  Court of Session.

(3) Rules made by the Secretary of State under this Act may make provision
empowering the registrar to require a person, in such cases as may be prescribed,
to give security for the costs of—

- (a) an application for [invalidation][126] of the registration of a design,
- (b) [...][127]
- (c) an appeal from any decision of the registrar under this Act,

and enabling the application or appeal to be treated as abandoned in default of
such security being given.

Evidence before registrar

31.—Rules made by the Secretary of State under this Act may make provi-   **A2–061**
sion—

- (a) as to the giving of evidence in proceedings before the registrar under this
  Act by affidavit or statutory declaration;
- (b) conferring on the registrar the powers of an official referee of the [Senior
  Courts][128] [or of the Court of Judicature][129] as regards the examination of
  witnesses on oath and the discovery and production of documents;
  and
- (c) applying in relation to the attendance of witness in proceedings before
  the registrar the rules applicable to the attendance of witnesses in
  proceedings before such a referee.

32.— ...   **A2–062**

Offences under s.5

33.—(1) If any person fails to comply with any direction given under section   **A2–063**
five of this Act or makes or causes to be made an application for the registration
of a design in contravention of that section, he shall be guilty of an offence and
liable—

- (a) on conviction on indictment to imprisonment for a term not exceeding
  two years or a fine, or both;
- (b) on summary conviction to imprisonment for a term not exceeding six
  months or a fine not exceeding the statutory maximum, or both.

(2) ...

[126] Substituted by the Registered Designs Regulations (SI 2001/3949) Sch.1, para.9.
[127] Repealed by the Registered Designs Regulations (SI 2001/3949) Sch.2.
[128] Substituted by the Constitutional Reform Act 2005, s.59(5) Sch.11, Pt.2, para.4.
[129] Inserted by the Constitutional Reform Act 2005 s.59(5) and Sch.11, Pt 4, para.18.

Falsification of register, etc

A2–064   34.—If any person makes or causes to be made a false entry in the register of designs, or a writing falsely purporting to be a copy of an entry in that register, or produces or tenders or causes to be produced or tendered in evidence any such writing, knowing the entry or writing to be false, he shall be guilty of an offence and liable—

(a) on conviction on indictment to imprisonment for a term not exceeding two years or a fine, or both;

(b) on summary conviction to imprisonment for a term not exceeding six months or a fine not exceeding the statutory maximum, or both.

Fine for falsely representing a design as registered

A2–065   35.—(1) If any person falsely represents that a design applied to[, or incorporated in, any product][130] sold by him is registered [. . .][131], he shall be liable on summary conviction to a fine not exceeding level 3 on the standard scale; and for the purposes of this provision a person who sells [a product][132] having stamped, engraved or impressed thereon or otherwise applied thereto the word "registered", or any other word expressing or implying that the design applied to[, or incorporated in, the product][133] is registered, shall be deemed to represent that the design applied to[, or incorporated in, the product][134] is registered [. . .].[135]

(2) If any person, after the right in a registered design has expired, marks [any product][136] to which the design has been applied [or in which it has been incorporated][137] with the word "registered", or any word or words implying that there is a subsisting right in the design under this Act, or causes any [such product][138] to be so marked, he shall be liable on summary conviction to a fine not exceeding level 1 on the standard scale.

[(3) For the purposes of this section, the use in the United Kingdom in relation to a design—

(a) of the word "registered", or

(b) of any other word or symbol importing a reference (express or implied) to registration,

shall be deemed to be a representation as to registration under this Act unless it is shown that the reference is to registration elsewhere than in the United Kingdom and that the design is in fact so registered.][139]

Offence by body corporate: liability of officers

A2–066   35A.—(1) Where an offence under this Act committed by a body corporate is proved to have been committed with the consent or connivance of a director, manager, secretary or other similar officer of the body, or a person purporting to

---

[130] Inserted by the Registered Designs Regulations (SI 2001/3949) Sch.1, para.10.
[131] Repealed by the Registered Designs Regulations (SI 2001/3949) Sch.1, para.10 and Sch.2.
[132] Substituted by the Registered Designs Regulations (SI 2001/3949) Sch.1, para.10.
[133] Substituted by the Registered Designs Regulations (SI 2001/3949) Sch.1, para.10.
[134] Substituted by the Registered Designs Regulations (SI 2001/3949) Sch.1, para.10.
[135] Repealed by the Registered Designs Regulations (SI 2001/3949) Sch.1, para.10 and Sch.2.
[136] Substituted by the Registered Designs Regulations (SI 2001/3949) Sch.1, para.10.
[137] Inserted by the Registered Designs Regulations (SI 2001/3949) Sch.1, para.10.
[138] Substituted by the Registered Designs Regulations (SI 2001/3949) Sch.1, para.10.
[139] Inserted by the Community Design Regulations 2005 (SI 2005/2339) reg.6.

act in any such capacity, he as well as the body corporate is guilty of the offence and liable to be proceeded against and punished accordingly.

(2) In relation to a body corporate whose affairs are managed by its members "director" means a member of the body corporate.

General power of Board of Trade to make rules, etc

36.—(1) Subject to the provisions of this Act, the Secretary of State may make such rules as he thinks expedient for regulating the business of the Patent Office in relation to designs and for regulating all matters by this Act placed under the direction or control of the registrar or the Secretary of State, **A2–067**

(1A) Rules may, in particular, make provision—

(a) prescribing the form of applications for registration of designs and of any representations or specimens of designs or other documents which may be filed at the Patent Office, and requiring copies to be furnished of any such representations, specimens or documents;

[(ab) requiring applications for registration of designs to specify—

(i) the products to which the designs are intended to be applied or in which they are intended to be incorporated;

(ii) the classification of the designs by reference to such test as may be prescribed;][140]

(b) regulating the procedure to be followed in connection with any application or request to the registrar or in connection with any proceeding before him, and authorising the rectification of irregularities of procedure;

(c) providing for the appointment of advisers to assist the registrar in proceedings before him;

(d) regulating the keeping of the register of designs;

(e) authorising the publication and sale of copies of representations of designs and other documents in the Patent Office;

(f) prescribing anything authorised or required by this Act to be prescribed by rules.

(1B) The remuneration of an adviser appointed to assist the registrar shall be determined by the Secretary of State with the consent of the Treasury and shall be defrayed out of money provided by Parliament.

(2) Rules made under this section may provide for the establishment of branch offices for designs and may authorise any document or thing required by or under this Act to be filed or done at the Patent Office to be filed or done at the branch office at Manchester or any other branch office established in pursuance of the rules.

Provisions as to rules and Orders

37.—(2) Any rules made by the Secretary of State in pursuance of [section 15 of this Act],[141] and any order made, direction given, or other action taken under the rules by the registrar, may be made, given or taken so as to have effect as respects things done or omitted to be done on or after such date, whether before or after the coming into operation of the rules or of this Act, as may be specified in the rules. **A2–068**

(3) Any power to make rules conferred by this Act on the Secretary of State or on the Appeal Tribunal shall be exercisable by statutory instrument; and the Statutory Instruments Act 1946, shall apply to a statutory instrument containing

---

[140] Added by the Registered Designs Regulations (SI 2001/3949) Sch.1, para.11.
[141] Substituted by the Registered Designs Regulations (SI 2001/3949) Sch.1, para.12.

rules made by the Appeal Tribunal in like manner as if the rules had been made by a Minister of the Crown.

(4) Any statutory instrument containing rules made by the Secretary of State under this Act shall be subject to annulment in pursuance of a resolution of either House of Parliament.

(5) Any Order in Council made under this Act may be revoked or varied by a subsequent Order in Council.

[Use of electronic communications

A2–069   **37A.**—(1) The registrar may give directions as to the form and manner in which documents to be delivered to the registrar—

    (a) in electronic form; or

    (b) using electronic communications,

are to be delivered to him.

(2) A direction under subsection (1) may provide that in order for a document to be delivered in compliance with the direction it shall be accompanied by one or more additional documents specified in the direction.

(3) Subject to subsections (11) and (12), if a document to which a direction under subsection (1) or (2) applies is delivered to the registrar in a form or manner which does not comply with the direction the registrar may treat the document as not having been delivered.

(4) Subsection (5) applies in relation to a case where—

    (a) a document is delivered using electronic communications, and

    (b) there is a requirement for a fee to accompany the document.

(5) The registrar may give directions specifying—

    (a) how the fee shall be paid; and

    (b) when the fee shall be deemed to have been paid.

(6) The registrar may give directions specifying that a person who delivers a document to the registrar in electronic form or using electronic communications cannot treat the document as having been delivered unless its delivery has been acknowledged.

(7) The registrar may give directions specifying how a time of delivery is to be accorded to a document delivered to him in electronic form or using electronic communications.

(8) A direction under this section may be given—

    (a) generally;

    (b) in relation to a description of cases specified in the direction;

    (c) in relation to a particular person or persons.

(9) A direction under this section may be varied or revoked by a subsequent direction under this section.

(10) The delivery using electronic communications to any person by the registrar of any document is deemed to be effected, unless the registrar has otherwise specified, by transmitting an electronic communication containing the document to an address provided or made available to the registrar by that person as an address of his for the receipt of electronic communications; and unless the contrary is proved such delivery is deemed to be effected immediately upon the transmission of the communication.

(11) A requirement of this Act that something must be done in the prescribed manner is satisfied in the case of something that is done—

    (a) using a document in electronic form, or

(b) using electronic communications,

only if the directions under this section that apply to the manner in which it is done are complied with.

(12) In the case of an application made as mentioned in subsection (11)(a) or (b) above, a reference in this Act to the application not having been made in accordance with rules under this Act includes a reference to its not having been made in accordance with any applicable directions under this section.

(13) This section applies—

(a) to delivery at the Patent Office as it applies to delivery to the registrar; and

(b) to delivery by the Patent Office as it applies to delivery by the registrar.][142]

Proceedings of Board of Trade

38.—(1) . . .   A2–070

Hours of business and excluded days

39.—(1) Rules made by the Secretary of State under this Act may specify the   A2–071
hour at which the Patent Office shall be deemed to be closed on any day for purposes of the transaction by the public of business under this Act or of any class of such business, and may specify days as excluded days for any such purposes.

(2) Any business done under this Act on any day after the hour specified as aforesaid in relation to business of that class, or an a day which is an excluded day in relation to business of that class, shall be deemed to have been done on the next following day not being an excluded day; and where the time for doing anything under this Act expires on an excluded day, that time shall be extended to the next following day not being an excluded day.

Fees

40.—There shall be paid in respect of the registration of designs and applica-   A2–072
tions therefor, and in respect of other matters relating to designs arising under this Act, such fees as may be prescribed by rules made by the Secretary of State with the consent of the Treasury.

Service of notices, etc, by post

41.—Any notice required or authorised to be given by or under this Act, and   A2–073
any application or other document so authorised or required to be made or filed, may be given, made or filed by post.

Annual report of registrar

42.—The Comptroller-General of Patents, Designs and Trade Marks shall, in his   A2–074
annual report with respect to the execution of the Patents Act 1977, include a report with respect to the execution of this Act as if it formed a part of or was included in that Act.

---

[142] Inserted by the Registered Designs Act 1949 and Patents Act 1977 (Electronic Communications) Order 2006 (SI 2006/1229) art.2.

Savings

A2–075   **43.**—(1) [. . .]¹⁴³

(2) Nothing in this Act shall affect the right of the Crown or of any person deriving title directly or indirectly from the Crown to sell or use [products]¹⁴⁴ forfeited under the laws relating to customs or excise.

Interpretation

A2–076   **44.**—(1) In this Act, except where the context otherwise requires, the following expressions have the meanings hereby respectively assigned by them, that is to say—

"Appeal Tribunal" means the Appeal Tribunal constituted and acting in accordance with section 28 of this Act as amended by the Administration of Justice Act 1969;
[. . .]¹⁴⁵
[. . .]¹⁴⁶
"assignee" includes the personal representative of a deceased assignee, and references to the assignee of any person include references to the assignee of the personal representative or assignee of that person;
"author" in relation to a design, has the meaning given by section 2(3) and (4);
["Community Design Regulation" means Council Regulation (EC) 6/2002 of 12th December 2001 on Community Designs;]¹⁴⁷
["complex product" has the meaning assigned to it by section 1(3) of this Act;]¹⁴⁸
[. . .]¹⁴⁹
"the court" shall be construed in accordance with section 27 of this Act;
"design" has the meaning assigned to it by [section 1(2)]¹⁵⁰ of this Act;
["electronic communication" has the same meaning as in the Electronic Communications Act 2000;]¹⁵¹
"employee", "employment" and "employer" refer to employment under a contract of service or of apprenticeship,
["national unregistered design right" means design right within the meaning of Part III of the Copyright, Designs and Patents Act 1988;]¹⁵²
"prescribed" means prescribed by rules made by the Secretary of State under this Act;
["product" has the meaning assigned to it by section 1(3) of this Act;]¹⁵³
"proprietor" has the meaning assigned to it by section two of this Act;
["registered Community design" means a design that complies with the conditions contained in, and is registered in the manner provided for in, the Community Design Regulation;]¹⁵⁴

---

¹⁴³ Repealed by the Registered Designs Regulations (SI 2001/3949) Sch.2.
¹⁴⁴ Substituted by the Registered Designs Regulations (SI 2001/3949) Sch.1, para.13.
¹⁴⁵ Repealed by the Registered Designs Regulations (SI 2001/3949) Sch.2.
¹⁴⁶ Repealed by the Registered Designs Regulations (SI 2001/3949) Sch.2.
¹⁴⁷ Inserted by the Registered Designs Regulations (SI 2003/550) reg.2.
¹⁴⁸ Inserted by the Registered Designs Regulations (SI 2001/3949) Sch.1, para.14.
¹⁴⁹ Repealed by the Registered Designs Regulations (SI 2001/3949) Sch.2.
¹⁵⁰ Substituted by the Registered Designs Regulations (SI 2001/3949) Sch.1, para.14.
¹⁵¹ Inserted by the Registered Designs Act 1949 and Patents Act 1977 (Electronic Communications) Order 2006 (SI 2006/1229) art.3.
¹⁵² Substituted by the Registered Designs Regulations (SI 2001/3949) Sch.1, para.14.
¹⁵³ Substituted by the Registered Designs Regulations (SI 2001/3949) Sch.1, para.14.
¹⁵⁴ Inserted by the Registered Designs Regulations (SI 2003/550) reg.2.

"registered proprietor" means the person or persons for the time being entered in the register of designs as proprietor of the design;

"registrar" means the Comptroller-General of Patents Designs and Trade Marks;

[...]¹⁵⁵

(2) [...]¹⁵⁶

(3) [...]¹⁵⁷

(4) For the purposes of subsection (1) of [section 14 of this Act]¹⁵⁸, the expression "personal representative", in relation to a deceased person, includes the legal representative of the deceased appointed in any country outside the United Kingdom.

[Application to Scotland

45.—(1) In the application of this Act to Scotland—   **A2–077**

"account of profits" means accounting and payment of profits;
"accounts" means count, reckoning and payment;
"arbitrator" means arbiter;
"assignment" means assignation;
"claimant" means pursuer;
"costs" means expenses;
"defendant" means defender;
"delivery up" means delivery;
"injunction" means interdict;
"interlocutory relief" means interim remedy.

(2) References to the Crown shall be construed as including references to the Crown in right of the Scottish Administration.]¹⁵⁹

Application to Northern Ireland

46.—In the application of this Act to Northern Ireland—   **A2–078**

(1) ...

(2) ...

(3) References to enactments include enactments comprised in Northern Ireland legislation:

(3A) References to the Crown include the Crown in right of Her Majesty's Government in Northern Ireland:

(4) References to a Government department shall be construed as including references to a Northern Ireland department and in relation to a Northern Ireland department references to the Treasury shall be construed as references to the Department of Finance and Personnel:

[(4A) Any reference to a claimant includes a reference to a plaintiff.]¹⁶⁰

(5) ...

Application to Isle of Man

47.—This Act extends to the Isle of Man, subject to any modifications contained   **A2–079**
in an Order made by Her Majesty in Council, and accordingly, subject to any such

---

¹⁵⁵ Repealed by the Registered Designs Regulations (SI 2001/3949) Sch.2.
¹⁵⁶ Repealed by the Registered Designs Regulations (SI 2001/3949) Sch.2.
¹⁵⁷ Repealed by the Registered Designs Regulations (SI 2001/3949) Sch.2.
¹⁵⁸ Substituted by the Registered Designs Regulations (SI 2001/3949) Sch.1, para.14.
¹⁵⁹ Substituted by the Intellectual Property (Enforcement, etc.) Regulations 2006 (SI 2006/1028) reg.2 and Sch.1, paras 1 and 5.
¹⁶⁰ Inserted by the Intellectual Property (Enforcement, etc.) Regulations 2006 (SI 2006/1028) reg.2 and Sch.1, paras 1 and 6.

Order, references in this Act to the United Kingdom shall be construed as including the Isle of Man.

Territorial waters and the Continental shelf

A2–080 **47A.**—(1) For the purposes of this Act the territorial waters of the United Kingdom shall be treated as part of the United Kingdom.

(2) This Act applies to things done in the United Kingdom sector of the continental shelf on a structure or vessel which is present there for purposes directly connected with the exploration of the sea bed or subsoil or the exploitation of their natural resources as it applies to things done in the United Kingdom.

(3) The United Kingdom sector of the continental shelf means the areas designated by order under section 1(7) of the Continental Shelf Act 1964.

Repeals, savings, and transitional provisions

A2–081 **48.**—(2) Subject to the provisions of this section, any Order in Council, rule, order, requirement, certificate, notice, decision, direction, authorisation, consent, application, request or thing made, issued, given or done under any enactment repealed by this Act shall, if in force at the commencement of this Act, and so far as it could have been made, issued, given or done under this Act, continue in force and have effect as if made, issued, given or done under the corresponding enactment of this Act.

(3) Any register kept under the Patents and Designs Act 1907, shall be deemed to form part of the corresponding register under this Act.

(4) Any design registered before the commencement of this Act shall be deemed to be registered under this Act in respect of articles of the class in which it is registered.

(5) [. . .][161]

(6) Any document referring to any enactment repealed by this Act shall be construed as referring to the corresponding enactment of this Act.

(7) Nothing in the foregoing provisions of this section shall be taken as prejudicing the operation of section 16(1) and section 17(2)(a) of the Interpretation Act 1978, (which relate to the effect of repeals).

Short title and commencement

A2–082 **49.**—(1) This Act may be cited as the Registered Designs Act 1949.

(2) This Act shall come into operation on the first day of January, nineteen hundred and fifty, immediately after the coming into operation of the Patents and Designs Act 1949.

[SCHEDULE A1]

GROUNDS FOR REFUSAL OF REGISTRATION IN RELATION TO EMBLEMS ETC

Grounds for refusal in relation to certain emblems etc

A2–083 **1.**—(1) A design shall be refused registration under this Act if it involves the use of—

  (a) the Royal arms, or any of the principal armorial bearings of the Royal arms, or any insignia or device so nearly resembling the Royal arms or any such armorial bearing as to be likely to be mistaken for them or it;

  (b) a representation of the Royal crown or any of the Royal flags;

  (c) a representation of Her Majesty or any member of the Royal family, or any colourable imitation thereof; or

[161] Repealed by the Registered Designs Regulations (SI 2001/3949) Sch.2.

(d)   words, letters or devices likely to lead persons to think that the applicant either has or recently has had Royal patronage or authorisation;

unless it appears to the registrar that consent for such use has been given by or on behalf of Her Majesty or (as the case may be) the relevant member of the Royal family.

(2) A design shall be refused registration under this Act if it involves the use of—

(a)   the national flag of the United Kingdom (commonly known as the Union Jack); or

(b)   the flag of England, Wales, Scotland, Northern Ireland or the Isle of Man,

and it appears to the registrar that the use would be misleading or grossly offensive.

(3) A design shall be refused registration under this Act if it involves the use of—

(a)   arms to which a person is entitled by virtue of a grant of arms by the Crown; or

(b)   insignia so nearly resembling such arms as to be likely to be mistaken for them;

unless it appears to the registrar that consent for such use has been given by or on behalf of the person concerned and the use is not in any way contrary to the law of arms.

(4) A design shall be refused registration under this Act if it involves the use of a controlled representation within the meaning of the Olympic Symbol etc. (Protection) Act 1995 unless it appears to the registrar that—

(a)   the application is made by the person for the time being appointed under section 1(2) of the Olympic Symbol etc. (Protection) Act 1995 (power of Secretary of State to appoint a person as the proprietor of the Olympics association right); or

(b)   consent for such use has been given by or on behalf of the person mentioned in paragraph (a) above.

Grounds for refusal in relation to emblems etc. of Paris Convention countries

2.—(1) A design shall be refused registration under this Act if it involves the use of the flag of a Paris Convention country unless—   **A2–084**

(a)   the authorisation of the competent authorities of that country has been given for the registration; or

(b)   it appears to the registrar that the use of the flag in the manner proposed is permitted without such authorisation.

(2) A design shall be refused registration under this Act if it involves the use of the armorial bearings or any other state emblem of a Paris Convention country which is protected under the Paris Convention unless the authorisation of the competent authorities of that country has been given for the registration.

(3) A design shall be refused registration under this Act if—

(a)   the design involves the use of an official sign or hallmark adopted by a Paris Convention country and indicating control and warranty;

(b)   the sign or hallmark is protected under the Paris Convention; and

(c)   the design could be applied to or incorporated in goods of the same, or a similar, kind as those in relation to which the sign or hallmark indicates control and warranty;

unless the authorisation of the competent authorities of that country has been given for the registration.

(4) The provisions of this paragraph as to national flags and other state emblems, and official signs or hallmarks, apply equally to anything which from a heraldic point of view imitates any such flag or other emblem, or sign or hallmark.

(5) Nothing in this paragraph prevents the registration of a design on the application of a national of a country who is authorised to make use of a state emblem, or official sign or hallmark, of that country, notwithstanding that it is similar to that of another country.

Grounds for refusal in relation to emblems etc. of certain international organisations

3.—(1) This paragraph applies to—   **A2–085**

(a)   the armorial bearings, flags or other emblems; and

(b)   the abbreviations and names,

of international intergovernmental organisations of which one or more Paris Convention countries are members.

(2) A design shall be refused registration under this Act if it involves the use of any such emblem, abbreviation or name which is protected under the Paris Convention unless—

(a)   the authorisation of the international organisation concerned has been given for the registration; or

(b)   it appears to the registrar that the use of the emblem, abbreviation or name in the manner proposed—

(i) is not such as to suggest to the public that a connection exists between the organisation and the design; or

(ii) is not likely to mislead the public as to the existence of a connection between the user and the organisation.

(3) The provisions of this paragraph as to emblems of an international organisation apply equally to anything which from a heraldic point of view imitates any such emblem.

(4) Nothing in this paragraph affects the rights of a person whose bona fide use of the design in question began before 4th January 1962 (when the relevant provisions of the Paris Convention entered into force in relation to the United Kingdom).

Paragraphs 2 and 3: supplementary

A2–086

4.—(1) For the purposes of paragraph 2 above state emblems of a Paris Convention country (other than the national flag), and official signs or hallmarks, shall be regarded as protected under the Paris Convention only if, or to the extent that—

(a) the country in question has notified the United Kingdom in accordance with Article 6ter(3) of the Convention that it desires to protect that emblem, sign or hallmark;

(b) the notification remains in force; and

(c) the United Kingdom has not objected to it in accordance with Article 6ter(4) or any such objection has been withdrawn.

(2) For the purposes of paragraph 3 above the emblems, abbreviations and names of an international organisation shall be regarded as protected under the Paris Convention only if, or to the extent that—

(a) the organisation in question has notified the United Kingdom in accordance with Article 6ter(3) of the Convention that it desires to protect that emblem, abbreviation or name;

(b) the notification remains in force; and

(c) the United Kingdom has not objected to it in accordance with Article 6ter(4) or any such objection has been withdrawn.

(3) Notification under Article 6ter(3) of the Paris Convention shall have effect only in relation to applications for the registration of designs made more than two months after the receipt of the notification.

Interpretation

A2–087

5.—In this Schedule—

"a Paris Convention country" means a country, other than the United Kingdom, which is a party to the Paris Convention; and

"the Paris Convention" means the Paris Convention for the Protection of Industrial Property of 20th March 1883.][162]

SCHEDULE 1

PROVISIONS AS TO THE USE OF REGISTERED DESIGNS FOR THE SERVICES OF THE CROWN AND AS TO THE RIGHTS OF THIRD PARTIES IN RESPECT OF SUCH USE

Use of registered designs for services of the Crown

A2–088

1.—(1) Notwithstanding anything in this Act, any Government department, and any person authorised in writing by a Government department, may use any registered design for the services of the Crown in accordance with the following provisions of this paragraph.

(2) If and so far as the design has before the date of registration thereof been duly recorded by or applied by or on behalf of a Government department otherwise than in consequence of the communication of the design directly or indirectly by the registered proprietor or any person from whom he derives title, any use of the design by virtue of this paragraph may be made free of any royalty or other payment to the registered proprietor.

(3) If and so far as the design has not been so recorded or applied as aforesaid, any use of the design made by virtue of this paragraph at any time after the date of registration thereof, or in consequence of any such communication as aforesaid, shall be made upon

---

[162] Added by the Registered Designs Regulations (SI 2001/3949) reg.3.

such terms as may be agreed upon, either before or after the use, between the Government department and the registered proprietor with the approval of the Treasury, or as may in default of agreement be determined by the court on a reference under paragraph 3 of this Schedule.

(4) The authority of a Government department in respect of a design may be given under this paragraph either before or after the design is registered and either before or after the acts in respect of which the authority is given are done, and may be given to any person whether or not he is authorised directly or indirectly by the registered proprietor to use the design.

(5) Where any use of a design is made by or with the authority of a Government department under this paragraph, then, unless it appears to the department that it would be contrary to the public interest so to do, the department shall notify the registered proprietor as soon as practicable after the use is begun, and furnish him with such information as to the extent of the use as he may from time to time require.

(6) For the purposes of this and the next following paragraph "the services of the Crown" shall be deemed to include—

(a) the supply to the government of any country outside the United Kingdom, in pursuance of an agreement or arrangement between Her Majesty's Government in the United Kingdom and the government of that country, of [products][163] required—
   (i) for the defence of that country; or
   (ii) for the defence of any other country whose government is party to any agreement or arrangement with Her Majesty's said Government in respect of defence matters;

(b) the supply to the United Nations, or to the government of any country belonging to that organisation, in pursuance of an agreement or arrangement between Her Majesty's Government and that organisation or government, of [products][164] required for any armed forced operating in pursuance of a resolution of that organisation or any organ of that organisation;

and the power of a Government department or a person authorised by a Government department under this paragraph to use a design shall include power to sell to any such government or to the said organisation any [products][165] the supply of which is authorised by this sub-paragraph, and to sell to any person any [products][166] made in the exercise of the powers conferred by this paragraph which are no longer required for the purpose for which they were made.

(7) The purchaser of any [products][167] sold in the exercise of powers conferred by this paragraph, and any person claiming through him, shall have power to deal with them in the same manner as if the rights in the registered design were held on behalf of His Majesty.

Rights of third parties in respect of Crown use

2.—(1) In relation to any use of a registered design, or a design in respect of which an **A2–089** application for registration is pending, made for the services of the Crown—

(a) by a Government department or a person authorised by a Government department under the last foregoing paragraph; or

(b) by the registered proprietor or applicant for registration to the order of a Government department,

the provisions of any licence, assignment or agreement made, whether before or after the commencement of this Act, between the registered proprietor or applicant for registration or any person who derives title from him or from whom he derives title and any person other than a Government department shall be of no effect so far as those provisions restrict or regulate the use of the design, or any model, document or information relating thereto, or provide for the making of payments in respect of any such use, or calculated by reference thereto; and the reproduction or publication of any model or document in connection with the said use shall not be deemed to be an infringement of any copyright or [national

[163] Substituted by the Registered Designs Regulations (SI 2001/3949) Sch.1, para.15.
[164] Substituted by the Registered Designs Regulations (SI 2001/3949) Sch.1, para.15.
[165] Substituted by the Registered Designs Regulations (SI 2001/3949) Sch.1, para.15.
[166] Substituted by the Registered Designs Regulations (SI 2001/3949) Sch.1, para.15.
[167] Substituted by the Registered Designs Regulations (SI 2001/3949) Sch.1, para.15.

unregistered design right][168] subsisting in the model or document or of any topography right.

(2) Where an exclusive licence granted otherwise than for royalties or other benefits determined by reference to the use of the design is in force under the registered design then—

    (a) in relation to any use of the design which, but for the provisions of this and the last foregoing paragraph, would constitute an infringement of the rights of the licensee, sub-paragraph (3) of the last foregoing paragraph shall have effect as if for the reference to the registered proprietor there were substituted a reference to the licensee; and

    (b) in relation to any use of the design by the licensee by virtue of an authority given under the last foregoing paragraph, that paragraph shall have effect as if the said sub-paragraph (3) were omitted.

(3) Subject to the provisions of the last foregoing sub-paragraph, where the registered design or the right to apply for or obtain registration of the design has been assigned to the registered proprietor in consideration of royalties or other benefits determined by reference to the use of the design, then—

    (a) in relation to any use of the design by virtue of paragraph 1 of this Schedule, sub-paragraph (3) of that paragraph shall have effect as if the reference to the registered proprietor included a reference to the assignor, and any sum payable by virtue of that sub-paragraph shall be divided between the registered proprietor and the assignor in such proportion as may be agreed upon between them or as may in default of agreement be determined by the court on a reference under the next following paragraph; and

    (b) in relation to any use of the design made for the services of the Crown by the registered proprietor to the order of a Government department, sub-paragraph (3) of paragraph 1 of this Schedule shall have effect as if that use were made by virtue of an authority given under that paragraph.

(4) Where, under sub-paragraph (3) of paragraph 1 of this Schedule, payments are required to be made by a Government department to a registered proprietor in respect of any use of a design, any person being the holder of an exclusive licence under the registered design (not being such a licence as is mentioned in sub-paragraph (2) of this paragraph) authorising him to make that use of the design shall be entitled to recover from the registered proprietor such part (if any) of those payments as may be agreed upon between that person and the registered proprietor, or as may in default of agreement be determined by the court under the next following paragraph to be just having regard to any expenditure incurred by that person—

    (a) in developing the said design; or

    (b) in making payments to the registered proprietor, other than royalties or other payments determined by reference to the use of the design, in consideration of the licence;

and if, at any time before the amount of any such payment has been agreed upon between the Government department and the registered proprietor, that person gives notice in writing of his interest to the department, any agreement as to the amount of that payment shall be of no effect unless it is made with his consent.

(5) In this paragraph "exclusive licence" means a licence from a registered proprietor which confers on the licensee, or on the licensee and persons authorised by him, to the exclusion of all other persons (including the registered proprietor), any right in respect of the registered design.

Compensation for loss of profit

A2–090   2A.—(1) Where Crown use is made of a registered design, the government department concerned shall pay—

    (a) to the registered proprietor, or

    (b) if there is an exclusive licence in force in respect of the design, to the exclusive licensee, compensation for any loss resulting from his not being awarded a contract

---

[168] Substituted by the Registered Designs Regulations (SI 2001/3949) Sch.1, para.5.

to supply the [products][169] to which the design is applied [or in which it is incorporated][170]

(2) Compensation is payable only to the extent that such a contract could have been fulfilled from his existing manufacturing capacity; but is payable notwithstanding the existence of circumstances rendering him ineligible for the award of such a contract.

(3) In determining the loss, regard shall be had to the profit which would have been made on such a contract and to the extent to which any manufacturing capacity was under used.

(4) No compensation is payable in respect of any failure to secure contracts for the supply of [products][171] to which the design is applied [or in which it is incorporated][172] otherwise than for the services of the Crown.

(5) The amount payable under this paragraph shall, if not agreed between the registered proprietor or licensee and the government department concerned with the approval of the Treasury, be determined by the court on a reference under paragraph 3, and it is in addition to any amount payable under paragraph 1 or 2 of this Schedule.

(6) In this paragraph—
"Crown use", in relation to a design, means the doing of anything by virtue of paragraph 1 which would otherwise be an infringement of the right in the design; and
"the government department concerned", in relation to such use, means the government department by whom or on whose authority the act was done.

Reference of disputes as to Crown use

A2–091

3.—(1) Any dispute as to—
  (a) the exercise by a Government department, or a person authorised by a Government department, of the powers conferred by paragraph 1 of this Schedule,
  (b) terms for the use of a design for the services of the Crown under that paragraph,
  (c) the right of any person to receive any part of a payment made under paragraph 1(3), or
  (d) the right of any person to receive a payment under paragraph 2A,
may be referred to the court by either party to the dispute.

(2) In any proceedings under this paragraph to which a Government department are a party, the department may—
  (a) if the registered proprietor is a party to the proceedings [and the department are a relevant person within the meaning of section 20 of this Act][173], apply for [invalidation][174] of the registration of the design upon any ground upon which the registration of a design may be [declared invalid][175] on an application to the court under section twenty of this Act;
  (b) in any case [and provided that the department would be the relevant person within the meaning of section 20 of this Act if they had made an application on the grounds for invalidity being raised][176], put in issue the validity of the registration of the design without applying for its [invalidation].[177]

(3) If in such proceedings as aforesaid any question arises whether a design has been recorded or applied as mentioned in paragraph 1 of this Schedule, and the disclosure of any document recording the design, or of any evidence of the application thereof, would in the opinion of the department be prejudicial to the public interest, the disclosure may be made confidentially to counsel for the other party or to an independent expert mutually agreed upon.

(4) In determining under this paragraph any dispute between a Government department and any person as to terms for the use of a design for the services of the Crown, the court

---

[169] Substituted by the Registered Designs Regulations (SI 2001/3949) Sch.1, para.15.
[170] Inserted by the Registered Designs Regulations (SI 2001/3949) Sch.1, para.15.
[171] Substituted by the Registered Designs Regulations (SI 2001/3949) Sch.1, para.15.
[172] Inserted by the Registered Designs Regulations (SI 2001/3949) Sch.1, para.15.
[173] Inserted by the Registered Designs Regulations (SI 2001/3949) Sch.1, para.15.
[174] Substituted by the Registered Designs Regulations (SI 2001/3949) Sch.1, para.15.
[175] Substituted by the Registered Designs Regulations (SI 2001/3949) Sch.1, para.15.
[176] Inserted by the Registered Designs Regulations (SI 2001/3949) Sch.1, para.15.
[177] Substituted by the Registered Designs Regulations (SI 2001/3949) Sch.1, para.15.

shall have regard to any benefit or compensation which that person or any person from whom he derives title may have received, or may be entitled to receive, directly or indirectly from any Government department in respect of the design in question.

(5) In any proceedings under this paragraph the court may at any time order the whole proceedings or any question or issue of fact arising therein to be referred to a special or official referee or an arbitrator on such terms as the court may direct; and references to the court in the foregoing provisions of this paragraph shall be construed accordingly.

Special provisions as to Crown use during emergency

A2–092   **4.**—(1) During any period of emergency within the meaning of this paragraph, the powers exercisable in relation to a design by a Government department, or a person authorised by a Government department under paragraph 1 of this Schedule shall include power to use the design for any purpose which appears to the department necessary or expedient—

    (a) for the efficient prosecution of any war in which His Majesty may be engaged;

    (b) for the maintenance of supplies and services essential to the life of the community;

    (c) for securing a sufficiency of supplies and services essential to the well-being of the community;

    (d) for promoting the productivity of industry, commerce and agriculture;

    (e) for fostering and directing exports and reducing imports, or imports of any classes, from all or any countries and for redressing the balance of trade;

    (f) generally for ensuring that the whole resources of the community are available for use, and are used, in a manner best calculated to serve the interests of the community; or

    (g) for assisting the relief of suffering and the restoration and distribution of essential supplies and services in any part of His Majesty's dominions or any foreign countries that are in grave distress as the result of war;

and any reference in this Schedule to the services of the Crown shall be construed as including a reference to the purposes aforesaid.

(2) In this paragraph the expression "period of emergency" means a period beginning on such date as may be declared by Order in Council to be the commencement, and ending on such date as may be so declared to be the termination, of a period of emergency for the purposes of this paragraph.

(3) No Order in Council under this paragraph shall be submitted to Her Majesty unless a draft of it has been laid before and approved by a resolution of each House of Parliament.

A3. The Registered Designs Regulations 2001 (SI 2001/3949)

Made   *8th December 2001*
Coming into force   *9th December 2001*

A3–001   Whereas a draft of the following Regulations has been approved by resolution of each House of Parliament:

Now, therefore, the Secretary of State, being designated (SI 2000/1813) for the purposes of section 2(2) of the European Communities Act 1972 (1972 c.68) in relation to measures relating to the legal protection of designs, in exercise of the powers conferred on her by the said section 2(2) hereby makes the following Regulations:

Citation, commencement and extent

A3–002   **1.**—(1) These Regulations may be cited as the Registered Designs Regulations 2001 and shall come into force on the day after the day on which they are made.

(2) Subject to paragraph (3), these Regulations extend to England and Wales, Scotland and Northern Ireland.

(3) The amendments made by these Regulations to the Chartered Associations (Protection of Names and Uniforms) Act 1926 do not extend to Northern Ireland.

Regulations 2 to 8 make amendments to the Registered Designs Act 1949. These amendments have been printed as part of the text of the Act as amended in App.A2.

Other modifications of enactments

9.—(1) The amendments specified in Schedule 1 (consequential amendments) shall have effect. **A3–003**

(2) The repeals specified in Schedule 2 shall have effect.

Transitional provisions: pending applications

10.—(1) This Regulation applies to applications for registration under the Registered Designs Act 1949 which have been made but not finally determined before the coming into force of these Regulations ("pending applications"). **A3–004**

(2) The Act of 1949 as it has effect immediately before the coming into force of these Regulations shall continue to apply in relation to pending applications so far as it relates to the determination of such applications.

(3) Accordingly the amendments and repeals made by these Regulations shall not apply in relation to the determination of such applications.

Transitional provisions: transitional registrations

11.—(1) This Regulation applies to any registration under the Registered Designs Act 1949 which results from the determination of a pending application (within the meaning of Regulation 10). **A3–005**

(2) The Act of 1949 as it has effect immediately before the coming into force of these Regulations shall continue to apply in relation to registrations to which this Regulation applies ("transitional registrations") so far as the Act relates to the cancellation or invalidation of such registrations (other than cancellation by virtue of section 11(3) of that Act).

(3) Accordingly the amendments and repeals made by these Regulations shall, so far as they relate to the cancellation or invalidation of registrations, not apply in relation to transitional registrations.

(4) The amendments and repeals made by these Regulations shall otherwise (and subject to paragraphs (5) to (9) and Regulation 14) apply in relation to transitional registrations.

(5) In the application by virtue of paragraph (4) of the amendments made by Regulation 5, the fact that transitional registrations are in respect of any articles, or sets of articles, shall be disregarded.

(6) The amendments made by Regulation 4[178] shall not operate so as to determine the dates of registration of designs to which transitional registrations apply; and these dates shall be determined by reference to the Act of 1949 as it has effect immediately before the coming into force of these Regulations.

(7) Where—

(a) any such date of registration for the purposes of calculating the period for which the right in a registered design subsists, or any extension of that period, under section 8 of the Act of 1949 is determined by virtue of section 14(2) of that Act; and

(b) that date is earlier than the date which would otherwise have been the date of registration for those purposes;

---

[178] Regulation 4 replaces s.3 of the Registered Designs Act 1949 with new ss.3, 3A, 3B, 3C and 3D, see A2. For the pre-amendment text of s.3, see para.XXX.

the difference between the two dates shall be added to the first period of five years for which the right in the registered design is to subsist.

(8) Any reference in section 8 of the Act of 1949 to a period of five years shall, in the case of any such period which is extended by virtue of paragraph (7), be treated as a reference to the extended period.

(9) The repeal by these Regulations of the proviso in section 4(1) of the Act of 1949 and of the reference to it in section 8 of that Act shall not apply to the right in a design to which a transitional registration applies.

Transitional provisions: post-1989 registrations

A3–006 **12.**—(1) This Regulation applies to—

    (a) any registration under the Registered Designs Act 1949 which—
        (i) has resulted from an application made on or after 1st August 1989 and before the coming into force of these Regulations; and
        (ii) has given rise to a right in a registered design which is in force at the coming into force of these Regulations;
    (b) any registration under the Act of 1949 which—
        (i) has resulted from an application made on or after 1st August 1989 and before the coming into force of these Regulations; and
        (ii) has given rise to a right in a registered design which is not in force at the coming into force of these Regulations but which is capable of being treated as never having ceased to be in force by virtue of section 8(4) of the Act of 1949 or of being restored by virtue of sections 8A and 8B of that Act; and
    (c) any registration which subsequently ceases to fall within sub-paragraph (b) because the right in the registered design has been treated or restored as mentioned in paragraph (ii) of that sub-paragraph.

(2) The Act of 1949 as it has effect immediately before the coming into force of these Regulations shall continue to apply in relation to registrations to which this Regulation applies ("post-1989 registrations") so far as the Act relates to the cancellation or invalidation of such registrations (other than cancellation by virtue of section 11(3) of that Act and by reference to an expiry of copyright occurring on or after the coming into force of these Regulations).

(3) Accordingly the amendments and repeals made by these Regulations shall, so far as they relate to the cancellation or invalidation of registrations, not apply in relation to post-1989 registrations.

(4) The amendments and repeals made by these Regulations shall otherwise apply (subject to paragraphs (5) to (9) and Regulation 14) in relation to post-1989 registrations.

(5) In the application by virtue of paragraph (4) of the amendments made by Regulation 5[179], the fact that post-1989 registrations are in respect of any articles, or sets of articles, shall be disregarded.

(6) The amendments made by Regulation 4[180] shall not operate so as to alter the dates of registration of designs to which post-1989 registrations apply.

(7) Where—

    (a) any such date of registration for the purposes of calculating the period for which the right in a registered design subsists, or any extension of

---

[179] Regulation 5 replaces s.7 of the Registered Designs Act 1949 with new ss.7 and 7A; see A2. For the pre-amendment text of s.7, see para.XXX.
[180] Regulation 4 replaces s.3 of the Registered Designs Act 1949 with new ss.3, 3A, 3B, 3C and 3D; see A2. For the pre-amendment text of s.3, see para.XXX.

that period, under section 8 of the Act of 1949 was determined by virtue of section 14(2) of that Act; and

(b) that date is earlier than the date which would otherwise have been the date of registration for those purposes;

the difference between the two dates shall be added to any period of five years which is current on the coming into force of these Regulations or, if no such period is current but a subsequent extension or restoration is effected under section 8, or sections 8A and 8B, of the Act of 1949, to the period resulting from that extension or restoration.

(8) Any reference in section 8 of the Act of 1949 to a period of five years shall, in the case of any such period which is extended by virtue of paragraph (7), be treated as a reference to the extended period.

(9) The repeal by these Regulations of the proviso in section 4(1) of the Act of 1949 and the reference to it in section 8 of that Act shall not apply to the right in a design to which a post-1989 registration applies.

Transitional provisions: pre-1989 registrations

13.—(1) This Regulation applies to—   A3–007

(a) any registration under the Registered Designs Act 1949 which—
   (i) has resulted from an application made before 1st August 1989; and
   (ii) has given rise to a copyright in a registered design which is in force at the coming into force of these Regulations;

(b) any registration under the Act of 1949 which—
   (i) has resulted from an application made before 1st August 1989; and
   (ii) has given rise to a copyright in a registered design which is not in force at the coming into force of these Regulations but which would be capable of coming back into force by virtue of an extension of the period of copyright under section 8(2) of the Act of 1949 if that provision were amended as set out in paragraph (8); and

(c) any registration which subsequently ceases to fall within sub-paragraph (b) because the copyright in the registered design has come back into force by virtue of an extension of the period of copyright under section 8(2) of the Act of 1949 as amended by paragraph (8).

(2) Subject as follows, the amendments and repeals made by these Regulations shall not apply to any provision of the Act of 1949 which only has effect in relation to applications for registration made before 1st August 1989 or any registrations resulting from such applications.

(3) Any such provision and any other provision of the Act of 1949 as it has effect immediately before the coming into force of these Regulations in relation to registrations which fall within paragraph (1) ("pre-1989 registrations") shall continue to apply so far as it relates to the cancellation or invalidation of pre-1989 registrations (other than cancellation by virtue of section 11(3) of that Act and by reference to an expiry of copyright occurring on or after the coming into force of these Regulations).

(4) Accordingly the amendments and repeals made by these Regulations shall, so far as they relate to the cancellation or invalidation of registrations, not apply in relation to pre-1989 registrations.

(5) The amendments and repeals made by these Regulations shall otherwise apply (subject to paragraphs (2) and (9) to (12) and Regulation 14) in relation to pre-1989 registrations.

(6) Amendments and repeals corresponding to the amendments and repeals made by these Regulations (other than those relating to the cancellation or invalidation of registrations) shall be treated as having effect, with necessary modifications and subject to Regulation 14, in relation to any provision of the Act of 1949 which only has effect in relation to applications for registration made before 1st August 1989 or any registrations resulting from such applications.

(7) In the application by virtue of paragraph (6) of amendments corresponding to those made by Regulation 5[181], the fact that pre-1989 registrations are in respect of any articles, or sets of articles, shall be disregarded.

(8) In section 8(2) of the Act of 1949 as it has effect in relation to pre-1989 registrations (period of copyright)—

(a) after the words "second period", where they appear for the second time, there shall be inserted "and for a fourth period of five years from the expiration of the third period and for a fifth period of five years from the expiration of the fourth period";

(b) after the words "second or third" there shall be inserted "or fourth or fifth"; and

(c) after the words "second period", where they appear for the third time, there shall be inserted "or the third period or the fourth period".

(9) The amendments made by Regulation 4[182] shall not operate so as to alter the dates of registration of designs to which pre-1989 registrations apply.

(10) Where—

(a) the date of registration for the purposes of calculating the period of copyright, or any extension of that period, under section 8(2) of the Act of 1949 as it has effect in relation to pre-1989 registrations was determined by virtue of section 14(2) of that Act; and

(b) that date is earlier than the date which would otherwise have been the date of registration for those purposes;

the difference between the two dates shall be added to any period of five years which is current on the coming into force of these Regulations or, if no such period is current but a subsequent extension is effected under section 8 of the Act of 1949 as amended by paragraph (8), to the period resulting from that extension.

(11) Any reference in section 8(2) of the Act of 1949 as amended by paragraph (8) to a period of five years shall, in the case of any such period which is extended by virtue of paragraph (10), be treated as a reference to the extended period.

(12) The repeal by these Regulations of the proviso in section 4(1) of the Act of 1949 shall not apply to the right in a design to which a pre-1989 registration applies.

Other transitional provisions

A3–008   14.—(1) Any licence which—

(a) permits anything which would otherwise be an infringement under the Registered Designs Act 1949 of the right in a registered design or the copyright in a registered design; and

(b) was granted by the registered proprietor of the design, or under section 10 or 11A of the Act of 1949, before the coming into force of these Regulations,

---

[181] Regulation 5 replaces s.7 of the Registered Designs Act 1949 with new ss.7 and 7A; see A2. For the pre-amendment text of s.7, see para.XXX.

[182] Regulation 4 replaces s.3 of the Registered Designs Act 1949 with new ss.3, 3A, 3B, 3C and 3D; see A2. For the pre-amendment text of s.3, see para.XXX.

shall continue in force, with necessary modifications, on or after the making of these Regulations.

(2) In determining the effect of any such licence on or after the coming into force of these Regulations, regard shall be had to the purpose for which the licence was granted; and, in particular, a licence granted for the full term or extent of the right in a registered design or the copyright in a registered design shall be treated as applying, subject to its other terms and conditions, to the full term or extent of that right as extended by virtue of these Regulations.

(3) The right in a registered design conferred by virtue of these Regulations in relation to registrations to which Regulation 11, 12 or 13 applies shall not enable the registered proprietor to prevent any person from continuing to carry out acts begun by him before the coming into force of these Regulations and which, at that time, the registered proprietor or, in the case of registrations to which Regulation 11 applies, a registered proprietor would have been unable to prevent.

(4) The right in a registered design conferred by virtue of these Regulations in relation to registrations to which Regulation 12 or 13 applies shall, in particular, not apply in relation to infringements committed in relation to those registrations before the coming into force of these Regulations.

(5) The repeals by these Regulations in section 5 of the Registered Designs Act 1949 shall not apply in relation to any evidence filed in support of an application made before the coming into force of these Regulations.

(6) The amendments and repeals made by these Regulations in section 22 of the Act of 1949 (other than the amendment to the proviso in subsection (2) of that section) shall not apply in relation to any registration which has resulted from an application made before the coming into force of these Regulations.

(7) The amendment to the proviso in section 22(2) of the Act of 1949 shall not apply where—

(a) the registration of the first-mentioned design resulted from an application made before the coming into force of these Regulations; and

(b) the application for the registration of the other design was also made before the coming into force of these Regulations.

(8) The amendments and repeals made by these Regulations in section 35 of the Act of 1949 shall not apply in relation to any offences committed before the coming into force of these Regulations.

(9) The repeal by these Regulations of provisions in section 44 of the Act of 1949 which relate to the meaning of a set of articles shall not apply so far as those provisions are required for the purposes of paragraph 6(2)(a) of Schedule 1 to the Copyright, Designs and Patents Act 1988.

(10) Any amendment or repeal by these Regulations of a provision in section 44 of the Act of 1949 or in any enactment other than the Act of 1949 shall not apply so far as that provision is required for the purposes of any other transitional provision made by these Regulations.

(11) The Act of 1949 as it has effect immediately before the coming into force of these Regulations shall continue to apply in relation to former registrations, whose registration resulted from an application made before the coming into force of these Regulations, so far as the Act relates to the cancellation or invalidation of such registrations.

(12) Paragraph (13) applies in relation to any registration to which Regulation 11, 12 or 13 applies which is in respect of any features of shape, configuration, pattern or ornament which do not fall within the new definition of "design" inserted into section 1 of the Act of 1949 by Regulation 2 of these Regulations.

(13) The Act of 1949 shall, so far as it applies in relation to any such registration, apply as if the features concerned were included within the new definition of "design" in that Act.

SCHEDULE 1

Consequential Amendments

Chartered Associations (Protection of Names and Uniforms) Act 1926

A3–009   **1.** In section 3 of the Chartered Associations (Protection of Names and Uniforms) Act 1926 (savings)—
  (a) for the word "article", in the first place where it appears, there shall be substituted "product";
  (b) for the words from "in respect of" to "1907", there shall be substituted "where a design is applied to, or incorporated in, the product and the design is protected by virtue of registration under the Registered Designs Act 1949";
  (c) for the words "such registered design", in both places where they appear, there shall be substituted "the design"; and
  (d) for the words "such article" there shall be substituted "the product".

Registered Designs Act 1949

A3–010   *Paragraphs 2 to 15 of the Schedule make amendments to the Registered Designs Act 1949. These amendments have been printed as part of the text of the Act as amended on the preceding pages of this Appendix.*

Copyright, Designs and Patents Act 1988

A3–011   **16.** In section 53(1)(b) of the Copyright, Designs and Patents Act 1988 (things done in reliance on registration of design) after the word "cancellation" there shall be inserted "or invalidation".

SCHEDULE 2

Repeals

A3–012   *The first part of Sch.2 repeals parts of the Registered Designs Act 1949. These repeals have been incorporated as part of the text of the Act as amended in App.A2.*

Chapter	Short title	Extent of repeal
1988 c.48.	The Copyright, Designs and Patents Act 1988.	Section 265. Section 268. In Schedule 3, paragraphs 1, 2, 3(4), 4, 6, 9 and 31(2) and (5).
1995 c.21.	The Merchant Shipping Act 1995.	In Schedule 13, paragraph 26.
1995 c.32.	The Olympic Symbol etc. (Protection) Act 1995.	Section 13(1).

A4. The Registered Designs Regulations 2003 (SI 2003/550)

Made — 6th March 2003
Laid before Parliament — 7th March 2003
Coming into force — 1st April 2003

A4–001   The Secretary of State, being designated (SI 2000/1813) for the purposes of section 2(2) of the European Communities Act 1972 (1972 c. 68) in relation to measures relating to the legal protection of designs, in exercise of powers conferred on her by the said section 2(2) hereby makes the following Regulations:

Citation, commencement and extent

1.—(1) These Regulations may be cited as the Registered Designs Regulations **A4–002** 2003 and shall come into force on 1st April 2003.

(2) These Regulations extend to England and Wales, Scotland and Northern Ireland.

Amendment to the Registered Designs Act 1949

2.—(1) The Registered Designs Act 1949 ("the Act") shall be amended as fol- **A4–003** lows.

(2) In section 1A(2)(b) of the Act, after "this Act" there shall be inserted "or the Community Design Regulation".

(3) In section 11ZB(4) of the Act—

(a) after "this Act" there shall be inserted "or the Community Design Regulation"; and

(b) after "the design" there shall be inserted ", the holder of the registered Community design".

(4) In section 20(1B) of the Act—

(a) after "this Act" there shall be inserted "or the Community Design Regulation"; and

(b) after "the design" there shall be inserted ", the holder of the registered Community design".

(5) In section 44(1) of the Act, at the appropriate places, there shall be inserted—

" 'Community Design Regulation' means Council Regulation (EC) 6/2002 of 12th December 2001 on Community Designs;";

" 'registered Community design' means a design that complies with the conditions contained in, and is registered in the manner provided for in, the Community Design Regulation;".

Transitional provisions: pending applications

3.—(1) This Regulation applies to applications for registration under the Act **A4–004** that have been made after the coming into force of the Registered Designs Regulations 2001 ("2001 Regulations") and before the coming into force of these Regulations but that have not been finally determined before the coming into force of these Regulations ("pending applications").

(2) The Act as it has effect immediately before the coming into force of these Regulations shall continue to apply in relation to pending applications.

(3) Accordingly the amendments made by these Regulations shall not apply in relation to such applications.

Transitional provisions: transitional registrations

4.—(1) This Regulation applies to any registration under the Act that results **A4–005** from the determination of a pending application (within the meaning of Regulation 3).

(2) The Act as it has effect immediately before the coming into force of these Regulations shall continue to apply in relation to registrations to which this Regulation applies ("transitional registrations").

(3) Accordingly the amendments made by these Regulations shall not apply in relation to transitional registrations.

Transitional provisions: resulting registrations

A4–006   5.—(1) This Regulation applies to any registration made under the Act before the coming into force of these Regulations that results from the determination of an application made under the Act after the coming into force of the 2001 Regulations.

(2) The Act as it has effect immediately before the coming into force of these Regulations shall continue to apply in relation to registrations to which this Regulation applies ("resulting registrations").

(3) Accordingly the amendments made by these Regulations shall not apply in relation to resulting registrations.

A5. The Registered Designs Act 1949 (version applying to pre-2001 registrations)

Registrable designs and proceedings for registration

Designs registrable under Act

A5–001   *1.—(1) Subject to the following provisions of this section, a design may, upon application made by the person claiming to be the proprietor, be registered under this Act in respect of any article or set of articles specified in the application.*

(2) Subject to the provisions of this Act, a design shall not be registered thereunder unless it is new or original and in particular shall not be so registered in respect of any article if it is the same as a design which before the date of the application for registration has been registered or published in the United Kingdom in respect of the same or any other article or differs from such a design only in immaterial details or in features which are variants commonly used in the trade.

(3) In this Act the expression "design" means features of shape, configuration, pattern or ornament applied to an article by any industrial process or means, being features which in the finished article appeal to and are judged solely by the eye, but does not include a method or principle of construction or features of shape or configuration which are dictated solely by the function which the article to be made in that shape or configuration has to perform.

(4) Rules made by the Board of Trade under this Act may provide for excluding from registration thereunder designs for such articles, being articles which are primarily literary or artistic in character, as the Board think fit.

[(1) In this Act "design" means features of shape, configuration, pattern or ornament applied to an article by any industrial process being features which in the finished article appeal to and are judged by the eye, but does not include—

    (a) a method or principle of construction, or

    (b) features of shape or configuration of an article which—

        (i) are dictated solely by the function which the article has to perform, or

        (ii) are dependent upon the appearance of another article of which the article is intended by the author of the design to form an integral part.]

(2) A design which is new may, upon application by the person claiming to be the proprietor, be registered under this Act in respect of any article, or set of articles, specified in the application.

(3) A design shall not be registered in respect of an article if the appearance of the article is not material, that is, if aesthetic considerations are not normally taken into account to a material extent by persons acquiring or using articles of that description, and would not be so taken into account if the design were to be applied to the article.

(4) A design shall not be regarded as new for the purposes of this Act if it is the same as a design—

(a) registered in respect of the same or any other article in pursuance of a prior application, or

(b) published in the United Kingdom in respect of the same or any other article before the date of the application,

or if it differs from such a design only in immaterial details or in features which are variants commonly used in the trade.

This subsection has effect subject to the provisions of sections 4, 6 and 16 of this Act.

(5) The Secretary of State may by rules provide for excluding from registration under this Act designs for such articles of a primarily literary or artistic character as the Secretary of State thinks fit.[183]

[(6) A design shall not be registered if it consists of or contains a controlled representation within the meaning of the Olympic Symbol etc. (Protection) Act 1995 unless it appears to the registrar—

(a) that the application is made by the person for the time being appointed under section 1(2) of the Olympic Symbol etc. (Protection) Act 1995 (power of Secretary of State to appoint a person as the proprietor of the Olympics association right), or

(b) that consent has been given by or on behalf of the person mentioned in paragraph (a) of this subsection][184]

Proprietorship of designs

2.—*(1) Subject to the provisions of this section, the author of a design shall be treated* **A5–002** *for the purposes of this Act as the proprietor of the design:*
Provided that where the design is executed by the author for another person for good consideration, that other person shall be treated for the purposes of this Act as the proprietor.

[(1) The author of a design shall be treated for the purposes of this Act as the original proprietor of the design, subject to the following provisions.

(1A) Where a design is created in pursuance of a commission for money or money's worth, the person commissioning the design shall be treated as the original proprietor of the design.

(1B) Where, in a case not falling within subsection (1A), a design is created by an employee in the course of his employment, his employer shall be treated as the original proprietor of the design.][185]

(2) Where a design, or the right to apply a design to any article, becomes vested, whether by assignment, transmission or operation of law, in any person other than the original proprietor, either alone or jointly with the original proprietor, that other person, or as the case may be the original proprietor and that other

---

[183] Substituted by the Copyright, Designs and Patents Act 1988 ss.265 and 266.
[184] Added by the Olympic Symbol, etc. (Protection) Act 1995 s.13(1).
[185] Substituted by the Copyright, Designs and Patents Act 1988 s.267.

person, shall be treated for the purposes of this Act as the proprietor of the design or as the proprietor of the design in relation to that article.

[(3) In this Act the "author" of a design means the person who creates it.

(4) In the case of a design generated by computer in circumstances such that there is no human author, the person by whom the arrangements necessary for the creation of the design are made shall be taken to be the author.][186]

Proceedings for registration

A5–003   **3.**—(1) An application for the registration of a design shall be made in the prescribed form and shall be filed at the Patent Office in the prescribed manner.

(2) For the purpose of deciding whether a design is new or original, the registrar may make such searches, if any, as he thinks fit.

(3) The registrar may refuse any application for the registration of a design or may register the design in pursuance of the application subject to such modifications, if any, as he thinks fit.

(4) An application which, owing to any default or neglect on the part of the applicant, has not been completed so as to enable registration to be effected within such time as may be prescribed shall be deemed to be abandoned.

[(2) An application for the registration of a design in which design right subsists shall not be entertained unless made by the person claiming to be the design right owner.

(3) For the purpose of deciding whether a design is new, the registrar may make such searches, if any, as he thinks fit.

(4) The registrar may, in such cases as may be prescribed, direct that for the purpose of deciding whether a design is new an application shall be treated as made on a date earlier or later than that on which it was in fact made.

(5) Except as otherwise expressly provided by this Act, a design when registered shall be registered as of the date on which the application for registration was made, or such other date (whether earlier or later than that date) as the registrar may in any particular case direct:

Provided that no proceedings shall be taken in respect of any infringement committed before the date on which the certificate of registration of the design under this Act is issued.

(6) An appeal shall lie from any decision of the registrar under subsection (3) of this section.

(5) The registrar may refuse an application for the registration of a design or may register the design in pursuance of the application subject to such modifications, if any, as he thinks fit; and a design when registered shall be registered as of the date on which the application was made or is treated as having been made.

(6) An application which, owing to any default or neglect on the part of the applicant, has not been completed so as to enable registration to be effected within such time as may be prescribed shall be deemed to be abandoned.

(7) An appeal lies from any decision of the registrar under this section.][187]

Registration of same design in respect of other articles, etc

A5–004   **4.**—(1) Where the registered proprietor of a design registered in respect of any article makes an application—

    (a) for registration in respect of one or more other articles, of the registered design, or

---

[186] Inserted by the Copyright, Designs and Patents Act 1988 s.267.
[187] Substituted by the Copyright, Designs and Patents Act 1988 s.272 and Sch.3 para.1.

(b) for registration in respect of the same or one or more other articles, of a design consisting of the registered design with modifications or variations not sufficient to alter the character or substantially to affect the identity thereof,

the application shall not be refused and the registration made on that application shall not be invalidated by reason only of the previous registration or publication of the registered design:

Provided that the period of copyright in a design registered by virtue of this section shall not extend beyond the expiration or the original and any extended period of copyright in the original registered design.

[Provided that the right in a design registered by virtue of this section shall not extend beyond the end of the period, and any extended period, for which the right subsists in the original registered design.][188]

(2) Where any person makes an application for the registration of a design in respect of any article and either—

(a) that design has been previously registered by another person in respect of some other article; or

(b) the design to which the application relates consists of a design previously registered by another person in respect of the same or some other article with modifications or variations not sufficient to alter the character or substantially to affect the identity thereof,

then, if at any time while the application is pending the applicant becomes the registered proprietor of the design previously registered, the foregoing provisions of this section shall apply as if at the time of making the application the applicant had been the registered proprietor of that design.

Provisions for secrecy of certain designs

5.—(1) Where, either before or after the commencement of this Act, an application for the registration of a design has been made, and it appears to the registrar that the design is one of a class notified to him by *a competent authority* [the Secretary of State][189] as relevant for defence purposes, he may give directions for prohibiting or restricting the publication of information with respect to the design, or the communication of such information to any person or class of persons specified in the directions.   **A5–005**

(2) *Rules shall be made by the Board of Trade under this Act for securing that the representation or specimen of a design in the case of which directions are given under this section shall not be open to inspection at the Patent Office during the continuance in force of the directions.*

[(2) The Secretary of State shall by rules make provision for securing that where such directions are given—

(a) the representation or specimen of the design, and

(b) any evidence filed in support of the applicant's contention that the appearance of an article is material (for the purposes of section 1(3) of this Act),

shall not be open to public inspection at the Patent Office during the continuance in force of the directions.][190]

(3) Where the registrar gives any such directions as aforesaid, he shall give notice of the application and of the directions to *a competent authority* [the

---

[188] Substituted by the Copyright, Designs and Patents Act 1988 s.272 and Sch.3 para.2.
[189] Substituted by the Copyright, Designs and Patents Act 1988 s.272 and Sch.3 para.3.
[190] Substituted by the Copyright, Designs and Patents Act 1988 s.272 and Sch.3 para.3.

Secretary of State][191], and thereupon the following provisions shall have effect, that is to say—

(a) *the competent authority* [the Secretary of State][192] shall, upon receipt of such notice, consider whether the publication of the design would be prejudicial to the defence of the realm and unless a notice under paragraph (c) of this subsection has previously been given by that authority to the registrar, shall reconsider that question before the expiration of nine months from the date of filing of the application for registration of the design and at least once in every subsequent year;

(b) for the purpose aforesaid, *the competent authority* [the Secretary of State][193] may, at any time after the design has been registered or, with the consent of the applicant, at any time before the design has been registered, inspect the representation or specimen of the design[, or any such evidence as is mentioned in subsection (2)(b) above,][194] filed in pursuance of the application;

(c) if upon consideration of the design at any time it appears to *the competent authority* [the Secretary of State][195] that the publication of the design would not, or would no longer, be prejudicial to the defence of the realm, *that authority* [he][196] shall give notice to the registrar to that effect;

(d) on the receipt of any such notice the registrar shall revoke the directions and may, subject to such conditions, if any, as he thinks fit, extend the time for doing anything required or authorised to be done by or under this Act in connection with the application or registration, whether or not that time has previously expired.

(4) No person resident in the United Kingdom shall, except under the authority of a written permit granted by or on behalf of the registrar, make or cause to be made any application outside the United Kingdom for the registration of a design of any class prescribed for the purposes of this subsection unless—

(a) an application for registration of the same design has been made in the United Kingdom not less than six weeks before the application outside the United Kingdom; and

(b) either no directions have been given under subsection (1) of this section in relation to the application in the United Kingdom or all such directions have been revoked:

Provided that this subsection shall not apply in relation to a design for which an application for protection has first been filed in a country outside the United Kingdom by a person resident outside the United Kingdom.

(5) *In this section the expression "competent authority" means a Secretary of State, the Admiralty or the Minister of Supply.*[197]

Provisions as to confidential disclosure, etc

A5–006   6.—(1) An application for the registration of a design shall not be refused, and the registration of a design shall not be invalidated, by reason only of—

---

[191] Substituted by the Copyright, Designs and Patents Act 1988 s.272 and Sch.3 para.3.
[192] Substituted by the Copyright, Designs and Patents Act 1988 s.272 and Sch.3 para.3.
[193] Substituted by the Copyright, Designs and Patents Act 1988 s.272 and Sch.3 para.3.
[194] Inserted by the Copyright, Designs and Patents Act 1988 s.272 and Sch.3 para.3.
[195] Substituted by the Copyright, Designs and Patents Act 1988 s.272 and Sch.3 para.3.
[196] Substituted by the Copyright, Designs and Patents Act 1988 s.272 and Sch.3 para.3.
[197] Repealed by the Copyright, Designs and Patents Act 1988 ss.272 and 303(2) and Sch.3, para.3(5) and Sch.8.

(a) the disclosure of the design by the proprietor to any other person in such circumstances as would make it contrary to good faith for that other person to use or publish the design;

(b) the disclosure of the design in breach of good faith by any person other than the proprietor of the design; or

(c) in the case of a new or original textile design intended for registration, the acceptance of a first and confidential order for goods bearing the design.

(2) An application for the registration of a design shall not be refused and the registration of a design shall not be invalidated by reason only—

(a) that a representation of the design, or any article to which the design has been applied, has been displayed, with the consent of the proprietor of the design, at an exhibition [certified by the Secretary of State][198] for the purposes of this subsection;

(b) that after any such display as aforesaid, and during the period of the exhibition, a representation of the design or any such article as aforesaid has been displayed by any person without the consent of the proprietor; or

(c) that a representation of the design has been published in consequence of any such display as is mentioned in paragraph (a) of this subsection,

if the application for registration of the design is made not later than six months after the opening of the exhibition.

(3) An application for the registration of a design shall not be refused, and the registration of a design shall not be invalidated, by reason only of the communication of the design by the proprietor thereof to a government department or to any person authorised by a government department to consider the merits of the design, or of anything done in consequence of such a communication.

(4) Where copyright under the Copyright Act 1956, subsists in an artistic work, and an application is made by, or with the consent of, the owner of that copyright for the registration of a corresponding design, that design shall not be treated for the purposes of this Act as being other than new or original by reason only of any use previously made of the artistic work, unless—

(a) the previous use consisted of or included the sale, letting for hire, or offer for sale or hire of articles to which the design in question (or a design differing from it only as mentioned in subsection (2) of section one of this Act) had been applied industrially, other than articles of a description specified in rules made under subsection (4) of section one of this Act, and

(b) that previous use was made by, or with the consent of, the owner of the copyright in the artistic work.[198a]

(5) Any rules made by virtue of subsection (5) of section ten of the Copyright Act 1956 (which relates to rules for determining the circumstances in which a design is to be taken to be applied industrially) shall apply for the purposes of the last foregoing subsection.[198b]

[(4) Where an application is made by or with the consent of the owner of copyright in an artistic work for the registration of a corresponding design, the design shall not be treated for the purposes of this Act as being other than new by reason only of any use previously made of the artistic work, subject to subsection (5).

[198] Substituted by the Copyright, Designs and Patents Act 1988 s.272 and Sch.3 para.4.
[198a] Inserted by the Copyright Act 1956 s.44(1).
[198b] Inserted by the Copyright Act 1956 s.44(1).

475

(5) Subsection (4) does not apply if the previous use consisted of or included the sale, letting for hire or offer or exposure for sale or hire of articles to which had been applied industrially—

    (a) the design in question, or

    (b) a design differing from it only in immaterial details or in features which are variants commonly used in the trade,

and that previous use was made by or with the consent of the copyright owner.

(6) The Secretary of State may make provision by rules as to the circumstances in which a design is to be regarded for the purposes of this section as "applied industrially" to articles, or any description of articles.][199]

Effect of registration, &c

Right given by registration

7.—(1) *The registration of a design under this Act shall give to the registered proprietor the copyright in the registered design, that is to say, the exclusive right in the United Kingdom and the Isle of Man to make or import for sale or for use for the purposes of any trade or business, or to sell, hire or offer for sale or hire, any article in respect of which the design is registered, being an article to which the article design or a design not substantially different from the article design has been applied, and to make anything for enabling any such article to be made as aforesaid, whether in the United Kingdom or the Isle of Man or elsewhere.*

(2) *Subject to the provisions of this Act and of subsection (3) of section three of the Crown Proceedings Act 1947, the registration of a design shall have the same effect against the Crown as it has against a subject.*

[Right given by registration

A5–007   **7.**—(1) The registration of a design under this Act gives the registered proprietor the exclusive right—

    (a) to make or import—
        (i) for sale or hire, or
        (ii) for use for the purposes of a trade or business, or
    (b) to sell, hire or offer or expose for sale or hire,

an article in respect of which the design is registered and to which that design or a design not substantially different from it has been applied.

(2) The right in the registered design is infringed by a person who without the licence of the registered proprietor does anything which by virtue of subsection (1) is the exclusive right of the proprietor.

(3) The right in the registered design is also infringed by a person who, without the licence of the registered proprietor makes anything for enabling any such article to be made, in the United Kingdom or elsewhere, as mentioned in subsection (1).

(4) The right in the registered design is also infringed by a person who without the licence of the registered proprietor—

    (a) does anything in relation to a kit that would be an infringement if done in relation to the assembled article (see subsection (1)), or

---

[199] Substituted by the Copyright, Designs and Patents Act 1988 s.272 and Sch.3, para.4.

(b) makes anything for enabling a kit to be made or assembled, in the United Kingdom or elsewhere, if the assembled article would be such an article as is mentioned in subsection (1);

and for this purpose a "kit" means a complete or substantially complete set of components intended to be assembled into an article.

(5) No proceedings shall be taken in respect of an infringement committed before the date on which the certificate of registration of the design under this Act is granted.

(6) The right in a registered design is not infringed by the reproduction of a feature of the design which, by virtue of section 1(1)(b), is left out of account in determining whether the design is registrable.][200]

Period of copyright

8.—(1) Copyright in a registered design shall, subject to the provisions of this Act, subsist for a period of five years from the date of registration.

(2) The registrar shall extend the period of copyright for a second period of five years from the expiration of the original period and for a third period of five years from the expiration of the second period if an application for extension of the period of copyright for the second or third period is made in the prescribed form before the expiration of the original period or the second period, as the case may be, and if the prescribed fee is paid before the expiration of the relevant period or [if such application is made and the said fee is paid][200a] within such further period (not exceeding [six months)][200b] as may be specified in a request made to the registrar and accompanied by the prescribed additional fee.

[(3) Where in the case of a registered design it is shown—

(a) *that the design, at the time when it was registered, was a corresponding design in relation to an artistic work in which copyright subsisted under the Copyright Act 1956;*

(b) *that, by reason of a previous use of that artistic work, the design would not have been registrable under this Act but for subsection (4) of section six of this Act; and*

(c) *that the copyright in that work under the Copyright Act 1956, expired before the date of expiry of the copyright in the design,*

the copyright in the design shall, notwithstanding anything in this section, be deemed to have expired at the same time as the copyright in the artistic work, and shall not be renewable after that time.][200c]

[Duration of right in registered design

8.—(1) The right in a registered design subsists in the first instance for a period of five years from the date of the registration of the design. **A5–008**

(2) The period for which the right subsists may be extended for a second, third, fourth and fifth period of five years, by applying to the registrar for an extension and paying the prescribed renewal fee.

(3) If the first, second, third or fourth period expires without such application and payment being made, the right shall cease to have effect; and the registrar shall, in accordance with rules made by the Secretary of State, notify the proprietor of that fact.

---

[200] Substituted by the Copyright, Designs and Patents Act 1988 s.268.

[200a] Words inserted by the Patents and Designs (Renewals, Extensions and Fees) Act 1961 s.1(2)(3)2.

[200b] Words inserted by the Patents and Designs (Renewals, Extensions and Fees) Act 1961 s.1(2)(3)2.

[200c] Inserted by the Copyright Act 1956 (c.74) s.44(2).

(4) If during the period of six months immediately following the end of that period an application for extension is made and the prescribed renewal fee and any prescribed additional fee is paid, the right shall be treated as if it had never expired, with the result that—

(a) anything done under or in relation to the right during that further period shall be treated as valid,

(b) an act which would have constituted an infringement of the right if it had not expired shall be treated as an infringement, and

(c) an act which would have constituted use of the design for the services of the Crown if the right had not expired shall be treated as such use.

(5) Where it is shown that a registered design—

(a) was at the time it was registered a corresponding design in relation to an artistic work in which copyright subsists, and

(b) by reason of a previous use of that work would not have been registrable but for section 6(4) of this Act (registration despite certain prior applications of design),

the right in the registered design expires when the copyright in that work expires, if that is earlier than the time at which it would otherwise expire, and it may not thereafter be renewed.

(6) The above provisions have effect subject to the proviso to section 4(1) (registration of same design in respect of other articles, &c.) [and, in the case of the right of the Secretary of State in any design forming part of the British mercantile marine uniform registered under this Act, to that right's subsisting so long as the design remains on the register].[201]][202]

[Restoration of lapsed right in design

A5–009   8A.—(1) Where the right in a registered design has expired by reason of a failure to extend, in accordance with section 8(2) or (4), the period for which the right subsists, an application for the restoration of the right in the design may be made to the registrar within the prescribed period.

(2) The application may be made by the person who was the registered proprietor of the design or by any other person who would have been entitled to the right in the design if it had not expired; and where the design was held by two or more persons jointly, the application may, with the leave of the registrar, be made by one or more of them without joining the others.

(3) Notice of the application shall be published by the registrar in the prescribed manner.

(4) If the registrar is satisfied that the proprietor took reasonable care to see that the period for which the right subsisted was extended in accordance with section 8(2) or (4), he shall, on payment of any unpaid renewal fee and any prescribed additional fee, order the restoration of the right in the design.

(5) The order may be made subject to such conditions as the registrar thinks fit, and if the proprietor of the design does not comply with any condition the registrar may revoke the order and give such consequential directions as he thinks fit.

(6) Rules altering the period prescribed for the purposes of subsection (1) may contain such transitional provisions and savings as appear to the Secretary of State to be necessary or expedient.][203]

---

[201] Inserted by the Merchant Shipping Act 1995 Sch.13, para.26.
[202] Substituted by the Copyright, Designs and Patents Act 1988 s.269.
[203] Substituted by the Copyright, Designs and Patents Act 1988 s.269.

[Effect of order for restoration of right

8B.—(1) The effect of an order under section 8A for the restoration of the right   **A5–010**
in a registered design is as follows.

(2) Anything done under or in relation to the right during the period between
expiry and restoration shall be treated as valid.

(3) Anything done during that period which would have constituted an
infringement if the right had not expired shall be treated as an infringement—

   (a) if done at a time when it was possible for an application for extension to
       be made under section 8(4); or
   (b) if it was a continuation or repetition of an earlier infringing act.

(4) If after it was no longer possible for such an application for extension to be
made, and before publication of notice of the application for restoration, a person—

   (a) began in good faith to do an act which would have constituted an
       infringement of the right in the design if it had not expired, or
   (b) made in good faith effective and serious preparations to do such an
       act,

he has the right to continue to do the act or, as the case may be, to do the act,
notwithstanding the restoration of the right in the design; but this does not extend
to granting a licence to another person to do the act.

(5) If the act was done, or the preparations were made, in the course of a
business, the person entitled to the right conferred by subsection (4) may—

   (a) authorise the doing of that act by any partners of his for the time being
       in that business, and
   (b) assign that right, or transmit it on death (or in the case of a body
       corporate on its dissolution), to any person who acquires that part of the
       business in the course of which the act was done or the preparations
       were made.

(6) Where an article is disposed of to another in exercise of the rights conferred
by subsection (4) or subsection (5), that other and any person claiming through
him may deal with the article in the same way as if it had been disposed of by the
registered proprietor of the design.

(7) The above provisions apply in relation to the use of a registered design for
the services of the Crown as they apply in relation to infringement of the right in
the design.][204]

Exemption of innocent infringer from liability for damages

9.—(1) In proceedings for the infringement of *copyright in a registered design* [the   **A5–011**
right in a registered design][205] damages shall not be awarded against a defendant
who proves that at the date of the infringement he was not aware, and had no
reasonable ground for supposing, that the design was registered; and a person
shall not be deemed to have been aware or to have had reasonable grounds for
supposing as aforesaid by reason only of the marking of an article with the word
"registered" or any abbreviation thereof, or any word or words expressing or
implying that the design applied to the article has been registered, unless the
number of the design accompanied the word or words or the abbreviation in
question.

---

[204] Substituted by the Copyright, Designs and Patents Act 1988 s.269.
[205] Substituted by the Copyright, Designs and Patents Act 1988 s.272 and Sch.3, para.5.

(2) Nothing in this section shall affect the power of the court to grant an injunction in any proceedings for infringement of *copyright in a registered design* [the right in a registered design].[205a]

Compulsory licence in respect of registered design

A5–012   **10.**—(1) At any time after a design has been registered any person interested may apply to the registrar for the grant of a compulsory licence in respect of the design on the ground that the design is not applied in the United Kingdom by any industrial process or means to the article in respect of which it is registered to such an extent as is reasonable in the circumstances of the case; and the registrar may make such order on the application as he thinks fit.

(2) An order for the grant of a licence shall, without prejudice to any other method of enforcement, have effect as if it were a deed executed by the registered proprietor and all other necessary parties, granting a licence in accordance with the order.

(3) No order shall be made under this section which would be at variance with any treaty, convention, arrangement or engagement applying to the United Kingdom and any convention country.

(4) An appeal shall lie from any order of the registrar under this section.

Cancellation of registration

A5–013   **11.**—(1) The registrar may, upon a request made in the prescribed manner by the registered proprietor, cancel the registration of a design.

(2) At any time after a design has been registered any person interested may apply to the registrar for the cancellation of the registration of the design on the ground that the design was not, at the date of the registration thereof, new or original[206], or on any other ground on which the registrar could have refused to register the design; and the registrar may make such order on the application as he thinks fit.

[(2A) At any time after a design has been registered, any person interested may apply to the registrar for the cancellation of the registration of the design on the grounds—

　　(a) *that the design, at the time when it was registered, was a corresponding design in relation to an artistic work in which copyright subsisted under the Copyright Act 1956;*

　　(b) *that, by reason of a previous use of that artistic work, the design would not have been registrable under this Act but for subsection (4) of section six of this Act; and*

　　(c) *that the copyright in that work under the Copyright Act 1956, has expired; and the registrar may make such order on the application as he thinks fit.][206a]*

(3) An appeal shall lie from any order of the registrar under the [either of the two][206b] last foregoing subsections.

[(3) At any time after a design has been registered, any person interested may apply to the registrar for the cancellation of the registration on the ground that—

　　(a) the design was at the time it was registered a corresponding design in relation to an artistic work in which copyright subsisted, and

　　(b) the right in the registered design has expired in accordance with section 8(4) of this Act (expiry of right in registered design on expiry of copyright in artistic work);

and the registrar may make such order on the application as he thinks fit.

(4) A cancellation under this section takes effect—

[205a] Substituted by the Copyright, Designs and Patents Act 1988 s.272 and Sch.3, para.5.

[206] Repealed by the Copyright, Designs and Patents Act 1988 ss.272 and 303(2), Sch.3 para.6(2) and Sch.8.

[206a] Inserted by the Copyright Act 1956 (c.74), s.44(3).

[206b] Words substituted by the Copyright Act 1956 (c.74) s.44(4).

(a) in the case of cancellation under subsection (1), from the date of the registrar's decision,

(b) in the case of cancellation under subsection (2), from the date of registration,

(c) in the case of cancellation under subsection (3), from the date on which the right in the registered design expired,

or, in any case, from such other date as the registrar may direct.

(5) An appeal lies from any order of the registrar under this section.][207]

[Powers exercisable for protection of the public interest

11A.—(1) Where a report of the [Competition Commission][208] has been laid   **A5–014** before Parliament containing conclusions to the effect—

(a) on a monopoly reference, that a monopoly situation exists and facts found by the Commission operate or may be expected to operate against the public interest,

(b) on a merger reference, that a merger situation qualifying for investigation has been created and the creation of the situation, or particular elements in or consequences of it specified in the report, operate or may be expected to operate against the public interest,

(c) on a competition reference, that a person was engaged in an anticompetitive practice which operated or may be expected to operate against the public interest, or

(d) on a reference under section 11 of the Competition Act 1980 (reference of public bodies and certain other persons), that a person is pursuing a course of conduct which operates against the public interest,

the appropriate Minister or Ministers may apply to the registrar to take action under this section.

(2) Before making an application the appropriate Minister or Ministers shall publish, in such manner as he or they think appropriate, a notice describing the nature of the proposed application and shall consider any representations which may be made within 30 days of such publication by persons whose interests appear to him or them to be affected.

(3) If on an application under this section it appears to the registrar that the matters specified in the Commission's report as being those which in the Commission's opinion operate, or operated or may be expected to operate, against the public interest include—

(a) conditions in licences granted in respect of a registered design by its proprietor restricting the use of the design by the licensee or the right of the proprietor to grant other licences, or

(b) a refusal by the proprietor of a registered design to grant licences on reasonable terms,

he may by order cancel or modify any such condition or may, instead or in addition, make an entry in the register to the effect that licences in respect of the design are to be available as of right.

(4) The terms of a licence available by virtue of this section shall, in default of agreement, be settled by the registrar on an application by the person requiring the licence; and terms so settled shall authorise the licensee to do everything

---

[207] Substituted by the Copyright, Designs and Patents Act 1988 ss.272 and 303(2) and Sch.3, para.6(2).

[208] Substituted by the Competition Act 1998 (Competition Commission) Transitional, Consequential and Supplemental Provisions Order (SI 1999/506) Pt II, art.9.

which would be an infringement of the right in the registered design in the absence of a licence.

(5) Where the terms of a licence are settled by the registrar, the licence has effect from the date on which the application to him was made.

(6) An appeal lies from any order of the registrar under this section.

(7) In this section "the appropriate Minister or Ministers" means the Minister or Ministers to whom the report of the [Competition Commission][209] was made.][210]

[Undertaking to take licence of right in infringement proceedings

A5–015   **11B.**—(1) If in proceedings for infringement of the right in a registered design in respect of which a licence is available as of right under section 11A of this Act the defendant undertakes to take a licence on such terms as may be agreed or, in default of agreement, settled by the registrar under that section—

   (a) no injunction shall be granted against him, and
   (b) the amount recoverable against him by way of damages or on an account of profits shall not exceed double the amount which would have been payable by him as licensee if such a licence on those terms had been granted before the earliest infringement.

(2) An undertaking may be given at any time before final order in the proceedings, without any admission of liability.

(3) Nothing in this section affects the remedies available in respect of an infringement committed before licences of right were available.][211]

Use for services of the Crown

A5–016   **12.**—The provisions of the First Schedule to this Act shall have effect with respect to the use of registered designs for the services of the Crown and the rights of third parties in respect of such use.

International Arrangements

Orders in Council as to convention countries

A5–017   **13.**—(1) His Majesty may, with a view to the fulfilment of a treaty, convention, arrangement or engagement, by Order in Council declare that any country specified in the Order is a convention country for the purposes of this Act:

Provided that a declaration may be made as aforesaid for the purposes either of all or of some only of the provisions of this Act, and a country in the case of which a declaration made for the purposes of some only of the provisions of this Act is in force shall be deemed to be a convention country for the purposes of those provisions only.

(2) His Majesty may by Order in Council direct that any of the Channel Islands, any colony, *any British protectorate or protected state, or any territory administered by His Majesty's Government in the United Kingdom under the trusteeship system of the United Nations,*[211a] shall be deemed to be a convention country for the purposes of all or any of the provisions of this Act; and an Order made under this subsection

---

[209] Substituted by the Competition Act 1998 (Competition Commission) Transitional, Consequential and Supplemental Provisions Order (SI 1999/506) Pt II, art.9.
[210] Inserted by the Copyright, Designs and Patents Act 1988 ss.266(5) and 270.
[211] Inserted by the Copyright, Designs and Patents Act 1988 ss.266(5) and 270.
[211a] Repealed by the Statute Law (Repeals) Act 1986 s.1(1) and Sch.1 Pt VI.

may direct that any such provisions shall have effect, in relation to the territory in question, subject to such conditions or limitations, if any, as may be specified in the Order.

(3) For the purposes of subsection (1) of this section, every colony, protectorate, territory subject to the authority or under the suzerainty of another country, and *territory administered by another country, and territory administered by another country in accordance with a mandate from the League of Nations or*[211b] under the trusteeship system of the United Nations, shall be deemed to be a country in the case of which a declaration may be made under that subsection.

Registration of design where application for protection in convention country has been made

14.—(1) An application for registration of a design in respect of which **A5–018** protection has been applied for in a convention country may be made in accordance with the provisions of this Act by the person by whom the application for protection was made or his personal representative or assignee:

Provided that no application shall be made by virtue of this section after the expiration of six months from the date of the application for protection in a convention country or, where more than one such application for protection has been made, from the date of the first application.

(2) *A design registered on an application made by virtue of this section shall be registered as of the date of the application for protection in the convention country or, where more than one such application for protection has been made, the date of the first such application:*

Provided that no proceedings shall be taken in respect of any infringement committed before the date on which the certificate of registration of the design under this Act is issued.

(3) *An application for the registration of a design made by virtue of this section shall not be refused, and the registration of a design on such an application shall not be invalidated, by reason only of the registration or publication of the design in the United Kingdom or the Isle of Man during the period specified in the proviso to subsection (1) of this section as that within which the application for registration may be made.*

[(2) Where an application for registration of a design is made by virtue of this section, the application shall be treated, for the purpose of determining whether that or any other design is new, as made on the date of the application for protection in the convention country or, if more than one such application was made, on the date of the first such application.

(3) Subsection (2) shall not be construed as excluding the power to give directions under section 3(4) of this Act in relation to an application made by virtue of this section.][212]

(4) Where a person has applied for protection for a design by an application which—

    (a) in accordance with the terms of a treaty subsisting between two or more convention countries, is equivalent to an application duly made in any one of those convention countries; or

    (b) in accordance with the law of any convention country, is equivalent to an application duly made in that convention country,

he shall be deemed for the purposes of this section to have applied in that convention country.

[211b] Repealed by the Statute Law (Repeals) Act 1986, s.1(1), Sch.1 Pt.VI.
[212] Substituted by the Copyright, Designs and Patents Act 1988 s.272 and Sch.3, para.7.

Extension of time for applications under s.14 in certain cases

A5–019 15.—(1) If *the Board of Trade* [the Secretary of State][213] is satisfied that provision substantially equivalent to the provision to be made by or under this section has been or will be made under the law of any convention country, *they* [he][214] may make rules empowering the registrar to extend the time for making application under subsection (1) of section 14 of this Act for registration of a design in respect of which protection has been applied for in that country in any case where the period specified in the proviso to that subsection expires during a period prescribed by the rules.

(2) Rules made under this section—

(a) may, where any agreement or arrangement has been made between His Majesty's Government in the United Kingdom and the government of the convention country for the supply or mutual exchange of information or articles, provide, either generally or in any class of case specified in the rules, that an extension of time shall not be granted under this section unless the design has been communicated in accordance with the agreement or arrangement;

(b) may, either generally or in any class of case specified in the rules, fix the maximum extension which may be granted under this section;

(c) may prescribe or allow any special procedure in connection with applications made by virtue of this section;

(d) may empower the registrar to extend, in relation to an application made by virtue of this section, the time limited by or under the foregoing provisions of this Act for doing any act, subject to such conditions, if any, as may be imposed by or under the rules;

(e) may provide for securing that the rights conferred by registration on an application made by virtue of this section shall be subject to such restrictions or conditions as may be specified by or under the rules and in particular to restrictions and conditions for the protection of persons (including persons acting on behalf of His Majesty) who, otherwise than as the result of a communication made in accordance with such an agreement or arrangement as is mentioned in paragraph (a) of this subsection, and before the date of the application in question or such later date as may be allowed by the rules, may have imported or made articles to which the design is applied or may have made any application for registration of the design.

Protection of designs communicated under international agreements

A5–020 16.—(1) Subject to the provisions of this section, *the Board of Trade* [the Secretary of State][215] may make rules for securing that, where a design has been communicated in accordance with an agreement or arrangement made between His Majesty's Government in the United Kingdom and the government of any other country for the supply or mutual exchange of information or articles,—

(a) an application for the registration of the design made by the person from whom the design was communicated or his personal representative or assignee shall not be prejudiced, and the registration of the design in pursuance of such an application shall not be invalidated, by reason only that the design has been communicated as aforesaid or that in consequence thereof—

[213] Substituted by the Copyright, Designs and Patents Act 1988 s.272 and Sch.3, para.8.
[214] Substituted by the Copyright, Designs and Patents Act 1988 s.272 and Sch.3, para.8.
[215] Substituted by the Copyright, Designs and Patents Act 1988 s.272 and Sch.3, para.9.

>   (i) the design has been published or applied, or
>
>   (ii) an application for registration of the design has been made by any other person, or the design has been registered on such an application;
>
>   (b) any application for the registration of a design made in consequence of such a communication as aforesaid may be refused and any registration of a design made on such an application may be cancelled.

(2) Rules made under subsection (1) of this section may provide that the publication or application of a design, or the making of any application for registration thereof shall, in such circumstances and subject to such conditions or exceptions as may be prescribed by the rules, be presumed to have been in consequence of such a communication as is mentioned in that subsection.

(3) The powers of *the Board of Trade* [the Secretary of State][216] under this section, so far as they are exercisable for the benefit of persons from whom designs have been communicated to His Majesty's Government in the United Kingdom by the government of any other country, shall only be exercised if and to the extent that *the Board are satisfied* [the Secretary of State is satisfied][217] that substantially equivalent provision has been or will be made under the law of that country for the benefit of persons from whom designs have been communicated by His Majesty's Government in the United Kingdom to the government of that country.

(4) References in the last foregoing subsection to the communication of a design to or by His Majesty's Government or the government of any other country shall be construed as including references to the communication of the design by or to any person authorised in that behalf by the government in question.

Register of designs, etc

17.—(1) There shall be kept at the Patent Office under the control of the registrar a register of designs, in which there shall be entered the names and addresses of proprietors of registered designs, notices of assignments and of transmissions of registered designs, and such other matters as may be prescribed or as the registrar may think fit.

(2) Subject to the provisions of this Act and to rules made by the Board of Trade thereunder, the register of designs shall, at all convenient times, be open to inspection by the public; and certified copies sealed with the seal of the Patent Office of any entry in the register shall be given to any persons requiring them on payment of the prescribed fee.

(3) The register of designs shall be prima facie evidence of any matters required or authorised by this Act to be entered therein.

(4) No notice of any trust, whether expressed, implied or constructive, shall be entered in the register of designs, and the registrar shall not be affected by any such notice.

[Register of designs

17.—(1) The registrar shall maintain the register of designs, in which shall be entered—

  (a) the names and addresses of proprietors of registered designs;

  (b) notices of assignments and of transmissions of registered designs; and

  (c) such other matters as may be prescribed or as the registrar may think fit.

A5–021

---

[216] Substituted by the Copyright, Designs and Patents Act 1988 s.272 and Sch.3, para.9.
[217] Substituted by the Copyright, Designs and Patents Act 1988 s.272 and Sch.3, para.9.

(2) No notice of any trust, whether express, implied or constructive, shall be entered in the register of designs, and the registrar shall not be affected by any such notice.

(3) The register need not be kept in documentary form.

(4) Subject to the provisions of this Act and to rules made by the Secretary of State under it, the public shall have a right to inspect the register at the Patent Office at all convenient times.

(5) Any person who applies for a certified copy of an entry in the register or a certified extract from the register shall be entitled to obtain such a copy or extract on payment of a fee prescribed in relation to certified copies and extracts; and rules made by the Secretary of State under this Act may provide that any person who applies for an uncertified copy or extract shall be entitled to such a copy or extract on payment of a fee prescribed in relation to uncertified copies and extracts.

(6) Applications under subsection (5) above or rules made by virtue of that subsection shall be made in such manner as may be prescribed.

(7) In relation to any portion of the register kept otherwise than in documentary form—

(a) the right of inspection conferred by subsection (4) above is a right to inspect the material on the register; and

(b) the right to a copy or extract conferred by subsection (5) above or rules is a right to a copy or extract in a form in which it can be taken away and in which it is visible and legible.

(8) Subject to subsection (11) below, the register shall be prima facie evidence of anything required or authorised to be entered in it and in Scotland shall be sufficient evidence of any such thing.

(9) A certificate purporting to be signed by the registrar and certifying that any entry which he is authorised by or under this Act to make has or has not been made, or that any other thing which he is so authorised to do has or has not been done, shall be prima facie evidence, and in Scotland shall be sufficient evidence, of the matters so certified.

(10) Each of the following—

(a) a copy of an entry in the register or an extract from the register which is supplied under subsection (5) above;

(b) a copy or any representation, specimen or document kept in the Patent Office or an extract from any such document,

which purports to be a certified copy or certified extract shall, subject to subsection (11) below, be admitted in evidence without further proof and without production of any original; and in Scotland such evidence shall be sufficient evidence.

(11) In the application of this section to England and Wales nothing in it shall be taken as detracting from section 69 or 70 of the Police and Criminal Evidence Act 1984 or any provision made by virtue of either of them.[218]

(12) In this section "certified copy" and "certified extract" means a copy and extract certified by the registrar and sealed with the seal of the Patent Office.][219]

Certificate of registration

A5–022   18.—(1) The registrar shall grant a certificate of registration in the prescribed form to the registered proprietor of a design when the design is registered.

---

[218] Repealed by the Youth Justice and Criminal Evidence Act 1999 Sch.6, para.1.
[219] Substituted by the Patents, Designs and Marks Act 1986 s.1 and Sch.1, para.3.

(2) The registrar may, in a case where he is satisfied that the certificate of registration has been lost or destroyed, or in any other case in which he thinks it expedient, furnish one or more copies of the certificate.

Registration of assignments, etc

19.—(1) Where any person becomes entitled by assignment, transmission or operation of law to a registered design or to a share in a registered design, or becomes entitled as mortgagee, licensee or otherwise to any other interest in a registered design, he shall apply to the registrar in the prescribed manner for the registration of his title as proprietor or co-proprietor or, as the case may be, of notice of his interest, in the register of designs.   **A5–023**

(2) Without prejudice to the provisions of the foregoing subsection, an application for the registration of the title of any person becoming entitled by assignment to a registered design or a share in a registered design, or becoming entitled by virtue of a mortgage, licence or other instrument to any other interest in a registered design, may be made in the prescribed manner by the assignor, mortgagor, licensor or other party to that instrument, as the case may be.

(3) Where application is made under this section for the registration of the title of any person, the registrar shall, upon proof of title to his satisfaction—

    (a) where that person is entitled to a registered design or a share in a registered design, register him in the register of designs as proprietor or co-proprietor of the design, and enter in that register particulars of the instrument or event by which he derives title; or

    (b) where that person is entitled to any other interest in the registered design, enter in that register notice of his interest, with particulars of the instrument (if any) creating it.

[(3A) Where design right subsists in a registered design, the registrar shall not register an interest under subsection (3) unless he is satisfied that the person entitled to that interest is also entitled to a corresponding interest in the design right.

(3B) Where design right subsists in a registered design and the proprietor of the registered design is also the design right owner, an assignment of the design right shall be taken to be also an assignment of the right in the registered design, unless a contrary intention appears.][220]

(4) Subject to any rights vested in any other person of which notice is entered in the register of designs, the person or persons registered as proprietor of a registered design shall have power to assign, grant licences under, or otherwise deal with the design, and to give effectual receipts for any consideration for any such assignment, licence or dealing.

Provided that any equities in respect of the design may be enforced in like manner as in respect of any other personal property.

(5) Except for the purposes of an application to rectify the register under the following provisions of this Act, a document in respect of which no entry has been made in the register of designs under subsection (3) of this section shall not be admitted in any court as evidence of the title of any person to a registered design or share of or interest in a registered design unless the court otherwise directs.

Rectification of register

20.—(1) The court may, on the application of any person aggrieved, order the register of designs to be rectified by the making of any entry therein or the variation or deletion of any entry therein.   **A5–024**

---

[220] Inserted by the Copyright, Designs and Patents Act 1988 s.272 and Sch.3, para.10.

(2) In proceedings under this section the court may determine any question which it may be necessary or expedient to decide in connection with the rectification of the register.

(3) Notice of any application to the court under this section shall be given in the prescribed manner to the registrar, who shall be entitled to appear and be heard on the application, and shall appear if so directed by the court.

(4) Any order made by the court under this section shall direct that notice of the order shall be served on the registrar in the prescribed manner; and the registrar shall, on receipt of the notice, rectify the register accordingly.

[(5) A rectification of the register under this section has effect as follows—

(a) an entry made has effect from the date on which it should have been made,

(b) an entry varied has effect as if it had originally been made in its varied form, and

(c) an entry deleted shall be deemed never to have had effect,

unless, in any case, the court directs otherwise.][221]

Power to correct clerical errors

A5–025   21.—(1) The registrar may, in accordance with the provisions of this section, correct any error in an application for the registration or in the representation of a design, or any error in the register of designs.

(2) A correction may be made in pursuance of this section either upon a request in writing made by any person interested and accompanied by the prescribed fee, or without such a request.

(3) Where the registrar proposes to make any such correction as aforesaid otherwise than in pursuance of a request made under this section, he shall give notice of the proposal to the registered proprietor or the applicant for registration of the design, as the case may be, and to any other person who appears to him to be concerned, and shall give them an opportunity to be heard before making the correction.

Inspection of registered designs

A5–026   22.—*(1) Subject to the following provisions of this section and to any rules made by the Board of Trade in pursuance of subsection (2) of section five of this Act, the representation or specimen of a design registered under this Act shall be open to inspection at the Patent Office on and after the day on which the certificate of registration is issued.*

[(1) Where a design has been registered under this Act, there shall be open to inspection at the Patent Office on and after the day on which the certificate of registration is issued—

(a) the representation or specimen of the design, and

(b) any evidence filed in support of the applicant's contention that the appearance of an article is material (for the purposes of section 1(3) of this Act).

This subsection has effect subject to the following provisions of this section and to any rules made under section 5(2) of this Act.][222]

(2) In the case of a design registered in respect of an article of any class prescribed for the purposes of this subsection, no *representation or specimen of the design* [representation, specimen or evidence][223] filed in pursuance of the application shall, until the expiration of such period after the day on which the certificate

---

[221] Inserted by the Copyright, Designs and Patents Act 1988 s.272 and Sch.3, para.11.
[222] Substituted by the Copyright, Designs and Patents Act 1988 s.272 and Sch.3, para.12.
[223] Substituted by the Copyright, Designs and Patents Act 1988 s.272 and Sch.3. para.12.

of registration is issued as may be prescribed in relation to articles of that class, be open to inspection at the Patent Office except by the registered proprietor, a person authorised in writing by the registered proprietor, or a person authorised by the registrar or by the court:

Provided that where the registrar proposes to refuse an application for the registration of any other design on the ground that it is the same as the first-mentioned design or differs from that design only in immaterial details or in features which are variants commonly used in the trade, the applicant shall be entitled to inspect the representation or specimen of the first-mentioned design filed in pursuance of the application for registration of that design.

(3) In the case of a design registered in respect of an article of any class prescribed for the purposes of the last foregoing subsection, the representation, specimen or evidence shall not, during the period prescribed as aforesaid, be inspected by any person by virtue of this section except in the presence of the registrar or of an officer acting under him; and except in the case of an inspection authorised by the proviso to that subsection, the person making the inspection shall not be entitled to take a copy of the representation, specimen or evidence or any part thereof.

(4) Where an application for the registration of a design has been abandoned or refused, neither the application for registration nor any representation, specimen or evidence filed in pursuance thereof shall at any time be open to inspection at the Patent Office or be published by the registrar.

Information as to existence of copyright

23.—*On the request of any person furnishing such information as may enable the registrar to identify the design, and on payment of the prescribed fee the registrar shall inform him whether the design is registered, and if so, in respect of what articles, and whether any extension of the period of copyright has been granted and shall state the date of registration and the name and address of the registered proprietor.*

[Information as to existence of right in registered design

23.—On the request of a person furnishing such information as may enable the registrar to identify the design, and on payment of the prescribed fee, the registrar shall inform him—

A5–027

(a) whether the design is registered and, if so, in respect of what articles, and

(b) whether any extension of the period of the right in the registered design has been granted,

and shall state the date of registration and the name and address of the registered proprietor.][224]

Evidence of entries, documents, etc

24.—*(1) A certificate purporting to be signed by the registrar and certifying that any entry which he is authorised by or under this Act to make has or has not been made, or that any other thing which he is so authorised to do has or has not been done shall be prima facie evidence of the matters so certified.*

(2) A copy of any entry in the register of designs or of any representation, specimen or document kept in the Patent Office or an extract from the register or any such document, purporting to be certified by the registrar and to be sealed with the seal of the Patent

---

[224] Substituted by the Copyright, Designs and Patents Act 1988 s.272 and Sch.3, para.13.

Office, shall be admitted in evidence without further proof and without production of the original.[224a]

Legal proceedings and appeals

Certificate of contested validity of registration

A5–028   **25.**—(1) If in any proceedings before the court the validity of the registration of a design is contested, and it is found by the court that the design is validly registered, the court may certify that the validity of the registration of the design was contested in those proceedings.

(2) Where any such certificate has been granted, then if in any subsequent proceedings before the court for infringement of *the copyright in the registered design* [the right in the registered design][225] or for cancellation of the registration of the design, a final order or judgment is made or given in favour of the registered proprietor, he shall, unless the court otherwise directs, be entitled to his costs as between solicitor and client:

Provided that this subsection shall not apply to the costs of any appeal in any such proceedings as aforesaid.

Remedy for groundless threats of infringement proceedings

A5–029   **26.**—(1) Where any person (whether entitled to or interested in a registered design or an application for registration of a design or not) by circulars, advertisements or otherwise threatens any other person with proceedings for infringement of *the copyright in a registered design* [the right in a registered design][225a], any person aggrieved thereby may bring an action against him for any such relief as is mentioned in the next following subsection.

(2) Unless in any action brought by virtue of this section the defendant proves that the acts in respect of which proceedings were threatened constitute or, if done, would constitute, an infringement of *the copyright in a registered design* [the right in a registered design][226] the registration of which is not shown by the plaintiff to be invalid, the plaintiff shall be entitled to the following relief, that is to say—

(a) a declaration to the effect that the threats are unjustifiable;
(b) an injunction against the continuance of the threats; and
(c) such damages, if any, as he has sustained thereby.

[(2A) Proceedings may not be brought under this section in respect of a threat to bring proceedings for an infringement alleged to consist of the making or importing of anything.][227]

(3) For the avoidance of doubt it is hereby declared that a mere notification that a design is registered does not constitute a threat of proceedings within the meaning of this section.

The Court

27.—*Subject to the provisions of this Act relating to Scotland, Northern Ireland and the Isle of Man, any reference or application to the court under this Act, shall, subject to*

[224a] Repealed by the Patents, Designs and Marks Act 1986 s.3(1) and Sch.3 Pt I.
[225] Substituted by the Copyright, Designs and Patents Act 1988 s.272 and Sch.3, para.14.
[225a] Substituted by Copyright, Designs and Patents Act 1988 s.272 and Sch.3, para.15.
[226] Substituted by the Copyright, Designs and Patents Act 1988 s.272 and Sch.3, para.15.
[227] Inserted by the Copyright, Designs and Patents Act 1988 s.272 and Sch.3, para.15.

rules of court, be dealt with by such judge of the High Court as the Lord Chancellor may select for the purpose.

[The court

27.—(1) In this Act "the court" means—

A5–030

    (a) in England and Wales, the High Court or any patents county court having jurisdiction by virtue of an order under section 287 of the Copyright, Designs and Patents Act 1988,

    (b) in Scotland, the Court of Session, and

    (c) in Northern Ireland, the High Court.

(2) Provision may be made by rules of court with respect to proceedings in the High Court in England and Wales for references and applications under this Act to be dealt with by such judge of that court as the Lord Chancellor may select for the purpose.][228]

The Appeal Tribunal

28.—(1) Any appeal from the registrar under this Act shall lie to the Appeal Tribunal.

A5–031

(2) The Appeal Tribunal shall be a judge of the High Court nominated for the purpose by the Lord Chancellor.

    [[(2) The Appeal Tribunal shall consist of—

    (a) one or more judges of the High Court nominated by the Lord Chancellor, and

    (b) one judge of the Court of Session nominated by the Lord President of that Court.][229]

(2A) At any time when it consists of two or more judges, the jurisdiction of the Appeal Tribunal—

    (a) where in the case of any particular appeal the senior of those judges so directs, shall be exercised in relation to that appeal by both of the judges, or (if there are more than two) by two of them, sitting together, and

    (b) in relation to any appeal in respect of which no such direction is given, may be exercised by any one of the judges;

and, in the exercise of that jurisdiction, different appeals may be heard at the same time by different judges.][230]

(3) The expenses of the Appeal Tribunal shall be defrayed and the fees to be taken therein may be fixed as if the Tribunal were a court of the High Court.

(4) The Appeal Tribunal may examine witnesses on oath and administer oaths for that purpose.

(5) Upon any appeal under this Act the Appeal Tribunal may by order award to any party such costs [or expenses][231] as the Tribunal may consider reasonable and direct how and by what parties the costs [or expenses][232] are to be paid; *and any such order may be a rule of court* [and any such order may be enforced—

    (a) in England and Wales or Northern Ireland, in the same way as an order of the High Court;

---

[228] Substituted by the Copyright, Designs and Patents Act 1988 s.272 and Sch.3, para.16.
[229] Substituted by the Copyright, Designs and Patents Act 1988 s.272 and Sch.3, para.17.
[230] Substituted by the Administration of Justice Act 1969 s.24.
[231] Inserted by the Copyright, Designs and Patents Act 1988 s.272 and Sch.3, para.17.
[232] Inserted by the Copyright, Designs and Patents Act 1988 s.272 and Sch.3, para.17.

(b) in Scotland, in the same way as a decree for expenses granted by the Court of Session.][233]

(6) The Appeal Tribunal shall, with regard to the right of audience, observe the same practice as before the first day of November, nineteen hundred and thirty-two, was observed in the hearing of appeals by the law officer.[234]

(7) Upon any appeal under this Act the Appeal Tribunal may exercise any power which could have been exercised by the registrar in the proceeding from which the appeal is brought.

(8) Subject to the foregoing provisions of this section the Appeal Tribunal may make rules for regulating all matters relating to proceedings before it under this Act[, including right of audience][235].

[(8A) At any time when the Appeal Tribunal consists of two or more judges, the power to make rules under subsection (8) of this section shall be exercisable by the senior of those judges:

Provided that another of those judges may exercise that power if it appears to him that it is necessary for rules to be made and that the judge (or, if more than one, each of the judges) senior to him is for the time being prevented by illness, absence or otherwise from making them.][236]

(9) An appeal to the Appeal Tribunal under this Act shall not be deemed to be a proceeding in the High Court.

[(10) For the purposes of this section the seniority of judges shall be reckoned by reference to the dates on which they were appointed judges of the High Court respectively.][236a]

[(10) In this section "the High Court" means the High Court in England and Wales; and for the purposes of this section the seniority of judges shall be reckoned by reference to the dates on which they were appointed judges of that court or the Court of Session.][237]

Powers and duties of Registrar

Exercise of discretionary powers of registrar

A5–032   29.—Without prejudice to any provisions of this Act requiring the registrar to hear any party to proceedings thereunder, or to give to any such party an opportunity to be heard, rules made by the Secretary of State under this Act shall require the registrar to give to any applicant for registration of a design an opportunity to be heard before exercising adversely to the applicant any discretion vested in the registrar by or under this Act.

Costs and security for costs

30.—(1) The registrar may, in any proceedings before him under this Act, by order award to any party such costs as he may consider reasonable, and direct how and by what parties they are to be paid; and any such order may be made a rule of court.

(2) If any party by whom application is made to the registrar for the cancellation of the registration of a design or for the grant of a licence in respect of a registered design, or by whom notice of appeal is given from any decision of the registrar under this Act, neither

---

[233] Substituted by the Copyright, Designs and Patents Act 1988 s.272 and Sch.3, para.17.
[234] Repealed by the Administration of Justice Act 1970 Sch.11.
[235] Inserted by the Administration of Justice Act 1970 s.10.
[236] Inserted by the Administration of Justice Act 1969 s.24.
[236a] Inserted by the Administration of Justice Act 1969 s.24(1) and (4).
[237] Substituted by the Copyright, Designs and Patents Act 1988 s.272 and Sch.3, para.17.

resides nor carries on business in the United Kingdom or the Isle of Man, the registrar, or, in the case of appeal, the Appeal Tribunal, may require him to give security for the costs of the proceedings or appeal, and in default of such security being given may treat the application or appeal as abandoned.

[Costs and security for costs

A5–033

30.—(1) Rules made by the Secretary of State under this Act may make provision empowering the registrar, in any proceedings before him under this Act—

    (a) to award any party such costs as he may consider reasonable, and

    (b) to direct how and by what parties they are to be paid.

(2) Any such order of the registrar may be enforced—

    (a) in England and Wales or Northern Ireland, in the same way as an order of the High Court;

    (b) in Scotland, in the same way as a decree for expenses granted by the Court of Session.

(3) Rules made by the Secretary of State under this Act may make provision empowering the registrar to require a person, in such cases as may be prescribed, to give security for the costs of—

    (a) an application for cancellation of the registration of a design,

    (b) an application for the grant of a licence in respect of a registered design, or

    (c) an appeal from any decision of the registrar under this Act,

and enabling the application or appeal to be treated as abandoned in default of such security being given.][238]

Evidence before registrar

31.—(1) Subject to rules made by the Board of Trade under this Act the evidence to be given in any proceedings before the registrar under this Act may be given by affidavit or statutory declaration; but the registrar may if he thinks fit in any particular case take oral evidence in lieu of or in addition to such evidence as aforesaid, and may allow any witness to be cross-examined on his affidavit or declaration.

(2) Subject to any such rules as aforesaid, the registrar shall in respect of the examination of witnesses on oath and the discovery and production of documents have all the powers of an official referee of the Supreme Court, and the rules applicable to the attendance of witnesses in proceedings before such a referee shall apply to the attendance of witnesses in proceedings before the registrar.

[Evidence before registrar

A5–034

31. Rules made by the Secretary of State under this Act may make provision—

    (a) as to the giving of evidence in proceedings before the registrar under this Act by affidavit or statutory declaration;

    (b) conferring on the registrar the powers of an official referee of the Supreme Court as regards the examination of witnesses on oath and the discovery and production of documents; and

---

[238] Substituted by the Copyright, Designs and Patents Act 1988 s.272 and Sch.3, para.19.

(c) applying in relation to the attendance of witnesses in proceedings before the registrar the rules applicable to the attendance of witnesses in proceedings before such a referee.][239]

Power of registrar to refuse to deal with certain agents

A5–035 32.—(1) *Rules made by the Board of Trade under this Act may authorise the registrar to refuse to recognise as agent in respect of any business under this Act—*

(a) *any individual whose name has been erased from, and not restored to, the register of patent agents kept in pursuance of rules made under the Patents Act 1949;*

(b) *any individual who is for the time being suspended in accordance with those rules from acting as a patent agent;*

(c) *any person who has been convicted of an offence under section eighty-eight of the Patents Act 1949;*

(d) *any person who is found by the Board of Trade (after being given an opportunity to be heard) to have been convicted of any offence or to have been guilty of any such misconduct as, in the case of an individual registered in the register of patent agents aforesaid, would render him liable to have his name erased therefrom;*

(e) *any person, not being registered as a patent agent, who in the opinion of the registrar is engaged wholly or mainly in acting as agent in applying for patents in the United Kingdom or elsewhere in the name or for the benefit of a person by whom he is employed;*

(f) *any company or firm, if any person whom the registrar could refuse to recognise as an agent in respect of any business under this Act is acting as a director or manager of the company or is a partner in the firm.*

(2) *The registrar shall refuse to recognise as agent in respect of any business under this Act any person who neither resides nor has a place of business in the United Kingdom or the Isle of Man.*[240]

Offences

Offences under s.5

A5–036 33.—(1) If any person fails to comply with any direction given under section five of this Act or makes or causes to be made an application for the registration of a design in contravention of that section, he shall be guilty of an offence and liable—

(a) *on summary conviction, to imprisonment for a term not exceeding three months or to a fine not exceeding one hundred pounds, or to both such imprisonment and such fine, or*

(b) *on conviction on indictment, to imprisonment for a term not exceeding two years or to a fine not exceeding five hundred pounds, or to both such imprisonment and such fine.*

[(a) on conviction on indictment to imprisonment for a term not exceeding two years or a fine, or both;

---

[239] Substituted by the Copyright, Designs and Patents Act 1988 s.272 and Sch.3, para.20.
[240] Repealed by the Copyright, Designs and Patents Act 1988 ss.272 and 303, Sch.3, para.21 and Sch.8.

(b)   on summary conviction to imprisonment for a term not exceeding six months or a fine not exceeding the statutory maximum, or both.][241]

(2) *Where an offence under section five of this Act is committed by a body corporate, every person who at the time of the commission of the offence is a director, general manager, secretary or other similar officer of the body corporate, or is purporting to act in any such capacity, shall be deemed to be guilty of that offence unless he proves that the offence was committed without his consent or connivance and that he exercised all such diligence to prevent the commission of the offence as he ought to have exercised having regard to the nature of his functions in that capacity and to all the circumstances.*[242]

Falsification of register, etc

34.—If any person makes or causes to be made a false entry in the register of designs, or a writing falsely purporting to be a copy of an entry in that register, or produces or tenders or causes to be produced or tendered in evidence any such writing, knowing the entry or writing to be false, he *shall be guilty of a misdemeanour* [shall be guilty of an offence and liable—

    A5–037

(a)   on conviction on indictment to imprisonment for a term not exceeding two years or a fine, or both;
(b)   on summary conviction to imprisonment for a term not exceeding six months or a fine not exceeding the statutory maximum, or both.][243]

Fine for falsely representing a design as registered

35.—(1) If any person falsely represents that a design applied to any article sold by him is registered in respect of that article, he shall be liable on summary conviction to *a fine not exceeding five pounds* [a fine not exceeding level 3 on the standard scale][244]; and for the purposes of this provision a person who sells an article having stamped, engraved or impressed thereon or otherwise applied thereto the word "registered", or any other word expressing or implying that the design applied to the article is registered, shall be deemed to represent that the design applied to the article is registered in respect of that article.

    A5–038

(2) If any person, after *the copyright in the design* [the right in a registered design][245] has expired, marks any article to which the design has been applied with the word "registered", or any word or words implying that there is a *subsisting copyright in the design* [subsisting right in the design under this Act][246], or causes any such article to be so marked, he shall be liable on summary conviction to *a fine not exceeding five pounds* [a fine not exceeding level 1 on the standard scale][247].

[Offence by body corporate: liability of officers

35A.—(1) Where an offence under this Act committed by a body corporate is proved to have been committed with the consent or connivance of a director, manager, secretary or other similar officer of the body, or a person purporting to act in any such capacity, he as well as the body corporate is guilty of the offence and liable to be proceeded against and punished accordingly.

    A5–039

---

[241] Substituted by the Copyright, Designs and Patents Act 1988 s.272 and Sch.3, para.22.
[242] Repealed by the Copyright, Designs and Patents Act 1988 s.272 and Sch.3, para.22.
[243] Substituted by the Copyright, Designs and Patents Act 1988 s.272 and Sch.3, para.23.
[244] Substituted by the Copyright, Designs and Patents Act 1988 s.272 and Sch.3, para.24.
[245] Substituted by the Copyright, Designs and Patents Act 1988 s.272 and Sch.3, para.24.
[246] Substituted by the Copyright, Designs and Patents Act 1988 s.272 and Sch.3, para.24.
[247] Substituted by the Copyright, Designs and Patents Act 1988 s.272 and Sch.3, para.24.

(2) In relation to a body corporate whose affairs are managed by its members "director" means a member of the body corporate.][248]

Rules, etc

General power of Secretary of State to make rules, etc

A5–040   36.—(1) Subject to the provisions of this Act, *the Board of Trade* [the Secretary of State][249] may make such rules *as they think expedient* [as he thinks expedient][250] for regulating the business of the Patent Office in relation to designs and for regulating all matters by this Act placed under the direction or control of the registrar or *the Board* [the Secretary of State][251].

and in particular, but without prejudice to the generality of the foregoing provision—

   (a) *for prescribing the form of applications for registration of designs and of any representations or specimens of designs or other documents which may be filed at the Patent Office, and for requiring copies to be furnished of any such representations, specimens or documents;*

   (b) *for regulating the procedure to be followed in connection with any application or request to the registrar or in connection with any proceeding before the registrar and for authorising the rectification of irregularities of procedure;*

   (c) *for regulating the keeping of the register of designs;*

   (d) *for authorising the publication and sale of copies of representations of designs and other documents in the Patent Office;*

   (e) *for prescribing anything authorised or required by this Act to be prescribed by rules made by the Board.*

[(1A) Rules may, in particular, make provision—

   (a) prescribing the form of applications for registration of designs and of any representations or specimens of designs or other documents which may be filed at the Patent Office, and requiring copies to be furnished of any such representations, specimens or documents;

   (b) regulating the procedure to be followed in connection with any application or request to the registrar or in connection with any proceeding before him, and authorising the rectification of irregularities of procedure;

   (c) providing for the appointment of advisers to assist the registrar in proceedings before him;

   (d) regulating the keeping of the register of designs;

   (e) authorising the publication and sale of copies of representations of designs and other documents in the Patent Office;

   (f) prescribing anything authorised or required by this Act to be prescribed by rules.

(1B) The remuneration of an adviser appointed to assist the registrar shall be determined by the Secretary of State with the consent of the Treasury and shall be defrayed out of money provided by Parliament.][252]

---

[248] Inserted by the Copyright, Designs and Patents Act 1988 s.272 and Sch.3, para.25.
[249] Substituted by the Copyright, Designs and Patents Act 1988 s.272 and Sch.3, para.26.
[250] Substituted by the Copyright, Designs and Patents Act 1988 s.272 and Sch.3, para.26.
[251] Substituted by the Copyright, Designs and Patents Act 1988 s.272 and Sch.3, para.26.
[252] Substituted by the Copyright, Designs and Patents Act 1988 s.272 and Sch.3, para.26.

(2) Rules made under this section may provide for the establishment of branch offices for designs and may authorise any document or thing required by or under this Act to be filed or done at the Patent Office to be filed or done at the branch office at Manchester or any other branch office established in pursuance of the rules.

Provisions as to rules and Orders

37.—(1) *Any rules made by the Board of Trade under this Act shall be advertised twice in the Journal.*[253]

A5–041

(2) Any rules made by *the Board of Trade* [the Secretary of State][254] in pursuance of section 15 or section 16 of this Act, and any order made, direction given, or other action taken under the rules by the registrar, may be made, given or taken so as to have effect as respects things done or omitted to be done on or after such date, whether before or after the coming into operation of the rules or of this Act, as may be specified in the rules.

(3) Any power to make rules conferred by this Act on *the Board of Trade* [the Secretary of State][255] or on the Appeal Tribunal shall be exercisable by statutory instrument; and the Statutory Instruments Act 1946 shall apply to a statutory instrument containing rules made by the Appeal Tribunal in like manner as if the rules had been made by a Minister of the Crown.

(4) Any statutory instrument containing rules made by *the Board of Trade* [the Secretary of State][256] under this Act shall be subject to annulment in pursuance of a resolution of either House of Parliament.

(5) Any Order in Council made under this Act may be revoked or varied by a subsequent Order in Council.

Proceedings of Board of Trade

38.—(1) *Anything required or authorised by this Act to be done by, to or before the Board of Trade may be done by, to or before the President of the Board of Trade, any secretary, under-secretary or assistant secretary of the Board, or any person authorised in that behalf by the President.*

A5–042

(2) *All documents purporting to be orders made by the Board of Trade and to be sealed with the seal of the Board, or to be signed by a secretary, under-secretary or assistant secretary of the Board, or by any person authorised in that behalf by the President of the Board, shall be received in evidence and shall be deemed to be such orders without further proof, unless the contrary is shown.*

(3) *A certificate, signed by the President of the Board of Trade, that any order made or act done is the order or act of the Board, shall be conclusive evidence of the fact so certified.*[257]

Supplemental

Hours of business and excluded days

39.—(1) Rules made by *the Board of Trade* [the Secretary of State][258] under this Act may specify the hour at which the Patent Office shall be deemed to be closed

A5–043

---

[253] Repealed by the Copyright, Designs and Patents Act 1988 ss.272 and 303, Sch.3, para.27(2) and Sch.8.

[254] Substituted by the Copyright, Designs and Patents Act 1988 s.272 and Sch.3, para.27.

[255] Substituted by the Copyright, Designs and Patents Act 1988 s.272 and Sch.3, para.27.

[256] Substituted by the Copyright, Designs and Patents Act 1988 s.272 and Sch.3, para.27.

[257] Repealed by the Copyright, Designs and Patents Act 1988 ss.272 and 303, Sch.3, para.28 and Sch.8.

[258] Substituted by the Copyright, Designs and Patents Act 1988 s.272 and Sch.3, para.29.

on any day for purposes of the transaction by the public of business under this Act or of any class of such business, and may specify days as excluded days for any such purposes.

(2) Any business done under this Act on any day after the hour specified as aforesaid in relation to business of that class, or on a day which is an excluded day in relation to business of that class, shall be deemed to have been done on the next following day not being an excluded day; and where the time for doing anything under this Act expires on an excluded day, that time shall be extended to the next following day not being an excluded day.

Fees

A5–044   **40.**—There shall be paid in respect of the registration of designs and applications therefor, and in respect of other matters relating to designs arising under this Act, such fees as may be prescribed by rules made by *the Board of Trade* [the Secretary of State][259] with the consent of the Treasury.

Service of notices, &c, by post

A5–045   **41.**—Any notice required or authorised to be given by or under this Act, and any application or other document so authorised or required to be made or filed, may be given, made or filed by post.

Annual report of registrar

A5–046   **42.**—The Comptroller-General of Patents, Designs and Trade Marks shall, in his annual report with respect to the execution of *the Patents Act 1949* [the Patents Act 1977][259a], include a report with respect to the execution of this Act as if it formed a part of or was included in that Act.

Savings

A5–047   **43.**—(1) Nothing in this Act shall be construed as authorising or requiring the registrar to register a design the use of which would, in his opinion, be contrary to law or morality.

(2) Nothing in this Act shall affect the right of the Crown or of any person deriving title directly or indirectly from the Crown to sell or use articles forfeited under the laws relating to customs or excise.

Interpretation

A5–048   **44.**—(1) In this Act, except where the context otherwise requires, the following expressions have the meanings hereby respectively assigned by them, that is to say—

> *Appeal Tribunal" means the judge nominated under section twenty-eight of this Act;* ["Appeal Tribunal" means the Appeal Tribunal constituted and acting in accordance with section 28 of this Act as amended by the Administration of Justice Act 1969;][260]
> article" means any article of manufacture and includes any part of an article if that part is made and sold separately;
> ["artistic work" has the same meaning as in *the Copyright Act 1956* [Part I of the Copyright, Designs and Patents Act 1988][261;][262]

[259] Substituted by the Copyright, Designs and Patents Act 1988 s.272 and Sch.3, para.30.
[259a] Substituted by the Patents Act 1977 Sch.5, para.3.
[260] Substituted by the Administration of Justice Act 1969 s.24.
[261] Substituted by the Copyright, Designs and Patents Act 1988 s.272 and Sch.3, para.31.
[262] Inserted by the Copyright Act 1956 s.44.

"assignee" includes the personal representative of a deceased assignee, and references to the assignee of any person include references to the assignee of the personal representative or assignee of that person;

["author" in relation to a design, has the meaning given by section 2(3) and (4);]263

copyright" has the meaning assigned it by subsection (1) of section seven of this Act;264

["corresponding design" has the same meaning as in section ten of the Copyright Act 1956 [, in relation to an artistic work, means a design which if applied to an article would produce something which would be treated for the purposes of Part I of the Copyright, Designs and Patents Act 1988 as a copy of that work;]265]266

"court" means the High Court; ["the court" shall be construed in accordance with section 27 of this Act;]267

design" has the meaning assigned to it by subsection (3) of section one of this Act [section 1(1) of this Act]268;

["employee", "employment" and "employer" refer to employment under a contract of service or of apprenticeship,]269

Journal" means the journal published by the comptroller under the Patents Act 1949;270

"prescribed" means prescribed by rules made by the Board of Trade [the Secretary of State]271 under this Act;

"proprietor" has the meaning assigned to it by section two of this Act;

"registered proprietor" means the person or persons for the time being entered in the register of designs as proprietor of the design;

"registrar" means the Comptroller-General of Patents Designs and Trade Marks;

"set of articles" means a number of articles of the same general character ordinarily on sale or intended to be used together, to each of which the same design, or the same design with modifications or variations not sufficient to alter the character or substantially to affect the identity thereof, is applied.

(2) Any reference in this Act to an article in respect of which a design is registered shall, in the case of a design registered in respect of a set of articles, be construed as a reference to any article of that set.

(3) Any question arising under this Act whether a number of articles constitute a set of articles shall be determined by the registrar; and notwithstanding anything in this Act any determination of the registrar under this subsection shall be final.

(4) For the purposes of subsection (1) of section 14 and of section 16 of this Act, the expression "personal representative", in relation to a deceased person, includes the legal representative of the deceased appointed in any country outside the United Kingdom.

---

263 Inserted by the Copyright, Designs and Patents Act 1988 s.272 and Sch.3, para.31.
264 Repealed by the Copyright, Designs and Patents Act 1988 ss.272 and 303, Sch.3, para.31 and Sch.8.
265 Substituted by the Copyright, Designs and Patents Act 1988 s.272 and Sch.3, para.31.
266 Inserted by the Copyright Act 1956 s.44.
267 Substituted by the Copyright, Designs and Patents Act 1988 s.272 and Sch.3, para.31.
268 Substituted by the Copyright, Designs and Patents Act 1988 s.272 and Sch.3, para.31.
269 Inserted by the Copyright, Designs and Patents Act 1988 s.272 and Sch.3, para.31.
270 Repealed by the Copyright, Designs and Patents Act 1988 ss.272 and 303, Sch.3, para.31 and Sch.8.
271 Substituted by the Copyright, Designs and Patents Act 1988 s.272 and Sch.3, para.31.

Application to Scotland

A5–049   **45.**—In the application of this Act to Scotland—

(1) The provisions of this Act conferring a special jurisdiction on the court as defined by this Act shall not, except so far as the jurisdiction extends, affect the jurisdiction of any court in Scotland in any proceedings relating to designs; and with reference to any such proceedings, the term "the Court" shall mean the Court of Session.[272]

(2) If any rectification of a register under this Act is required in pursuance of any proceeding in a court, a copy of the order, decree, or other authority for the rectification, shall be served on the registrar, and he shall rectify the register accordingly.[273]

(3) The expression "injunction" means "interdict" the expression "arbitrator" means "arbiter" the expression "plaintiff" means "pursuer" the expression "defendant" means "defender".

[(4) References to the Crown shall be construed as including references to the Crown in right of the Scottish Administration.][274]

Application to Northern Ireland

A5–050   **46.** In the application of this Act to Northern Ireland—

(1) The provisions of this Act conferring a special jurisdiction on the court, as defined by this Act, shall not, except so far as the jurisdiction extends, affect the jurisdiction of any court in Northern Ireland in any proceedings relating to designs; and with reference to any such proceedings the term "the Court" means the High Court in Northern Ireland.[275]

(2) If any rectification of a register under this Act is required in pursuance of any proceedings in a court, a copy of the order, decree, or other authority for the rectification shall be served on the registrar, and he shall rectify the register accordingly.[276]

(3) References to enactments of the Parliament of the United Kingdom shall be construed as references of those enactments as they apply in Northern Ireland.

[(3) References to enactments include enactments comprised in Northern Ireland legislation.][277]

[(3A) References to the Crown include the Crown in right of Her Majesty's Government in Northern Ireland.][278]

(4) References to a government department shall be construed as including references to *a department of the Governance of Northern Ireland* [a Northern Ireland department][279], [and in relation to a Northern Ireland department references to the Treasury shall be construed as references to the Department of Finance and Personnel][280].

(5) The expression "summary conviction" shall be construed as meaning conviction subject to, and in accordance with, the Petty Sessions (Ireland) Act 1851, and any Act (including any Act of the Parliament of Northern Ireland) amending that Act.[281]

---

[272] Repealed by the Copyright, Designs and Patents Act 1988 ss.272 and 303, Sch.3, para.32 and Sch.8.

[273] Repealed by the Copyright, Designs and Patents Act 1988 ss.272 and 303, Sch.3, para.32 and Sch.8.

[274] Added by Scotland Act 1998 (Consequential Modifications) (No.2) Order (SI 1999/1820) Sch.2, para.25.

[275] Repealed by the Copyright, Designs and Patents Act 1988 ss.272 and 303, Sch.3, para.33 and Sch.8.

[276] Repealed by the Copyright, Designs and Patents Act 1988 ss.272 and 303, Sch.3, para.33 and Sch.8.

[277] Substituted by the Copyright, Designs and Patents Act 1988 s.272 and Sch.3, para.33.

[278] Inserted by the Copyright, Designs and Patents Act 1988 s.272 and Sch.3, para.33.

[279] Substituted by the Copyright, Designs and Patents Act 1988 s.272 and 305, and Sch.3, para.33.

[280] Inserted by the Copyright, Designs and Patents Act 1988 s.272 and Sch.3, para.33.

[281] Repealed by the Northern Ireland Act 1962 Sch.4, Pt IV.

Isle of Man

47.—This Act shall extend to the Isle of Man subject to the following modifica-tions—

(1) Nothing in this Act shall affect the jurisdiction of the courts in the Isle of Man in proceedings for infringement or in any action or proceeding respecting a design competent to those courts;

(2) The punishment for a misdemeanour under this Act in the Isle of Man shall be imprisonment for any term not exceeding two years, with or without hard labour, and with or without a fine not exceeding one hundred pounds, at the discretion of the court;

(3) Any offence under this Act committed in the Isle of Man which would in England be punishable on summary conviction may be prosecuted, and any fine in respect thereof recovered, at the instance of any person aggrieved, in the manner in which offences punishable on summary conviction may for the time being be prosecuted.

[Application to Isle of Man

47.—This Act extends to the Isle of Man, subject to any modifications contained in an Order made by Her Majesty in Council, and accordingly, subject to any such Order, references in this Act to the United Kingdom shall be construed as including the Isle of Man.][282]   **A5–051**

[Territorial waters and the continental shelf

47A.—(1) For the purposes of this Act the territorial waters of the United Kingdom shall be treated as part of the United Kingdom.   **A5–052**

(2) This Act applies to things done in the United Kingdom sector of the continental shelf on a structure or vessel which is present there for purposes directly connected with the exploration of the sea bed or subsoil or the exploitation of their natural resources as it applies to things done in the United Kingdom.

(3) The United Kingdom sector of the continental shelf means the areas designated by order under section 1(7) of the Continental Shelf Act 1964.][283]

Repeals, savings, and transitional provisions

48.—*(1) Subject to the provisions of this section the enactments specified in the Second Schedule to this Act are hereby repealed to the extent specified in the third column of that Schedule.*[284]   **A5–053**

(2) Subject to the provisions of this section, any Order in Council, rule, order, requirement, certificate, notice, decision, direction, authorisation, consent, application, request or thing made, issued, given or done under any enactment repealed by this Act shall, if in force at the commencement of this Act, and so far as it could have been made, issued, given or done under this Act, continue in force and have effect as if made, issued, given or done under the corresponding enactment of this Act.

(3) Any register kept under the Patents and Designs Act 1907 shall be deemed to form part of the corresponding register under this Act.

(4) Any design registered before the commencement of this Act shall be deemed to be registered under this Act in respect of articles of the class in which it is registered.

[282] Substituted by the Copyright, Designs and Patents Act 1988 s.272 and Sch.3, para.34.
[283] Inserted by the Copyright, Designs and Patents Act 1988 s.272 and Sch.3, para.35.
[284] Repealed by the Copyright, Designs and Patents Act 1988 ss.272 and 303, Sch.3, para.36 and Sch.8.

(5) Where, in relation to any design, the time for giving notice to the registrar under section 59 of the Patents and Designs Act 1907 expired before the commencement of this Act and the notice was not given, subsection (2) of section 6 of this Act shall not apply in relation to that design or any registration of that design.

(6) Any document referring to any enactment repealed by this Act shall be construed as referring to the corresponding enactment of this Act.

(7) Nothing in the foregoing provisions of this section shall be taken as prejudicing the operation of *section thirty-eight of the Interpretation Act 1889* [section 16(1) and section 17(2)(a) of the Interpretation Act 1978][285] (which *relates* [relate][286] to the effect of repeals).

Short title and commencement

A5–054　**49.**—(1) This Act may be cited as the Registered Designs Act 1949.

(2) This Act shall come into operation on the first day of January, nineteen hundred and fifty, immediately after the coming into operation of the Patents and Designs Act 1949.

FIRST SCHEDULE

PROVISIONS AS TO THE USE OF REGISTERED DESIGNS FOR THE SERVICES OF THE CROWN AND AS TO THE RIGHTS OF THIRD PARTIES IN RESPECT OF SUCH USE

Use of registered designs for services of the Crown

A5–055　**1.**—(1) Notwithstanding anything in this Act, any Government department, and any person authorised in writing by a Government department, may use any registered design for the services of the Crown in accordance with the following provisions of this paragraph.

(2) If and so far as the design has before the date of registration thereof been duly recorded by or applied by or on behalf of a Government department otherwise than in consequence of the communication of the design directly or indirectly by the registered proprietor or any person from whom he derives title, any use of the design by virtue of this paragraph may be made free of any royalty or other payment to the registered proprietor.

(3) If and so far as the design has not been so recorded or applied as aforesaid, any use of the design made by virtue of this paragraph at any time after the date of registration thereof, or in consequence of any such communication as aforesaid, shall be made upon such terms as may be agreed upon, either before or after the use, between the Government department and the registered proprietor with the approval of the Treasury, or as may in default of agreement be determined by the court on a reference under paragraph 3 of this Schedule.

(4) The authority of a Government department in respect of a design may be given under this paragraph either before or after the design is registered and either before or after the acts in respect of which the authority is given are done, and may be given to any person whether or not he is authorised directly or indirectly by the registered proprietor to use the design.

(5) Where any use of a design is made by or with the authority of a Government department under this paragraph, then, unless it appears to the department that it would be contrary to the public interest so to do, the department shall notify the registered proprietor as soon as practicable after the use is begun, and furnish him with such information as to the extent of the use as he may from time to time require.

(6) *For the purposes of this and the next following paragraph, any use of a design for the supply to the government of any country outside the United Kingdom, in pursuance of any agreement or arrangement between His Majesty's Government in the United Kingdom and the government of that*

---

[285] Substituted by the Interpretation Act 1978 s.25.
[286] Substituted by the Interpretation Act 1978 s.25.

country, of articles required for the defence of that country shall be deemed to be a use of the design for the services of the Crown; and the power of a Government department or a person authorised by a Government department under this paragraph to use a design shall include power—

   (a)   *to sell such articles to the government of any country in pursuance of any such agreement or arrangement as aforesaid; and*

   (b)   *to sell to any person any articles made in the exercise of the powers conferred by this paragraph which are no longer required for the purpose for which they were made.*

[(6) For the purposes of this and the next following paragraph "the services of the Crown" shall be deemed to include—

   (a)   the supply to the government of any country outside the United Kingdom, in pursuance of an agreement or arrangement between Her Majesty's Government in the United Kingdom and the government of that country, of articles required—

        (i)   for the defence of that country; or

        (ii) for the defence of any other country whose government is party to any agreement or arrangement with Her Majesty's said Government in respect of defence matters;

   (b)   the supply to the United Nations, or the government of any country belonging to that organisation, in pursuance of an agreement or arrangement between Her Majesty's Government and that organisation or government, of articles required for any armed forces operating in pursuance of a resolution of that organisation or any organ of that organisation;

and the power of a Government department or a person authorised by a Government department under this paragraph to use a design shall include power to sell to any such government or to the said organisation any articles the supply of which is authorised by this sub-paragraph, and to sell to any person any articles made in the exercise of the powers conferred by this paragraph which are no longer required for the purpose for which they were made.][287]

(7) The purchaser of any articles sold in the exercise of powers conferred by this paragraph, and any person claiming through him, shall have power to deal with them in the same manner as if the rights in the registered design were held on behalf of His Majesty.

***Rights of third parties in respect of Crown use

2.—(1) In relation to any use of a registered design, or a design in respect of which an application for registration is pending, made for the services of the Crown—   **A5–056**

   (a)   by a Government department or a person authorised by a Government department under the last foregoing paragraph; or

   (b)   by the registered proprietor or applicant for registration to the order of a Government department,

the provisions of any licence, assignment or agreement made, whether before or after the commencement of this Act, between the registered proprietor or applicant for registration or any person who derives title from him or from whom he derives title and any person other than a Government department shall be of no effect so far as those provisions restrict or regulate the use of the design, or any model, document or information relating thereto, or provide for the making of payments in respect of any such use, or calculated by reference thereto; and the reproduction or publication of any model or document in connection with the said use shall not be deemed to be an infringement of any copyright [or design right][288] subsisting in the model or document [or of any topography right][289].

(2) Where an exclusive licence granted otherwise than for royalties or other benefits determined by reference to the use of the design is in force under the registered design then—

   (a)   in relation to any use of the design which, but for the provisions of this and the last foregoing paragraph, would constitute an infringement of the rights of the licensee, sub-paragraph (3) of the last foregoing paragraph shall have effect as if for the reference to the registered proprietor there were substituted a reference to the licensee; and

---

[287] Substituted by the Defence Contracts Act 1958 s.1.

[288] Inserted by the Copyright, Designs and Patents Act 1988 s.272 and Sch.3, para.37.

[289] Inserted by the Semiconductor Products (Protection of Topography) Regulations 1987 (SI 1987/1497) reg.9.

(b) in relation to any use of the design by the licensee by virtue of an authority given under the last foregoing paragraph, that paragraph shall have effect as if the said sub-paragraph (3) were omitted.

(3) Subject to the provisions of the last foregoing sub-paragraph, where the registered design or the right to apply for or obtain registration of the design has been assigned to the registered proprietor in consideration of royalties or other benefits determined by reference to the use of the design, then—

(a) in relation to any use of the design by virtue of paragraph 1 of this Schedule, sub-paragraph (3) of that paragraph shall have effect as if the reference to the registered proprietor included a reference to the assignor, and any sum payable by virtue of that sub-paragraph shall be divided between the registered proprietor and the assignor in such proportion as may be agreed upon between them or as may in default of agreement be determined by the court on a reference under the next following paragraph; and

(b) in relation to any use of the design made for the services of the Crown by the registered proprietor to the order of a Government department, sub-paragraph (3) of paragraph 1 of this Schedule shall have effect as if that use were made by virtue of an authority given under that paragraph.

(4) Where, under sub-paragraph (3) of paragraph 1 of this Schedule, payments are required to be made by a Government department to a registered proprietor in respect of any use of a design, any person being the holder of an exclusive licence under the registered design (not being such a licence as is mentioned in sub-paragraph (2) of this paragraph) authorising him to make that use of the design shall be entitled to recover from the registered proprietor such part (if any) of those payments as may be agreed upon between that person and the registered proprietor, or as may in default of agreement be determined by the court under the next following paragraph to be just having regard to any expenditure incurred by that person—

(a) in developing the said design; or

(b) in making payments to the registered proprietor, other than royalties or other payments determined by reference to the use of the design, in consideration of the licence;

and if, at any time before the amount of any such payment has been agreed upon between the Government department and the registered proprietor, that person gives notice in writing of his interest to the department, any agreement as to the amount of that payment shall be of no effect unless it is made with his consent.

(5) In this paragraph "exclusive licence" means a licence from a registered proprietor which confers on the licensee, or on the licensee and persons authorised by him, to the exclusion of all other persons (including the registered proprietor), any right in respect of the registered design.

Compensation for loss of profit

A5–057   [2A.—(1) Where Crown use is made of a registered design, the government department concerned shall pay—

(a) to the registered proprietor, or

(b) if there is an exclusive licence in force in respect of the design, to the exclusive licensee,

compensation for any loss resulting from his not being awarded a contract to supply the articles to which the design is applied.

(2) Compensation is payable only to the extent that such a contract could have been fulfilled from his existing manufacturing capacity; but is payable notwithstanding the existence of circumstances rendering him ineligible for the award of such a contract.

(3) In determining the loss, regard shall be had to the profit which would have been made on such a contract and to the extent to which any manufacturing capacity was under-used.

(4) No compensation is payable in respect of any failure to secure contracts for the supply of articles to which the design is applied otherwise than for the services of the Crown.

(5) The amount payable under this paragraph shall, if not agreed between the registered proprietor or licensee and the government department concerned with the approval of the Treasury, be determined by the court on a reference under paragraph 3; and it is in addition to any amount payable under paragraph 1 or 2 of this schedule.

(6) In this paragraph—

"Crown use", in relation to a design, means the doing of anything by virtue of paragraph 1 which would otherwise be an infringement of the right in the design; and

"the government department concerned", in relation to such use, means the government department by whom or on whose authority the act was done.][290]

Reference of disputes as to Crown use

3.—*(1) Any dispute as to the exercise by a Government department or a person authorised by a Government department of the powers conferred by paragraph 1 of this Schedule, or as to terms for the use of a design for the services of the Crown thereunder, or as to the right of any person to receive any part of a payment made in pursuance of sub-paragraph (3) of that paragraph, may be referred to the court by either party to the dispute in such manner as may be prescribed by rules of court.* **A5–058**

[(1) Any dispute as to—

(a) the exercise by a Government department, or a person authorised by a Government department, of the powers conferred by paragraph 1 of this Schedule,

(b) terms for the use of a design for the services of the Crown under that paragraph,

(c) the right of any person to receive any part of a payment made under paragraph 1(3), or

(d) the right of any person to receive a payment under paragraph 2A,

may be referred to the court by either party to the dispute.][291]

(2) In any proceedings under this paragraph to which a Government department are a party, the department may—

(a) if the registered proprietor is a party to the proceedings, apply for cancellation of the registration of the design upon any ground upon which the registration of a design may be cancelled on an application to the court under section twenty of this Act;

(b) in any case, put in issue the validity of the registration of the design without applying for its cancellation.

(3) If in such proceedings as aforesaid any question arises whether a design has been recorded or applied as mentioned in paragraph 1 of this Schedule, and the disclosure of any document recording the design, or of any evidence of the application thereof, would in the opinion of the department be prejudicial to the public interest, the disclosure may be made confidentially to counsel for the other party or to an independent expert mutually agreed upon.

(4) In determining under this paragraph any dispute between a Government department and any person as to terms for the use of a design for the services of the Crown, the court shall have regard to any benefit or compensation which that person or any person from whom he derives title may have received, or may be entitled to receive, directly or indirectly from any Government department in respect of the design in question.

(5) In any proceedings under this paragraph the court may at any time order the whole proceedings or any question or issue of fact arising therein to be referred to a special or official referee or an arbitrator on such terms as the court may direct; and references to the court in the foregoing provisions of this paragraph shall be construed accordingly.

Special provisions as to Crown use during emergency

4.—(1) During any period of emergency within the meaning of this paragraph, the powers exercisable in relation to a design by a Government department, or a person authorised by a Government department under paragraph 1 of this Schedule shall include power to use the design for any purpose which appears to the department necessary or expedient— **A5–059**

(a) for the efficient prosecution of any war in which His Majesty may be engaged;

---

[290] Inserted by the Copyright, Designs and Patents Act 1988 s.271.
[291] Substituted by the Copyright, Designs and Patents Act 1988 s.271.

(b) for the maintenance of supplies and services essential to the life of the community;

(c) for securing a sufficiency of supplies and services essential to the well-being of the community;

(d) for promoting the productivity of industry, commerce and agriculture;

(e) for fostering and directing exports and reducing imports, or imports of any classes, from all or any countries and for redressing the balance of trade;

(f) generally for ensuring that the whole resources of the community are available for use, and are used, in a manner best calculated to serve the interests of the community; or

(g) for assisting the relief of suffering and the restoration and distribution of essential supplies and services in any part of His Majesty's dominions or any foreign countries that are in grave distress as the result of war;

and any reference in this Schedule to the services of the Crown shall be construed as including a reference to the purposes aforesaid.

(2) In this paragraph the expression "period of emergency" means a period beginning on such date as may be declared by Order in Council to be the commencement, and ending on such date as may be so declared to be the termination, of a period of emergency for the purposes of this paragraph.

(3) *A draft of any Order in Council under this paragraph shall be laid before Parliament; and the draft shall not be submitted to His Majesty except in pursuance of an Address presented by each House of Parliament praying that the Order be made.*

(3) No Order in Council under this paragraph shall be submitted to Her Majesty unless a draft of it has been laid before and approved by a resolution of each House of Parliament.]ˣˣˣ

ˣˣˣ Substituted by the Copyright, Designs and Patents Act 1988 s.272 and Sch.3, para.37(5).

A6. Section 266 of the Copyright, Designs and Patents Act 1988 (transitional provisions relating to designs applied for between January 12, 1988 and August 1, 1989)

Provisions with respect to certain designs registered in pursuance of application made before commencement

A6–001   **266.**—(1) Where a design is registered under the Registered Designs Act 1949 in pursuance of an application made after 12th January 1988 and before the commencement of this Part which could not have been registered under section 1 of that Act as substituted by section 265 above[292]—

(a) the right in the registered design expires ten years after the commencement of this Part, if it does not expire earlier in accordance with the 1949 Act, and

(b) any person is, after the commencement of this Part, entitled as of right to a licence to do anything which would otherwise infringe the right in the registered design.

---

[292] Section 265 amended s.1 of the Registered Designs Act 1949. For the effect of the amendment, compare s.1 before this amendment with s.1 after amendment in App.A5, para.A5–001 above.

(2) The terms of a licence available by virtue of this section shall, in default of agreement, be settled by the registrar on an application by the person requiring the licence; and the terms so settled shall authorise the licensee to do everything which would be an infringement of the right in the registered design in the absence of a licence.

(3) In settling the terms of a licence the registrar shall have regard to such factors as may be prescribed by the Secretary of State by order made by statutory instrument.

No such order shall be made unless a draft of it has been laid before and approved by a resolution of each House of Parliament.

(4) Where the terms of a licence are settled by the registrar, the licence has effect from the date on which the application to the registrar was made.

(5) Section 11B of the 1949 Act (undertaking to take licence of right in infringement proceedings), as inserted by section 270 below, applies where a licence is available as of right under this section, as it applies where a licence is available as of right under section 11A of that Act.

(6) Where a licence is available as of right under this section, a person to whom a licence was granted before the commencement of this Part may apply to the registrar for an order adjusting the terms of that licence.

(7) An appeal lies from any decision of the registrar under this section.

(8) This section shall be construed as one with the Registered Designs Act 1949.

A7. The Patents and Designs Acts 1907 and 1919 (consolidated—extracts)

Threats

36.—Where any person claiming [*to be the patentee of an invention*] **to have an interest in a patent,** by circulars, advertisements, or otherwise, threatens any other person with any legal proceedings or liability in respect of any alleged infringement of the patent, any person aggrieved thereby may bring an action against him, and may obtain an injunction against the continuance of such threats, and may recover such damage (if any) as he has sustained thereby, if the alleged infringement to which the threats related was not in fact an infringement of [*any legal rights of the person making such threats*] **the patent.**

[*Provided that this section shall not apply if the person making such threats with due diligence commences and prosecutes an action for infringement of his patent.*]

Provided that this section shall not apply if an action for infringement of the patent is commenced and prosecuted with due diligence.

A7–001

PART II

DESIGNS

Registration of Designs

Application for registration of designs

49.—(1) The comptroller may, on the application made in the prescribed form and manner of any person claiming to be the proprietor of any new or original

A7–002

design not previously published in the United Kingdom, register the design under this Part of this Act.

(2) The same design may be registered in more than one class, and, in case of doubt as to the class in which a design ought to be registered, the comptroller may decide the question.

[...]

(5) A design when registered shall be registered as of the date of the application for registration.

A7–003   50.—Where a design has been registered in one or more classes of goods the application of the proprietor of the design to register it in some one or more other classes shall not be refused, nor shall the registration thereof be invalidated—

(a) on the grounds of the design not being a [*new and original*] **new or original** design, by reason only that it was so previously registered; or

(b) on the ground of the design having been previously published in the United Kingdom, by reason only that it has been applied to goods of any class in which it was so previously registered.

Legal Proceedings

Piracy of registered design

A7–004   60.—(1) During the existence of copyright in any design it shall not be lawful for any person—

(a) For the purposes of sale to apply or cause to be applied to any article in any class of goods in which the design is registered the design or any fraudulent or obvious imitation thereof, except with the licence or written consent of the registered proprietor, or to do anything with a view to enable the design to be so applied; or

(b) Knowing that the design or any fraudulent or obvious imitation thereof has been applied to any article without the consent of the registered proprietor to publish or expose or cause to be published or exposed for sale that article.

(2) If any person acts in contravention of this section he shall be liable for every contravention to pay to the registered proprietor of the design a sum not exceeding fifty pounds, recoverable as a simple contract debt, or if the proprietor elects to bring an action for the recovery of damages for such contravention, and for an injunction against the repetition thereof, he shall be liable to pay such damages as may be awarded and to be restrained by injunction accordingly:

Provided that the total sum recoverable as a simple contract debt in respect of any one design shall not exceed one hundred pounds.

Definitions

A7–005   93.—In this Act, unless the context otherwise requires,—

[*"Design" means any design (not being a design for a sculpture or other thing within the protection of the Sculpture Copyright Act, 1814) applicable to any article, whether the design is applicable for the pattern, or for the shape or configuration, or for the ornament thereof, or for any two or more of such purposes, and by whatever means it is applicable, whether by printing, painting, embroidering, weaving, sewing, modelling, casting, embossing, engraving, staining, or any other means whatever, manual, mechanical, or chemical, separate or combined*:]

"Design" means only the features of shape, configuration, pattern, or ornament applied to any article by any industrial process or means, whether manual, mechanical, or chemical, separate or combined, which in the finished article appeal to and are judged solely by the eye; but does not include any mode or principle of construction, or anything which is in substance a mere mechanical device:

"Article" means (as respects designs) any article of manufacture and any substance artificial or natural, or partly artificial and partly natural:

"Copyright" means the exclusive right to apply a design to any article in any class in which the design is registered:

[*"Proprietor of a new and original design,"*]—

"Proprietor of a new or original design,"]—

(a) Where the author of the design, for good consideration, executes the work for some other person, means the person for whom the design is so executed; and

(b) Where any person acquires the design or the right to apply the design to any article either exclusively of any other person or otherwise, means, in the respect and to the extent in and to which the design or right has been so acquired, the person by whom the design or right is so acquired; and

(c) In any other case, means the author of the defendant;

and where the property in, or the right to apply, the design has devolved from the original proprietor upon any other person, includes that other person:

[*Note*: Words in square brackets in italics are as originally enacted in the Patents and Designs Act 1907. The text in bold is as amended by the Patents and Designs Act 1919 s.19 and Schedule.]

A8. The Patents, Designs and Trade Marks Act 1883 (c.57)

An Act to amend and consolidate the Law relating to Patents for Inventions, Registration of Designs, and of Trade Marks.   **A8–001**

[25TH AUGUST 1883]

Be it enacted by the Queen's most Excellent Majesty, by and with the advice and consent of the Lords Spiritual and Temporal, and Commons, in this present Parliament assembled, and by the authority of the same, as follows:

PART I

PRELIMINARY

1.—This Act may be cited as the Patents, Designs, and Trade Marks Act, 1883.   **A8–002**

PART II

DESIGNS

Registration of Designs

Application for registration of designs

A8–003   **47.**—(1) The comptroller may, on application by or on behalf of any person claiming to be the proprietor of any new or original design not previously published in the United Kingdom, register the design under this part of this Act.

(2) The application must be made in the form set forth in the First Schedule to this Act, or in such other form as may be from time to time prescribed, and must be left at, or sent by post to, the patent office in the prescribed manner.

(3) The application must contain a statement of the nature of the design, and the class or classes of goods in which the applicant desires that the design be registered.

(4) The same design may be registered in more than one class.

(5) In case of doubt as to the class in which a design ought to be registered, the comptroller may decide the question.

(6) The comptroller may, if he thinks fit, refuse to register any design presented to him for registration, but any person aggrieved by any such refusal may apply therefrom to the Board of Trade.

(7) The Board of Trade shall, if required, hear the applicant and the comptroller, and may make an order determining whether, and subject to what conditions, if any, registration is to be permitted.

Legal Proceedings

Penalty on piracy of registered design

A8–004   **58.**—During the existence of copyright in any design—

(a) It shall not be lawful for any person without the license or written consent of the registered proprietor to apply such design or any fraudulent or obvious imitation thereof, in the class or classes of goods in which such design is registered, for purposes of sale to any article of manufacture or to any substance artificial or natural or partly artificial and partly natural; and

(b) It shall not be lawful for any person to publish or expose for sale any article of manufacture or any substance to which such design or any fraudulent or obvious imitation thereof shall have been so applied, knowing that the same has been so applied without the consent of the registered proprietor.

Any person who acts in contravention of this section shall be liable for every offence to forfeit a sum not exceeding fifty pounds to the registered proprietor of the design, who may recover such sum as a simple contract debt by action in any court of competent jurisdiction.

Action for damages

A8–005   **59.**—Notwithstanding the remedy given by this Act for the recovery of such penalty as aforesaid, the registered proprietor of any design may (if he elects to do so) bring an action for the recovery of any damages arising from the application of any such design, or of any fraudulent or obvious imitation thereof for the purpose of sale, to any article of manufacture or substance, or from the publication sale or exposure for sale by any person of any article or substance to which such design or any fraudulent or obvious imitation thereof shall have been so applied, such person knowing that the proprietor had not given his consent to such application.

Definitions

Definition of "design", "copyright"

60.—In and for the purposes of this Act—   A8–006

"Design" means any design applicable to any article of manufacture, or to any substance artificial or natural, or partly artificial and partly natural, whether the design is applicable for the pattern, or for the shape or configuration, or for the ornament thereof, or for any two or more of such purposes, and by whatever means it is applicable, whether by printing, painting, embroidering, weaving, sewing, modelling, casting, embossing, engraving, straining, or any other means whatever, manual, mechanical, or chemical, separate or combined, not being a design for a sculpture, or other thing within the protection of the Sculpture Copyright Act of the year 1814 (fifty-fourth George the Third, chapter fifty-six).

"Copyright" means the exclusive right to apply a design to any article of manufacture or to any such substance as aforesaid in the class or classes in which the design is registered.

Definition of proprietor

61.—The author of any new and original design shall be considered the   A8–007
proprietor thereof, unless he executed the work on behalf of another person for a good or valuable consideration, in which case such person shall be considered the proprietor, and every person acquiring for a good or valuable consideration a new and original design, or the right to apply the same to any such article or substance as aforesaid, either exclusively of any other person or otherwise, and also every person on whom the property in such defendant or such right in the application thereof shall devolve, shall be considered the proprietor of the design in the respect in which the same may have been so acquired, and to that extent, but not otherwise.

A9. The Regulatory Reform (Registered Designs) Order 2006 (SI 2006/1974)

Introductory

1.—(1) This Order may be cited as the Regulatory Reform (Registered Designs)   A9–001
Order 2006 and it shall come into force on 1st October 2006.

(2) This Order extends to England and Wales, Scotland and Northern Ireland.

2.—The Registered Designs Act 1949 shall be amended as follows.

(Rules 3–17 make amendments to the Registered Designs Act 1949. These amendments have been printed as part of the text of the Act as amended on the preceding pages of this Appendix.)

Transitional provisions

A9–002   **18.**—(1) The amendments made to the Registered Designs Act 1949 by articles 7 to 10 shall not apply to post-1989 registrations or pre-1989 registrations.

(2) In paragraph (1)—

"post-1989 registrations" means registrations to which regulation 12 of the Registered Designs Regulations 2001 applies;
"pre-1989 registrations" means registrations which fall within regulation 13(1) of those Regulations.

19.—The amendments made to section 22 of the Registered Designs Act 1949 by article 16(2)(b) and (3) shall not apply to any registration under the Act which has resulted from an application made before the coming into force of this Order.

A10. The Registered Designs Rules 2006 (SI 2006/1975)

PART 1

INTRODUCTORY

Citation and commencement

A10–001   **1.**—These Rules may be cited as the Registered Designs Rules 2006 and shall come into force on 1st October 2006.

Interpretation

A10–002   **2.**—(1) In these Rules—

"the Act" means the Registered Designs Act 1949;
"the journal" means the journal published under rule 44(1); and
"section" means a section of the Act.

(2) Where a time or period has been altered under rules 19(1) or 39 to 41, any reference in these Rules to the time or period shall be construed as a reference to the time or period as altered.

Forms

A10–003   **3.**—(1) The forms of which the use is required by these Rules are those set out in Schedule 1.

(2) Such a requirement to use a form is satisfied by the use of a form which is acceptable to the registrar and contains the information required by the form as so set out.

PART 2

APPLICATIONS FOR REGISTRATION

Applications for registration and formal requirements

Applications

4.—(1) An application for the registration of a design or designs shall be made on Form DF2A and—

    (a) shall include the identity of the person making the application; and

    (b) in relation to each design, shall either—

        (i) include a representation of the design; or

        (ii) be accompanied by a specimen of the design,

and it shall be accompanied by the prescribed fee.

(2) But an application for the registration of a design or designs, which is a subsequent application for the purposes of section 3B(3), shall be made on Form DF2B and be accompanied by the prescribed fee.

(3) Where an application includes a representation of the design, the applicant may give his consent for its publication on Form DF2A or Form DF2B.

(4) Where a person purports to file something under section 3(1) and—

    (a) it is not in the form prescribed by either paragraph (1) or (2); or

    (b) it is not accompanied by the prescribed fee,

the registrar shall notify that person accordingly.

(5) A representation or specimen filed under paragraph (1)(b) may be accompanied by a brief description of the design.

(6) A specimen may not be filed under paragraph (1)(b) if it is hazardous or perishable; and where such a specimen is so filed it shall be disregarded.

(7) An application for the registration of a design which is a repeating surface pattern shall only be treated as such if—

    (a) the representation or specimen filed under paragraph (1)(b) includes the complete pattern and a sufficient portion of the repeat in length and width to show how the pattern repeats; and

    (b) the application contains a statement that it relates to a repeating surface pattern.

Formal requirements

5.—(1) An application for the registration of a design shall comply with the first and second requirement.

(2) The first requirement is that the applicant has specified the product to which the design is intended to be applied or in which it is intended to be incorporated.

(3) The second requirement is that the dimensions of any specimen of the design filed under rule 4(1)(b)(ii) shall not exceed 29.7cm × 21cm × 1cm.

(4) Where the applicant files a representation of the design after being notified under rule 8(1) that the application does not comply with the second requirement—

    (a) that representation shall be deemed to have been filed under rule 4(1)(b)(i); and

A10–004

A10–005

513

(b) any specimen filed under rule 4(1)(b)(ii) shall be treated as not having been filed.

(5) Nothing done to comply with the first requirement shall be taken to affect the scope of the protection conferred by the registration of a design.

Disclaimers

Partial disclaimers

A10–006   6.—An application for the registration of a design may be accompanied by a disclaimer which—

(a) limits the scope or extent of protection being applied for in relation to the design; or

(b) Indicates that the application for registration relates to a design that forms only a part of the appearance of a product.

Convention applications

Convention applications

A10–007   7.—(1) Where an application for the registration of a design or designs is made by virtue of section 14 the applicant shall comply with the following provisions.

(2) The application shall contain a declaration specifying—

(a) the date of making of each convention application; and

(b) the country it was made in or in respect of.

(3) The applicant shall, before the end of the period of 3 months beginning with the date on which the application was filed, file at the Patent Office a copy of the representation of the design that was the subject of each convention application.

(4) A copy of the representation filed under paragraph (3) shall be—

(a) duly certified by the authority with which it was filed; or

(b) verified to the satisfaction of the registrar.

(5) Paragraph (3) shall not apply where a copy of the convention application is kept at the Patent Office.

(6) Where any document relating to the convention application is in a language other than English or Welsh, the registrar may direct the applicant to provide a translation of the whole or any part of that document.

(7) The translation shall be filed before the end of the period of 3 months beginning with the date of the direction.

(8) Where the applicant—

(a) fails to file a copy of the representation of the design which has been certified or verified in accordance with paragraph (4); or

(b) fails to comply with a direction given under paragraph (6),

the convention application shall be disregarded for the purposes of section 14(2).

(9) In this rule "convention application" means an application for the protection of a design which has been made in a convention country.

Examination of application, representations for publication and time limits

Substantive and formal examination of application

8.—(1) Where it appears to the registrar that he should refuse to register a design included in an application— **A10–008**

    (a) by reason of the application for the registration of that design not being made in accordance with any of these Rules, other than rule 9(2) (see section 3A(2)); or

    (b) by reason of section 3A(3) or (4),

he shall notify the applicant accordingly.

(2) The notification shall include a statement of why it appears to the registrar that he should refuse to register the design (for the purposes of this rule the "statement of objections").

(3) The applicant may, before the end of the period of 2 months beginning with the date of the notification, send his written observations on the statement of objections to the registrar.

(4) The registrar shall give the applicant an opportunity to be heard.

(5) Where the registrar refuses to register a design included in an application, he shall send to the applicant the written reasons for his decision.

(6) The date on which the written reasons were sent to the applicant shall be deemed to be the date of the decision for the purposes of any appeal.

Representation of design for publication

9.—(1) Where the registrar decides that he should not refuse to register the design for the reasons mentioned in rule 8(1)(a) or (b) and— **A10–009**

    (a) no representation of the design has been filed; or

    (b) a representation has been filed but it is not suitable for publication,

the registrar shall direct the applicant to provide a suitable representation.

(2) Where a direction is given, the applicant shall, before the end of the period of 3 months beginning with the date of the direction, file a suitable representation (otherwise the registrar may refuse to register the design: see section 3A(2)).

(3) Where a suitable representation has been filed, the applicant shall file his consent for its publication on Form DF2C

(4) But paragraph (3) shall not apply where the applicant consented to publication in accordance with rule 4(3).

(5) In this rule "suitable representation" means a representation of the design which is suitable for publication.

Time limits under section 3(5) and section 3B

10.—(1) The time prescribed for the purposes of section 3(5) shall be 12 months beginning with the date on which the application for registration of the design was made or treated as made (disregarding section 14). **A10–010**

(2) The period prescribed for the purposes of section 3B(3) shall be the period of 2 months beginning with the date on which the earlier application was modified under section 3B(3).

PART 3

DESIGNS AFTER REGISTRATION

Publication

Publication

A10–011   11.—(1) When a design has been registered, the registrar shall publish a representation of that design in the journal as soon as possible after the certificate of registration is granted.

(2) When the registrar publishes the representation, he may also publish any other information he thinks is relevant to that design.

(3) The representation published under paragraph (1) shall be the representation filed under rule 4(1)(b)(i) or 9(2) or as mentioned in rule 5(4).

Duration of rights and surrender

Extension of duration of right in registered design

A10–012   12.—(1) An application for an extension under section 8(2) or 8(4) shall be made on Form DF9A.

(2) An application under section 8(2) may only be made during the period of 6 months ending with the date on which the relevant period of 5 years expires.

(3) On receipt of the prescribed renewal fee the registrar shall notify the registered proprietor of the extension of the right in the registered design.

(4) Where the right in a registered design has ceased to have effect by reason of section 8(3), the registrar shall, before the end of the period of 6 weeks beginning with the date on which the right ceased, send written notice to the registered proprietor of that fact.

(5) But paragraph (4) shall not apply where the renewal fee and the prescribed additional fee is paid before a notice is sent.

Restoration of a lapsed right in a design under section 8A

A10–013   13.—(1) An application for the restoration of the right in a design under section 8A shall—

(a) be made on Form DF29; and
(b) be supported by evidence of the statements made in the application.

(2) The period prescribed for the purposes of section 8A(1) shall be the period of 12 months beginning with the date on which the registered design ceased to have effect.

(3) The notice of the application shall be published in the journal.

(4) Where, upon consideration of that evidence, the registrar is not satisfied that a case for an order under section 8A has been made out, he shall notify the applicant accordingly.

(5) The applicant may, before the end of the period of 1 month beginning with the date of that notification, request to be heard by the registrar.

(6) Where the applicant requests a hearing, the registrar shall give him an opportunity to be heard; after which the registrar shall determine whether the application under section 8A shall be granted or refused.

(7) Where the registrar decides not to make the order he shall give the applicant written reasons for his refusal.

Cancellation of registration

14.—A request under section 11 to cancel the registration of a design shall be made on Form DF19C   **A10–014**

PART 4

PROCEEDINGS HEARD BEFORE THE REGISTRAR

Conduct of proceedings

Procedure for applying for a declaration of invalidity

15.—(1) An application for a declaration of invalidity under section 11ZB shall—   **A10–015**

  (a) be made on Form DF19A; and

  (b) include a statement of the grounds on which the application is made.

(2) The statement of grounds shall include a concise statement of the facts and grounds on which the applicant relies and shall be verified by a statement of truth.

(3) The registrar shall send a copy of Form DF19A and the statement of case to the registered proprietor.

(4) The registrar shall specify a period within which the registered proprietor shall file a counter-statement.

(5) The registered proprietor, within that period, shall—

  (a) file his counter-statement on Form DF19B; and

  (b) send a copy of it to the applicant,

otherwise the registrar may treat him as not opposing the application.

(6) In his counter-statement the registered proprietor shall—

  (a) include a concise statement of the facts on which he relies;

  (b) state which of the allegations in the statement of grounds he denies;

  (c) state which of the allegations he is unable to admit or deny, but which he requires the applicant to prove;

  (d) state which allegations he admits,

and it shall be verified by a statement of truth.

(7) In this Part—

  (a) "statement of case" means the statement of grounds filed by the applicant or the counter-statement filed by the registered proprietor; and

  (b) references to the statement of case include part of the statement of case.

Evidence rounds

16.—(1) When the period specified under rule 15(4) has expired, the registrar shall specify the periods within which evidence may be filed by the parties.   **A10–016**

(2) Where the applicant for a declaration of invalidity files no evidence (other than his statement of grounds) in support of his application, the registrar may treat him as having withdrawn his application.

(3) The registrar may, at any time if he thinks fit, give leave to either party to file evidence upon such terms as he thinks fit.

(4) Under this rule, evidence shall only be considered to be filed when—

(a) it has been received by the registrar; and

(b) it has been sent to all other parties to the proceedings.

(5) The registrar shall give the parties an opportunity to be heard.

(6) Where any party requests to be heard, the registrar shall send to the parties notice of a date for the hearing.

Decision of registrar on invalidity

A10–017   **17.**—(1) When the registrar has made a decision on the application for a declaration of invalidity, he shall send to the parties written notice of it, stating the reasons for his decision.

(2) The date on which the decision was sent to the applicant shall be deemed to be the date of the decision for the purposes of any appeal.

Exercise of discretionary powers of registrar

A10–018   **18.**—The registrar shall give to any applicant for registration of a design an opportunity to be heard before exercising adversely to the applicant any discretion vested in the registrar by or under the Act.

General powers of registrar in relation to proceedings before him

A10–019   **19.**—(1) The registrar may extend or shorten (or further extend or shorten) any period which has been specified under any provision of this Part.

(2) At any stage of proceedings before him, the registrar may direct that the parties to the proceedings attend a case management conference or pre-hearing review.

(3) Except where the Act or these Rules otherwise provide, the registrar may give such directions as to the management of the proceedings as he thinks fit, and in particular he may—

(a) require a document, information or evidence to be filed;

(b) require a translation of any document;

(c) require a party or a party's legal representative to attend a hearing;

(d) hold a hearing and receive evidence by telephone or by using any other method of direct oral communication;

(e) allow a statement of case to be amended;

(f) stay the whole, or any part, of the proceedings either generally or until a specified date or event;

(g) consolidate proceedings;

(h) direct that part of any proceedings be dealt with as separate proceedings.

(4) The registrar may control the evidence by giving directions as to—

(a) the issues on which he requires evidence;

(b) the nature of the evidence which he requires to decide those issues; and

(c) the way in which the evidence is to be placed before him,

and the registrar may use his power under this paragraph to exclude evidence which would otherwise be admissible.

(5) When the registrar gives directions under any provision of this Part, he may—

(a) make them subject to conditions; and

(b) specify the consequences of failure to comply with the directions or a condition.

Hearings in public

20.—(1) Subject to paragraphs (3) and (4), any hearing before the registrar of proceedings between two or more parties relating to an application for a registered design or a registered design, shall be held in public. **A10–020**

(2) Any party to the proceedings may apply to the registrar for the hearing to be held in private.

(3) The registrar shall only grant an application under paragraph (2) where—

(a) it is in the interests of justice for the hearing to be in held in private; and

(b) all the parties to the proceedings have had an opportunity to be heard on the matter,

and where the application is granted the hearing shall be in private.

(4) Any hearing of an application under paragraph (2) shall be held in private.

(5) In this rule a reference to a hearing includes any part of a hearing.

(6) [. . .][293]

Evidence in proceedings before the registrar

21.—(1) Subject as follows, evidence filed under this Part may be given— **A10–021**

(a) by witness statement, statement of case, affidavit, statutory declaration; or

(b) in any other form which would be admissible as evidence in proceedings before the court.

(2) A witness statement or a statement of case may only be given in evidence if it includes a statement of truth.

(3) The general rule is that evidence at hearings is to be by witness statement unless the registrar or any enactment requires otherwise.

(4) For the purposes of this Part, a statement of truth—

(a) means a statement that the person making the statement believes that the facts stated in a particular document are true; and

(b) shall be dated and signed by—

(i) in the case of a witness statement, the maker of the statement,

(ii) in any other case, the party or his legal representative.

(5) In this Part, a witness statement is a written statement signed by a person that contains the evidence which that person would be allowed to give orally.

Miscellaneous

Costs of proceedings

22.—The registrar may, in any proceedings before him under the Act, award to any party by order such costs as he considers reasonable, and direct how and by what parties they are to be paid. **A10–022**

---

[293] Revoked by the Tribunals, Courts and Enforcement Act 2007 (Transitional and Consequential Provisions) Order 2008 (SI 2008/2683) art.6(1) and Sch.1, para.31.

Security for costs

A10–023   **23.**—(1) The registrar may require a person to give security for the costs of any application or appeal mentioned in section 30(3) if—

    (a) he is satisfied, having regard to all the circumstances of the case, that it is just to require such security; and

    (b) one or more of the conditions in paragraph (2) applies.

(2) The conditions are—

    (a) the person is resident outside the United Kingdom but—

      (i) not resident in a Brussels Contracting State,

      (ii) a Lugano Contracting State, or

      (iii) a Regulation State,

    as defined in section 1(3) of the Civil Jurisdiction and Judgments Act 1982;

    (b) the person is a company or other body (whether incorporated inside or outside the United Kingdom) and there is reason to believe that it will be unable to pay the other person's costs if ordered to do so;

    (c) the person has changed his address since filing an address for service with a view to evading the consequences of the proceedings;

    (d) the person has furnished an incorrect address for service;

    (e) the person has taken steps in relation to his assets that would make it difficult to enforce an order for costs against him;

    (f) the person has failed to pay a costs order in relation to previous proceedings before the registrar or a court (whether or not the proceedings were between the same parties).

(3) In default of such security being given the registrar may treat the application or appeal as abandoned.

Registrar shall have the powers of official referee

A10–024   **24.**—The registrar shall have the powers of an official referee of the Supreme Court as regards—

    (a) the attendance of witnesses and their examination on oath; and

    (b) the discovery and production of documents,

but he shall have no power to punish summarily for contempt.

Minimum notice of hearing

A10–025   **25.**—The registrar shall not give a person less than 14 days notice of any hearing under the Act.

PART 5

THE REGISTER AND OTHER INFORMATION

Certificate of registration and registrable interests

Certificate of registration

A10–026   **26.**—(1) The certificate of registration of a design shall include—

    (a) the name of the registered proprietor;

    (b) the date of registration; and

(c) the registration number of the design.

(2) Any request by the registered proprietor for a copy of the certificate of registration shall—

    (a) be in writing; and

    (b) be accompanied by the prescribed fee.

(3) Before considering the request, the registrar may require the person making the request to provide such information or evidence as the registrar thinks fit.

Registration of interests

27.—(1) The following matters are prescribed for the purposes of section 17(1)(c)—   **A10–027**

    (a) the registered proprietor's address for service;

    (b) the grant or cancellation of a licence under a registered design;

    (c) the granting or cancelling of a security interest (whether fixed or floating) over a registered design or any right in or under it;

    (d) an order of a court or other competent authority transferring a registered design or any right in or under it.

(2) An application to the registrar to enter in the register a matter not mentioned in section 17(1)(a) or (b) or paragraph (1) shall be made in writing.

(3) An application under section 19(1) or (2) shall be made on Form DF12A.

(4) Where the registrar has doubts about whether he should enter a matter in the register—

    (a) he shall inform the person making the application of the reasons for his doubts; and

    (b) he may require that person to furnish evidence in support of the application.

Inspection and information about registered designs

Inspection of register, representations and specimens

28.—(1) The register and any representation or specimen of a registered design shall be open for inspection at the Patent Office during the hours the Patent Office is open for all classes of public business (see rule 45(2)).   **A10–028**

(2) Whilst a direction under section 5(1) in respect of a design remains in force, no representation or specimen of the design shall be open to inspection.

Inspection of documents

29.—(1) Where a design has been registered under the Act, there shall be open to inspection at the Patent Office on and after the date on which the certificate of registration is granted every document kept at the Patent Office in connection with that design.   **A10–029**

(2) But no document may be inspected—

    (a) before the end of the period of 14 days beginning with the day—

        (i) it was filed at the Patent Office; or

        (ii) received by the registrar or the Patent Office;

    (b) where that document was prepared by the registrar or the Patent Office for internal use only;

    (c) where the document includes matter—

        (i) which in the registrar's opinion disparages any person in a way likely to damage him; or

(ii) the inspection of which would in his opinion be generally expected to encourage offensive, immoral or anti-social behaviour.

(3) Unless, in a particular case, the registrar otherwise directs, no document may be inspected—

(a) where—
(i) the document was prepared by the registrar or the Patent Office other than for internal use; and
(ii) it contains information which the registrar considers should remain confidential;
(b) where it is treated as a confidential document (under rule 30).

(4) In this rule and rule 30 references to a document include part of a document.

Confidential information

A10–030   30.—(1) Where a person files a document at the Patent Office or sends it to the registrar or the Patent Office, any person may request that the document be treated as a confidential document.

(2) A request to treat a document as confidential shall—

(a) be made before the end of the period of 14 days beginning with the date on which the document was filed at the Patent Office or received by the registrar or at the Patent Office;
(b) include reasons for the request.

(3) Where a request has been made under paragraph (1), the document shall be treated as confidential until the registrar refuses that request or makes a direction under paragraph (4).

(4) Where it appears that there is good reason for the document to remain confidential, the registrar may direct that the document shall be treated as a confidential document; otherwise he shall refuse the request made under paragraph (1).

(5) But, where the registrar believes there is no longer a good reason for the direction under paragraph (4) to remain in force, he shall revoke it.

Information about rights in registered designs

A10–031   31.—(1) A request for information under section 23 shall be made on Form DF21 and be accompanied by the prescribed fee.

(2) The request shall—

(a) where the registration number is known by the person making the request, include that number; or
(b) in any other case, be accompanied by a representation or specimen of the product—
(i) in which the design has been incorporated; or
(ii) to which the design has been applied.

Copies of documents

Copies of entries in, or extracts from, the register

A10–032   32.—An application under section 17(5) for a certified copy of an entry in the register or a certified extract from the register shall be made on Form DF23 and be accompanied by the prescribed fee.

Copies of representations and specimens

33.—(1) A person may apply to the registrar for a certified copy of any representation or specimen of a design; and that person shall be entitled to such a copy.

(2) An application under paragraph (1) shall be made in writing and be accompanied by the prescribed fee.

A10–033

Alterations and rectification

Alteration of name or address

34.—(1) Any person may request that an alteration to his name or address—

(a) be entered in the register; or

(b) be made to any application or other document filed at the Patent Office.

(2) A request under paragraph (1) shall in relation to an alteration to—

(a) his name, be made on Form DF16A; and

(b) his address, be made on Form DF16A or in writing.

(3) Where the registrar has doubts about whether he should make the alteration to a name or address—

(a) he shall inform the person making the request of the reason for his doubts; and

(b) he may require that person to furnish evidence in support of the request.

(4) Where the registrar has no doubts (or no longer has doubts) about whether he should make the alteration, it shall be entered in the register or made to the application or document.

A10–034

Notice of rectification of the register

35.—(1) The prescribed manner of giving notice to the registrar for the purposes of section 20(3) is by giving written notice.

(2) The prescribed manner of service on the registrar for the purposes of section 20(4) is by filing a copy of the order at the Patent Office.

A10–035

PART 6

MISCELLANEOUS

Agents and advisers

Agents

36.—(1) Any act required or authorised by the Act to be done by or to any person in connection with the registration of a design, or any procedure relating to a registered design, may be done by or to an agent authorised by that person orally or in writing.

A10–036

523

(2) But an agent shall only be treated as authorised under paragraph (1) where—

    (a) he was nominated by the applicant at the time of—
        (i) making his application for registration;
        (ii) making his application for a declaration of invalidity under section 11ZB; or
        (iii) making his application under section 19(1) or (2); or
    (b) he has filed Form DF1A.

(3) Where an agent has been authorised under paragraph (1), the registrar may, if he thinks fit in any particular case, require the signature or presence of his principal.

Appointing advisers

A10–037   **37.**—(1) The registrar may appoint an adviser to assist him in any proceedings before him.

(2) the registrar shall settle any question or instructions to be submitted or given to the adviser.

Correction of irregularities and extensions of time

Correction of irregularities

A10–038   **38.**—Where the registrar thinks fit, he may rectify any irregularity of procedure—

    (a) after giving the parties such notice, and
    (b) subject to such conditions,

as he may direct.

Extension of times or periods prescribed by Rules

A10–039   **39.**—(1) The registrar may, if he thinks fit, extend (or further extend) any time or period prescribed by these Rules, except the periods prescribed by—

    (a) rule 10(1) (period prescribed for the purposes of section 3(5)); and
    (b) rule 13(2) (period for making an application for restoration),

(but those periods may be extended under rules 38, 40 and 41).

(2) Any extension under paragraph (1) shall be made—

    (a) after giving the parties such notice, and
    (b) subject to such conditions,

as the registrar may direct.

(3) An extension may be granted under paragraph (1) notwithstanding that the time or period prescribed by the relevant rule has expired.

Interrupted days

A10–040   **40.**—(1) The registrar may certify any day as an interrupted day where—

    (a) there is an event or circumstance causing an interruption in the normal operation of the Patent Office; or
    (b) there is a general interruption or subsequent dislocation in the postal services of the United Kingdom.

(2) Any certificate of the registrar made under paragraph (1) shall be posted in the Patent Office and advertised in the journal.

(3) The registrar shall, where the time for doing anything under these Rules expires on an interrupted day, extend that time to the next following day not being an interrupted day (or an excluded day).

(4) In this rule—

"interrupted day" means a day which has been certified as such under paragraph (1); and
"excluded day" means a day specified as such by rule 46.

Delays in communication services

41.—(1) The registrar shall extend any time or period in these Rules where he is satisfied that the failure to do something under these Rules was wholly or mainly attributed to a delay in, or failure of, a communication service.　**A10–041**

(2) Any extension under paragraph (1) shall be—

(a) made after giving the parties such notice; and
(b) subject to such conditions,

as the registrar may direct.

(3) In this rule "communication service" means a service by which documents may be sent and delivered and includes post, electronic communications and courier.

Address for service

Address for service

42.—(1) For the purposes of any proceedings under the Act, an address for service shall be furnished by—　**A10–042**

(a) an applicant for the registration of a design;
(b) a person who makes an application under section 11ZB for a declaration of invalidity of a registered design;
(c) the registered proprietor of the design who opposes such an application.

(2) The proprietor of a registered design, or any person who has registered any interest in a registered design, may furnish an address for service on Form DF1A.

(3) Where a person has furnished an address for service under paragraph (1) or (2), he may substitute a new address for service by notifying the registrar on Form DF1A.

[(4) An address for service furnished under this Rule shall be an address in the United Kingdom, another EEA state or the Channel Islands.][294]

(5) [. . .][295]

(6) In this rule "EEA State" means a member State, Iceland, Liechtenstein or Norway.

---

[294] Substituted by the Patents, Trade Marks and Designs (Address for Service) Rules 2009 (SI 2009/546) rr.5 and 6.
[295] Revoked by the Patents, Trade Marks and Designs (Address for Service) Rules 2009 (SI 2009/546) rr.5 and 6.

Failure to furnish an address for service

A10–043   43.—(1) Where—

(a) a person has failed to furnish an address for service under rule 42(1); and

(b) the registrar has sufficient information enabling him to contact that person,

the registrar shall direct that person to furnish an address for service.

(2) Where a direction has been given under paragraph (1), the person directed shall, before the end of the period of 2 months beginning with the date of the direction, furnish an address for service.

(3) Paragraph (4) applies where—

(a) a direction was given under paragraph (1) and the period prescribed by paragraph (2) has expired; or

(b) the registrar had insufficient information to give a direction under paragraph (1),

and the person has failed to furnish an address for service.

(4) Where this paragraph applies—

(a) in the case of an applicant for the registration of a design, the application shall be treated as withdrawn;

(b) in the case of a person applying under section 11ZB for a declaration of invalidity, his application shall be treated as withdrawn; and

(c) in the case of the proprietor who is opposing an application under section 11ZB, he shall be deemed to have withdrawn from the proceedings.

(5) In this rule an "address for service" means an address which complies with the requirements of rule 42(4) [. . . .][296]

Miscellaneous

The journal

A10–044   44.—(1) The registrar shall publish a journal which shall contain—

(a) everything which is required by the Act or these Rules to be published; and

(b) any other information that the registrar may consider to be generally useful or important.

(2) In these Rules "the journal" means the journal published under paragraph (1).

Hours of business

A10–045   45.—(1) For the transaction of relevant business by the public the Patent Office shall be open—

(a) on Monday to Friday between 9.00am and midnight; and

(b) on Saturday between 9.00am and 1.00pm.

---

[296] Revoked by the Patents, Trade Marks and Designs (Address for Service) Rules 2009 (SI 2009/546) rr.5 and 7.

(2) For the transaction of all other business by the public under the Act the Patent Office shall be open between 9.00am and 5.00pm.

(3) In this Part "relevant business" means the filing of any application or other document except—

(a) an application for an extension under section 8; or

(b) an application for the registration of a design or designs made by virtue of section 14.

Excluded days

46.—(1) The following shall be excluded days for the transaction by the public of business under the Act—

A10–046

(a) a Sunday;

(b) Good Friday;

(c) Christmas day; or

(d) a day which is specified or proclaimed to be a bank holiday by or under section 1 of the Banking and Financial Dealings Act 1971.

(2) A Saturday shall be an excluded day for the transaction by the public of business under the Act, except relevant business (see rule 45(1)).

Transitional provisions and revocation

47.—(1) Schedule 2 (transitional provisions) shall have effect.

A10–047

(2) The instruments set out in Schedule 3 (revocations) are revoked to the extent specified.

SCHEDULE 1

FORMS

A10–048

Form number	Title	Rule
DF1A	Appointment or change of agent or contact address	36 and 42
DF2A	Application to register one or more designs	4
DF2B	Application to register one or more designs divided from an earlier application	4
DF2C	Application to publish one or more designs	9
DF9A	Renewal of design registration	12
DF12A	Application to record a change of ownership or to record or cancel a licence or security	27
DF16A	Change of proprietor's name or address	34
DF19A	Request to invalidate a design registration	15
DF19B	Notice of counter-statement	15
DF19C	Notice by proprietor to cancel a registration	14
DF21	Request for a search of the UK designs register	31
DF23	Request for a Certified Copy	32
DF29	Request to restore a registration	13

INTELLECTUAL
PROPERTY OFFICE

Designs Form DF1A

Appointment or change of agent or contact address

Concept House
Cardiff Road
Newport
South Wales
NP10 8QQ

Please read the guidance note below about filling in this form.

1. Your reference.	
2. Design number or numbers affected. (List on a separate sheet if there is not enough space on this form.)	
3. Full name of the applicant or proprietor.	
4. Full name and address (including postcode) of the new agent or contact address. Designs ADP number (if you know it).	
5. Have you been authorised to act in all matters relating to the above design or designs? If 'no' please give details of the extent of your appointment.	
6. Declaration. Signature of the applicant or their representative.	We have been appointed by the above applicant or proprietor.
Name in BLOCK CAPITALS.	
Date.	
7. Name and daytime phone number of the person we should contact in case of query. You may also provide your e-mail address.	
Number of sheets attached to this form.	

Note:

We suggest you check the proprietor's name and the designs they own by doing a proprietor search on our website www.ipo.gov.uk before you fill in the form.

(REV OCT06)   Intellectual Property Office is an operating name of the Patent Office   **Form DF1A**

INTELLECTUAL
PROPERTY OFFICE

Designs Form DF2A
Official fee due with this form

Application to register one or more designs

Concept House
Cardiff Road
Newport
South Wales
NP10 8QQ

Please read the guidance note below about filling in this form.

1.	Your reference:	
2.	If you are applying for more than one design, please state the total number.	
	How many of these designs do you wish to have published and registered immediately?	
3.	**Full name and address (including postcode) of the applicant.**	
	Your application details, including your name and address, will appear on our records both in the office and on the electronic register which is searchable by the public.	
	Designs ADP number (if you know it).	
	If you are applying in the name of a company, where is it incorporated?	
	If incorporated in the USA, in which state is it incorporated?	
4.	Full name and address (including postcode) of your agent or your contact address if not the same as in section 3 above.	
	Designs ADP number (if you know it).	
5.	**Fees enclosed.**	
6.	**Signature of the applicant or their representative.**	
	Name in BLOCK CAPITALS.	
	Date.	
7	**Name and daytime phone number of the person we should contact in case of query. You may also provide your e-mail address.**	
	How many pages are you sending us?	This is sheet 1 of

Note:

Section 5: If this application contains more than one design, attach a Designs Ready Reckoner sheet.

(REV Jun 10)   Intellectual Property Office is an operating name of the Patent Office   **Form DF2A**

This is the _____ (for example, first) design out of a total of _____ designs

You must answer these questions for each design in a multiple application, so copy this sheet as many times as you need.

A.	**Name of the applicant.**	
B.	**Which product or products is the design for?**	
C.	**How many illustration sheets are there for this design?**	
D.	Write "RSP" if this is the design of a pattern which repeats across the surface of a product, for example, wallpaper.	
E.	If you wish, you may give a brief description of the design shown in the illustration or sample.	
F.	List any limitations or disclaimers you want to record.	
G.	**Do you agree that we should publish this design as soon as possible? Please state yes or no.**	
H.	If you are claiming priority from an earlier application to register this design, give these details.	Priority date Country Application number
I.	If the earlier application was made in a different name, say how the current applicant has a right to apply. If, for example, by assignment of the earlier application, give the date of the transaction.	

Notes: **You MUST answer all of the questions above which are shown in BOLD print.**

Please phone us on 08459 500 505 if you need help to fill in this form.

Checklist   Tick the box if you have included priority documents with this application ☐

(REV Jun 10)   **Form DF2A**

Illustration sheet

This is the   (for example, first) design out of a total of   designs

INTELLECTUAL
PROPERTY OFFICE

Designs Form DF2B
Official fee due with this form

Application to register one or more designs
divided from an earlier application

Please read the guidance note below about filling in this form.

Concept House
Cardiff Road
Newport
South Wales
NP10 8QQ

1. Your reference:	
2. Design number of earlier application.	
3. If you are applying for more than one design, please state the total number. How many of these designs do you wish to have published and registered immediately?	
4. Full name of the applicant. Designs ADP number (if you know it). If you are applying in the name of a company, where is it incorporated? If incorporated in the USA, in which state is it incorporated? <small>Your application details, including your name and address, will appear on our records both in the office and on the electronic register which is searchable by the public.</small>	
5. Full name and address (including postcode) of your agent or your contact address (including postcode) if not the same as in section 4 above.	
Designs ADP number (if you know it).	
6. Fees enclosed.	
7. Signature of the applicant or their representative.	
Name in BLOCK CAPITALS.	
Date.	
8. Name and daytime phone number of the person we should contact in case of query. You may also provide your e-mail address.	
How many pages are you sending us?	This is sheet 1 of

Note:

Section 6: If this application contains more than one design, attach a Designs Ready Reckoner sheet.

(REV Jun 10)   Intellectual Property Office is an operating name of the Patent Office   **Form DF2B**

This is the _____ (for example, first) design out of a total of _____ designs

You must answer these questions for each design in a multiple application, so copy this sheet as many times as you need.

A. Name of the applicant.	
B. Which product or products is the design for?	
C. How many illustration sheets are there for this design?	
D. Write "RSP" if this is the design of a pattern which repeats across the surface of a product, for example, wallpaper.	
E. If you wish, you may give a brief description of the design shown in the illustration or sample.	
F. List any limitations or disclaimers you want to record.	
G. Do you agree that we should publish this design as soon as possible? Please state yes or no.	
H. If you are claiming priority from an earlier application to register this design, give these details.	Priority date Country Application number
I. If the earlier application was made in a different name, say how the current applicant has a right to apply. If, for example, by assignment of the earlier application, give the date of the transaction.	

Notes: **You MUST answer all of the questions above which are shown in BOLD print.**

Please phone us on 08459 500 505 if you need help to fill in this form.

Checklist   Tick the box if you have included priority documents with this application ☐

(REV Jun 10)   **Form DF2B**

Illustration sheet

This is the   (for example, first) design out of a total of   designs

INTELLECTUAL
PROPERTY OFFICE

Designs Form DF2C
Offical fee for each design due with this form

Application to publish one or more designs

Concept House
Cardiff Road
Newport
South Wales
NP10 8QQ

Please read the guidance notes below about filling in this form

1. Your reference.	
2. Design application number or numbers.	
3. Filing date of application.	
4. Full name of the applicant.	
Designs ADP number (if you know it).	
5. Full name and address (including postcode) of your agent (if any).	
Designs ADP number (if you know it).	
6. Fees enclosed.	£
7. Signature of the applicant or their representative.	
Name in BLOCK CAPITALS.	
Date.	
8. Name and daytime phone number of the person we should contact in case of query. You may also provide your e-mail address.	

Notes:

You must apply for your design to be published within one year of applying to register the design. If you do not do so, we will treat your application as abandoned.

You need only complete this form if you did not consent to publication in the original application form.

(REV OCT06)   Intellectual Property Office is an operating name of the Patent Office   **Form DF2C**

INTELLECTUAL
PROPERTY OFFICE

Designs Form DF9A
Offical fee due with this form

Renewal of Design Registration

Concept House
Cardiff Road
Newport
South Wales
NP10 8QQ

1. Your reference.	
2. Design number.	
3. Full name of the registered proprietor.	
4. Renewal date.	
5. Fees: Amount of renewal fee.	£
Amount of late renewal fee. (You must pay this if you are renewing up to six months after the renewal date.)	£
Total fees.	£
6. If you would like confirmation of renewal sent to an address that is not the address of the registered proprietor, please give details here. Designs ADP number (if you know it).	
7. Signature.	
Name in BLOCK CAPITALS.	
Date.	
8. Name and daytime phone number of the person we should contact in case of query. You may also provide your e-mail address.	

(REV OCT06)   Intellectual Property Office is an operating name of the Patent Office   **Form DF9A**

INTELLECTUAL
PROPERTY OFFICE

Designs Form DF12A

Application to record a change of ownership
or to record or cancel a licence or security

Please read the guidance notes on the back about filling in this form

Concept House
Cardiff Road
Newport
South Wales
NP10 8QQ

1. Your reference.	
2. Design numbers affected. (List on a separate sheet if there is not enough space on this form.)	
3. Full name of the applicant or proprietor showing on the register.	
To record a change of ownership 4. Full name and address (including postcode) of the new applicant or proprietor.	
To record or cancel a licence or security Write "R" to record or "C" to cancel 5. (a) A licence. (b) A security.	
6. Full name and address (including postcode) of the licensee, or person granted a security against the design.	
All cases 7. If the new proprietor or the person named in section 6 above is a corporate body, in what country is it incorporated?	
8. Date of the transfer, licence or security.	
9. Give us the name, address and telephone number of the person to write to with confirmation that the transaction has been recorded if different to that shown in Section 3.	
10. Authorisation. Signature of the person applying to record the transaction, or their representative. Name in BLOCK CAPITALS.	
Date.	

(REV OCT06)   Intellectual Property Office is an operating name of the Patent Office   **Form DF12A**

11. Name and daytime phone number of the person we should contact in case of query. You may also provide your e-mail address.	
Number of sheets attached to this form.	

Notes

Use this form to ask us to record changes in the ownership of designs, including company mergers, or to record or cancel a licence or security interest against a design. It is not a substitute for the assignment document or other proof of the transaction. We may ask you to provide written proof of the transaction.

If the applicant or proprietor has merely changed their name, use Form DF16A, not this one.

We suggest you check the proprietor's name and the designs they own by doing a proprietor search on our website www.ipo.gov.uk before you fill in the form.

(REV OCT06)   **Form DF12A**

INTELLECTUAL
PROPERTY OFFICE

Designs Form DF16A

Change of proprietor's name or address

Concept House
Cardiff Road
Newport
South Wales
NP10 8QQ

Please read the guidance note below about filling in this form.

1. Your reference.	
2. Design numbers affected. (List on a separate sheet if there is not enough space on this form.)	
3. Full name of the applicant or proprietor as now shown on our records. Designs ADP number (if you know it).	
4. New name or address (including postcode) to be recorded.	
5. Name and address (including postcode) of agent (if any), or your contact address (including postcode) if not the same as in section 3 above.	
6. Declaration.	I declare there has been no change in the ownership of the designs.
Signature of the proprietor or their representative.	
Name in BLOCK CAPITALS.	
Date.	
7. Name and daytime phone number of the person we should contact in case of query. You may also provide your e-mail address.	
Number of sheets attached to this form.	

Note:

We suggest you check the proprietor's name and the designs they own by doing a proprietor search on our website www.ipo.gov.uk before you fill in the form.

If the ownership of the designs has changed, use Form DF12A, not this one.

INTELLECTUAL
PROPERTY OFFICE

Designs Form DF19A
Official fee due with this form

Request to invalidate a design registration

Concept House
Cardiff Road
Newport
South Wales
NP10 8QQ

Please read the guidance notes below about filling in this form.

1. Your reference.	
2. Design number.	
3. Full name of the proprietor.	
4. Full name and address (including postcode) of the applicant for invalidation.	
5. Full name and address (including postcode) of your agent (if any).	
6. Declaration. Signature of the applicant or their representative.	I believe that the facts in the attached statement of case are true.
Name in BLOCK CAPITALS.	
Date.	
7. Name and daytime phone number of the person we should contact in case of query. You may also provide your e-mail address.	
Number of sheets attached to this form.	This is sheet 1 of

Notes:

You can use this form to apply for:

- the invalidation of the registration of a design.
- the cancellation of the registration of a design which was applied for before the Registered Designs Act 1949 was amended by the Registered Designs Regulations 2001.
- You must attach a Statement of Case with this form. You do not have to file evidence at this stage, but if you wish to do so, please tick the box.

Please phone us on 08459 500 505 if you need help to fill in this form.

Checklist   Statement of Case   ☐

Evidence (optional)   ☐

(REV OCT06)   Intellectual Property Office is an operating name of the Patent Office   **Form DF19A**

INTELLECTUAL
PROPERTY OFFICE

Designs Form DF19B

Notice of counter-statement

Concept House
Cardiff Road
Newport
South Wales
NP10 8QQ

Please read the guidance note below about filling in this form.

1. Your reference.	
2. Design number.	
3. Full name of the proprietor.	
4. Full name and address (including postcode) of your agent (if any).	
5. Full name of the applicant for invalidation.	
6. Declaration. Signature of the proprietor or their representative.	I believe that the facts in the attached counter-statement are true.
Name in BLOCK CAPITALS.	
Date.	
7. Name and daytime phone number of the person we should contact in case of query. You may also provide your e-mail address.	
Number of sheets attached to this form.	This is sheet 1 of

Notes: You must attach a counter-statement with this form. You do not have to file evidence at this stage, but if you wish to do so, please tick the box.

Please phone us on 08459 500 505 if you need help to fill in this form.

Checklist -   Counter-statement   ☐

Evidence (optional)   ☐

(REV OCT06)   Intellectual Property Office is an operating name of the Patent Office   **Form DF19B**

Designs Form DF19C

Notice by proprietor to cancel a registration

Please read the guidance note below about filling in this form.

Concept House
Cardiff Road
Newport
South Wales
NP10 8QQ

1. Your reference.	
2. Design number.	
3. Full name of the proprietor. Designs ADP number (if you know it).	
4. Name and address (including postcode) of your agent (if any).	
5. Signature of the proprietor or their representative.	
Name in BLOCK CAPITALS.	
Date.	
6. Name and daytime phone number of the person we should contact in case of query. You may also provide your e-mail address.	

Note:

Use this form to give up all your legal rights in a design registration. Once we action it, the registered proprietor cannot decide to reinstate the registration. Please use a separate form for each registration.

INTELLECTUAL
PROPERTY OFFICE

Designs Form DF21
Official fee due with this form

Request for a search of the UK designs register

Please read the guidance notes below about filling in this form.

Concept House
Cardiff Road
Newport
South Wales
NP10 8QQ

1. Your reference.	
2. Full name and address (including postcode) where we should send the result of the search.	
3. In relation to which product or products (up to a maximum of three) do you want us to carry out a search for the attached design?	
4. Signature.	
Name in BLOCK CAPITALS.	
Date.	
5. Name and daytime phone number of the person we should contact in case of query. You may also provide your e-mail address.	

Notes:

You must tell us which product or products you want us to search for and send us an illustration of the design you want us to look for.

You must use a separate form and pay a separate fee for each different design that you want us to look for.

(REV OCT06)   Intellectual Property Office is an operating name of the Patent Office   **Form DF21**

Designs Form DF23
Offical fee due with this form

Request for a Certified Copy

Concept House
Cardiff Road
Newport
South Wales
NP10 8QQ

Please read the guidance notes below about filling in this form.

1. Your reference.	
2. Design number.	
3. How many copies do you want?	
4. Tick if certificate will later be legalised.	
5. Do you want us to certify: a) the design as it was applied for; or b) the design as it is registered.	
6. Full name and address (including postcode) where we should send the certificate.	
7. Signature.	
Name in BLOCK CAPITALS.	
Date.	
8. Name and daytime phone number of the person we should contact in case of query. You may also provide your e-mail address.	

Notes:

Section 4   We need to know if the certificate will be legalised by the Foreign & Commonwealth Office, so that we can provide an original signature.

We do not certify Registered Community Designs. You must apply to OHIM for these.

(REV OCT06)   Intellectual Property Office is an operating name of the Patent Office   **Form DF23**

INTELLECTUAL
PROPERTY OFFICE

Designs Form DF29
Offical fee due with this form

Request to restore a registration

Concept House
Cardiff Road
Newport
South Wales
NP10 8QQ

Please read the guidance notes below about filling in this form.

1. Your reference.	
2. Design number.	
3. Full name of the registered proprietor.	
4. When should the design have been renewed?	
5. Your name and address (including postcode), if you are not the proprietor, or your agent's name and address, if you have one.	
6. Signature of the applicant or his representative.	
Name in BLOCK CAPITALS.	
Date.	
7. Name and daytime phone number of the person we should contact in case of query. You may also provide your e-mail address.	
Number of sheets attached to this form.	This is sheet 1 of

Notes:

You can apply to restore a design up to twelve months after it should have been renewed.
You can check the renewal date by doing a design search on our website www.ipo.gov.uk

If it is now 6 months or later since the date when the design should have been renewed, use this form. If however it is less than 6 months since the due date of renewal, use Form DF9A instead.

You do not have to send us a renewal request with this Form, but you must send us a renewal request (Form DF9A) and pay the correct renewal fees if we agree to restore the design.

You must attach a statement and additional evidence (if any), fully explaining why you did not renew the design in time.

(REV OCT06)   Intellectual Property Office is an operating name of the Patent Office   **Form DF29**

SCHEDULE 2

TRANSITIONAL PROVISIONS

Part 1

Provisions Relating to Pending Applications

Interpretation

A10–049   1.—In this Part—

"the old Rules" means the Registered Designs Rules 1995 as they had effect immediately before the coming into force of these Rules; and

"the RRO" means the Regulatory Reform (Registered Designs) Order 2006.

Statement of objections

A10–050   2.—Where—

(a) the registrar sent the applicant a statement of objections under rule 29 of the old Rules; and

(b) the applicant has not sent to the registrar his observations in writing on the objections,

the objections shall be treated as the "statement of objections" under rule 8 of these Rules and the date on which the objections were sent shall be treated as the date on which the applicant was notified under rule 8(1).

Period prescribed for the purposes of section 3B(3)

A10–051   3.—Where—

(a) the period prescribed by rule 10 of these Rules has expired before the date on which these Rules come into force; and

(b) the period prescribed for the purposes of section 3B by rule 36A of the old Rules has not expired before the date on which these Rules come into force,

the period prescribed for the purposes of section 3B(3) shall be that mentioned in rule 36A of the old Rules.

Publication

4.—Rules 9 and 11 shall not apply where the application for registration of a design under the Act was made before these Rules come into force.

Restoration

5.—An application made in accordance with rule 41(2) of the old Rules shall be treated as made in accordance with rule 13(1) of these Rules.

Inspection of register

6.—Where the amendments made to section 22, by article 16(2)(b) and (3) of the RRO, do not apply to a registration under the Act (by reason of article 19 of the RRO), rule 69 of the old Rules shall continue to have effect in relation to that registration.

Inspection of documents

A10–052   7.—Rules 29 and 30 shall not apply to any document filed at the Patent Office before these Rules come into force.

Requests for certified copies

8.—A request under rule 72 of the old Rules for a certified copy of any representation, specimen or document kept at the Patent Office shall be treated as an application under rule 33(1) of these Rules.

Invalidity proceedings

A10–053   9.—(1) The time the registrar allowed under rule 53 of the old Rules for the filing of the counter-statement shall be treated as the period specified under rule 15(4) of these Rules.

(2) Where—

(a) an application for a declaration of invalidity which was made before these Rules came into force; and

(b) a counter-statement has been filed by the registered proprietor,

the registrar shall, within 28 days of these Rules coming into force, specify the periods within which any evidence may be filed, in accordance with rule 16(1).

Part 2

Provisions Relating to Applications under the Old Act

Interpretation
A10–054
10.—In this Part, "the old Act" means the Registered Designs Act 1949 as it had effect on 27th October 2001.

Application of this Part
A10–055
11.—This Part applies to—
    (a) transitional registrations, within the meaning of regulation 11 of the Registered Designs Regulations 2001;
    (b) post-1989 registrations, within the meaning of regulation 12 of those Regulations; and
    (c) pre-1989 registrations, within the meaning of regulation 13 of those Regulations.

Meaning of applied industrially
A10–056
12.—For the purposes of section 6 of the old Act, the circumstances in which a design shall be regarded as "applied industrially" are—
    (a) where the design is applied to more than fifty articles, which do not all together constitute a single set of articles (within the meaning of section 44(1) of the old Act); or
    (b) where the design is applied to goods manufactured in lengths or pieces, not being hand-made goods.

Applications under section 11(2) of old Act
13.—(1) Part 4 of these Rules applies to an application under section 11(2) of the old Act for the cancellation of registration as it applies to an application for a declaration of invalidity under section 11ZB of the Act.

(2) Where an application is made under section 11(2) of the old Act, any reference in rule 15(1) to an application for a declaration of invalidity under section 11ZB of the Act shall be construed as a reference to an application under the relevant provision of the old Act.

(3) For the purposes of rule 23(1), an application under section 11(2) of the old Act shall be treated as if it were mentioned in section 30(3) of the Act.

SCHEDULE 3

REVOCATIONS

A10–057

Title and number	Extent of revocation
Registered Designs Rules 1995 (SI 1995/2912)	The whole rules.
Registered Designs (Amendment) Rules 1999 (SI 1999/3196)	The whole rules.
Registered Designs (Amendment) Rules 2001 (SI 2001/3950)	The whole rules.
Patents, Trade Marks and Designs (Address For Service, etc) Rules 2006 (SI 2006/760)	Rules 10 to 14.
Trade Marks and Designs (Address For Service) (Amendment) Rules 2006 (2006/1029)	Rule 2.

A11. The Designs (Convention Countries) Order 2007 (SI 2007/277)

A11–001 **1.**—(1) This Order may be cited as the Designs (Convention Countries) Order 2007 and shall come into force on 6th April 2007.

(2) The Designs (Convention Countries) Order 2006 is revoked.

2.—The countries specified in the Schedule are declared to be convention countries for the purposes of all the provisions of the Registered Designs Act 1949.

SCHEDULE

CONVENTION COUNTRIES

A11–002

Albania
Algeria
Andorra
Angola
Antigua and Barbuda
Argentina
Armenia
Australia
Austria
Azerbaijan
Bahamas
Bahrain
Bangladesh
Barbados
Belarus
Belgium
Belize
Benin
Bhutan
Bolivia
Bosnia and Herzegovina
Botswana
Brazil
Brunei Darussalam
Bulgaria
Burkina Faso
Burundi
Cambodia
Cameroon
Canada
[Cape Verde]²⁹⁷
Central African Republic
Chad
Chile
China
Colombia
Congo
Congo, Democratic Republic of the
Costa Rica

Côte d'Ivoire
Croatia
Cuba
Cyprus
Czech Republic
Denmark
Djibouti
Dominica
Dominican Republic
Ecuador
Eygpt
El Salvador
Equatorial Guinea
Estonia
Faeroe Islands
Fiji
Finland
France (including all Overseas Departments and Territories)
Gabon
Gambia
Georgia
Germany
Ghana
Greece
Grenada
Guatemala
Guinea
Guinea-Bissau
Guyana
Haiti
Holy See
Honduras
Hong Kong
Hungary
Iceland
India
Indonesia

---

²⁹⁷ Inserted by the Designs (Convention Countries) (Amendment) Order 2009 (SI 2009/2747) art.2.

Iran, Islamic Republic of
Iraq
Ireland
Israel
Italy
Jamaica
Japan
Jordan
Kazakhstan
Kenya
Korea, Democratic Republic of
Korea, Republic of
Kuwait
Kyrgyzstan
Lao Peoples Democratic Republic
Latvia
Lebanon
Lesotho
Liberia
Libyan Arab Jamahiriya
Liechtenstein
Lithuania
Luxembourg
Macau
Macedonia, the former Yugoslav Republic
  of
Madagascar
Malawi
Malaysia
Maldives
Mali
Malta
Mauritania
Mauritius
Mexico
Moldova
Monaco
Mongolia
Montenegro
Morocco
Mozambique
Myanmar
Namibia
Nepal
Netherlands
Netherlands Antilles and Aruba
New Zealand (including the Cook Islands,
  Niue and Tokelau)
Nicaragua
Niger
Nigeria
Norway
Oman
Pakistan
Panama

Papua New Guinea
Paraguay
Peru
Philippines
Poland
Portugal
Qatar
Romania
Russian Federation
Rwanda
Saint Kitts and Nevis
Saint Lucia
Saint Vincent and the Grenadines
San Marino
Sao Tome and Principe
Saudi Arabia
Senegal
Serbia
Seychelles
Sierra Leone
Singapore
Slovakia
Slovenia
Solomon Islands
South Africa
Spain
Sri Lanka
Sudan
Suriname
Swaziland
Sweden
Switzerland
Syrian Arab Republic
Taiwan
Tajikistan
Tanzania, United Republic of
Thailand
Togo
Tonga
Trinidad and Tobago
Tunisia
Turkey
Turkmenistan
Uganda
Ukraine
United Arab Emirates
United States of America (including Puerto
  Rico and all territories and possessions)
Uruguay
Uzbekistan
Venezuela
Viet Nam
Yemen
Zambia
Zimbabwe

APPENDIX B

COMMUNITY DESIGNS

Contents

B1. Council Regulation (EC) No 6/2002 of 12 December 2001 on Community designs

THE COUNCIL OF THE EUROPEAN UNION,

B1–001   Having regard to the Treaty establishing the European Community, and in particular Article 308 thereof,

Having regard to the proposal from the Commission,[1]

Having regard to the opinion of the European Parliament,[2]

Having regard to the opinion of the Economic and Social Committee,[3]

Whereas:

(1) A unified system for obtaining a Community design to which uniform protection is given with uniform effect throughout the entire territory of the Community would further the objectives of the Community as laid down in the Treaty.

(2) Only the Benelux countries have introduced a uniform design protection law. In all the other Member States the protection of designs is a matter for the relevant national law and is confined to the territory of the Member State concerned. Identical designs may be therefore protected differently in different

[1] OJ C 29, 31.1.1994, p.20 and OJ C 248, 29.8.2000, p.3.
[2] OJ C 67, 1.3.2001, p.318.
[3] OJ C 110, 2.5.1995 and OJ C 75, 15.3.2000, p.35.

Member States and for the benefit of different owners. This inevitably leads to conflicts in the course of trade between Member States.

(3) The substantial differences between Member States' design laws prevent and distort Community-wide competition. In comparison with domestic trade in, and competition between, products incorporating a design, trade and competition within the Community are prevented and distorted by the large number of applications, offices, procedures, laws, nationally circumscribed exclusive rights and the combined administrative expense with correspondingly high costs and fees for the applicant. Directive 98/71/EC of the European Parliament and of the Council of 13 October 1998 on the legal protection of designs[4] contributes to remedying this situation.

(4) The effect of design protection being limited to the territory of the individual Member States whether or not their laws are approximated, leads to a possible division of the internal market with respect to products incorporating a design which is the subject of national rights held by different individuals, and hence constitutes an obstacle to the free movement of goods.

(5) This calls for the creation of a Community design which is directly applicable in each Member State, because only in this way will it be possible to obtain, through one application made to the Office for Harmonisation in the Internal Market (Trade Marks and Design) in accordance with a single procedure under one law, one design right for one area encompassing all Member States.

(6) Since the objectives of the proposed action, namely, the protection of one design right for one area encompassing all the Member States, cannot be sufficiently achieved by the Member States by reason of the scale and the effects of the creation of a Community design and a Community design authority and can therefore, and can therefore be better achieved at Community level, the Community may adopt measures, in accordance with the principle of subsidiarity as set out in Article 5 of the Treaty. In accordance with the principle of proportionality, as set out in that Article, this Regulation does not go beyond what is necessary in order to achieve those objectives.

(7) Enhanced protection for industrial design not only promotes the contribution of individual designers to the sum of Community excellence in the field, but also encourages innovation and development of new products and investment in their production.

(8) Consequently a more accessible design-protection system adapted to the needs of the internal market is essential for Community industries.

(9) The substantive provisions of this Regulation on design law should be aligned with the respective provisions in Directive 98/71/EC.

(10) Technological innovation should not be hampered by granting design protection to features dictated solely by a technical function. It is understood that this does not entail that a design must have an aesthetic quality. Likewise, the interoperability of products of different makes should not be hindered by extending protection to the design of mechanical fittings. Consequently, those features of a design which are excluded from protection for those reasons should not be taken into consideration for the purpose of assessing whether other features of the design fulfil the requirements for protection.

(11) The mechanical fittings of modular products may nevertheless constitute an important element of the innovative characteristics of modular products and present a major marketing asset, and therefore should be eligible for protection.

(12) Protection should not be extended to those component parts which are not visible during normal use of a product, nor to those features of such part which are not visible when the part is mounted, or which would not, in themselves, fulfil

---

[4] OJ L 289, 28.10.1998, p.28.

the requirements as to novelty and individual character. Therefore, those features of design which are excluded from protection for these reasons should not be taken into consideration for the purpose of assessing whether other features of the design fulfil the requirements for protection.

(13) Full-scale approximation of the laws of the Member States on the use of protected designs for the purpose of permitting the repair of a complex product so as to restore its original appearance, where the design is applied to or incorporated in a product which constitutes a component part of a complex product upon whose appearance the protected design is dependent, could not be achieved through Directive 98/71/EC. Within the framework of the conciliation procedure on the said Directive, the Commission undertook to review the consequences of the provisions of that Directive three years after the deadline for transposition of the Directive in particular for the industrial sectors which are most affected. Under these circumstances, it is appropriate not to confer any protection as a Community design for a design which is applied to or incorporated in a product which constitutes a component part of a complex product upon whose appearance the design is dependent and which is used for the purpose of the repair of a complex product so as to restore its original appearance, until the Council has decided its policy on this issue on the basis of a Commission proposal.

(14) The assessment as to whether a design has individual character should be based on whether the overall impression produced on an informed user viewing the design clearly differs from that produced on him by the existing design corpus, taking into consideration the nature of the product to which the design is applied or in which it is incorporated, and in particular the industrial sector to which it belongs and the degree of freedom of the designer in developing the design.

(15) A Community design should, as far as possible, serve the needs of all sectors of industry in the Community.

(16) Some of those sectors produce large numbers of designs for products frequently having a short market life where protection without the burden of registration formalities is an advantage and the duration of protection is of lesser significance. On the other hand, there are sectors of industry which value the advantages of registration for the greater legal certainty it provides and which require the possibility of a longer term of protection corresponding to the foreseeable market life of their products.

(17) This calls for two forms of protection, one being a short-term unregistered design and the other being a longer term registered design.

(18) A registered Community design requires the creation and maintenance of a register in which will be registered all those applications which comply with formal conditions and which have been accorded a date of filing. This registration system should in principle not be based upon substantive examination as to compliance with requirements for protection prior to registration, thereby keeping to a minimum the registration and other procedural burdens on applicants.

(19) A Community design should not be upheld unless the design is new and unless it also possesses an individual character in comparison with other designs.

(20) It is also necessary to allow the designer or his successor in title to test the products embodying the design in the market place before deciding whether the protection resulting from a registered Community design is desirable. To this end it is necessary to provide that disclosures of the design by the designer or his successor in title, or abusive disclosures during a period of 12 months prior to the date of the filing of the application for a registered Community design should not

be prejudicial in assessing the novelty or the individual character of the design in question.

(21) The exclusive nature of the right conferred by the registered Community design is consistent with its greater legal certainty. It is appropriate that the unregistered Community design should, however, constitute a right only to prevent copying. Protection could not therefore extend to design products which are the result of a design arrived at independently by a second designer. This right should also extend to trade in products embodying infringing designs.

(22) The enforcement of these rights is to be left to national laws. It is necessary therefore to provide for some basic uniform sanctions in all Member States. These should make it possible, irrespective of the jurisdiction under which enforcement is sought, to stop the infringing acts.

(23) Any third person who can establish that he has in good faith commenced use even for commercial purposes within the Community, or has made serious and effective preparations to that end, of a design included within the scope of protection of a registered Community design, which has not been copied from the latter, may be entitled to a limited exploitation of that design.

(24) It is a fundamental objective of this Regulation that the procedure for obtaining a registered Community design should present the minimum cost and difficulty to applicants, so as to make it readily available to small and medium-sized enterprises as well as to individual designers.

(25) Those sectors of industry producing large numbers of possibly short-lived designs over short periods of time of which only some may be eventually commercialised will find advantage in the unregistered Community design. Furthermore, there is also a need for these sectors to have easier recourse to the registered Community design. Therefore, the option of combining a number of designs in one multiple application would satisfy that need. However, the designs contained in a multiple application may be dealt with independently of each other for the purposes of enforcement of rights, licensing, rights in rem, levy of execution, insolvency proceedings, surrender, renewal, assignment, deferred publication or declaration of invalidity.

(26) The normal publication following registration of a Community design could in some cases destroy or jeopardise the success of a commercial operation involving the design. The facility of a deferment of publication for a reasonable period affords a solution in such cases.

(27) A procedure for hearing actions concerning validity of a registered Community design in a single place would bring savings in costs and time compared with procedures involving different national courts.

(28) It is therefore necessary to provide safeguards including a right of appeal to a Board of Appeal, and ultimately to the Court of Justice. Such a procedure would assist the development of uniform interpretation of the requirements governing the validity of Community designs.

(29) It is essential that the rights conferred by a Community design can be enforced in an efficient manner throughout the territory of the Community.

(30) The litigation system should avoid as far as possible "forum shopping". It is therefore necessary to establish clear rules of international jurisdiction.

(31) This Regulation does not preclude the application to designs protected by Community designs of the industrial property laws or other relevant laws of the Member States, such as those relating to design protection acquired by registration or those relating to unregistered designs, trade marks, patents and utility models, unfair competition or civil liability.

(32) In the absence of the complete harmonisation of copyright law, it is important to establish the principle of cumulation of protection under the Community design and under copyright law, whilst leaving Member States free

to establish the extent of copyright protection and the conditions under which such protection is conferred.

(33) The measures necessary for the implementation of this Regulation should be adopted in accordance with Council Decision 1999/468/EC of 28 June 1999 laying down the procedures for the exercise of implementing powers conferred on the Commission,[5]

HAS ADOPTED THIS REGULATION:

TITLE I

GENERAL PROVISIONS

Article 1

Community design

B1–002   1. A design which complies with the conditions contained in this Regulation is hereinafter referred to as a "Community design".

2. A design shall be protected:

    (a) by an "unregistered Community design", if made available to the public in the manner provided for in this Regulation;

    (b) by a "registered Community design", if registered in the manner provided for in this Regulation.

3. A Community design shall have a unitary character. It shall have equal effect throughout the Community. It shall not be registered, transferred or surrendered or be the subject of a decision declaring it invalid, nor shall its use be prohibited, save in respect of the whole Community. This principle and its implications shall apply unless otherwise provided in this Regulation.

Article 2

Office

B1–003   The Office for Harmonisation in the Internal Market (Trade Marks and Designs), hereinafter referred to as "the Office", instituted by Council Regulation (EC) No.40/94 of 20 December 1993 on the Community trade mark,[6] hereinafter referred to as the "Regulation on the Community trade mark", shall carry out the tasks entrusted to it by this Regulation.

---

[5] OJ L 184, 17.7.1999, p.23.
[6] OJ L 11, 14.1.1994, p.1. Regulation as last amended by Regulation (EC) No.3288/94 (OJ L 349, 31.12.1994, p.83).

TITLE II

THE LAW RELATING TO DESIGNS

SECTION 1

REQUIREMENTS FOR PROTECTION

Article 3

Definitions

For the purposes of this Regulation: **B1–004**

    (a) "design" means the appearance of the whole or a part of a product resulting from the features of, in particular, the lines, contours, colours, shape, texture and/or materials of the product itself and/or its ornamentation;

    (b) "product" means any industrial or handicraft item, including *inter alia* parts intended to be assembled into a complex product, packaging, get-up, graphic symbols and typographic typefaces, but excluding computer programs;

    (c) "complex product" means a product which is composed of multiple components which can be replaced permitting disassembly and re-assembly of the product.

Article 4

Requirements for protection

1. A design shall be protected by a Community design to the extent that it is **B1–005** new and has individual character.

2. A design applied to or incorporated in a product which constitutes a component part of a complex product shall only be considered to be new and to have individual character:

    (a) if the component part, once it has been incorporated into the complex product, remains visible during normal use of the latter; and

    (b) to the extent that those visible features of the component part fulfil in themselves the requirements as to novelty and individual character.

3. "Normal use" within the meaning of paragraph (2)(a) shall mean use by the end user, excluding maintenance, servicing or repair work.

Article 5

Novelty

1. A design shall be considered to be new if no identical design has been made **B1–006** available to the public:

(a) in the case of an unregistered Community design, before the date on which the design for which protection is claimed has first been made available to the public;

(b) in the case of a registered Community design, before the date of filing of the application for registration of the design for which protection is claimed, or, if priority is claimed, the date of priority.

2. Designs shall be deemed to be identical if their features differ only in immaterial details.

Article 6

Individual character

B1–007 1. A design shall be considered to have individual character if the overall impression it produces on the informed user differs from the overall impression produced on such a user by any design which has been made available to the public:

(a) in the case of an unregistered Community design, before the date on which the design for which protection is claimed has first been made available to the public;

(b) in the case of a registered Community design, before the date of filing the application for registration or, if a priority is claimed, the date of priority.

2. In assessing individual character, the degree of freedom of the designer in developing the design shall be taken into consideration.

Article 7

Disclosure

B1–008 1. For the purpose of applying Articles 5 and 6, a design shall be deemed to have been made available to the public if it has been published following registration or otherwise, or exhibited, used in trade or otherwise disclosed, before the date referred to in Articles 5(1)(a) and 6(1)(a) or in Articles 5(1)(b) and 6(1)(b), as the case may be, except where these events could not reasonably have become known in the normal course of business to the circles specialised in the sector concerned, operating within the Community. The design shall not, however, be deemed to have been made available to the public for the sole reason that it has been disclosed to a third person under explicit or implicit conditions of confidentiality.

2. A disclosure shall not be taken into consideration for the purpose of applying Articles 5 and 6 and if a design for which protection is claimed under a registered Community design has been made available to the public:

(a) by the designer, his successor in title, or a third person as a result of information provided or action taken by the designer or his successor in title; and

(b) during the 12-month period preceding the date of filing of the application or, if a priority is claimed, the date of priority.

3. Paragraph 2 shall also apply if the design has been made available to the public as a consequence of an abuse in relation to the designer or his successor in title.

Article 8

Designs dictated by their technical function and designs of interconnections

1. A Community design shall not subsist in features of appearance of a product which are solely dictated by its technical function.

2. A Community design shall not subsist in features of appearance of a product which must necessarily be reproduced in their exact form and dimensions in order to permit the product in which the design is incorporated or to which it is applied to be mechanically connected to or placed in, around or against another product so that either product may perform its function.

3. Notwithstanding paragraph 2, a Community design shall under the conditions set out in Articles 5 and 6 subsist in a design serving the purpose of allowing the multiple assembly or connection of mutually interchangeable products within a modular system.

B1–009

Article 9

Designs contrary to public policy or morality

A Community design shall not subsist in a design which is contrary to public policy or to accepted principles of morality.

B1–010

SECTION 2

SCOPE AND TERM OF PROTECTION

Article 10

Scope of protection

1. The scope of the protection conferred by a Community design shall include any design which does not produce on the informed user a different overall impression.

2. In assessing the scope of protection, the degree of freedom of the designer in developing his design shall be taken into consideration.

B1–011

Article 11

Commencement and term of protection of the unregistered Community design

1. A design which meets the requirements under Section 1 shall be protected by an unregistered Community design for a period of three years as from the date on which the design was first made available to the public within the Community.

2. For the purpose of paragraph 1, a design shall be deemed to have been made available to the public within the Community if it has been published, exhibited, used in trade or otherwise disclosed in such a way that, in the normal course of business, these events could reasonably have become known to the circles

B1–012

specialised in the sector concerned, operating within the Community. The design shall not, however, be deemed to have been made available to the public for the sole reason that it has been disclosed to a third person under explicit or implicit conditions of confidentiality.

Article 12

Commencement and term of protection of the registered Community design

B1–013   Upon registration by the Office, a design which meets the requirements under Section 1 shall be protected by a registered Community design for a period of five years as from the date of the filing of the application. The right holder may have the term of protection renewed for one or more periods of five years each, up to a total term of 25 years from the date of filing.

Article 13

Renewal

B1–014   1. Registration of the registered Community design shall be renewed at the request of the right holder or of any person expressly authorised by him, provided that the renewal fee has been paid.

2. The Office shall inform the right holder of the registered Community design and any person having a right entered in the register of Community designs, referred to in Article 72, hereafter referred to as the "register" in respect of the registered Community design, of the expiry of the registration in good time before the said expiry. Failure to give such information shall not involve the responsibility of the Office.

3. The request for renewal shall be submitted and the renewal fee paid within a period of six months ending on the last day of the month in which protection ends. Failing this, the request may be submitted and the fee paid within a further period of six months from the day referred to in the first sentence, provided that an additional fee is paid within this further period.

4. Renewal shall take effect from the day following the date on which the existing registration expires. The renewal shall be entered in the register.

SECTION 3

RIGHT TO THE COMMUNITY DESIGN

Article 14

Right to the Community design

B1–015   1. The right to the Community design shall vest in the designer or his successor in title.

2. If two or more persons have jointly developed a design, the right to the Community design shall vest in them jointly.

3. However, where a design is developed by an employee in the execution of his duties or following the instructions given by his employer, the right to the

Community design shall vest in the employer, unless otherwise agreed or specified under national law.

Article 15

Claims relating to the entitlement to a Community design

1. If an unregistered Community design is disclosed or claimed by, or a **B1–016** registered Community design has been applied for or registered in the name of, a person who is not entitled to it under Article 14, the person entitled to it under that provision may, without prejudice to any other remedy which may be open to him, claim to become recognised as the legitimate holder of the Community design.

2. Where a person is jointly entitled to a Community design, that person may, in accordance with paragraph 1, claim to become recognised as joint holder.

3. Legal proceedings under paragraphs 1 or 2 shall be barred three years after the date of publication of a registered Community design or the date of disclosure of an unregistered Community design. This provision shall not apply if the person who is not entitled to the Community design was acting in bad faith at the time when such design was applied for or disclosed or was assigned to him.

4. In the case of a registered Community design, the following shall be entered in the register:

   (a) the mention that legal proceedings under paragraph 1 have been instituted;

   (b) the final decision or any other termination of the proceedings;

   (c) any change in the ownership of the registered Community design resulting from the final decision.

Article 16

Effects of a judgement on entitlement to a registered Community design

1. Where there is a complete change of ownership of a registered Community **B1–017** design as a result of legal proceedings under Article 15(1), licences and other rights shall lapse upon the entering in the register of the person entitled.

2. If, before the institution of the legal proceedings under Article 15(1) has been registered, the holder of the registered Community design or a licensee has exploited the design within the Community or made serious and effective preparations to do so, he may continue such exploitation provided that he requests within the period prescribed by the implementing regulation a non-exclusive licence from the new holder whose name is entered in the register. The licence shall be granted for a reasonable period and upon reasonable terms.

3. Paragraph 2 shall not apply if the holder of the registered Community design or the licensee was acting in bad faith at the time when he began to exploit the design or to make preparations to do so.

Article 17

Presumption in favour of the registered holder of the design

The person in whose name the registered Community design is registered or, **B1–018** prior to registration, the person in whose name the application is filed, shall be deemed to be the person entitled in any proceedings before the Office as well as in any other proceedings.

Article 18

Right of the designer to be cited

B1–019   The designer shall have the right, in the same way as the applicant for or the holder of a registered Community design, to be cited as such before the Office and in the register. If the design is the result of teamwork, the citation of the team may replace the citation of the individual designers.

SECTION 4

EFFECTS OF THE COMMUNITY DESIGN

Article 19

Rights conferred by the Community design

B1–020   1. A registered Community design shall confer on its holder the exclusive right to use it and to prevent any third party not having his consent from using it. The aforementioned use shall cover, in particular, the making, offering, putting on the market, importing, exporting or using of a product in which the design is incorporated or to which it is applied, or stocking such a product for those purposes.

2. An unregistered Community design shall, however, confer on its holder the right to prevent the acts referred to in paragraph 1 only if the contested use results from copying the protected design.

The contested use shall not be deemed to result from copying the protected design if it results from an independent work of creation by a designer who may be reasonably thought not to be familiar with the design made available to the public by the holder.

3. Paragraph 2 shall also apply to a registered Community design subject to deferment of publication as long as the relevant entries in the register and the file have not been made available to the public in accordance with Article 50(4).

Article 20

Limitation of the rights conferred by a Community design

B1–021   1. The rights conferred by a Community design shall not be exercised in respect of:

(a) acts done privately and for non-commercial purposes;
(b) acts done for experimental purposes;
(c) acts of reproduction for the purpose of making citations or of teaching, provided that such acts are compatible with fair trade practice and do not unduly prejudice the normal exploitation of the design, and that mention is made of the source.

2. In addition, the rights conferred by a Community design shall not be exercised in respect of:

    (a) the equipment on ships and aircraft registered in a third country when these temporarily enter the territory of the Community;

    (b) the importation in the Community of spare parts and accessories for the purpose of repairing such craft;

    (c) the execution of repairs on such craft.

Article 21

Exhaustion of rights

The rights conferred by a Community design shall not extend to acts relating to a product in which a design included within the scope of protection of the Community design is incorporated or to which it is applied, when the product has been put on the market in the Community by the holder of the Community design or with his consent.

B1–022

Article 22

Rights of prior use in respect of a registered Community design

1. A right of prior use shall exist for any third person who can establish that before the date of filing of the application, or, if a priority is claimed, before the date of priority, he has in good faith commenced use within the Community, or has made serious and effective preparations to that end, of a design included within the scope of protection of a registered Community design, which has not been copied from the latter.

B1–023

2. The right of prior use shall entitle the third person to exploit the design for the purposes for which its use had been effected, or for which serious and effective preparations had been made, before the filing or priority date of the registered Community design.

3. The right of prior use shall not extend to granting a licence to another person to exploit the design.

4. The right of prior use cannot be transferred except, where the third person is a business, along with that part of the business in the course of which the act was done or the preparations were made.

Article 23

Government use

Any provision in the law of a Member State allowing use of national designs by or for the government may be applied to Community designs, but only to the extent that the use is necessary for essential defence or security needs.

B1–024

SECTION 5

INVALIDITY

Article 24

Declaration of invalidity

1. A registered Community design shall be declared invalid on application to the Office in accordance with the procedure in Titles VI and VII or by a

B1–025

Community design court on the basis of a counterclaim in infringement proceedings.

2. A Community design may be declared invalid even after the Community
design has lapsed or has been surrendered.

3. An unregistered Community design shall be declared invalid by a Community design court on application to such a court or on the basis of a counterclaim
in infringement proceedings.

Article 25

Grounds for invalidity

B1–026   1. A Community design may be declared invalid only in the following cases:

(a) if the design does not correspond to the definition under Article 3(a);

(b) if it does not fulfil the requirements of Articles 4 to 9;

(c) if, by virtue of a court decision, the right holder is not entitled to the
Community design under Article 14;

(d) if the Community design is in conflict with a prior design which has been
made available to the public after the date of filing of the application or,
if priority is claimed, the date of priority of the Community design, and
which is protected from a date prior to the said date

(i) by a registered Community design or an application for such a
design, or

(ii) by a registered design right of a Member State, or by an application
for such a right, or

(iii) by a design right registered under the Geneva Act of the Hague
Agreement concerning the international registration of industrial
designs, adopted in Geneva on 2 July 1999, hereinafter referred to as
"the Geneva Act94, which was approved by Council Decision
954/2006 and which has effect in the Community, or by an application for such a right;[7]

(e) if a distinctive sign is used in a subsequent design, and Community law
or the law of the Member State governing that sign confers on the right
holder of the sign the right to prohibit such use;

(f) if the design constitutes an unauthorised use of a work protected under
the copyright law of a Member State;

(g) if the design constitutes an improper use of any of the items listed in
Article 6ter of the "Paris Convention" for the Protection of Industrial
Property hereafter referred to as the "Paris Convention", or of badges,
emblems and escutcheons other than those covered by the said Article
6ter and which are of particular public interest in a Member State.

2. The ground provided for in paragraph (1)(c) may be invoked solely by the
person who is entitled to the Community design under Article 14.

3. The grounds provided for in paragraph (1)(d), (e) and (f) may be invoked
solely by the applicant for or holder of the earlier right.

4. The ground provided for in paragraph (1)(g) may be invoked solely by the
person or entity concerned by the use.

5. Paragraphs 3 and 4 shall be without prejudice to the freedom of Member
States to provide that the grounds provided for in paragraphs 1(d) and (g) may
also be invoked by the appropriate authority of the Member State in question on
its own initiative.

---

[7] Substituted by Regulation (EC) No.1891/2006 (OJ L 386/14, 29.12.2006).

6. A registered Community design which has been declared invalid pursuant to paragraph (1)(b), (e), (f) or (g) may be maintained in an amended form, if in that form it complies with the requirements for protection and the identity of the design is retained. "Maintenance" in an amended form may include registration accompanied by a partial disclaimer by the holder of the registered Community design or entry in the register of a court decision or a decision by the Office declaring the partial invalidity of the registered Community design.

Article 26

Consequences of invalidity

1. A Community design shall be deemed not to have had, as from the outset, the effects specified in this Regulation, to the extent that it has been declared invalid. **B1–027**

2. Subject to the national provisions relating either to claims for compensation for damage caused by negligence or lack of good faith on the part of the holder of the Community design, or to unjust enrichment, the retroactive effect of invalidity of the Community design shall not affect:

(a) any decision on infringement which has acquired the authority of a final decision and been enforced prior to the invalidity decision;

(b) any contract concluded prior to the invalidity decision, in so far as it has been performed before the decision; however, repayment, to an extent justified by the circumstances, of sums paid under the relevant contract may be claimed on grounds of equity.

TITLE III

COMMUNITY DESIGNS AS OBJECTS OF PROPERTY

Article 27

Dealing with Community designs as national design rights

1. Unless Articles 28, 29, 30, 31 and 32 provide otherwise, a Community design as an object of property shall be dealt with in its entirety, and for the whole area of the Community, as a national design right of the Member State in which: **B1–028**

(a) the holder has his seat or his domicile on the relevant date; or

(b) where point (a) does not apply, the holder has an establishment on the relevant date.

2. In the case of a registered Community design, paragraph 1 shall apply according to the entries in the register.

3. In the case of joint holders, if two or more of them fulfil the condition under paragraph 1, the Member State referred to in that paragraph shall be determined:

(a) in the case of an unregistered Community design, by reference to the relevant joint holder designated by them by common agreement;

(b) in the case of a registered Community design, by reference to the first of the relevant joint holders in the order in which they are mentioned in the register.

563

4. Where paragraphs 1, 2 and 3 do not apply, the Member State referred to in paragraph 1 shall be the Member State in which the seat of the Office is situated.

Article 28

Transfer of the registered Community design

B1–029   The transfer of a registered Community design shall be subject to the following provisions:

(a) at the request of one of the parties, a transfer shall be entered in the register and published;

(b) until such time as the transfer has been entered in the register, the successor in title may not invoke the rights arising from the registration of the Community design;

(c) where there are time limits to be observed in dealings with the Office, the successor in title may make the corresponding statements to the Office once the request for registration of the transfer has been received by the Office;

(d) all documents which by virtue of Article 66 require notification to the holder of the registered Community design shall be addressed by the Office to the person registered as holder or his representative, if one has been appointed.

Article 29

Rights in rem on a registered Community design

B1–030   1. A registered Community design may be given as security or be the subject of rights *in rem*.

2. On request of one of the parties, the rights mentioned in paragraph 1 shall be entered in the register and published.

Article 30

Levy of execution

B1–031   1. A registered Community design may be levied in execution.

2. As regards the procedure for levy of execution in respect of a registered Community design, the courts and authorities of the Member State determined in accordance with Article 27 shall have exclusive jurisdiction.

3. On request of one of the parties, levy of execution shall be entered in the register and published.

Article 31

Insolvency proceedings

B1–032   1. The only insolvency proceedings in which a Community design may be involved shall be those opened in the Member State within the territory of which the centre of a debtor's main interests is situated.

2. In the case of joint proprietorship of a Community design, paragraph 1 shall apply to the share of the joint proprietor.

3. Where a Community design is involved in insolvency proceedings, on request of the competent national authority an entry to this effect shall be made in the register and published in the Community Designs Bulletin referred to in Article 73(1).

Article 32

Licensing

1. A Community design may be licensed for the whole or part of the Community. A licence may be exclusive or non-exclusive. **B1–033**

2. Without prejudice to any legal proceedings based on the law of contract, the holder may invoke the rights conferred by the Community design against a licensee who contravenes any provision in his licensing contract with regard to its duration, the form in which the design may be used, the range of products for which the licence is granted and the quality of products manufactured by the licensee.

3. Without prejudice to the provisions of the licensing contract, the licensee may bring proceedings for infringement of a Community design only if the right holder consents thereto. However, the holder of an exclusive licence may bring such proceedings if the right holder in the Community design, having been given notice to do so, does not himself bring infringement proceedings within an appropriate period.

4. A licensee shall, for the purpose of obtaining compensation for damage suffered by him, be entitled to intervene in an infringement action brought by the right holder in a Community design.

5. In the case of a registered Community design, the grant or transfer of a licence in respect of such right shall, at the request of one of the parties, be entered in the register and published.

Article 33

Effects vis-à-vis third parties

1. The effects vis-à-vis third parties of the legal acts referred to in Articles 28, 29, 30 and 32 shall be governed by the law of the Member State determined in accordance with Article 27. **B1–034**

2. However, as regards registered Community designs, legal acts referred to in Articles 28, 29 and 32 shall only have effect vis-à-vis third parties in all the Member States after entry in the register. Nevertheless, such an act, before it is so entered, shall have effect vis-à-vis third parties who have acquired rights in the registered Community design after the date of that act but who knew of the act at the date on which the rights were acquired.

3. Paragraph 2 shall not apply to a person who acquires the registered Community design or a right concerning the registered Community design by way of transfer of the whole of the undertaking or by any other universal succession.

4. Until such time as common rules for the Member States in the field of insolvency enter into force, the effects vis-à-vis third parties of insolvency proceedings shall be governed by the law of the Member State in which such

proceedings are first brought under the national law or the regulations applicable in this field.

Article 34

The application for a registered Community design as an object of property

B1–035   1. An application for a registered Community design as an object of property shall be dealt with in its entirety, and for the whole area of the Community, as a national design right of the Member State determined in accordance with Article 27.

2. Articles 28, 29, 30, 31, 32 and 33 shall apply *mutatis mutandis* to applications for registered Community designs. Where the effect of one of these provisions is conditional upon an entry in the register, that formality shall be performed upon registration of the resulting registered Community design.

TITLE IV

APPLICATION FOR A REGISTERED COMMUNITY DESIGN

SECTION 1

FILING OF APPLICATIONS AND THE CONDITIONS WHICH GOVERN THEM

Article 35

Filing and forwarding of applications

B1–036   1. An application for a registered Community design shall be filed, at the option of the applicant:

(a) at the Office; or
(b) at the central industrial property office of a Member State; or
(c) in the Benelux countries, at the Benelux Design Office.

2. Where the application is filed at the central industrial property office of a Member State or at the Benelux Design Office, that office shall take all steps to forward the application to the Office within two weeks after filing. It may charge the applicant a fee which shall not exceed the administrative costs of receiving and forwarding the application.

3. As soon as the Office has received an application which has been forwarded by a central industrial property office of a Member State or by the Benelux Design Office, it shall inform the applicant accordingly, indicating the date of its receipt at the Office.

4. No less than 10 years after the entry into force of this Regulation, the Commission shall draw up a report on the operation of the system of filing applications for registered Community designs, accompanied by any proposals for revision that it may deem appropriate.

Article 36

Conditions with which applications must comply

1. An application for a registered Community design shall contain:

(a) a request for registration;
(b) information identifying the applicant;
(c) a representation of the design suitable for reproduction. However, if the object of the application is a two-dimensional design and the application contains a request for deferment of publication in accordance with Article 50, the representation of the design may be replaced by a specimen.

2. The application shall further contain an indication of the products in which the design is intended to be incorporated or to which it is intended to be applied.

3. In addition, the application may contain:

(a) a description explaining the representation or the specimen;
(b) a request for deferment of publication of the registration in accordance with Article 50;
(c) information identifying the representative if the applicant has appointed one;
(d) the classification of the products in which the design is intended to be incorporated or to which it is intended to be applied according to class;
(e) the citation of the designer or of the team of designers or a statement under the applicant's responsibility that the designer or the team of designers has waived the right to be cited.

4. The application shall be subject to the payment of the registration fee and the publication fee. Where a request for deferment under paragraph 3(b) is filed, the publication fee shall be replaced by the fee for deferment of publication.

5. The application shall comply with the conditions laid down in the implementing regulation.

6. The information contained in the elements mentioned in paragraph 2 and in paragraph 3(a) and (d) shall not affect the scope of protection of the design as such.

Article 37

Multiple applications

1. Several designs may be combined in one multiple application for registered Community designs. Except in cases of ornamentation, this possibility is subject to the condition that the products in which the designs are intended to be incorporated or to which they are intended to be applied all belong to the same class of the International Classification for Industrial Designs.

2. Besides the fees referred to in Article 36(4), the multiple application shall be subject to payment of an additional registration fee and an additional publication fee. Where the multiple application contains a request for deferment of publication, the additional publication fee shall be replaced by the additional fee for deferment of publication. The additional fees shall correspond to a percentage of the basic fees for each additional design.

3. The multiple application shall comply with the conditions of presentation laid down in the implementing regulation.

4. Each of the designs contained in a multiple application or registration may be dealt with separately from the others for the purpose of applying this Regulation. It may in particular, separately from the others, be enforced, licensed, be the subject of a right *in rem*, a levy of execution or insolvency proceedings, be surrendered, renewed or assigned, be the subject of deferred publication or be declared invalid. A multiple application or registration may be divided into separate applications or registrations only under the conditions set out in the implementing regulation.

Article 38

Date of filing

B1–039   1. The date of filing of an application for a registered Community design shall be the date on which documents containing the information specified in Article 36(1) are filed with the Office by the applicant, or, if the application has been filed with the central industrial property office of a Member State or with the Benelux Design Office, with that office.

2. By derogation from paragraph 1, the date of filing of an application filed with the central industrial property office of a Member State or with the Benelux Design Office and reaching the Office more than two months after the date on which documents containing the information specified in Article 36(1) have been filed shall be the date of receipt of such documents by the Office.

Article 39

Equivalence of Community filing with national filing

B1–040   An application for a registered Community design which has been accorded a date of filing shall, in the Member States, be equivalent to a regular national filing, including where appropriate the priority claimed for the said application.

Article 40

Classification

B1–041   For the purpose of this Regulation, use shall be made of the Annex to the Agreement establishing an International Classification for Industrial Designs, signed at Locarno on 8 October 1968.

SECTION 2

PRIORITY

Article 41

Right of priority

B1–042   1. A person who has duly filed an application for a design right or for a utility model in or for any State party to the Paris Convention for the Protection of

Industrial Property, or to the Agreement establishing the World Trade Organisation, or his successors in title, shall enjoy, for the purpose of filing an application for a registered Community design in respect of the same design or utility model, a right of priority of six months from the date of filing of the first application.

2. Every filing that is equivalent to a regular national filing under the national law of the State where it was made or under bilateral or multilateral agreements shall be recognised as giving rise to a right of priority.

3. "Regular national filing" means any filing that is sufficient to establish the date on which the application was filed, whatever may be the outcome of the application.

4. A subsequent application for a design which was the subject of a previous first application, and which is filed in or in respect of the same State, shall be considered as the first application for the purpose of determining priority, provided that, at the date of the filing of the subsequent application, the previous application has been withdrawn, abandoned or refused without being open to public inspection and without leaving any rights outstanding, and has not served as a basis for claiming priority. The previous application may not thereafter serve as a basis for claiming a right of priority.

5. If the first filing has been made in a State which is not a party to the Paris Convention, or to the Agreement establishing the World Trade Organisation, paragraphs 1 to 4 shall apply only in so far as that State, according to published findings, grants, on the basis of a filing made at the Office and subject to conditions equivalent to those laid down in this Regulation, a right of priority having equivalent effect.

Article 42

Claiming priority

An applicant for a registered Community design desiring to take advantage of the priority of a previous application shall file a declaration of priority and a copy of the previous application. If the language of the latter is not one of the languages of the Office, the Office may require a translation of the previous application in one of those languages.　**B1–043**

Article 43

Effect of priority right

The effect of the right of priority shall be that the date of priority shall count as the date of the filing of the application for a registered Community design for the purpose of Articles 5, 6, 7, 22, 25(1)(d) and 50(1).　**B1–044**

Article 44

Exhibition priority

1. If an applicant for a registered Community design has disclosed products in which the design is incorporated, or to which it is applied, at an official or officially recognised international exhibition falling within the terms of the Convention on International Exhibitions signed in Paris on 22 November 1928　**B1–045**

and last revised on 30 November 1972, he may, if he files the application within a period of six months from the date of the first disclosure of such products, claim a right of priority from that date within the meaning of Article 43.

2. An applicant who wishes to claim priority pursuant to paragraph 1, under the conditions laid down in the implementing regulation, must file evidence that he has disclosed at an exhibition the products in or to which the design is incorporated or applied.

3. An exhibition priority granted in a Member State or in a third country does not extend the period of priority laid down in Article 41.

TITLE V

REGISTRATION PROCEDURE

Article 45

Examination as to formal requirements for filing

B1–046   1. The Office shall examine whether the application complies with the requirements laid down in Article 36(1) for the accordance of a date of filing.

2. The Office shall examine whether:

(a) the application complies with the other requirements laid down in Article 36(2), (3), (4) and (5) and, in the case of a multiple application, Article 37(1) and (2);

(b) the application meets the formal requirements laid down in the implementing regulation for the implementation of Articles 36 and 37;

(c) the requirements of Article 77(2) are satisfied;

(d) the requirements concerning the claim to priority are satisfied, if a priority is claimed.

3. The conditions for the examination as to the formal requirements for filing shall be laid down in the implementing regulation.

Article 46

Remediable deficiencies

B1–047   1. Where, in carrying out the examination under Article 45, the Office notes that there are deficiencies which may be corrected, the Office shall request the applicant to remedy them within the prescribed period.

2. If the deficiencies concern the requirements referred to in Article 36(1) and the applicant complies with the Office's request within the prescribed period, the Office shall accord as the date of filing the date on which the deficiencies are remedied. If the deficiencies are not remedied within the prescribed period, the application shall not be dealt with as an application for a registered Community design.

3. If the deficiencies concern the requirements, including the payment of fees, as referred to in Article 45(2)(a), (b) and (c) and the applicant complies with the Office's request within the prescribed period, the Office shall accord as the date of filing the date on which the application was originally filed. If the deficiencies or

the default in payment are not remedied within the prescribed period, the Office shall refuse the application.

4. If the deficiencies concern the requirements referred to in Article 45(2)(d), failure to remedy them within the prescribed period shall result in the loss of the right of priority for the application.

Article 47

Grounds for non-registrability

1. If the Office, in carrying out the examination pursuant to Article 45, notices **B1–048** that the design for which protection is sought:

(a) does not correspond to the definition under Article 3(a); or
(b) is contrary to public policy or to accepted principles of morality, it shall refuse the application.

2. The application shall not be refused before the applicant has been allowed the opportunity of withdrawing or amending the application or of submitting his observations.

Article 48

Registration

If the requirements that an application for a registered Community design must **B1–049** satisfy have been fulfilled and to the extent that the application has not been refused by virtue of Article 47, the Office shall register the application in the Community design Register as a registered Community design. The registration shall bear the date of filing of the application referred to in Article 38.

Article 49

Publication

Upon registration, the Office shall publish the registered Community design in **B1–050** the Community Designs Bulletin as mentioned in Article 73(1). The contents of the publication shall be set out in the implementing regulation.

Article 50

Deferment of publication

1. The applicant for a registered Community design may request, when filing **B1–051** the application, that the publication of the registered Community design be deferred for a period of 30 months from the date of filing the application or, if a priority is claimed, from the date of priority.

2. Upon such request, where the conditions set out in Article 48 are satisfied, the registered Community design shall be registered, but neither the representation of the design nor any file relating to the application shall, subject to Article 74(2), be open to public inspection.

3. The Office shall publish in the Community Designs Bulletin a mention of the deferment of the publication of the registered Community design. The mention shall be accompanied by information identifying the right holder in the registered Community design, the date of filing the application and any other particulars prescribed by the implementing regulation.

4. At the expiry of the period of deferment, or at any earlier date on request by the right holder, the Office shall open to public inspection all the entries in the register and the file relating to the application and shall publish the registered Community design in the Community Designs Bulletin, provided that, within the time limit laid down in the implementing regulation:

- (a) the publication fee and, in the event of a multiple application, the additional publication fee are paid;
- (b) where use has been made of the option pursuant to Article 36(1)(c), the right holder has filed with the Office a representation of the design.

If the right holder fails to comply with these requirements, the registered Community design shall be deemed from the outset not to have had the effects specified in this Regulation.

5. In the case of multiple applications, paragraph 4 need only be applied to some of the designs included therein.

6. The institution of legal proceedings on the basis of a registered Community design during the period of deferment of publication shall be subject to the condition that the information contained in the register and in the file relating to the application has been communicated to the person against whom the action is brought.

TITLE VI

SURRENDER AND INVALIDITY OF THE REGISTERED COMMUNITY DESIGN

Article 51

Surrender

B1–052   1. The surrender of a registered Community design shall be declared to the Office in writing by the right holder. It shall not have effect until it has been entered in the register.

2. If a Community design which is subject to deferment of publication is surrendered it shall be deemed from the outset not to have had the effects specified in this Regulation.

3. A registered Community design may be partially surrendered provided that its amended form complies with the requirements for protection and the identity of the design is retained.

4. Surrender shall be registered only with the agreement of the proprietor of a right entered in the register. If a licence has been registered, surrender shall be entered in the register only if the right holder in the registered Community design proves that he has informed the licensee of his intention to surrender. This entry shall be made on expiry of the period prescribed by the implementing regulation.

5. If an action pursuant to Article 14 relating to the entitlement to a registered Community design has been brought before a Community design court, the

Office shall not enter the surrender in the register without the agreement of the claimant.

Article 52

Application for a declaration of invalidity

1. Subject to Article 25(2), (3), (4) and (5), any natural or legal person, as well as **B1–053** a public authority empowered to do so, may submit to the Office an application for a declaration of invalidity of a registered Community design.

2. The application shall be filed in a written reasoned statement. It shall not be deemed to have been filed until the fee for an application for a declaration of invalidity has been paid.

3. An application for a declaration of invalidity shall not be admissible if an application relating to the same subject matter and cause of action, and involving the same parties, has been adjudicated on by a Community design court and has acquired the authority of a final decision.

Article 53

Examination of the application

1. If the Office finds that the application for a declaration of invalidity is **B1–054** admissible, the Office shall examine whether the grounds for invalidity referred to in Article 25 prejudice the maintenance of the registered Community design.

2. In the examination of the application, which shall be conducted in accordance with the implementing regulation, the Office shall invite the parties, as often as necessary, to file observations, within a period to be fixed by the Office, on communications from the other parties or issued by itself.

3. The decision declaring the registered Community design invalid shall be entered in the register upon becoming final.

Article 54

Participation in the proceedings of the alleged infringer

1. In the event of an application for a declaration of invalidity of a registered **B1–055** Community design being filed, and as long as no final decision has been taken by the Office, any third party who proves that proceedings for infringement of the same design have been instituted against him may be joined as a party in the invalidity proceedings on request submitted within three months of the date on which the infringement proceedings were instituted.

The same shall apply in respect of any third party who proves both that the right holder of the Community design has requested that he cease an alleged infringement of the design and that he has instituted proceedings for a court ruling that he is not infringing the Community design.

2. The request to be joined as a party shall be filed in a written reasoned statement. It shall not be deemed to have been filed until the invalidity fee, referred to in Article 52(2), has been paid. Thereafter the request shall, subject to

any exceptions laid down in the implementing regulation, be treated as an application for a declaration of invalidity.

TITLE VII

APPEALS

Article 55

Decisions subject to appeal

B1–056 1. An appeal shall lie from decisions of the examiners, the Administration of Trade Marks and Designs and Legal Division and Invalidity Divisions. It shall have suspensive effect.

2. A decision which does not terminate proceedings as regards one of the parties can only be appealed together with the final decision, unless the decision allows separate appeal.

Article 56

Persons entitled to appeal and to be parties to appeal proceedings

B1–057 Any party to proceedings adversely affected by a decision may appeal. Any other parties to the proceedings shall be parties to the appeal proceedings as of right.

Article 57

Time limit and form of appeal

B1–058 Notice of appeal must be filed in writing at the Office within two months after the date of notification of the decision appealed from. The notice shall be deemed to have been filed only when the fee for appeal has been paid. Within four months after the date of notification of the decision, a written statement setting out the grounds of appeal must be filed.

Article 58

Interlocutory revision

B1–059 1. If the department whose decision is contested considers the appeal to be admissible and well founded, it shall rectify its decision. This shall not apply where the appellant is opposed by another party to the proceedings.

2. If the decision is not rectified within one month after receipt of the statement of grounds, the appeal shall be remitted to the Board of Appeal without delay and without comment as to its merits.

Article 59

Examination of appeals

1. If the appeal is admissible, the Board of Appeal shall examine whether the appeal is to be allowed.

B1–060

2. In the examination of the appeal, the Board of Appeal shall invite the parties, as often as necessary, to file observations, within a period to be fixed by the Board of Appeal, on communications from the other parties or issued by itself.

Article 60

Decisions in respect of appeals

1. Following the examination as to the merits of the appeal, the Board of Appeal shall decide on the appeal. The Board of Appeal may either exercise any power within the competence of the department which was responsible for the decision appealed against or remit the case to that department for further prosecution.

B1–061

2. If the Board of Appeal remits the case for further prosecution to the department whose decision was appealed, that department shall be bound by the *ratio decidendi* of the Board of Appeal, in so far as the facts are the same.

3. The decisions of the Boards of Appeal shall take effect only from the date of expiry of the period referred to in Article 61(5) or, if an action has been brought before the Court of Justice within that period, from the date of rejection of such action.

Article 61

Actions before the Court of Justice

1. Actions may be brought before the Court of Justice against decisions of the Boards of Appeal on appeals.

B1–062

2. The action may be brought on grounds of lack of competence, infringement of an essential procedural requirement, infringement of the Treaty, of this Regulation or of any rule of law relating to their application or misuse of power.

3. The Court of Justice has jurisdiction to annul or to alter the contested decision.

4. The action shall be open to any party to proceedings before the Board of Appeal adversely affected by its decision.

5. The action shall be brought before the Court of Justice within two months of the date of notification of the decision of the Board of Appeal.

6. The Office shall be required to take the necessary measures to comply with the judgment of the Court of Justice.

TITLE VIII

PROCEDURE BEFORE THE OFFICE

SECTION 1

GENERAL PROVISIONS

Article 62

Statement of reasons on which decisions are based

B1–063   Decisions of the Office shall state the reasons on which they are based. They shall be based only on reasons or evidence on which the parties concerned have had an opportunity to present their comments.

Article 63

Examination of the facts by the Office of its own motion

B1–064   1. In proceedings before it the Office shall examine the facts of its own motion. However, in proceedings relating to a declaration of invalidity, the Office shall be restricted in this examination to the facts, evidence and arguments provided by the parties and the relief sought.

2. The Office may disregard facts or evidence which are not submitted in due time by the parties concerned.

Article 64

Oral proceedings

B1–065   1. If the Office considers that oral proceedings would be expedient, they shall be held either at the instance of the Office or at the request of any party to the proceedings.

2. Oral proceedings, including delivery of the decision, shall be public, unless the department before which the proceedings are taking place decides otherwise in cases where admission of the public could have serious and unjustified disadvantages, in particular for a party to the proceedings.

Article 65

Taking of evidence

B1–066   1. In any proceedings before the Office the means of giving or obtaining evidence shall include the following:

(a) hearing the parties;

(b) requests for information;

(c) the production of documents and items of evidence;

(d) hearing witnesses;

(e) opinions by experts;

(f) statements in writing, sworn or affirmed or having a similar effect under the law of the State in which the statement is drawn up.

2. The relevant department of the Office may commission one of its members to examine the evidence adduced.

3. If the Office considers it necessary for a party, witness or expert to give evidence orally, it shall issue a summons to the person concerned to appear before it.

4. The parties shall be informed of the hearing of a witness or expert before the Office. They shall have the right to be present and to put questions to the witness or expert.

Article 66

Notification

The Office shall, as a matter of course, notify those concerned of decisions and summonses and of any notice or other communication from which a time limit is reckoned, or of which those concerned must be notified under other provisions of this Regulation or of the implementing regulation, or of which notification has been ordered by the President of the Office.

B1–067

Article 67

Restitutio in integrum

1. The applicant for or holder of a registered Community design or any other party to proceedings before the Office who, in spite of all due care required by the circumstances having been taken, was unable to observe a time limit vis-à-vis the Office shall, upon application, have his rights re-established if the non-observance in question has the direct consequence, by virtue of the provisions of this Regulation, of causing the loss of any rights or means of redress.

B1–068

2. The application must be filed in writing within two months of the removal of the cause of non-compliance with the time limit. The omitted act must be completed within this period. The application shall only be admissible within the year immediately following the expiry of the unobserved time limit. In the case of non-submission of the request for renewal of registration or of non-payment of a renewal fee, the further period of six months provided for in the second sentence of Article 13(3) shall be deducted from the period of one year.

3. The application must state the grounds on which it is based and must set out the facts on which it relies. It shall not be deemed to be filed until the fee for the re-establishment of rights has been paid.

4. The department competent to decide on the omitted act shall decide upon the application.

5. The provisions of this Article shall not be applicable to the time limits referred to in paragraph 2 and Article 41(1).

6. Where the applicant for or holder of a registered Community design has his rights re-established, he may not invoke his rights vis-à-vis a third party who, in good faith, in the course of the period between the loss of rights in the application

for or registration of the registered Community design and publication of the mention of re-establishment of those rights, has put on the market products in which a design included within the scope of protection of the registered Community design is incorporated or to which it is applied.

7. A third party who may avail himself of the provisions of paragraph 6 may bring third party proceedings against the decision re-establishing the rights of the applicant for or holder of the registered Community design within a period of two months as from the date of publication of the mention of re-establishment of those rights.

8. Nothing in this Article shall limit the right of a Member State to grant *restitutio in integrum* in respect of time limits provided for in this Regulation and to be complied with vis-à-vis the authorities of such State.

Article 68

Reference to general principles

B1–069   In the absence of procedural provisions in this Regulation, the implementing regulation, the fees regulation or the rules of procedure of the Boards of Appeal, the Office shall take into account the principles of procedural law generally recognised in the Member States.

Article 69

Termination of financial obligations

B1–070   1. Rights of the Office to the payment of fees shall be barred four years from the end of the calendar year in which the fee fell due.

2. Rights against the Office for the refunding of fees or sums of money paid in excess of a fee shall be barred after four years from the end of the calendar year in which the right arose.

3. The periods laid down in paragraphs 1 and 2 shall be interrupted, in the case covered by paragraph 1, by a request for payment of the fee and, in the case covered by paragraph 2, by a reasoned claim in writing. On interruption it shall begin again immediately and shall end at the latest six years after the end of the year in which it originally began, unless in the meantime judicial proceedings to enforce the right have begun. In this case the period shall end at the earliest one year after the judgment has acquired the authority of a final decision.

SECTION 2

COSTS

Article 70

Apportionment of costs

B1–071   1. The losing party in proceedings for a declaration of invalidity of a registered Community design or appeal proceedings shall bear the fees incurred by the other party as well as all costs incurred by him essential to the proceedings, including travel and subsistence and the remuneration of an agent, adviser or advocate, within the limits of scales set for each category of costs under the conditions laid down in the implementing regulation.

2. However, where each party succeeds on some and fails on other heads, or if reasons of equity so dictate, the Invalidity Division or Board of Appeal shall decide a different apportionment of costs.

3. A party who terminates the proceedings by surrendering the registered Community design or by not renewing its registration or by withdrawing the application for a declaration of invalidity or the appeal, shall bear the fees and the costs incurred by the other party as stipulated in paragraphs 1 and 2.

4. Where a case does not proceed to judgment, the costs shall be at the discretion of the Invalidity Division or Board of Appeal.

5. Where the parties conclude before the Invalidity Division or Board of Appeal a settlement of costs differing from that provided for in paragraphs 1, 2, 3 and 4, the body concerned shall take note of that agreement.

6. On request, the registry of the Invalidity Division or Board of Appeal shall fix the amount of the costs to be paid pursuant to the preceding paragraphs. The amount so determined may be reviewed by a decision of the Invalidity Division or Board of Appeal on a request filed within the period prescribed by the implementing regulation.

Article 71

Enforcement of decisions fixing the amount of costs

1. Any final decision of the Office fixing the amount of costs shall be enforceable. **B1–072**

2. Enforcement shall be governed by the rules of civil procedure in force in the State in the territory of which it is carried out. The order for its enforcement shall be appended to the decision, without any other formality than verification of the authenticity of the decision, by the national authority which the government of each Member State shall designate for this purpose and shall make known to the Office and to the Court of Justice.

3. When these formalities have been completed on application by the party concerned, the latter may proceed to enforcement in accordance with the national law, by bringing the matter directly before the competent authority.

4. Enforcement may be suspended only by a decision of the Court of Justice. However, the courts of the Member State concerned shall have jurisdiction over complaints that enforcement is being carried out in an irregular manner.

SECTION 3

INFORMING THE PUBLIC AND THE OFFICIAL AUTHORITIES OF THE MEMBER STATES

Article 72

Register of Community designs

The Office shall keep a register to be known as the register of Community **B1–073** designs, which shall contain those particulars of which the registration is provided for by this Regulation or by the implementing regulation. The register shall be open to public inspection, except to the extent that Article 50(2) provides otherwise.

Article 73

Periodical publications

B1–074   1. This Office shall periodically publish a Community Designs Bulletin containing entries open to public inspection in the register as well as other particulars the publication of which is prescribed by this Regulation or by the implementing regulation.

2. Notices and information of a general character issued by the President of the Office, as well as any other information relevant to this Regulation or its implementation, shall be published in the Official Journal of the Office.

Article 74

Inspection of files

B1–075   1. The files relating to applications for registered Community designs which have not yet been published or the files relating to registered Community designs which are subject to deferment of publication in accordance with Article 50 or which, being subject to such deferment, have been surrendered before or on the expiry of that period, shall not be made available for inspection without the consent of the applicant for or the right holder in the registered Community design.

2. Any person who can establish a legitimate interest may inspect a file without the consent of the applicant for or holder of the registered Community design prior to the publication or after the surrender of the latter in the case provided for in paragraph 1.

This shall in particular apply if the interested person proves that the applicant for or the holder of the registered Community design has taken steps with a view to invoking against him the right under the registered Community design.

3. Subsequent to the publication of the registered Community design, the file may be inspected on request.

4. However, where a file is inspected pursuant to paragraph 2 or 3, certain documents in the file may be withheld from inspection in accordance with the provisions of the implementing regulation.

Article 75

Administrative cooperation

B1–076   Unless otherwise provided in this Regulation or in national laws, the Office and the courts or authorities of the Member States shall on request give assistance to each other by communicating information or opening files for inspection.

Where the Office opens files to inspection by courts, public prosecutors' offices or central industrial property offices, the inspection shall not be subject to the restrictions laid down in Article 74.

Article 76

Exchange of publications

1. The Office and the central industrial property offices of the Member States shall despatch to each other on request and for their own use one or more copies of their respective publications free of charge.

2. The Office may conclude agreements relating to the exchange or supply of publications.

B1–077

SECTION 4

REPRESENTATION

Article 77

General principles of representation

1. Subject to paragraph 2, no person shall be compelled to be represented before the Office.

B1–078

2. Without prejudice to the second subparagraph of paragraph 3, natural or legal persons not having either their domicile or their principal place of business or a real and effective industrial or commercial establishment in the Community must be represented before the Office in accordance with Article 78(1) in all proceedings before the Office established by this Regulation, other than in filing an application for a registered Community design; the implementing regulation may permit other exceptions.

3. Natural or legal persons having their domicile or principal place of business or a real and effective industrial or commercial establishment in the Community may be represented before the Office by one of their employees, who must file with it a signed authorisation for inclusion in the files, the details of which are set out in the implementing regulation. An employee of a legal person to which this paragraph applies may also represent other legal persons which have economic connections with the first legal person, even if those other legal persons have neither their domicile nor their principal place of business nor a real and effective industrial or commercial establishment within the Community.

Article 78

Professional representation

1. Representation of natural or legal persons in proceedings before the Office under this Regulation may only be undertaken by:

B1–079

(a) any legal practitioner qualified in one of the Member States and having his place of business within the Community, to the extent that he is entitled, within the said State, to act as a representative in industrial property matters; or

(b) any professional representatives whose name has been entered on the list of professional representatives referred to in Article 89(1)(b) of the Regulation on the Community trade mark; or

(c) persons whose names are entered on the special list of professional representatives for design matters referred to in paragraph 4.

2. The persons referred to in paragraph 1(c) shall only be entitled to represent third persons in proceedings on design matters before the Office.

3. The implementing regulation shall provide whether and under what conditions representatives must file with the Office a signed authorisation for insertion on the files.

4. Any natural person may be entered on the special list of professional representatives in design matters, if he fulfils the following conditions:

(a) he must be a national of one of the Member States;
(b) he must have his place of business or employment in the Community;
(c) he must be entitled to represent natural or legal persons in design matters before the central industrial property office of a Member State or before the Benelux Design Office. Where, in that State, the entitlement to represent in design matters is not conditional upon the requirement of special professional qualifications, persons applying to be entered on the list must have habitually acted in design matters before the central industrial property office of the said State for at least five years. However, persons whose professional qualification to represent natural or legal persons in design matters before the central industrial property office of one of the Member States is officially recognised in accordance with the regulations laid by such State shall not be subject to the condition of having exercised the profession.

5. Entry on the list referred to in paragraph 4 shall be effected upon request, accompanied by a certificate furnished by the central industrial property office of the Member State concerned, which must indicate that the conditions laid down in the said paragraph are fulfilled.

6. The President of the Office may grant exemption from:

(a) the requirement of paragraph 4(a) in special circumstances;
(b) the requirement of paragraph 4(c), second sentence, if the applicant furnishes proof that he has acquired the requisite qualification in another way.

7. The conditions under which a person may be removed from the list shall be laid down in the implementing regulation.

TITLE IX

JURISDICTION AND PROCEDURE IN LEGAL ACTIONS RELATING TO COMMUNITY DESIGNS

SECTION 1

JURISDICTION AND ENFORCEMENT

Article 79

Application of the Convention on Jurisdiction and Enforcement

B1–080   1. Unless otherwise specified in this Regulation, the Convention on Jurisdiction and the Enforcement of Judgements in Civil and Commercial Matters, signed in

Brussels on 27 September 1968[8], hereinafter referred to as the 'Convention on Jurisdiction and Enforcement', shall apply to proceedings relating to Community designs and applications for registered Community designs, as well as to proceedings relating to actions on the basis of Community designs and national designs enjoying simultaneous protection.

2. The provisions of the Convention on Jurisdiction and Enforcement which are rendered applicable by the paragraph 1 shall have effect in respect of any Member State solely in the text which is in force in respect of that State at any given time.

3. In the event of proceedings in respect of the actions and claims referred to in Article 85:

(a) Articles 2, 4, 5(1), (3), (4) and (5), 16(4) and 24 of the Convention on Jurisdiction and Enforcement shall not apply;

(b) Articles 17 and 18 of that Convention shall apply subject to the limitations in Article 82(4) of this Regulation;

(c) the provisions of Title II of that Convention which are applicable to persons domiciled in a Member State shall also be applicable to persons who do not have a domicile in any Member State but have an establishment therein.

4. The provisions of the Convention on Jurisdiction and Enforcement shall not have effect in respect of any Member State for which that Convention has not yet entered into force. Until such entry into force, proceedings referred to in paragraph 1 shall be governed in such a Member State by any bilateral or multilateral convention governing its relationship with another Member State concerned, or, if no such convention exists, by its domestic law on jurisdiction, recognition and enforcement of decisions.

SECTION 2

DISPUTES CONCERNING THE INFRINGEMENT AND VALIDITY OF COMMUNITY DESIGNS

Article 80

Community design courts

1. The Member States shall designate in their territories as limited a number as possible of national courts and tribunals of first and second instance (Community design courts) which shall perform the functions assigned to them by this Regulation.   **B1–081**

2. Each Member State shall communicate to the Commission not later than 6 March 2005 a list of Community design courts, indicating their names and their territorial jurisdiction.

3. Any change made after communication of the list referred to in paragraph 2 in the number, names or territorial jurisdiction of the Community design courts shall be notified without delay by the Member State concerned to the Commission.

---

[8] OJ L 299, 31.12.1972, p.32. Convention as amended by the Conventions on the Accession to that Convention of the States acceding to the European Communities.

4. The information referred to in paragraphs 2 and 3 shall be notified by the Commission to the Member States and published in the *Official Journal of the European Communities*.

5. As long as a Member State has not communicated the list as stipulated in paragraph 2, jurisdiction for any proceedings resulting from an action covered by Article 81 for which the courts of that State have jurisdiction pursuant to Article 82 shall lie with that court of the State in question which would have jurisdiction *ratione loci* and *ratione materiae* in the case of proceedings relating to a national design right of that State.

Article 81

Jurisdiction over infringement and validity

B1–082   The Community design courts shall have exclusive jurisdiction:

   (a) for infringement actions and—if they are permitted under national law—actions in respect of threatened infringement of Community designs;
   (b) for actions for declaration of non-infringement of Community designs, if they are permitted under national law;
   (c) for actions for a declaration of invalidity of an unregistered Community design;
   (d) for counterclaims for a declaration of invalidity of a Community design raised in connection with actions under (a).

Article 82

International jurisdiction

B1–083   1. Subject to the provisions of this Regulation and to any provisions of the Convention on Jurisdiction and Enforcement applicable by virtue of Article 79, proceedings in respect of the actions and claims referred to in Article 81 shall be brought in the courts of the Member State in which the defendant is domiciled or, if he is not domiciled in any of the Member States, in any Member State in which he has an establishment.

2. If the defendant is neither domiciled nor has an establishment in any of the Member States, such proceedings shall be brought in the courts of the Member State in which the plaintiff is domiciled or, if he is not domiciled in any of the Member States, in any Member State in which he has an establishment.

3. If neither the defendant nor the plaintiff is so domiciled or has such an establishment, such proceedings shall be brought in the courts of the Member State where the Office has its seat.

4. Notwithstanding paragraphs 1, 2 and 3:

   (a) Article 17 of the Convention on Jurisdiction and Enforcement shall apply if the parties agree that a different Community design court shall have jurisdiction;
   (b) Article 18 of that Convention shall apply if the defendant enters an appearance before a different Community design court.

5. Proceedings in respect of the actions and claims referred to in Article 81(a) and (d) may also be brought in the courts of the Member State in which the act of infringement has been committed or threatened.

Article 83

Extent of jurisdiction on infringement

1. A Community design court whose jurisdiction is based on Article 82(1), (2) **B1–084** (3) or (4) shall have jurisdiction in respect of acts of infringement committed or threatened within the territory of any of the Member States.

2. A Community design court whose jurisdiction is based on Article 82(5) shall have jurisdiction only in respect of acts of infringement committed or threatened within the territory of the Member State in which that court is situated.

Article 84

Action or counterclaim for a declaration of invalidity of a Community design

1. An action or a counterclaim for a declaration of invalidity of a Community **B1–085** design may only be based on the grounds for invalidity mentioned in Article 25.

2. In the cases referred to in Article 25(2), (3), (4) and (5) the action or the counterclaim may be brought solely by the person entitled under those provisions.

3. If the counterclaim is brought in a legal action to which the right holder of the Community design is not already a party, he shall be informed thereof and may be joined as a party to the action in accordance with the conditions set out in the law of the Member State where the court is situated.

4. The validity of a Community design may not be put in issue in an action for a declaration of non-infringement.

Article 85

Presumption of validity—defence as to the merits

1. In proceedings in respect of an infringement action or an action for **B1–086** threatened infringement of a registered Community design, the Community design court shall treat the Community design as valid. Validity may be challenged only with a counter-claim for a declaration of invalidity. However, a plea relating to the invalidity of a Community design, submitted otherwise than by way of counterclaim, shall be admissible in so far as the defendant claims that the Community design could be declared invalid on account of an earlier national design right, within the meaning of Article 25(1)(d), belonging to him.

2. In proceedings in respect of an infringement action or an action for threatened infringement of an unregistered Community design, the Community design court shall treat the Community design as valid if the right holder produces proof that the conditions laid down in Article 11 have been met and indicates what constitutes the individual character of his Community design. However, the defendant may contest its validity by way of a plea or with a counterclaim for a declaration of invalidity.

Article 86

Judgements of invalidity

B1–087   1. Where in a proceeding before a Community design court the Community design has been put in issue by way of a counterclaim for a declaration of invalidity:

(a) if any of the grounds mentioned in Article 25 are found to prejudice the maintenance of the Community design, the court shall declare the Community design invalid;

(b) if none of the grounds mentioned in Article 25 is found to prejudice the maintenance of the Community design, the court shall reject the counterclaim.

2. The Community design court with which a counterclaim for a declaration of invalidity of a registered Community design has been filed shall inform the Office of the date on which the counterclaim was filed. The latter shall record this fact in the register.

3. The Community design court hearing a counterclaim for a declaration of invalidity of a registered Community design may, on application by the right holder of the registered Community design and after hearing the other parties, stay the proceedings and request the defendant to submit an application for a declaration of invalidity to the Office within a time limit which the court shall determine. If the application is not made within the time limit, the proceedings shall continue; the counterclaim shall be deemed withdrawn. Article 91(3) shall apply.

4. Where a Community design court has given a judgment which has become final on a counterclaim for a declaration of invalidity of a registered Community design, a copy of the judgment shall be sent to the Office. Any party may request information about such transmission. The Office shall mention the judgment in the register in accordance with the provisions of the implementing regulation.

5. No counterclaim for a declaration of invalidity of a registered Community design may be made if an application relating to the same subject matter and cause of action, and involving the same parties, has already been determined by the Office in a decision which has become final.

Article 87

Effects of the judgement on invalidity

B1–088   When it has become final, a judgment of a Community design court declaring a Community design invalid shall have in all the Member States the effects specified in Article 26.

Article 88

Applicable law

B1–089   1. The Community design courts shall apply the provisions of this Regulation.

2. On all matters not covered by this Regulation, a Community design court shall apply its national law, including its private international law.

3. Unless otherwise provided in this Regulation, a Community design court shall apply the rules of procedure governing the same type of action relating to a national design right in the Member State where it is situated.

Article 89

Sanctions in actions for infringement

1. Where in an action for infringement or for threatened infringement a **B1–090** Community design court finds that the defendant has infringed or threatened to infringe a Community design, it shall, unless there are special reasons for not doing so, order the following measures:

- (a) an order prohibiting the defendant from proceeding with the acts which have infringed or would infringe the Community design;
- (b) an order to seize the infringing products;
- (c) an order to seize materials and implements predominantly used in order to manufacture the infringing goods, if their owner knew the effect for which such use was intended or if such effect would have been obvious in the circumstances;
- (d) any order imposing other sanctions appropriate under the circumstances which are provided by the law of the Member State in which the acts of infringement or threatened infringement are committed, including its private international law.

2. The Community design court shall take such measures in accordance with its national law as are aimed at ensuring that the orders referred to in paragraph 1 are complied with.

Article 90

Provisional measures, including protective measures

1. Application may be made to the courts of a Member State, including **B1–091** Community design courts, for such provisional measures, including protective measures, in respect of a Community design as may be available under the law of that State in respect of national design rights even if, under this Regulation, a Community design court of another Member State has jurisdiction as to the substance of the matter.

2. In proceedings relating to provisional measures, including protective measures, a plea otherwise than by way of counterclaim relating to the invalidity of a Community design submitted by the defendant shall be admissible. Article 85(2) shall, however, apply *mutatis mutandis*.

3. A Community design court whose jurisdiction is based on Article 82(1), (2), (3) or (4) shall have jurisdiction to grant provisional measures, including protective measures, which, subject to any necessary procedure for recognition and enforcement pursuant to Title III of the Convention on Jurisdiction and Enforcement, are applicable in the territory of any Member State. No other court shall have such jurisdiction.

Article 91

Specific rules on related actions

B1–092   1. A Community design court hearing an action referred to in Article 81, other than an action for a declaration of non-infringement, shall, unless there are special grounds for continuing the hearing, of its own motion after hearing the parties, or at the request of one of the parties and after hearing the other parties, stay the proceedings where the validity of the Community design is already in issue before another Community design court on account of a counterclaim or, in the case of a registered Community design, where an application for a declaration of invalidity has already been filed at the Office.

2. The Office, when hearing an application for a declaration of invalidity of a registered Community design, shall, unless there are special grounds for continuing the hearing, of its own motion after hearing the parties, or at the request of one of the parties and after hearing the other parties, stay the proceedings where the validity of the registered Community design is already in issue on account of a counterclaim before a Community design court. However, if one of the parties to the proceedings before the Community design court so requests, the court may, after hearing the other parties to these proceedings, stay the proceedings. The Office shall in this instance continue the proceedings pending before it.

3. Where the Community design court stays the proceedings it may order provisional measures, including protective measures, for the duration of the stay.

Article 92

Jurisdiction of Community design courts of second instance—further appeal

B1–093   1. An appeal to the Community design courts of second instance shall lie from judgments of the Community design courts of first instance in respect of proceedings arising from the actions and claims referred to in Article 81.

2. The conditions under which an appeal may be lodged with a Community design court of second instance shall be determined by the national law of the Member State in which that court is located.

3. The national rules concerning further appeal shall be applicable in respect of judgments of Community design courts of second instance.

S<small>ECTION</small> 3

O<small>THER</small> <small>DISPUTES CONCERNING</small> C<small>OMMUNITY DESIGNS</small>

Article 93

Supplementary provisions on the jurisdiction of national courts other than Community design courts

B1–094   1. Within the Member State whose courts have jurisdiction under Article 79(1) or (4), those courts shall have jurisdiction for actions relating to Community designs other than those referred to in Article 81 which would have jurisdiction *ratione loci* and *ratione materiae* in the case of actions relating to a national design right in that State.

2. Actions relating to a Community design, other than those referred to in Article 81, for which no court has jurisdiction pursuant to Article 79(1) and (4) and paragraph 1 of this Article may be heard before the courts of the Member State in which the Office has its seat.

Article 94

Obligation of the national court

A national court which is dealing with an action relating to a Community design other than the actions referred to in Article 81 shall treat the design as valid. Articles 85(2) and 90(2) shall, however, apply *mutatis mutandis*.   B1–095

Title X

Effects on the Laws of the Member States

Article 95

Parallel actions on the basis of Community designs and national design rights

1. Where actions for infringement or for threatened infringement involving the   B1–096
same cause of action and between the same parties are brought before the courts of different Member States, one seized on the basis of a Community design and the other seized on the basis of a national design right providing simultaneous protection, the court other than the court first seized shall of its own motion decline jurisdiction in favour of that court. The court which would be required to decline jurisdiction may stay its proceedings if the jurisdiction of the other court is contested.

2. The Community design court hearing an action for infringement or threatened infringement on the basis of a Community design shall reject the action if a final judgment on the merits has been given on the same cause of action and between the same parties on the basis of a design right providing simultaneous protection.

3. The court hearing an action for infringement or for threatened infringement on the basis of a national design right shall reject the action if a final judgment on the merits has been given on the same cause of action and between the same parties on the basis of a Community design providing simultaneous protection.

4. Paragraphs 1, 2 and 3 shall not apply in respect of provisional measures, including protective measures.

Article 96

Relationship to other forms of protection under national law

1. The provisions of this Regulation shall be without prejudice to any provisions   B1–097
of Community law or of the law of the Member States concerned relating to

589

unregistered designs, trade marks or other distinctive signs, patents and utility models, typefaces, civil liability and unfair competition.

2. A design protected by a Community design shall also be eligible for protection under the law of copyright of Member States as from the date on which the design was created or fixed in any form. The extent to which, and the conditions under which, such a protection is conferred, including the level of originality required, shall be determined by each Member State.

TITLE XI

SUPPLEMENTARY PROVISIONS CONCERNING THE OFFICE

SECTION 1

GENERAL PROVISIONS

Article 97

General provision

B1–098   Unless otherwise provided in this Title, Title XII of the Regulation on the Community trade mark shall apply to the Office with regard to its tasks under this Regulation.

Article 98

Language of proceedings

B1–099   1. The application for a registered Community design shall be filed in one of the official languages of the Community.

2. The applicant must indicate a second language which shall be a language of the Office the use of which he accepts as a possible language of proceedings before the Office.

If the application was filed in a language which is not one of the languages of the Office, the Office shall arrange to have the application translated into the language indicated by the applicant.

3. Where the applicant for a registered Community design is the sole party to proceedings before the Office, the language of proceedings shall be the language used for filing the application. If the application was made in a language other then the languages of the Office, the Office may send written communications to the applicant in the second language indicated by the applicant in his application.

4. In the case of invalidity proceedings, the language of proceedings shall be the language used for filing the application for a registered Community design if this is one of the languages of the Office. If the application was made in a language other than the languages of the Office, the language of proceedings shall be the second language indicated in the application.

The application for a declaration of invalidity shall be filed in the language of proceedings.

Where the language of proceedings is not the language used for filing the application for a registered Community design, the right holder of the Community design may file observations in the language of filing. The Office shall arrange to have those observations translated into the language of proceedings.

The implementing regulation may provide that the translation expenses to be borne by the Office may not, subject to a derogation granted by the Office where justified by the complexity of the case, exceed an amount to be fixed for each category of proceedings on the basis of the average size of statements of case received by the Office. Expenditure in excess of this amount may be allocated to the losing party in accordance with Article 70.

5. Parties to invalidity proceedings may agree that a different official language of the Community is to be the language of the proceedings.

Article 99

Publication and register

1. All information the publication of which is prescribed by this Regulation or the implementing regulation shall be published in all the official languages of the Community.

2. All entries in the Register of Community designs shall be made in all the official languages of the Community.

3. In cases of doubt, the text in the language of the Office in which the application for a registered Community design was filed shall be authentic. If the application was filed in an official language of the Community other than one of the languages of the Office, the text in the second language indicated by the applicant shall be authentic.

B1–100

Article 100

Supplementary powers of the President

In addition to the functions and powers conferred on the President of the Office by Article 119 of the Regulation on the Community trade mark, the President may place before the Commission any proposal to amend this Regulation, the implementing regulation, the fees regulation and any other rule to the extent that they apply to registered Community designs, after consulting the Administrative Board and, in the case of the fees regulation, the Budget Committee.

B1–101

Article 101

Supplementary powers of the Administrative Board

In addition to the powers conferred on it by Article 121 *et seq* of the Regulation on the Community trade mark or by other provisions of this Regulation, the Administrative Board;

(a) shall set the date for the first filing of applications for registered Community designs pursuant to Article 111(2);

(b) shall be consulted before adoption of the guidelines for examination as to formal requirements, examination as to grounds for refusal of registration and invalidity proceedings in the Office and in the other cases provided for in this Regulation.

B1–102

SECTION 2

PROCEDURES

Article 102

Competence

B1–103   For taking decisions in connection with the procedures laid down in this Regulation the following shall be competent:

    (a) examiners;
    (b) the Administration of Trade Marks and Designs and Legal Division;
    (c) Invalidity Divisions;
    (d) Boards of Appeal.

Article 103

Examiners

B1–104   An examiner shall be responsible for taking decisions on behalf of the Office in relation to an application for a registered Community design.

Article 104

The Administration of Trade Marks and Designs and Legal Division

B1–105   1. The Administration of Trade Marks and Legal Division provided for by Article 128 of the Regulation on the Community trade mark shall become the Administration of Trade Marks and Designs and Legal Division.

2. In addition to the powers conferred upon it by the Regulation on the Community trade mark, it shall be responsible for taking those decisions required by this Regulation which do not fall within the competence of an examiner or an Invalidity Division. It shall in particular be responsible for decisions in respect of entries in the register.

Article 105

Invalidity Divisions

B1–106   1. An Invalidity Division shall be responsible for taking decisions in relation to applications for declarations of invalidity of registered Community designs.

2. An Invalidity Division shall consist of three members. At least one of the members must be legally qualified.

Article 106

Boards of Appeal

B1–107   In addition to the powers conferred upon it by Article 131 of the Regulation on the Community trade mark, the Boards of Appeal instituted by that Regulation shall be responsible for deciding on appeals from decisions of the examiners, the Invalidity Divisions and from the decisions of the Administration of Trade Marks and Designs and Legal Division as regards their decisions concerning Community designs.

TITLE XIA[8a]

INTERNATIONAL REGISTRATION OF DESIGNS

SECTION 1

GENERAL PROVISIONS

Article 106a

Application of provisions

1. Unless otherwise specified in this title, this Regulation and any Regulations   **B1–108**
implementing this Regulation adopted pursuant to Article 109 shall apply, mutatis mutandis, to registrations of industrial designs in the international register maintained by the International Bureau of the World Intellectual Property Organisation (hereinafter referred to as "international registration" and "the International Bureau") designating the Community, under the Geneva Act.

2. Any recording of an international registration designating the Community in the International Register shall have the same effect as if it had been made in the register of Community designs of the Office, and any publication of an international registration designating the Community in the Bulletin of the International Bureau shall have the same effect as if it had been published in the Community Designs Bulletin.

SECTION 2

INTERNATIONAL REGISTRATIONS DESIGNATING THE COMMUNITY

Article 106b

Procedure for filing the international application

International applications pursuant to Article 4(1) of the Geneva Act shall be   **B1–109**
filed directly at the International Bureau.

[8a] This title and arts 105a to 106f inserted by Council Regulation (EC) No.1891/2006.

Article 106c

Designation fees

B1–110   The prescribed designation fees referred to in Article 7(1) of the Geneva Act are replaced by an individual designation fee.

Article 106d

Effects of international registration designating the European Community

B1–111   1. An international registration designating the Community shall, from the date of its registration referred to in Article 10(2) of the Geneva Act, have the same effect as an application for a registered Community design.

2. If no refusal has been notified or if any such refusal has been withdrawn, the international registration of a design designating the Community shall, from the date referred to in paragraph 1, have the same effect as the registration of a design as a registered Community design.

3. The Office shall provide information on international registrations referred to in paragraph 2, in accordance with the conditions laid down in the Implementing Regulation.

Article 106e

Refusal

B1–112   1. The Office shall communicate to the International Bureau a notification of refusal not later than six months from the date of publication of the international registration, if in carrying out an examination of an international registration, the Office notices that the design for which protection is sought does not correspond to the definition under Article 3(a), or is contrary to public policy or to accepted principles of morality.

The notification shall state the grounds on which the refusal is based.

2. The effects of an international registration in the Community shall not be refused before the holder has been allowed the opportunity of renouncing the international registration in respect of the Community or of submitting observations.

3. The conditions for the examination as to the grounds for refusal shall be laid down in the Implementing Regulation.

Article 106f

Invalidation of the effects of an international registration

B1–113   1. The effects of an international registration in the Community may be declared invalid partly or in whole in accordance with the procedure in Titles VI and VII or by a Community design court on the basis of a counterclaim in infringement proceedings.

2. Where the Office is aware of the invalidation, it shall notify it to the International Bureau.[9]

TITLE XII

FINAL PROVISIONS

Article 107

Implementing regulation

1. The rules implementing this Regulation shall be adopted in an implementing **B1–114** regulation.

2. In addition to the fees already provided for in this Regulation, fees shall be charged, in accordance with the detailed rules of application laid down in the implementing regulation and in a fees regulation, in the cases listed below:

(a) late payment of the registration fee;
(b) late payment of the publication fee;
(c) late payment of the fee for deferment of publication;
(d) late payment of additional fees for multiple applications;
(e) issue of a copy of the certificate of registration;
(f) registration of the transfer of a registered Community design;
(g) registration of a licence or another right in respect of a registered Community design;
(h) cancellation of the registration of a licence or another right;
(i) issue of an extract from the register;
(j) inspection of the files;
(k) issue of copies of file documents;
(l) communication of information in a file;
(m) review of the determination of the procedural costs to be refunded;
(n) issue of certified copies of the application.

3. The implementing regulation and the fees regulation shall be adopted and amended in accordance with the procedure laid down in Article 109(2).

Article 108

Rules of procedure of the Boards of Appeal

The rules of procedure of the Boards of Appeal shall apply to appeals heard by **B1–115** those Boards under this Regulation, without prejudice to any necessary adjustment or additional provision, adopted in accordance with the procedure laid down in Article 109(2).

---

[9] Title XIa inserted by Regulation (EC) No.1891/2006 (OJ L 386/14, 29.12.2006).

Article 109

Committee

B1–116   1. The Commission shall be assisted by a Committee.

2. Where reference is made to this paragraph, Articles 5 and 7 of Decision 1999/468/EC shall apply.

The period laid down in Article 5(6) of Decision 1999/468/EC shall be set at three months.

3. The Committee shall adopt its rules of procedure.

Article 110

Transitional provision

B1–117   1. Until such time as amendments to this Regulation enter into force on a proposal from the Commission on this subject, protection as a Community design shall not exist for a design which constitutes a component part of a complex product used within the meaning of Article 19(1) for the purpose of the repair of that complex product so as to restore its original appearance.

2. The proposal from the Commission referred to in paragraph 1 shall be submitted together with, and take into consideration, any changes which the Commission shall propose on the same subject pursuant to Article 18 of Directive 98/71/EC.

Provisions relating to the enlargement of the Community

B1–118   1. As from the date of accession of the Czech Republic, Estonia, Cyprus, Latvia, Lithuania, Hungary, Malta, Poland, Slovenia and Slovakia (hereinafter referred to as "new Member State(s)"), a Community design protected or applied for pursuant to this Regulation before the date of accession shall be extended to the territory of those Member States in order to have equal effect throughout the Community.

2. The application for a registered Community design may not be refused on the basis of any of the grounds for non-registrability listed in Article 47(1), if these grounds became applicable merely because of the accession of a new Member State.

3. A Community design as referred to in paragraph 1 may not be declared invalid pursuant to Article 25(1) if the grounds for invalidity became applicable merely because of the accession of a new Member State.

4. The applicant or the holder of an earlier right in a new Member State may oppose the use of a Community design falling under Article 25(1)(d), (e) or (f) within the territory where the earlier right is protected. For the purpose of this provision, "earlier right" means a right acquired or applied for in good faith before accession.

5. Paragraphs 1, 3 and 4 above shall also apply to unregistered Community designs. Pursuant to Article 11, a design which has not been made public within the territory of the Community shall not enjoy protection as an unregistered Community design.[10]

---

[10] Inserted by the Annex II of the Act of Accession—4. Company law—C. Industrial property rights—III. Community design. (OJ L236, 23/09/2003, p.344.)

Article 111

Entry into force

1. This Regulation shall enter into force on the 60th day following its **B1–119**
publication in the *Official Journal of the European Communities*.

2. Applications for registered Community designs may be filed at the Office
from the date fixed by the Administrative Board on the recommendation of the
President of the Office.

3. Applications for registered Community designs filed within three months
before the date referred to in paragraph 2 shall be deemed to have been filed on
that date.

This Regulation shall be binding in its entirety and directly applicable in all
Member States.

Done at Brussels, 12 December 2001.

For the Council
The President
M. AELVOET

B2. Commission Regulation (EC) No 2245/2002 of 21 October 2002 implementing Council Regulation (EC) No 6/2002 on Community Designs

THE COMMISSION OF THE EUROPEAN COMMUNITIES

Having regard to the Treaty establishing the European Community, **B2–001**
Having regard to Council Regulation (EC) No.6/2002 of 12 December 2001 on
Community designs,[11] and in particular Article 107(3) thereof,
Whereas:

(1) Regulation (EC) No.6/2002 creates a system enabling a design having effect
throughout the Community to be obtained on the basis of an application to the
Office for Harmonisation in the Internal Market (trade marks and designs)
(hereinafter "the Office").

(2) For this purpose, Regulation (EC) No.6/2002 contains the necessary
provisions for a procedure leading to the registration of a Community design, as
well as for the administration of registered Community designs, for appeals
against decisions of the Office and for proceedings for the invalidation of a
Community design.

(3) The present Regulation lays down the necessary measures for implementing
the provisions of Regulation (EC) No.6/2002.

(4) This Regulation should ensure the smooth and efficient operation of design
proceedings before the Office.

(5) The measures provided for in this Regulation are in accordance with the
opinion of the Committee established under Article 109 of Regulation (EC)
No.6/2002,

---

[11] OJ L 3, 5.1.2002, p.1.

597

HAS ADOPTED THIS REGULATION

CHAPTER 1

APPLICATION PROCEDURE

Article 1

Content of the application

B2–002   1. The application for a registered Community design shall contain:

(a) a request for registration of the design as a registered Community design;

(b) the name, address and nationality of the applicant and the State in which the applicant is domiciled or in which it has its seat or establishment. Names of natural persons shall take the form of the family name and the given name(s). Names of legal entities shall be indicated by their official designation, which may be abbreviated in a customary manner, furthermore, the State whose law governs such entities shall be indicated.
    The telephone numbers as well as fax numbers and details of other data-communications links, such as electronic mail, may be given. Only one address shall, in principle, be indicated for each applicant; where several addresses are indicated, only the address mentioned first shall be taken into account, except where the applicant designates one of the addresses as an address for service. If the Office has given the applicant an identification number, it shall be sufficient to mention that number together with the name of the applicant;

(c) a representation of the design in accordance with Article 4 of this Regulation or, if the application concerns a two-dimensional design and contains a request for deferment of publication in accordance with Article 50 of Regulation (EC) No.6/2002, a specimen in accordance with Article 5 of this Regulation;

(d) an indication, in accordance with Article 3(3), of the products in which the design is intended to be incorporated or to which it is intended to be applied;

(e) if the applicant has appointed a representative, the name of that representative and the address of his/her place of business in accordance with point (b); if the representative has more than one business address or if there are two or more representatives with different business addresses, the application shall indicate which address shall be used as an address for service: where no such indication is made, only the first-mentioned address shall be taken into account as an address for service. If there is more than one applicant, the application may indicate the appointment of one applicant or representative as common representative. If an appointed representative has been given an identification number by the Office, it shall be sufficient to mention that number together with the name of the representative;

(f) if applicable, a declaration that priority of a previous application is claimed pursuant to Article 42 of Regulation (EC) No.6/2002, stating the date on which the previous application was filed and the country in which or for which it was filed;

(g) if applicable, a declaration that exhibition priority is claimed pursuant to Article 44 of Regulation (EC) No.6/2002, stating the name of the exhibition and the date of the first disclosure of the products in which the design is incorporated or to which it is applied;

(h) a specification of the language in which the application is filed, and of the second language pursuant to Article 98(2) of Regulation (EC) No.6/2002;

(i) the signature of the applicant or his/her representative in accordance with Article 65.

2. The application may contain:

(a) a single description per design not exceeding 100 words explaining the representation of the design or the specimen; the description must relate only to those features which appear in the reproductions of the design or the specimen; it shall not contain statements as to the purported novelty or individual character of the design or its technical value;

(b) a request for deferment of publication of registration in accordance with Article 50(1) of Regulation (EC) No.6/2002;

(c) an indication of the 'Locarno classification' of the products contained in the application, that is to say, of the class or classes and the subclass or subclasses to which they belong in accordance with the Annex to the Agreement establishing an international classification for industrial designs, signed at Locarno on 8 October 1968 (hereinafter 'the Locarno Agreement'), referred to in Article 3 and subject to Article 2(2);

(d) the citation of the designer or of the team of designers or a statement signed by the applicant to the effect that the designer or team of designers has waived the right to be cited under Article 36(3)(e) of Regulation (EC) No.6/2002.

Article 2

Multiple application

1. An application may be a multiple application requesting the registration of several designs.   **B2–003**

2. When several designs other than ornamentation are combined in a multiple application, the application shall be divided if the products in which the designs are intended to be incorporated or to which they are intended to be applied belong to more than one class of the Locarno Classification.

3. For each design contained in the multiple application the application shall provide a representation of the design in accordance with Article 4 and the indication of the product in which the design is intended to be incorporated or to be applied.

4. The applicant shall number the designs contained in the multiple application consecutively, using arabic numerals.

Article 3

Classification and indication of products

1. Products shall be classified in accordance with Article 1 of the Locarno   **B2–004**
Agreement, as amended and in force at the date of filing of the design.

2. The classification of products shall serve exclusively administrative purposes.

3. The indication of products shall be worded in such a way as to indicate clearly the nature of the products and to enable each product to be classified in only one class of the Locarno classification, preferably using the terms appearing in the list of products set out therein.

4. The products shall be grouped according to the classes of the Locarno classification, each group being preceded by the number of the class to which that group of products belongs and presented in the order of the classes and subclasses under that classification.

Article 4

Representation of the design

B2–005   1. The representation of the design shall consist in a graphic or photographic reproduction of the design, either in black and white or in colour. It shall meet the following requirements:

- (a) save where the application is filed by electronic means pursuant to Article 67, the representation must be filed on separate sheets of paper or reproduced on the page provided for that purpose in the form made available by the Office pursuant to Article 68:
- (b) in the case of separate sheets of paper, the design shall be reproduced on opaque white paper and either pasted or printed directly on it. Only one copy shall be filed and the sheets of paper shall not be folded or stapled;
- (c) the size of the separate sheet shall be DIN A4 size (29,7 cm × 21 cm) and the space used for the reproduction shall be no larger than 26,2 cm × 17 cm. A margin of at least 2,5 cm shall be left on the left-hand side; at the top of each sheet of paper the number of views shall be indicated pursuant to paragraph 2 and, in the case of a multiple application, the consecutive number of the design; no explanatory text, wording or symbols, other than the indication 'top' or the name or address of the applicant, may be displayed thereon;
- (d) where the application is filed by electronic means, the graphic or photographic reproduction of the designs shall be in a data format determined by the President of the Office; the manner of identifying the different designs contained in a multiple application, or the different views, shall be determined by the President of the Office;
- (e) the design shall be reproduced on a neutral background and shall not be retouched with ink or correcting fluid. It shall be of a quality permitting all the details of the matter for which protection is sought to be clearly distinguished and permitting it to be reduced or enlarged to a size no greater than 8 cm by 16 cm per view for entry in the Register of Community Designs provided for in Article 72 of Regulation (EC) No.6/2002, hereinafter 'the Register', and for direct publishing in the *Community Designs Bulletin* referred to in Article 73 of that Regulation.

2. The representation may contain no more than seven different views of the design. Any one graphic or photographic reproduction may contain only one view. The applicant shall number each view using arabic numerals. The number shall consist of separate numerals separated by a point, the numeral to the left of the point indicating the number of the design, that to the right indicating the number of the view.

In cases where more than seven views are provided, the Office may disregard for registration and publication any of the extra views. The Office shall take the views in the consecutive order in which the views are numbered by the applicant.

3. Where an application concerns a design that consists in a repeating surface pattern, the representation of the design shall show the complete pattern and a sufficient portion of the repeating surface.

The size limits set out in paragraph 1(c) shall apply.

4. Where an application concerns a design consisting in a typographic typeface, the representation of the design shall consist in a string of all the letters of the alphabet, in both upper and lower case, and of all the arabic numerals, together with a text of five lines produced using that typeface, both letters and numerals being in the size pitch 16.

Article 5

Specimens

1. Where the application concerns a two-dimensional design and contains a request for a deferment of publication, in accordance with Article 50(1) of Regulation (EC) No.6/2002, the representation of the design may be replaced by a specimen pasted on a sheet of paper.   **B2–006**

Applications for which a specimen is submitted must be sent by a single mail or directly delivered to the office of filing.

Both the application and the specimen shall be submitted at the same time.

2. The specimens shall not exceed 26,2 cm × 17 cm in size, 50 grams in weight or 3 mm in thickness. The specimen shall be capable of being stored, unfolded, alongside documents of the size prescribed in Article 4(1)(c).

3. Specimens that are perishable or dangerous to store shall not be filed.

The specimen shall be filed in five copies; in the case of a multiple application, five copies of the specimen shall be filed for each design.

4. Where the design concerns a repeating surface pattern, the specimen shall show the complete pattern and a sufficient portion of the repeating surface in length and width. The limits set out in paragraph 2 shall apply.

Article 6

Fees for the application

1. The following fees shall be paid at the time when the application is submitted to the Office: **B2–007**

(a) the registration fee;
(b) the publication fee or a deferment fee if deferment of publication has been requested;
(c) an additional registration fee in respect of each additional design included in a multiple application;
(d) an additional publication fee in respect of each additional design included in a multiple application, or an additional deferment fee in respect of each additional design included in a multiple application if deferment of publication has been requested.

2. Where the application includes a request for deferment of publication of registration, the publication fee and any additional publication fee in respect of each additional design included in a multiple application shall be paid within the time limits specified in Article 15(4).

Article 7

Filing of the application

B2–008   1. The Office shall mark the documents making up the application with the date of its receipt and the file number of the application.

Each design contained in a multiple application shall be numbered by the Office in accordance with a system determined by the President.

The Office shall issue to the applicant without delay a receipt which shall specify the file number, the representation, description or other identification of the design, the nature and the number of the documents and the date of their receipt.

In the case of a multiple application, the receipt issued by the Office shall specify the first design and the number of designs filed.

2. If the application is filed with the central industrial property office of a Member State or at the Benelux Design Office in accordance with Article 35 of Regulation (EC) No.6/2002, the office of filing shall number each page of the application, using arabic numerals. The office of filing shall mark the documents making up the application with the date of receipt and the number of pages before forwarding the application to the Office.

The office of filing shall issue to the applicant without delay a receipt specifying the nature and the number of the documents and the date of their receipt.

3. If the Office receives an application forwarded by the central industrial property office of a Member State or the Benelux Design Office, it shall mark the application with the date of receipt and the file number and shall issue to the applicant without delay a receipt in accordance with the third and fourth subparagraphs of paragraph 1, indicating the date of receipt at the Office.

Article 8

Claiming priority

B2–009   1. Where the priority of one or more previous applications is claimed in the application pursuant to Article 42 of Regulation (EC) No.6/2002, the applicant shall indicate the file number of the previous application and file a copy of it within three months of the filing date referred to in Article 38 of that Regulation. The President of the Office shall determine the evidence to be provided by the applicant.

2. Where, subsequent to the filing of the application, the applicant wishes to claim the priority of one or more previous applications pursuant to Article 42 of Regulation (EC) No.6/2002, he/she shall submit, within one month of the filing date, the declaration of priority, stating the date on which and the country in or for which the previous application was made.

The applicant shall submit to the Office the indications and evidence referred to in paragraph 1 within three months of receipt of the declaration of priority.

Article 9

Exhibition priority

1. Where exhibition priority has been claimed in the application pursuant to Article 44 of Regulation (EC) No.6/2002, the applicant shall, together with the application or at the latest within three months of the filing date, file a certificate issued at the exhibition by the authority responsible for the protection of industrial property at the exhibition.

B2–010

That certificate shall declare that the design was incorporated in or applied to the product and disclosed at the exhibition, and shall state the opening date of the exhibition and, where the first disclosure of the product did not coincide with the opening date of the exhibition, the date of such first disclosure. The certificate shall be accompanied by an identification of the actual disclosure of the product, duly certified by that authority.

2. Where the applicant wishes to claim an exhibition priority subsequent to the filing of the application, the declaration of priority, indicating the name of the exhibition and the date of the first disclosure of the product in which the design was incorporated or to which it was applied, shall be submitted within one month of the filing date. The indications and evidence referred to in paragraph 1 shall be submitted to the Office within three months of receipt of the declaration of priority.

Article 10

Examination of requirements for a filing date and of formal requirements

1. The Office shall notify the applicant that a date of filing cannot be granted if the application does not contain:

B2–011

    (a) a request for registration of the design as a registered Community design;

    (b) information identifying the applicant;

    (c) a representation of the design pursuant to Article 4(1)(d) and (e) or, where applicable, a specimen.

2. If the deficiencies indicated in paragraph 1 are remedied within two months of receipt of the notification, the date on which all the deficiencies are remedied shall determine the date of filing.

If the deficiencies are not remedied before the time limit expires, the application shall not be dealt with as a Community design application. Any fees paid shall be refunded.

3. The Office shall call upon the applicant to remedy the deficiencies noted within a time limit specified by it where, although a date of filing has been granted, the examination reveals that:

    (a) the requirements set out in Articles 1, 2, 4 and 5 or the other formal requirements for applications laid down in the Regulation (EC) No.6/2002 or in this Regulation have not been complied with;

    (b) the full amount of the fees payable pursuant to Article 6(1), read in conjunction with Commission Regulation (EC) No.2246/2002[12] has not been received by the Office;

---

[12] See page 54 of this Official Journal.

(c) where priority has been claimed pursuant to Articles 8 and 9, either in the application itself or within one month after the date of filing, the other requirements set out in those Articles have not been complied with;

(d) in the case of a multiple application, the products in which the designs are intended to be incorporated or to which they are intended to be applied belong to more than one class of the Locarno classification.

In particular, the Office shall call upon the applicant to pay the required fees within two months of the date of notification, together with the late payment fees provided for in Article 107(2)(a) to (d) of Regulation (EC) No.6/2002 and as set out in Regulation (EC) No.2246/2002.

In the case of the deficiency referred to in point (d) of the first subparagraph, the Office shall call upon the applicant to divide the multiple application in order to ensure compliance with the requirements under Article 2(2). It shall also call upon the applicant to pay the total amount of the fees for all the applications resulting from the separation of the multiple application, within such a time limit as it may specify.

After the applicant has complied with the request to divide the application within the time limit set, the date of filing of the resulting application or applications shall be the date of filing granted to the multiple application initially filed.

4. If the deficiencies referred to in paragraph 3(a) and (d) are not remedied before the time limit expires, the Office shall reject the application.

5. If the fees payable pursuant to Article 6(1)(a) and (b) are not paid before the time limit expires, the Office shall reject the application.

6. If any additional fees payable pursuant to Article 6(1)(c) or (d) in respect of multiple applications are not paid or not paid in full before the time limit expires, the Office shall reject the application in respect of all the additional designs which are not covered by the amount paid.

In the absence of any criteria for determining which designs are intended to be covered, the Office shall take the designs in the numerical order in which they are represented in accordance with Article 2(4). The Office shall reject the application in so far as it concerns designs for which additional fees have not been paid or have not been paid in full.

7. If the deficiencies referred to in paragraph 3(c) are not remedied before the time limit expires, the right of priority for the application shall be lost.

8. If any of the deficiencies referred to in paragraph 3 is not remedied before the time limit expires and such deficiency concerns only some of the designs contained in a multiple application, the Office shall reject the application, or the right of priority shall be lost, only in so far as those designs are concerned.

Article 11

Examination of grounds for non-registrability

B2–012   1. Where, pursuant to Article 47 of Regulation (EC) No.6/2002, the Office finds, in the course of carrying out the examination under Article 10 of this Regulation, that the design for which protection is sought does not correspond to the definition of design provided in Article 3(a) of Regulation (EC) No.6/2002 or that the design is contrary to public policy or to accepted principles of morality, it shall inform the applicant that the design is non-registrable, specifying the ground for non-registrability.

2. The Office shall specify a time limit within which the applicant may submit his/her observations, withdraw the application or amend it by submitting an

amended representation of the design, provided that the identity of the design is retained.

3. Where the applicant fails to overcome the grounds for non-registrability within the time limit, the Office shall refuse the application. If those grounds concern only some of the designs contained in a multiple application, the Office shall refuse the application only in so far as those designs are concerned.

Article 11a

Examination of grounds for refusal

1. Where, pursuant to Article 106e(1) of Regulation (EC) No 6/2002, the Office finds, in the course of carrying out an examination of an international registration, that the design for which protection is sought does not correspond to the definition of design provided for in Article 3(a) of that Regulation or that the design is contrary to public policy or to accepted principles of morality, it shall send to the International Bureau of the World Intellectual Property Organisation (hereinafter "the International Bureau") a notification of refusal not later than six months from the date of publication of the international registration, specifying the grounds for refusal pursuant to Article 12(2) of the Geneva Act of the Hague Agreement concerning the International Registration of Industrial Designs adopted on 2 July 1999 (hereinafter "the Geneva Act") approved by Council Decision 2006/954/EC[13].

B2–013

2. The Office shall specify a time limit within which the holder of the international registration has the possibility, pursuant to Article 106e(2) of Regulation (EC) No 6/2002, to renounce the international registration in respect of the Community, to limit the international registration to one or some of the industrial designs in respect of the Community or to submit observations.

3. Where the holder of the international registration is obliged to be represented in proceedings before the Office pursuant to Article 77(2) of Regulation (EC) No 6/2002, the notification shall contain a reference to the obligation of the holder to appoint a representative as referred to in Article 78(1) of that Regulation.

The time limit specified in paragraph 2 of this Article shall apply mutatis mutandis.

4. If the holder fails to appoint a representative within the specified time limit, the Office shall refuse the protection of the international registration.

5. Where the holder submits observations that would satisfy the Office within the specified time limit, the Office shall withdraw the refusal and notify the International Bureau in accordance with Article 12(4) of the Geneva act.

Where, pursuant to Article 12(2) of the Geneva act, the holder does not submits observations that would satisfy the Office within the specified time limit, the Office shall confirm the decision refusing protection for the international registration. That decision is subject to appeal in accordance with Title VII of Regulation (EC) No 6/2002.

6. Where the holder renounces the international registration or limits the international registration to one or some of the industrial designs in respect of the Community, he shall inform the International Bureau by way of recording

[13] OJ L 386, 29.12.2006, P 28.

procedure in accordance with Article 16(1)(iv) and (v) of the Geneva Act. The holder can inform the Office submitting a corresponding statement.[14]

Article 12

Withdrawal or correction of the application

B2–014
1. The applicant may at any time withdraw a Community design application or, in the case of a multiple application, withdraw some of the designs contained in the application.

2. Only the name and address of the applicant, errors of wording or of copying, or obvious mistakes may be corrected, at the request of the applicant and provided that such correction does not change the representation of the design.

3. An application for the correction of the application pursuant to paragraph 2 shall contain:

(a) the file number of the application;
(b) the name and the address of the applicant in accordance with Article 1(1)(b);
(c) where the applicant has appointed a representative, the name and the business address of the representative in accordance with Article 1(1)(e);
(d) the indication of the element of the application to be corrected and that element in its corrected version.

4. If the requirements for the correction of the application are not fulfilled, the Office shall communicate the deficiency to the applicant. If the deficiency is not remedied within the time limits specified by the Office, the Office shall reject the application for correction.

5. A single application may be made for the correction of the same element in two or more applications submitted by the same applicant.

6. Paragraphs 2 to 5 shall apply *mutatis mutandis* to applications to correct the name or the business address of a representative appointed by the applicant.

CHAPTER II

REGISTRATION PROCEDURE

Article 13

Registration of the design

B2–015
1. If the application satisfies the requirements referred to in Article 48 of Regulation (EC) No.6/2002, the design contained in that application and the particulars set out in Article 69(2) of this Regulation shall be recorded in the Register.

2. If the application contains a request for deferment of publication pursuant to Article 50 of Regulation (EC) No.6/2002, that fact and the date of expiry of the period of deferment shall be recorded.

[14] Inserted by the Regulation (EC) No.876/2007 (OJ L 193, 25/07/2007, p.13).

3. The fees payable pursuant to Article 6(1) shall not be refunded even if the design applied for is not registered.

Article 14

Publication of the registration

1. The registration of the design shall be published in the *Community Designs* **B2–016**
Bulletin.

2. Subject to paragraph 3, the publication of the registration shall contain:

(a) the name and address of the holder of the Community design (hereinafter "the holder");

(b) where applicable, the name and business address of the representative appointed by the holder other than a representative falling within the first subparagraph of Article 77(3) of Regulation (EC) No.6/2002; if more than one representative has the same business address, only the name and business address of the first-named representative shall be published, the name being followed by the words 'et al'; if there are two or more representatives with different business addresses, only the address for service determined pursuant to Article 1(1)(e) of this Regulation shall be published; where an association of representatives is appointed pursuant to Article 62(9) only the name and business address of the association shall be published;

(c) the representation of the design pursuant to Article 4; where the representation of the design is in colour, the publication shall be in colour;

(d) where applicable, an indication that a description has been filed pursuant to Article 1(2)(a);

(e) an indication of the products in which the design is intended to be incorporated or to which it is intended to be applied, preceded by the number of the relevant classes and subclasses of the Locarno classification, and grouped accordingly;

(f) where applicable, the name of the designer or the team of designers;

(g) the date of filing and the file number and, in the case of a multiple application, the file number of each design;

(h) where applicable, particulars of the claim of priority pursuant to Article 42 of Regulation (EC) No.6/2002;

(i) where applicable, particulars of the claim of exhibition priority pursuant to Article 44 of Regulation (EC) No.6/2002;

(j) the date and the registration number and the date of the publication of the registration;

(k) the language in which the application was filed and the second language indicated by the applicant pursuant to Article 98(2) of Regulation (EC) No.6/2002.

3. If the application contains a request for deferment of publication pursuant to Article 50 of Regulation (EC) No.6/2002, a mention of the deferment shall be published in the *Community Designs Bulletin*, together with the name of the holder, the name of the representative, if any, the date of filing and registration, and the file number of the application. Neither the representation of the design nor any particulars identifying its appearance shall be published.

Article 15

Deferment of publication

B2–017   1. Where the application contains a request for deferment of publication pursuant to Article 50 of Regulation (EC) No.6/2002, the holder shall, together with the request or at the latest three months before the 30-month deferment period expires:

   (a) pay the publication fee referred to in Article 6(1)(b);
   (b) in the case of a multiple registration, pay the additional publication fees, referred to in Article 6(1)(d);
   (c) in cases where a representation of the design has been replaced by a specimen in accordance with Article 5, file a representation of the design in accordance with Article 4. This applies to all the designs contained in a multiple application for which publication is requested;
   (d) in the case of a multiple registration, clearly indicate which of the designs contained therein is to be published or which of the designs are to be surrendered, or, if the period of deferment has not yet expired, for which designs deferment is to be continued.

Where the holder requests publication before the expiry of the 30-month deferment period, he/she shall, at the latest three months before the requested date of publication, comply with the requirements set out in points (a) to (d) of the first paragraph.

2. If the holder fails to comply with the requirements set out in paragraph 1(c) or (d), the Office shall call upon him/her to remedy the deficiencies within a specified time limit which shall in no case expire after the 30-month deferment period.

3. If the holder fails to remedy the deficiencies referred to in paragraph 2 within the applicable time limit:

   (a) the registered Community design shall be deemed from the outset not to have had the effects specified in Regulation (EC) No.6/2002;
   (b) where the holder has requested earlier publication as provided for under the second subparagraph of paragraph 1, the request shall be deemed not to have been filed.

4. If the holder fails to pay the fees referred to in paragraph 1(a) or (b), the Office shall call upon him/her to pay those fees together with the fees for late payment provided for in Article 107(2)(b) or (d) of Regulation (EC) No.6/2002 and as set out in Regulation (EC) No.2246/2002, within a specified time limit which shall in no case expire after the 30-month deferment period.

If no payment has been made within that time limit, the Office shall notify the holder that the registered Community design has from the outset not had the effects specified in Regulation (EC) No.6/2002.

If, in respect of a multiple registration, a payment is made within that time limit but is insufficient to cover all the fees payable pursuant to paragraph 1(a) and (b), as well as the applicable fee for late payment, all the designs in respect of which the fees have not been paid shall be deemed from the outset not to have had the effects specified in Regulation (EC) No.6/2002.

Unless it is clear which designs the amount paid is intended to cover, and in the absence of other criteria for determining which designs are intended to be covered, the Office shall take the designs in the numerical order in which they are represented in accordance with Article 2(4).

All designs for which the additional publication fee has not been paid or has not been paid in full, together with the applicable fee for late payment, shall be deemed from the outset not to have had the effects specified in Regulation (EC) No.6/2002.

Article 16

Publication after the period for deferment

1. Where the holder has complied with the requirements laid down in Article 15, the Office shall, at the expiry of the period for deferment or in the case of a request for earlier publication, as soon as is technically possible: **B2–018**

   (a) publish the registered Community design in the *Community Designs Bulletin*, with the indications set out in Article 14(2), together with an indication of the fact that the application contained a request for deferment of publication pursuant to Article 50 of Regulation (EC) No.6/2002 and, where applicable, that a specimen was filed in accordance with Article 5 of this Regulation;

   (b) make available for public inspection any file relating to the design;

   (c) open to public inspection all the entries in the Register, including any entries withheld from inspection pursuant to Article 73.

2. Where Article 15(4) applies, the actions referred to in paragraph 1 of this Article shall not take place in respect of those designs contained in the multiple registration which are deemed from the outset not to have had the effects specified in Regulation (EC) No.6/2002.

Article 17

Certificate of registration

1. After publication, the Office shall issue to the holder a certificate of registration which shall contain the entries in the Register provided for in Article 69(2) and a statement to the effect that those entries have been recorded in the Register.   **B2–019**

2. The holder may request that certified or uncertified copies of the certificate of registration be supplied to him/her upon payment of a fee.

Article 18

Maintenance of the design in an amended form

1. Where, pursuant to Article 25(6) of Regulation (EC) No.6/2002, the registered Community design is maintained in an amended form, the Community design in its amended form shall be entered in the Register and published in the *Community Designs Bulletin*.   **B2–020**

2. Maintenance of a design in an amended form may include a partial disclaimer, not exceeding 100 words, by the holder or an entry in the Register of

Community Designs of a court decision or a decision by the Office declaring the partial invalidity of the design right.

Article 19

Change of the name or address of the holder or of his/her registered representative

B2–021   1. A change of the name or address of the holder which is not the consequence of a transfer of the registered design shall, at the request of the holder, be recorded in the Register.

2. An application for a change of the name or address of the holder shall contain:

    (a) the registration number of the design;

    (b) the name and the address of the holder as recorded in the Register. If the holder has been given an identification number by the Office, it shall be sufficient to indicate that number together with the name of the holder;

    (c) the indication of the name and address of the holder, as changed, in accordance with Article 1(1)(b);

    (d) where the holder has appointed a representative, the name and business address of the representative, in accordance with Article 1(1)(e).

3. The application referred to in paragraph 2 shall not be subject to payment of a fee.

4. A single application may be made for a change of the name or address in respect of two or more registrations of the same holder.

5. If the requirements set out in paragraphs 1 and 2 are not fulfilled, the Office shall communicate the deficiency to the applicant.

If the deficiency is not remedied within the time limits specified by the Office, the Office shall reject the application.

6. Paragraphs 1 to 5 shall apply *mutatis mutandis* to a change of the name or address of the registered representative.

7. Paragraphs 1 to 6 shall apply *mutatis mutandis* to applications for Community designs. The change shall be recorded in the files kept by the Office concerning the Community design application.

Article 20

Correction of mistakes and errors in the Register and in the publication of the registration

B2–022   Where the registration of a design or the publication of the registration contains a mistake or error attributable to the Office, the Office shall correct the error or mistake of its own motion or at the request of the holder.

Where such a request is made by the holder, Article 19 shall apply *mutatis mutandis*. The request shall not be subject to payment of a fee.

The Office shall publish the corrections made pursuant to this Article.

CHAPTER III

RENEWAL OF REGISTRATION

Article 21

Notification of expiry of registration

At least six months before expiry of the registration, the Office shall inform the **B2–023** holder, and any person having a right entered in the Register, including a licence, in respect of the Community design, that the registration is approaching expiry. Failure to give notification shall not affect the expiry of the registration.

Article 22

Renewal of Community design registration

1. An application for renewal of registration shall contain: **B2–024**

    (a) the name of the person requesting renewal;
    (b) the registration number;
    (c) where applicable, an indication that renewal is requested for all the designs covered by a multiple registration or, if the renewal is not requested for all such designs, an indication of those designs for which renewal is requested.

2. The fees payable pursuant to Article 13 of Regulation (EC) No 6/2002 for the renewal of a registration shall consist of:

    (a) renewal fee, which, in cases where several designs are covered by a multiple registration, shall be proportionate to the number of designs covered by the renewal;
    (b) here applicable, the additional fee for late payment of the renewal fee or late submission of the request for renewal, pursuant to Article 13 of Regulation (EC) No 6/2002, as specified in Regulation (EC) No 2246/2002.

3. If the payment referred to in paragraph 2 of this Article is made according to the provisions of Article 5(1) of the Regulation (EC) No 2246/2002, this shall be deemed to constitute a request for renewal provided that it contains all the indications required under points (a) and (b) of paragraph 1, of this Article and Article 6(1) of that Regulation.

4. Where the application for renewal is filed within the time limits provided for in Article 13(3) of Regulation (EC) No 6/2002, but the other conditions for renewal provided for in Article 13 thereof and in this Regulation are not satisfied, the Office shall inform the applicant of the deficiencies.

5. Where an application for renewal is not submitted or is submitted after expiry of the time limit provided for in the second sentence of Article 13(3) of Regulation (EC) No 6/2002, or if the fees are not paid or are paid only after expiry of the relevant time limit, or if the deficiencies are not remedied within the time limit specified by the Office, the Office shall determine that the registration has expired and shall notify the holder accordingly.

In the case of a multiple registration, where the fees paid are insufficient to cover all the designs for which renewal is requested, such a determination shall be made only after the Office has established which designs the amount paid is intended to cover.

In the absence of other criteria for determining which designs are intended to be covered, the Office shall take the designs in the numerical order in which they are represented in accordance with Article 2(4).

The Office shall determine that the registration has expired with regard to all designs for which the renewal fees have not been paid or have not been paid in full.

6. Where the determination made pursuant to paragraph 5 has become final, the Office shall cancel the design from the Register with effect from the day following the day on which the existing registration expired.

7. Where the renewal fees provided for in paragraph 2 have been paid but the registration is not renewed, those fees shall be refunded.

8. A single application for renewal may be submitted for two or more designs, whether or not part of the same multiple registration, upon payment of the required fees for each of the designs, provided that the holders or the representatives are the same in each case.[15]

Article 22a

Renewals of international registration designating the Community

B2–025   The international registration shall be renewed directly at the International Bureau in compliance with Article 17 of the Geneva Act.[16]

CHAPTER IV

TRANSFER, LICENCES AND OTHER RIGHTS, CHANGES

Article 23

Transfer

B2–026   1. An application for registration of a transfer pursuant to Article 28 of Regulation (EC) No.6/2002 shall contain:

    (a) the registration number of the Community design;
    (b) particulars of the new holder in accordance with Article 1(1)(b);
    (c) where not all of the designs covered by a multiple registration are included in the transfer, particulars of the registered designs to which the transfer relates;
    (d) documents duly establishing the transfer.

2. The application may contain, where applicable, the name and business address of the representative of the new holder, to be set out in accordance with Article 1(1)(e).

3. The application shall not be deemed to have been filed until the required fee has been paid. If the fee is not paid or is not paid in full, the Office shall notify the applicant accordingly.

---

[15] Substituted by Regulation (EC) No.876/2007 (OJ L 193, 25/07/2007, p.13).
[16] Inserted by the Regulation (EC) No.876/2007 (OJ L 193, 25/07/2007, p.13).

4. The following shall constitute sufficient proof of transfer under paragraph 1(d):

(a) the application for registration of the transfer is signed by the registered holder or his/her representative and by the successor in title or his/her representative; or

(b) the application, if submitted by the successor in title, is accompanied by a declaration, signed by the registered holder or his/her representative, that he/she agrees to the registration of the successor in title; or

(c) the application is accompanied by a completed transfer form or document, signed by the registered holder or his/her representative and by the successor in title or his/her representative.

5. Where the conditions applicable to the registration of a transfer are not fulfilled, the Office shall notify the applicant of the deficiencies.

If the deficiencies are not remedied within the time limit specified by the Office, it shall reject the application for registration of the transfer.

6. A single application for registration of a transfer may be submitted for two or more registered Community designs, provided that the registered holder and the successor in title are the same in each case.

7. Paragraphs 1 to 6 shall apply *mutatis mutandis* to the transfer of applications for registered Community designs. The transfer shall be recorded in the files kept by the Office concerning the Community design application.

Article 24

Registration of licences and other rights

1. Article 23(1)(a), (b) and (c) and Article 23(2), (3), (5) and (6) shall apply *mutatis mutandis* to the registration of the grant or transfer of a licence, to registration of the creation or transfer of a right *in rem* in respect of a registered Community design, and to registration of enforcement measures. However, where a registered Community design is involved in insolvency proceedings, the request of the competent national authority for an entry in the Register to this effect shall not be subject to payment of a fee.

B2–027

In the case of a multiple registration, each registered Community design may, separately from the others, be licensed, the subject of a right *in rem*, levy of execution or insolvency proceedings.

2. Where the registered Community design is licensed for only a part of the Community, or for a limited period of time, the application for registration of the licence shall indicate the part of the Community or the period of time for which the licence is granted.

3. Where the conditions applicable to registration of licences and other rights, set out in Articles 29, 30 or 32 of Regulation (EC) No.6/2002, in paragraph 1 of this Article, and in the other applicable Articles of this Regulation are not fulfilled, the Office shall notify the applicant of the deficiencies.

If the deficiencies are not remedied within a time limit specified by the Office, it shall reject the application for registration.

4. Paragraphs 1, 2 and 3 shall apply *mutatis mutandis* to licences and other rights concerning applications for registered Community designs. Licences, rights *in rem* and enforcement measures shall be recorded in the files kept by the Office concerning the Community design application.

5. The request for a non-exclusive licence pursuant to Article 16(2) of Regulation (EC) No.6/2002 shall be made within three months of the date of the entry in the Register of the newly entitled holder.

Article 25

Special provisions for the registration of a licence

B2–028   1. A licence in respect of a registered Community design shall be recorded in the Register as an exclusive licence if the holder of the design or the licensee so requests.

2. A licence in respect of a registered Community design shall be recorded in the Register as a sub-licence where it is granted by a licensee whose licence is recorded in the Register.

3. A licence in respect of a registered Community design shall be recorded in the Register as a territorially limited licence if it is granted for a part of the Community.

4. A licence in respect of a registered Community design shall be recorded in the Register as a temporary licence if it is granted for a limited period of time.

Article 26

Cancellation or modification of the registration of licences and other rights

B2–029   1. A registration effected under Article 24 shall be cancelled upon application by one of the persons concerned.

2. The application shall contain:

    (a) the registration number of the registered Community design, or in the case of a multiple registration, the number of each design; and

    (b) particulars of the right whose registration is to be cancelled.

3. Application for cancellation of the registration of a licence or other right shall not be deemed to have been filed until the required fee has been paid.

If the fee is not paid or is not paid in full, the Office shall notify the applicant accordingly. A request from a competent national authority for cancellation of an entry where a registered Community design is involved in insolvency proceedings shall not be subject to payment of a fee.

4. The application shall be accompanied by documents showing that the registered right no longer exists or by a statement by the licensee or the holder of another right to the effect that he/she consents to cancellation of the registration.

5. Where the requirements for cancellation of the registration are not satisfied, the Office shall notify the applicant of the deficiencies. If the deficiencies are not remedied within the time limit specified by the Office, it shall reject the application for cancellation of the registration.

6. Paragraphs 1, 2, 4 and 5 shall apply *mutatis mutandis* to a request for modification of a registration effected pursuant to Article 24.

7. Paragraphs 1 to 6 shall apply *mutatis mutandis* to entries made in the files pursuant to Article 24(4).

CHAPTER V

SURRENDER AND INVALIDITY

Article 27

Surrender

1. A declaration of surrender pursuant to Article 51 of Regulation (EC) **B2–030**
No.6/2002 shall contain:

   (a) the registration number of the registered Community design:
   (b) the name and address of the holder in accordance with Article 1(1)(b);
   (c) where a representative has been appointed, the name and business
        address of the representative in accordance with Article 1(1)(e);
   (d) where surrender is declared only for some of the designs contained in a
        multiple registration, an indication of the designs for which the sur-
        render is declared or the designs which are to remain registered;
   (e) where, pursuant to Article 51(3) of Regulation (EC) No.6/2002, the
        registered Community design is partially surrendered, a representation
        of the amended design in accordance with Article 4 of this Regulation.

2. Where a right of a third party relating to the registered Community design is
entered in the Register, it shall be sufficient proof of his/her agreement to the
surrender that a declaration of consent to the surrender is signed by the holder of
that right or his/her representative.

Where a licence has been registered, surrender of the design shall be registered
three months after the date on which the holder satisfies the Office that he/she
has informed the licensee of his/her intention to surrender it. If the holder proves
to the Office before the expiry of that period that the licensee has given his/her
consent, the surrender shall be registered forthwith.

3. Where a claim relating to the entitlement to a registered Community design
has been brought before a court pursuant to Article 15 of Regulation (EC)
No.6/2002, a declaration of consent to the surrender, signed by the claimant or
his/her representative, shall be sufficient proof of his/her agreement to the
surrender.

4. If the requirements governing surrender are not fulfilled, the Office shall
communicate the deficiencies to the declarant. If the deficiencies are not remedied
within the time limit specified by the Office, the Office shall reject the entry of the
surrender in the Register.

Article 28

Application for a declaration of invalidity

1. An application to the Office for a declaration of invalidity pursuant to Article   **B2–031**
52 of Regulation (EC) No.6/2002 shall contain:

   (a) as concerns the registered Community design for which the declaration
        of invalidity is sought:
        (i) its registration number;
        (ii) the name and address of its holder;
   (b) as regards the grounds on which the application is based:

(i) a statement of the grounds on which the application for a declaration of invalidity is based;

(ii) additionally, in the case of an application pursuant to Article 25(1)(d) of Regulation (EC) No.6/2002, the representation and particulars identifying the prior design on which the application for a declaration of invalidity is based and showing that the applicant is entitled to invoke the earlier design as a ground for invalidity pursuant to Article 25(3) of that Regulation;

(iii) additionally, in the case of an application pursuant to Article 25(1)(e) or (f) of Regulation (EC) No.6/2002, the representation and particulars identifying the distinctive sign or the work protected by copyright on which the application for a declaration of invalidity is based and particulars showing that the applicant is the holder of the earlier right pursuant to Article 25(3) of that Regulation;

(iv) additionally, in the case of an application pursuant to Article 25(1)(g) of the Regulation (EC) No.6/2002, the representation and particulars of the relevant item as referred to in that Article and particulars showing that the application is filed by the person or entity concerned by the improper use pursuant to Article 25(4) of that Regulation;

(v) where the ground for invalidity is that the registered Community design does not fulfil the requirements set out in Article 5 or 6 of Regulation (EC) No.6/2002, the indication and the reproduction of the prior designs that could form an obstacle to the novelty or individual character of the registered Community design, as well as documents proving the existence of those earlier designs;

(vi) an indication of the facts, evidence and arguments submitted in support of those grounds;

(c) as concerns the applicant:

(i) his/her name and address in accordance with Article 1(1)(b);

(ii) if the applicant has appointed a representative, the name and the business address of the representative, in accordance with Article 1(1)(e);

(iii) additionally, in the case of an application pursuant to Article 25(1)(c) of Regulation (EC) No.6/2002, particulars showing that the application is made by a person or by persons duly entitled pursuant to Article 25(2) of that Regulation.

2. The application shall be subject to the fee referred to in Article 52(2) of Regulation (EC) No.6/2002.

3. The Office shall inform the holder that an application for declaration of invalidity has been filed.

Article 29

Languages used in invalidity proceedings

B2–032   1. The application for a declaration of invalidity shall be filed in the language of proceedings pursuant to Article 98(4) of Regulation (EC) No.6/2002.

2. Where the language of proceedings is not the language used for filing the application and the holder has filed his/her observations in the language of filing, the Office shall arrange to have those observations translated into the language of proceedings.

3. Three years after the date fixed in accordance with Article 111(2) of Regulation (EC) No.6/2002, the Commission will submit to the Committee

mentioned in Article 109 of Regulation (EC) No.6/2002 a report on the application of paragraph 2 of this Article and, if appropriate, proposals for fixing a limit for the expenses borne by the Office in this respect as provided for in the fourth subparagraph of Article 98(4) of Regulation (EC) No.6/2002.

4. The Commission may decide to submit the report and possible proposals referred to in paragraph 3 at an earlier date, and the Committee shall discuss them as a matter of priority if the facilities in paragraph 2 lead to disproportionate expenditure.

5. Where the evidence in support of the application is not filed in the language of the invalidity proceedings, the applicant shall file a translation of that evidence into that language within two months of the filing of such evidence.

6. Where the applicant for a declaration of invalidity or the holder informs the Office, within two months of receipt by the holder of the communication referred to in Article 31(1) of this Regulation, that they have agreed on a different language of proceedings pursuant to Article 98(5) of Regulation (EC) No.6/2002, the applicant shall, where the application was not filed in that language, file a translation of the application in that language within one month of the said date.

Article 30

Rejection of the application for declaration of invalidity as inadmissible

1. If the Office finds that the application for declaration of invalidity does not **B2–033** comply with Article 52 of Regulation (EC) No.6/2002, Article 28(1) of this Regulation or any other provision of Regulation (EC) No.6/2002 or this Regulation, it shall inform the applicant accordingly and shall call upon him/her to remedy the deficiencies within such time limit as it may specify.

If the deficiencies are not remedied within the specified time limit, the Office shall reject the application as inadmissible.

2. Where the Office finds that the required fees have not been paid, it shall inform the applicant accordingly and shall inform him/her that the application will be deemed not to have been filed if the required fees are not paid within a specified time limit.

If the required fees are paid after the expiry of the time limit specified, they shall be refunded to the applicant.

3. Any decision to reject an application for a declaration of invalidity pursuant to paragraph 1 shall be communicated to the applicant.

Where, pursuant to paragraph 2, an application is deemed not to have been filed, the applicant shall be informed accordingly.

Article 31

Examination of the application for a declaration of invalidity

1. If the Office does not reject the application for declaration of invalidity in **B2–034** accordance with Article 30, it shall communicate such application to the holder and shall request him/her to file his/her observations within such time limits as it may specify.

2. If the holder files no observations, the Office may base its decision concerning invalidity on the evidence before it.

3. Any observations filed by the holder shall be communicated to the applicant, who may be called upon by the Office to reply within specified time limits.

4. All communications pursuant to Article 53(2) of Regulation (EC) No.6/2002 and all observations filed in that respect shall be sent to the parties concerned.

5. The Office may call upon the parties to make a friendly settlement.

6. Where the Office declares invalid the effects of an international registration in the territory of the Community; it shall notify its decision to the International Bureau upon becoming final.[17]

Article 32

Multiple applications for a declaration of invalidity

B2–035   1. Where a number of applications for a declaration of invalidity have been filed relating to the same registered Community design, the Office may deal with them in one set of proceedings.

The Office may subsequently decide no longer to deal with them in that way.

2. If a preliminary examination of one or more applications reveals that the registered Community design may be invalid, the Office may suspend the other invalidity proceedings.

The Office shall inform the remaining applicants of any relevant decisions taken during such proceedings as are continued.

3. Once a decision declaring the invalidity of the design has become final, the applications in respect of which the proceedings have been suspended in accordance with paragraph 2 shall be deemed to have been disposed of and the applicants concerned shall be informed accordingly. Such disposition shall be considered to constitute a case which has not proceeded to judgment for the purposes of Article 70(4) of Regulation (EC) No.6/2002.

4. The Office shall refund 50% of the invalidity fee referred to in Article 52(2) of Regulation (EC) No.6/2002 paid by each applicant whose application is deemed to have been disposed of in accordance with paragraphs 1, 2 and 3 of this Article.

Article 33

Participation of an alleged infringer

B2–036   Where, pursuant to Article 54 of Regulation (EC) No.6/2002, an alleged infringer seeks to join the proceedings, he/she shall be subject to the relevant provisions of Articles 28, 29 and 30 of this Regulation, and shall in particular file a reasoned statement and pay the fee referred to in Article 52(2) of Regulation (EC) No.6/2002.

---

[17] Inserted by the Regulation (EC) No.876/2007 (OJ L 193, 25/07/2007, p.13).

CHAPTER VI

APPEALS

Article 34

Content of the notice of appeal

1. The notice of appeal shall contain: **B2–037**

   (a) the name and address of the appellant in accordance with Article 1(1)(b);

   (b) where the appellant has appointed a representative, the name and the business address of the representative in accordance with Article 1(1)(e);

   (c) a statement identifying the decision which is contested and the extent to which amendment or cancellation of the decision is requested.

2. The notice of appeal shall be filed in the language of the proceedings in which the decision subject to the appeal was taken.

Article 35

Rejection of the appeal as inadmissible

1. If the appeal does not comply with Articles 55, 56 and 57 of Regulation (EC)   **B2–038**
No.6/2002 and Article 34(1)(c) and (2) of this Regulation, the Board of Appeal shall reject it as inadmissible, unless each deficiency has been remedied before the relevant time limit laid down in Article 57 of Regulation (EC) No.6/2002 has expired.

2. If the Board of Appeal finds that the appeal does not comply with other provisions of Regulation (EC) No.6/2002 or other provisions of this Regulation, in particular with Article 34(1)(a) and (b), it shall inform the appellant accordingly and shall request him/her to remedy the deficiencies noted within such time limit as it may specify. If the deficiencies are not remedied in good time, the Board of Appeal shall reject the appeal as inadmissible.

3. If the fee for appeal has been paid after expiry of the time limits for the filing of an appeal pursuant to Article 57 of Regulation (EC) No.6/2002, the appeal shall be deemed not to have been filed and the appeal fee shall be refunded to the appellant.

Article 36

Examination of appeals

1. Save as otherwise provided, the provisions relating to proceedings before the   **B2–039**
department which has made the decision against which the appeal is brought shall be applicable to appeal proceedings *mutatis mutandis*.

2. The Board of Appeal's decision shall contain:

   (a) a statement that it is delivered by the Board;

   (b) the date when the decision was taken;

    (c) the names of the Chairman and the other members of the Board of Appeal taking part;

    (d) the name of the competent employee of the registry;

    (e) the names of the parties and of their representatives;

    (f) a statement of the issues to be decided;

    (g) a summary of the facts;

    (h) the reasons;

    (i) the order of the Board of Appeal, including, where necessary, a decision on costs.

3. The decision shall be signed by the Chairman and the other members of the Board of Appeal and by the employee of the registry of the Board of Appeal.

Article 37

Reimbursement of appeal fees

B2–040   The reimbursement of appeal fees shall be ordered in the event of interlocutory revision or where the Board of Appeal deems an appeal to be allowable, if such reimbursement is equitable by reason of a substantial procedural violation. In the event of interlocutory revision, reimbursement shall be ordered by the department whose decision has been impugned, and in other cases by the Board of Appeal.

CHAPTER VII

DECISIONS AND COMMUNICATIONS OF THE OFFICE

Article 38

Form of decisions

B2–041   1. Decisions of the Office shall be in writing and shall state the reasons on which they are based.

Where oral proceedings are held before the Office, the decision may be given orally. Subsequently, the decision in writing shall be notified to the parties.

2. Decisions of the Office which are open to appeal shall be accompanied by a written communication indicating that notice of appeal must be filed in writing at the Office within two months of the date of notification of the decision from which appeal is to be made. The communications shall also draw the attention of the parties to the provisions laid down in Articles 55, 56 and 57 of Regulation (EC) No.6/2002.

The parties may not plead any failure to communicate the availability of such appeal proceedings.

Article 39

Correction of errors in decisions

B2–042   In decisions of the Office, only linguistic errors, errors of transcription and obvious mistakes may be corrected. They shall be corrected by the department which took the decision, acting of its own motion or at the request of an interested party.

Article 40

Nothing of loss of rights

1. If the Office finds that the loss of any rights results from Regulation (EC) **B2–043** No.6/2002 or this Regulation without any decision having been taken, it shall communicate this to the person concerned in accordance with Article 66 of Regulation (EC) No.6/2002, and shall draw his/her attention to the legal remedies set out in paragraph 2 of this Article.

2. If the person concerned considers that the finding of the Office is inaccurate, he/she may, within two months of notification of the communication referred to in paragraph 1, apply for a decision on the matter by the Office.

Such decision shall be given only if the Office disagrees with the person requesting it; otherwise the Office shall amend its finding and inform the person requesting the decision.

Article 41

Signature, name, seal

1. Any decision, communication or notice from the Office shall indicate the **B2–044** department or division of the Office as well as the name or the names of the official or officials responsible. They shall be signed by the official or officials, or, instead of a signature, carry a printed or stamped seal of the Office.

2. The President of the Office may determine that other means of identifying the department or division of the Office and the name of the official or officials responsible or an identification other than a seal may be used where decisions, communications or notices are transmitted by fax or any other technical means of communication.

CHAPTER VIII

ORAL PROCEEDINGS AND TAKING OF EVIDENCE

Article 42

Summons to oral proceedings

1. The parties shall be summoned to oral proceedings provided for in Article 64 **B2–045** of Regulation (EC) No.6/2002 and their attention shall be drawn to paragraph 3 of this Article. At least one month's notice of the summons shall be given unless the parties agree to a shorter time limit.

2. When issuing the summons, the Office shall draw attention to the points which in its opinion need to be discussed in order for the decision to be taken.

3. If a party who has been duly summoned to oral proceedings before the Office does not appear as summoned, the proceedings may continue without him/her.

Article 43

Taking of evidence by the Office

B2–046   1. Where the Office considers it necessary to hear the oral evidence of parties, of witnesses or of experts or to carry out an inspection, it shall take a decision to that end, stating the means by which it intends to obtain evidence, the relevant facts to be proved and the date, time and place of the hearing or inspection.

If oral evidence from witnesses and experts is requested by a party, the decision of the Office shall determine the period of time within which the party filing the request must make known to the Office the names and addresses of the witnesses and experts whom the party wishes to be heard.

2. The period of notice given in the summons of a party, witness or expert to give evidence shall be at least one month, unless they agree to a shorter time limit.

The summons shall contain:

(a) an extract from the decision mentioned in the first subparagraph of paragraph 1, indicating in particular the date, time and place of the hearing ordered and stating the facts regarding which the parties, witnesses and experts are to be heard;

(b) the names of the parties to proceedings and particulars of the rights which the witnesses or experts may invoke pursuant to Article 45(2) to (5).

Article 44

Commissioning of experts

B2–047   1. The Office shall decide in what form the report made by an expert whom it appoints shall be submitted.

2. The terms of reference of the expert shall include:

(a) a precise description of his/her task;

(b) the time limit laid down for the submission of the expert's report;

(c) the names of the parties to the proceedings;

(d) particulars of the claims which the expert may invoke pursuant to Article 45(2), (3) and (4).

3. A copy of any written report shall be submitted to the parties.

4. The parties may object to an expert on grounds of incompetence or on the same grounds as those on which objection may be made to an examiner or to a member of a Division or Board of Appeal pursuant to Article 132(1) and (3) of Council Regulation (EC) No.40/94[18]. The department of the Office concerned shall rule on the objection.

Article 45

Costs of taking of evidence

B2–048   1. The taking of evidence by the Office may be made conditional upon deposit with it, by the party who has requested the evidence to be taken, of a sum which shall be fixed by reference to an estimate of the costs.

[18] OJ L 11, 14.1.1994, P 1.

2. Witnesses and experts who are summoned by and appear before the Office shall be entitled to reimbursement of reasonable expenses for travel and subsistence. An advance for those expenses may be granted to them by the Office. The first sentence shall apply also to witnesses and experts who appear before the Office without being summoned by it and who are heard as witnesses or experts.

3. Witnesses entitled to reimbursement under paragraph 2 shall also be entitled to appropriate compensation for loss of earnings, and experts shall be entitled to fees for their services. Those payments shall be made to the witnesses and experts after they have fulfilled their duties or tasks, where such witnesses and experts have been summoned by the Office on its own initiative.

4. The amounts and the advances for expenses to be paid pursuant to paragraphs 1, 2 and 3 shall be determined by the President of the Office and shall be published in the Official Journal of the Office.

The amounts shall be calculated on the same basis as the compensation and salaries received by officials in grades A 4 to A 8 as laid down in the Staff Regulations of officials of the European Communities and in Annex VII thereto.

5. Final liability for the amounts due or paid pursuant to paragraphs 1 to 4 shall lie with:

(a) the Office where the Office, on its own initiative, considered it necessary to hear the oral evidence of witnesses or experts; or

(b) the party concerned where that party requested the giving of oral evidence by witnesses or experts, subject to the decision on apportionment and fixing of costs pursuant to Articles 70 and 71 of Regulation (EC) No.6/2002 and Article 79 of this Regulation.

The party referred to in point (b) of the first subparagraph shall reimburse the Office for any advances duly paid.

Article 46

Minutes of oral proceedings and of evidence

1. Minutes of oral proceedings or the taking of evidence shall be drawn up, containing the essentials of the oral proceedings or of the taking of evidence, the relevant statements made by the parties, the testimony of the parties, witnesses or experts and the result of any inspection. **B2–049**

2. The minutes of the testimony of a witness, expert or party shall be read out or submitted to him/her so that he/she may examine them. It shall be noted in the minutes that this formality has been carried out and that the person who gave the testimony approved the minutes. Where his/her approval is not given, his/her objections shall be noted.

3. The minutes shall be signed by the employee who drew them up and by the employee who conducted the oral proceedings or taking of evidence.

4. The parties shall be provided with a copy of the minutes.

5. Upon request, the Office shall make available to the parties transcripts of recordings of the oral proceedings, in typescript or in any other machine-readable form.

The release of transcripts of those recordings shall be subject to the payment of the costs incurred by the Office in making such transcript. The amount to be charged shall be determined by the President of the Office.

CHAPTER IX

NOTIFICATIONS

Article 47

General provisions on notifications

B2–050   1. In proceedings before the Office, any notifications to be made by the Office shall take the form of the original document, of a copy thereof certified by, or bearing the seal of, the Office or of a computer print-out bearing such seal. Copies of documents emanating from the parties themselves shall not require such certification.

2. Notifications shall be made:

  (a) by post in accordance with Article 48;
  (b) by hand delivery in accordance with Article 49;
  (c) by deposit in a post box at the Office in accordance with Article 50;
  (d) by fax and other technical means in accordance with Article 51;
  (e) by public notification in accordance with Article 52.

3. Communications between the Office and the International Bureau shall be in a mutually agreed manner and format, where possible by electronic means. Any reference to forms shall be construed as including forms available in electronic format.[19]

Article 48

Notification by post

B2–051   1. Decisions subject to a time limit for appeal, summonses and other documents as determined by the President of the Office shall be notified by registered letter with acknowledgement of delivery.

Decisions and communications subject to another time limit shall be notified by registered letter, unless the President of the Office determines otherwise.

All other communications shall be ordinary mail.

2. Notifications to addressees having neither their domicile nor their principal place of business nor an establishment in the Community and who have not appointed a representative in accordance with Article 77(2) of Regulation (EC) No.6/2002 shall be effected by posting the document requiring notification by ordinary mail to the last address of the addressee known to the Office.

Notification shall be deemed to have been effected when the posting has taken place.

3. Where notification is effected by registered letter, whether or not with acknowledgement of delivery, it shall be deemed to be delivered to the addressee on the 10th day following that of its posting, unless the letter has failed to reach the addressee or has reached him/her at a later date.

In the event of any dispute, it shall be for the Office to establish that the letter has reached its destination or to establish the date on which it was delivered to the addressee, as the case may be.

[19] Inserted by the Regulation (EC) No.876/2007 (OJ L 193, 25/07/2007, p.13).

4. Notification by registered letter, with or without acknowledgement of delivery, shall be deemed to have been effected even if the addressee refuses to accept the letter.

5. To the extent that notification by post is not covered by paragraphs 1 to 4, the law of the State on the territory of which notification is made shall apply.

Article 49

Notification by hand delivery

Notification may be effected on the premises of the Office by hand delivery of the document to the addressee, who shall on delivery acknowledge its receipt. **B2–052**

Article 50

Notification by deposit in a post box at the Office

Notification may also be effected to addressees who have been provided with a post box at the Office, by depositing the document therein. A written notification of deposit shall be inserted in the files. The date of deposit shall be recorded on the document. Notification shall be deemed to have taken place on the fifth day following deposit of the document in the post box at the Office. **B2–053**

Article 51

Notification by fax and other technical means

1. Notification by fax shall be effected by transmitting either the original or a copy, as provided for in Article 47(1), of the document to be notified. The details of such transmission shall be determined by the President of the Office. **B2–054**

2. Details of notification by other technical means of communication shall be determined by the President of the Office.

Article 52

Public notification

1. If the address of the addressee cannot be established, or if notification in accordance with Article 48(1) has proved to be impossible even after a second attempt by the Office, notification shall be effected by public notice. **B2–055**

Such notice shall be published at least in the *Community Designs Bulletin*.

2. The President of the Office shall determine how the public notice is to be given and shall fix the beginning of the time limit of one month on the expiry of which the document shall be deemed to have been notified.

Article 53

Notification to representatives

1. If a representative has been appointed or where the applicant first named in a common application is considered to be the common representative pursuant to **B2–056**

Article 61(1), notifications shall be addressed to that appointed or common representative.

2. If several representatives have been appointed for a single interested party, notification to any one of them shall be sufficient, unless a specific address for service has been indicated in accordance with Article 1(1)(e).

3. If several interested parties have appointed a common representative, notification of a single document to the common representative shall be sufficient.

Article 54

Irregularities in notification

B2–057   Where a document has reached the addressee, if the Office is unable to prove that it has been duly notified or if provisions relating to its notification have not been observed, the document shall be deemed to have been notified on the date established by the Office as the date of receipt.

Article 55

Notification of documents in the case of several parties

B2–058   Documents emanating from parties which contain substantive proposals, or a declaration of withdrawal of a substantive proposal, shall be notified to the other parties as a matter of course. Notification may be dispensed with where the document contains no new pleadings and the matter is ready for decision.

CHAPTER X

TIME LIMITS

Article 56

Calculation of time limits

B2–059   1. Time limits shall be laid down in terms of full years, months, weeks or days.

2. The beginning of any time limit shall be calculated starting on the day following the day on which the relevant event occurred, the event being either a procedural step or the expiry of another time limit. Where that procedural step is a notification, the event considered shall be the receipt of the document notified, unless otherwise provided.

3. Where a time limit is expressed as one year or a certain number of years, it shall expire in the relevant subsequent year in the month having the same name and on the day having the same number as the month and the day on which the relevant event occurred. Where the relevant month has no day with the same number the time limit shall expire on the last day of that month.

4. Where a time limit is expressed as one month or a certain number of months, it shall expire in the relevant subsequent month on the day which has the same

number as the day on which the relevant event occurred. Where the day on which the relevant event occurred was the last day of a month or where the relevant subsequent month has no day with the same number the time limit shall expire on the last day of that month.

5. Where a time limit is expressed as one week or a certain number of weeks, it shall expire in the relevant subsequent week on the day having the same name as the day on which the relevant event occurred.

Article 57

Duration of time limits

1. Where Regulation (EC) No.6/2002 or this Regulation provide for a time limit **B2–060** to be specified by the Office, such time limit shall, when the party concerned has its domicile or its principal place of business or an establishment within the Community, be not less than one month, or, when those conditions are not fulfilled, not less than two months, and no more than six months.

The Office may, when this is appropriate under the circumstances, grant an extension of a time limit specified if such extension is requested by the party concerned and the request is submitted before the original time limit expires.

2. Where there are two or more parties, the Office may make the extension of a time limit subject to the agreement of the other parties.

Article 58

Expiry of time limits in special cases

1. If a time limit expires on a day on which the Office is not open for receipt of **B2–061** documents or on which, for reasons other than those referred to in paragraph 2, ordinary mail is not delivered in the locality in which the Office is located, the time limit shall extend until the first day thereafter on which the Office is open for receipt of documents and on which ordinary mail is delivered.

The days on which the Office is not open for receipt of documents shall be determined by the President of the Office before the commencement of each calendar year.

2. If a time limit expires on a day on which there is a general interruption or subsequent dislocation in the delivery of mail in a Member State or between a Member State and the Office, the time limit shall extend until the first day following the end of the period of interruption or dislocation, for parties having their residence or registered office in the State concerned or who have appointed representatives with a place of business in that State.

In the event of the Member State concerned being the State in which the Office is located, the first subparagraph shall apply to all parties.

The period referred to in the first subparagraph shall be as determined by the President of the Office.

3. Paragraphs 1 and 2 shall apply *mutatis mutandis* to the time limits provided for in Regulation (EC) No.6/2002 or this Regulation in the case of transactions to be carried out with the competent authority within the meaning of Article 35(1)(b) and (c) of Regulation (EC) No.6/2002.

4. If an exceptional occurrence such as natural disaster or strike interrupts or dislocates the proper functioning of the Office so that any communication from the Office to parties concerning the expiry of a time limit is delayed, acts to be

completed within such a time limit may still be validly completed within one month of the notification of the delayed communication.

The date of commencement and the end of any such interruption or dislocation shall be as determined by the President of the Office.

CHAPTER XI

INTERRUPTION OF PROCEEDINGS AND WAIVING OF ENFORCED RECOVERY PROCEDURES

Article 59

Interruption of proceedings

B2–062   1. Proceedings before the Office shall be interrupted:

(a) in the event of the death or legal incapacity of the applicant for or holder of a registered Community design or of the person authorised by national law to act on his/her behalf;

(b) in the event that the applicant for or holder of a registered Community design is, as a result of some action taken against his/her property, prevented for legal reasons from continuing the proceedings before the Office;

(c) in the event of the death or legal incapacity of the representative of an applicant for or holder of a registered Community design or of his/her being prevented for legal reasons resulting from action taken against his/her property from continuing the proceedings before the Office.

To the extent that the events referred to in point (a) of the first subparagraph do not affect the authorisation of a representative appointed under Article 78 of Regulation (EC) No.6/2002, proceedings shall be interrupted only on application by such representative.

2. When, in the cases referred to in points (a) and (b) of the first subparagraph of paragraph 1, the Office has been informed of the identity of the person authorised to continue the proceedings before the Office, the Office shall communicate to such person and to any interested third parties that the proceedings shall be resumed as from a date to be fixed by the Office.

3. In the case referred to in paragraph 1(c), the proceedings shall be resumed when the Office has been informed of the appointment of a new representative of the applicant or when the Office has notified to the other parties the communication of the appointment of a new representative of the holder of the design.

If, three months after the beginning of the interruption of the proceedings, the Office has not been informed of the appointment of a new representative, it shall communicate that fact to the applicant for or holder of the registered Community design:

(a) where Article 77(2) of Regulation (EC) No.6/2002 is applicable, that the Community design application will be deemed to be withdrawn if the information is not submitted within two months after that communication is notified; or

(b) where Article 77(2) of Regulation (EC) No.6/2002 is not applicable, that the proceedings will be resumed with the applicant for or holder as from the date on which that communication is notified.

4. The time limits, other than the time limit for paying the renewal fees, in force as regards the applicant for or holder of the Community design at the date of

interruption of the proceedings, shall begin again as from the day on which the proceedings are resumed.

Article 60

Waiving of enforced recovery procedures

The President of the Office may waive action for the enforced recovery of any sum due where the sum to be recovered is minimal or where such recovery is too uncertain. **B2–063**

CHAPTER XII

REPRESENTATION

Article 61

Appointment of a common representative

1. If there is more than one applicant and the application for a registered Community design does not name a common representative, the applicant first named in the application shall be considered to be the common representative. **B2–064**

However, if one of the applicants is obliged to appoint a professional representative, such representative shall be considered to be the common representative unless the applicant named first in the application has also appointed a professional representative.

The first and second subparagraphs shall apply *mutatis mutandis* to third parties acting in common in applying for a declaration of invalidity, and to joint holders of a registered Community design.

2. If, during the course of proceedings, transfer is made to more than one person, and such persons have not appointed a common representative, paragraph 1 shall apply.

If such application is not possible, the Office shall require such persons to appoint a common representative within two months. If this request is not complied with, the Office shall appoint the common representative.

Article 62

Authorisations

1. Legal practitioners and professional representatives entered on the lists maintained by the Office pursuant to Article 78(1)(b) or (c) of Regulation (EC) No.6/2002 may file with the Office a signed authorisation for inclusion in the files. **B2–065**

Such authorisation shall be filed if the Office expressly requires it or, where there are several parties to the proceedings in which the representative acts before the Office, one of the parties expressly request it.

2. Employees acting on behalf of natural or legal persons pursuant to Article 77(3) of Regulation (EC) No.6/2002 shall file with the Office a signed authorisation for insertion in the files.

3. The authorisation may be filed in any of the official languages of the Community. It may cover one or more applications or registered Community designs or may be in the form of a general authorisation allowing the representative to act in respect of all proceedings before the Office to which the person who has issued it is a party.

4. Where, pursuant to paragraphs 1 or 2, an authorisation has to be filed, the Office shall specify a time limit within which such authorisation shall be filed. If the authorisation is not filed in due time, proceedings shall be continued with the represented person. Any procedural steps other than the filing of the application taken by the representative shall be deemed not to have been taken if the represented person does not approve them. The application of Article 77(2) of Regulation (EC) No.6/2002 shall remain unaffected.

5. Paragraphs 1, 2 and 3 shall apply *mutatis mutandis* to a document withdrawing an authorisation.

6. Any representative who has ceased to be authorised shall continue to be regarded as the representative until the termination of his/her authorisation has been communicated to the Office.

7. Subject to any provisions to the contrary contained therein, an authorisation shall not terminate vis-à-vis the Office upon the death of the person who gave it.

8. Where several representatives are appointed by the same party, they may, notwithstanding any provisions to the contrary in their authorisations, act either collectively or individually.

9. The authorisation of an association of representatives shall be deemed to be an authorisation of any representative who can establish that he/she practises within that association.

Article 63

Representation

B2–066   Any notification or other communication addressed by the Office to the duly authorised representative shall have the same effect as if it had been addressed to the represented person.

Any communication addressed to the Office by the duly authorised representative shall have the same effect as if it originated from the represented person.

Article 64

Amendment of the special list of professional representatives for design matters

B2–067   1. The entry of a professional representative in the special list of professional representatives for design matters, as referred to in Article 78(4) of Regulation (EC) No.6/2002, shall be deleted at his/her request.

2. The entry of a professional representative shall be deleted automatically:

  (a) in the event of the death or legal incapacity of the professional representative;

  (b) where the professional representative is no longer a national of a Member State, unless the President of the Office has granted an exemption pursuant to Article 78(6)(a) of Regulation (EC) No.6/2002;

  (c) where the professional representative no longer has his/her place of business or employment in the Community;

(d) where the professional representative no longer possesses the entitlement referred to in the first sentence of Article 78(4)(c) of Regulation (EC) No.6/2002.

3. The entry of a professional representative shall be suspended of the Office's own motion where his/her entitlement to represent natural or legal persons before the Benelux Design Office or the central industrial property office of the Member State as referred to in the first sentence of Article 78(4)(c) of Regulation (EC) No.6/2002 has been suspended.

4. A person whose entry has been deleted shall, upon request pursuant to Article 78(5) of Regulation (EC) No.6/2002, be reinstated in the list of professional representatives if the conditions for deletion no longer exist.

5. The Benelux Design Office and the central industrial property offices of the Member States concerned shall, where they are aware thereof, promptly inform the Office of any relevant events referred to in paragraphs 2 and 3.

6. The amendments of the special list of professional representatives for design matters shall be published in the Official Journal of the Office.

CHAPTER XIII

WRITTEN COMMUNICATIONS AND FORMS

Article 65

Communication in writing or by other means

1. Subject to paragraph 2, applications for the registration of a Community **B2–068** design as well as any other application or declaration provided for in Regulation (EC) No.6/2002 and all other communications addressed to the Office shall be submitted as follows:

(a) by submitting a signed original of the document in question to the Office, by post, personal delivery, or by any other means; annexes to documents submitted need not be signed;

(b) by transmitting a signed original by fax in accordance with Article 66; or

(c) by transmitting the contents of the communication by electronic means in accordance with Article 67.

2. Where the applicant avails himself of the possibility provided for in Article 36(1)(c) of Regulation (EC) No.6/2002 of filing a specimen of the design, the application and the specimen shall be submitted to the Office by a single mail in the form prescribed in paragraph 1(a) of this Article. If the application and the specimen, or specimens in the case of a multiple application, are not submitted by a single mail the Office shall not give a filing date until the last item has been received pursuant to Article 10(1) of this Regulation.

Article 66

Communication by fax

1. Where an application for registration of a Community design is submitted by **B2–069** fax and the application contains a reproduction of the design pursuant to Article

4(1) which does not satisfy the requirements of that Article, the required reproduction suitable for registration and publication shall be submitted to the Office in accordance with Article 65(1)(a).

Where the reproduction is received by the Office within a time limit of one month from the date of the receipt of the fax, the application shall be deemed to have been received by the Office on the date on which the fax was received.

Where the reproduction is received by the Office after the expiry of that time limit, the application shall be deemed to have been received by the Office on the date on which the reproduction was received.

2. Where a communication received by fax is incomplete or illegible, or where the Office has reasonable doubts as to the accuracy of the transmission, the Office shall inform the sender accordingly and shall call upon him/her, within a time limit to be specified by the Office, to retransmit the original by fax or to submit the original in accordance with Article 65(1)(a).

Where that request is complied with within the time limit specified, the date of the receipt of the retransmission or of the original shall be deemed to be the date of the receipt of the original communication, provided that where the deficiency concerns the granting of a filing date for an application to register a Community design, the provisions on the filing date shall apply.

Where the request is not complied with within the time limit specified, the communication shall be deemed not to have been received.

3. Any communication submitted to the Office by fax shall be considered to be duly signed if the reproduction of the signature appears on the printout produced by the fax.

4. The President of the Office may determine additional requirements for communication by fax, such as the equipment to be used, technical details of communication, and methods of identifying the sender.

Article 67

Communication by electronic means

B2–070   1. Applications for registration of a Community design may be submitted by electronic means, including the representation of the design, and notwithstanding Article 65(2) in the case of filing a specimen.

The conditions shall be laid down by the President of the Office.

3. In addition to the entries set out in paragraph 2 the Register shall contain the following entries, each accompanied by the date of recording such entry:

(a) changes in the name, the address or the nationality of the holder or in the State in which he/she is domiciled or has his/her seat or establishment;

(b) changes in the name or business address of the representative, other than a representative falling within the first subparagraph of Article 77(3) of Regulation (EC) No.6/2002;

(c) when a new representative is appointed, the name and business address of that representative;

(d) a mention that a multiple application or registration has been divided into separate applications or registrations pursuant to Article 37(4) of Regulation (EC) No.6/2002;

(e) the notice of an amendment to the design pursuant to Article 25(6) of Regulation (EC) No.6/2002, including, if applicable, a reference to the disclaimer made or the court decision or the decision by the Office declaring the partial invalidity of the design right, as well as corrections of mistakes and errors pursuant to Article 20 of this Regulation;

(f) a mention that entitlement proceedings have been instituted under Article 15(1) of Regulation (EC) No.6/2002 in respect of a registered Community design;

(g) the final decision or other termination of proceedings pursuant to Article 15(4)(b) of Regulation (EC) No.6/2002 concerning entitlement proceedings;

(h) a change of ownership pursuant to Article 15(4)(c) of Regulation (EC) No.6/2002;

(i) transfers pursuant to Article 28 of Regulation (EC) No.6/2002;

(j) the creation or transfer of a right *in rem* pursuant to Article 29 of Regulation (EC) No.6/2002 and the nature of the right *in rem*;

(k) levy of execution pursuant to Article 30 of Regulation (EC) No.6/2002 and insolvency proceedings pursuant to Article 31 of that Regulation;

(l) the grant or transfer of a licence pursuant to Article 16(2) or Article 32 of Regulation (EC) No.6/2002 and, where applicable, the type of licence pursuant to Article 25 of this Regulation;

(m) renewal of the registration pursuant to Article 13 of Regulation (EC) No.6/2002 and the date from which it takes effect;

(n) a record of the determination of the expiry of the registration;

(o) a declaration of total or partial surrender by the holder pursuant to Article 51(1) and (3) of Regulation (EC) No.6/2002;

(p) the date of submission of an application or of the filing of a counterclaim for a declaration of invalidity pursuant, respectively, to Article 52 or Article 86(2) of Regulation (EC) No.6/2002;

(q) the date and content of the decision on the application or counterclaim for declaration of invalidity or any other termination of proceedings pursuant, respectively, to Article 53 or Article 86(4) of Regulation (EC) No.6/2002;

(r) a mention pursuant to Article 50(4) of Regulation (EC) No.6/2002 that the registered Community design is deemed from the outset not to have had the effects specified in that Regulation;

(s) the cancellation of the representative recorded pursuant to paragraph 2(e);

(t) the modification or cancellation from the Register of the items referred to in points (j), (k) and (l).

4. The President of the Office may determine that items other than those referred to in paragraphs 2 and 3 shall be entered in the Register.

5. The holder shall be notified of any change in the Register.

6. Subject to Article 73, the Office shall provide certified or uncertified extracts from the Register on request, on payment of a fee.

CHAPTER XV

COMMUNITY DESIGNS BULLETIN AND DATA BASE

Article 70

Community Designs Bulletin

1. The Office shall determine the frequency of the publication of the *Community Designs Bulletin* and the manner in which such publication shall take place.   **B2–071**

2. Without prejudice to the provisions of Article 50(2) of Regulation (EC) No.6/2002 and subject to Articles 14 and 16 of this Regulation relating to deferment of publication, the *Community Designs Bulletin* shall contain publications of registration and of entries made in the Register as well as other particulars relating to registrations of designs whose publication is prescribed by Regulation (EC) No.6/2002 or by this Regulation.

3. Where particulars whose publication is prescribed in Regulation (EC) No.6/2002 or in this Regulation are published in the *Community Designs Bulletin*, the date of issue shown on the Bulletin shall be taken as the date of publication of the particulars.

4. The information the publication of which is prescribed in Articles 14 and 16 shall, where appropriate, be published in all the official languages of the Community.

Article 71

Database

B2–072   1. The Office shall maintain an electronic database with the particulars of applications for registration of Community designs and entries in the Register. The Office may, subject to the restrictions prescribed by Article 50(2) and (3) of Regulation (EC) No.6/2002, make available the contents of that database for direct access or on CD-ROM or in any other machine-readable form.

2. The President of the Office shall determine the conditions of access to the database and the manner in which the contents of this database may be made available in machine-readable form, including the charges for those acts.

3. The Office shall provide information on international registrations of designs designating the Community in the form of an electronic link to the searchable database maintained by the International Bureau.[20]

CHAPTER XVI

INSPECTION OF FILES AND KEEPING OF FILES

Article 72

Parts of the file excluded from inspection

B2–073   The parts of the file which shall be excluded from inspection pursuant to Article 74(4) of Regulation (EC) No.6/2002 shall be:

    (a) documents relating to exclusion or objection pursuant to Article 132 of Regulation (EC) No.40/94, the provisions of that Article being considered for this purpose as applying *mutatis mutandis* to registered Community designs and to applications for these;

    (b) draft decisions and opinions, and all other internal documents used for the preparation of decisions and opinions;

---

[20] Inserted by the Regulation (EC) No.876/2007 (OJ L 193, 25/07/2007, p.13).

(c) parts of the file which the party concerned showed a special interest in keeping confidential before the application for inspection of the files was made, unless inspection of such part of the file is justified by overriding legitimate interests of the party seeking inspection.

Article 73

Inspection of the Register of Community Designs

Where the registration is subject to a deferment of publication pursuant to Article 50(1) of Regulation (EC) No.6/2002:

    B2–074

(a) access to the Register to persons other than the holder shall be limited to the name of the holder, the name of any representative, the date of filing and registration, the file number of the application and the mention that publication is deferred;

(b) the certified or uncertified extracts from the Register shall contain only the name of the holder, the name of any representative, the date of filing and registration, the file number of the application and the mention that publication is deferred, except where the request has been made by the holder or his/her representative.

Article 74

Procedures for the inspection of files

1. Inspection of the files of registered Community designs shall either be of the original document, or of copies thereof, or of technical means of storage if the files are so stored.

    B2–075

The request for inspection of the files shall not be deemed to have been made until the required fee has been paid.

The means of inspection shall be determined by the President of the Office.

2. Where inspection of the files relates to an application for a registered Community design or to a registered Community design which is subject to deferment of publication, which, being subject to such deferment, has been surrendered before or on the expiry of that period or which, pursuant to Article 50(4) of Regulation (EC) No.6/2002, is deemed from the outset not to have had the effects specified in that Regulation, the request shall contain an indication and evidence to the effect that:

(a) the applicant for or holder of the Community design has consented to the inspection; or

(b) the person requesting the inspection has established a legitimate interest in the inspection of the file, in particular where the applicant for or holder of the Community design has stated that after the design has been registered he/she will invoke the rights under it against the person requesting the inspection.

3. Inspection of the files shall take place on the premises of the Office.

4. On request, inspection of the files shall be effected by means of issuing copies of file documents. Such copies shall incur fees.

5. The Office shall issue on request certified or uncertified copies of the application for a registered Community design or of those file documents of which copies may be issued pursuant to paragraph 4 upon payment of a fee.

Article 75

Communication of information contained in the files

B2–076   Subject to the restrictions provided for in Article 74 of Regulation (EC) No.6/2002 and Articles 72 and 73 of this Regulation, the Office may, upon request, communicate information from any file of a Community design applied for or of a registered Community design, subject to payment of a fee.

However, the Office may require the applicant to inspect the file *in situ*, should it deem that to be appropriate in view of the quantity of information to be supplied.

Article 76

Keeping of files

B2–077   1. The Office shall keep the files relating to Community design applications and to registered Community designs for at least five years from the end of the year in which:

  (a) the application is rejected or withdrawn;
  (b) the registration of the registered Community design expires definitively;
  (c) the complete surrender of the registered Community design is registered pursuant to Article 51 of Regulation (EC) No.6/2002;
  (d) the registered Community design is definitively removed from the Register;
  (e) the registered Community design is deemed not to have had the effects specified in Regulation (EC) No.6/2002 pursuant to Article 50(4) thereof.

2. The President of the Office shall determine the form in which the files shall be kept.

CHAPTER XVII

ADMINISTRATIVE COOPERATION

Article 77

Exchange of information and communications between the Office and the authorities of the Member States

B2–078   1. The Office and the central industrial property offices of the Member States and the Benelux Design Office shall, upon request, communicate to each other relevant information about the filing of applications for registered Community designs, Benelux designs or national registered designs and about proceedings relating to such applications and the designs registered as a result thereof. Such communications shall not be subject to the restrictions provided for in Article 74 of Regulation (EC) No.6/2002.

2. Communications between the Office and the courts or authorities of the Member States which arise out of the application of Regulation (EC) No.6/2002 or this Regulation shall be effected directly between those authorities.

Such communication may also be effected through the central industrial property offices of the Member States or the Benelux Design Office.

3. Expenditure in respect of communications pursuant to paragraphs 1 and 2 shall be chargeable to the authority making the communications, which shall be exempt from fees.

Article 78

Inspection of files by or via courts or authorities of the Member States

1. Inspection of files relating to Community designs applied for or registered   **B2–079**
Community designs by courts or authorities of the Member States shall if so requested be of the original documents or of copies thereof. Article 74 shall not apply.

2. Courts or public prosecutors' offices of the Member States may, in the course of proceedings before them, open files or copies thereof transmitted by the Office to inspection by third parties. Such inspection shall be subject to Article 74 of Regulation (EC) No.6/2002.

3. The Office shall not charge any fee for inspections pursuant to paragraphs 1 and 2.

4. The Office shall, at the time of transmission of the files or copies thereof to the courts or public prosecutors' offices of the Member States, indicate the restrictions to which the inspection of files relating to Community designs applied for or registered Community designs is subject pursuant to Article 74 of Regulation (EC) No.6/2002 and Article 72 of this Regulation.

CHAPTER XVIII

COSTS

Article 79

Apportionment and fixing of costs

1. Apportionment of costs pursuant to Article 70(1) and (2) of Regulation (EC)   **B2–080**
No.6/2002 shall be dealt with in the decision on the application for a declaration of invalidity of a registered Community design, or in the decision on the appeal.

2. Apportionment of costs pursuant to Article 70(3) and (4) of Regulation (EC) No.6/2002 shall be dealt with in a decision on costs by the Invalidity Division or the Board of Appeal.

3. A bill of costs, with supporting evidence, shall be attached to the request for the fixing of costs provided for in the first sentence of Article 70(6) of Regulation (EC) No.6/2002.

The request shall be admissible only if the decision in respect of which the fixing of costs is required has become final. Costs may be fixed once their credibility is established.

4. The request provided for in the second sentence of Article 70(6) of Regulation (EC) No.6/2002 for a review of the decision of the registry on the fixing of costs, stating the reasons on which it is based, must be filed at the Office within one month of the date of notification of the awarding of costs.

It shall not be deemed to be filed until the fee for reviewing the amount of the costs has been paid.

5. The Invalidity Division or the Board of Appeal, as the case may be, shall take a decision on the request referred to in paragraph 4 without oral proceedings.

6. The fees to be borne by the losing party pursuant to Article 70(1) of Regulation (EC) No.6/2002 shall be limited to the fees incurred by the other party for the application for a declaration of invalidity and/or for the appeal.

7. Costs essential to the proceedings and actually incurred by the successful party shall be borne by the losing party in accordance with Article 70(1) of Regulation (EC) No.6/2002 on the basis of the following maximum rates:

(a) travel expenses of one party for the outward and return journey between the place of residence or the place of business and the place where oral proceedings are held or where evidence is taken, as follows:
  (i) the cost of the first-class rail fare including usual transport supplements where the total distance by rail does not exceed 800 km;
  (ii) the cost of the tourist-class air fare where the total distance by rail exceeds 800 km or the route includes a sea crossing;

(b) subsistence expenses of one party equal to the daily subsistence allowance for officials in grades A4 to A8 as laid down in Article 13 of Annex VII to the Staff Regulations of officials of the European Communities;

(c) travel expenses of representatives within the meaning of Article 78(1) of Regulation (EC) No.6/2002 and of witnesses and of experts, at the rates provided for in point (a);

(d) subsistence expenses of representatives within the meaning of Article 78(1) of Regulation (EC) No.6/2002 and of witnesses and experts, at the rates referred to in point (b);

(e) costs entailed in the taking of evidence in the form of examination of witnesses, opinions by experts or inspection, up to EUR 300 per proceedings;

(f) costs of representation, within the meaning of Article 78(1) of Regulation (EC) No.6/2002:
  (i) of the applicant in proceedings relating to invalidity of a registered Community design up to EUR 400;
  (ii) of the holder in proceedings relating to invalidity of a registered Community design up to EUR 400;
  (iii) of the appellant in appeal proceedings up to EUR 500;
  (iv) of the defendant in appeal proceedings up to EUR 500;

(g) where the successful party is represented by more than one representative within the meaning of Article 78(1) of the Regulation (EC) No.6/2002, the losing party shall bear the costs referred to in points (c), (d) and (f) for one such person only;

(h) the losing party shall not be obliged to reimburse the successful party for any costs, expenses and fees other than those referred to in points (a) to (g).

Where the taking of evidence in any of the proceedings referred to in point (f) of the first subparagraph involves the examination of witnesses, opinions by experts or inspection, an additional amount shall be granted for representation costs of up to EUR 600 per proceedings.

CHAPTER XIX

LANGUAGES

Article 80

Applications and declarations

Without prejudice to Article 98(4) of Regulation (EC) No.6/2002:   **B2–081**

(a) any application or declaration relating to an application for a registered Community design may be filed in the language used for filing the application or in the second language indicated by the applicant in his/her application;

(b) any application or declaration other than an application for declaration of invalidity pursuant to Article 52 of Regulation (EC) No.6/2002, or declaration of surrender pursuant to Article 51 of that Regulation relating to a registered Community design may be filed in one of the languages of the Office;

(c) when any of the forms provided by the Office pursuant to Article 68 is used, such forms may be used in any of the official languages of the Community, provided that the form is completed in one of the languages of the Office, as far as textual elements are concerned.

Article 81

Written proceedings

1. Without prejudice to Article 98(3) and (5) of Regulation (EC) No.6/2002 and   **B2–082**
save as otherwise provided in this Regulation, in written proceedings before the Office a party may use any language of the Office.

If the language chosen is not the language of the proceedings, the party shall supply a translation into that language within one month of the date of the submission of the original document.

Where the applicant for a registered Community design is the sole party to proceedings before the Office and the language used for the filing of the application for the registered Community design is not one of the languages of the Office, the translation may also be filed in the second language indicated by the applicant in his/her application.

2. Save as otherwise provided in this Regulation, documents to be used in proceedings before the Office may be filed in any official language of the Community.

Where the language of such documents is not the language of the proceedings the Office may require that a translation be supplied, within a time limit specified by it, in that language or, at the choice of the party to the proceeding, in any language of the Office.

Article 82

Oral proceedings

1. Any party to oral proceedings before the Office may, in place of the language   **B2–083**
of proceedings, use one of the other official languages of the Community, on

condition that he/she makes provision for interpretation into the language of proceedings.

Where the oral proceedings are held in a proceeding concerning the application for registration of a design the applicant may use either the language of the application or the second language indicated by him/her.

2. In oral proceedings concerning the application for registration of a design, the staff of the Office may use either the language of the application or the second language indicated by the applicant.

In all other oral proceedings, the staff of the Office may use, in place of the language of the proceedings, one of the other languages of the Office, on condition that the party or parties to the proceedings agree(s) to such use.

3. With regard to the taking of evidence, any party to be heard, witness or expert who is unable to express himself/herself adequately in the language of proceedings, may use any of the official languages of the Community.

Where the taking of evidence is decided upon following a request by a party to the proceedings, parties to be heard, witnesses or experts who express themselves in languages other than the language of proceedings may be heard only if the party who made the request makes provision for interpretation into that language.

In proceedings concerning the application for registration of a design, in place of the language of the application, the second language indicated by the applicant may be used.

In any proceedings with only one party, the Office may at the request of the party concerned permit derogation from the provisions in this paragraph.

4. If the parties and the Office so agree, any official language of the Community may be used in oral proceedings.

5. The Office shall, if necessary, make provision at its own expense for interpretation into the language of proceedings, or, where appropriate, into its other languages, unless this interpretation is the responsibility of one of the parties to the proceedings.

6. Statements by staff of the Office, by parties to the proceedings and by witnesses and experts, made in one of the languages of the Office during oral proceedings shall be entered in the minutes in the language employed. Statements made in any other language shall be entered in the language of proceedings.

Corrections to the application for or the registration of a Community design shall be entered in the minutes in the language of proceedings.

Article 83

Certification of translations

B2–084   1. When a translation of any document is to be filed, the Office may require the filing, within a time limit to be specified by it, of a certificate that the translation corresponds to the original text.

Where the certificate relates to the translation of a previous application pursuant to Article 42 of Regulation (EC) No.6/2002, such time limit shall not be less than three months after the date of filing of the application.

Where the certificate is not filed within that time limit, the document shall be deemed not to have been received.

2. The President of the Office may determine the manner in which translations are certified.

Article 84

Legal authenticity of translations

In the absence of evidence to the contrary, the Office may assume that a translation corresponds to the relevant original text. **B2–085**

CHAPTER XX

RECIPROCITY, TRANSITION PERIOD AND ENTRY INTO FORCE

Article 85

Publication of reciprocity

1. If necessary, the President of the Office shall request the Commission to enquire whether a State which is not party to the Paris Convention for the Protection of Industrial Property or to the Agreement establishing the World Trade Organisation grants reciprocal treatment within the meaning of Article 41(5) Regulation (EC) No.6/2002. **B2–086**

2. If the Commission determines that reciprocal treatment in accordance with paragraph 1 is granted, it shall publish a communication to that effect in the *Official Journal of the European Communities*.

3. Article 41(5) of Regulation (EC) No.6/2002 shall apply from the date of publication in the *Official Journal of the European Communities* of the communication referred to in paragraph 2, unless the communication states an earlier date from which it is applicable.

Article 41(5) of Regulation (EC) No.6/2002 shall cease to be applicable from the date of publication in the *Official Journal of the European Communities* of a communication of the Commission stating that reciprocal treatment is no longer granted, unless the communication states an earlier date from which it is applicable.

4. Communications referred to in paragraphs 2 and 3 shall also be published in the Official Journal of the Office.

Article 86

Transition period

1. Any application for registration of a Community design filed no more than three months before the date fixed pursuant to Article 111(2) of Regulation (EC) No.6/2002 shall be marked by the Office with the filing date determined pursuant to that provision and with the actual date of receipt of the application. **B2–087**

2. With regard to the application, the priority period of six months provided for in Articles 41 and 44 of Regulation (EC) No.6/2002 shall be calculated from the date fixed pursuant to Article 111(2) of that Regulation.

3. The Office may issue a receipt to the applicant prior to the date fixed pursuant to Article 111(2) of Regulation (EC) No.6/2002.

4. The Office may examine the applications prior to the date fixed pursuant to Article 111(2) of Regulation (EC) No.6/2002 and communicate with the applicant with a view to remedying any deficiencies prior to that date.

Any decisions with regard to such applications may be taken only after that date.

5. Where the date of receipt of an application for the registration of a Community design by the Office, by the central industrial property office of a Member State or by the Benelux Design Office is before the commencement of the three-month period specified in Article 111(3) of Regulation (EC) No.6/2002 the application shall be deemed not to have been filed.

The applicant shall be informed accordingly and the application shall be sent back to him/her.

Article 87

Entry into force

B2–088   This Regulation shall enter into force on the seventh day following its publication in the *Official Journal of the European Communities*.

This Regulation shall be binding in its entirety and directly applicable in all Member States.

Done at Brussels, 21 October 2002.

For the Commission
Frederik BOLKESTEIN
Member of the Commission

B3. Commission Regulation (EC) No 2246/2002 of 16 December 2002 on the fees payable to the Office for Harmonization in the Internal Market (Trade Marks and Designs) in respect of the registration of Community designs

THE COMMISSION OF THE EUROPEAN COMMUNITIES,

B3–001   Having regard to the Treaty establishing the European Community,
Having regard to Council Regulation (EC) No.6/2002 of 12 December 2001 on Community designs[21] and in particular Article 107 thereof,
Whereas:
(1) In the light of Article 139 of Council Regulation (EC) No.40/94 of 20 December 1993 on the Community trade mark[22], as amended by Regulation (EC) No.3288/94[23] which by virtue of Article 97 of Regulation (EC) No.6/2002 is also applicable to this Regulation the amounts of the fees should be fixed at such a level as to ensure that the revenue in respect thereof is in principle sufficient for the budget of the Office to be balanced.

---

[21] OJ L 3, 5.1.2002, P 1.
[22] OJ L 11, 14.1.1994, p.1.
[23] OJ L 349, 31.12.1994, p.83.

(2) Commission Regulation (EC) No.2245/2002 of 21 October 2002 implementing Council Regulation (EC) No.6/2002 on Community designs[24] also deals with the conditions under which the fees established by Regulation (EC) No.6/2002 have to be paid to the Office.

(3) To ensure the necessary flexibility, the President of the Office should be empowered, subject to certain conditions, to lay down the charges which may be payable to the Office in respect of services it may render, the charges for access to the Office databases and the making available of the contents of these databases in machine-readable form, and to set charges for the sale of the Office's publications.

(4) In order to facilitate the payment of fees and charges, the President should be empowered to authorise methods of payment which are additional to those explicitly provided for in this Regulation.

(5) The measures provided for in this Regulation are in accordance with the opinion of the Committee established under Article 109 of Regulation (EC) No.6/2002,

HAS ADOPTED THIS REGULATION

Article 1

Subject matter

This Regulation lays down the amounts and rules for payment of the following: **B3–002**

1. fees payable to:

   (a) the Office for Harmonization in the Internal Market (Trade Marks and Designs) (hereinafter the "Office") on the basis of Regulation (EC) No 6/2002 and Regulation (EC) No 2245/2002;

   (b) the International Bureau of the World Intellectual Property Organisation on the basis of the Geneva Act of the Hague Agreement concerning the International Registration of Industrial Designs adopted on 2 July 1999 (hereinafter "the Geneva Act") approved by Council Decision 2006/954/EC[25];

2. charges laid down by the President of the Office.[26]

Article 2

Fees

1. The fees payable to the Office on the basis of Regulation (EC) No 6/2002 and **B3–003** Regulation (EC) No 2245/2002 are set out in the Annex to this Regulation.

2. Individual designation fees payable to the International Bureau on the basis of Article 7(2) of the Geneva Act in conjunction with Article 106c of Regulation (EC) No 6/2002 and Article 13(1) of that Regulation and Article 22(2)(a) of Regulation (EC) No 2245/2002 are set out in the Annex to this Regulation.[27]

[24] See p.26 of this Official Journal.
[25] OJ L 386, 29.12.2006, p.28.
[26] Substituted by Regulation (EC) No.877/2007 (OJ L 193, 25/07/2007 p.16).
[27] Substituted by Regulation (EC) No.877/2007 (OJ L 193, 25/07/2007 p.16).

Article 3

Charges laid down by the President

B3–004   1. The President shall lay down the amount to be charged for any services rendered by the Office other than those specified in the Annex.

2. The President shall lay down the amount to be charged for the Community Designs Bulletin as well as any other publications issued by the Office.

3. The amounts of the charges shall be laid down in euro.

4. The amounts of the charges laid down by the President in accordance with paragraphs 1 and 2 shall be published in the Official Journal of the Office.

Article 4

Due date for fees and charges

B3–005   1. Fees and charges in respect of which the due date is not specified in Regulation (EC) No.6/2002 or in Regulation (EC) No.2245/2002 shall be due on the date of receipt of the request for the service for which the fee or the charge is incurred.

2. The President may decide not to make services mentioned in paragraph 1 dependent upon the advance payment of the corresponding fees or charges.

Article 5

Payment of fees and charges

B3–006   1. Fees and charges due to the Office shall be paid in euro by payment or transfer to a bank account held by the Office.[28]

2. The President may determine methods of payment other than those set out in paragraph 1, in particular by means of deposits in current accounts held with the Office. Those methods shall be published in the Official journal of the Office.

Article 6

Particulars concerning payment

B3–007   1. Every payment shall indicate the name of the person making the payment and shall contain the necessary information to enable the Office to establish immediately the purpose of the payment. In particular, the following information shall be provided:

  (a) when the registration fee is paid, the purpose of the payment, namely "registration fee" and, where appropriate, the reference provided by the applicant in the application for the registration of a Community design;

---

[28] Substituted by Regulation (EC) No.877/2007 (OJ L 193, 25/07/2007 p.16).

(b) when the publication fee is paid, the purpose of the payment, namely "publication fee" and, where appropriate, the reference provided by the applicant in the application for the registration of a Community design;

(c) when the publication fee is paid as provided for in Article 50(4) of Regulation (EC) No.6/2002, the purpose of the payment, namely "publication fee" and the registration number;

(d) when the fee for the deferment of publication is paid, the purpose of the payment, namely "deferment fee" and, where appropriate, the reference provided by the applicant in the application for the registration of a Community design;

(e) when the invalidity fee is paid, the registration number and the name of the holder of the registered Community design against which the application is directed, and the purpose of the payment, namely "invalidity fee".

2. If the purpose of the payment cannot immediately be established, the Office shall require the person making the payment to notify it in writing of this purpose within such period as it may specify. If the person does not comply with the request in due time, the payment shall be considered not to have been made. The amount which has been paid shall be refunded.

Article 7

Deemed date of payment

1. The date on which any payment shall be considered to have been made to the Office shall be the date on which the amount of the payment is actually entered in a bank account held by the Office.[29]   **B3–008**

2. Where the President allows, in accordance with the provisions of Article 5(2), other methods of paying fees than those set out in Article 5(1), he shall also lay down the date on which such payments shall be considered to have been made.

3. Where, pursuant to paragraphs 1 and 2, payment of a fee is not considered to have been made until after the expiry of the period in which it was due, it shall be considered that this period has been observed if evidence is provided to the Office that the person who made the payment:

(a) duly gave an order to a banking establishment to transfer the amount of the payment in a Member State within the period within which the payment should have been made; and[30]

    (i) effected payment through a banking establishment;

    (ii) duly gave an order to a banking establishment to transfer the amount of the payment; or

    (iii) dispatched at a post office or otherwise a letter bearing the address of the Office and containing a cheque within the meaning of Article 5(1)(b), provided that the cheque is met, and

(b) paid a surcharge of 10% on the relevant fee or fees, but not exceeding EUR 200;

no surcharge is payable if a condition according to subparagraph a has been fulfilled not later than 10 days before the expiry of the period for payment.

[29] Substituted by Regulation (EC) No.877/2007 (OJ L 193, 25/07/2007 p.16).
[30] Substituted by Regulation (EC) No.877/2007 (OJ L 193, 25/07/2007 p.16).

4. The Office may request the person who made the payment to produce evidence as to the date on which a condition according to paragraph 3(a) was fulfilled and, where required, to pay the surcharge referred to in paragraph 3(b), within a period to be specified by it. If the person fails to comply with this request or if the evidence is insufficient, or if the required surcharge is not paid in due time, the period for payment shall be considered not to have been observed.

Article 8

Insufficiency of the amount paid

B3–009

1. A time limit for payment shall, in principle, be considered to have been observed only if the full amount of the fee has been paid in due time. If the fee is not paid in full, the amount which has been paid shall be refunded after the period for payment has expired.

2. The Office may, however, in so far as this is possible within the time remaining before the end of the period, give the person making the payment the opportunity to pay the amount lacking or, where this is considered justified, forego any small amounts lacking without prejudice to the rights of the person making the payment.

Article 9

Refund of insignificant amounts

B3–010

1. Where an excessive sum is paid to cover a fee or a charge, the excess shall not be refunded if the amount is insignificant and the party concerned has not expressly requested a refund.

The President shall determine what constitutes an insignificant amount.

2. Determinations by the President pursuant to paragraph 1 shall be published in the Official Journal of the Office.

Article 10

Entry into force

B3–011

This Regulation shall enter into force on the seventh day following its publication in the *Official Journal of the European Communities*.

This Regulation shall be binding in its entirety and directly applicable in all Member States.

Done at Brussels, 16 December 2002.

For the Commission
Frederik BOLKESTEIN
Member of the Commission

ANNEX

B3–012

	(in euro)
1. Registration fee (Article 36(4) of Regulation (EC) No 6/2002; Article 6(1)(a) of Regulation (EC) No 2245/2002)	230
1A. Individual Designation fee for an international registration (Article 106c of Regulation (EC) No 6/2002; Article 7(2) of the Geneva Act—(per design)	62[31]
2. Additional registration fee in respect of each additional design included in a multiple application (Article 37(2) of Regulation (EC) No 6/2002; Article 6(1)(c) of Regulation (EC) No 2245/2002):	
(a) for each design from the second to the 10th design;	115
(b) for each design from the 11th design onwards	50
3. Publication fee (Article 36(4) of Regulation (EC) No 6/2002; Article 6(1)(b) of Regulation (EC) 2245/2002):	120
4. Additional publication fee in respect of each additional design included in a multiple application (Article 37(2) of Regulation (EC) No 6/2002; Article 6(1)(d) of Regulation (EC) No 2245/2002):	
(a) for each design from the 2nd to the 10th design;	60
(b) for each design from the 11th design onwards	30
5. Fee for deferment of publication (Article 36(4) of Regulation (EC) No 6/2002; Article 6(1)(b) of Regulation (EC) No 2245/2002);	40
6. Additional fee for deferment of publication in respect of each additional design included in a multiple application subject to deferment of publication (Article 37(2) of Regulation (EC) No 6/2002; Article 6(1)(d) of Regulation (EC) No 2245/2002):	
(a) for each design from the 2nd to the 10th design;	20
(b) for each design from the 11th design onwards	10
7. Fee for the late payment of the registration fee (Article 107(2)(a) of Regulation (EC) No 6/2002; Article 10(3) of Regulation (EC) No 2245/2002)	60
8. Fee for the late payment of the publication fee (Article 107(2)(b) of Regulation (EC) No 6/2002; Article 10(3) and Article 15(4) of Regulation (EC) No 2245/2002	30
9. Fee for the late payment of the fee for deferment of publication (Article 107(2)(c) of Regulation (EC) No 6/2002; Article 10(3) of Regulation (EC) No 2245/2002)	10
10. Fee for the late payment of additional fees for multiple applications as referred to in 2, 4 and 6 of this annex (Article 107(2)(d) of Regulation (EC) No 6/2002; Article 10(3) and Article 15(4) of Regulation (EC) No 2245/2002	25% of the additional fees
11. Renewal fee (Article 13(1) of Regulation (EC) No 6/2002; Article 22(2)(a) of Regulation (EC) No 2245/2002) per design, included or not in a multiple registration:	
(a) for the first period of renewal;	90
(b) for the second period of renewal;	120
(c) for the third period of renewal;	150
(d) for the fourth period of renewal	180

[31] Inserted by the Regulation (EC) No.877/2007 (OJ L 193, 25/07/2007 p.16).

	(in euro)
11a.Individual renewal fee for an international registration (Article 13(1) and 106c of Regulation (EC) No 6/2002; Article 22(2)(a) of Regulation (EC) No 2245/2002) per design:	
(a) for the first period of renewal—(per design)	31
(b) for the second period of renewal—(per design)	31
(c) for the third period of renewal—(per design)	31
(d) for the fourth period of renewal—(per design)	31[32]
12. Fee for the late payment of the renewal fee or the late submission of the request for renewal (Article 13(3) of Regulation (EC) No 6/2002; Article 22(2)(b) of Regulation (EC) No 2245/2002)	25% of the renewal fee
13. Fee for the application for a declaration of invalidity (Article 52(2) of Regulation (EC) No 6/2002; Article 28(2) of Regulation (EC) No 2245/2002):	350
14. Appeal fee (Article 57 of Regulation (EC) No 6/2002; Article 35(3) of Regulation (EC) No 2245/2002)	800
15. Fee for *restitutio in integrum* (Article 67(3) of Regulation (EC) No 6/2002)	200
16. Fee for the recording of the transfer of an application for a Commuity design (Article 34(2) and 107(2)(f) of Regulation (EC) No 6/2002; Article 23(7) of Regulation (EC) No 2245/2002)	200 per design subject to a maximum of 1 000 where multiple requests are submitted in the same application for recording of the transfer or at the same time
17. Fee for the registration of the transfer of a registered Community design (Article 107(2)(f) of Regulation (EC) No 6/2002; Article 23(3) of Regulation (EC) No 2245/2002)	200 per design subject to a maximum of 1 000 where multiple requests are submitted in the same application for registration of the transfer or at the same time
18. Fee for the registration of a licence or another right in respect of a registered Community design (Article 107(2)(g) of Regulation (EC) No 6/2002; Article 23(3) and Article 24(1) of Regulation (EC) No 2245/2002) or an application for a Community design (Articles 34(2) and 107(2)(g) of Regulation (EC) No 6/2002; Article 23(3); Article 24(1) and Article 24(4) of Regulation (EC) No 2245/2002):	200 per design subject to a maximum of 1 000 where multiple requests are submitted in the same application for registration of a licence or another right or at the same time
(a) grant of a licence;	
(b) transfer of a licence;	
(c) creation of a right in rem;	
(d) transfer of a right in rem;	
(e) levy of execution	

[32] Inserted by the Regulation (EC) No.877/2007 (OJ L 193, 25/07/2007 p.16).

	(in euro)
19. Fee for the cancellation of the registration of a licence or other right (Article 107(2)(h) of Regulation (EC) No 6/2002; Article 26(3) of Regulation (EC) No 2245/2002)	200 per cancellation subject to a maximum of 1 000 where multiple requests are submitted in the same application for cancellation of the registration of a licence or other right or at the same time
20. Fee for the issue of a copy of the application for a registered Community design (Article 107(2)(n) of Regulation (EC) No 6/2002; Article 74(5) of Regulation (EC) No 2245/2002), a copy of the certificate of registration (Article 107(2)(e) of Regulation (EC) No 6/2002; Article 17(2) of Regulation (EC) No 2245/2002), or an extract from the register (Article 107(2)(i) of Regulation (EC) No 6/2002; Article 69(6) of Regulation (EC) No 2245/2002);	
(a) uncertified copy or extract;	10
(b) certified copy or extract	30
21. Fee for the inspection of the files (Article 107(2)(j) of Regulation (EC) No 6/2002; Article 74(1) of Regulation (EC) No 2245/2002)	30
22. Fee for the issue of copies of file documents (Article 107(2)(k) of Regulation (EC) No 6/2002; Article 74(5) of Regulation (EC) No 2245/2002):	
(a) uncertified copy;	10
(b) certified copy,	30
plus per page, exceeding 10	1
23. Fee for the communication of information in a file (Article 107(2)(l) of Regulation (EC) No 6/2002; Article 75 of Regulation (EC) No 2245/2002):	10
plus per page exceeding 10	1
24. Fee for the review of the determination of the procedural costs to be refunded (Article 107(2)(m) of Regulation (EC) No 6/2002; Article 79(4) of Regulation (EC) No 2245/2002).	100

B4. Council Regulation (EC) No 1891/2006 of 18 December 2006 amending Regulations (EC) No 6/2002 and (EC) No 40/94 to give effect to the accession of the European Community to the Geneva Act of the Hague Agreement concerning the international registration of industrial designs

THE COUNCIL OF THE EUROPEAN UNION,

Having regard to the Treaty establishing the European Community, and in particular Article 308 thereof,   **B4-001**

Having regard to the proposal from the Commission,

Having regard to the opinion of the European Economic and Social Committee,

Having regard to the opinion of the European Parliament,

Whereas:

(1) Council Regulation (EC) No 6/2002 of 12 December 2001 on Community designs[33] created the Community design system whereby undertakings can by means of one procedural system obtain Community designs to which uniform protection is given and which produce their effects throughout the entire area of the Community.

(2) Following preparations initiated and carried out by the World Intellectual Property Organisation (WIPO) with the participation of the Member States which are members of the Hague Union, the Member States which are not members of the Hague Union and the European Community, the Diplomatic Conference, convened for that purpose at Geneva, adopted the Geneva Act of the Hague Agreement concerning the international registration of industrial designs (hereinafter referred to as the "Geneva Act") on 2 July 1999.

(3) The Council, by Council Decision 954 approved the accession of the European Community to the Geneva Act of the Hague Agreement concerning the international registration of industrial designs and authorised the President of the Council to deposit the instrument of accession with the Director-General of WIPO as from the date on which the Council has adopted the measures which are necessary to give effect to the accession of the Community to the Geneva Act. This Regulation contains those measures.

(4) The appropriate measures should be incorporated in Regulation (EC) No 6/2002 through the inclusion of a new title on "International registration of designs".

(5) The rules and procedures relating to international registrations designating the Community should, in principle, be the same as the rules and procedures which apply to Community designs applications. According to this principle, an international registration designating the Community should be subject to the examination as to the grounds for non-registrability before it takes the same effect as a registered Community design. Likewise, an international registration having the same effect as a registered Community design should be subject to the same rules on invalidation as a registered Community design.

(6) Regulation (EC) No 6/2002 should therefore be amended accordingly.

(7) The accession of the Community to the Geneva Act will create a new source of revenues for the Office for the Harmonisation in the Internal Market (Trade Marks and Designs). Council Regulation (EC) No 40/94 of 20 December 1993 on the Community trade mark[34] should therefore be amended accordingly,

HAS ADOPTED THIS REGULATION:

Article 1

B4–002   Article 134(3) of Regulation (EC) No 40/94 is replaced by the following:

"3. Revenue shall comprise, without prejudice to other types of income, total fees payable under the fees regulations, total fees payable under the Madrid Protocol referred to in Article 140 of this Regulation for an international registration designating the European Communities and other payments made to Contracting Parties to the Madrid Protocol, total fees payable under the Geneva Act referred to in Article 106c of Regulation (EC) No 6/2002 for an international registration designating the European Community and other payments made to Contracting Parties to the Geneva Act, and, to the extend

---

[33] OJ L 3, 5.1.2002, p.1. Regulation as last amended by 2005 Act of Accession.
[34] OJ L 11, 14.1.1994, p.1. Regulation as last amended by 2005 Act of Accession.

necessary, a subsidy entered against a specific heading of the general budget of the European Communities, Commission section.".

Article 2

Regulation (EC) No 6/2002 is amended as follows: **B4–003**
1. Article 25(1)(d) is replaced by the following:

(For text substituted by this provision, see App.B, para.B1–026, above.)

2. The following title is inserted after title XI:

(For text inserted by this provision (Title XIA and arts 106a–106f), see App.B, paras B1–026–B1–113.)

Article 3

This Regulation shall enter into force on the date on which the Geneva Act **B4–004**
enters into force with respect to the European Community.

The date of entry into force of this Regulation shall be published in the *Official Journal of the European Union.*

This Regulation shall be binding in its entirety and directly applicable in all Member States.

Done at Brussels, 18 December 2006.

For the Council
The President
J.-E. Enestam

B5. The Community Design Regulations 2005 (SI 2005/2339)

Made	*15th August 2005*
Laid before Parliament	*23rd August 2005*
Coming into force	*1st October 2005*

The Secretary of State, being a Minister designated for the purposes of section **B5–001**
2(2) of the European Communities Act 1972 in relation to measures relating to the legal protection of designs, in exercise of the powers conferred on him by that section makes the following Regulations:

Introductory and interpretation

1.—(1) These Regulations may be cited as the Community Design Regulations **B5–002**
2005 and shall come into force on 1st October 2005.

(2) In these Regulations

["Community design court" means a court designated as such by the Community Designs (Designation of Community Design Courts) Regulations 2005;][35]

---

[35] Inserted by the Intellectual Property (Enforcement, etc.) Regulations 2006 (SI 2006/1028) reg.2(3) and Sch.3, paras 7 and 8.

"the Community Design Regulation" means Council Regulation (EC) 6/2002 of 12th December 2001 on Community Designs;[...]³⁶
"Community design", "registered Community design" and "unregistered Community design" have the same meanings as in the Community Design Regulation[; and
"international registration" has the same meaning as in Articles 106a to 106f of the Community Design Regulation]³⁷.

[(3) In addition, references to a Community design and a registered Community design include a reference to a design protected by virtue of an international registration designating the Community.]³⁸

[Infringement proceedings

B5–003   **1A.**—(1) This regulation and regulations 1B to 1D are without prejudice to the duties of the Community design court under the provisions of Article 89(1)(a) to (c) of the Community Design Regulation.
(2) In an action for infringement of a Community design all such relief by way of damages, injunctions, accounts or otherwise is available to the holder of the Community design as is available in respect of the infringement of any other property right.]³⁹

[Order for delivery up

B5–004   **1B.**—(1) Where a person—

(a) has in his possession, custody or control for commercial purposes an infringing article, or
(b) has in his possession, custody or control anything specifically designed or adapted for making articles to a particular design which is a Community design, knowing or having reason to believe that it has been or is to be used to make an infringing article,

the holder of the Community design in question may apply to the Community design court for an order that the infringing article or other thing be delivered up to him or to such other person as the court may direct.
(2) An application shall not be made after the end of the period specified in the following provisions of this regulation; and no order shall be made unless the court also makes, or it appears to the court that there are grounds for making, an order under regulation 1C (order as to disposal of infringing articles, &c).
(3) An application for an order under this regulation may not be made after the end of the period of six years from the date on which the article or thing in question was made, subject to paragraph (4).
(4) If during the whole or any part of that period the holder of the Community design—

(a) is under a disability, or
(b) is prevented by fraud or concealment from discovering the facts entitling him to apply for an order,

---

³⁶ Revoked by the Designs (International Registrations Designating the European Community) Regulations 2007 (SI 2007/3378) reg.3(1) and (2)(a).
³⁷ Inserted by the Designs (International Registrations Designating the European Community) Regulations 2007 (SI 2007/3378) reg.3(1) and (2)(a).
³⁸ Inserted by the Designs (International Registrations Designating the European Community) Regulations 2007 (SI 2007/3378) reg.3(1) and (2)(a).
³⁹ Inserted by the Intellectual Property (Enforcement, etc.) Regulations 2006 (SI 2006/1028) reg.2(3) and Sch.3, paras 7 and 9.

an application may be made at any time before the end of the period of six years from the date on which he ceased to be under a disability or, as the case may be, could with reasonable diligence have discovered those facts.

(5) In paragraph (4) "disability"—

(a) in England and Wales, has the same meaning as in the Limitation Act 1980;
(b) in Scotland, means legal disability within the meaning of the Prescription and Limitation (Scotland) Act 1973;
(c) in Northern Ireland, has the same meaning as in the Statute of Limitations (Northern Ireland) 1958.

(6) A person to whom an infringing article or other thing is delivered up in pursuance of an order under this regulation shall, if an order under regulation 1C is not made, retain it pending the making of an order, or the decision not to make an order, under that regulation.

(7) The reference in paragraph (1) to an act being done in relation to an article for "commercial purposes" are to its being done with a view to the article in question being sold or hired in the course of a business.

(8) Nothing in this regulation affects any other power of the court.][40]

[Order as to disposal of infringing articles, &c

1C.—(1) An application may be made to the Community design court for an order that an infringing article or other thing delivered up in pursuance of an order under regulation 1B shall be—   **B5–005**

(a) forfeited to the holder of the Community design, or
(b) destroyed or otherwise dealt with as the court may think fit,
or for a decision that no such order should be made.

(2) In considering what order (if any) should be made, the court shall consider whether other remedies available in an action for infringement of the right in a Community design would be adequate to compensate the holder and to protect his interests.

(3) Where there is more than one person interested in an article or other thing, the court shall make such order as it thinks just and may (in particular) direct that the thing be sold, or otherwise dealt with, and the proceeds divided.

(4) If the court decides that no order should be made under this regulation, the person in whose possession, custody or control the article or other thing was before being delivered up is entitled to its return.

(5) References in this regulation to a person having an interest in an article or other thing include any person in whose favour an order could be made in respect of it—

(a) under this regulation;
(b) under section 24D of the Registered Designs Act 1949;
(c) under section 114, 204 or 231 of the Copyright, Designs and Patents Act 1988; or
(d) under section 19 of the Trade Marks Act 1994 (including that section as applied by regulation 4 of the Community Trade Mark Regulations 2006 (SI 2006/1027)).][41]

---

[40] Inserted by the Intellectual Property (Enforcement, etc.) Regulations 2006 (SI 2006/1028) reg.2(3) and Sch.3, paras 7 and 9.
[41] Inserted by the Intellectual Property (Enforcement, etc.) Regulations 2006 (SI 2006/1028) reg.2(3) and Sch.3, paras 7 and 9.

[Meaning of "infringing article"

B5–006   **1D.**—(1) In these Regulations "infringing article", in relation to a design, shall be construed in accordance with this regulation.

(2) An article is an infringing article if its making to that design was an infringement of a Community design.

(3) An article is also an infringing article if—

(a) it has been or is proposed to be imported into the United Kingdom, and

(b) its making to that design in the United Kingdom would have been an infringement of a Community design or a breach of an exclusive licensing agreement relating to that Community design.

(4) Where it is shown that an article is made to a design which is or has been a Community design, it shall be presumed until the contrary is proved that the article was made at a time when the right in the Community design subsisted.

(5) Nothing in paragraph (3) shall be construed as applying to an article which may be lawfully imported into the United Kingdom by virtue of an enforceable Community right within the meaning of section 2(1) of the European Communities Act 1972.][42]

Remedy for groundless threats of infringement proceedings

B5–007   **2.**—(1) Where any person (whether entitled to or interested in a Community design or not) by circulars, advertisements or otherwise threatens any other person with proceedings for infringement of a Community design, any person aggrieved thereby may bring an action against him for any such relief as is mentioned in paragraph (2).

(2) Subject to paragraphs (3) and (4), the claimant shall be entitled to the following relief—

(a) a declaration to the effect that the threats are unjustifiable;
(b) an injunction against the continuance of the threats; and
(c) such damages, if any, as he has sustained by reason of the threats.

(3) If the defendant proves that the acts in respect of which proceedings were threatened constitute or, if done, would constitute an infringement of a registered Community design the claimant shall be entitled to the relief claimed only if he shows that the registration is invalid.

(4) If the defendant proves that the acts in respect of which proceedings were threatened constitute or, if done, would constitute an infringement of an unregistered Community design the claimant shall not be entitled to the relief claimed.

(5) Proceedings may not be brought under this regulation in respect of a threat to bring proceedings for an infringement alleged to consist of the making or importing of anything.

(6) Mere notification that a design is—

(a) a registered Community design; or
(b) protected as an unregistered Community design,

does not constitute a threat of proceedings for the purpose of this regulation.

[(6A) In relation to a design protected by virtue of an international registration designating the Community, the reference in paragraph (3) to a registration being invalid includes a reference to the effects of the international registration being

---

[42] Inserted by the Intellectual Property (Enforcement, etc.) Regulations 2006 (SI 2006/1028) reg.2(3) and Sch.3, paras 7 and 9.

declared invalid in accordance with Article 106f of the Community Design Regulation.][43]

(7) [. . .][44]

Falsely representing a design as a registered Community design

3.—(1) It is an offence for a person falsely to represent that a design applied to, or incorporated in, any product sold by him is a registered Community design.

B5–008

(2) It is an offence for a person, after a registered Community design has expired, to represent (expressly or by implication) that a design applied to, or incorporated in, any product sold is still registered in the manner provided for in the Community Design Regulation.

(3) A person guilty of an offence under paragraph (1) is liable on summary conviction to a fine not exceeding level 3 on the standard scale.

(4) A person guilty of an offence under paragraph (2) is liable on summary conviction to a fine not exceeding level 1 on the standard scale.

Privilege for communications with those on the special list of professional design representatives

4.—(1) This regulation applies to communications as to any matter relating to the protection of any design.

B5–009

(2) Any such communication—

(a) between a person and his professional designs representative, or

(b) for the purposes of obtaining, or in response to a request for, information which a person is seeking for the purpose of instructing his professional designs representative,

is privileged from, or in Scotland protected against, disclosure in legal proceedings in the same way as a communication between a person and his solicitor or, as the case may be, a communication for the purpose of obtaining, or in response to a request for, information which a person is seeking for the purpose of instructing his solicitor.

(3) In paragraph (2) "professional designs representative" means a person who is on the special list of professional representatives for design matters referred to in Article 78 of the Community Design Regulation.

Use of Community design for services of the Crown

5.—The provisions of the Schedule to these Regulations shall have effect with respect to the use of registered Community designs and unregistered Community designs for the services of the Crown and the rights of third parties in respect of such use.

B5–010

[Application to Scotland and Northern Ireland

5A.—(1) In the application of these Regulations to Scotland—

B5–011

"accounts" means count, reckoning and payment;
"claimant" means pursuer;
"defendant" means defender;
"delivery up" means delivery;
"injunction" means interdict.

---

[43] Inserted by the Designs (International Registrations Designating the European Community) Regulations 2007 (SI 2007/3378) reg.3(1) and (3).

[44] Revoked by the Intellectual Property (Enforcement, etc.) Regulations 2006 (SI 2006/1028) reg.2(4) and Sch.4.

(2) In the application of these Regulations to Northern Ireland, "claimant" includes plaintiff.][45]

(Regulation 6 makes amendments to the Registered Designs Act 1949 s.35. These amendments have been printed as part of the text of the Act as amended on the preceding pages of App.A2. The Schedule to these Regulations is not included in this publication.)

[45] Inserted by the Intellectual Property (Enforcement, etc.) Regulations 2006 (SI 2006/1028) reg.2(3) and Sch.3, paras 7 and 10.

Appendix C

UK UNREGISTERED DESIGN RIGHT

Contents

C1. The Copyright, Designs and Patents Act 1988 (c.48) Part III (as amended)

PART III

DESIGN RIGHT

CHAPTER I

DESIGN RIGHT IN ORIGINAL DESIGNS

Introductory

Design right

213.—(1) Design right is a property right which subsists in accordance with this Part in an original design.   **C1–001**

(2) In this Part "design" means the design of any aspect of the shape or configuration (whether internal or external) of the whole or part of an article.

(3) Design right does not subsist in—

(a) a method or principle of construction,

(b) features of shape or configuration of an article which—

(i) enable the article to be connected to, or placed in, around or against, another article so that either article may perform its function, or

(ii) are dependent upon the appearance of another article of which the article is intended by the designer to form an integral part, or

(c) surface decoration.

(4) A design is not "original" for the purposes of this Part if it is commonplace in the design field in question at the time of its creation.

(5) Design right subsists in a design only if the design qualifies for design right protection by reference to—

(a) the designer or the person by whom the design was commissioned or the designer employed (see section 218 and 219), or

(b) the person by whom and country in which articles made to the design were first marketed (see section 220),

or in accordance with any Order under section 221 (power to make further provision with respect to qualification).

[(5A) Design right does not subsist in a design which consists of or contains a controlled representation within the meaning of the Olympic Symbol etc (Protection) Act 1995.][1]

(6) Design right does not subsist unless and until the design has been recorded in a design document or an article has been made to the design.

(7) Design right does not subsist in a design which was so recorded, or to which an article was made, before the commencement of this Part.

The designer

C1–002   **214.**—(1) In this Part the "designer", in relation to a design, means the person who creates it.

(2) In the case of a computer-generated design the person by whom the arrangements necessary for the creation of the design are undertaken shall be taken to be the designer.

Ownership of design right

C1–003   **215.**—(1) The designer is the first owner of any design right in a design which is not created in pursuance of a commission or in the course of employment.

(2) Where a design is created in pursuance of a commission, the person commissioning the design is the first owner of any design right in it.

(3) Where, in a case not falling within subsection (2) a design is created by an employee in the course of his employment, his employer is the first owner of any design right in the design.

(4) If a design qualifies for design right protection by virtue of section 220 (qualification by references to first marketing of articles made to the design), the above rules do not apply and the person by whom the articles in question are marketed is the first owner of the design right.

Duration of design right

C1–004   **216.**—(1) Design right expires—

(a) fifteen years from the end of the calendar year in which the design was first recorded in a design document or an article was first made to the design, whichever first occurred, or

[1] Inserted by the Olympic Symbol, etc. (Protection) Act 1995 s.14.

(b) if articles made to the design are made available for sale or hire within five years from the end of that calendar year, ten years from the end of the calendar year in which that first occurred.

(2) The reference in subsection (1) to articles being made available for sale or hire is to their being made so available anywhere in the world by or with the licence of the design right owner.

Qualification for design right protection

Qualifying individuals and qualifying persons

217.—(1) In this Part—   C1–005

"qualifying individual" means a citizen or subject of, or an individual habitually resident in, a qualifying country; and
"qualifying person" means a qualifying individual or a body corporate or other body having legal personality which—
   (a) is formed under the law of a part of the United Kingdom or another qualifying country, and
   (b) has in any qualifying country a place of business at which substantial business activity is carried on.

(2) References in this Part to a qualifying person include the Crown and the government of any other qualifying country.
(3) In this section "qualifying country" means—

   (a) the United Kingdom,
   (b) a country to which this part extends by virtue of an Order under section 255,
   (c) another member State of the European Economic Community, or
   (d) to the extent that an Order under section 256 so provides, a country designated under that section as enjoying reciprocal protection.

(4) The reference in the definition of "qualifying individual" to a person's being a citizen or subject of a qualifying country shall be construed—

   (a) in relation to the United Kingdom, as a reference to his being a British citizen, and
   (b) in relation to a colony of the United Kingdom, as a reference to his being a [British overseas territories' citizen][2] by connection with that colony.

(5) In determining for the purpose of the definition of "qualifying person" whether substantial business activity is carried on at a place of business in any country, no account shall be taken of dealings in goods which are at all material times outside that country.

Qualification by reference to designer

218.—(1) This section applies to a design which is not created in pursuance of   C1–006
a commission or in the course of employment.
(2) A design to which this section applies qualifies for design right protection if the designer is a qualifying individual or, in the case of a computer-generated design, a qualifying person.

---

[2] Substituted by the the British Overseas Territories Act 2002 s.2(3).

(3) A joint design to which this section applies qualifies for design right protection if any of the designers is a qualifying individual or, as the case may be, a qualifying person.

(4) Where a joint design qualifies for design right protection under this section, only those designers who are qualifying individuals of qualifying persons are entitled to design right under section 215(1) (first ownership of design right entitlement of designer).

Qualification by reference to commissioner or employer

C1–007   219.—(1) A design qualifies for design right protection if it is created in pursuance of a commission from, or in the course of employment with, a qualifying person.

(2) In the case of a joint commission or joint employment a design qualifies for design right protection if any of the commissioners or employers is a qualifying person.

(3) Where a design which is jointly commissioned or created in the course of joint employment qualifies for design right protection under this section, only those commissioners or employers who are qualifying persons are entitled to design right under section 215(2) or (3) (first ownership of design right: entitlement of commissioner or employer).

Qualification by reference to first marketing

C1–008   220.—(1) A design which does not qualify for design right protection under section 218 or 219 (qualification by reference to designer, commissioner or employer) qualifies for design right protection if the first marketing of articles made to the design—

(a) is by a qualifying person who is exclusively authorised to put such articles on the market in the United Kingdom, and

(b) takes place in the United Kingdom, another country to which this Part extends by virtue of an Order under section 255, or another member State of the European Economic Community.

(2) If the first marketing of articles made to the design is done jointly by two or more persons, the design qualifies for design right protection if any of those persons meets the requirements specified in subsection (1)(a).

(3) In such a case only the persons who meet those requirements are entitled to design right under section 215(4) (first ownership of design right: entitlement of first marketer of articles made to the design).

(4) In subsection (1)(a) "exclusively authorised" refers—

(a) to authorisation by the person who would have been first owner of design right as designer, commissioner of the design or employer of the designer if he had been a qualifying person, or by a person lawfully claiming under such a person, and

(b) to exclusivity capable of being enforced by legal proceedings in the United Kingdom.

Power to make further provision as to qualification

C1–009   221.—(1) Her Majesty may, with a view to fulfilling an international obligation of the United Kingdom, by Order in Council provide that a design qualifies for design right protection if such requirements as are specified in the Order are met.

(2) An Order may make different provision for different descriptions of design or article; and may make such consequential modifications of the operation of

sections 215 (ownership of design right) and sections 218 to 220 (other means of qualification) as appear to Her Majesty to be appropriate.

(3) A statutory instrument containing an Order in Council under this section shall be subject to annulment in pursuance of a resolution of either House of Parliament.

Dealings with design right

Assignment and licences

222.—(1) Design right is transmissible by assignment, by testamentary disposi-   **C1–010** tion or by operation of law, as personal or moveable property.

(2) An assignment of other transmission of design right may be partial, that is, limited so as to apply—

(a) to one or more, but not all, of the things the design right owner has the exclusive right to do;

(b) to part, but not the whole, of the period for which the right is to subsist.

(3) An assignment of design right is not effective unless it is in writing signed by or on behalf of the assignor.

(4) A licence granted by the owner of design right is binding on every successor in title to his interest in the right, except a purchaser in good faith for valuable consideration and without notice (actual or constructive) of the licence or a person deriving title from such a purchaser; and references in this Part to doing anything with, or without, the licence of the design right owner shall be construed accordingly.

Prospective ownership of design right

223.—(1) Where by an agreement made in relation to future design right, and   **C1–011** signed by or on behalf of the prospective owner of the design right, the prospective owner purports to assign the future design right (wholly or partially) to another person, then if, on the right coming into existence, the assignee or another person claiming under him would be entitled as against all other persons to require the right to be vested in him, the right shall vest in him by virtue of this section.

(2) In this section—

"future design right" means design right which will or may come into existence in respect of a future design or class of designs or on the occurrence of a future event; and

"prospective owner" shall be construed accordingly, and includes a person who is prospectively entitled to design right by virtue of such an agreement as is mentioned in subsection (1).

(3) A licence granted by a prospective owner of design right is binding on every successor in title to this interest (or prospective interest) in the right, except a purchaser in good faith for valuable consideration and without notice (actual or constructive) of the licence or a person deriving title from such a purchaser; and references in this Part to doing anything with, or without, the licence of the design right owner shall be construed accordingly.

Assignment of right in registered design presumed to carry with it design right

C1–012   224.—Where a design consisting of a design in which design right subsists is registered under the Registered Designs Act 1949 and the proprietor of the registered design is also the design right owner, an assignment of the right in the registered design shall be taken to be also an assignment of the design right, unless a contrary intention appears.

Exclusive licences

C1–013   225.—(1) In this Part an "exclusive licence" means a licence in writing signed by or on behalf of the design right owner authorising the licensee to the exclusion of all other persons, including the person granting the licence, to exercise a right which would otherwise be exercisable exclusively by the design right owner.

(2) The licensee under an exclusive licence has the same rights against any successor in title who is bound by the licence as he has against the person granting the licence.

CHAPTER II

RIGHTS OF DESIGN RIGHT OWNER AND REMEDIES

Infringement of design right

Primary infringement of design right

C1–014   226.—(1) The owner of design right in a design has the exclusive right to reproduce the design for commercial purposes—

(a) by making articles to that design, or

(b) by making a design document recording the design for the purpose of enabling such articles to be made.

(2) Reproduction of a design by making articles to the design means copying the design so as to produce articles exactly or substantially to that design, and references in this Part to making articles to a design shall be construed accordingly.

(3) Design right is infringed by a person who without the licence of the design right owner does, or authorises another to do, anything which by virtue of this section is the exclusive right of the design right owner.

(4) For the purposes of this section reproduction may be direct or indirect, and it is immaterial whether any intervening acts themselves infringe the design right.

(5) This section has effect subject to the provisions of Chapter III (exceptions to rights of design right owner).

Secondary infringement: importing or dealing with infringing article

C1–015   227.—(1) Design right is infringed by a person who is, without the licence of the design right owner—

(a) imports into the United Kingdom for commercial purposes, or

(b) has in his possession for commercial purposes, or

(c) sells, lets for hire, or offers or exposes for sale or hire, in the course of a business, an article which is, and which he knows or has reason to believe is, an infringing article.

(2) This subsection has effect subject to the provisions of Chapter III (exceptions to rights of design right owner).

Meaning of "infringing article"

228.—(1) In this Part "infringing article", in relation to a design, shall be construed in accordance with this section.

(2) An article is an infringing article if its making to that design was an infringement of design right in the design.

(3) An article is also an infringing article if—

(a) it has been or is proposed to be imported into the United Kingdom, and
(b) its making to that design in the United Kingdom would have been an infringement of design right in the design or a breach of an exclusive licence agreement relating to the design.

(4) Where it is shown that an article is made to a design in which design right subsists or has subsisted at any time, it shall be presumed until the contrary is proved that the article was made at a time when design right subsisted.

(5) Nothing in subsection (3) shall be construed as applying to an article which may lawfully be imported into the United Kingdom by virtue of any enforceable Community right within the meaning of section 2(1) of the European Communities Act 1972.

(6) The expression "infringing article" does not include a design document, notwithstanding that its making was or would have been an infringement of design right.

Remedies for infringement

Rights and remedies of design right owner

229.—(1) An infringement of design right is actionable by the design right owner.

(2) In an action for infringement of design right all such relief by way of damages, injunctions, accounts or otherwise is available to the plaintiff as is available in respect of the infringement of any other property right.

(3) The court may in an action for infringement of design right, having regard to all the circumstances and in particular to—

(a) the flagrancy of the infringement, and
(b) any benefit accruing to the defendant by reason of the infringement,

award such additional damages as the justice of the case may require.

(4) This section has effect subject to section 233 (innocent infringement).

Order for delivery up

230.—(1) Where a person—

(a) has in his possession, custody or control for commercial purposes an infringing article, or
(b) has in his possession, custody or control anything specifically designed or adapted for making articles to a particular design, knowing or having

C1–016

C1–017

C1–018

reason to believe that it has been or is to be used to make an infringing article,

the owner of the design right in the design in question may apply to the court for an order that the infringing article or other thing be delivered up to him or to such other person as the court may direct.

(2) An application shall not be made after the end of the period specified in the following provisions of this section; and no order shall be made unless the court also makes, or it appears to the court that there are grounds for making, an order under section 231 (order as to disposal of infringing article, &c.).

(3) An application for an order under this section may not be made after the end of the period of six years from the date on which the article or thing in question was made, subject to subsection (4).

(4) If during the whole or any part of that period the design right owner—

(a) is under a disability, or
(b) is prevented by fraud or concealment from discovering the facts entitling him to apply for an order,

an application may be made at any time before the end of the period of six years from the date on which he ceased to be under a disability or, as the case may be, could with reasonable diligence have discovered those facts.

(5) In subsection (4) "disability"—

(a) in England and Wales, has the same meaning as in the Limitation Act 1980;
(b) in Scotland, means legal disability within the meaning of the Prescription and Limitations (Scotland) Act 1973;
(c) in Northern Ireland, has the same meaning as in the Statute of Limitations (Northern Ireland) 1958.

(6) A person to whom an infringing article or other thing is delivered up in pursuance of an order under this section shall, if an order under section 231 is not made, retain it pending the making of an order, or the decision not to make an order, under that section.

(7) Nothing in this section affects any other power of the court.

Order as to disposal of infringing articles, &c

C1–019   **231.**—(1) An application may be made to the court for an order that an infringing article or other thing delivered up in pursuance of an order under section 230 shall be—

(a) forfeited to the design right owner, or
(b) destroyed or otherwise dealt with as the court may think fit,

or for a decision that no such order should be made.

(2) In considering what order (if any) should be made, the court shall consider whether other remedies available in an action for infringement of design right would be adequate to compensate the design right owner and to protect his interests.

(3) Provision shall be made by rules of court as to the service of notice on persons having an interest in the article or other thing, and any such person is entitled—

(a) to appear in proceedings for an order under this section, whether or not he was served with notice, and

(b) to appeal against any order made, whether or not he appeared;

and an order shall not take effect until the end of the period within which notice of an appeal may be given or, if before the end of that period notice of appeal is duly given, until the final determination or abandonment of the proceedings on the appeal.

(4) Where there is more than one person interested in an article or other thing, the court shall make such order as it thinks just and may (in particular) direct that the thing be sold, or otherwise dealt with, and the proceeds divided.

(5) If the court decides that no order should be made under this section, the person in whose possession, custody or control the article or other thing was before being delivered up [. . .]³ is entitled to its return.

(6) References in this section to a person having an interest in an article or other thing include any person in whose favour an order could be made in respect of—

[(a) under this section or under section 114 or 204 of this Act;
(b) under section 24D of the Registered Designs Act 1949;
(c) under section 19 of Trade Marks Act 1994 (including that section as applied by regulation 4 of the Community Trade Mark Regulations 2006 (SI 2006/1027)); or
(d) under regulation 1C of the Community Design Regulations 2005 (SI 2005/2339)]⁴.

Jurisdiction of county court and sheriff court

232.—(1) In England, Wales and Northern Ireland a county court may entertain proceedings under—   **C1–020**

section 230 (order for delivery up of infringing article, &c.),
section 231 (order as to disposal of infringing article, &c.), or
section 235(5) (application by exclusive licensee having concurrent rights),

[save that, in Northern Ireland, a county court may entertain such proceedings only]⁵ where the value of the infringing articles and other things in question does not exceed the county court limit for actions in tort.

(2) In Scotland proceedings for an order under any of those provisions may be brought in the sheriff court.

(3) Nothing in this section shall be construed as affecting the jurisdiction of the High Court or, in Scotland, the Court of Session.

Innocent infringement

233.—(1) Where in an action for infringement of design right brought by virtue of section 226 (primary infringement) it is shown that at the time of the infringement the defendant did not know, and had no reason to believe, that design right subsisted in the design to which the action relates, the plaintiff is not entitled to damages against him, but without prejudice to any other remedy.   **C1–021**

---

³ Words repealed by the Intellectual Property (Enforcement, etc.) Regulations 2006 (SI 2006/1028) Sch.4.
⁴ Substituted by the the Intellectual Property (Enforcement, etc.) Regulations 2006 (SI 2006/1028) Sch.2, paras 6 and 14.
⁵ Inserted (for all proceedings except family proceedings within the meaning of Pt V of 1984 c.42 and proceedings to which s.27(1) of 1984 c.28 (Admiralty jurisdiction) applies) by the High Court and County Courts Jurisdiction Order (SI 1991/724) Sch.1.

(2) Where in an action for infringement of design right brought by virtue of section 227 (secondary infringement) a defendant shows that the infringing article was innocently acquired by him or a predecessor in title of his, the only remedy available against him in respect of the infringement is damages not exceeding a reasonable royalty in respect of the act complained of.

(3) In subsection (2) "innocently acquired" means that the person acquiring the article did not know and had no reason to believe that it was an infringing article.

Rights and remedies of exclusive licensee

C1–022   234.—(1) An exclusive licensee has, except against the design right owner, the same rights and remedies in respect of matters occurring after the grant of the licence as if the licence had been an assignment.

(2) His rights and remedies are concurrent with those of the design right owner; and references in the relevant provisions of this Part to the design right owner shall be construed accordingly.

(3) In an action brought by an exclusive licensee by virtue of this section a defendant may avail himself of any defence which would have been available to him if the action had been brought by the design right owner.

Exercise of concurrent rights

C1–023   235.—(1) Where an action for infringement of design right brought by the design right owner or an exclusive licensee relates (wholly or partly) to an infringement in respect of which they have concurrent rights of action, the design right owner or, as the case may be, the exclusive licensee may not, without the leave of the court, proceed with the action unless the other is either joined as a plaintiff or added as a defendant.

(2) A design right owner or exclusive licensee who is added as a defendant in pursuance of subsection (1) is not liable for any costs in the action unless he takes part in the proceedings.

(3) The above provisions do not affect the granting of interlocutory relief on the application of the design right owner or an exclusive licensee.

(4) Where an action for infringement of design right is brought which relates (wholly or partly) to an infringement in respect of which the design right owner and an exclusive licensee have concurrent rights of action—

   (a) the court shall, in assessing damages, take into account—
       (i) the terms of the licence, and
       (ii) any pecuniary remedy already awarded or available to either of them in respect of the infringement;
   (b) no account of profits shall be directed if an award of damages has been made, or an account of profits has been directed, in favour of the other of them in respect of the infringement; and
   (c) the court shall if an account of profits is directed apportion the profits between them as the court considers just, subject to any agreement between them;

and these provisions apply whether or not the design right owner and the exclusive licensee are both parties to the action.

(5) The design right owner shall notify any exclusive licensee having concurrent rights before applying for an order under section 230 (order for delivery up of infringing article, &c.); and the court may on the application of the licensee make such order under that section as it thinks fit having regard to the terms of the licence.

CHAPTER III

EXCEPTIONS TO RIGHTS OF DESIGN RIGHT OWNERS

Infringement of copyright

Infringement of copyright

236.—Where copyright subsists in a work which consists of or includes a design   C1–024
in which design right subsists, it is not an infringement of design right in the
design to do anything which is an infringement of the copyright in that work.

Availability of licences of right

Licences available in last five years of design right

237.—(1) Any person is entitled as of right to a licence to do in the last five years   C1–025
of the design right term anything which would otherwise infringe the design
right.

(2) The terms of the licence shall, in default of agreement, be settled by the
comptroller.

(3) The Secretary of State may if it appears to hi necessary in order to—

(a) comply with an international obligation of the United Kingdom, or
(b) secure or maintain reciprocal protection for British designs in other
   countries,

by order exclude from the operation of subsection (1) designs of a description
specified in the order or designs applied to articles of a description so specified.

(4) An order shall be made by statutory instrument; and no order shall be made
unless a draft of it has been laid before and approved by a resolution of each
House of Parliament.

Powers exercisable for protection of the public interest

238.—[(1) Subsection (1A) applies where whatever needs to be remedied,   C1–026
mitigated or prevented by the Secretary of State, the Competition Commission or
(as the case may be) the Office of Fair Trading under section 12(5) of the
Competition Act 1980 or section 41(2), 55(2), 66(6), 75(2), 83(2), 138(2), 147(2) or
160(2) of, or paragraph 5(2) or 10(2) of Schedule 7 to, the Enterprise Act 2002
(powers to take remedial action following references to the Commission in
connection with public bodies and certain other persons, mergers or market
investigations etc.) consists of or includes—

(a) conditions in licences granted by a design right owner restricting the use
   of the design by the licensee or the right of the design right owner to
   grant other licences, or
(b) a refusal of a design right owner to grant licences on reasonable terms.

(1A) The powers conferred by Schedule 8 to the Enterprise Act 2002 include
power to cancel or modify those conditions and, instead or in addition, to provide
that licences in respect of the design right shall be available as of right.

(2) The references to anything permitted by Schedule 8 to the Enterprise Act 2002 in section 12(5A) of the Competition Act 1980 and in sections 75(4)(a), 83(4)(a), 84(2)(a), 89(1), 160(4)(a), 161(3)(a) and 164(1) of, and paragraphs 5, 10 and 11 of Schedule 7 to, the Act of 2002 shall be construed accordingly.][6]

(3) The terms of a licence available by virtue of this section shall, in default of agreement, be settled by the comptroller.

Undertaking to take licence of right in infringement proceedings

C1–027   239.—(1) If in proceedings for infringement of design right in a design in respect of which a licence is available as of right under section 237 or 238 the defendant undertakes to take a licence on such terms as may be agreed or, in default of agreement, settled by the comptroller under that section—

  (a) no injunction shall be granted against him,
  (b) no order for delivery up shall be made under section 230, and
  (c) the amount recoverable against him by way of damages or on an account of profits shall not exceed double the amount which would have been payable by him as licensee if such a licence on those terms had been granted before the earliest infringement.

(2) An undertaking may be given at any time before final order in the proceedings, without any admission of liability.

(3) Nothing in this section affects the remedies available in respect of an infringement committed before licences of right were available.

Crown use of designs

Crown use of designs

C1–028   240.—(1) A government department, or a person authorised in writing by a government department, may without the licence of the design right owner—

  (a) do anything for the purpose of supplying articles for the services of the Crown, or
  (b) dispose of articles no longer required for the services of the Crown;

and nothing done by virtue of this section infringes the design right.

(2) References in this Part to "the services of the Crown" are to—

  (a) the defence of the realm,
  (b) foreign defence purposes, and
  (c) health service purposes.

(3) The reference to the supply of articles for "foreign defence purposes" is to their supply—

  (a) for the defence of a country outside the realm in pursuance of an agreement or arrangement to which the government of that country and Her Majesty's Government in the United Kingdom are parties; or
  (b) for use by armed forces operating in pursuance of a resolution of the United Nations or one of its organs.

(4) The reference to the supply of articles for "health service purposes" are to their supply for the purpose of providing—

---

[6] Substituted (subject to savings specified in SI 2003/1397 arts 3(1) and 8) by Enterprise Act 2002, Sch 25, para.18.

[(za) primary medical services or primary dental services under [the National Health Service Act 2006 or the National Health Service (Wales) Act 2006,][7] [or primary medical services under Part 1 of the National Health Service (Scotland) Act 1978][8]][9]

    (a) pharmaceutical services, general medical services or general dental services under—

        (i) Chapter 1 of Part 7 of the National Health Service Act 2006, or Chapter 1 of Part 7 of the National Health Service (Wales) Act 2006 (in the case of pharmaceutical services),][10]

        (ii) Part II of the National Health Service (Scotland) Act 1978 [(in the case of pharmaceutical services or general dental services)][11], or

        (iii) the corresponding provisions of the law in force in Northern Ireland; or

    (b) personal medical services or personal dental services in accordance with arrangements made under—

        (ii) section 17C of the 1978 Act [(in the case of personal dental services)][12], or

        (iii) the corresponding provisions of the law in force in Northern Ireland, [or

    (c) local pharmaceutical services provided under [the National Health Service Act 2006 or the National Health Service (Wales) Act 2006.][13]

(5) In this Part—

"Crown use", in relation to a design, means the doing of anything by virtue of this section which would otherwise be an infringement of design right in the design; and

"the government department concerned", in relation to such use, means the government department by whom or on whose authority the act was done.

(6) The authority of a government department in respect of Crown use of a design may be given to a person either before or after the use and whether or not he is authorised, directly or indirectly, by the design right owner to do anything in relation to the design.

(7) A person acquiring anything sold in the exercise of powers conferred by this section, and any person claiming under him, may deal with it in the same manner as if the design right were held on behalf of the Crown.

Settlement of terms for Crown use

241.—(1) Where Crown use is made of a design, the government department concerned shall—

C1–029

---

[7] Substituted by the the National Health Service (Consequential Provisions) Act 2006 Sch.1, paras 111 and 113.

[8] Inserted by the Primary Medical Services (Scotland) Act 2004 (Consequential Modifications) Order (SI 2004/957) Sch.1, para.5.

[9] Inserted by the Health and Social Care (Community Health and Standards) Act 2003 Sch.11, para.52.

[10] Substituted by the National Health Service (Consequential Provisions) Act 2006 Sch.1, paras 111 and 113.

[11] Inserted by the Primary Medical Services (Scotland) Act 2004 (Consequential Modifications) Order (SI 2004/957) Sch.1, para.5.

[12] Inserted by the Primary Medical Services (Scotland) Act 2004 (Consequential Modifications) Order (SI 2004/957) Sch.1, para.5.

[13] Substituted by the the National Health Service (Consequential Provisions) Act 2006 Sch.1, paras 111 and 113.

(a) notify the design right owner as soon as practicable, and
(b) give him such information as to the extent of the use as he may from time to time require,

unless it appears to the department that it would be contrary to the public interest to do so or the identity of the design right owner cannot be ascertained on reasonable inquiry.

(2) Crown use of a design shall be on such terms as, either before or after the use, are agreed between the government department concerned and the design right owner with the approval of the Treasury or, in default of agreement, are determined by the court.

In the application of this subsection to Northern Ireland the reference to the Treasury shall, where the government department referred to in that subsection is a Northern Ireland department, be construed as a reference to the Department of Finance and Personnel.

[In the application of this subsection to Scotland, where the government department referred to in that subsection is any part of the Scottish Administration, the words "with the approval of the Treasury" are omitted.][14]

(3) Where the identity of the design right owner cannot be ascertained on reasonable inquiry, the government department concerned may apply to the court who may order that no royalty or other sum shall be payable in respect of Crown use of the design until the owner agrees terms with the department or refers the matter to the court for determination.

Rights of third parties in case of Crown use

C1–030   242.—(1) The provisions of any licence, assignment or agreement made between the design right owner (or anyone deriving title from him or from whom he derives title) and any person other than a government department are of no effect in relation to Crown use of a design, or any act incidental to Crown use, so far as they—

(a) restrict or regulation anything done in relation to the design, or the use of any model, document or other information relating to it, or
(b) provide for the making of payments in respect of, or calculated by reference to such use;

and the copying or issuing to the public of copies of any such model or document in connection with the thing done, or any such use, shall be deemed not to be an infringement of any copyright in the model or document.

(2) Subsection (1) shall not be construed as authorising the disclosure of any such model, document or information in contravention of the licence, assignment or agreement.

(3) Where an exclusive licence is in force in respect of the design—

(a) if the licence was granted for royalties—
(i) any agreement between the design right owner and a government department under section 241 (settlement of terms for Crown use) requires the consent of the licensee, and
(ii) the licensee is entitled to recover from the design right owner such part of the payment for Crown use as may be agreed between them or, in default of agreement, determined by the court;
(b) if the licence was granted otherwise than for royalties—
(i) section 241 applies in relation to anything done which but for section 240 (Crown use) and subsection (1) above would be an

[14] Inserted by the Scotland Act 1998 (Consequential Modifications) (No.2) Order (SI 1999/1820) Sch.2, para.93.

infringement of the rights of the licensee with the substitution for references to the design right owner of references to the licensee, and

(ii) section 241 does not apply in relation to anything done by the licensee by virtue of an authority given under section 240.

(4) Where the design right has been assigned to the design right owner in consideration of royalties—

(a) section 241 applies in relation to Crown use of the design as if the references to the design right owner included the assignor, and any payment for Crown use shall be divided between them in such proportion as may be agreed or, in default of agreement, determined by the court; and

(b) section 241 applies in relation to any act incidental to Crown use as it applies in relation to Crown use of the design.

(5) Where any model, document or other information relating to a design is used in connection with Crown use of the design, or any act incidental to Crown use, section 241 applies to the use of the model, document or other information with the substitution for the references to the design right owner of references to the person entitled to the benefit of any provision of an agreement rendered inoperative by subsection (1) above.

(6) In this section—

"act incidental to Crown use" means anything done for the services of the Crown to the order of a government department by the design right owner in respect of a design;

"payment for Crown use" means such amount as is payable by the government department concerned by virtue of section 241; and

"royalties" includes any benefit determined by reference to the use of the design.

Crown use: compensation for loss of profit

243.—(1) Where Crown use is made of a design, the government department concerned shall pay—   **C1–031**

(a) to the design right owner, or

(b) if there is an exclusive licence in force in respect of the design, to the exclusive licensee,

compensation for any loss resulting from his not being awarded a contract to supply the articles made to the design.

(2) Compensation is payable only to the extent that such a contract could have been fulfilled from his existing manufacturing capacity; but is payable notwithstanding the existence of circumstances rendering him ineligible for the award of such a contract.

(3) In determining the loss, regard shall be had to the profit which would have been made on such a contract and to the extent to which any manufacturing capacity was under-used.

(4) No compensation is payable in respect of any failure to secure contracts for the supply of articles made to the design otherwise than for the services of the Crown.

(5) The amount payable shall, if not agreed between the design right owner or licensee and the government department concerned with the approval of the Treasury, be determined by the court on a reference under section 252; and it is in addition to any amount payable under section 241 or 242.

(6) In the application of this section to Northern Ireland, the reference in subsection (5) to the Treasury shall, where the government department concerned is a Northern Ireland department, be construed as a reference to the Department of Finance and Personnel.

[(7) In the application of this section to Scotland, where the government department referred to in subsection (5) is any part of the Scottish Administration, the words "with the approval of the Treasury" in that subsection are omitted.][15]

Special provision for Crown use during emergency

C1–032   244.—(1) During a period of emergency the powers exercisable in relation to a design by virtue of section 240 (Crown use) include power to do any act which would otherwise be an infringement of design right for any purpose which appears to the government department concerned necessary or expedient—

(a) for the efficient prosecution of any war in which Her Majesty may be engaged;

(b) for the maintenance of supplies and services essential to the life of the community;

(c) for securing a sufficiency of supplies and services essential to the well-being of the community;

(d) for promoting the productivity of industry, commerce and agriculture;

(e) for fostering and directing exports and reducing imports, or imports of any classes, from all or any countries and for redressing the balance of trade;

(f) generally for ensuring that the whole resources of the community are available for use, and are used, in a manner best calculated to serve the interests of the community; or

(g) for assisting the relief of suffering and the restoration and distribution of essential supplies and services in any country outside the United Kingdom which is in grave distress as the result of war.

(2) References in this Part to the services of the Crown include, as respects a period of emergency, those purposes; and references to "Crown use" include any act which would apart from this section be an infringement of design right.

(3) In this section "period of emergency" means a period beginning with such date as may be declared by Order in Council to be the beginning, and ending with such date as may be so declared to be the end, of a period of emergency for the purposes of this section.

(4) No Order in Council under this section shall be submitted to Her Majesty unless a draft of it has been laid before and approved by a resolution of each House of Parliament.

General

Power to provide for further exceptions

C1–033   245.—(1) The Secretary of State may if it appears to him necessary in order to—

(a) comply with an international obligation of the United Kingdom, or

---

[15] Added by the Scotland Act 1998 (Consequential Modifications) (No.2) Order (SI 1999/1820) Sch.2, para.93.

(b) secure or maintain reciprocal protection for British designs in other countries,

by order provide that acts of a description specified in the order do not infringe design right.

(2) An order may make different provision for different descriptions of design or article.

(3) An order shall be made by statutory instrument and no order shall be made unless a draft of it has been laid before and approved by a resolution of each House of Parliament.

CHAPTER IV

JURISDICTION OF THE COMPTROLLER AND THE COURT

Jurisdiction of the comptroller

Jurisdiction to decide matters relating to design right

246.—(1) A party to a dispute as to any of the following matters may refer the dispute to the comptroller for his decision—   **C1–034**

    (a) the subsistence of design right,
    (b) the term of design right, or
    (c) the identity of the person in whom design right first vested;

and the comptroller's decision on the reference is binding on the parties to the dispute.

(2) No other court or tribunal shall decide any such matter except—

    (a) on a reference or appeal from the comptroller,
    (b) in infringement or other proceedings in which the issue arises incidentally, or
    (c) in proceedings brought with the agreement of the parties or the leave of the comptroller.

(3) The comptroller has jurisdiction to decide any incidental question of fact or law arising in the course of a reference under this section.

Application to settle terms of licence of right

247.—(1) A person requiring a licence which is available as of right by virtue of—   **C1–035**

    (a) section 237 (licences available in the last five years of design right), or
    (b) an order under section 238 (licences made available in the public interest), may apply to the comptroller to settle the terms of the licence.

(2) No application for the settlement of the terms of a licence available by virtue of section 237 may be made earlier than one year before the earliest date on which the licence may take effect under that section.

(3) The terms of a licence settled by the comptroller shall authorise the licensee to do—

    (a) in the case of licence available by virtue of section 237, everything which would be an infringement of the design right in the absence of a licence;

(b) in the case of a licence available by virtue of section 238, everything in respect of which a licence is so available.

(4) In settling the terms of a licence of the comptroller shall have regard to such factors as may be prescribed by the Secretary of State by order made by statutory instrument.

(5) No such order shall be made unless a draft of it has been laid before and approved by a resolution of each House of Parliament.

(6) Where the terms of a licence are settled by the comptroller, the licence has effect—

(a) in the case of an application in respect of a licence available by virtue of section 237 made before the earliest date on which the licence may take effect under that section, from that date;

(b) in any other case, from the date on which the application to the comptroller was made.

Settlement of terms where design right owner unknown

C1–036   **248.**—(1) This section applies where a person making an application under section 247 (settlement of terms of licence of right) is unable on reasonable inquiry to discover the identity of the design right owner.

(2) The comptroller may in settling the terms of the licence order that the licence shall be free of any obligation as to royalties or other payments.

(3) If such an order is made the design right owner may apply to the comptroller to vary the terms of the licence with effect from the date on which his application is made.

(4) If the terms of a licence are settled by the comptroller and it is subsequently established that a licence was not available as of right, the licensee shall not be liable in damages for, or for an account of profits in respect of, anything done before he was aware of any claim by the design right owner that a licence was not available.

Appeals as to terms of licence of right

C1–037   **249.**—(1) An appeal lies from any decision of the comptroller under section 247 or 248 (settlement of terms of licence of right) to the Appeal Tribunal constituted under section 28 of the Registered Designs Act 1949.

(2) Section 28 of that Act applies to appeals from the comptroller under this section as it applies to appeals from the registrar under that Act; but rules made under that section may make different provision for appeals under this section.

Rules

C1–038   **250.**—(1) The Secretary of State may make rules for regulating the procedure to be followed in connection with any proceeding before the comptroller under this Part.

(2) Rules may, in particular, make provision—

(a) prescribing forms;

(b) requiring fees to be paid;

(c) authorising the rectification of irregularities of procedure;

(d) regulating the mode of giving evidence and empowering the comptroller to compel the attendance of witnesses and the discovery of and production of documents;

(e) providing for the appointment of advisers to assist the comptroller in proceedings before him;

(f) prescribing time limits for doing anything required to be done (and providing for the alteration of any such limit); and

(g) empowering the comptroller to award costs and to direct how, to what party and from what parties, costs are to be paid.

(3) Rules prescribing fees require the consent of the Treasury.

(4) The remuneration of an adviser appointed to assist the comptroller shall be determined by the Secretary of State with the consent of the Treasury and shall be defrayed out of money provided by Parliament.

(5) Rules shall be made by statutory instrument which shall be subject to annulment in pursuance of a resolution of either House of Parliament.

Jurisdiction of the court

References and appeals on design right matters

251.—(1) In any proceedings before him under section 246 (reference of matter relating to design right), the comptroller may at any time order the whole proceedings or any question or issue (whether of fact or law) to be referred, on such terms as he may direct, to the High Court or, in Scotland, the Court of Session.

(2) The comptroller shall make such an order if the parties to the proceedings agree that he should do so.

(3) On a reference under this section the court may exercise any power available to the comptroller by virtue of this Part as respects the matter referred to it and, following its determination, may refer any matter back to the comptroller.

(4) An appeal lies from any decision of the comptroller in proceedings before him under section 246 (decisions on matters relating to design right) to the High Court or, in Scotland, the Court of Session.

Reference of disputes relating to Crown use

252.—(1) A dispute as to any matter which falls to be determined by the court in default of agreement under—

(a) section 241 (settlement of terms for Crown use),
(b) section 242 (rights of third parties in case of Crown use), or
(c) section 243 (Crown use: compensation for loss of profit),

may be referred to the court by any party to the dispute.

(2) In determining a dispute between a government department and any person as to the terms for Crown use of a design the court shall have regard to—

(a) any sums which that person or a person from whom he derives title has received or is entitled to receive, directly or indirectly, from any government department in respect of the design; and
(b) whether that person or a person from whom he derives title has in the court's opinion without reasonable cause failed to comply with a request of the department for the use of the design on reasonable terms.

(3) One of two or more joint owners of design right may, without the concurrence of the others, refer a dispute to the court under this section, but shall not do so unless the others are made parties; and none of those others is liable for any costs unless he takes part in the proceedings.

(4) Where the consent of an exclusive licensee is required by section 242(3)(a)(i) to the settlement by agreement of the terms for Crown use of a design, a determination by the court of the amount of any payment to be made for such use

C1–039

C1–040

is of no effect unless the licensee has been notified of the reference and given an opportunity to be heard.

(5) On the reference of a dispute as to the amount recoverable as mentioned in section 242(3)(a)(ii) (right of exclusive licensee to recover part of amount payable to design right owner) the court shall determine what is just having regard to any expenditure incurred by the licensee—

> (a) in developing the design, or
> (b) in making payments to the design right owner in consideration of the licence (other than royalties or other payments determined by reference to the use of the design).

(6) In this section "the court" means—

> (a) in England and Wales, the High Court or any patents county court having jurisdiction by virtue of an order under section 287 of this Act,
> (b) in Scotland, the Court of Session, and
> (c) in Northern Ireland, the High Court.

CHAPTER V

MISCELLANEOUS AND GENERAL

Miscellaneous

Remedy for groundless threats of infringement proceedings

C1–041   253.—(1) Where a person threatens another person with proceedings for infringement of design right, a person aggrieved by the threats may bring an action against him claiming—

> (a) a declaration to the effect that the threats are unjustifiable;
> (b) an injunction against the continuance of the threats;
> (c) damages in respect of any loss which he has sustained by the threats.

(2) If the plaintiff proves that the threats were made and that he is a person aggrieved by them, he is entitled to the relief claimed unless the defendant shows that the acts in respect of which proceedings were threatened did constitute, or if done would have constituted, an infringement of the design right concerned.

(3) Proceedings may not be brought under this section in respect of a threat to bring proceedings for an infringement alleged to consist of making or importing anything.

(4) Mere notification that a design is protected by design right does not constitute a threat of proceedings for the purposes of this section.

Licensee under licence of right not to claim connection with design right owner

C1–042   254.—(1) A person who has a licence in respect of a design by virtue of section 237 or 238 (licences of right) shall not, without the consent of the design right owner—

> (a) apply to goods which he is marketing, or proposes to market, in reliance on that licence a trade description indicating that he is the licensee of the design right owner, or

(b) use any such trade description in an advertisement in relation to such goods.

(2) A contravention of subsection (1) is actionable by the design right owner.

(3) In this section "trade description", the reference to applying a trade description to goods and "advertisement" have the same meaning as in the Trade Descriptions Act 1968.

Extent of operation of this part

Countries to which this Part extends

255.—(1) This Part extends to England and Wales, Scotland and Northern   **C1–043**
Ireland.

(2) Her Majesty may by Order in Council direct that this Part shall extend, subject to such exceptions and modifications as may be specified in the Order to—

(a) any of the Channel Islands,
(b) the Isle of Man, or
(c) any colony.

(3) That power includes power to extend, subject to such exceptions and modifications as may be specified in the Order, any Order in Council made under section 221 (further provision as to qualification for design right protection) or section 256 (countries enjoying reciprocal protection).

(4) The legislature of a country to which this Part has been extended may modify or add to the provisions of this Part, in their operation as part of the law of that country, as the legislature may consider necessary to adapt the provisions to the circumstances of that country; but not so as to deny design right protection in a case where it would otherwise exist.

(5) Where a country to which this Part extends ceases to be a colony of the United Kingdom, it shall continue to be treated as such a country for the purposes of this Part until—

(a) an Order in Council is made under section 256 designating it as a country enjoying reciprocal protection, or
(b) an Order in Council is made declaring that it shall cease to be so treated by reason of the fact that the provisions of this Part as part of the law of that country have been amended or repealed.

(6) A statutory instrument containing an Order in Council under subsection (5)(b) shall be subject to annulment in pursuance of a resolution of either House of Parliament.

Countries enjoying reciprocal protection

256.—(1) Her Majesty may, if it appears to Her that the law of a country   **C1–044**
provides adequate protection for British designs, by Order in Council designate that country as one enjoying reciprocal protection under this Part.

(2) If the law of a country provides adequate protection only for certain classes of British design, or only for designs applied to certain classes of article, any Order designating that country shall contain provision limiting, to a corresponding extent, the protection afforded by this Part in relation to designs connected with that country.

(3) An Order under this section shall be subject to annulment in pursuance of a resolution of either House of Parliament.

Territorial waters and the continental shelf

C1–045   **257.**—(1) For the purposes of this Part the territorial waters of the United Kingdom shall be treated as part of the United Kingdom.

(2) This Part applies to things done in the United Kingdom sector of the continental shelf on a structure or vessel which is present there for purposes directly connected with the exploration of the sea bed or subsoil or the exploitation of their natural resources as it applies to things done in the United Kingdom.

(3) The United Kingdom sector of the continental shelf means the areas designated by order under section 1(7) of the Continental Shelf Act 1946.

Interpretation

Construction of references to design right owner

C1–046   **258.**—(1) Where different persons are (whether in consequence of a partial assignment or otherwise) entitled to different aspects of design right in a work, the design right owner for any purpose of this Part is the person who is entitled to the right in the respect relevant for that purpose.

(2) Where design right (or any aspect of design right) is owned by more than one person jointly, references in this Part to the design right owner are to all the owners, so that, in particular, any requirement of the licence of the design right owner requires the licence of all of them.

Joint designs

C1–047   **259.**—(1) In this Part a "joint design" means a design produced by the collaboration of two or more designers in which the contribution of each is not distinct from that of the other or others.

(2) References in this Part to the designer of a design shall, except as otherwise provided, be construed in relation to a joint design as references to all the designers of the design.

Application of provisions to articles in kit form

C1–048   **260.**—(1) The provisions of this Part apply in relation to a kit, that is, a complete or substantially complete set of components intended to be assembled into an article, as they apply in relation to the assembled article.

(2) Subsection (1) does not affect the question whether design right subsists in any aspect of the design of the components of a kit as opposed to the design of the assembled article.

Requirement of signature: application in relation to body corporate

C1–049   **261.**—The requirement in the following provisions that an instrument be signed by or on behalf of a person is also satisfied in the case of a body corporate by the affixing of its seal—

> section 222(3) (assignment of design right),
> section 223(1) (assignment of future design right),
> section 225(1) (grant of exclusive licence).

Adaptation of expressions in relation to Scotland

C1–050   **262.**—In the application of this Part to Scotland—

> "account of profits" means accounting and payment of profits;

"accounts" means count, reckoning and payment;
"assignment" means assignation;
"costs" means expenses;
"defendant" means defender;
"delivery up" means delivery;
"injunction" means interdict;
"interlocutory relief" means interim remedy; and
"plaintiff" means pursuer.

Minor definitions

263.—(1) In this Part—   C1–051

"British design" means a design which qualifies for design right protection
by reason of a connection with the United Kingdom of the designer or the
person by whom the design is commissioned or the designer is employed;
"business" includes a trade or profession;
"commission" means a commission for money or money's worth;
"the comptroller" means the Comptroller-General of Patents, Designs and
Trade Marks;
"computer-generated", in relation to a design, means that the design is
generated by computer in circumstances such that there is no human
designer,
"country" includes any territory;
"the Crown" includes the Crown in right of Her Majesty's Government in
Northern Ireland[and the Crown in right of the Scottish Administration][16]
[and the Crown in right of the Welsh Assembly Government][17];
"design document" means any record of a design, whether in the form of a
drawing, a written description, a photograph, data stored in a computer or
otherwise;
"employee", "employment" and "employer" refer to employment under a
contract of service or of apprenticeship;
"government department" includes a Northern Ireland department [and any
part of the Scottish Administration][18] [and any part of the Welsh Assembly
Government][19].

(2) References in this Part to "marketing", in relation to an article, are to its
being sold or let for hire, or offered or exposed for sale or hire, in the course of a
business, and related expressions shall be construed accordingly; but no account
shall be taken for the purposes of this Part of marketing which is merely
colourable and not intended to satisfy the reasonable requirements of the public.

(3) References in this Part to an act being done in relation to an article for
"commercial purposes" are to its being done with a view to the article in question
being sold or hired in the course of a business.

Index of defined expressions

264.—The following Table shows provisions defining or otherwise explaining   C1–052
expressions used in this Part (other than provisions defining or explaining an
expression used only in the same section)—

[16] Inserted by the Scotland Act 1998 (Consequential Modifications) (No.2) Order (SI
1999/1820) Sch.2, para.93.
[17] Inserted by the Government of Wales Act 2006 Sch.10, paras 22 and 31.
[18] Inserted by the Scotland Act 1998 (Consequential Modifications) (No.2) Order (SI
1999/1820) Sch.2, para.93.
[19] Inserted by the Government of Wales Act 2006 Sch.10, paras 22 and 31.

account of profits and accounts (in Scotland)	section 262
assignment (in Scotland)	section 262
British designs	section 263(1)
business	section 263(1)
commercial purposes	section 263(3)
commission	section 263(1)
the comptroller	section 263(1)
computer-generated	section 263(1)
costs (in Scotland)	section 262
country	section 263(1)
the Crown	section 263(1)
Crown use	sections 240(5) and 244(2)
defendant (in Scotland)	section 262
delivery up (in Scotland)	section 262
design	section 213(2)
design document	section 263(1)
designer	sections 214 and 259(2)
design right	section 213(1)
design right owner	sections 234(2) and 258
employee, employment and employer	section 263(1)
exclusive licence	section 225(1)
government department	section 263(1)
government department concerned (in relation to Crown use)	section 240(5)
infringing article	section 228
injunction (in Scotland)	section 262
interlocutory relief (in Scotland)	section 262
joint design	section 259(1)
licence (of the design right owner)	sections 222(4), 223(3) and 258
making articles to a design	section 226(2)
marketing (and related expressions)	section 263(2)
original	section 213(4)
plaintiff (in Scotland)	section 262
qualifying individual	section 217(1)
qualifying person	section 217(1) and (2)
signed	section 261

C2. Council Decision of 22 December 1994 on the Extension of the Legal Protection of Topographies of Semiconductor Products to Persons from a Member of the World Trade Organization (94/824/EC)

THE COUNCIL OF THE EUROPEAN UNION,

C2–001 Having regard to the Treaty establishing the European Community,
Having regard to Council Directive 87/54/EEC of 16 December 1986 on the legal protection of topographies of semiconductor products[20] and in particular Article 3(7) thereof,

[20] OJ No L 24, 27.1.1987, p.36.

Having regard to the proposal from the Commission,

Whereas the Agreement establishing the World Trade Organization (hereinafter, 'WTO Agreement') was signed on behalf of the Community; whereas the Agreement on Trade-Related Aspects of Intellectual Property Rights (hereinafter, 'the TRIPs Agreement'), annexed to the WTO Agreement, contains detailed provisions on the protection of intellectual property rights whose purpose is the establishment of international disciplines in this area in order to promote international trade and prevent trade distortions and friction due to the lack of adequate and effective intellectual property protection;

Whereas in order to ensure that all relevant Community legislation is in full compliance with the TRIPs Agreement, the Community must take certain measures in relation to current Community acts on the protection of intellectual property rights; whereas these measures entail in some respects the amendment or modification of Community acts; whereas these measures also entail complementing current Community acts;

Whereas Directive 87/54/EEC concerns the legal protection of topographies of semiconductor products; whereas Articles 35 to 38 of the TRIPs Agreement set out the obligations of WTO Members in relation to the protection of layout-designs (topographies) of integrated circuits; whereas in accordance with Article 1(3) and Article 3 of the TRIPs Agreement, the Community must ensure that nationals of all other WTO Members benefit from such protection and from the application of national treatment; whereas it is therefore necessary to extend the protection under Directive 87/54/EEC to nationals of WTO Members, without any reciprocity requirement; whereas it is adequate to use the procedure of Article 3(7) of the Directive to this end,

HAS DECIDED AS FOLLOWS:

Article 1

C2–002

Member States shall extend the legal protection for topographies of semiconductor products provided for under Directive 87/54/EEC as follows:

    (a) natural persons who are nationals of, or are domiciled in the territory of, a Member of the WTO Agreement, shall be treated as nationals of a Member State;

    (b) legal entities which or natural persons who have a real and effective establishment for the creation of topographies or the production of integrated circuits in the territory of a Member of the WTO Agreement shall be treated as legal entities or natural persons having a real and effective industrial or commercial establishment in the territory of a Member State.

Article 2

C2–003

1. This Decision shall enter into force on 1 January 1995.

2. It shall apply from 1 January 1996.

3. Council Decision 90/510/EEC of 9 October 1990 on the extension of the legal protection of topographies of semiconductor products to persons from certain countries and territories[21] is replaced as from the date of application of the present

---

[21] OJ No L 258, 17.10.1990, p.29. Decision as amended by Decision 93/17/EEC (OJ No L 11, 19.1.1993, p.22).

Decision, in so far as it concerns the extension of the protection under Directive 87/54/EEC to countries or territories Members of the WTO Agreement.

Article 3

C2–004 This Decision is addressed to the Member States.

Done at Brussels, 22 December 1994.

For the Council
The President
H. SEEHOFER

C3. The Design Right (Proceedings before Comptroller) Rules 1989 (SI 1989/1130)

C3–001 The Secretary of State, in exercise of the powers conferred upon him by section 250 of the Copyright, Designs and Patents Act 1988, with the consent of the Treasury pursuant to subsection (3) of that section as to the fees prescribed under these Rules, and after consultation with the Council on Tribunals in accordance with section 10(1) of the Tribunal and Inquiries Act 1971, hereby makes the following Rules—

Citation and commencement

C3–002 **1.**—These Rules may be cited as the Design Right (Proceedings before Comptroller) Rules 1989 and shall come into force on 1 August 1989.

Interpretation

C3–003 **2.**—(1) In these Rules, unless the context otherwise requires—

"the Act" means the Copyright, Designs and Patents Act 1988;
"applicant" means a person who has referred a dispute or made an application to the Comptroller;
"application" means an application to the Comptroller to settle or vary the terms of a licence of right or to adjust the terms of a licence;
"dispute" means a dispute as to any of the matters referred to in rule 3(1); and
"proceedings" means proceedings before the Comptroller in respect of a dispute or application.

(2) A rule or schedule referred to by number means the rule or schedule so numbered in these Rules; and a requirement under these Rules to use a form set out in Schedule 1 is satisfied by the use either of a replica of that form or of a form which contains the information required by the form set out in the said Schedule and which is acceptable to the Comptroller.

Proceedings in respect of a dispute

C3–004 **3.**—(1) Proceedings under section 246 of the Act in respect of a dispute as to—

(a) the subsistence of design right,
(b) the term of design right, or

(c) the identity of the person in whom design right first vested,

shall be commenced by the service by the applicant on the Comptroller of a notice in Form 1 in Schedule 1. There shall be served with that notice a statement in duplicate setting out the name and address of the other party to the dispute (hereinafter in this rule referred to as the respondent) the issues in dispute, the applicant's case and the documents relevant to his case.

(2) Within 14 days of the receipt of the notice the Comptroller shall send a copy of the notice, together with a copy of the applicant's statement, to the respondent.

(3) Within 28 days of the receipt by him of the documents referred to in paragraph (2) above, the respondent shall serve on the Comptroller a counter-statement and shall at the same time serve a copy of it on the applicant. Such counter-statement shall set out full particulars of the grounds on which he contests the applicant's case, any issues on which he and the applicant are in agreement and the documents relevant to his case.

(4) Within 21 days of the service on him of the counter-statement, the applicant may serve a further statement on the Comptroller setting out the grounds on which he contests the respondent's case, and shall at the same time serve a copy of it on the respondent.

(5) No amended statement or further statement shall be served by either party except by leave or direction of the Comptroller.

Comptroller's directions

4.—(1) The Comptroller shall give such directions as to the further conduct of   **C3–005**
proceedings as he considers appropriate [including directing the party or parties to attend a case management conference or a pre-hearing review or both][22].

(2) If a party fails to comply with any direction given under this rule, the Comptroller may in awarding costs take account of such default.

Procedure and evidence at hearing

5.—(1) Unless the Comptroller otherwise directs, all evidence in the proceed-   **C3–006**
ings shall be by statutory declaration [, witness statement][23] or affidavit.

(2) Where the Comptroller thinks fit in any particular case to take oral evidence in lieu of or in addition to evidence by statutory declaration [, witness statement][24] or affidavit he may so direct and, unless he directs otherwise, shall allow any witness to be cross-examined on his evidence.

(3) A party to the proceedings who desires to make oral representations shall so notify the Comptroller and the Comptroller shall, unless he and the parties agree to a shorter period, give at least 14 days' notice of the time and place of the hearing to the parties.

(4) If a party intends to refer at a hearing to any document not already referred to in the proceedings, he shall, unless the Comptroller and the other party agree to a shorter period, give 14 days' notice of his intention, together with particulars of every document to which he intends to refer, to the Comptroller and the other party.

---

[22] Added by the Design Right (Proceedings before Comptroller) (Amendment) Rules (SI 1999/3195) r.3.

[23] Added by the Design Right (Proceedings before Comptroller) (Amendment) Rules (SI 1999/3195) r.4.

[24] Added by Design Right (Proceedings before Comptroller) (Amendment) Rules (SI 1999/3195) r.4.

(5) At any stage of the proceedings the Comptroller may direct that such documents, information or evidence as he may require shall be filed within such time as he may specify.

(6) The hearing of any proceedings, or part of proceedings, under this rule shall be in public, unless the Comptroller, after consultation with the parties, otherwise directs.

[(7) The Comptroller may give a direction as he thinks fit in any particular case that evidence shall be given by affidavit or statutory declaration instead of or in addition to a witness statement.

(8) Where in proceedings before the Comptroller, a party adduces evidence of a statement made by a person otherwise than while giving oral evidence in the proceedings and does not call that person as a witness, the Comptroller may, if he thinks fit, permit any other party to the proceedings to call that person as a witness and cross-examine him on the statement as if he had been called by the first-mentioned party and as if the statement were his evidence in chief.][25]

Representation and rights of audience

C3–007   **6.**—(1) Any party to the proceedings may appear in person or be represented by counsel or a solicitor (of any part of the United Kingdom) or, subject to paragraph (4) below, a patent [attorney][26] or any other person whom he desires to represent him.

(2) Anything required or authorised by these Rules to be done by or in relation to any person may be done by or in relation to his agent.

(3) Where after a person has become a party to the proceedings he appoints an agent for the first time or appoints an agent in substitution for another, the newly appointed agent shall give written notice of his appointment to the Comptroller and to every other party to the proceedings.

(4) The Comptroller may refuse to recognise as such an agent in respect of any proceedings before him—

    (a) a person who has been convicted of an offences under section 88 of the Patents Act 1949 or section 114 of the Patents Act 1977 or section 276 of the Act;

    (b) [a person][27] whose name has been erased from and not restored to, or who is suspended from, the register of patent [attorneys][28] (kept [in accordance with][29] [section 275 of the Act][30]) on the ground of misconduct;

    (c) a person who is found by the Secretary of State to have been guilty of such conduct as would, in the case of [a person][31] registered in the

---

[25] Added by Design Right (Proceedings before Comptroller) (Amendment) Rules (SI 1999/3195) r.4.

[26] Substituted by the Legal Services Act 2007 (Consequential Amendments) Order 2009 (SI 2009/3348) art.8.

[27] Substituted by the Legal Services Act 2007 (Consequential Amendments) Order 2009 (SI 2009/3348) art.8.

[28] Substituted by the Legal Services Act 2007 (Consequential Amendments) Order 2009 (SI 2009/3348) art.8.

[29] Substituted by the Legal Services Act 2007 (Consequential Amendments) Order 2009 (SI 2009/3348) art.8.

[30] Substituted by the Design Right (Proceedings before Comptroller) (Amendment) Rules (SI 1990/1453) r.2.

[31] Substituted by the Legal Services Act 2007 (Consequential Amendments) Order 2009 (SI 2009/3348) art.8.

register of patent [attorneys][32], render [the person][33] liable to have [the person's][34] name erased from the register on the ground of misconduct;

(d) a partnership or body corporate of which one of the partners or directors is a person whom the Comptroller could refuse to recognise under sub-paragraphs (a), (b), or (c) above.

Application to be made a party to proceedings

7.—(1) A person who claims to have a substantial interest in a dispute in respect of which proceedings have been commenced may apply to the Comptroller to be made a party to the dispute in Form 2 in Schedule 1, supported by a statement of his interest. He shall serve a copy of his application, together with his statement, on every party to the proceedings.

(2) The Comptroller shall, upon being satisfied of the substantial interest of that person in the dispute, grant the application and shall give such directions or further directions under rule 4(1) as may be necessary to enable that person to participate in the proceedings as a party to the dispute.

C3–008

Withdrawal of reference

8.—A party (including a person made a party to the proceedings under rule 7) may at any time before the Comptroller's decision withdraw from the proceedings by serving a notice to that effect on the Comptroller and every other party to the proceedings, but such withdrawal shall be without prejudice to the Comptroller's power to make an order as to the payment of costs incurred up to the time of service of the notice.

C3–009

Decision of the Comptroller

9.—After hearing the party or parties desiring to be heard, or if none of the parties so desires, then without a hearing, the Comptroller shall decide the dispute and notify his decision to the parties, giving written reasons for his decision if so required by any party.

C3–010

Proceedings in respect of application to settle terms of licence of right or adjust terms of licence

10.—(1) Proceedings in respect of an application to the Comptroller—

C3–011

(a) under section 247 of the Act, to settle the terms of a licence available as of right by virtue of section 237 or under an order under section 238 of the Act, or

(b) under paragraph 19(2) of Schedule 1 to the Act, to settle the terms of a licence available as of right in respect of a design recorded or embodied in a design document or model before 1 August 1989, or

(c) adjust the terms of a licence granted before 1 August 1989 in respect of a design referred to in sub-paragraph (b) above,

shall be commenced by the service by the applicant on the Comptroller of a notice in Form 3 in Schedule 1.

---

[32] Substituted by the Legal Services Act 2007 (Consequential Amendments) Order 2009 (SI 2009/3348) art.8.

[33] Substituted by the Legal Services Act 2007 (Consequential Amendments) Order 2009 (SI 2009/3348) art.8.

[34] Substituted by the Legal Services Act 2007 (Consequential Amendments) Order 2009 (SI 2009/3348) art.8.

(2) There shall be served with the notice a statement in duplicate setting out—

    (a) in the case of an application referred to in paragraph (1)(a) or (b) above, the terms of the licence which the applicant requires the Comptroller to settle and, unless the application is one to which rule 13 relates, the name and address of the owner of the design right or, as the case may be, the copyright owner of the design;

    (b) in the case of an application referred to in paragraph (1)(c) above, the date and terms of the licence and the grounds on which the applicant requires the Comptroller to adjust those terms and the name and address of the grantor of the licence.

(3) Within 14 days of the receipt of the notice the Comptroller shall send a copy of it, together with a copy of the applicant's statement, to the person (hereinafter in this rule referred to as the respondent) shown in the application as the design right owner, copyright owner or grantor of the licence, as appropriate.

(4) Within 6 weeks of the receipt by him of the notice sent under paragraph (3) above the respondent shall, if he does not agree to the terms of the licence required by the applicant to be settled or, as the case may be, adjusted, serve a notice of objection on the Comptroller with a statement setting out the grounds of his objection and at the same time shall serve a copy of the same on the applicant.

(5) Within 4 weeks of the receipt of the notice of objection the applicant may serve on the Comptroller a counter-statement and at the same time serve a copy of it on the respondent.

(6) No amended statement or further statement shall be served by either party except by leave or direction of the Comptroller.

11.—Rules 4, 5, 6 and 8 shall apply in respect of proceedings under rule 10 as they apply in respect of proceedings under rule 3.

C3–012   **12.**—After hearing the party or parties desiring to be heard, or if none of the parties so desires, then without a hearing, the Comptroller shall decide the application and notify his decision to the parties, giving written reasons for his decision if so required by any party.

Settlement of terms where design right owner unknown

C3–013   **13.**—(1) Where a person making an application under rule 10(1)(a) or (b) is unable (after making such inquiries as he considers reasonable) to discover the identity of the design right owner or, as the case may be, the copyright owner, he shall serve with his notice under that rule a statement to that effect, setting out particulars of the inquiries made by him as to the identity of the owner of the right and the result of those inquiries.

(2) The Comptroller may require the applicant to make such further inquiries into the identity of the owner of the right as he thinks fit and, may for that purpose, require him to publish in such a manner as the Comptroller considers appropriate particulars of the application.

(3) The Comptroller shall, upon being satisfied from the applicant's statement or the further inquiries made under paragraph (2) above the identity of the owner of the right cannot be discovered, consider the application and settle the terms of the licence.

Proceedings in respect of application by design right owner to vary terms of licence

C3–014   **14.**—(1) Where the Comptroller has, in settling the terms of the licence under rule 13, ordered that the licence shall be free of any obligation as to royalties or other payments, the design right owner or copyright owner (as the case may be) may serve on the Comptroller a notice in Form 4 in Schedule 1 applying for the terms of the licence to be varied from the date of his application. There shall be served with the notice a statement in duplicate setting out the particulars of the grounds for variation and the terms required to be varied.

(2) Within 14 days of the receipt of the notice the Comptroller shall send a copy of the notice, together with the design right or copyright owner's statement, to the applicant under rule 10 (hereinafter in this rule referred to as the licensee).

(3) The licensee shall, if he does not agree to the terms as required to be varied by the design right or copyright owner, within 6 weeks of the receipt of the notice serve notice of objection on the Comptroller with a statement setting out the grounds of his objection and at the same time shall serve a copy of the same on the design right or copyright owner, as the case may be.

(4) Within 4 weeks of the receipt of the notice of objection the design right or copyright owner may serve on the Comptroller a counter-statement, and at the same time shall serve a copy of it on the licensee.

(5) No amended statement or further statement shall be served by either party except by leave or direction of the Comptroller.

15.—Rules 4, 5, 6 and 8 shall apply in respect of proceedings under rule 14 as they apply in respect of proceedings under rule 3. **C3–015**

16.—After hearing the party or parties desiring to be heard, or if none of the parties so desires, then without a hearing, the Comptroller shall decide the application and notify his decision to the parties, giving written reasons for his decision if so required by any party. **C3–016**

General

17.—Any document filed in any proceedings may, if the Comptroller thinks fit, be amended, and any irregularity in procedure may be rectified by the Comptroller on such terms as he may direct. **C3–017**

18.—(1) Any statutory declaration or affidavit filed in any proceedings shall be made and subscribed as follows— **C3–018**

(a) in the United Kingdom, before any justice of the peace or any commissioner or other officer authorised by law in any part of the United Kingdom to administer an oath for the purpose of any legal proceedings;

(b) in any other part of Her Majesty's dominions or in the Republic of Ireland, before any court, judge, justice of the peace or any officer authorised by law to administer an oath there for the purpose of any legal proceedings; and

(c) elsewhere, before a British Minister, or person exercising the functions of a British Minister, or a Consul, Vice-Consul or other person exercising the functions of a British Consul or before a notary public, judge or magistrate.

(2) Any document purporting to have fixed, impressed or subscribed thereto or thereon the seal or signature of any person authorised by paragraph (1) above to take a declaration may be admitted by the Comptroller without proof of the genuineness of the seal or signature or of the official character of the person or his authority to take the declaration.

(3) In England and Wales, the Comptroller shall, in relation to the giving of evidence (including evidence on oath), the attendance of witnesses and the discovery and production of documents, have all the powers of a judge of the High Court, other than the power to punish summarily for contempt of court.

(4) In Scotland, the Comptroller shall, in relation to the giving of evidence (including evidence on oath), have all the powers which a Lord Ordinary of the

Court of Session has in an action before him, other than the power to punish summarily for contempt of court, and, in relation to the attendance of witnesses and the recovery and production of documents, have all the powers of the Court of Session.

C3–019   **18(A).**—Any witness statement filed under these Rules shall—

    (a) be a written statement signed and dated by a person which contains the evidence which the person signing it would be allowed to give orally; and

    (b) include a statement by the intended witness that he believes the facts in it are true.][35]

C3–020   **19.**—The Comptroller may appoint an adviser to assist him in any proceedings and shall settle the question or instructions to be submitted or given to such an adviser.

C3–021   **20.**—[(1) The times or periods prescribed by these Rules for doing any act or taking any proceedings thereunder may be extended or shortened by the Comptroller if he thinks fit, upon such notice and upon such terms as he may direct, and an extension may be granted although the time for doing such act or taking such proceedings has already expired.][36]

(2) Where the last day for the doing of any act falls on a day on which the Patent Office is closed and by reason thereof the act cannot be done on that day, it may be done on the next day on which the Office is open.

C3–022   **21.**—For the purposes of these Rules the Patent Office shall be open Monday to Friday—

    (a) between [9.00 a.m.][37] and midnight, for the filing of applications, forms and other documents, and

    (b) between [9.00 a.m.][38] and [5.00 p.m.][39] for all other purposes,

excluding Good Friday, Christmas Day[, Tuesday 4th January 2000][40] and any day specified or proclaimed to be a bank holiday under section 1 of the Banking and Financial Dealings Act 1971.

C3–023   **22.**—(1) The Comptroller may, in respect of any proceedings, by order award such costs or, in Scotland, such expenses as he considers reasonable and direct how, to what party and from what parties they are to be paid.

(2) Where any applicant or a person making an application under rule 7 neither resides nor carries on business in the United Kingdom or another member State of the European Economic Community the Comptroller may require him to give security for the costs or expenses of the proceedings and in default of such security being given may treat the references or application as abandoned.

C3–024   **23.**—(1) Every person concerned in any proceedings to which these Rules relate shall furnish to the Comptroller an address for service [. . .][41], and that address

---

[35] Added by the Design Right (Proceedings before Comptroller) (Amendment) Rules (SI 1999/3195) r.5.

[36] Substituted by the Design Right (Proceedings before Comptroller) (Amendment) Rules (SI 1999/3195) r.6.

[37] Substituted by the Design Right (Proceedings before Comptroller) (Amendment) Rules (SI 1999/3195) r.7.

[38] Substituted by the Design Right (Proceedings before Comptroller) (Amendment) Rules (SI 1999/3195) r.7.

[39] Substituted by the Design Right (Proceedings before Comptroller) (Amendment) Rules (SI 1999/3195) r.7.

[40] Inserted by the Design Right (Proceedings before Comptroller) (Amendment) Rules (SI 1999/3195) r.7.

[41] Revoked by Patents, Trade Marks and Designs (Address For Service and Time Limits, etc) Rules 2006 (SI 2006/760), rr.2 and 3.

may be treated for all purposes connected with such proceedings as the address of the person concerned.

[(1A) The address for service shall be an address in the United Kingdom, another EEA state or the Channel Islands.][42] Patents, Trade Marks and Designs (Address For Service and Time Limits, etc) Rules 2006

(2) Where any document or part of a document which is in a language other than English is served on the Comptroller or any party to proceeding or filed with the Comptroller in pursuance of these Rules, it shall be accompanied by a translation into English of the document or part, verified to the satisfaction of the Comptroller as corresponding to the original text.

24.—The fees specified in Schedule 2 shall be payable in respect of the matters there mentioned.

C3–025

SCHEDULE 1

Rules 3(1), 7(1), 10(1) and 14(1)

List of Design Right Forms

C3–026

1   Reference of dispute to comptroller
2   Application to be made a party to proceedings
3   Application to settle terms of licence of right or to adjust terms of licence granted before 1 August 1989
4   Application by design right or copyright owner to vary terms of licence of right

SCHEDULE 2

Rule 24

Fees

C3–027

[On reference of dispute (Form 1) under rule 3(1)	£65	
On application (Form 2) under rule 7(1)	£40	
On application (Form 3) under rule 10(1)	£65	
On application (Form 4) under rule 14(1)	£65][43]	

C4. Council Directive of 16 December 1986 on the Legal Protection of Topographies of Semiconductor Products (87/54/EEC)

THE COUNCIL OF THE EUROPEAN COMMUNITIES,

Having regard to the Treaty establishing the European Economic Community and in particular Article 100 thereof,

C4–001

Having regard to the proposal from the Commission,[44]
Having regard to the opinion of the European Parliament,[45]
Having regard to the opinion of the Economic and Social Committee,[46]

---

[42] Inserted by the Patents, Trade Marks and Designs (Address for Service) Rules 2009 (SI 2009/546), rr.2 and 3.
[43] Substituted by the Design Right (Proceedings before Comptroller) (Amendment) Rules (SI 1992/615) r.2.
[44] OJ No C 360, 31.12.1985, p.14.
[45] OJ No C 255, 13.10.1986, p.249.
[46] OJ No C 189, 28.7.1986, p.5.

Whereas semiconductor products are playing an increasingly important role in a broad range of industries and semiconductor technology can accordingly be considered as being of fundamental importance for the Community's industrial development;

Whereas the functions of semiconductor products depend in large part on the topographies of such products and whereas the development of such topographies requires the investment of considerable resources, human, technical and financial, while topographies of such products can be copied at a fraction of the cost needed to develop them independently;

Whereas topographies of semiconductor products are at present not clearly protected in all Member States by existing legislation and such protection, where it exists, has different attributes;

Whereas certain existing differences in the legal protection of semiconductor products offered by the laws of the Member States have direct and negative effects on the functioning of the common market as regards semiconductor products and such differences could well become greater as Member States introduce new legislation on this subject;

Whereas existing differences having such effects need to be removed and new ones having a negative effect on the common market prevented from arising;

Whereas, in relation to extension of protection to persons outside the Community, Member States should be free to act on their own behalf in so far as Community decisions have not been taken within a limited period of time;

Whereas the Community's legal framework on the protection of topographies of semiconductor products can, in the first instance, be limited to certain basic principles by provisions specifying whom and what should be protected, the exclusive rights on which protected persons should be able to rely to authorize or prohibit certain acts, exceptions to these rights and for how long the protection should last;

Whereas other matters can for the time being be decided in accordance with national law, in particular, whether registration or deposit is required as a condition for protection and, subject to an exclusion of licences granted for the sole reason that a certain period of time has elapsed, whether and on what conditions non-voluntary licences may be granted in respect of protected topographies;

Whereas protection of topographies of semiconductor products in accordance with this Directive should be without prejudice to the application of some other forms of protection;

Whereas further measures concerning the legal protection of topographies of semiconductor products in the Community can be considered at a later stage, if necessary, while the application of common basic principles by all Member States in accordance with the provisions of this Directive is an urgent necessity, HAS ADOPTED THIS DIRECTIVE:

CHAPTER 1

DEFINITIONS

Article 1

C4–002   1. For the purposes of this Directive:

(a) a 'semiconductor product' shall mean the final or an intermediate form of any product:

     (i) consisting of a body of material which includes a layer of semi-conducting material; and

     (ii) having one or more other layers composed of conducting, insulating or semiconducting material, the layers being arranged in accordance with a predetermined three-dimensional pattern; and

     (iii) intended to perform, exclusively or together with other functions, an electronic function;

  (b) the 'topography' of a semiconductor product shall mean a series of related images, however fixed or encoded;

     (i) representing the three-dimensional pattern of the layers of which a semiconductor product is composed; and

     (ii) in which series, each image has the pattern or part of the pattern of a surface of the semiconductor product at any stage of its manufacture;

  (c) 'commercial exploitation' means the sale, rental, leasing or any other method of commercial distribution, or an offer for these purposes. However, for the purposes of Articles 3(4), 4(1), 7(1), (3) and (4) 'commercial exploitation' shall not include exploitation under conditions of confidentiality to the extent that no further distribution to third parties occurs, except where exploitation of a topography takes place under conditions of confidentiality required by a measure taken in conformity with Article 223(1)(b) of the Treaty.

2. The Council acting by qualified majority on a proposal from the Commission, may amend paragraph 1(a)(i) and (ii) in order to adapt these provisions in the light of technical progress.

CHAPTER 2

PROTECTION OF TOPOGRAPHIES OF SEMICONDUCTOR PRODUCTS

Article 2

1. Member States shall protect the topographies of semiconductor products by   **C4–003** adopting legislative provisions conferring exclusive rights in accordance with the provisions of the Directive.

2. The topography of a semiconductor product shall be protected in so far as it satisfies the conditions that it is the result of its creator's own intellectual effort and is not commonplace in the semiconductor industry. Where the topography of a semiconductor product consists of elements that are commonplace in the semiconductor industry, it shall be protected only to the extent that the combination of such elements, taken as a whole, fulfils the above mentioned conditions.

Article 3

1. Subject to paragraphs 2 to 5, the right to protection shall apply in favour of   **C4–004** persons who are the creators of the topographies of semiconductor products.

2. Member States may provide that,

  (a) where a topography is created in the course of the creator's employment, the right to protection shall apply in favour of the creator's employer unless the terms of employment provide to the contrary;

691

(b) where a topography is created under a contract other than a contract of employment, the right to protection shall apply in favour of a party to the contract by whom the topography has been commissioned, unless the contract provides to the contrary.

3. (a) As regards the persons referred to in paragraph 1, the right to protection shall apply in favour of natural persons who are nationals of a Member State or who have their habitual residence on the territory of a Member State.

(b) Where Member States make provision in accordance with paragraph 2, the right to protection shall apply in favour of:

(i) natural persons who are nationals of a Member State or who have their habitual residence on the territory of a Member State;

(ii) companies or other legal persons which have a real and effective industrial or commercial establishment on the territory of a Member State.

4. Where no right to protection exists in accordance with other provisions of this Article, the right to protection shall also apply in favour of the persons referred to in paragraph 3(b)(i) and (ii) who:

(a) first commercially exploit within a Member State a topography which has not yet been exploited commercially anywhere in the world; and

(b) have been exclusively authorized to exploit commercially the topography throughout the Community by the person entitled to dispose of it.

5. The right to protection shall also apply in favour of the successors in title of the persons mentioned in paragraphs 1 to 4.

6. Subject to paragraph 7, Member States may negotiate and conclude agreements or understandings with third States and multilateral Conventions concerning the legal protection of topographies of semiconductor products whilst respecting Community law and in particular the rules laid down in this Directive.

7. Member States may enter into negotiations which third States with a view to extending the right to protection to persons who do not benefit from the right to protection according to the provisions of this Directive. Member States who enter into such negotiations shall inform the Commission thereof.

When a Member State wishes to extend protection to persons who otherwise do not benefit from the right to protection according to the provisions of this Directive or to conclude an agreement or understanding on the extension of protection with a non-Member State it shall notify the Commission. The Commission shall inform the other Member States thereof. The Member State shall hold the extension of protection or the conclusion of the agreement or understanding in abeyance for one month from the date on which it notifies the Commission. However, if within that period the Commission notifies the Member State concerned of its intention to submit a proposal to the Council for all Member States to extend protection in respect of the persons or non-Member State concerned, the Member State shall hold the extension of protection or the conclusion of the agreement or understanding in abeyance for a period of two months from the date of the notification by the Member State.

Where, before the end of this two-month period, the Commission submits such a proposal to the Council, the Member State shall hold the extension of protection or the conclusion of the agreement or understanding in abeyance for a further period of four months from the date on which the proposal was submitted.

In the absence of a Commission notification or proposal or a Council decision within the time limits prescribed above, the Member State may extend protection or conclude the agreement or understanding.

A proposal by the Commission to extend protection, whether or not it is made following a notification by a Member State in accordance with the preceding paragraphs shall be adopted by the Council acting by qualified majority.

A Decision of the Council on the basis of a Commission proposal shall not prevent a Member State from extending protection to persons, in addition to those to benefit from protection in all Member States, who were included in the envisaged extension, agreement or understanding as notified, unless the Council acting by qualified majority has decided otherwise.

8. Commission proposals and Council decisions pursuant to paragraph 7 shall be published for information in the Official Journal of the European Communities.

Article 4

1. Member States may provide that the exclusive rights conferred in conformity **C4–005** with Article 2 shall not come into existence or shall no longer apply to the topography of a semiconductor product unless an application for registration in due form has been filed with a public authority within two years of its first commercial exploitation. Member States may require in addition to such registration that material identifying or exemplifying the topography or any combination thereof has been deposited with a public authority, as well as a statement as to the date of first commercial exploitation of the topography where it precedes the date of the application for registration.

2. Member States shall ensure that material deposited in conformity with paragraph 1 is not made available to the public where it is a trade secret. This provision shall be without prejudice to the disclosure of such material pursuant to an order of a court or other competent authority to persons involved in litigation concerning the validity or infringement of the excusive rights referred to in Article 2.

3. Member States may require that transfers of rights in protected topographies be registered.

4. Member States may subject registration and deposit in accordance with paragraphs 1 and 3 to the payment of fees not exceeding their administrative costs.

5. Conditions prescribing the fulfilment of additional formalities for obtaining or maintaining protection shall not be admitted.

6. Member States which require registration shall provide for legal remedies in favour of a person having the right to protection in accordance with the provisions of this Directive who can prove that another person has applied for or obtained the registration of a topography without his authorization.

Article 5

1. The exclusive rights referred to in Article 2 shall include the rights to **C4–006** authorize or prohibit any of the following acts:

    (a) reproduction of a topography in so far as it is protected under Article 2(2);

    (b) commercial exploitation or the importation for that purpose of a topography or of a semiconductor product manufactured by using the topography.

2. Notwithstanding paragraph 1, a Member State pay permit the reproduction of a topography privately for non commercial aims.

3. The exclusive rights referred to in paragraph 1(a) shall not apply to reproduction for the purpose of analyzing, evaluating or teaching the concepts, processes, systems or techniques embodied in the topography or the topography itself.

4. The exclusive rights referred to in paragraph 1 shall not extend to any such act in relation to a topography meeting the requirements of Article 2(2) and created on the basis of an analysis and evaluation of another topography, carried out in conformity with paragraph 3.

5. The exclusive rights to authorize or prohibit the acts specified in paragraph 1(b) shall not apply to any such act committed after the topography or the semiconductor product has been put on the market in a Member State by the person entitled to authorize its marketing or with his consent. 6. A person who, when he acquires a semiconductor product, does not know, or has no reasonable grounds to believe, that the product is protected by an exclusive right conferred by a Member State in conformity with this Directive shall not be prevented from commercially exploiting that product.

However, for acts committed after that person knows, or has reasonable grounds to believe, that the semiconductor product is so protected, Member States shall ensure that on the demand of the rightholder a tribunal may require, in accordance with the provisions of the national law applicable, the payment of adequate remuneration.

7. The provisions of paragraph 6 shall apply to the successors in title of the person referred to in the first sentence of that paragraph.

Article 6

C4–007   Member States shall not subject the exclusive rights referred to in Article 2 to licences granted, for the sole reason that a certain period of time has elapsed, automatically, and by operation of law.

Article 7

C4–008   1. Member States shall provide that the exclusive rights referred to in Article 2 shall come into existence:

    (a) where registration is the condition for the coming into existence of the exclusive rights in accordance with Article 4, on the earlier of the following dates:
        (i) the date when the topography is first commercially exploited anywhere in the world;
        (ii) the date when an application or registration has been filed in due form; or
    (b) when the topography is first commercially exploited anywhere in the world; or
    (c) when the topography is first fixed or encoded.

2. Where the exclusive rights come into existence in accordance with paragraph 1(a) or (b), the Member States shall provide, for the period prior to those rights

coming into existence, legal remedies in favour of a person having the right to protection in accordance with the provisions of this Directive who can prove that another person has fraudulently reproduced or commercially exploited or imported for that purpose a topography. This paragraph shall be without prejudice to legal remedies made available to enforce the exclusive rights conferred in conformity with Article 2.

3. The exclusive rights shall come to an end 10 years from the end of the calendar year in which the topography is first commercially exploited anywhere in the world or, where registration is a condition for the coming into existence or continuing application of the exclusive rights, 10 years from the earlier of the following dates:

    (a) the end of the calendar year in which the topography is first commercially exploited anywhere in the world;

    (b) the end of the calendar year in which the application for registration has been filed in due form.

4. Where a topography has not been commercially exploited anywhere in the world within a period of 15 years from its first fixation or encoding, any exclusive rights in existence pursuant to paragraph 1 shall come to an end and no new exclusive rights shall come into existence unless an application for registration in due form has been filed within that period in those Member States where registration is a condition for the coming into existence or continuing application of the exclusive rights.

Article 8

The protection granted to the topographies of semiconductor products in accordance with Article 2 shall not extend to any concept, process, system, technique or encoded information embodied in the topography other than the topography itself.   **C4–009**

Article 9

Where the legislation of Member States provides that semiconductor products manufactured using protected topographies may carry an indication, the indication to be used shall be a capital T as follows: T, 'T', [T], T, T* or T.   **C4–010**

CHAPTER 3

CONTINUED APPLICATION OF OTHER LEGAL PROVISIONS

Article 10

1. The provisions of this Directive shall be without prejudice to legal provisions concerning patent and utility model rights.

2. The provisions of this Directive shall be without prejudice: **C4–011**

    (a) to rights conferred by the Member States in fulfilment of their obligations under international agreements, including provisions extending such rights to nationals of, or residents in, the territory of the Member State concerned;

    (b) to the law of copyright in Member States, restricting the reproduction of drawing or other artistic representations of topographies by copying them in two dimensions.

3. Protection granted by national law to topographies of semiconductor products fixed or encoded before the entry into force of the national provisions enacting the Directive, but no later than the date set out in Article 11(1), shall not be affected by the provisions of this Directive.

CHAPTER 4

FINAL PROVISIONS

Article 11

C4–012   1. Member States shall bring into force the laws, regulations or administrative provisions necessary to comply with this Directive by 7 November 1987.

2. Member States shall ensure that they communicate to the Commission the texts of the main provisions of national law which they adopt in the field covered by this Directive.

Article 12

C4–013   This Directive is addressed to the Member States.

Done at Brussels, 16 December 1986.

For the Council
The President
G. HOWE

C5. The Design Right (Reciprocal Protection) (No.2) Order 1989 (SI 1989/1294)

C5–001   Whereas, it appears to Her Majesty that the laws of the countries mentioned in article 2 of this Order provide adequate protection for British designs:

Now, therefore, Her Majesty, by virtue of the authority conferred upon Her by section 256(1) of the Copyright, Designs and Patents Act 1988, is pleased, by and with the advice of Her Privy Council, to order, and it is hereby ordered, as follows:

C5–002   **1.**—This Order may be cited as the Design Right (Reciprocal Protection) (No. 2) Order 1989 and shall come into force on 1 August 1989.

C5–003   **2.**—The following countries are hereby designated as enjoying reciprocal protection under Part III of the Copyright, Designs and Patents Act 1988 (design right)—

Anguilla
Bermuda
British Indian Ocean Territory
British Virgin Islands
Cayman Islands
Channel Islands
Falklands Islands
Gibraltar
Hong Kong
Isle of Man
Montserrat
New Zealand
Pitcairn, Henderson, Ducie and Oeno Islands
St Helena and Dependencies
South Georgia and the South Sandwich Islands
Turks and Caicos Islands.

3.—The Design Right (Reciprocal Protection) Order 1989 is hereby revoked.   **C5–004**

C6. The Design Right (Semiconductor Topographies) Regulations 1989 (SI 1989/1100)

Whereas a draft of the following Regulations has been approved by resolution   **C6–001**
of each House of Parliament:
Now, therefore, the Secretary of State, being designated for the purposes of
section 2(2) of the European Communities Act 1972 in relation to the conferment
and protection of exclusive rights in the topographies of semiconductor products,
in exercise of the powers conferred on him by the said section 2(2) hereby makes
the following Regulations:

Citation and commencement

1.—These Regulations may be cited as the Design Right (Semiconductor   **C6–002**
Topographies) Regulations 1989 and shall come into force on 1 August 1989.

Interpretation

2.—(1) In these Regulations—   **C6–003**

"the Act" means the Copyright, Designs and Patents Act 1988;
"semiconductor product" means an article the purpose, or one of the
purposes, of which is the performance of an electronic function and which
consists of two or more layers, at least one of which is composed of
semiconducting material and in or upon one or more of which is fixed a
pattern appertaining to that or another function; and
"semiconductor topography" means a design within the meaning of section
213(2) of the Act which is a design of either of the following:
  (a) the pattern fixed, or intended to be fixed, in or upon—
     (i) a layer of a semiconductor product, or
     (ii) a layer of material in the course of and for the purpose of the
      manufacture of a semiconductor product, or
  (b) the arrangement of the patterns fixed, or intended to be fixed, in or
    upon the layers of a semiconductor product in relation to one
    another.

697

(2) Except where the context otherwise requires, these Regulations shall be construed as one with Part III of the Act (design right).

Application of Copyright, Designs and Patents Act 1988, Part III

C6–004   3.—In its application to a design which is a semiconductor topography, Part III of the Act shall have effect subject to regulations 4 to 9 below.

Qualification

C6–005   4.—(1) Section 213(5) of the Act has effect subject to paragraphs (2) to (4) below.

[(2) Part III of the Act has effect as if for section 217(3) there was substituted the following—

"(3) In this section "qualifying country" means—
(a)   the United Kingdom,
(b)   another member State,
(c)   the Isle of Man, Gibraltar, the Channel Islands or any colony,
(d)   a country listed in the Schedule to the Design Right (Semiconductor Topographies) Regulations 1989.".][47]

(3) Where a semiconductor topography is created in pursuance of a commission or in the course of employment and the designer of the topography is, by virtue of section 215 of the Act (as substituted by regulation 5 below), the first owner of design right in that topography, section 219 of the Act does not apply and section 218(2) to (4) of the Act shall apply to the topography as if it had not been created in pursuance of a commission or in the course of employment.

(4) Section 220 of the Act has effect subject to regulation 7 below and as if for subsection (1) there was substituted the following:

"220.—(1) A design which does not qualify for design right protection under section 218 or 219 (as modified by regulation 4(3) of the Design Right (Semiconductor Topographies) Regulations 1989) or under the said regulation 4(3) qualifies for design right protection if the first marketing of applications made to the design—
(a)   is by a qualifying person who is exclusively authorised to put such articles on the market in every member State of the European Economic Community, and
(b)   takes place within the territory of any member State.";

and subsection (4) of section 220 accordingly has effected as if the words "in the United Kingdom" were omitted.

Ownership of design right

C6–006   5.—Part III of the Act has effect as if for section 215 of the Act there was substituted the following:

"215.—(1) The designer is the first owner of any design right in a design which is not created in pursuance of a commission or in the course of employment.

(2) Where a design is created in pursuance of a commission, the person commissioning the design is the first owner of any design right in it subject to any agreement in writing to the contrary.

[47] Substituted by the Design Right (Semiconductor Topographies) (Amendment) Regulations 2006 (SI 2006/1833) regs 2 and 3.

(3) Where, in a case not falling within subsection (2) a design is created by an employee in the course of his employment, his employer is the first owner of any design right in the design subject to any agreement in writing to the contrary.

(4) If a design qualifies for design right protection by virtue of section 220 (as modified by regulation 4(4) of the Design Right (Semiconductor Topographies) Regulations 1989), the above rules do not apply and, subject to regulation 7 of the said Regulations, the person by whom the articles in question are marketed is the first owner of the design right.".

Duration of design right

6.—(1) Part III of the Act has effect as if for section 216 of the Act there was substituted the following: **C6–007**

"216. The design right in a semiconductor topography expires—
- (a) ten years from the end of the calendar year in which the topography or articles made to the topography were first made available for sale or hire anywhere in the world by or with the licence of the design right owner, or
- (b) if neither the topography nor articles made to the topography are so made available within a period of fifteen years commencing with the earlier of the time when the topography was first recorded in a design document or the time when an article was first made to the topography, at the end of that period.".

(2) Subsection (2) of section 263 of the Act has effect as if the words "or a semiconductor topography" were inserted after the words "in relation to an article".

(3) The substitute provision set out in paragraph (1) above has effect subject to regulation 7 below.

Confidential information

7.—In determining, for the purposes of section 215(4), 216 or 220 of the Act (as modified by these Regulations), whether there has been any marketing, or anything has been made available for sale or hire, no account shall be taken of any sale or ire, or any offer or exposure for sale or hire, which is subject to an obligation of confidence in respect of information about the semiconductor topography in question unless either— **C6–008**

- (a) the article or semiconductor topography sold or hired or offered or exposed for sale or hire has been sold or hired on a previous occasion (whether or not subject to an obligation of confidence), or
- (b) the obligation is imposed at the behest of the Crown, or of the government of any country outside the United Kingdom, for the protection of security in connection with the production of arms, munitions or war material.

Infringement

8.—(1) Section 226 of the Act has effect as if for subsection (1) there was substituted the following: **C6–009**

"226.—(1) Subject to subsection (1A), the owner of design right in a design has the exclusive right to reproduce the design—
- (a) by making articles to that design, or
- (b) by making a design document recording the design for the purpose of enabling such articles to be made.
(1A) Subsection (1) does not apply to—

    (a) the reproduction of a design privately for non-commercial aims; or

    (b) the reproduction of a design for the purpose of analysing or evaluat-
ing the design or analysing, evaluating or teaching the concepts,
processes, systems or techniques embodied in it."

(2) Section 227 of the Act does not apply if the article in question has previously
been sold or hired within—

    (a) the United Kingdom by or with the licence of the owner of design right
in the semiconductor topography in question, or

    (b) the territory of any other member State of the European Economic
Community or the territory of Gibraltar by or with the consent of the
person for the time being entitled to import it into or sell or hire it within
that territory.

(3) Section 228(6) of the Act does not apply.

(4) It is not an infringement of design right in a semiconductor topography
to—

    (a) create another original semiconductor topography as a result of an
analysis or evaluation of the first topography or of the concepts,
processes, systems or techniques embodied in it, or

    (b) reproduce that other topography.

(5) Anything which would be an infringement of the design right in a
semiconductor topography if done in relation to the topography as a whole is an
infringement of the design right in the topography if done in relation to a
substantial part of the topography.

Licences of right

C6–010   **9.**—Section 237 of this Act does not apply.

Revocation and transitional provisions

C6–011   **10.**—(1) The Semiconductor Products (Protection of Topography) Regulations
1987 are hereby revoked.

(2) Sub-paragraph (1) of paragraph 19 of Schedule 1 to the Act shall not apply
in respect of a semiconductor topography created between 7 November 1987 and
31 July 1989.

(3) In its application to copyright in a semiconductor topography created before
7 November 1987, sub-paragraph (2) of the said paragraph 19 shall have effect as
if the reference to sections 237 to 239 were a reference to sections 238 and 239; and
sub-paragraph (3) of that paragraph accordingly shall not apply to such copyright.

SCHEDULE Regulation 4(2)

C6–012   Albania[48]
Angola
Antigua and Barbuda
Argentina
Armenia
Australia
Bahrain, Kingdom of
Bangladesh
Barbados

---

[48] Substituted by the Design Right (Semiconductor Topographies) (Amendment) Regulations 2006 (SI 2006/1833) regs 2 and 4 and Sch.1.

Belize
Benin
Bolivia
Botswana
Brazil
Brunei Darussalam
Bulgaria
Burkina Faso
Burundi
Cambodia
Cameroon
Canada
Central African Republic
Chad
Chile
China
Colombia
Congo
Costa Rica
Côte d'Ivoire
Croatia
Cuba
Democratic Republic of the Congo
Djibouti
Dominica
Dominican Republic
Ecuador
Egypt
El Salvador
Fiji
Former Yugoslav Republic of Macedonia
French overseas territories
Gabon
The Gambia
Georgia
Ghana
Grenada
Guatemala
Guinea
Guinea Bissau
Guyana
Haiti
Honduras
Hong Kong
Iceland
India
Indonesia
Israel
Jamaica
Japan
Jordan
Kenya
Korea, Republic of
Kuwait
Kyrgyz Republic
Lesotho
Liechtenstein
Macao, China
Madagascar
Malawi
Malaysia

Maldives
Mali
Mauritania
Mauritius
Mexico
Moldova
Mongolia
Morocco
Mozambique
Myanmar
Namibia
Nepal
Netherlands Antilles
New Zealand
Nicaragua
Niger
Nigeria
Norway
Oman
Pakistan
Panama
Papua New Guinea
Paraguay
Peru
Philippines
Qatar
Romania
Rwanda
Saint Kitts and Nevis
Saint Lucia
Saint Vincent & the Grenadines
Saudi Arabia
Senegal
Sierra Leone
Singapore
Solomon Islands
South Africa
Sri Lanka
Suriname
Swaziland
Switzerland
Chinese Taipei
Tanzania
Thailand
Togo
Trinidad and Tobago
Tunisia
Turkey
Uganda
United Arab Emirates
United States of America
Uruguay
Venezuela
Zambia
Zimbabwe][49]

---

[49] Substituted by the Design Right (Semiconductor Topographies) (Amendment) Regulations 2006 (SI 2006/1833) regs 2 and 4 and Sch.1.

PART II

[Albania
Angola
Antigua and Barbuda
Argentina
Armenia
Australia
Bahrain, Kingdom of
Bangladesh
Barbados
Belize
Benin
Bolivia
Botswana
Brazil
Brunei Darussalam
Bulgaria
Burkina Faso
Burundi
Cambodia
Cameroon
Canada
Central African Republic
Chad
Chile
China
Colombia
Congo
Costa Rica
Côte d'Ivoire
Croatia
Cuba
Democratic Republic of the Congo
Djibouti
Dominica
Dominican Republic
Ecuador
Egypt
El Salvador
Fiji
Former Yugoslav Republic of Macedonia
French overseas territories
Gabon
The Gambia
Georgia
Ghana
Grenada
Guatemala
Guinea
Guinea Bissau
Guyana
Haiti
Honduras
Hong Kong
Iceland
India
Indonesia
Israel
Jamaica
Japan

703

Jordan
Kenya
Korea, Republic of
Kuwait
Kyrgyz Republic
Lesotho
Liechtenstein
Macao, China
Madagascar
Malawi
Malaysia
Maldives
Mali
Mauritania
Mauritius
Mexico
Moldova
Mongolia
Morocco
Mozambique
Myanmar
Namibia
Nepal
Netherlands Antilles
New Zealand
Nicaragua
Niger
Nigeria
Norway
Oman
Pakistan
Panama
Papua New Guinea
Paraguay
Peru
Philippines
Qatar
Romania
Rwanda
Saint Kitts and Nevis
Saint Lucia
Saint Vincent & the Grenadines
Saudi Arabia
Senegal
Sierra Leone
Singapore
Solomon Islands
South Africa
Sri Lanka
Suriname
Swaziland
Switzerland
Chinese Taipei
Tanzania
Thailand
Togo
[Tonga][50]
Trinidad and Tobago

---

[50] Inserted by the Design Right (Semiconductor Topographies) (Amendment) (No 2) Regulations 2008 (SI 2008/1434) reg.3.

Tunisia
Turkey
Uganda
[Ukraine][51]
United Arab Emirates
United States of America
Uruguay
Venezuela
[Vietnam][52]
Zambia
Zimbabwe][53]

[51] Inserted by the Design Right (Semiconductor Topographies) (Amendment) (No 2) Regulations 2008 (SI 2008/1434) reg.3.
[52] Inserted by the Design Right (Semiconductor Topographies) (Amendment) (No 2) Regulations 2008 (SI 2008/1434) reg.3.
[53] Substituted by the Design Right (Semiconductor Topographies) (Amendment) Regulations 2006 (SI 2006/1833) regs 2 and 4 and Sch.1.

APPENDIX D

COPYRIGHT

Contents

Para.

D1. The Copyright, Designs and Patents Act 1988 (c.48) (extracts relating to copyright)

PART I

COPYRIGHT

CHAPTER I

SUBSISTENCE, OWNERSHIP AND DURATION OF COPYRIGHT

Introductory

Copyright and Copyright Works

D1–001   **1.**—(1) Copyright is a property right which subsists in accordance with this Part in the following descriptions of work—

(a) original literary, dramatic, musical or artistic works,
(b) sound recordings, films [or broadcasts][1] and

[1] Substituted, subject to the savings specified in SI 2003/2498 reg.32, by the Copyright and Related Rights Regulations (SI 2003/2498) reg.5.

706

(c) the typographical arrangement of published editions.

(2) In this Part "copyright work" means a work of any of those descriptions in which copyright subsists.

(3) Copyright does not subsist in a work unless the requirements of this Part with respect to qualification for copyright protection are met (see section 153 and the provisions referred to there).

Rights subsisting in copyright works

2.—(1) The owner of the copyright in a work of any description has the exclusive right to do the acts specified in Chapter II as the acts restricted by the copyright in a work of that description.

D1–002

(2) In relation to certain descriptions of copyright work the following rights conferred by Chapter IV (moral rights) subsist in favour of the author, director or commissioner of the work, whether or not he is the owner of the copyright—

(a) section 77 (right to be identified as author or director),
(b) section 80 (right to object to derogatory treatment of work), and
(c) section 85 (right to privacy of certain photographs and films).

Descriptions of work and related provisions

Literary, dramatic and musical works

3.—(1) In this Part—

D1–003

"literary work" means any work, other than a dramatic or musical work, which is written, spoken or sung, and accordingly includes—
  (a) a table or compilation other than a database,
  (b) a computer program;
  (c) preparatory design material for a computer program; and
  [(d) a database;]²
"dramatic work" includes a work of dance or mime; and
"musical work" means a work consisting of music, exclusive of any words or action intended to be sung, spoken or performed with the music.

(2) Copyright does not subsist in a literary, dramatic or musical work unless and until it is recorded, in writing or otherwise; and references in this Part to the time at which such a work is made are to the time at which it is so recorded.

(3) It is immaterial for the purposes of subsection (2) whether the work is recorded by or with the permission of the author; and where it is not recorded by the author, nothing in that subsection affects the question whether copyright subsists in the record as distinct from the work recorded.

Databases

[**3A.**—(1) In this Part "database" means a collection of independent works, data or other materials which—

D1–004

(a) are arranged in a systematic or methodical way, and
(b) are individually accessible by electronic or other means.

(2) For the purposes of this Part a literary work consisting of a database is original if, and only if, by reason of the selection or arrangement of the contents of the database the database constitutes the author's own intellectual creation.]³

---

² Added by the Copyright and Rights in Databases Regulations (SI 1997/3032) reg.5.
³ Added by the Copyright and Rights in Databases Regulations (SI 1997/3032) reg.6.

Artistic works

D1–005

4.—(1) In this Part "artistic work" means—

  (a) a graphic work, photograph, sculpture or collage, irrespective of artistic quality,

  (b) a work of architecture being a building or a model for a building, or

  (c) a work of artistic craftsmanship.

  (2) In this Part—

"building" includes any fixed structure, and a part of a building or fixed structure;

"graphic work" includes—

  (a) any painting, drawing, diagram, map, chart or plan, and

  (b) any engraving, etching, lithograph, woodcut or similar work;

"photograph" means a recording of light or other radiation on any medium on which an image is produced or from which an image may by any means be produced, and which is not part of a film;

"sculpture" includes a cast or model made for purposes of sculpture.

Authorship and ownership of copyright

Authorship of works

D1–006

9.—(1) In this Part "author", in relation to a work, means the person who creates it.

  (2) That person shall be taken to be—

  (aa) in the case of a sound recording, the producer;

  (ab) in the case of a film, the producer and the principal director;

  (b) in the case of a broadcast, the person making the broadcast (see section 6(3)) or, in the case of a broadcast which relays another broadcast by reception and immediate re-transmission, the person making that other broadcast;

    [. . .][4]

  (d) in the case of the typographical arrangement of a published edition, the publisher.

  (3) In the case of a literary, dramatic, musical or artistic work which is computer-generated, the author shall be taken to be the person by whom the arrangements necessary for the creation of the work are undertaken.

  (4) For the purposes of this Part a work is of "unknown authorship" if the identity of the author is unknown or, in the case of a work of joint authorship, if the identity of none of the authors is known.

  (5) For the purposes of this Part the identity of an author shall be regarded as unknown if it is not possible for a person to ascertain his identity by reasonable inquiry; but if his identity is once known it shall not subsequently be regarded as unknown.

Works of joint authorship

D1–007

10.—(1) In this Part a "work of joint authorship" means a work produced by the collaboration of two or more authors in which the contribution of each author is not distinct from that of the other author or authors.

---

[4] Repealed, subject to the savings specified in SI 2003/2498 reg.32, by the Copyright and Related Rights Regulations (SI 2003/2498) Sch.2, para.1.

[(1A) A film shall be treated as a work of joint authorship unless the producer and the principal director are the same person.][5]

(2) A broadcast shall be treated as a work of joint authorship in any case where more than one person is to be taken as making the broadcast (see section 6(3)).

(3) References in this Part to the author of a work shall, except as otherwise provided, be construed in relation to a work of joint authorship as references to all the authors of the work.

First ownership of copyright

11.—(1) The author of a work is the first owner of any copyright in it, subject to the following provisions.

(2) Where a literary, dramatic, musical or artistic work[, or a film,][6] is made by an employee in the course of his employment, his employer is the first owner of any copyright in the work subject to any agreement to the contrary.

(3) This section does not apply to Crown copyright or Parliamentary copyright (see sections 163 and 165) or to copyright which subsists by virtue of section 168 (copyright of certain international organisations).

D1–008

Duration of copyright

Duration of copyright in literary, dramatic, musical or artistic works

12.—(1) The following provisions have effect with respect to the duration of copyright in a literary, dramatic, musical or artistic work.

(2) Copyright expires at the end of the period of 70 years from the end of the calendar year in which the author dies, subject as follows.

(3) If the work is of unknown authorship, copyright expires—

(a) at the end of the period of 70 years from the end of the calendar year in which the work was made, or

(b) if during that period the work is made available to the public, at the end of the period of 70 years from the end of the calendar year in which it is first so made available,

subject as follows.

(4) Subsection (2) applies if the identity of the author becomes known before the end of the period specified in paragraph (a) or (b) of subsection (3).

(5) For the purposes of subsection (3) making available to the public includes—

(a) in the case of a literary, dramatic or musical work—
  (i) performance in public, or
  (ii) communication to the public;

(b) in the case of an artistic work—
  (i) exhibition in public,
  (ii) a film including the work being shown in public, or
  [(iii) communication to the public;][7]

but in determining generally for the purposes of that subsection whether a work has been made available to the public no account shall be taken of any unauthorised act.

D1–009

[5] Added by the Copyright and Related Rights Regulations (SI 1996/2967) reg.18.
[6] Inserted by the Copyright and Related Rights Regulations (SI 1996/2967) reg.18.
[7] Substituted, subject to the savings specified in SI 2003/2498 reg.32, by the Copyright and Related Rights Regulations (SI 2003/2498) Sch.1, para.4.

(6) Where the country of origin of the work is not an EEA state and the author of the work is not a national of an EEA state, the duration of copyright is that to which the work is entitled in the country of origin, provided that does not exceed the period which would apply under subsections (2) to (5).

(7) If the work is computer-generated the above provisions do not apply and copyright expires at the end of the period of 50 years from the end of the calendar year in which the work was made.

(8) The provisions of this section are adapted as follows in relation to a work of joint authorship—

- (a) the reference in subsection (2) to the death of the author shall be construed—
  - (i) if the identity of all the authors is known, as a reference to the death of the last of them to die, and
  - (ii) if the identity of one or more of the authors is known and the identity of one or more others is not, as a reference to the death of the last whose identity is known;
- (b) the reference in subsection (4) to the identity of the author becoming known shall be construed as a reference to the identity of any of the authors becoming known;
- (c) the reference in subsection (6) to the author not being a national of an EEA state shall be construed as a reference to none of the authors being a national of an EEA state.

(9) This section does not apply to Crown copyright or Parliamentary copyright (see sections 163 to [166D][8]) or to copyright which subsists by virtue of section 168 (copyright of certain international organisations).

CHAPTER II

RIGHTS OF COPYRIGHT OWNER

The acts restricted by copyright

The acts restricted by copyright in a work

D1–010   16.—(1) The owner of the copyright in a work has, in accordance with the following provisions of this Chapter, the exclusive right to do the following acts in the United Kingdom—

- (a) to copy the work (see section 17);
- (b) to issue copies of the work to the public (see section 18);
- (ba) to rent or lend the work to the public (see section 18A);
- (c) to perform, show or play the work in public (see section 19);
- [(d) to communicate the work to the public (see section 20);][9]
- (e) to make an adaptation of the work or do any of the above in relation to an adaptation (see section 21);

---

[8] Substituted by the Government of Wales Act 2006 s.160(1) and Sch.10, paras 22 and 23.

[9] Substituted, subject to the savings specified in SI 2003/2498 reg.32, by the Copyright and Related Rights Regulations (SI 2003/2498) reg.6.

and those acts are referred to in this Part as the "acts restricted by the copy-right".

(2) Copyright in a work is infringed by a person who without the licence of the copyright owner does, or authorises another to do, any of the acts restricted by the copyright.

(3) References in this Part to the doing of an act restricted by the copyright in a work are to the doing of it—

(a) in relation to the work as a whole or any substantial part of it, and

(b) either directly or indirectly;

and it is immaterial whether any intervening acts themselves infringe copy-right.

(4) This Chapter has effect subject to—

(a) the provisions of Chapter III (acts permitted in relation to copyright works), and

(b) the provisions of Chapter VII (provisions with respect to copyright licensing).

Infringement of copyright by copying

17.—(1) The copying of the work is an act restricted by the copyright in every **D1–011** description of copyright work; and references in this Part to copying and copies shall be construed as follows.

(2) Copying in relation to a literary, dramatic, musical or artistic work means reproducing the work in any material form.
This includes storing the work in any medium by electronic means.

(3) In relation to an artistic work copying includes the making of a copy in three dimensions of a two-dimensional work and the making of a copy in two dimensions of a three-dimensional work.

(4) Copying in relation to a film [or broadcast][10] includes making a photograph of the whole or any substantial part of any image forming part of the film [or broadcast][11].

(5) Copying in relation to the typographical arrangement of a published edition means making a facsimile copy of the arrangement.

(6) Copying in relation to any description of work includes the making of copies which are transient or are incidental to some other use of the work.

Infringement by issue of copies to the public

18.—(1) The issue to the public of copies of the work is an act restricted by the **D1–012** copyright in every description of copyright work.

(2) *References in this Part to the issue to the public of copies of a work are to—*

(a) the act of putting into circulation in the EEA copies not previously put into circulation in the EEA by or with the consent of the copyright owner, or

(b) the act of putting into circulation outside the EEA copies not previously put into circulation in the EEA or elsewhere.

(4) References in this Part to the issue of copies of a work include the issue of the original.

---

[10] Substituted, subject to the savings specified in SI 2003/2498 reg.32, by the Copyright and Related Rights Regulations (SI 2003/2498) reg.5.

[11] Substituted, subject to the savings specified in SI 2003/2498 reg.32, by the Copyright and Related Rights Regulations (SI 2003/2498) reg.5.

[*NOTE: The Above amendments were purportedly made to this section by the Copyright and Related Rights Regulations 1996 (SI 1996/2967). The opinion is expressed in the text of this work (paras 9.14 to 9.17 ante) that this amendment is ultra vires and void, and that the original text of the Act as passed by Parliament still has effect, at least in the industrial design field. The original text of s.18(2) is as follows:*

"18.—(2) References in this Part to the issue to the public of copies of a work are to the act of putting into circulation copies not previously put into circulation, in the United Kingdom or elsewhere, and not to—

(a) any subsequent distribution, sale, hiring or loan of those copies, or

(b) any subsequent importation of those copies into the United Kingdom;

except that in relation to sound recordings, films and computer programs the restricted act of issuing copies to the public includes any rental of copies to the public."]

Infringement by rental or lending of work to the public

D1–013   **18A.**—(1) The rental or lending of copies of the work to the public is an act restricted by the copyright in—

(a) a literary, dramatic or musical work,

(b) an artistic work, other than—

  (i) a work of architecture in the form of a building or a model for a building, or

  (ii) a work of applied art, or

(c) a film or a sound recording.

(2) In this Part, subject to the following provisions of this section—

(a) "rental" means making a copy of the work available for use, on terms that it will or may be returned, for direct or indirect economic or commercial advantage, and

(b) "lending" means making a copy of the work available for use, on terms that it will or may be returned, otherwise than for direct or indirect economic or commercial advantage, through an establishment which is accessible to the public.

(3) The expressions "rental" and "lending" do not include—

(a) making available for the purpose of public performance, playing or showing in public, [or communication to the public][12];

(b) making available for the purpose of exhibition in public; or

(c) making available for on-the-spot reference use.

(4) The expression "lending" does not include making available between establishments which are accessible to the public.

(5) Where lending by an establishment accessible to the public gives rise to a payment the amount of which does not go beyond what is necessary to cover the operating costs of the establishment, there is no direct or indirect economic or commercial advantage for the purposes of this section.

(6) References in this Part to the rental or lending of copies of a work include the rental or lending of the original.

---

[12] Substituted, subject to the savings specified in SI 2003/2498 reg.32, by the Copyright and Related Rights Regulations (SI 2003/2498) Sch.1, para.6.

Secondary infringement of copyright

Secondary infringement: importing infringing copy

22.—The copyright in a work is infringed by a person who, without the licence **D1–014**
of the copyright owner, imports into the United Kingdom, otherwise than for his
private and domestic use, an article which is, and which he knows or has reason
to believe is, an infringing copy of the work.

Secondary infringement: possessing or dealing with infringing copy

23.—The copyright in a work is infringed by a person who, without the licence **D1–015**
of the copyright owner—

    (a) possesses in the course of a business,
    (b) sells or lets for hire, or offers or exposes for sale or hire,
    (c) in the course of a business exhibits in public or distributes, or
    (d) distributes otherwise than in the course of a business to such an extent as
        to affect prejudicially the owner of the copyright,

an article which is, and which he knows or has reason to believe is, an infringing
copy of the work.

Secondary infringement: providing means for making infringing copies

24.—(1) Copyright in a work is infringed by a person who, without the licence **D1–016**
of the copyright owner—

    (a) makes,
    (b) imports into the United Kingdom,
    (c) possesses in the course of a business, or
    (d) sells or lets for hire, or offers or exposes for sale or hire,

an article specifically designed or adapted for making copies of that work,
knowing or having reason to believe that it is to be used to make infringing
copies.

(2) Copyright in a work is infringed by a person who without the licence of the
copyright owner transmits the work by means of a telecommunications system
(otherwise than by [communication to the public][13]), knowing or having reason to
believe that infringing copies of the work will be made by means of the reception
of the transmission in the United Kingdom or elsewhere.

Infringing copies

Meaning of "infringing copy"

27.—(1) In this Part "infringing copy", in relation to a copyright work, shall be **D1–017**
construed in accordance with this section.

(2) An article is an infringing copy if its making constituted an infringement of
the copyright in the work in question.

(3) An article is also an infringing copy if—

    (a) it has been or is proposed to be imported into the United Kingdom,
        and

---

[13] Substituted, subject to the savings specified in SI 2003/2498 reg.32, by the Copyright and
   Related Rights Regulations (SI 2003/2498) Sch.1, para.5.

(b) its making in the United Kingdom would have constituted an infringement of the copyright in the work in question, or a breach of an exclusive licence agreement relating to that work.

(4) Where in any proceedings the question arises whether an article is an infringing copy and it is shown—

(a) that the article is a copy of the work, and
(b) that copyright subsists in the work or has subsisted at any time,

it shall be presumed until the contrary is proved that the article was made at a time when copyright subsisted in the work.

(5) Nothing in subsection (3) shall be construed as applying to an article which may lawfully be imported into the United Kingdom by virtue of any enforceable Community right within the meaning of section 2(1) of the European Communities Act 1972.

(6) In this Part "infringing copy" includes a copy falling to be treated as an infringing copy by virtue of any of the following provisions—

[section 31A(6) and (9) (making a single accessible copy for personal use),
section 31B(9) and (10) (multiple copies for visually impaired persons),
section 31C(2) (intermediate copies held by approved bodies),][14]
section 32(5) (copies made for purposes of instruction or examination),
section 35(3) (recordings made by educational establishments for educational purposes),
section 36(5) (reprographic copying by educational establishments for purposes of instruction),
section 37(3)(b) (copies made by librarian or archivist in reliance on false declaration),
section 56(2) (further copies, adaptations, &c. of work in electronic form retained on transfer of principal copy),
section 63(2) (copies made for purpose of advertising artistic work for sale),
section 68(4) (copies made for purpose of broadcast),
section 70(2) (recording for the purposes of time-shifting),
section 71(2) (photographs of broadcasts), or
any provision of an order under section 141 (statutory licence for certain reprographic copying by educational establishments).

CHAPTER III

ACTS PERMITTED IN RELATION TO COPYRIGHT WORKS

Introductory

Introductory provisions

D1–018   28.—(1) The provisions of this Chapter specify acts which may be done in relation to copyright works notwithstanding the subsistence of copyright; they relate only to the question of infringement of copyright and do not affect any other right or obligation restricting the doing of any of the specified acts.

---

[14] Inserted by the Copyright (Visually Impaired Persons) Act 2002 s.7(1).

(2) Where it is provided by this Chapter that an act does not infringe copyright, or may be done without infringing copyright, and no particular description of copyright work is mentioned, the act in question does not infringe the copyright in a work of any description.

(3) No inference shall be drawn from the description of any act which may by virtue of this Chapter be done without infringing copyright as to the scope of the acts restricted by the copyright in any description of work.

(4) The provisions of this Chapter are to be construed independently of each other, so that the fact that an act does not fall within one provision does not mean that it is not covered by another provision.

Making of temporary copies

[28A.—Copyright in a literary work, other than a computer program or a **D1–019** database, or in a dramatic, musical or artistic work, the typographical arrangement of a published edition, a sound recording or a film, is not infringed by the making of a temporary copy which is transient or incidental, which is an integral and essential part of a technological process and the sole purpose of which is to enable—

(a) a transmission of the work in a network between third parties by an intermediary; or

(b) a lawful use of the work;

and which has no independent economic significance.][15]

General

Research and private study

29.—(1) Fair dealing with a literary, dramatic, musical or artistic work for the **D1–020** purposes of research for a non-commercial purpose does not infringe any copyright in the work provided that it is accompanied by a sufficient acknowledgement.

(1B) No acknowledgement is required in connection with fair dealing for the purposes mentioned in subsection (1) where this would be impossible for reasons of practicality or otherwise.

(1C) Fair dealing with a literary, dramatic, musical or artistic work for the purposes of private study does not infringe any copyright in the work.

(2) Fair dealing with the typographical arrangement of a published edition for the purposes of research or private study does not infringe any copyright in the arrangement.

(3) Copying by a person other than the researcher or student himself is not fair dealing if—

(a) in the case of a librarian, or a person acting on behalf of a librarian, he does anything which regulations under section 40 would not permit to be done under section 38 or 39 (articles or parts of published works: restriction on multiple copies of same material), or

(b) in any other case, the person doing the copying knows or has reason to believe that it will result in copies of substantially the same material being provided to more than one person at substantially the same time and for substantially the same purpose.

[15] Inserted, subject to the savings specified in SI 2003/2498 reg.32, by the Copyright and Related Rights Regulations (SI 2003/2498) reg.8.

(4) It is not fair dealing—

    (a) to convert a computer program expressed in a low level language into a version expressed in a higher level language, or

    (b) incidentally in the course of so converting the program, to copy it, (these acts being permitted if done in accordance with section 50B (decompilation)).

(4A) It is not fair dealing to observe, study or test the functioning of a computer program in order to determine the ideas and principles which underlie any element of the program (these acts being permitted if done in accordance with section 50BA (observing, studying and testing)).

    [. . .][16]

Criticism, review and news reporting

D1–021   **30.**—(1) Fair dealing with a work for the purpose of criticism or review, of that or another work or of a performance of a work, does not infringe any copyright in the work provided that it is accompanied by a sufficient acknowledgement and provided that the work has been made available to the public.

(1A) For the purposes of subsection (1) a work has been made available to the public if it has been made available by any means, including—

    (a) the issue of copies to the public;

    (b) making the work available by means of an electronic retrieval system;

    (c) the rental or lending of copies of the work to the public;

    (d) the performance, exhibition, playing or showing of the work in public;

    (e) the communication to the public of the work,

but in determining generally for the purposes of that subsection whether a work has been made available to the public no account shall be taken of any unauthorised act.

(2) Fair dealing with a work (other than a photograph) for the purpose of reporting current events does not infringe any copyright in the work provided that (subject to subsection (3)) it is accompanied by a sufficient acknowledgement.

(3) No acknowledgement is required in connection with the reporting of current events by means of a sound recording, film [or broadcast where this would be impossible for reasons of practicality or otherwise].[17]

Incidental inclusion of copyright material

D1–022   **31.**—(1) Copyright in a work is not infringed by its incidental inclusion in an artistic work, sound recording, film or broadcast.

(2) Nor is the copyright infringed by the issue to the public of copies, or the playing, showing or communication to the public, of anything whose making was, by virtue of subsection (1), not an infringement of the copyright.

(3) A musical work, words spoken or sung with music, or so much of a sound recording [or broadcast][18] as includes a musical work or such words, shall not be regarded as incidentally included in another work if it is deliberately included.

---

[16] Repealed, subject to the savings specified in SI 2003/2498 reg.32, by the Copyright and Related Rights Regulations (SI 2003/2498) Sch.2, para.1.

[17] Substituted, subject to the savings specified in SI 2003/2498 reg.32, by the Copyright and Related Rights Regulations (SI 2003/2498) reg.10.

[18] Substituted, subject to the savings specified in SI 2003/2498 reg.32, by the Copyright and Related Rights Regulations (SI 2003/2498) Sch.1, para.3.

Designs

Design documents and models

51.—(1) It is not an infringement of any copyright in a design document or model recording or embodying a design for anything other than an artistic work or a typeface to make an article to the design or to copy an article made to the design.

(2) Nor is it an infringement of the copyright to issue to the public, or include in a film[or communicate to the public][19], anything the making of which was, by virtue of subsection (1), not an infringement of that copyright.

(3) In this section—

 "design" means the design of any aspect of the shape or configuration (whether internal or external) of the whole or part of an article, other than surface decoration; and

 "design document" means any record of a design, whether in the form of a drawing, a written description, a photograph, data stored in a computer or otherwise.

D1–023

Effect of exploitation of design derived from artistic work

52.—(1) This section applies where an artistic work has been exploited, by or with the licence of the copyright owner, by—

 (a) making by an industrial process articles falling to be treated for the purposes of this Part as copies of the work, and

 (b) marketing such articles, in the United Kingdom or elsewhere.

(2) After the end of the period of 25 years from the end of the calendar year in which such articles are first marketed, the work may be copied by making articles of any description, or doing anything for the purpose of making articles of any description, and anything may be done in relation to articles so made, without infringing copyright in the work.

(3) Where only part of an artistic work is exploited as mentioned in subsection (1), subsection (2) applies only in relation to that part.

(4) The Secretary of State may by order make provision—

 (a) as to the circumstances in which an article, or any description of an article, is to be regarded for the purposes of this section as made by an industrial process;

 (b) excluding from the operation of this section such articles of a primarily literary or artistic character as he thinks fit.

(5) An order shall be made by statutory instrument which shall be subject to annulment in pursuance of a resolution of either House of Parliament.

(6) In this section—

 (a) references to articles do not include films; and

 (b) references to the marketing of an article are to its being sold or let for hire or offered or exposed for sale or hire.

D1–024

Things done in reliance on registration of designs

53.—(1) The copyright in an artistic work is not infringed by anything done—

D1–025

---

[19] Substituted, subject to the savings specified in SI 2003/2498 reg.32, by the Copyright and Related Rights Regulations (SI 2003/2498) Sch.1, para.8.

(a) in pursuance of an assignment or licence made or granted by a person registered under the Registered Designs Act 1949 as the proprietor of a corresponding design, and

(b) in good faith in reliance on the registration and without notice of any proceedings for the cancellation[or invalidation][20] of the registration or for rectifying the relevant entry in the register of designs;
and this is so notwithstanding that the person registered as the proprietor was not the proprietor of the design for the purposes of the 1949 Act.

(2) In subsection (1) a "corresponding design", in relation to an artistic work, means a design within the meaning of the 1949 Act which if applied to an article would produce something which would be treated for the purposes of this Part as a copy of the artistic work.

Works in electronic form

Transfers of copies of works in electronic form

D1–026   **56.**—(1) This section applies where a copy of a work in electronic form has been purchased on terms which, expressly or impliedly or by virtue of any rule of law, allow the purchaser to copy the work, or to adapt it or make copies of an adaptation, in connection with his use of it.
(2) If there are no express terms—

(a) prohibiting the transfer of the copy by the purchaser, imposing obligations which continue after a transfer, prohibiting the assignment of any licence or terminating any licence on a transfer, or

(b) providing for the terms on which a transferee may do the things which the purchaser was permitted to do,
anything which the purchaser was allowed to do may also be done without infringement of copyright by a transferee; but any copy, adaptation or copy of an adaptation made by the purchaser which is not also transferred shall be treated as an infringing copy for all purposes after the transfer.

(3) The same applies where the original purchased copy is no longer usable and what is transferred is a further copy used in its place.
(4) The above provisions also apply on a subsequent transfer, with the substitution for references in subsection (2) to the purchaser of references to the subsequent transferor.

Representation of certain artistic works on public display

D1–027   **62.**—(1) This section applies to—

(a) buildings, and

(b) sculptures, models for buildings and works of artistic craftsmanship, if permanently situated in public place or in premises open to the public.

(2) The copyright in such a work is not infringed by—

(a) making a graphic work representing it,

(b) making a photograph or film of it, or

[20] Inserted by the Registered Designs Regulations (SI 2001/3949) Sch.1, para.16.

718

(c) making a broadcast of a visual image of it.

(3) Nor is the copyright infringed by the issue to the public of copies, or the [communication to the public],[21] of anything whose making was, by virtue of this section, not an infringement of the copyright.

Advertisement of sale of artistic work

63.—(1) It is not an infringement of copyright in an artistic work to copy it, or to issue copies to the public, for the purpose of advertising the sale of the work.

D1–028

(2) Where a copy which would otherwise be an infringing copy is made in accordance with this section but is subsequently dealt with for any other purpose, it shall be treated as an infringing copy for the purposes of that dealing, and if that dealing infringes copyright for all subsequent purposes. For this purpose "dealt with" means sold or let for hire, offered or exposed for sale or hire, exhibited in public[, distributed or communicated to the public].[22]

Making of subsequent works by the same artist

64.—Where the author of an artistic work is not the copyright owner, he does not infringe the copyright by copying the work in making another artistic work, provided he does not repeat or imitate the main design of the earlier work.

D1–029

Reconstruction of buildings

65.—Anything done for the purposes of reconstructing a building does not infringe any copyright—

D1–030

- (a) in the building, or
- (b) in any drawings or plans in accordance with which the building was, by or with the licence of the copyright owner, constructed.

CHAPTER V

DEALINGS WITH RIGHTS IN COPYRIGHT WORKS

Copyright

Assignment and Licences

90.—(1) Copyright is transmissible by assignment, by testamentary disposition or by operation of law, as personal or moveable property.

D1–031

(2) An assignment or other transmission of copyright may be partial, that is, limited so as to apply—

- (a) to one or more, but not all, of the things the copyright owner has the exclusive right to do;
- (b) to part, but not the whole, of the period for which the copyright is to subsist.

---

[21] Substituted, subject to the savings specified in SI 2003/2498 reg.32, by the Copyright and Related Rights Regulations (SI 2003/2498) Sch.1, para.5.
[22] Substituted, subject to the savings specified in SI 2003/2498 reg.32, by the Copyright and Related Rights Regulations (SI 2003/2498) reg.17.

(3) An assignment of copyright is not effective unless it is in writing signed by or on behalf of the assignor.

(4) A licence granted by a copyright owner is binding on every successor in title to his interest in the copyright, except a purchaser in good faith for valuable consideration and without notice (actual or constructive) of the licence or a person deriving title from such a purchaser; and references in this Part to doing anything with, or without, the licence of the copyright owner shall be construed accordingly.

Prospective ownership of copyright

D1–032   91.—(1) Where by an agreement made in relation to future copyright, signed by or on behalf of the prospective owner of the copyright, the prospective owner purports to assign the future copyright (wholly or partially) to another person, then if, on the copyright coming into existence, the assignee or another person claiming under him would be entitled as against all other persons to require the copyright to be vested in him, the copyright shall vest in the assignee or his successor in title by virtue of this subsection.

(2) In this Part—

"future copyright" means copyright which will or may come into existence in respect of a future work or class of works or on the occurrence of a future event; and

"prospective owner" shall be construed accordingly, and includes a person who is prospectively entitled to copyright by virtue of such an agreement as is mentioned in subsection (1).

(3) A licence granted by a prospective owner of copyright is binding on every successor in title to his interest (or prospective interest) in the right, except a purchaser in good faith for valuable consideration and without notice (actual or constructive) of the licence or a person deriving title from such a purchaser; and references in this Part to doing anything with, or without, the licence of the copyright owner shall be construed accordingly.

Exclusive licences

D1–033   92.—(1) In this Part an "exclusive licence" means a licence in writing signed by or on behalf of the copyright owner authorising the licensee to the exclusion of all other persons, including the person granting the licence, to exercise a right which would otherwise be exercisable exclusively by the copyright owner.

(2) The licensee under an exclusive licence has the same rights against a successor in title who is bound by the licence as he has against the person granting the licence.

Copyright to pass under will with unpublished work

D1–034   93. Where under a bequest (whether specific or general) a person is entitled, beneficially or otherwise, to—

(a) an original document or other material thing recording or embodying a literary, dramatic, musical or artistic work which was not published before the death of the testator, or

(b) an original material thing containing a sound recording or film which was not published before the death of the testator,

the bequest shall, unless a contrary intention is indicated in the testator's will or a codicil to it, be construed as including the copyright in the work in so far as the testator was the owner of the copyright immediately before his death.

CHAPTER VI

REMEDIES FOR INFRINGEMENT

Rights and remedies of copyright owner

Infringement actionable by copyright owner

96.—(1) An infringement of copyright is actionable by the copyright owner.   **D1–035**
(2) In an action for infringement of copyright all such relief by way of damages, injunctions, accounts or otherwise is available to the plaintiff as is available in respect of the infringement of any other property right.
(3) This section has effect subject to the following provisions of this Chapter.

Provisions as to damages in infringement action

97.—(1) Where in an action for infringement of copyright it is shown that at the   **D1–036**
time of the infringement the defendant did not know, and had no reason to believe, that copyright subsisted in the work to which the action relates, the plaintiff is not entitled to damages against him, but without prejudice to any other remedy.
(2) The court may in an action for infringement of copyright having regard to all the circumstances, and in particular to—

(a) the flagrancy of the infringement, and
(b) any benefit accruing to the defendant by reason of the infringement,

award such additional damages as the justice of the case may require.

[Injunctions against service providers

97A.—(1) The High Court (in Scotland, the Court of Session) shall have power   **D1–037**
to grant an injunction against a service provider, where that service provider has actual knowledge of another person using their service to infringe copyright.
(2) In determining whether a service provider has actual knowledge for the purpose of this section, a court shall take into account all matters which appear to it in the particular circumstances to be relevant and, amongst other things, shall have regard to—

(a) whether a service provider has received a notice through a means of contact made available in accordance with regulation 6(1)(c) of the Electronic Commerce (EC Directive) Regulations 2002 (SI 2002/2013); and
(b) the extent to which any notice includes—
    (i) the full name and address of the sender of the notice;
    (ii) details of the infringement in question.

(3) In this section "service provider" has the meaning given to it by regulation 2 of the Electronic Commerce (EC Directive) Regulations 2002.][23]

---

[23] Inserted, subject to the savings specified SI 2003/2498 reg.32, by Copyright and Related Rights Regulations (SI 2003/2498) reg.27.

Undertaking to take licence of right in infringement proceedings

D1–038   **98.**—(1) If in proceedings for infringement of copyright in respect of which a licence is available as of right under section 144 (powers exercisable in consequence of report of [Competition Commission][24]) the defendant undertakes to take a licence on such terms as may be agreed or, in default of agreement, settled by the Copyright Tribunal under that section—

(a) no injunction shall be granted against him,

(b) no order for delivery up shall be made under section 99, and

(c) the amount recoverable against him by way of damages or on an account of profits shall not exceed double the amount which would have been payable by him as licensee if such a licence on those terms had been granted before the earliest infringement.

(2) An undertaking may be given at any time before final order in the proceedings, without any admission of liability.

(3) Nothing in this section affects the remedies available in respect of an infringement committed before licences of right were available.

Order for delivery up

D1–039   **99.**—(1) Where a person—

(a) has an infringing copy of a work in his possession, custody or control in the course of a business, or

(b) has in his possession, custody or control an article specifically designed or adapted for making copies of a particular copyright work, knowing or having reason to believe that it has been or is to be used to make infringing copies,

the owner of the copyright in the work may apply to the court for an order that the infringing copy or article be delivered up to him or to such other person as the court may direct.

(2) An application shall not be made after the end of the period specified in section 113 (period after which remedy of delivery up not available); and no order shall be made unless the court also makes, or it appears to the court that there are grounds for making, an order under section 114 (order as to disposal of infringing copy or other article).

(3) A person to whom an infringing copy or other article is delivered up in pursuance of an order under this section shall, if an order under section 114 is not made, retain it pending the making of an order, or the decision not to make an order, under that section.

(4) Nothing in this section affects any other power of the court.

Right to seize infringing copies and other articles

D1–040   **100.**—(1) An infringing copy of a work which is found exposed or otherwise immediately available for sale or hire, and in respect of which the copyright owner would be entitled to apply for an order under section 99, may be seized and detained by him or a person authorised by him. The right to seize and detain is exercisable subject to the following conditions and is subject to any decision of the court under section 114.

(2) Before anything is seized under this section notice of the time and place of the proposed seizure must be given to a local police station.

---

[24] Substituted by the Competition Act 1998 (Competition Commission) Transitional, Consequential and Supplemental Provisions Order (SI 1999/506) art.23.

(3) A person may for the purpose of exercising the right conferred by this section enter premises to which the public have access but may not seize anything in the possession, custody or control of a person at a permanent or regular place of business of his, and may not use any force.

(4) At the time when anything is seized under this section there shall be left at the place where it was seized a notice in the prescribed form containing the prescribed particulars as to the person by whom or on whose authority the seizure is made and the grounds on which it is made.

(5) In this section—

"premises" includes land, buildings, moveable structures, vehicles, vessels, aircraft and hovercraft; and
"prescribed" means prescribed by order of the Secretary of State.

(6) An order of the Secretary of State under this section shall be made by statutory instrument which shall be subject to annulment in pursuance of a resolution of either House of Parliament.

Rights and remedies of exclusive licensee

Rights and remedies of exclusive licensee

101.—(1) An exclusive licensee has, except against the copyright owner, the   **D1–041**
same rights and remedies in respect of matters occurring after the grant of the licence as if the licence had been an assignment.

(2) His rights and remedies are concurrent with those of the copyright owner; and references in the relevant provisions of this Part to the copyright owner shall be construed accordingly.

(3) In an action brought by an exclusive licensee by virtue of this section a defendant may avail himself of any defence which would have been available to him if the action had been brought by the copyright owner.

[Certain infringements actionable by a non-exclusive licensee

101A.—(1) A non-exclusive licensee may bring an action for infringement of   **D1–042**
copyright if—

    (a) the infringing act was directly connected to a prior licensed act of the licensee; and
    (b) the licence—
        (i) is in writing and is signed by or on behalf of the copyright owner; and
        (ii) expressly grants the non-exclusive licensee a right of action under this section.

(2) In an action brought under this section, the non-exclusive licensee shall have the same rights and remedies available to him as the copyright owner would have had if he had brought the action.

(3) The rights granted under this section are concurrent with those of the copyright owner and references in the relevant provisions of this Part to the copyright owner shall be construed accordingly.

(4) In an action brought by a non-exclusive licensee by virtue of this section a defendant may avail himself of any defence which would have been available to him if the action had been brought by the copyright owner.

(5) Subsections (1) to (4) of section 102 shall apply to a non-exclusive licensee who has a right of action by virtue of this section as it applies to an exclusive licensee.

(6) In this section a "non-exclusive licensee" means the holder of a licence authorising the licensee to exercise a right which remains exercisable by the copyright owner.][25]

Exercise of concurrent rights

D1–043   **102.**—(1) Where an action for infringement of copyright brought by the copyright owner or an exclusive licensee relates (wholly or partly) to an infringement in respect of which they have concurrent rights of action, the copyright owner or, as the case may be, the exclusive licensee may not, without the leave of the court, proceed with the action unless the other is either joined as a plaintiff or added as a defendant.

(2) A copyright owner or exclusive licensee who is added as a defendant in pursuance of subsection (1) is not liable for any costs in the action unless he takes part in the proceedings.

(3) The above provisions do not affect the granting of interlocutory relief on an application by a copyright owner or exclusive licensee alone.

(4) Where an action for infringement of copyright is brought which relates (wholly or partly) to an infringement in respect of which the copyright owner and an exclusive licensee have or had concurrent rights of action—

(a) the court shall in assessing damages take into account—
    (i) the terms of the licence, and
    (ii) any pecuniary remedy already awarded or available to either of them in respect of the infringement;
(b) no account of profits shall be directed if an award of damages has been made, or an account of profits has been directed, in favour of the other of them in respect of the infringement; and
(c) the court shall if an account of profits is directed apportion the profits between them as the court considers just, subject to any agreement between them;

and these provisions apply whether or not the copyright owner and the exclusive licensee are both parties to the action.

(5) The copyright owner shall notify any exclusive licensee having concurrent rights before applying for an order under section 99 (order for delivery up) or exercising the right conferred by section 100 (right of seizure); and the court may on the application of the licensee make such order under section 99 or, as the case may be, prohibiting or permitting the exercise by the copyright owner of the right conferred by section 100, as it thinks fit having regard to the terms of the licence.

Presumptions

Presumptions relevant to literary, dramatic, musical and artistic works

D1–044   **104.**—(1) The following presumptions apply in proceedings brought by virtue of this Chapter with respect to a literary, dramatic, musical or artistic work.

(2) Where a name purporting to be that of the author appeared on copies of the work as published or on the work when it was made, the person whose name appeared shall be presumed, until the contrary is proved—

(a) to be the author of the work;

---

[25] Inserted subject to the savings specified SI 2003/2498, reg.32 by Copyright and Related Rights Regulations (SI 2003/2498) reg.28.

    (b) to have made it in circumstances not falling within section 11(2), 163, 165 or 168 (works produced in course of employment, Crown copyright, Parliamentary copyright or copyright of certain international organisations).

(3) In the case of a work alleged to be a work of joint authorship, subsection (2) applies in relation to each person alleged to be one of the authors.

(4) Where no name purporting to be that of the author appeared as mentioned in subsection (2) but

    (a) the work qualifies for copyright protection by virtue of section 155 (qualification by reference to country of first publication), and

    (b) a name purporting to be that of the publisher appeared on copies of the work as first published,
        the person whose name appeared shall be presumed, until the contrary is proved, to have been the owner of the copyright at the time of publication.

(5) If the author of the work is dead or the identity of the author cannot be ascertained by reasonable inquiry, it shall be presumed, in the absence of evidence to the contrary—

    (a) that the work is an original work, and

    (b) that the plaintiff's allegations as to what was the first publication of the work and as to the country of first publication are correct.

Offences

Criminal liability for making or dealing with infringing articles &c.

107.—(1) A person commits an offence who, without the licence of the copyright owner—   **D1–045**

    (a) makes for sale or hire, or

    (b) imports into the United Kingdom otherwise than for his private and domestic use, or

    (c) possesses in the course of a business with a view to committing any act infringing the copyright, or

    (d) in the course of a business—
        (i) sells or lets for hire, or
        (ii) offers or exposes for sale or hire, or
        (iii) exhibits in public, or
        (iv) distributes, or

    (e) distributes otherwise than in the course of a business to such an extent as to affect prejudicially the owner of the copyright,

an article which is, and which he knows or has reason to believe is, an infringing copy of a copyright work.

(2) A person commits an offence who—

    (a) makes an article specifically designed or adapted for making copies of a particular copyright work, or

    (b) has such an article in his possession,

knowing or having reason to believe that it is to be used to make infringing copies for sale or hire or for use in the course of a business.

(2A) A person who infringes copyright in a work by communicating the work to the public—

(a) in the course of a business, or

(b) otherwise than in the course of a business to such an extent as to affect prejudicially the owner of the copyright,

commits an offence if he knows or has reason to believe that, by doing so, he is infringing copyright in that work.

(3) Where copyright is infringed (otherwise than by reception of a communication to the public)—

(a) by the public performance of a literary, dramatic or musical work, or

(b) by the playing or showing in public of a sound recording or film,

any person who caused the work to be so performed, played or shown is guilty of an offence if he knew or had reason to believe that copyright would be infringed.

(4) A person guilty of an offence under subsection (1)(a), (b), (d)(iv) or (e) is liable—

(a) on summary conviction to imprisonment for a term not exceeding six months or a fine not exceeding [£50,000][26], or both;

(b) on conviction on indictment to a fine or imprisonment for a term not exceeding ten years, or both.

[(4A) A person guilty of an offence under subsection (2A) is liable—

(a) on summary conviction to imprisonment for a term not exceeding three months or a fine not exceeding [£50,000][27], or both;

(b) on conviction on indictment to a fine or imprisonment for a term not exceeding two years, or both.][28]

(5) A person guilty of any other offence under this section is liable on summary conviction to imprisonment for a term not exceeding six months or a fine not exceeding level 5 on the standard scale, or both.

(6) Sections 104 to 106 (presumptions as to various matters connected with copyright) do not apply to proceedings for an offence under this section; but without prejudice to their application in proceedings for an order under section 108 below.

Order for delivery up in criminal proceedings

D1–046   108.—(1) The court before which proceedings are brought against a person for an offence under section 107 may, if satisfied that at the time of his arrest or charge—

(a) he had in his possession, custody or control in the course of a business an infringing copy of a copyright work, or

(b) he had in his possession, custody or control an article specifically designed or adapted for making copies of a particular copyright work, knowing or having reason to believe that it had been or was to be used to make infringing copies,

order that the infringing copy or article be delivered up to the copyright owner or to such other person as the court may direct.

(2) For this purpose a person shall be treated as charged with an offence—

---

[26] Substituted by the Digital Economy Act 2010 s.42(1) and (2).

[27] Substituted by the Digital Economy Act 2010 s.42(1) and (2).

[28] Inserted, subject to the savings specified SI 2003/2498 reg.32, by the Copyright and Related Rights Regulations (SI 2003/2498) reg.26.

(a) in England, Wales and Northern Ireland, when he is orally charged or is served with a summons or indictment;

(b) in Scotland, when he is cautioned, charged or served with a complaint or indictment.

(3) An order may be made by the court of its own motion or on the application of the prosecutor (or, in Scotland, the Lord Advocate or procurator-fiscal), and may be made whether or not the person is convicted of the offence, but shall not be made—

(a) after the end of the period specified in section 113 (period after which remedy of delivery up not available), or

(b) if it appears to the court unlikely that any order will be made under section 114 (order as to disposal of infringing copy or other article).

(4) An appeal lies from an order made under this section by a magistrates' court—

(a) in England and Wales, to the Crown Court, and

(b) in Northern Ireland, to the county court;

and in Scotland, where an order has been made under this section, the person from whose possession, custody or control the infringing copy or article has been removed may, without prejudice to any other form of appeal under any rule of law, appeal against that order in the same manner as against sentence.

(5) A person to whom an infringing copy or other article is delivered up in pursuance of an order under this section shall retain it pending the making of an order, or the decision not to make an order, under section 114.

(6) Nothing in this section affects the powers of the court under [section 143 of the Powers of Criminal Courts (Sentencing) Act 2000][29], Part II of the Proceeds of Crime (Scotland) Act 1995 or Article 7 of the Criminal Justice (Northern Ireland) Order 1980 (general provisions as to forfeiture in criminal proceedings).

Search Warrants

109.—(1) Where a justice of the peace (in Scotland, a sheriff or justice of the **D1–047** peace) is satisfied by information on oath given by a constable (in Scotland, by evidence on oath) that there are reasonable grounds for believing—

(a) that an offence under section [107(1), (2) or (2A)][30] has been or is about to be committed in any premises, and

(b) that evidence that such an offence has been or is about to be committed is in those premises, he may issue a warrant authorising a constable to enter and search the premises, using such reasonable force as is necessary.

(2) The power conferred by subsection (1) does not, in England and Wales, extend to authorising a search for material of the kinds mentioned in section 9(2) of the Police and Criminal Evidence Act 1984 (certain classes of personal or confidential material).

(3) A warrant under this section—

(a) may authorise persons to accompany any constable executing the warrant, and

---

[29] Substituted by the Powers of Criminal Courts (Sentencing) Act 2000 Sch.9, para.115.
[30] Substituted, subject to the savings specified SI 2003/2498 reg.32, by the Copyright and Related Rights Regulations (SI 2003/2498) reg.26.

(b) remains in force for [three months][31] from the date of its issue.

(4) In executing a warrant issued under this section a constable may seize an article if he reasonably believes that it is evidence that any offence under [section 107(1), (2) or (2A)][32] has been or is about to be committed.

(5) In this section "premises" includes land, buildings, fixed or moveable structures, vehicles, vessels, aircraft and hovercraft.

Offence by body corporate: liability of officers

D1–048   **110.**—(1) Where an offence under section 107 committed by a body corporate is proved to have been committed with the consent connivance of a director, manager, secretary or other similar officer of the body, or a person purporting to act in any such capacity, he as well as the body corporate is guilty of the offence and liable to be proceeded against and punished accordingly.

(2) In relation to a body corporate whose affairs are managed by its members "director" means a member of the body corporate.

Provision for preventing importation of infringing copies

Infringing copies may be treated as prohibited goods

D1–049   **111.**—(1) The owner of the copyright in a published literary, dramatic or musical work may give notice in writing to the Commissioners of Customs and Excise—

  (a) that he is the owner of the copyright in the work, and
  (b) that he requests the Commissioners, for a period specified in the notice, to treat as prohibited goods printed copies of the work which are infringing copies.

(2) The period specified in a notice under subsection (1) shall not exceed five years and shall not extend beyond the period for which copyright is to subsist.

(3) The owner of the copyright in a sound recording or film may give notice in writing to the Commissioners of Customs and Excise—

  (a) that he is the owner of the copyright in the work,
  (b) that infringing copies of the work are expected to arrive in the United Kingdom at a time and a place specified in the notice, and
  (c) that he requests the Commissioners to treat the copies as prohibited goods.

(3A) The Commissioners may treat as prohibited goods only infringing copies of works which arrive in the United Kingdom—

  (a) from outside the European Economic Area, or
  (b) from within that Area but not having been entered for free circulation.

[(3B) This section does not apply to goods placed in, or expected to be placed in, one of the situations referred to in Article 1(1), in respect of which an application may be made under Article 5(1), of Council Regulation (EC) No 1383/2003 concerning customs action against goods suspected of infringing

---

[31] Substituted, in relation to England and Wales, by the Serious Organised Crime and Police Act 2005 s.174(2) and Sch.16, paras 6(1) and (2).
[32] Substituted, subject to the savings specified SI 2003/2498 reg.32 by the Copyright and Related Rights Regulations (SI 2003/2498) reg.26.

certain intellectual property rights and the measures to be taken against goods found to have infringed such rights.][33]

(4) When a notice is in force under this section the importation of goods to which the notice relates, otherwise than by a person for his private and domestic use, [subject to subsections (3A) and (3B), is prohibited][34]; but a person is not by reason of the prohibition liable to any penalty other than forfeiture of the goods.

Power of Commissioners of Customs and Excise to make regulations

112.—(1) The Commissioners of Customs and Excise may make regulations prescribing the form in which notice is to be given under section 111 and requiring a person giving notice— **D1–050**

(a) to furnish the Commissioners with such evidence as may be specified in the regulations, either on giving notice or when the goods are imported, or at both those times, and

(b) to comply with such other conditions as may be specified in the regulations.

(2) The regulations may, in particular, require a person giving such a notice—

(a) to pay such fees in respect of the notice as may be specified by the regulations;

(b) to give such security as may be so specified in respect of any liability or expense which the Commissioners may incur in consequence of the notice by reason of the detention of any article or anything done to an article detained;

(c) to indemnify the Commissioners against any such liability or expense, whether security has been given or not.

(3) The regulations may make different provision as respects different classes of case to which they apply and may include such incidental and supplementary provisions as the Commissioners consider expedient.

(4) Regulations under this section shall be made by statutory instrument which shall be subject to annulment in pursuance of a resolution of either House of Parliament.

(5) [. .][35]

Supplementary

Period after which remedy of delivery up not available

113.—(1) An application for an order under section 99 (order for delivery up in civil proceedings) may not be made after the end of the period of six years from the date on which the infringing copy or article in question was made, subject to the following provisions. **D1–051**

(2) If during the whole or any part of that period the copyright owner—

---

[33] Substituted by the Goods Infringing Intellectual Property Rights (Customs) Regulations 2004 (SI 2004/1473) reg.12.
[34] Substituted by the Copyright (EC Measures Relating to Pirated Goods and Abolition of Restrictions on the Import of Goods) Regulations (SI 1995/1445) reg.2.
[35] Repealed by the Commissioners for Revenue and Customs Act 2005 ss.50(6) and 52(2), Sch.4, para.38 and Sch.5.

(a) is under a disability, or

(b) is prevented by fraud or concealment from discovering the fact is entitling him to apply for an order,

an application may be made at any time before the end of the period of six years from the date on which he ceased to be under a disability or, as the case may be, could with reasonable diligence have discovered those facts.

(3) In subsection (2) "disability"—

(a) in England and Wales, has the same meaning as the Limitation Act 1980;

(b) in Scotland, means legal disability within the meaning of the Prescription and Limitations (Scotland) Act 1973;

(c) in Northern Ireland, has the same meaning as in the Statute of Limitations (Northern Ireland) 1958.

(4) An order under section 108 (order for delivery up in criminal proceedings) shall not, in any case, be made after the end of the period of six years from the date on which the infringing copy or article in question was made.

Order as to disposal of infringing copy or other article

D1–052   **114.**—(1) An application may be made to the court for an order that an infringing copy or other article delivered up in pursuance of an order under section 99 or 108, or seized and detained in pursuance of the right conferred by section 100, shall be—

(a) forfeited to the copyright owner, or

(b) destroyed or otherwise dealt with as the court may think fit,

or for a decision that no such order should be made.

(2) In considering what order (if any) should be made, the court shall consider whether other remedies available in an action for infringement of copyright would be adequate to compensate the copyright owner and to protect his interests.

(3) Provision shall be made by rules of court as to the service of notice on persons having an interest in the copy or other articles, and any such person is entitled—

(a) to appear in proceedings for an order under this section, whether or not he was served with notice, and

(b) to appeal against any order made, whether or not he appeared;

and an order shall not take effect until the end of the period within which notice of an appeal may be given or, if before the end of that period notice of appeal is duly given, until the final determination or abandonment of the proceedings on the appeal.

(4) Where there is more than one person interested in a copy or other article, the court shall make such order as it thinks just and may (in particular) direct that the article be sold, or otherwise dealt with, and the proceeds divided.

(5) If the court decides that no order should be made under this section, the person in whose possession, custody or control the copy or other article was before being delivered up or seized is entitled to its return.

(6) References in this section to a person having an interest in a copy or other article include any person in whose favour an order could be made in respect of it—

[(a)   under this section or under section 204 or 231 of this Act;

(b)   under section 24D of the Registered Designs Act 1949;

- (c) under section 19 of Trade Marks Act 1994 (including that section as applied by regulation 4 of the Community Trade Mark Regulations 2006 (SI 2006/1027)); or
- (d) under regulation 1C of the Community Design Regulations 2005 (SI 2005/2339)][36].

Forfeiture of infringing copies, etc.: England and Wales or Northern Ireland

114A.—(1) In England and Wales or Northern Ireland where there have come **D1–053** into the possession of any person in connection with the investigation or prosecution of a relevant offence—

- (a) infringing copies of a copyright work, or
- (b) articles specifically designed or adapted for making copies of a particular copyright work,

that person may apply under this section for an order for the forfeiture of the infringing copies or articles.

(2) For the purposes of this section "relevant offence" means—

- (a) an offence under [section 107(1), (2) or (2A)][37] (criminal liability for making or dealing with infringing articles, etc.),
- (b) an offence under the Trade Descriptions Act 1968 (c. 29),
- [(ba) an offence under the Business Protection from Misleading Marketing Regulations 2008,
- (bb) an offence under the Consumer Protection from Unfair Trading Regulations 2008, or][38]
- (c) an offence involving dishonesty or deception.

(3) An application under this section may be made—

- (a) where proceedings have been brought in any court for a relevant offence relating to some or all of the infringing copies or articles, to that court, or
- (b) where no application for the forfeiture of the infringing copies or articles has been made under paragraph (a), by way of complaint to a magistrates' court.

(4) On an application under this section, the court shall make an order for the forfeiture of any infringing copies or articles only if it is satisfied that a relevant offence has been committed in relation to the infringing copies or articles.

(5) A court may infer for the purposes of this section that such an offence has been committed in relation to any infringing copies or articles if it is satisfied that such an offence has been committed in relation to infringing copies or articles which are representative of the infringing copies or articles in question (whether by reason of being of the same design or part of the same consignment or batch or otherwise).

(6) Any person aggrieved by an order made under this section by a magistrates' court, or by a decision of such a court not to make such an order, may appeal against that order or decision—

- (a) in England and Wales, to the Crown Court, or

---

[36] Substituted by the Intellectual Property (Enforcement, etc.) Regulations 2006 (SI 2006/1028) reg.2(2) and Sch.2, paras 6 and 7.

[37] Substituted, subject to the savings specified SI 2003/2498 reg.32, by the Copyright and Related Rights Regulations (SI 2003/2498) reg.26.

[38] Substituted by the Consumer Protection from Unfair Trading Regulations 2008 (SI 2008/1277) reg.30(1) and Sch.2, Pt 1, paras 39 and 40.

(b) in Northern Ireland, to the county court.

(7) An order under this section may contain such provision as appears to the court to be appropriate for delaying the coming into force of the order pending the making and determination of any appeal (including any application under section 111 of the Magistrates' Courts Act 1980 (c. 43) or Article 146 of the Magistrates' Courts (Northern Ireland) Order 1981 (S.I. 1981/1675 (N.I. 26)) (statement of case)).

(8) Subject to subsection (9), where any infringing copies or articles are forfeited under this section they shall be destroyed in accordance with such directions as the court may give.

(9) On making an order under this section the court may direct that the infringing copies or articles to which the order relates shall (instead of being destroyed) be forfeited to the owner of the copyright in question or dealt with in such other way as the court considers appropriate.

Forfeiture of infringing copies, etc.: Scotland

D1–054   **114B.**—(1) In Scotland the court may make an order under this section for the forfeiture of any—

(a) infringing copies of a copyright work, or
(b) articles specifically designed or adapted for making copies of a particular copyright work.

(2) An order under this section may be made—

(a) on an application by the procurator-fiscal made in the manner specified in section 134 of the Criminal Procedure (Scotland) Act 1995 (c. 46), or
(b) where a person is convicted of a relevant offence, in addition to any other penalty which the court may impose.

(3) On an application under subsection (2)(a), the court shall make an order for the forfeiture of any infringing copies or articles only if it is satisfied that a relevant offence has been committed in relation to the infringing copies or articles.

(4) The court may infer for the purposes of this section that such an offence has been committed in relation to any infringing copies or articles if it is satisfied that such an offence has been committed in relation to infringing copies or articles which are representative of the infringing copies or articles in question (whether by reason of being of the same design or part of the same consignment or batch or otherwise).

(5) The procurator-fiscal making the application under subsection (2)(a) shall serve on any person appearing to him to be the owner of, or otherwise to have an interest in, the infringing copies or articles to which the application relates a copy of the application, together with a notice giving him the opportunity to appear at the hearing of the application to show cause why the infringing copies or articles should not be forfeited.

(6) Service under subsection (5) shall be carried out, and such service may be proved, in the manner specified for citation of an accused in summary proceedings under the Criminal Procedure (Scotland) Act 1995.

(7) Any person upon whom notice is served under subsection (5) and any other person claiming to be the owner of, or otherwise to have an interest in, infringing copies or articles to which an application under this section relates shall be entitled to appear at the hearing of the application to show cause why the infringing copies or articles should not be forfeited.

(8) The court shall not make an order following an application under subsection (2)(a)—

(a) if any person on whom notice is served under subsection (5) does not appear, unless service of the notice on that person is proved, or

(b) if no notice under subsection (5) has been served, unless the court is satisfied that in the circumstances it was reasonable not to serve such notice.

(9) Where an order for the forfeiture of any infringing copies or articles is made following an application under subsection (2)(a), any person who appeared, or was entitled to appear, to show cause why infringing copies or articles should not be forfeited may, within 21 days of the making of the order, appeal to the High Court by Bill of Suspension.

(10) Section 182(5)(a) to (e) of the Criminal Procedure (Scotland) Act 1995 (c. 46) shall apply to an appeal under subsection (9) as it applies to a stated case under Part 2 of that Act.

(11) An order following an application under subsection (2)(a) shall not take effect—

(a) until the end of the period of 21 days beginning with the day after the day on which the order is made, or

(b) if an appeal is made under subsection (9) above within that period, until the appeal is determined or abandoned.

(12) An order under subsection (2)(b) shall not take effect—

(a) until the end of the period within which an appeal against the order could be brought under the Criminal Procedure (Scotland) Act 1995, or

(b) if an appeal is made within that period, until the appeal is determined or abandoned.

(13) Subject to subsection (14), infringing copies or articles forfeited under this section shall be destroyed in accordance with such directions as the court may give.

(14) On making an order under this section the court may direct that the infringing copies or articles to which the order relates shall (instead of being destroyed) be forfeited to the owner of the copyright in question or dealt with in such other way as the court considers appropriate.

(15) For the purposes of this section—

["relevant offence" means—

(a) an offence under section 107(1), (2) or (2A) (criminal liability for making or dealing with infringing articles, etc),

(b) an offence under the Trade Descriptions Act 1968,

(c) an offence under the Business Protection from Misleading Marketing Regulations 2008,

(d) an offence under the Consumer Protection from Unfair Trading Regulations 2008, or

(e) any offence involving dishonesty or deception;][39]

"the court" means—

(a) in relation to an order made on an application under subsection (2)(a), the sheriff, and

(b) in relation to an order made under subsection (2)(b), the court which imposed the penalty.

[39] Substituted by the Consumer Protection from Unfair Trading Regulations 2008 (SI 2008/1277) reg.30(1) and Sch.2, Pt 1, paras 39 and 41.

Jurisdiction of county court and sheriff court

D1–055 **115.**—(1) In England, Wales and Northern Ireland a county court may entertain proceedings under—

section 99 (order for delivery up of infringing copy or other article),
section 102(5) (order as to exercise of rights by copyright owner where exclusive licensee has concurrent rights), or
section 114 (order as to disposal of infringing copy or other article), [save that, in Northern Ireland, a county court may entertain such proceedings only][40]

where the value of the infringing copies and other articles in question does not exceed the county court limit for actions in tort.

(2) In Scotland proceedings for an order under any of those provisions may be brought in the sheriff court.

(3) Nothing in this section shall be construed as affecting the jurisdiction of the High Court or, in Scotland, the Court of Session.

Chapter IX

Qualification for and Extent of Copyright Protection

Qualification for copyright protection

Qualification for copyright protection

D1–056 **153.**—(1) Copyright does not subsist in a work unless the qualification requirements of this Chapter are satisfied as regards—

(a) the author (see section 154), or
(b) the country in which the work was first published (see section 155), or
(c) in the case of a broadcast[. . .][41], the country from which the broadcast was made[. . .][42] (see section 156).

(2) Subsection (1) does not apply in relation to Crown copyright or Parliamentary copyright (see sections 163 to [166D][43]) or to copyright subsisting by virtue of section 168 (copyright of certain international organisations).

(3) If the qualification requirements of this Chapter, or section 163, 165 or 168, are once satisfied in respect of a work, copyright does not cease to subsist by reason of any subsequent event.

Qualification by reference to author

D1–057 **154.**—(1) A work qualifies for copyright protection if the author was at the material time a qualifying person, that is—

[40] Inserted, for all proceedings except family proceedings within the meaning of Pt V of 1984 c.42 and proceedings to which s.27(1) of 1984 c.28 (Admiralty jurisdiction) applies, by the High Court and County Courts Jurisdiction Order (SI 1991/724) Sch.1, para.1.

[41] Repealed, subject to the savings specified in SI 2003/2498 reg.32 by the Copyright and Related Rights Regulations (SI 2003/2498) Sch.2, para.1.

[42] Repealed, subject to the savings specified in SI 2003/2498 reg.32 by the Copyright and Related Rights Regulations (SI 2003/2498) Sch.2, para.1.

[43] Substituted by the Government of Wales Act 2006 s.160(1) and Sch.10, paras 22 and 25.

(a) a British citizen, a British overseas territories citizen, a British National (Overseas), a British Overseas citizen, a British subject or a British protected person within the meaning of the British Nationality Act 1981, or

(b) an individual domiciled or resident in the United Kingdom or another country to which the relevant provisions of this Part extend, or

(c) a body incorporated under the law of a part of the United Kingdom or of another country to which the relevant provisions of this Part extend.

(2) Where, or so far as, provision is made by Order under section 159 (application of this Part to countries to which it does not extend), a work also qualifies for copyright protection if at the material time the author was a citizen or subject of, an individual domiciled or resident in, or a body incorporated under the law of, a country to which the Order relates.

(3) A work of joint authorship qualifies for copyright protection if at the material time any of the authors satisfies the requirements of subsection (1) or (2); but where a work qualifies for copyright protection only under this section, only those authors who satisfy those requirements shall be taken into account for the purposes of—

section 11(1) and (2) (first ownership of copyright; entitlement of author or author's employer),
section 12 (duration of copyright), and section 9(4) (meaning of "unknown authorship") so far as it applies for the purposes of section 12, and
section 57 (anonymous or pseudonymous works: acts permitted on assumptions as to expiry of copyright or death of author).

(4) The material time in relation to a literary, dramatic, musical or artistic work is—

(a) in the case of an unpublished work, when the work was made or, if the making of the work extended over a period, a substantial part of that period;

(b) in the case of a published work, when the work was first published or, if the author had died before that time, immediately before his death.

(5) The material time in relation to other descriptions of work is as follows—

(a) in the case of a sound recording or film, when it was made;

(b) in the case of a broadcast, when the broadcast was made;

[. . .]⁴⁴

(d) in the case of the typographical arrangement of a published edition, when the edition was first published.

Qualification by reference to country of first publication

155.—(1) A literary, dramatic, musical or artistic work, a sound recording or film, or the typographical arrangement of a published edition, qualifies for copyright protection if it is first published—   **D1–058**

(a) in the United Kingdom, or

(b) in another country to which the relevant provisions of this Part extend.

(2) Where, or so far as, provision is made by Order under section 159 (application of this Part to countries to which it does not extend), such work also

---

⁴⁴ Repealed, subject to the savings specified in SI 2003/2498 reg.32, by the Copyright and Related Rights Regulations (SI 2003/2498) Sch.2, para.1.

qualifies for copyright protection if it is first published in a country to which the Order relates.

(3) For the purposes of this section, publication in one country shall not be regarded as other than the first publication by reason of simultaneous publication elsewhere; and for this purpose publication elsewhere within the previous 30 days shall be treated as simultaneous.

Extent and application of this Part

Countries to which this Part extends

D1–059 **157.**—(1) This Part extends to England and Wales, Scotland and Northern Ireland.

(2) Her Majesty may by Order in Council direct that this Part shall extend, subject to such exceptions and modifications as may be specified in the Order, to—

(a) any of the Channel Islands,
(b) the Isle of Man, or
(c) any colony.

(3) That power includes power to extend, subject to such exceptions and modifications as may be specified in the Order, any Order in Council made under the following provisions of this Chapter.

(4) The legislature of a country to which this Part has been extended may modify or add to the provisions of this Part, in their operation as part of the law of that country, as the legislature may consider necessary to adapt the provisions to the circumstances of that country—

(a) as regards procedure and remedies, or
(b) as regards works qualifying for copyright protection by virtue of a connection with that country.

(5) Nothing in this section shall be construed as restricting the extent of paragraph 36 of Schedule 1 (transitional provisions: dependent territories where the Copyright Act 1956 or the Copyright Act 1911 remains in force) in relation to the law of a dependent territory to which this Part does not extend.

Countries ceasing to be colonies

D1–060 **158.**—(1) The following provisions apply where a country to which this Part has been extended ceases to be a colony of the United Kingdom.

(2) As from the date on which it ceases to be a colony it shall cease to be regarded as a country to which this Part extends for the purposes of—

(a) section 160(2)(a) (denial of copyright protection to citizens of countries not giving adequate protection to British works), and
(b) sections 163 and 165 (Crown and Parliamentary copyright).

(3) But it shall continue to be treated as a country to which this Part extends for the purposes of sections 154 to 156 (qualification for copyright protection) until—

(a) an Order in Council is made in respect of that country under section 159 (application of this Part to countries to which it does not extend), or
(b) an Order in Council is made declaring that it shall cease to be so treated by reason of the fact that the provisions of this Part as part of the law of that country have been repealed or amended.

(4) A statutory instrument containing an Order in Council under subsection (3)(b) shall be subject to annulment in pursuance of a resolution of either House of Parliament.

Application of this Part to countries to which it does not extend

159.—(1) Her Majesty may be Order in Council make provision for applying in relation to a country to which this Part does not extend any of the provisions of this Part specified in the Order, so as to secure that those provisions— **D1–061**

- (a) apply in relation to persons who are citizens or subjects of that country or are domiciled or resident there, as they apply to persons who are British citizens or are domiciled or resident in the United Kingdom, or
- (b) apply in relation to bodies incorporated under the law of that country as they apply in relation to bodies incorporated under the law of a part of the United Kingdom, or
- (c) apply in relation to works first published in that country as they apply in relation to works first published in the United Kingdom, or
- (d) apply in relation to broadcasts made from[...][45] that country as they apply in relation to broadcasts made from [...][46] the United Kingdom.

(2) An Order may make provision for all or any of the matters mentioned in subsection (1) and may—

- (a) apply any provisions of this Part subject to such exceptions and modifications as are specified in the Order; and
- (b) direct that any provisions of this Part apply either generally or in relation to such classes or works, or other classes of case, as are specified in the Order.

(3) Except in the case of a Convention country or another member State of the European Economic Community, Her Majesty shall not make an Order in Council under this section in relation to a country unless satisfied that provision has been or will be made under the law of that country, in respect of the class of works to which the Order relates, giving adequate protection to the owners of copyright under this Part.

(4) In subsection (3) "Convention country" means a country which is a party to a Convention relating to copyright to which the United Kingdom is also a party.

(5) A statutory instrument containing an Order in Council under this section shall be subject to annulment in pursuance of a resolution of either House of Parliament.

Denial of copyright protection to citizens of countries not giving adequate protection to British works

160.—(1) If it appears to Her Majesty that the law of a country fails to give adequate protection to British works to which this section applies, or to one or more classes of such works, Her Majesty may make provision by Order in Council **D1–062**

---

[45] Repealed, subject to the savings specified in SI 2003/2498 reg.32, by the Copyright and Related Rights Regulations (SI 2003/2498) Sch.2, para.1.
[46] Repealed, subject to the savings specified in SI 2003/2498 reg.32, by the Copyright and Related Rights Regulations (SI 2003/2498) Sch.2, para.1.

in accordance with this section restricting the rights conferred by this Part in relation to works of authors connected with that country.

(2) An Order in Council under this section shall designate the country concerned and provide that, for the purposes specified in the Order, works first published after a date specified in the Order shall not be treated as qualifying for copyright protection by virtue of such publication if at that time the authors are—

(a) citizens are subjects of that country (not domiciled or resident in the United Kingdom or another country to which the relevant provisions of this Part extend), or

(b) bodies incorporated under the law of that country;

and the Order may make such provision for all the purposes of this Part or for such purposes as are specified in the Order, and either generally or in relation to such class of cases as are specified in the Order, having regard to the nature and extent of that failure referred to in subsection (1).

(3) This section applies to literary, dramatic, musical and artistic works, sound recordings and films; and "British works" means works of which the author was a qualifying person at the material time within the meaning of section 154.

(4) A statutory instrument containing an Order in Council under this section shall be subject to annulment in pursuance of a resolution of either House of Parliament.

Supplementary

Territorial waters and the continental shelf

D1–063   161.—(1) For the purposes of this Part the territorial waters of the United Kingdom shall be treated as part of the United Kingdom.

(2) This Part applies to things done in the United Kingdom sector of the continental shelf on a structure or vessel which is present there for purposes directly connected with the exploration of the sea bed or subsoil or the exploitation of their natural resources as it applies to things done in the United Kingdom.

(3) The United Kingdom sector of the continental shelf means the areas designated by order under section 1(7) of the Continental Shelf Act 1946.

British ships, aircraft and hovercraft

D1–064   162.—(1) This Part applies to things done on a British ship, aircraft or hovercraft as it applies to things done in the United Kingdom.

(2) In this section—

"British ship" means a ship which is a British ship for the purposes of the [Merchant Shipping Act 1995][47] otherwise than by virtue of registration in a country outside the United Kingdom; and "British aircraft" and "British hovercraft" mean an aircraft or hovercraft registered in the United Kingdom.

---

[47] Substituted in definition by the Merchant Shipping Act 1995 Sch.13, para.84.

CHAPTER X

MISCELLANEOUS AND GENERAL

Crown and Parliamentary copyright

Crown copyright

163.—(1) Where a work is made by Her Majesty or by an officer or servant of   **D1–065**
the Crown in the course of his duties—

    (a) the work qualifies for copyright protection notwithstanding section
       153(1) (ordinary requirement as to qualification for copyright protection),
       and
    (b) Her Majesty is the first owner of any copyright in the work.

  (1A) [. . .][48]
  (2) Copyright in such a work is referred to in this Part as "Crown copyright",
notwithstanding that it may be, or have been, assigned to another person.
  (3) Crown copyright in a literary, dramatic, musical or artistic work continues
to subsist—

    (a) until the end of the period of 125 years from the end of the calendar year
       in which the work was made, or
    (b) if the work is published commercially before the end of the period of 75
       years from the end of the calendar year in which it was made, until the
       end of the period of 50 years from the end of the calendar year in which
       it was first so published.

  (4) In the case of a work of joint authorship where one or more but not all of the
authors are persons falling within subsection (1), this section applies only in
relation to those authors and the copyright subsisting by virtue of their contribution to the work.
  (5) Except as mentioned above, and subject to any express exclusion elsewhere
in this Part, the provisions of this Part apply in relation to Crown copyright as to
other copyright.
  (6) This section does not apply to a work if, or to the extent that, Parliamentary
copyright subsists in the work (see sections 165 to [166D][49]).

Interpretation

General provisions as to construction

172.—(1) This Part restates and amends the law of copyright, that is, the   **D1–066**
provisions of the Copyright Act 1956, as amended.
  (2) A provision of this Part which corresponds to a provision of the previous
law shall not be construed as departing from the previous law merely because of
a change of expression.

---

[48] Repealed by the Government of Wales Act 2006 ss.160(1) and 163, Sch.10, paras 22, 26(1)
   and (2) and Sch.12.
[49] Substituted by the Government of Wales Act 2006 s.160(1) and Sch.10, paras 22 and
   26.

(3) Decisions under the previous law may be referred to the for the purpose of establishing whether a provision of this Part departs from the previous law, or otherwise for establishing the true construction of this Part.

Meaning of EEA and related expressions

D1–067   172A.—(1) In this part—

"the EEA" means the European Economic Area; and
"EEA state" means a member state, Iceland, Liechtenstein or Norway.[50]

(2) References in this Part to a person being [a national of an EEA State][51] shall be construed in relation to a body corporate as references to its being incorporated under the law of an EEA state.

(3) [. . .].[52–53]

Construction of references to copyright owner

D1–068   173.—(1) Where different persons are (whether in consequence of a partial assignment or otherwise) entitled to different aspects of copyright in a work, the copyright owner for any purpose of this Part is the person who is entitled to the aspect of copyright relevant for that purpose.

(2) Where copyright (or any aspect of copyright) is owned by more than one person jointly, references in this Part to the copyright owner are to all the owners, so that, in particular, any requirement of the licence of the copyright owner requires the licence of all of them.

Meaning of publication and commercial publication

D1–069   175.—(1) In this Part "publication", in relation to a work—

(a) means the issue of copies to the public, and
(b) includes, in the case of a literary, dramatic, musical or artistic work, making it available to the public by means of an electronic retrieval system;

and related expressions shall be construed accordingly.

(2) In this Part "commercial publication", in relation to a literary, dramatic, musical or artistic work means—

(a) issuing copies of the work to the public at a time when copies made in advance of the receipt of orders are generally available to the public, or
(b) making the work available to the public by means of an electronic retrieval system;

and related expressions shall be construed accordingly.

(3) In the case of a work of architecture in the form of a building, or an artistic work incorporated in a building, construction of the building shall be treated as equivalent to publication of the work.

(4) The following do not constitute publication for the purposes of this Part and references to commercial publication shall be construed accordingly—

(a) in the case of a literary, dramatic or musical work—

---

[50] Substituted by the Copyright and Related Rights Regulations (SI 1996/2967) reg.9.
[51] Substituted by the Intellectual Property (Enforcement, etc.) Regulations 2006 (SI 2006/1028) reg.2(2) and Sch.2, paras 6 and 8.
[52–53] Repealed by the Intellectual Property (Enforcement, etc.) Regulations 2006 (SI 2006/1028) reg.2(4) and Sch.4.

    (i) the performance of the work, or

    (ii) the communication to the public of the work (otherwise than for the purposes of an electronic retrieval system);

  (b) in the case of an artistic work—

    (i) the exhibition of the work,

    (ii) the issue to the public of copies of a graphic work representing, or of photographs of, a work of architecture in the form of a building or a model for a building, a sculpture or a work of artistic craftsmanship,

    (iii) the issue to the public of copies of a film including the work, or

    (iv) the communication to the public of the work (otherwise than for the purposes of an electronic retrieval system);

  (c) in the case of a sound recording or film—

    (i) the work being played or shown in public, or

    (ii) the [communication to the public of the work].[54]

(5) References in this Part to publication or commercial publication do not include publication which is merely colourable and not intended to satisfy the reasonable requirements of the public.

(6) No account shall be taken for the purposes of this section of any unauthorised act.

Requirement of signature: application in relation to body corporate

176. The requirement in the following provisions that an instrument be signed by or on behalf of a person is also satisfied in the case of a body corporate by the affixing of its seal—   **D1–070**

section 78(3)(b) (assertion by licensor of right to identification of author in case of public exhibition of copy made in pursuance of the licence),
section 90(3) (assignment of copyright),
section 91(1) (assignment of future copyright), section 92(1) (grant of exclusive licence).

(2) The requirement in the following provisions that an instrument be signed by a person is satisfied in the case of a body corporate by signature on behalf of the body or by the affixing of its seal—

section 78(2)(b) (assertion by instrument in writing of right to have author identified),
section 87(2) (waiver of moral rights).

Adaption of expressions for Scotland

177. In the application of this Part to Scotland—   **D1–071**

"account of profits" means accounting and payment of profits;
"accounts" means count, reckoning and payment;
"assignment" means assignation;
"costs" means expenses;
"defendant" means defender;
"delivery up" means delivery;
"estoppel" means personal bar;
"injunction" means interdict;

---

[54] Substituted, subject to the savings specified in SI 2003/2498 reg.32, by the Copyright and Related Rights Regulations (SI 2003/2498) Sch.1, para.6.

"interlocutory relief" means interim remedy; and
"plaintiff" means pursuer.

Minor definitions

D1–072   **178.**—In this Part—

"article", in the context of an article in a periodical, includes an item of any description;
"business" includes a trade or profession;
"collective work" means—

    (a) a work of joint authorship, or

    (b) a work in which there are distinct contributions by different authors or in which works or parts of works of different authors are incorporated;

"computer-generated", in relation to a work, means that the work is generated by computer in circumstances such that there is no human author of the work;
"country" includes any territory;
"the Crown" includes the Crown in right of the Scottish Administration[, of the Welsh Assembly Government][55] or of Her Majesty's Government in Northern Ireland or in any country outside the United Kingdom to which this Part extends;
"electronic" means actuated by electric, magnetic, electro-magnetic, electro-chemical or electro-mechanical energy, and "in electronic form" means in a form usable only by electronic means;
"employed", "employee", "employer" and "employment" refer to employment under a contract of service or of apprenticeship;
"facsimile copy" includes a copy which is reduced or enlarged in scale;
"international organisation" means an organisation the members of which include one or more states;
"judicial proceedings" includes proceedings before any court, tribunal or person having authority to decide any matter affecting a person's legal rights or liabilities;
"parliamentary proceedings" includes proceedings of the Northern Ireland Assembly of the Scottish Parliament or of the European Parliament [and Assembly proceedings within the meaning of section 1(5) of the Government of Wales Act 2006][56];
"private study" does not include any study which is directly or indirectly for a commercial purpose;
"producer", in relation to a sound recording or a film, means the person by whom the arrangements necessary for the making of the sound recording or film are undertaken;
"public library" means a library administered by or on behalf of—

    (a) in England and Wales, a library authority within the meaning of the Public Libraries and Museums Act 1964;

    (b) in Scotland, a statutory library authority within the meaning of the Public Libraries (Scotland) Act 1955;

    (c) in Northern Ireland, an Education and Library Board within the meaning of the Education and Libraries (Northern Ireland) Order 1986;

---

[55] Inserted by the Government of Wales Act 2006 s.160(1) Sch.10, paras 22 and 29.
[56] Inserted by the Government of Wales Act 2006 s.160(1) and Sch.10, paras 22 and 29.

"rental right" means the right of a copyright owner to authorise or prohibit the rental of copies of the work (see section 18A);

"reprographic copy" and "reprographic copying" refer to copying by means of a reprographic process;

"reprographic process" means a process—

   (a) for making facsimile copies, or

   (b) involving the use of an appliance for making multiple copies, and includes, in relation to a work held in electronic form, any copying by electronic means, but does not include the making of a film or sound recording;

"sufficient acknowledgement" means an acknowledgement identifying the work in question by its title or other description, and identifying the author unless—

   (a) in the case of a published work, it is published anonymously;

   (b) in the case of an unpublished work, it is not possible for a person to ascertain the identity of the author by reasonable inquiry;

"sufficient disclaimer", in relation to an act capable of infringing the right conferred by section 80 (right to object to derogatory treatment of work), means a clear and reasonably prominent indication—

   (a) given at the time of the act, and

   (b) if the author or director is then identified, appearing along with the identification, that the work has been subjected to treatment to which the author or director has not consented;

"telecommunications system" means a system for conveying visual images, sounds or other information by electronic means;

"typeface" includes an ornamental motif used in printing;

"unauthorised", as regards anything done in relation to a work, means done otherwise than—

   (a) by or with the licence of the copyright owner, or

   (b) if copyright does not subsist in the work, by or with the licence of the author or, in a case where section 11(2) would have applied, the author's employer or, in either case, persons lawfully claiming under him, or

   (c) in pursuance of section 48 (copying, &c. of certain material by the Crown);

["wireless broadcast" means a broadcast by means of wireless telegraphy;][57]

"wireless telegraphy" means the sending of electro-magnetic energy over paths not provided by a material substance constructed or arranged for that purpose, but does not include the transmission of microwave energy between terrestrial fixed points;

"writing" includes any form of notation or code, whether by hand or otherwise and regardless of the method by which, or medium in or on which, it is recorded, and "written" shall be construed accordingly.

Index of defined expressions

179. The following Table shows provisions defining or otherwise explaining **D1–073** expressions used in this Part (other than provisions defining or explaining an expression used only in the same section)—

---

[57] Inserted, subject to the savings specified in SI 2003/2498 reg.32 by the Copyright and Related Rights Regulations (SI 2003/2498) Sch.1, para.15.

[accessible copy	section 31F(3)][58]
account of profits and accounts (in Scotland)	section 177
acts restricted by copyright	section 16(1)
adaptation	section 21(3)[
[approved body	section 31B(12)]2
archivist (in sections 37 to 43)	section 37(6)
article (in a periodical)	section 178
artistic work	section 4(1)
assignment (in Scotland)	section 177
author	sections 9 and 10(3)
broadcast (and related expressions)	section 6
building	section 4(2)
business	section 178
collective work	section 178
commencement (in Schedule 1)	paragraph 1(2) of that Schedule
commercial publication	section 175
communication to the public	section 20"
computer-generated	section 178
copy and copying	section 17
copyright (generally)	section 1
copyright (in Schedule 1)	paragraph 2(2) of that Schedule
copyright owner	sections 101(2) and 173
Copyright Tribunal	section 145
copyright work	section 1(2)
costs (in Scotland)	section 177
country	section 178
country of origin	section 15A
the Crown	section 178
Crown copyright	sections 163(2) and 164(3)
database	section 3A(1)
defendant (in Scotland)	section 177
delivery up (in Scotland)	section 177
dramatic work	section 3(1)
[the EEA, EEA state and national of an EEA state][59]	section 172A
educational establishment	sections 174(1) to (4)
electronic and electronic form	section 178
employed, employee, employer and employment	section 178
excepted sound recording	section 72(1A)
exclusive licence	section 92(1)
existing works (in Schedule 1)	paragraph 1(3) of that Schedule
facsimile copy	section 178
film	section 5B

[58] This section was amended by the British Nationality (Modification of Enactments) Order 1982 (1982 SI/1832) and is printed as amended. As to "British subject" see British Nationality Act 1981 (c.61) s.51(1) and *Milltronics Ltd v Hycontrol Ltd* [1990] F.S.R. 273.
[59] Substituted by the Intellectual Property (Enforcement, etc.) Regulations 2006 (SI 2006/1028) reg.2(2) and Sch.2, paras 6 and 9.

future copyright	section 91(2)
general licence (in sections 140 and 141)	section 140(7)
graphic work	section 4(2)
infringing copy	section 27
injunction (in Scotland)	section 177
interlocutory relief (in Scotland)	section 177
international organisation	section 178
issue of copies to the public	section 18(2)
joint authorship (work of)	sections 10(1) and (2)
judicial proceedings	section 178
lawful user (in sections 50A to 50C)	section 50A(2)
lending	section 18A(2) to (6)
librarian (in sections 37 to 43)	section 37(6)
licence (in sections 125 to 128)	section 124
licence of copyright owner	sections 90(4), 91(3) and 173
licensing body (in Chapter VII)	section 116(2)
licensing scheme (generally)	section 116(1)
licensing scheme (in sections 118 to 121)	section 117
literary work	section 3(1)
made (in relation to a literary, dramatic or musical work)	section 3(2)
musical work	section 3(1)
needletime	section 135A
the new copyright provisions (in Schedule 1)	paragraph 1(1) of that Schedule
the 1911 Act (in Schedule 1)	paragraph 1(1) of that Schedule
the 1956 Act (in Schedule 1)	paragraph 1(1) of that Schedule
on behalf of (in relation to an educational establishment)	section 174(5)
original (in relation to a database)	section 3A(2).
Parliamentary copyright	sections 165(2) and (7) and 166(6), 166A(3)[, 166B(3), 166C(3) and 166D(3)][60]
parliamentary proceedings	section 178
performance	section 19(2)
photograph	section 4(2)
plaintiff (in Scotland)	section 177
prescribed conditions (in sections 38 to 43)	section 37(1)(b)
prescribed library or archive (in sections 38 to 43)	section 37(1)(a)
private study	section 178
producer (in relation to a sound recording or film)	section 178
programme (in the context of broadcasting)	section 6(3)
prospective owner (of copyright)	section 91(2)
public library	section 178

---

[60] Substituted by the Government of Wales Act 2006 s.160(1) and Sch.10, paras 22 and 30.

D2. The Copyright Act 1956 (c.74) (extracts—as amended)

PART I

COPYRIGHT IN ORIGINAL WORKS

Nature of copyright under this Act

D2–001   **1.**—(1) In this Act "copyright" in relation to a work (except where the context otherwise requires) means the exclusive right, by virtue and subject to the provisions of this Act, to do, and to authorise other persons to do, certain acts in relation to that work in the United Kingdom or in any other country to which the relevant provision of this Act extends.

The said acts, in relation to a work of any description, are those acts which, in the relevant provision of this Act, are designated as the acts restricted by the copyright in a work of that description.

(2) In accordance with the preceding subsection, but subject to the following provisions of this Act, the copyright in a work is infringed by any person who, not being the owner of the copyright, and without the licence of the owner thereof, does, or authorises another person to do, any of the said acts in relation to the work in the United Kingdom or in any other country to which the relevant provision of this Act extends.

(3) In the preceding subsections references to the relevant provision of this Act, in relation to a work of any description, are references to the provision of this Act whereby it is provided that (subject to compliance with the conditions specified therein) copyright shall subsist in works of that description.

(4) The preceding provisions of this section shall apply, in relation to any subject-matter (other than a work) of a description to which any provision of Part II of this Act relates, as they apply in relation to a work.

(5) For the purposes of any provision of this Act which specifies the conditions under which copyright may subsist in any description of work or other subject-matter, "qualified person"—

- (a) in the case of an individual, means a person who is a British subject or British protected person or a citizen of the Republic of Ireland or (not being a British subject or British protected person or a citizen of the Republic of Ireland) is domiciled or resident in the United Kingdom or in another country to which that provision extends, and
- (b) in the case of a body corporate, means a body incorporated under the laws of any part of the United Kingdom or of another country to which that provision extends.

In this subsection "British protected person" has the same meaning as in [the British Nationality Act, 1981.]

Copyright in artistic works

3.—(1) In this Act "artistic work" means a work of any of the following descriptions, that is to say,— **D2–002**

- (a) the following, irrespective of artistic quality, namely paintings, sculptures, drawings, engravings and photographs;
- (b) works of architecture, being either buildings or models for buildings;
- (c) works of artistic craftsmanship, not falling within either of the preceding paragraphs.

(2) Copyright shall subsist, subject to the provisions of this Act, in every original artistic work which is unpublished, and of which the author was a qualified person at the time when the work was made, or, if the making of the work extended over a period, was a qualified person for a substantial part of that period.

(3) Where an original artistic work has been published, then, subject to the provisions of this Act, copyright shall subsist in the work (or, if copyright in the work subsisted immediately before its first publication, shall continue to subsist) if, but only if,—

- (a) the first publication of the work took place in the United Kingdom, or in another country to which this section extends, or
- (b) the author of the work was a qualified person at the time when the work was first published, or
- (c) the author had died before that time, but was a qualified person immediately before his death.

(4) Subject to the last preceding subsection, copyright subsisting in a work by virtue of this section shall continue to subsist until the end of the period of fifty years from the end of the calendar year in which the author died, and shall then expire:
Provided that—

- (a) in the case of an engraving, if before the death of the author the engraving had not been published, the copyright shall continue to subsist until the end of the period of fifty years from the end of the calendar year in which it is first published;

(b) the copyright in a photograph shall continue to subsist until the end of the period of fifty years from the end of the calendar year in which the photograph is first published, and shall then expire.

(5) The acts restricted by the copyright in an artistic work are—

(a) reproducing the work in any material form;

(b) publishing the work;

(c) including the work in a television broadcast;

[(d) including the work in a cable programme.][61]

Ownership of copyright in literary, dramatic, musical and artistic works

D2–003   4.—(1) Subject to the provisions of this section, the author of a work shall be entitled to any copyright subsisting in the work by virtue of this Part of the Act.

(3) Subject to the last preceding subsection, where a person commissions the taking of a photograph, or the painting or drawing of a portrait, or the making of an engraving, and pays or agrees to pay for it in money or money's worth, and the work is made in pursuance of that commission, the person who so commissioned the work shall be entitled to any copyright subsisting therein by virtue of this Part of this Act.

(4) Where, in a case not falling within either of the two last preceding subsections, a work is made in the course of the author's employment by another person under a contract of service or apprenticeship, that other person shall be entitled to any copyright subsisting in the work by virtue of this Part of this Act.

(5) Each of the last three preceding subsections shall have effect subject, in any particular case, to any agreement excluding the operation thereof in that case.

(6) The preceding provisions of this section shall all have effect subject to the provisions of Part VI of this Act.

Infringements by importation, sale and other dealings

D2–004   5.—(1) Without prejudice to the general provisions of section one of this Act as to infringements of copyright, the provisions of this section shall have effect in relation to copyright subsisting by virtue of this Part of this Act.

(2) The copyright in a literary, dramatic, musical or artistic work is infringed by any person who, without the licence of the owner of the copyright, imports an article (otherwise than for his private and domestic use) into the United Kingdom, or into any other country to which this section extends, if to his knowledge the making of that article constituted an infringement of that copyright, or would have constituted such an infringement if the article had been made in the place into which it is so imported.

(3) The copyright in a literary, dramatic, musical or artistic work is infringed by any person who, in the United Kingdom, or in any other country to which this section extends, and without the licence of the owner of the copyright—

(a) sells, lets for hire, or by way of trade offers or exposes for sale or hire any article, or

(b) by way of trade exhibits any article in public,

---

[61] This section was amended by the Cable and Broadcasting Act 1984 (c.46) and is printed as amended.

if to his knowledge the making of the article constituted an infringement of that copyright, or (in the case of an imported article) would have constituted an infringement of that copyright if the article had been made in the place into which it was imported.

(4) The last preceding subsection shall apply in relation to the distribution of any articles either—

(a) for purposes of trade, or
(b) for other purposes, but to such an extent as to affect prejudicially the owner of the copyright in question,

as it applies in relation to the sale of an article.

(5) The copyright in a literary, dramatic or musical work is also infringed by any person who permits a place of public entertainment to be used for a performance in public of the work, where the performance constitutes an infringement of the copyright in the work:

Provided that this subsection shall not apply in a case where the person permitting the place to be so used—

(a) was not aware, and had no reasonable grounds for suspecting, that the performance would be an infringement of the copyright, or
(b) gave the permission gratuitously, or for a consideration which was only nominal or (if more than nominal) did not exceed a reasonable estimate of the expenses to be incurred by him in consequence of the use of the place for the performance.

(6) In this section "place of public entertainment" includes any premises which are occupied mainly for other purposes, but are from time to time made available for hire to such persons as may desire to hire them for purposes of public entertainment.

General exceptions from protection of artistic works

9.—(1) No fair dealing with an artistic work for purposes of research or private study shall constitute an infringement of the copyright in the work. **D2–005**

(2) no fair dealing with an artistic work shall constitute an infringement of the copyright in the work if it is for purposes of criticism or review, whether of that work or of another work, and is accompanied by a sufficient acknowledgment.

(3) The copyright in a work to which this subsection applies which is permanently situated in a public place, or in premises open to the public, is not infringed by the making of a painting, drawing, engraving or photograph of the work, or the inclusion of the work in a cinematograph film or in a television broadcast.

This subsection applies to sculptures, and to such works of artistic craftsmanship as are mentioned in paragraph (c) of subsection (1) of section three of this Act.

(4) The copyright in a work of architecture is not infringed by the making of a painting, drawing, engraving or photograph of the work, or the inclusion of the work in a cinematograph film on in a television broadcast.

(5) Without prejudice to the two last preceding subsections, the copyright in an artistic work is not infringed by the inclusion of the work in a cinematograph film or in a television broadcast, if its inclusion therein is only by way of background or is otherwise only incidental to the principal matters represented in the film or broadcast.

(6) The copyright in an artistic work is not infringed by the publication of a painting, drawing, engraving, photograph or cinematograph film, if by virtue of any of the three last preceding subsections the making of that painting, drawing,

engraving, photograph or film did not constitute an infringement of the copyright.

(7) The copyright in an artistic work is not infringed by reproducing it for the purposes of a judicial proceeding or for the purposes of a report of a judicial proceeding.

(8) The making of an object of any description which is in three dimensions shall not be taken to infringe the copyright in an artistic work in two dimensions, if the object would not appear, to persons who are not experts in relation to objects of that description, to be a reproduction of the artistic work.

(9) The copyright in a artistic work is not infringed by the making of a subsequent artistic work by the same author, notwithstanding that part of the earlier work—

(a) is reproduced in the subsequent work, and
(b) is so reproduced by the use of a mould, cast, sketch, plan, model or study made for the purposes of the earlier work,

if in making the subsequent work the author does not repeat or imitate the main design of the earlier work.

(10) Where copyright subsists in a building as a work of architecture, the copyright is not infringed by any reconstruction of that building; and where a building has been constructed in accordance with architectural drawings or plans in which copyright subsists, and has been so constructed by, or with the licence of, the owner of that copyright, any subsequent reconstruction of the building by reference to those drawings or plans shall not constitute an infringement of that copyright.

(11) The provisions of this section shall apply in relation to a [cable programme] as they apply in relation to a television broadcast.

Special exception in respect of industrial designs

D2–006   10.—(1) ...

(2) Where copyright subsists in an artistic work, and—

(a) a corresponding design is applied industrially by or with the licence of the owner of the copyright in the work, and
(b) articles to which the design has been so applied are sold, let for hire, or offered for sale or hire [whether in the United Kingdom or elsewhere], and
(c) ...

(2) Where copyright subsists in an artistic work, and—

(a) *a corresponding design is applied industrially by or with the licence of the owner of the copyright in the work, and*
(b) *articles to which the design has been so applied are sold, let for hire or offered for sale or hire, and*
(c) *at the time when those articles are sold, let for hire, or offered for sale or hire, they are not articles in respect of which the design has been registered under the Act of 1949, the following provisions of this section shall apply.*

(3) Subject to the next following subsection,—

(a) *during the relevant period of fifteen years, it shall not be an infringement of the copyright in the work to do anything which, at the time when it is done, would have been within the scope of the copyright in the design if the design had, immediately before that time, been registered in respect of all relevant articles; and*
(b) *after the end of the relevant period of fifteen years, it shall not be an infringement of the copyright in the work to do anything which, at the time when it is done,*

would, if the design had been registered immediately before that time, have been within the scope of the copyright in the design as extended to all associated designs and articles.

In this subsection "the relevant period of fifteen years" means the period of fifteen years beginning with the date on which articles, such as are mentioned in paragraph (b) of the last preceding subsection, were first sold, let for hire, or offered for sale or hire in the circumstances mentioned in paragraph (c) of that subsection; and "all relevant articles", in relation to any time within that period, means all articles falling within the said paragraph (b) which had before that time been sold, let for hire, or offered for sale or hire in those circumstances.

[(3) Subject to the next following subsection, after the end of the relevant period of 15 years it shall not be an infringement of the copyright in the work to do anything which at the time when it is done would, if a corresponding design had been registered under the Registered Designs Act 1949 (in this section referred to as "the Act of 1949") immediately before that time, have been within the scope of the copyright in the design as extended to all associated designs and articles.

In this subsection "the relevant period of 15 years" means the period of 15 years beginning with the date on which articles, such as are mentioned in paragraph (b) of the last preceding subsection, were first sold, let for hire or offered for sale or hire, whether in the United Kingdom or elsewhere.]

(4) For the purposes of subsections (2) and (3) of this section, no account shall be taken of any articles in respect of which, at the time when they were sold, let for hire, or offered for sale or hire, the design in question was excluded from registration under the Act of 1949 by rules made under subsection (4) of section one of that Act (which relates to the exclusion of designs for articles which are primarily literary or artistic in character); and for the purposes of any proceedings under this Act a design shall be conclusively presumed to have been so excluded if—

(a) before the commencement of those proceedings, an application for the registration of the design under the Act of 1949 in respect of those articles had been refused;

(b) the reason or one of the reasons stated for the refusal was that the design was excluded from such registration by rules made under the said subsection (4); and

(c) no appeal against that refusal had been allowed before the date of the commencement of the proceedings or was pending on that date.

(5) The power of the Board of Trade to make rules under section thirty-six of the Act of 1949 shall include power to make rules for the purposes of this section for determining the circumstances in which a design is to be taken to be applied industrially.

(6) In this section, references to the scope of the copyright in a registered design are references to the aggregate of the things, which, by virtue of section seven of the Act of 1949, the registered proprietor of the design has the exclusive right to do, and references to the scope of the copyright in a registered design as extended to all associated designs and articles are references to the aggregate of the things which, by virtue of that section, the registered proprietor would have had the exclusive right to do if—

(a) when that design was registered, there had at the same time been registered every possible design consisting of that design with modifications or variations not sufficient to alter the character or substantially to affect the identity thereof, and the said proprietor had been registered as the proprietor of every such design, and

(b) the design in question, and every other design such as is mentioned in the preceding paragraph, had been registered in respect of all the articles to which it was capable of being applied.[62]

(7) In this section "corresponding design", in relation to an artistic work, means a design which, when applied to an article, results in a reproduction of that work.

Provisions as to anonymous and pseudonymous works, and works of joint authorship

D2–007   11.—(1) The preceding provisions of this Part of this Act shall have effect subject to the modifications specified in the Second Schedule to this Act in the case of works published anonymously or pseudonymously.

(2) The provisions of the Third Schedule to this Act shall have effect with respect to works of joint authorship.

(3) In this Act "work of joint authorship" means a work produced by the collaboration of two or more authors in which the contribution of each author is not separate from the contribution of the other author or authors.

PART VI

MISCELLANEOUS AND SUPPLEMENTARY PROVISIONS

Amendments of Registered Designs Act, 1949

D2–008   44.—(1) In section six of the Registered Designs Act, 1949, (under which the disclosure of a design in certain circumstances is not to be a reason for refusing registration), the following subsections shall be inserted after subsection (3):

"(4) Where copyright under the Copyright Act, 1956, subsists in an artistic work, and an application is made by, or with the consent of, the owner of that copyright for the registration of a corresponding design, that design shall not be treated for the purposes of this Act as being other than new or original by reason only of any use previously made of the artistic work, unless—

(a) the previous use consisted of or included the sale, letting for hire, or offer for sale or hire of articles to which the design in question (or a design differing from it only as mentioned in subsection (2) of section one of this Act) had been applied industrially, other than articles of a description specified in rules made under subsection (4) of section one of this Act, and

(b) that previous use was made by, or with the consent of, the owner of the copyright in the artistic work.

(5) Any rules made by virtue of subsection (5) of section ten of the Copyright Act, 1956 (which relates to rules for determining the circumstances in which a design is to be taken to be applied industrially) shall apply for the purposes of the last foregoing subsection."

(2) The following subsection shall be added at the end of section eight of the said Act of 1949 (which relates to the period of copyright in registered designs):

"(3) Where in the case of a registered design it is shown—

---

[62] Subsections (1) and (2)(c) were repealed, the words in square brackets in subs.(2)(b) were inserted, and subs.(3) was substituted, by the Design Copyright Act 1968 s.1(1).

(a) that the design, at the time when it was registered, was a corresponding design in relation to an artistic work in which copyright subsisted under the Copyright Act, 1956;

(b) that, by reason of a previous use of that artistic work, the design would not have been registrable under this Act but for subsection (4) of section six of this Act; and

(c) that the copyright in that work under the Copyright Act, 1956, expired before the date of expiry of the copyright in the design,

the copyright in the design shall, notwithstanding anything in this section, be deemed to have expired at the same time as the copyright in the artistic work, and shall not be renewable after that time."

(3) In section eleven of the said Act of 1949 (which relates to cancellation of the registration of designs), the following subsection shall be inserted after subsection (2):

"(2A) At any time after a design has been registered, any person interested may apply to the registrar for the cancellation of the article of the design on the grounds—

(a) that the design, at the time when it was registered, was a corresponding design in relation to an artistic work in which copyright subsisted under the Copyright Act, 1956;

(b) that, by reason of a previous use of that artistic work, the design would not have been registrable under this Act but for subsection (4) of section six of this Act; and

(c) that the copyright in that work under the Copyright Act, 1956, has expired; and the registrar may make such order on the application as he thinks fit."

(4) In subsection (3) of the said section eleven, for the words "the last foregoing subsection" there shall be substituted the words "either of the two last foregoing subsections."

(5) In subsection (1) of section forty-four of the said Act of 1949 (which relates to the interpretation of that Act)—

(a) after the definition of "article" there shall be inserted the words "'artistic work' has the same meaning as in the Copyright Act, 1956"; and

(b) after the definition of "copyright" there shall be inserted the words "'corresponding design' has the same meaning as in section ten of the Copyright Act, 1956."

Interpretation

48.—(1) In this Act, except in so far as the context otherwise requires, the **D2–009** following expressions have the meanings hereby assigned to them respectively, that is to say:

"building" includes any structure;

"construction" includes erection, and references to reconstruction shall be construed accordingly;

"drawing" includes any diagram, map, chart or plan;

"engraving" includes any etching, lithograph, woodcut, print or similar work, not being a photograph;

"photograph" means any product of photograph or of any process akin to photography, other than a part of a cinematograph film, and "author", in relation to a photograph, means the person who, at the time when the photograph is taken, is the owner of the material on which it is taken;

"reproduction", in the case of a literary, dramatic or musical work, includes a reproduction in the form of a record or of a cinematograph film, and, in the case of an artistic work, includes a version produced by converting the work into a three-dimensional form, or, if it is in three dimensions, by converting it into a two-dimensional form, and references to reproducing a work shall be construed accordingly;

"sculpture" includes any cast or model made for purposes of sculpture.

SCHEDULES

Section 10   FIRST SCHEDULE

False Registration of Industrial Designs

D2–010   1. The provisions of this Schedule shall have effect where—
  (a) copyright subsists in an artistic work, and proceedings are brought under this Act relating to that work;
  (b) a corresponding design has been registered under the Act of 1949, and the copyright in the design subsisting by virtue of that registration has not expired by effluxion of time before the commencement of those proceedings; and
  (c) it is proved or admitted in the proceedings that the person registered as the proprietor of the design was not the proprietor thereof for the purposes of the Act of 1949, and was so registered without the knowledge of the owner of the copyright in the artistic work.

  2. For the purposes of those proceedings (but subject to the next following paragraph) the registration shall be treated as never having been effected, and accordingly, in relation to that registration, [subsection (1) of section ten of this Act shall not apply, and] nothing in section seven of the Act of 1949 shall be construed as affording any defence in those proceedings.

  3. Notwithstanding anything in the last preceding paragraph, if in the proceedings it is proved or admitted that any act to which the proceedings relate—
  (a) was done in pursuance of an assignment or licence made or granted by the person registered as proprietor of the design, and
  (b) was so done in good faith in reliance upon the registration, and without notice of any proceedings for the cancellation of the registration or for rectifying the entry in the register of designs relating thereto,
[subsection (1) of section ten of this Act shall apply in relation to that act for the purposes of the first-mentioned proceedings] [this shall be a good defence to such proceedings].

  4. In this Schedule "the Act of 1949" means the Registered Designs Act, 1949, and "corresponding design" has the meaning assigned to it by subsection (7) of section ten of this Act.

Section 59   SEVENTH SCHEDULE

Transitional Provisions

Part I

Provisions Relating to Part I of Act

D2–011   8.—(1) Section ten and the First Schedule to this Act do not apply to artistic works made before the commencement of that section.

(2) Copyright shall not subsist by virtue of this Act in any artistic work made before the commencement of section ten which, at the time when the work was made, constituted a design capable of registration under the Registered Designs Act, 1949, or under the enactments repealed by that Act, and was used, or intended to be used, as a model or pattern to be multiplied by any industrial process.

(3) The provisions set out in paragraph 2 of the Eighth Schedule to this Act (being the relevant provisions of the Copyright (Industrial Designs) Rules, 1949) shall apply for the purposes of the last preceding sub-paragraph.

9.—(1) Where, before the repeal by this Act of section three of the Act of 1911, a person **D2–012**
has, in the case of a work, given the notice requisite under the proviso set out in paragraph
3 of the Eighth Schedule to this Act (being the proviso to the said section three), then, as
respects reproductions by that person of that work after the repeal of that section by this Act,
that proviso shall have effect as if it had been re-enacted in this Act as a proviso to
subsection (2) of section one:

Provided that the said proviso shall so have effect subject to the provisions set out in
paragraphs 4 and 5 of the Eighth Schedule to this Act (being so much of subsection (1) of
sections sixteen and seventeen respectively of the Act of 1911 as is applicable to the said
proviso), as if those provisions had also been re-enacted in this Act.

(2) For the purposes of the operation of the said proviso in accordance with the preceding
sub-paragraph, any regulations made by the Board of Trade thereunder before the repeal of
section three of the Act of 1911 shall have effect as if they had been made under this Act, and
the power of the Board of Trade to make further regulations thereunder shall apply as if the
proviso had been re-enacted as mentioned in the preceding sub-paragraph.

Section 50   EIGHTH SCHEDULE

Provisions of Copyright Act, 1911, and Rules, referred to in Seventh Schedule

2. *Rule 2 of the Copyright (Industrial Designs) Rules, 1949 (referred to in paragraph 8 of*   **D2–013**
Seventh Schedule):

A design shall be deemed to be used as a model or pattern to be multiplied by any
industrial process—
  (a) when the design is reproduced or is intended to be reproduced on more than fifty
      single articles, unless all the articles in which the design is reproduced or is
      intended to be reproduced together form only a single set of articles as defined in
      subsection (1) of section 44 of the Registered Designs Act, 1949, or
  (b) when the design is to be applied to—
      (i) printed paper hangings,
      (ii) carpets, floor cloths or oil cloths, manufactured or sold in lengths or pieces,
      (iii) textile piece goods, or textile goods manufactured or sold in lengths or pieces,
            or
      (iv) lace, not made by hand.

D3. The Copyright Act 1911 (extracts)

(1 & 2 GEO. 5, C.46)

An Act to amend and consolidate the Law relating to Copyright.
[16TH DECEMBER, 1911]

PART I

IMPERIAL COPYRIGHT

Rights

Copyright

1.—(1) Subject to the provisions of this Act, copyright shall subsist throughout   **D3–001**
the parts of His Majesty's dominions to which this Act extends for the term

755

hereinafter mentioned in every original literary dramatic musical and artistic work, if—

    (a) in the case of a published work, the work was first published within such parts of His Majesty's dominions as aforesaid; and

    (b) in the case of an unpublished work, the author was at the date of the making of the work a British subject or resident within such parts of His Majesty's dominions as aforesaid;

but in no other works, except so far as the protection conferred by this Act is extended by Orders in Council thereunder relating to self-governing dominions to which this Act does not extend and to foreign countries.

(2) For the purposes of this Act, "copyright" means the sole right to produce or reproduce the work or any substantial part thereof in any material form whatsoever, to perform, or in the case of a lecture to deliver, the work or any substantial part thereof in public; if the work is unpublished, to publish the work or any substantial part thereof; and shall include the sole right,—

    (a) to produce, reproduce, perform, or publish any translation of the work;

    (b) in the case of a dramatic work, to convert it into a novel or other non-dramatic work;

    (c) in the case of a novel or other non-dramatic work, or of an artistic work, to convert it into a dramatic work, by way of performance in public or otherwise;

    (d) in the case of a literary, dramatic, or musical work, to make any record, perforated roll, cinematograph film, or other contrivance by means of which the work may be mechanically performed or delivered,

and to authorise any such acts as aforesaid.

(3) For the purposes of this Act, publication, in relation to any work, means the issue of copies of the work to the public, and does not include the performance in public of a dramatic or musical work, the delivery in public of a lecture, the exhibition in public of an artistic work, or the construction of an architectural work of art, but, for the purposes of this provision, the issue of photographs and engravings of works of sculpture and architectural works of an art shall not be deemed to be publication of such works.

Infringement of copyright

D3–002   **2.**—(1) Copyright in a work shall be deemed to be infringed by any person who, without the consent of the owner of the copyright, does anything the sole right to do which is by this Act conferred on the owner of the copyright: Provided that the following acts shall not constitute an infringement of copyright:

    (i) Any fair dealing with any work or the purposes of private study, research, criticism, review, or newspaper summary:

    (ii) Where the author of an artistic work is not the owner of the copyright therein, the use by the author of any mould, cast, sketch, plan, model, or study made by him for the purpose of the work, provided that he does not thereby repeat or imitate the main design of that work:

    (iii) The making or publishing of paintings, drawings, engravings, or photographs of a work of sculpture or artistic craftsmanship, if permanently situate in a public place or building, or the making or publishing of paintings, drawings, engravings, or photographs (which are not in the nature of architectural drawings or plans) if any architectural work of art:

    (iv) The publication in a collection, mainly composed of non-copyright matter, bona fide intended for the use of schools, and so described in the title and in any advertisements issued by the publisher, of short passages from published literary works not themselves published for the use of schools in which copyright subsists: provided that not more than two of such passages from works by the same author are published by the same publisher within five years, and that the source from which such passages are taken is acknowledged:

(v) The publication in a newspaper of a report of a lecture lectured in public, unless the report is prohibited by conspicuous written or printed notice affixed before and maintained during the lecture at or about the main entrance of the building in which the lecture is given, and, except whilst the building is being used for public worship, in a position near the lecturer; but nothing in this paragraph shall affect the provisions in paragraph (i) as to newspaper summaries:

(vi) the reading or recitation in public by one person of any reasonable extract from any published work.

(2) Copyright in a work shall also be deemed to be infringed by any person who—

(a) sells or lets for hire, or by way of trade exposes or offers for sale or hire; or

(b) distributes either for the purposes of trade or to such an extent as to affect prejudicially the owner of the copyright; or

(c) by way of trade exhibits in public; or

(d) imports for sale or hire into any part of His Majesty's dominions to which this Act extends,

any work which to his knowledge infringes copyright or would infringe copyright if it had been made within the part of His Majesty's dominions in or into which the sale or hiring, exposure, offering for sale or hire, distribution, exhibition, or importation took place.

(3) Copyright in a work shall also be deemed to be infringed by any person who for his private profit permits a theatre or other place of entertainment to be used for the performance in public of the work without the consent of the owner of the copyright, unless he was not aware, and had no reasonable ground for suspecting, that the performance would be an infringement of copyright.

Term of copyright

3. The term for which copyright shall subsist shall, except as otherwise **D3–003** expressly provided by this Act, be the life of the author and a period of fifty years after his death:

Provided that at any time after the expiration of twenty-five years, or in the case of a work in which copyright subsists at the passing of this Act thirty years, from the death of the author of a published work, copyright in the work shall not be deemed to be infringed by the reproduction of the work for sale if the person reproducing the work proves that he has given the prescribed notice in writing of his intention to reproduce the work, and that he has paid in the prescribed manner to, or for he benefit of, the owner of the copyright royalties in respect of all copies of the work sold by him calculated at the rate of ten per cent on the price at which he publishes the work; and, for the purposes of this proviso, the Board of Trade may make regulations prescribing the mode in which notices are to be given, and the particulars to be given in such notices, and the mode, time, and frequency of the payment of royalties, including (if they think fit) regulations requiring payment in advance or otherwise securing the payment of royalties.

Ownership of copyright, etc

D3–004   **5.**—(1) Subject to the provisions of this Act, the author of a work shall be the first owner of the copyright therein:
Provided that—

(a) where, in the case of an engraving, photograph, or portrait, the plate or other original was ordered by some other person and was made for valuable consideration in pursuance of that order, then, in the absence of any agreement to the contrary, the person by whom such plate or other original was ordered shall be the first owner of the copyright; and

(b) where the author was in the employment of some other person under a contract of service or apprenticeship and the work was made in the course of his employment by that person, the person by whom the author was employed shall, in the absence of any agreement to the contrary, be the first owner of the copyright, but where the work is an article or other contribution to a newspaper, magazine, or similar periodical, there shall, in the absence of any agreement to the contrary, be deemed to be reserved to the author a right to restrain the publication of the work, otherwise than as part of a newspaper, magazine, or similar periodical.

(2) The owner of the copyright in any work may assign the right, either wholly or partially, and either generally or subject to limitations to the United Kingdom or any self-governing dominion or other part of His Majesty's dominions to which this Act extends, and either for the whole term of the copyright or for any part thereof, and may grant any interest in the right by licence, but no such assignment

Provisions as to photographs

D3–005   **21.** The term for which copyright shall subsist in photographs shall be fifty years from the making of the original negative from which the photograph was directly or indirectly derived, and the person who was the owner of such negative at the time when such negative was made shall be deemed to be the author of the work, and, where such owner is a body corporate, the body corporate shall be deemed for the purposes of this Act to reside within the parts of His Majesty's dominions to which this Act extends if it has established a place of business within such parts.

Provisions as to designs registrable under 7 Edw. 7, c. 29

D3–006   **22.**—(1) This Act shall not apply to designs capable of being registered under the Patents and Designs Act, 1907, except designs which, though capable of being so registered, are not used or intended to be used as models or patterns to be multiplied by any industrial process.

(2) General rules under section eighty-six of the Patents and Designs Act, 1907, may be made for determining the conditions under which as design shall be deemed to be used for such purposes as aforesaid.

Interpretation

D3–007   **35.**—(1) In this Act, unless the context otherwise requires—

"Artistic work" includes works of painting, drawing, sculpture and artistic craftsmanship, and architectural works of art and engravings and photographs;
"Work of sculpture" includes casts and models;

"Architectural work of art" means any building or structure having an artistic character or design, in respect of such character or design, or any model for such building or structure, provided that the protection afforded by this Act shall be confined to the artistic character and design, and shall not extend to processes or methods of construction;

"Engravings" include etchings, lithographs, wood-cuts, prints, and other similar works, not being photographs;

"Photograph" includes photo-lithograph and any work produced by any process analogous to photography;

"Plate" includes any stereotype or other plate, stone, block, mould, matrix, transfer, or negative used or intended to be used for printing or reproducing copies of any work, and any matrix or other appliance by which records, perforated rolls or other contrivances for the acoustic representation of the work are or are intended to be made.

D4. The Copyright and Performances (Application to Other Countries) Order 2008 (SI 2008/677)

Her Majesty is satisfied that provision has been or will be made giving adequate protection to the owners of the copyright in British sound recordings and wireless broadcasts under the laws of Algeria, Georgia and Vietnam, to the owners of the copyright in British sound recordings under the laws of China, to the owners of the copyright in British wireless broadcasts under the laws of Tonga and to performances and persons having recording rights in relation to performances under the laws of Algeria, Vietnam, Georgia, China and Tonga.   **D4–001**

Accordingly, Her Majesty, by and with the advice of Her Privy Council, in exercise of the powers conferred upon Her by sections 159 and 208 of the Copyright, Designs and Patents Act 1988 and by section 2(2) of the European Communities Act 1972, makes the following Order:

Introductory

1.—(1) This Order may be cited as the Copyright and Performances (Application to Other Countries) Order 2008 and shall come into force on 6th April 2008.   **D4–002**

(2) In this Order "the Act" means the Copyright, Designs and Patents Act 1988.

(3) The Copyright and Performances (Application to Other Countries) Order 2007 is revoked.

Literary, dramatic, musical and artistic works, films and the typographical arrangement of published editions

2.—(1) All the provisions of Part 1 of the Act, insofar as they relate to literary, dramatic, musical and artistic works, films and the typographical arrangement of published editions, apply in relation to the countries indicated in the second column of the table set out in the Schedule so that those provisions apply—   **D4–003**

(a) in relation to persons who are citizens or subjects of, or are domiciled or resident in, those countries as they apply to persons who are British citizens or are domiciled or resident in the United Kingdom,

(b) in relation to bodies incorporated under the laws of those countries as they apply in relation to bodies incorporated under the law of a part of the United Kingdom, and

    (c) in relation to works first published in those countries as they apply in relation to works first published in the United Kingdom,

subject to paragraph (2).

(2) Where a literary, dramatic, musical or artistic work was first published before 1st June 1957 it shall not qualify for copyright protection by reason of section 154 (qualification by reference to author).

Sound recordings

D4–004   3.—(1) Except for the provisions listed in paragraph (2)(a), all the provisions of Part 1 of the Act, insofar as they relate to sound recordings, apply in relation to the countries indicated in the third column of the table set out in the Schedule so that those provisions apply—

    (a) in relation to persons who are citizens or subjects of, or are domiciled or resident in, those countries as they apply to persons who are British citizens or are domiciled or resident in the United Kingdom,

    (b) in relation to bodies incorporated under the laws of those countries as they apply in relation to bodies incorporated under the law of a part of the United Kingdom, and

    (c) in relation to works first published in those countries as they apply in relation to works first published in the United Kingdom.

(2) Where in the third column of the table set out in the Schedule the entry for a country—

    (a) includes an asterisk (*), the following provisions of Part 1 of the Act, insofar as they relate to sound recordings, also apply to that country—
        (i) section 18A (infringement by rental or lending of work to the public) insofar as it applies to lending;
        (ii) section 19 (infringement by playing of work in public);
        (iii) section 20 (infringement by communication to the public);
        (iv) section 26 (secondary infringement: provision of apparatus for infringing performance, &c; and
        (v) section 107(2A) and (3) (criminal liability for communicating to the public or playing a sound recording);

    (b) includes a hash (£), the following provisions of Part 1 of the Act, insofar as they relate to sound recordings, also apply to that country—
        (i) section 20 (infringement by communication to the public), except that references to communication to the public do not include the broadcasting of a sound recording; and
        (ii) section 107(2A) (criminal liability for communicating to the public), except that it does not apply in relation to the broadcasting of a sound recording.

Wireless broadcasts

D4–005   4.—(1) Except for the provisions listed in paragraph (2), all the provisions of Part 1 of the Act, insofar as they relate to wireless broadcasts, apply in relation to the countries indicated in the fourth column of the table set out in the Schedule so that those provisions apply—

    (a) in relation to persons who are citizens or subjects of, or are domiciled or resident in, those countries as they apply to persons who are British citizens or are domiciled or resident in the United Kingdom,

    (b) in relation to bodies incorporated under the laws of those countries as they apply in relation to bodies incorporated under the law of a part of the United Kingdom, and

(c) in relation to broadcasts made from those countries as they apply in relation to broadcasts made from the United Kingdom,

subject to paragraphs (3) to (5).

(2) The following provisions of Part 1 of the Act, insofar as they relate to wireless broadcasts, also apply in relation to a country where its entry in the fourth column of the table set out in the Schedule does not include an asterisk (*)—

(a) section 18A (infringement by rental or lending of work to the public);
(b) section 19 (infringement by showing or playing of work in public), but only insofar as it relates to broadcasts other than television broadcasts;
(c) section 20 (infringement by communication to the public), except in relation to broadcasting by wireless telegraphy;
(d) section 26 (secondary infringement: provision of apparatus for infringing performance, &c), but only insofar as it relates to broadcasts other than television broadcasts;
(e) section 107(2A) (criminal liability for communicating to the public), except in relation to broadcasting by wireless telegraphy.

(3) The provisions of Part 1 of the Act do not apply in relation to a wireless broadcast made from a place in a country, referred to in paragraph (4), before the relevant date.

(4) The relevant date in relation to a country—

(a) where its entry in the fourth column of the table set out in the Schedule includes an "(X)", is 1st June 1957;
(b) where its entry in the fourth column of the table set out in the Schedule includes a "(Y)", is 1st January 1996; or
(c) where there is a date next to its entry in the fourth column of the table set out in the Schedule, is that date.

(5) For the purposes of section 14(5) of the Act (duration of copyright in repeats) any wireless broadcast which does not qualify for copyright protection shall be disregarded.

Other broadcasts

5.—All the provisions of Part 1 of the Act, insofar as they relate to broadcasts **D4–006** (other than wireless broadcasts), apply in relation to the countries indicated in the fifth column of the table set out in the Schedule so that those provisions apply—

(a) in relation to persons who are citizens or subjects of, or are domiciled or resident in, those countries as they apply to persons who are British citizens or are domiciled or resident in the United Kingdom,
(b) in relation to bodies incorporated under the laws of those countries as they apply in relation to bodies incorporated under the law of a part of the United Kingdom, and
(c) in relation to broadcasts made from those countries as they apply in relation to broadcasts made from the United Kingdom.

Performances

6.—(1) The countries in respect of which the word "designated" is included in **D4–007** the sixth column of the table set out in the Schedule are designated as enjoying reciprocal protection under Part 2 of the Act.

(2) The countries in respect of which the word "deemed" is included in the sixth column of the table set out in the Schedule shall be treated as if they were designated as enjoying reciprocal protection under Part 2 of the Act, except that—

(a) in that Part the term "recording" shall be construed as applying only to sound recordings (and not to films);
(b) the following provisions of Part 2 of the Act shall not apply—
   (i) section 182C (consent required for rental or lending of copies to public), insofar as it relates to lending;
   (ii) section 182D (right to equitable remuneration for exploitation of sound recording);
   (iii) section 183 (infringement of performer's rights by use of recording made without consent);
   (iv) sections 185 to 188 (rights of person having recording rights);
   (v) section 198(2) (criminal liability for playing or communicating to the public); and
(c) where in the sixth column of the table set out in the Schedule the entry for a country includes an asterisk (*), the following provisions of Part 2 of the Act shall also not apply—
   (i) section 182CA (consent required for making available to the public);
   (ii) section 198(1A) (criminal liability for making available to the public).

Savings

D4–008   7.—(1) For the purposes of this article an act is an "excluded act" where—

(a) a person (A) has incurred any expenditure or liability in connection with the act; and
(b) he—
   (i) began in good faith to do the act, or
   (ii) made in good faith effective and serious preparations to do the act,

at a time when the act neither infringed nor was restricted by the relevant rights in the work or performance.

(2) Where another person (B) acquires those relevant rights pursuant to this Order, A has the right—

(a) to continue to do the excluded act, or
(b) to do the excluded act,

notwithstanding that the excluded act infringes or is restricted by those relevant rights.

(3) Where B, or his exclusive licensee, pays reasonable compensation to A paragraph (2) no longer applies.

(4) Where—

(a) B offers to pay compensation to A under paragraph (3); but
(b) A and B cannot agree on what compensation is reasonable,

either person may refer the matter to arbitration.

(5) In this article "relevant rights" means copyright, the rights conferred by Chapter 4 of Part 1 of the Act and the rights conferred by Part 2 of the Act.

SCHEDULE

D4–009

Country	Article 2 (literary, dramatic, musical and artistic works, films and typographical arrangements)	Article 3 (sound recordings)	Article 4 (wireless broadcasts)	Article 5 (other broadcasts)	Article 6 (performances)
Albania	Applies	Applies (*)	Applies (1st September 2000)		Designated
Algeria	Applies	Applies (*)	Applies (22nd April 2007)		Designated
Andorra	Applies	Applies (*)	Applies (25th May 2004)		Designated
Angola	Applies	Applies	Applies (*) (23rd November 1996)		Deemed (*)
Antigua and Barbuda	Applies	Applies	Applies (*)(Y)		Deemed (*)
Argentina	Applies	Applies(*)	Applies (2nd March 1992)		Designated
Armenia	Applies	Applies (*)	Applies (31st January 2003)		Designated
Australia (including Norfolk Island)	Applies	Applies (*)	Applies (30th September 1992)		Designated
Austria	Applies	Applies (*)	Applies (X)	Applies	
Azerbaijan	Applies	Applies (*)	Applies (5th October 2005)		Designated
Bahamas	Applies	Applies			
Bahrain	Applies	Applies (*)	Applies (Y)		Designated
Bangladesh	Applies	Applies (*)	Applies (*)(Y)		Deemed (*)
[Bermuda	Applies	Applies (*)	Applies (6th August 1962)	Applies	Designated][63]
Barbados	Applies	Applies (*)	Applies (18th September 1983)		Designated
Belarus	Applies	Applies (*)	Applies (27th May 2003)		Designated
Belgium	Applies	Applies (*)	Applies (X)	Applies	
Belize	Applies	Applies	Applies (*)(Y)		Deemed (*)
Benin	Applies	Applies (£)	Applies (*) (22nd February 1996)		Deemed
Bhutan	Applies	Applies			
Bolivia	Applies	Applies (*)	Applies (24th November 1993)		Designated
Bosnia and Herzegovina	Applies	Applies			
Botswana	Applie	Applies (£)	Applies (*)(Y)		Deemed
Brazil	Applies	Applies (*)	Applies (29th September 1965)		Designated
Brunei Darussalam	Applies	Applies	Applies (*)(Y)		Deemed (*)
Bulgaria	Applies	Applies (*)	Applies (X)	Applies	
Burkina Faso	Applies	Applies (*)	Applies (14th January 1988)		Designated
Burundi	Applies	Applies	Applies (*)(Y)		Deemed (*)
Cambodia	Applies	Applies	Applies (*) (13th October 2004)		Deemed (*)
Cameroon	Applies	Applies	Applies (*)(Y)		Deemed (*)

[63] Inserted by the Copyright and Performances (Application to Other Countries) (Amendment) Order 2009 (SI 2009/2745) art.2.

Country	Article 2 (literary, dramatic, musical and artistic works, films and typographical arrangements)	Article 3 (sound recordings)	Article 4 (wireless broadcasts)	Article 5 (other broadcasts)	Article 6 (performances)
Canada	Applies	Applies (*)	Applies (Y)		Designated
Cape Verde	Applies	Applies (*)	Applies (3rd July 1997)		Designated
Central African Republic	Applies	Applies	Applies (*)(Y)		Deemed (*)
Chad	Applies	Applies	Applies (*) (19th October 1996)		Deemed (*)
Chile	Applies	Applies (*)	Applies (5th September 1974)		Designated
China	Applies	Applies (£)	Applies (*) (11th December 2001)		Deemed
Columbia	Applies	Applies (*)	Applies (17th September 1976)		Designated
Comoros	Applies	Applies			
Congo	Applies	Applies (*)	Applies (18th May 1964)		Designated
Costa Rica	Applies	Applies (*)	Applies (9th September 1971)		Designated
Cote d'Ivoire	Applies	Applies	Applies (*)(Y)		Deemed (*)
Croatia	Applies	Applies (*)	Applies (20th April 2000)		Designated
Cuba	Applies	Applies	Applies (*)(Y)		Deemed (*)
Cyprus	Applies	Applies (*)	Applies (X)	Applies	
Czech Republic	Applies	Applies (*)	Applies (X)	Applies	
Democratic Republic of the Congo	Applies	Applies	Applies (*) (1st January 1997)		Deemed (*)
Denmark	Applies	Applies (*)	Applies (X)	Applies	
Djibouti	Applies	Applies	Applies (*)(Y)		Deemed (*)
Dominica	Applies	Applies (*)	Applies (Y)		Designated
Dominican Republic	Applies	Applies (*)	Applies (27th January 1987)		Designated
Ecuador	Applies	Applies (*)	Applies (18th May 1964)		Designated
Egypt	Applies	Applies	Applies (*)(Y)		Deemed (*)
El Salvador	Applies	Applies (*)	Applies (29th June 1979)		Designated
Equatorial Guinea	Applies	Applies			
Estonia	Applies	Applies (*)	Applies (X)	Applies	
Faeroe Islands	Applies	Applies	Applies (1st February 1962)		Designated
Fiji	Applies	Applies (*)	Applies (11th April 1972)		Designated
Finland	Applies	Applies (*)	Applies (X)	Applies	
France (including overseas departments and territories)	Applies	Applies (*)	Applies (X)	Applies	
Gabon	Applies	Applies (#)	Applies (*)(Y)		Deemed
Gambia	Applies	Applies	Applies (*) (23rd October 1996)		Deemed (*)
Georgia	Applies	Applies (*)	Applies (14th August 2004)		Designated
Germany	Applies	Applies (*)	Applies (X)	Applies	

764

Country	Article 2 (literary, dramatic, musical and artistic works, films and typographical arrangements)	Article 3 (sound recordings)	Article 4 (wireless broadcasts)	Article 5 (other broadcasts)	Article 6 (performances)
Ghana	Applies	Applies (*)	Applies (*)(Y)		Deemed (*)
Gibraltar	Applies	Applies (*)	Applies (X)	Applies	Designated
Greece	Applies	Applies (*)	Applies (X)	Applies	
Greenland	Applies	Applies	Applies (1st February 1962)		Designated
Grenada	Applies	Applies	Applies (*) (22nd February 1996)		Deemed (*)
Guatemala	Applies	Applies (*)	Applies (14th January 1977)		Designated
Guinea	Applies	Applies (#)	Applies (*)(Y)		Deemed
Guinea-Bissau	Applies	Applies	Applies (*)(Y)		Deemed (*)
Guyana	Applies	Applies	Applies (*)(Y)		Deemed (*)
Haiti	Applies	Applies	Applies (*) (30th January 1996)		Deemed (*)
Holy See	Applies	Applies			
Honduras	Applies	Applies (*)	Applies (16th February 1990)		Designated
Hong Kong	Applies	Applies (*)	Applies (X)		Deemed (*)
Hungary	Applies	Applies (*)	Applies (X)	Applies	
Iceland	Applies	Applies (*)	Applies(X)	Applies	Designated
India	Applies	Applies (*)	Applies (*)(Y)		Deemed (*)
Indonesia	Applies	Applies (*)	Applies (X)	Applies	Deemed
Ireland	Applies	Applies (*)	Applies (X)	Applies	
Isle of Man	Applies	Applies (*)	Applies (X)	Applies	Designated
Israel	Applies	Applies (*)	Applies (Y)		Designated
Italy	Applies	Applies (*)	Applies (X)	Applies	
Jamaica	Applies	Applies (*)	Applies (27th January 1994)		Designated
Japan	Applies	Applies (*)	Applies (26th October 1989)		Designated
Jordan	Applies	Applies (#)	Applies (*) (11th April 2000)		Deemed
Kazakhstan	Applies	Applies (#)		Deemed	
Kenya	Applies	Applies	Applies (*)(Y)		Deemed (*)
Korea, Democratic People's Republic of	Applies	Applies			
Korea, Republic of	Applies	Applies	Applies (*)(Y)		Deemed (*)
Kuwait	Applies	Applies	Applies (*)(Y)		Deemed (*)
Kyrgyzstan	Applies	Applies (*)	Applies (20th December 1998)		Designated
Lao People's Democratic Republic	Applies	Applies			
Latvia	Applies	Applies (*)	Applies (X)	Applies	
Lebanon	Applies	Applies (*)	Applies (12th August 1997)		Designated
Lesotho	Applies	Applies (*)	Applies (26th January 1990)		Designated
Liberia	Applies	Applies			
Libyan Arab Jamahiriya	Applies	Applies			
Liechtenstein	Applies	Applies (*)	Applies (X)	Applies	Designated
Lithuania	Applies	Applies (*)	Applies (X)	Applies	
Luxembourg	Applies	Applies (*)	Applies (X)	Applies	

Country	Article 2 (literary, dramatic, musical and artistic works, films and typographical arrangements)	Article 3 (sound recordings)	Article 4 (wireless broadcasts)	Article 5 (other broadcasts)	Article 6 (performances)
Macao	Applies	Applies	Applies (*)(Y)		Deemed (*)
Macedonia, the former Yugoslav Republic of	Applies	Applies (*)	Applies (2nd March 1998)		Designated
Madagascar	Applies	Applies	Applies (*)(Y)		Deemed (*)
Malawi	Applies	Applies (*)	Applies (22nd June 1989)		Deemed (*)
Malaysia	Applies	Applies (*)	Applies (X)		Deemed (*)
Maldives	Applies	Applies	Applies (*)(Y)		Deemed (*)
Mali	Applies	Applies (#)	Applies (*)(Y)		Deemed
Malta	Applies	Applies (*)	Applies (X)	Applies	
Mauritania	Applies	Applies	Applies (*)(Y)		Deemed (*)
Mauritius	Applies	Applies	Applies (*)(Y)		Deemed (*)
Mexico	Applies	Applies (*)	Applies (18th May 1964)		Designated
Micronesia, Federated States of	Applies	Applies			
Moldova, Republic of	Applies	Applies (*)	Applies (5th December 1995)		Designated
Monaco	Applies	Applies (*)	Applies (6th December 1985)		Designated
Mongolia	Applies	Applies (#)	Applies (*) (29th January 1997)		Deemed
Montenegro	Applies	Applies (*)	Applies (10th June 2003)		Designated
Morocco	Applies	Applies	Applies (*)(Y)		Deemed (*)
Mozambique	Applies	Applies	Applies (*)(Y)		Deemed (*)
Myanmar	Applies	Applies	Applies (*)(Y)		Deemed (*)
Namibia	Applies	Applies	Applies (*)(Y)		Deemed (*)
Nepal	Applies	Applies	Applies (*) (23rd April 2004)		Deemed (*)
Netherlands	Applies	Applies (*)	Applies (X)	Applies	
Netherlands Antilles and Aruba	Applies	Applies	Applies (*)(Y)		Deemed
New Zealand	Applies	Applies (*)	Applies (*)(Y)		Deemed (*)
Nicaragua	Applies	Applies (*)	Applies (Y)		Designated
Niger	Applies	Applies (*)	Applies (18th May 1964)		Designated
Nigeria	Applies	Applies (*)	Applies (29th October 1993)		Designated
Norway	Applies	Applies (*)	Applies (X)	Applies	Designated
Oman	Applies	Applies	Applies (*) (9th November 2000)		Deemed
Pakistan	Applies	Applies (*)	Applies (*)(Y)		Deemed (*)
Panama	Applies	Applies (*)	Applies (2nd September 1983)		Designated
Papua New Guinea	Applies	Applies	Applies (*) (9th June 1996)		Deemed (*)
Paraguay	Applies	Applies (*)	Applies (26th February 1970)		Designated
Peru	Applies	Applies (*)	Applies (7th August 1985)		Designated
Philippines	Applies	Applies (*)	Applies (25th September 1984)		Designated
Poland	Applies	Applies (*)	Applies (X)	Applies	

Country	Article 2 (literary, dramatic, musical and artistic works, films and typographical arrangements)	Article 3 (sound recordings)	Article 4 (wireless broadcasts)	Article 5 (other broadcasts)	Article 6 (performances)
Portugal	Applies	Applies (*)	Applies (X)	Applies	
Qatar	Applies	Applies	Applies (*) (13th January 1996)		Deemed
Romania	Applies	Applies (*)	Applies (X)	Applies	
Russian Federation	Applies	Applies (*)	Applies (26th May 2003)		Designated
Rwanda	Applies	Applies	Applies (*) (22nd May 1996)		Deemed (*)
Saint Kitts and Nevis	Applies	Applies	Applies (*) (21st February 1996)		Deemed (*)
Saint Lucia	Applies	Applies (*)	Applies (Y)		Designated
Saint Vincent and the Grenadines	Applies	Applies	Applies (*)(Y)		Deemed (*)
Samoa	Applies	Applies			
Saudi Arabia	Applies	Applies			
Senegal	Applies	Applies (#)	Applies (*)(Y)		Deemed
Serbia	Applies	Applies (*)	Applies (10th June 2003)		Designated
Sierra Leone	Applies	Applies	Applies (*)(Y)		Deemed (*)
Singapore	Applies	Applies (#)	Applies (X)	Applies	Deemed
Slovak Republic	Applies	Applies (*)	Applies (X)	Applies	
Slovenia	Applies	Applies (*)	Applies (X)	Applies	
Solomon Islands	Applies	Applies	Applies (*) (26th July 1996)		Deemed
South Africa	Applies	Applies	Applies (*)(Y)		Deemed (*)
Spain	Applies	Applies (*)	Applies (X)	Applies	
Sri Lanka	Applies	Applies	Applies (*)(Y)		Deemed (*)
Sudan	Applies	Applies			
Suriname	Applies	Applies	Applies (*)(Y)		Deemed (*)
Swaziland	Applies	Applies	Applies (*)(Y)		Deemed (*)
Sweden	Applies	Applies (*)	Applies (X)	Applies	
Switzerland	Applies	Applies (*)	Applies (X)	Applies	Designated
Syrian Arab Republic	Applies	Applies (*)	Applies (13th May 2006)		Designated
Taiwan	Applies	Applies (*)	Applies (*) (1st January 2002)		Deemed (*)
Tajikistan	Applies	Applies			
Tanzania, United Republic of	Applies	Applies	Applies (*)(Y)		Deemed (*)
Thailand	Applies	Applies (*)	Applies (*)(Y)		Deemed (*)
Togo	Applies	Applies (*)	Applies (Y)		Designated
Tonga	Applies	Applies	Applies (*) (27th July 2007)		Deemed (*)
Trinidad and Tobago	Applies	Applies	Applies (*)(Y)		Deemed (*)
Tunisia	Applies	Applies	Applies (*)(Y)		Deemed (*)
Turkey	Applies	Applies (*)	Applies (Y)		Designated
Uganda	Applies	Applies	Applies (*)(Y)		Deemed (*)
Ukraine	Applies	Applies (*)	Applies (12th June 2002)		Designated
United Arab Emirates	Applies	Applies (*)	Applies (10th April 1996)		Designated

Country	Article 2 (literary, dramatic, musical and artistic works, films and typographical arrangements)	Article 3 (sound recordings)	Article 4 (wireless broadcasts)	Article 5 (other broadcasts)	Article 6 (performances)
United States of America (including Puerto Rico and all territories and possessions)	Applies	Applies (#)	Applies (*)(Y)		Deemed
Uruguay	Applies	Applies (*)	Applies (4th July 1977)		Designated
Uzbekistan	Applies	Applies			
Venezuela	Applies	Applies (*)	Applies (Y)		Designated
Vietnam	Applies	Applies (*)	Applies (1st March 2007)		Designated
Zambia	Applies	Applies	Applies (*)(Y)		Deemed (*)
Zimbabwe	Applies	Applies	Applies (*)(Y)		Deemed (*)

D5. The Copyright (Industrial Process and Excluded Articles) (No.2) Order 1989 (SI 1989/1070)

D5–001 The Secretary of State, in exercise of the powers conferred upon him by section 52(4) of the Copyright, Designs and Patents Act 1988 ("the Act"), hereby makes the following Order:

D5–002 1.—This Order may be cited as the Copyright (Industrial Process and Excluded Articles) (No.2) Order 1989 and shall come into force on 1st August 1989.

D5–003 2.—An article is to be regarded for the purposes of section 52 of the Act (limitation of copyright protection for design derived from artistic work) as made by an industrial process if—

 (a) it is one of more than fifty articles which—
  (i) all fall to be treated for the purposes of Part I of the Act as copies of a particular artistic work, but
  (ii) do not all together constitute a single set of articles as defined in section 44(1) of the Registered Designs Act 1949; or
 (b) it consists of goods manufactured in lengths or pieces, not being hand-made goods.

D5–004 3.—(1) There are excluded from the operation of section 52 of the Act—

 (a) works of sculpture, other than casts or models used or intended to be used as models or patterns to be multiplied by any industrial process;
 (b) wall plaques, medals and medallions; and
 (c) printed matter primarily of a literary or artistic character, including book jackets, calendars, certificates, coupons, dress-making patterns, greetings cards, labels, leaflets, maps, plans, playing cards, postcards, stamps, trade advertisements, trade forms and cars, transfers and similar articles.

 (2) Nothing in article 2 of this Order shall be taken to limit the meaning of "industrial process" in paragraph (1)(a) of this article.

4.—The Copyright (Industrial Designs) Rules 1957 and the Copyright (Industrial Processa and Excluded Articles) Order 1989 are hereby revoked. **D5–005**

D6. The Copyright (Industrial Designs) Rules 1957 (SI 1957/867)

The Board of Trade, in pursuance of the powers conferred upon them by section **D6–001**
36 of the Registered Designs Act, 1949, and subsection (5) of section 10 of the
Copyright Act, 1956, hereby make the following rules—

Industrial Application of Designs

1.—A design shall be taken to be applied industrially for the purposes of **D6–002**
section 10 of the Copyright Act, 1956, if it is applied—

(a) to more than fifty articles all of which do not together constitute a single
set of articles as defined in subsection (1) of section 44 of the Registered
Designs Act, 1949; or
(b) to goods manufactured in lengths or pieces, other than hand-made
goods.

Interpretation

2.—(1) Reference in these Rules to the application of a design to any articles or **D6–003**
goods means the application of the design to those articles or goods by a process
of printing or embossing or by any other process whatsoever, and shall be
deemed to include a reference to the reproduction of the design on or in those
articles or goods in the course of their production.

(2) The Interpretation Act, 1889(a), shall apply to the interpretation of these
Rules as it applies to the interpretation of an Act of Parliament, and as if these
Rules and the Rules hereby revoked were Acts of Parliament.

Revocation, Citation and Commencement

3.—(1) The Copyright (Industrial Designs) Rules, 1949(b), are hereby **D6–004**
revoked.

(2) These Rules may be cited as the Copyright (Industrial Designs) Rules, 1957,
and shall come into operation on the 1st day of June, 1957.

Dated this 17th day of May, 1957.

APPENDIX E

COURT, TRIBUNAL AND PROCEDURAL RULES

Contents

E1. CPR Part 63—Patents and Other Intellectual Property Claims

[Scope of this Part and interpretation

E1–001   **63.1.**—(1) This Part applies to all intellectual property claims including—

(a) registered intellectual property rights such as—
  (i) patents;
  (ii) registered designs; and
  (iii) registered trade marks; and
(b) unregistered intellectual property rights such as—
  (i) copyright;
  (ii) design right;
  (iii) the right to prevent passing off; and
  (iv) the other rights set out in [Practice Direction 63][1].

(2) In this Part—

(a) "the 1977 Act" means the Patents Act 1977;
(b) "the 1988 Act" means the Copyright, Designs and Patents Act 1988;
(c) "the 1994 Act" means the Trade Marks Act 1994;

[1] Substituted by the Civil Procedure (Amendment No.2) Rules 2009 (SI 2009/3390) r.38.

(d) "the Comptroller" means the Comptroller General of Patents, Designs and Trade Marks;

(e) "patent" means a patent under the 1977 Act or a supplementary protection certificate granted by the Patent Office under Article 10(1) of Council Regulation (EEC) No 1768/92 or of Regulation (EC) No 1610/96 of the European Parliament and the Council and includes any application for a patent or supplementary protection certificate;

(f) "Patents Court" means the Patents Court of the High Court constituted as part of the Chancery Division by section 6(1) of the Senior Courts Act 1981;

(g) "patents county court" means a county court designated as a patents county court under section 287(1) of the 1988 Act;

(h) "patents judge" means a person nominated under section 291(1) of the 1988 Act as the patents judge of a patents county court;

(i) [...][2]

(j) "the register" means whichever of the following registers is appropriate—

(i) patents maintained by the Comptroller under section 32 of the 1977 Act;

(ii) designs maintained by the registrar under section 17 of the Registered Designs Act 1949;

(iii) trade marks maintained by the registrar under section 63 of the 1994 Act;

(iv) Community trade marks maintained by the Office for Harmonisation in the Internal Market under Article 83 of Council Regulation (EC) No 40/94;

(v) Community designs maintained by the Office for Harmonisation in the Internal Market under Article 72 of Council Regulation (EC) No 6/2002; and

(vi) plant varieties maintained by the Controller under regulation 12 of the Plant Breeders' Rights Regulations 1998; and

(k) "the registrar" means—

(i) the registrar of trade marks; or

(ii) the registrar of registered designs,

whichever is appropriate.

(3) Claims to which this Part applies are allocated to the multi-track.][3]

I Patents and Registered Designs

[Scope of Section I and allocation

63.2.—(1) This Section applies to—

E1–002

(a) any claim under—
(i) the 1977 Act;
(ii) the Registered Designs Act 1949;
(iii) the Defence Contracts Act 1958; and

(b) any claim relating to—
(i) Community registered designs;
(ii) semiconductor topography rights; or

---

[2] Revoked by the Civil Procedure (Amendment No.2) Rules 2009 (SI 2009/3390) r.38.
[3] Substituted by the Civil Procedure (Amendment) Rules 2009 (SI 2009/2092) r.12 and Sch.1.

(iii) plant varieties.

(2) Claims to which this Section applies must be started in—

    (a) the Patents Court; or

    (b) a patents county court.][4]

[Specialist list

E1–003 **63.3.**—Claims in the Patents Court and a patents county court form specialist lists for the purpose of rule 30.5.][5]

[Patents judge

E1–004 **63.4.**—(1) Subject to paragraph (2), proceedings in a patents county court will be dealt with by the patents judge of that court.

(2) When a matter needs to be dealt with urgently and it is not practicable or appropriate for the patents judge to deal with such a matter, the matter may be dealt with by another judge with appropriate specialist experience nominated by the Chancellor of the High Court.][6]

[Starting the claim

E1–005 **63.5.**—Claims to which this Section applies must be started—

    (a) by a Part 7 claim form; or

    (b) in existing proceedings under Part 20.][7]

[Claim for infringement or challenge to validity of a patent or registered design

E1–006 **63.6.**—A statement of case in a claim for infringement or a claim in which the validity of a patent or registered design is challenged must contain particulars as set out in [Practice Direction 63][8].][9]

[Defence and reply

E1–007 **63.7.**—Part 15 applies with the modification—

    (a) to rule 15.4(1)(b) that in a claim for infringement under rule 63.6, the period for filing a defence where the defendant files an acknowledgment of service under Part 10 is 42 days after service of the particulars of claim;

    (b) that where rule 15.4(2) provides for a longer period to file a defence than in rule 63.7(a), then the period of time in rule 15.4(2) will apply; and

    (c) to rule 15.8 that the claimant must—

      (i) file any reply to a defence; and

      (ii) serve it on all other parties,

[4] Substituted by the Civil Procedure (Amendment) Rules 2009 (SI 2009/2092) r.12 and Sch.1.
[5] Substituted by the Civil Procedure (Amendment) Rules 2009 (SI 2009/2092) r.12 and Sch.1.
[6] Substituted by the Civil Procedure (Amendment) Rules 2009 (SI 2009/2092) r.12 and Sch.1.
[7] Substituted by the Civil Procedure (Amendment) Rules 2009 (SI 2009/2092) r.12 and Sch.1.
[8] Substituted by the Civil Procedure (Amendment No.2) Rules 2009 (SI 2009/3390) r.38.
[9] Substituted by the Civil Procedure (Amendment) Rules 2009 (SI 2009/2092) r.12 and Sch.1.

within 21 days of service of the defence.][10]

[Case management

63.8.—(1) Parties do not need to file an allocation questionnaire.

E1–008

(2) The following provisions only of Part 29 apply—

    (a) rule 29.3(2) (legal representatives to attend case management conferences);

    (b) rule 29.4 (the court's approval of agreed proposals for the management of proceedings); and

    (c) rule 29.5 (variation of case management timetable) with the exception of paragraph (1)(b) and (c).

(3) As soon as practicable the court will hold a case management conference which must be fixed in accordance with [Practice Direction 63][11].][12]

[Disclosure and inspection

63.9.—Part 31 is modified to the extent set out in [Practice Direction 63][13].][14]

E1–009

II Registered Trade Marks And Other Intellectual Property Rights

[Allocation

63.13.—Claims relating to matters arising out of the 1994 Act and other intellectual property rights set out in [Practice Direction 63][15] must be started in—

E1–010

    (a) the Chancery Division;

    (b) a patents county court; or

    (c) save as set out in [Practice Direction 63][16], a county court where there is also a Chancery District Registry.][17]

III Service Of Documents And Participation by the Comptroller

[Service of documents

63.14.—(1) Subject to paragraph (2), Part 6 applies to service of a claim form and any document in any proceedings under this Part.

E1–011

(2) A claim form relating to a registered right may be served—

---

[10] Substituted by the Civil Procedure (Amendment) Rules 2009 (SI 2009/2092) r.12 and Sch.1.

[11] Substituted by the Civil Procedure (Amendment No.2) Rules 2009 (SI 2009/3390) r.38.

[12] Substituted by the Civil Procedure (Amendment) Rules 2009 (SI 2009/2092) r.12 and Sch.1.

[13] Substituted by the Civil Procedure (Amendment No.2) Rules 2009 (SI 2009/3390) r.38.

[14] Substituted by the Civil Procedure (Amendment) Rules 2009 (SI 2009/2092) r.12 and Sch.1.

[15] Substituted by the Civil Procedure (Amendment No.2) Rules 2009 (SI 2009/3390) r.38.

[16] Substituted by the Civil Procedure (Amendment No.2) Rules 2009 (SI 2009/3390) r.38.

[17] Substituted by the Civil Procedure (Amendment) Rules 2009 (SI 2009/2092) r.12 and Sch.1.

    (a) on a party who has registered the right at the address for service given for that right in the United Kingdom Patent Office register, provided the address is within the United Kingdom; or

    (b) in accordance with rule 6.32(1), 6.33(1) or 6.33(2) on a party who has registered the right at the address for service given for that right in the appropriate register at—

      (i) the United Kingdom Patent Office; or

      (ii) the Office for Harmonisation in the Internal Market.

(3) Where a party seeks any remedy (whether by claim form, counterclaim or application notice), which would if granted affect an entry in any United Kingdom Patent Office register, that party must serve on the Comptroller or registrar—

    (a) the claim form, counterclaim or application notice;

    (b) any other statement of case where relevant (including any amended statement of case); and

    (c) any accompanying documents.][18]

[Participation by the Comptroller

E1–012   **63.15.**—Where the documents set out in rule 63.14(3) are served, the Comptroller or registrar—

    (a) may take part in proceedings; and

    (b) need not serve a defence or other statement of case unless the court orders otherwise.][19]

IV Appeals

[Appeals from decisions of the Comptroller or the registrar

E1–013   **63.16.**—(1) Part 52 applies to appeals from decisions of the Comptroller and the registrar.

(2) Appeals about patents must be made to the Patents Court, and other appeals to the Chancery Division.

(3) Where Part 52 requires a document to be served, it must also be served on the Comptroller or registrar, as appropriate.][20]

E2. Practice Direction 63—Intellectual Property Claims (supplementing CPR Part 63)

E2–001   **1.1.** This practice direction is divided into four sections—

    • Section I—Provisions about patents and those other rights within the scope of Section I of Part 63

---

[18] Substituted by the Civil Procedure (Amendment) Rules 2009 (SI 2009/2092) r.12 and Sch.1.

[19] Substituted by the Civil Procedure (Amendment) Rules 2009 (SI 2009/2092) r.12 and Sch.1.

[20] Substituted by the Civil Procedure (Amendment) Rules 2009 (SI 2009/2092) r.12 and Sch.1.

- Section II—Provisions about registered trade marks and other intellectual property rights
- Section III—Provisions about appeals
- Section IV—Provisions about final orders

SECTION I—PROVISIONS ABOUT PATENTS AND THOSE OTHER RIGHTS WITHIN THE SCOPE OF SECTION I OF PART 63

Scope of Section I

2.1. This Section applies to claims within the scope of Section 1 of Part 63.   E2–002

Starting the claim (rule 63.5)

3.1. A claim form to which this Section applies must—   E2–003

  (a) be marked 'Chancery Division Patents Court' or 'Patents County Court' as the case may be, in the top right hand corner below the title of the court, and

  (b) state the number of any patent or registered design to which the claim relates.

Claim for infringement or challenge to validity (rule 63.6)

4.1. In a claim for infringement of a patent—   E2–004

  (1) the statement of case must—
    (a) show which of the claims in the specification of the patent are alleged to be infringed; and
    (b) give at least one example of each type of infringement alleged; and
  (2) a copy of each document referred to in the statement of case, and where necessary a translation of the document, must be served with the statement of case.

4.2. Where the validity of a patent or registered design is challenged—

  (1) the statement of case must contain particulars of—
    (a) the remedy sought; and
    (b) the issues except those relating to validity of the patent or registered design;
  (2) the statement of case must have a separate document attached to and forming part of it headed 'Grounds of Invalidity' which must—
    (a) specify the grounds on which validity of the patent or registered design is challenged; and
    (b) include particulars that will clearly define every issue (including any challenge to any claimed priority date) which it is intended to raise; and
  (3) a copy of each document referred to in the Grounds of Invalidity, and where necessary a translation of the document, must be served with the Grounds of Invalidity.

4.3. Where in an application in which the validity of a patent or a registered design is challenged, the Grounds of Invalidity include an allegation—

  (1) that the invention is not a patentable invention because it is not new or does not include an inventive step, the particulars must specify details of the matter in the state of the art relied on, as set out in paragraph 4.4;

(2) that the specification of the patent does not disclose the invention clearly enough and completely enough for it to be performed by a person skilled in the art, the particulars must state, if appropriate, which examples of the invention cannot be made to work and in which respects they do not work or do not work as described in the specification; or

(3) that the registered design is not new or lacks individual character, the particulars must specify details of any prior design relied on, as set out in paragraph 4.4.

4.4. The details required under paragraphs 4.3(1) and 4.3(3) are—

(1) in the case of matter or a design made available to the public by written description, the date on which and the means by which it was so made available, unless this is clear from the fact of the matter; and

(2) in the case of matter or a design made available to the public by use—
  (a) the date or dates of such use;
  (b) the name of all persons making such use;
  (c) the place of such use;
  (d) any written material which identifies such use;
  (e) the existence and location of any apparatus employed in such use; and
  (f) all facts and matters relied on to establish that such matter was made available to the public.

4.5. In any proceedings in which the validity of a patent is challenged, where a party alleges that machinery or apparatus was used before the priority date of the claim the court may order inspection of that machinery or apparatus.

4.6. If the validity of a patent is challenged on the ground that the invention did not involve an inventive step, a party who wishes to rely on the commercial success of the patent must state in the statement of case the grounds on which that party so relies.

Case management (rule 63.8)

E2–005 **5.1.** The following paragraphs only of Practice Direction 29 apply—

(1) paragraph 5 (case management conferences)
  (a) excluding paragraph 5.9; and
  (b) modified so far as is made necessary by other specific provisions of this practice direction; and

(2) paragraph 7 (failure to comply with case management directions).

5.2. Case management will be dealt with by—

(1) a judge of the Patents Court, a patents judge or a Master, but
(2) a Master may only deal with the following matters—
  (a) orders by way of settlement, except settlement of procedural disputes;
  (b) applications for extension of time;
  (c) applications for permission to serve out of the jurisdiction;
  (d) applications for security for costs;
  (e) other matters as directed by a judge of the court; and
  (f) enforcement of money judgments.

5.3. The claimant must apply for a case management conference within 14 days of the date when all defendants who intend to file and serve a defence have done so.

5.4. Where the claim has been transferred, the claimant must apply for a case management conference within 14 days of the date of the order transferring the claim, unless the court held or gave directions for a case management conference when it made the order transferring the claim.

5.5 Any party may, at a time earlier than that provided in paragraphs 5.3 and 5.4, apply in writing to the court to fix a case management conference.

5.6. If the claimant does not make an application in accordance with paragraphs 5.3 and 5.4, any other party may apply for a case management conference.

5.7. The court may fix a case management conference at any time on its own initiative.

5.8. Not less than 4 days before a case management conference, each party must file and serve an application notice for any order which that party intends to seek at the case management conference.

5.9. Unless the court orders otherwise, the claimant, or the party who makes an application under paragraph 5.6, in consultation with the other parties, must prepare a case management bundle containing—

(1) the claim form;
(2) all other statements of case (excluding schedules), except that, if a summary of a statement of case has been filed, the bundle must contain the summary, and not the full statement of case;
(3) a pre-trial timetable, if one has been agreed or ordered;
(4) the principal orders of the court; and
(5) any agreement in writing made by the parties as to disclosure,

and provide copies of the case management bundle for the court and the other parties at least 4 days before the first case management conference or any earlier hearing at which the court may give case management directions.

5.10. At the case management conference the court may direct that—

(1) a scientific adviser under section 70(3) of the Senior Courts Act 1981 or under section 63(1) of the County Courts Act 1984 be appointed; and
(2) a document setting out basic undisputed technology should be prepared.

(Rule 35.15 applies to scientific advisers.)

5.11. Where a trial date has not been fixed by the court, a party may apply for a trial date by filing a certificate which must—

(1) state the estimated length of the trial, agreed if possible by all parties;
(2) detail the time required for the judge to consider the documents;
(3) identify the area of technology; and
(4) assess the complexity of the technical issues involved by indicating the complexity on a scale of 1 to 5 (with 1 being the least and 5 the most complex).

5.12. The claimant, in consultation with the other parties, must revise and update the documents, referred to in paragraph 5.9 appropriately as the case proceeds. This must include making all necessary revisions and additions at least 7 days before any subsequent hearing at which the court may give case management directions.

Disclosure and inspection (rule 63.9)

(Paragraphs 6.1 and 6.2 are omitted.) E2–006

6.3. Where the issue of commercial success arises, the patentee must, within such time limit as the court may direct, serve a schedule containing—

(1) where the commercial success relates to an article or product—
    (a) an identification of the article or product (for example by product code number) which the patentee asserts has been made in accordance with the claims of the patent;

    (b) a summary by convenient periods of sales of any such article or product;

    (c) a summary for the equivalent periods of sales, if any, of any equivalent prior article or product marketed before the article or product in sub-paragraph (a); and

    (d) a summary by convenient periods of any expenditure on advertising and promotion which supported the marketing of the articles or products in sub-paragraphs (a) and (c); or

(2) where the commercial success relates to the use of a process—

    (a) an identification of the process which the patentee asserts has been used in accordance with the claims of the patent;

    (b) a summary by convenient periods of the revenue received from the use of such process;

    (c) a summary for the equivalent periods of the revenues, if any, received from the use of any equivalent prior art process; and

    (d) a summary by convenient periods of any expenditure which supported the use of the process in sub-paragraphs (a) and (c).

Experiments

E2–007   **7.1.** A party seeking to establish any fact by experimental proof conducted for the purpose of litigation must, at least 21 days before service of the application notice for directions under paragraph 7.3, or within such other time as the court may direct, serve on all parties a notice—

(1) stating the facts which the party seeks to establish; and

(2) giving full particulars of the experiments proposed to establish them.

7.2. A party served with a notice under paragraph 7.1—

(1) must within 21 days after such service, serve on the other party a notice stating whether or not each fact is admitted; and

(2) may request the opportunity to inspect a repetition of all or a number of the experiments identified in the notice served under paragraph 7.1.

7.3. Where any fact which a party seeks to establish by experimental proof is not admitted, that party must apply to the court for permission and directions by application notice.

Use of models or apparatus

E2–008   **8.1.** A party that intends to rely on any model or apparatus must apply to the court for directions at the first case management conference.

Time estimates for trial, trial bundle, reading guide and detailed trial timetable

E2–009   **9.1.** Not less than one week before the beginning of the trial, each party must inform the court in writing of the estimated length of its—

(1) oral submissions;

(2) examination in chief, if any, of its own witnesses; and

(3) cross-examination of witnesses of any other party.

9.2. At least four days before the date fixed for the trial, the claimant must file—

(1) the trial bundle;

(2) a reading guide for the judge; and

(3) a detailed trial timetable which should be agreed, if possible.

9.3. The reading guide filed under paragraph 9.2 must—

(1) be short and, if possible, agreed;
(2) set out the issues, the parts of the documents that need to be read on each issue and the most convenient order in which they should be read;
(3) identify the relevant passages in text books and cases, if appropriate; and
(4) not contain argument.

(Paragraphs 10.1 to 13.2 are omitted.)

Order affecting entry in the register of patents or designs

14.1. Where any order of the court affects the validity of an entry in the register, the party in whose favour the order is made, must serve a copy of such order on the Comptroller within 14 days.   **E2–010**

14.2. Where the order is in favour of more than one party, a copy of the order must be served by such party as the court directs.

European Community designs

15.1. The Patents Court and the patents county court at the Central London County Court are the designated Community design courts under Article 80(5) of Council Regulation (EC) 6/2002.   **E2–011**

15.2. Where a counterclaim is filed at the Community design court, for a declaration of invalidity of a registered Community design, the Community design court will inform the Office for Harmonisation in the Internal Market of the date on which the counterclaim was filed, in accordance with Article 86(2) of Council Regulation (EC) 6/2002.

15.3. On filing a counterclaim under paragraph 15.2, the party filing it must inform the Community design court in writing that it is a counterclaim to which paragraph 15.2 applies and that the Office for Harmonisation in the Internal Market needs to be informed of the date on which the counterclaim was filed.

15.4. Where a Community design court has given a judgment which has become final on a counterclaim for a declaration of invalidity of a registered Community design, the Community design court will send a copy of the judgment to the Office for Harmonisation in the Internal Market, in accordance with Article 86(4) of Council Regulation (EC) 6/2002.

15.5. The party in whose favour judgment is given under paragraph 15.4 must inform the Community design court at the time of judgment that paragraph 15.4 applies and that the Office for Harmonisation in the Internal Market needs to be sent a copy of the judgment.

SECTION II—PROVISIONS ABOUT REGISTERED TRADE MARKS AND OTHER
INTELLECTUAL PROPERTY RIGHTS

Allocation (rule 63.13)

16.1. The other intellectual property rights referred to in rule 63.13 are—   **E2–012**

(1) copyright;
(2) rights in performances;
(3) rights conferred under Part VII of the 1988 Act;
(4) design right;
(5) Community design right;
(6) association rights;
(7) moral rights;

(8) database rights;

(9) unauthorised decryption rights;

(10) hallmarks;

(11) technical trade secrets litigation;

(12) passing off;

(13) protected designations of origin, protected geographical indications and traditional speciality guarantees;

(14) registered trade marks; and

(15) Community trade marks.

16.2. There are Chancery district registries at Birmingham, Bristol, Caernarfon, Cardiff, Leeds, Liverpool, Manchester, Mold, Newcastle upon Tyne and Preston.

16.3. The county courts at Caernarfon, Mold and Preston do not have jurisdiction in relation to registered trade marks and Community trade marks.

Starting the claim

E2–013   **17.1.** A claim form to which Section II of Part 63 applies must be marked in the top right hand corner 'Intellectual Property' below the title of the court in which it is issued.

17.2. In the case of claims concerning registered trade marks and Community trade marks, the claim form must state the registration number of any trade mark to which the claim relates.

Reference to the court by the registrar or the Comptroller

E2–014   **18.1.** This paragraph applies where—

(1) an application is made to the registrar under the 1994 Act and the registrar refers the application to the court; or

(2) a reference is made to the Comptroller under section 246 of the 1988 Act and the Comptroller refers the whole proceedings or a particular question or issue to the court under section 251(1) of that Act.

18.2. Where paragraph 18.1 applies, the applicant under the 1994 Act or the person making the reference under section 246 of the 1988 Act, as the case may be, must start a claim seeking the court's determination of the reference within 14 days of receiving notification of the decision to refer.

18.3. If the person referred to in paragraph 18.2 does not start a claim within the period prescribed by that paragraph, that person will be deemed to have abandoned the reference.

18.4. The period prescribed under paragraph 18.2 may be extended by—

(1) the registrar or the Comptroller as the case may be; or

(2) the court

where a party so applies, even if the application is not made until after the expiration of that period.

Application to the court under section 19 of the 1994 Act

E2–015   **19.1.** Where an application is made under section 19 of the 1994 Act, the applicant must serve the claim form or application notice on all identifiable persons having an interest in the goods, materials or articles within the meaning of section 19 of the 1994 Act.

Order affecting entry in the register of trade marks

20.1. Where any order of the court affects the validity of an entry in the register, the provisions of paragraphs 14.1 and 14.2 apply.   **E2–016**

European Community trade marks

21.1. The Chancery Division, the patents county court at the Central London   **E2–017** County Court and the county courts where there is also a Chancery district registry, except Caernarfon, Mold and Preston, are designated Community trade mark courts for the purposes of Article 91(1) of Council Regulation (EC) 40/94.

21.2. Where a counterclaim is filed at the Community trade mark court, for revocation or for a declaration of invalidity of a Community trade mark, the Community trade mark court will inform the Office for Harmonisation in the Internal Market of the date on which the counterclaim was filed, in accordance with Article 96(4) of Council Regulation (EC) 40/94.

21.3. On filing a counterclaim under paragraph 21.2, the party filing it must inform the Community trade mark court in writing that it is a counterclaim to which paragraph 21.2 applies and that the Office for Harmonisation in the Internal Market needs to be informed of the date on which the counterclaim was filed.

21.4. Where the Community trade mark court has given a judgment which has become final on a counterclaim for revocation or for a declaration of invalidity of a Community trade mark, the Community trade mark court will send a copy of the judgment to the Office for Harmonisation in the Internal Market, in accordance with Article 96(6) of Council Regulation (EC) 40/94.

21.5. The party in whose favour judgment is given under paragraph 21.4 must inform the Community trade mark court at the time of judgment that paragraph 21.4 applies and that the Office for Harmonisation in the Internal Market needs to be sent a copy of the judgment.

Claim for additional damages under section 97(2), section 191J(2) or section 229(3) of the 1988 Act

22.1. Where a claimant seeks to recover additional damages under section 97(2),   **E2–018** section 191J(2) or section 229(3) of the 1988 Act, the particulars of claim must include—

(1) a statement to that effect; and
(2) the grounds for claiming them.

Application for delivery up or forfeiture under the 1988 Act

23.1. An applicant who applies under section 99, 114, 195, 204, 230 or 231 of the   **E2–019** 1988 Act for delivery up or forfeiture must serve—

(1) the claim form; or
(2) application notice, where appropriate,

on all identifiable persons who have an interest in the goods, material or articles within the meaning of section 114, 204 or 231 of the 1988 Act.

Association rights

24.1. Where an application is made under regulations made under section 7 of   **E2–020** the Olympic Symbol etc (Protection) Act 1995, the applicant must serve the claim form or application notice on all identifiable persons having an interest in the goods, materials or articles within the meaning of the regulations.

Section III—Provisions About Appeals

Reference to the court by an appointed person

E2–021　**25.1.** This paragraph applies where a person appointed by the Lord Chancellor to hear and decide appeals under section 77 of the 1994 Act, refers an appeal to the Chancery Division under section 76(3) of the 1994 Act.

25.2. The appellant must file a claim form seeking the court's determination of the appeal within 14 days of receiving notification of the decision to refer.

25.3. The appeal will be deemed to have been abandoned if the appellant does not file a claim form within the period prescribed by paragraph 25.2.

25.4. The period prescribed under paragraph 25.2 may be extended by—

(1) the person appointed by the Lord Chancellor; or
(2) the court

where the appellant so applies, even if such application is not made until after the expiration of that period.

Section IV—Provisions About Final Orders

Costs

E2–022　**26.1**. Where the court makes an order for delivery up or destruction of infringing goods, or articles designed or adapted to make such goods, the person against whom the order is made must pay the costs of complying with that order unless the court orders otherwise.

26.2. Where the court finds that an intellectual property right has been infringed, the court may, at the request of the applicant, order appropriate measures for the dissemination and publication of the judgment to be taken at the expense of the infringer.

E3. The Patents County Court (Designation and Jurisdiction) Order 1994 (SI 1994/1609)

The Lord Chancellor, in exercise of the powers conferred on him by section 287 of the Copyright, Designs and Patents Act 1988, hereby makes the following Order—

Citation and commencement

E3–001　**1.**—This Order may be cited as the Patents County Court (Designation and Jurisdiction) Order 1994 and shall come into force on 11 July 1994.

Designation as Patents County Court

E3–002　**2.**—The Central London County Court is hereby designated as a patents county court.

3.—As a patents county court, the Central London County Court shall have jurisdiction, subject to [article 4 below—

(a)][21] to hear and determine any action or matter relating to patents or designs over which the High Court would have jurisdiction, together

---

[21] Substituted by the High Court and County Courts Jurisdiction (Amendment) Order 2005 (SI 2005/587) art.5.

with any claims or matters ancillary to, or arising from, such proceedings[; and

(b) under the following provisions of the Trade Marks Act 1994—
   (i) sections 15, 16, 19, 23(5), 25(4)(b), 30, 31, 46, 47, 64, 73 and 74;
   (ii) paragraph 12 of Schedule 1; and
   (ii) paragraph 14 of Schedule 2,

to include jurisdiction to hear and determine any claims or matters ancillary to, or arising from proceedings brought under such provisions][22].

4.—The jurisdiction conferred by article 3 above shall not include jurisdiction to hear appeals from the comptroller.

Discontinuance and transitional provision

5.—(1) The Edmonton County Court shall cease to be a patents county court and accordingly the Patents County Court (Designation and Jurisdiction) Order 1990 is hereby revoked.

(2) The patents county court at the Central London County Court shall have jurisdiction in proceedings commenced in the patents county court at the Edmonton County Court before the coming into force of this Order.

E3–003

E4. The Community Designs (Designation of Community Design Courts) Regulations (SI 2005/696)

The Secretary of State, being a Minister designated for the purposes of section 2(2) of the European Communities Act 1972 in relation to measures relating to the legal protection of designs, in exercise of powers conferred on her by that section makes the following Regulations:

1.—These Regulations may be cited as the Community Designs (Designation of Community Design Courts) Regulations 2005 and shall come into force on 6th April 2005.

2.—(1) For the purposes of Article 80 of the Council Regulation (EC) No 6/2002 of 12th December 2001 on Community designs, the following courts are designated as Community design courts—

(a) in England and Wales—
   (i) the High Court; and
   (ii) any county court designated as a patents county court under section 287(1) of the Copyright, Designs and Patents Act 1988;
(b) in Scotland, the Court of Session; and
(c) in Northern Ireland, the High Court.

(2) For the purpose of hearing appeals from judgments of the courts designated by paragraph (1), the following courts are designated as Community design courts—

(a) in England and Wales, the Court of Appeal;
(b) in Scotland, the Court of Session;
(c) in Northern Ireland, the Court of Appeal.

E4–001

---

[22] Inserted by the the High Court and County Courts Jurisdiction (Amendment) Order 2005 (SI 2005/587) art.5.

E5. The Registered Designs Appeal Tribunal Rules (SI 1950/430) (as amended)

E5-001 [**1.**—(1) Any person who desires to appeal to the Registered Designs Appeal Tribunal from a decision of the Comptroller-General of Patents, Designs and Trade Marks (in these Rules referred to as "the Registrar") in any case in which a right of appeal is given by the Registered Designs Act 1949 (in these Rules referred to as "the Act") shall file with the registrar of the Appeal Tribunal at the Royal Courts of Justice, London, a notice of appeal in the form set out in the schedule to these Rules.

(2) The notice of appeal shall be filed—

   (a) in the case of a decision on a matter of procedure, within 14 days after the date of the decision; and

   (b) in any other case, within six weeks after the date of the decision.

(3) The Registrar may determine whether any decision is on a matter of procedure and any such determination shall itself be a decision on a matter of procedure.][23]

2.—The appellant shall [within two days of filing the notice of appeal send a copy thereof][24] to the Registrar and to any person or persons who appeared, or gave notice of opposition, on the proceedings before the Registrar.

3.—On receiving the notice of appeal the Registrar shall forthwith transmit to the registrar of the Appeal Tribunal all the papers relating to the matter which is the subject of the appeal.

[**4.**—Except by leave of the Appeal Tribunal, no appeal shall be entertained unless notice of appeal has been given within the period specified in rule 1(2) or within such further time as the Registrar may allow upon request made to him prior to the expiry of that period.][25]

5.—The registrar of the Appeal Tribunal shall give to the appellant and the Registrar and to any opposing party not less than seven days' notice of the time and place appointed for the hearing of the appeal, unless the Appeal Tribunal expressly directs that shorter notice may be given.

[**5A.**—(1) A party to an appeal before the Appeal Tribunal may appear and be heard either in person or by a patent agent, a solicitor, or counsel.

(2) In this Rule—

   "counsel" means a member of the Bar of England and Wales or of Northern Ireland or a member of the Faculty of Advocates in Scotland; and

   "patent agent" has the same meaning as it has in the Patents Act 1949.][26]

6.—The evidence used on appeal to the Appeal Tribunal shall be the same as that used before the Registrar and no further evidence shall be given, except with the leave of the Appeal Tribunal given upon application made for that purpose.

7.—The regulations applicable to the filing of documentary evidence on proceedings before the Registrar shall apply to documentary evidence filed on an appeal to the Appeal Tribunal.

---

[23] Substituted by the Registered Designs Appeal Tribunal (Amendment) Rules (SI 1970/1075) r.2.

[24] Substituted by the Registered Designs Appeal Tribunal (Amendment) Rules (SI 1970/1075) r.3.

[25] Substituted by the Registered Designs Appeal Tribunal (Amendment) Rules (SI 1970/1075) r.4.

[26] Added by the Registered Designs Appeal Tribunal (Amendment) Rules (SI 1970/1075) r.5.

8.—The Appeal Tribunal may, at the request of any party, order the attendance at the hearing for the purpose of cross-examination of any person who has made a declaration in the matter to which the appeal relates.

9.—Any person requiring the attendance of a witness for cross-examination shall tender to the witness whose attendance is required a reasonable sum for conduct money.

10.—The Appeal Tribunal may, in awarding costs, either fix the amount thereof or direct by whom and in what manner the amount of the costs is to be ascertained.

11.—If any costs awarded are not paid within fourteen days after the amount thereof has been fixed or ascertained, or within such shorter period as may be directed by the Appeal Tribunal, the party to whom the costs are payable may apply to the Appeal Tribunal for an order for payment under the provisions of section 28(5) of the Act.

12.—Any notice or other document required to be filed with or sent to the registrar of the Appeal Tribunal under these Rules may be sent by prepaid letter through the post.

13.—The Interpretation Act 1889, shall apply to the interpretation of these Rules as it applies to the interpretation of an Act of Parliament.

14.—These Rules may be cited as the Registered Designs Appeal Tribunal Rules 1950, and shall come into force on the first day of April, 1950.

Notice of Appeal

SCHEDULE 1, PARAGRAPH 1

(Form of Notice of Appeal is omitted.)

[NOTE:—This notice must be sent to the Registrar of the Registered Designs Appeal Tribunal, Royal Courts of Justice, London, WC2A 2LL and must bear an impressed judicature fee stamp for £6. An unstamped copy of the notice must be sent to the Comptroller-General of Patents, Designs and Trade Marks at the Patent Office, 25 Southampton Buildings, London, W.C.2, and to any person who appeared or gave notice of opposition on the proceedings from which the appeal is brought, within the period prescribed by the Registered Designs Appeal Tribunal Rules.][27]

E5–002

E6. Commission Regulation (EC) No 216/96 of 5 February 1996 laying down the rules of procedure of the Boards of Appeal of the Office for Harmonization in the Internal Market (Trade Marks and Designs)

THE COMMISSION OF THE EUROPEAN COMMUNITIES,

Having regard to the Treaty establishing the European Community,

Having regard to Council Regulation (EC) No.40/94 of 20 December 1994 on the Community trade mark (1), as amended by Regulation (EC) No.3288/94 (2), and in particular Article 140(3) thereof,

E6–001

[27] Substituted by the Registered Designs Appeal Tribunal (Amendment) Rules (SI 1970/1075) r.6.

Whereas Regulation (EC) No.40/94 (hereinafter "the Regulation") creates a new trade mark system allowing a trade mark having effect throughout the Community to be obtained on the basis of an application to the Office for Harmonization in the Internal Market (Trade Marks and Designs) ("the Office");

Whereas for this purpose the Regulation contains in particular the necessary provisions for a procedure leading to the registration of a Community trade marks, as well as for the administration of Community trade marks, for appeals against decisions of the Office and for proceedings in relation to revocation or invalidity of a Community trade mark;

Whereas under Article 130 of the Regulation, the Boards of Appeal are to be responsible for deciding on appeals from decisions of the examiners, the Opposition Divisions, the Administration of Trade Marks and Legal Division and the Cancellation Divisions;

Whereas Title VII of the Regulation contains basic principles regarding appeals against decisions of examiners, the Opposition Divisions, the Administration of Trade Marks and Legal Division and the Cancellation Divisions;

Whereas Title X of Commission Regulation (EC) No.2868/95 of 13 December 1995 implementing Council Regulation No.40/94 on the Community Trade Mark (3) contains implementing rules to Title VII of the Regulation;

Whereas this Regulation supplements those other rules, in particular as regards the organization of the Boards and the oral procedure;

Whereas before the beginning of each working year a scheme should be established for the distribution of business between the Boards of Appeal by an Authority established for that purpose; whereas to this end the said Authority should apply objective criteria such as classes of products and services or initial letters of the names of applicants;

Whereas to facilitate the handling and disposal of appeals, a rapporteur should be designated for each case, who should be responsible inter alia for preparing communications with the parties and drafting decisions;

Whereas the parties to proceedings before the Boards of Appeal may not be in a position or may not be willing to bring questions of general relevance to a pending case to the attention of the Boards of Appeal; whereas, therefore, the Boards of Appeal should have the power, of their own motion or pursuant to a request by the President, to invite the President of the Office, to submit comments on questions of general interest in relation to a case pending before the Boards of Appeal;

Whereas the measures provided for in this Regulation are in accordance with the opinion of the Committee established under Article 141 of the Regulation, HAS ADOPTED THIS REGULATION

Article 1

Presidium of the Boards of Appeal

E6–002   1. The authority referred to in Articles 130 and 131 of the Regulation shall be the Presidium of the Boards of Appeal (referred to hereinafter as "the Presidium").

2. The Presidium shall comprise the President of the Boards of Appeal, who shall chair it, the chairmen of the Boards and Board members elected for each calendar year by and from among all the members of the Boards other than the President of the Boards of Appeal and the chairmen of the Boards. The number of Board members so elected shall be a quarter of the number of Board members, other than the President of the Boards of Appeal and the chairmen of the Boards, rounded up if necessary.

3. If the President of the Boards of Appeal is unable to act or if the post of President is vacant, the Presidium shall be chaired by:

(a) the chairman of the Board having the longest service on the Boards of Appeal; or

(b) where chairmen have the same length of service, by the eldest of those qualifying under the preceding subparagraph.

4. The Presidium may validly deliberate only if at least two-thirds of its members are present, including its chairman and two Board chairmen. Decisions of the Presidium shall be taken by a majority vote. In the event of a tie, the vote of the chairman shall be decisive.

5. Before the beginning of each calendar year, and without prejudice to Article 1(b), the Presidium shall decide on objective criteria for allocating cases among the Boards for the calendar year in question and shall designate the full and alternate members of each of the Boards for that year. Each member of the Boards of Appeal may be assigned to several Boards as a full or alternate member. These measures may be modified, as necessary, in the course of the calendar year in question. Decisions adopted by the Presidium pursuant to this paragraph shall be published in the Official Journal of the Office.

6. The Presidium shall also be competent to:

(a) lay down such rules of a procedural nature as are necessary for the processing of cases brought before the Boards and such rules as are necessary on the organisation of the Boards' work;

(b) rule on any conflict concerning the allocation of cases among the Boards of Appeal;

(c) lay down its internal rules;

(d) lay down practical instructions of a procedural nature for parties involved in proceedings before the Boards of Appeal, for example, with regard to the submission of written statements and to oral proceedings;

(e) exercise any other powers as are conferred to it by the present Regulation.

7. The President of the Boards of Appeal shall consult the Presidium on the expenditure requirements of the Boards, which he shall communicate to the President of the Office with a view to drawing up the expenditure estimates and where he considers it appropriate, on any other question relating to the management of the Boards of Appeal.][28]

[Article 1(a)

Grand Board

1. The enlarged Board set up by Article 130(3) of the Regulation shall be the Grand Board. **E6–003**

2. The Grand Board shall comprise nine members, including the President of the Boards of Appeal, who shall chair it, the chairmen of the Boards, the rapporteur designated prior to referral to the Grand Board, if applicable, and members drawn in rotation from a list comprising the names of all members of the Boards of Appeal other than the President of the Boards of Appeal and the chairmen of the Boards.

[28] Substituted by Regulation (EC) No 2082/2004 (OJ L 360, 07/12/2004 p.8).

The Presidium shall draw up the list referred to in the first paragraph and establish the rules according to which members are drawn from that list on the basis of objective criteria. The list and such rules shall be published in the Official Journal of the Office. If a rapporteur has not been designated prior to referral to the Grand Board, the chairman of the Grand Board shall designate a rapporteur from among the members of the Grand Board.

3. If the President of the Boards of Appeal is unable to act or if the post of President is vacant, or in the event of exclusion or objection within the meaning of Article 132 of the Regulation, the Grand Board shall be chaired by:

(a) the chairman having the longest service on the Boards of Appeal; or
(b) where chairmen have the same length of service, by the eldest of those qualifying under the preceding subparagraph 4.

4. If another member of the Grand Board is unable to act or in the event of exclusion or objection within the meaning of Article 132 of the Regulation, he or she shall be replaced by the person highest on the list referred to in paragraph 2 of this Article.

5. The Grand Board may not hear cases and oral proceedings may not take place before it unless seven of its members are present, including its chairman and the rapporteur.

If the Grand Board hears a case in the presence of only eight of its members, the member with the least seniority in the Boards of Appeal shall not take part in the vote, unless that member is the chairman or the rapporteur, in which case the member with the next highest seniority to that of the chairman or rapporteur shall not vote.][29]

[Article 1(b)]

Referral to the Grand Board

E6–004   1. A Board may refer a case allocated to it to the Grand Board if it believes that this is justified by the legal difficulty or importance of the case or by special circumstances, for example, if Boards of Appeal have issued diverging decisions on a point of law raised by that case.

2. A Board shall refer a case allocated to it to the Grand Board if it believes that it must deviate from an interpretation of the relevant legislation given in an earlier decision of the Grand Board.

3. The Presidium may, on a proposal made by the President of the Boards of Appeal on his or her own initiative or at the request of a member of the Presidium, refer to the Grand Board a case allocated to a Board if it believes that this is justified by the legal difficulty or importance of the case or by special circumstances, for example, if Boards of Appeal have issued diverging decisions on a point of law raised by that case.

4. The Grand Board shall, without delay, refer the case back to the Board to which it was originally allocated if it believes that the conditions for the original referral are not met.

5. All decisions relating to referral to the Grand Board shall be reasoned and shall be communicated to the parties to the case.][30]

---

[29] Inserted by Regulation (EC) No 2082/2004 (OJ L 360, 07/12/2004 p.8).
[30] Inserted by Regulation (EC) No 2082/2004 (OJ L 360, 07/12/2004 p.8).

[Article 1(c)

Decisions by a single member

1. The Presidium shall draw up an indicative list of the types of cases which the   **E6–005**
Boards may, unless special circumstances apply, devolve to a single member, such
as decisions closing the proceedings following agreement between the parties,
and decisions on the award of costs and the admissibility of the appeal.

The Presidium may also draw up a list of the types of cases which may not be
devolved to a single member.

2. A Board may delegate to its chairman the decision to allocate to a single
member cases falling within the types of cases defined by the Presidium in
accordance with paragraph 1.

3. The decision to devolve the case upon a single member shall be communicated to the parties.

The member to whom the case has been devolved shall refer it to the Board if
he finds that the conditions for devolution are no longer met.][31]

[Article 1(d)

Referral of a case following a ruling of the Court of Justice

1. If, pursuant to Article 63(6) of the Regulation, the measures necessary to   **E6–006**
comply with a judgment of the Court of Justice annulling all or part of a decision
of a Board of Appeal or of the Grand Board include re-examination by the Boards
of Appeal of the case which was the subject of that decision, the Presidium shall
decide if the case shall be referred to the Board which adopted that decision, or to
another Board, or to the Grand Board.

2. If the case is referred to another Board, that Board shall not comprise
members who were party to the contested decision. This provision shall not apply
if the case is referred to the Grand Board.][32]

Article 2

Replacement of members

1. Reasons for replacement by alternates shall in particular include leave,   **E6–007**
sickness, inescapable commitments and the grounds of exclusion set out in Article
132 of the Regulation.

2. Any member asking to be replaced by an alternate shall without delay inform
the Chairman of the Board concerned of his unavailability.

Article 3

Exclusion and objection

1. If a Board has knowledge of a possible reason for exclusion or objection   **E6–008**
under Article 132 (3) of the Regulation which does not originate from a member

[31] Inserted by Regulation (EC) No 2082/2004 (OJ L 360, 07/12/2004 p.8).
[32] Inserted by Regulation (EC) No 2082/2004 (OJ L 360, 07/12/2004 p.8).

himself or from any party to the proceedings, the procedure of Article 132 (4) of the Regulation shall be applied.

2. The member concerned shall be invited to present his comments as to whether there is a reason for exclusion or objection.

3. Before a decision is taken on the action to be taken pursuant to Article 132 (4) of the Regulation, there shall be no further proceedings in the case.

Article 4

Rapporteurs

E6–009   1. The Chairman of each Board shall for each appeal designate a member of his Board, or himself, as rapporteur.

2. The rapporteur shall carry out a preliminary study of the appeal. He may prepare communications to the parties subject to the direction of the Chairman of the Board. Communications shall be signed by the rapporteur on behalf of the Board.

3. [...][33]

[3].[34] The rapporteur shall draft decisions.

Article 5

Registry

E6–010   1. A Registry shall be set up at the Boards of Appeal, and shall, inter alia, be responsible, under the authority of the President of the Boards of Appeal, for the receipt, dispatch, safekeeping and notification of all documents relating to the proceedings before the Boards of Appeal, and for compilation of the relevant files.

2. The Registry shall be headed by a Registrar. The President of the Boards of Appeal shall appoint a Registry agent who shall perform the tasks of the Registrar when the latter is absent or unable to act or if the post of Registrar is vacant.

3. The Registrar shall, in particular, ensure that the deadlines and other formal conditions relating to the presentation of the appeal and of the statement of grounds are respected.

If an irregularity is detected which is liable to make the appeal inadmissible, the Registrar shall, without delay, send a reasoned opinion to the chairman of the Board concerned.

4. The minutes of oral proceedings and of the taking of evidence shall be drawn up by the Registrar or, if the President of the Boards of Appeal agrees, by such agent of the Boards of Appeal as the chairman of the Board concerned may designate.

5. The President of the Boards of Appeal may delegate to the Registrar the task of allocating cases to the Boards of Appeal in accordance with allocation criteria laid down by the Presidium.

The Presidium may, upon a proposal by the President of the Boards of Appeal, delegate to the Registry other tasks relating to the conduct of proceedings before the Boards of Appeal.][35]

---

[33] Repealed by Regulation (EC) No 2082/2004 (OJ L 360, 07/12/2004 p.8).
[34] Renumbered by Regulation (EC) No 2082/2004 (OJ L 360, 07/12/2004 p.8).
[35] Substituted by Regulation (EC) No 2082/2004 (OJ L 360, 07/12/2004 p.8).

Article 6

Change in the composition of a Board

1. If the composition of a Board is changed after oral proceedings, the parties to the proceedings shall be informed that, at the request of any party, fresh oral proceedings shall be held before the Board in its new composition. Fresh oral proceedings shall also be held if so requested by the new member and if the other members of the Board have given their agreement.

2. The new member shall be bound to the same extent as the other members by an interim decision which has already been taken.

3. If, when a Board has already reached a final decision, a member is unable to act, he shall not be replaced by an alternate. If the Chairman is unable to act, then the member of the Board concerned having the longer service on the Board, or where members have the same length of service, the older member, shall sign the decision on behalf of the Chairman.

E6–011

Article 7

Joinder of appeal proceedings

1. If several appeals are filed against a decision, those appeals shall be considered in the same proceedings.

2. If appeals are filed against separate decisions and all the appeals are designated to be examined by one Board having the same composition, that Board may deal with those appeals in joined proceedings with the consent of the parties.

E6–012

Article 8

Procedure

1. If the Registrar sends the chairman of a Board of Appeal an opinion on the admissibility of an appeal in accordance with Article 5(3), second paragraph, the chairman of the Board in question may either suspend the proceedings and request the Board to rule on the admissibility of the appeal, or reserve judgement on the admissibility of the appeal for the decision to end the proceedings before the Board of Appeal.

2. In inter partes proceedings, and without prejudice to Article 61(2) of the Regulation, the statement setting out the grounds of appeal and the response to it may be supplemented by a reply from the appellant, lodged within two months of the notification of the response, and a rejoinder by the defendant, lodged within two months of notification of the reply.

3. In inter partes proceedings, the defendant may, in his or her response, seek a decision annulling or altering the contested decision on a point not raised in the appeal. Such submissions shall cease to have effect should the appellant discontinue the proceedings.][36]

E6–013

---

[36] Substituted by Regulation (EC) No 2082/2004 (OJ L 360, 07/12/2004 p.8).

Article 9

Oral proceedings

E6–014   1. If oral proceedings are to take place, the Board shall ensure that the parties have provided all relevant information and documents before the hearing.

2. The Board may, when issuing the summons to attend oral proceedings, add a communication drawing attention to matters which seem to be of special significance, or to the fact that certain questions appear no longer to be contentious, or containing other observations that may help to concentrate on essentials during the oral proceedings.

3. The Board shall ensure that the case is ready for decision at the conclusion of the oral proceedings, unless there are special reasons to the contrary.

Article 10

Communications to the parties

E6–015   If a Board deems it expedient to communicate with the parties regarding a possible appraisal of substantive or legal matters, such communication shall be made in such a way as not to imply that the Board is in any way bound by it.

Article 11

Comments on questions of general interest

E6–016   The Board may, on its own initiative or at the written, reasoned request of the President of the Office, invite him to comment in writing or orally on questions of general interest which arise in the course of proceedings pending before it. The parties shall be entitled to submit their observations on the President's comments.

Article 12

Deliberations preceding decisions

E6–017   The rapporteur shall submit to the other members of the Board a draft of the decision to be taken and shall set a reasonable time-limit within which to oppose it or to ask for changes. The Board shall meet to deliberate on the decision to be taken if it appears that the members of a Board are not all of the same opinion. Only members of the Board shall participate in the deliberations; the Chairman of the Board concerned may, however, authorize other officers such as registrars or interpreters to attend. Deliberations shall be secret.

Article 13

Order of voting

E6–018   1. During the deliberations between members of a Board, the opinion of the rapporteur shall be heard first, and, if the rapporteur is not the Chairman, the Chairman last.

2. If voting is necessary, votes shall be taken in the same sequence, save that if the Chairman is also the rapporteur, be shall vote last. Abstentions shall not be permitted.

Article 14

Entry into force

This Regulation shall enter into force the third day following its publication in the Official Journal of the European Communities.

E6–019

This Regulation shall be binding in its entirety and directly applicable in all Member States.

Done at Brussels, 5 February 1996.

For the Commission
Mario MONTI
Member of the Commission

E7. Rules of Procedure of the General Court of the European Union (extracts—as amended on March 26, 2010)

(OJ L 136 OF 30 MAY 1991; CORRIGENDUM PUBLISHED IN OJ L 317 OF 19.11.1991, P.34)

TITLE IV[37]

PROCEEDINGS RELATING TO INTELLECTUAL PROPERTY RIGHTS

Article 130[38]

1. Subject to the special provisions of this Title, the provisions of these Rules of Procedure shall apply to proceedings brought against the Office for Harmonisation in the Internal Market (Trade Marks and Designs) and against the Community Plant Variety Office (both hereinafter referred to as "the Office"), and concerning the application of the rules relating to an intellectual property regime.

E7–001

2. The provisions of this Title shall not apply to actions brought directly against the Office without prior proceedings before a Board of Appeal.

Article 131[39]

1. The application shall be drafted in one of the languages described in Article 35(1), according to the applicant's choice.

E7–002

---

[37] As amended on July 6, 1995 (OJ L172 of 22.7.1995, p.3).
[38] As amended on July 6, 1995 (OJ L172 of 22.7.1995, p.3).
[39] As amended on July 6, 1995 (OJ L172 of 22.7.1995, p.3).

2. The language in which the application is drafted shall become the language of the case if the applicant was the only party to the proceedings before the Board of Appeal or if another party to those proceedings does not object to this within a period laid down for that purpose by the Registrar after the application has been lodged.

If, within that period, the parties to the proceedings before the Board of Appeal inform the Registrar of their agreement on the choice, as the language of the case, of one of the languages referred to in Article 35(1), that language shall become the language of the case before the General Court.

In the event of an objection to the choice of the language of the case made by the applicant within the period referred to above and in the absence of an agreement on the matter between the parties to the proceedings before the Board of Appeal, the language in which the application for registration in question was filed at the Office shall become the language of the case. If, however, on a reasoned request by any party and after hearing the other parties, the President finds that the use of that language would not enable all parties to the proceedings before the Board of Appeal to follow the proceedings and defend their interests and that only the use of another language from among those mentioned in Article 35(1) makes it possible to remedy that situation, he may designate that other language as the language of the case; the President may refer the matter to the General Court.

3. In the pleadings and other documents addressed to the General Court and during the oral procedure, the applicant may use the language chosen by him in accordance with paragraph 1 and each of the other parties may use a language chosen by that party from those mentioned in Article 35(1).

4. If, by virtue of paragraph 2, a language other than that in which the application is drafted becomes the language of the case, the Registrar shall cause the application to be translated into the language of the case.

Each party shall be required, within a reasonable period to be prescribed for that purpose by the Registrar, to produce a translation into the language of the case of the pleadings or documents other than the application that are lodged by that party in a language other than the language of the case pursuant to paragraph 3. The party producing the translation, which shall be authentic within the meaning of Article 37, shall certify its accuracy. If the translation is not produced within the period prescribed, the pleading or the procedural document in question shall be removed from the file.

The Registrar shall cause everything said during the oral procedure to be translated into the language of the case and, at the request of any party, into the language used by that party in accordance with paragraph 3.

Article 132[40]

E7–003　1. Without prejudice to Article 44, the application shall contain the names of all the parties to the proceedings before the Board of Appeal and the addresses which they had given for the purposes of the notifications to be effected in the course of those proceedings.

The contested decision of the Board of Appeal shall be appended to the application. The date on which the applicant was notified of that decision must be indicated.

2. If the application does not comply with paragraph 1, Article 44(6) shall apply.

[40] As amended on July 6, 1995 (OJ L172 of 22.7.1995, p.3).

Article 133[41]

1. The Registrar shall inform the Office and all the parties to the proceedings **E7–004** before the Board of Appeal of the lodging of the application. He shall arrange for service of the application after determining the language of the case in accordance with Article 131(2).

2. The application shall be served on the Office, as defendant, and on the parties to the proceedings before the Board of Appeal other than the applicant. Service shall be effected in the language of the case.

Service of the application on a party to the proceedings before the Board of Appeal shall be effected by registered post with a form of acknowledgment of receipt at the address given by the party concerned for the purposes of the notifications to be effected in the course of the proceedings before the Board of Appeal.

3. Once the application has been served, the Office shall forward to the General Court the file relating to the proceedings before the Board of Appeal.

Article 134[42]

1. The parties to the proceedings before the Board of Appeal other than the **E7–005** applicant may participate, as interveners, in the proceedings before the General Court.

2. The interveners referred to in paragraph 1 shall have the same procedural rights as the main parties.

They may support the form of order sought by a main party and they may apply for a form of order and put forward pleas in law independently of those applied for and put forward by the main parties.

3. An intervener, as referred to in paragraph 1, may, in his response lodged in accordance with Article 135(1), seek an order annulling or altering the decision of the Board of Appeal on a point not raised in the application and put forward pleas in law not raised in the application.

Such submissions seeking orders or putting forward pleas in law in the intervener's response shall cease to have effect should the applicant discontinue the proceedings.

4. In derogation from Article 122, the default procedure shall not apply where an intervener, as referred to in paragraph 1 of this Article, has responded to the application in the manner and within the period prescribed.

Article 135[43]

1. The Office and the interveners referred to in Article 134(1) may submit **E7–006** responses to the application within a period of two months from the service of the application.

Article 46 shall apply to the responses.

2. The application and the responses may be supplemented by replies and rejoinders by the parties, including the interveners referred to in Article 134(1),

[41] As amended on July 6, 1995 (OJ L172 of 22.7.1995, p.3).
[42] As amended on July 6, 1995 (OJ L172 of 22.7.1995, p.3).
[43] As amended on July 6, 1995 (OJ L172 of 22.7.1995, p.3).

where the President, on a reasoned application made within two weeks of service of the responses or replies, considers such further pleading necessary and allows it in order to enable the party concerned to put forward its point of view.

The President shall prescribe the period within which such pleadings are to be submitted.

3. Without prejudice to the foregoing, in the cases referred to in Article 134(3), the other parties may, within a period of two months of service upon them of the response, submit a pleading confined to responding to the form of order sought and the pleas in law submitted for the first time in the response of an intervener. That period may be extended by the President on a reasoned application from the party concerned.

4. The parties' pleadings may not change the subject-matter of the proceedings before the Board of Appeal.

Article 136[44]

E7–007   1. Where an action against a decision of a Board of Appeal is successful, the General Court may order the Office to bear only its own costs.

2. Costs necessarily incurred by the parties for the purposes of the proceedings before the Board of Appeal and costs incurred for the purposes of the production, prescribed by the second subparagraph of Article 131(4), of translations of pleadings or other documents into the language of the case shall be regarded as recoverable costs.

In the event of inaccurate translations being produced, the second subparagraph of Article 87(3) shall apply.

[44] As amended on July 6, 1995 (OJ L172 of 22.7.1995, p.3).

APPENDIX F

INTERNATIONAL MATERIALS

Contents

F1. Paris Convention for the Protection of Industrial Property of 20 March 1883 (as amended on October 2, 1979)

Article 1

Establishment of the Union; Scope of Industrial Property

(1) The countries to which this Convention applies constitute a Union for the protection of industrial property. **F1–001**

(2) The protection of industrial property has as its object patents, utility models, industrial designs, trademarks, service marks, trade names, indications of source or appellations of origin, and the repression of unfair competition.

(3) Industrial property shall be understood in the broadest sense and shall apply not only to industry and commerce proper, but likewise to agricultural and extractive industries and to all manufactured or natural products, for example, wines, grain, tobacco leaf, fruit, cattle, minerals, mineral waters, beer, flowers, and flour.

(4) Patents shall include the various kinds of industrial patents recognised by the laws of the countries of the Union, such as patents of importation, patents of improvement, patents and certificates of addition, etc.

Article 2

National Treatment for Nationals of Countries of the Union

F1–002   (1) Nationals of any country of the Union shall, as regards the protection of industrial property, enjoy in all the other countries of the Union the advantages that their respective laws now grant, or may hereafter grant, to nationals; all without prejudice to the rights specially provided for by this Convention. Consequently, they shall have the same protection as the latter, and the same legal remedy against any infringement of their rights, provided that the conditions and formalities imposed upon nationals are complied with.

(2) However, no requirement as to domicile or establishment in the country where protection is claimed may be imposed upon nationals of countries of the Union for the enjoyment of any industrial property rights.

(3) The provisions of the laws of each of the countries of the Union relating to judicial and administrative procedure and to jurisdiction, and to the designation of an address for service or the appointment of an agent, which may be required by the laws on industrial property are expressly reserved.

Article 3

Same Treatment for Certain Categories of Persons as for Nationals of Countries of the Union

F1–003   Nationals of countries outside the Union who are domiciled or who have real and effective industrial or commercial establishments in the territory of one of the countries of the Union shall be treated in the same manner as nationals of the countries of the Union.

Article 4

A to I: Patents, Utility Models, Industrial Designs, Marks, Inventors' Certificates: Right of Priority

G: Patents: Division of the Application

F1–004   A. (1) Any person who has duly filed an application for a patent, or for the registration of a utility model, or of an industrial design, or of a trademark, in one of the countries of the Union, or his successor in title, shall enjoy, for the purpose of filing in the other countries, a right of priority during the periods hereinafter fixed.

(2) Any filing that is equivalent to a regular national filing under the domestic legislation of any country of the Union or under bilateral or multilateral treaties concluded between countries of the Union shall be recognised as giving rise to the right of priority.

(3) By a regular national filing is meant any filing that is adequate to establish the date on which the application was filed in the country concerned, whatever may be the subsequent fate of the application.

B. Consequently, any subsequent filing in any of the other countries of the Union before the expiration of the periods referred to above shall not be invalidated by reason of any acts accomplished in the interval, in particular, another filing, the publication or exploitation of the invention, the putting on sale of copies of the design, or the use of the mark, and such acts cannot give rise to any third-party right or any right of personal possession. Rights acquired by third parties before the date of the first application that serves as the basis for the right of priority are reserved in accordance with the domestic legislation of each country of the Union.

C. (1) The periods of priority referred to above shall be twelve months for patents and utility models, and six months for industrial designs and trademarks.

(2) These periods shall start from the date of filing of the first application; the day of filing shall not be included in the period.

(3) If the last day of the period is an official holiday, or a day when the Office is not open for the filing of applications in the country where protection is claimed, the period shall be extended until the first following working day.

(4) A subsequent application concerning the same subject as a previous first application within the meaning of paragraph (2), above, filed in the same country of the Union shall be considered as the first application, of which the filing date shall be the starting point of the period of priority, if, at the time of filing the subsequent application, the said previous application has been withdrawn, abandoned, or refused, without having been laid open to public inspection and without leaving any rights outstanding, and if it has not yet served as a basis for claiming a right of priority. The previous application may not thereafter serve as a basis for claiming a right of priority.

D. (1) Any person desiring to take advantage of the priority of a previous filing shall be required to make a declaration indicating the date of such filing and the country in which it was made. Each country shall determine the latest date on which such declaration must be made.

(2) These particulars shall be mentioned in the publications issued by the competent authority, and in particular in the patents and the specifications relating thereto.

(3) The countries of the Union may require any person making a declaration of priority to produce a copy of the application (description, drawings, etc.) previously filed. The copy, certified as correct by the authority which received such application, shall not require any authentication, and may in any case be filed, without fee, at any time within three months of the filing of the subsequent application. They may require it to be accompanied by a certificate from the same authority showing the date of filing, and by a translation.

(4) No other formalities may be required for the declaration of priority at the time of filing the application. Each country of the Union shall determine the consequences of failure to comply with the formalities prescribed by this Article, but such consequences shall in no case go beyond the loss of the right of priority.

(5) Subsequently, further proof may be required. Any person who avails himself of the priority of a previous application shall be required to specify the number of that application; this number shall be published as provided for by paragraph (2), above.

E. (1) Where an industrial design is filed in a country by virtue of a right of priority based on the filing of a utility model, the period of priority shall be the same as that fixed for industrial designs.

(2) Furthermore, it is permissible to file a utility model in a country by virtue of a right of priority based on the filing of a patent application, and vice versa.

Article 5

B. Industrial Designs: Failure to Work; Importation of Articles.

D. Patents, Utility Models, Marks, Industrial Designs: Marking

F1–005   B. The protection of industrial designs shall not, under any circumstance, be subject to any forfeiture, either by reason of failure to work or by reason of the importation of applications corresponding to those which are protected.

D. No indication or mention of the patent, of the utility model, of the registration of the trademark, or of the deposit of the industrial design, shall be required upon the goods as a condition of recognition of the right to protection.

Article 5bis

All Industrial Property Rights: Period of Grace for the Payment of Fees for the Maintenance of Rights; Patents: Restoration

F1–006   (1) A period of grace of not less than six months shall be allowed for the payment of the fees prescribed for the maintenance of industrial property rights, subject, if the domestic legislation so provides, to the payment of a surcharge.

(2) The countries of the Union shall have the right to provide for the restoration of patents which have lapsed by reason of non-payment of fees.

Article 5quinquies

Industrial Designs

F1–007   Industrial designs shall be protected in all the countries of the Union.

Article 11

Inventions, Utility Models, Industrial Designs, Marks: Temporary Protection at Certain International Exhibitions

F1–008   (1) The countries of the Union shall, in conformity with their domestic legislation, grant temporary protection to patentable inventions, utility models, industrial designs, and trademarks, in respect of goods exhibited at official or officially recognised international exhibitions held in the territory of any of them.

(2) Such temporary protection shall not extend the periods provided by Article 4. If, later, the right of priority is invoked, the authorities of any country may provide that the period shall start from the date of introduction of the goods into the exhibition.

(3) Each country may require, as proof of the identity of the article exhibited and of the date of its introduction, such documentary evidence as it considers necessary.

Article 12

Special National Industrial Property Services

(1) Each country of the Union undertakes to establish a special industrial **F1–009**
property service and a central office for the communication to the public of
patents, utility models, industrial designs, and trademarks.

(2) This service shall publish an official periodical journal. It shall publish
regularly:

    (a) the names of the proprietors of patents granted, with a brief designation
          of the inventions patented;

    (b) the reproduction of registered trademarks.

F2. Agreement on Trade Related Aspects of Intellectual Property Rights, including Trade in Counterfeit Goods (extracts)

Part I

General Provisions and Basic Principles

Article 1

Nature and Scope of Obligations

1. Members shall give effect to the provisions of this Agreement. Members may, **F2–001**
but shall not be obliged to, implement in their domestic law more extensive
protection than is required by this Agreement, provided that such protection does
not contravene the provisions of this Agreement. Members shall be free to
determine the appropriate method of implementing the provisions of this
Agreement within their own legal system and practice.

2. For the purposes of this Agreement, the term "intellectual property" refers to
all categories of intellectual property that are the subject of Sections 1 to 7 of Part
II.

3. Members shall accord the treatment provided for in this Agreement to the
nationals of other Members. In respect of the relevant intellectual property right,
the nationals of other Members shall be understood as those natural or legal
persons that would meet the criteria for eligibility for protection provided for in
the Paris Convention (1967), the Berne Convention (1971), the Rome Convention
and the Treaty on Intellectual Property in Respect of Integrated Circuits, were all
Members of the WTO members of those conventions. Any Member availing itself
of the possibilities provided in paragraph 3 of Article 5 or paragraph 2 of Article
6 of the Rome Convention shall make a notification as foreseen in those provisions
to the Council for Trade-Related Aspects of Intellectual Property Rights.

Article 2

Intellectual Property Conventions

1. In respect of Parts II, III and IV of this Agreement, Members shall comply **F2–002**
with Articles 1–12 and 19 of the Paris Convention (1967).

2. Nothing in Parts I to IV of this Agreement shall derogate from existing obligations that Members may have to each other under the Paris Convention, the Berne Convention, the Rome Convention and the Treaty on Intellectual Property in Respect of Integrated Circuits.

Article 3

National Treatment

F2–003   1. Each Member shall accord to the nationals of other Members treatment no less favourable than that it accords to its own nationals with regard to the protection of intellectual property, subject to the exceptions already provided in, respectively, Paris Convention (1967), the Berne Convention (1971), the Rome Convention and the Treaty on Intellectual Property in Respect of Integrated Circuits. In respect of performers, producers of phonograms and broadcasting organisations, this obligation only applies in respect of the rights provided under this Agreement. Any Member availing itself of the possibilities provided in Article 6 of the Berne Convention and paragraph 1(b) of Article 16 of the Rome Convention shall make a notification as foreseen in those provisions to the Council for Trade-Related Aspects of Intellectual Property Rights.

2. Members may avail themselves of the exceptions permitted under paragraph 1 above in relation to judicial and administrative procedures, including the designation of an address for service or the appointment of an agent within the jurisdiction of a Member, only where such exceptions are necessary to secure compliance with laws and regulations which are not inconsistent with the provisions of this Agreement and where such practices are not applied in a manner which would constitute a disguised restriction on trade.

Article 4

Most-Favoured-Nation Treatment

F2–004   With regard to the protection of intellectual property, an advantage, favour, privilege or immunity granted by a Member to the nationals of any other country shall be accorded immediately and unconditionally to the nationals of all other Members. Exempted from this obligation are any advantage, favour, privilege or immunity accorded by a Member:

(a) deriving from international agreements on judicial assistance and law enforcement of a general nature and not particularly confined to the protection of intellectual property;

(b) granted in accordance with the provisions of the Berne Convention (1971) or the Rome Convention authorising that the treatment according to a function not of national treatment but of the treatment accorded in another country;

(c) in respect of the rights of performers, producers of phonograms and broadcasting organisations not provided under this Agreement;

(d) deriving from international agreements related to the protection of intellectual property which entered into force prior to the entry into force of the Agreement Establishing the WTO, provided that such agreements are notified to the Council for Trade-Related Aspects of Intellectual Property Rights and do not constitute an arbitrary or unjustifiable discrimination against nationals of other Members.

Article 5

Multilateral Agreements on Acquisition or Maintenance of Protection

The obligations under Articles 3 and 4 above do not apply to procedures provided in multilateral agreements concluded under the auspices of the World Intellectual Property Organisation relating to the acquisition or maintenance of intellectual property rights.

F2–005

Article 6

Exhaustion

For the purposes of dispute settlement under this Agreement, subject to the provisions of Articles 3 and 4 above nothing in this Agreement shall be used to address the issue of the exhaustion of intellectual property rights.

F2–006

Article 7

Objectives

The protection and enforcement of intellectual property rights should contribute to the promotion of technological innovation and to the transfer and dissemination of technology, to the mutual advantage of producers and users of technical knowledge and in a manner conducive to social and economic welfare, and to a balance of rights and obligations.

F2–007

Article 8

Principles

1. Members may, in formulating or amending their national laws and regulations, adopt measures necessary to protect public health and nutrition, and to promote the public interest in sectors of vital importance to their socio-economic and technological development, provided that such measures are consistent with the provisions of this Agreement.

F2–008

2. Appropriate measures, provided that they are consistent with the provisions of this Agreement, may be needed to prevent the abuse of intellectual property rights by right holders or the resort to practices which unreasonably restrain trade or adversely affect the international transfer of technology.

Part II

Standards Concerning the Availability, Scope and Use of Intellectual Property Rights

Section 1: Copyright and Related Rights

Article 9

Relation to Berne Convention

F2–009   1. Members shall comply with Articles 1–21 and the Appendix of the Berne Convention (1971). However, Members shall not have rights or obligations under this Agreement in respect of the rights conferred under Article 6bis of that Convention or of the rights derived therefrom.

2. Copyright protection shall extend to expressions and not to ideas, procedures, methods of operation or mathematical concepts as such.

Article 12

Term of Protection

F2–010   Whenever the term of protection of a work, other than a photographic work or a work of applied art, is calculated on a basis other than the life of a natural person, such term shall be no less than fifty years from the end of the calendar year of authorised publication, or, failing such authorised publication within fifty years from the making of the work, fifty years from the end of the calendar year of making.

Article 13

Limitations and Exceptions

F2–011   Members shall confine limitations or exceptions to exclusive rights to certain special cases which do not conflict with a normal exploitation of the work and do not unreasonably prejudice the legitimate interests of the right holder.

Section 4: Industrial Designs

Article 25

Requirements for Protection

F2–012   1. Members shall provide for the protection of independently created industrial designs that are new or original. Members may provide that designs are not new or original if they do not significantly differ from known designs or combinations of known design features. Members may provide that such protection shall not extend to designs dictated essentially by technical or functional considerations.

2. Each Member shall ensure that requirements for securing protection for textile designs, in particular in regard to any cost, examination or publication, do not unreasonably impair the opportunity to seek and obtain such protection.

Members shall be free to meet this obligation through industrial design law or through copyright law.

Article 26

Protection

1. The owner of a protected industrial design shall have the right to prevent third parties not having his consent from making, selling or importing articles bearing or embodying a design which is a copy, or substantially a copy, of the protected design, when such acts are undertaken for commercial purposes.   **F2–013**

2. Members may provide limited exceptions to the protection of industrial designs, provided that such exceptions do not unreasonably conflict with the normal exploitation of protected industrial designs and do not unreasonably prejudice the legitimate interests of the owner of the protected design, taking account of the legitimate interests of third parties.

3. The duration of protection available shall amount to at least ten years.

Section 6: Layout-Designs (Topographies) of Integrated Circuits

Article 35

Relation to IPIC Treaty

Members agree to provide protection to the layout-designs (topographies) of integrated circuits (hereinafter referred to as "layout-designs") in accordance with Articles 2–7 (other than paragraph 3 of Article 6), Article 12 and paragraph 3 of Article 16 of the Treaty on Intellectual Property in Respect of Integrated Circuits and, in addition, to comply with the following provisions.   **F2–014**

Article 36

Scope of the Protection

Subject to the provisions of paragraph 1 of Article 37 below, Members shall consider unlawful the following acts if performed without the authorisation of the right holder: importing, selling, or otherwise distributing for commercial purposes a protected layout-design, an integrated circuit in which a protected layout-design is incorporated, or an article incorporating such an integrated circuit only insofar as it continues to contain an unlawfully reproduced layout-design.   **F2–015**

Article 37

Acts not Requiring the Authorisation of the Right Holder

1. Notwithstanding Article 36 above, no Member shall consider unlawful the performance of any of the acts referred to in that Article in respect of an integrated circuit incorporating an unlawfully reproduced layout-design or any article incorporating such an integrated circuit where the person performing or ordering such acts did not know and had no reasonable ground to know, when acquiring   **F2–016**

the integrated circuit or application incorporating such an integrated circuit, that it incorporated an unlawfully reproduced layout-design. Members shall provide that, after the time that such person has received sufficient notice that the layout-design was unlawfully reproduced, he may perform any of the acts with respect to the stock on hand or ordered before such time, but shall be liable to pay to the right holder a sum equivalent to a reasonable royalty such as would be payable under a freely negotiated licence in respect of such a layout-design.

2. The conditions set out in sub-paragraphs (a)–(k) of Article 31 above shall apply mutatis mutandis in the event of any non-voluntary licensing of a layout-design or of its use by or for the government without the authorisation of the right holder.

Article 38

Term of Protection

F2–017   1. In Members requiring registration as a condition of protection, the term of protection of layout-designs shall not end before the expiration of a period of ten years counted from the date of filing an application for registration or from the first commercial exploitation wherever in the world it occurs.

2. In Members not requiring registration as a condition for protection, layout-designs shall be protected for a term of no less than ten years from the date of the first commercial exploitation wherever in the world it occurs.

3. Notwithstanding paragraphs 1 and 2 above, a Member may provide that protection shall lapse fifteen years after the creation of the layout-design.

Part III

Enforcement Of Intellectual Property Right

Section 1: General Obligations

Article 41

F2–018   1. Members shall ensure that enforcement procedures as specified in this Part are available under their national laws so as to permit effective action against any act of infringement of intellectual property rights covered by this Agreement, including expeditious remedies to prevent infringements and remedies which constitute a deterrent to further infringements. These procedures shall be applied in such a manner as to avoid the creation of barriers to legitimate trade and to provide for safeguards against their abuse.

2. Procedures concerning the enforcement of intellectual property rights shall be fair and equitable. They shall not be unnecessarily complicated or costly, or entail unreasonable time-limits or unwarranted delays.

3. Decisions on the merits of a case shall preferably be in writing and reasoned. They shall be made available at least to the parties to the proceeding without undue delay. Decisions on the merits of a case shall be based only on evidence in respect of which parties were offered the opportunity to be heard.

4. Parties to a proceeding shall have an opportunity for review by a judicial authority of final administrative decisions and, subject to jurisdictional provisions in national laws concerning the importance of a case, of at least the legal aspects

of initial judicial decisions on the merits of a case. However, there shall be no obligation to provide an opportunity for review of acquittals in criminal cases.

5. It is understood that this Part does not create any obligation to put in place a judicial system for the enforcement of intellectual property rights distinct from that for the enforcement of laws in general, nor does it affect the capacity of Members to enforce their laws in general. Nothing in this Part creates any obligation with respect to the distribution of resources as between enforcement of intellectual property rights and the enforcement of laws in general.

Section 2: Civil and Administrative Procedures and Remedies

Article 42

Fair and Equitable Procedures

Members shall make available to right holders civil judicial procedures **F2–019** concerning the enforcement of any intellectual property right covered by this Agreement. Defendants shall have the right to written notice which is timely and contains sufficient detail, including the basis of the claims. Parties shall be allowed to be represented by independent legal counsel, and procedures shall not impose overly burdensome requirements concerning mandatory personal appearances. All parties to such procedures shall be duly entitled to substantiate their claims and to present all relevant evidence. The procedure shall provide a means to identify and protect confidential information, unless this would be contrary to existing constitutional requirements.

Article 43

Evidence

1. The judicial authorities shall have the authority, where a party has presented **F2–020** reasonably available evidence sufficient to support its claims and has specified evidence relevant to substantiation of its claims which lies in the control of the opposing party, to order that this evidence be produced by the opposing party, subject in appropriate cases to conditions which ensure the protection of confidential information.

2. In cases in which a party to a proceeding voluntarily and without good reason refuses access to, or otherwise does not provide necessary information within a reasonable period, or significantly impedes a procedure relating to an enforcement action, a Member may accord judicial authorities the authority to make preliminary and final determinations, affirmative or negative, on the basis of the information presented to them, including the complaint or the allegation presented by the party adversely affected by the denial of access to information, subject to providing the parties an opportunity to be heard on the allegations of evidence.

Article 44

Injunctions

1. The judicial authorities shall have the authority to order a party to desist **F2–021** from an infringement, inter alia to prevent the entry into the channels of commerce in their jurisdiction of imported goods that involve the infringement of

an intellectual property right, immediately after customs clearance of such goods. Members are not obliged to accord such authority in respect of protected subject matter acquired or ordered by a person prior to knowing or having reasonable grounds to know that dealing in such subject matter would entail the infringement of an intellectual property right.

2. Notwithstanding the other provisions of this Part and provided that the provisions of Part II specifically addressing use by governments, or by third parties authorised by a government, without the authorisation of the right holder are complied with, Members may limit the remedies available against such use to payment of remuneration in accordance with sub-paragraph (h) of Article 31 above. In other cases, the remedies under this Part shall apply or, where these remedies are inconsistent with national law, declaratory judgments and adequate compensation shall be available.

Article 45

Damages

F2–022   1. The judicial authorities shall have the authority to order the infringer to pay the right holder damage adequate to compensate for the injury the right holder has suffered because of an infringement of his intellectual property right by an infringer who knew or had reasonable grounds to know that he was engaged in infringing activity.

2. The judicial authorities shall also have the authority to order the infringer to pay the right holder expenses, which may include appropriate attorney's fees. In appropriate cases, Members may authorise the judicial authorities to order recovery of profits and/or payment of pre-established damages even where the infringer did not know or had no reasonable grounds to know that he was engaged in infringing activity.

Article 46

Other Remedies

F2–023   In order to create an effective deterrent to infringement, the judicial authorities shall have the authority to order that goods that they have found to be infringing be, without compensation of any sort, disposed of outside the channels of commerce in such a manner as to avoid any harm caused to the right holder, or, unless this would be contrary to existing constitutional requirements, destroyed. The judicial authorities shall also have the authority to order that materials and implements the predominant use of which has been in the creation of the infringing goods be, without compensation of any sort, disposed of outside the channels of commerce in such a manner as to minimise the risks of further infringements. In considering such requests, the need for proportionality between the seriousness of the infringement and the remedies ordered as well as the interests of third parties shall be taken into account. In regard to counterfeit trademark goods, the simple removal of the trademark unlawfully affixed shall not be sufficient, other than in exceptional cases, to permit release of the goods into the channels of commerce.

Article 47

Right of Information

Members may provide that the judicial authorities shall have the authority, **F2–024** unless this would be out of proportion to the seriousness of the infringement, to order the infringer to inform the right holder of the identity of third persons involved in the production and distribution of the infringing goods or services and of their channels of distribution.

Article 48

Indemnification of the Defendant

1. The judicial authorities shall have the authority to order a party at whose **F2–025** request measures were taken and who has abused enforcement procedures to provide a party wrongfully enjoined or restrained adequate compensation for the injury suffered because of such abuse. The judicial authorities shall also have the authority to order the applicant to pay the defendant expenses, which may include appropriate attorney's fees.

2. In respect of the administration of any law pertaining to the protection or enforcement of intellectual property rights, members shall only exempt both public authorities and officials from liability to appropriate remedial measures where actions are taken or intended in good faith in the course of the administration of such laws.

Article 49

Administrative Procedures

To the extent that any civil remedy can be ordered as a result of administrative **F2–026** procedures on the merits of a case, such procedures shall conform to principles equivalent in substance to those set forth in this Section.

Section 3: Provisional Measures
Article 50

1. The judicial authorities shall have the authority to order prompt and effective **F2–027** provisional measures:

    (a) to prevent an infringement of any intellectual property right from occurring, and in particular to prevent the entry into the channels of commerce in their jurisdiction of goods, including imported goods immediately after customs clearance;

    (b) to preserve relevant evidence in regard to the alleged infringement.

2. The judicial authorities shall have the authority to adopt provisional measures inaudita altera parte where appropriate, in particular where any delay is likely to cause irreparable harm to the right holder, or where there is a demonstrable risk of evidence being destroyed.

3. The judicial authorities shall have the authority to require the applicant to provide any reasonably available evidence in order to satisfy themselves with a

sufficient degree of certainty that the applicant is the right holder and that his right is being infringed or that such infringement is imminent, and to order the applicant to provide a security or equivalent assurance sufficient to protect the defendant and to prevent abuse.

4. Where provisional measures have been adopted inaudita altera parte, the parties affected shall be given notice, within delay after the execution of the measures at the latest. A review, including a right to be heard, shall take place upon request of the defendant with a view to deciding, within a reasonable period after the modification of the measures, whether these measures shall be modified, revoked or confirmed.

5. The applicant may be required to supply other information necessary for the identification of the goods concerned by the authority that will execute the provisional measures.

6. Without prejudice to paragraph 4 above, provisional measures taken on the basis of paragraphs 1 and 2 above shall, upon request by the defendant, be revoked or otherwise cease to have effect, if proceedings leading to a decision on the merits of the case are not initiated within a reasonable period, to be determined by the judicial authority ordering the measures where national law so permits or, in the absence of such a determination, not to exceed twenty working days or thirty-one calendar days, whichever is the longer.

7. Where the provisional measures are revoked or where they lapse due to any act or omission by the applicant, or where it is subsequently found that there has been no infringement or threat of infringement of an intellectual property right, the judicial authorities shall have the authority to order the applicant, upon request of the defendant, to provide the defendant appropriate compensation for any injury caused by these measures.

8. To the extent that any provisional measure can be ordered as a result of administrative procedures, such procedures shall conform to principles equivalent in substance to those set forth in this Section.

PART IV

ACQUISITION AND MAINTENANCE OF INTELLECTUAL PROPERTY RIGHTS AND RELATED INTER-PARTES PROCEDURES

Article 62

F2–028 1. Members may require, as a condition of the acquisition or maintenance of the intellectual property rights provided for under Section 2–6 of Part II of this Agreement, compliance with reasonable procedures and formalities. Such procedures and formalities shall be consistent with the provisions of this Agreement.

2. Where the acquisition of an intellectual property right is subject to the right being granted or registered, Members shall ensure that the procedures for grant or registration, subject to compliance with the substantive conditions for acquisition of the right, permit the granting or registration of the right within a reasonable period of time so as to avoid unwarranted curtailment of the period of protection.

3. Article 4 of the Paris Convention (1967) shall apply mutatis mutandis to service marks.

4. Procedures concerning the acquisition or maintenance of intellectual property rights and, where the national law provides for such procedures, administrative revocation and inter partes procedures such as opposition, revocation

and cancellation, shall be governed by the general principles set out in paragraphs 2 and 3 of Article 41.

5. Final administrative decisions in any of the procedures referred to under paragraph 4 above shall be subject to review by a judicial or quasi-judicial authority. However, there shall be no obligation to provide an opportunity for such review in decisions in cases of unsuccessful opposition or administrative revocation, provided that the grounds for such procedures can be the subject of invalidation procedures.

F3. Washington Treaty on Intellectual Property in Respect of Integrated Circuits (of May 26, 1989)

Article 1

Establishment of a Union

The Contracting Parties constitute themselves into a Union for the purposes of this Treaty.   **F3–001**

Article 2

Definitions

For the purposes of this Treaty: **F3–002**

 (i) "integrated circuit" means a product, in its final form or an intermediate form, in which the elements, at least one of which is an active element, and some or all of the interconnections are integrally formed in and/or on a piece of material and which is intended to perform an electronic function,

 (ii) "layout-design (topography)" means the three-dimensional disposition, however expressed, of the elements, at least one of which is an active element, and of some or all of the interconnections of an integrated circuit, or such a three-dimensional disposition prepared for an integrated circuit intended for manufacture,

 (iii) "holder of the right" means the natural person who, or the legal entity which, according to the applicable law, is to be regarded as the beneficiary of the protection referred to in Article 6,

 (iv) "protected layout-design (topography)" means a layout-design (topography) in respect of which the conditions of protection referred to in this Treaty are fulfilled,

 (v) "Contracting Party" means a State, or an Intergovernmental Organisation meeting the requirements of item (x), party to this Treaty,

 (vi) "territory of a Contracting Party" means, where the Contracting Party is a State, the territory of that State and, where the Contracting Party is an Intergovernmental Organisation, the territory in which the consulting treaty of that Intergovernmental Organisation applies,

 (vii) "Union" means the Union referred to in Article 1,

 (viii) "Assembly" means the Assembly referred to in Article 9,

 (ix) "Director General" means the Director General of the World Intellectual Property Organisation,

811

(x) "Intergovernmental Organisation" means an organisation constituted by, and composed of, States of any region of the world, which has competence in respect of matters governed by this Treaty, has its own legislation providing for intellectual property protection in respect of layout-designs (topographies) and binding on all its member States, and has been duly authorised, in accordance with its internal procedures, to sign, ratify, accept, approve or accede to this Treaty.

Article 3

The Subject Matter of the Treaty

F3–003   (1) (a) Each Contracting Party shall have the obligation to secure, throughout its territory, intellectual property protection in respect of layout-designs (topographies) in accordance with this Treaty. It shall, in particular, secure adequate measures to ensure the prevention of acts considered unlawful under Article 6 and appropriate legal remedies where such acts have been committed.

(b) The right of the holder of the right in respect of an integrated circuit applies whether or not the integrated circuit is incorporated in an article.

(c) Notwithstanding article 2(i), any Contracting Party whose law limits the protection of layout-designs (topographies) to layout-designs (topographies) of semiconductor integrated circuits shall be free to apply that limitation as long as its law contains such limitation.

(2) (a) The obligation referred to in paragraph (1)(a) shall apply to layout-designs (topographies) that are original in the sense that they are the result of their creators' own intellectual effort and are not commonplace among creators of layout-designs (topographies) and manufacturers of integrated circuits at the time of their creation.

(b) A layout-design (topography) that consists of a combination of elements and interconnections that are commonplace shall be protected only if the combination, taken as a whole, fulfills the conditions referred to in subparagraph (a).

Article 4

The Legal Form of the Protection

F3–004   Each Contracting Party shall be free to implement its obligations under this Treaty through a special law on layout-designs (topographies) or its law on copyright, patents, utility models, industrial designs, unfair competition or any other law or a combination of any of those laws.

Article 5

National Treatment

F3–005   (1) Subject to compliance with its obligation referred to in Article 3(1)(a), each Contracting Party shall, in respect of the intellectual property protection of layout-designs (topographies), accord, within its territory,

> (i) to natural persons who are nationals of, or are domiciled in the territory of, any of the other Contracting Parties, and
> (ii) to legal entities which or natural persons who, in the territory of any of the other Contracting Parties, have a real and effective establishment for the creation of layout-designs (topographies) or the production of integrated circuits, the same treatment that it accords to its own nationals.

(2) Notwithstanding paragraph (1), any Contracting Party is free not to apply national treatment as far as any obligations to appoint an agent or to designate an address for service are concerned or as far as the special rules applicable to foreigners in court proceedings are concerned.

(3) Where the Contracting party is an Intergovernmental Organisation, "nationals" in paragraph (1) means nationals of any of the States members of that Organisation.

Article 6

The Scope of the Protection

> (1) (a) Any Contracting Party shall consider unlawful the following acts if **F3–006** performed without the authorisation of the holder of the right,
> > (i) the act of reproducing, whether by incorporation in an integrated circuit or otherwise, a protected layout-design (topography) in its entirety or any part thereof, except the act of reproducing any part that does not comply with the requirement of originality referred to in Article 3(2).
> > (ii) the act of importing, selling or otherwise distributing for commercial purposes a protected layout-design (topography) or an integrated circuit in which a layout-design (topography) is incorporated.
> > (b) Any Contracting Party shall be free to consider unlawful acts other than those specified in subparagraph (a) if performed without the authorisation of the holder of the right.
> (2) (a) Notwithstanding paragraph (1), no Contracting Party shall consider unlawful the performance, without the authorisation of the holder of the right, of the act of reproduction referred to in paragraph (1)(a)(i) where that act is performed by a third party for private purposes or for the sole purpose of evaluation, analysis, research or teaching.
> > (b) Where the third party referred to in subparagraph (a), on the basis of evaluation or analysis of the protected layout-design (topography) ("the first layout-design (topography)"), creates a layout-design (topography) complying with the requirement of originality referred to in Article 3(2) ("the second layout-design (topography)"), that third party may incorporate the second layout-design (topography) in an integrated circuit or perform any of the acts referred to in paragraph (1) in respect of the second layout-design (topography) without being regarded as infringing the rights of the holder of the right in the first layout-design (topography).
> > (c) The holder of the right may not exercise his right in respect of an identical original layout-design (topography) that was independently created by a third party.
> (3) (a) Notwithstanding paragraph (1), any Contracting Party may, in its legislation, provide for the possibility of its executive or judicial

authority granting a non-exclusive license, in circumstances that are not ordinary, for the performance of any of the acts referred to in paragraph (1) by a third party without the authorisation of the holder of the right ("non-voluntary license"), after unsuccessful efforts, made by the said third party in line with normal commercial practices, to obtain such authorisation, where the granting of the non-voluntary license is found, by the granting authority, to be necessary to safeguard a national purpose deemed to be vital by that authority, the non-voluntary license shall be available for exploitation only in the territory of that country and shall be subject to the payment of an equitable remuneration by the third party to the holder of the right.

(b) The provisions of this Treaty shall not affect the freedom of any Contracting party to apply measures, including the granting, after a formal proceeding by its executive or judicial authority, of a non-voluntary license, in application of its laws in order to secure free competition and to prevent abuses by the holder of the right.

(c) The granting of any non-voluntary license referred to in subparagraph (a) or subparagraph (b) shall be subject to judicial review. Any non-voluntary license referred to in subparagraph (a) shall be revoked when the conditions referred to in that subparagraph cease to exist.

(4) Notwithstanding paragraph (1)(a)(ii), no Contracting Party shall be obliged to consider unlawful the performance of any of the acts referred to in that paragraph in respect of an integrated circuit incorporating an unlawfully reproduced layout-design (topography) where the person performing or ordering such acts did not know and had no reasonable ground to know, when acquiring the said integrated circuit, that it incorporates an unlawfully reproduced layout-design (topography).

(5) Notwithstanding paragraph (1)(a)(ii), any Contracting party may consider lawful the performance, without the authorisation of the holder of the right, of any of the acts referred to in that paragraph where the act is performed in respect of a protected layout-design (topography), or in respect of an integrated circuit in which such a layout-design (topography) is incorporated, that has been put on the market by, or with the consent of, the holder of the right.

Article 7

Exploitation, Registration, Disclosure

F3–007   (1) Any Contracting Party shall be free not to protect a layout-design (topography) until it has been ordinarily commercially exploited, separately or as incorporated in an integrated circuit, somewhere in the world.

(2) (a) Any Contracting Party shall be free not to protect a layout-design (topography) until the layout-design (topography) has been the subject of an application for registration, filed in due form with the competent public authority, or of a registration with that authority, it may be required that the application be accompanied by the filing of a copy or drawing of the layout-design (topography) and, where the integrated circuit has been commercially exploited, of a sample of that integrated circuit, along with information defining the electronic function which the integrated circuit is intended to perform, however, the applicant may exclude such parts of the copy or drawing that relate to the manner of manufacture of the integrated circuit, provided that the parts

submitted are sufficient to allow the identification of the layout-design (topography).

(b) Where the filing of an application for registration according for subparagraph (a) is required, the Contracting Party may require that such filing be effected within a certain period of time from the date on which the holder of the right first exploits ordinarily commercially anywhere in the world the layout-design (topography) of an integrated circuit, such period shall not be less than two years counted from the said date.

(c) Registration under subparagraph (a) may be subject to the payment of a fee.

Article 8

The Duration of the Protection

Protection shall last at least eight years.   **F3–008**

Article 9

Assembly

(1) (a) The Union shall have an Assembly consisting of the Contracting Parties.   **F3–009**

(b) Each Contracting Party shall be represented by one delegate who may be assisted by alternate delegates, advisors and experts.

(c) Subject to subparagraph (d), the expenses of each delegation shall be borne by the Contracting Party that has appointed the delegation.

(d) The Assembly may ask the World Intellectual Property Organisation to grant financial assistance to facilitate the participation of delegations of Contracting Parties that are regarded as developing countries in conformity with the established practice of the General Assembly of the United Nations.

(2) (a) The Assembly shall deal with matters concerning the maintenance and development of the Union and the application and operation of this Treaty.

(b) The Assembly shall decide the convocation of any diplomatic conference for the revision of this Treaty and give the necessary instructions to the Director General for the preparation of such diplomatic conference.

(c) The Assembly shall perform the functions allocated to it under Article 14 and shall establish the details of the procedures provided for in that Article, including the financing of such procedures.

(3) (a) Each Contracting Party that is a State shall have one vote and shall vote only in its own name.

(b) Any Contracting Party that is an Intergovernmental Organisation shall exercise its right to vote, in place of its member States, with a number of votes equal to the number of its member States which are party to this Treaty and which are present at the time the vote is taken. No such Intergovernmental Organisation shall exercise its right to vote if any of its member States participates in the vote.

(4) The Assembly shall meet in ordinary session once every two years upon convocation by the Director General.

(5) The Assembly shall establish its own rules of procedure, including the convocation of extraordinary sessions, the requirements of a quorum and, subject to the provisions of this Treaty, the required majority for various kinds of decisions.

Article 10

International Bureau

F3–010   (1) (a) The International Bureau of the World Intellectual Property Organisation shall,

(i) perform the administrative tasks concerning the Union, as well as any tasks specially assigned to it by the Assembly,

(ii) subject to the availability of funds, provide technical assistance, on request, to the Governments of Contracting Parties that are States and are regarded as developing countries in conformity with the established practice of the General Assembly of the United Nations.

(b) No Contracting Party shall have any financial obligations, in particular, no Contracting Party shall be required to pay any contributions to the International Bureau on account of its membership in the Union.

(2) The Director General shall be the chief executive of the Union and shall represent the Union.

Article 11

Amendment of Certain Provisions of the Treaty

F3–011   (1) The Assembly may amend the definitions contained in Article 2(i) and (ii), as well as Articles 3(1)(c), 9(1)(b) and (d), 9(4), 10(1)(a) and 14.

(2) (a) Proposals under this Article for amendment of the provisions of this Treaty referred to in paragraph (1) may be initiated by any Contracting Party or by the Director General.

(b) Such proposals shall be communicated by the Director General to the Contracting Parties at least six months in advance of their consideration by the Assembly.

(c) No such proposal shall be made before the expiration of five years from the date of entry into force of this Treaty under Article 16(1).

(3) Adoption by the Assembly of any amendment under paragraph (1) shall require four-fifths of the votes cast.

(4) (a) Any amendment to the provisions of this Treaty referred to in paragraph (1) shall enter into force three months after written notifications of acceptance, effected in accordance with their respective constitutional processes, having been received by the Director General from three-fourths of the Contracting Parties members of the Assembly at the time the Assembly adopted the amendment. Any amendment to the said provisions thus accepted shall bind all States and Intergovernmental Organisations that were Contracting Parties at the time the amendment was adopted by the Assembly or that become Contracting Parties thereafter, except Contracting Parties which have notified their

    denunciation of this Treaty in accordance with Article 17 before the
entry into force of the amendment.

(b) In establishing the required three-fourths referred to in subparagraph
(a), a notification made by an Intergovernmental Organisation shall
only be taken into account if no notification has been made by any of its
member States.

Article 12

Safeguard of Paris and Berne Convention

This Treaty shall not affect the obligations that any Contracting Party may have   **F3–012**
under the Paris Convention for the Protection of Industrial Property or the Berne
Convention for the Protection of Literary and Artistic Works.

Article 13

Reservations

No reservations to this Treaty shall be made.   **F3–013**

Article 14

Settlement of Disputes

(1) (a) Where any dispute arises concerning the interpretation or implementa-   **F3–014**
tion of this Treaty, a Contracting Party may bring the matter to the
attention of another Contracting Party and request the latter to enter
into consultations with it.

(b) The Contracting Party so requested shall provide promptly an adequate
opportunity for the requested consultations.

(c) The Contracting Parties engaged in consultations shall attempt to reach,
within a reasonable period of time, a mutually satisfactory solution of
the dispute.

(2) If a mutually satisfactory solution is not reached within a reasonable period
of time through the consultations referred to in paragraph (1), the parties to the
dispute may agree to resort to other means designed to lead to an amicable
settlement of their dispute, such as good offices, conciliation, mediation and
arbitration.

(3) (a) If the dispute is not satisfactorily settled through the consultations
referred to in paragraph (1), or if the means referred to in paragraph (2)
are not resorted to, or do not lead to an amicable settlement within a
reasonable period of time, the Assembly, at the written request of either
of the parties to the dispute, shall convene a panel of three members to
examine the matter. The members of the panel shall not, unless the
parties to the dispute agree otherwise, be from either party to the
dispute. They shall be selected from a list of designated governmental
experts established by the Assembly. The terms of reference for the
panel shall be agreed upon by the parties to the dispute. If such

agreement is not achieved within three months, the Assembly shall set the terms of reference for the panel after having consulted the parties to the dispute and the members of the panel. The panel shall give full opportunity to the parties to the dispute and any other interested Contracting Parties to present to it their views. If both parties to the dispute so request, the panel shall stop its proceedings.

(b) The Assembly shall adopt rules for the establishment of the said list of experts, and the manner of selecting the members of the panel, who shall be governmental experts of the Contracting Parties, and for the conduct of the panel proceedings, including provisions to safeguard the confidentiality of the proceedings and of any material designated as confidential by any participant in the proceedings.

(c) Unless the parties to the dispute reach an agreement between themselves prior to the panel's concluding its proceedings, the panel shall promptly prepare a written report and provide it to the parties to the dispute for their review. The parties to the dispute shall have a reasonable period of time, whose length will be fixed by the panel, to submit any comments on the report to the panel, unless they agree to a longer time in their attempts to reach a mutually satisfactory resolution to their dispute. The panel shall take into account the comments and shall promptly transmit its report to the Assembly. The report shall contain the facts and recommendations for the resolution of the dispute, and shall be accompanied by the written comments, if any of the parties to the dispute.

(4) The Assembly shall give the report of the panel prompt consideration. The Assembly shall, by consensus, make recommendations to the parties to the dispute, based upon its interpretation of this Treaty and the report of the panel.

Article 15

Becoming Party to the Treaty

F3–015   (1) (a) Any State member of the World Intellectual Property Organisation or of the United Nations may become party to this Treaty.

(b) Any Intergovernmental Organisation which meets the requirements of Article 2(x) may become party to this Treaty. The Organisation shall inform the Director General of its competence, and any subsequent changes in its competence, with respect to the matters governed by this Treaty. The Organisation and its member States may, without, however, any derogation from the obligations under this Treaty, decide on their respective responsibilities for the performance of their obligations under this Treaty.

(2) A State or Intergovernmental Organisation shall become party to this Treaty by:

(i) signature followed by the deposit of an instrument of ratification, acceptance or approval, or

(ii) the deposit of an instrument of accession.

(3) The instruments referred to in paragraph (2) shall be deposited with the Director General.

Article 16

Entry Into Force of the Treaty

(1) This Treaty shall enter into force, with respect to each of the first five States **F3–016** or Intergovernmental Organisations which have deposited their instruments of ratification, acceptance, approval or accession, three months after the date on which the fifth instrument of ratification, acceptance, approval or accession has been deposited.

(2) This Treaty shall enter into force with respect to any State or Intergovernmental Organisation not covered by paragraph (1) three months after the date on which that State or Intergovernmental Organisation has deposited its instrument of ratification, acceptance, approval or accession unless a later date has been indicated in the instrument; in the latter case, this Treaty shall enter into force with respect to the said State or Intergovernmental Organisation on the date thus indicated.

(3) Any Contracting party shall have the right not to apply this Treaty to any layout-design (topography) that exists at the time this Treaty enters into force in respect of that Contracting party, provided that this provision does not affect any protection that such layout-design (topography) may, at that time, enjoy in the territory of that Contracting Party by virtue of international obligations other than those resulting from this Treaty or the legislation of the said Contracting Party.

Article 17

Denunciation of the Treaty

(1) Any Contracting Party may denounce this Treaty by notification addressed **F3–017** to the Director General.

(2) Denunciation shall take effect one year after the day on which the Director General has received the notification of denunciation.

Article 18

Texts of the Treaty

(1) This Treaty is established in a single original in the English, Arabic, Chinese, **F3–018** French, Russian and Spanish language, all texts being equally authentic.

(2) Official texts shall be established by the Director General, after consultation with the interested Governments, in such other languages as the Assembly may designate.

Article 19

Depositary

The Director General shall be the depositary of this Treaty. **F3–019**

Article 20

Signature

F3–020   This Treaty shall be open for signature between 26 May 1989, and 25 August 1989, with the Government of the United States of America, and between 26 August 1989 and 25 May 1990, at the headquarters of WIPO.

In Witness Whereof the undersigned, being duly authorised thereto, have signed this Treaty.

Done at Washington, this twenty-sixth day of May one thousand nine hundred and eighty-nine.

F4. Locarno Agreement Establishing an International Classification for Industrial Designs (signed at Locarno on October 8, 1968 and as amended on September 28, 1979)

Article 1

Establishment of a Special Union; Adoption of an International Classification

F4–001   (1) The countries to which this Agreement applies constitute a Special Union.

(2) They adopt a single classification for industrial designs (hereinafter designated as "the international classification").

(3) The international classification shall comprise:

    (i) a list of classes and subclasses;

    (ii) an alphabetical list of goods in which industrial designs are incorporated, with an indication of the classes and subclasses into which they fall;

    (iii) explanatory notes.

(4) The list of classes and subclasses is the list annexed to the present Agreement, subject to such amendments and additions as the Committee of Experts set up under Article 3 (hereinafter designated as "the Committee of Experts") may make to it.

(5) The alphabetical list of goods and the explanatory notes shall be adopted by the Committee of Experts in accordance with the procedure laid down in Article 3.

(6) The international classification may be amended or supplemented by the Committee of Experts, in accordance with the procedure laid down in Article 3.

(7) (a) The international classification shall be established in the English and French languages.

    (b) Official texts of the international classification, in such other languages as the Assembly referred to in Article 5 may designate, shall be established, after consultation with the interested Governments, by the International Bureau of Intellectual Property (hereinafter designated as "the International Bureau") referred to in the Convention Establishing the World Intellectual Property Organization (hereinafter designated as "the Organization").

Article 2

Use and Legal Scope of the International Classification

(1) Subject to the requirements prescribed by this Agreement, the international classification shall be solely of an administrative character. Nevertheless, each country may attribute to it the legal scope which it considers appropriate. In particular, the international classification shall not bind the countries of the Special Union as regards the nature and scope of the protection afforded to the design in those countries.

F4–002

(2) Each country of the Special Union reserves the right to use the international classification as a principal or as a subsidiary system.

(3) The Offices of the countries of the Special Union shall include in the official documents for the deposit or registration of designs, and, if they are officially published, in the publications in question, the numbers of the classes and subclasses of the international classification into which the goods incorporating the designs belong.

(4) In selecting terms for inclusion in the alphabetical list of goods, the Committee of Experts shall exercise reasonable care to avoid using terms in which exclusive rights may exist. The inclusion of any word in the alphabetical index, however, is not an expression of opinion of the Committee of Experts on whether or not it is subject to exclusive rights.

Article 3

Committee of Experts

(1) A Committee of Experts shall be entrusted with the tasks referred to in Article 1(4), 1(5) and 1(6). Each country of the Special Union shall be represented on the Committee of Experts, which shall be organized according to rules of procedure adopted by a simple majority of the countries represented.

F4–003

(2) The Committee of Experts shall adopt the alphabetical list and explanatory notes by a simple majority of the votes of the countries of the Special Union.

(3) Proposals for amendments or additions to the international classification may be made by the Office of any country of the Special Union or by the International Bureau. Any proposal emanating from an Office shall be communicated by that Office to the International Bureau. Proposals from Offices and from the International Bureau shall be transmitted by the latter to the members of the Committee of Experts not later than two months before the session of the Committee at which the said proposals are to be considered.

(4) The decisions of the Committee of Experts concerning the adoption of amendments and additions to be made in the international classification shall be by a simple majority of the countries of the Special Union. Nevertheless, if such decisions entail the setting up of a new class or any transfer of goods from one class to another, unanimity shall be required.

(5) Each expert shall have the right to vote by mail.

(6) If a country does not appoint a representative for a given session of the Committee of Experts, or if the expert appointed has not expressed his vote during the session or within a period to be prescribed by the rules of procedure of the Committee of Experts, the country concerned shall be considered to have accepted the decision of the Committee.

Article 4

Notification and Publication of the Classification and of Amendments and Additions Thereto

F4–004   (1) The alphabetical list of goods and the explanatory notes adopted by the Committee of Experts, as well as any amendment or addition to the international classification decided by the Committee, shall be communicated to the Offices of the countries of the Special Union by the International Bureau. The decisions of the Committee of Experts shall enter into force as soon as the communication is received. Nevertheless, if such decisions entail the setting up of a new class or any transfer of goods from one class to another, they shall enter into force within a period of six months from the date of the said communication.

(2) The International Bureau, as depositary of the international classification, shall incorporate therein the amendments and additions which have entered into force. Announcements of the amendments and additions shall be published in the periodicals to be designated by the Assembly.

Article 5

Assembly of the Special Union

F4–005   (1) (a) The Special Union shall have an Assembly consisting of the countries of the Special Union.

(b) The Government of each country of the Special Union shall be represented by one delegate, who may be assisted by alternate delegates, advisors, and experts.

(c) The expenses of each delegation shall be borne by the Government which has appointed it.

(2) (a) Subject to the provisions of Article 3, the Assembly shall:

(i) deal with all matters concerning the maintenance and development of the Special Union and the implementation of this Agreement;

(ii) give directions to the International Bureau concerning the preparation for conferences of revision;

(iii) review and approve the reports and activities of the Director General of the Organization (hereinafter designated as "the Director General") concerning the Special Union, and give him all necessary instructions concerning matters within the competence of the Special Union;

(iv) determine the program and adopt the biennial budget of the Special Union, and approve its final accounts;

(v) adopt the financial regulations of the Special Union;

(vi) decide on the establishment of official texts of the international classification in languages other than English and French;

(vii) establish, in addition to the Committee of Experts set up under Article 3, such other committees of experts and working groups as it deems appropriate to achieve the objectives of the Special Union;

(viii) determine which countries not members of the Special Union and which intergovernmental and international non-governmental organizations shall be admitted to its meetings as observers;

(ix) adopt amendments to Articles 5 to 8;

        (x) take any other appropriate action designed to further the objectives of the Special Union;

        (xi) perform such other functions as are appropriate under this Agreement.

  (b) With respect to matters which are of interest also to other Unions administered by the Organization, the Assembly shall make its decisions after having heard the advice of the Coordination Committee of the Organization.

(3) (a) Each country member of the Assembly shall have one vote.

  (b) One-half of the countries members of the Assembly shall constitute a quorum.

  (c) Notwithstanding the provisions of subparagraph *(b)*, if, in any session, the number of countries represented is less than one-half but equal to or more than one-third of the countries members of the Assembly, the Assembly may make decisions but, with the exception of decisions concerning its own procedure, all such decisions shall take effect only if the conditions set forth hereinafter are fulfilled. The International Bureau shall communicate the said decisions to the countries members of the Assembly which were not represented and shall invite them to express in writing their vote or abstention within a period of three months from the date of the communication. If, at the expiration of this period, the number of countries having thus expressed their vote or abstention attains the number of countries which was lacking for attaining the quorum in the session itself, such decisions shall take effect provided that at the same time the required majority still obtains.

  (d) Subject to the provisions of Article 8(2), the decisions of the Assembly shall require two-thirds of the votes cast.

  (e) Abstentions shall not be considered as votes.

  (f) A delegate may represent, and vote in the name of, one country only.

(4) (a) The Assembly shall meet once in every second calendar year in ordinary session upon convocation by the Director General and, in the absence of exceptional circumstances, during the same period and at the same place as the General Assembly of the Organization.

  (b) The Assembly shall meet in extraordinary session upon convocation by the Director General, at the request of one-fourth of the countries members of the Assembly.

  (c) The agenda of each session shall be prepared by the Director General.

(5) The Assembly shall adopt its own rules of procedure.

Article 6

International Bureau

(1) (a) Administrative tasks concerning the Special Union shall be performed by the International Bureau.   **F4–006**

  (b) In particular, the International Bureau shall prepare the meetings and provide the secretariat of the Assembly, the Committee of Experts, and such other committees of experts and working groups as may have been established by the Assembly or the Committee of Experts.

  (c) The Director General shall be the chief executive of the Special Union and shall represent the Special Union.

(2) The Director General and any staff member designated by him shall participate, without the right to vote, in all meetings of the Assembly, the Committee of Experts, and such other committees of experts or working groups as may have been established by the Assembly or the Committee of Experts. The Director General, or a staff member designated by him, shall be *ex officio* secretary of those bodies.

(3) (a) The International Bureau shall, in accordance with the directions of the Assembly, make the preparations for the conferences of revision of the provisions of the Agreement other than Articles 5 to 8.

(b) The International Bureau may consult with intergovernmental and international non-governmental organizations concerning preparations for conferences of revision.

(c) The Director General and persons designated by him shall take part, without the right to vote, in the discussions at those conferences.

(4) The International Bureau shall carry out any other tasks assigned to it.

Article 7

Finances

F4–007 (1) (a) The Special Union shall have a budget.

(b) The budget of the Special Union shall include the income and expenses proper to the Special Union, its contribution to the budget of expenses common to the Unions, and, where applicable, the sum made available to the budget of the Conference of the Organization.

(c) Expenses not attributable exclusively to the Special Union but also to one or more other Unions administered by the Organization shall be considered as expenses common to the Unions. The share of the Special Union in such common expenses shall be in proportion to the interest the Special Union has in them.

(2) The budget of the Special Union shall be established with due regard to the requirements of coordination with the budgets of the other Unions administered by the Organization.

(3) The budget of the Special Union shall be financed from the following sources:

(i) contributions of the countries of the Special Union;

(ii) fees and charges due for services rendered by the International Bureau in relation to the Special Union;

(iii) sale of, or royalties on, the publications of the International Bureau concerning the Special Union;

(iv) gifts, bequests, and subventions;

(v) rents, interests, and other miscellaneous income.

(4) (a) For the purpose of establishing its contribution referred to in paragraph (3)(i), each country of the Special Union shall belong to the same class as it belongs to in the Paris Union for the Protection of Industrial Property, and shall pay its annual contributions on the basis of the same number of units as is fixed for that class in that Union.[1]

[1] With effect from January 1, 1994, the Governing Bodies of WIPO and the Unions administered by WIPO adopted a new contribution system that replaces the corresponding provisions of this Agreement. Details concerning that system may be obtained from the International Bureau of WIPO (Editor's note).

(b) The annual contribution of each country of the Special Union shall be an amount in the same proportion to the total sum to be contributed to the budget of the Special Union by all countries as the number of its units is to the total of the units of all contributing countries.

(c) Contributions shall become due on the first of January of each year.

(d) A country which is in arrears in the payment of its contributions may not exercise its right to vote in any organ of the Special Union if the amount of its arrears equals or exceeds the amount of the contributions due from it for the preceding two full years. However, any organ of the Special Union may allow such a country to continue to exercise its right to vote in that organ if, and as long as, it is satisfied that the delay in payment is due to exceptional and unavoidable circumstances.

(e) If the budget is not adopted before the beginning of a new financial period, it shall be at the same level as the budget of the previous year, as provided in the financial regulations.

(5) The amount of the fees and charges due for services rendered by the International Bureau in relation to the Special Union shall be established, and shall be reported to the Assembly, by the Director General.

(6) (a) The Special Union shall have a working capital fund which shall be constituted by a single payment made by each country of the Special Union. If the fund becomes insufficient, the Assembly shall decide to increase it.

(b) The amount of the initial payment of each country to the said fund or of its participation in the increase thereof shall be a proportion of the contribution of that country for the year in which the fund is established or the decision to increase it is made.

(c) The proportion and the terms of payment shall be fixed by the Assembly on the proposal of the Director General and after it has heard the advice of the Coordination Committee of the Organization.

(7) (a) In the headquarters agreement concluded with the country on the territory of which the Organization has its headquarters, it shall be provided that, whenever the working capital fund is insufficient, such country shall grant advances. The amount of those advances and the conditions on which they are granted shall be the subject of separate agreements, in each case, between such country and the Organization.

(b) The country referred to in subparagraph (a) and the Organization shall each have the right to denounce the obligation to grant advances, by written notification. Denunciation shall take effect three years after the end of the year in which it has been notified.

(8) The auditing of the accounts shall be effected by one or more of the countries of the Special Union or by external auditors, as provided in the financial regulations. They shall be designated, with their agreement, by the Assembly.

Article 8

Amendment of Articles 5 to 8

(1) Proposals for the amendment of Articles 5, 6, 7, and the present Article, may be initiated by any country of the Special Union or by the Director General. Such proposals shall be communicated by the Director General to the countries of the Special Union at least six months in advance of their consideration by the Assembly.

F4–008

(2) Amendments to the Articles referred to in paragraph (1) shall be adopted by the Assembly. Adoption shall require three-fourths of the votes cast, provided that any amendment to Article 5, and to the present paragraph, shall require four-fifths of the votes cast.

(3) Any amendment to the Articles referred to in paragraph (1) shall enter into force one month after written notifications of acceptance, effected in accordance with their respective constitutional processes, have been received by the Director General from three-fourths of the countries members of the Special Union at the time the amendment was adopted. Any amendment to the said Articles thus accepted shall bind all the countries which are members of the Special Union at the time the amendment enters into force, or which become members thereof at a subsequent date, provided that any amendment increasing the financial obligations of countries of the Special Union shall bind only those countries which have notified their acceptance of such amendment.

Article 9

Ratification and Accession; Entry Into Force

F4–009   (1) Any country party to the Paris Convention for the Protection of Industrial Property which has signed this Agreement may ratify it, and, if it has not signed it, may accede to it.

(2) Instruments of ratification and accession shall be deposited with the Director General.

(3) (a) With respect to the first five countries which have deposited their instruments of ratification or accession, this Agreement shall enter into force three months after the deposit of the fifth such instrument.

(b) With respect to any other country, this Agreement shall enter into force three months after the date on which its ratification or accession has been notified by the Director General, unless a subsequent date has been indicated in the instrument of ratification or accession. In the latter case, this Agreement shall enter into force with respect to that country on the date thus indicated.

(4) Ratification or accession shall automatically entail acceptance of all the clauses and admission to all the advantages of this Agreement.

Article 10

Force and Duration of the Agreement

F4–010   This Agreement shall have the same force and duration as the Paris Convention for the Protection of Industrial Property.

Article 11

Revision of Articles 1 to 4 and 9 to 15

F4–011   (1) Articles 1 to 4 and 9 to 15 of this Agreement may be submitted to revision with a view to the introduction of desired improvements.

(2) Every revision shall be considered at a conference which shall be held among the delegates of the countries of the Special Union.

Article 12

Denunciation

(1) Any country may denounce this Agreement by notification addressed to the **F4–012** Director General. Such denunciation shall affect only the country making it, the Agreement remaining in full force and effect as regards the other countries of the Special Union.

(2) Denunciation shall take effect one year after the day on which the Director General has received the notification.

(3) The right of denunciation provided by this Article shall not be exercised by any country before the expiration of five years from the date upon which it becomes a member of the Special Union.

Article 13

Territories

The provisions of Article 24 of the Paris Convention for the Protection of **F4–013** Industrial Property shall apply to this Agreement.

Article 14

Signature, Languages, Notifications

(1) (a) This Agreement shall be signed in a single copy in the English and **F4–014** French languages, both texts being equally authentic, and shall be deposited with the Government of Switzerland.

(b) This Agreement shall remain open for signature at Berne until June 30, 1969.

(2) Official texts shall be established by the Director General, after consultation with the interested Governments, in such other languages as the Assembly may designate.

(3) The Director General shall transmit two copies, certified by the Government of Switzerland, of the signed text of this Agreement to the Governments of the countries that have signed it and, on request, to the Government of any other country.

(4) The Director General shall register this Agreement with the Secretariat of the United Nations.

(5) The Director General shall notify the Governments of all countries of the Special Union of the date of entry into force of the Agreement, signatures, deposits of instruments of ratification or accession, acceptances of amendments to this Agreement and the dates on which such amendments enter into force, and notifications of denunciation.

Article 15

Transitional Provision

F4–015   Until the first Director General assumes office, references in this Agreement to the International Bureau of the Organization or to the Director General shall be deemed to be references to the United International Bureaux for the Protection of Intellectual Property (BIRPI) or its Director, respectively.

ANNEX

LIST OF CLASSES AND SUBCLASSES OF THE INTERNATIONAL CLASSIFICATION SEVENTH EDITION (AS IN FORCE FROM JANUARY 1, 1999)

Class 01—Foodstuffs

F4–016   01) BAKERS' PRODUCTS, BISCUITS, PASTRY, MACARONI AND OTHER CEREAL PRODUCTS, CHOCOLATES, CONFECTIONERY, ICES
02) FRUIT AND VEGETABLES
03) CHEESES, BUTTER AND BUTTER SUBSTITUTES, OTHER DAIRY PRODUCE
04) BUTCHERS' MEAT (INCLUDING PORK PRODUCTS), FISH
05) [VACANT]
06) ANIMAL FOODSTUFFS
99) MISCELLANEOUS

Class 02—Articles of clothing and haberdashery

F4–017   01) UNDERGARMENTS, LINGERIE, CORSETS, BRASSIERES, NIGHTWEAR
02) GARMENTS
03) HEADWEAR
04) FOOTWEAR, SOCKS AND STOCKINGS
05) NECKTIES, SCARVES, NECKERCHIEFS AND HANDKERCHIEFS
06) GLOVES
07) HABERDASHERY AND CLOTHING ACCESSORIES
99) MISCELLANEOUS

Class 03—Travel goods, cases, parasols and personal belongings, not elsewhere specified

F4–018   01) TRUNKS, SUITCASES, BRIEFCASES, HANDBAGS, KEYHOLDERS, CASES SPECIALLY DESIGNED FOR THEIR CONTENTS, WALLETS AND SIMILAR ARTICLES
02) [VACANT]
03) UMBRELLAS, PARASOLS, SUNSHADES AND WALKING STICKS
04) FANS
99) MISCELLANEOUS

Class 04—Brushware

F4–019   01) BRUSHES AND BROOMS FOR CLEANING
02) TOILET BRUSHES, CLOTHES BRUSHES AND SHOE BRUSHES
03) BRUSHES FOR MACHINES

04) PAINTBRUSHES, BRUSHES FOR USE IN COOKING
99) MISCELLANEOUS

Class 05—Textile piecegoods, artificial and natural sheet material

01) SPUN ARTICLES   F4–020
02) LACE
03) EMBROIDERY
04) RIBBONS, BRAIDS AND OTHER DECORATIVE TRIMMINGS
05) TEXTILE FABRICS
06) ARTIFICIAL OR NATURAL SHEET MATERIAL
99) MISCELLANEOUS

Class 06—Furnishing

01) BEDS AND SEATS   F4–021
02) [VACANT]
03) TABLES AND SIMILAR FURNITURE
04) STORAGE FURNITURE
05) COMPOSITE FURNITURE
06) OTHER FURNITURE AND FURNITURE PARTS
07) MIRRORS AND FRAMES
08) CLOTHES HANGERS
09) MATTRESSES AND CUSHIONS
10) CURTAINS AND INDOOR BLINDS
11) CARPETS, MATS AND RUGS
12) TAPESTRIES
13) BLANKETS AND OTHER COVERING MATERIALS, HOUSEHOLD
LINEN AND NAPERY
99) MISCELLANEOUS

Class 07—Household goods, not elsewhere specified

01) CHINA, GLASSWARE, DISHES AND OTHER ARTICLES OF A SIMILAR   F4–022
NATURE
02) COOKING APPLIANCES, UTENSILS AND CONTAINERS
03) TABLES KNIVES, FORKS AND SPOONS
04) APPLIANCES AND UTENSILS, HAND-MANIPULATED, FOR PREPAR-
ING FOOD OR DRINK
05) FLATIRONS AND WASHING, CLEANING AND DRYING EQUIPMENT
06) OTHER TABLE UTENSILS
07) OTHER HOUSEHOLD RECEPTACLES
08) FIREPLACE IMPLEMENTS
99) MISCELLANEOUS

Class 08—Tools and hardware

01) TOOLS AND IMPLEMENTS FOR DRILLING, MILLING OR DIGGING   F4–023
02) HAMMERS AND OTHER SIMILAR TOOLS AND IMPLEMENTS
03) CUTTING TOOLS AND IMPLEMENTS
04) SCREWDRIVERS AND OTHER SIMILAR TOOLS AND IMPLEMENTS
05) OTHER TOOLS AND IMPLEMENTS
06) HANDLES, KNOBS AND HINGES
07) LOCKING OR CLOSING DEVICES
08) FASTENING, SUPPORTING OR MOUNTING DEVICES NOT INCLUDED
IN OTHER CLASSES
09) METAL FITTINGS AND MOUNTINGS FOR DOORS, WINDOWS AND
FURNITURE, AND SIMILAR ARTICLES

10) BICYCLE RACKS
99) MISCELLANEOUS

Class 09—Packages and containers for the transport or handling of goods

F4–024   01) BOTTLES, FLASKS, POTS, CARBOYS, DEMIJOHNS, AND CONTAINERS WITH DYNAMIC DISPENSING MEANS
02) STORAGE CANS, DRUMS AND CASKS
03) BOXES, CASES, CONTAINERS, (PRESERVE) TINS OR CANS
04) HAMPERS, CRATES AND BASKETS
05) BAGS, SACHETS, TUBES AND CAPSULES
06) ROPES AND HOOPING MATERIALS
07) CLOSING MEANS AND ATTACHMENTS
08) PALLETS AND PLATFORMS FOR FORKLIFTS
09) REFUSE AND TRASH CONTAINERS AND STANDS THEREFOR
99) MISCELLANEOUS

Class 10—Clocks and watches and other measuring instruments, checking and signalling instruments

F4–025   01) CLOCKS AND ALARM CLOCKS
02) WATCHES AND WRIST WATCHES
03) OTHER TIME-MEASURING INSTRUMENTS
04) OTHER MEASURING INSTRUMENTS, APPARATUS AND DEVICES
05) INSTRUMENTS, APPARATUS AND DEVICES FOR CHECKING, SECURITY OR TESTING
06) SIGNALLING APPARATUS AND DEVICES
07) CASINGS, DIALS, HANDS AND ALL OTHER PARTS AND ACCESSORIES OF INSTRUMENTS FOR MEASURING, CHECKING AND SIGNALLING
99) MISCELLANEOUS

Class 11—Articles of adornment

F4–026   01) JEWELLERY
02) TRINKETS, TABLE, MANTEL AND WALL ORNAMENTS, FLOWER VASES AND POTS
03) MEDALS AND BADGES
04) ARTIFICIAL FLOWERS, FRUIT AND PLANTS
05) FLAGS, FESTIVE DECORATIONS
99) MISCELLANEOUS

Class 12—Means of transport or hoisting

F4–027   01) VEHICLES DRAWN BY ANIMALS
02) HANDCARTS, WHEELBARROWS
03) LOCOMOTIVES AND ROLLING STOCK FOR RAILWAYS AND ALL OTHER RAIL VEHICLES
04) TELPHER CARRIERS, CHAIR LIFTS AND SKI LIFTS
05) ELEVATORS AND HOISTS FOR LOADING OR CONVEYING
06) SHIPS AND BOATS
07) AIRCRAFT AND SPACE VEHICLES
08) MOTOR CARS, BUSES AND LORRIES
09) TRACTORS
10) ROAD VEHICLE TRAILERS
11) CYCLES AND MOTORCYCLES
12) PERAMBULATORS, INVALID CHAIRS, STRETCHERS
13) SPECIAL-PURPOSE VEHICLES
14) OTHER VEHICLES

15) TYRES AND ANTI-SKID CHAINS FOR VEHICLES

16) PARTS, EQUIPMENT AND ACCESSORIES FOR VEHICLES, NOT INCLUDED IN OTHER CLASSES OR SUBCLASSES

99) MISCELLANEOUS

Class 13—Equipment for production, distribution or transformation of electricity

01) GENERATORS AND MOTORS   **F4–028**

02) POWER TRANSFORMERS, RECTIFIERS, BATTERIES AND ACCUMU-LATORS

03) EQUIPMENT FOR DISTRIBUTION OR CONTROL OF ELECTRIC POWER

99) MISCELLANEOUS

Class 14—Recording, communication or information retrieval equipment

01) EQUIPMENT FOR THE RECORDING OR REPRODUCTION OF SOUNDS   **F4–029** OR PICTURES

02) DATA PROCESSING EQUIPMENT AS WELL AS PERIPHERAL APPARA-TUS AND DEVICES

03) COMMUNICATIONS EQUIPMENT, WIRELESS REMOTE CONTROLS AND RADIO AMPLIFIERS

99) MISCELLANEOUS

Class 15—Machines, not elsewhere specified

01) ENGINES   **F4–030**

02) PUMPS AND COMPRESSORS

03) AGRICULTURAL MACHINERY

04) CONSTRUCTION MACHINERY

05) WASHING, CLEANING AND DRYING MACHINES

06) TEXTILE, SEWING, KNITTING AND EMBROIDERING MACHINES INCLUDING THEIR INTEGRAL PARTS

07) REFRIGERATION MACHINERY AND APPARATUS

08) [VACANT]

09) MACHINE TOOLS, ABRADING AND FOUNDING MACHINERY

99) MISCELLANEOUS

Class 16—Photographic, cinematographic and optical apparatus

01) PHOTOGRAPHIC CAMERAS AND FILM CAMERAS   **F4–031**

02) PROJECTORS AND VIEWERS

03) PHOTOCOPYING APPARATUS AND ENLARGERS

04) DEVELOPING APPARATUS AND EQUIPMENT

05) ACCESSORIES

06) OPTICAL ARTICLES

99) MISCELLANEOUS

Class 17—Musical instruments

01) KEYBOARD INSTRUMENTS   **F4–032**

02) WIND INSTRUMENTS

03) STRINGED INSTRUMENTS

04) PERCUSSION INSTRUMENTS

05) MECHANICAL INSTRUMENTS

99) MISCELLANEOUS

Class 18—Printing and office machinery

F4–033
01) TYPEWRITERS AND CALCULATING MACHINES
02) PRINTING MACHINES
03) TYPE AND TYPE FACES
04) BOOKBINDING MACHINES, PRINTERS' STAPLING MACHINES, GUILLOTINES AND TRIMMERS (FOR BOOKBINDING)
99) MISCELLANEOUS

Class 19—Stationery and office equipment, artists' and teaching materials

F4–034
01) WRITING PAPER, CARDS FOR CORRESPONDENCE AND ANNOUNCEMENTS
02) OFFICE EQUIPMENT
03) CALENDARS
04) BOOKS AND OTHER OBJECTS OF SIMILAR OUTWARD APPEARANCE
05) [VACANT]
06) MATERIALS AND INSTRUMENTS FOR WRITING BY HAND, FOR DRAWING, FOR PAINTING, FOR SCULPTURE, FOR ENGRAVING AND FOR OTHER ARTISTIC TECHNIQUES
07) TEACHING MATERIALS
08) OTHER PRINTED MATTER
99) MISCELLANEOUS

Class 20—Sales and advertising equipment, signs

F4–035
01) AUTOMATIC VENDING MACHINES
02) DISPLAY AND SALES EQUIPMENT
03) SIGNS, SIGNBOARDS AND ADVERTISING DEVICES
99) MISCELLANEOUS

Class 21—Games, toys, tents and sports goods

F4–036
01) GAMES AND TOYS
02) GYMNASTICS AND SPORTS APPARATUS AND EQUIPMENT
03) OTHER AMUSEMENT AND ENTERTAINMENT ARTICLES
04) TENTS AND ACCESSORIES THEREOF
99) MISCELLANEOUS

Class 22—Arms, pyrotechnic articles, articles for hunting, fishing and pest killing

F4–037
01) PROJECTILE WEAPONS
02) OTHER WEAPONS
03) AMMUNITION, ROCKETS AND PYROTECHNIC ARTICLES
04) TARGETS AND ACCESSORIES
05) HUNTING AND FISHING EQUIPMENT
06) TRAPS, ARTICLES FOR PEST KILLING
99) MISCELLANEOUS

Class 23—Fluid distribution equipment, sanitary, heating, ventilation and air-conditioning equipment, solid fuel

F4–038
01) FLUID DISTRIBUTION EQUIPMENT
02) SANITARY APPLIANCES
03) HEATING EQUIPMENT
04) VENTILATION AND AIR-CONDITIONING EQUIPMENT

05) SOLID FUEL
99) MISCELLANEOUS

Class 24—Medical and laboratory equipment

01) APPARATUS AND EQUIPMENT FOR DOCTORS, HOSPITALS AND   **F4–039**
LABORATORIES
02) MEDICAL INSTRUMENTS, INSTRUMENTS AND TOOLS FOR LABO-
RATORY USE
03) PROSTHETIC ARTICLES
04) MATERIALS FOR DRESSING WOUNDS, NURSING AND MEDICAL
CARE
99) MISCELLANEOUS

Class 25—Building units and construction elements

01) BUILDING MATERIALS   **F4–040**
02) PREFABRICATED OR PRE-ASSEMBLED BUILDING PARTS
03) HOUSES, GARAGES AND OTHER BUILDINGS
04) STEPS, LADDERS AND SCAFFOLDS
99) MISCELLANEOUS

Class 26—Lighting apparatus

01) CANDLESTICKS AND CANDELABRA   **F4–041**
02) TORCHES AND HAND LAMPS AND LANTERNS
03) PUBLIC LIGHTING FIXTURES
04) LUMINOUS SOURCES, ELECTRICAL OR NOT
05) LAMPS, STANDARD LAMPS, CHANDELIERS, WALL AND CEILING
FIXTURES, LAMPSHADES, REFLECTORS, PHOTOGRAPHIC AND CINE-
MATOGRAPHIC PROJECTOR LAMPS
06) LUMINOUS DEVICES FOR VEHICLES
99) MISCELLANEOUS

Class 27—Tobacco and smokers' supplies

01) TOBACCO, CIGARS AND CIGARETTES   **F4–042**
02) PIPES, CIGAR AND CIGARETTE HOLDERS
03) ASHTRAYS
04) MATCHES
05) LIGHTERS
06) CIGAR CASES, CIGARETTE CASES, TOBACCO JARS AND POUCHES
99) MISCELLANEOUS

Class 28—Pharmaceutical and cosmetic products, toilet articles and apparatus

01) PHARMACEUTICAL PRODUCTS   **F4–043**
02) COSMETIC PRODUCTS
03) TOILET ARTICLES AND BEAUTY PARLOR EQUIPMENT
04) WIGS, FALSE HAIRPIECES
99) MISCELLANEOUS

Class 29—Devices and equipment against fire hazards, for accident prevention and for rescue

01) DEVICES AND EQUIPMENT AGAINST FIRE HAZARDS   **F4–044**
02) DEVICES AND EQUIPMENT FOR ACCIDENT PREVENTION AND FOR
RESCUE, NOT ELSEWHERE SPECIFIED
99) MISCELLANEOUS

Class 30—Articles for the care and handling of animals

F4–045 01) ANIMAL CLOTHING
02) PENS, CAGES, KENNELS AND SIMILAR SHELTERS
03) FEEDERS AND WATERERS
04) SADDLERY
05) WHIPS AND PRODS
06) BEDS AND NESTS
07) PERCHES AND OTHER CAGE ATTACHMENTS
08) MARKERS, MARKS AND SHACKLES
09) HITCHING POSTS
99) MISCELLANEOUS

Class 31—Machines and appliances for preparing food or drink, not elsewhere specified

F4–046 00) MACHINES AND APPLIANCES FOR PREPARING FOOD OR DRINK, NOT ELSEWHERE SPECIFIED

Class 99—Miscellaneous

F4–047 00) MISCELLANEOUS

F5. Geneva Act of the Hague Agreement Concerning the International Registration of Industrial Designs (adopted by the Diplomatic Conference on July 2, 1999)

Agreed Statements by the Diplomatic Conference Regarding the Geneva Act and the Regulations under the Geneva Act

INTRODUCTORY PROVISIONS

Article 1

Abbreviated Expressions

F5–001 For the purposes of this Act:

(i) "the Hague Agreement" means the Hague Agreement Concerning the International Deposit of Industrial Designs, henceforth renamed the Hague Agreement Concerning the International Registration of Industrial Designs;
(ii) "this Act" means the Hague Agreement as established by the present Act;
(iii) "Regulations" means the Regulations under this Act;
(iv) "prescribed" means prescribed in the Regulations;
(v) "Paris Convention" means the Paris Convention for the Protection of Industrial Property, signed at Paris on March 20, 1883, as revised and amended;
(vi) "international registration" means the international registration of an industrial design effected according to this Act;

834

(vii) "international application" means an application for international registration;

(viii) "International Register" means the official collection of data concerning international registrations maintained by the International Bureau, which data this Act or the Regulations require or permit to be recorded, regardless of the medium in which such data are stored;

(ix) "person" means a natural person or a legal entity;

(x) "applicant" means the person in whose name an international application is filed;

(xi) "holder" means the person in whose name an international registration is recorded in the International Register;

(xii) "intergovernmental organization" means an intergovernmental organization eligible to become party to this Act in accordance with Article 27(1)(ii);

(xiii) "Contracting Party" means any State or intergovernmental organization party to this Act;

(xiv) "applicant's Contracting Party" means the Contracting Party or one of the Contracting Parties from which the applicant derives its entitlement to file an international application by virtue of satisfying, in relation to that Contracting Party, at least one of the conditions specified in Article 3; where there are two or more Contracting Parties from which the applicant may, under Article 3, derive its entitlement to file an international application, "applicant's Contracting Party" means the one which, among those Contracting Parties, is indicated as such in the international application;

(xv) "territory of a Contracting Party" means, where the Contracting Party is a State, the territory of that State and, where the Contracting Party is an intergovernmental organization, the territory in which the constituent treaty of that intergovernmental organization applies;

(xvi) "Office" means the agency entrusted by a Contracting Party with the grant of protection for industrial designs with effect in the territory of that Contracting Party;

(xvii) "Examining Office" means an Office which *ex officio* examines applications filed with it for the protection of industrial designs at least to determine whether the industrial designs satisfy the condition of novelty;

(xviii) "designation" means a request that an international registration have effect in a Contracting Party; it also means the recording, in the International Register, of that request;

(xix) "designated Contracting Party" and "designated Office" means the Contracting Party and the Office of the Contracting Party, respectively, to which a designation applies;

(xx) "1934 Act" means the Act signed at London on June 2, 1934, of the Hague Agreement;

(xxi) "1960 Act" means the Act signed at The Hague on November 28, 1960, of the Hague Agreement;

(xxii) "1961 Additional Act" means the Act signed at Monaco on November 18, 1961, additional to the 1934 Act;

(xxiii) "Complementary Act of 1967" means the Complementary Act signed at Stockholm on July 14, 1967, as amended, of the Hague Agreement;

(xxiv) "Union" means the Hague Union established by the Hague Agreement of November 6, 1925, and maintained by the 1934 and 1960

Acts, the 1961 Additional Act, the Complementary Act of 1967 and this Act;

(xxv) "Assembly" means the Assembly referred to in Article 21(1)(a) or any body replacing that Assembly;

(xxvi) "Organization" means the World Intellectual Property Organization;

(xxvii) "Director General" means the Director General of the Organization;

(xxviii) "International Bureau" means the International Bureau of the Organization;

(xxix) "instrument of ratification" shall be construed as including instruments of acceptance or approval.

Article 2

Applicability of Other Protection Accorded by Laws of Contracting Parties and by Certain International Treaties

F5–002   (1) [*Laws of Contracting Parties and Certain International Treaties*] The provisions of this Act shall not affect the application of any greater protection which may be accorded by the law of a Contracting Party, nor shall they affect in any way the protection accorded to works of art and works of applied art by international copyright treaties and conventions, or the protection accorded to industrial designs under the Agreement on Trade-Related Aspects of Intellectual Property Rights annexed to the Agreement Establishing the World Trade Organization.

(2) [*Obligation to Comply with the Paris Convention*] Each Contracting Party shall comply with the provisions of the Paris Convention which concern industrial designs.

CHAPTER I

INTERNATIONAL APPLICATION AND INTERNATIONAL REGISTRATION

Article 3

Entitlement to File an International Application

F5–003   Any person that is a national of a State that is a Contracting Party or of a State member of an intergovernmental organization that is a Contracting Party, or that has a domicile, a habitual residence or a real and effective industrial or commercial establishment in the territory of a Contracting Party, shall be entitled to file an international application.

Article 4

Procedure for Filing the International Application

F5–004   (1) [*Direct or Indirect Filing*]

(a) The international application may be filed, at the option of the applicant, either directly with the International Bureau or through the Office of the applicant's Contracting Party.

(b) Notwithstanding subparagraph (a), any Contracting Party may, in a declaration, notify the Director General that international applications may not be filed through its Office.

(2) [*Transmittal Fee in Case of Indirect Filing*] The Office of any Contracting Party may require that the applicant pay a transmittal fee to it, for its own benefit, in respect of any international application filed through it.

Article 5

Contents of the International Application

(1) [*Mandatory Contents of the International Application*] The international applica- **F5–005**
tion shall be in the prescribed language or one of the prescribed languages and shall contain or be accompanied by

  (i) a request for international registration under this Act;
 (ii) the prescribed data concerning the applicant;
(iii) the prescribed number of copies of a reproduction or, at the choice of the applicant, of several different reproductions of the industrial design that is the subject of the international application, presented in the prescribed manner; however, where the industrial design is two-dimensional and a request for deferment of publication is made in accordance with paragraph (5), the international application may, instead of containing reproductions, be accompanied by the prescribed number of specimens of the industrial design;
 (iv) an indication of the product or products which constitute the industrial design or in relation to which the industrial design is to be used, as prescribed;
  (v) an indication of the designated Contracting Parties;
 (vi) the prescribed fees;
(vii) any other prescribed particulars.

(2) [*Additional Mandatory Contents of the International Application*]

  (a) Any Contracting Party whose Office is an Examining Office and whose law, at the time it becomes party to this Act, requires that an application for the grant of protection to an industrial design contain any of the elements specified in subparagraph (b) in order for that application to be accorded a filing date under that law may, in a declaration, notify the Director General of those elements.
  (b) The elements that may be notified pursuant to subparagraph (a) are the following:
     (i) indications concerning the identity of the creator of the industrial design that is the subject of that application;
    (ii) a brief description of the reproduction or of the characteristic features of the industrial design that is the subject of that application;
   (iii) a claim.
  (c) Where the international application contains the designation of a Contracting Party that has made a notification under subparagraph (a), it shall also contain, in the prescribed manner, any element that was the subject of that notification.

(3) [*Other Possible Contents of the International Application*] The international application may contain or be accompanied by such other elements as are specified in the Regulations.

(4) [*Several Industrial Designs in the Same International Application*] Subject to such conditions as may be prescribed, an international application may include two or more industrial designs.

(5) [*Request for Deferred Publication*] The international application may contain a request for deferment of publication.

Article 6

Priority

F5–006   (1) [*Claiming of Priority*]

(a) The international application may contain a declaration claiming, under Article 4 of the Paris Convention, the priority of one or more earlier applications filed in or for any country party to that Convention or any Member of the World Trade Organization.

(b) The Regulations may provide that the declaration referred to in subparagraph (a) may be made after the filing of the international application. In such case, the Regulations shall prescribe the latest time by which such declaration may be made.

(2) [*International Application Serving as a Basis for Claiming Priority*] The international application shall, as from its filing date and whatever may be its subsequent fate, be equivalent to a regular filing within the meaning of Article 4 of the Paris Convention.

Article 7

Designation Fees

F5–007   (1) [*Prescribed Designation Fee*] The prescribed fees shall include, subject to paragraph (2), a designation fee for each designated Contracting Party.

(2) [*Individual Designation Fee*] Any Contracting Party whose Office is an Examining Office and any Contracting Party that is an intergovernmental organization may, in a declaration, notify the Director General that, in connection with any international application in which it is designated, and in connection with the renewal of any international registration resulting from such an international application, the prescribed designation fee referred to in paragraph (1) shall be replaced by an individual designation fee, whose amount shall be indicated in the declaration and can be changed in further declarations. The said amount may be fixed by the said Contracting Party for the initial term of protection and for each term of renewal or for the maximum period of protection allowed by the Contracting Party concerned. However, it may not be higher than the equivalent of the amount which the Office of that Contracting Party would be entitled to receive from an applicant for a grant of protection for an equivalent period to the same number of industrial designs, that amount being diminished by the savings resulting from the international procedure.

(3) [*Transfer of Designation Fees*] The designation fees referred to in paragraphs (1) and (2) shall be transferred by the International Bureau to the Contracting Parties in respect of which those fees were paid.

Article 8

Correction of Irregularities

(1) [*Examination of the International Application*] If the International Bureau finds **F5–008** that the international application does not, at the time of its receipt by the International Bureau, fulfill the requirements of this Act and the Regulations, it shall invite the applicant to make the required corrections within the prescribed time limit.

(2) [*Irregularities Not Corrected*]

> (a) If the applicant does not comply with the invitation within the prescribed time limit, the international application shall, subject to subparagraph (b), be considered abandoned.
>
> (b) In the case of an irregularity which relates to Article 5(2) or to a special requirement notified to the Director General by a Contracting Party in accordance with the Regulations, if the applicant does not comply with the invitation within the prescribed time limit, the international application shall be deemed not to contain the designation of that Contracting Party.

Article 9

Filing Date of the International Application

(1) [*International Application Filed Directly*] Where the international application is **F5–009** filed directly with the International Bureau, the filing date shall, subject to paragraph (3), be the date on which the International Bureau receives the international application.

(2) [*International Application Filed Indirectly*] Where the international application is filed through the Office of the applicant's Contracting Party, the filing date shall be determined as prescribed.

(3) [*International Application with Certain Irregularities*] Where the international application has, on the date on which it is received by the International Bureau, an irregularity which is prescribed as an irregularity entailing a postponement of the filing date of the international application, the filing date shall be the date on which the correction of such irregularity is received by the International Bureau.

Article 10

International Registration, Date of the International Registration, Publication and Confidential Copies of the International Registration

(1) [*International Registration*] The International Bureau shall register each **F5–010** industrial design that is the subject of an international application immediately upon receipt by it of the international application or, where corrections are invited under Article 8, immediately upon receipt of the required corrections. The registration shall be effected whether or not publication is deferred under Article 11.

(2) [*Date of the International Registration*]

> (a) Subject to subparagraph (b), the date of the international registration shall be the filing date of the international application.

839

(b) Where the international application has, on the date on which it is received by the International Bureau, an irregularity which relates to Article 5(2), the date of the international registration shall be the date on which the correction of such irregularity is received by the International Bureau or the filing date of the international application, whichever is the later.

(3) [*Publication*]

    (a) The international registration shall be published by the International Bureau. Such publication shall be deemed in all Contracting Parties to be sufficient publicity, and no other publicity may be required of the holder.

    (b) The International Bureau shall send a copy of the publication of the international registration to each designated Office.

(4) [*Maintenance of Confidentiality Before Publication*] Subject to paragraph (5) and Article 11(4)(b), the International Bureau shall keep in confidence each international application and each international registration until publication.

(5) [*Confidential Copies*]

    (a) The International Bureau shall, immediately after registration has been effected, send a copy of the international registration, along with any relevant statement, document or specimen accompanying the international application, to each Office that has notified the International Bureau that it wishes to receive such a copy and has been designated in the international application.

    (b) The Office shall, until publication of the international registration by the International Bureau, keep in confidence each international registration of which a copy has been sent to it by the International Bureau and may use the said copy only for the purpose of the examination of the international registration and of applications for the protection of industrial designs filed in or for the Contracting Party for which the Office is competent. In particular, it may not divulge the contents of any such international registration to any person outside the Office other than the holder of that international registration, except for the purposes of an administrative or legal proceeding involving a conflict over entitlement to file the international application on which the international registration is based. In the case of such an administrative or legal proceeding, the contents of the international registration may only be disclosed in confidence to the parties involved in the proceeding who shall be bound to respect the confidentiality of the disclosure.

Article 11

Deferment of Publication

F5–011   (1) [*Provisions of Laws of Contracting Parties Concerning Deferment of Publication*]

    (a) Where the law of a Contracting Party provides for the deferment of the publication of an industrial design for a period which is less than the prescribed period, that Contracting Party shall, in a declaration, notify the Director General of the allowable period of deferment.

    (b) Where the law of a Contracting Party does not provide for the deferment of the publication of an industrial design, the Contracting Party shall, in a declaration, notify the Director General of that fact.

(2) [*Deferment of Publication*] Where the international application contains a request for deferment of publication, the publication shall take place,

    (i) where none of the Contracting Parties designated in the international application has made a declaration under paragraph (1), at the expiry of the prescribed period or,

    (ii) where any of the Contracting Parties designated in the international application has made a declaration under paragraph (1)(a), at the expiry of the period notified in such declaration or, where there is more than one such designated Contracting Party, at the expiry of the shortest period notified in their declarations.

(3) [*Treatment of Requests for Deferment Where Deferment Is Not Possible Under Applicable Law*] Where deferment of publication has been requested and any of the Contracting Parties designated in the international application has made a declaration under paragraph (1)(b) that deferment of publication is not possible under its law,

    (i) subject to item (ii), the International Bureau shall notify the applicant accordingly; if, within the prescribed period, the applicant does not, by notice in writing to the International Bureau, withdraw the designation of the said Contracting Party, the International Bureau shall disregard the request for deferment of publication;

    (ii) where, instead of containing reproductions of the industrial design, the international application was accompanied by specimens of the industrial design, the International Bureau shall disregard the designation of the said Contracting Party and shall notify the applicant accordingly.

(4) [*Request for Earlier Publication or for Special Access to the International Registration*]

    (a) At any time during the period of deferment applicable under paragraph (2), the holder may request publication of any or all of the industrial designs that are the subject of the international registration, in which case the period of deferment in respect of such industrial design or designs shall be considered to have expired on the date of receipt of such request by the International Bureau.

    (b) The holder may also, at any time during the period of deferment applicable under paragraph (2), request the International Bureau to provide a third party specified by the holder with an extract from, or to allow such a party access to, any or all of the industrial designs that are the subject of the international registration.

(5) [*Renunciation and Limitation*]

    (a) If, at any time during the period of deferment applicable under paragraph (2), the holder renounces the international registration in respect of all the designated Contracting Parties, the industrial design or designs that are the subject of the international registration shall not be published.

    (b) If, at any time during the period of deferment applicable under paragraph (2), the holder limits the international registration, in respect of all of the designated Contracting Parties, to one or some of the industrial designs that are the subject of the international registration, the other industrial design or designs that are the subject of the international registration shall not be published.

(6) [*Publication and Furnishing of Reproductions*]

(a) At the expiration of any period of deferment applicable under the provisions of this Article, the International Bureau shall, subject to the payment of the prescribed fees, publish the international registration. If such fees are not paid as prescribed, the international registration shall be canceled and publication shall not take place.

(b) Where the international application was accompanied by one or more specimens of the industrial design in accordance with Article 5(1)(iii), the holder shall submit the prescribed number of copies of a reproduction of each industrial design that is the subject of that application to the International Bureau within the prescribed time limit. To the extent that the holder does not do so, the international registration shall be canceled and publication shall not take place.

Article 12

Refusal

F5–012   (1) [*Right to Refuse*] The Office of any designated Contracting Party may, where the conditions for the grant of protection under the law of that Contracting Party are not met in respect of any or all of the industrial designs that are the subject of an international registration, refuse the effects, in part or in whole, of the international registration in the territory of the said Contracting Party, provided that no Office may refuse the effects, in part or in whole, of any international registration on the ground that requirements relating to the form or contents of the international application that are provided for in this Act or the Regulations or are additional to, or different from, those requirements have not been satisfied under the law of the Contracting Party concerned.

(2) [*Notification of Refusal*]

(a) The refusal of the effects of an international registration shall be communicated by the Office to the International Bureau in a notification of refusal within the prescribed period.

(b) Any notification of refusal shall state all the grounds on which the refusal is based.

(3) [*Transmission of Notification of Refusal; Remedies*]

(a) The International Bureau shall, without delay, transmit a copy of the notification of refusal to the holder.

(b) The holder shall enjoy the same remedies as if any industrial design that is the subject of the international registration had been the subject of an application for the grant of protection under the law applicable to the Office that communicated the refusal. Such remedies shall at least consist of the possibility of a re-examination or a review of the refusal or an appeal against the refusal.

(4) [*Withdrawal of Refusal*] Any refusal may be withdrawn, in part or in whole, at any time by the Office that communicated it.

Article 13

Special Requirements Concerning Unity of Design

F5–013   (1) [*Notification of Special Requirements*] Any Contracting Party whose law, at the time it becomes party to this Act, requires that designs that are the subject of the same application conform to a requirement of unity of design, unity of production or unity of use, or belong to the same set or composition of items, or that only one independent and distinct design may be claimed in a single application, may, in a declaration, notify the Director General accordingly. However, no such declaration shall affect the right of an applicant to include two or more industrial designs in an international application in accordance with Article 5(4), even if the application designates the Contracting Party that has made the declaration.

(2) [*Effect of Declaration*] Any such declaration shall enable the Office of the Contracting Party that has made it to refuse the effects of the international registration pursuant to Article 12(1) pending compliance with the requirement notified by that Contracting Party.

(3) [*Further Fees Payable on Division of Registration*] Where, following a notification of refusal in accordance with paragraph (2), an international registration is divided before the Office concerned in order to overcome a ground of refusal stated in the notification, that Office shall be entitled to charge a fee in respect of each additional international application that would have been necessary in order to avoid that ground of refusal.

Article 14

Effects of the International Registration

(1) [*Effect as Application Under Applicable Law*] The international registration shall, from the date of the international registration, have at least the same effect in each designated Contracting Party as a regularly-filed application for the grant of protection of the industrial design under the law of that Contracting Party.   **F5–014**

(2) [*Effect as Grant of Protection Under Applicable Law*]

    (a) In each designated Contracting Party the Office of which has not communicated a refusal in accordance with Article 12, the international registration shall have the same effect as a grant of protection for the industrial design under the law of that Contracting Party at the latest from the date of expiration of the period allowed for it to communicate a refusal or, where a Contracting Party has made a corresponding declaration under the Regulations, at the latest at the time specified in that declaration.

    (b) Where the Office of a designated Contracting Party has communicated a refusal and has subsequently withdrawn, in part or in whole, that refusal, the international registration shall, to the extent that the refusal is withdrawn, have the same effect in that Contracting Party as a grant of protection for the industrial design under the law of the said Contracting Party at the latest from the date on which the refusal was withdrawn.

    (c) The effect given to the international registration under this paragraph shall apply to the industrial design or designs that are the subject of that registration as received from the International Bureau by the designated Office or, where applicable, as amended in the procedure before that Office.

(3) [*Declaration Concerning Effect of Designation of Applicant's Contracting Party*]

    (a) Any Contracting Party whose Office is an Examining Office may, in a declaration, notify the Director General that, where it is the applicant's Contracting Party, the designation of that Contracting Party in an international registration shall have no effect.

(b) Where a Contracting Party having made the declaration referred to in subparagraph (a) is indicated in an international application both as the applicant's Contracting Party and as a designated Contracting Party, the International Bureau shall disregard the designation of that Contracting Party.

Article 15

Invalidation

F5–015   (1) [*Requirement of Opportunity of Defense*] Invalidation, by the competent authorities of a designated Contracting Party, of the effects, in part or in whole, in the territory of that Contracting Party, of the international registration may not be pronounced without the holder having, in good time, been afforded the opportunity of defending his rights.

(2) [*Notification of Invalidation*] The Office of the Contracting Party in whose territory the effects of the international registration have been invalidated shall, where it is aware of the invalidation, notify it to the International Bureau.

Article 16

Recording of Changes and Other Matters Concerning International Registrations

F5–016   (1) [*Recording of Changes and Other Matters*] The International Bureau shall, as prescribed, record in the International Register

(i) any change in ownership of the international registration, in respect of any or all of the designated Contracting Parties and in respect of any or all of the industrial designs that are the subject of the international registration, provided that the new owner is entitled to file an international application under Article 3,

(ii) any change in the name or address of the holder,

(iii) the appointment of a representative of the applicant or holder and any other relevant fact concerning such representative,

(iv) any renunciation, by the holder, of the international registration, in respect of any or all of the designated Contracting Parties,

(v) any limitation, by the holder, of the international registration, in respect of any or all of the designated Contracting Parties, to one or some of the industrial designs that are the subject of the international registration,

(vi) any invalidation, by the competent authorities of a designated Contracting Party, of the effects, in the territory of that Contracting Party, of the international registration in respect of any or all of the industrial designs that are the subject of the international registration,

(vii) any other relevant fact, identified in the Regulations, concerning the rights in any or all of the industrial designs that are the subject of the international registration.

(2) [*Effect of Recording in International Register*] Any recording referred to in items (i), (ii), (iv), (v), (vi) and (vii) of paragraph (1) shall have the same effect as if it had been made in the Register of the Office of each of the Contracting Parties concerned, except that a Contracting Party may, in a declaration, notify the Director General that a recording referred to in item (i) of paragraph (1) shall not

have that effect in that Contracting Party until the Office of that Contracting Party has received the statements or documents specified in that declaration.

(3) [*Fees*] Any recording made under paragraph (1) may be subject to the payment of a fee.

(4) [*Publication*] The International Bureau shall publish a notice concerning any recording made under paragraph (1). It shall send a copy of the publication of the notice to the Office of each of the Contracting Parties concerned.

Article 17

Initial Term and Renewal of the International Registration and Duration of Protection

(1) [*Initial Term of the International Registration*] The international registration shall be effected for an initial term of five years counted from the date of the international registration. **F5–017**

(2) [*Renewal of the International Registration*] The international registration may be renewed for additional terms of five years, in accordance with the prescribed procedure and subject to the payment of the prescribed fees.

(3) [*Duration of Protection in Designated Contracting Parties*]

(a) Provided that the international registration is renewed, and subject to subparagraph (b), the duration of protection shall, in each of the designated Contracting Parties, be 15 years counted from the date of the international registration.

(b) Where the law of a designated Contracting Party provides for a duration of protection of more than 15 years for an industrial design for which protection has been granted under that law, the duration of protection shall, provided that the international registration is renewed, be the same as that provided for by the law of that Contracting Party.

(c) Each Contracting Party shall, in a declaration, notify the Director General of the maximum duration of protection provided for by its law.

(4) [*Possibility of Limited Renewal*] The renewal of the international registration may be effected for any or all of the designated Contracting Parties and for any or all of the industrial designs that are the subject of the international registration.

(5) [*Recording and Publication of Renewal*] The International Bureau shall record renewals in the International Register and publish a notice to that effect. It shall send a copy of the publication of the notice to the Office of each of the Contracting Parties concerned.

Article 18

Information Concerning Published International Registrations

(1) [*Access to Information*] The International Bureau shall supply to any person applying therefor, upon the payment of the prescribed fee, extracts from the International Register, or information concerning the contents of the International Register, in respect of any published international registration. **F5–018**

(2) [*Exemption from Legalization*] Extracts from the International Register supplied by the International Bureau shall be exempt from any requirement of legalization in each Contracting Party.

CHAPTER II

ADMINISTRATIVE PROVISIONS

Article 19

Common Office of Several States

F5–019   (1) [*Notification of Common Office*] If several States intending to become party to this Act have effected, or if several States party to this Act agree to effect, the unification of their domestic legislation on industrial designs, they may notify the Director General

(i) that a common Office shall be substituted for the national Office of each of them, and

(ii) that the whole of their respective territories to which the unified legislation applies shall be deemed to be a single Contracting Party for the purposes of the application of Articles 1, 3 to 18 and 31 of this Act.

(2) [*Time at Which Notification Is to Be Made*] The notification referred to in paragraph (1) shall be made,

(i) in the case of States intending to become party to this Act, at the time of the deposit of the instruments referred to in Article 27(2);

(ii) in the case of States party to this Act, at any time after the unification of their domestic legislation has been effected.

(3) [*Date of Entry into Effect of the Notification*] The notification referred to in paragraphs (1) and (2) shall take effect,

(i) in the case of States intending to become party to this Act, at the time such States become bound by this Act;

(ii) in the case of States party to this Act, three months after the date of the communication thereof by the Director General to the other Contracting Parties or at any later date indicated in the notification.

Article 20

Membership of the Hague Union

F5–020   The Contracting Parties shall be members of the same Union as the States party to the 1934 Act or the 1960 Act.

Article 21

Assembly

F5–021   (1) [*Composition*]

(a) The Contracting Parties shall be members of the same Assembly as the States bound by Article 2 of the Complementary Act of 1967.

(b) Each member of the Assembly shall be represented in the Assembly by one delegate, who may be assisted by alternate delegates, advisors and experts, and each delegate may represent only one Contracting Party.

(c) Members of the Union that are not members of the Assembly shall be admitted to the meetings of the Assembly as observers.

(2) [*Tasks*]

  (a) The Assembly shall

    (i) deal with all matters concerning the maintenance and development of the Union and the implementation of this Act;

    (ii) exercise such rights and perform such tasks as are specifically conferred upon it or assigned to it under this Act or the Complementary Act of 1967;

    (iii) give directions to the Director General concerning the preparations for conferences of revision and decide the convocation of any such conference;

    (iv) amend the Regulations;

    (v) review and approve the reports and activities of the Director General concerning the Union, and give the Director General all necessary instructions concerning matters within the competence of the Union;

    (vi) determine the program and adopt the biennial budget of the Union, and approve its final accounts;

    (vii) adopt the financial regulations of the Union;

    (viii) establish such committees and working groups as it deems appropriate to achieve the objectives of the Union;

    (ix) subject to paragraph (1)(c), determine which States, intergovernmental organizations and non-governmental organizations shall be admitted to its meetings as observers;

    (x) take any other appropriate action to further the objectives of the Union and perform any other functions as are appropriate under this Act.

  (b) With respect to matters which are also of interest to other Unions administered by the Organization, the Assembly shall make its decisions after having heard the advice of the Coordination Committee of the Organization.

(3) [*Quorum*]

  (a) One-half of the members of the Assembly which are States and have the right to vote on a given matter shall constitute a quorum for the purposes of the vote on that matter.

  (b) Notwithstanding the provisions of subparagraph (a), if, in any session, the number of the members of the Assembly which are States, have the right to vote on a given matter and are represented is less than one-half but equal to or more than one-third of the members of the Assembly which are States and have the right to vote on that matter, the Assembly may make decisions but, with the exception of decisions concerning its own procedure, all such decisions shall take effect only if the conditions set forth hereinafter are fulfilled. The International Bureau shall communicate the said decisions to the members of the Assembly which are States, have the right to vote on the said matter and were not represented and shall invite them to express in writing their vote or abstention within a period of three months from the date of the communication. If, at the expiration of this period, the number of such members having thus expressed their vote or abstention attains the number of the members which was lacking for attaining the quorum in the session itself, such decisions shall take effect provided that at the same time the required majority still obtains.

(4) [*Taking Decisions in the Assembly*]

    (a) The Assembly shall endeavor to take its decisions by consensus.

    (b) Where a decision cannot be arrived at by consensus, the matter at issue shall be decided by voting. In such a case,

        (i) each Contracting Party that is a State shall have one vote and shall vote only in its own name, and

        (ii) any Contracting Party that is an intergovernmental organization may vote, in place of its Member States, with a number of votes equal to the number of its Member States which are party to this Act, and no such intergovernmental organization shall participate in the vote if any one of its Member States exercises its right to vote, and *vice versa*.

    (c) On matters concerning only States that are bound by Article 2 of the Complementary Act of 1967, Contracting Parties that are not bound by the said Article shall not have the right to vote, whereas, on matters concerning only Contracting Parties, only the latter shall have the right to vote.

(5) [*Majorities*]

    (a) Subject to Articles 24(2) and 26(2), the decisions of the Assembly shall require two-thirds of the votes cast.

    (b) Abstentions shall not be considered as votes.

(6) [*Sessions*]

    (a) The Assembly shall meet once in every second calendar year in ordinary session upon convocation by the Director General and, in the absence of exceptional circumstances, during the same period and at the same place as the General Assembly of the Organization.

    (b) The Assembly shall meet in extraordinary session upon convocation by the Director General, either at the request of one-fourth of the members of the Assembly or on the Director General's own initiative.

    (c) The agenda of each session shall be prepared by the Director General.

(7) [*Rules of Procedure*] The Assembly shall adopt its own rules of procedure.

Article 22

International Bureau

F5–022   (1) [*Administrative Tasks*]

    (a) International registration and related duties, as well as all other administrative tasks concerning the Union, shall be performed by the International Bureau.

    (b) In particular, the International Bureau shall prepare the meetings and provide the secretariat of the Assembly and of such committees of experts and working groups as may be established by the Assembly.

(2) [*Director General*] The Director General shall be the chief executive of the Union and shall represent the Union.

(3) [*Meetings Other than Sessions of the Assembly*] The Director General shall convene any committee and working group established by the Assembly and all other meetings dealing with matters of concern to the Union.

(4) [*Role of the International Bureau in the Assembly and Other Meetings*]

    (a) The Director General and persons designated by the Director General shall participate, without the right to vote, in all meetings of the Assembly, the committees and working groups established by the Assembly, and any other meetings convened by the Director General under the aegis of the Union.

    (b) The Director General or a staff member designated by the Director General shall be *ex officio* secretary of the Assembly, and of the committees, working groups and other meetings referred to in subparagraph (a).

(5) [*Conferences*]

    (a) The International Bureau shall, in accordance with the directions of the Assembly, make the preparations for any revision conferences.

    (b) The International Bureau may consult with intergovernmental organizations and international and national non-governmental organizations concerning the said preparations.

    (c) The Director General and persons designated by the Director General shall take part, without the right to vote, in the discussions at revision conferences.

(6) [*Other Tasks*] The International Bureau shall carry out any other tasks assigned to it in relation to this Act.

Article 23

Finances

(1) [*Budget*]

    F5–023

    (a) The Union shall have a budget.

    (b) The budget of the Union shall include the income and expenses proper to the Union and its contribution to the budget of expenses common to the Unions administered by the Organization.

    (c) Expenses not attributable exclusively to the Union but also to one or more other Unions administered by the Organization shall be considered to be expenses common to the Unions. The share of the Union in such common expenses shall be in proportion to the interest the Union has in them.

(2) [*Coordination with Budgets of Other Unions*] The budget of the Union shall be established with due regard to the requirements of coordination with the budgets of the other Unions administered by the Organization.

(3) [*Sources of Financing of the Budget*] The budget of the Union shall be financed from the following sources:

    (i) fees relating to international registrations;

    (ii) charges due for other services rendered by the International Bureau in relation to the Union;

    (iii) sale of, or royalties on, the publications of the International Bureau concerning the Union;

    (iv) gifts, bequests and subventions;

    (v) rents, interests and other miscellaneous income.

(4) [*Fixing of Fees and Charges; Level of the Budget*]

    (a) The amounts of the fees referred to in paragraph (3)(i) shall be fixed by the Assembly on the proposal of the Director General. Charges referred to in paragraph 3(ii) shall be established by the Director General and shall be provisionally applied subject to approval by the Assembly at its next session.

(b) The amounts of the fees referred to in paragraph (3)(i) shall be so fixed that the revenues of the Union from fees and other sources shall be at least sufficient to cover all the expenses of the International Bureau concerning the Union.

(c) If the budget is not adopted before the beginning of a new financial period, it shall be at the same level as the budget of the previous year, as provided in the financial regulations.

(5) [*Working Capital Fund*] The Union shall have a working capital fund which shall be constituted by the excess receipts and, if such excess does not suffice, by a single payment made by each member of the Union. If the fund becomes insufficient, the Assembly shall decide to increase it. The proportion and the terms of payment shall be fixed by the Assembly on the proposal of the Director General.

(6) [*Advances by Host State*]

(a) In the headquarters agreement concluded with the State on the territory of which the Organization has its headquarters, it shall be provided that, whenever the working capital fund is insufficient, such State shall grant advances. The amount of those advances and the conditions on which they are granted shall be the subject of separate agreements, in each case, between such State and the Organization.

(b) The State referred to in subparagraph (a) and the Organization shall each have the right to denounce the obligation to grant advances, by written notification. Denunciation shall take effect three years after the end of the year in which it has been notified.

(7) [*Auditing of Accounts*] The auditing of the accounts shall be effected by one or more of the States members of the Union or by external auditors, as provided in the financial regulations. They shall be designated, with their agreement, by the Assembly.

Article 24

Regulations

F5–024   (1) [*Subject Matter*] The Regulations shall govern the details of the implementation of this Act. They shall, in particular, include provisions concerning

(i) matters which this Act expressly provides are to be prescribed;

(ii) further details concerning, or any details useful in the implementation of, the provisions of this Act;

(iii) any administrative requirements, matters or procedures.

(2) [*Amendment of Certain Provisions of the Regulations*]

(a) The Regulations may specify that certain provisions of the Regulations may be amended only by unanimity or only by a four-fifths majority.

(b) In order for the requirement of unanimity or a four-fifths majority no longer to apply in the future to the amendment of a provision of the Regulations, unanimity shall be required.

(c) In order for the requirement of unanimity or a four-fifths majority to apply in the future to the amendment of a provision of the Regulations, a four-fifths majority shall be required.

(3) [*Conflict Between This Act and the Regulations*] In the case of conflict between the provisions of this Act and those of the Regulations, the former shall prevail.

CHAPTER III

REVISION AND AMENDMENT

Article 25

Revision of This Act

(1) [*Revision Conferences*] This Act may be revised by a conference of the Contracting Parties.   **F5–025**

(2) [*Revision or Amendment of Certain Articles*] Articles 21, 22, 23 and 26 may be amended either by a revision conference or by the Assembly according to the provisions of Article 26.

Article 26

Amendment of Certain Articles by the Assembly

(1) [*Proposals for Amendment*]   **F5–026**

   (a) Proposals for the amendment by the Assembly of Articles 21, 22, 23 and this Article may be initiated by any Contracting Party or by the Director General.

   (b) Such proposals shall be communicated by the Director General to the Contracting Parties at least six months in advance of their consideration by the Assembly.

(2) [*Majorities*] Adoption of any amendment to the Articles referred to in paragraph (1) shall require a three-fourths majority, except that adoption of any amendment to Article 21 or to the present paragraph shall require a four-fifths majority.

(3) [*Entry into Force*]

   (a) Except where subparagraph (b) applies, any amendment to the Articles referred to in paragraph (1) shall enter into force one month after written notifications of acceptance, effected in accordance with their respective constitutional processes, have been received by the Director General from three-fourths of those Contracting Parties which, at the time the amendment was adopted, were members of the Assembly and had the right to vote on that amendment.

   (b) Any amendment to Article 21(3) or (4) or to this subparagraph shall not enter into force if, within six months of its adoption by the Assembly, any Contracting Party notifies the Director General that it does not accept such amendment.

   (c) Any amendment which enters into force in accordance with the provisions of this paragraph shall bind all the States and intergovernmental organizations which are Contracting Parties at the time the amendment enters into force, or which become Contracting Parties at a subsequent date.

CHAPTER IV

FINAL PROVISIONS

Article 27

Becoming Party to This Act

F5–027   (1) [*Eligibility*] Subject to paragraphs (2) and (3) and Article 28,

(i) any State member of the Organization may sign and become party to this Act;

(ii) any intergovernmental organization which maintains an Office in which protection of industrial designs may be obtained with effect in the territory in which the constituting treaty of the intergovernmental organization applies may sign and become party to this Act, provided that at least one of the member States of the intergovernmental organization is a member of the Organization and provided that such Office is not the subject of a notification under Article 19.

(2) [*Ratification or Accession*] Any State or intergovernmental organization referred to in paragraph (1) may deposit

(i) an instrument of ratification if it has signed this Act, or

(ii) an instrument of accession if it has not signed this Act.

(3) [*Effective Date of Deposit*]

(a) Subject to subparagraphs (b) to (d), the effective date of the deposit of an instrument of ratification or accession shall be the date on which that instrument is deposited.

(b) The effective date of the deposit of the instrument of ratification or accession of any State in respect of which protection of industrial designs may be obtained only through the Office maintained by an intergovernmental organization of which that State is a member shall be the date on which the instrument of that intergovernmental organization is deposited if that date is later than the date on which the instrument of the said State has been deposited.

(c) The effective date of the deposit of any instrument of ratification or accession containing or accompanied by the notification referred to in Article 19 shall be the date on which the last of the instruments of the States members of the group of States having made the said notification is deposited.

(d) Any instrument of ratification or accession of a State may contain or be accompanied by a declaration making it a condition to its being considered as deposited that the instrument of one other State or one intergovernmental organization, or the instruments of two other States, or the instruments of one other State and one intergovernmental organization, specified by name and eligible to become party to this Act, is or are also deposited. The instrument containing or accompanied by such a declaration shall be considered to have been deposited on the day on which the condition indicated in the declaration is fulfilled. However, when an instrument specified in the declaration itself contains, or is itself accompanied by, a declaration of the said kind, that instrument shall be considered as deposited on the day on which the condition specified in the latter declaration is fulfilled.

(e) Any declaration made under paragraph (d) may be withdrawn, in its entirety or in part, at any time. Any such withdrawal shall become effective on the date on which the notification of withdrawal is received by the Director General.

Article 28

Effective Date of Ratifications and Accessions

(1) [*Instruments to Be Taken into Consideration*] For the purposes of this Article, **F5–028** only instruments of ratification or accession that are deposited by States or intergovernmental organizations referred to in Article 27(1) and that have an effective date according to Article 27(3) shall be taken into consideration.

(2) [*Entry into Force of This Act*] This Act shall enter into force three months after six States have deposited their instruments of ratification or accession, provided that, according to the most recent annual statistics collected by the International Bureau, at least three of those States fulfill at least one of the following conditions:

(i) at least 3,000 applications for the protection of industrial designs have been filed in or for the State concerned, or

(ii) at least 1,000 applications for the protection of industrial designs have been filed in or for the State concerned by residents of States other than that State.

(3) [*Entry into Force of Ratifications and Accessions*]

(a) Any State or intergovernmental organization that has deposited its instrument of ratification or accession three months or more before the date of entry into force of this Act shall become bound by this Act on the date of entry into force of this Act.

(b) Any other State or intergovernmental organization shall become bound by this Act three months after the date on which it has deposited its instrument of ratification or accession or at any later date indicated in that instrument.

Article 29

Prohibition of Reservations

No reservations to this Act are permitted. **F5–029**

Article 30

Declarations Made by Contracting Parties

(1) [*Time at Which Declarations May Be Made*] Any declaration under Articles **F5–030** 4(1)(b), 5(2)(a), 7(2), 11(1), 13(1), 14(3), 16(2) or 17(3)(c) may be made

(i) at the time of the deposit of an instrument referred to in Article 27(2), in which case it shall become effective on the date on which the State or intergovernmental organization having made the declaration becomes bound by this Act, or

(ii) after the deposit of an instrument referred to in Article 27(2), in which case it shall become effective three months after the date of its receipt by the Director General or at any later date indicated in the declaration but shall apply only in respect of any international registration whose date of international registration is the same as, or is later than, the effective date of the declaration.

(2) [*Declarations by States Having a Common Office*] Notwithstanding paragraph (1), any declaration referred to in that paragraph that has been made by a State which has, with another State or other States, notified the Director General under Article 19(1) of the substitution of a common Office for their national Offices shall become effective only if that other State or those other States makes or make a corresponding declaration or corresponding declarations.

(3) [*Withdrawal of Declarations*] Any declaration referred to in paragraph (1) may be withdrawn at any time by notification addressed to the Director General. Such withdrawal shall take effect three months after the date on which the Director General has received the notification or at any later date indicated in the notification. In the case of a declaration made under Article 7(2), the withdrawal shall not affect international applications filed prior to the coming into effect of the said withdrawal.

Article 31

Applicability of the 1934 and 1960 Acts

F5–031   (1) [*Relations Between States Party to Both This Act and the 1934 or 1960 Acts*] This Act alone shall be applicable as regards the mutual relations of States party to both this Act and the 1934 Act or the 1960 Act. However, such States shall, in their mutual relations, apply the 1934 Act or the 1960 Act, as the case may be, to industrial designs deposited at the International Bureau prior to the date on which this Act becomes applicable as regards their mutual relations.

(2) [*Relations Between States Party to Both This Act and the 1934 or 1960 Acts and States Party to the 1934 or 1960 Acts Without Being Party to This Act*]

(a) Any State that is party to both this Act and the 1934 Act shall continue to apply the 1934 Act in its relations with States that are party to the 1934 Act without being party to the 1960 Act or this Act.

(b) Any State that is party to both this Act and the 1960 Act shall continue to apply the 1960 Act in its relations with States that are party to the 1960 Act without being party to this Act.

Article 32

Denunciation of This Act

F5–032   (1) [*Notification*] Any Contracting Party may denounce this Act by notification addressed to the Director General.

(2) [*Effective Date*] Denunciation shall take effect one year after the date on which the Director General has received the notification or at any later date indicated in the notification. It shall not affect the application of this Act to any

international application pending and any international registration in force in respect of the denouncing Contracting Party at the time of the coming into effect of the denunciation.

Article 33

Languages of This Act; Signature

(1) [*Original Texts; Official Texts*]   **F5–033**

    (a) This Act shall be signed in a single original in the English, Arabic, Chinese, French, Russian and Spanish languages, all texts being equally authentic.

    (b) Official texts shall be established by the Director General, after consultation with the interested Governments, in such other languages as the Assembly may designate.

(2) [*Time Limit for Signature*] This Act shall remain open for signature at the headquarters of the Organization for one year after its adoption.

Article 34

Depositary

The Director General shall be the depositary of this Act.   **F5–034**

AGREED STATEMENTS BY THE DIPLOMATIC CONFERENCE REGARDING THE GENEVA ACT
AND THE REGULATIONS UNDER THE GENEVA ACT

1. When adopting Article 12(4), Article 14(2)(b) and Rule 18(4), the Diplomatic   **F5–035** Conference understood that a withdrawal of refusal by an Office that has communicated a notification of refusal may take the form of a statement to the effect that the Office concerned has decided to accept the effects of the international registration in respect of the industrial designs, or some of the industrial designs, to which the notification of refusal related. It was also understood that an Office may, within the period allowed for communicating a notification of refusal, send a statement to the effect that it has decided to accept the effects of the international registration even where it has not communicated such a notification of refusal.

2. When adopting Article 10, the Diplomatic Conference understood that nothing in this Article precludes access to the international application or the international registration by the applicant or the holder or a person having the consent of the applicant or the holder.

INDEX

Abuse of rights
Community registered designs
abuse of designer's rights, 2–082
Abuse of procedure
and see **Groundless threats**
groundless threats
threat of proceedings,
7–001—7–002, 7–021—7–029
Account of profits
infringement proceedings,
6–061—6–064
Additional damages
infringement proceedings, and,
6–057—6–060
Aesthetic appearance
Community registered designs
meaning, 2–018
registrability, 3–075—3–076
Aircraft
Community registered designs
ships and aircraft from another
country, 2–088—2–089
Anonymous works
copyright, D2–007
Appeals
and see **Registered Designs Appeal
Tribunal**
Community registered designs,
B1–056—B1–062, B1–115,
B2–037—B2–040
Comptroller of Patents Designs and
Trade Marks
appeals from decisions, E1–013
patents, E2–021
Registered Designs Appeal Tribunal
appeals from decisions,
2–137—2–138
appeals to, 2–133—2–136
registered designs (pre-2001)
appeals from RDAT's decisions,
2–137—2–138
registration of Community design
appeals against OHIM decisions,
2–151
trade marks, E2–021

Applications
Hague system, under
Contracting Parties, 2–153
Paris Convention applications
compared, 2–155
procedure, 2–154
statutory provisions, 2–152
registered designs (pre-2001)
appeals from RDAT's decisions,
2–137—2–138
appeals from decision,
2–133—2–136
application method, 2–123—2–125
Designs Form DF2A,
2–123—2–124
Designs Registry, functions of,
2–122
examination, 2–130—2–131
generally, 2–121
grant of certificate, 2–139
hearing of objections, 2–132
illegal designs, 2–129
immoral designs, 2–129
inspection of registration, 2–140
Office objections, 2–130—2–131
Paris Convention applications,
2–141—2–142, 2–155
specimens of design,
2–126—2–128
registration of Community design
appeals against OHIM decisions,
2–151
application system, 2–143—2–144
completion of registration, 2–150
filing form, 2–145—2–146
formal examination only,
2–148—2–149
multiple applications, 2–147
Artistic works
buildings, D1–005
categories, 5–004—5–005
Copyright Act 1956, under, D2–002
exceptions, D2–005
graphic works, 5–006—5–018
meaning, D1–005
physical existence, 5–045—5–046

Registered designs (before December 9, 2001)—*cont.*
eye appeal—*cont.*
functional articles, and, 3–061—3–066
functional articles
design features with functional purpose, 3–067—3–070
eye appeal, and, 3–061—3–066
historical development of exclusion, 3–071—3–074
"mere mechanical device", 3–071—3–073
statutory exclusion, 3–054—3–060
industrial process, 3–045—3–046
infringement
article for which design registered, 3–181—3–183
comparison of design on register, 3–189—3–190
comparison of designs as a whole, 3–211—3–213
essential features, difference in, 3–194—3–195
features constituting design, 3–191—3–193
identification by reference to prior art, 3–196—3–202
kits of parts, 3–173—3–176
making moulds and tools, 3–170—3–172
primary acts, 3–168—3–169
requirements, 3–164—3–167
resemblance, degree of, 3–184—3–187
statement of novelty, impact of, 3–214—3–215
substantiality of differences, 3–206—3–210
temporal limits, 3–180
territorial limits, 3–177—3–179
test for substantial difference, 3–188
very well known subject, 3–203—3–205
letters, 3–084
licences
exclusive licences, 3–244—3–245
generally, 3–238—3–243
registration, 3–246—3–247
method of construction
scope of exclusion, 3–077—3–083
novelty
assessment against prior design, 3–145—3–147

Registered designs (before December 9, 2001)—*cont.*
novelty—*cont.*
class of articles, 3–162—3–163
conflicting registrations, 3–094—3–096
date of assessment, 3–091—3–093
difference in immaterial details, 3–151—3–153
"new or original", 3–160—3–161
prior publication, 3–097—3–144
statutory requirement, 3–089—3–090
trade variants, 3–154—3–159
whole design need not be new, 3–148—3–150
numerals, 3–084
parts of articles
generally, 3–038—3–040
"must-match" exclusion, 3–041—3–044
pattern, 3–021—3–024
pre-CDPA 1988 designs
"design", 3–271—3–273
infringement, 3–274
maximum term of protection, 3–275
pre- and post-1988 registered designs, 3–270
registrability, 3–271—3–273
transitional provisions, 3–270—3–275
principle of construction
scope of exclusion, 3–077—3–083
prior publication
see also **Disclosure; Documents**
breach of good faith, 3–135—3–138
confidential disclosures, 3–131—3–134
disclosure of design applied to article, 3–118—3–124
disclosure to a single person, 3–129—3–130
disclosure to government department, 3–139
documents, in, 3–108—3–124
exhibition display, 3–140—3–141
exploitation of artistic copyright, 3–125—3–128
extent of publication, 3–112—3–117
meaning, 3–097—3–099
prior use, 3–100—3–104